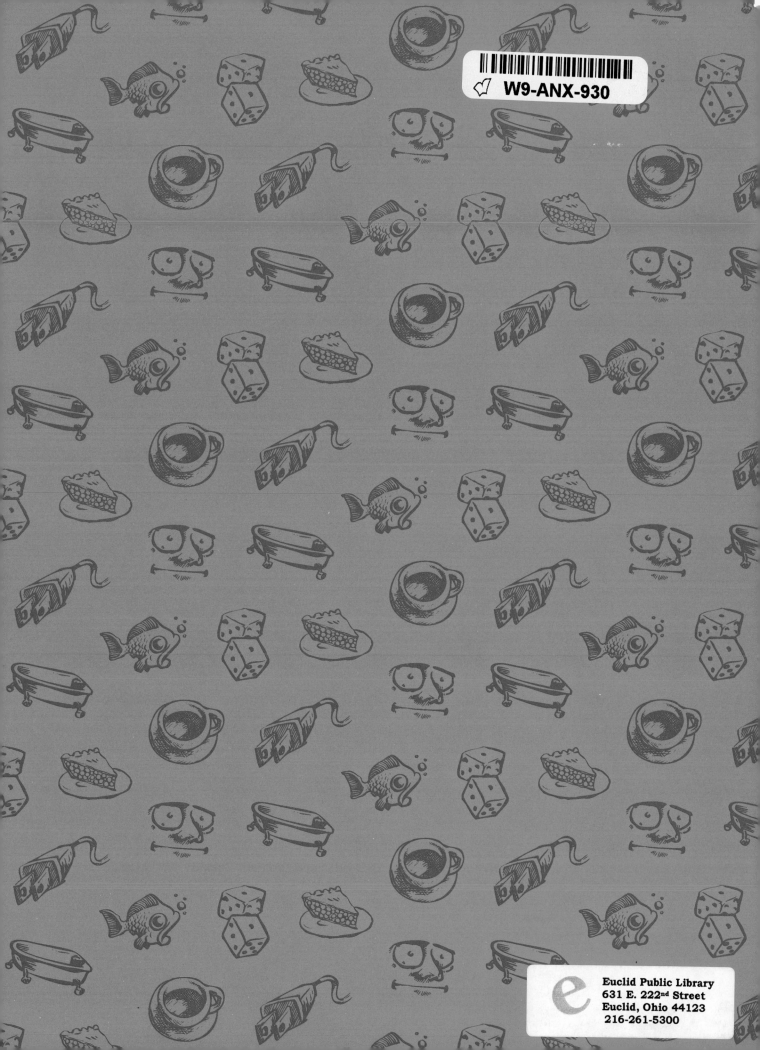

publisher
MIKE RICHARDSON

the first too much coffee man *editor*
BOB SCHRECK

dark horse presents *story editors*
MIKE RICHARDSON & **BRENDAN WRIGHT**

original trade collection editors
SHAWNA GORE, JAMIE S. RICH
& **DIANA SCHUTZ** *with* **JEREMY BARLOW**

original omnibus editors
SHAWNA GORE *with*
JEMIAH JEFFERSON
& **JAY (RACHEL) EDIDIN**

omnibus plus editors
PHILIP R. SIMON *with*
HANNAH MEANS-SHANNON
& **MEGAN WALKER**

designer
SARAH TERRY

cover artist
SHANNON WHEELER

original cover colorist
MARTIN THOMAS

cover colorist and digital art technician
MELISSA MARTIN

Special thanks to **Patricia Wheeler, Richard Epstein, Austin Wheeler, Berkeley Wheeler, Thelonious Xavier Tiberius Wheeler, Rani Vivathanachai,** *and* **Maximilian Gore Perez**

TOO MUCH COFFEE MAN OMNIBUS PLUS

This volume collects *Too Much Coffee Man's Guide for the Perplexed*, published in 1998; *Too Much Coffee Man's Parade of Tirade*, published in 1999; *Too Much Coffee Man's Amusing Musings*, published in 2001; *Too Much Coffee Man: How to Be Happy*, published in 2005; *Screw Heaven, When I Die I'm Going to Mars*, published in 2007; *Too Much Coffee Man Omnibus*, published in 2011; the *Dark Horse Presents* Volume 3 #33 cover, featuring *Too Much Coffee Man*; and "Too Much Coffee Man vs. The Squirrel."

Published by
Dark Horse Books
A division of Dark Horse Comics, Inc.
10956 SE Main Street | Milwaukie, OR 97222

DarkHorse.com | TMCM.com

Library of Congress Cataloging-in-Publication data on file.

First edition: June 2017 | ISBN 978-1-50670-402-9

1 3 5 7 9 10 8 6 4 2
Printed in China

TOO MUCH COFFEE MAN

by SHANNON WHEELER

Dark Horse Books

TABLE OF CONTENTS

AMUSING MUSINGS

CHAPTER 1

CHAPTER 2

CHAPTER 3

CHAPTER 4

CHAPTER 5

CHAPTER 6

CHAPTER 7

HOW TO BE HAPPY

SCREW HEAVEN, WHEN I DIE I'M GOING TO MARS

OMNIBUS PLUS (BONUS) COLOR SECTION

INTRODUCTION

In a coffee shop, I'm reading through a stack of papers that represent twenty-three years of *Too Much Coffee Man* cartoons, the contents of this book. My emotions are mixed. No, they're not really mixed. They *flip*. I'm amazed at the cartoon I drew. I am a genius. I turn the page, and I wince. The idea is recycled, and the drawing is bad. Idiot. Back and forth. I often don't even turn the page. The same cartoon is great and terrible. Idiot and genius. Faster and faster, like a strobe light.

If that isn't evidence of mental problems, I don't know what is.

Every page is a diary. I don't necessarily remember drawing a certain cartoon, but I do remember what was happening in my life at the time. Happy. Sad. Heartbroken. In love. Drunk. Hung over. On deadline and unenthusiastic, inspired and exuberant . . . I cartooned through it all.

And I sacrificed to meet deadlines. Here's an example that easily fits as a metaphor. I dated my neighbor. After we broke up, I watched her continue to date. My drawing table was at a window that looked out on to her house. Why didn't I move my drawing table? I could have. But I would have gone to the window to check on her anyway, and I would waste time getting up from my table. Easier to keep the table at the window. I could tell myself I didn't care. But really, I wanted the pain. When someone stabs you, and you want them to twist the knife.

Her date picks her up. I draw. Hours later, they come back. I draw. Downstairs lights go on. Draw. Kitchen lights go on. Draw. Upstairs lights go on. Draw. Then off. Draw. Bathroom lights. Draw. He'd leave, and all the lights would go off. I draw and think, "This agony better be worth it."

I put comics before relationships, health (mental and physical), and wealth. Is it worth it? Probably not. I should have taken care of my relationships. I should have taken care of my body and my mind. I should always sleep more. I like sleep. I should probably put in the time and money and go to therapy. I wasted my youth drawing.

I should have dated more, gone to more parties, taken more drugs, and attended orgies back when I was still healthy and attractive. Of course, my friends who did all that stuff have perma-fried brains and sexual diseases, but maybe they're better artists because they have a wealth of life experiences to tap from. Bukowski, Burroughs, and other writers whose names begin with "b" benefited from their indulgences.

I barely hold on without the added burden of crippling addiction.

The work it takes maintaining my marginal life makes the thought of adding an addiction or two unimaginable. But who knows. The amount of stuff I don't know could fill a bucket with a hole in it. The only thing I know for sure is never doubt yourself . . . except maybe sometimes.

—Shannon Wheeler, January 2017

PARADE OF TIRADE

PARADE OF TIRADE INTRODUCTION

by Henry Rollins

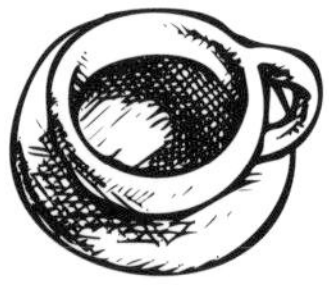

How many times have you sat alone in a coffee house and stared into the liquid black abyss of your coffee cup to see the blasted reflection of your own mortal futility staring back at you as you sit still while being jettisoned toward the end of your life? Your thoughts ricochet like wild bullets fired into an iron-walled room. Getting older. Every day closer to death. Never took advantage of your youth. Squandered your resources. Old relationships come back to haunt you as you reference them against the one you're trapped in now or the one you wish you were. Your obsessions scream and taunt you from the corners of your eyes. Your thoughts smash down like a neural hammer on your cranial anvil. One thing becomes clear as you look at the tables full of people chattering away like dolphins on speed—only the strong dare to drink from the bottomless black insomnia mother pool alone. That would be you.

As the diner so aptly depicted in Edward Hopper's *Nighthawks*, the coffee house sits like a lit oasis in the desolate nocturnal city sprawl. Inside is hope and respite from your headlong pitch into oblivion. The first cup makes sense. The second makes more. On you go. As you pick up speed, everything around you seems to slow down slightly. Perfection. You are now traveling at life's frantic and banal velocity. The canvas of another night shot full of holes. The slow commute back to the room to wait it out until you are released from the teeth and cast into twitching sleep: never deep and never long as your mind slams down the rails. The sun comes up; the noise level skyrockets as the city lurches forward with metal-on-metal desperation. Too Much Coffee Man is the embodiment of our stressed urban intellectual overload smashing into a wall. He sits, grinding his teeth in the eye of the storm, deeply entrenched in the battlefield of a world gone mad.

As you pass your days in that job you hate, as you pummel yourself into distraction from the excruciating reality that it's all slipping away, Too Much Coffee Man must stay awake to ponder and process our collective psychosis. We must sympathize with his neuroses as if they were our very own. Because indeed, they are. As you sleep uneasily, Too Much Coffee Man is on point, doing . . . well, not much of anything to qualify him as a superhero. His eyes, however, are fixed on the Abyss, his thoughts ceaselessly cast into the Void. Enough vast darkness for you? I thought so.

Too Much Coffee Man and his loyal comrades—Underwater Guy, Too Much Espresso Guy, and Too Much German White Chocolate Woman With Almonds—walk the wall for us even though it only looks like they're just absent-mindedly watching television. They are, in fact, worthy constituents and useful propellants, compelling Too Much Coffee Man ever onward. Perfection manifests itself in many ways.

What a mess we have made. All we can do is thank them. They deserve so much more.

About the artist: The creator of Too Much Coffee Man is not the man of mystery that you would have hoped. He does not speak in oblique pithy verse. He does not live in mansioned solitude overlooking a distant sparkling metropolis. He does not go from port to port under the cover of night, sending panels to nervous and furious editors who anxiously pace office floors long after closing time awaiting his next artistic spasm. Don't we wish. No, friends, he's Shannon Wheeler, a slave to the grind, be it the bean or the common working stone against which so many of us throw ourselves daily. When friends were asked to talk about him for this short bio, they all demanded anonymity. Many of them used the term "long suffering" to describe the relationship. When I phoned the artist to ask what he wanted said on his behalf, he replied, "Something about me being lashed to the mast of a ship in a raging sea of creative impulse, that the roiling forces of genius that constantly course through my . . ." That's when I hung up and got sick of this job. Enjoy the work, but don't try to understand Mr. Wheeler. Thankfully, that's his job.

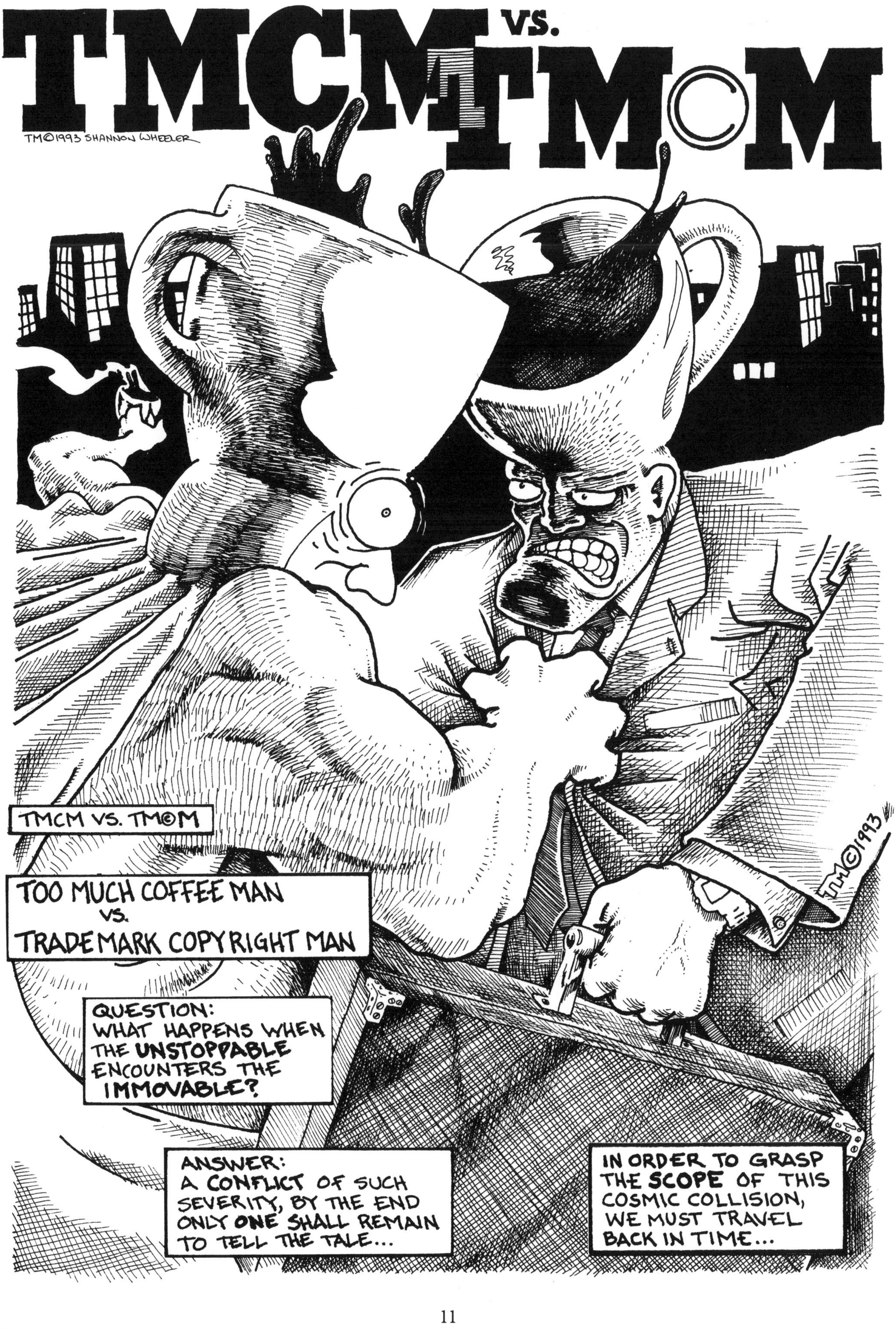
TMCM VS. TM©M
TM©1993 SHANNON WHEELER
TMCM VS. TM©M
TOO MUCH COFFEE MAN VS. TRADEMARK COPYRIGHT MAN
QUESTION: WHAT HAPPENS WHEN THE UNSTOPPABLE ENCOUNTERS THE IMMOVABLE?
TM©1993
ANSWER: A CONFLICT OF SUCH SEVERITY, BY THE END ONLY ONE SHALL REMAIN TO TELL THE TALE...
IN ORDER TO GRASP THE SCOPE OF THIS COSMIC COLLISION, WE MUST TRAVEL BACK IN TIME...

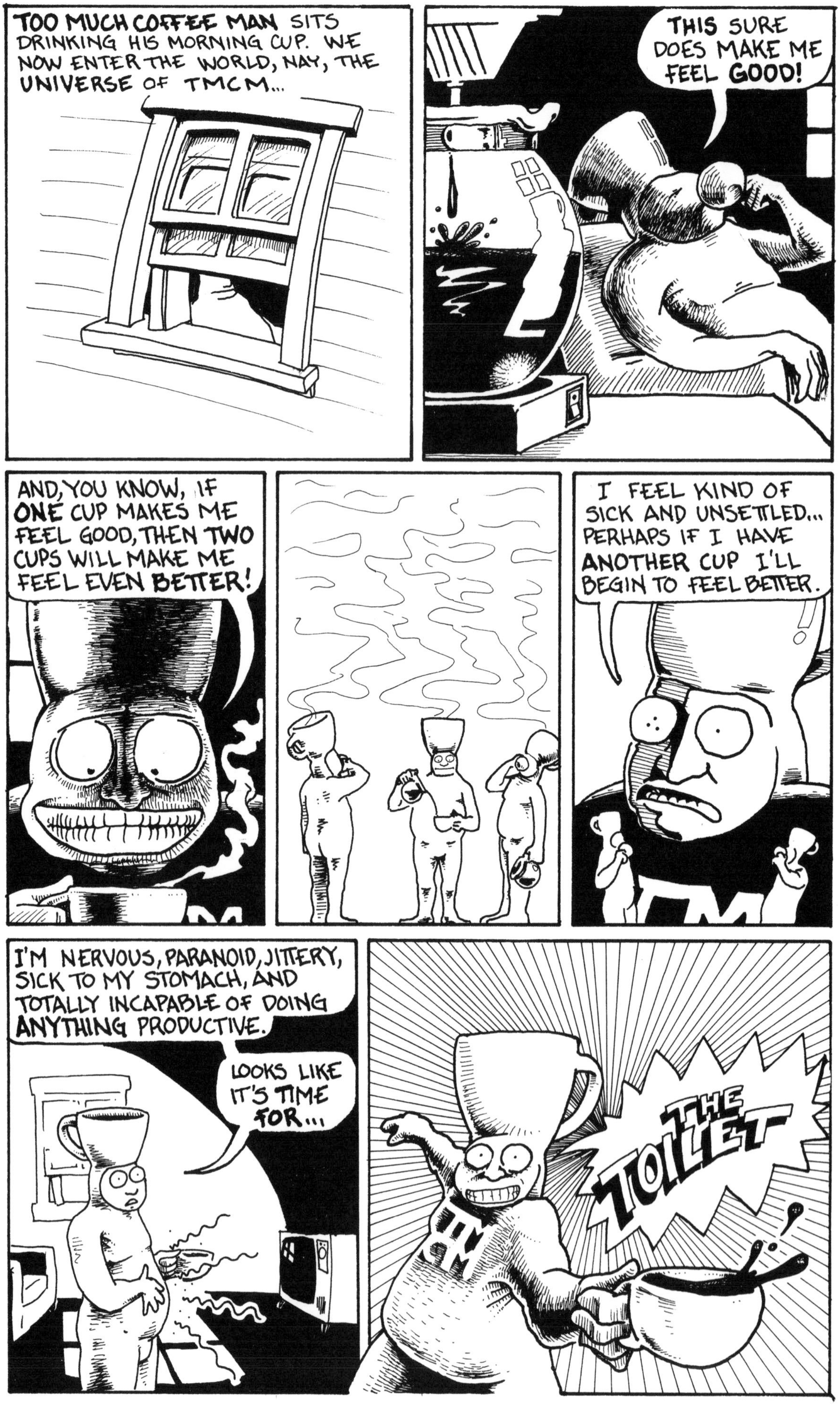
TOO MUCH COFFEE MAN SITS DRINKING HIS MORNING CUP. WE NOW ENTER THE WORLD, NAY, THE UNIVERSE OF TMCM...
THIS SURE DOES MAKE ME FEEL GOOD!
AND, YOU KNOW, IF ONE CUP MAKES ME FEEL GOOD, THEN TWO CUPS WILL MAKE ME FEEL EVEN BETTER!
I FEEL KIND OF SICK AND UNSETTLED... PERHAPS IF I HAVE ANOTHER CUP I'LL BEGIN TO FEEL BETTER.
I'M NERVOUS, PARANOID, JITTERY, SICK TO MY STOMACH, AND TOTALLY INCAPABLE OF DOING ANYTHING PRODUCTIVE.
LOOKS LIKE IT'S TIME FOR...
THE TOILET

TIME TO SIT AND CONTEMPLATE **LIFE.**

AS I SIT AND CON-TEMPLATE, I BEGIN TO REALIZE HOW SHORT OUR LIVES ACTUALLY ARE.

I NEED TO **DO** SOMETHING... BUT WHEN I'M INVOLVED WITH A PROJECT, I LOSE TRACK OF TIME. I TURN AROUND AND YEARS OF MY LIFE ARE SUDDENLY **GONE.**

IF...I SIT AND DO NOTHING...THEN... TIME SEEMS TO SLOW...TO A CRAWL...

BUT...I ACCOMPLISH NOTHING.

IF I COULD MANAGE TO DO SOMETHING **AND** NOTHING AT THE **SAME** TIME, IT'LL SEEM LIKE LIFE LASTS **FOREVER.**

BUT I'M WASTING TIME THINKING ABOUT WASTING TIME.

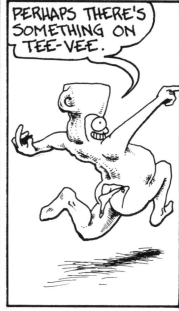

PERHAPS THERE'S SOMETHING ON TEE-VEE.

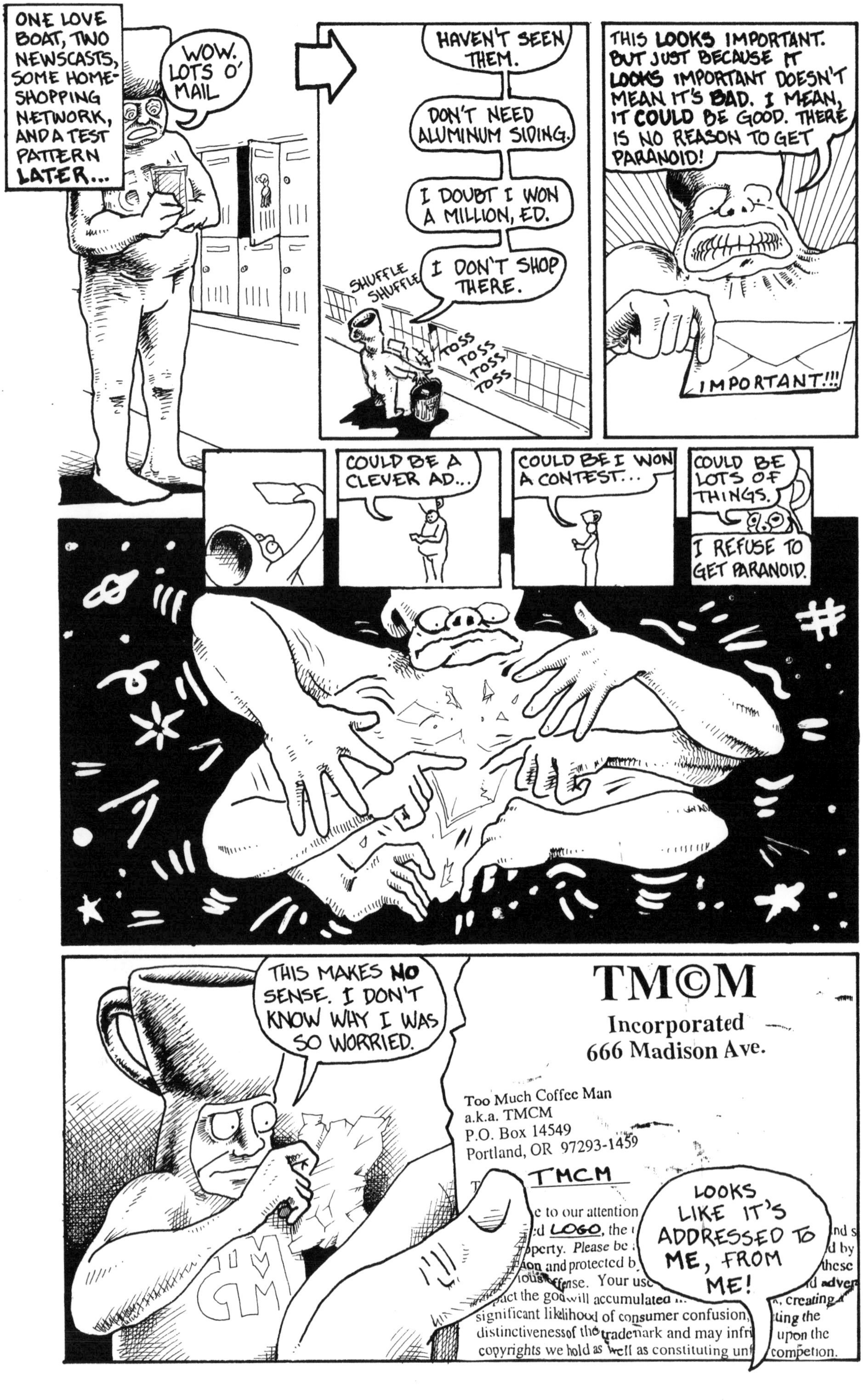
ONE LOVE BOAT, TWO NEWSCASTS, SOME HOME-SHOPPING NETWORK, AND A TEST PATTERN LATER...
WOW. LOTS O' MAIL
HAVEN'T SEEN THEM.
DON'T NEED ALUMINUM SIDING.
I DOUBT I WON A MILLION, ED.
I DON'T SHOP THERE.
SHUFFLE SHUFFLE
TOSS TOSS TOSS TOSS
THIS LOOKS IMPORTANT. BUT JUST BECAUSE IT LOOKS IMPORTANT DOESN'T MEAN IT'S BAD. I MEAN, IT COULD BE GOOD. THERE IS NO REASON TO GET PARANOID!
IMPORTANT!!!
COULD BE A CLEVER AD...
COULD BE I WON A CONTEST...
COULD BE LOTS OF THINGS.
I REFUSE TO GET PARANOID.
THIS MAKES NO SENSE. I DON'T KNOW WHY I WAS SO WORRIED.
TM©M
Incorporated
666 Madison Ave.
Too Much Coffee Man
a.k.a. TMCM
P.O. Box 14549
Portland, OR 97293-1459
TMCM
LOOKS LIKE IT'S ADDRESSED TO ME, FROM ME!

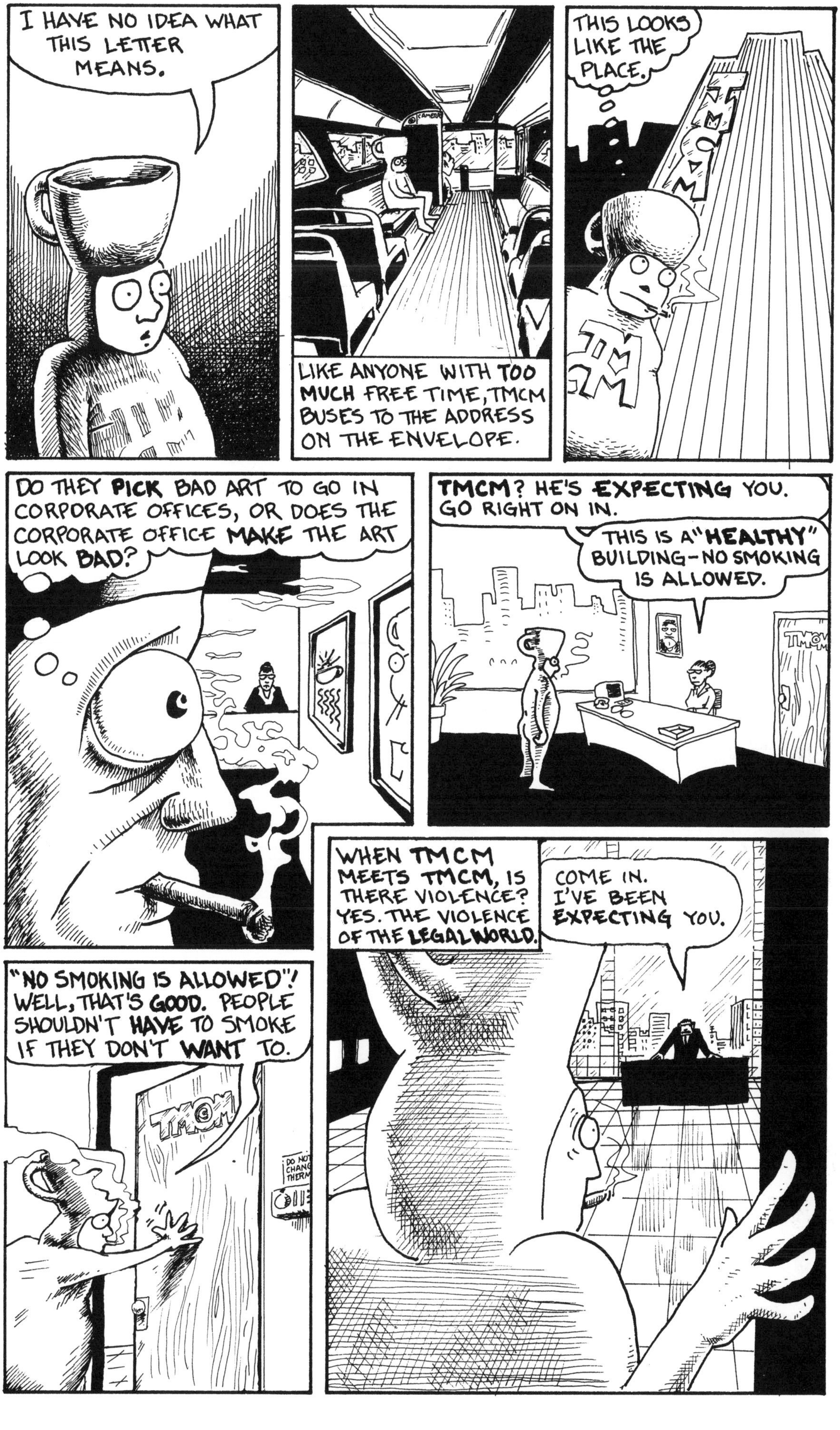
I HAVE NO IDEA WHAT THIS LETTER MEANS.
LIKE ANYONE WITH TOO MUCH FREE TIME, TMCM BUSES TO THE ADDRESS ON THE ENVELOPE.
THIS LOOKS LIKE THE PLACE.
TMCM
DO THEY PICK BAD ART TO GO IN CORPORATE OFFICES, OR DOES THE CORPORATE OFFICE MAKE THE ART LOOK BAD?
TMCM? HE'S EXPECTING YOU. GO RIGHT ON IN.
THIS IS A "HEALTHY" BUILDING—NO SMOKING IS ALLOWED.
WHEN TMCM MEETS TMCM, IS THERE VIOLENCE? YES. THE VIOLENCE OF THE LEGAL WORLD.
COME IN. I'VE BEEN EXPECTING YOU.
"NO SMOKING IS ALLOWED"! WELL, THAT'S GOOD. PEOPLE SHOULDN'T HAVE TO SMOKE IF THEY DON'T WANT TO.
TMCM

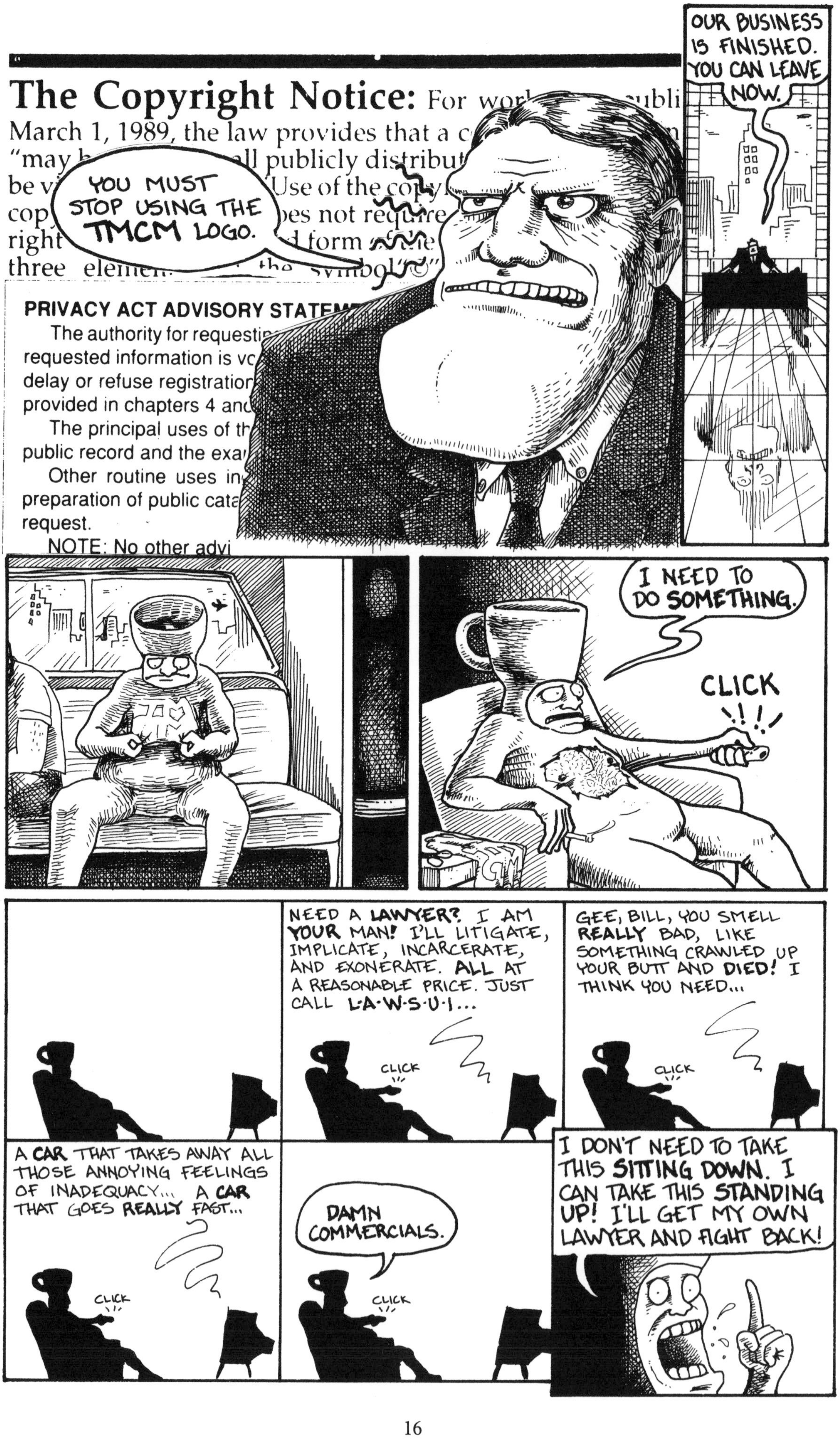
The Copyright Notice: For wor ubli
March 1, 1989, the law provides that a c
"may b all publicly distribut
be v Use of the co
cop oes not require
right l form
three elemen the symbol "©"
YOU MUST STOP USING THE TMCM LOGO.
PRIVACY ACT ADVISORY STATEM
The authority for requestin
requested information is vo
delay or refuse registration
provided in chapters 4 and
The principal uses of th
public record and the exa
Other routine uses in
preparation of public cata
request.
NOTE: No other advi
OUR BUSINESS IS FINISHED. YOU CAN LEAVE NOW.
I NEED TO DO SOMETHING.
CLICK
NEED A LAWYER? I AM YOUR MAN! I'LL LITIGATE, IMPLICATE, INCARCERATE, AND EXONERATE. ALL AT A REASONABLE PRICE. JUST CALL L·A·W·S·U·I...
CLICK
GEE, BILL, YOU SMELL REALLY BAD, LIKE SOMETHING CRAWLED UP YOUR BUTT AND DIED! I THINK YOU NEED...
CLICK
A CAR THAT TAKES AWAY ALL THOSE ANNOYING FEELINGS OF INADEQUACY... A CAR THAT GOES REALLY FAST...
CLICK
DAMN COMMERCIALS.
CLICK
I DON'T NEED TO TAKE THIS SITTING DOWN. I CAN TAKE THIS STANDING UP! I'LL GET MY OWN LAWYER AND FIGHT BACK!

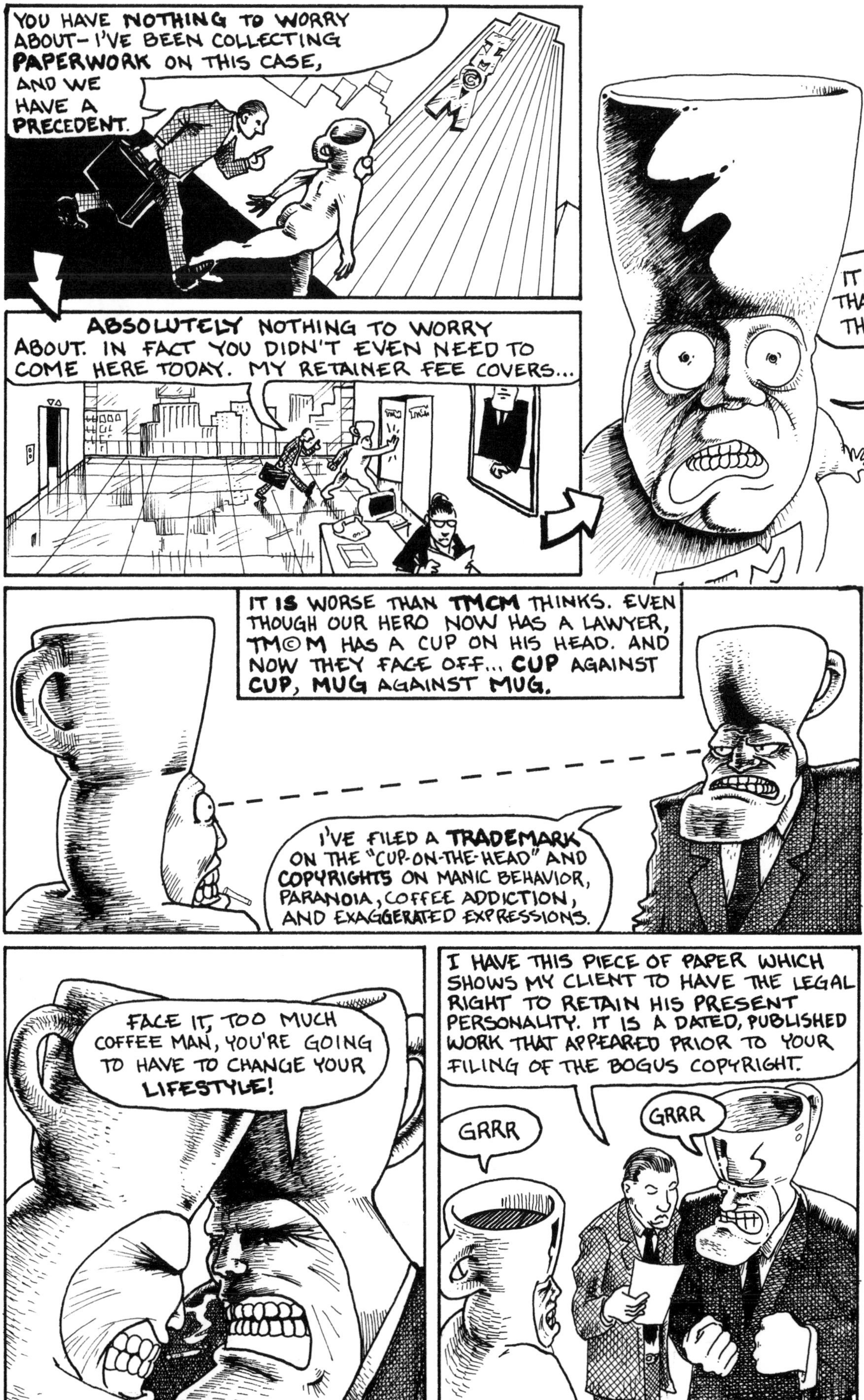
YOU HAVE NOTHING TO WORRY ABOUT– I'VE BEEN COLLECTING PAPERWORK ON THIS CASE, AND WE HAVE A PRECEDENT.
ABSOLUTELY NOTHING TO WORRY ABOUT. IN FACT YOU DIDN'T EVEN NEED TO COME HERE TODAY. MY RETAINER FEE COVERS...
IT'S WORSE THAN I THOUGHT!
IT IS WORSE THAN TMCM THINKS. EVEN THOUGH OUR HERO NOW HAS A LAWYER, TM©M HAS A CUP ON HIS HEAD. AND NOW THEY FACE OFF... CUP AGAINST CUP, MUG AGAINST MUG.
I'VE FILED A TRADEMARK ON THE "CUP-ON-THE-HEAD" AND COPYRIGHTS ON MANIC BEHAVIOR, PARANOIA, COFFEE ADDICTION, AND EXAGGERATED EXPRESSIONS.
FACE IT, TOO MUCH COFFEE MAN, YOU'RE GOING TO HAVE TO CHANGE YOUR LIFESTYLE!
I HAVE THIS PIECE OF PAPER WHICH SHOWS MY CLIENT TO HAVE THE LEGAL RIGHT TO RETAIN HIS PRESENT PERSONALITY. IT IS A DATED, PUBLISHED WORK THAT APPEARED PRIOR TO YOUR FILING OF THE BOGUS COPYRIGHT.
GRRR
GRRR

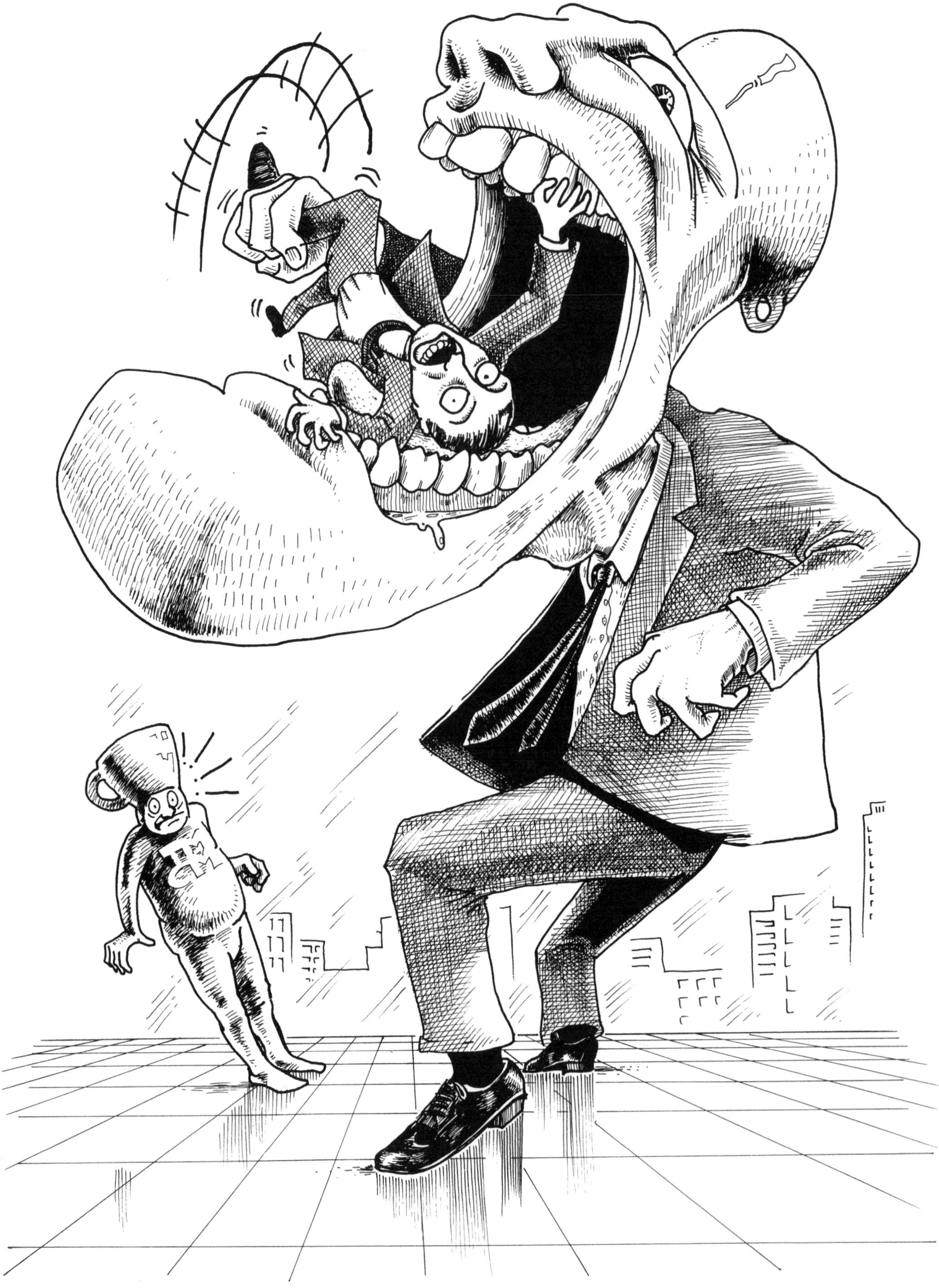

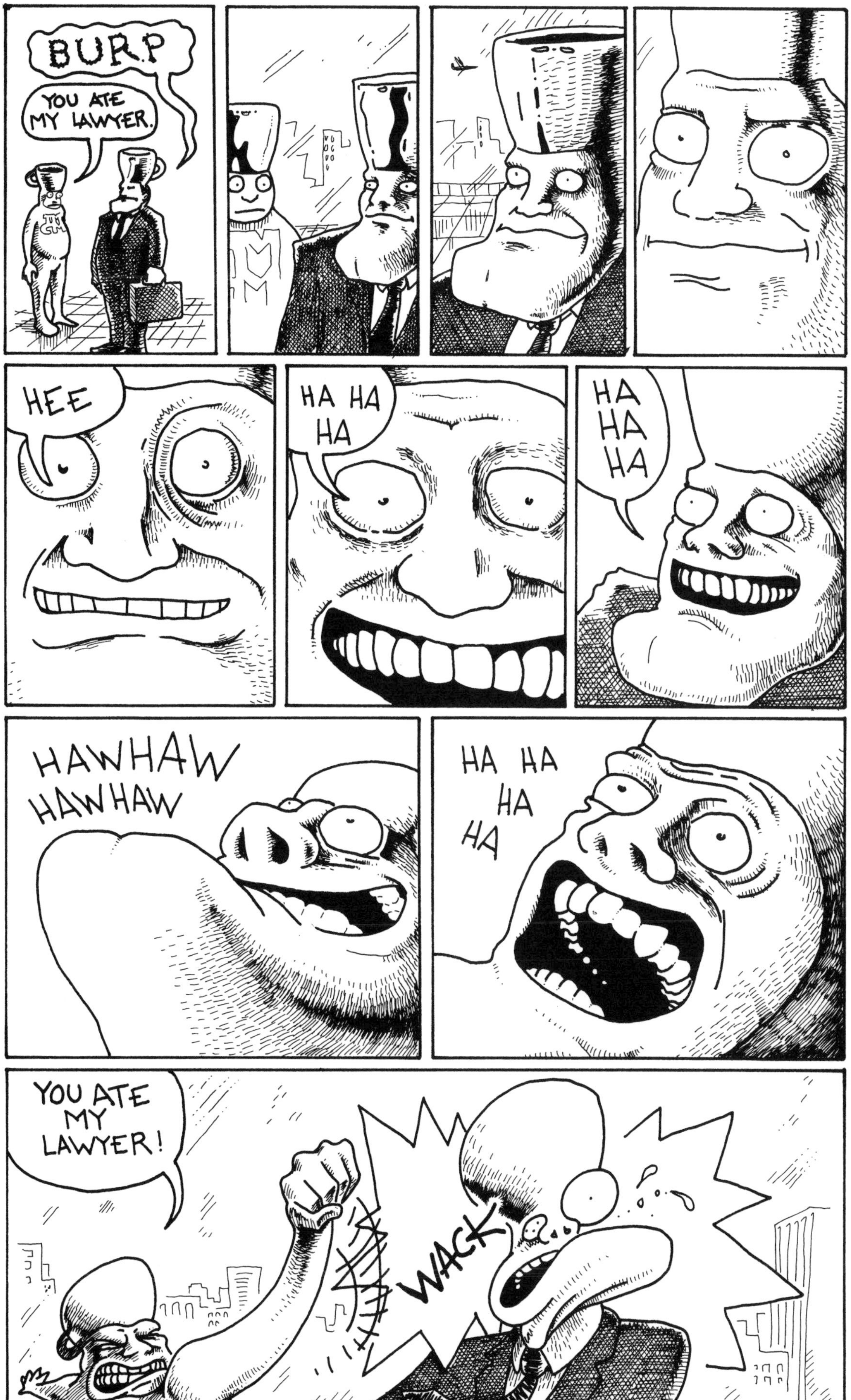
BURP
YOU ATE MY LAWYER.
HEE
HA HA HA
HA HA HA
HAWHAW HAWHAW
HA HA HA HA
YOU ATE MY LAWYER!
WACK

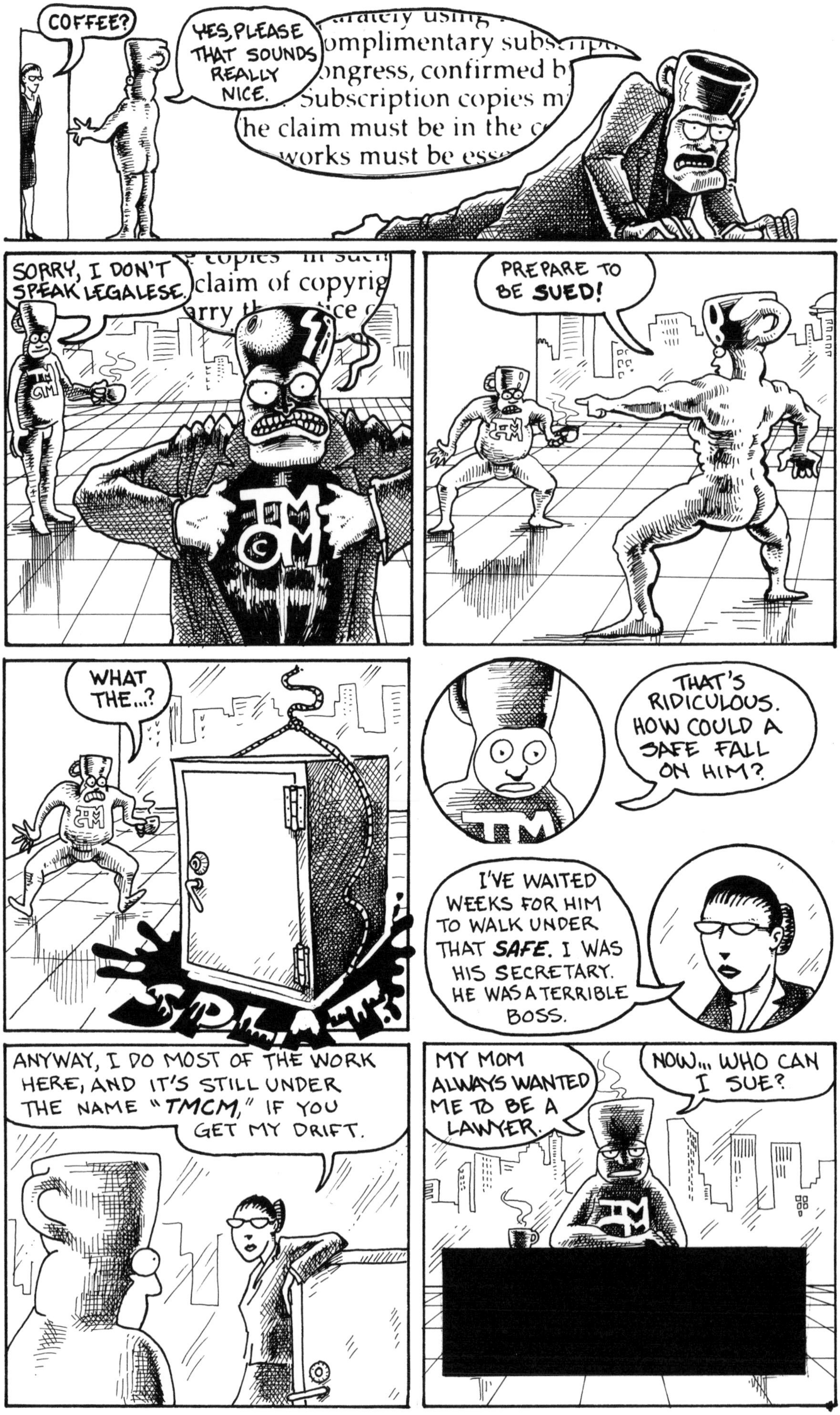
COFFEE?
YES, PLEASE THAT SOUNDS REALLY NICE.
omplimentary subsc
ongress, confirmed b
Subscription copies m
he claim must be in the c
works must be ess
SORRY, I DON'T SPEAK LEGALESE.
claim of copyrig
PREPARE TO BE SUED!
WHAT THE...?
SPLAT
THAT'S RIDICULOUS. HOW COULD A SAFE FALL ON HIM?
I'VE WAITED WEEKS FOR HIM TO WALK UNDER THAT SAFE. I WAS HIS SECRETARY. HE WAS A TERRIBLE BOSS.
ANYWAY, I DO MOST OF THE WORK HERE, AND IT'S STILL UNDER THE NAME "TMCM," IF YOU GET MY DRIFT.
MY MOM ALWAYS WANTED ME TO BE A LAWYER.
NOW... WHO CAN I SUE?

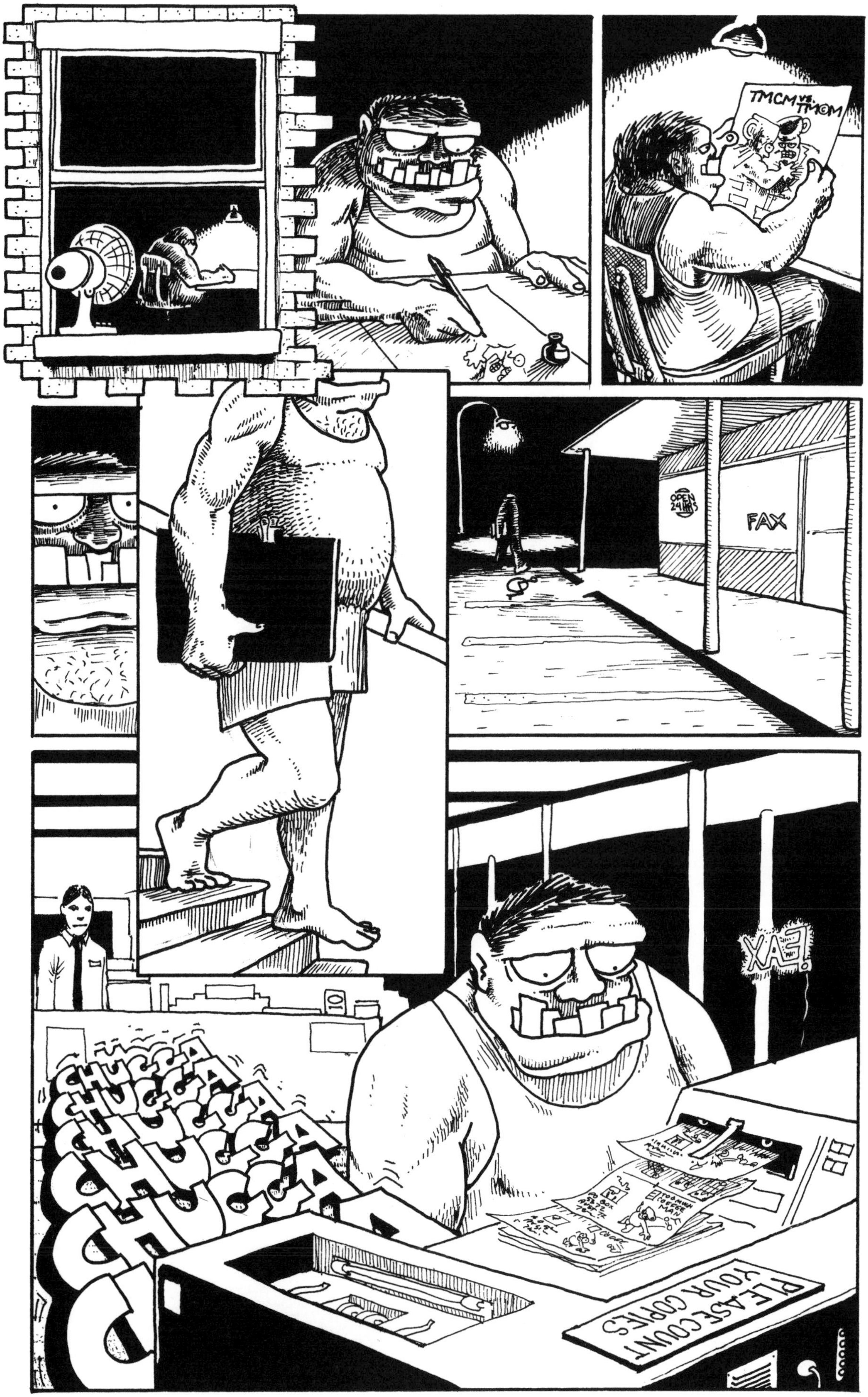
TMCM vs. TMOM
OPEN 24 HRS
FAX
CHUGGA
CHUGGA
CHUGGA
CHUGGA
CHUGGA
C
PLEASE COUNT YOUR COPIES

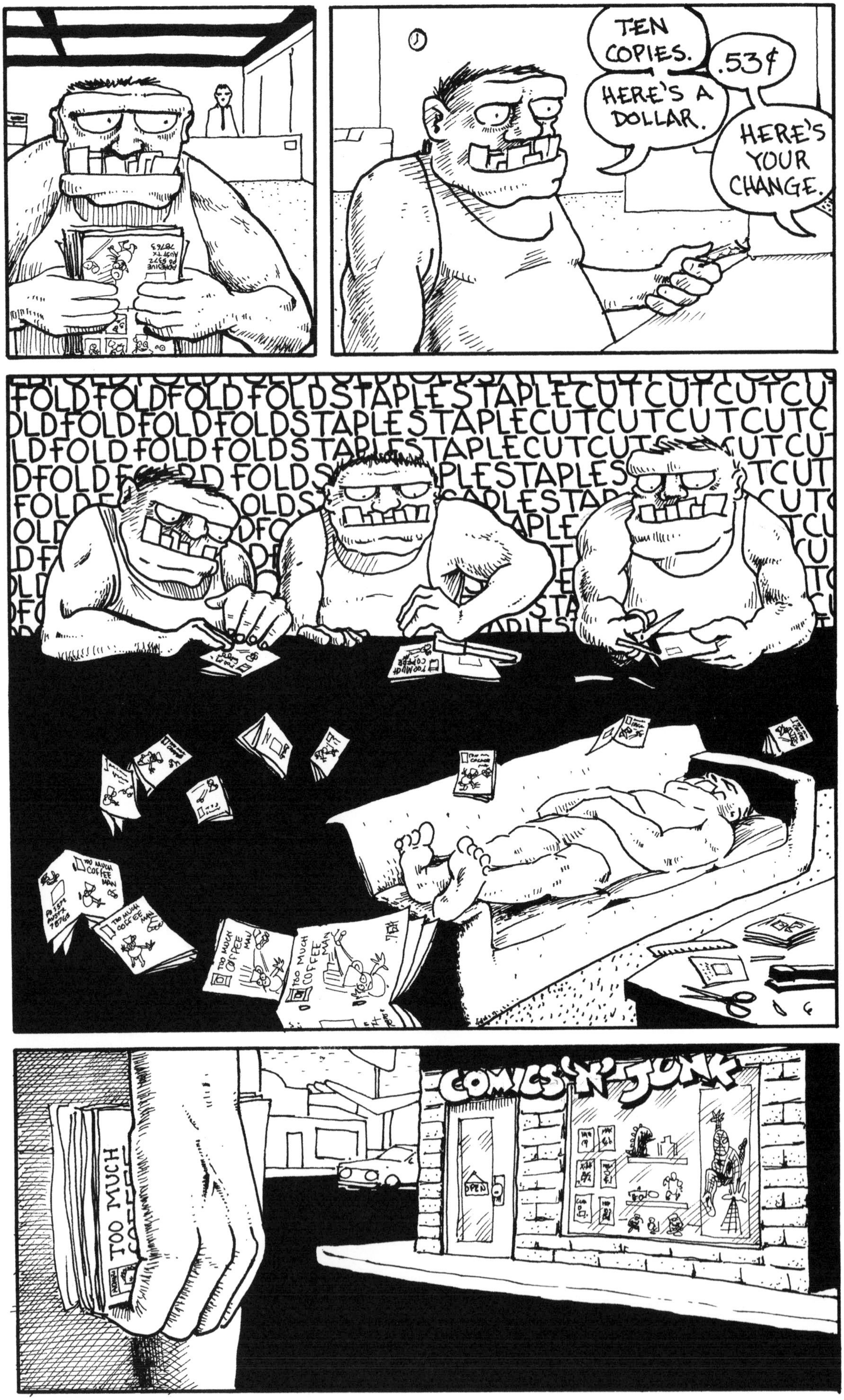
TEN COPIES.
HERE'S A DOLLAR.
.53¢
HERE'S YOUR CHANGE.
FOLD FOLD FOLD FOLD STAPLE STAPLE CUT CUT CUT CUT
TOO MUCH COFFEE MAN
COMICS 'N' JUNK
OPEN
TOO MUCH

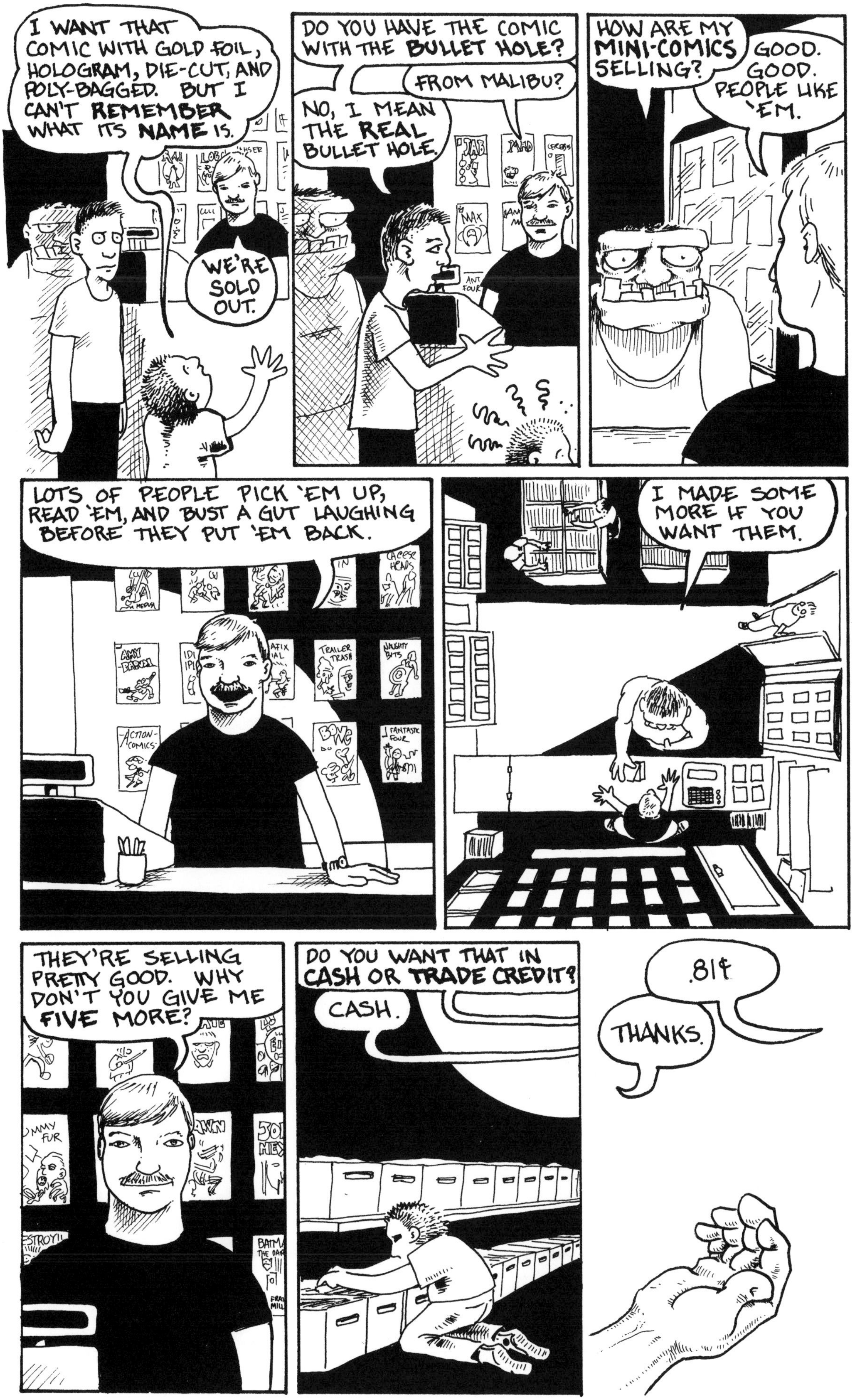
I WANT THAT COMIC WITH GOLD FOIL, HOLOGRAM, DIE-CUT, AND POLY-BAGGED. BUT I CAN'T REMEMBER WHAT ITS NAME IS.
WE'RE SOLD OUT.
DO YOU HAVE THE COMIC WITH THE BULLET HOLE?
FROM MALIBU?
NO, I MEAN THE REAL BULLET HOLE.
HOW ARE MY MINI-COMICS SELLING?
GOOD. GOOD. PEOPLE LIKE 'EM.
LOTS OF PEOPLE PICK 'EM UP, READ 'EM, AND BUST A GUT LAUGHING BEFORE THEY PUT 'EM BACK.
I MADE SOME MORE IF YOU WANT THEM.
THEY'RE SELLING PRETTY GOOD. WHY DON'T YOU GIVE ME FIVE MORE?
DO YOU WANT THAT IN CASH OR TRADE CREDIT?
CASH.
.81¢
THANKS.

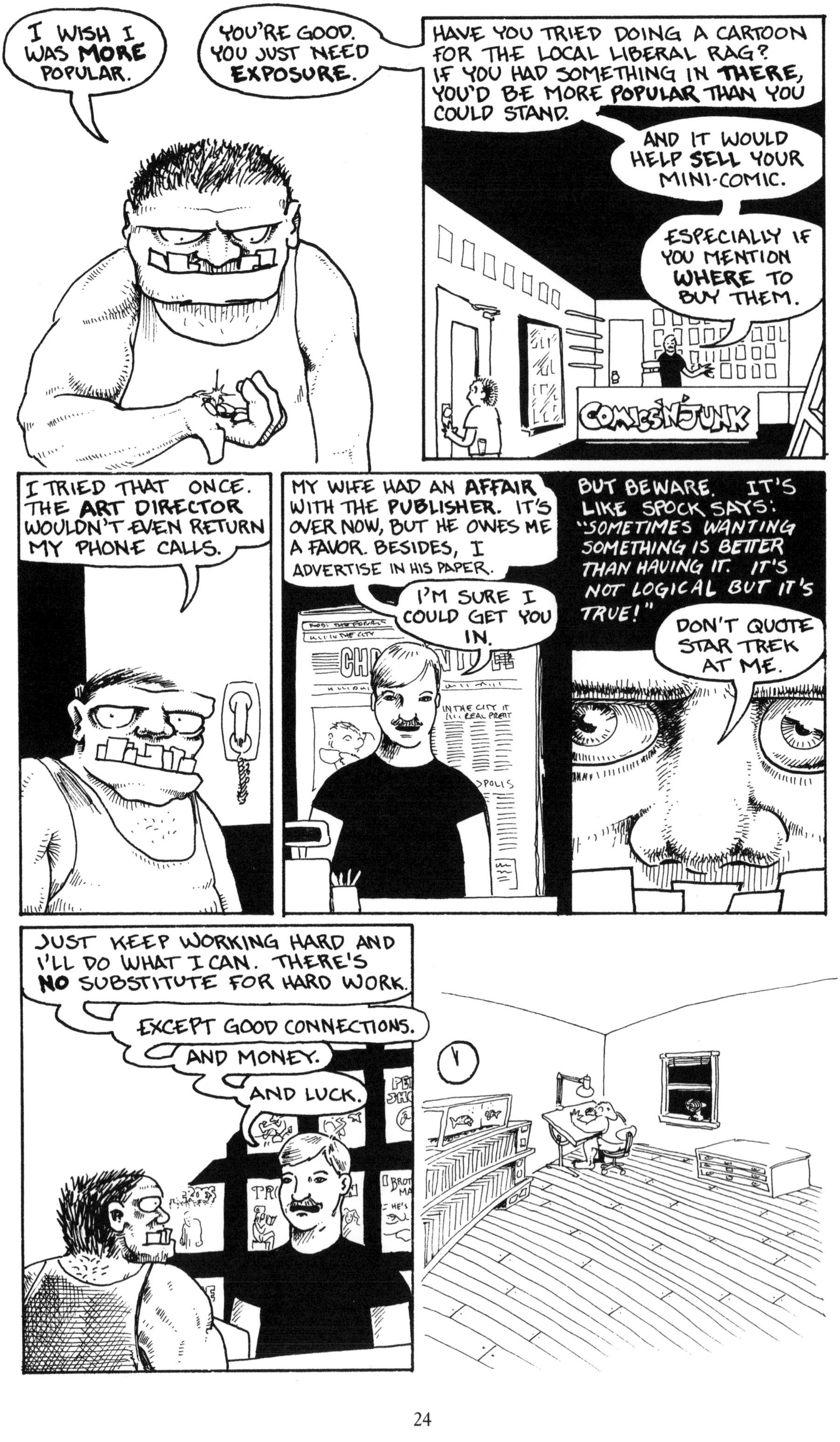
I WISH I WAS MORE POPULAR.
YOU'RE GOOD. YOU JUST NEED EXPOSURE.
HAVE YOU TRIED DOING A CARTOON FOR THE LOCAL LIBERAL RAG? IF YOU HAD SOMETHING IN THERE, YOU'D BE MORE POPULAR THAN YOU COULD STAND.
AND IT WOULD HELP SELL YOUR MINI-COMIC.
ESPECIALLY IF YOU MENTION WHERE TO BUY THEM.
COMICS'N'JUNK
I TRIED THAT ONCE. THE ART DIRECTOR WOULDN'T EVEN RETURN MY PHONE CALLS.
MY WIFE HAD AN AFFAIR WITH THE PUBLISHER. IT'S OVER NOW, BUT HE OWES ME A FAVOR. BESIDES, I ADVERTISE IN HIS PAPER.
I'M SURE I COULD GET YOU IN.
BUT BEWARE. IT'S LIKE SPOCK SAYS: "SOMETIMES WANTING SOMETHING IS BETTER THAN HAVING IT. IT'S NOT LOGICAL BUT IT'S TRUE!"
DON'T QUOTE STAR TREK AT ME.
JUST KEEP WORKING HARD AND I'LL DO WHAT I CAN. THERE'S NO SUBSTITUTE FOR HARD WORK.
EXCEPT GOOD CONNECTIONS.
AND MONEY.
AND LUCK.

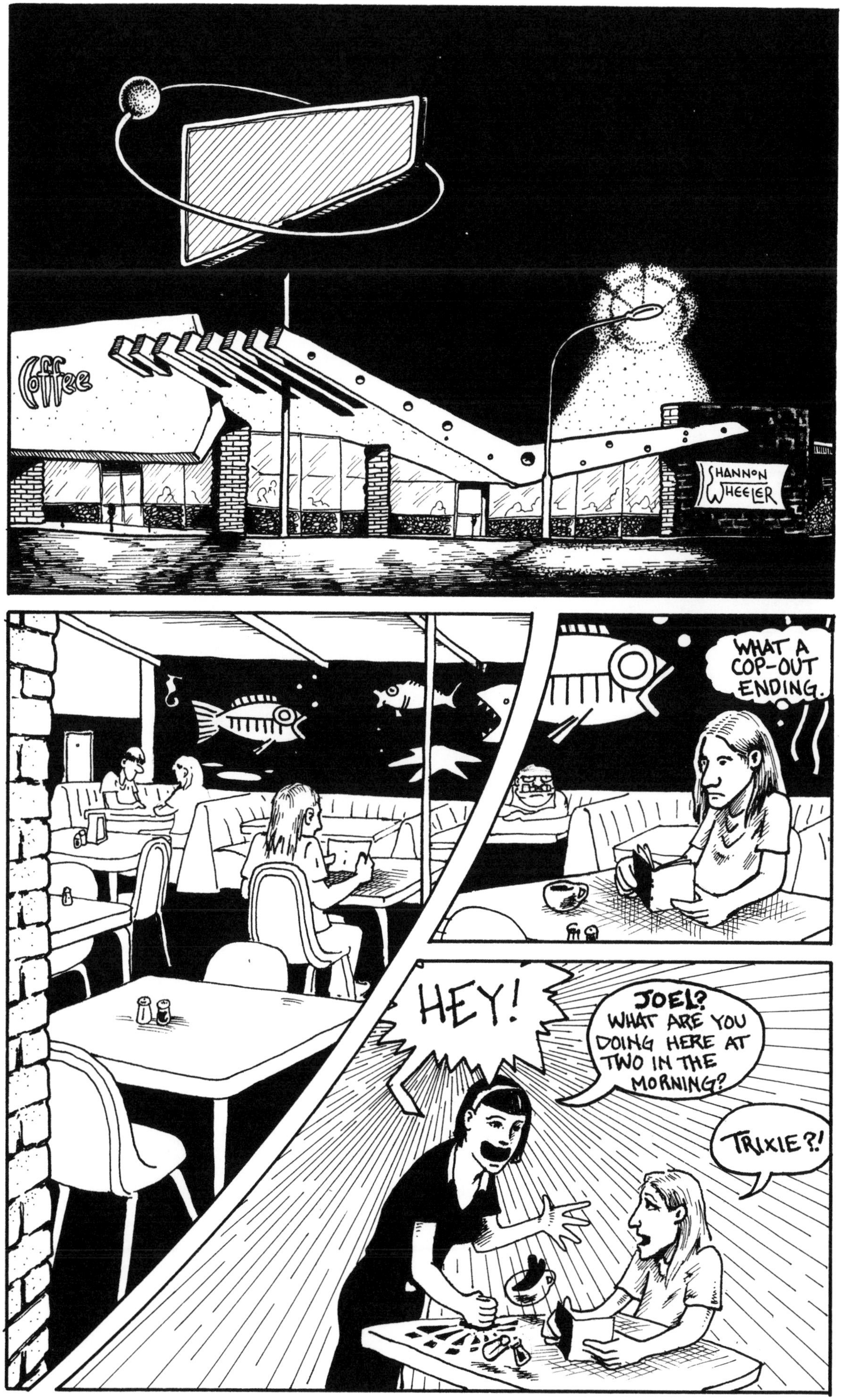
Coffee
SHANNON WHEELER
WHAT A COP-OUT ENDING.
HEY!
JOEL? WHAT ARE YOU DOING HERE AT TWO IN THE MORNING?
TRIXIE?!

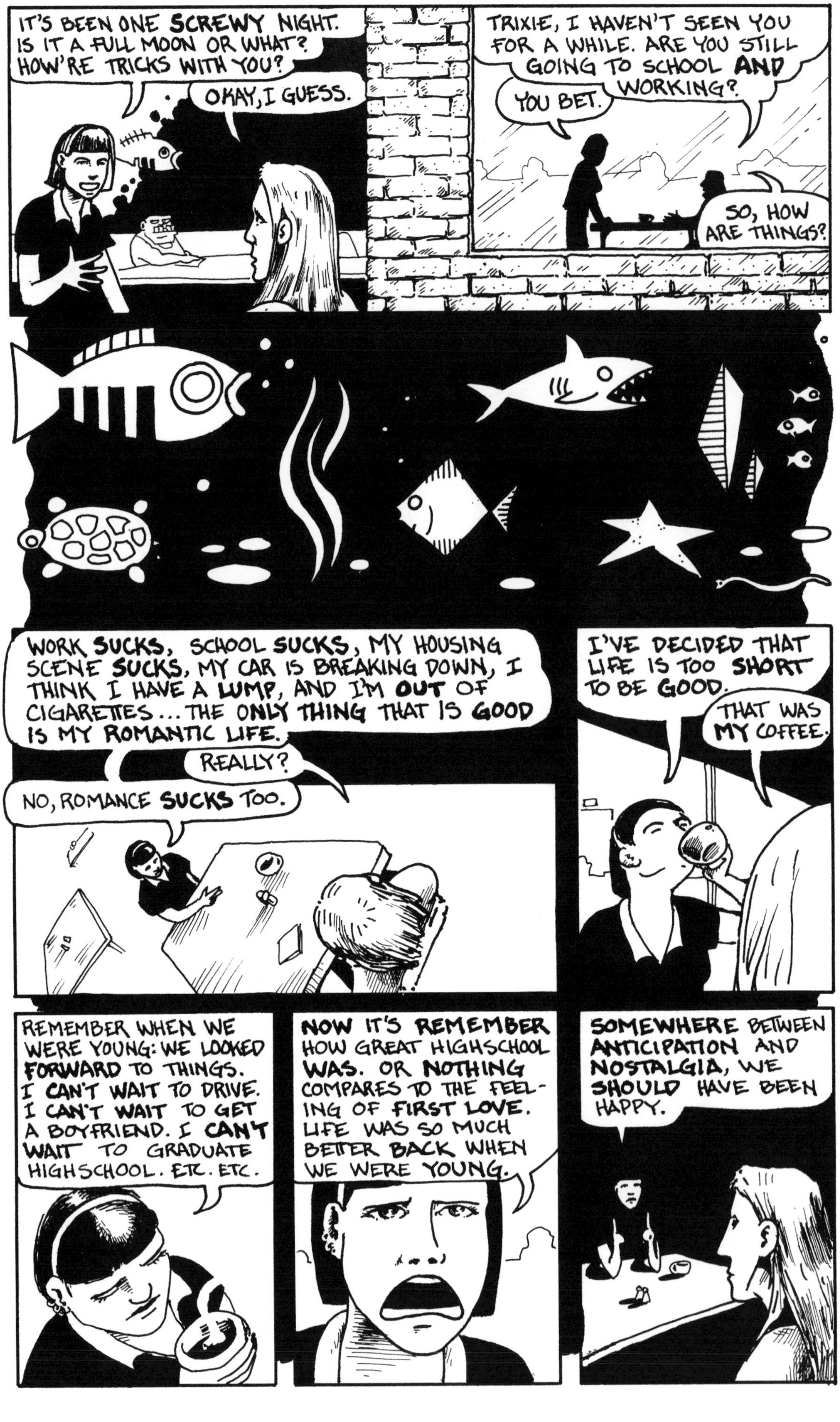

IT'S BEEN ONE SCREWY NIGHT. IS IT A FULL MOON OR WHAT? HOW'RE TRICKS WITH YOU?
OKAY, I GUESS.
TRIXIE, I HAVEN'T SEEN YOU FOR A WHILE. ARE YOU STILL GOING TO SCHOOL AND WORKING?
YOU BET.
SO, HOW ARE THINGS?
WORK SUCKS, SCHOOL SUCKS, MY HOUSING SCENE SUCKS, MY CAR IS BREAKING DOWN, I THINK I HAVE A LUMP, AND I'M OUT OF CIGARETTES... THE ONLY THING THAT IS GOOD IS MY ROMANTIC LIFE.
REALLY?
NO, ROMANCE SUCKS TOO.
I'VE DECIDED THAT LIFE IS TOO SHORT TO BE GOOD.
THAT WAS MY COFFEE.
REMEMBER WHEN WE WERE YOUNG: WE LOOKED FORWARD TO THINGS. I CAN'T WAIT TO DRIVE. I CAN'T WAIT TO GET A BOYFRIEND. I CAN'T WAIT TO GRADUATE HIGHSCHOOL. ETC. ETC.
NOW IT'S REMEMBER HOW GREAT HIGHSCHOOL WAS. OR NOTHING COMPARES TO THE FEELING OF FIRST LOVE. LIFE WAS SO MUCH BETTER BACK WHEN WE WERE YOUNG.
SOMEWHERE BETWEEN ANTICIPATION AND NOSTALGIA, WE SHOULD HAVE BEEN HAPPY.

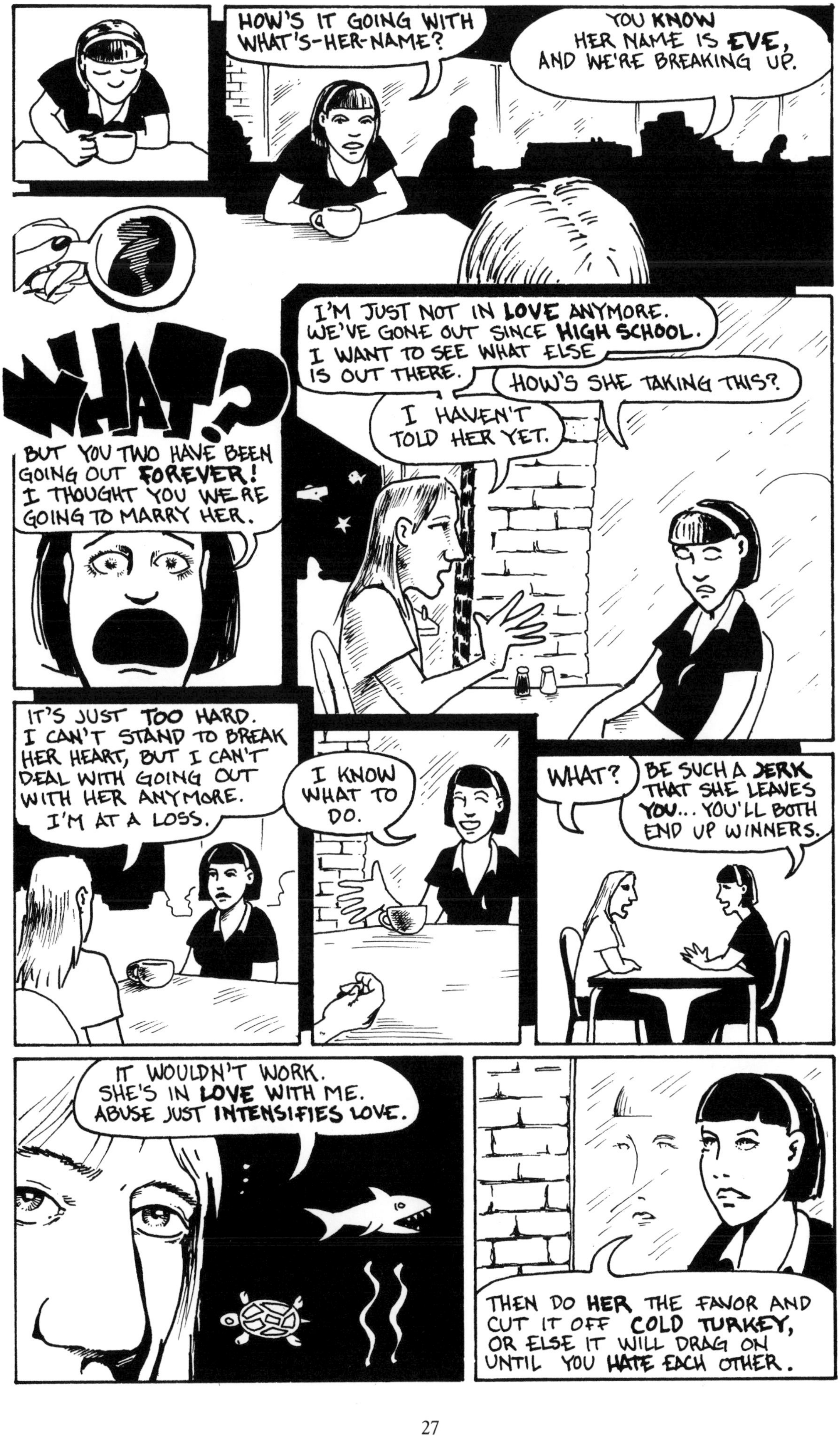
HOW'S IT GOING WITH WHAT'S-HER-NAME?
YOU KNOW HER NAME IS EVE, AND WE'RE BREAKING UP.
WHAT?
BUT YOU TWO HAVE BEEN GOING OUT FOREVER! I THOUGHT YOU WERE GOING TO MARRY HER.
I'M JUST NOT IN LOVE ANYMORE. WE'VE GONE OUT SINCE HIGH SCHOOL. I WANT TO SEE WHAT ELSE IS OUT THERE.
HOW'S SHE TAKING THIS?
I HAVEN'T TOLD HER YET.
IT'S JUST TOO HARD. I CAN'T STAND TO BREAK HER HEART, BUT I CAN'T DEAL WITH GOING OUT WITH HER ANYMORE. I'M AT A LOSS.
I KNOW WHAT TO DO.
WHAT?
BE SUCH A JERK THAT SHE LEAVES YOU... YOU'LL BOTH END UP WINNERS.
IT WOULDN'T WORK. SHE'S IN LOVE WITH ME. ABUSE JUST INTENSIFIES LOVE.
THEN DO HER THE FAVOR AND CUT IT OFF COLD TURKEY, OR ELSE IT WILL DRAG ON UNTIL YOU HATE EACH OTHER.

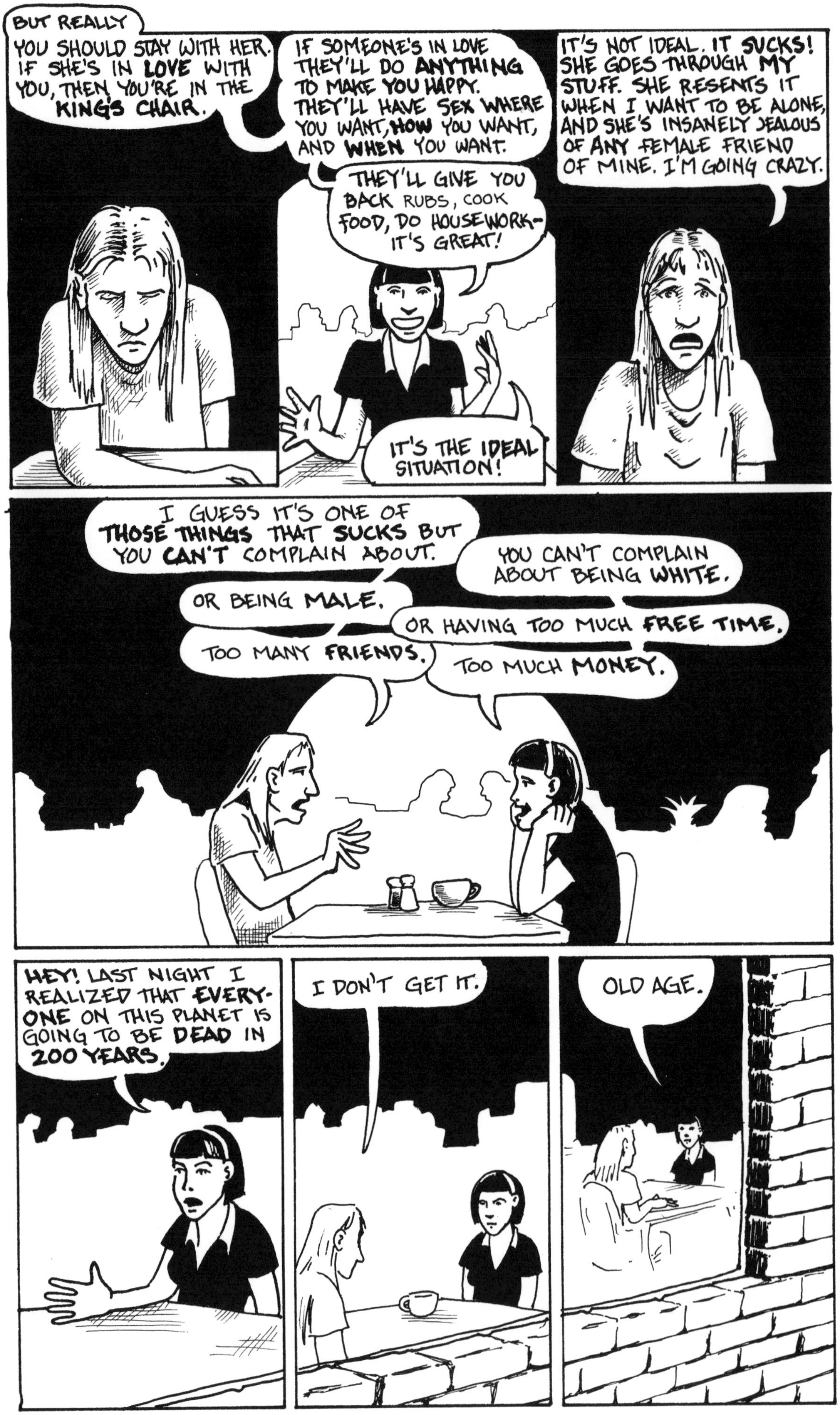

BUT REALLY
YOU SHOULD STAY WITH HER. IF SHE'S IN LOVE WITH YOU, THEN YOU'RE IN THE KING'S CHAIR.
IF SOMEONE'S IN LOVE THEY'LL DO ANYTHING TO MAKE YOU HAPPY. THEY'LL HAVE SEX WHERE YOU WANT, HOW YOU WANT, AND WHEN YOU WANT.
THEY'LL GIVE YOU BACK RUBS, COOK FOOD, DO HOUSEWORK- IT'S GREAT!
IT'S THE IDEAL SITUATION!
IT'S NOT IDEAL. IT SUCKS! SHE GOES THROUGH MY STUFF. SHE RESENTS IT WHEN I WANT TO BE ALONE, AND SHE'S INSANELY JEALOUS OF ANY FEMALE FRIEND OF MINE. I'M GOING CRAZY.
I GUESS IT'S ONE OF THOSE THINGS THAT SUCKS BUT YOU CAN'T COMPLAIN ABOUT.
YOU CAN'T COMPLAIN ABOUT BEING WHITE.
OR BEING MALE.
OR HAVING TOO MUCH FREE TIME.
TOO MANY FRIENDS.
TOO MUCH MONEY.
HEY! LAST NIGHT I REALIZED THAT EVERY-ONE ON THIS PLANET IS GOING TO BE DEAD IN 200 YEARS.
I DON'T GET IT.
OLD AGE.

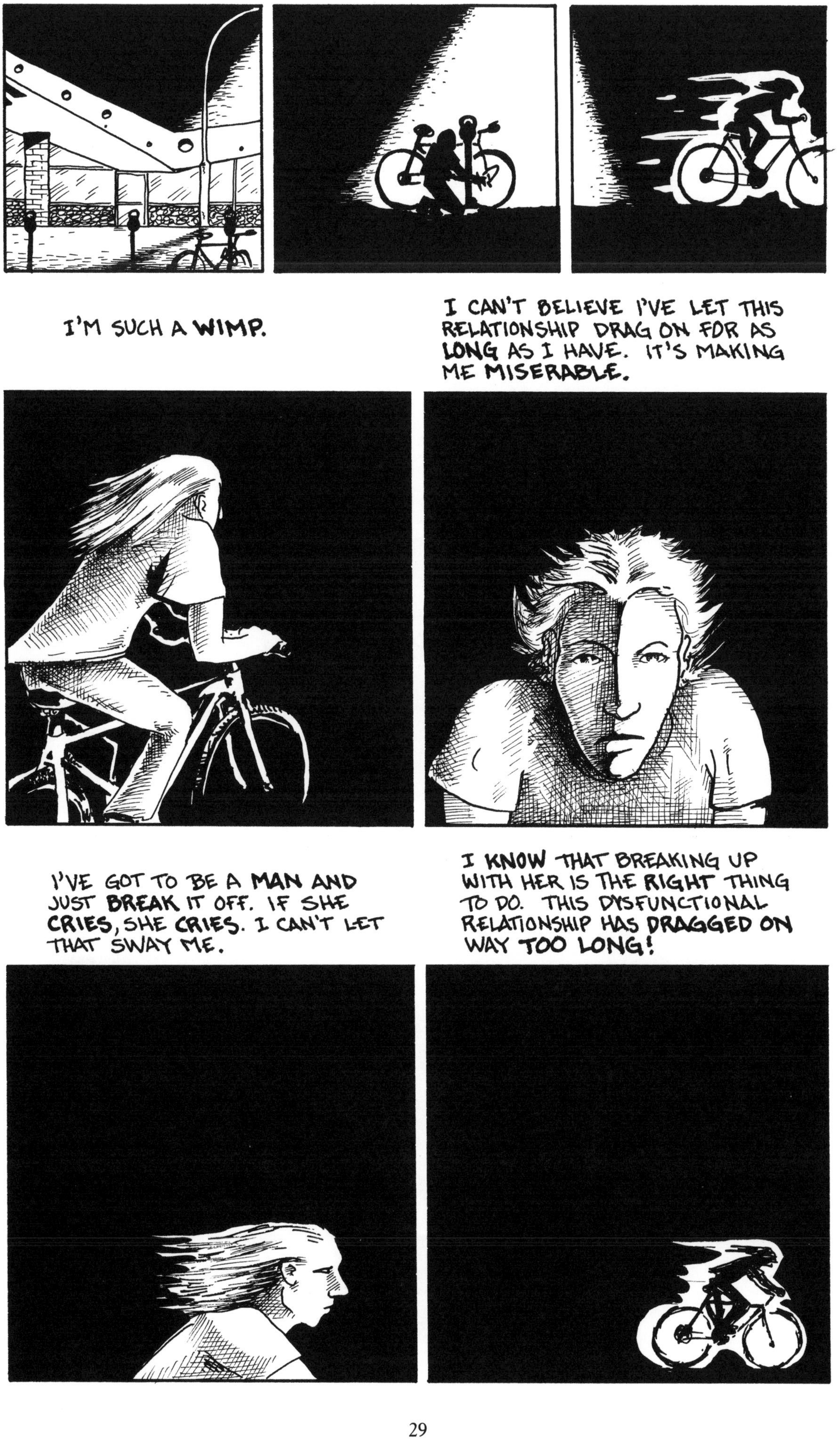
I'M SUCH A WIMP.
I CAN'T BELIEVE I'VE LET THIS RELATIONSHIP DRAG ON FOR AS LONG AS I HAVE. IT'S MAKING ME MISERABLE.
I'VE GOT TO BE A MAN AND JUST BREAK IT OFF. IF SHE CRIES, SHE CRIES. I CAN'T LET THAT SWAY ME.
I KNOW THAT BREAKING UP WITH HER IS THE RIGHT THING TO DO. THIS DYSFUNCTIONAL RELATIONSHIP HAS DRAGGED ON WAY TOO LONG!

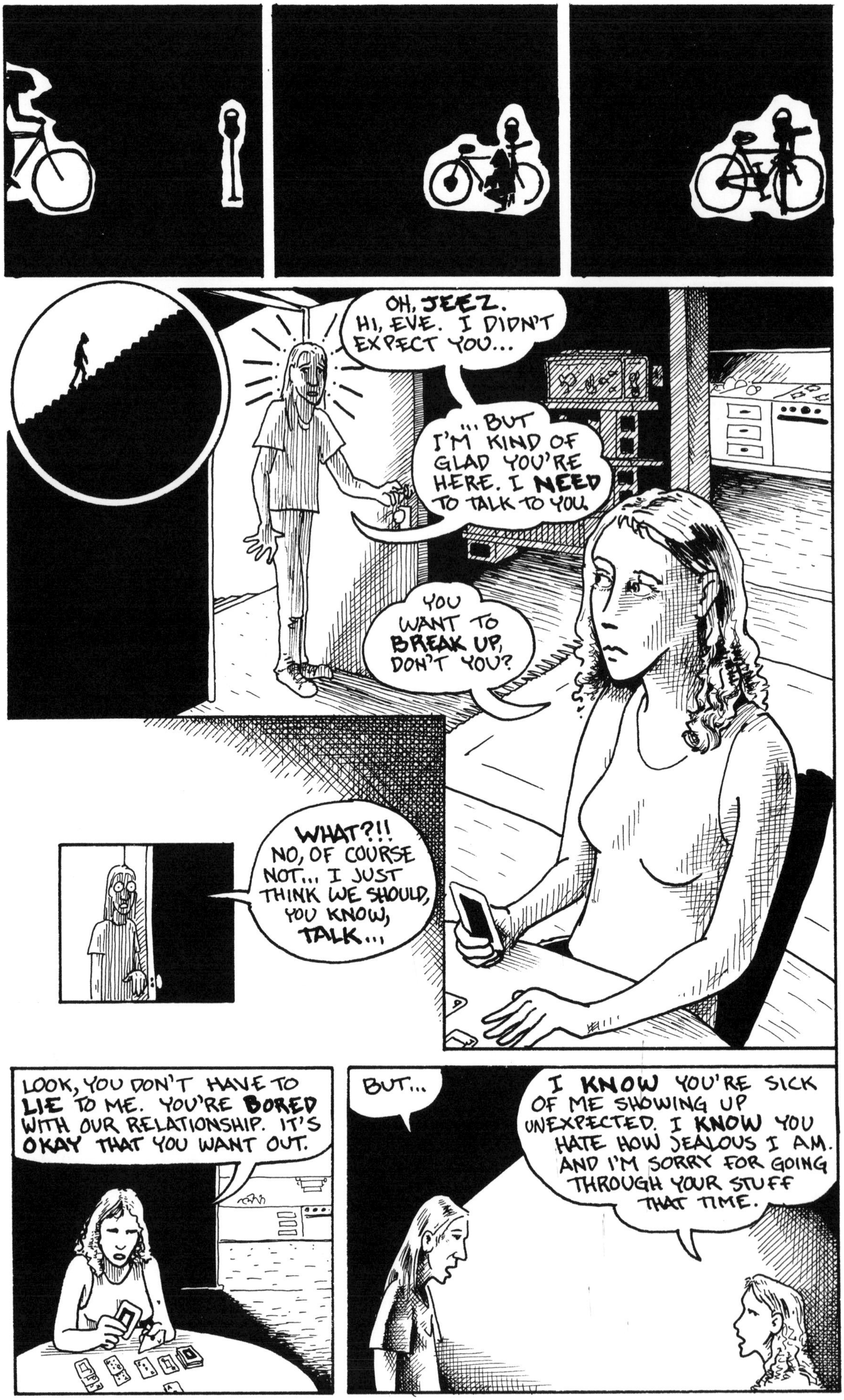
OH, JEEZ. HI, EVE. I DIDN'T EXPECT YOU...
...BUT I'M KIND OF GLAD YOU'RE HERE. I NEED TO TALK TO YOU.
YOU WANT TO BREAK UP, DON'T YOU?
WHAT?!! NO, OF COURSE NOT... I JUST THINK WE SHOULD, YOU KNOW, TALK...
LOOK, YOU DON'T HAVE TO LIE TO ME. YOU'RE BORED WITH OUR RELATIONSHIP. IT'S OKAY THAT YOU WANT OUT.
BUT...
I KNOW YOU'RE SICK OF ME SHOWING UP UNEXPECTED. I KNOW YOU HATE HOW JEALOUS I AM. AND I'M SORRY FOR GOING THROUGH YOUR STUFF THAT TIME.

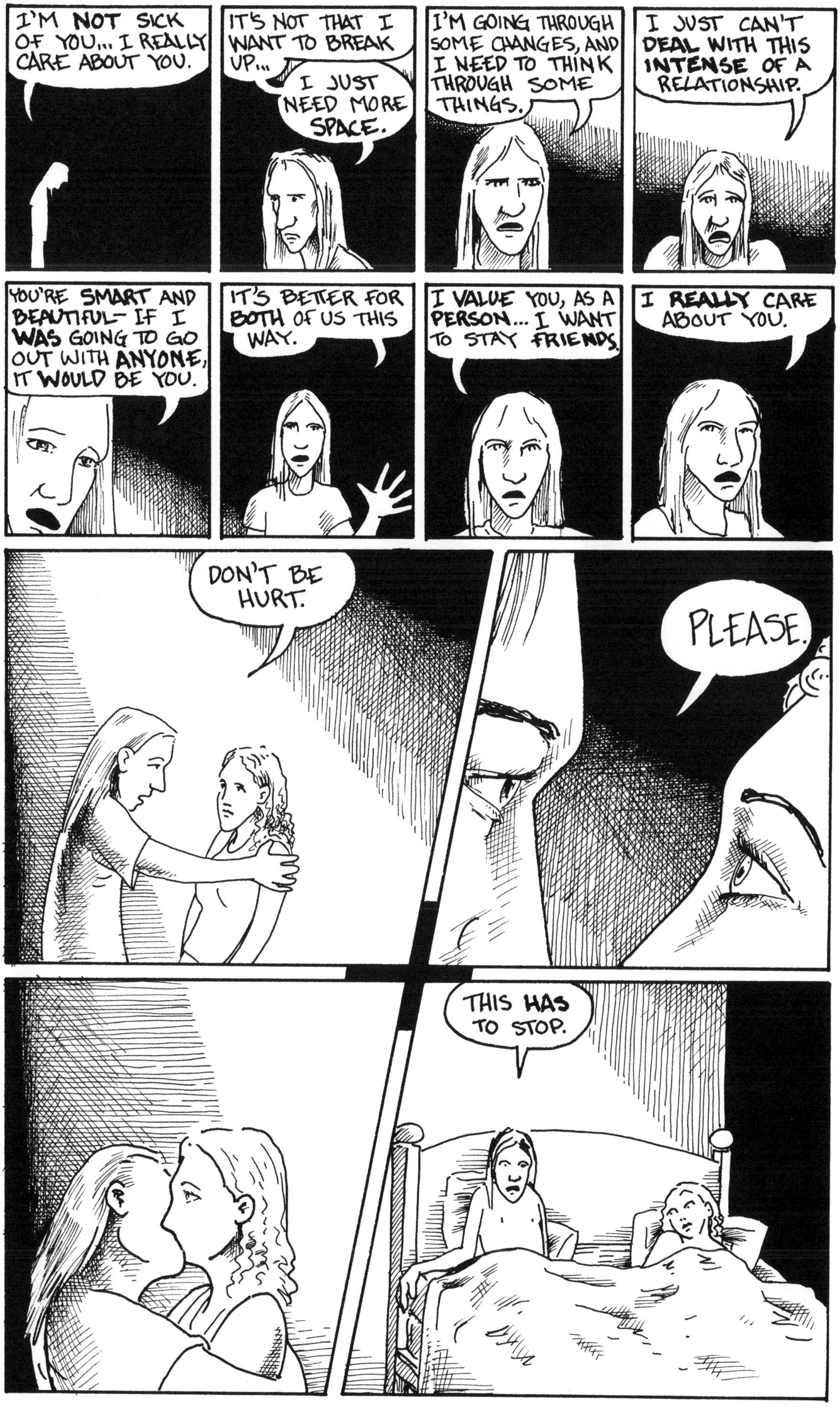
I'M NOT SICK OF YOU... I REALLY CARE ABOUT YOU.
IT'S NOT THAT I WANT TO BREAK UP...
I JUST NEED MORE SPACE.
I'M GOING THROUGH SOME CHANGES, AND I NEED TO THINK THROUGH SOME THINGS.
I JUST CAN'T DEAL WITH THIS INTENSE OF A RELATIONSHIP.
YOU'RE SMART AND BEAUTIFUL- IF I WAS GOING TO GO OUT WITH ANYONE, IT WOULD BE YOU.
IT'S BETTER FOR BOTH OF US THIS WAY.
I VALUE YOU, AS A PERSON... I WANT TO STAY FRIENDS.
I REALLY CARE ABOUT YOU.
DON'T BE HURT.
PLEASE.
THIS HAS TO STOP.

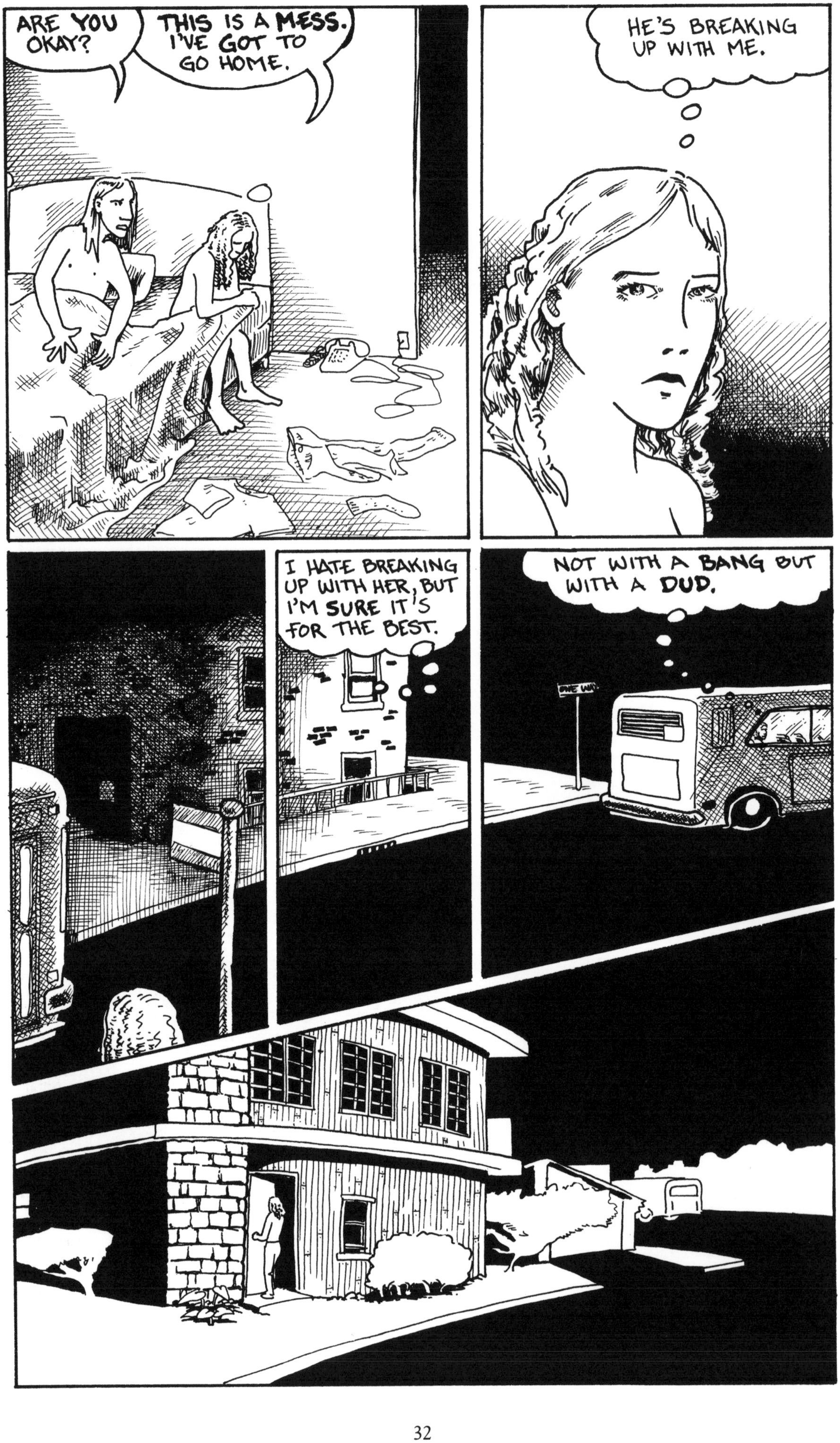
ARE YOU OKAY?
THIS IS A MESS. I'VE GOT TO GO HOME.
HE'S BREAKING UP WITH ME.
I HATE BREAKING UP WITH HER, BUT I'M SURE IT'S FOR THE BEST.
NOT WITH A BANG BUT WITH A DUD.

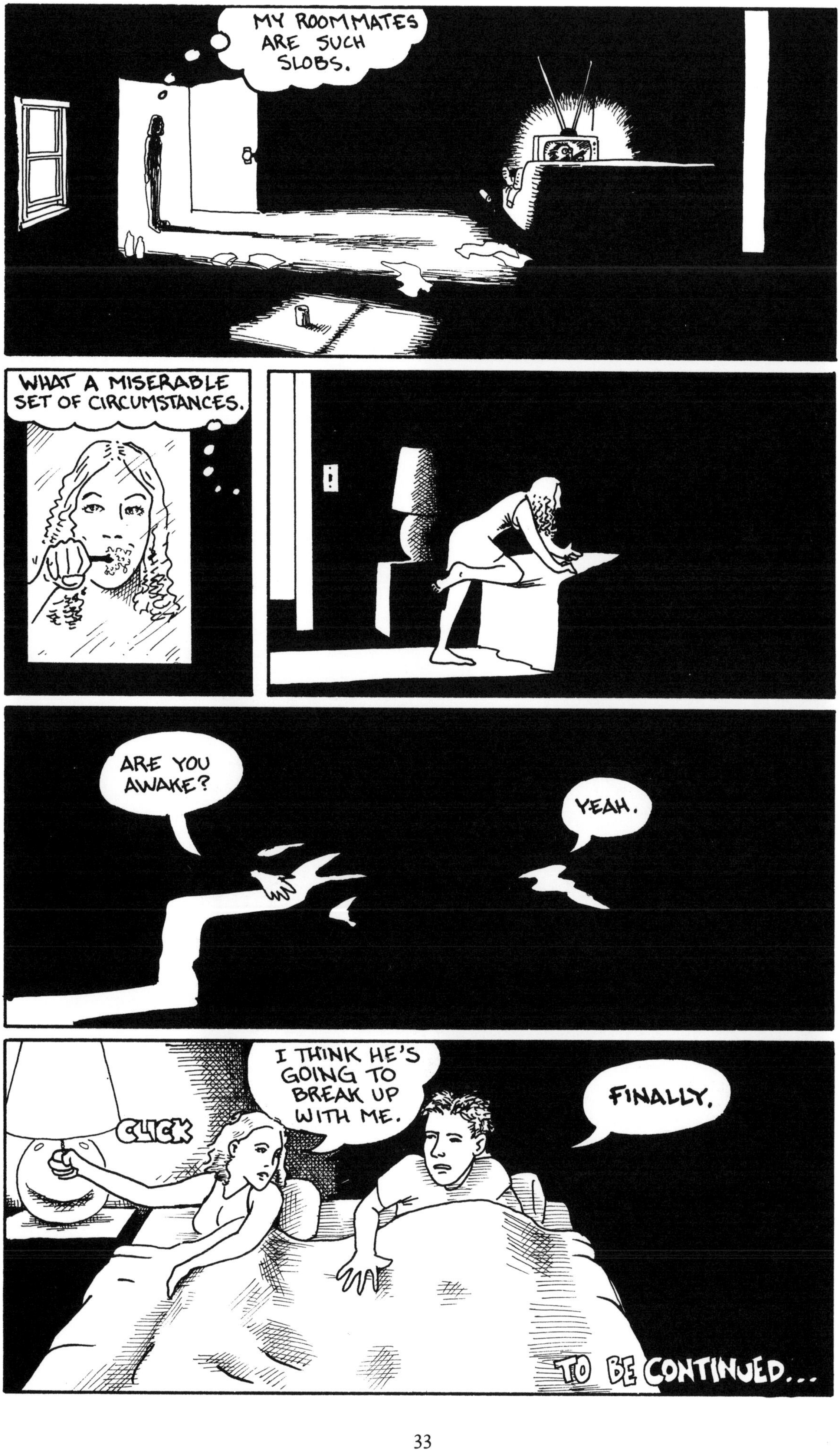
MY ROOMMATES ARE SUCH SLOBS.
WHAT A MISERABLE SET OF CIRCUMSTANCES.
ARE YOU AWAKE?
YEAH.
CLICK
I THINK HE'S GOING TO BREAK UP WITH ME.
FINALLY.
TO BE CONTINUED...

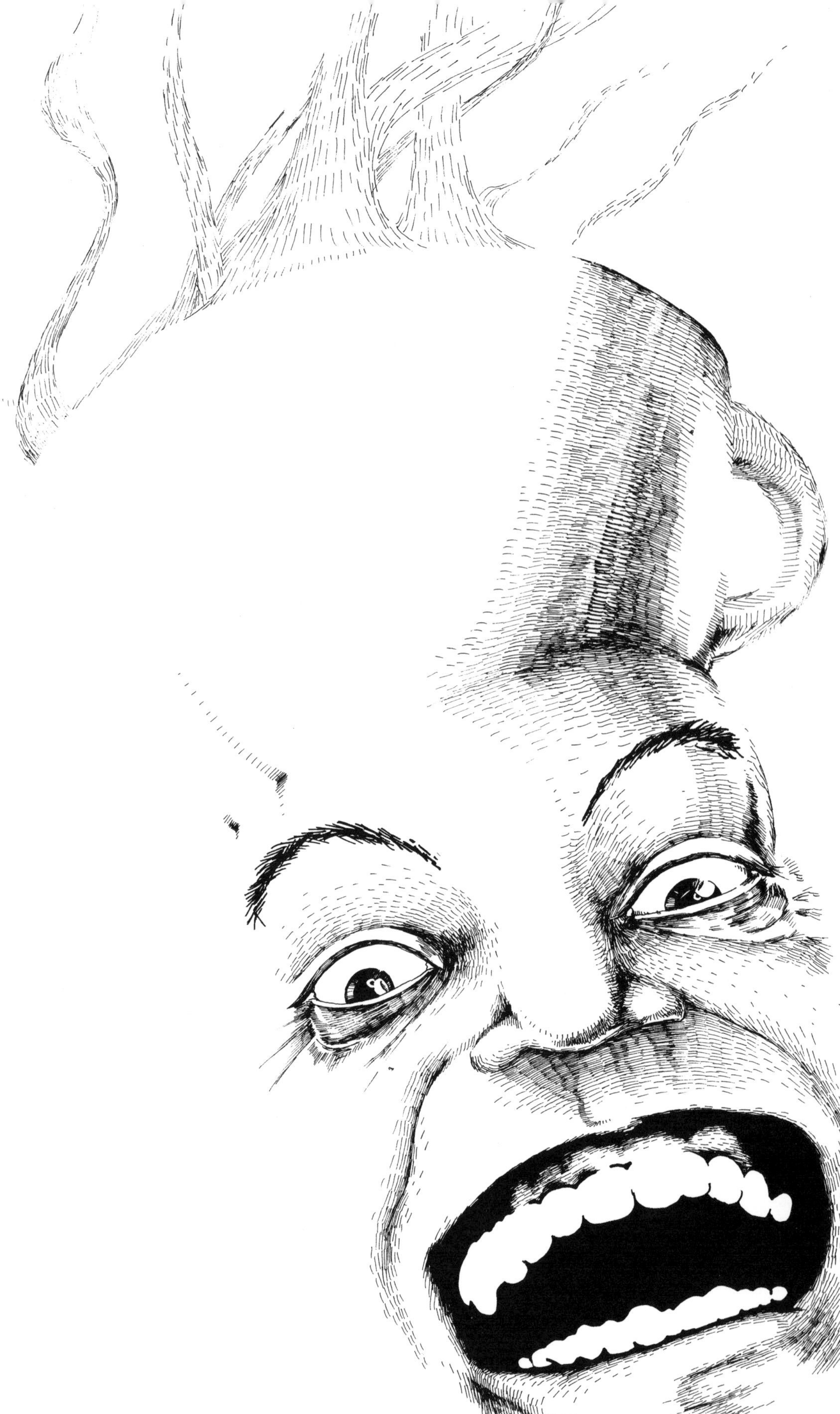
SHANNON WHEELER 1994©

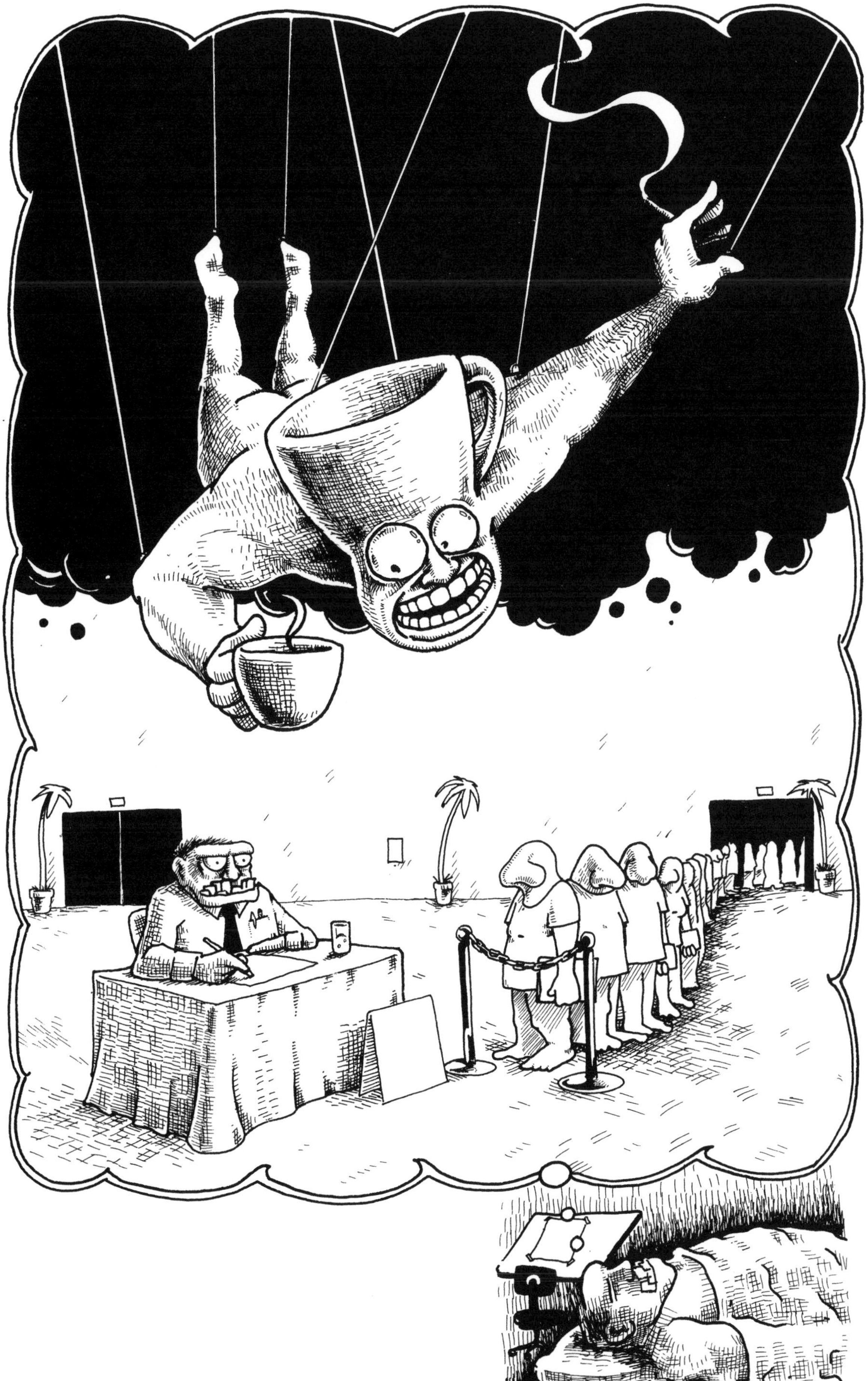

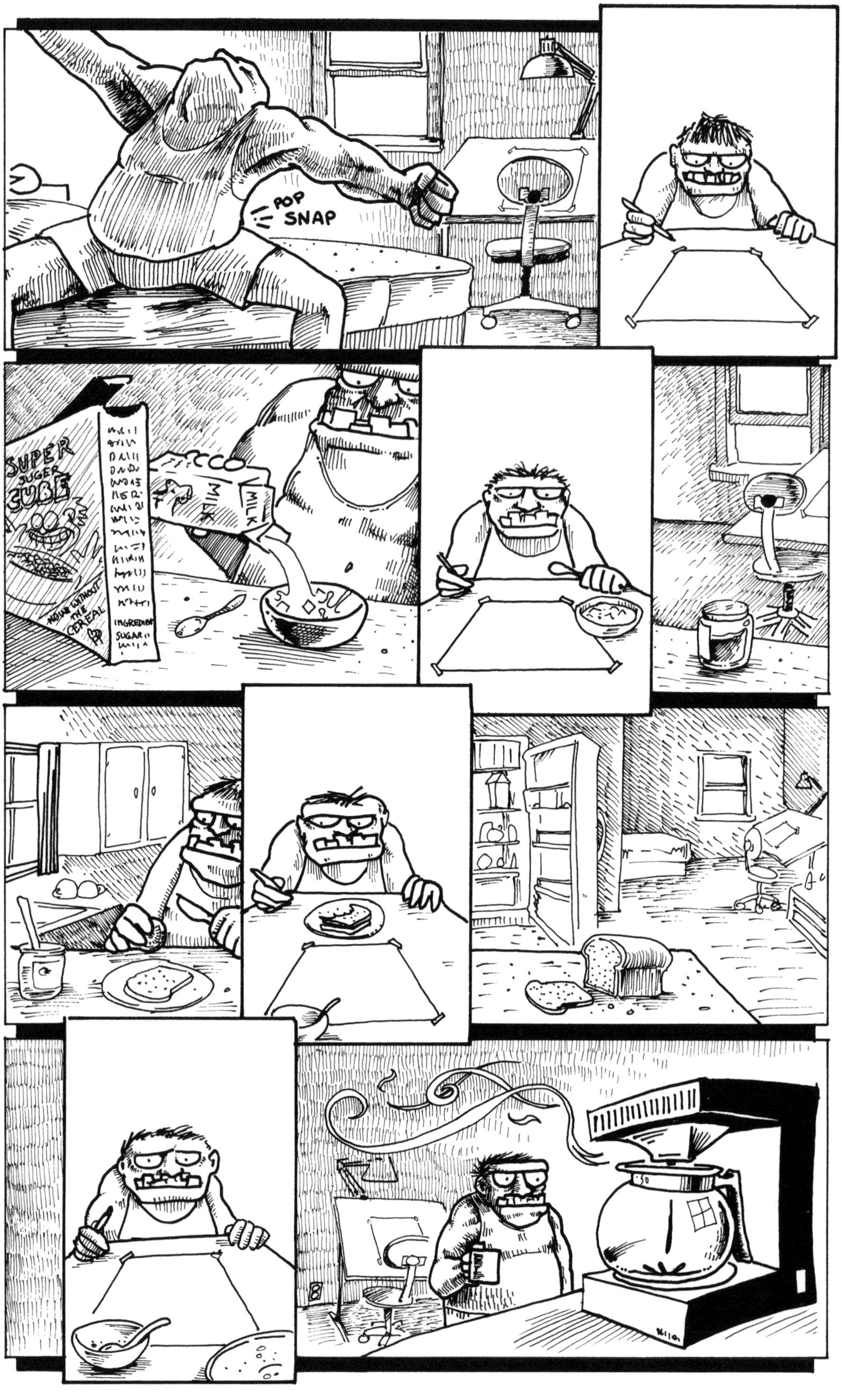

POP
SNAP
SUPER SUGER CUBE
NOW WITHOUT THE CEREAL
INGREDIENT
SUGAR
MILK
MILK

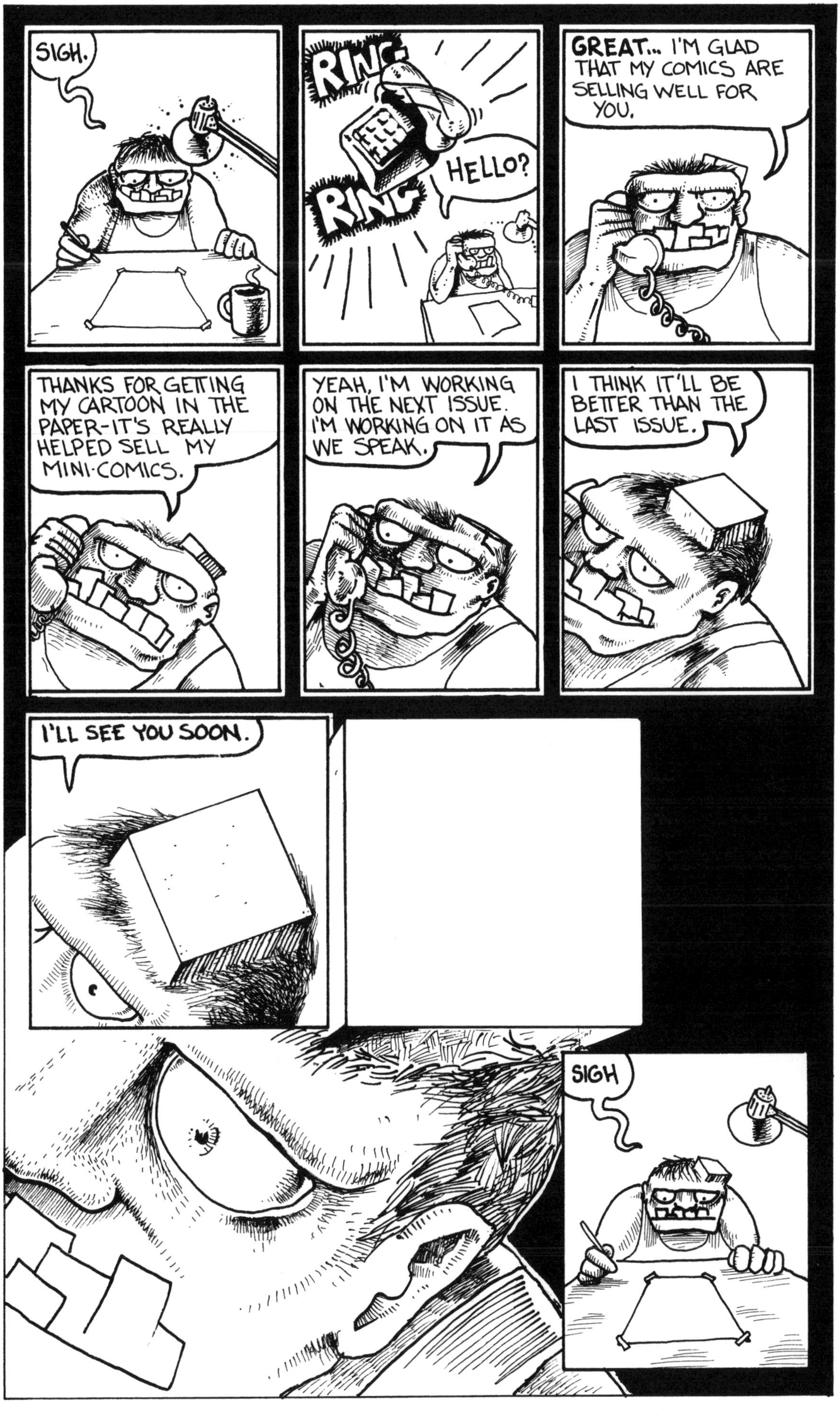
SIGH.
RING
RING
HELLO?
GREAT... I'M GLAD THAT MY COMICS ARE SELLING WELL FOR YOU.
THANKS FOR GETTING MY CARTOON IN THE PAPER-IT'S REALLY HELPED SELL MY MINI-COMICS.
YEAH, I'M WORKING ON THE NEXT ISSUE. I'M WORKING ON IT AS WE SPEAK.
I THINK IT'LL BE BETTER THAN THE LAST ISSUE.
I'LL SEE YOU SOON.
SIGH

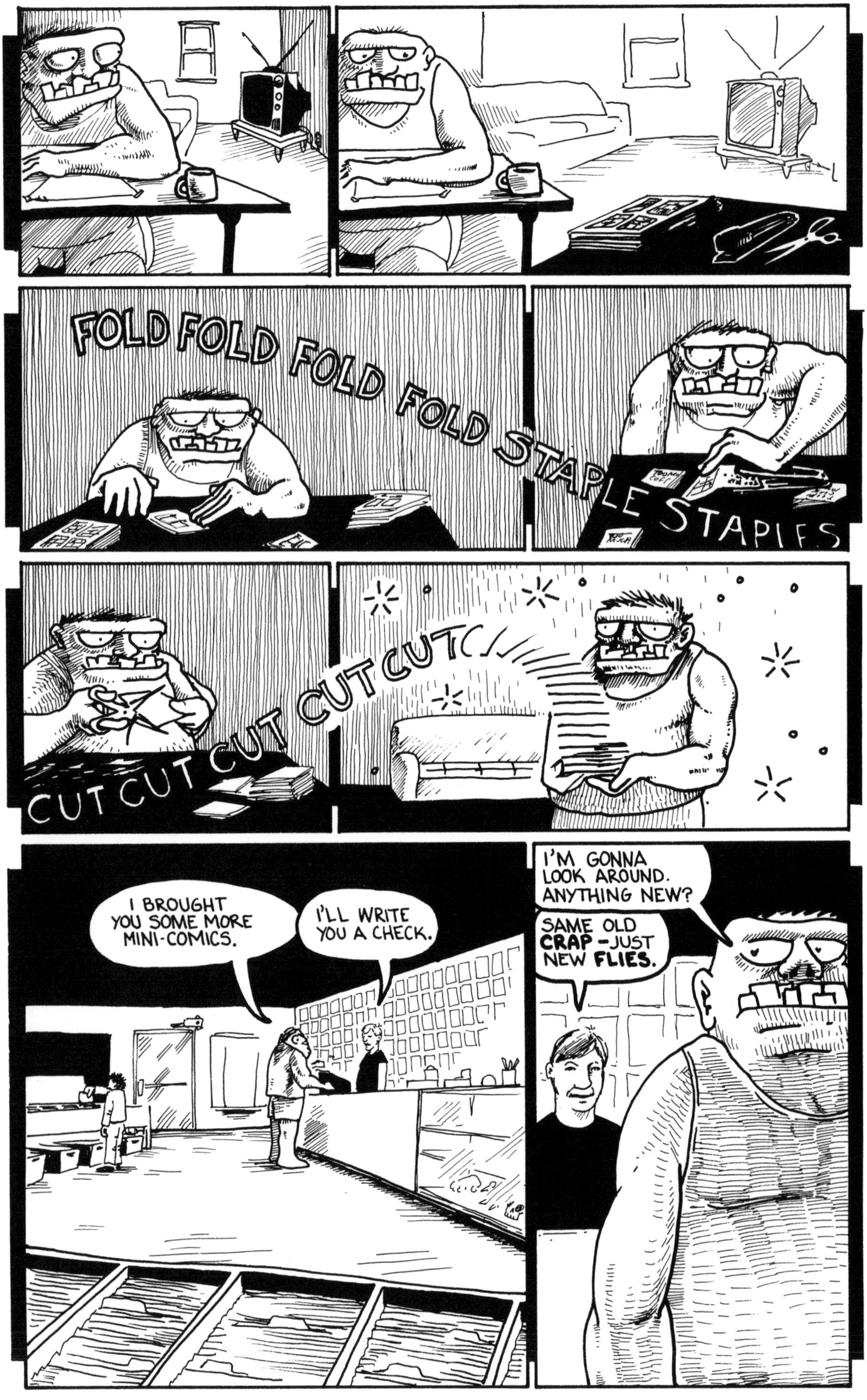
FOLD FOLD FOLD FOLD STAPLE STAPLES
CUT CUT CUT CUT CUT CUTC
I BROUGHT YOU SOME MORE MINI-COMICS.
I'LL WRITE YOU A CHECK.
I'M GONNA LOOK AROUND. ANYTHING NEW?
SAME OLD **CRAP** –JUST NEW **FLIES.**

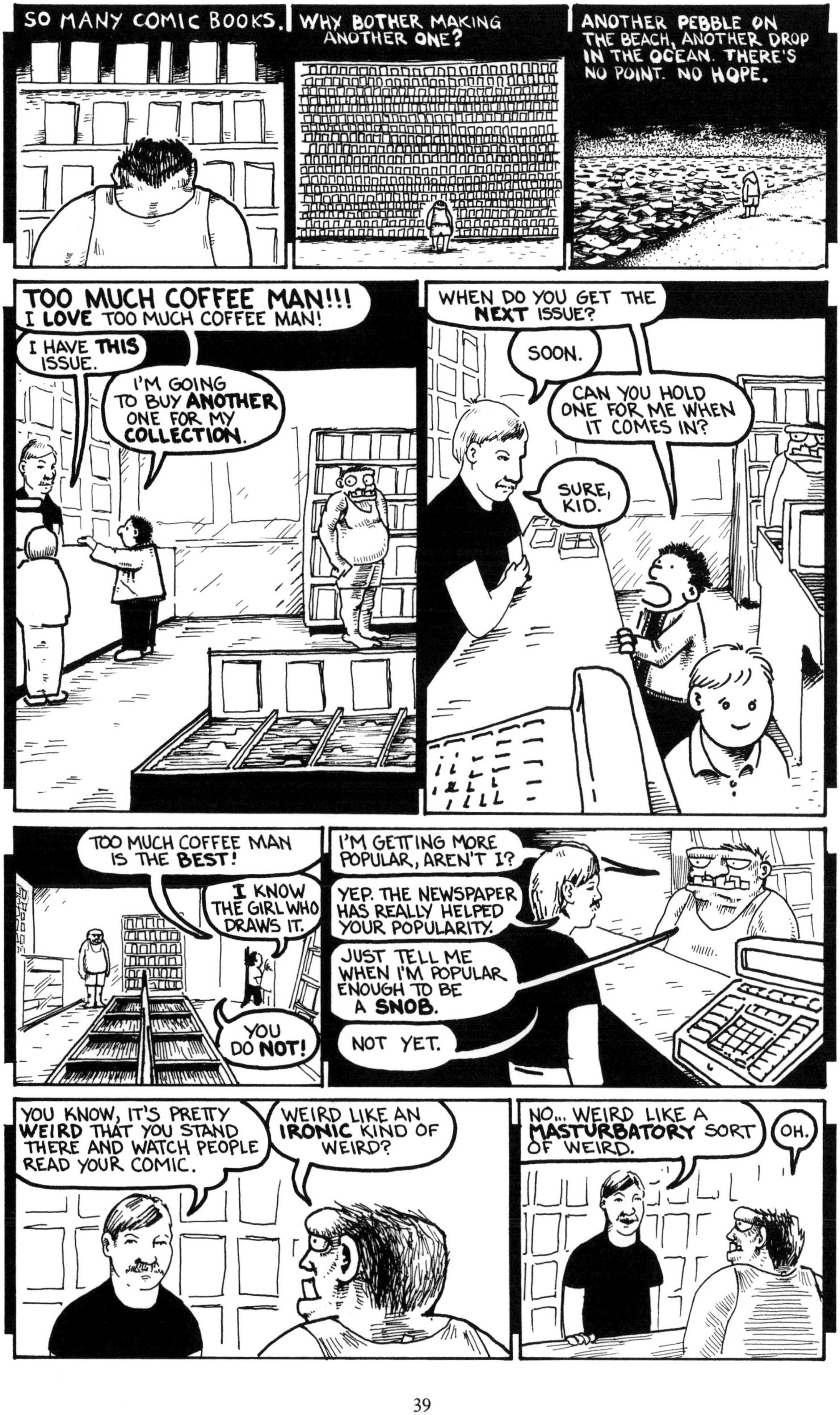
SO MANY COMIC BOOKS.
WHY BOTHER MAKING ANOTHER ONE?
ANOTHER PEBBLE ON THE BEACH, ANOTHER DROP IN THE OCEAN. THERE'S NO POINT. NO HOPE.
TOO MUCH COFFEE MAN!!! I LOVE TOO MUCH COFFEE MAN!
I HAVE THIS ISSUE.
I'M GOING TO BUY ANOTHER ONE FOR MY COLLECTION.
WHEN DO YOU GET THE NEXT ISSUE?
SOON.
CAN YOU HOLD ONE FOR ME WHEN IT COMES IN?
SURE, KID.
TOO MUCH COFFEE MAN IS THE BEST!
I KNOW THE GIRL WHO DRAWS IT.
YOU DO NOT!
I'M GETTING MORE POPULAR, AREN'T I?
YEP. THE NEWSPAPER HAS REALLY HELPED YOUR POPULARITY.
JUST TELL ME WHEN I'M POPULAR ENOUGH TO BE A SNOB.
NOT YET.
YOU KNOW, IT'S PRETTY WEIRD THAT YOU STAND THERE AND WATCH PEOPLE READ YOUR COMIC.
WEIRD LIKE AN IRONIC KIND OF WEIRD?
NO... WEIRD LIKE A MASTURBATORY SORT OF WEIRD.
OH.

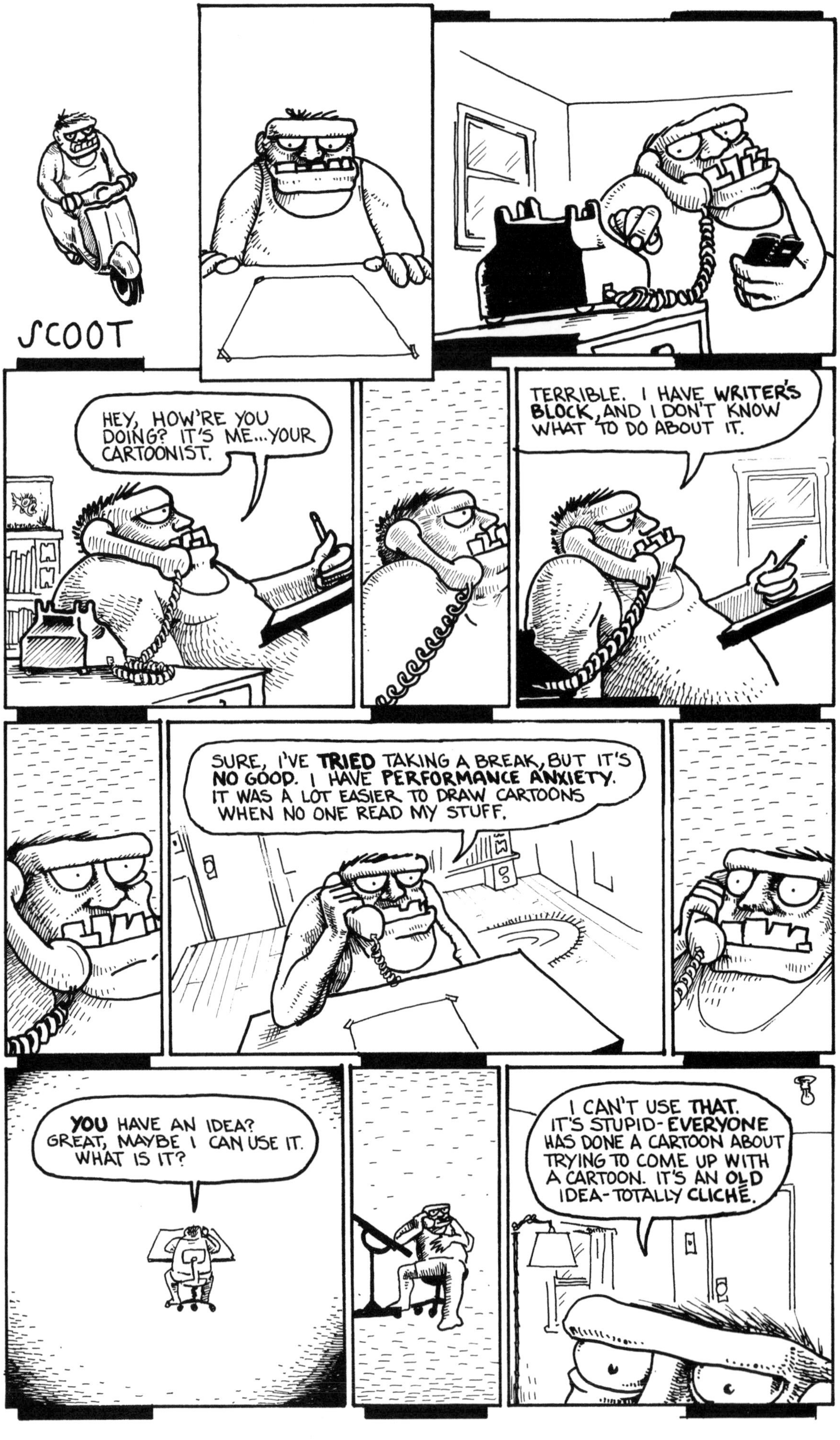
SCOOT
HEY, HOW'RE YOU DOING? IT'S ME...YOUR CARTOONIST.
TERRIBLE. I HAVE WRITER'S BLOCK, AND I DON'T KNOW WHAT TO DO ABOUT IT.
SURE, I'VE TRIED TAKING A BREAK, BUT IT'S NO GOOD. I HAVE PERFORMANCE ANXIETY. IT WAS A LOT EASIER TO DRAW CARTOONS WHEN NO ONE READ MY STUFF.
YOU HAVE AN IDEA? GREAT, MAYBE I CAN USE IT. WHAT IS IT?
I CAN'T USE THAT. IT'S STUPID-EVERYONE HAS DONE A CARTOON ABOUT TRYING TO COME UP WITH A CARTOON. IT'S AN OLD IDEA-TOTALLY CLICHÉ.

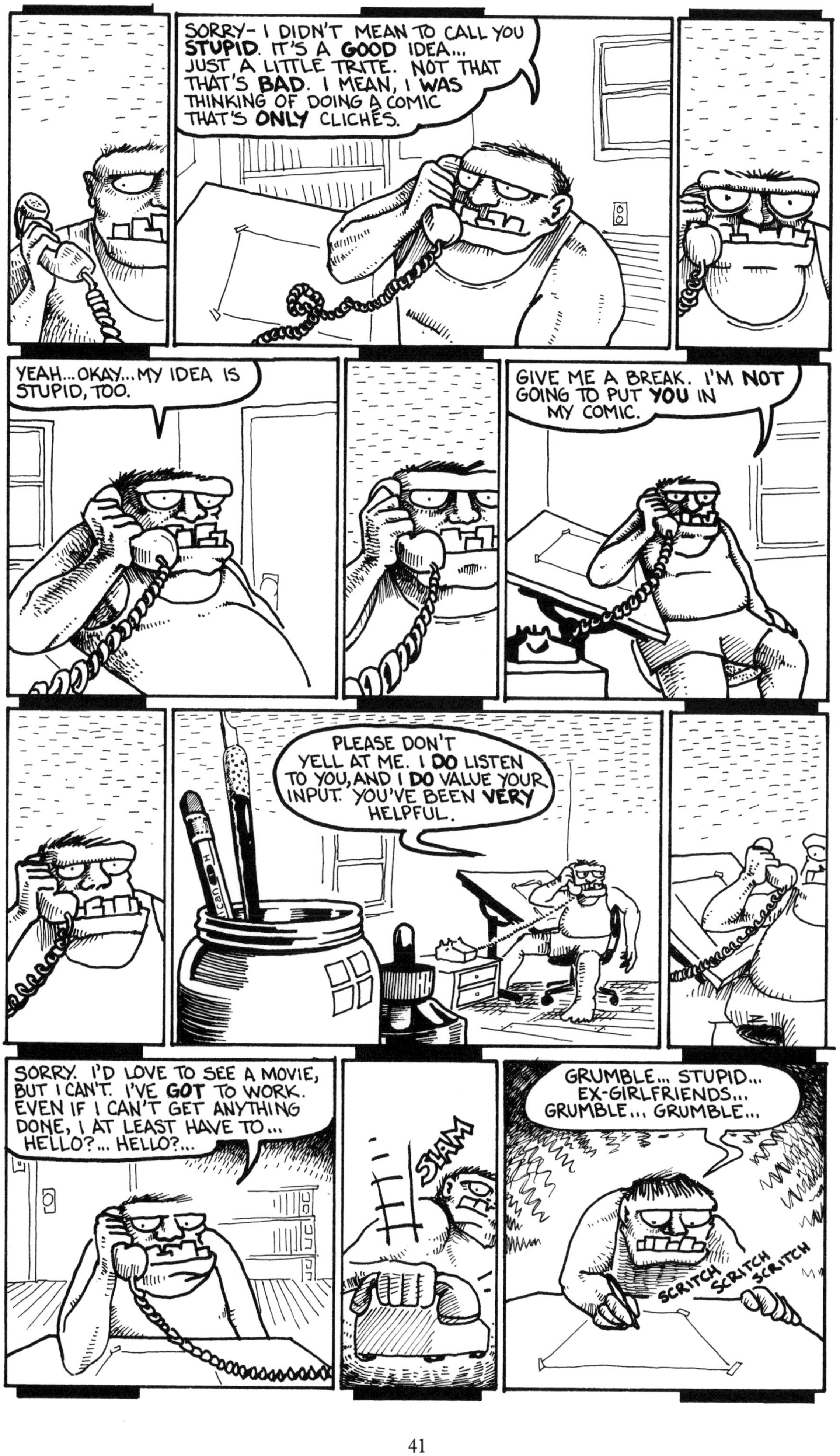
SORRY- I DIDN'T MEAN TO CALL YOU STUPID. IT'S A GOOD IDEA... JUST A LITTLE TRITE. NOT THAT THAT'S BAD. I MEAN, I WAS THINKING OF DOING A COMIC THAT'S ONLY CLICHÉS.
YEAH...OKAY...MY IDEA IS STUPID, TOO.
GIVE ME A BREAK. I'M NOT GOING TO PUT YOU IN MY COMIC.
PLEASE DON'T YELL AT ME. I DO LISTEN TO YOU, AND I DO VALUE YOUR INPUT. YOU'VE BEEN VERY HELPFUL.
SORRY. I'D LOVE TO SEE A MOVIE, BUT I CAN'T. I'VE GOT TO WORK. EVEN IF I CAN'T GET ANYTHING DONE, I AT LEAST HAVE TO... HELLO?... HELLO?...
SLAM
GRUMBLE... STUPID... EX-GIRLFRIENDS... GRUMBLE... GRUMBLE...
SCRITCH SCRITCH SCRITCH

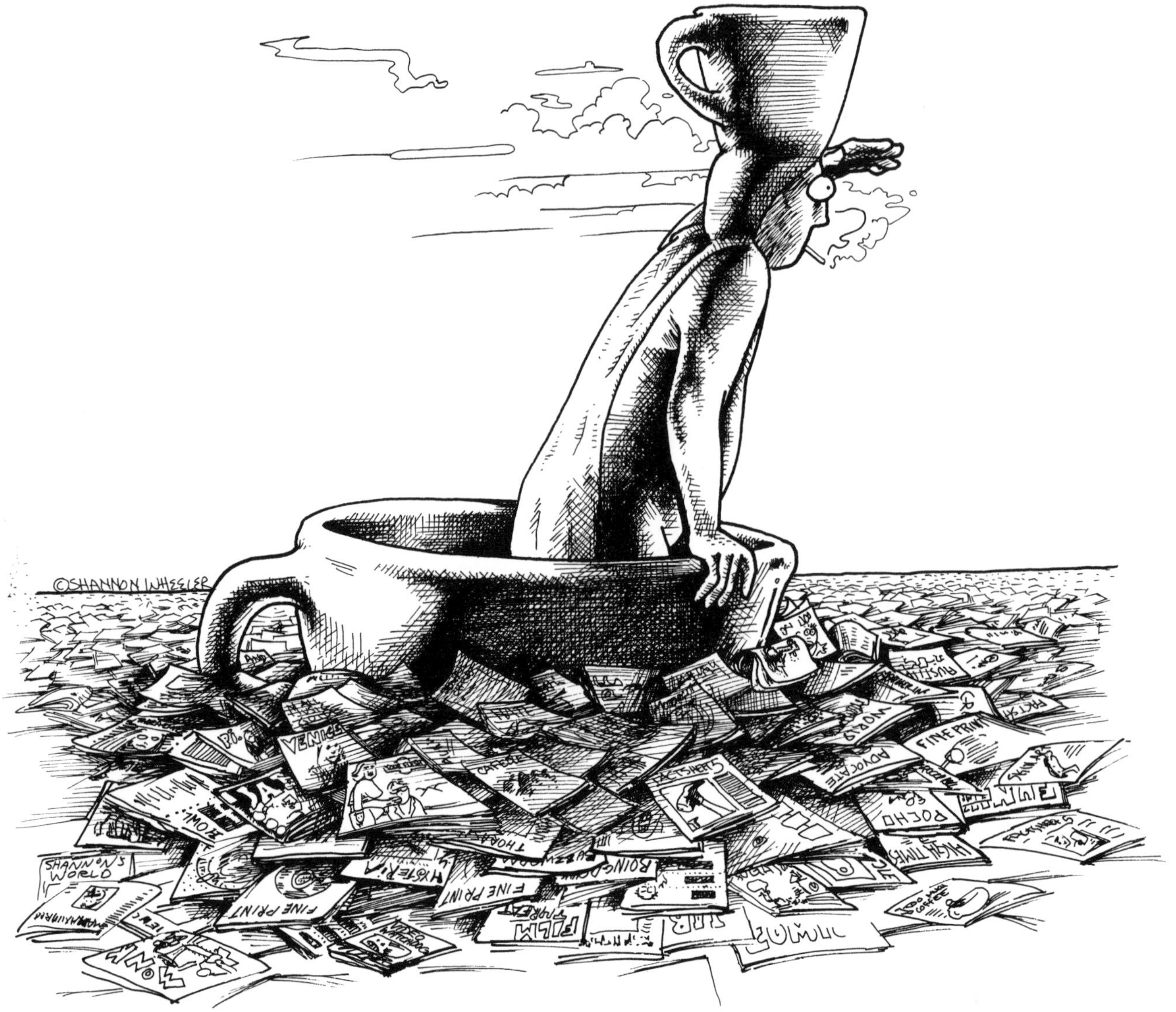
©SHANNON WHEELER
SHANNON'S WORLD
VENICE
FINE PRINT
FINE PRINT
FINE PRINT
ADVOCATE
HYSTERIA
BOING BOING
FILM

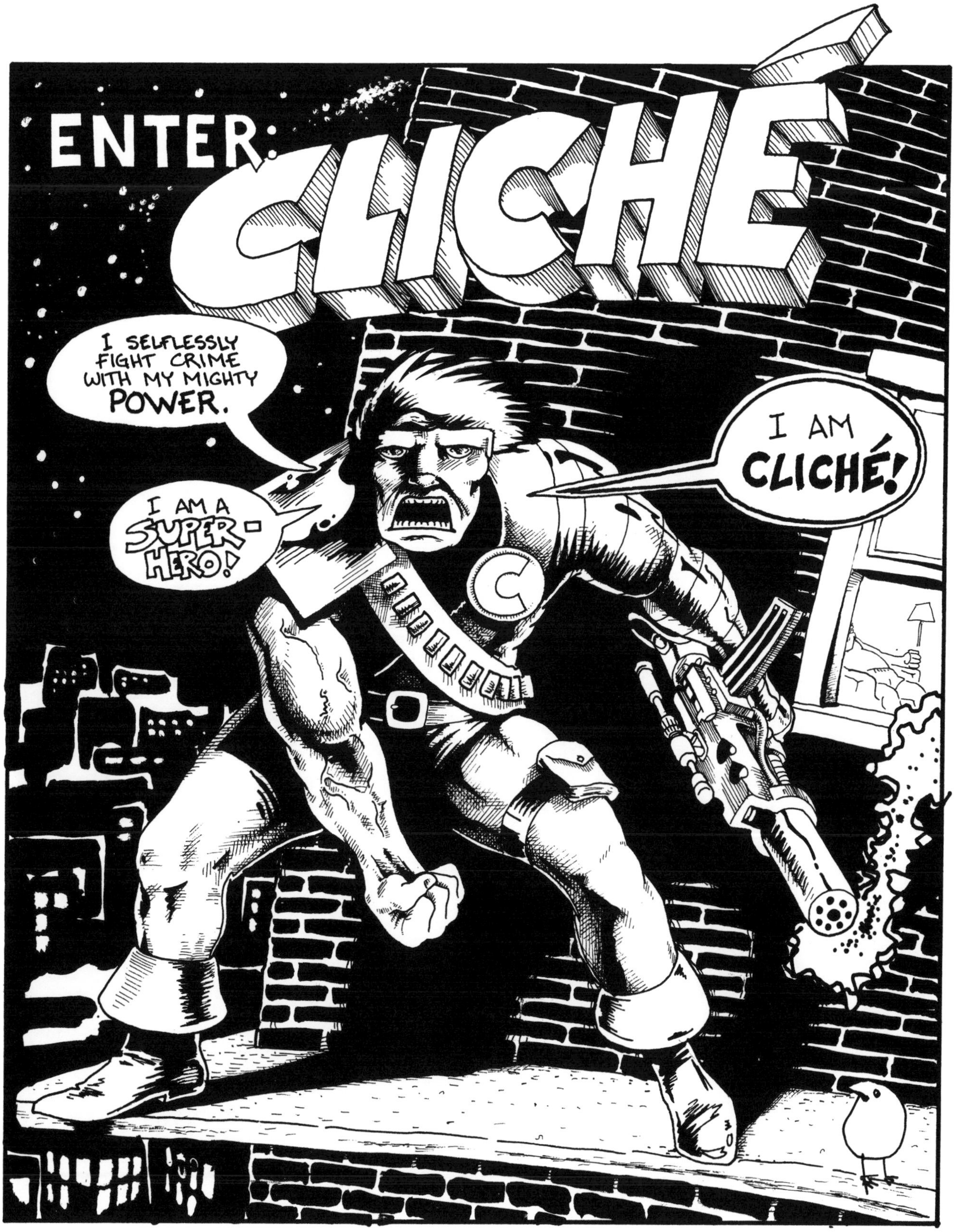
ENTER: CLICHÉ
I SELFLESSLY FIGHT CRIME WITH MY MIGHTY POWER.
I AM A SUPER-HERO!
I AM CLICHÉ!

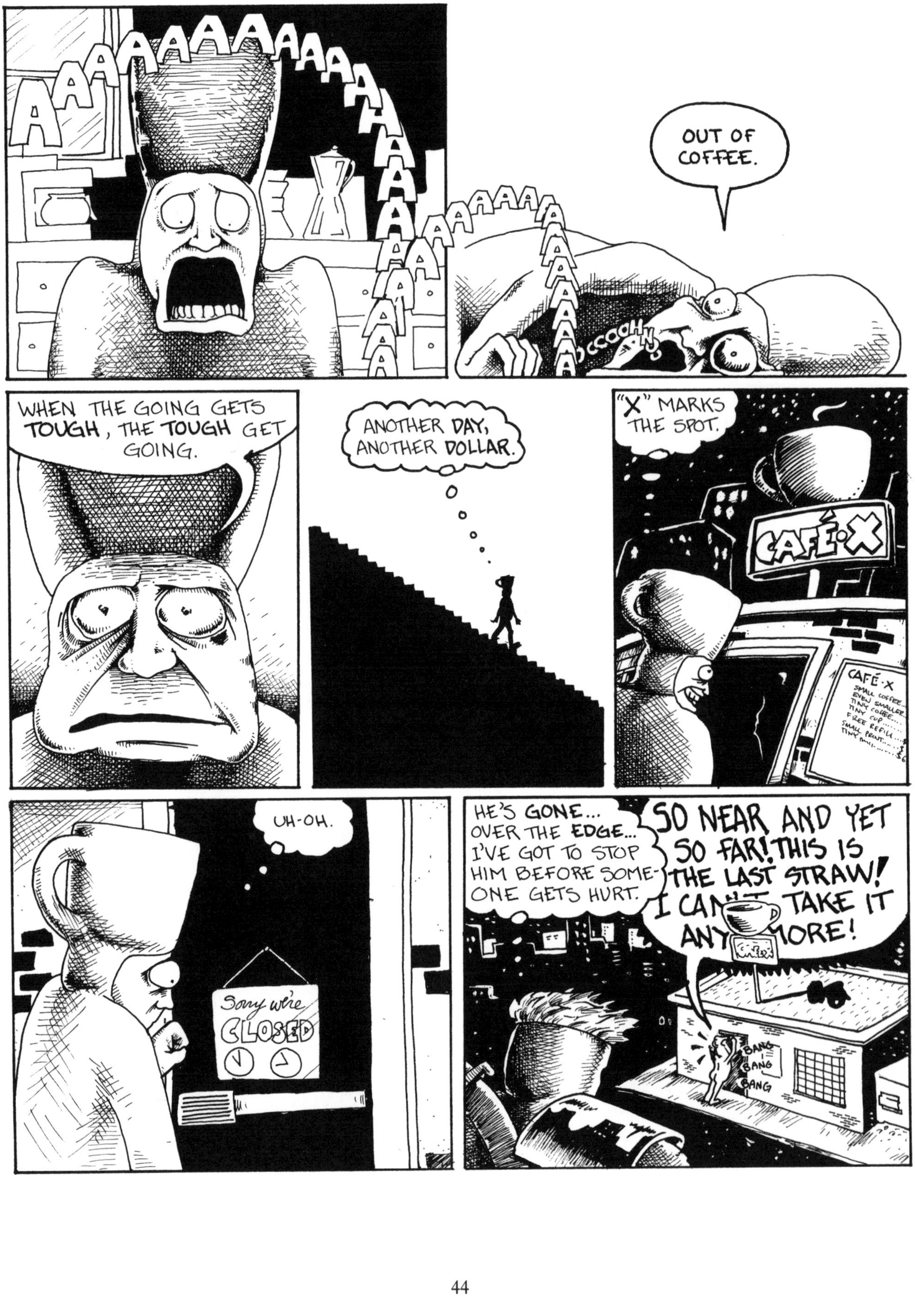
AAAAAAAAAAAAAAAAAAAAAAAAAAAAAAAAAAAAAAA
OUT OF COFFEE.
WHEN THE GOING GETS TOUGH, THE TOUGH GET GOING.
ANOTHER DAY, ANOTHER DOLLAR.
"X" MARKS THE SPOT.
CAFÉ·X
UH-OH.
Sorry we're CLOSED
HE'S GONE... OVER THE EDGE... I'VE GOT TO STOP HIM BEFORE SOME-ONE GETS HURT.
SO NEAR AND YET SO FAR! THIS IS THE LAST STRAW! I CA TAKE IT ANY ORE!
BANG BANG BANG

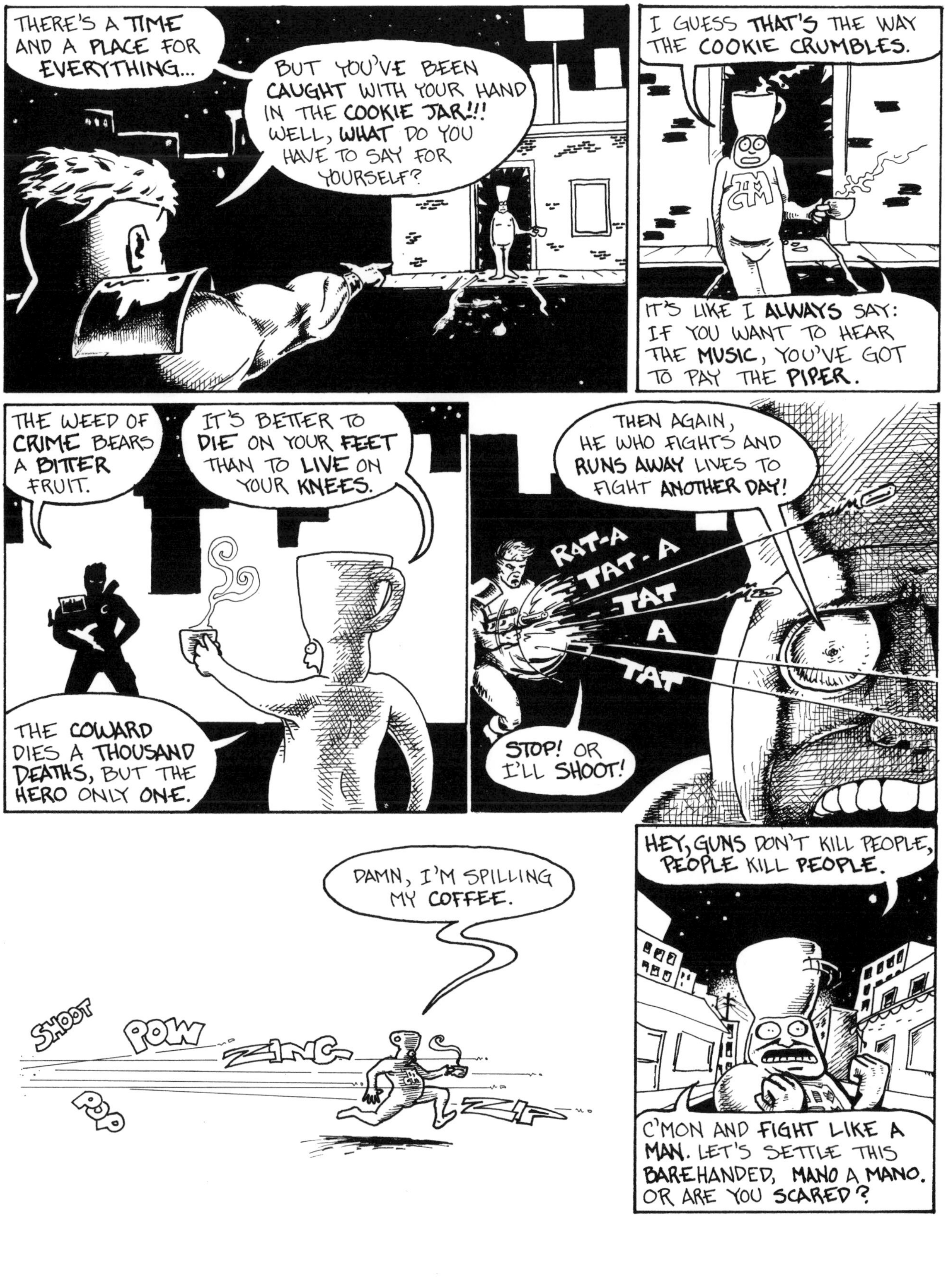
THERE'S A TIME AND A PLACE FOR EVERYTHING...
BUT YOU'VE BEEN CAUGHT WITH YOUR HAND IN THE COOKIE JAR!!! WELL, WHAT DO YOU HAVE TO SAY FOR YOURSELF?
I GUESS THAT'S THE WAY THE COOKIE CRUMBLES.
CM
IT'S LIKE I ALWAYS SAY: IF YOU WANT TO HEAR THE MUSIC, YOU'VE GOT TO PAY THE PIPER.
THE WEED OF CRIME BEARS A BITTER FRUIT.
IT'S BETTER TO DIE ON YOUR FEET THAN TO LIVE ON YOUR KNEES.
THE COWARD DIES A THOUSAND DEATHS, BUT THE HERO ONLY ONE.
THEN AGAIN, HE WHO FIGHTS AND RUNS AWAY LIVES TO FIGHT ANOTHER DAY!
RAT-A TAT-A TAT A TAT
STOP! OR I'LL SHOOT!
DAMN, I'M SPILLING MY COFFEE.
SHOOT
POW
ZING
POP
ZIP
HEY, GUNS DON'T KILL PEOPLE, PEOPLE KILL PEOPLE.
C'MON AND FIGHT LIKE A MAN. LET'S SETTLE THIS BAREHANDED, MANO A MANO. OR ARE YOU SCARED?

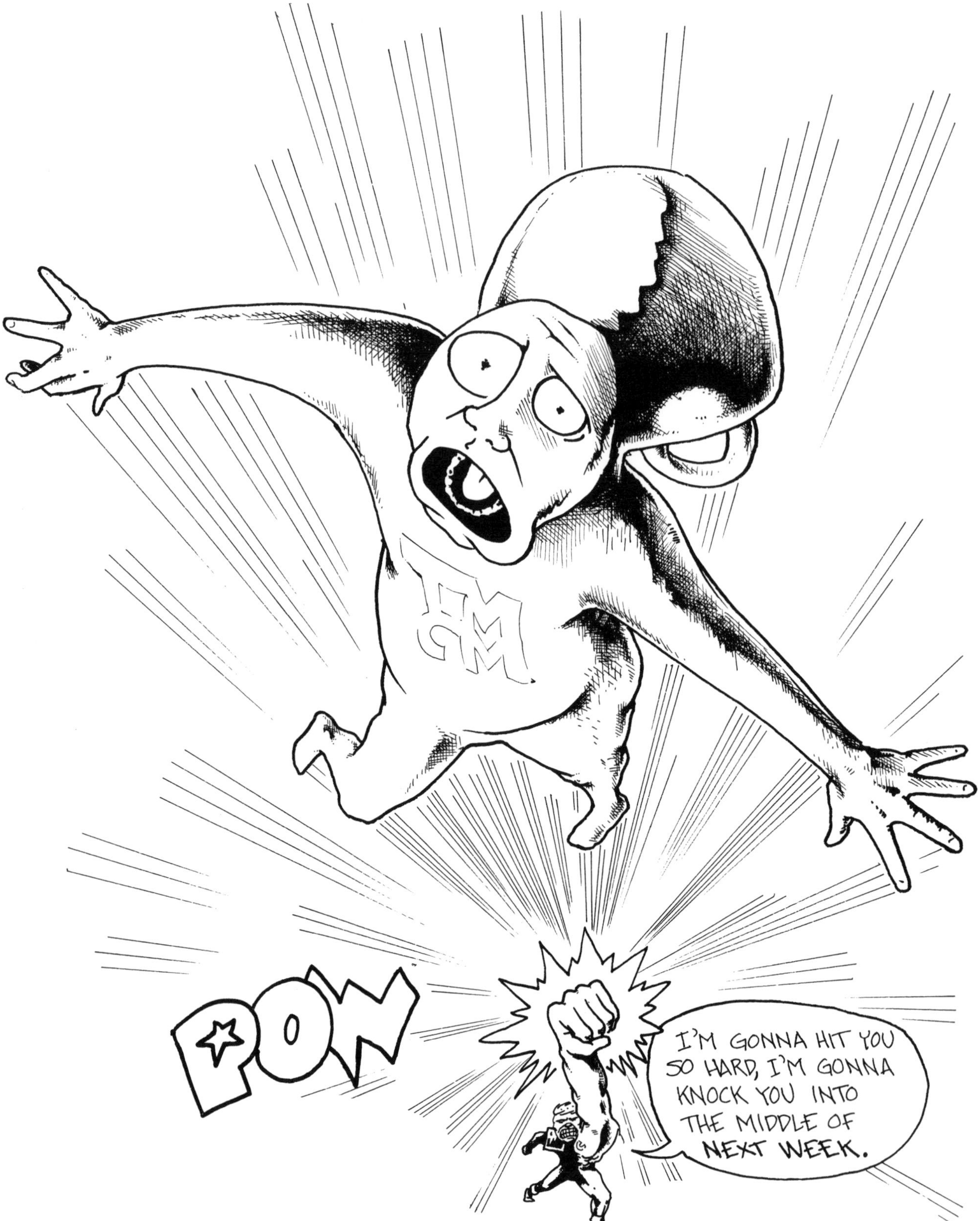

PON
I'M GONNA HIT YOU SO HARD, I'M GONNA KNOCK YOU INTO THE MIDDLE OF NEXT WEEK.

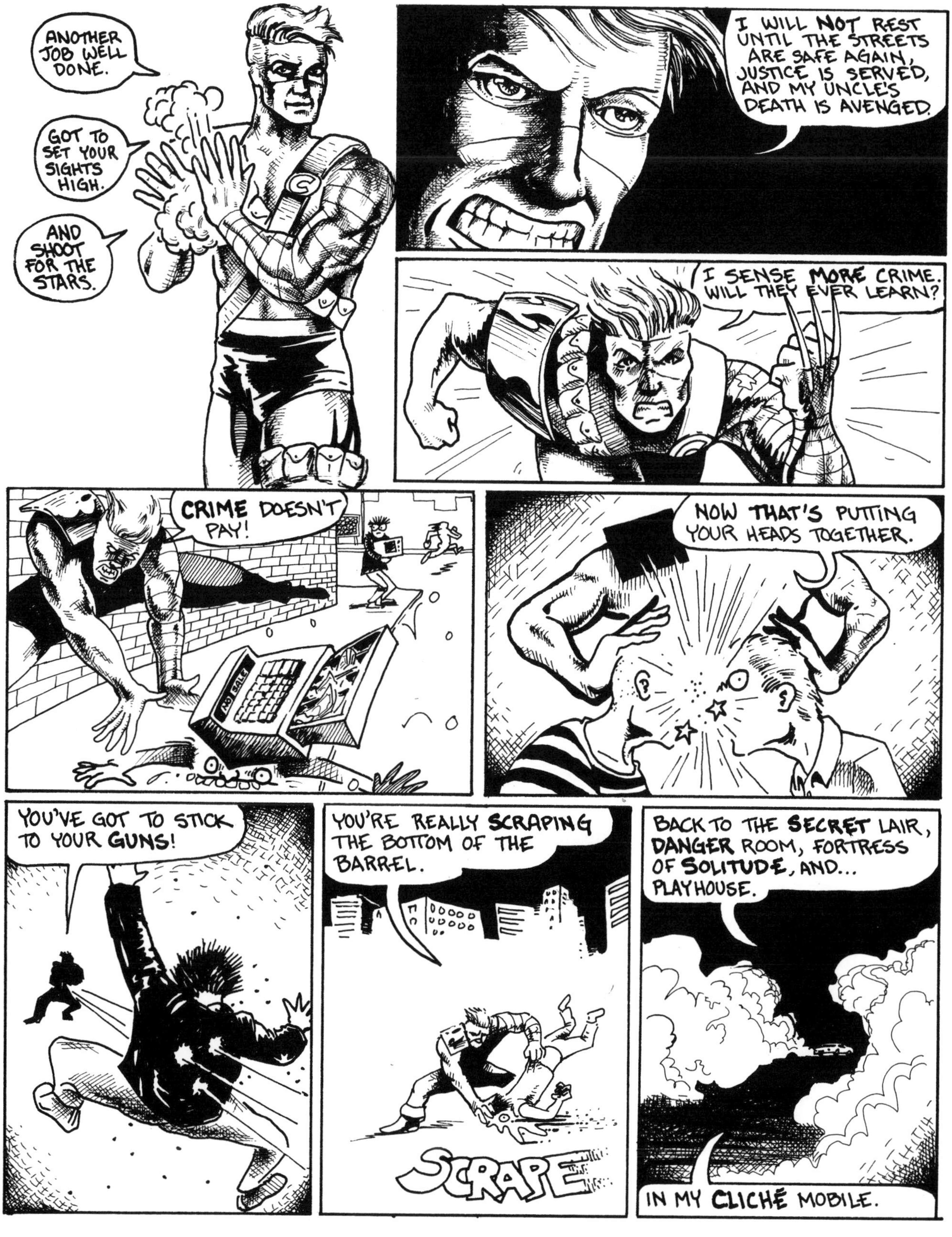
ANOTHER JOB WELL DONE.
GOT TO SET YOUR SIGHTS HIGH.
AND SHOOT FOR THE STARS.
I WILL NOT REST UNTIL THE STREETS ARE SAFE AGAIN, JUSTICE IS SERVED, AND MY UNCLE'S DEATH IS AVENGED.
I SENSE MORE CRIME. WILL THEY EVER LEARN?
CRIME DOESN'T PAY!
NOW THAT'S PUTTING YOUR HEADS TOGETHER.
YOU'VE GOT TO STICK TO YOUR GUNS!
YOU'RE REALLY SCRAPING THE BOTTOM OF THE BARREL.
SCRAPE
BACK TO THE SECRET LAIR, DANGER ROOM, FORTRESS OF SOLITUDE, AND... PLAYHOUSE.
IN MY CLICHÉ MOBILE.

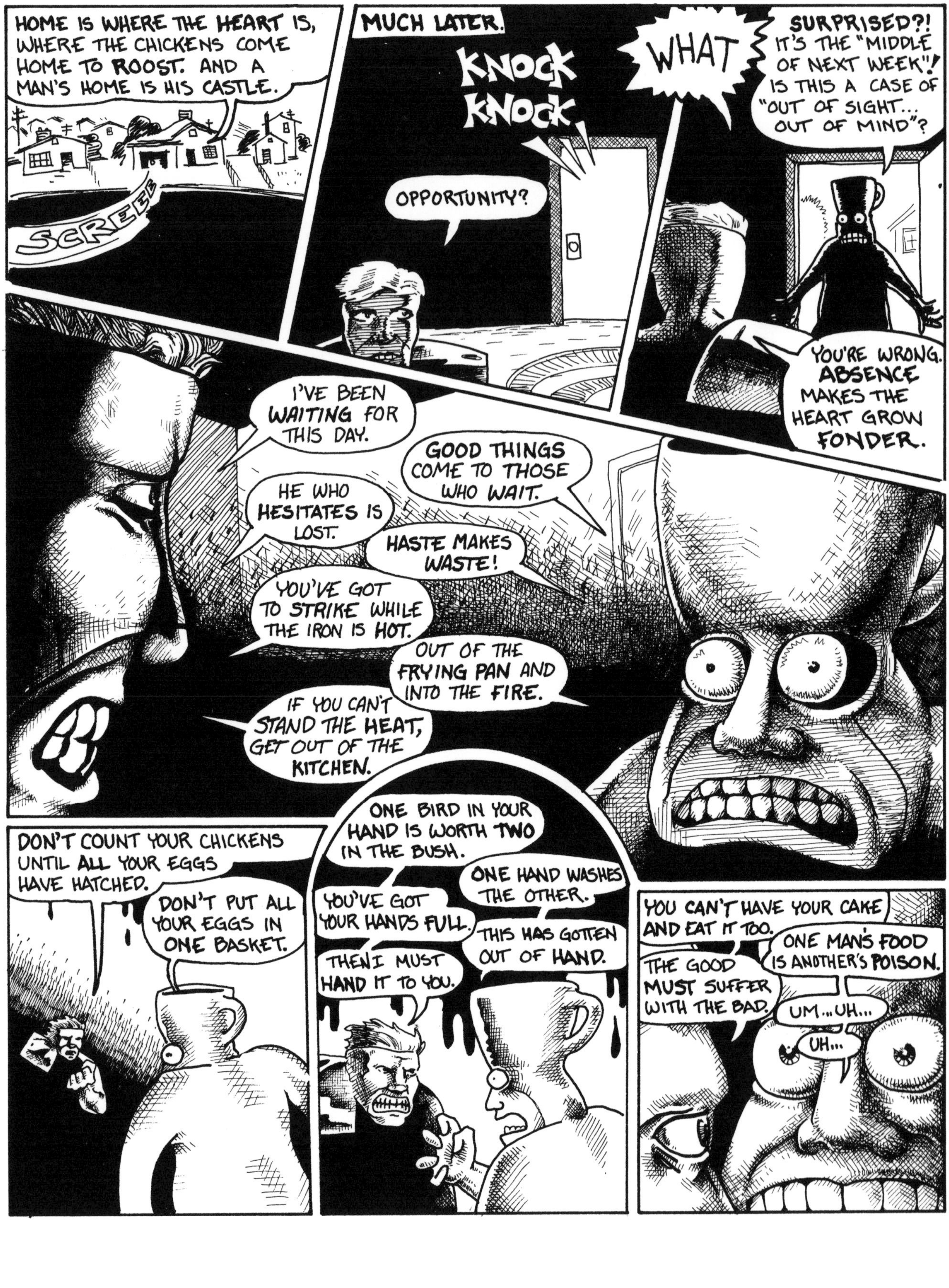
HOME IS WHERE THE HEART IS, WHERE THE CHICKENS COME HOME TO ROOST. AND A MAN'S HOME IS HIS CASTLE.
SCREEE
MUCH LATER.
KNOCK KNOCK
OPPORTUNITY?
WHAT
SURPRISED?! IT'S THE "MIDDLE OF NEXT WEEK"! IS THIS A CASE OF "OUT OF SIGHT... OUT OF MIND"?
YOU'RE WRONG. ABSENCE MAKES THE HEART GROW FONDER.
I'VE BEEN WAITING FOR THIS DAY.
GOOD THINGS COME TO THOSE WHO WAIT.
HE WHO HESITATES IS LOST.
HASTE MAKES WASTE!
YOU'VE GOT TO STRIKE WHILE THE IRON IS HOT.
OUT OF THE FRYING PAN AND INTO THE FIRE.
IF YOU CAN'T STAND THE HEAT, GET OUT OF THE KITCHEN.
DON'T COUNT YOUR CHICKENS UNTIL ALL YOUR EGGS HAVE HATCHED.
DON'T PUT ALL YOUR EGGS IN ONE BASKET.
ONE BIRD IN YOUR HAND IS WORTH TWO IN THE BUSH.
ONE HAND WASHES THE OTHER.
YOU'VE GOT YOUR HANDS FULL.
THIS HAS GOTTEN OUT OF HAND.
THEN I MUST HAND IT TO YOU.
YOU CAN'T HAVE YOUR CAKE AND EAT IT TOO.
ONE MAN'S FOOD IS ANOTHER'S POISON.
THE GOOD MUST SUFFER WITH THE BAD.
UM...UH...
UH...

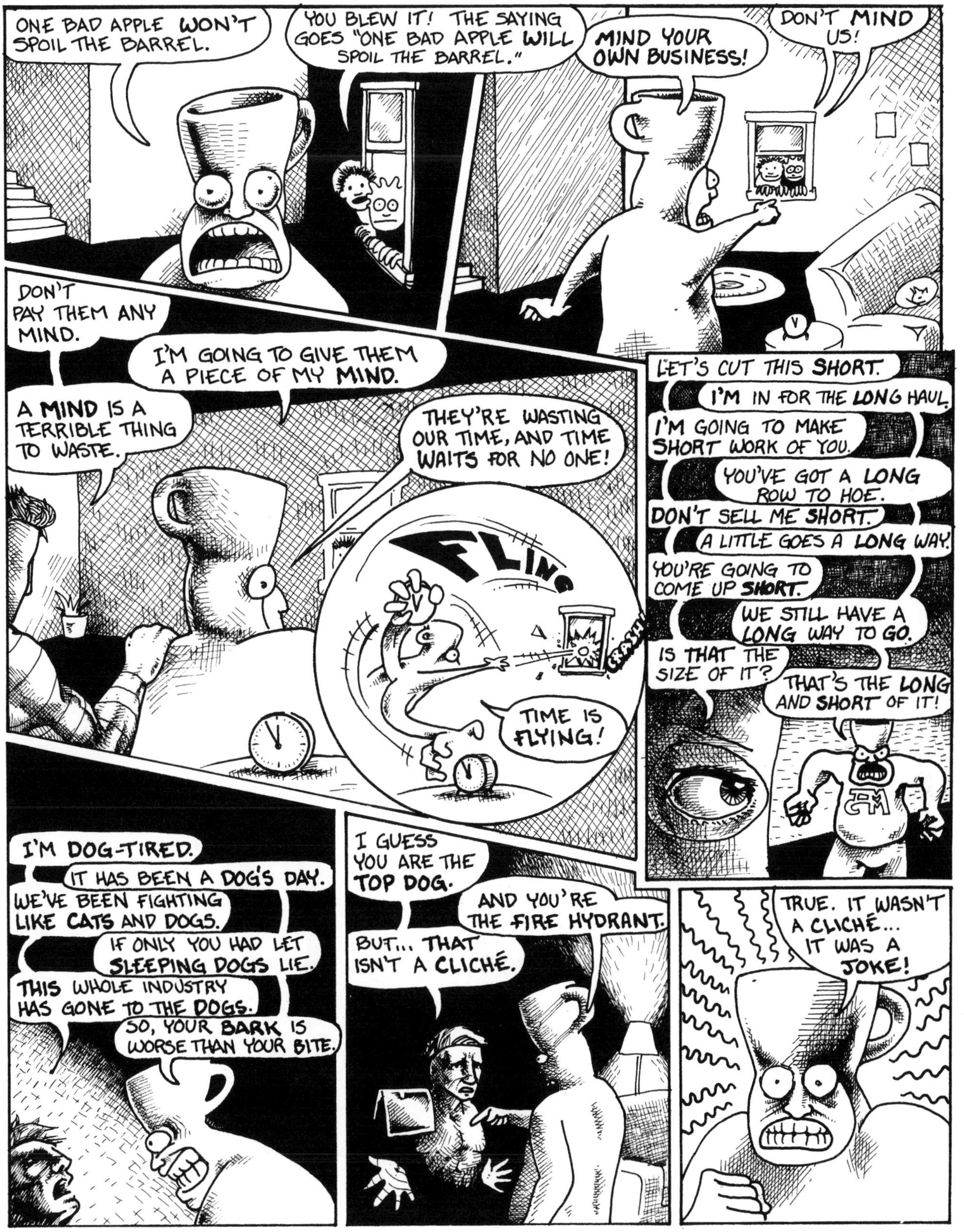
ONE BAD APPLE WON'T SPOIL THE BARREL.
YOU BLEW IT! THE SAYING GOES "ONE BAD APPLE WILL SPOIL THE BARREL."
MIND YOUR OWN BUSINESS!
DON'T MIND US!
DON'T PAY THEM ANY MIND.
I'M GOING TO GIVE THEM A PIECE OF MY MIND.
A MIND IS A TERRIBLE THING TO WASTE.
THEY'RE WASTING OUR TIME, AND TIME WAITS FOR NO ONE!
FLING
CRASH!
TIME IS FLYING!
LET'S CUT THIS SHORT.
I'M IN FOR THE LONG HAUL.
I'M GOING TO MAKE SHORT WORK OF YOU.
YOU'VE GOT A LONG ROW TO HOE.
DON'T SELL ME SHORT.
A LITTLE GOES A LONG WAY.
YOU'RE GOING TO COME UP SHORT.
WE STILL HAVE A LONG WAY TO GO.
IS THAT THE SIZE OF IT?
THAT'S THE LONG AND SHORT OF IT!
I'M DOG-TIRED.
IT HAS BEEN A DOG'S DAY.
WE'VE BEEN FIGHTING LIKE CATS AND DOGS.
IF ONLY YOU HAD LET SLEEPING DOGS LIE.
THIS WHOLE INDUSTRY HAS GONE TO THE DOGS.
SO, YOUR BARK IS WORSE THAN YOUR BITE.
I GUESS YOU ARE THE TOP DOG.
AND YOU'RE THE FIRE HYDRANT.
BUT... THAT ISN'T A CLICHÉ.
TRUE. IT WASN'T A CLICHÉ... IT WAS A JOKE!

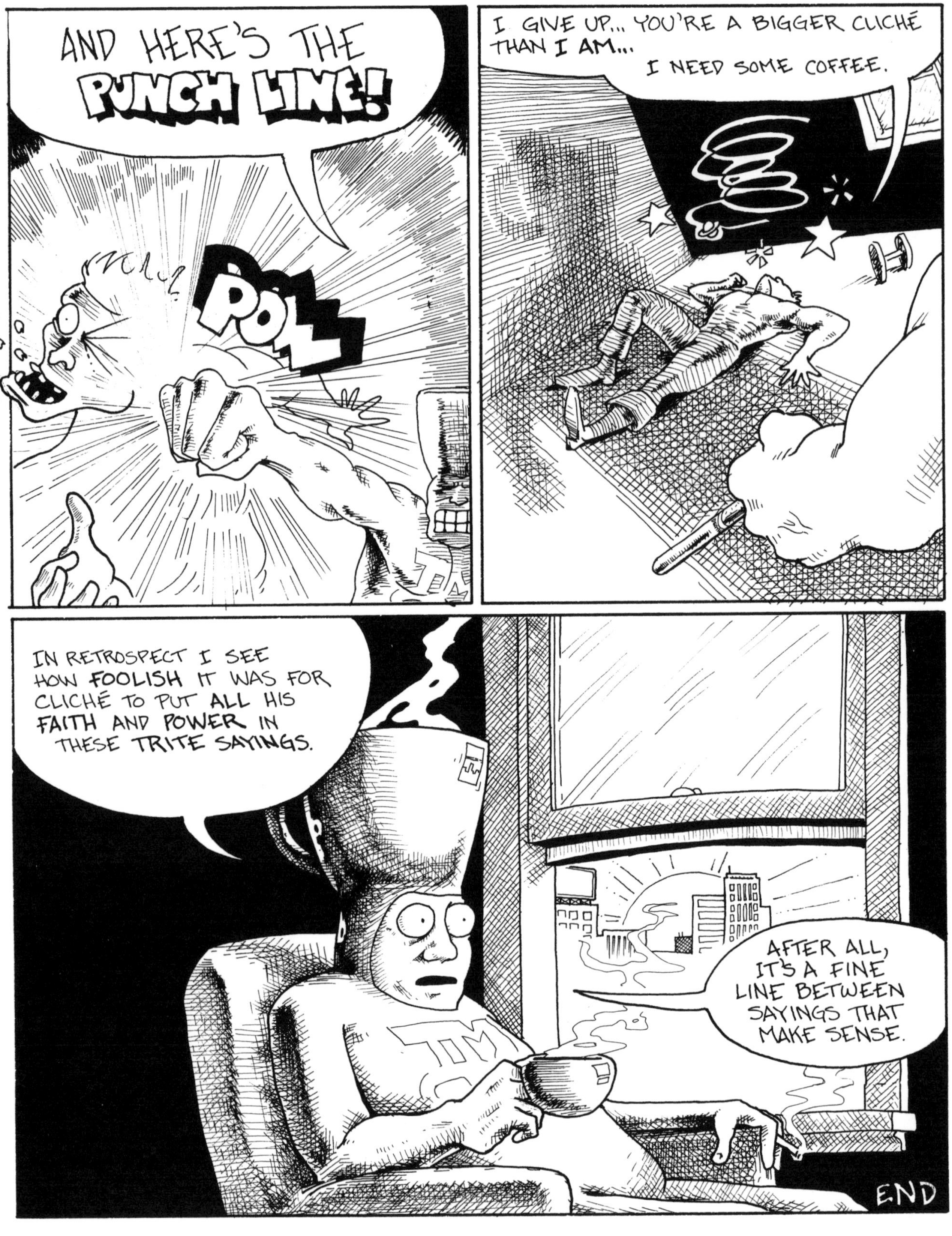
AND HERE'S THE PUNCH LINE!
POW
I GIVE UP... YOU'RE A BIGGER CLICHÉ THAN I AM...
I NEED SOME COFFEE.
IN RETROSPECT I SEE HOW FOOLISH IT WAS FOR CLICHÉ TO PUT ALL HIS FAITH AND POWER IN THESE TRITE SAYINGS.
AFTER ALL, IT'S A FINE LINE BETWEEN SAYINGS THAT MAKE SENSE.
END

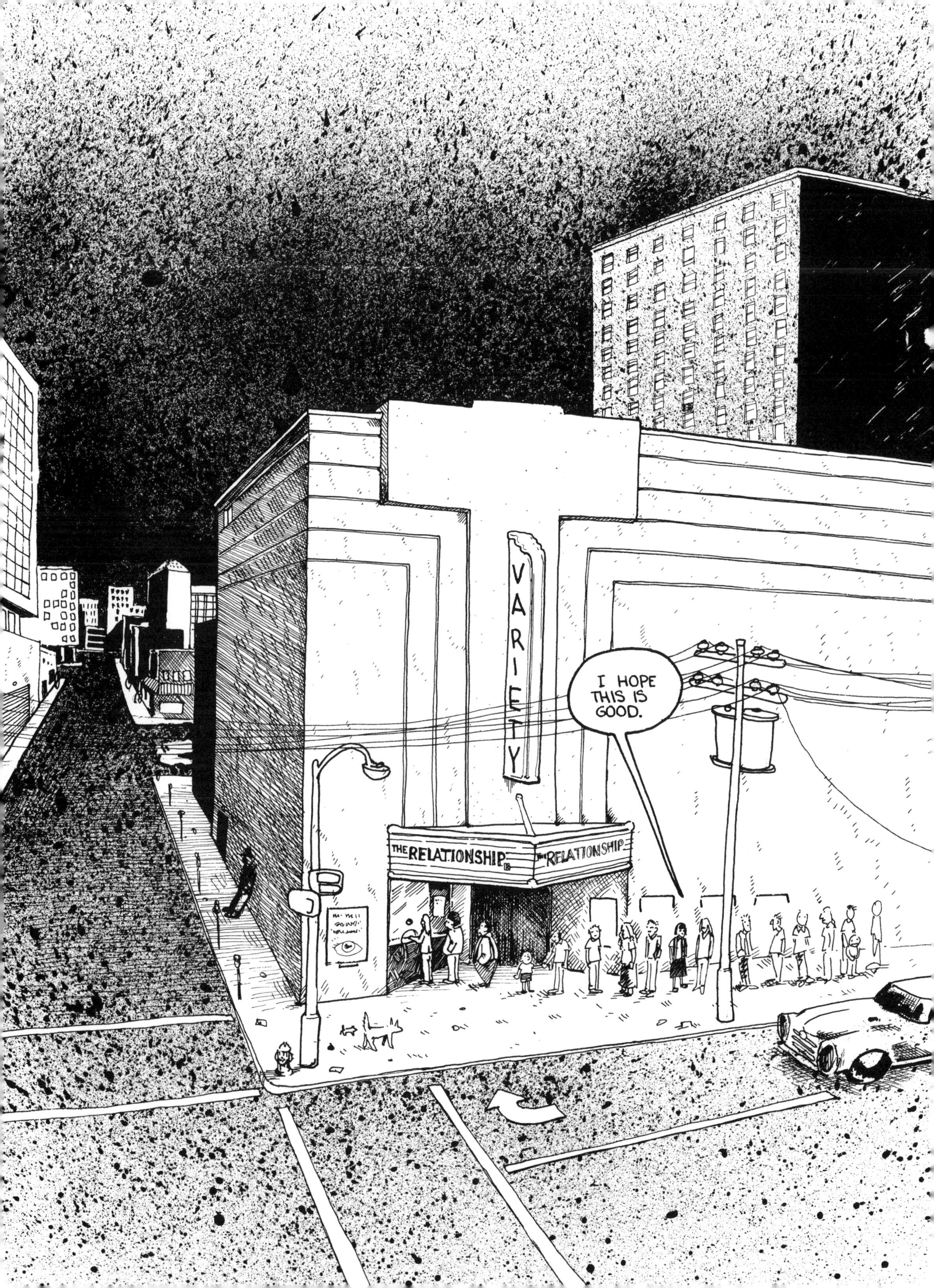
VARIETY
THE RELATIONSHIP
THE RELATIONSHIP
I HOPE THIS IS GOOD.

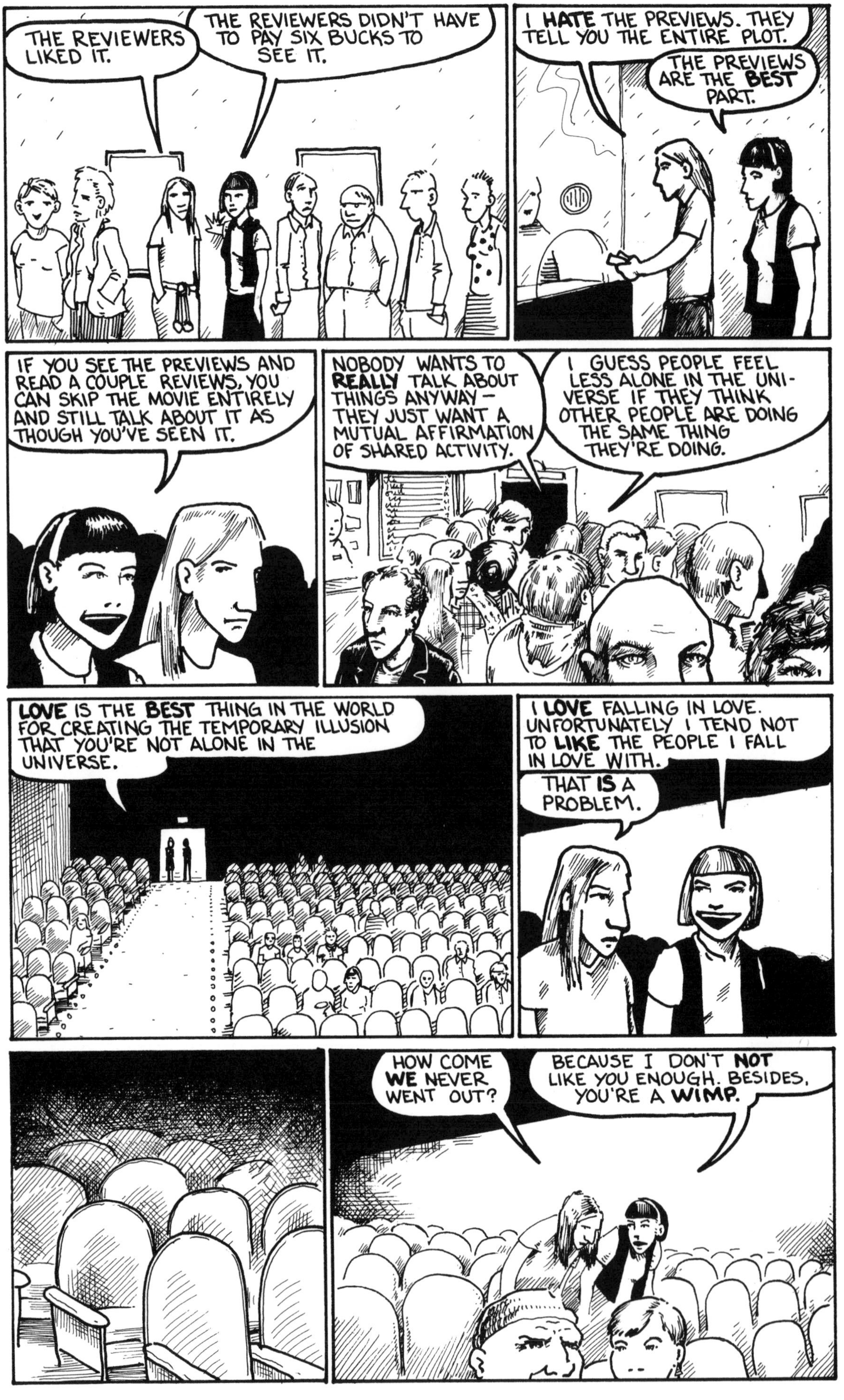
THE REVIEWERS LIKED IT.
THE REVIEWERS DIDN'T HAVE TO PAY SIX BUCKS TO SEE IT.
I HATE THE PREVIEWS. THEY TELL YOU THE ENTIRE PLOT.
THE PREVIEWS ARE THE BEST PART.
IF YOU SEE THE PREVIEWS AND READ A COUPLE REVIEWS, YOU CAN SKIP THE MOVIE ENTIRELY AND STILL TALK ABOUT IT AS THOUGH YOU'VE SEEN IT.
NOBODY WANTS TO REALLY TALK ABOUT THINGS ANYWAY — THEY JUST WANT A MUTUAL AFFIRMATION OF SHARED ACTIVITY.
I GUESS PEOPLE FEEL LESS ALONE IN THE UNIVERSE IF THEY THINK OTHER PEOPLE ARE DOING THE SAME THING THEY'RE DOING.
LOVE IS THE BEST THING IN THE WORLD FOR CREATING THE TEMPORARY ILLUSION THAT YOU'RE NOT ALONE IN THE UNIVERSE.
I LOVE FALLING IN LOVE. UNFORTUNATELY I TEND NOT TO LIKE THE PEOPLE I FALL IN LOVE WITH.
THAT IS A PROBLEM.
HOW COME WE NEVER WENT OUT?
BECAUSE I DON'T NOT LIKE YOU ENOUGH. BESIDES, YOU'RE A WIMP.

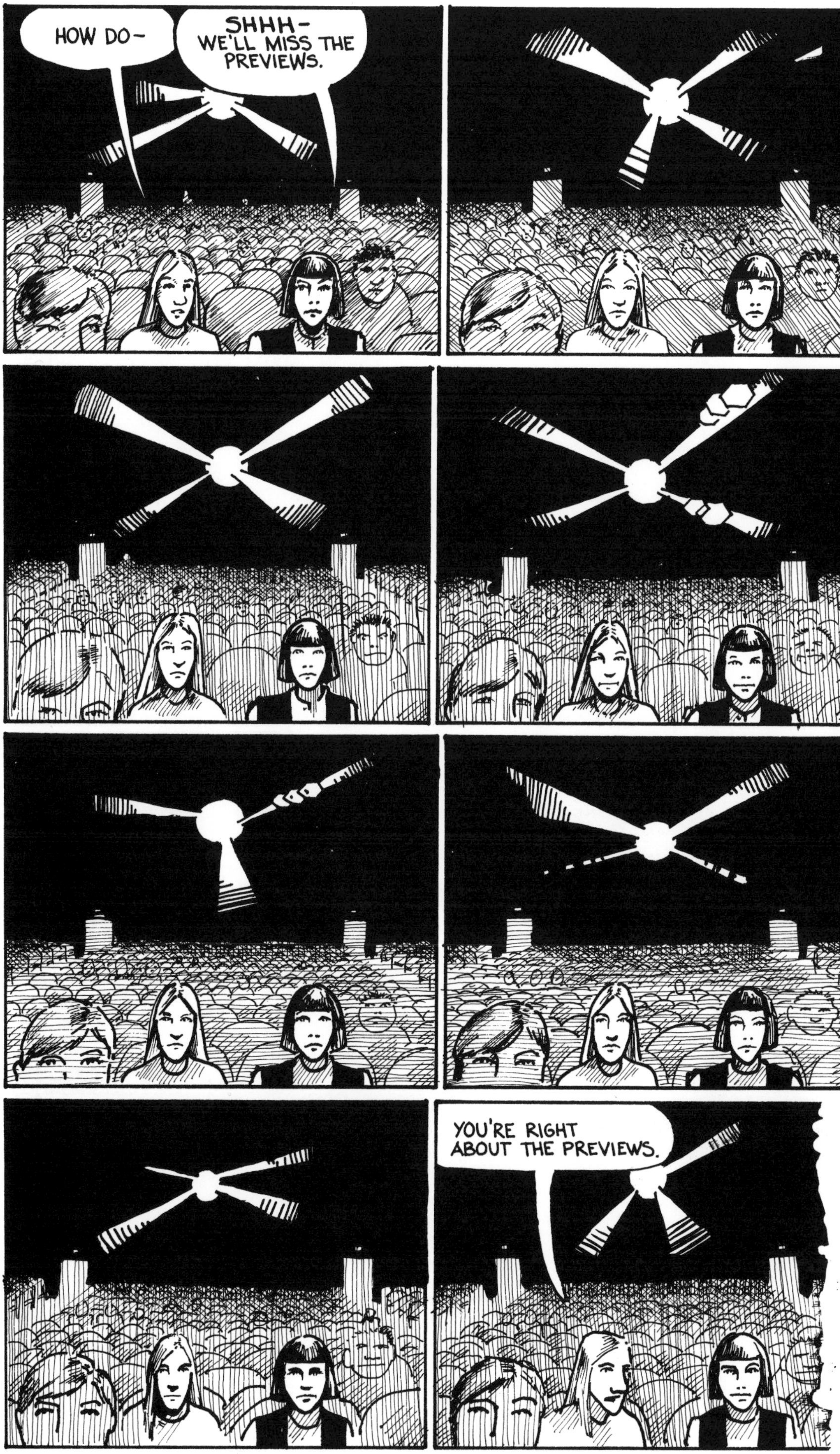
HOW DO-
SHHH- WE'LL MISS THE PREVIEWS.
YOU'RE RIGHT ABOUT THE PREVIEWS.

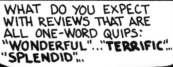

THAT SURE DID **SUCK**.

"WONDERFUL"
"GREAT"
"THE BEST"

NOW SHOWING

THE **RELA**

WHAT DO YOU EXPECT WITH REVIEWS THAT ARE ALL ONE-WORD QUIPS: "WONDERFUL"..."TERRIFIC"... "SPLENDID"...

YOU **KNOW** THEY DID A **LOT** OF EDITING TO GET THOSE "**GLOWING**" REVIEWS.

SOMETIMES I **HATE** MOVIES.

IF I WERE A VILLAIN AND **HAD** THE HERO, I WOULDN'T FOLLOW THE **RULE** AND **TALK** OR **GLOAT.** I'D JUST **KILL** HIM. AND I WOULDN'T DO IT IN SOME **WEIRD** OR **FANCY** WAY. I'D JUST SHOOT HIM IN THE **HEAD** QUICK 'N' EASY.

WHENEVER A KILLER IS KILLED, EVERYONE RELAXES... THEN SUDDENLY -BAM- HE'S BACK ON THE SET, EVERYONE IS SHOCKED, THEY KILL HIM FOR GOOD, AND EVERYONE RELAXES AGAIN, AND THE MOVIE'S OVER.

THAT'S WHAT'S CALLED A FAUX-FINIS.

WHAT'S THAT?

THE FAKE FINISH.

DID YOU LEARN THAT IN YOUR FILM CLASS?

NO, I MADE IT UP.

BURN BOOKS

FLIGHTPATH coff·

5011

THERE ARE **SO MANY** THINGS THAT ARE THE SAME IN **EVERY** MOVIE BUT **NEVER** OCCUR IN REAL LIFE.

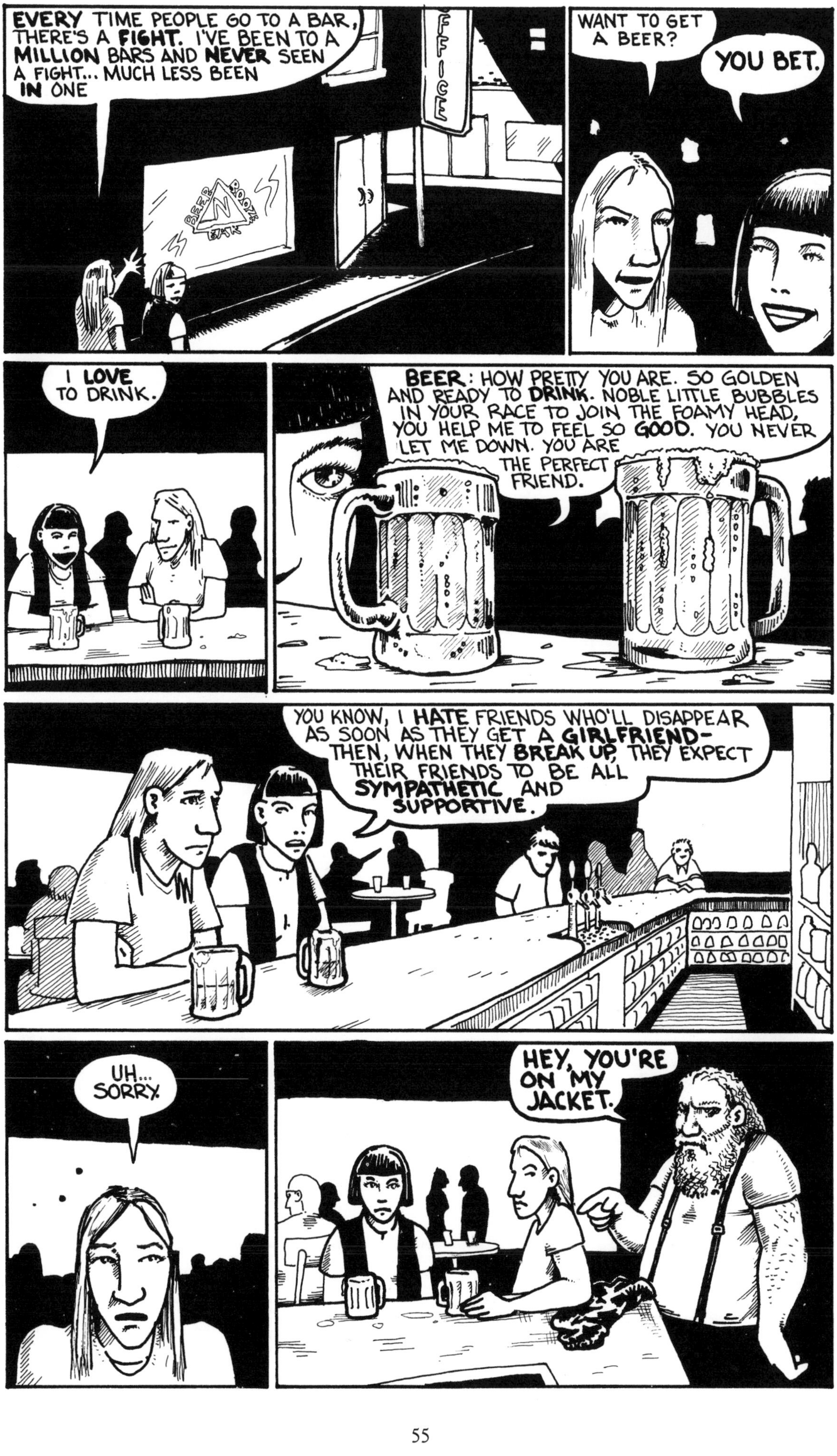
EVERY TIME PEOPLE GO TO A BAR, THERE'S A FIGHT. I'VE BEEN TO A MILLION BARS AND NEVER SEEN A FIGHT... MUCH LESS BEEN IN ONE
OFFICE
BEER N BOOZE BAR
WANT TO GET A BEER?
YOU BET.
I LOVE TO DRINK.
BEER: HOW PRETTY YOU ARE. SO GOLDEN AND READY TO DRINK. NOBLE LITTLE BUBBLES IN YOUR RACE TO JOIN THE FOAMY HEAD, YOU HELP ME TO FEEL SO GOOD. YOU NEVER LET ME DOWN. YOU ARE THE PERFECT FRIEND.
YOU KNOW, I HATE FRIENDS WHO'LL DISAPPEAR AS SOON AS THEY GET A GIRLFRIEND- THEN, WHEN THEY BREAK UP, THEY EXPECT THEIR FRIENDS TO BE ALL SYMPATHETIC AND SUPPORTIVE.
UH... SORRY.
HEY, YOU'RE ON MY JACKET.

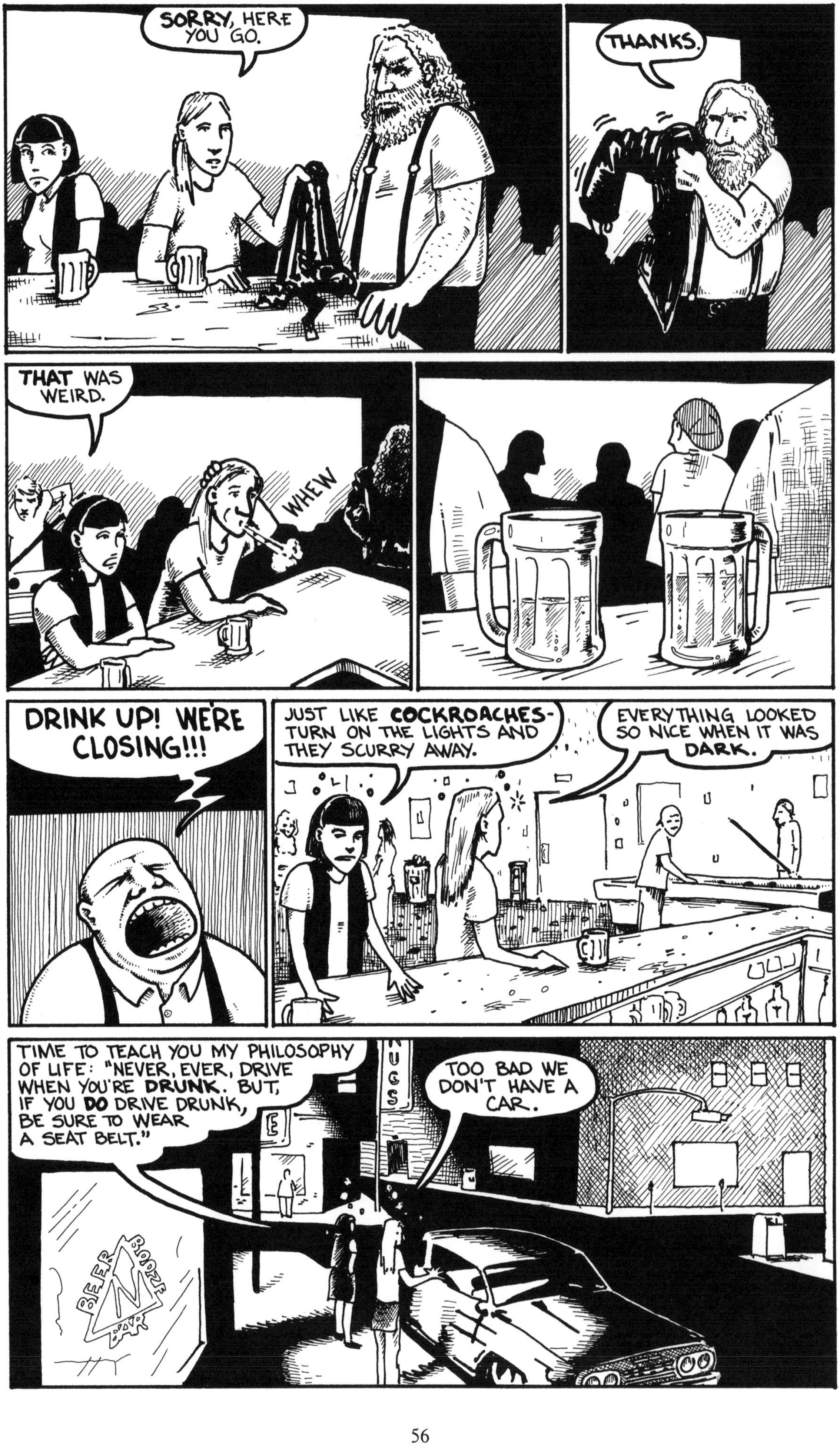
SORRY, HERE YOU GO.
THANKS.
THAT WAS WEIRD.
WHEW
DRINK UP! WE'RE CLOSING!!!
JUST LIKE COCKROACHES- TURN ON THE LIGHTS AND THEY SCURRY AWAY.
EVERYTHING LOOKED SO NICE WHEN IT WAS DARK.
TIME TO TEACH YOU MY PHILOSOPHY OF LIFE: "NEVER, EVER, DRIVE WHEN YOU'RE DRUNK. BUT, IF YOU DO DRIVE DRUNK, BE SURE TO WEAR A SEAT BELT."
TOO BAD WE DON'T HAVE A CAR.
BEER BOOZE BAR

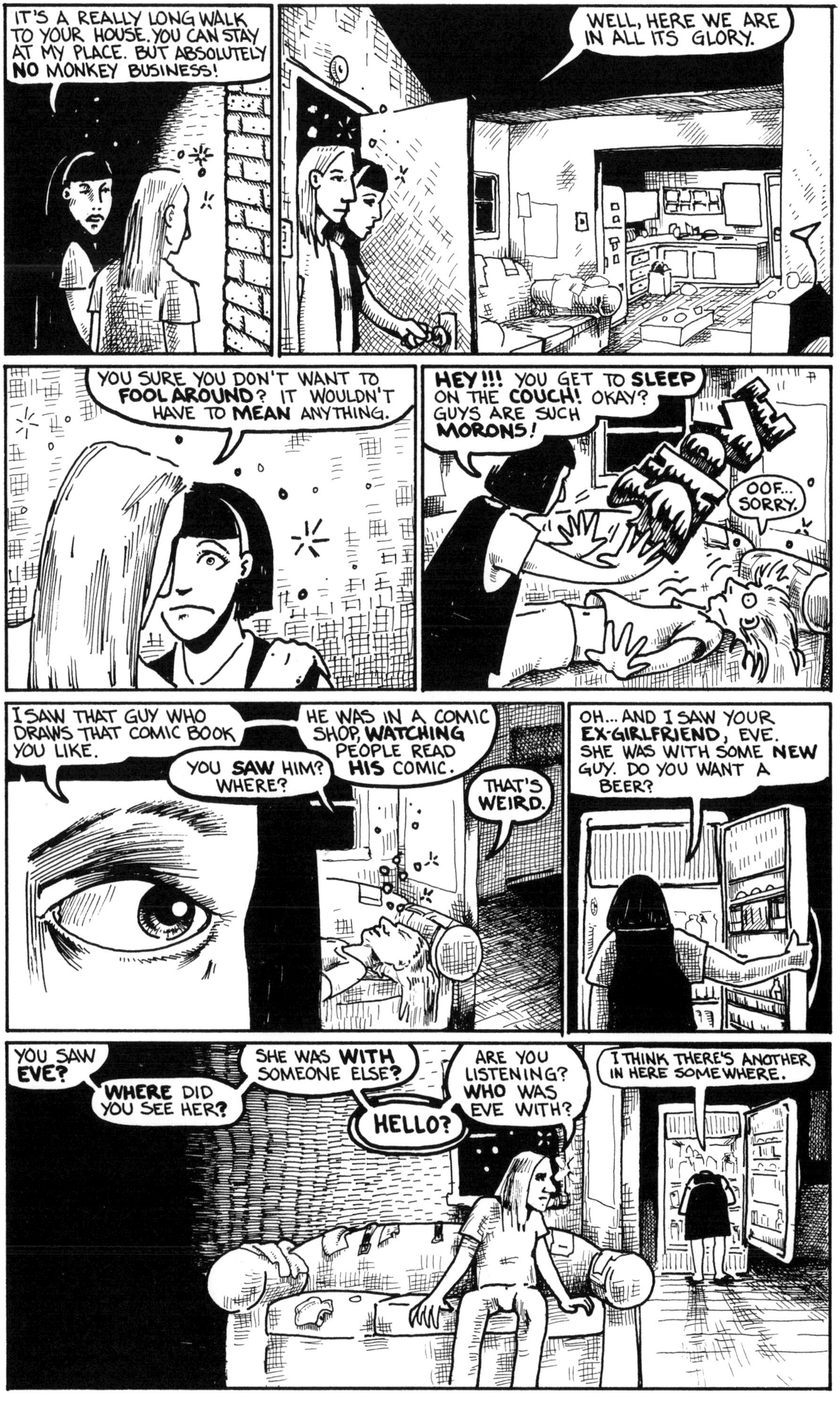
IT'S A REALLY LONG WALK TO YOUR HOUSE. YOU CAN STAY AT MY PLACE. BUT ABSOLUTELY NO MONKEY BUSINESS!
WELL, HERE WE ARE IN ALL ITS GLORY.
YOU SURE YOU DON'T WANT TO FOOL AROUND? IT WOULDN'T HAVE TO MEAN ANYTHING.
HEY!!! YOU GET TO SLEEP ON THE COUCH! OKAY? GUYS ARE SUCH MORONS!
SHOVE
OOF... SORRY.
I SAW THAT GUY WHO DRAWS THAT COMIC BOOK YOU LIKE.
YOU SAW HIM? WHERE?
HE WAS IN A COMIC SHOP, WATCHING PEOPLE READ HIS COMIC.
THAT'S WEIRD.
OH... AND I SAW YOUR EX-GIRLFRIEND, EVE. SHE WAS WITH SOME NEW GUY. DO YOU WANT A BEER?
YOU SAW EVE?
WHERE DID YOU SEE HER?
SHE WAS WITH SOMEONE ELSE?
HELLO?
ARE YOU LISTENING? WHO WAS EVE WITH?
I THINK THERE'S ANOTHER IN HERE SOMEWHERE.

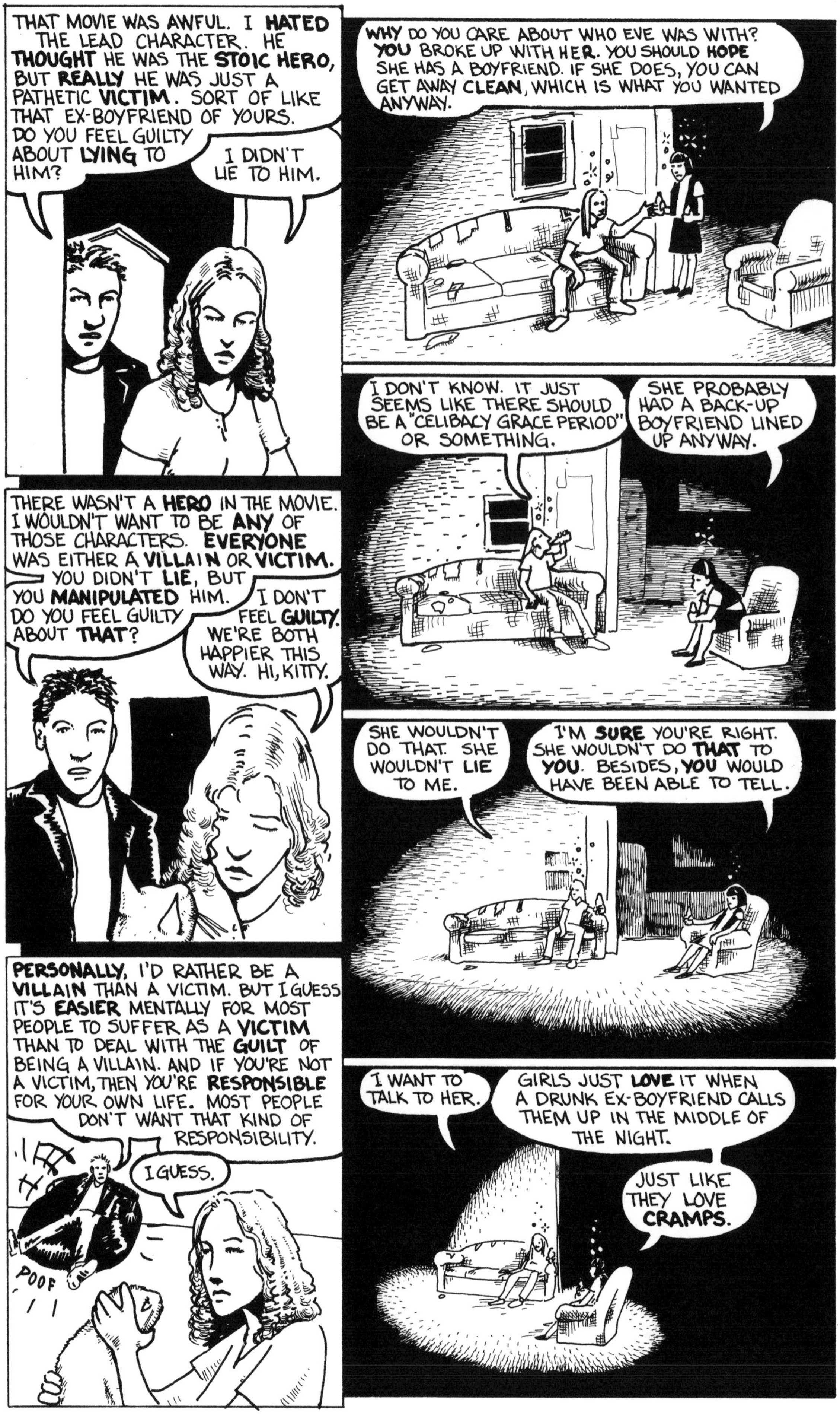
THAT MOVIE WAS AWFUL. I HATED THE LEAD CHARACTER. HE THOUGHT HE WAS THE STOIC HERO, BUT REALLY HE WAS JUST A PATHETIC VICTIM. SORT OF LIKE THAT EX-BOYFRIEND OF YOURS. DO YOU FEEL GUILTY ABOUT LYING TO HIM?
I DIDN'T LIE TO HIM.
THERE WASN'T A HERO IN THE MOVIE. I WOULDN'T WANT TO BE ANY OF THOSE CHARACTERS. EVERYONE WAS EITHER A VILLAIN OR VICTIM.
YOU DIDN'T LIE, BUT YOU MANIPULATED HIM. DO YOU FEEL GUILTY ABOUT THAT?
I DON'T FEEL GUILTY. WE'RE BOTH HAPPIER THIS WAY. HI, KITTY.
PERSONALLY, I'D RATHER BE A VILLAIN THAN A VICTIM. BUT I GUESS IT'S EASIER MENTALLY FOR MOST PEOPLE TO SUFFER AS A VICTIM THAN TO DEAL WITH THE GUILT OF BEING A VILLAIN. AND IF YOU'RE NOT A VICTIM, THEN YOU'RE RESPONSIBLE FOR YOUR OWN LIFE. MOST PEOPLE DON'T WANT THAT KIND OF RESPONSIBILITY.
I GUESS.
POOF
WHY DO YOU CARE ABOUT WHO EVE WAS WITH? YOU BROKE UP WITH HER. YOU SHOULD HOPE SHE HAS A BOYFRIEND. IF SHE DOES, YOU CAN GET AWAY CLEAN, WHICH IS WHAT YOU WANTED ANYWAY.
I DON'T KNOW. IT JUST SEEMS LIKE THERE SHOULD BE A "CELIBACY GRACE PERIOD" OR SOMETHING.
SHE PROBABLY HAD A BACK-UP BOYFRIEND LINED UP ANYWAY.
SHE WOULDN'T DO THAT. SHE WOULDN'T LIE TO ME.
I'M SURE YOU'RE RIGHT. SHE WOULDN'T DO THAT TO YOU. BESIDES, YOU WOULD HAVE BEEN ABLE TO TELL.
I WANT TO TALK TO HER.
GIRLS JUST LOVE IT WHEN A DRUNK EX-BOYFRIEND CALLS THEM UP IN THE MIDDLE OF THE NIGHT.
JUST LIKE THEY LOVE CRAMPS.

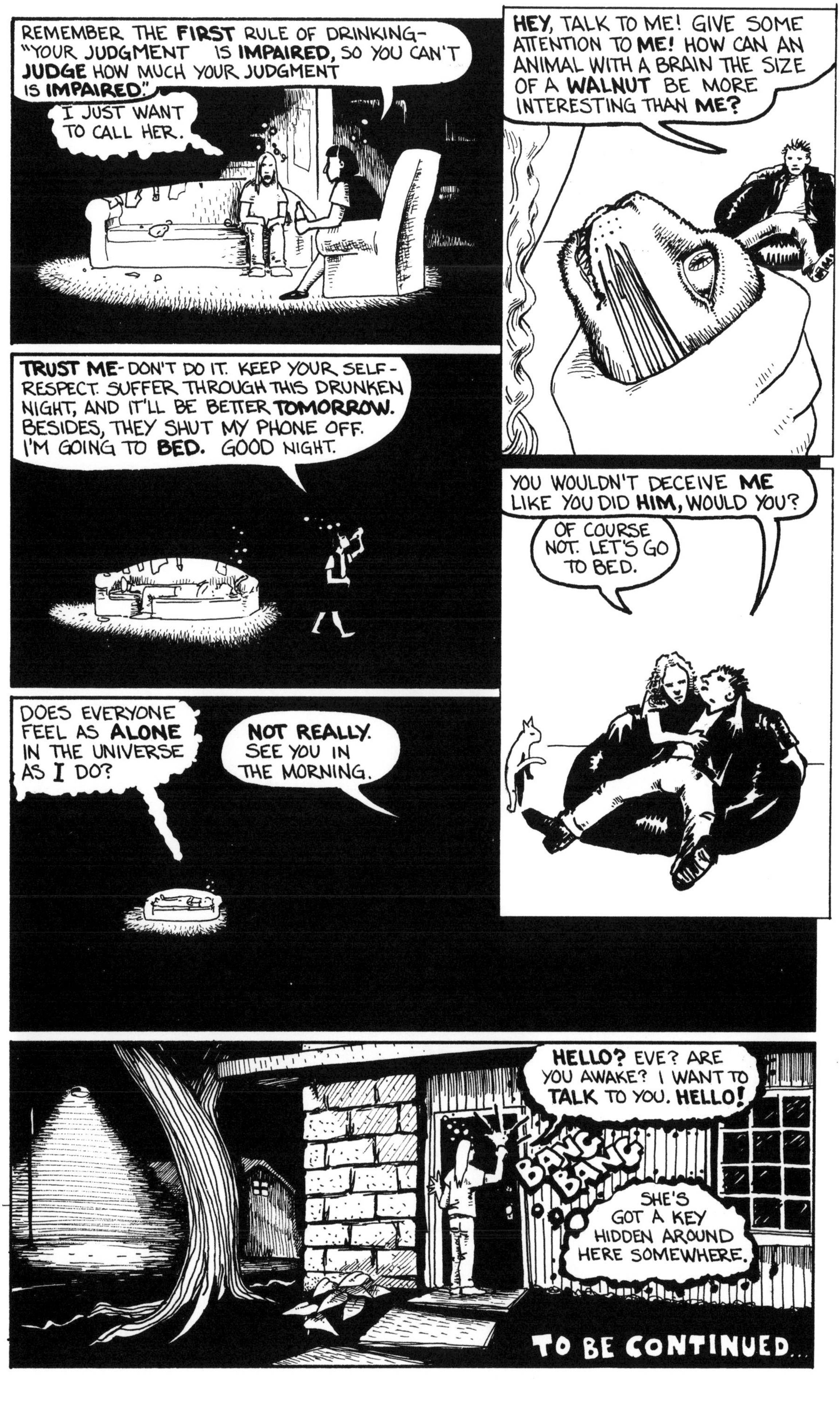

REMEMBER THE FIRST RULE OF DRINKING- "YOUR JUDGMENT IS IMPAIRED, SO YOU CAN'T JUDGE HOW MUCH YOUR JUDGMENT IS IMPAIRED."
I JUST WANT TO CALL HER.
HEY, TALK TO ME! GIVE SOME ATTENTION TO ME! HOW CAN AN ANIMAL WITH A BRAIN THE SIZE OF A WALNUT BE MORE INTERESTING THAN ME?
TRUST ME- DON'T DO IT. KEEP YOUR SELF-RESPECT. SUFFER THROUGH THIS DRUNKEN NIGHT, AND IT'LL BE BETTER TOMORROW. BESIDES, THEY SHUT MY PHONE OFF. I'M GOING TO BED. GOOD NIGHT.
YOU WOULDN'T DECEIVE ME LIKE YOU DID HIM, WOULD YOU?
OF COURSE NOT. LET'S GO TO BED.
DOES EVERYONE FEEL AS ALONE IN THE UNIVERSE AS I DO?
NOT REALLY. SEE YOU IN THE MORNING.
HELLO? EVE? ARE YOU AWAKE? I WANT TO TALK TO YOU. HELLO!
BANG BANG
SHE'S GOT A KEY HIDDEN AROUND HERE SOMEWHERE.
TO BE CONTINUED...

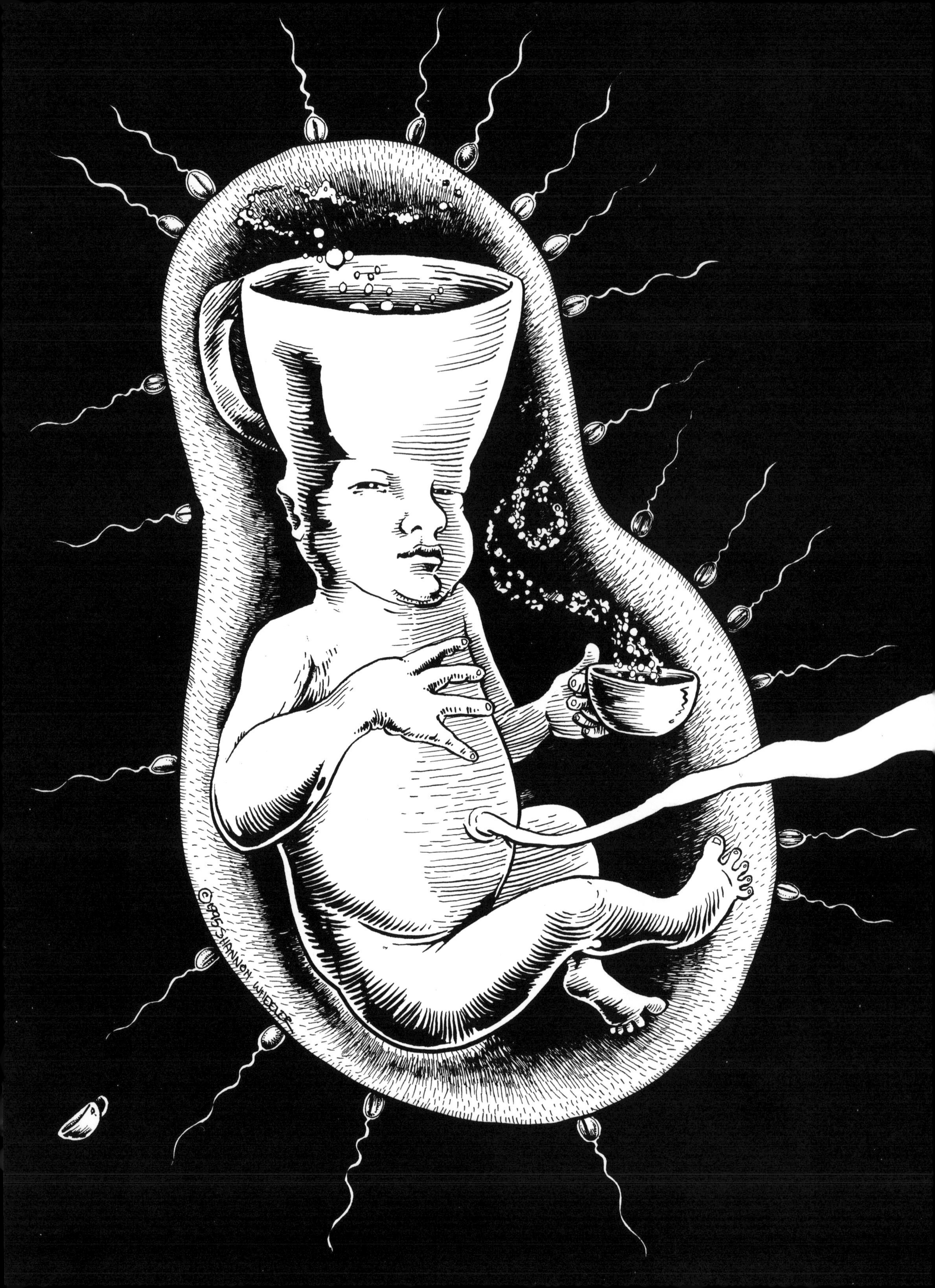
©1995 SHANNON WHEELER

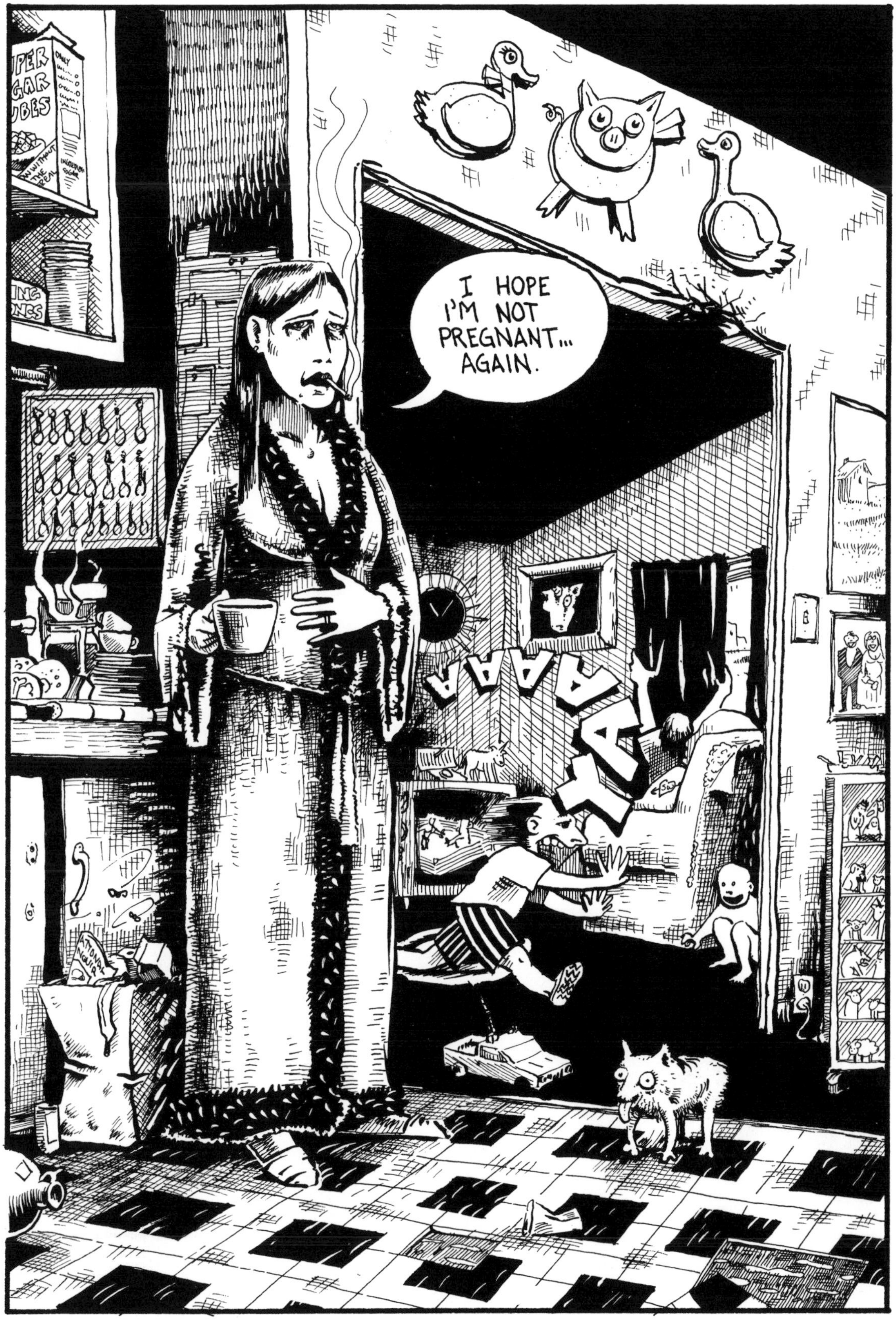
I HOPE I'M NOT PREGNANT... AGAIN.

NO! HE DID *NOT* BEGIN AS A *PRE-NATAL* TRAILER PARK *TRAGEDY!* NOR WAS IT A *GOVERNMENT EXPERIMENT* THAT SIRED *TOO MUCH COFFEE MAN*. OUR STORY IS MORE *COMPLICATED* THAN THAT.

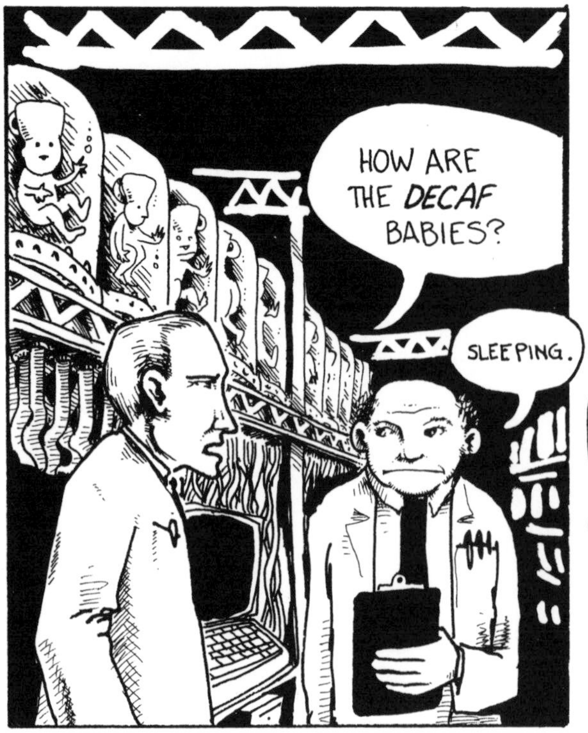
HOW ARE THE DECAF BABIES?
SLEEPING.

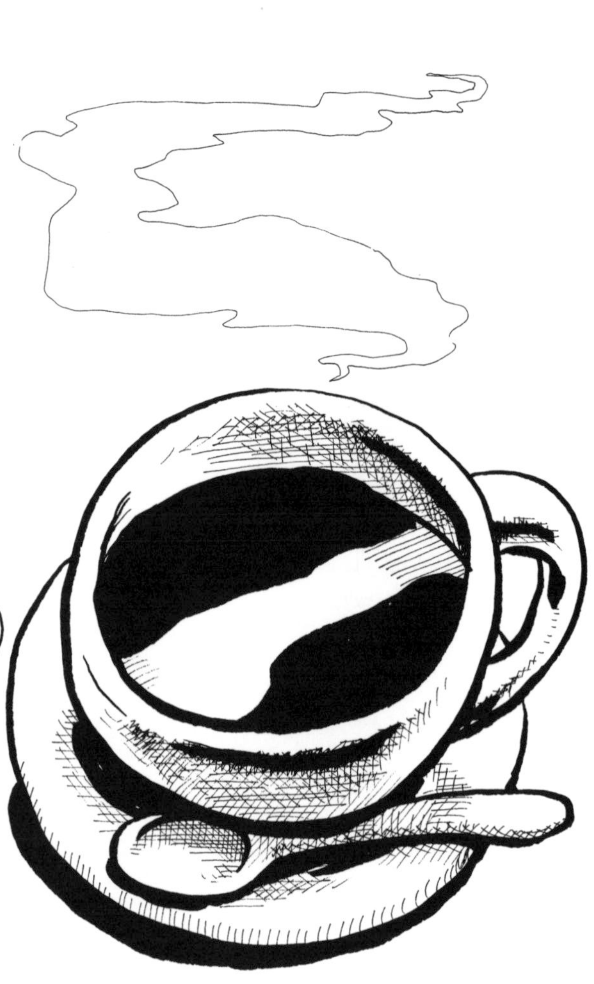

NO ALIENS WERE INVOLVED. EVEN THOUGH SOME PEOPLE THINK *COFFEE BEANS* ARE FROM *OUTER SPACE*.

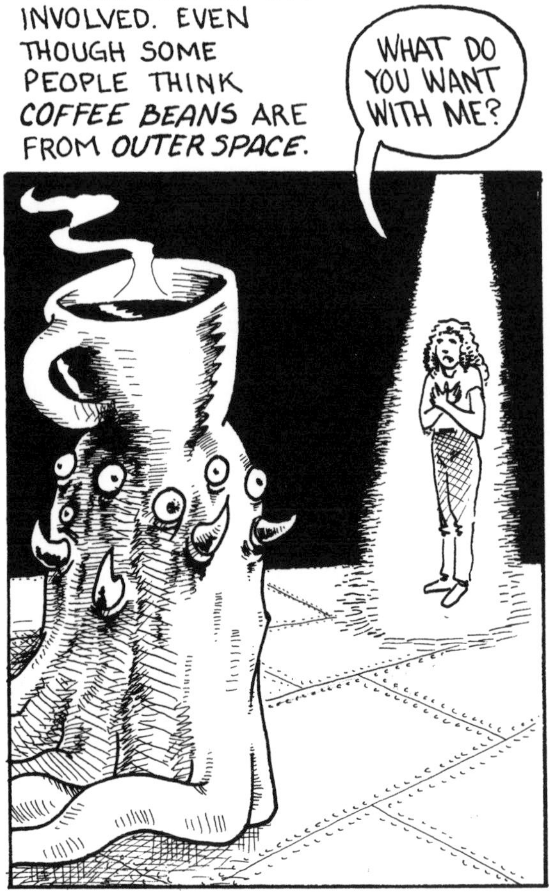
WHAT DO YOU WANT WITH ME?

COULD HE HAVE BEEN A *STUDENT*, TRYING TO *MEMORIZE* COUNTLESS FACTS: *OVERWHELMING* TODAY AND *IRRELEVANT* TOMORROW. COULD ONE *MORE* CUP OF *COFFEE* MAKE ACADEMIA SEEM *SIGNIFICANT*? PERHAPS...

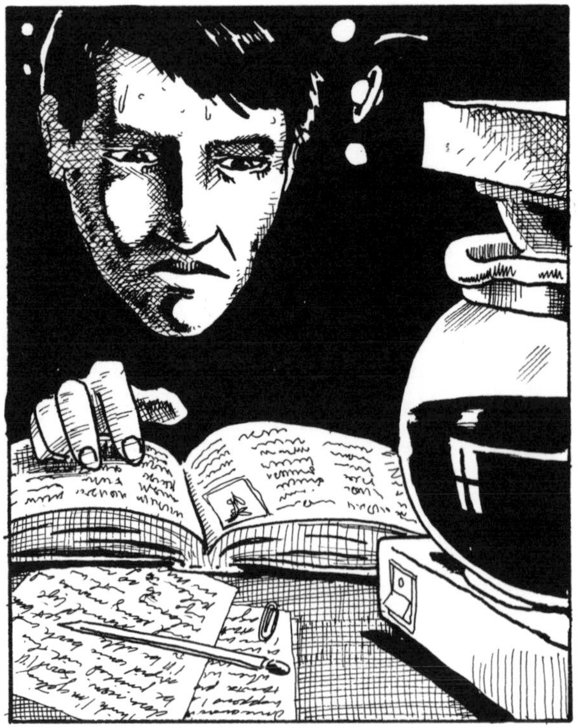

BUT *THAT* IS *NOT* HOW OUR HERO BEGAN. ***HOW*** DID ***TOO MUCH COFFEE MAN*** COME INTO BEING? WAS IT THE ***CIA?***

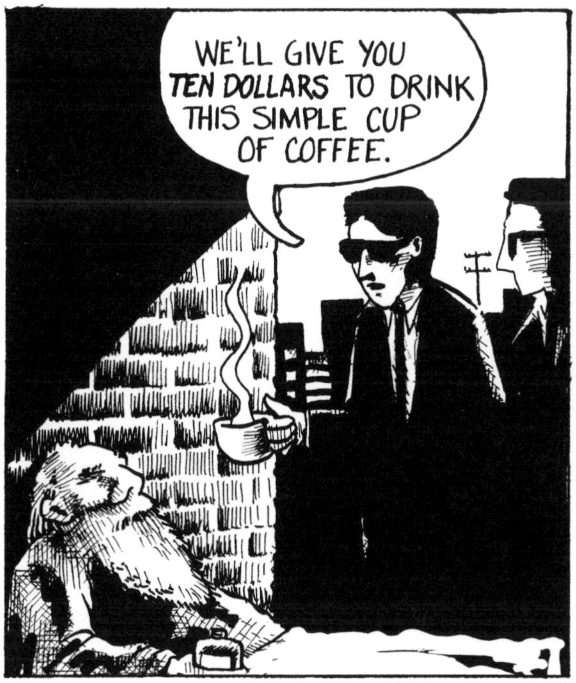
WE'LL GIVE YOU TEN DOLLARS TO DRINK THIS SIMPLE CUP OF COFFEE.

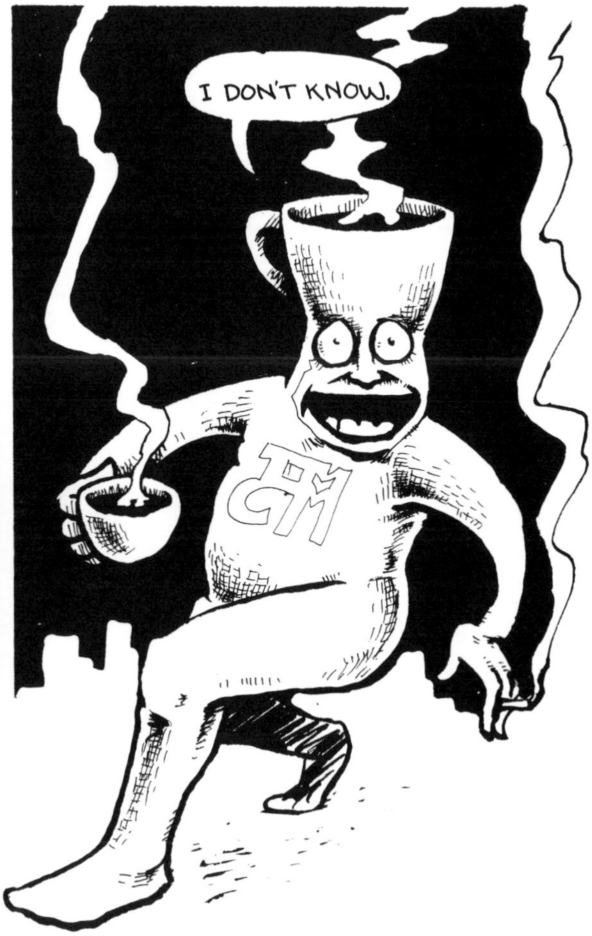
I DON'T KNOW.

OR, WAS IT ***DIVINE INSPIRATION?***

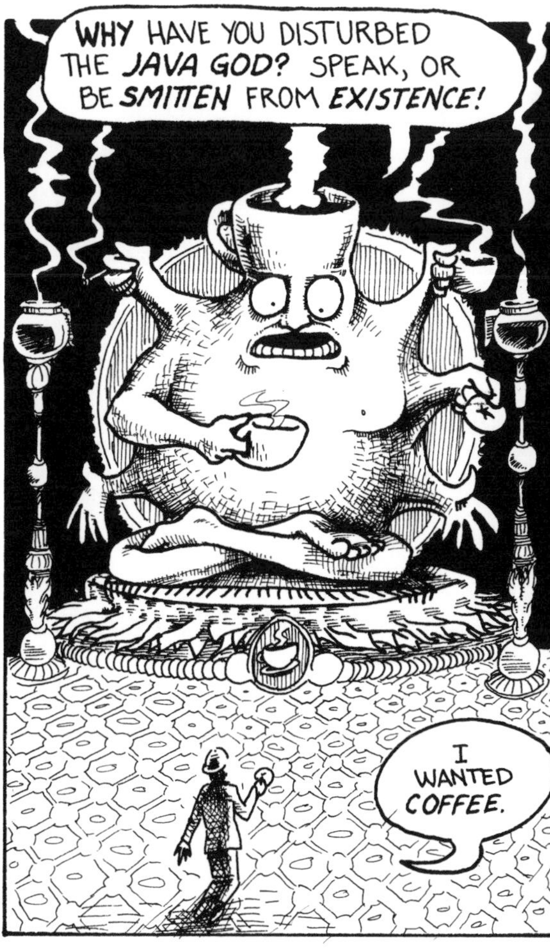
WHY HAVE YOU DISTURBED THE JAVA GOD? SPEAK, OR BE SMITTEN FROM EXISTENCE!
I WANTED COFFEE.

OUR STORY ***DOES*** BEGIN, FINALLY, ***HERE,*** IN A CAFÉ JUST OUTSIDE A SMALL TOWN.

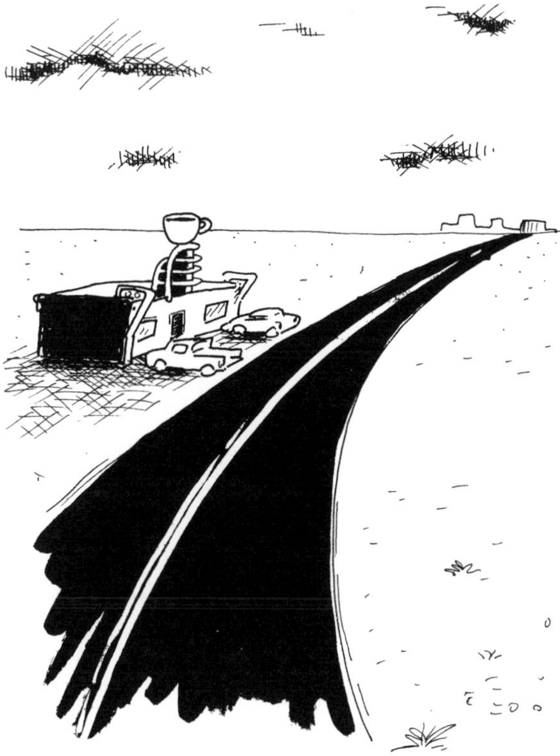

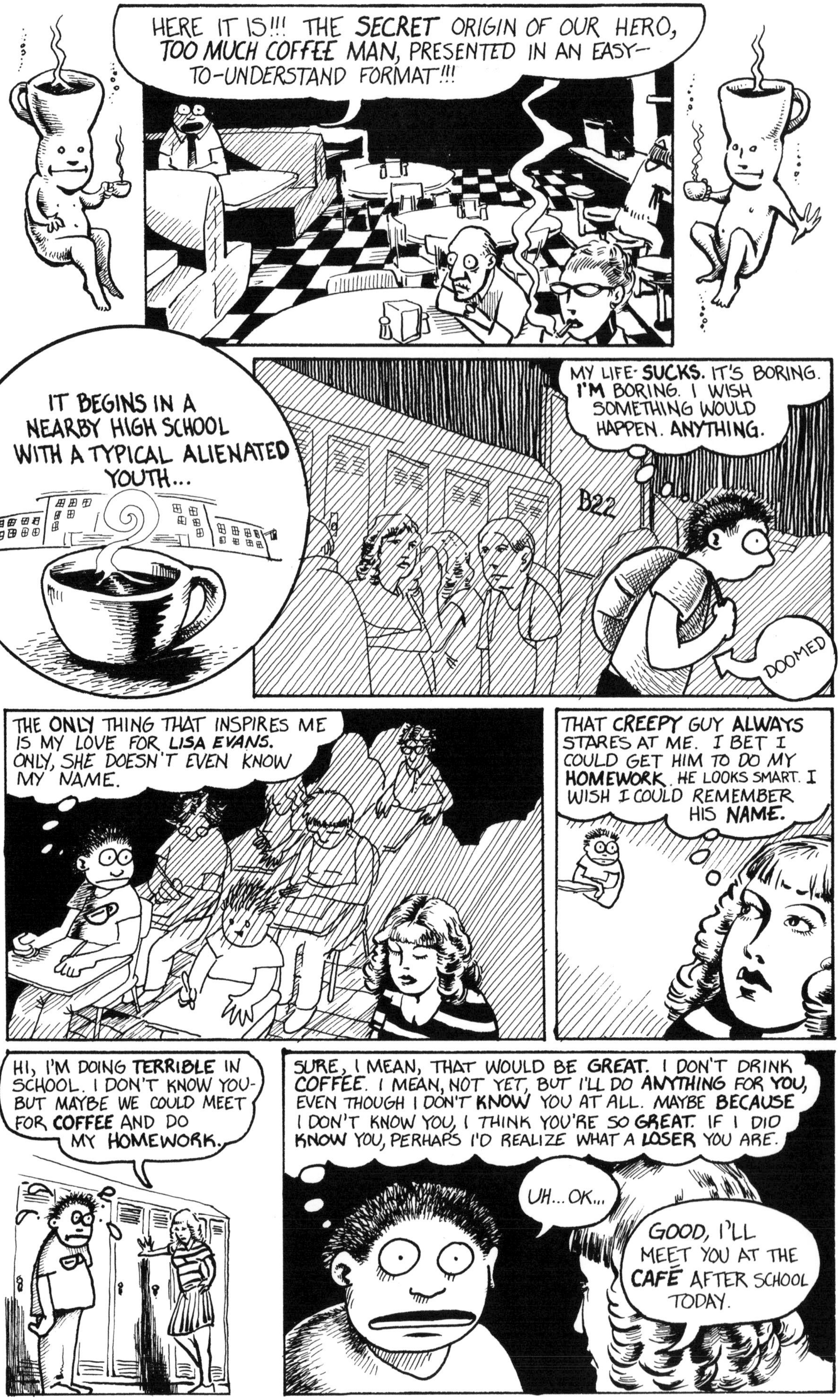
HERE IT IS!!! THE SECRET ORIGIN OF OUR HERO, TOO MUCH COFFEE MAN, PRESENTED IN AN EASY-TO-UNDERSTAND FORMAT!!!
IT BEGINS IN A NEARBY HIGH SCHOOL WITH A TYPICAL ALIENATED YOUTH...
MY LIFE SUCKS. IT'S BORING. I'M BORING. I WISH SOMETHING WOULD HAPPEN. ANYTHING.
B22
DOOMED
THE ONLY THING THAT INSPIRES ME IS MY LOVE FOR LISA EVANS. ONLY, SHE DOESN'T EVEN KNOW MY NAME.
THAT CREEPY GUY ALWAYS STARES AT ME. I BET I COULD GET HIM TO DO MY HOMEWORK. HE LOOKS SMART. I WISH I COULD REMEMBER HIS NAME.
HI, I'M DOING TERRIBLE IN SCHOOL. I DON'T KNOW YOU-BUT MAYBE WE COULD MEET FOR COFFEE AND DO MY HOMEWORK.
SURE, I MEAN, THAT WOULD BE GREAT. I DON'T DRINK COFFEE. I MEAN, NOT YET, BUT I'LL DO ANYTHING FOR YOU, EVEN THOUGH I DON'T KNOW YOU AT ALL. MAYBE BECAUSE I DON'T KNOW YOU, I THINK YOU'RE SO GREAT. IF I DID KNOW YOU, PERHAPS I'D REALIZE WHAT A LOSER YOU ARE.
UH...OK...
GOOD, I'LL MEET YOU AT THE CAFÉ AFTER SCHOOL TODAY.

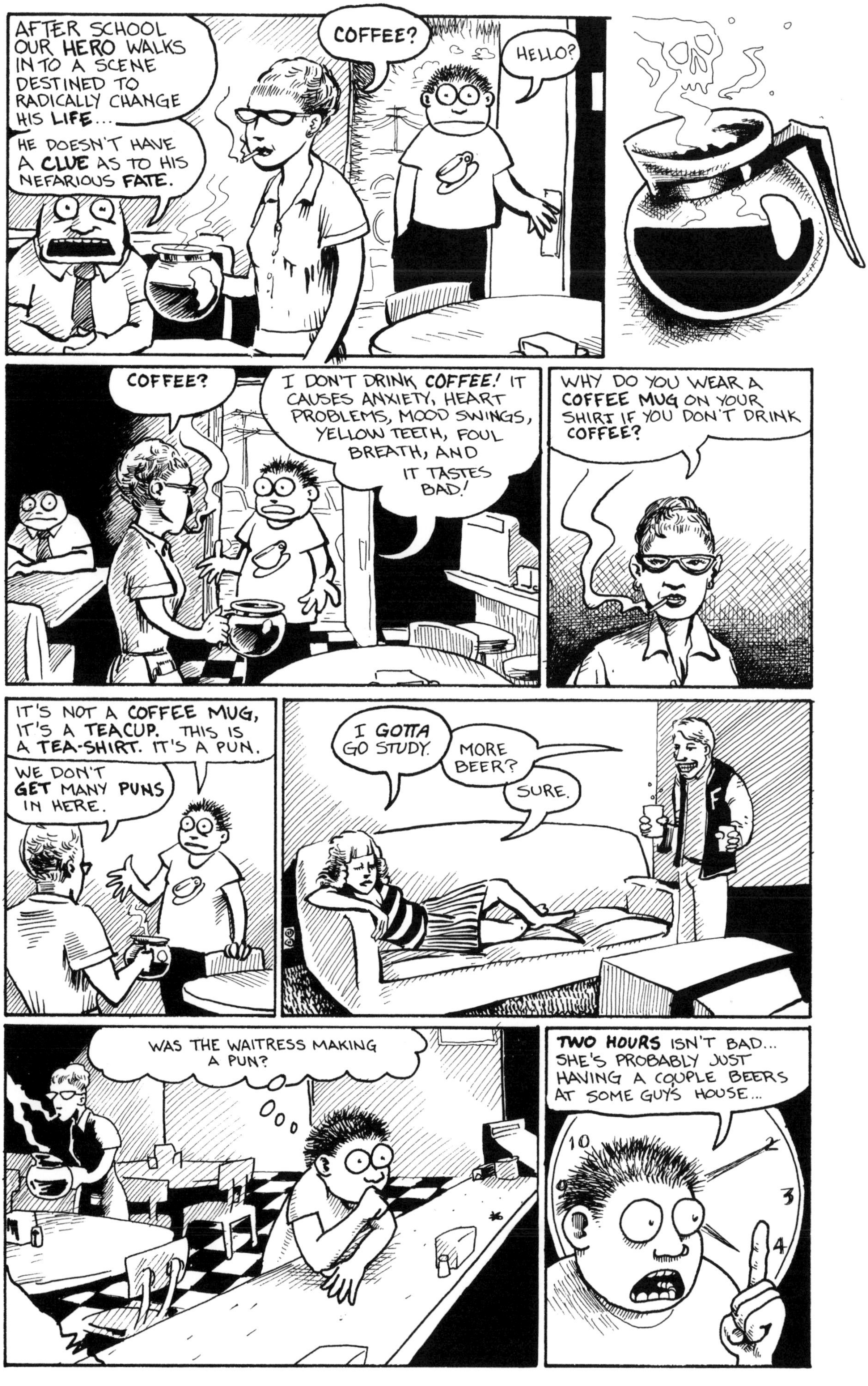

AFTER SCHOOL OUR HERO WALKS IN TO A SCENE DESTINED TO RADICALLY CHANGE HIS LIFE...
HE DOESN'T HAVE A CLUE AS TO HIS NEFARIOUS FATE.
COFFEE?
HELLO?
COFFEE?
I DON'T DRINK COFFEE! IT CAUSES ANXIETY, HEART PROBLEMS, MOOD SWINGS, YELLOW TEETH, FOUL BREATH, AND
IT TASTES BAD!
WHY DO YOU WEAR A COFFEE MUG ON YOUR SHIRT IF YOU DON'T DRINK COFFEE?
IT'S NOT A COFFEE MUG, IT'S A TEACUP. THIS IS A TEA-SHIRT. IT'S A PUN.
WE DON'T GET MANY PUNS IN HERE.
I GOTTA GO STUDY.
MORE BEER?
SURE.
WAS THE WAITRESS MAKING A PUN?
TWO HOURS ISN'T BAD... SHE'S PROBABLY JUST HAVING A COUPLE BEERS AT SOME GUY'S HOUSE...

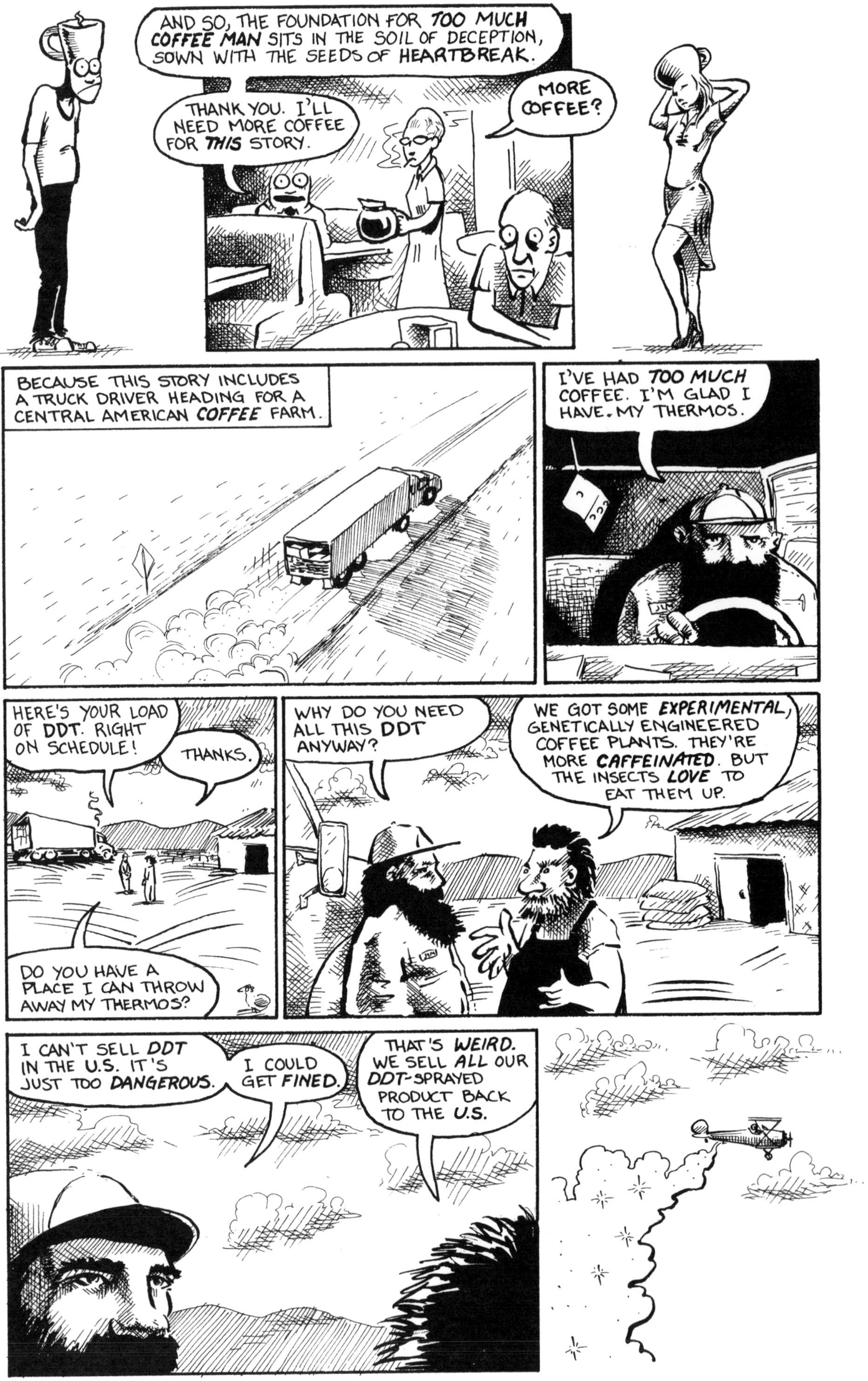
AND SO, THE FOUNDATION FOR TOO MUCH COFFEE MAN SITS IN THE SOIL OF DECEPTION, SOWN WITH THE SEEDS OF HEARTBREAK.
THANK YOU. I'LL NEED MORE COFFEE FOR THIS STORY.
MORE COFFEE?
BECAUSE THIS STORY INCLUDES A TRUCK DRIVER HEADING FOR A CENTRAL AMERICAN COFFEE FARM.
I'VE HAD TOO MUCH COFFEE. I'M GLAD I HAVE MY THERMOS.
HERE'S YOUR LOAD OF DDT. RIGHT ON SCHEDULE!
THANKS.
DO YOU HAVE A PLACE I CAN THROW AWAY MY THERMOS?
WHY DO YOU NEED ALL THIS DDT ANYWAY?
WE GOT SOME EXPERIMENTAL, GENETICALLY ENGINEERED COFFEE PLANTS. THEY'RE MORE CAFFEINATED. BUT THE INSECTS LOVE TO EAT THEM UP.
I CAN'T SELL DDT IN THE U.S. IT'S JUST TOO DANGEROUS.
I COULD GET FINED.
THAT'S WEIRD. WE SELL ALL OUR DDT-SPRAYED PRODUCT BACK TO THE U.S.

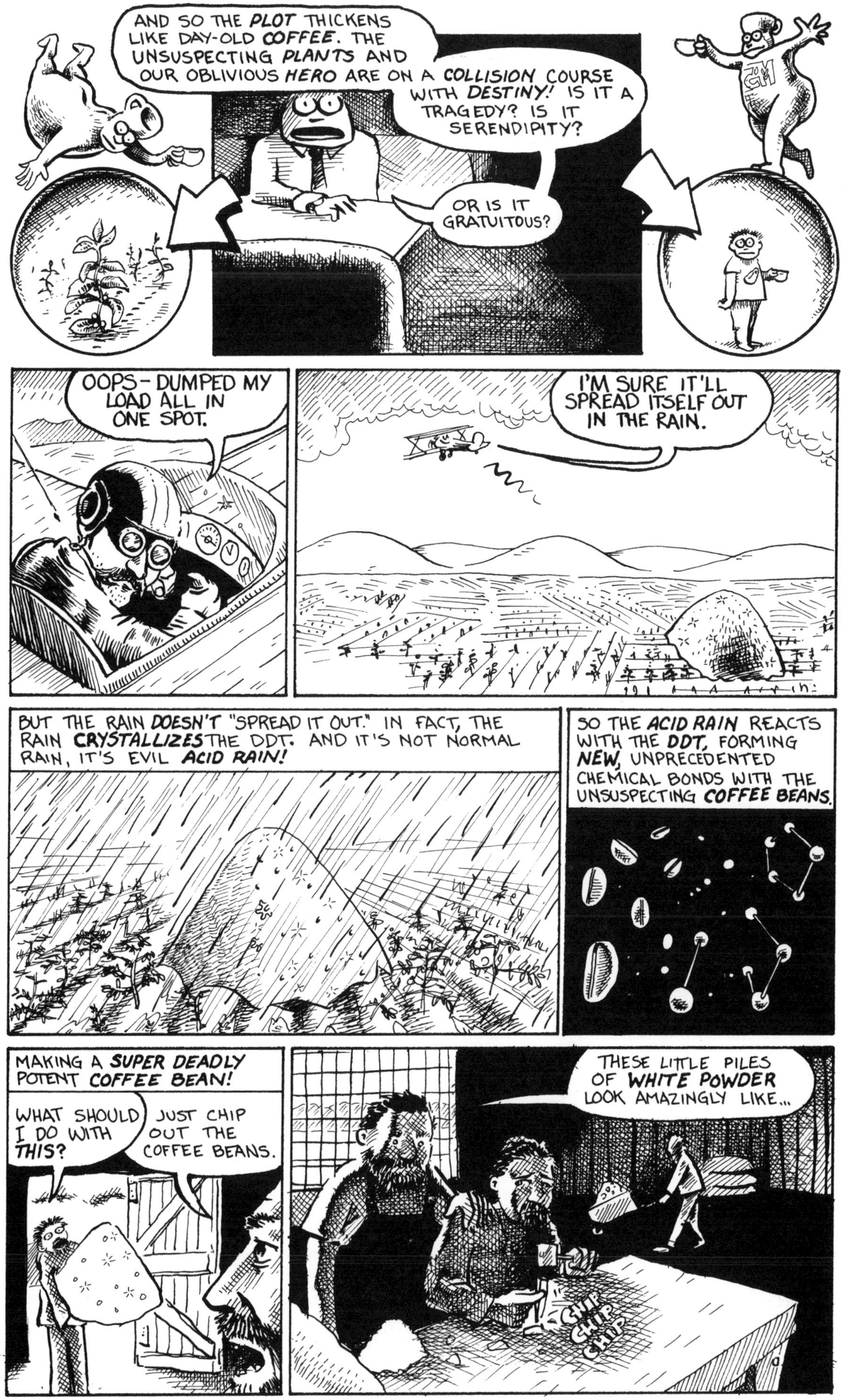
AND SO THE PLOT THICKENS LIKE DAY-OLD COFFEE. THE UNSUSPECTING PLANTS AND OUR OBLIVIOUS HERO ARE ON A COLLISION COURSE WITH DESTINY! IS IT A TRAGEDY? IS IT SERENDIPITY?
OR IS IT GRATUITOUS?
OOPS- DUMPED MY LOAD ALL IN ONE SPOT.
I'M SURE IT'LL SPREAD ITSELF OUT IN THE RAIN.
BUT THE RAIN DOESN'T "SPREAD IT OUT." IN FACT, THE RAIN CRYSTALLIZES THE DDT. AND IT'S NOT NORMAL RAIN, IT'S EVIL ACID RAIN!
SO THE ACID RAIN REACTS WITH THE DDT, FORMING NEW, UNPRECEDENTED CHEMICAL BONDS WITH THE UNSUSPECTING COFFEE BEANS.
MAKING A SUPER DEADLY POTENT COFFEE BEAN!
WHAT SHOULD I DO WITH THIS?
JUST CHIP OUT THE COFFEE BEANS.
THESE LITTLE PILES OF WHITE POWDER LOOK AMAZINGLY LIKE...
CHIP CHIP CHIP

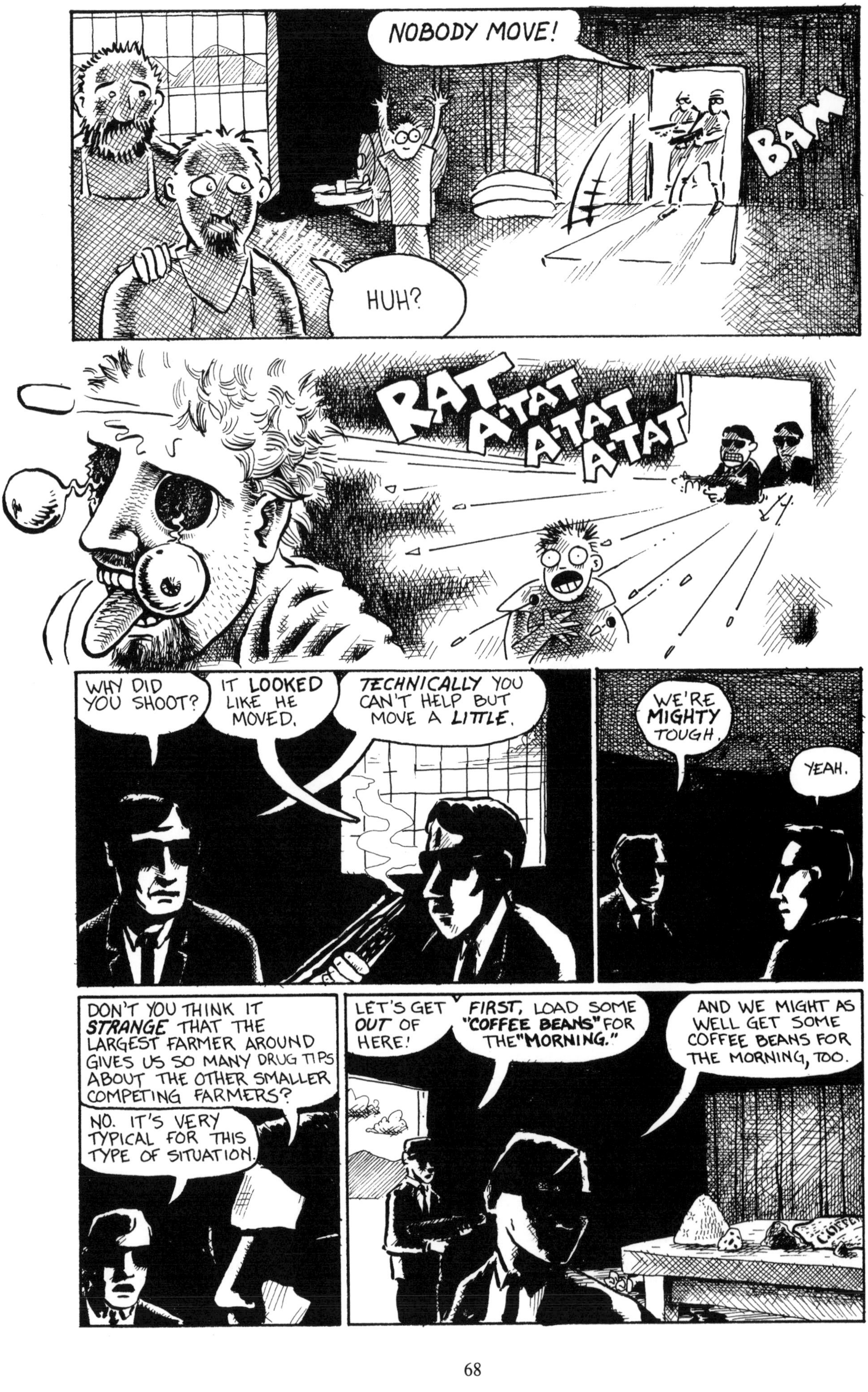
NOBODY MOVE!
BAM
HUH?
RAT-A-TAT A-TAT A-TAT
WHY DID YOU SHOOT?
IT LOOKED LIKE HE MOVED.
TECHNICALLY YOU CAN'T HELP BUT MOVE A LITTLE.
WE'RE MIGHTY TOUGH.
YEAH.
DON'T YOU THINK IT STRANGE THAT THE LARGEST FARMER AROUND GIVES US SO MANY DRUG TIPS ABOUT THE OTHER SMALLER COMPETING FARMERS?
NO. IT'S VERY TYPICAL FOR THIS TYPE OF SITUATION.
LET'S GET OUT OF HERE!
FIRST, LOAD SOME "COFFEE BEANS" FOR THE "MORNING."
AND WE MIGHT AS WELL GET SOME COFFEE BEANS FOR THE MORNING, TOO.

WHAT'S THAT TICKING NOISE?
I DON'T KNOW, BUT IT SOUNDS LIKE...
TICK TICK TICK TICK TICK TICK
COSMIC RADIATION!!!
I-I FEEL AS IF A MILLION TINY NEEDLES ARE PIERCING MY BODY...
NO TIME TO BE TRENDY! WE'VE GOT TO TAKE THIS COPTER DOWN FAST!
ARG! WE'VE FLOWN TOO LOW TOO FAST! WE'VE ACCIDENTALLY FLOWN INTO... A...
A NEVADA NUCLEAR TESTING SITE!!!
FOOMP
THAT WAS TOO CLOSE FOR COMFORT!
I'M UNCOMFORTABLE.
MEANWHILE
UH, WAITRESS, I'VE CHANGED MY MIND. I THINK I WILL HAVE THAT COFFEE.
WE JUST RAN OUT. I'LL MAKE A NEW POT. IT'LL JUST BE A SEC.

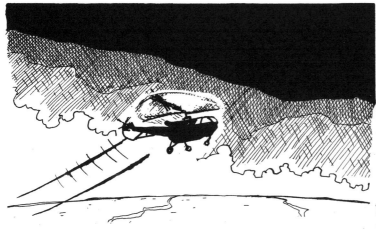

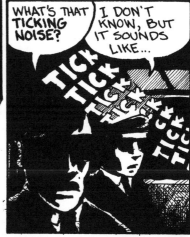

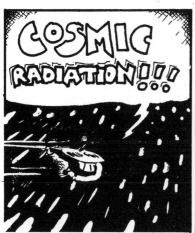

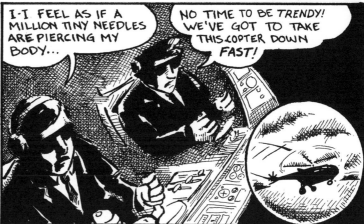

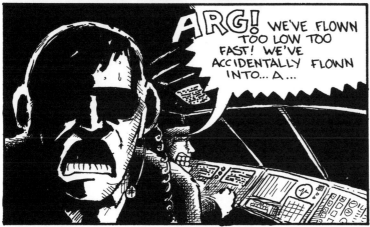

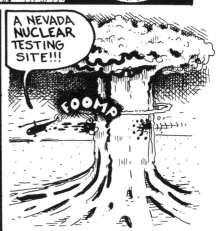

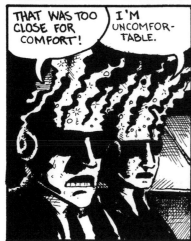

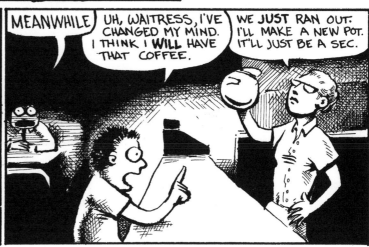

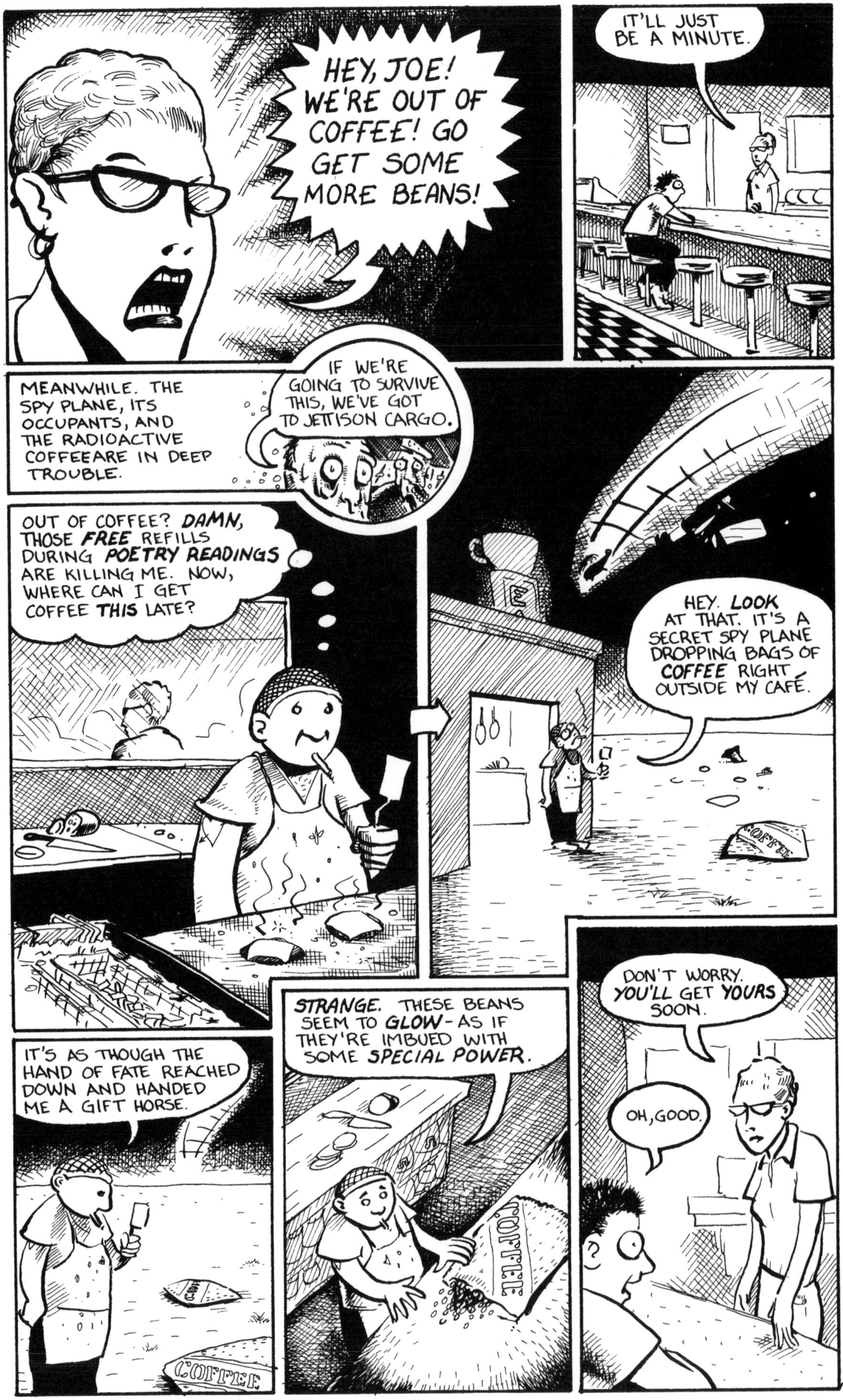
HEY, JOE! WE'RE OUT OF COFFEE! GO GET SOME MORE BEANS!
IT'LL JUST BE A MINUTE.
MEANWHILE. THE SPY PLANE, ITS OCCUPANTS, AND THE RADIOACTIVE COFFEEARE IN DEEP TROUBLE.
IF WE'RE GOING TO SURVIVE THIS, WE'VE GOT TO JETTISON CARGO.
OUT OF COFFEE? DAMN, THOSE FREE REFILLS DURING POETRY READINGS ARE KILLING ME. NOW, WHERE CAN I GET COFFEE THIS LATE?
HEY. LOOK AT THAT. IT'S A SECRET SPY PLANE DROPPING BAGS OF COFFEE RIGHT OUTSIDE MY CAFÉ.
COFFEE
IT'S AS THOUGH THE HAND OF FATE REACHED DOWN AND HANDED ME A GIFT HORSE.
COFFEE
STRANGE. THESE BEANS SEEM TO GLOW- AS IF THEY'RE IMBUED WITH SOME SPECIAL POWER.
COFFEE
DON'T WORRY. YOU'LL GET YOURS SOON.
OH, GOOD.

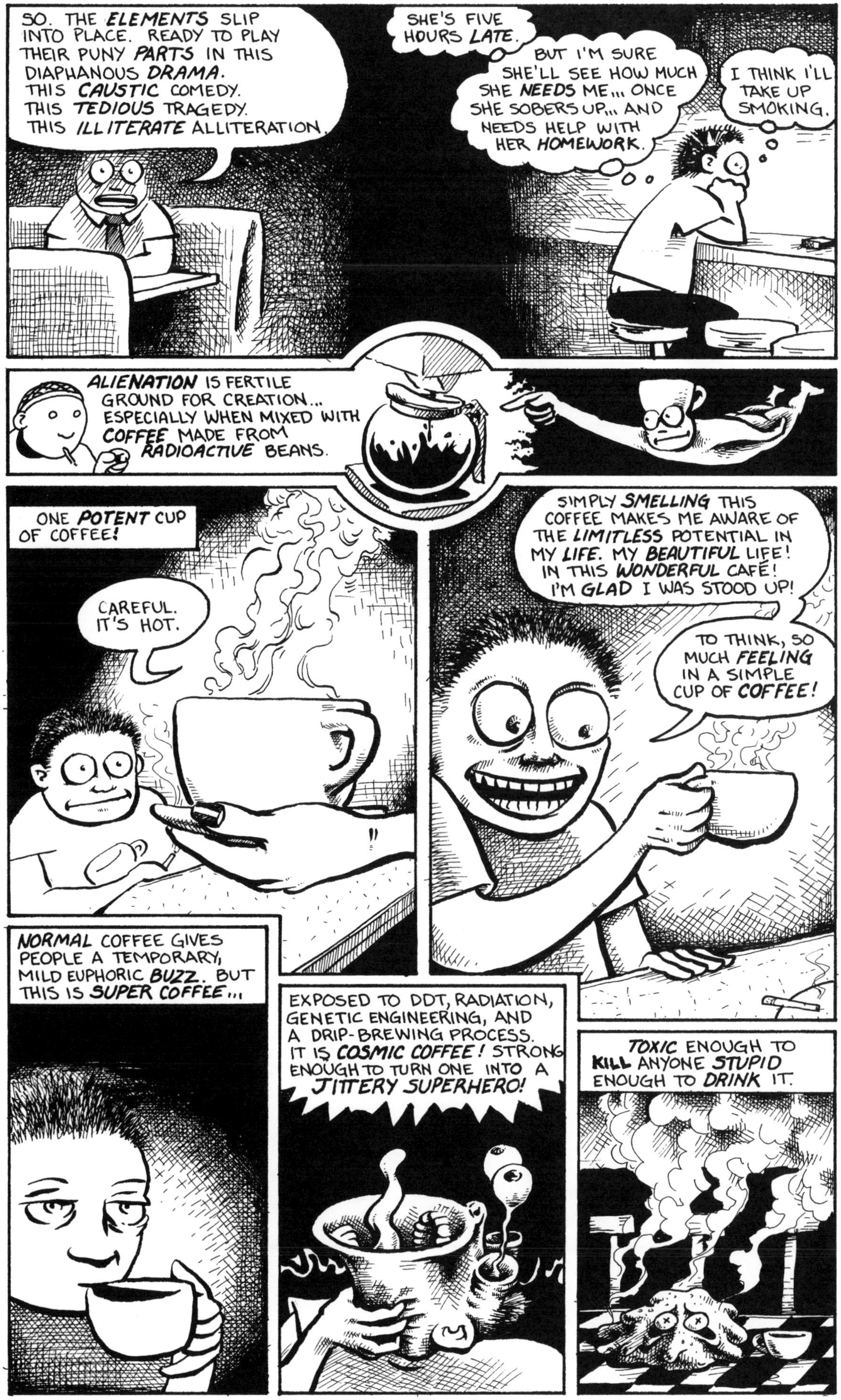

SO. THE ELEMENTS SLIP INTO PLACE. READY TO PLAY THEIR PUNY PARTS IN THIS DIAPHANOUS DRAMA. THIS CAUSTIC COMEDY. THIS TEDIOUS TRAGEDY. THIS ILLITERATE ALLITERATION.
SHE'S FIVE HOURS LATE.
BUT I'M SURE SHE'LL SEE HOW MUCH SHE NEEDS ME... ONCE SHE SOBERS UP... AND NEEDS HELP WITH HER HOMEWORK.
I THINK I'LL TAKE UP SMOKING.
ALIENATION IS FERTILE GROUND FOR CREATION... ESPECIALLY WHEN MIXED WITH COFFEE MADE FROM RADIOACTIVE BEANS.
ONE POTENT CUP OF COFFEE!
CAREFUL. IT'S HOT.
SIMPLY SMELLING THIS COFFEE MAKES ME AWARE OF THE LIMITLESS POTENTIAL IN MY LIFE. MY BEAUTIFUL LIFE! IN THIS WONDERFUL CAFÉ! I'M GLAD I WAS STOOD UP!
TO THINK, SO MUCH FEELING IN A SIMPLE CUP OF COFFEE!
NORMAL COFFEE GIVES PEOPLE A TEMPORARY, MILD EUPHORIC BUZZ. BUT THIS IS SUPER COFFEE...
EXPOSED TO DDT, RADIATION, GENETIC ENGINEERING, AND A DRIP-BREWING PROCESS. IT IS COSMIC COFFEE! STRONG ENOUGH TO TURN ONE INTO A JITTERY SUPERHERO!
TOXIC ENOUGH TO KILL ANYONE STUPID ENOUGH TO DRINK IT.

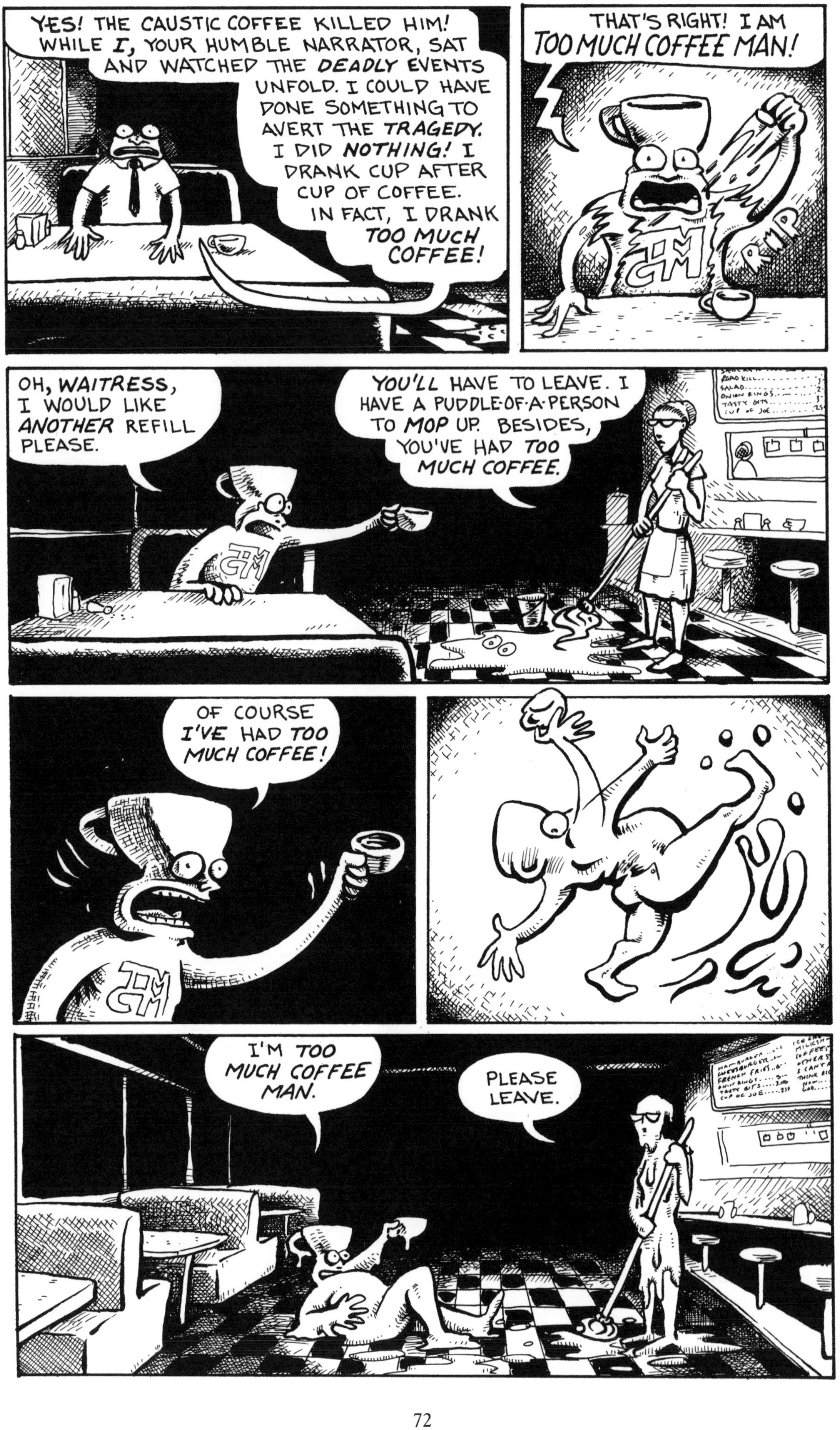
YES! THE CAUSTIC COFFEE KILLED HIM! WHILE I, YOUR HUMBLE NARRATOR, SAT AND WATCHED THE DEADLY EVENTS UNFOLD. I COULD HAVE DONE SOMETHING TO AVERT THE TRAGEDY. I DID NOTHING! I DRANK CUP AFTER CUP OF COFFEE. IN FACT, I DRANK TOO MUCH COFFEE!
THAT'S RIGHT! I AM TOO MUCH COFFEE MAN!
RIP
TM CM
OH, WAITRESS, I WOULD LIKE ANOTHER REFILL PLEASE.
YOU'LL HAVE TO LEAVE. I HAVE A PUDDLE-OF-A-PERSON TO MOP UP. BESIDES, YOU'VE HAD TOO MUCH COFFEE.
OF COURSE I'VE HAD TOO MUCH COFFEE!
I'M TOO MUCH COFFEE MAN.
PLEASE LEAVE.

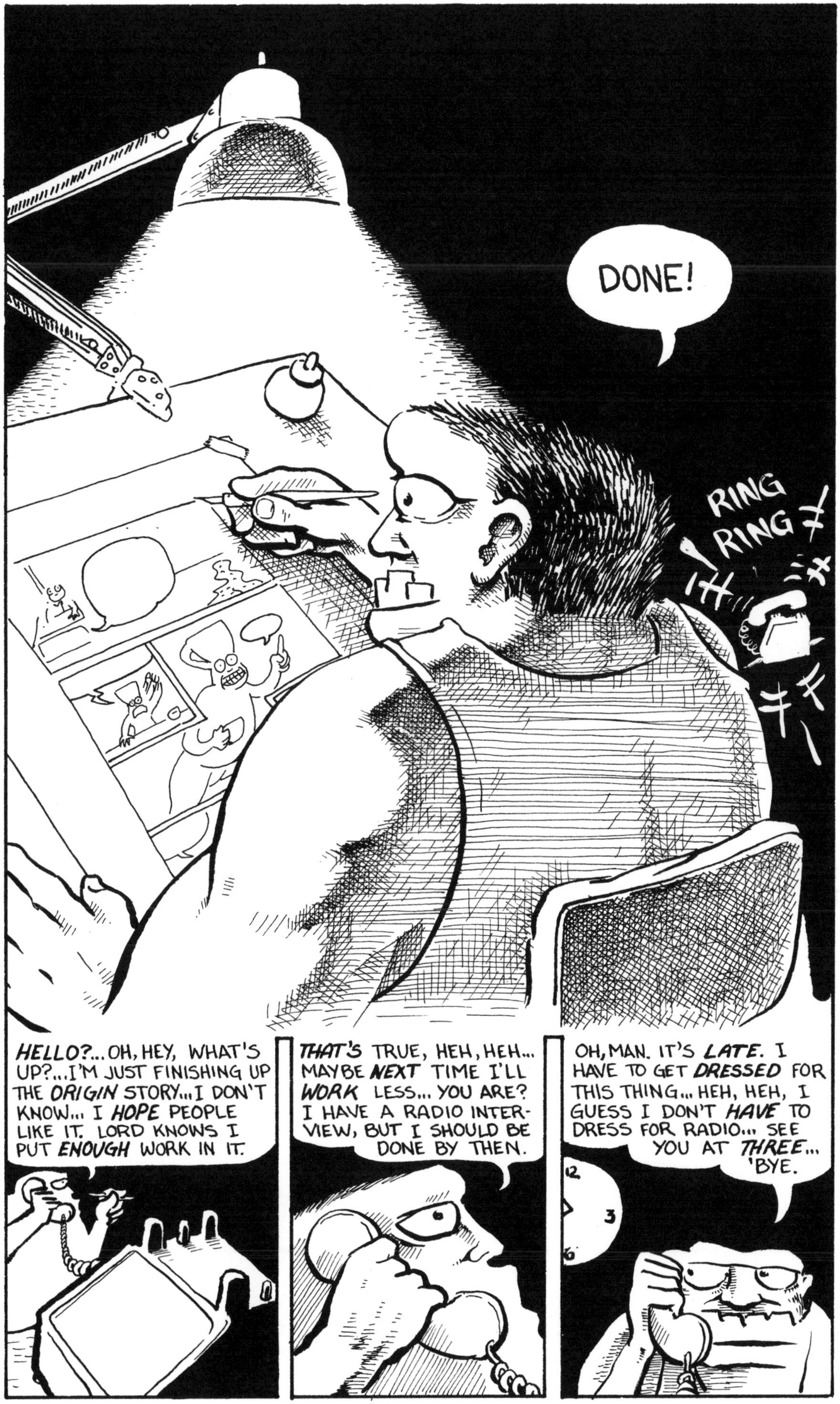
DONE!
RING RING
HELLO?...OH, HEY, WHAT'S UP?...I'M JUST FINISHING UP THE ORIGIN STORY...I DON'T KNOW... I HOPE PEOPLE LIKE IT. LORD KNOWS I PUT ENOUGH WORK IN IT.
THAT'S TRUE, HEH, HEH... MAYBE NEXT TIME I'LL WORK LESS... YOU ARE? I HAVE A RADIO INTER-VIEW, BUT I SHOULD BE DONE BY THEN.
OH, MAN. IT'S LATE. I HAVE TO GET DRESSED FOR THIS THING... HEH, HEH, I GUESS I DON'T HAVE TO DRESS FOR RADIO... SEE YOU AT THREE... 'BYE.

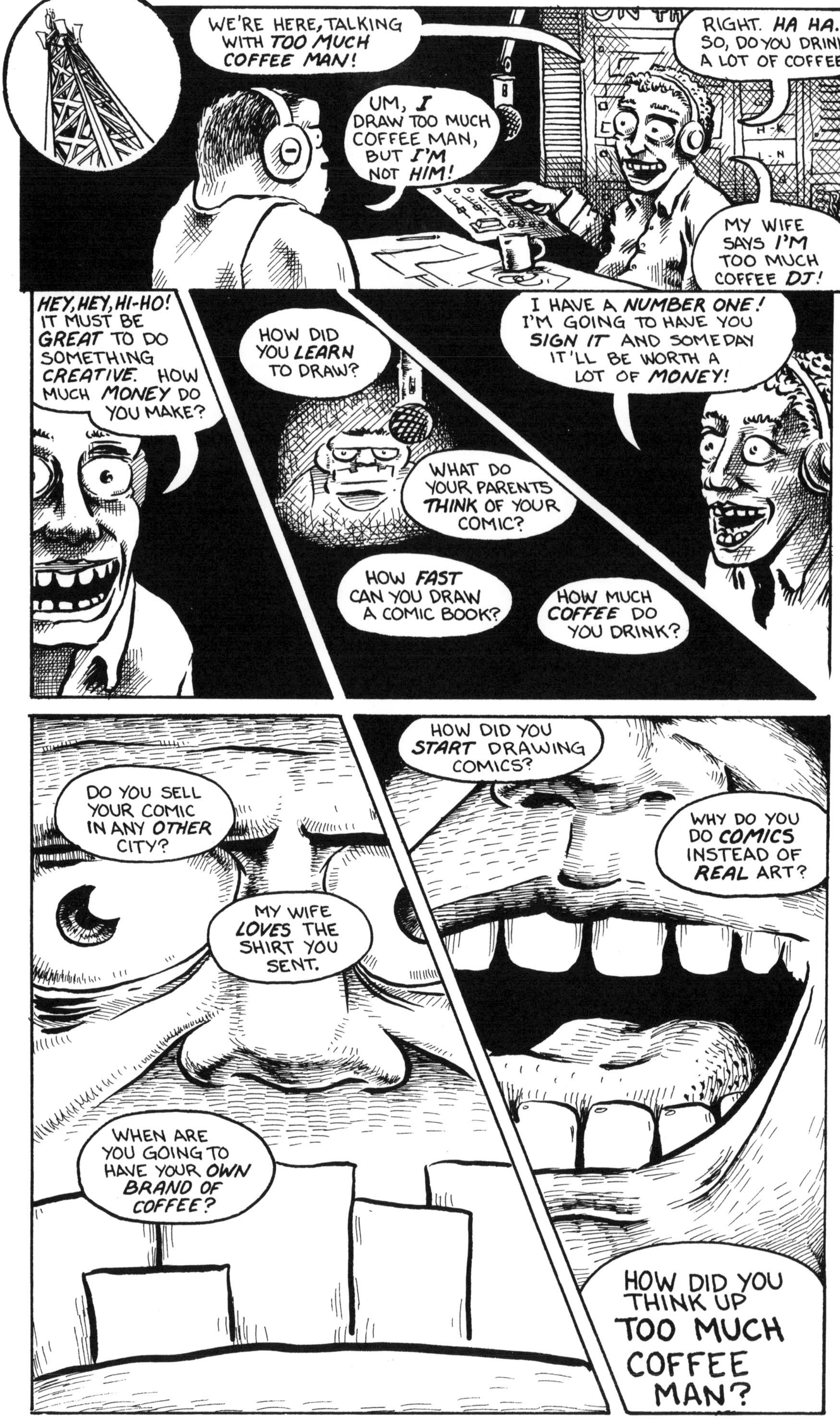
WE'RE HERE, TALKING WITH TOO MUCH COFFEE MAN!
UM, I DRAW TOO MUCH COFFEE MAN, BUT I'M NOT HIM!
RIGHT. HA HA. SO, DO YOU DRINK A LOT OF COFFEE?
MY WIFE SAYS I'M TOO MUCH COFFEE DJ!
HEY, HEY, HI-HO! IT MUST BE GREAT TO DO SOMETHING CREATIVE. HOW MUCH MONEY DO YOU MAKE?
HOW DID YOU LEARN TO DRAW?
I HAVE A NUMBER ONE! I'M GOING TO HAVE YOU SIGN IT AND SOMEDAY IT'LL BE WORTH A LOT OF MONEY!
WHAT DO YOUR PARENTS THINK OF YOUR COMIC?
HOW FAST CAN YOU DRAW A COMIC BOOK?
HOW MUCH COFFEE DO YOU DRINK?
DO YOU SELL YOUR COMIC IN ANY OTHER CITY?
MY WIFE LOVES THE SHIRT YOU SENT.
WHEN ARE YOU GOING TO HAVE YOUR OWN BRAND OF COFFEE?
HOW DID YOU START DRAWING COMICS?
WHY DO YOU DO COMICS INSTEAD OF REAL ART?
HOW DID YOU THINK UP TOO MUCH COFFEE MAN?

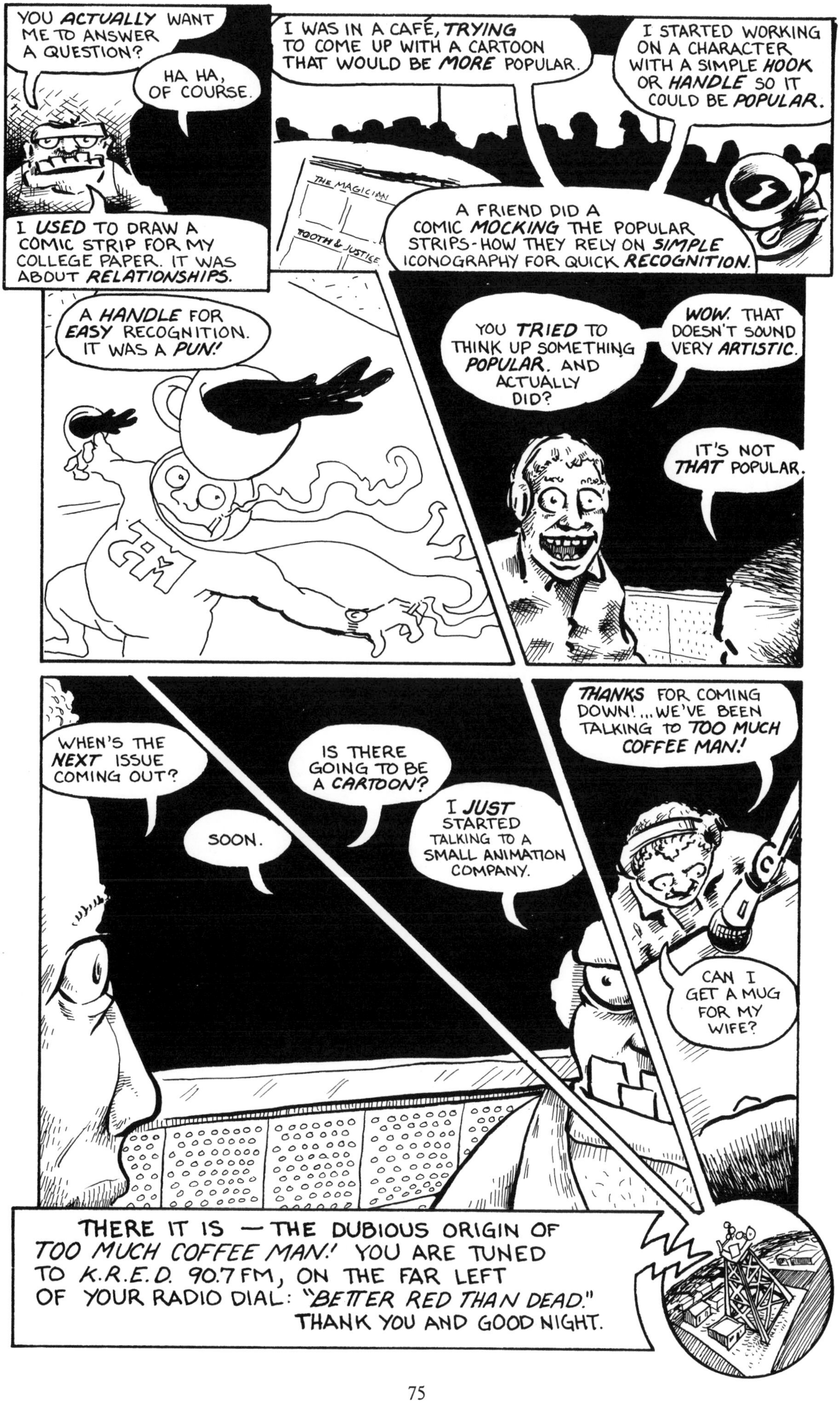
YOU ACTUALLY WANT ME TO ANSWER A QUESTION?
HA HA, OF COURSE.
I USED TO DRAW A COMIC STRIP FOR MY COLLEGE PAPER. IT WAS ABOUT RELATIONSHIPS.
I WAS IN A CAFÉ, TRYING TO COME UP WITH A CARTOON THAT WOULD BE MORE POPULAR.
I STARTED WORKING ON A CHARACTER WITH A SIMPLE HOOK OR HANDLE SO IT COULD BE POPULAR.
THE MAGICIAN
TOOTH & JUSTICE
A FRIEND DID A COMIC MOCKING THE POPULAR STRIPS- HOW THEY RELY ON SIMPLE ICONOGRAPHY FOR QUICK RECOGNITION.
A HANDLE FOR EASY RECOGNITION. IT WAS A PUN!
TCM
YOU TRIED TO THINK UP SOMETHING POPULAR, AND ACTUALLY DID?
WOW. THAT DOESN'T SOUND VERY ARTISTIC.
IT'S NOT THAT POPULAR.
WHEN'S THE NEXT ISSUE COMING OUT?
SOON.
IS THERE GOING TO BE A CARTOON?
I JUST STARTED TALKING TO A SMALL ANIMATION COMPANY.
THANKS FOR COMING DOWN!...WE'VE BEEN TALKING TO TOO MUCH COFFEE MAN!
CAN I GET A MUG FOR MY WIFE?
THERE IT IS — THE DUBIOUS ORIGIN OF TOO MUCH COFFEE MAN! YOU ARE TUNED TO K.R.E.D. 90.7 FM, ON THE FAR LEFT OF YOUR RADIO DIAL: "BETTER RED THAN DEAD." THANK YOU AND GOOD NIGHT.

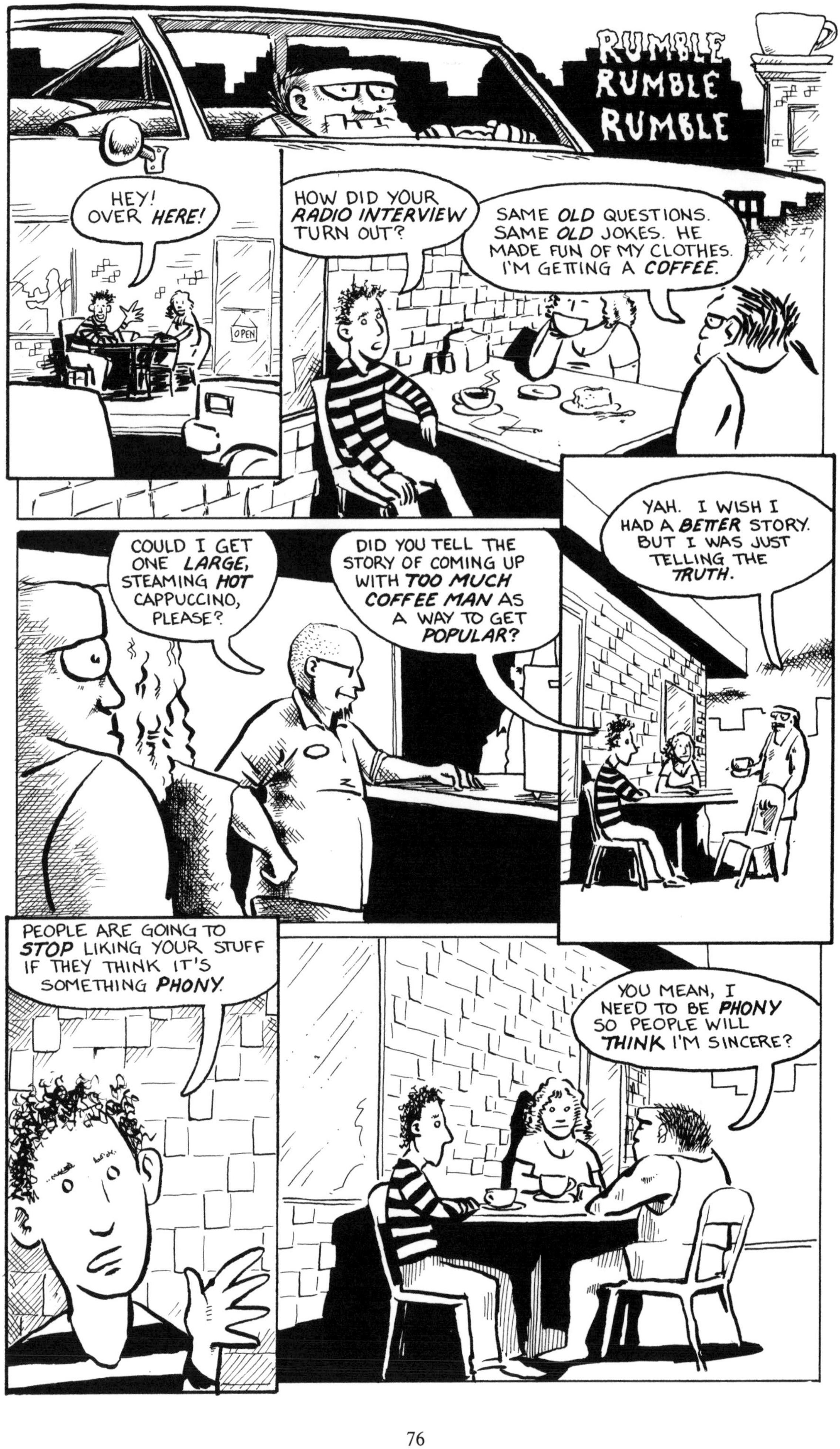
RUMBLE RUMBLE RUMBLE
HEY! OVER HERE!
OPEN
HOW DID YOUR RADIO INTERVIEW TURN OUT?
SAME OLD QUESTIONS. SAME OLD JOKES. HE MADE FUN OF MY CLOTHES. I'M GETTING A COFFEE.
COULD I GET ONE LARGE, STEAMING HOT CAPPUCCINO, PLEASE?
DID YOU TELL THE STORY OF COMING UP WITH TOO MUCH COFFEE MAN AS A WAY TO GET POPULAR?
YAH. I WISH I HAD A BETTER STORY. BUT I WAS JUST TELLING THE TRUTH.
PEOPLE ARE GOING TO STOP LIKING YOUR STUFF IF THEY THINK IT'S SOMETHING PHONY.
YOU MEAN, I NEED TO BE PHONY SO PEOPLE WILL THINK I'M SINCERE?

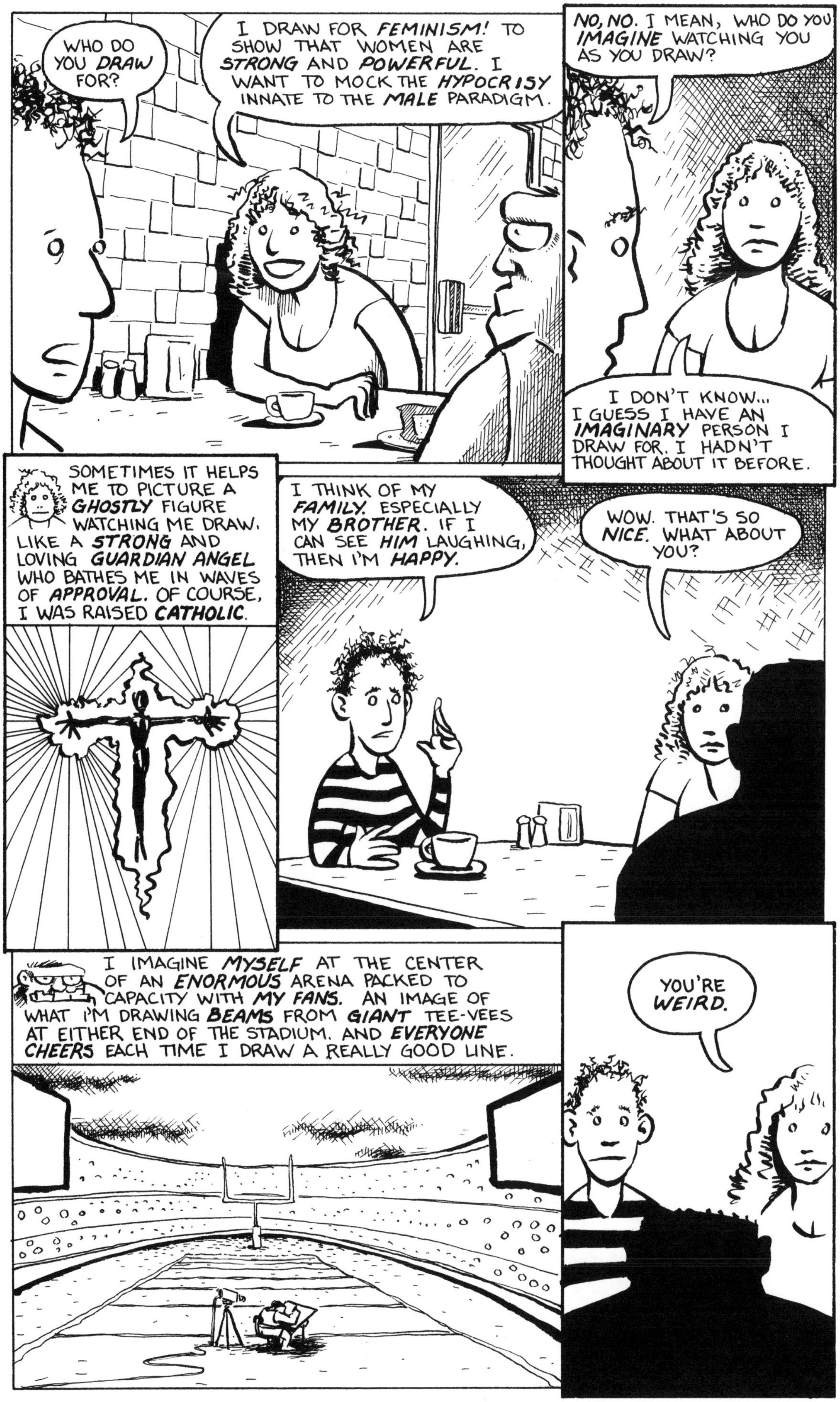
WHO DO YOU DRAW FOR?
I DRAW FOR FEMINISM! TO SHOW THAT WOMEN ARE STRONG AND POWERFUL. I WANT TO MOCK THE HYPOCRISY INNATE TO THE MALE PARADIGM.
NO, NO. I MEAN, WHO DO YOU IMAGINE WATCHING YOU AS YOU DRAW?
I DON'T KNOW... I GUESS I HAVE AN IMAGINARY PERSON I DRAW FOR. I HADN'T THOUGHT ABOUT IT BEFORE.
SOMETIMES IT HELPS ME TO PICTURE A GHOSTLY FIGURE WATCHING ME DRAW. LIKE A STRONG AND LOVING GUARDIAN ANGEL WHO BATHES ME IN WAVES OF APPROVAL. OF COURSE, I WAS RAISED CATHOLIC.
I THINK OF MY FAMILY. ESPECIALLY MY BROTHER. IF I CAN SEE HIM LAUGHING, THEN I'M HAPPY.
WOW. THAT'S SO NICE. WHAT ABOUT YOU?
I IMAGINE MYSELF AT THE CENTER OF AN ENORMOUS ARENA PACKED TO CAPACITY WITH MY FANS. AN IMAGE OF WHAT I'M DRAWING BEAMS FROM GIANT TEE-VEES AT EITHER END OF THE STADIUM. AND EVERYONE CHEERS EACH TIME I DRAW A REALLY GOOD LINE.
YOU'RE WEIRD.

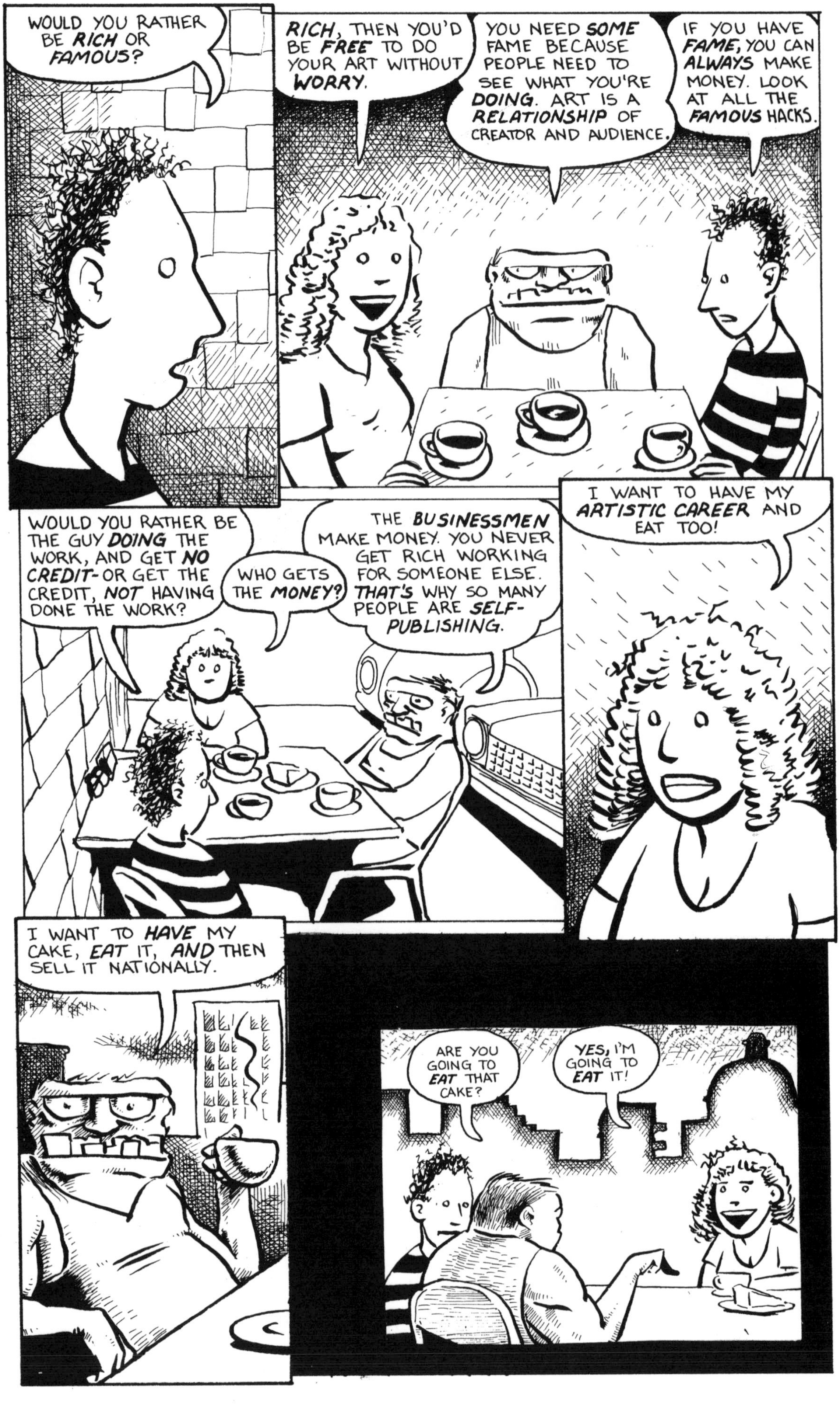
WOULD YOU RATHER BE RICH OR FAMOUS?
RICH, THEN YOU'D BE FREE TO DO YOUR ART WITHOUT WORRY.
YOU NEED SOME FAME BECAUSE PEOPLE NEED TO SEE WHAT YOU'RE DOING. ART IS A RELATIONSHIP OF CREATOR AND AUDIENCE.
IF YOU HAVE FAME, YOU CAN ALWAYS MAKE MONEY. LOOK AT ALL THE FAMOUS HACKS.
WOULD YOU RATHER BE THE GUY DOING THE WORK, AND GET NO CREDIT- OR GET THE CREDIT, NOT HAVING DONE THE WORK?
WHO GETS THE MONEY?
THE BUSINESSMEN MAKE MONEY. YOU NEVER GET RICH WORKING FOR SOMEONE ELSE. THAT'S WHY SO MANY PEOPLE ARE SELF-PUBLISHING.
I WANT TO HAVE MY ARTISTIC CAREER AND EAT TOO!
I WANT TO HAVE MY CAKE, EAT IT, AND THEN SELL IT NATIONALLY.
ARE YOU GOING TO EAT THAT CAKE?
YES, I'M GOING TO EAT IT!

I FEEL
SICK.

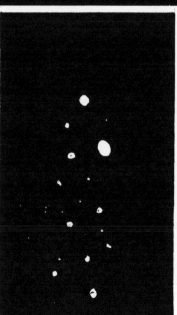

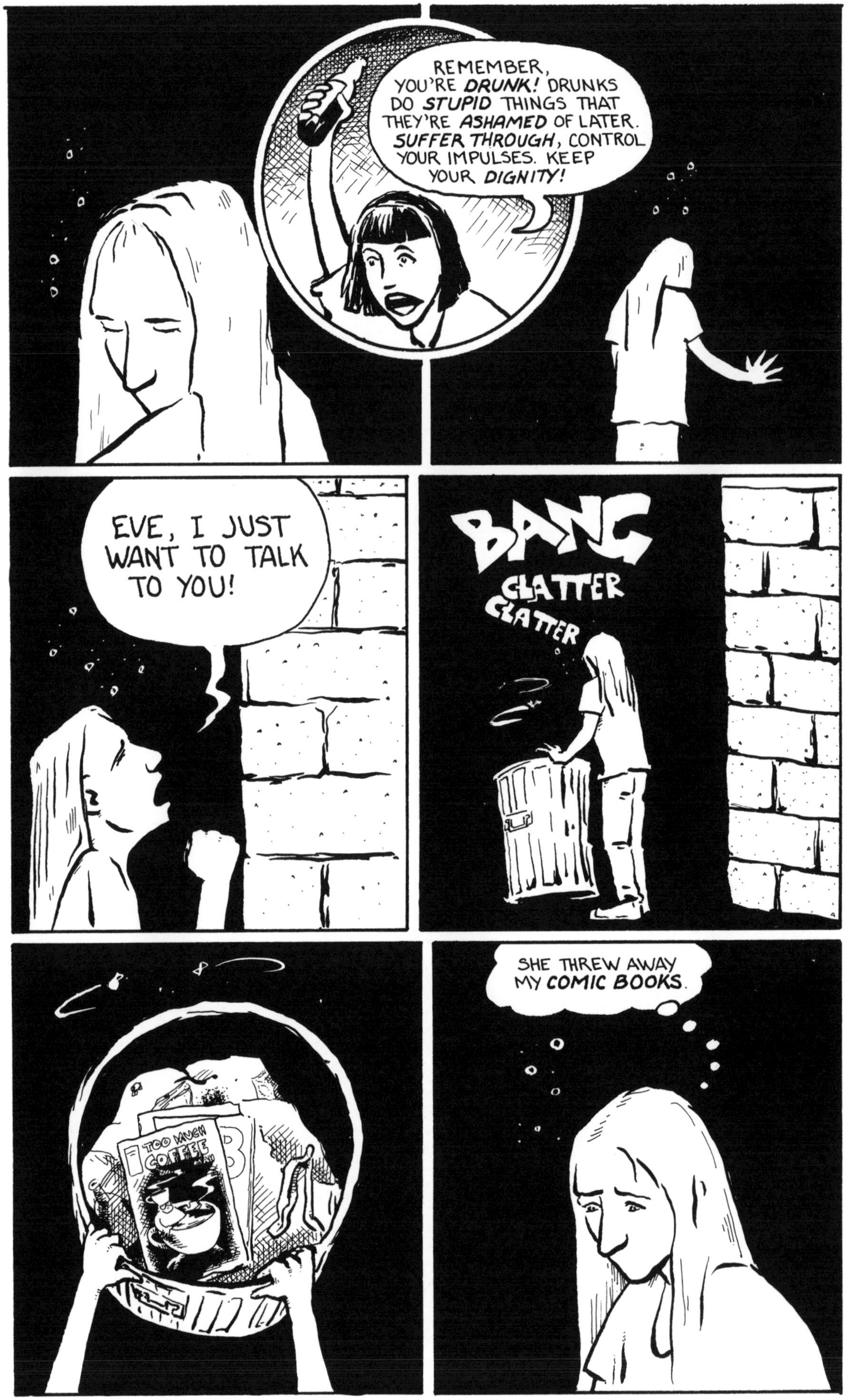
REMEMBER, YOU'RE DRUNK! DRUNKS DO STUPID THINGS THAT THEY'RE ASHAMED OF LATER. SUFFER THROUGH, CONTROL YOUR IMPULSES. KEEP YOUR DIGNITY!
EVE, I JUST WANT TO TALK TO YOU!
BANG
CLATTER
CLATTER
TOO MUCH COFFEE
SHE THREW AWAY MY COMIC BOOKS.

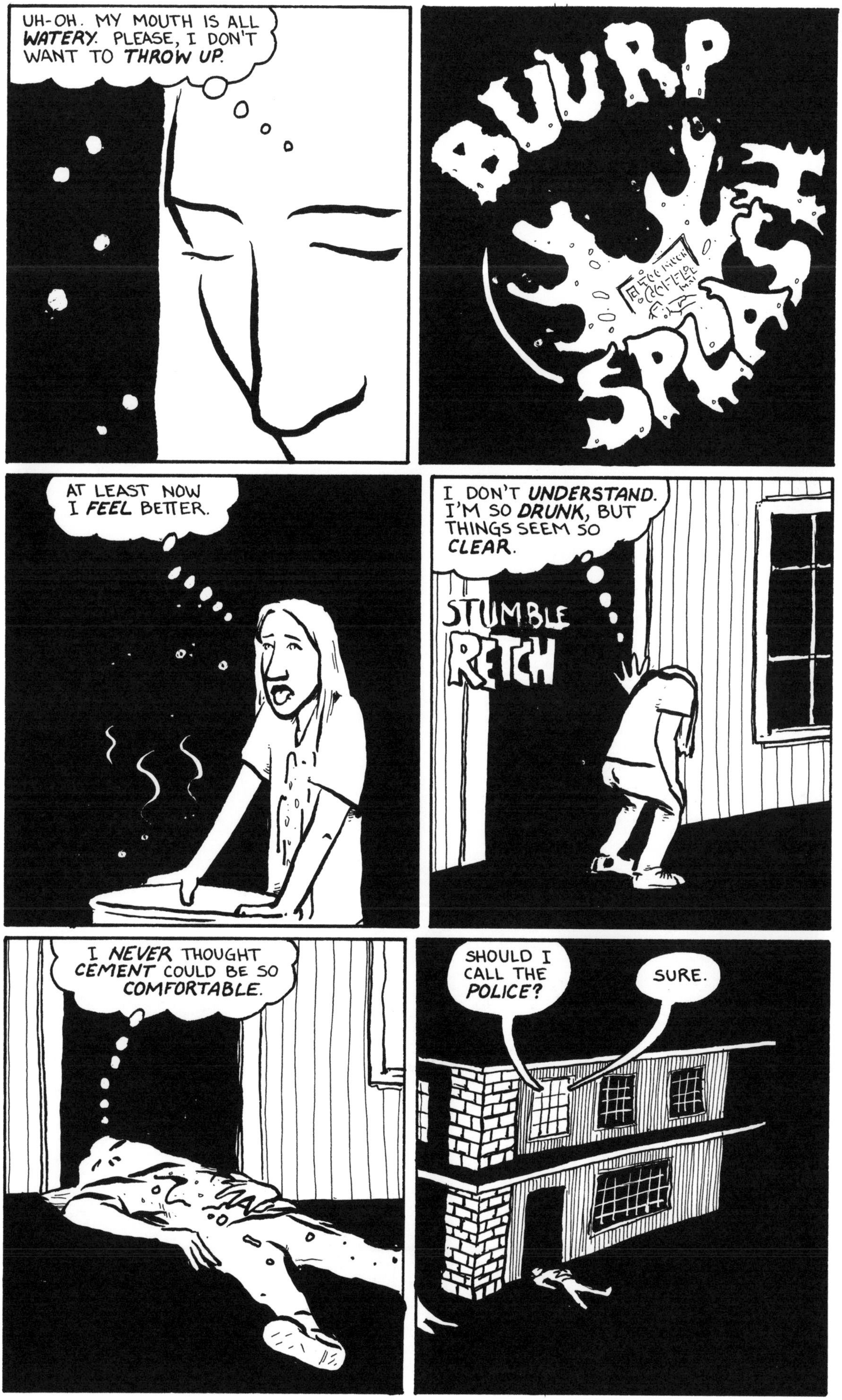
UH-OH. MY MOUTH IS ALL WATERY. PLEASE, I DON'T WANT TO THROW UP.
BUURP
SPLASH
AT LEAST NOW I FEEL BETTER.
I DON'T UNDERSTAND. I'M SO DRUNK, BUT THINGS SEEM SO CLEAR.
STUMBLE
RETCH
I NEVER THOUGHT CEMENT COULD BE SO COMFORTABLE.
SHOULD I CALL THE POLICE?
SURE.

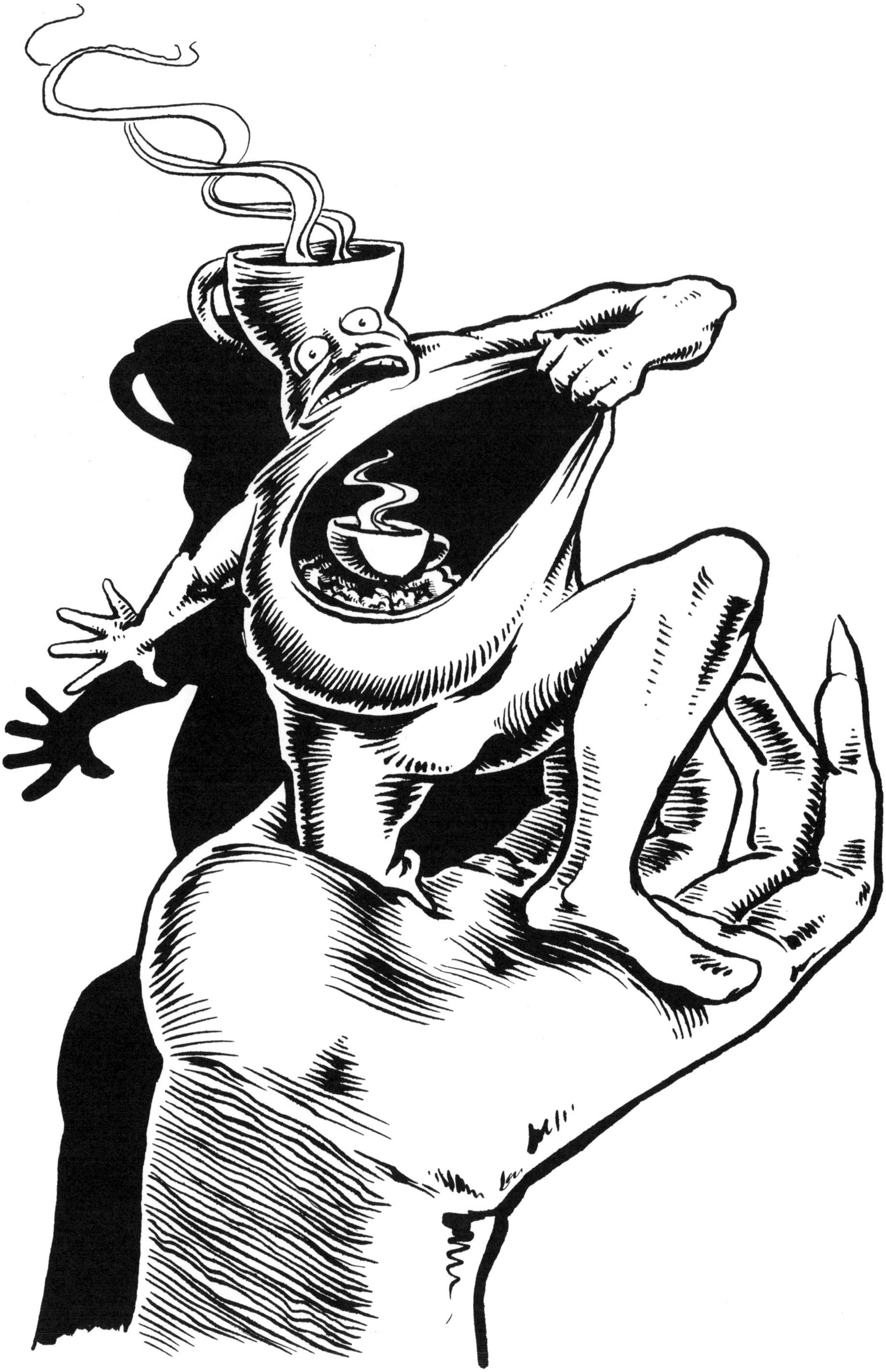

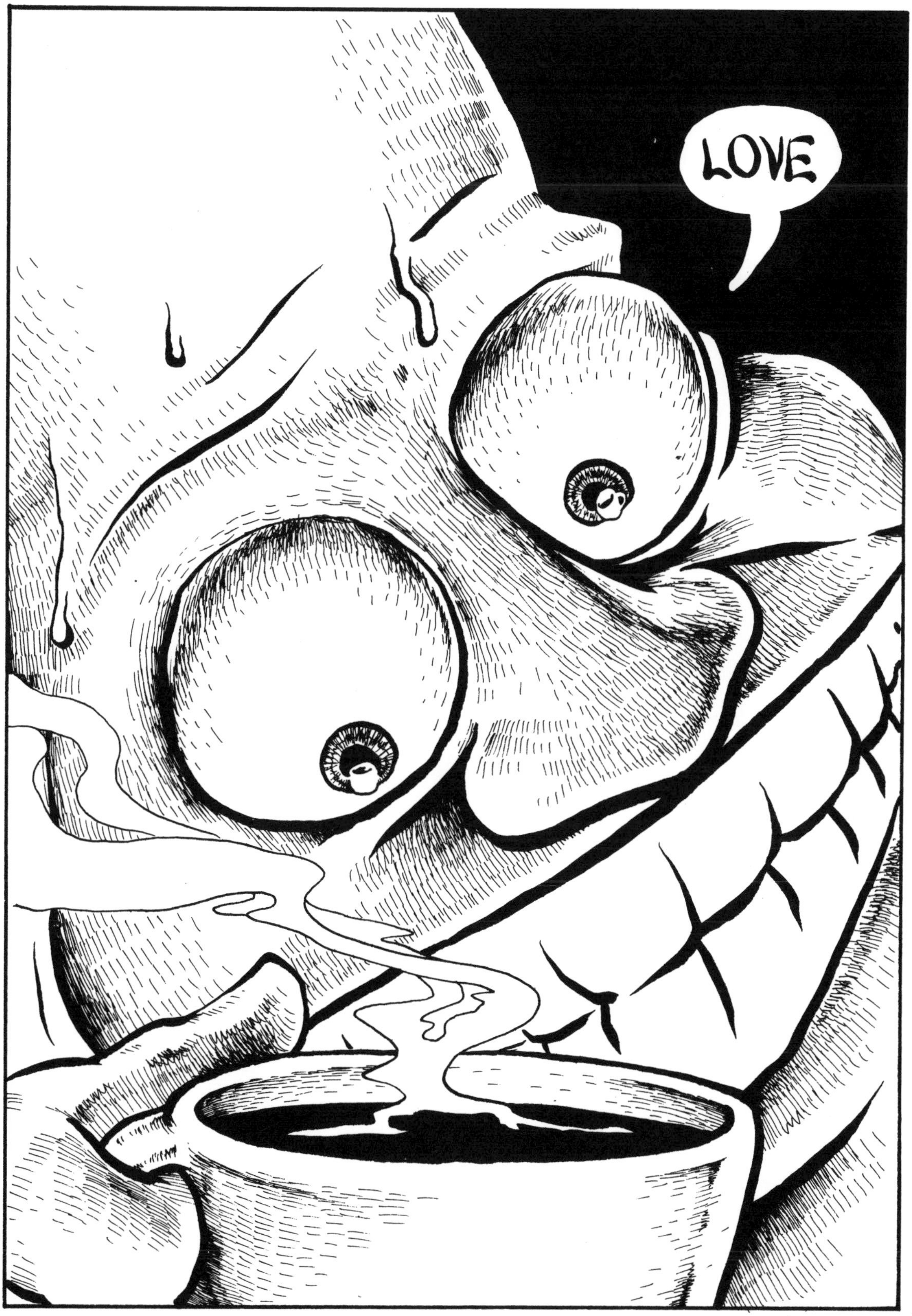
LOVE

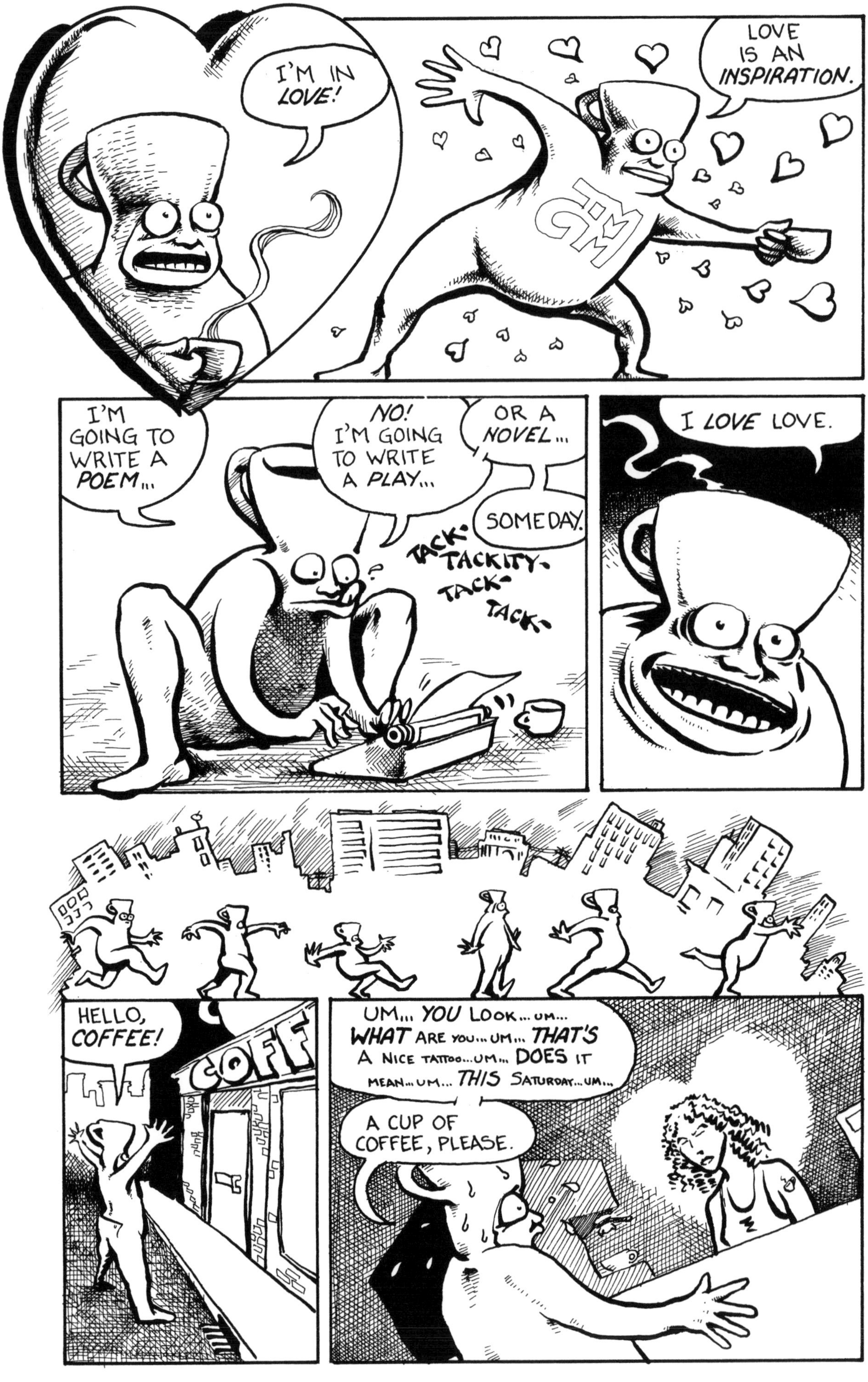
I'M IN LOVE!
LOVE IS AN INSPIRATION.
I'M GOING TO WRITE A POEM...
NO! I'M GOING TO WRITE A PLAY...
OR A NOVEL...
SOMEDAY.
TACK-TACKITY-TACK-TACK-
I LOVE LOVE.
HELLO, COFFEE!
COFF
UM... YOU LOOK... UM... WHAT ARE YOU... UM... THAT'S A NICE TATTOO... UM... DOES IT MEAN... UM... THIS SATURDAY... UM...
A CUP OF COFFEE, PLEASE.

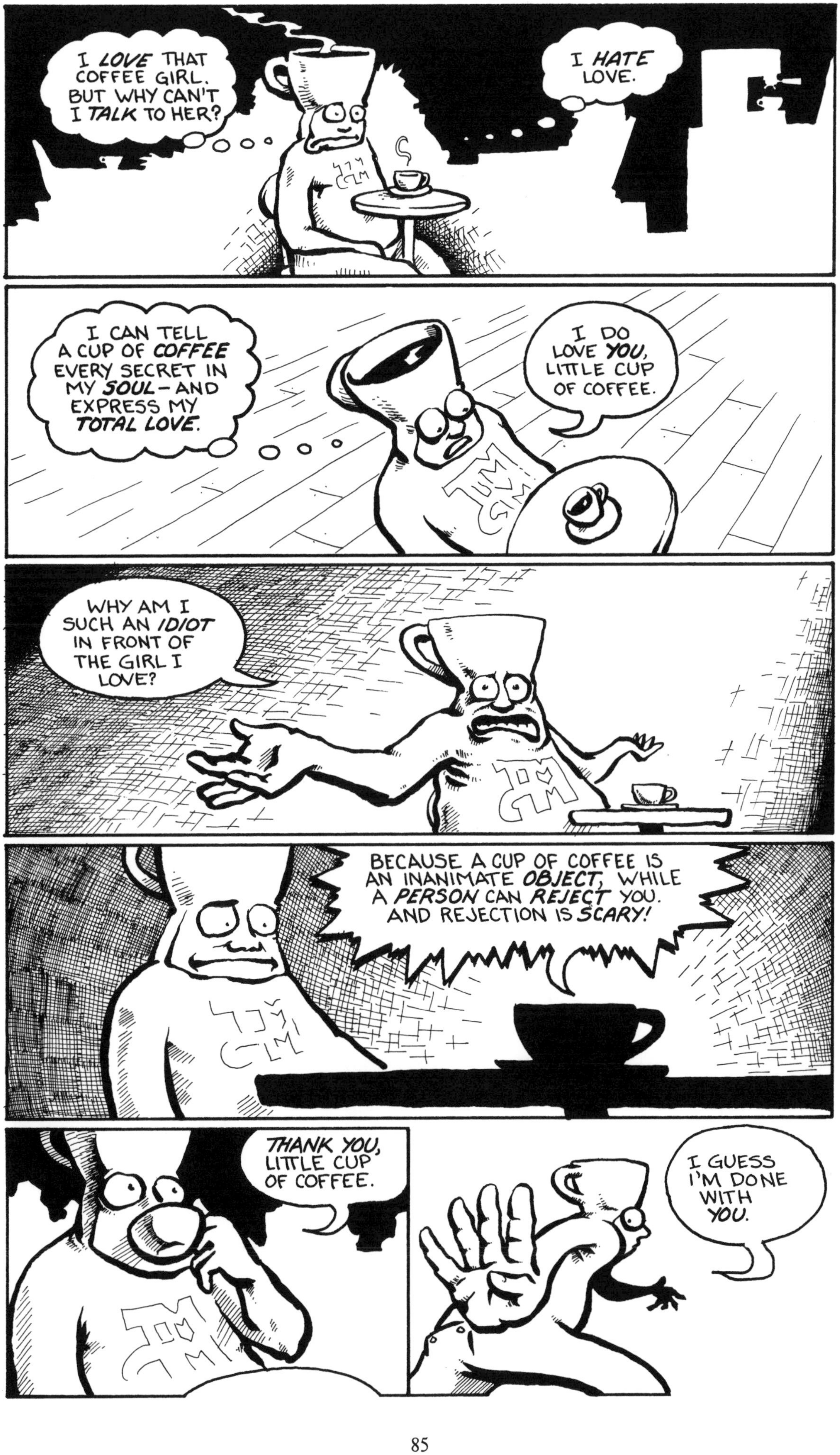
I LOVE THAT COFFEE GIRL. BUT WHY CAN'T I TALK TO HER?
I HATE LOVE.
I CAN TELL A CUP OF COFFEE EVERY SECRET IN MY SOUL—AND EXPRESS MY TOTAL LOVE.
I DO LOVE YOU, LITTLE CUP OF COFFEE.
WHY AM I SUCH AN IDIOT IN FRONT OF THE GIRL I LOVE?
BECAUSE A CUP OF COFFEE IS AN INANIMATE OBJECT, WHILE A PERSON CAN REJECT YOU. AND REJECTION IS SCARY!
THANK YOU, LITTLE CUP OF COFFEE.
I GUESS I'M DONE WITH YOU.

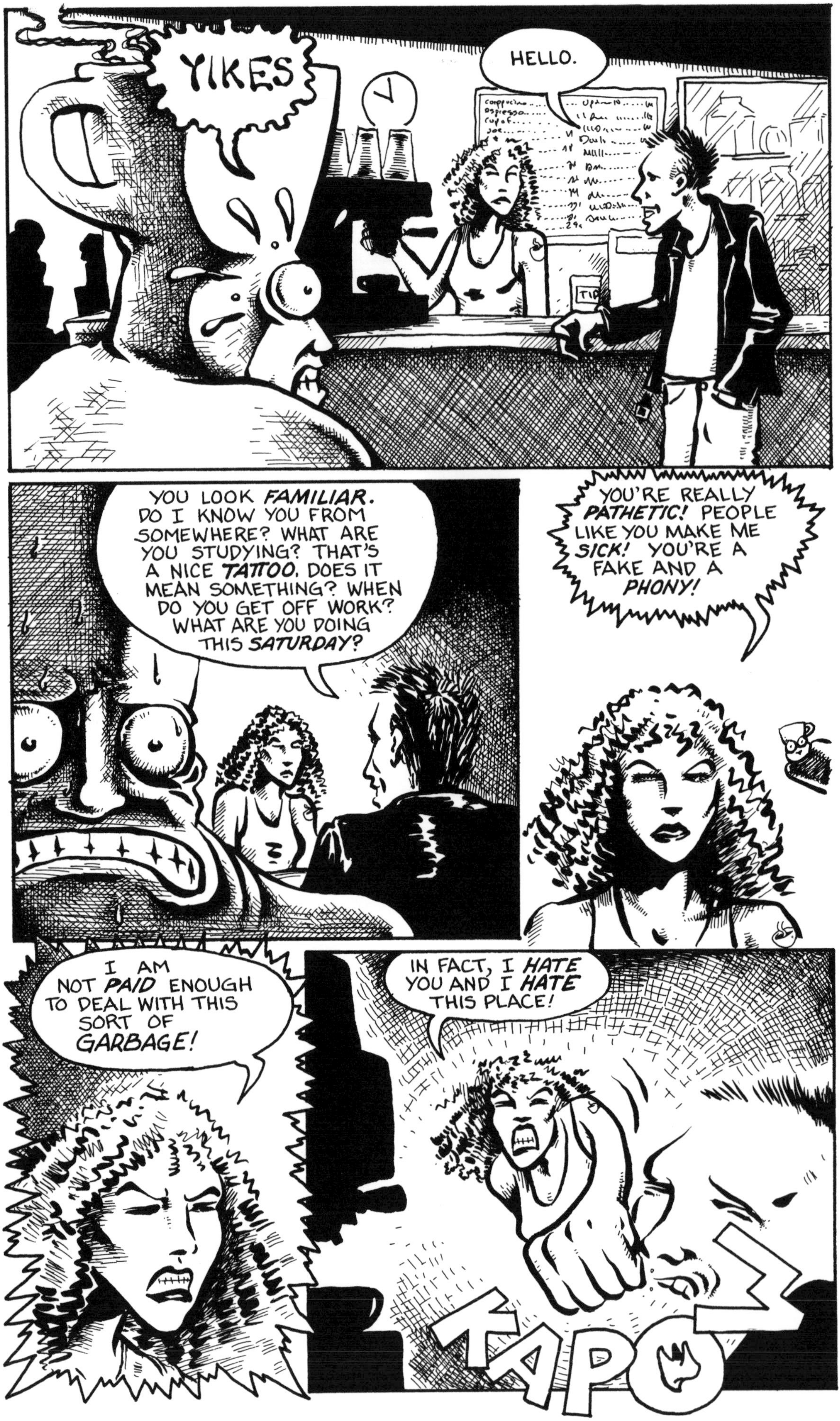
YIKES
HELLO.
YOU LOOK FAMILIAR. DO I KNOW YOU FROM SOMEWHERE? WHAT ARE YOU STUDYING? THAT'S A NICE TATTOO. DOES IT MEAN SOMETHING? WHEN DO YOU GET OFF WORK? WHAT ARE YOU DOING THIS SATURDAY?
YOU'RE REALLY PATHETIC! PEOPLE LIKE YOU MAKE ME SICK! YOU'RE A FAKE AND A PHONY!
I AM NOT PAID ENOUGH TO DEAL WITH THIS SORT OF GARBAGE!
IN FACT, I HATE YOU AND I HATE THIS PLACE!
KAPOW

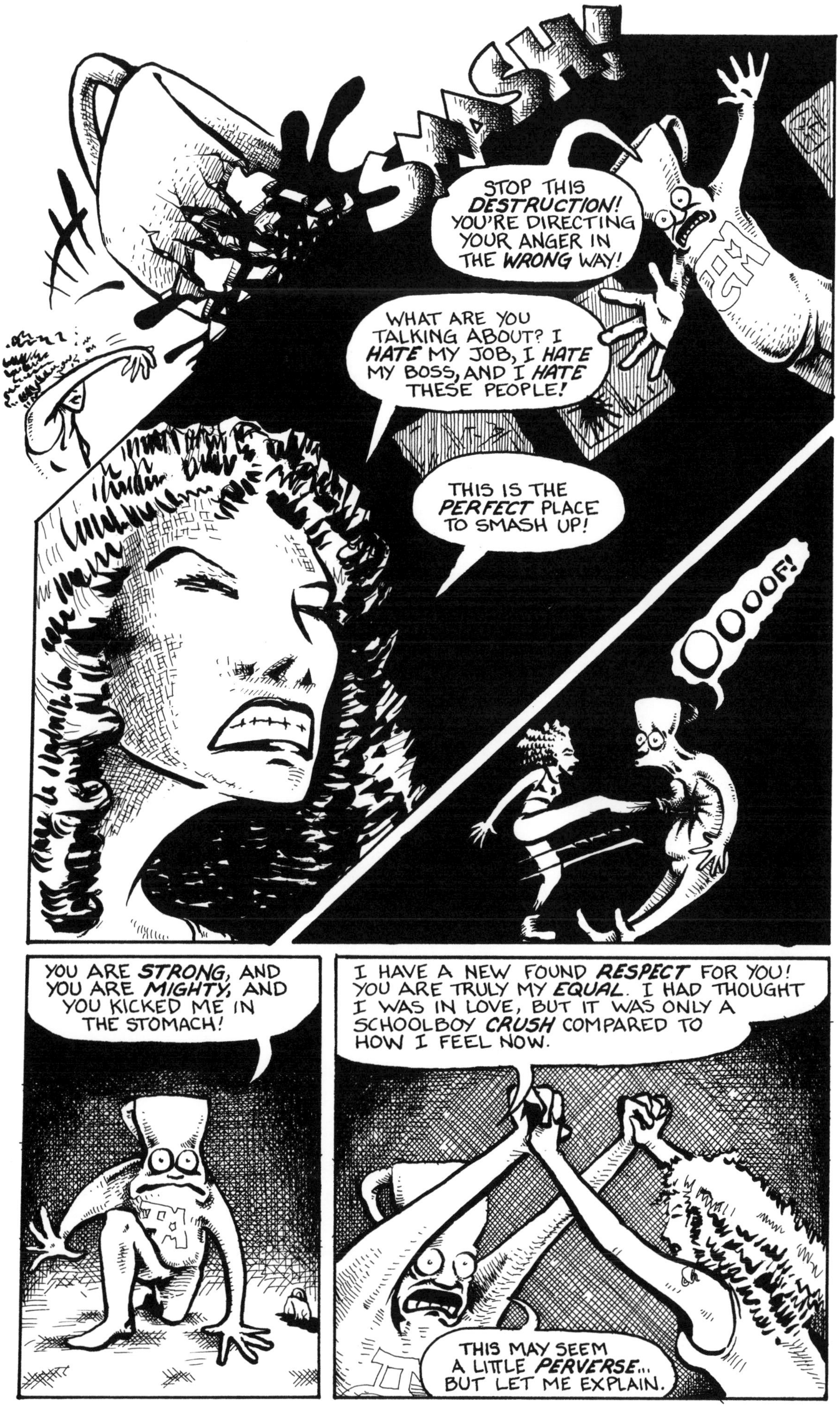
SMASH!
STOP THIS DESTRUCTION! YOU'RE DIRECTING YOUR ANGER IN THE WRONG WAY!
WHAT ARE YOU TALKING ABOUT? I HATE MY JOB, I HATE MY BOSS, AND I HATE THESE PEOPLE!
THIS IS THE PERFECT PLACE TO SMASH UP!
OOOOOF!
YOU ARE STRONG, AND YOU ARE MIGHTY, AND YOU KICKED ME IN THE STOMACH!
I HAVE A NEW FOUND RESPECT FOR YOU! YOU ARE TRULY MY EQUAL. I HAD THOUGHT I WAS IN LOVE, BUT IT WAS ONLY A SCHOOLBOY CRUSH COMPARED TO HOW I FEEL NOW.
THIS MAY SEEM A LITTLE PERVERSE... BUT LET ME EXPLAIN.

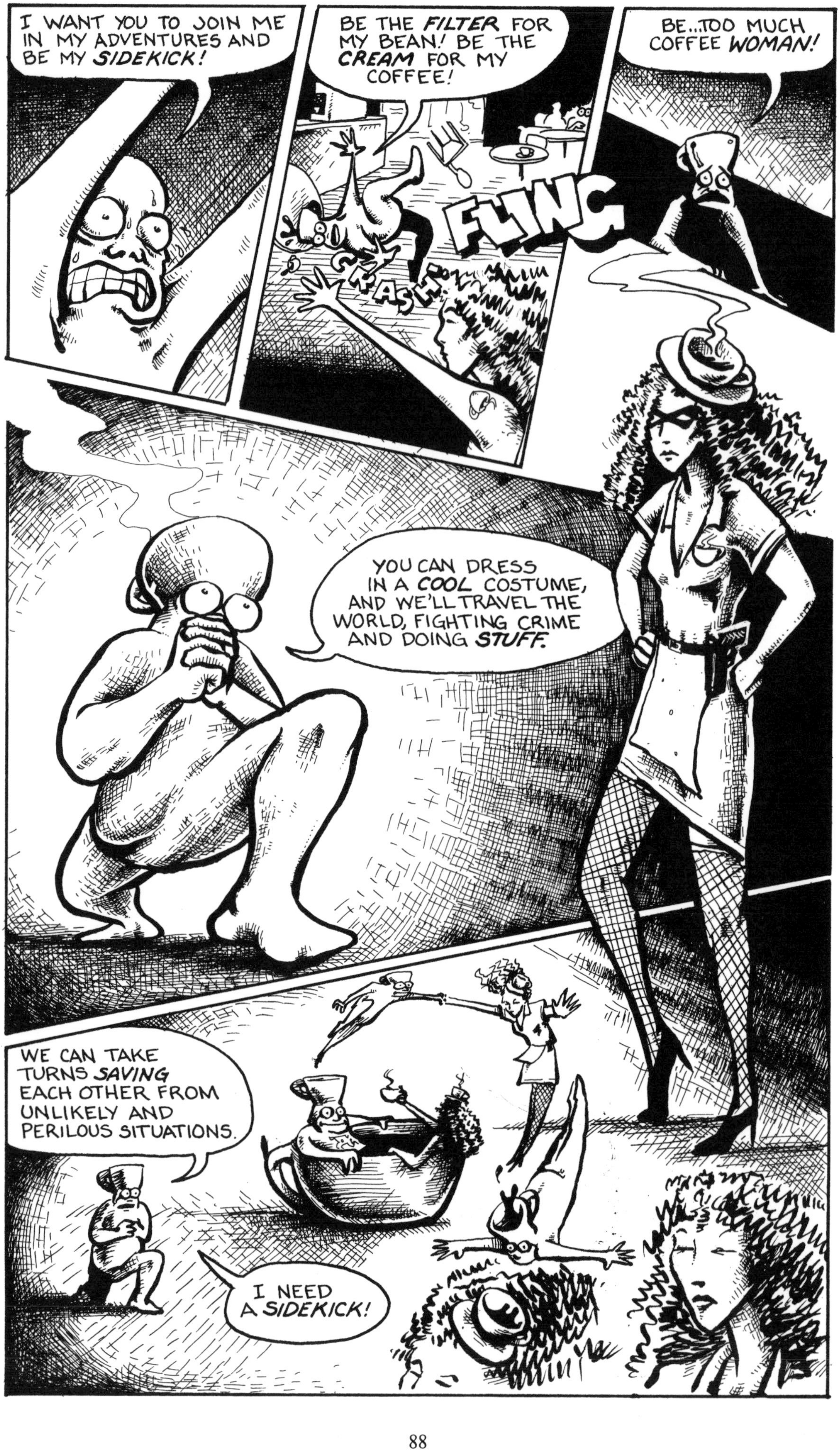
I WANT YOU TO JOIN ME IN MY ADVENTURES AND BE MY SIDEKICK!
BE THE FILTER FOR MY BEAN! BE THE CREAM FOR MY COFFEE!
FLING
CRASH
BE...TOO MUCH COFFEE WOMAN!
YOU CAN DRESS IN A COOL COSTUME, AND WE'LL TRAVEL THE WORLD, FIGHTING CRIME AND DOING STUFF.
WE CAN TAKE TURNS SAVING EACH OTHER FROM UNLIKELY AND PERILOUS SITUATIONS.
I NEED A SIDEKICK!

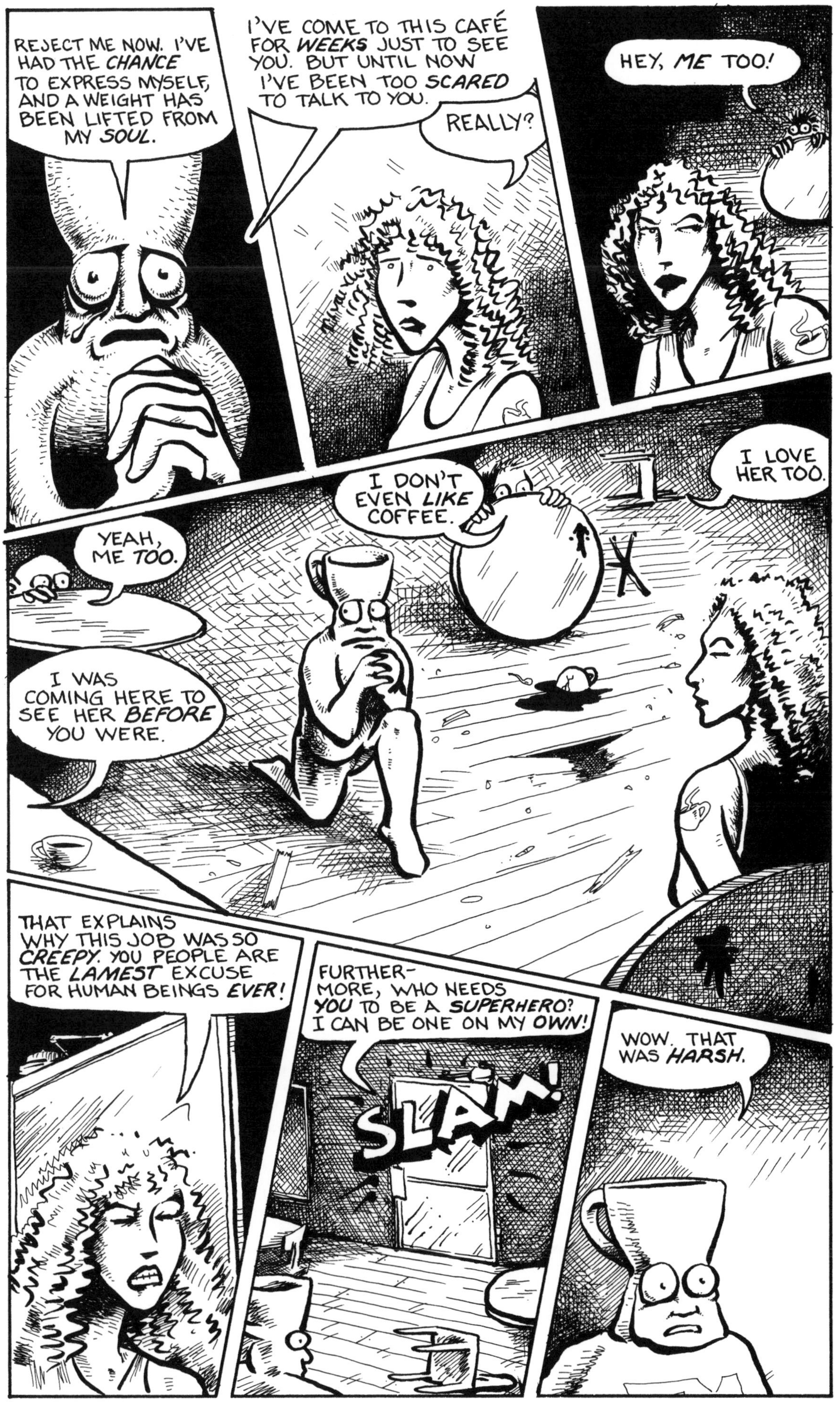
REJECT ME NOW. I'VE HAD THE CHANCE TO EXPRESS MYSELF, AND A WEIGHT HAS BEEN LIFTED FROM MY SOUL.
I'VE COME TO THIS CAFÉ FOR WEEKS JUST TO SEE YOU. BUT UNTIL NOW I'VE BEEN TOO SCARED TO TALK TO YOU.
REALLY?
HEY, ME TOO!
I DON'T EVEN LIKE COFFEE.
I LOVE HER TOO.
YEAH, ME TOO.
I WAS COMING HERE TO SEE HER BEFORE YOU WERE.
THAT EXPLAINS WHY THIS JOB WAS SO CREEPY. YOU PEOPLE ARE THE LAMEST EXCUSE FOR HUMAN BEINGS EVER!
FURTHER-MORE, WHO NEEDS YOU TO BE A SUPERHERO? I CAN BE ONE ON MY OWN!
SLAM!
WOW. THAT WAS HARSH.

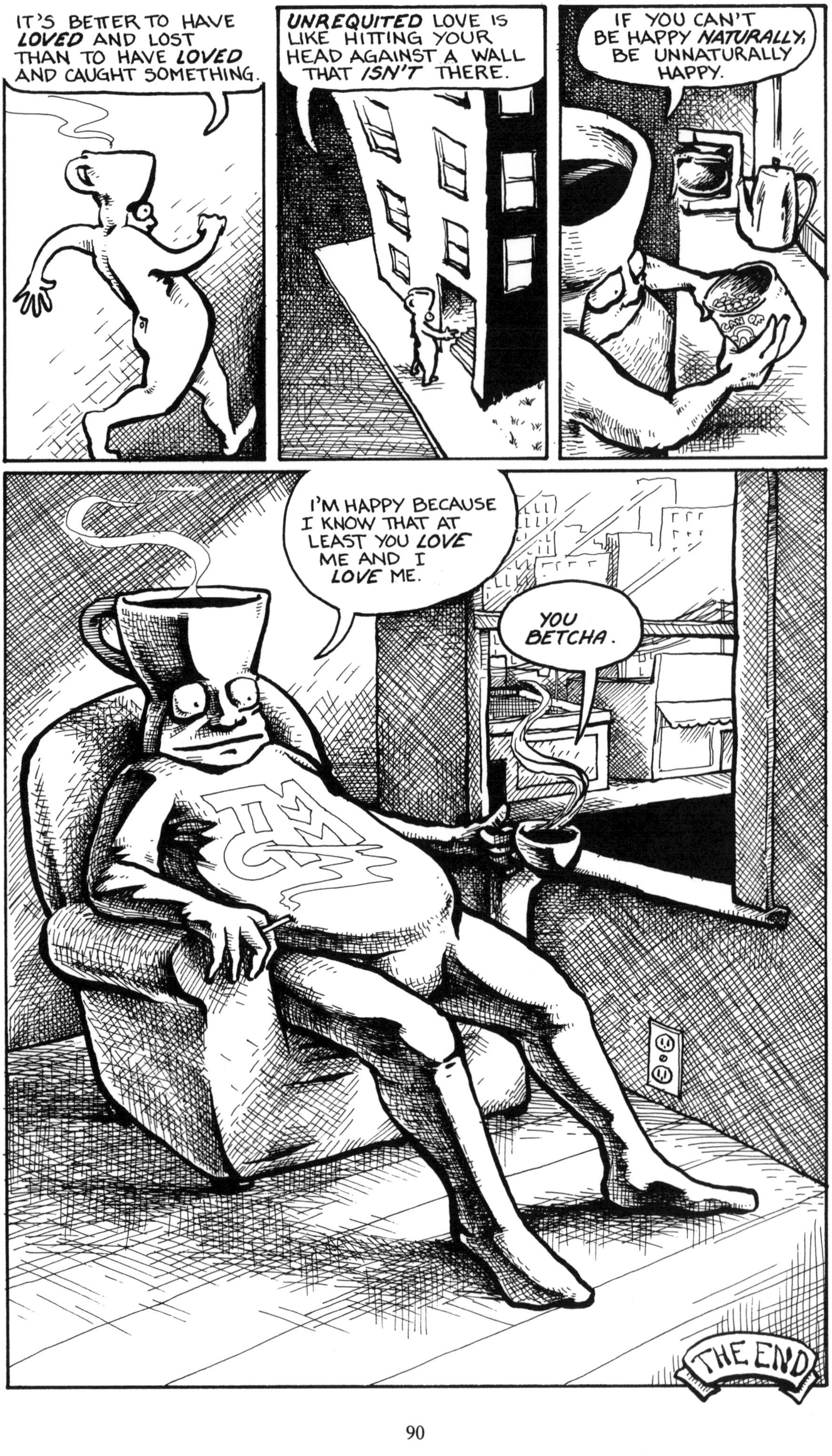
IT'S BETTER TO HAVE LOVED AND LOST THAN TO HAVE LOVED AND CAUGHT SOMETHING.
UNREQUITED LOVE IS LIKE HITTING YOUR HEAD AGAINST A WALL THAT ISN'T THERE.
IF YOU CAN'T BE HAPPY NATURALLY, BE UNNATURALLY HAPPY.
I'M HAPPY BECAUSE I KNOW THAT AT LEAST YOU LOVE ME AND I LOVE ME.
YOU BETCHA.
THE END

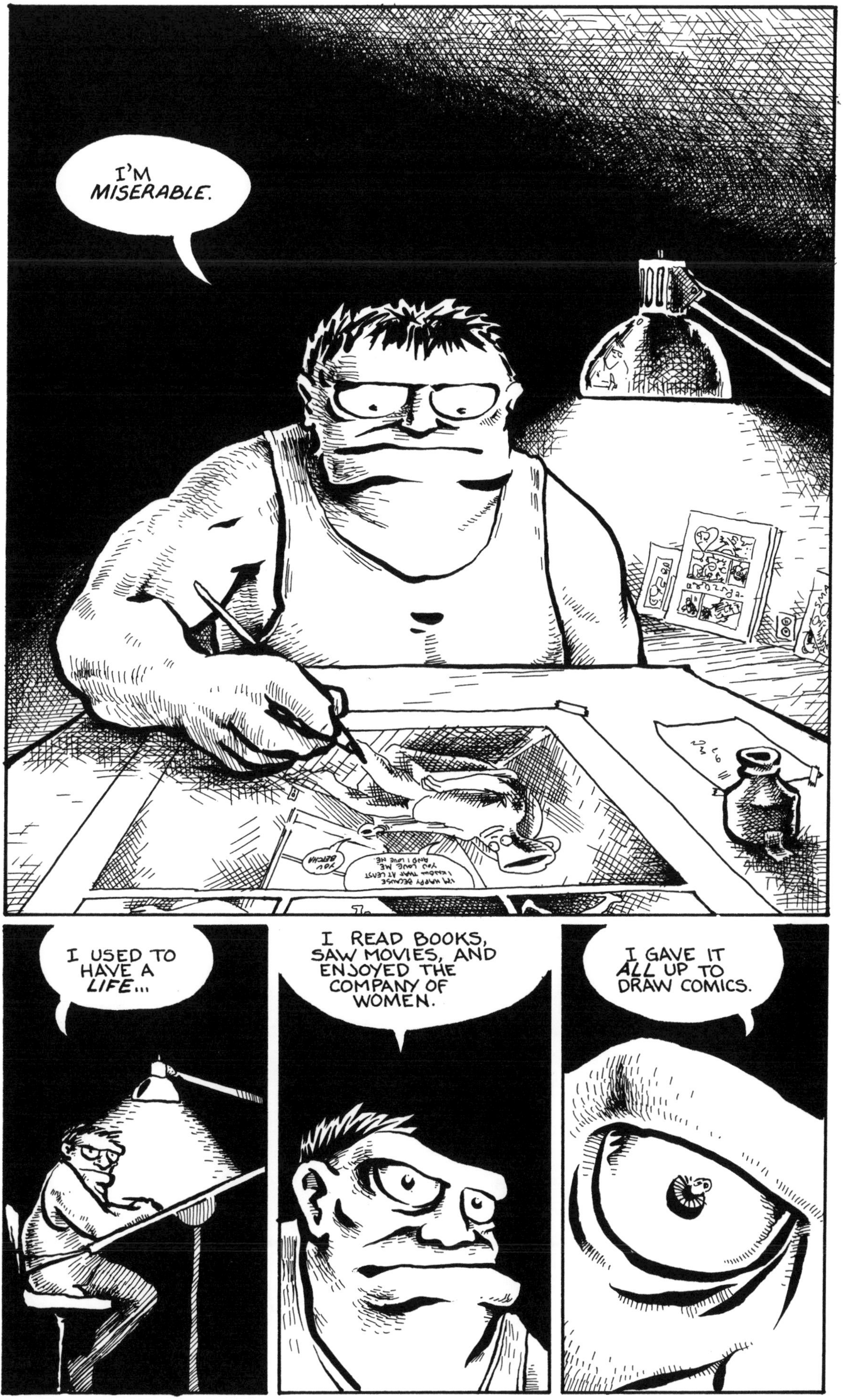
I'M MISERABLE.
I USED TO HAVE A LIFE...
I READ BOOKS, SAW MOVIES, AND ENJOYED THE COMPANY OF WOMEN.
I GAVE IT ALL UP TO DRAW COMICS.

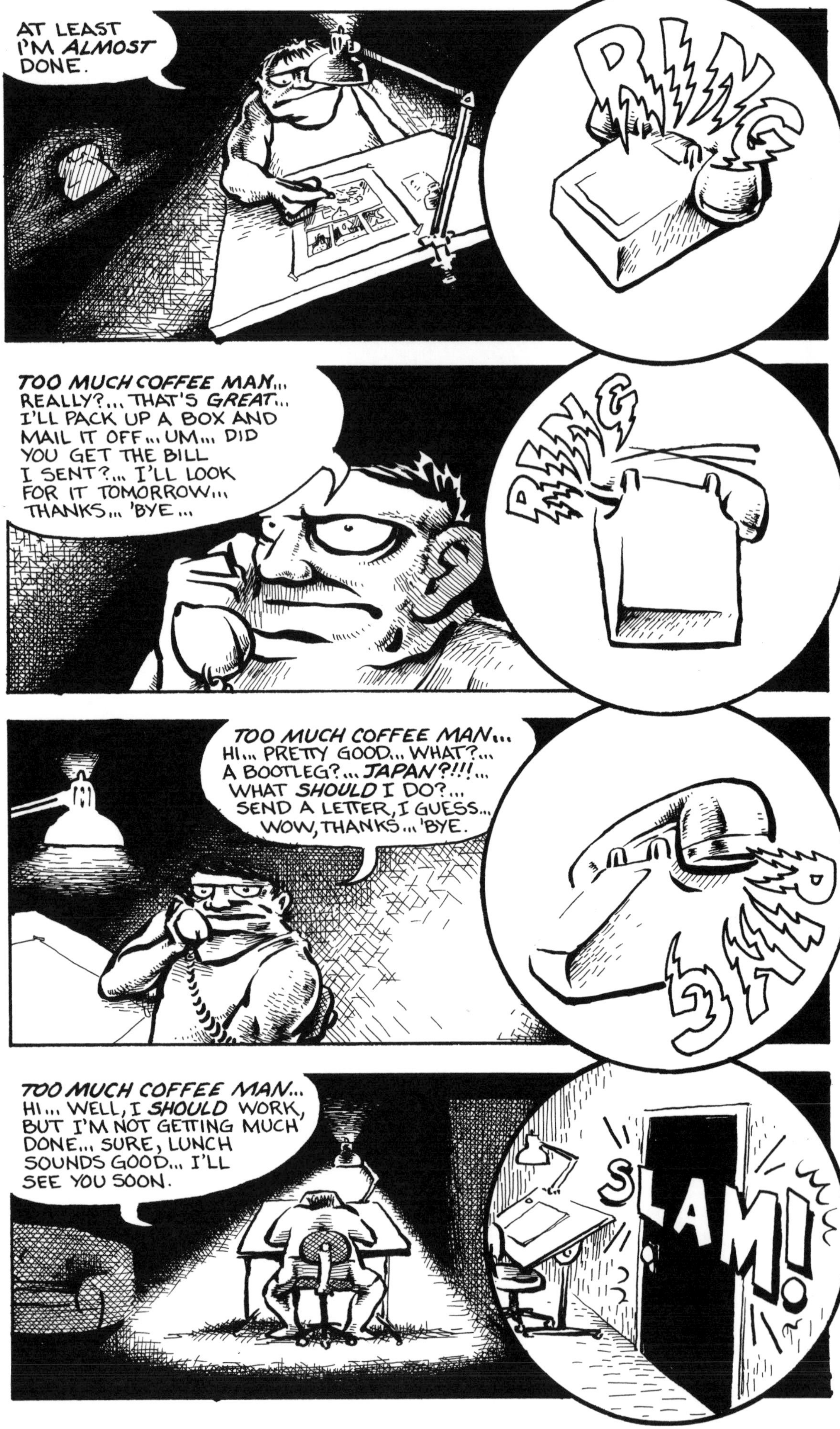
AT LEAST I'M ALMOST DONE.
RING
TOO MUCH COFFEE MAN... REALLY?... THAT'S GREAT... I'LL PACK UP A BOX AND MAIL IT OFF... UM... DID YOU GET THE BILL I SENT?... I'LL LOOK FOR IT TOMORROW... THANKS... 'BYE...
RING
TOO MUCH COFFEE MAN... HI... PRETTY GOOD... WHAT?... A BOOTLEG?... JAPAN?!!!... WHAT SHOULD I DO?... SEND A LETTER, I GUESS... WOW, THANKS... 'BYE.
RING
TOO MUCH COFFEE MAN... HI... WELL, I SHOULD WORK, BUT I'M NOT GETTING MUCH DONE... SURE, LUNCH SOUNDS GOOD... I'LL SEE YOU SOON.
SLAM!

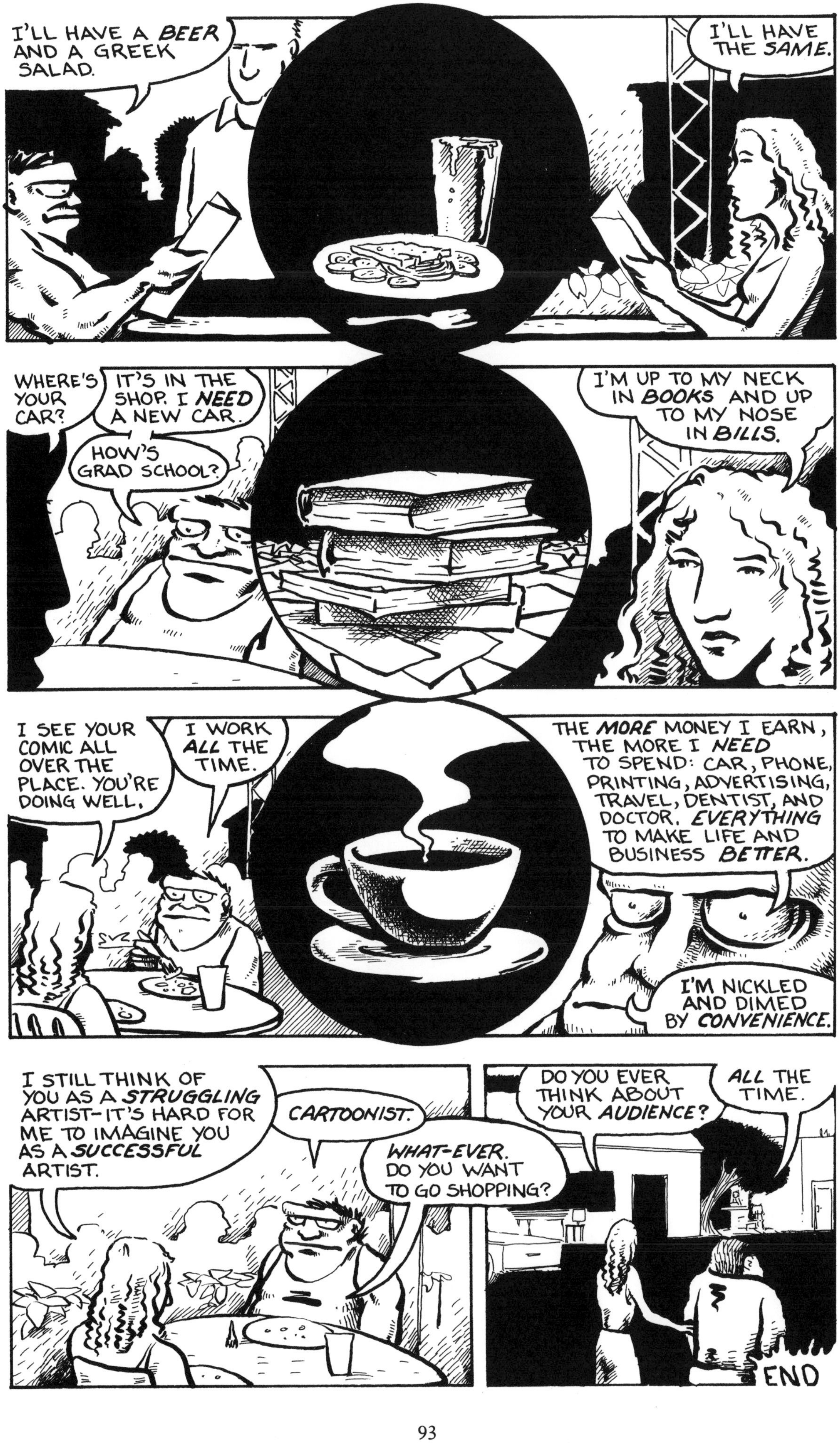
I'LL HAVE A BEER AND A GREEK SALAD.
I'LL HAVE THE SAME.
WHERE'S YOUR CAR?
IT'S IN THE SHOP. I NEED A NEW CAR.
HOW'S GRAD SCHOOL?
I'M UP TO MY NECK IN BOOKS AND UP TO MY NOSE IN BILLS.
I SEE YOUR COMIC ALL OVER THE PLACE. YOU'RE DOING WELL.
I WORK ALL THE TIME.
THE MORE MONEY I EARN, THE MORE I NEED TO SPEND: CAR, PHONE, PRINTING, ADVERTISING, TRAVEL, DENTIST, AND DOCTOR. EVERYTHING TO MAKE LIFE AND BUSINESS BETTER.
I'M NICKLED AND DIMED BY CONVENIENCE.
I STILL THINK OF YOU AS A STRUGGLING ARTIST-IT'S HARD FOR ME TO IMAGINE YOU AS A SUCCESSFUL ARTIST.
CARTOONIST.
WHAT-EVER. DO YOU WANT TO GO SHOPPING?
DO YOU EVER THINK ABOUT YOUR AUDIENCE?
ALL THE TIME.
END

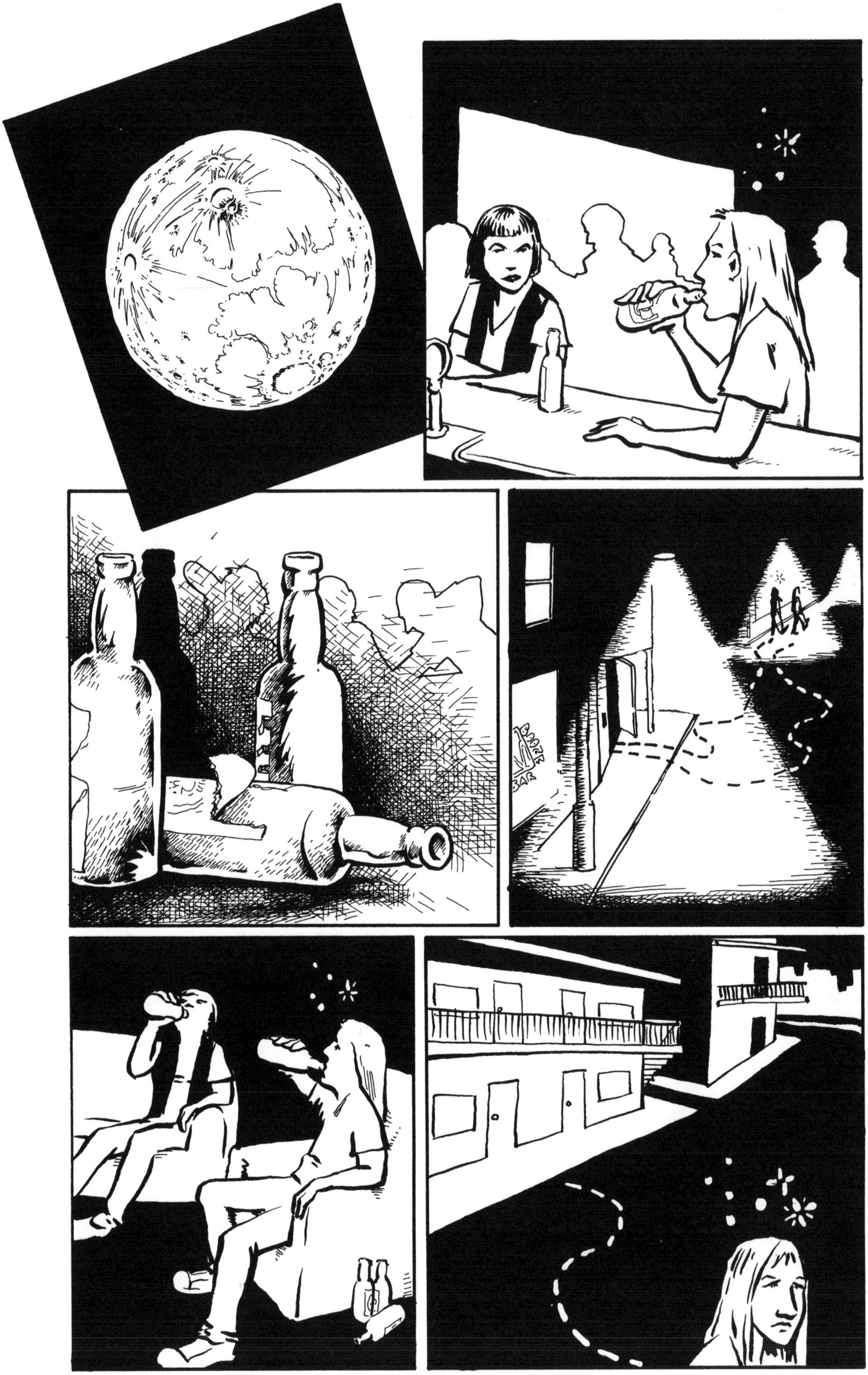
BOOZE
BAR

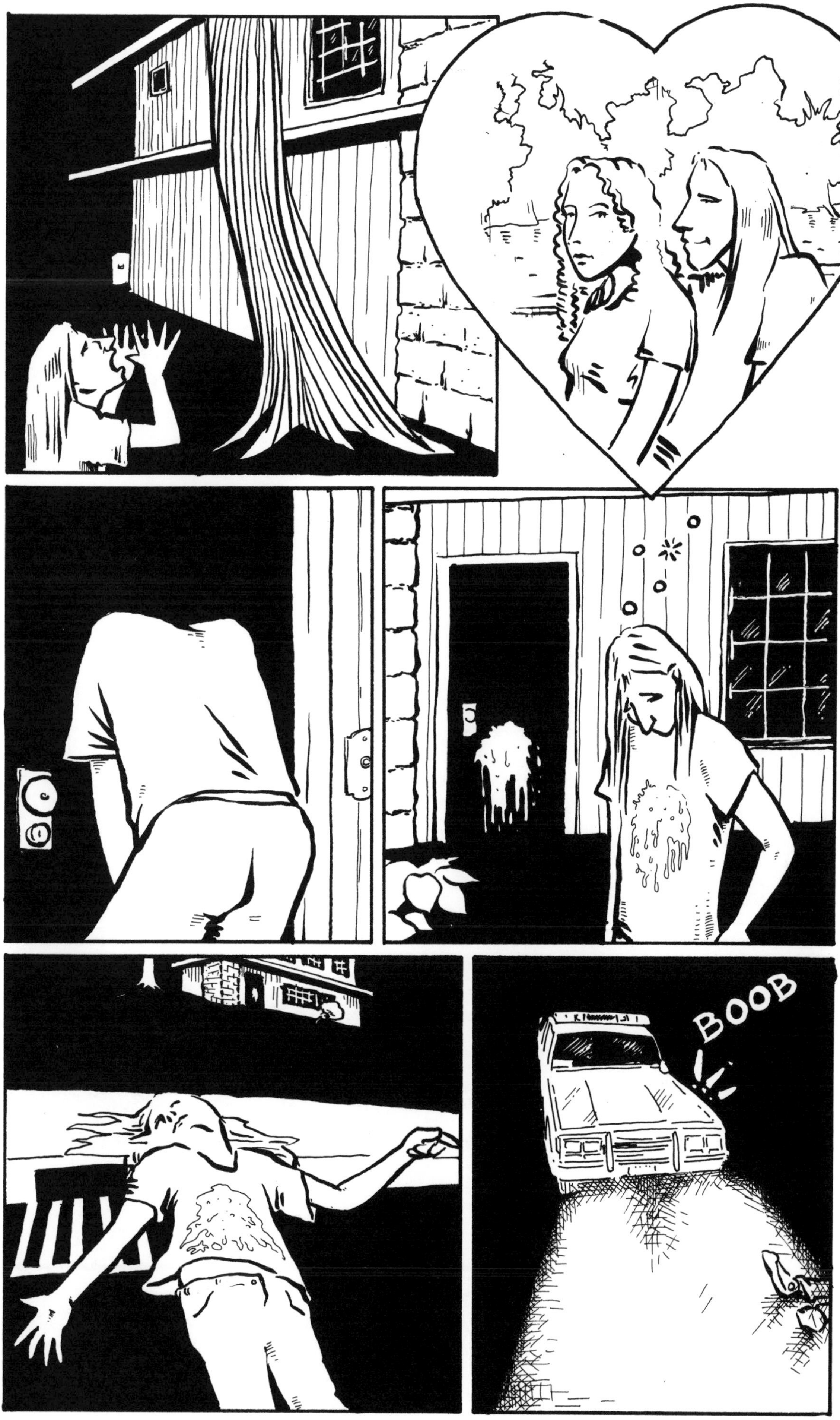
BOOB

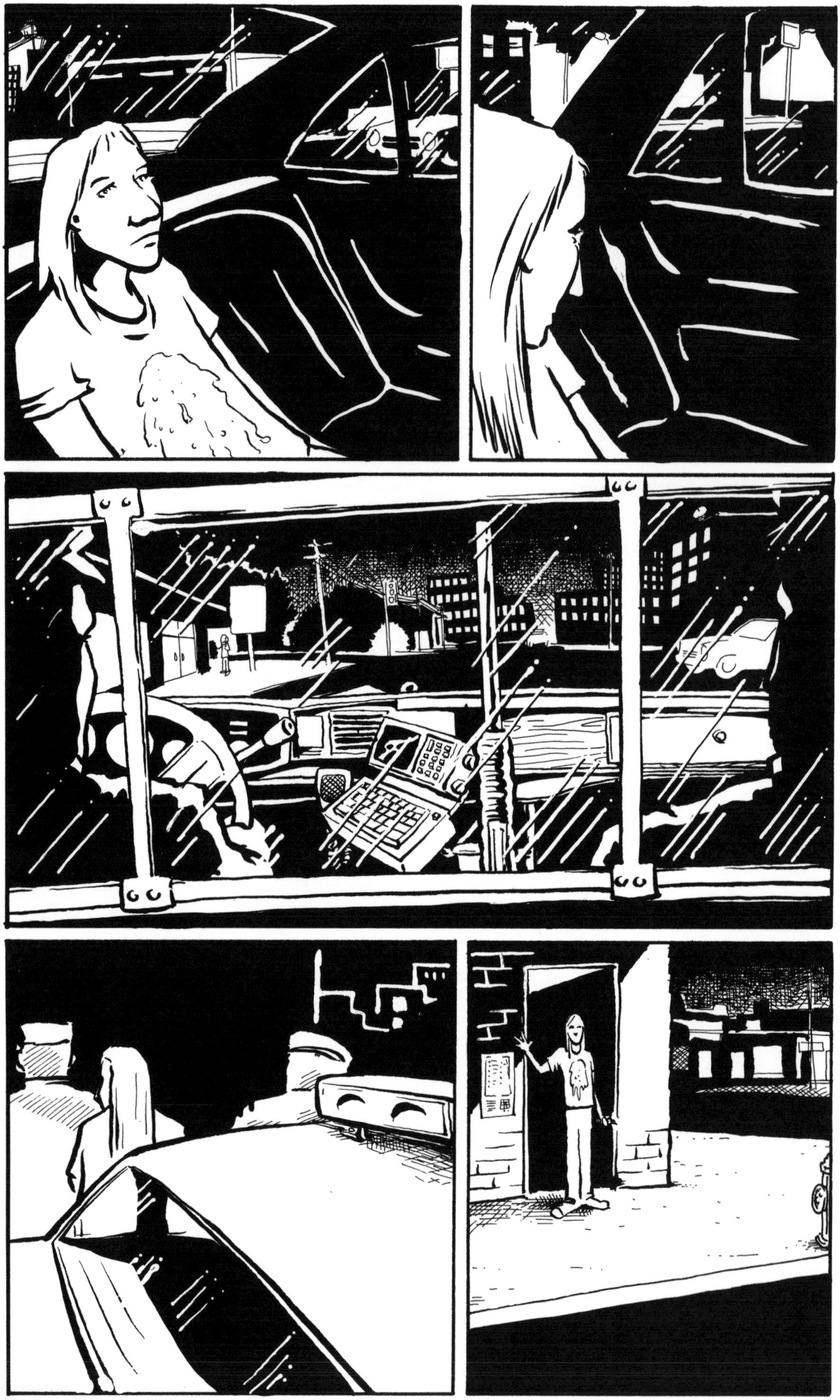

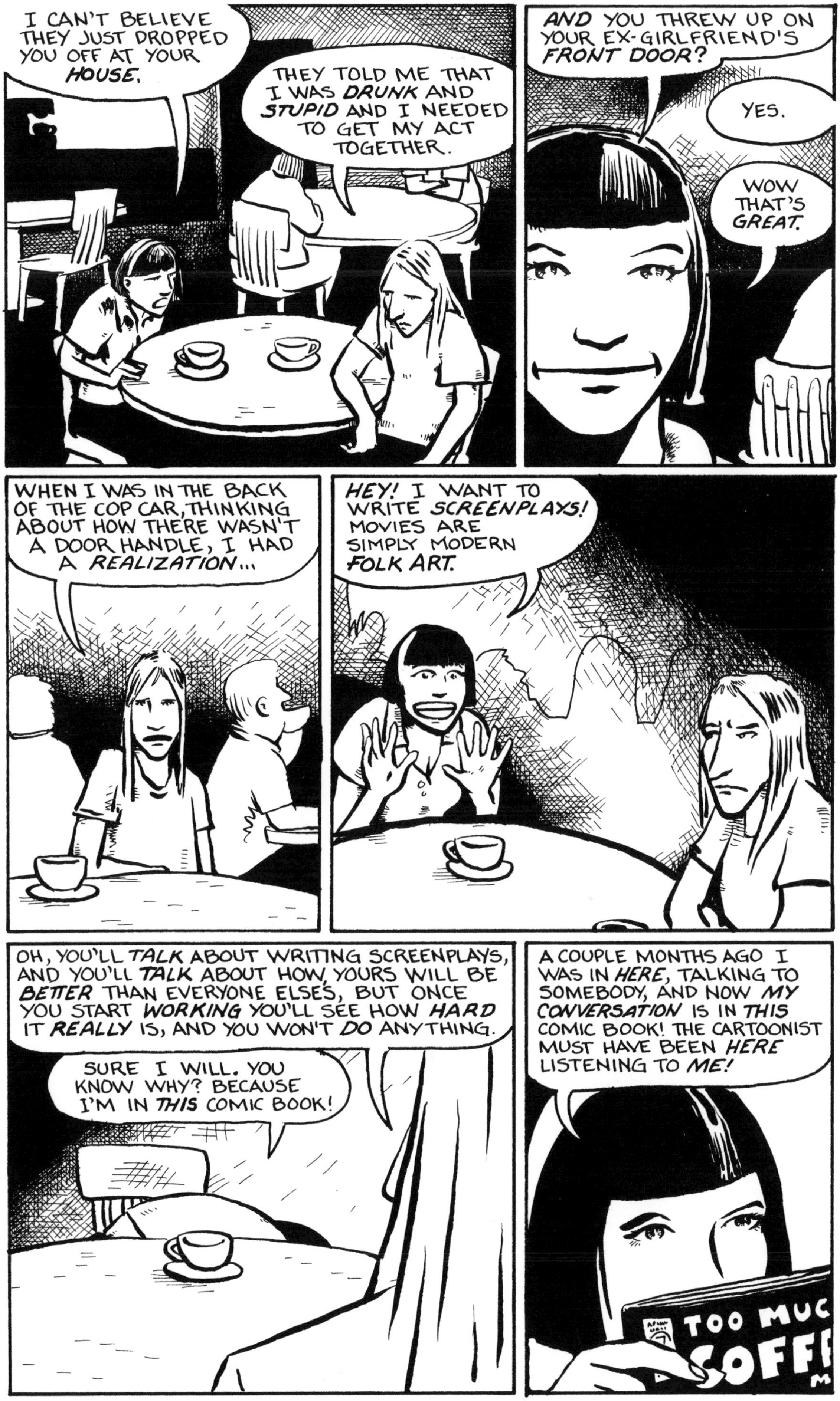
I CAN'T BELIEVE THEY JUST DROPPED YOU OFF AT YOUR HOUSE.
THEY TOLD ME THAT I WAS DRUNK AND STUPID AND I NEEDED TO GET MY ACT TOGETHER.
AND YOU THREW UP ON YOUR EX-GIRLFRIEND'S FRONT DOOR?
YES.
WOW THAT'S GREAT.
WHEN I WAS IN THE BACK OF THE COP CAR, THINKING ABOUT HOW THERE WASN'T A DOOR HANDLE, I HAD A REALIZATION...
HEY! I WANT TO WRITE SCREENPLAYS! MOVIES ARE SIMPLY MODERN FOLK ART.
OH, YOU'LL TALK ABOUT WRITING SCREENPLAYS, AND YOU'LL TALK ABOUT HOW, YOURS WILL BE BETTER THAN EVERYONE ELSE'S, BUT ONCE YOU START WORKING YOU'LL SEE HOW HARD IT REALLY IS, AND YOU WON'T DO ANYTHING.
SURE I WILL. YOU KNOW WHY? BECAUSE I'M IN THIS COMIC BOOK!
A COUPLE MONTHS AGO I WAS IN HERE, TALKING TO SOMEBODY, AND NOW MY CONVERSATION IS IN THIS COMIC BOOK! THE CARTOONIST MUST HAVE BEEN HERE LISTENING TO ME!
TOO MUC
COFF

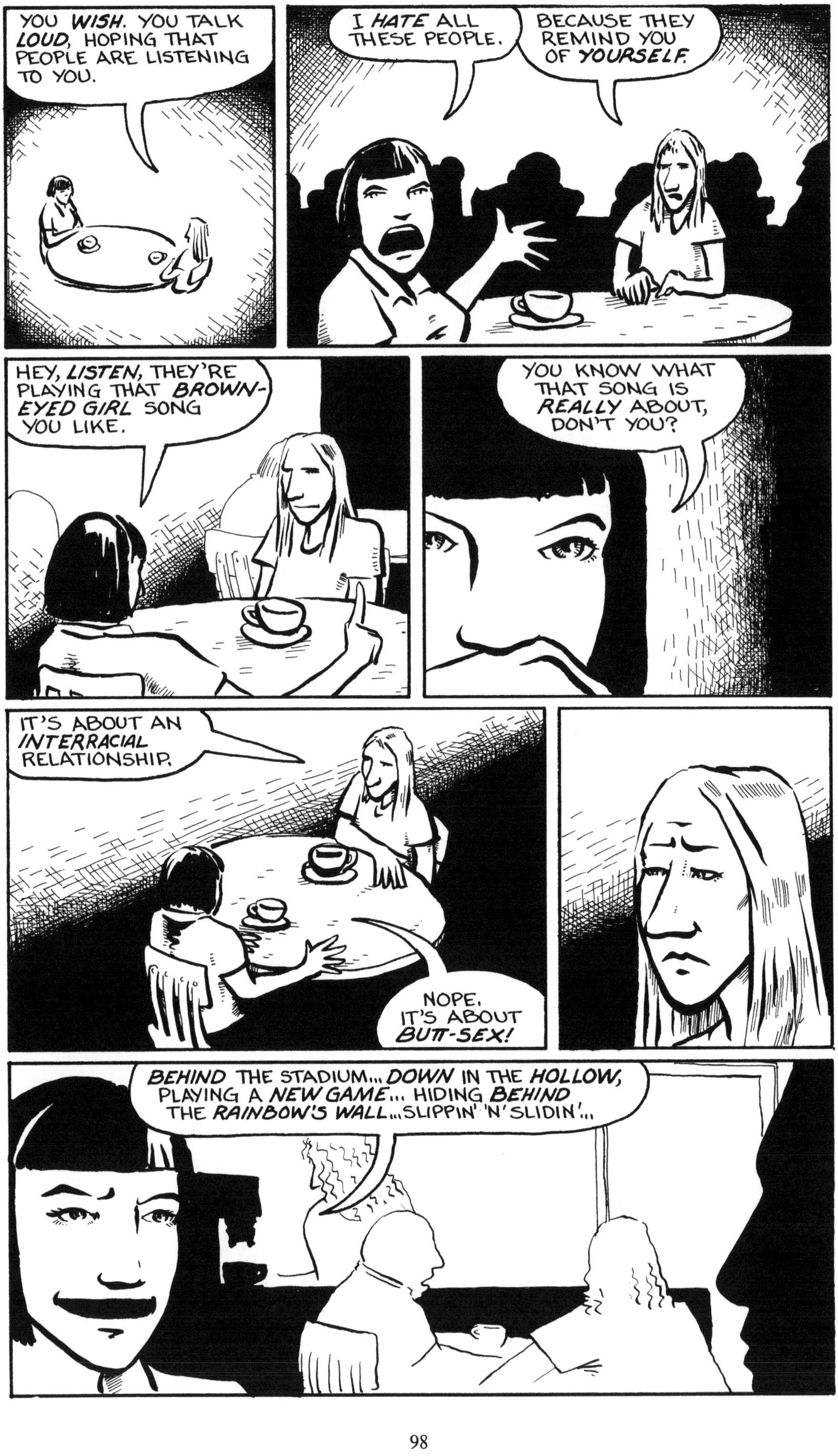
YOU WISH. YOU TALK LOUD, HOPING THAT PEOPLE ARE LISTENING TO YOU.
I HATE ALL THESE PEOPLE.
BECAUSE THEY REMIND YOU OF YOURSELF.
HEY, LISTEN, THEY'RE PLAYING THAT BROWN-EYED GIRL SONG YOU LIKE.
YOU KNOW WHAT THAT SONG IS REALLY ABOUT, DON'T YOU?
IT'S ABOUT AN INTERRACIAL RELATIONSHIP.
NOPE. IT'S ABOUT BUTT-SEX!
BEHIND THE STADIUM... DOWN IN THE HOLLOW, PLAYING A NEW GAME... HIDING BEHIND THE RAINBOW'S WALL... SLIPPIN' 'N' SLIDIN'...

WHAT'S *THE OLD MAN WITH A TRANSISTOR RADIO* MEAN?

I DON'T KNOW.

I *REFUSE* TO BELIEVE THAT THAT SONG IS ABOUT *THAT.*

IT DOESN'T MATTER WHAT *YOU* BELIEVE, BECAUSE *NOW* EVERY TIME YOU HEAR THAT SONG YOU *WILL* THINK OF...

THAT *WAS* ONE OF MY FAVORITE SONGS.

IT STILL *COULD* BE.

THAT WAS A *MEAN* TRICK.

IT'S ALL IN *YOUR* HEAD.

BUT, ANYWAY, I WASN'T FINISHED WITH MY STORY WHEN YOU INTERRUPTED.

IN THE BACK OF THE COP CAR, I REALIZED I'M STILL IN *LOVE* WITH MY GIRLFRIEND.

YOU'RE A FOOL.

TO BE CONTINUED...

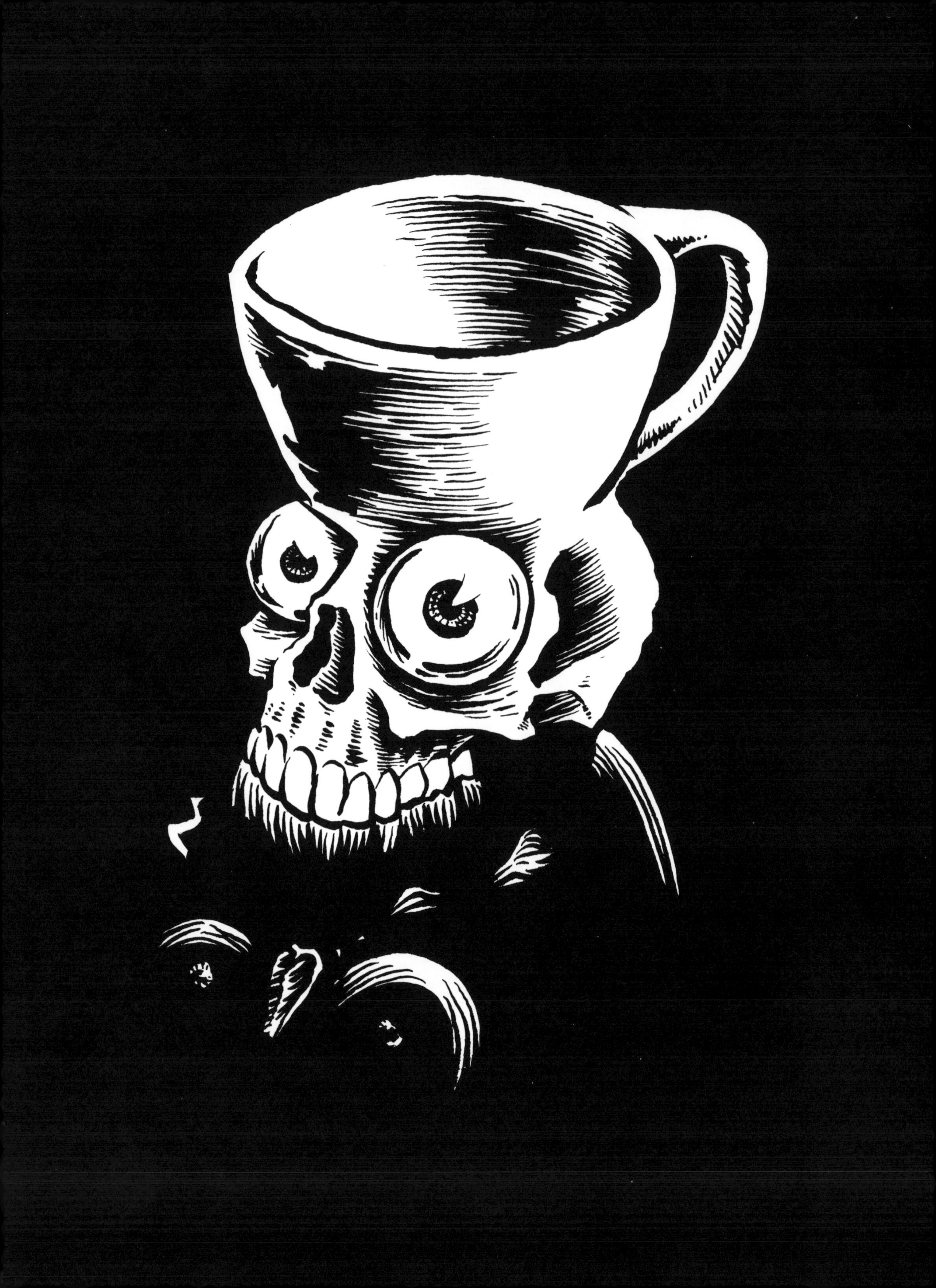

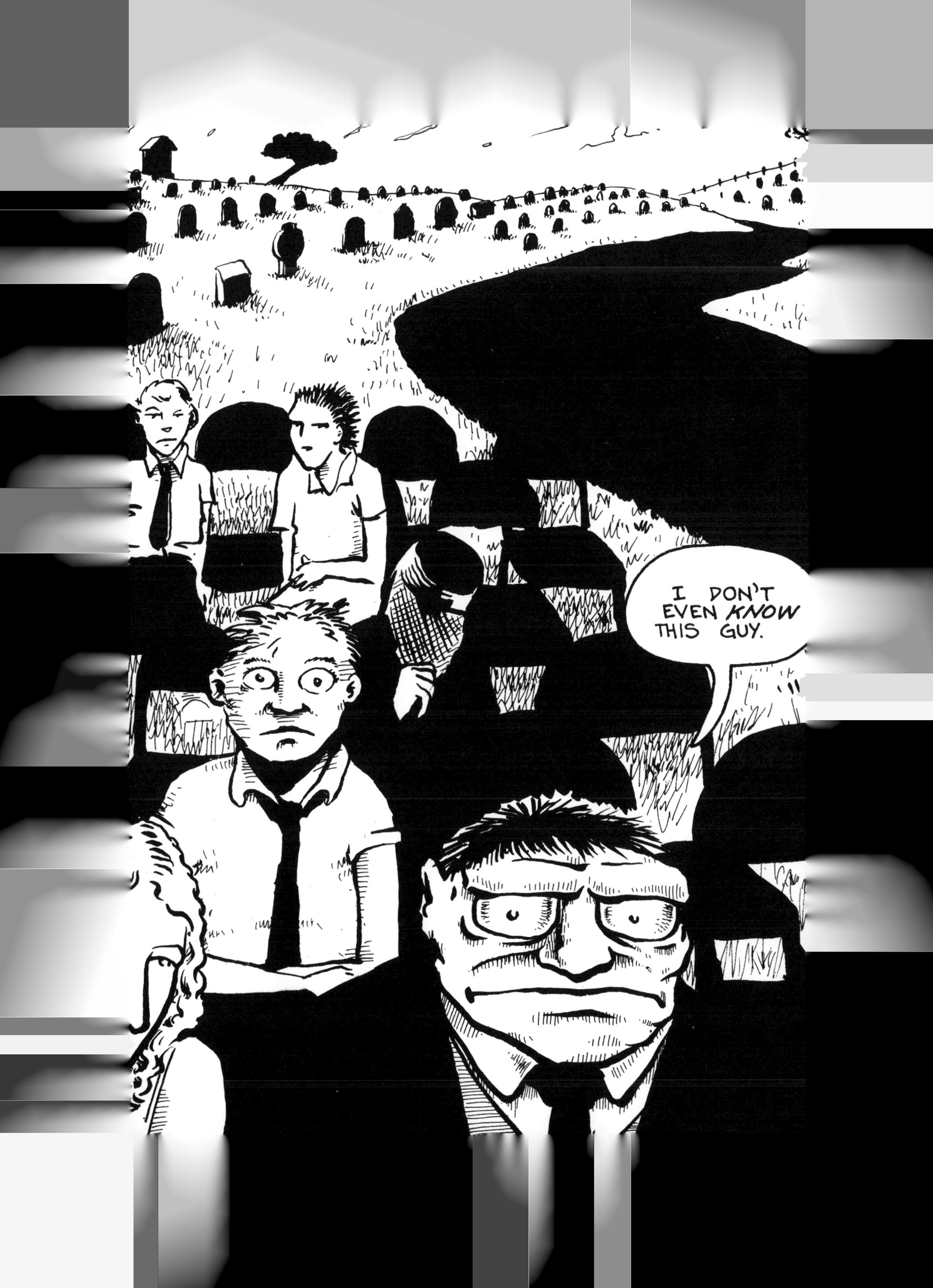
I DON'T EVEN KNOW THIS GUY.

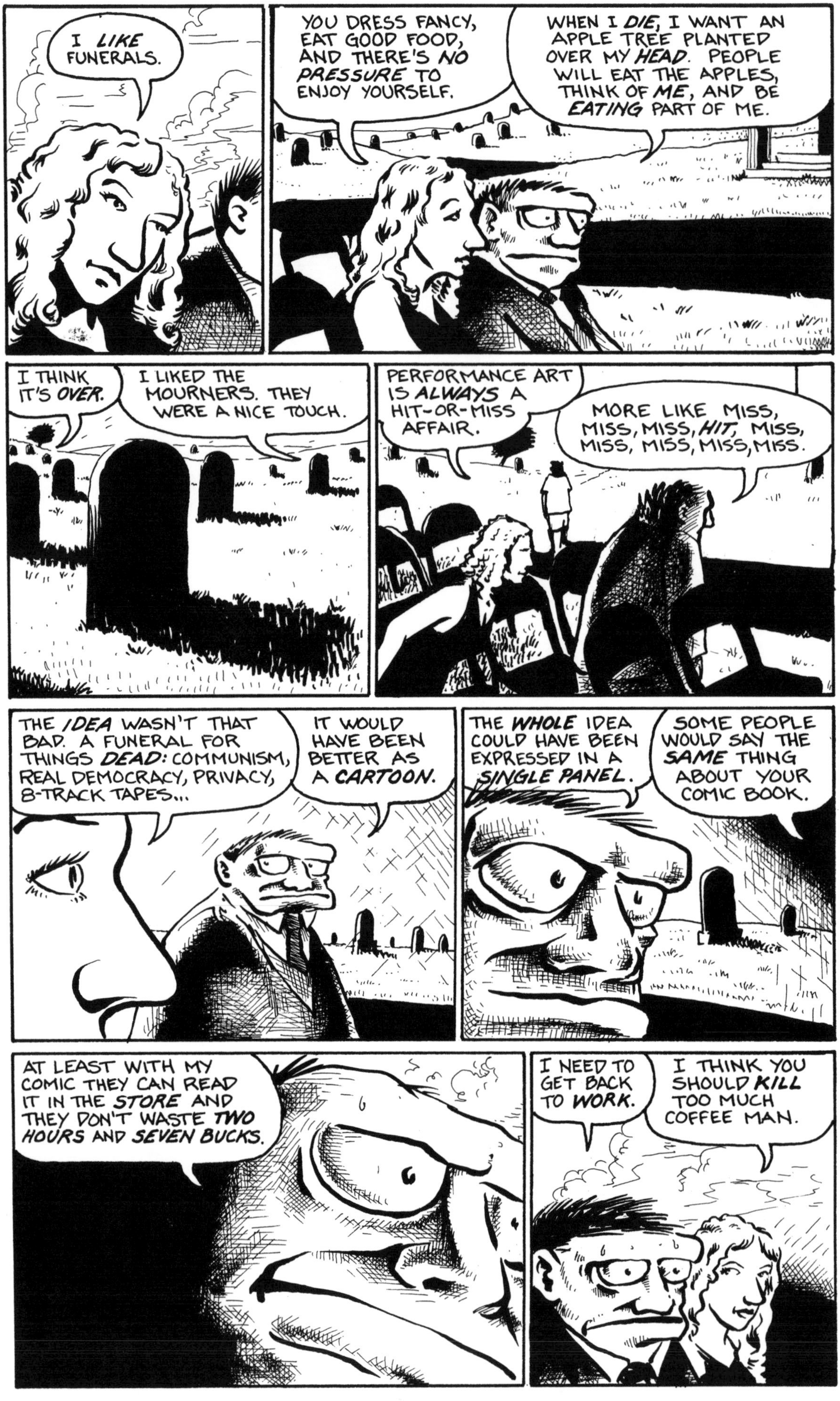
I LIKE FUNERALS.
YOU DRESS FANCY, EAT GOOD FOOD, AND THERE'S NO PRESSURE TO ENJOY YOURSELF.
WHEN I DIE, I WANT AN APPLE TREE PLANTED OVER MY HEAD. PEOPLE WILL EAT THE APPLES, THINK OF ME, AND BE EATING PART OF ME.
I THINK IT'S OVER.
I LIKED THE MOURNERS. THEY WERE A NICE TOUCH.
PERFORMANCE ART IS ALWAYS A HIT-OR-MISS AFFAIR.
MORE LIKE MISS, MISS, MISS, HIT, MISS, MISS, MISS, MISS, MISS, MISS.
THE IDEA WASN'T THAT BAD. A FUNERAL FOR THINGS DEAD: COMMUNISM, REAL DEMOCRACY, PRIVACY, 8-TRACK TAPES...
IT WOULD HAVE BEEN BETTER AS A CARTOON.
THE WHOLE IDEA COULD HAVE BEEN EXPRESSED IN A SINGLE PANEL.
SOME PEOPLE WOULD SAY THE SAME THING ABOUT YOUR COMIC BOOK.
AT LEAST WITH MY COMIC THEY CAN READ IT IN THE STORE AND THEY DON'T WASTE TWO HOURS AND SEVEN BUCKS.
I NEED TO GET BACK TO WORK.
I THINK YOU SHOULD KILL TOO MUCH COFFEE MAN.

THE DEATH OF TOO MUCH COFFEE MAN

AAAAARG!!! MY HEART!

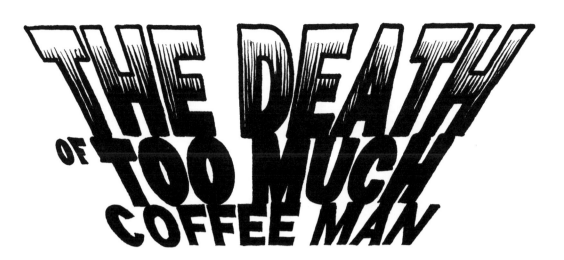

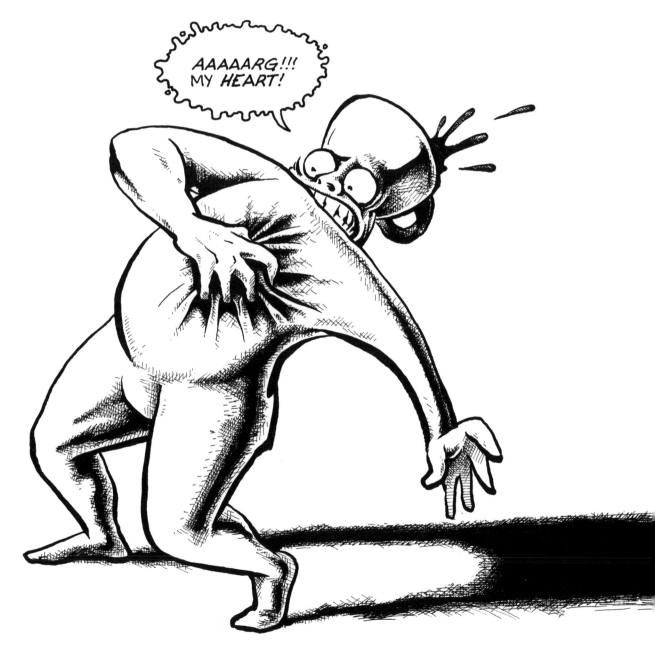

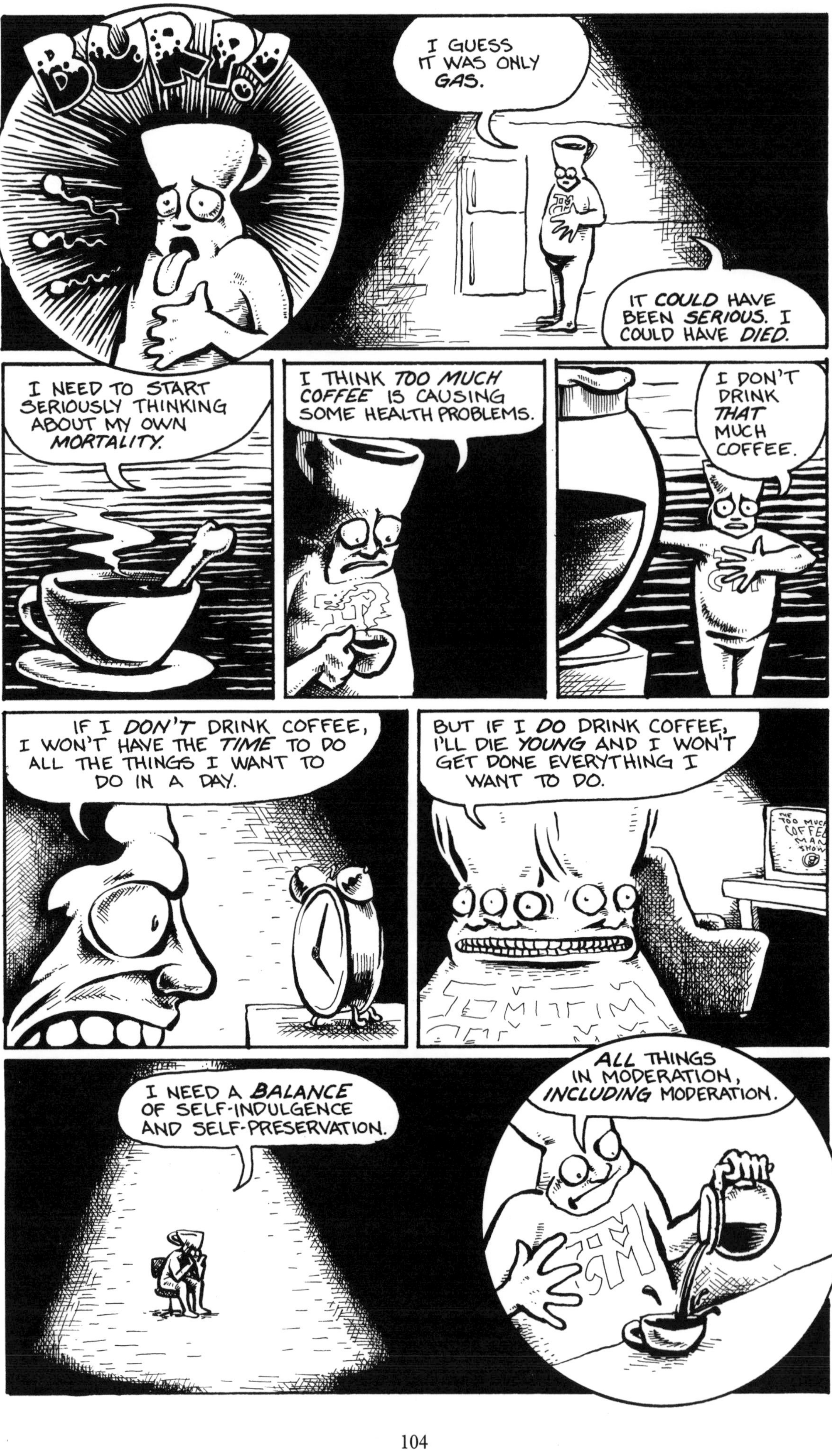
BURP!
I GUESS IT WAS ONLY GAS.
IT COULD HAVE BEEN SERIOUS. I COULD HAVE DIED.
I NEED TO START SERIOUSLY THINKING ABOUT MY OWN MORTALITY.
I THINK TOO MUCH COFFEE IS CAUSING SOME HEALTH PROBLEMS.
I DON'T DRINK THAT MUCH COFFEE.
IF I DON'T DRINK COFFEE, I WON'T HAVE THE TIME TO DO ALL THE THINGS I WANT TO DO IN A DAY.
BUT IF I DO DRINK COFFEE, I'LL DIE YOUNG AND I WON'T GET DONE EVERYTHING I WANT TO DO.
I NEED A BALANCE OF SELF-INDULGENCE AND SELF-PRESERVATION.
ALL THINGS IN MODERATION, INCLUDING MODERATION.

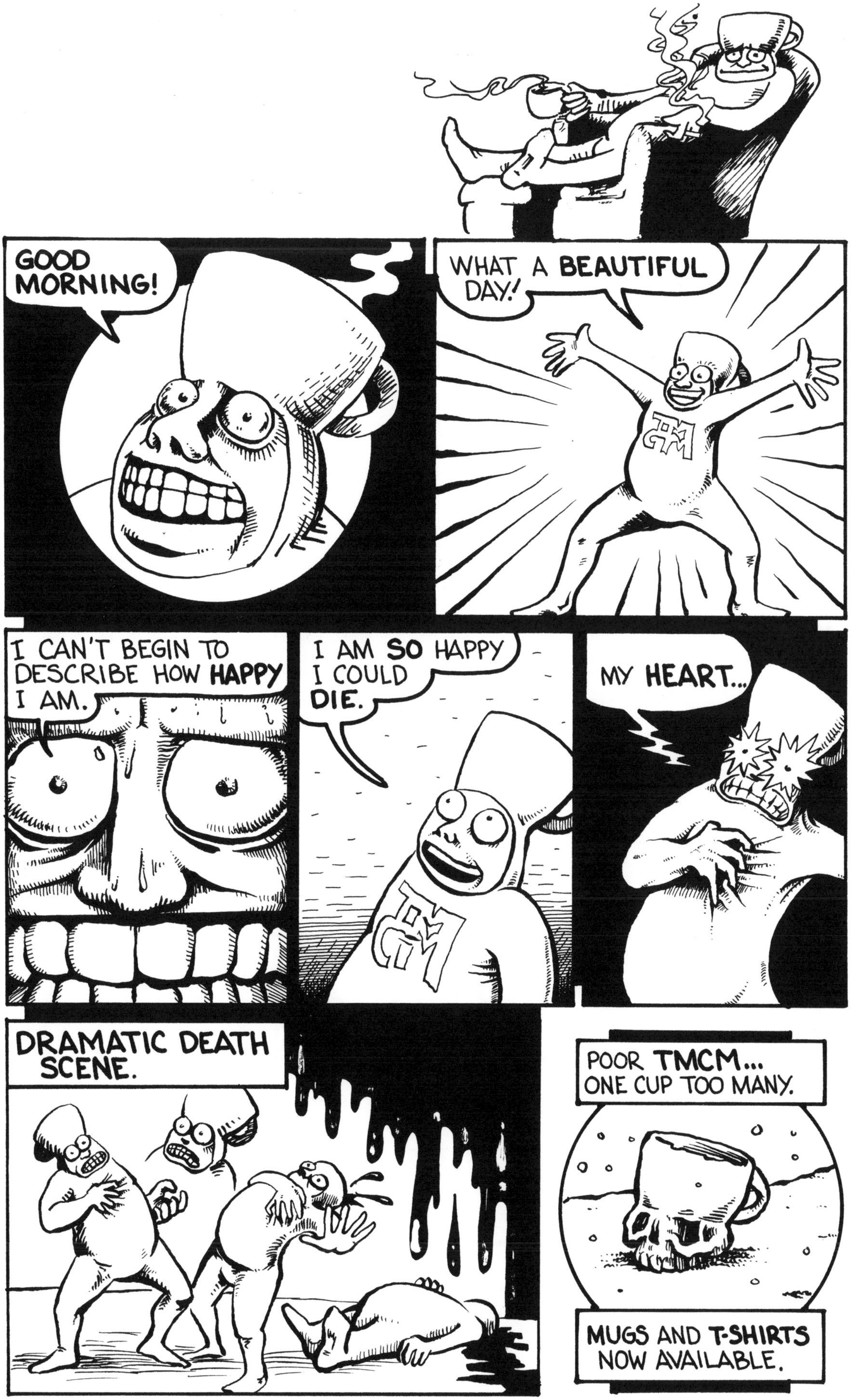
GOOD MORNING!
WHAT A BEAUTIFUL DAY!
I CAN'T BEGIN TO DESCRIBE HOW HAPPY I AM.
I AM SO HAPPY I COULD DIE.
MY HEART...
DRAMATIC DEATH SCENE.
POOR TMCM... ONE CUP TOO MANY.
MUGS AND T-SHIRTS NOW AVAILABLE.

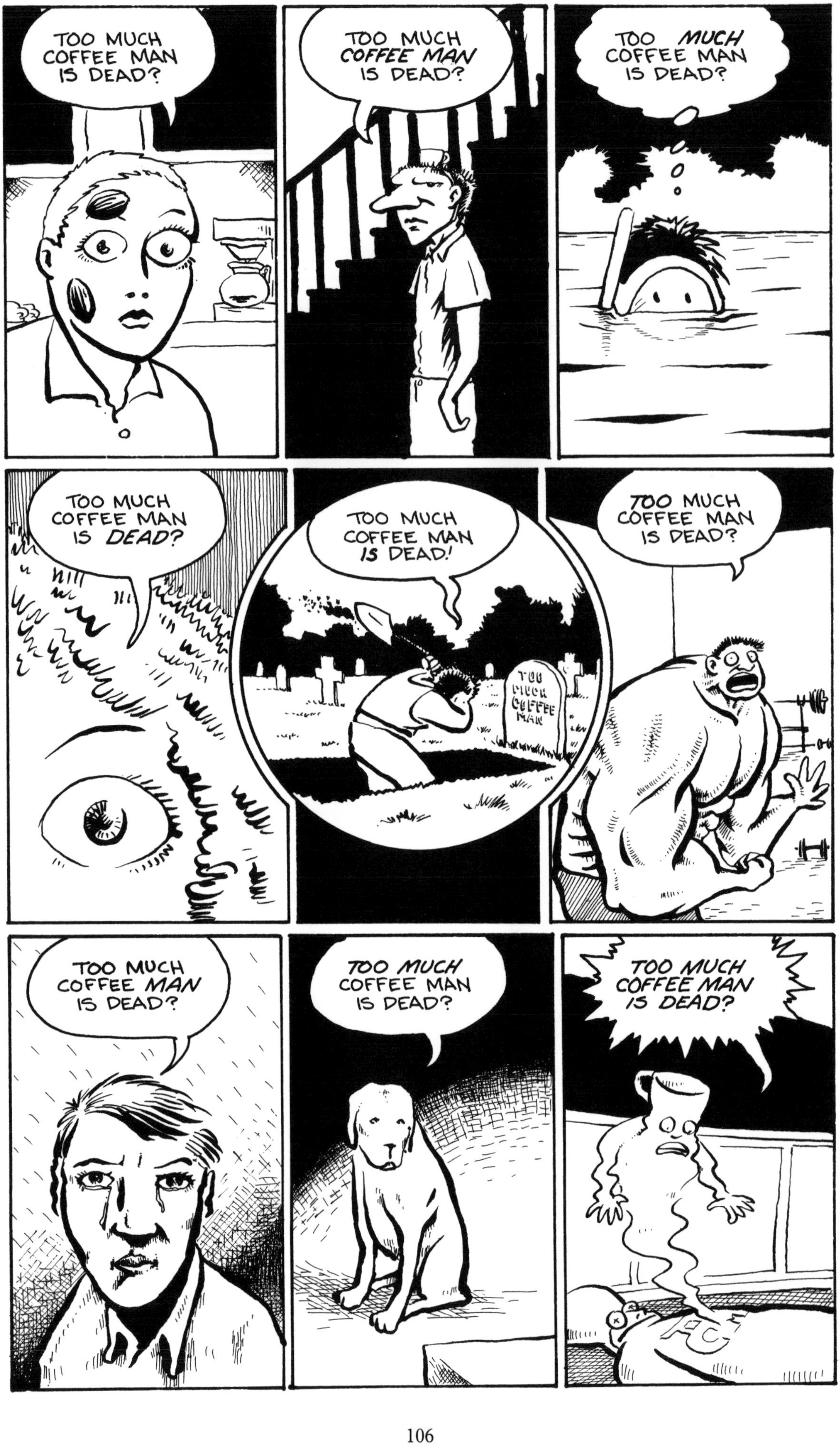
TOO MUCH COFFEE MAN IS DEAD?
TOO MUCH COFFEE MAN IS DEAD?
TOO MUCH COFFEE MAN IS DEAD?
TOO MUCH COFFEE MAN IS DEAD?
TOO MUCH COFFEE MAN IS DEAD!
TOO MUCH COFFEE MAN
TOO MUCH COFFEE MAN IS DEAD?
TOO MUCH COFFEE MAN IS DEAD?
TOO MUCH COFFEE MAN IS DEAD?
TOO MUCH COFFEE MAN IS DEAD?

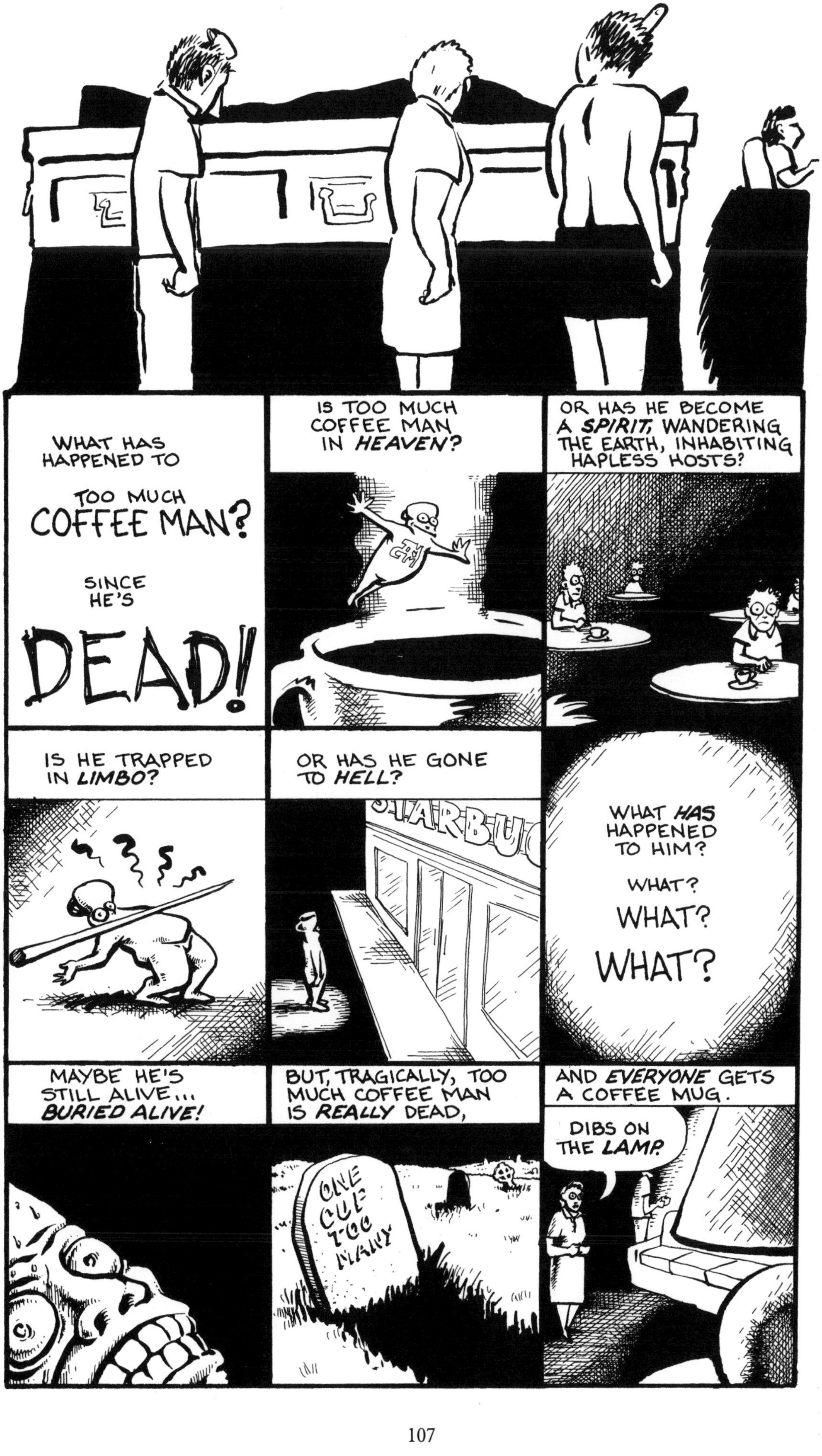
WHAT HAS HAPPENED TO
TOO MUCH COFFEE MAN?
SINCE HE'S
DEAD!
IS TOO MUCH COFFEE MAN IN HEAVEN?
OR HAS HE BECOME A SPIRIT, WANDERING THE EARTH, INHABITING HAPLESS HOSTS?
IS HE TRAPPED IN LIMBO?
OR HAS HE GONE TO HELL?
WHAT HAS HAPPENED TO HIM?
WHAT?
WHAT?
WHAT?
MAYBE HE'S STILL ALIVE... BURIED ALIVE!
BUT, TRAGICALLY, TOO MUCH COFFEE MAN IS REALLY DEAD,
ONE CUP TOO MANY
AND EVERYONE GETS A COFFEE MUG.
DIBS ON THE LAMP.

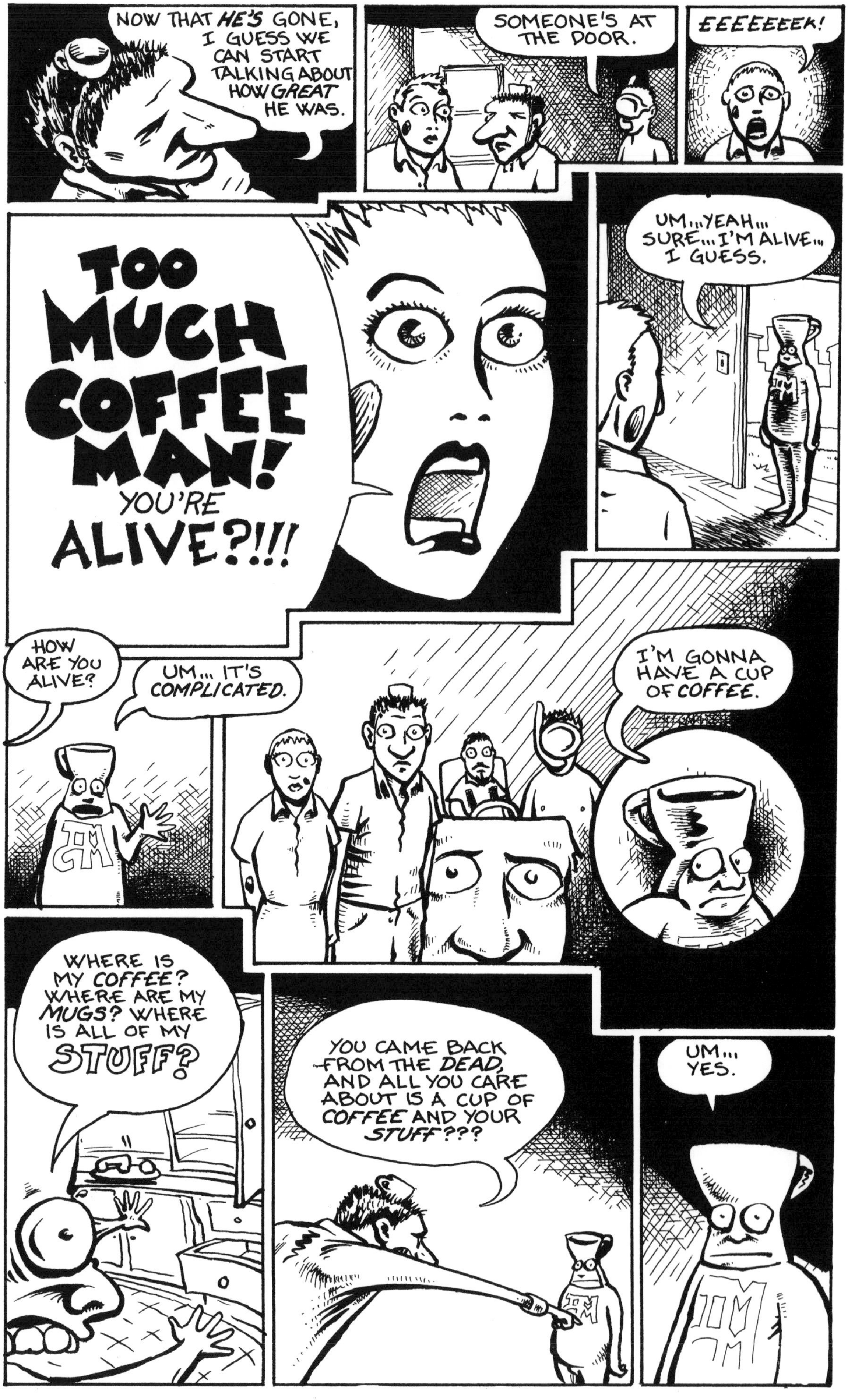
NOW THAT HE'S GONE, I GUESS WE CAN START TALKING ABOUT HOW GREAT HE WAS.
SOMEONE'S AT THE DOOR.
EEEEEEEK!
TOO MUCH COFFEE MAN! YOU'RE ALIVE?!!!
UM... YEAH... SURE... I'M ALIVE... I GUESS.
HOW ARE YOU ALIVE?
UM... IT'S COMPLICATED.
I'M GONNA HAVE A CUP OF COFFEE.
WHERE IS MY COFFEE? WHERE ARE MY MUGS? WHERE IS ALL OF MY STUFF?
YOU CAME BACK FROM THE DEAD, AND ALL YOU CARE ABOUT IS A CUP OF COFFEE AND YOUR STUFF???
UM... YES.

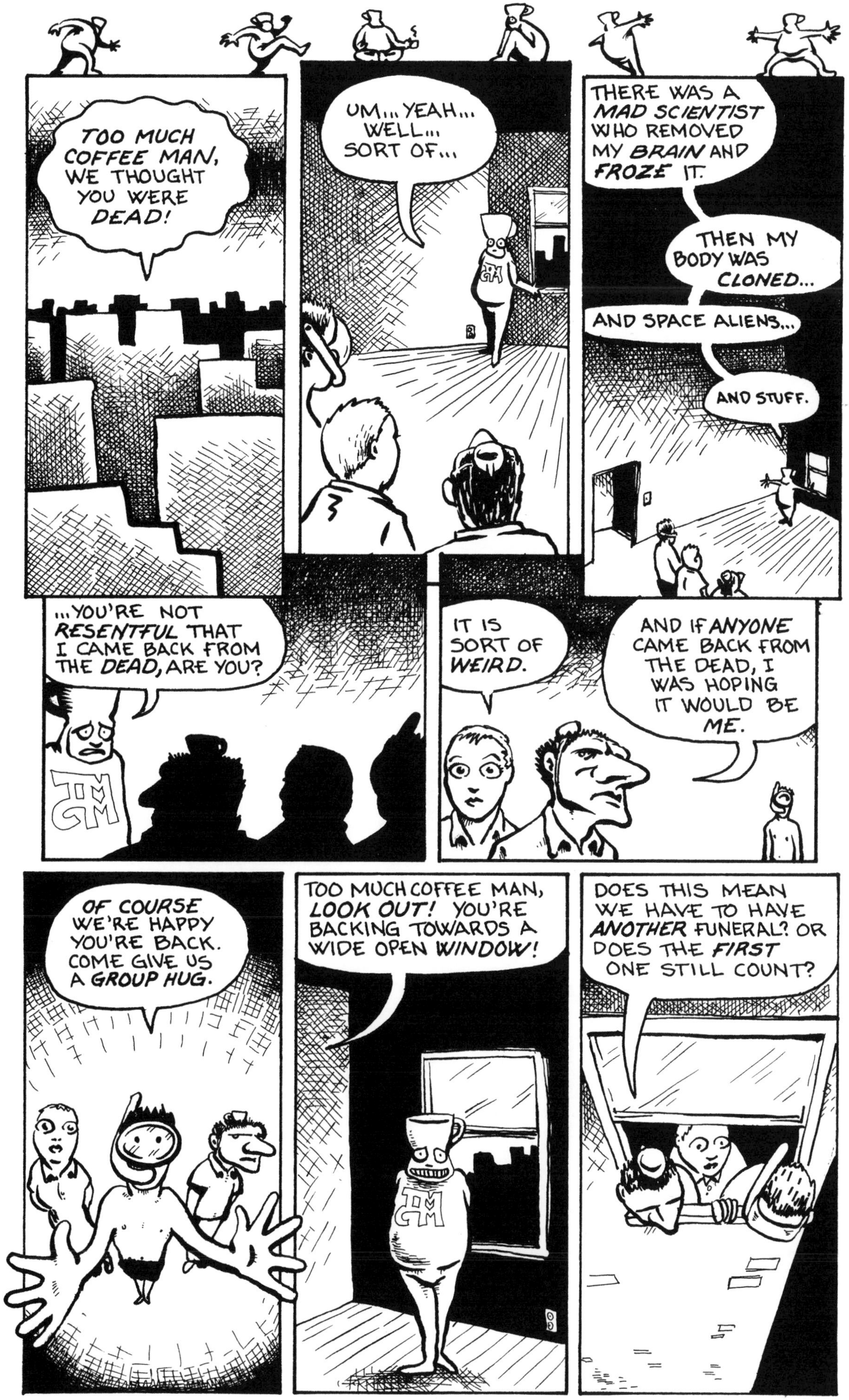
TOO MUCH COFFEE MAN, WE THOUGHT YOU WERE DEAD!
UM... YEAH... WELL... SORT OF...
THERE WAS A MAD SCIENTIST WHO REMOVED MY BRAIN AND FROZE IT.
THEN MY BODY WAS CLONED...
AND SPACE ALIENS...
AND STUFF.
...YOU'RE NOT RESENTFUL THAT I CAME BACK FROM THE DEAD, ARE YOU?
IT IS SORT OF WEIRD.
AND IF ANYONE CAME BACK FROM THE DEAD, I WAS HOPING IT WOULD BE ME.
OF COURSE WE'RE HAPPY YOU'RE BACK. COME GIVE US A GROUP HUG.
TOO MUCH COFFEE MAN, LOOK OUT! YOU'RE BACKING TOWARDS A WIDE OPEN WINDOW!
DOES THIS MEAN WE HAVE TO HAVE ANOTHER FUNERAL? OR DOES THE FIRST ONE STILL COUNT?

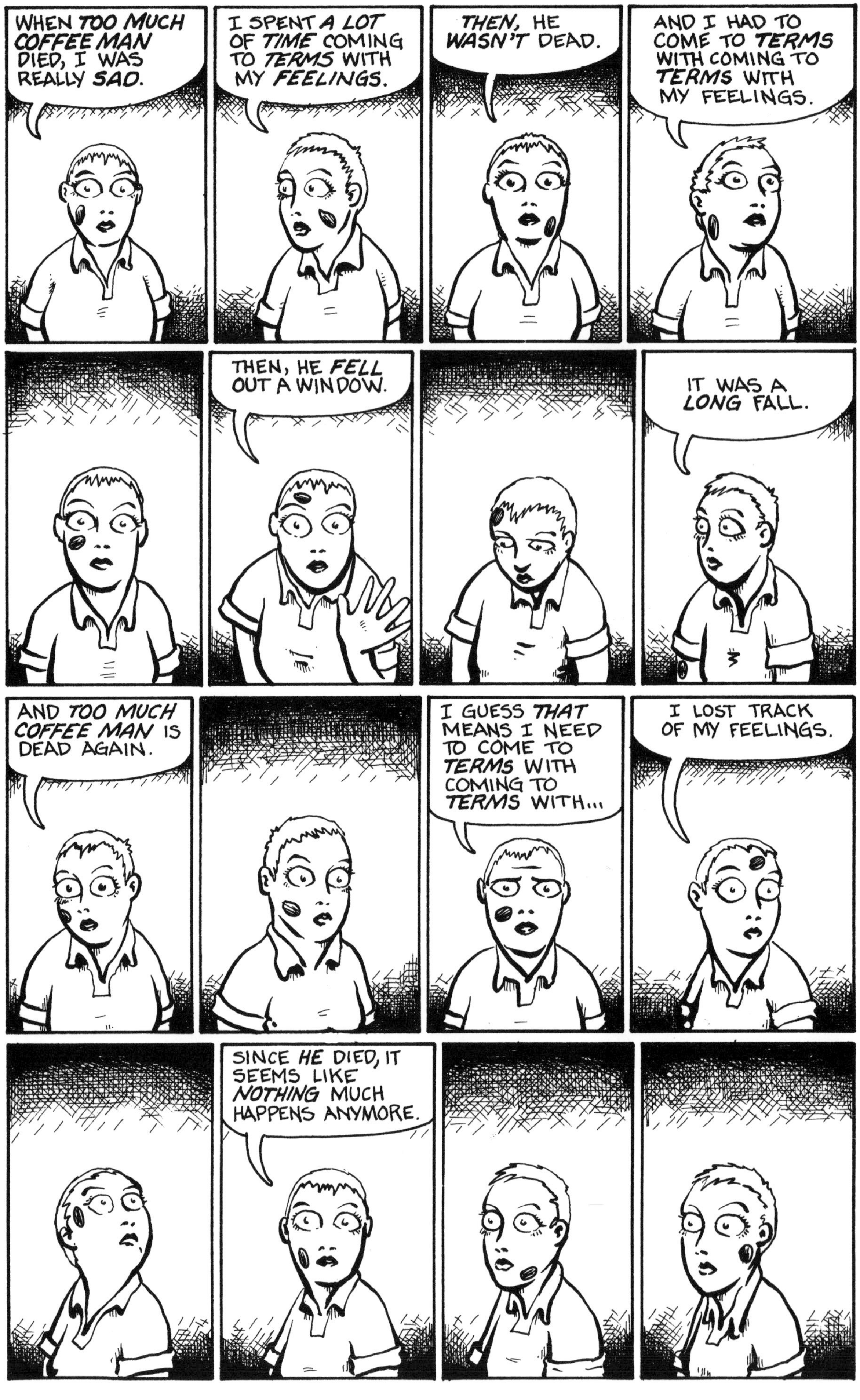
WHEN TOO MUCH COFFEE MAN DIED, I WAS REALLY SAD.
I SPENT A LOT OF TIME COMING TO TERMS WITH MY FEELINGS.
THEN, HE WASN'T DEAD.
AND I HAD TO COME TO TERMS WITH COMING TO TERMS WITH MY FEELINGS.
THEN, HE FELL OUT A WINDOW.
IT WAS A LONG FALL.
AND TOO MUCH COFFEE MAN IS DEAD AGAIN.
I GUESS THAT MEANS I NEED TO COME TO TERMS WITH COMING TO TERMS WITH...
I LOST TRACK OF MY FEELINGS.
SINCE HE DIED, IT SEEMS LIKE NOTHING MUCH HAPPENS ANYMORE.

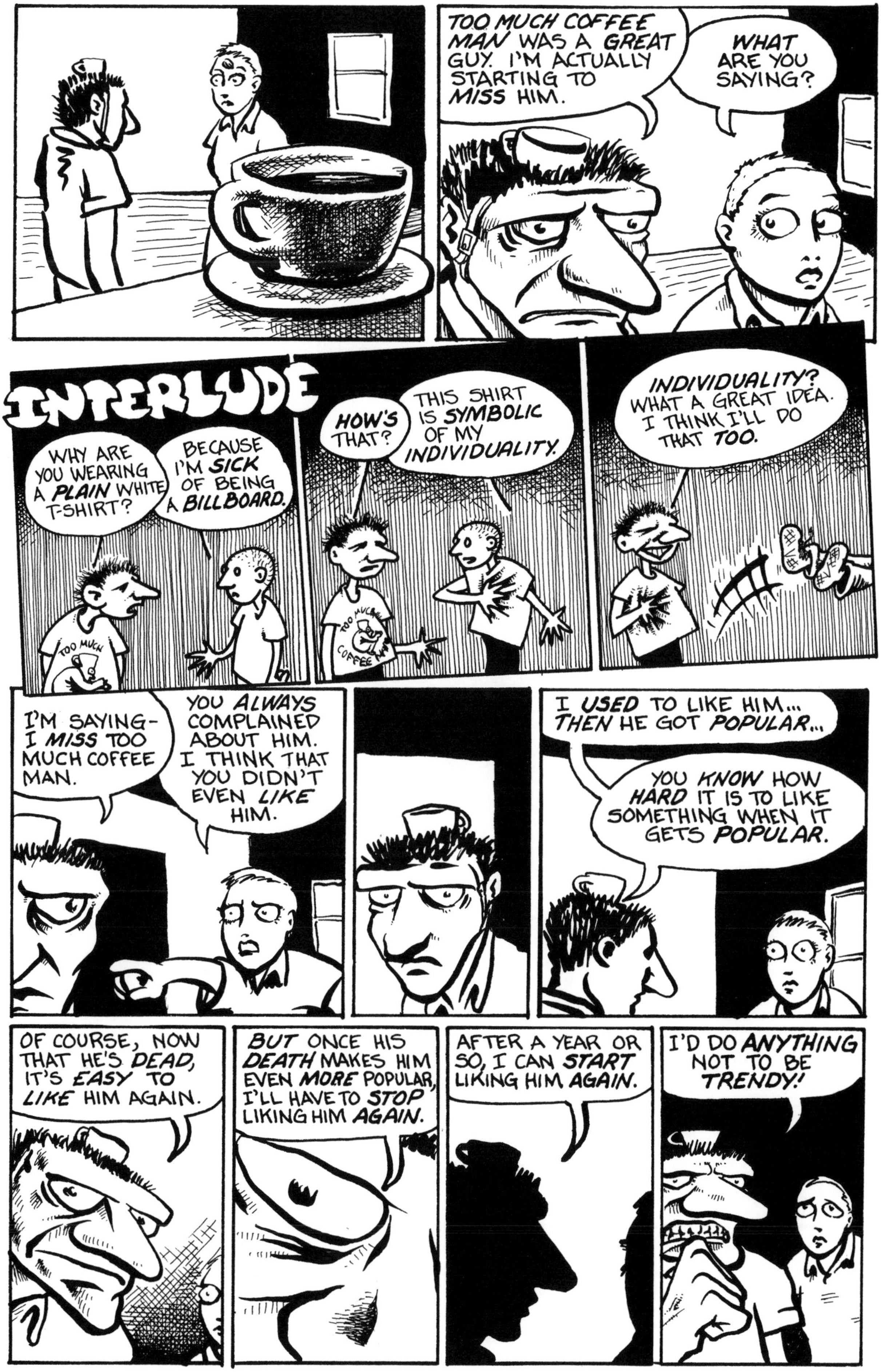
TOO MUCH COFFEE MAN WAS A GREAT GUY. I'M ACTUALLY STARTING TO MISS HIM.
WHAT ARE YOU SAYING?
INTERLUDE
WHY ARE YOU WEARING A PLAIN WHITE T-SHIRT?
BECAUSE I'M SICK OF BEING A BILLBOARD.
TOO MUCH
HOW'S THAT?
THIS SHIRT IS SYMBOLIC OF MY INDIVIDUALITY.
TOO MUCH COFFEE MAN
INDIVIDUALITY? WHAT A GREAT IDEA. I THINK I'LL DO THAT TOO.
I'M SAYING- I MISS TOO MUCH COFFEE MAN.
YOU ALWAYS COMPLAINED ABOUT HIM. I THINK THAT YOU DIDN'T EVEN LIKE HIM.
I USED TO LIKE HIM... THEN HE GOT POPULAR...
YOU KNOW HOW HARD IT IS TO LIKE SOMETHING WHEN IT GETS POPULAR.
OF COURSE, NOW THAT HE'S DEAD, IT'S EASY TO LIKE HIM AGAIN.
BUT ONCE HIS DEATH MAKES HIM EVEN MORE POPULAR, I'LL HAVE TO STOP LIKING HIM AGAIN.
AFTER A YEAR OR SO, I CAN START LIKING HIM AGAIN.
I'D DO ANYTHING NOT TO BE TRENDY!

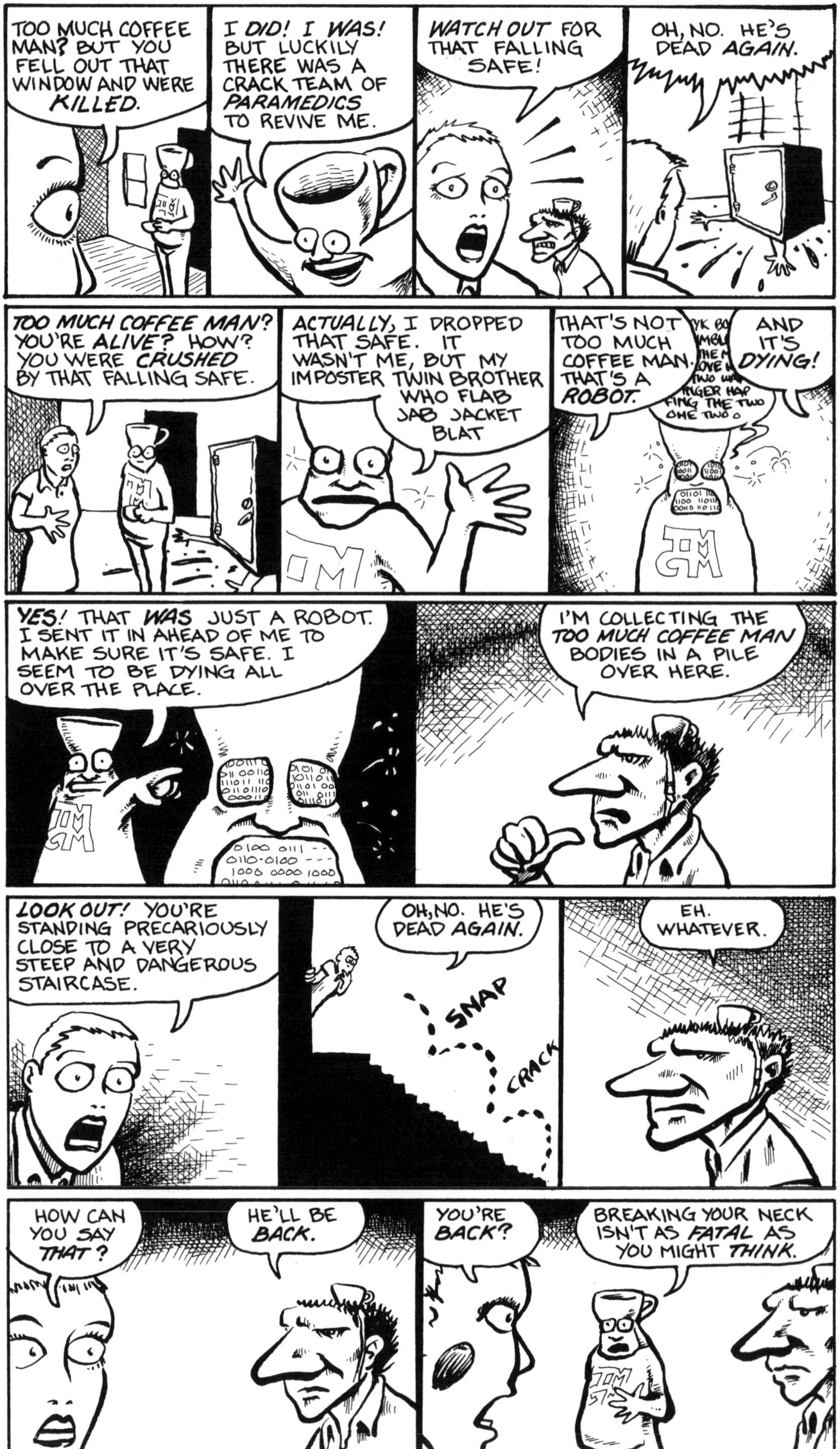
TOO MUCH COFFEE MAN? BUT YOU FELL OUT THAT WINDOW AND WERE KILLED.
I DID! I WAS! BUT LUCKILY THERE WAS A CRACK TEAM OF PARAMEDICS TO REVIVE ME.
WATCH OUT FOR THAT FALLING SAFE!
OH, NO. HE'S DEAD AGAIN.
TOO MUCH COFFEE MAN? YOU'RE ALIVE? HOW? YOU WERE CRUSHED BY THAT FALLING SAFE.
ACTUALLY, I DROPPED THAT SAFE. IT WASN'T ME, BUT MY IMPOSTER TWIN BROTHER WHO FLAB JAB JACKET BLAT
THAT'S NOT TOO MUCH COFFEE MAN. THAT'S A ROBOT.
AND IT'S DYING!
YES! THAT WAS JUST A ROBOT. I SENT IT IN AHEAD OF ME TO MAKE SURE IT'S SAFE. I SEEM TO BE DYING ALL OVER THE PLACE.
I'M COLLECTING THE TOO MUCH COFFEE MAN BODIES IN A PILE OVER HERE.
LOOK OUT! YOU'RE STANDING PRECARIOUSLY CLOSE TO A VERY STEEP AND DANGEROUS STAIRCASE.
OH, NO. HE'S DEAD AGAIN.
SNAP
CRACK
EH. WHATEVER.
HOW CAN YOU SAY THAT?
HE'LL BE BACK.
YOU'RE BACK?
BREAKING YOUR NECK ISN'T AS FATAL AS YOU MIGHT THINK.

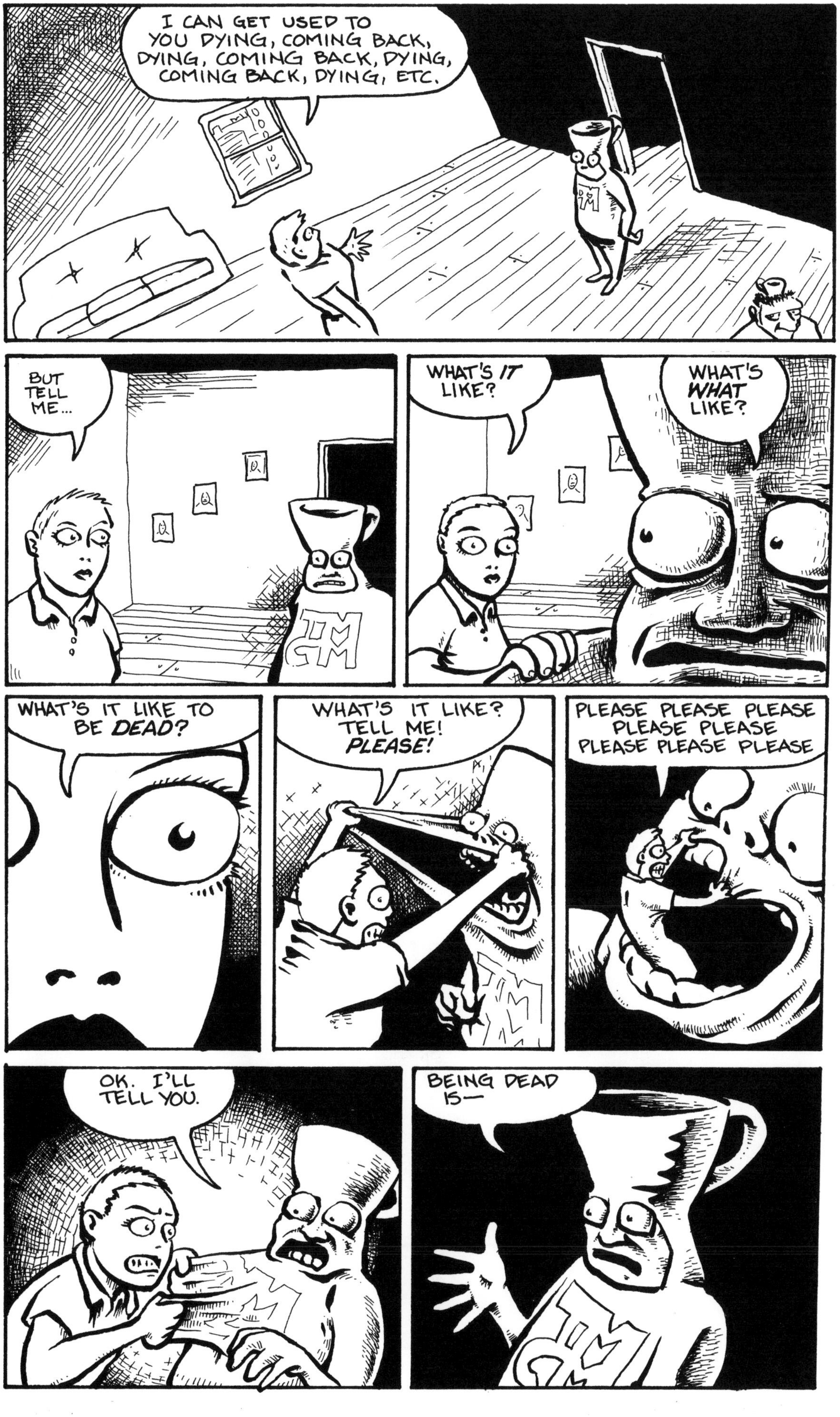
I CAN GET USED TO YOU DYING, COMING BACK, DYING, COMING BACK, DYING, COMING BACK, DYING, ETC.
BUT TELL ME...
WHAT'S IT LIKE?
WHAT'S WHAT LIKE?
WHAT'S IT LIKE TO BE DEAD?
WHAT'S IT LIKE? TELL ME! PLEASE!
PLEASE PLEASE PLEASE PLEASE PLEASE PLEASE PLEASE PLEASE
OK. I'LL TELL YOU.
BEING DEAD IS—

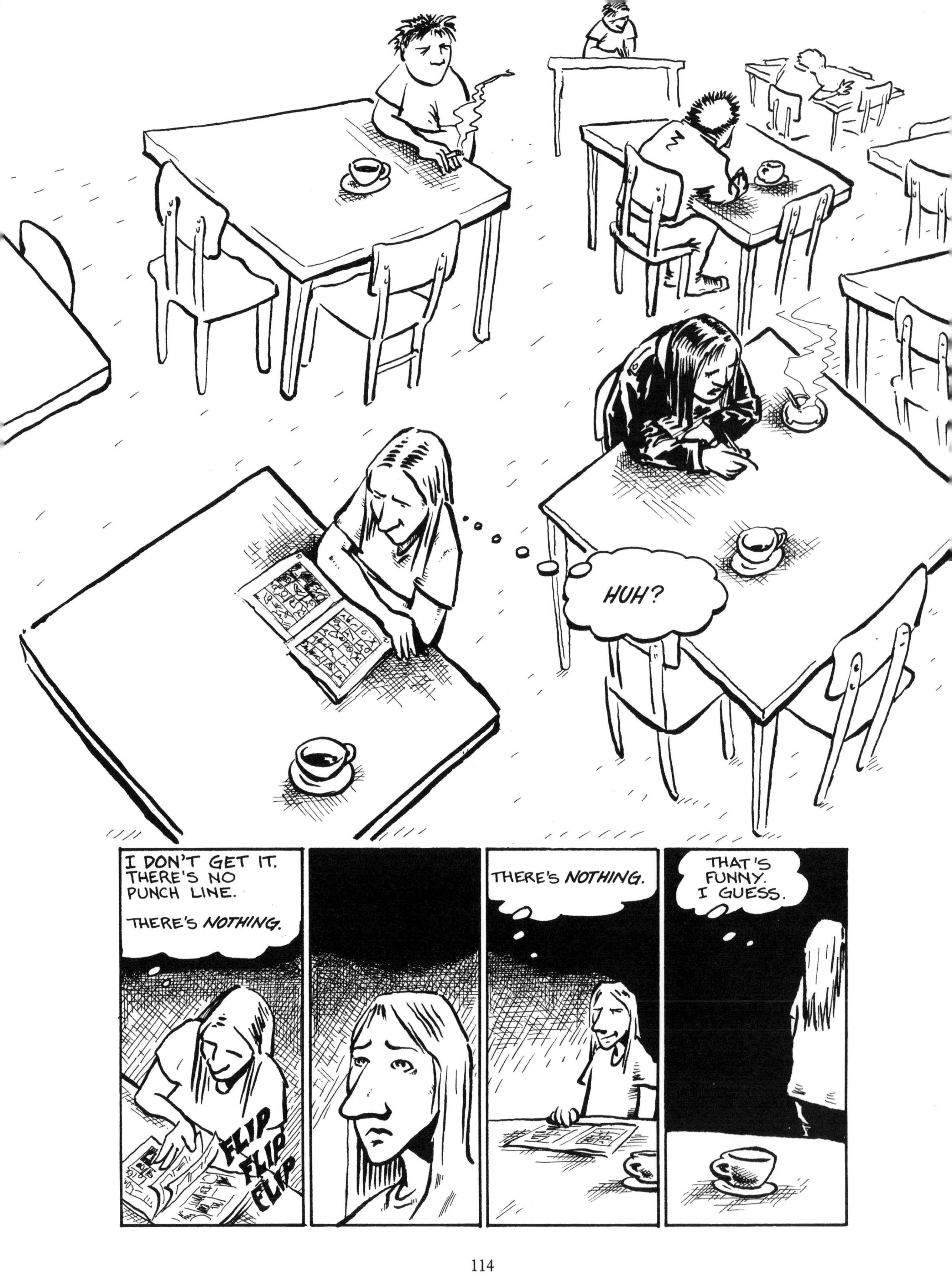
HUH?
I DON'T GET IT. THERE'S NO PUNCH LINE.
THERE'S NOTHING.
FLIP FLIP FLIP
THERE'S NOTHING.
THAT'S FUNNY. I GUESS.

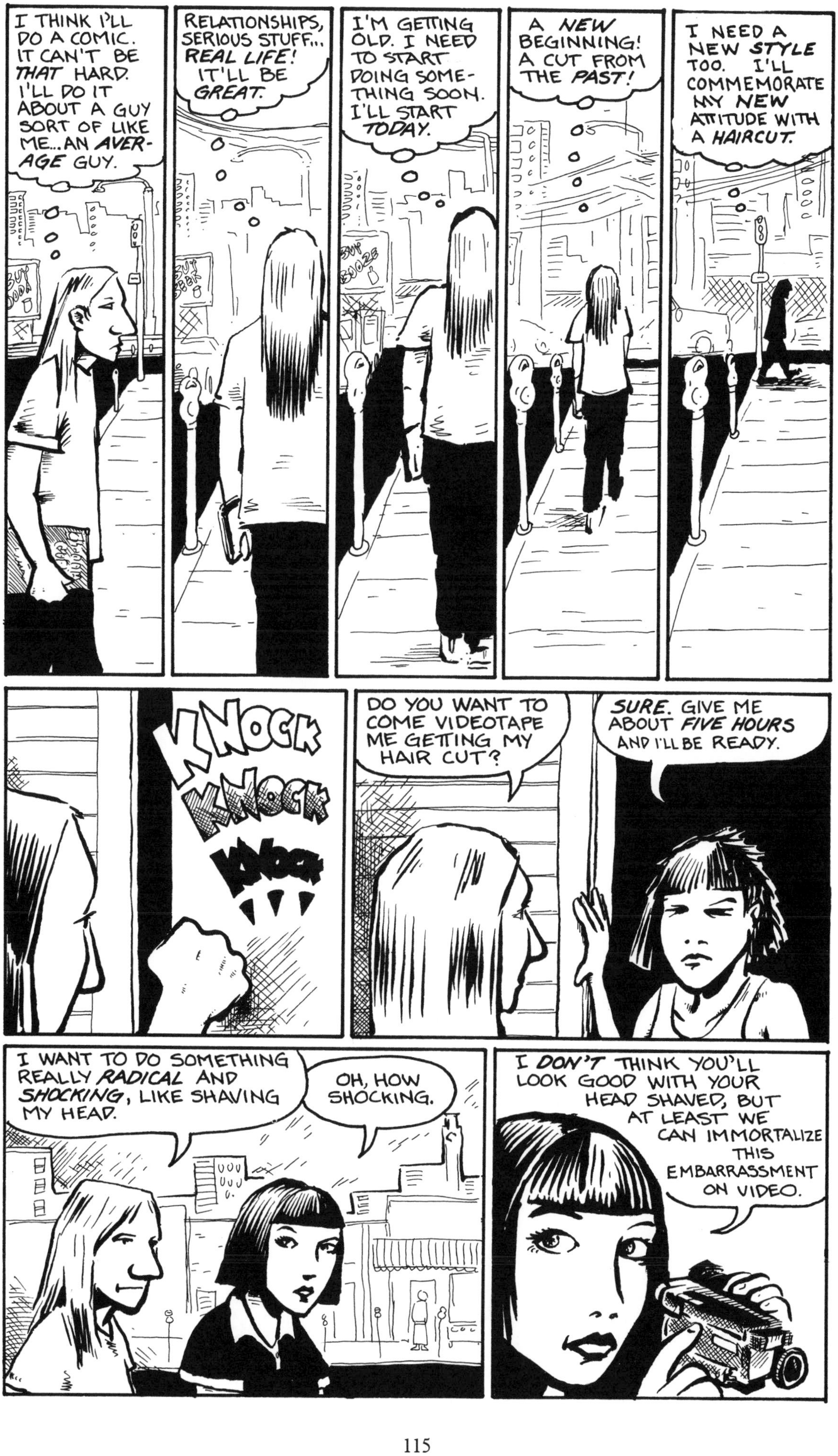
I THINK I'LL DO A COMIC. IT CAN'T BE THAT HARD. I'LL DO IT ABOUT A GUY SORT OF LIKE ME...AN AVERAGE GUY.
RELATIONSHIPS, SERIOUS STUFF... REAL LIFE! IT'LL BE GREAT.
I'M GETTING OLD. I NEED TO START DOING SOMETHING SOON. I'LL START TODAY.
A NEW BEGINNING! A CUT FROM THE PAST!
I NEED A NEW STYLE TOO. I'LL COMMEMORATE MY NEW ATTITUDE WITH A HAIRCUT.
KNOCK KNOCK KNOCK!!!
DO YOU WANT TO COME VIDEOTAPE ME GETTING MY HAIR CUT?
SURE. GIVE ME ABOUT FIVE HOURS AND I'LL BE READY.
I WANT TO DO SOMETHING REALLY RADICAL AND SHOCKING, LIKE SHAVING MY HEAD.
OH, HOW SHOCKING.
I DON'T THINK YOU'LL LOOK GOOD WITH YOUR HEAD SHAVED, BUT AT LEAST WE CAN IMMORTALIZE THIS EMBARRASSMENT ON VIDEO.

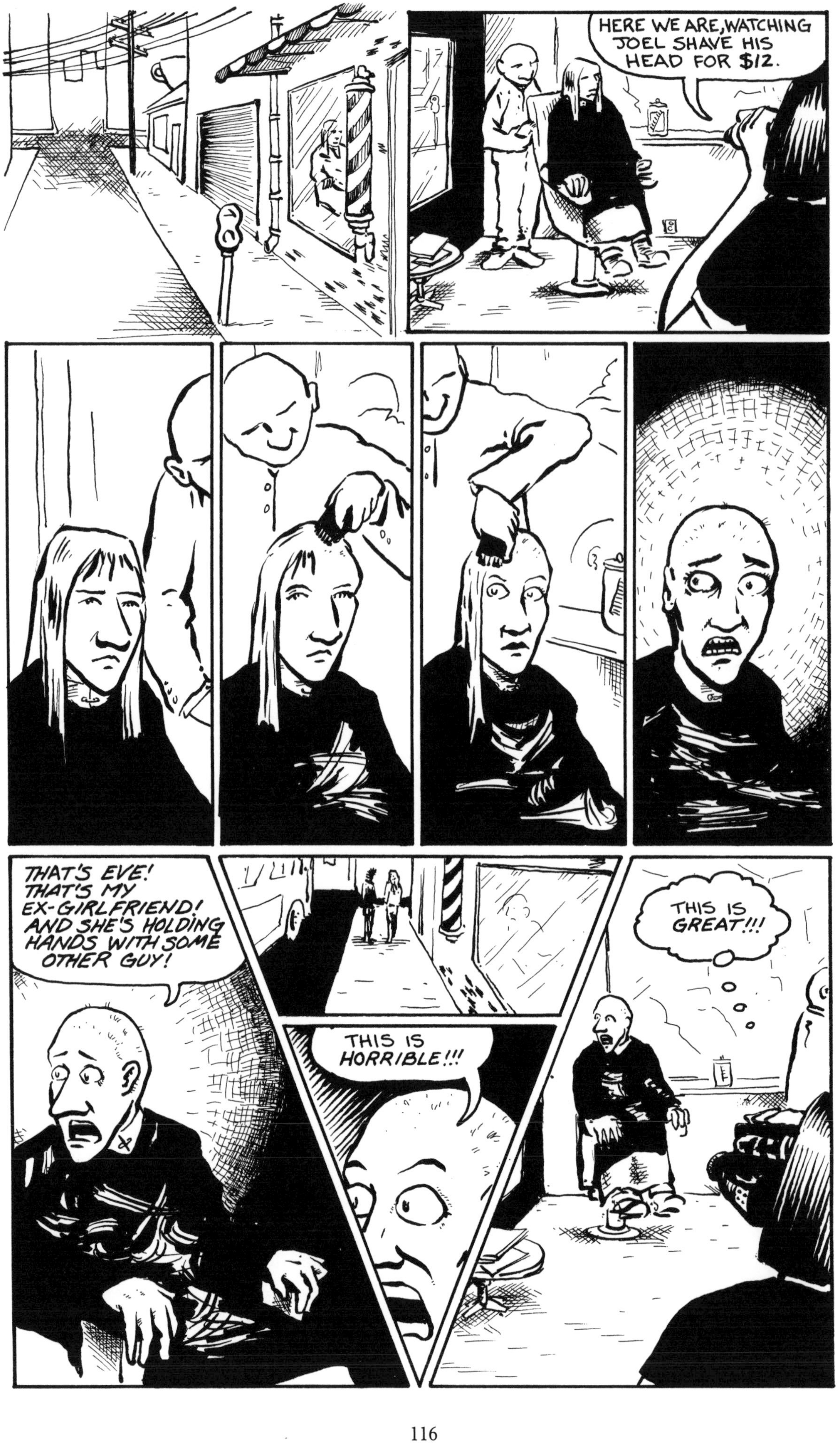
HERE WE ARE, WATCHING JOEL SHAVE HIS HEAD FOR $12.
THAT'S EVE! THAT'S MY EX-GIRLFRIEND! AND SHE'S HOLDING HANDS WITH SOME OTHER GUY!
THIS IS HORRIBLE!!!
THIS IS GREAT!!!

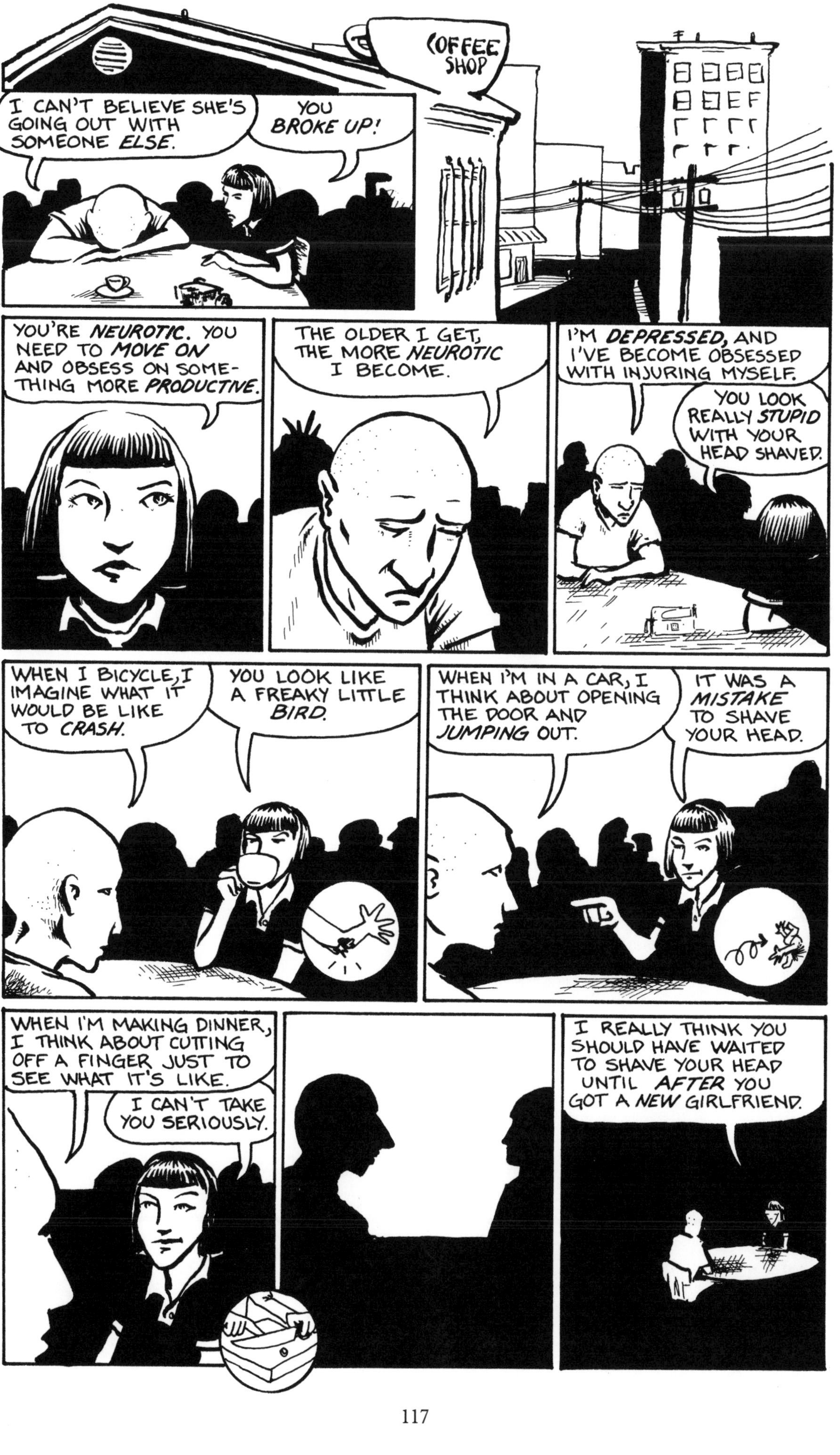

COFFEE SHOP
I CAN'T BELIEVE SHE'S GOING OUT WITH SOMEONE *ELSE*.
YOU *BROKE UP!*
YOU'RE *NEUROTIC*. YOU NEED TO *MOVE ON* AND OBSESS ON SOMETHING MORE *PRODUCTIVE*.
THE OLDER I GET, THE MORE *NEUROTIC* I BECOME.
I'M *DEPRESSED*, AND I'VE BECOME OBSESSED WITH INJURING MYSELF.
YOU LOOK REALLY *STUPID* WITH YOUR HEAD SHAVED.
WHEN I BICYCLE, I IMAGINE WHAT IT WOULD BE LIKE TO *CRASH*.
YOU LOOK LIKE A FREAKY LITTLE *BIRD*.
WHEN I'M IN A CAR, I THINK ABOUT OPENING THE DOOR AND *JUMPING* OUT.
IT WAS A *MISTAKE* TO SHAVE YOUR HEAD.
WHEN I'M MAKING DINNER, I THINK ABOUT CUTTING OFF A FINGER JUST TO SEE WHAT IT'S LIKE.
I CAN'T TAKE YOU SERIOUSLY.
I REALLY THINK YOU SHOULD HAVE WAITED TO SHAVE YOUR HEAD UNTIL *AFTER* YOU GOT A *NEW* GIRLFRIEND.

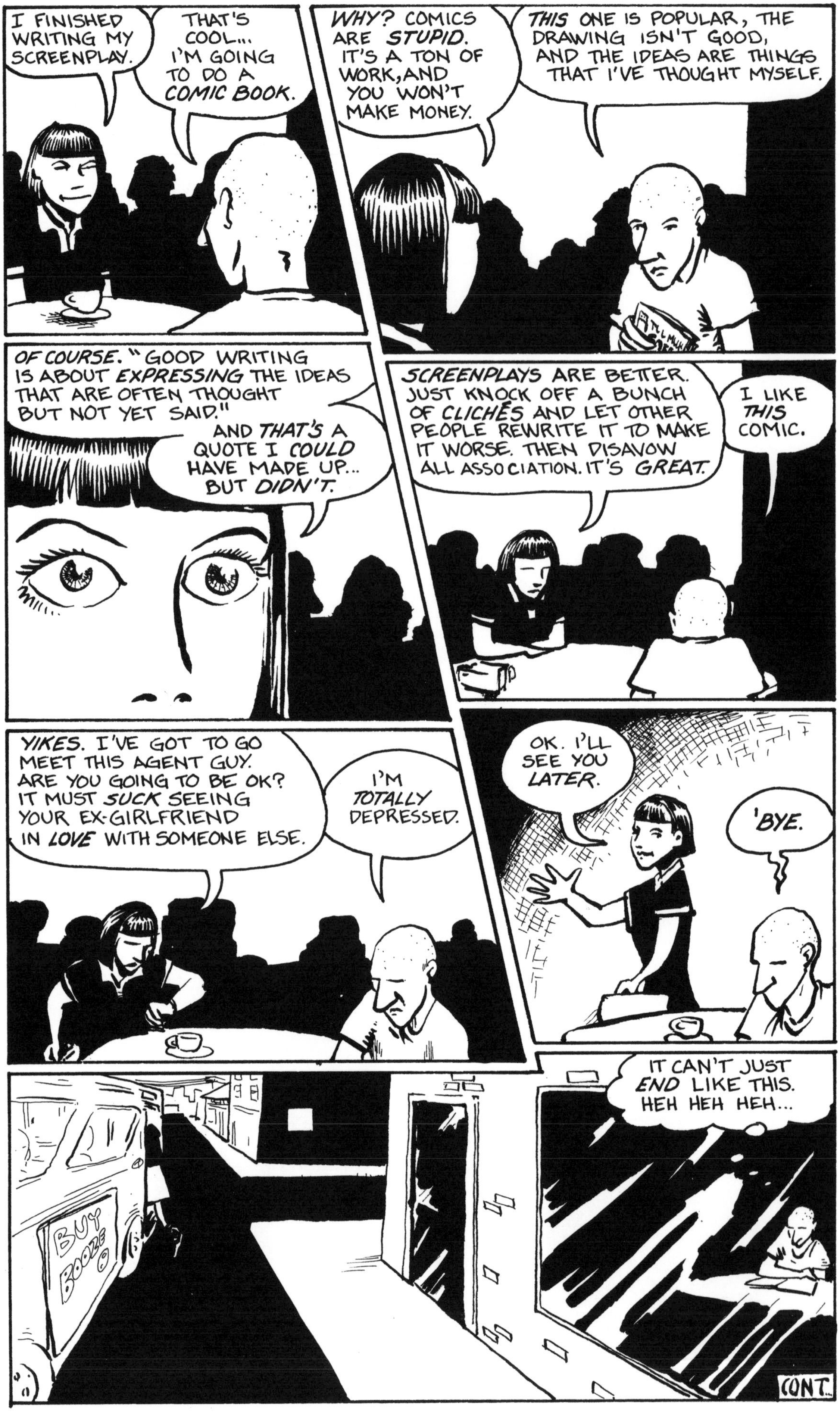
I FINISHED WRITING MY SCREENPLAY.
THAT'S COOL... I'M GOING TO DO A COMIC BOOK.
WHY? COMICS ARE STUPID. IT'S A TON OF WORK, AND YOU WON'T MAKE MONEY.
THIS ONE IS POPULAR, THE DRAWING ISN'T GOOD, AND THE IDEAS ARE THINGS THAT I'VE THOUGHT MYSELF.
OF COURSE. "GOOD WRITING IS ABOUT EXPRESSING THE IDEAS THAT ARE OFTEN THOUGHT BUT NOT YET SAID."
AND THAT'S A QUOTE I COULD HAVE MADE UP... BUT DIDN'T.
SCREENPLAYS ARE BETTER. JUST KNOCK OFF A BUNCH OF CLICHÉS AND LET OTHER PEOPLE REWRITE IT TO MAKE IT WORSE. THEN DISAVOW ALL ASSOCIATION. IT'S GREAT.
I LIKE THIS COMIC.
YIKES. I'VE GOT TO GO MEET THIS AGENT GUY. ARE YOU GOING TO BE OK? IT MUST SUCK SEEING YOUR EX-GIRLFRIEND IN LOVE WITH SOMEONE ELSE.
I'M TOTALLY DEPRESSED.
OK. I'LL SEE YOU LATER.
'BYE.
BUY BOOZE
IT CAN'T JUST END LIKE THIS. HEH HEH HEH...
CONT...

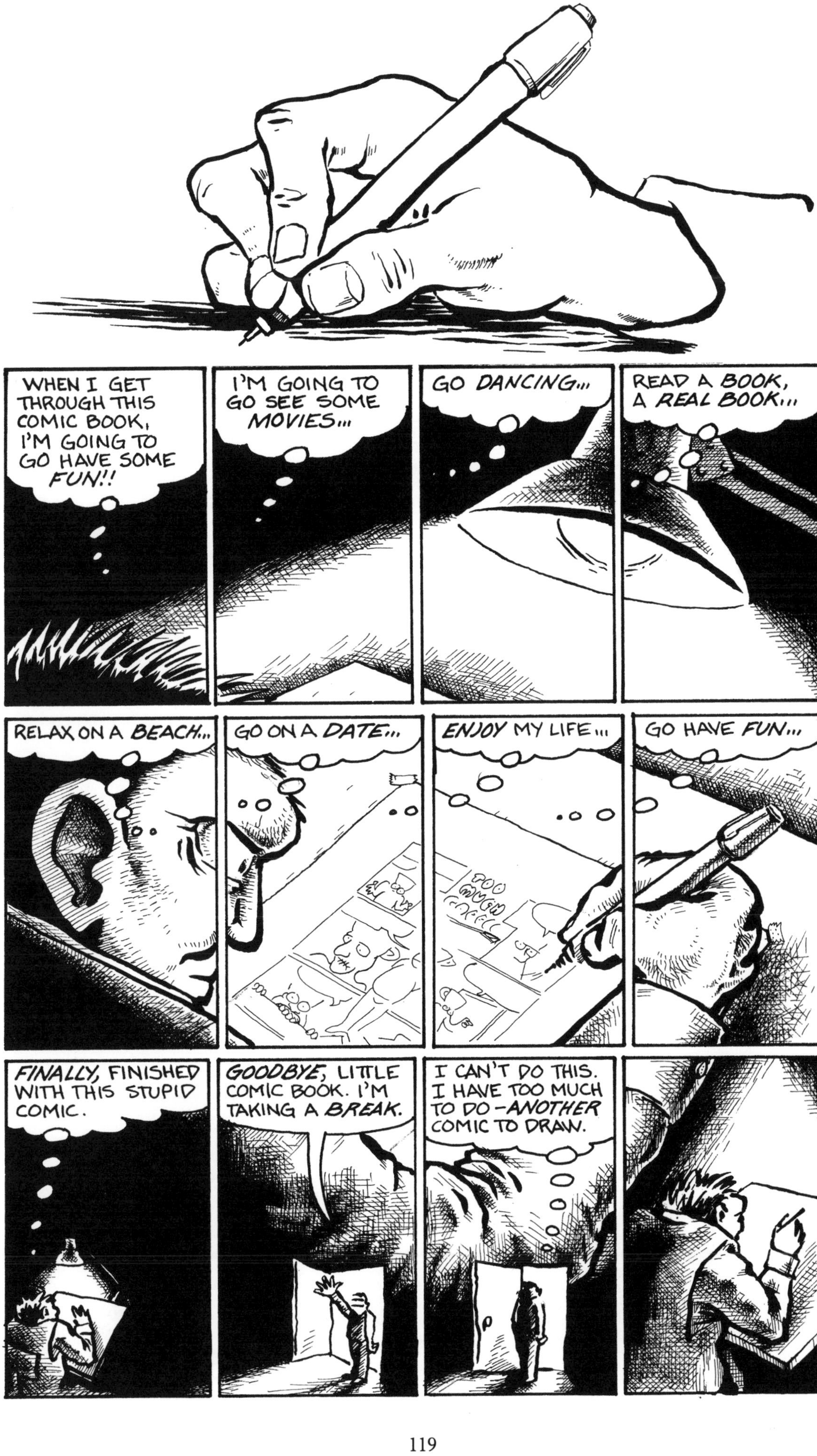
WHEN I GET THROUGH THIS COMIC BOOK, I'M GOING TO GO HAVE SOME FUN!!
I'M GOING TO GO SEE SOME MOVIES...
GO DANCING...
READ A BOOK, A REAL BOOK...
RELAX ON A BEACH...
GO ON A DATE...
ENJOY MY LIFE...
GO HAVE FUN...
FINALLY, FINISHED WITH THIS STUPID COMIC.
GOODBYE, LITTLE COMIC BOOK. I'M TAKING A BREAK.
I CAN'T DO THIS. I HAVE TOO MUCH TO DO—ANOTHER COMIC TO DRAW.

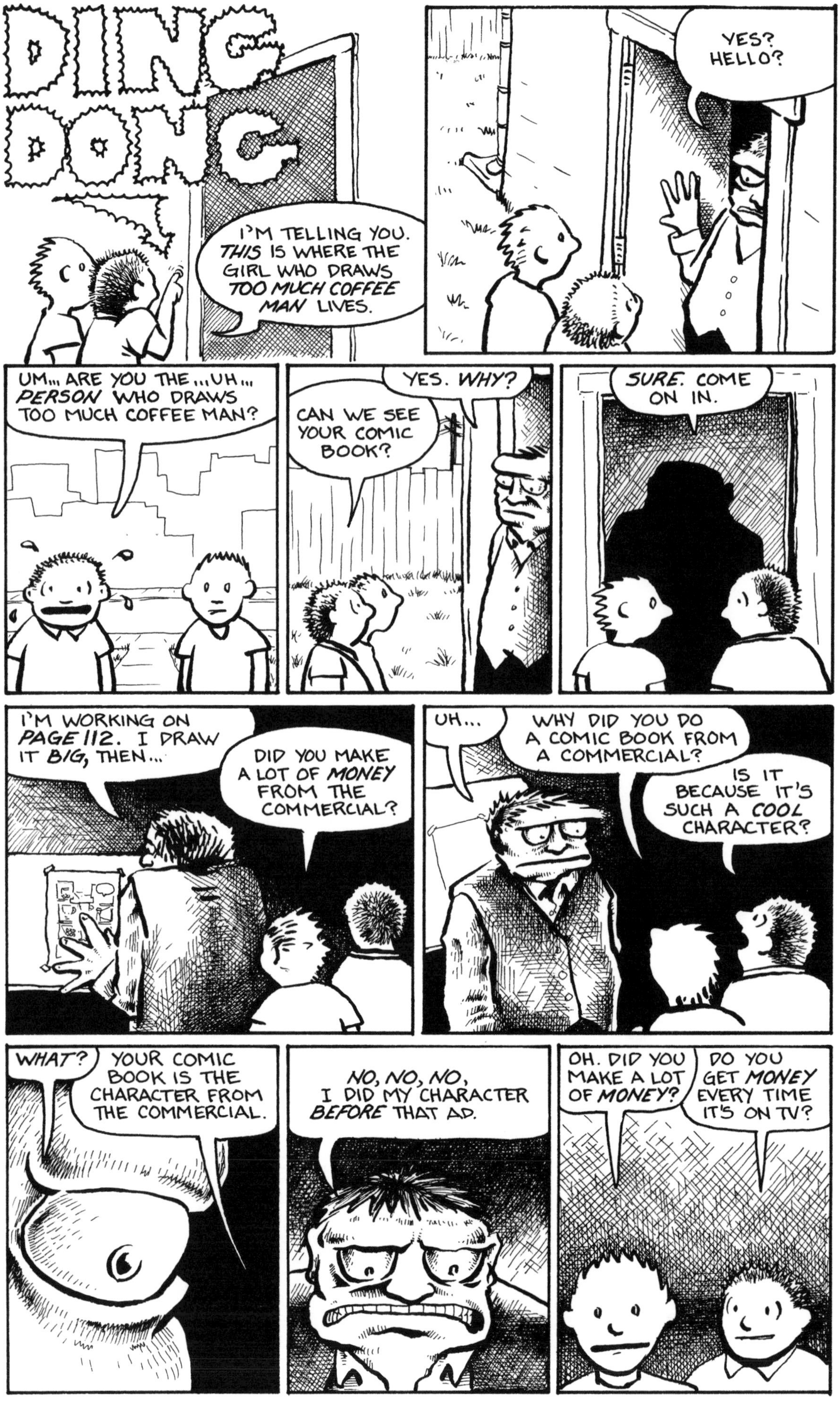

DING DONG
I'M TELLING YOU. THIS IS WHERE THE GIRL WHO DRAWS TOO MUCH COFFEE MAN LIVES.
YES? HELLO?
UM... ARE YOU THE...UH... PERSON WHO DRAWS TOO MUCH COFFEE MAN?
YES. WHY?
CAN WE SEE YOUR COMIC BOOK?
SURE. COME ON IN.
I'M WORKING ON PAGE 112. I DRAW IT BIG, THEN...
DID YOU MAKE A LOT OF MONEY FROM THE COMMERCIAL?
UH...
WHY DID YOU DO A COMIC BOOK FROM A COMMERCIAL?
IS IT BECAUSE IT'S SUCH A COOL CHARACTER?
WHAT?
YOUR COMIC BOOK IS THE CHARACTER FROM THE COMMERCIAL.
NO, NO, NO, I DID MY CHARACTER BEFORE THAT AD.
OH. DID YOU MAKE A LOT OF MONEY?
DO YOU GET MONEY EVERY TIME IT'S ON TV?

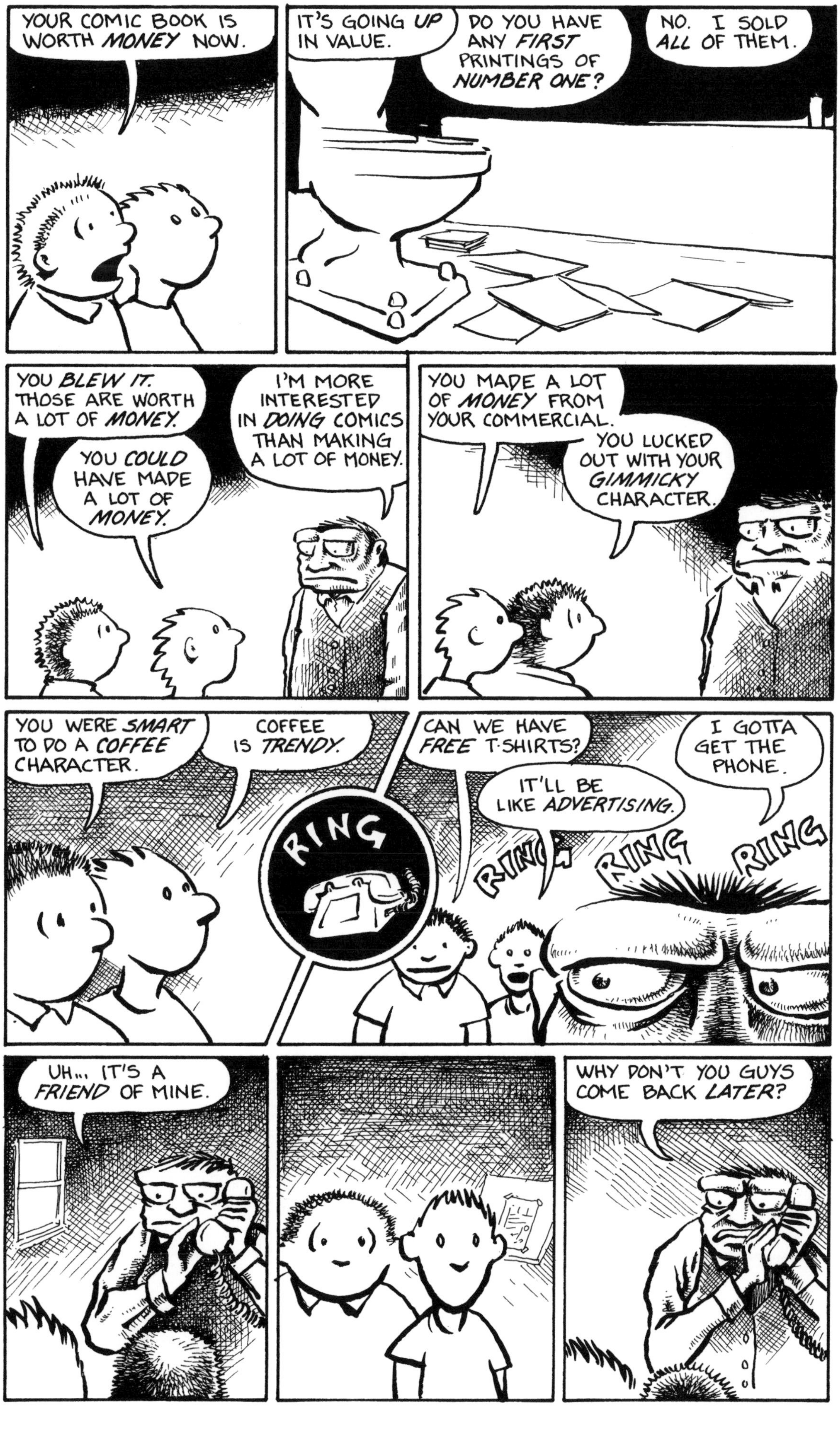
YOUR COMIC BOOK IS WORTH MONEY NOW.
IT'S GOING UP IN VALUE.
DO YOU HAVE ANY FIRST PRINTINGS OF NUMBER ONE?
NO. I SOLD ALL OF THEM.
YOU BLEW IT. THOSE ARE WORTH A LOT OF MONEY.
YOU COULD HAVE MADE A LOT OF MONEY.
I'M MORE INTERESTED IN DOING COMICS THAN MAKING A LOT OF MONEY.
YOU MADE A LOT OF MONEY FROM YOUR COMMERCIAL.
YOU LUCKED OUT WITH YOUR GIMMICKY CHARACTER.
YOU WERE SMART TO DO A COFFEE CHARACTER.
COFFEE IS TRENDY.
RING
CAN WE HAVE FREE T-SHIRTS?
IT'LL BE LIKE ADVERTISING.
RING
RING
RING
I GOTTA GET THE PHONE.
UH... IT'S A FRIEND OF MINE.
WHY DON'T YOU GUYS COME BACK LATER?

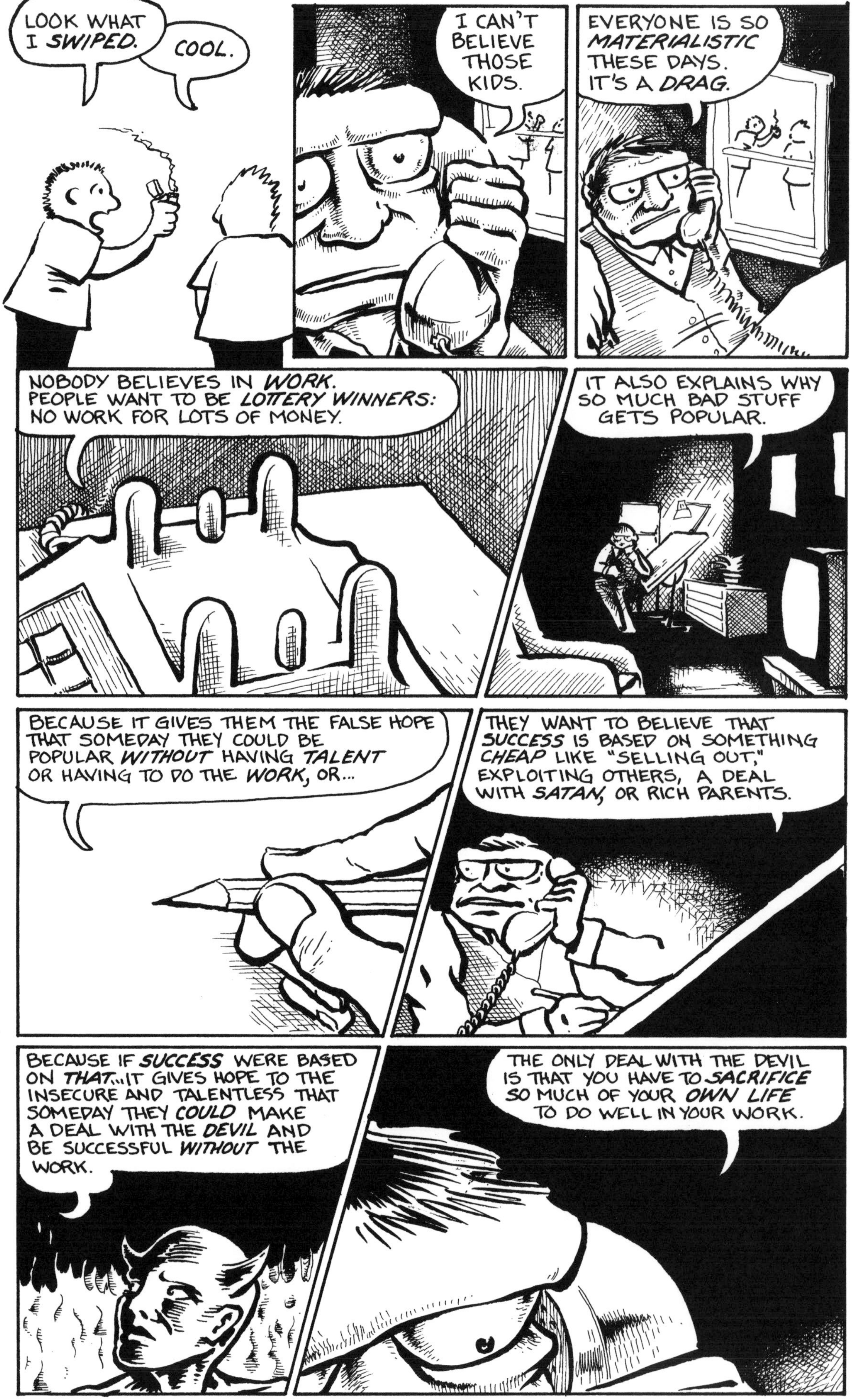
LOOK WHAT I SWIPED.
COOL.
I CAN'T BELIEVE THOSE KIDS.
EVERYONE IS SO MATERIALISTIC THESE DAYS. IT'S A DRAG.
NOBODY BELIEVES IN WORK. PEOPLE WANT TO BE LOTTERY WINNERS: NO WORK FOR LOTS OF MONEY.
IT ALSO EXPLAINS WHY SO MUCH BAD STUFF GETS POPULAR.
BECAUSE IT GIVES THEM THE FALSE HOPE THAT SOMEDAY THEY COULD BE POPULAR WITHOUT HAVING TALENT OR HAVING TO DO THE WORK, OR...
THEY WANT TO BELIEVE THAT SUCCESS IS BASED ON SOMETHING CHEAP LIKE "SELLING OUT," EXPLOITING OTHERS, A DEAL WITH SATAN, OR RICH PARENTS.
BECAUSE IF SUCCESS WERE BASED ON THAT...IT GIVES HOPE TO THE INSECURE AND TALENTLESS THAT SOMEDAY THEY COULD MAKE A DEAL WITH THE DEVIL AND BE SUCCESSFUL WITHOUT THE WORK.
THE ONLY DEAL WITH THE DEVIL IS THAT YOU HAVE TO SACRIFICE SO MUCH OF YOUR OWN LIFE TO DO WELL IN YOUR WORK.

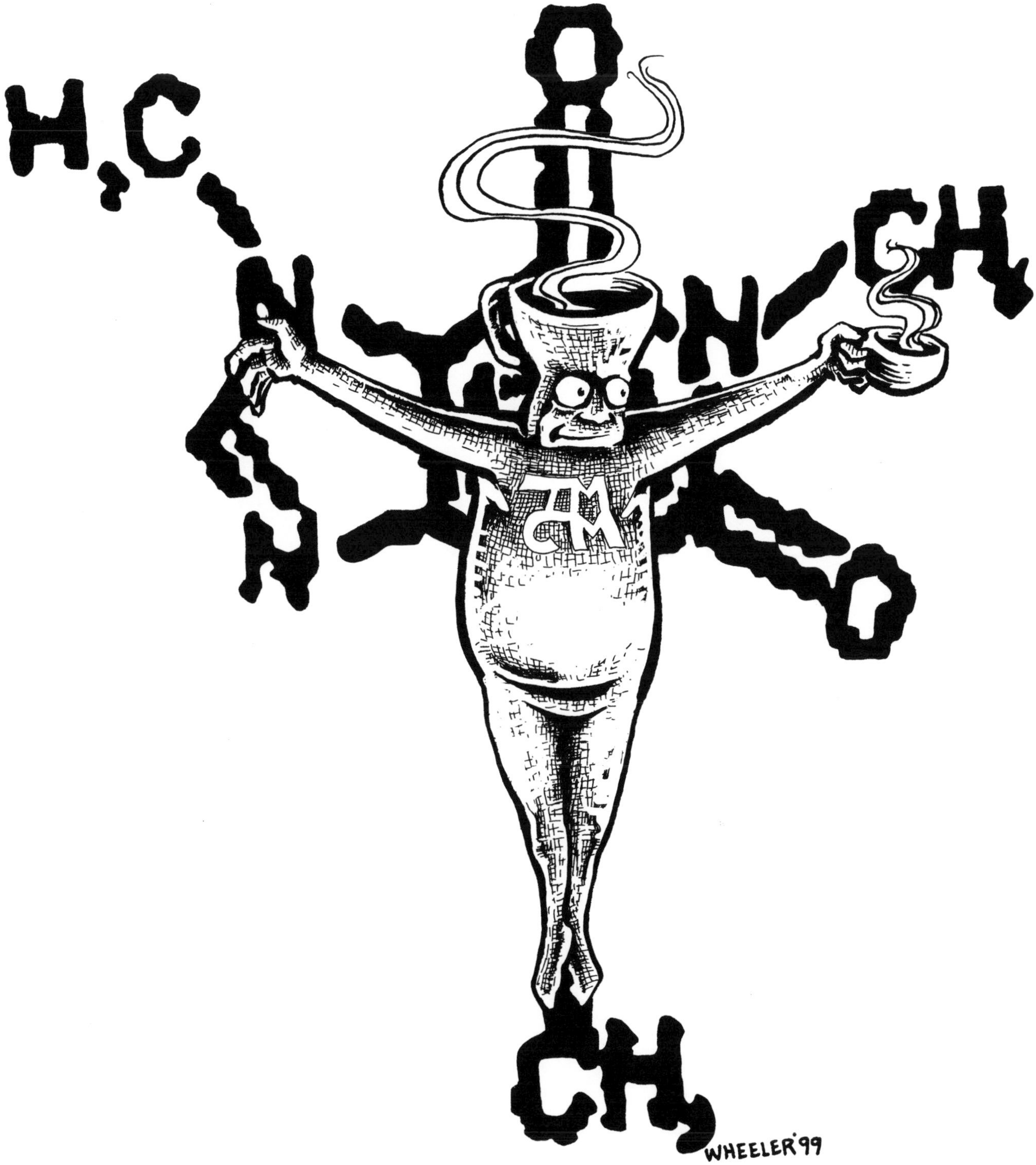
WHEELER'99

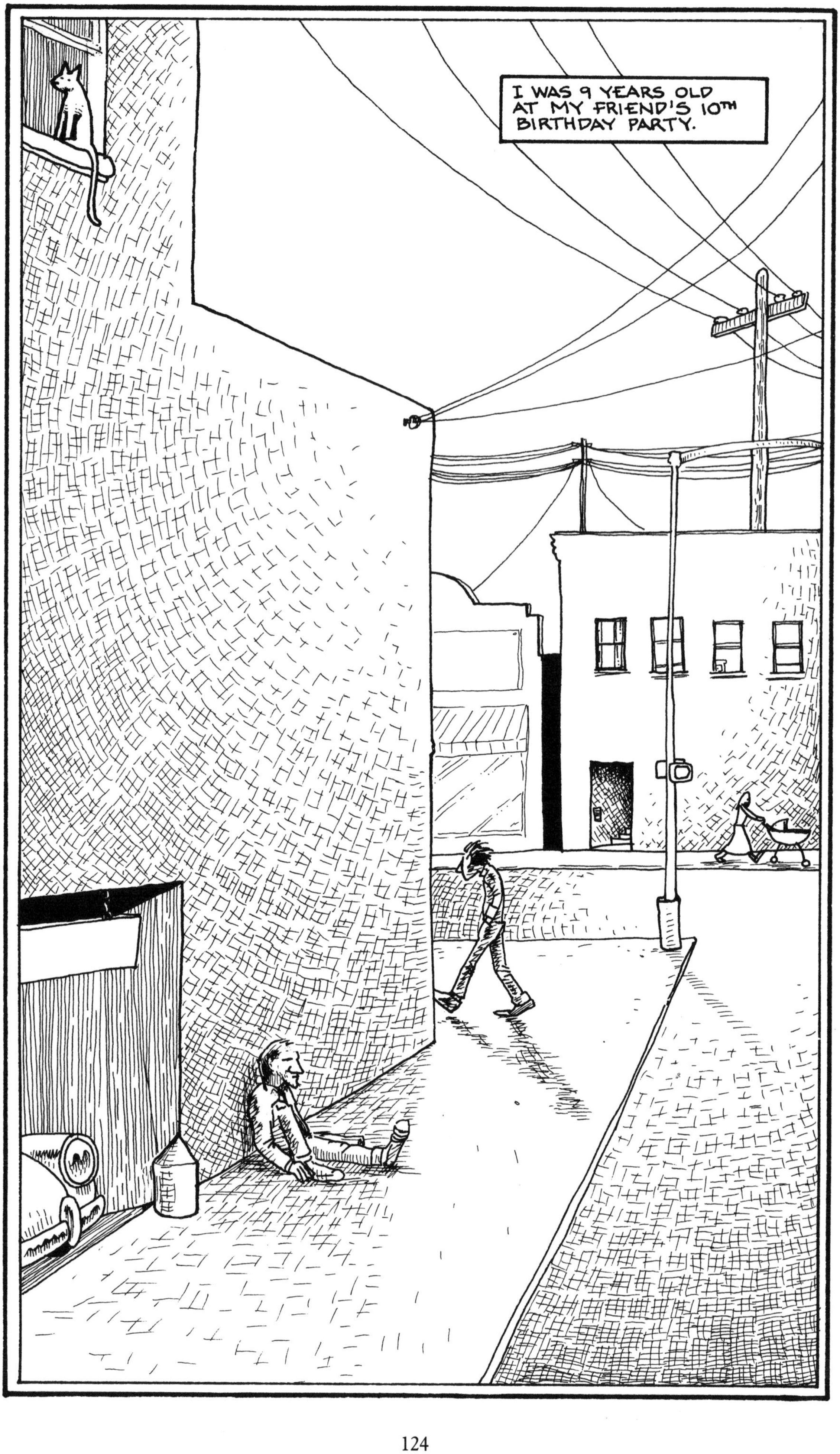
I WAS 9 YEARS OLD AT MY FRIEND'S 10TH BIRTHDAY PARTY.

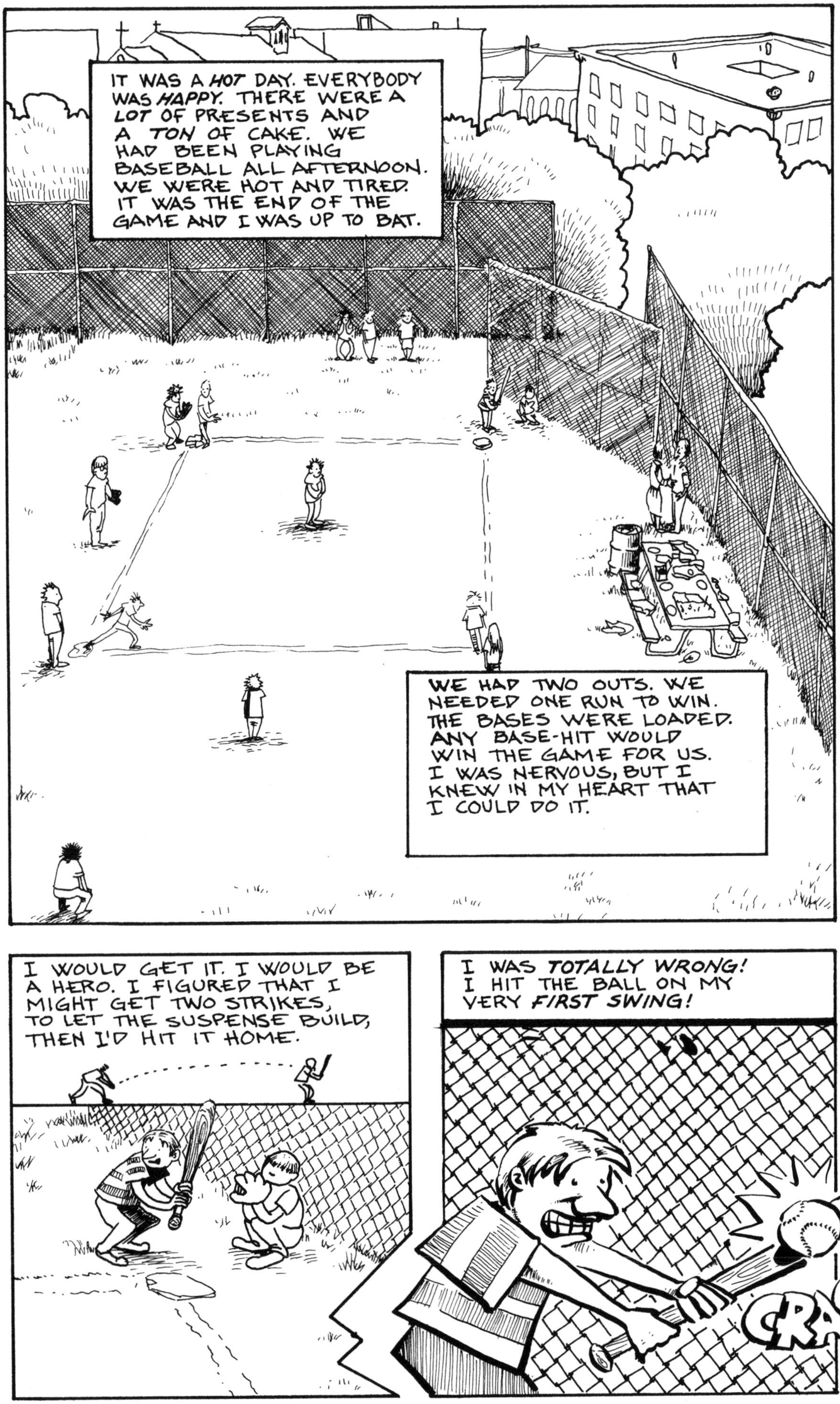
IT WAS A HOT DAY. EVERYBODY WAS HAPPY. THERE WERE A LOT OF PRESENTS AND A TON OF CAKE. WE HAD BEEN PLAYING BASEBALL ALL AFTERNOON. WE WERE HOT AND TIRED. IT WAS THE END OF THE GAME AND I WAS UP TO BAT.
WE HAD TWO OUTS. WE NEEDED ONE RUN TO WIN. THE BASES WERE LOADED. ANY BASE-HIT WOULD WIN THE GAME FOR US. I WAS NERVOUS, BUT I KNEW IN MY HEART THAT I COULD DO IT.
I WOULD GET IT. I WOULD BE A HERO. I FIGURED THAT I MIGHT GET TWO STRIKES, TO LET THE SUSPENSE BUILD, THEN I'D HIT IT HOME.
I WAS TOTALLY WRONG! I HIT THE BALL ON MY VERY FIRST SWING!
CRACK

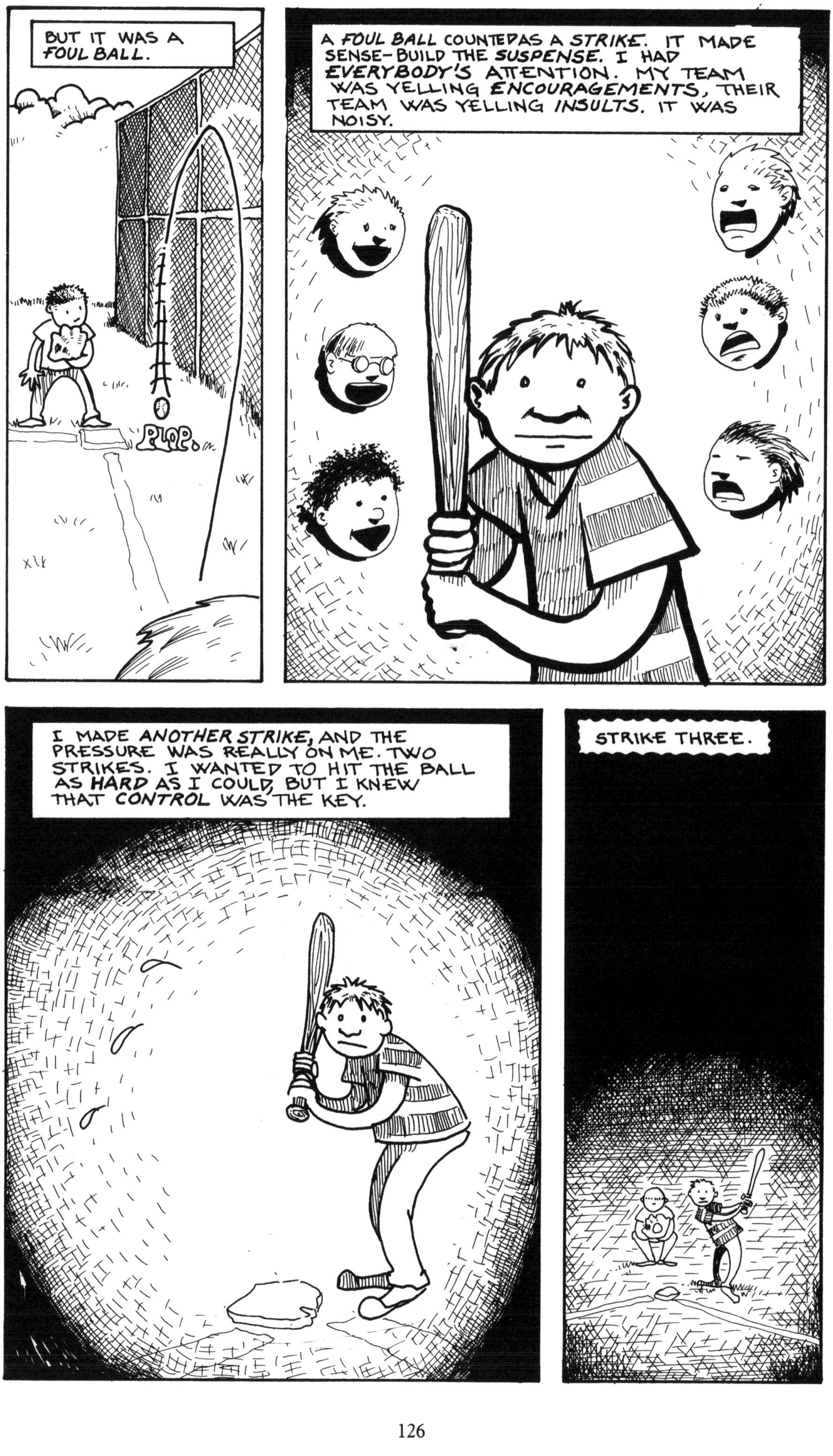
BUT IT WAS A FOUL BALL.
PLOP.
A FOUL BALL COUNTED AS A STRIKE. IT MADE SENSE-BUILD THE SUSPENSE. I HAD EVERYBODY'S ATTENTION. MY TEAM WAS YELLING ENCOURAGEMENTS, THEIR TEAM WAS YELLING INSULTS. IT WAS NOISY.
I MADE ANOTHER STRIKE, AND THE PRESSURE WAS REALLY ON ME. TWO STRIKES. I WANTED TO HIT THE BALL AS HARD AS I COULD, BUT I KNEW THAT CONTROL WAS THE KEY.
STRIKE THREE.

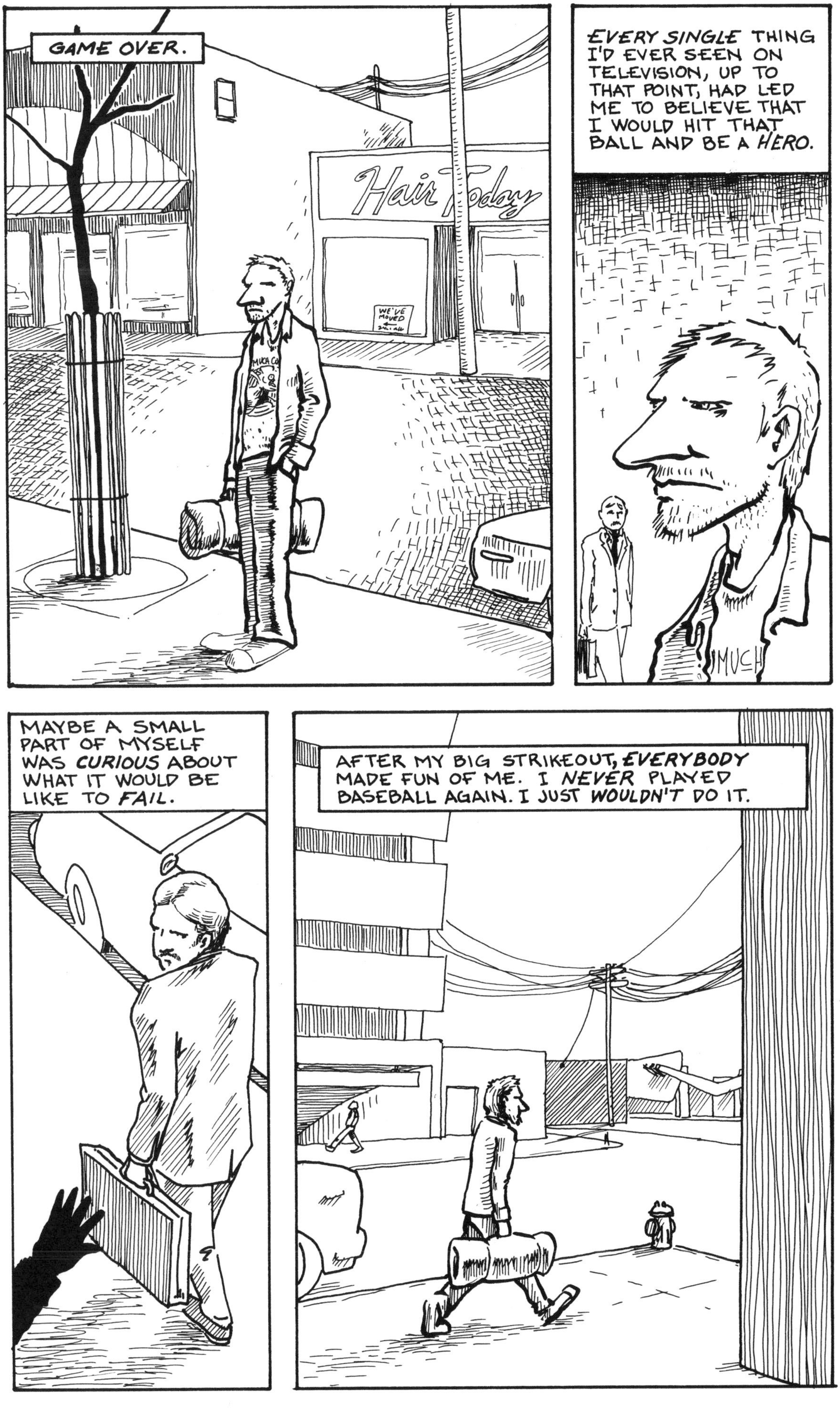
GAME OVER.
Hair Today
EVERY SINGLE THING I'D EVER SEEN ON TELEVISION, UP TO THAT POINT, HAD LED ME TO BELIEVE THAT I WOULD HIT THAT BALL AND BE A HERO.
MUCH
MAYBE A SMALL PART OF MYSELF WAS CURIOUS ABOUT WHAT IT WOULD BE LIKE TO FAIL.
AFTER MY BIG STRIKEOUT, EVERYBODY MADE FUN OF ME. I NEVER PLAYED BASEBALL AGAIN. I JUST WOULDN'T DO IT.

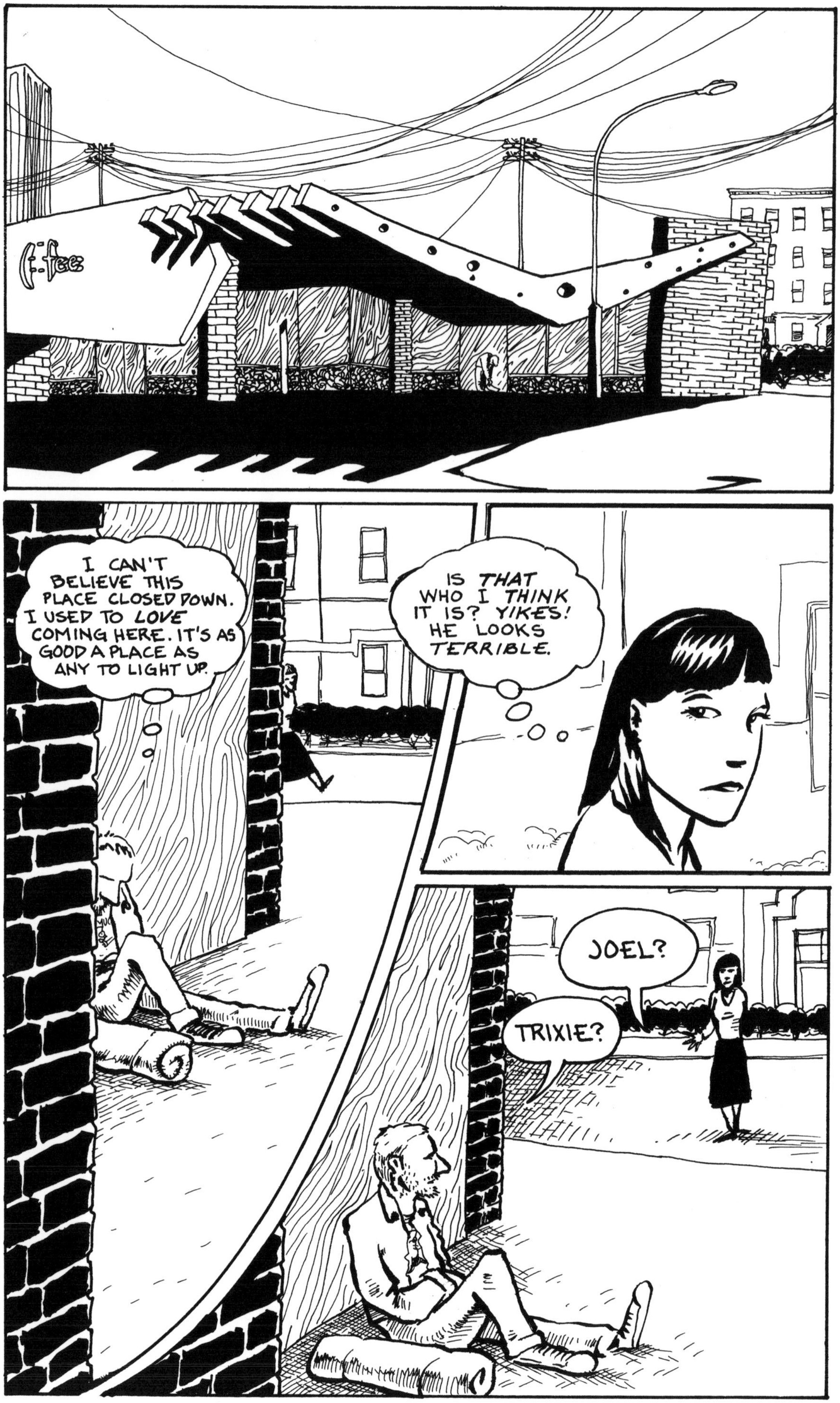
C-fee
I CAN'T BELIEVE THIS PLACE CLOSED DOWN. I USED TO LOVE COMING HERE. IT'S AS GOOD A PLACE AS ANY TO LIGHT UP.
IS THAT WHO I THINK IT IS? YIKES! HE LOOKS TERRIBLE.
JOEL?
TRIXIE?

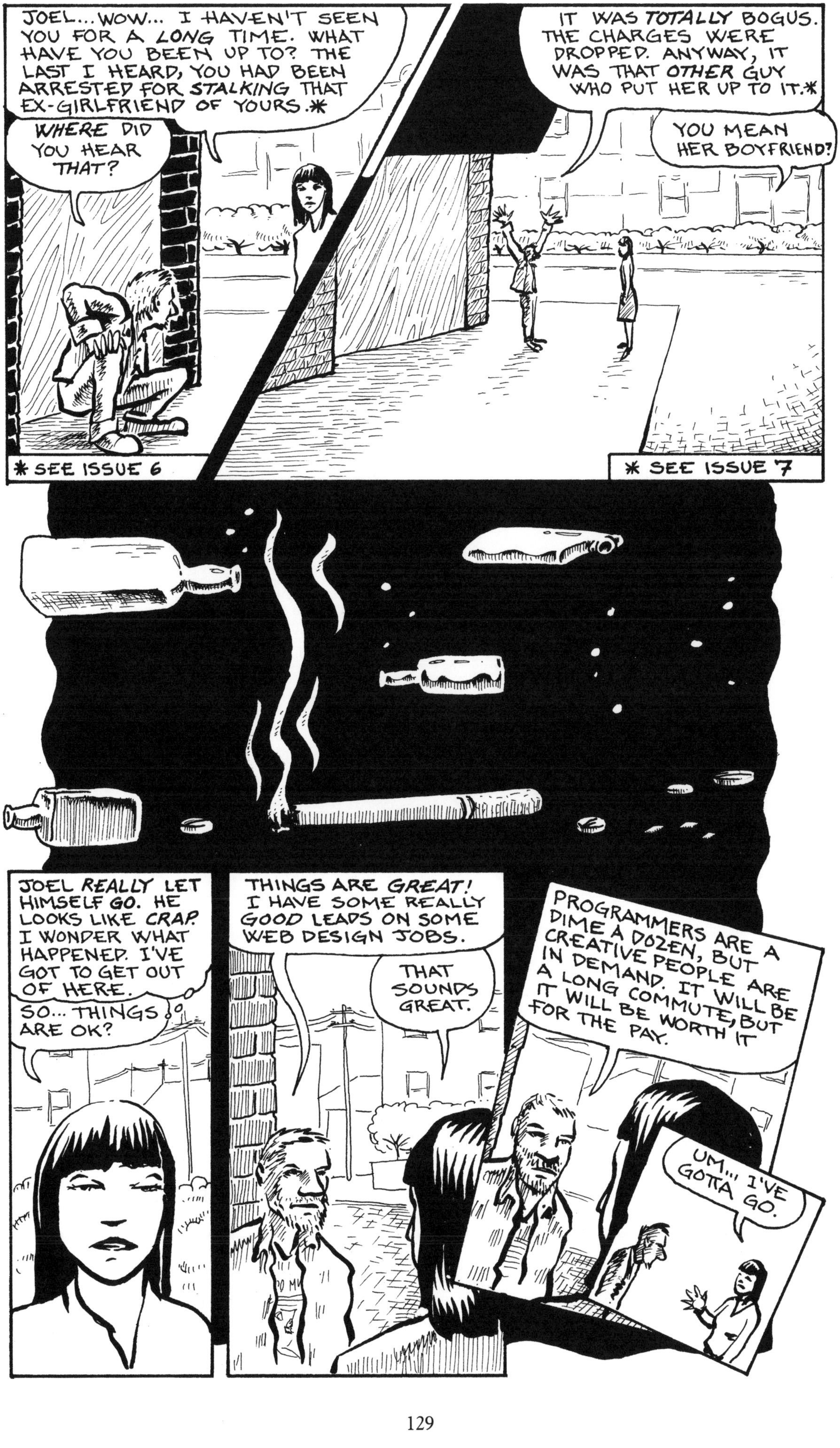
JOEL... WOW... I HAVEN'T SEEN YOU FOR A *LONG* TIME. WHAT HAVE YOU BEEN UP TO? THE LAST I HEARD, YOU HAD BEEN ARRESTED FOR *STALKING* THAT EX-GIRLFRIEND OF YOURS.*
WHERE DID YOU HEAR *THAT*?
* SEE ISSUE 6
IT WAS *TOTALLY* BOGUS. THE CHARGES WERE DROPPED. ANYWAY, IT WAS THAT *OTHER* GUY WHO PUT HER UP TO IT.*
YOU MEAN HER BOYFRIEND?
* SEE ISSUE 7
JOEL *REALLY* LET HIMSELF *GO*. HE LOOKS LIKE *CRAP*. I WONDER WHAT HAPPENED. I'VE GOT TO GET OUT OF HERE.
SO... THINGS ARE OK?
THINGS ARE *GREAT*! I HAVE SOME REALLY *GOOD* LEADS ON SOME WEB DESIGN JOBS.
THAT SOUNDS GREAT.
PROGRAMMERS ARE A DIME A DOZEN, BUT CREATIVE PEOPLE ARE IN DEMAND. IT WILL BE A LONG COMMUTE, BUT IT WILL BE WORTH IT FOR THE PAY.
UM... I'VE GOTTA GO.

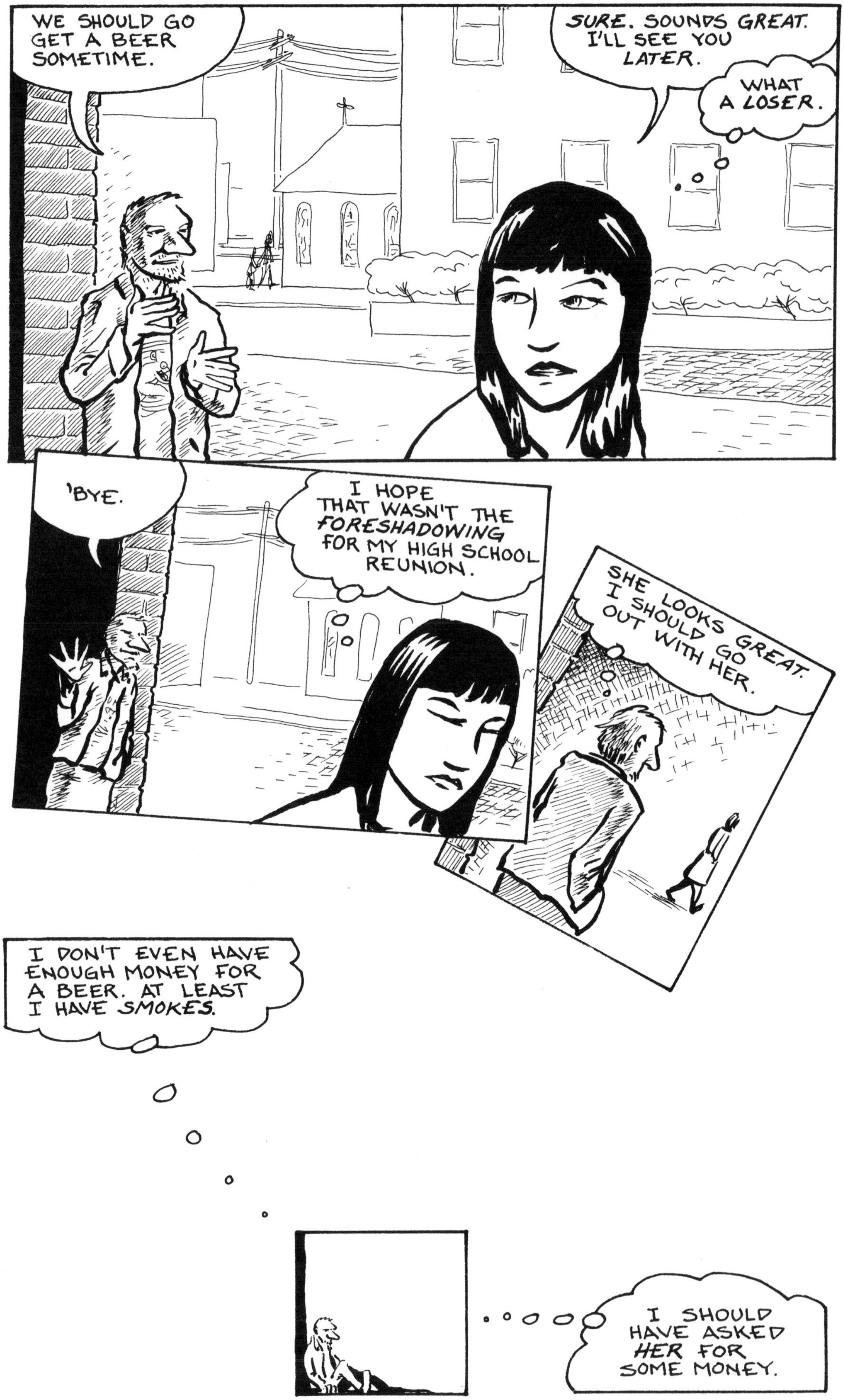
WE SHOULD GO GET A BEER SOMETIME.
SURE. SOUNDS GREAT. I'LL SEE YOU LATER.
WHAT A LOSER.
'BYE.
I HOPE THAT WASN'T THE FORESHADOWING FOR MY HIGH SCHOOL REUNION.
SHE LOOKS GREAT. I SHOULD GO OUT WITH HER.
I DON'T EVEN HAVE ENOUGH MONEY FOR A BEER. AT LEAST I HAVE SMOKES.
I SHOULD HAVE ASKED HER FOR SOME MONEY.

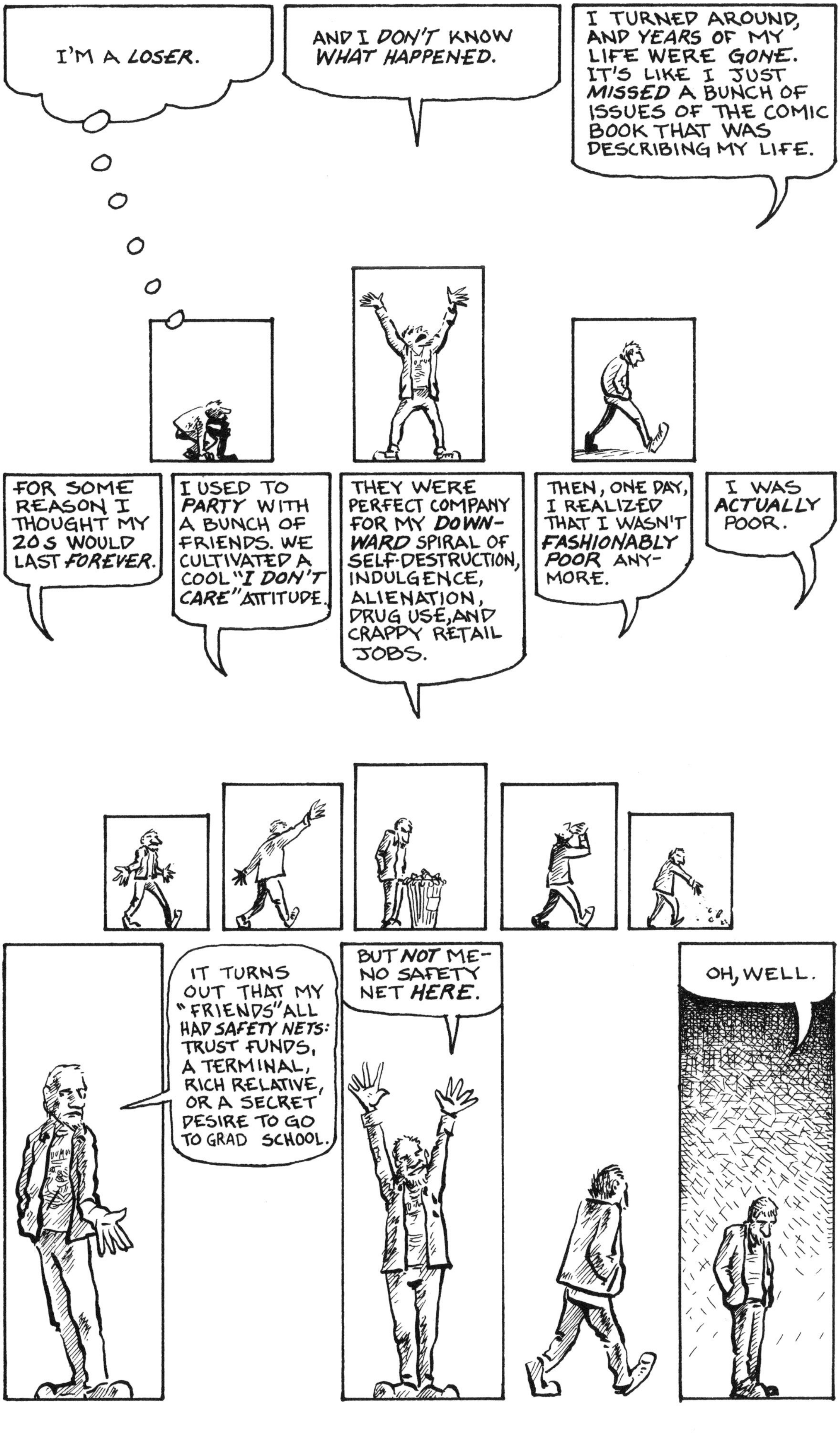
I'M A LOSER.
AND I DON'T KNOW WHAT HAPPENED.
I TURNED AROUND, AND YEARS OF MY LIFE WERE GONE. IT'S LIKE I JUST MISSED A BUNCH OF ISSUES OF THE COMIC BOOK THAT WAS DESCRIBING MY LIFE.
FOR SOME REASON I THOUGHT MY 20S WOULD LAST FOREVER.
I USED TO PARTY WITH A BUNCH OF FRIENDS. WE CULTIVATED A COOL "I DON'T CARE" ATTITUDE.
THEY WERE PERFECT COMPANY FOR MY DOWNWARD SPIRAL OF SELF-DESTRUCTION, INDULGENCE, ALIENATION, DRUG USE, AND CRAPPY RETAIL JOBS.
THEN, ONE DAY, I REALIZED THAT I WASN'T FASHIONABLY POOR ANYMORE.
I WAS ACTUALLY POOR.
IT TURNS OUT THAT MY "FRIENDS" ALL HAD SAFETY NETS: TRUST FUNDS, A TERMINAL, RICH RELATIVE, OR A SECRET DESIRE TO GO TO GRAD SCHOOL.
BUT NOT ME- NO SAFETY NET HERE.
OH, WELL.

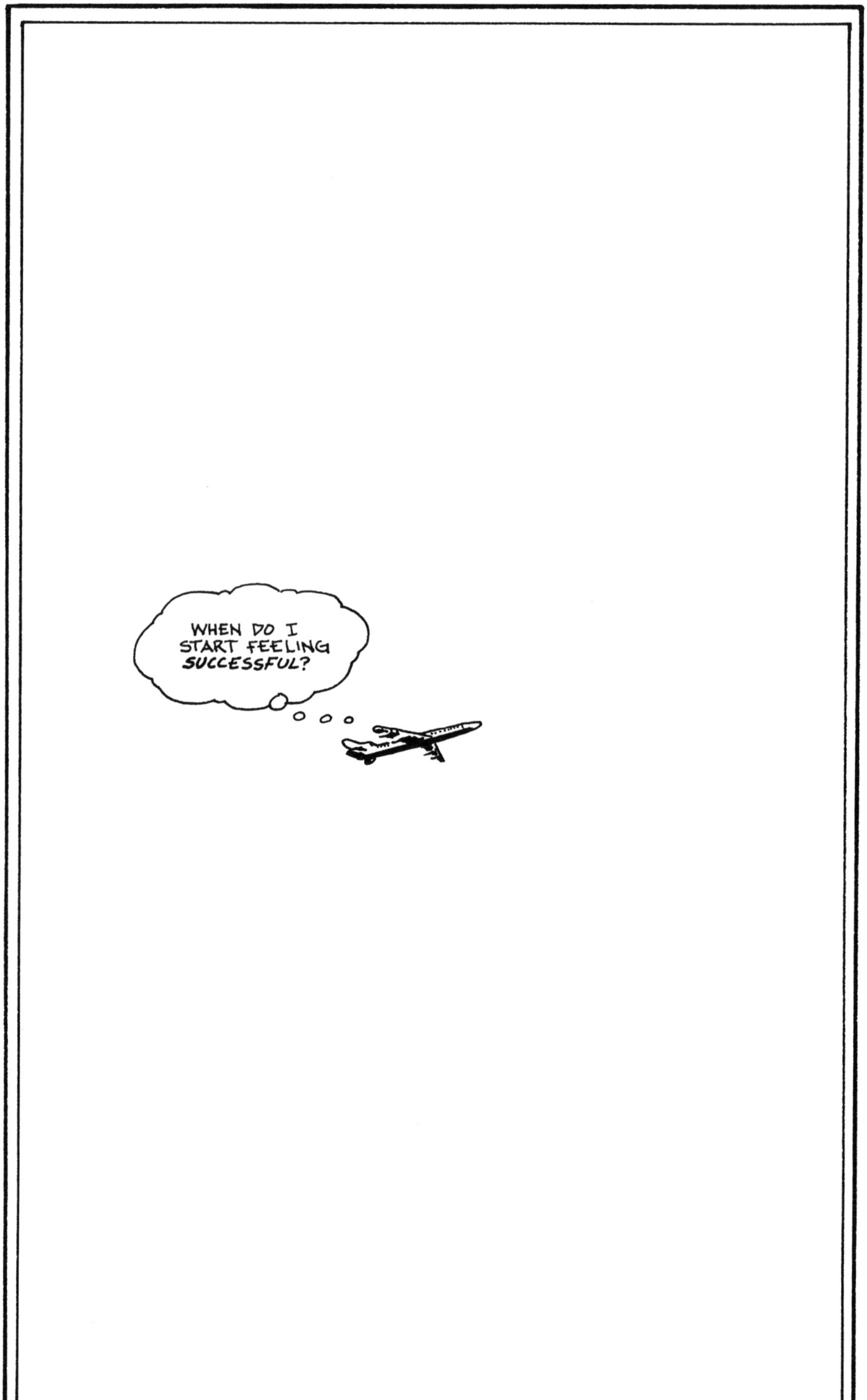
WHEN DO I START FEELING SUCCESSFUL?

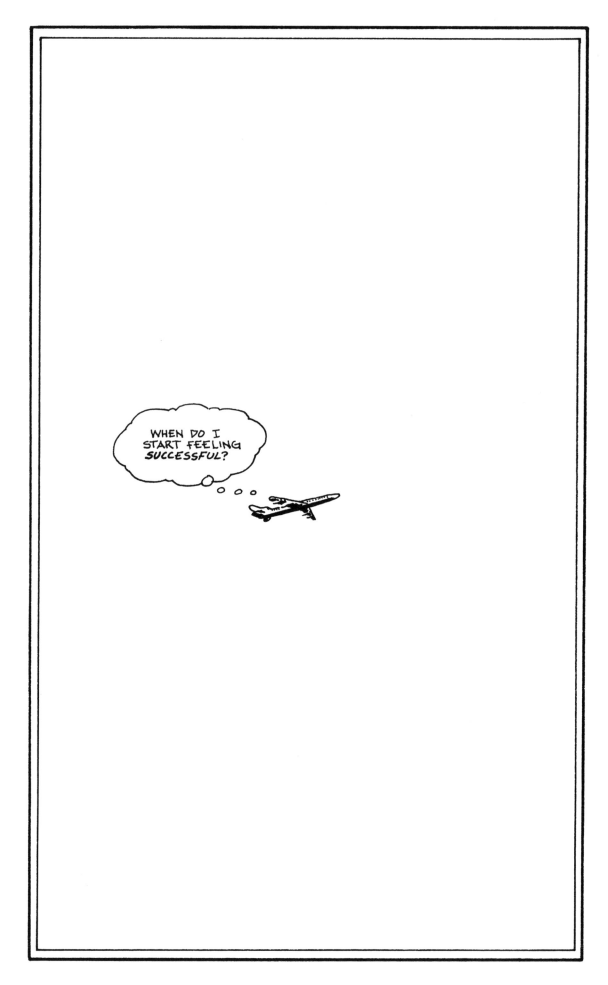

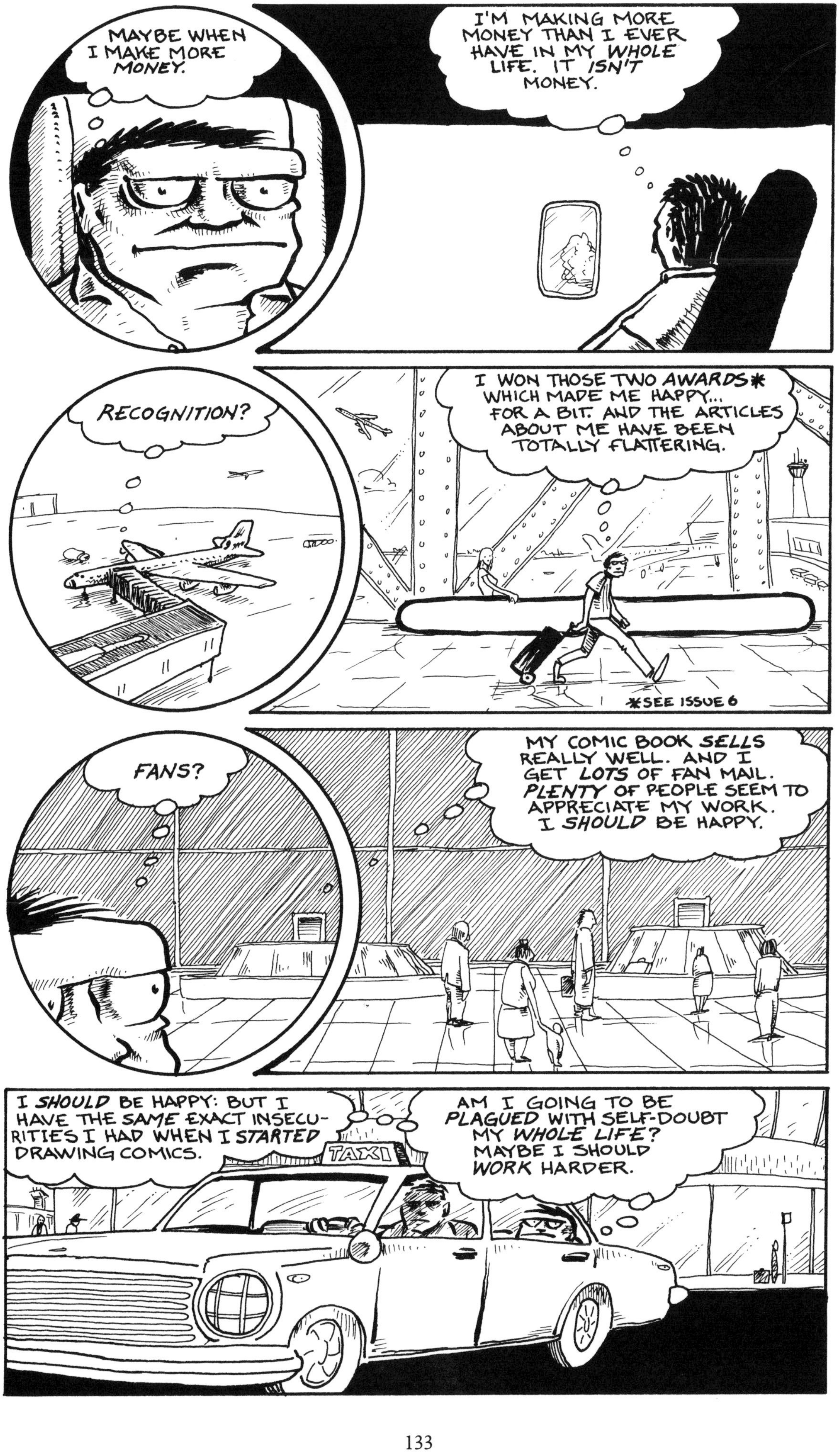
MAYBE WHEN I MAKE MORE *MONEY*.
I'M MAKING MORE MONEY THAN I EVER HAVE IN MY *WHOLE* LIFE. IT *ISN'T* MONEY.
RECOGNITION?
I WON THOSE TWO *AWARDS*✱ WHICH MADE ME HAPPY... FOR A BIT. AND THE ARTICLES ABOUT ME HAVE BEEN TOTALLY FLATTERING.
✱SEE ISSUE 6
FANS?
MY COMIC BOOK *SELLS* REALLY WELL. AND I GET *LOTS* OF FAN MAIL. *PLENTY* OF PEOPLE SEEM TO APPRECIATE MY WORK. I *SHOULD* BE HAPPY.
I *SHOULD* BE HAPPY: BUT I HAVE THE *SAME EXACT* INSECURITIES I HAD WHEN I *STARTED* DRAWING COMICS.
TAXI
AM I GOING TO BE *PLAGUED* WITH SELF-DOUBT MY *WHOLE LIFE*? MAYBE I SHOULD *WORK* HARDER.

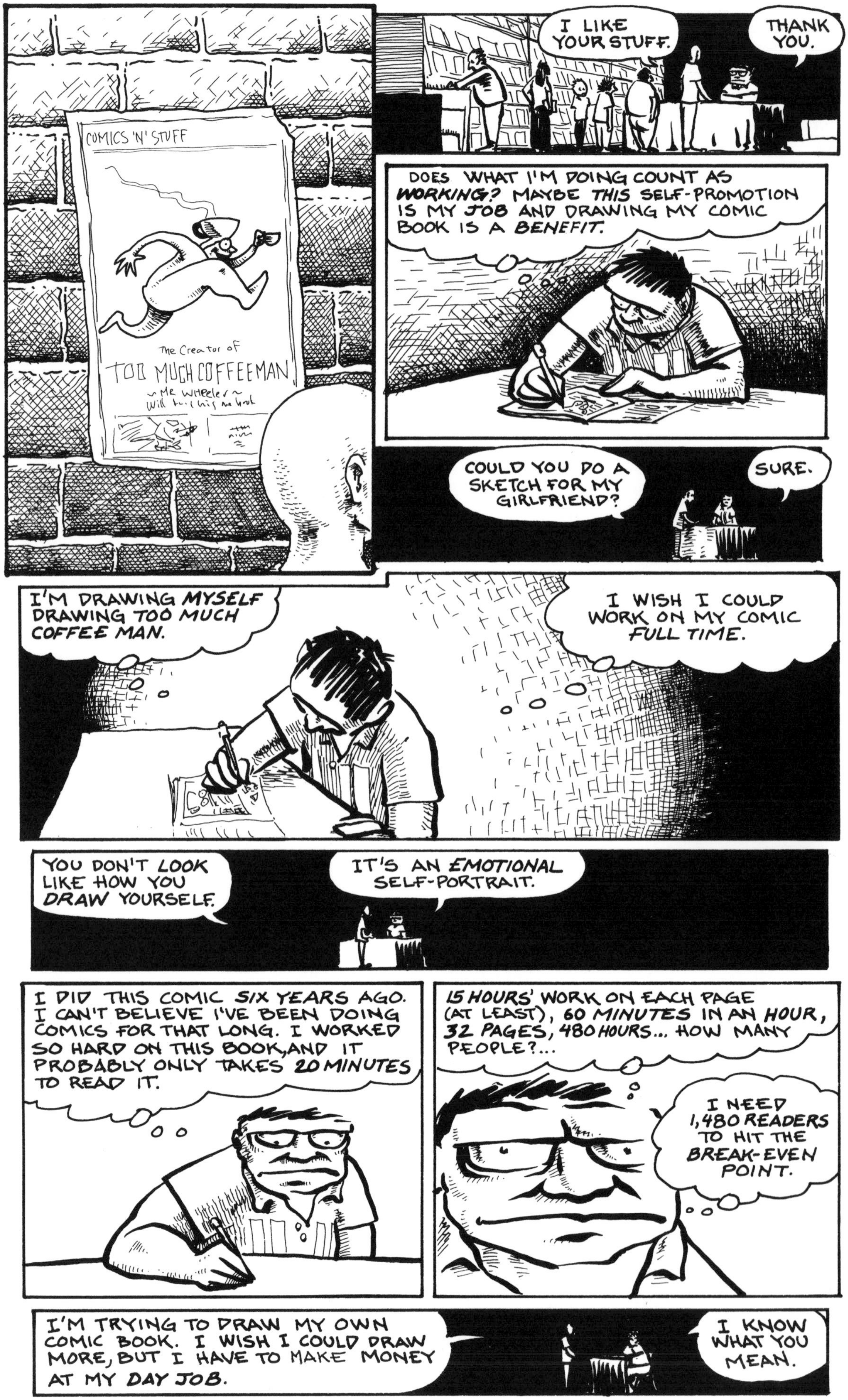
COMICS 'N' STUFF
The Creator of
TOO MUCH COFFEEMAN
I LIKE YOUR STUFF.
THANK YOU.
DOES WHAT I'M DOING COUNT AS WORKING? MAYBE THIS SELF-PROMOTION IS MY JOB AND DRAWING MY COMIC BOOK IS A BENEFIT.
COULD YOU DO A SKETCH FOR MY GIRLFRIEND?
SURE.
I'M DRAWING MYSELF DRAWING TOO MUCH COFFEE MAN.
I WISH I COULD WORK ON MY COMIC FULL TIME.
YOU DON'T LOOK LIKE HOW YOU DRAW YOURSELF.
IT'S AN EMOTIONAL SELF-PORTRAIT.
I DID THIS COMIC SIX YEARS AGO. I CAN'T BELIEVE I'VE BEEN DOING COMICS FOR THAT LONG. I WORKED SO HARD ON THIS BOOK, AND IT PROBABLY ONLY TAKES 20 MINUTES TO READ IT.
15 HOURS' WORK ON EACH PAGE (AT LEAST), 60 MINUTES IN AN HOUR, 32 PAGES, 480 HOURS... HOW MANY PEOPLE?...
I NEED 1,480 READERS TO HIT THE BREAK-EVEN POINT.
I'M TRYING TO DRAW MY OWN COMIC BOOK. I WISH I COULD DRAW MORE, BUT I HAVE TO MAKE MONEY AT MY DAY JOB.
I KNOW WHAT YOU MEAN.

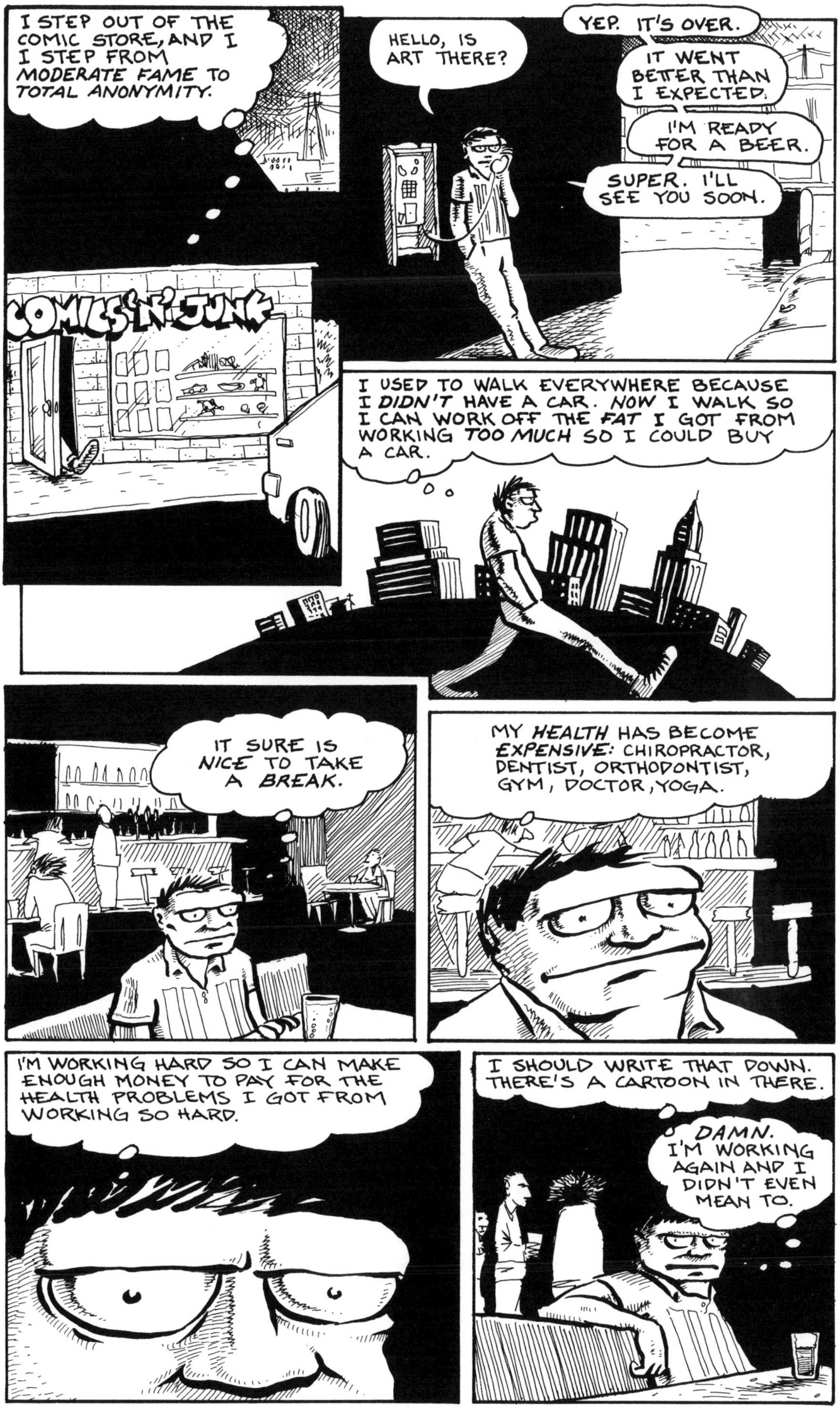
I STEP OUT OF THE COMIC STORE, AND I STEP FROM MODERATE FAME TO TOTAL ANONYMITY.
COMICS 'N' JUNK
HELLO, IS ART THERE?
YEP. IT'S OVER.
IT WENT BETTER THAN I EXPECTED.
I'M READY FOR A BEER.
SUPER. I'LL SEE YOU SOON.
I USED TO WALK EVERYWHERE BECAUSE I DIDN'T HAVE A CAR. NOW I WALK SO I CAN WORK OFF THE FAT I GOT FROM WORKING TOO MUCH SO I COULD BUY A CAR.
IT SURE IS NICE TO TAKE A BREAK.
MY HEALTH HAS BECOME EXPENSIVE: CHIROPRACTOR, DENTIST, ORTHODONTIST, GYM, DOCTOR, YOGA.
I'M WORKING HARD SO I CAN MAKE ENOUGH MONEY TO PAY FOR THE HEALTH PROBLEMS I GOT FROM WORKING SO HARD.
I SHOULD WRITE THAT DOWN. THERE'S A CARTOON IN THERE.
DAMN. I'M WORKING AGAIN AND I DIDN'T EVEN MEAN TO.

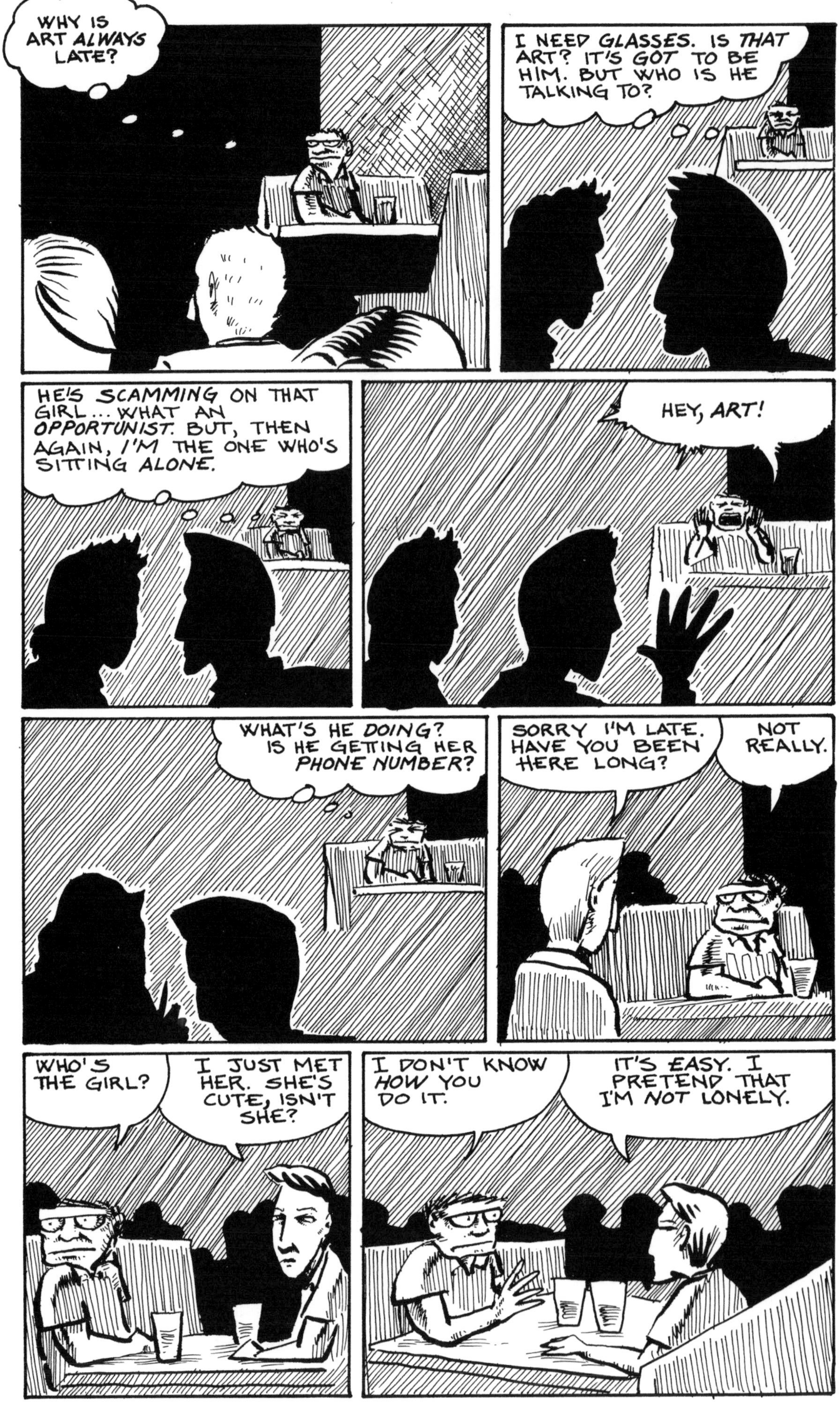
WHY IS ART ALWAYS LATE?
I NEED GLASSES. IS THAT ART? IT'S GOT TO BE HIM. BUT WHO IS HE TALKING TO?
HE'S SCAMMING ON THAT GIRL... WHAT AN OPPORTUNIST. BUT, THEN AGAIN, I'M THE ONE WHO'S SITTING ALONE.
HEY, ART!
WHAT'S HE DOING? IS HE GETTING HER PHONE NUMBER?
SORRY I'M LATE. HAVE YOU BEEN HERE LONG?
NOT REALLY.
WHO'S THE GIRL?
I JUST MET HER. SHE'S CUTE, ISN'T SHE?
I DON'T KNOW HOW YOU DO IT.
IT'S EASY. I PRETEND THAT I'M NOT LONELY.

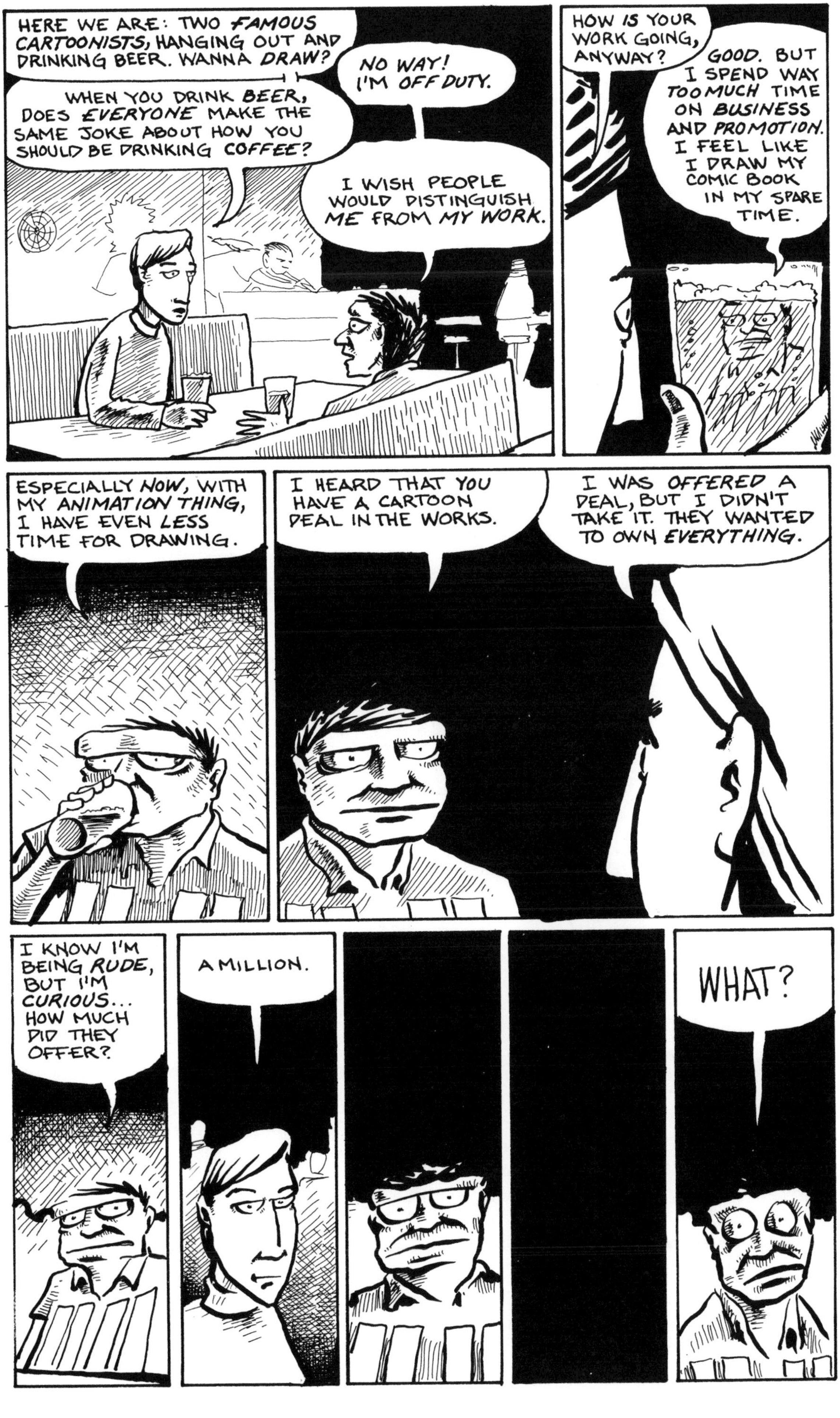
HERE WE ARE: TWO FAMOUS CARTOONISTS, HANGING OUT AND DRINKING BEER. WANNA DRAW?
NO WAY! I'M OFF DUTY.
WHEN YOU DRINK BEER, DOES EVERYONE MAKE THE SAME JOKE ABOUT HOW YOU SHOULD BE DRINKING COFFEE?
I WISH PEOPLE WOULD DISTINGUISH ME FROM MY WORK.
HOW IS YOUR WORK GOING, ANYWAY?
GOOD. BUT I SPEND WAY TOO MUCH TIME ON BUSINESS AND PROMOTION. I FEEL LIKE I DRAW MY COMIC BOOK IN MY SPARE TIME.
ESPECIALLY NOW, WITH MY ANIMATION THING, I HAVE EVEN LESS TIME FOR DRAWING.
I HEARD THAT YOU HAVE A CARTOON DEAL IN THE WORKS.
I WAS OFFERED A DEAL, BUT I DIDN'T TAKE IT. THEY WANTED TO OWN EVERYTHING.
I KNOW I'M BEING RUDE, BUT I'M CURIOUS... HOW MUCH DID THEY OFFER?
A MILLION.
WHAT?

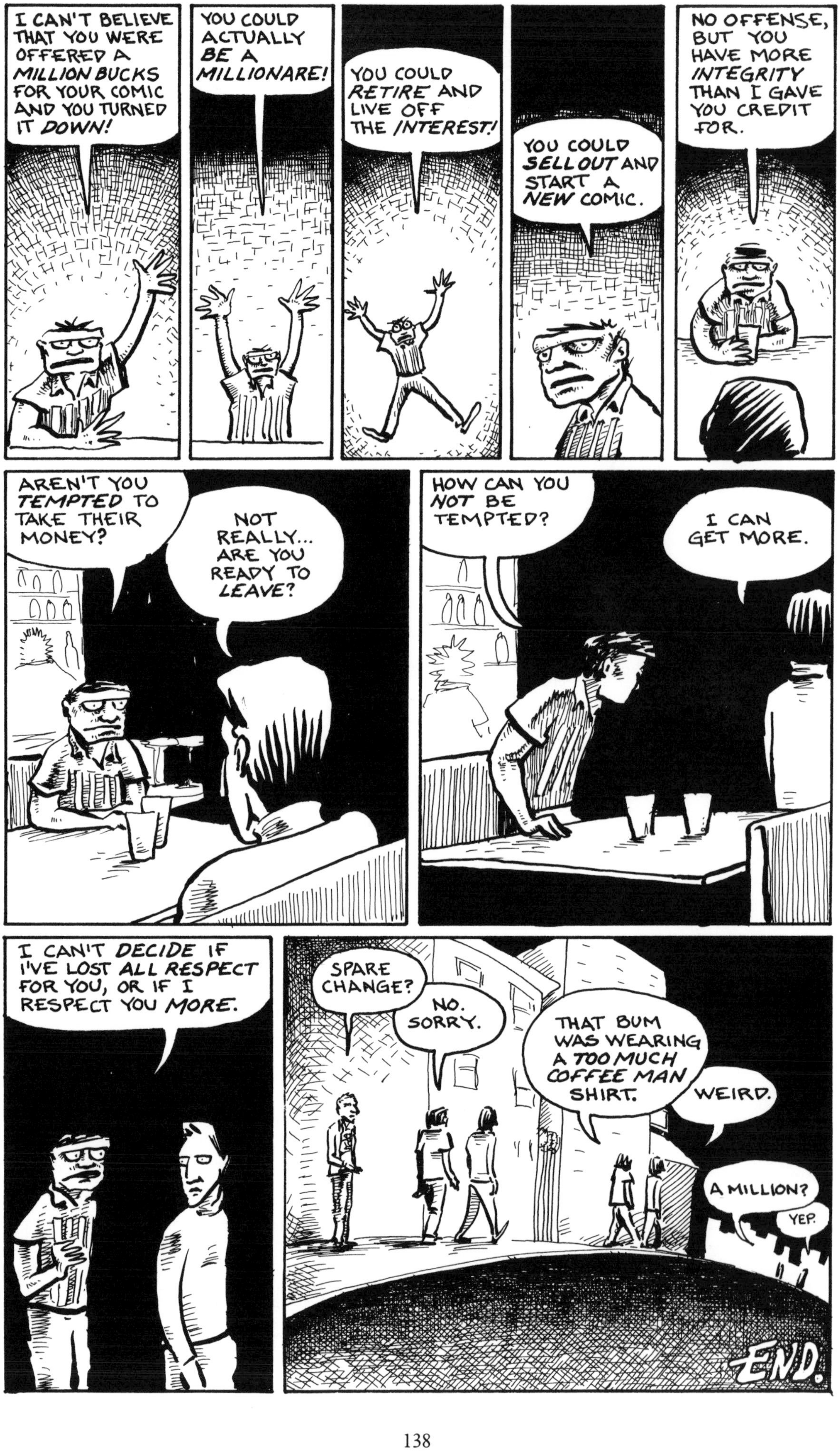

I CAN'T BELIEVE THAT YOU WERE OFFERED A MILLION BUCKS FOR YOUR COMIC AND YOU TURNED IT DOWN!
YOU COULD ACTUALLY BE A MILLIONARE!
YOU COULD RETIRE AND LIVE OFF THE INTEREST!
YOU COULD SELL OUT AND START A NEW COMIC.
NO OFFENSE, BUT YOU HAVE MORE INTEGRITY THAN I GAVE YOU CREDIT FOR.
AREN'T YOU TEMPTED TO TAKE THEIR MONEY?
NOT REALLY... ARE YOU READY TO LEAVE?
HOW CAN YOU NOT BE TEMPTED?
I CAN GET MORE.
I CAN'T DECIDE IF I'VE LOST ALL RESPECT FOR YOU, OR IF I RESPECT YOU MORE.
SPARE CHANGE?
NO. SORRY.
THAT BUM WAS WEARING A TOO MUCH COFFEE MAN SHIRT.
WEIRD.
A MILLION?
YEP.
END.

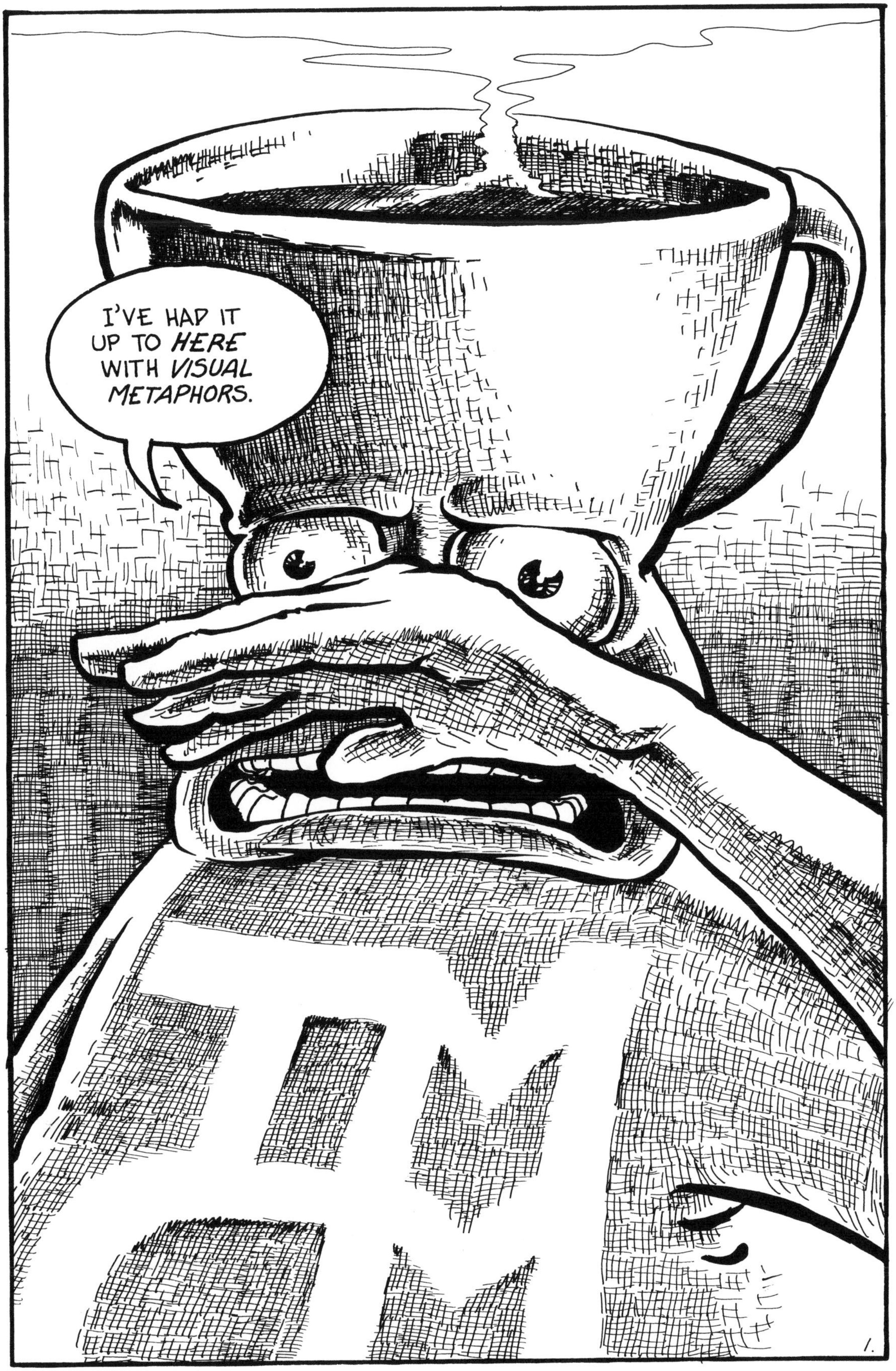
I'VE HAD IT UP TO HERE WITH VISUAL METAPHORS.
1.

THAT WAS A *PRETTY FUNNY PUN,* MISTER TOO MUCH COFFEE MAN.

I'M SICK OF *SARCASM* BEING PASSED OFF AS *HUMOR!*

IF YOU'RE MAKING A *JOKE,* YOU SHOULD TRY TO BE *CLEVER!*

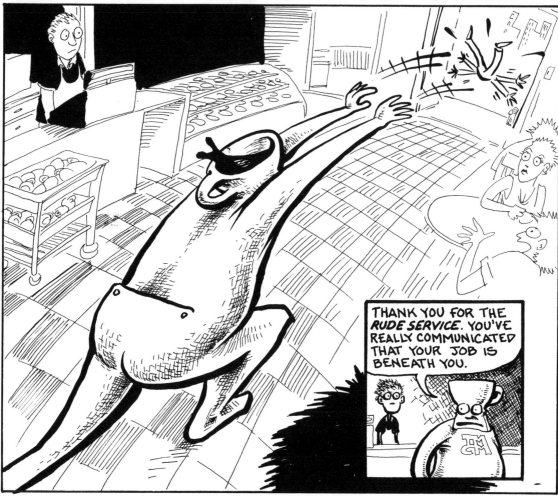

THANK YOU FOR THE *RUDE SERVICE.* YOU'VE REALLY COMMUNICATED THAT YOUR JOB IS BENEATH YOU.

I *HATE* COFFEE SHOPS. EVERYBODY SITS AROUND AND *PRETENDS* TO HAVE AN OPINION.

DISLIKING EVERYTHING IS *NOT* THE SAME THING AS HAVING AN *OPINION!*

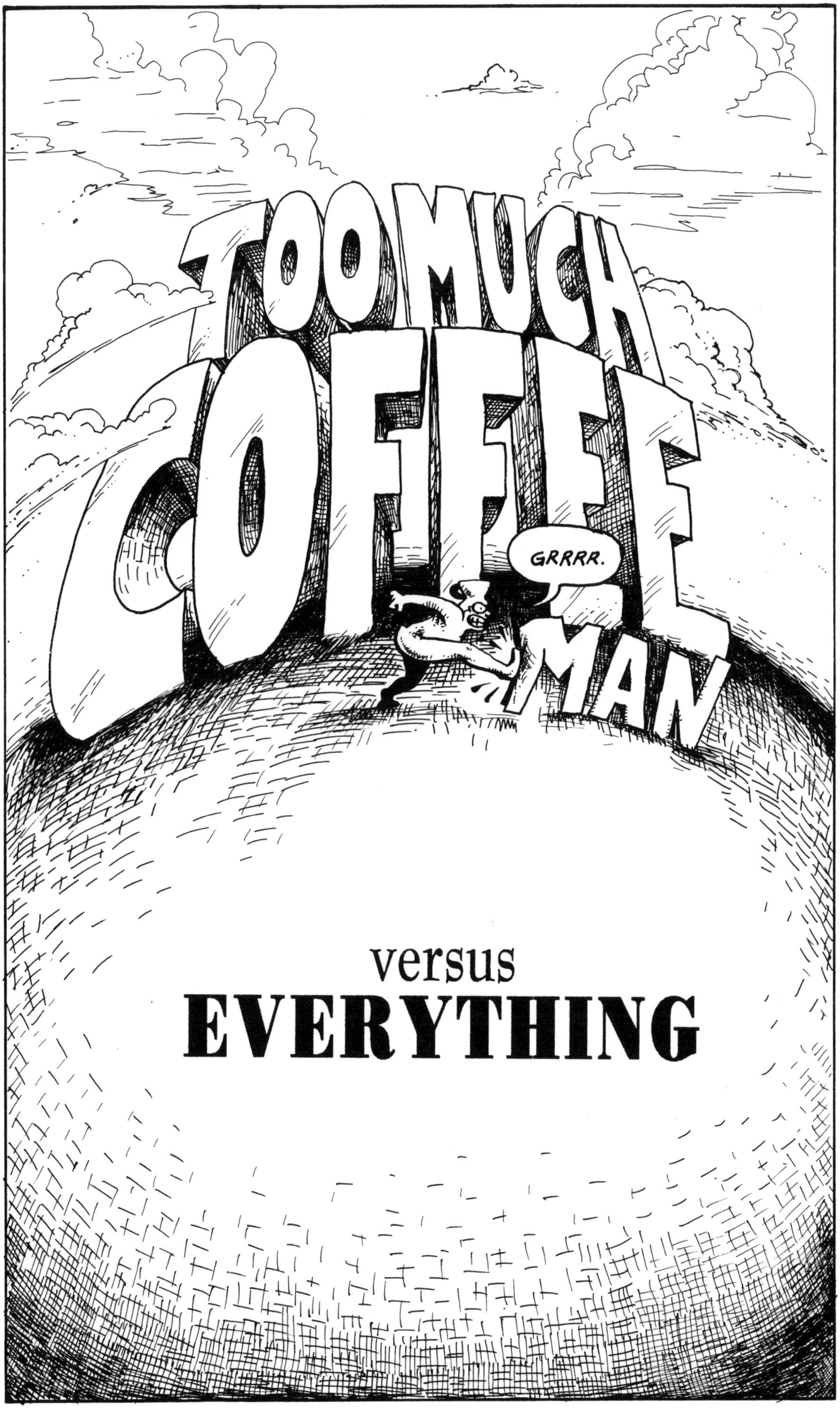
TOO MUCH
COFFEE
GRRRR.
MAN
versus
EVERYTHING

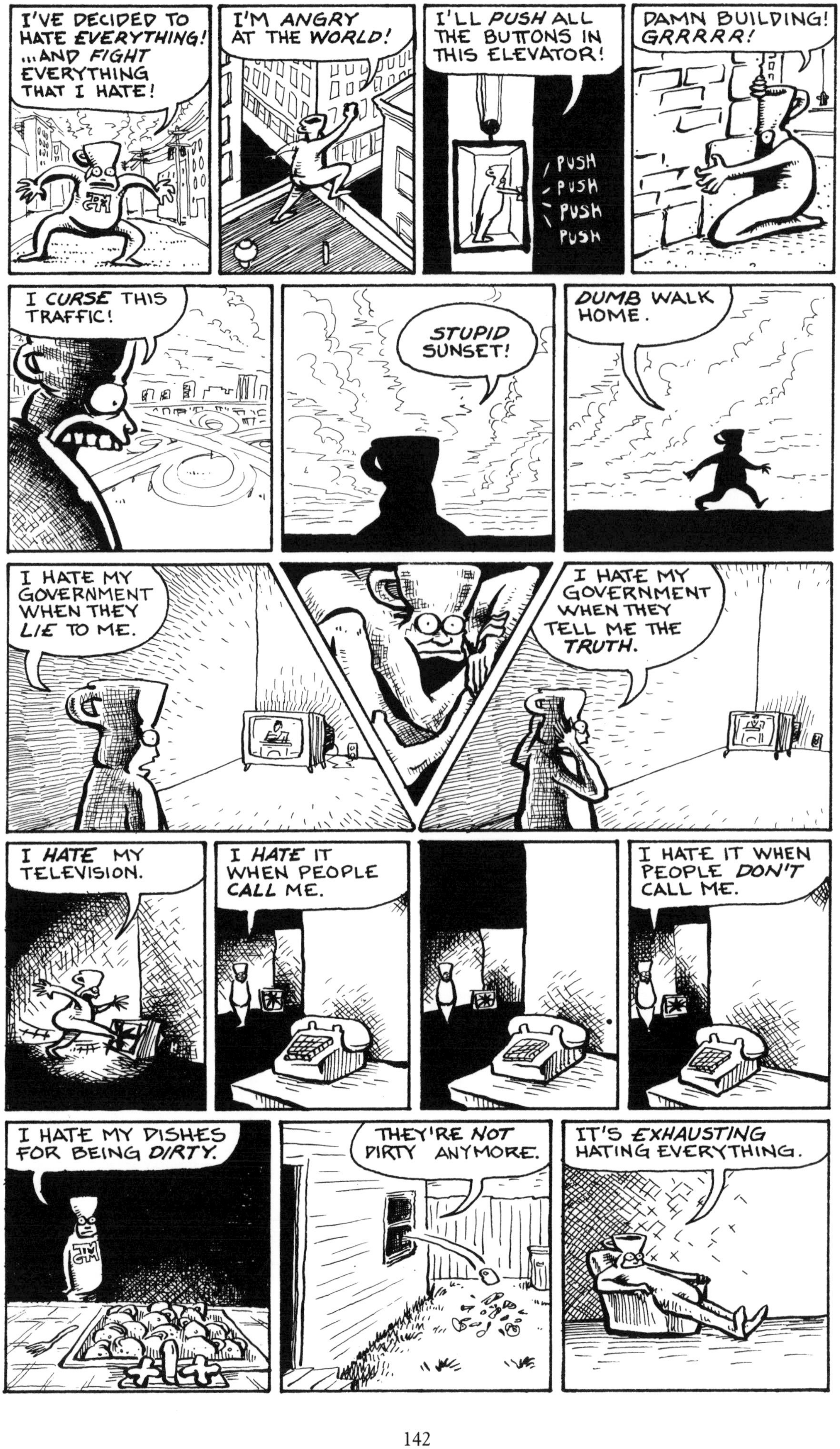
I'VE DECIDED TO HATE EVERYTHING! ...AND FIGHT EVERYTHING THAT I HATE!
I'M ANGRY AT THE WORLD!
I'LL PUSH ALL THE BUTTONS IN THIS ELEVATOR!
PUSH
PUSH
PUSH
PUSH
DAMN BUILDING! GRRRRR!
I CURSE THIS TRAFFIC!
STUPID SUNSET!
DUMB WALK HOME.
I HATE MY GOVERNMENT WHEN THEY LIE TO ME.
I HATE MY GOVERNMENT WHEN THEY TELL ME THE TRUTH.
I HATE MY TELEVISION.
I HATE IT WHEN PEOPLE CALL ME.
I HATE IT WHEN PEOPLE DON'T CALL ME.
I HATE MY DISHES FOR BEING DIRTY.
THEY'RE NOT DIRTY ANYMORE.
IT'S EXHAUSTING HATING EVERYTHING.

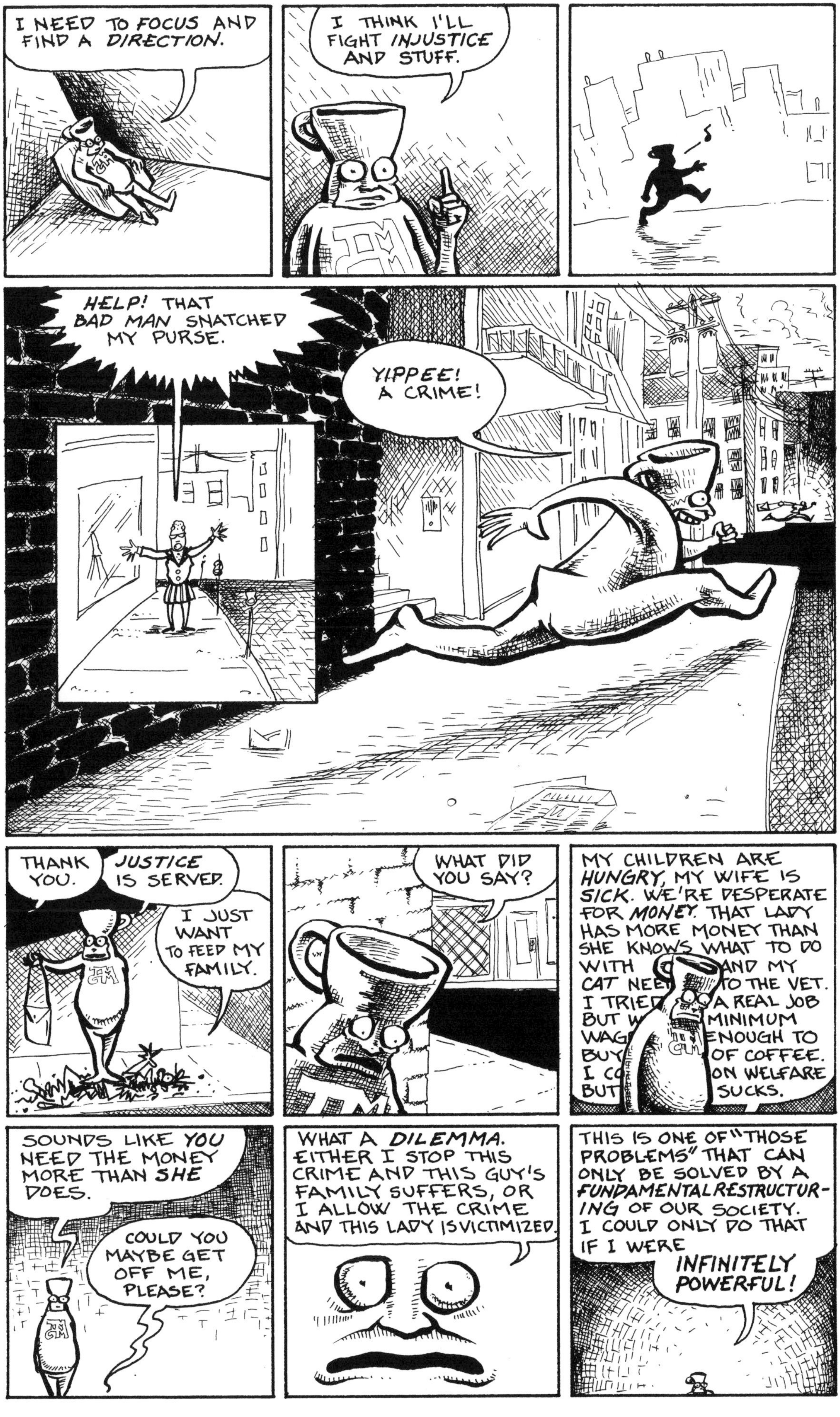
I NEED TO FOCUS AND FIND A DIRECTION.
I THINK I'LL FIGHT INJUSTICE AND STUFF.
HELP! THAT BAD MAN SNATCHED MY PURSE.
YIPPEE! A CRIME!
THANK YOU.
JUSTICE IS SERVED.
I JUST WANT TO FEED MY FAMILY.
WHAT DID YOU SAY?
MY CHILDREN ARE HUNGRY, MY WIFE IS SICK. WE'RE DESPERATE FOR MONEY. THAT LADY HAS MORE MONEY THAN SHE KNOWS WHAT TO DO WITH AND MY CAT NEE TO THE VET. I TRIED A REAL JOB BUT W MINIMUM WAG ENOUGH TO BUY OF COFFEE. I CO ON WELFARE BUT SUCKS.
SOUNDS LIKE YOU NEED THE MONEY MORE THAN SHE DOES.
COULD YOU MAYBE GET OFF ME, PLEASE?
WHAT A DILEMMA. EITHER I STOP THIS CRIME AND THIS GUY'S FAMILY SUFFERS, OR I ALLOW THE CRIME AND THIS LADY IS VICTIMIZED.
THIS IS ONE OF "THOSE PROBLEMS" THAT CAN ONLY BE SOLVED BY A FUNDAMENTAL RESTRUCTURING OF OUR SOCIETY. I COULD ONLY DO THAT IF I WERE
INFINITELY POWERFUL!

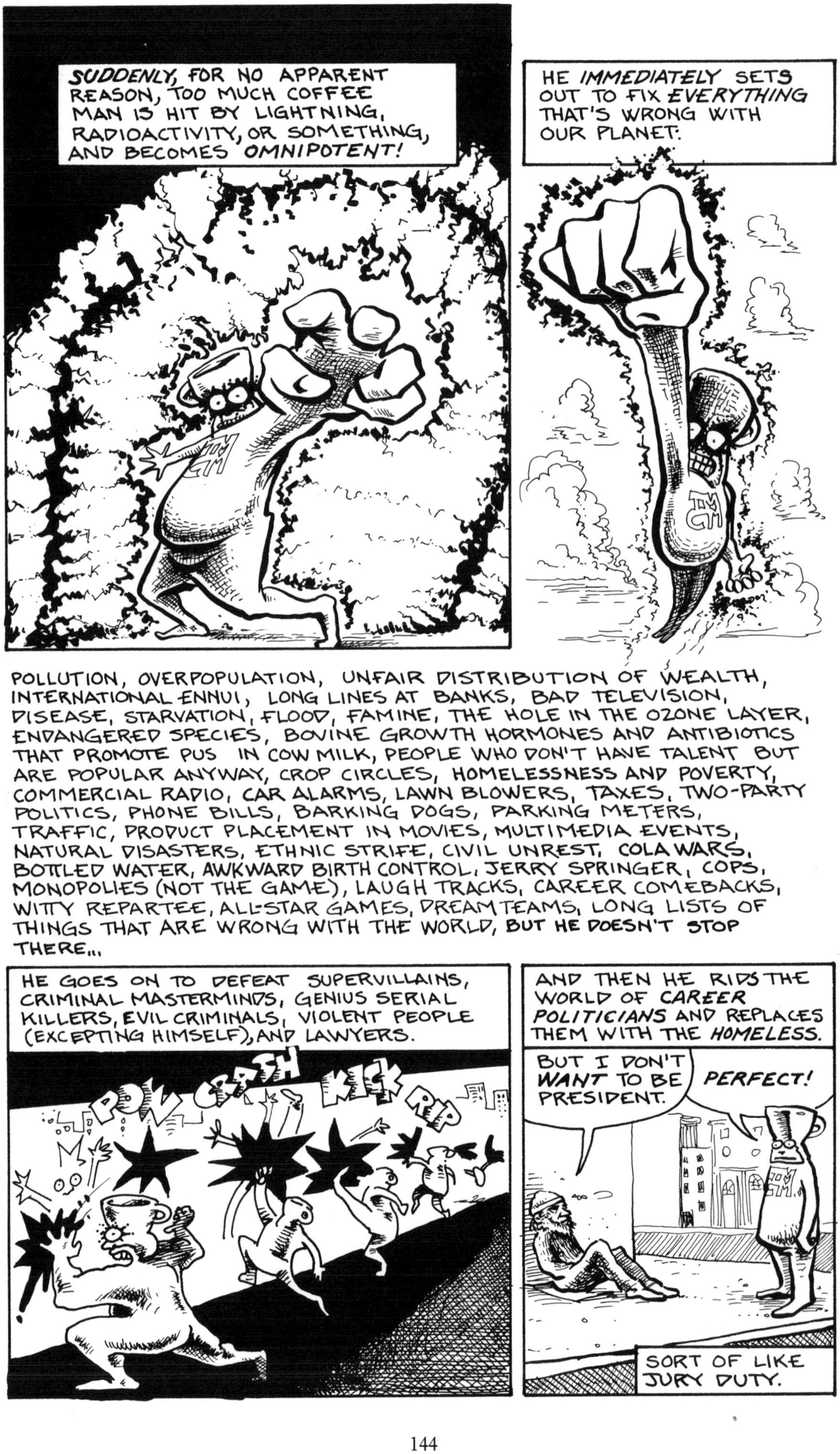
SUDDENLY, FOR NO APPARENT REASON, TOO MUCH COFFEE MAN IS HIT BY LIGHTNING, RADIOACTIVITY, OR SOMETHING, AND BECOMES OMNIPOTENT!
HE IMMEDIATELY SETS OUT TO FIX EVERYTHING THAT'S WRONG WITH OUR PLANET:
POLLUTION, OVERPOPULATION, UNFAIR DISTRIBUTION OF WEALTH, INTERNATIONAL ENNUI, LONG LINES AT BANKS, BAD TELEVISION, DISEASE, STARVATION, FLOOD, FAMINE, THE HOLE IN THE OZONE LAYER, ENDANGERED SPECIES, BOVINE GROWTH HORMONES AND ANTIBIOTICS THAT PROMOTE PUS IN COW MILK, PEOPLE WHO DON'T HAVE TALENT BUT ARE POPULAR ANYWAY, CROP CIRCLES, HOMELESSNESS AND POVERTY, COMMERCIAL RADIO, CAR ALARMS, LAWN BLOWERS, TAXES, TWO-PARTY POLITICS, PHONE BILLS, BARKING DOGS, PARKING METERS, TRAFFIC, PRODUCT PLACEMENT IN MOVIES, MULTIMEDIA EVENTS, NATURAL DISASTERS, ETHNIC STRIFE, CIVIL UNREST, COLA WARS, BOTTLED WATER, AWKWARD BIRTH CONTROL, JERRY SPRINGER, COPS, MONOPOLIES (NOT THE GAME), LAUGH TRACKS, CAREER COMEBACKS, WITTY REPARTEE, ALL-STAR GAMES, DREAM TEAMS, LONG LISTS OF THINGS THAT ARE WRONG WITH THE WORLD, BUT HE DOESN'T STOP THERE...
HE GOES ON TO DEFEAT SUPERVILLAINS, CRIMINAL MASTERMINDS, GENIUS SERIAL KILLERS, EVIL CRIMINALS, VIOLENT PEOPLE (EXCEPTING HIMSELF), AND LAWYERS.
POW
KICK
RIP
AND THEN HE RIDS THE WORLD OF CAREER POLITICIANS AND REPLACES THEM WITH THE HOMELESS.
BUT I DON'T WANT TO BE PRESIDENT.
PERFECT!
SORT OF LIKE JURY DUTY.

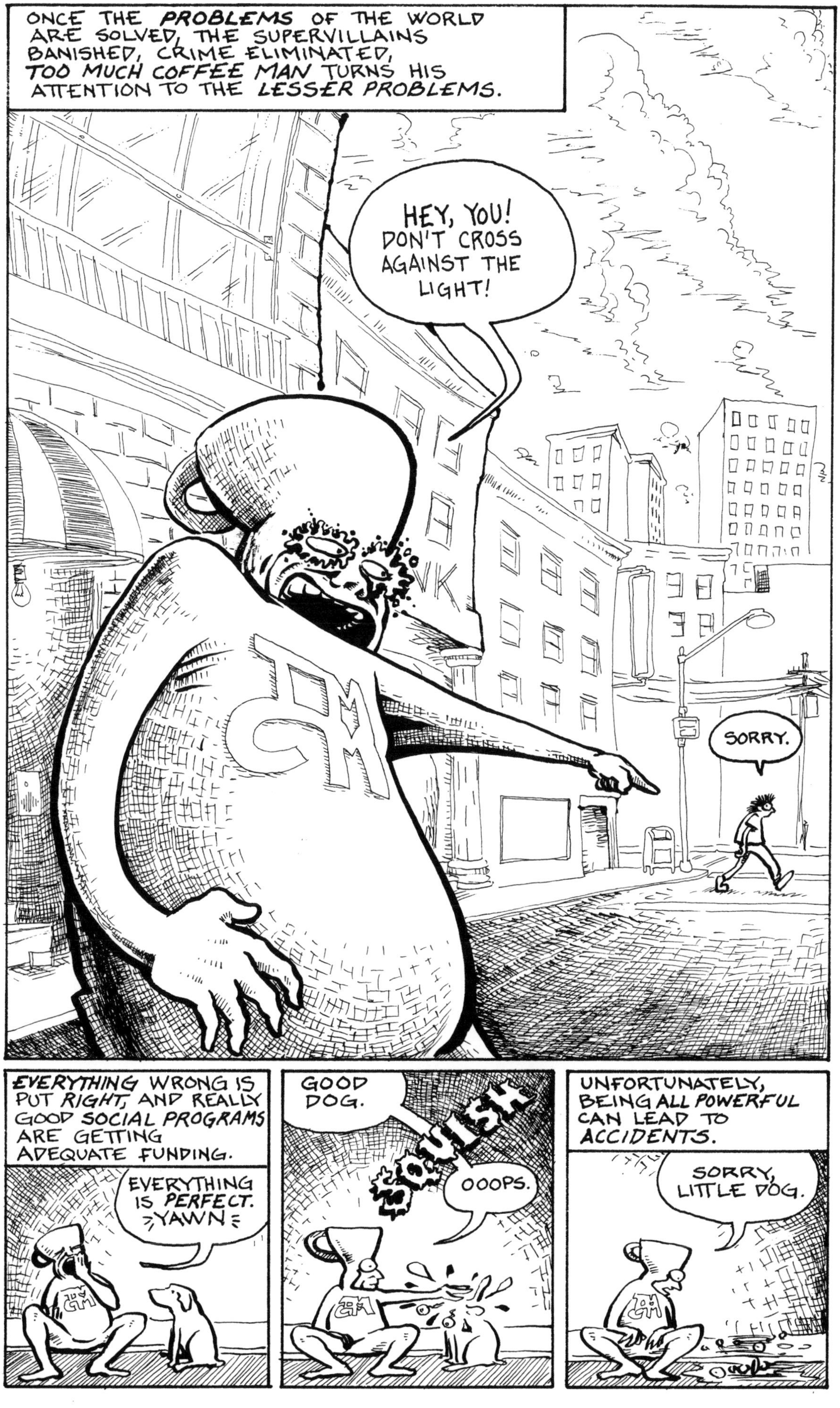
ONCE THE PROBLEMS OF THE WORLD ARE SOLVED, THE SUPERVILLAINS BANISHED, CRIME ELIMINATED, TOO MUCH COFFEE MAN TURNS HIS ATTENTION TO THE LESSER PROBLEMS.
HEY, YOU! DON'T CROSS AGAINST THE LIGHT!
SORRY.
EVERYTHING WRONG IS PUT RIGHT, AND REALLY GOOD SOCIAL PROGRAMS ARE GETTING ADEQUATE FUNDING.
EVERYTHING IS PERFECT. YAWN
GOOD DOG.
SQUISH
OOOPS.
UNFORTUNATELY, BEING ALL POWERFUL CAN LEAD TO ACCIDENTS.
SORRY, LITTLE DOG.

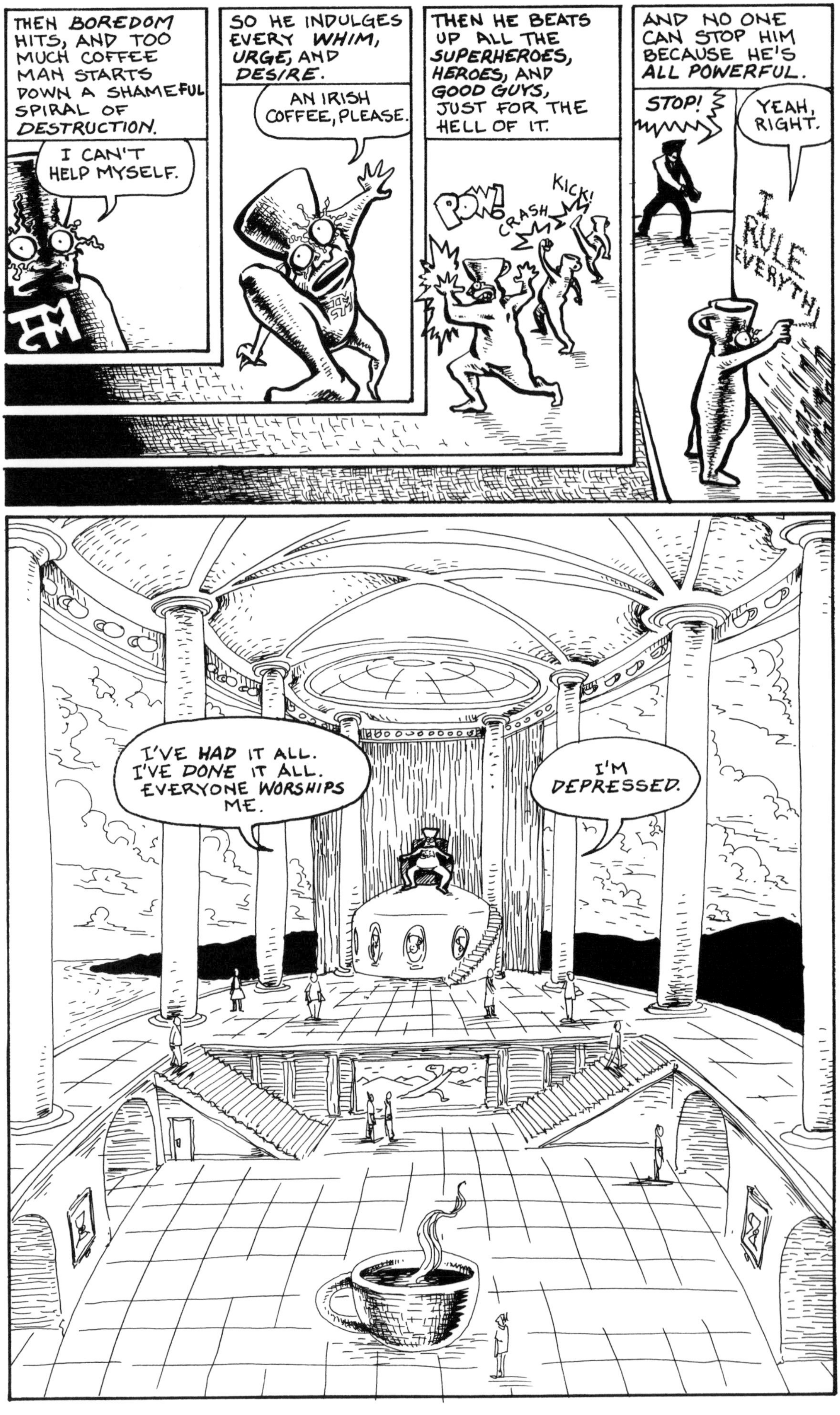
THEN BOREDOM HITS, AND TOO MUCH COFFEE MAN STARTS DOWN A SHAMEFUL SPIRAL OF DESTRUCTION.
I CAN'T HELP MYSELF.
SO HE INDULGES EVERY WHIM, URGE, AND DESIRE.
AN IRISH COFFEE, PLEASE.
THEN HE BEATS UP ALL THE SUPERHEROES, HEROES, AND GOOD GUYS, JUST FOR THE HELL OF IT.
POW!
CRASH
KICK!
AND NO ONE CAN STOP HIM BECAUSE HE'S ALL POWERFUL.
STOP!
YEAH, RIGHT.
I RULE EVERYTHI
I'VE HAD IT ALL. I'VE DONE IT ALL. EVERYONE WORSHIPS ME.
I'M DEPRESSED.

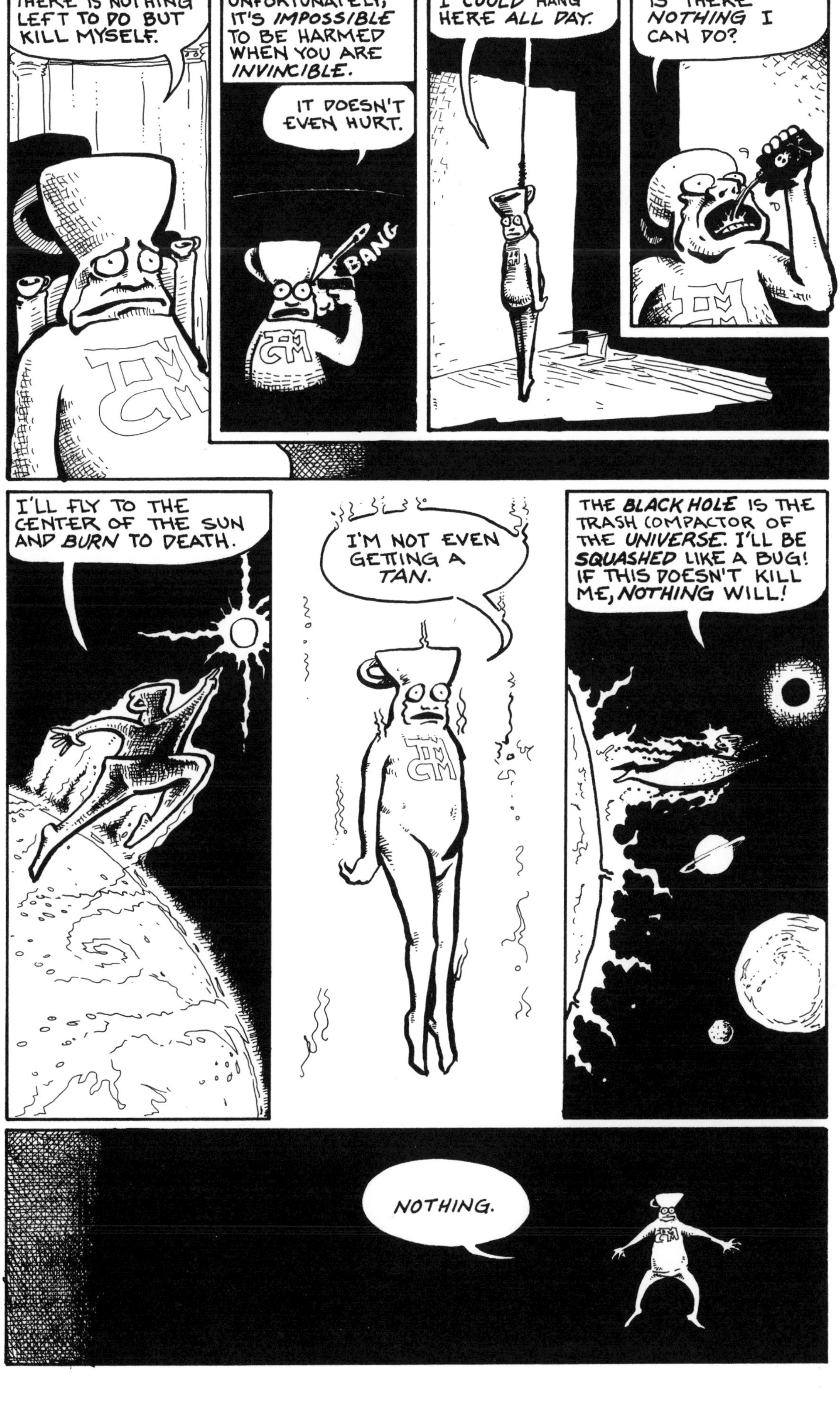
THERE IS NOTHING LEFT TO DO BUT KILL MYSELF.
UNFORTUNATELY, IT'S IMPOSSIBLE TO BE HARMED WHEN YOU ARE INVINCIBLE.
IT DOESN'T EVEN HURT.
BANG
I COULD HANG HERE ALL DAY.
IS THERE NOTHING I CAN DO?
I'LL FLY TO THE CENTER OF THE SUN AND BURN TO DEATH.
I'M NOT EVEN GETTING A TAN.
THE BLACK HOLE IS THE TRASH COMPACTOR OF THE UNIVERSE. I'LL BE SQUASHED LIKE A BUG! IF THIS DOESN'T KILL ME, NOTHING WILL!
NOTHING.

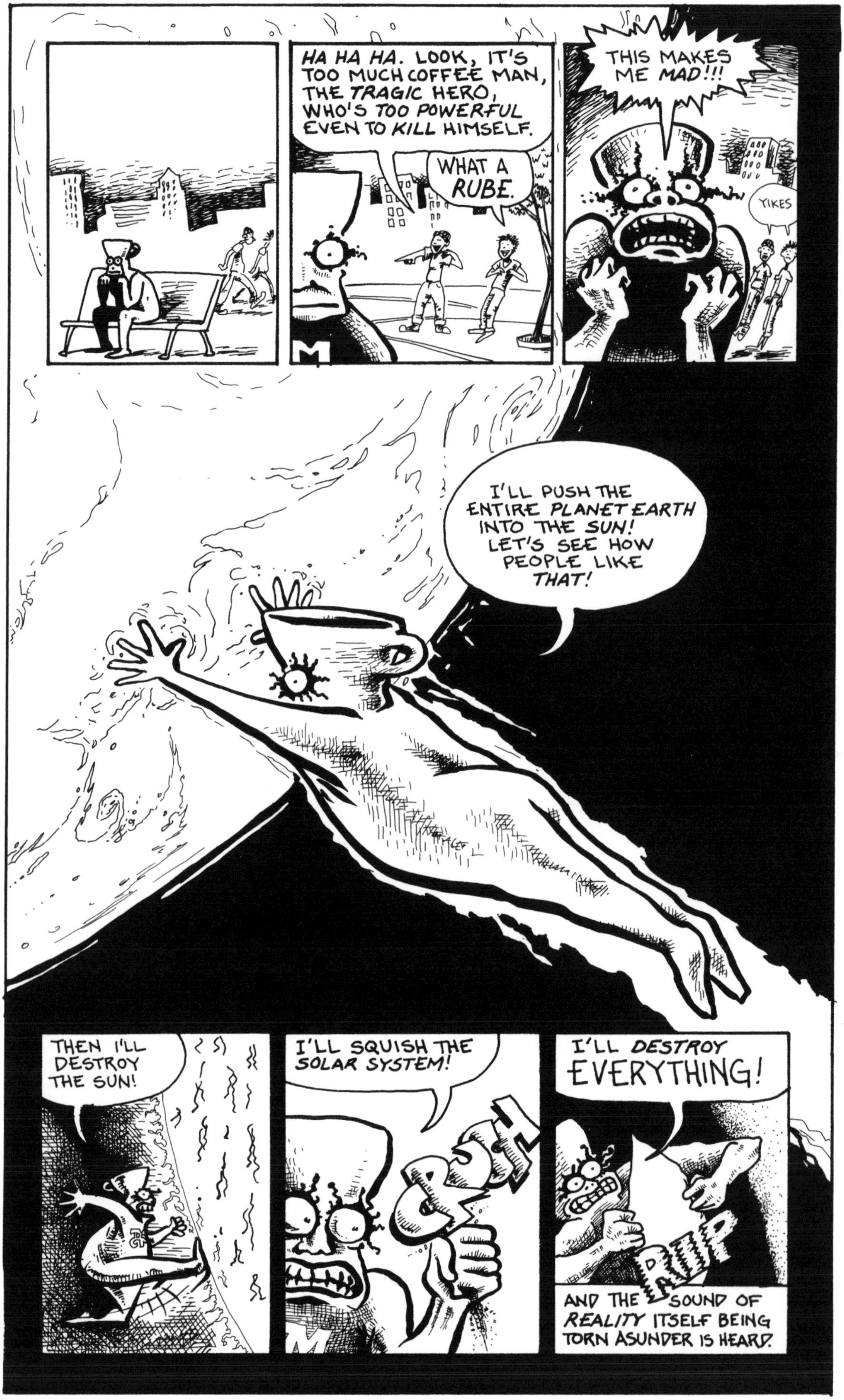
HA HA HA. LOOK, IT'S TOO MUCH COFFEE MAN, THE TRAGIC HERO, WHO'S TOO POWERFUL EVEN TO KILL HIMSELF.
WHAT A RUBE.
THIS MAKES ME MAD!!!
YIKES
I'LL PUSH THE ENTIRE PLANET EARTH INTO THE SUN! LET'S SEE HOW PEOPLE LIKE THAT!
THEN I'LL DESTROY THE SUN!
I'LL SQUISH THE SOLAR SYSTEM!
CRUSH
I'LL DESTROY EVERYTHING!
RRIIP
AND THE SOUND OF REALITY ITSELF BEING TORN ASUNDER IS HEARD.

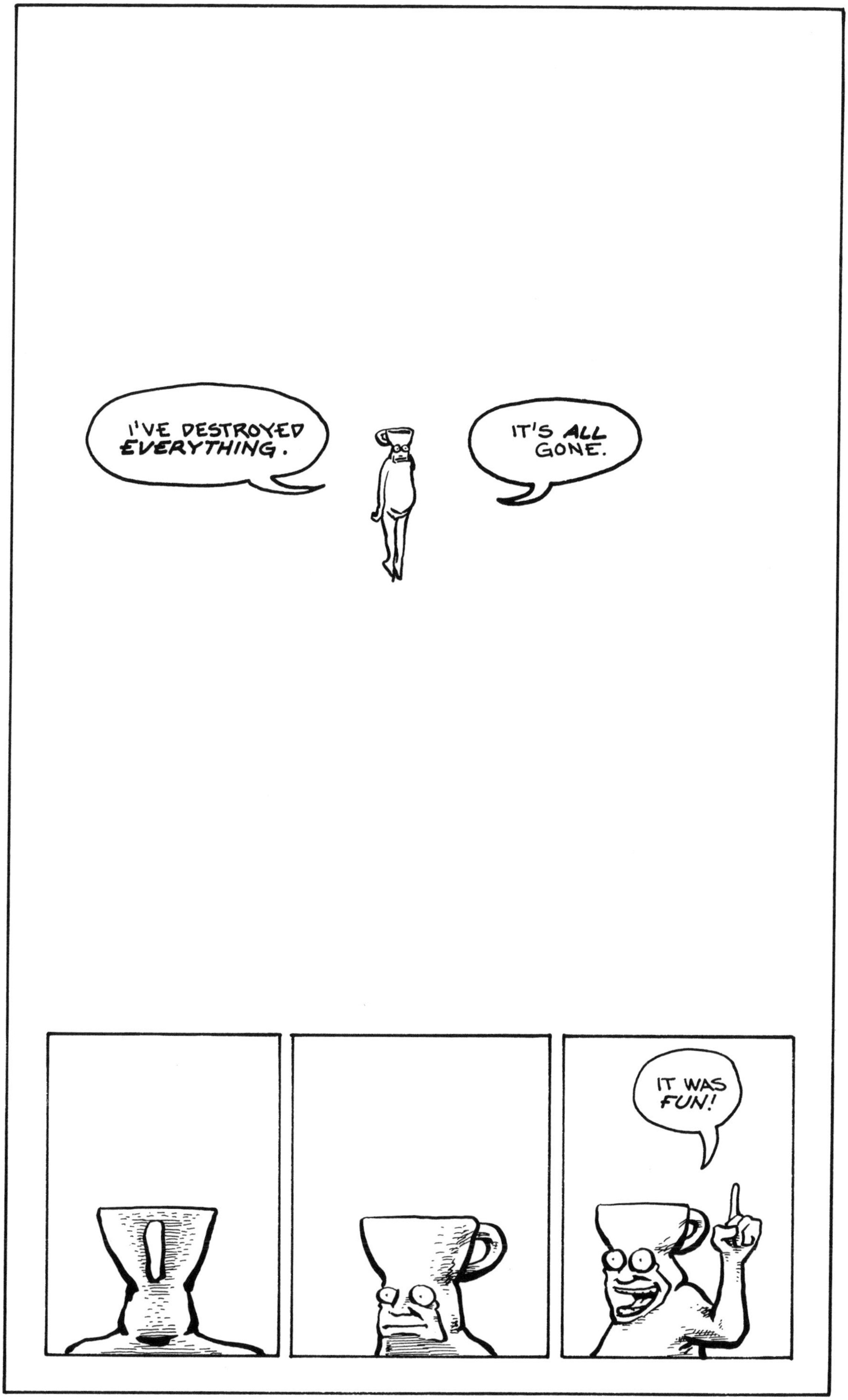
I'VE DESTROYED EVERYTHING.
IT'S ALL GONE.
IT WAS FUN!

PARADE OF TIRADE AFTERWORD

by Shannon Wheeler

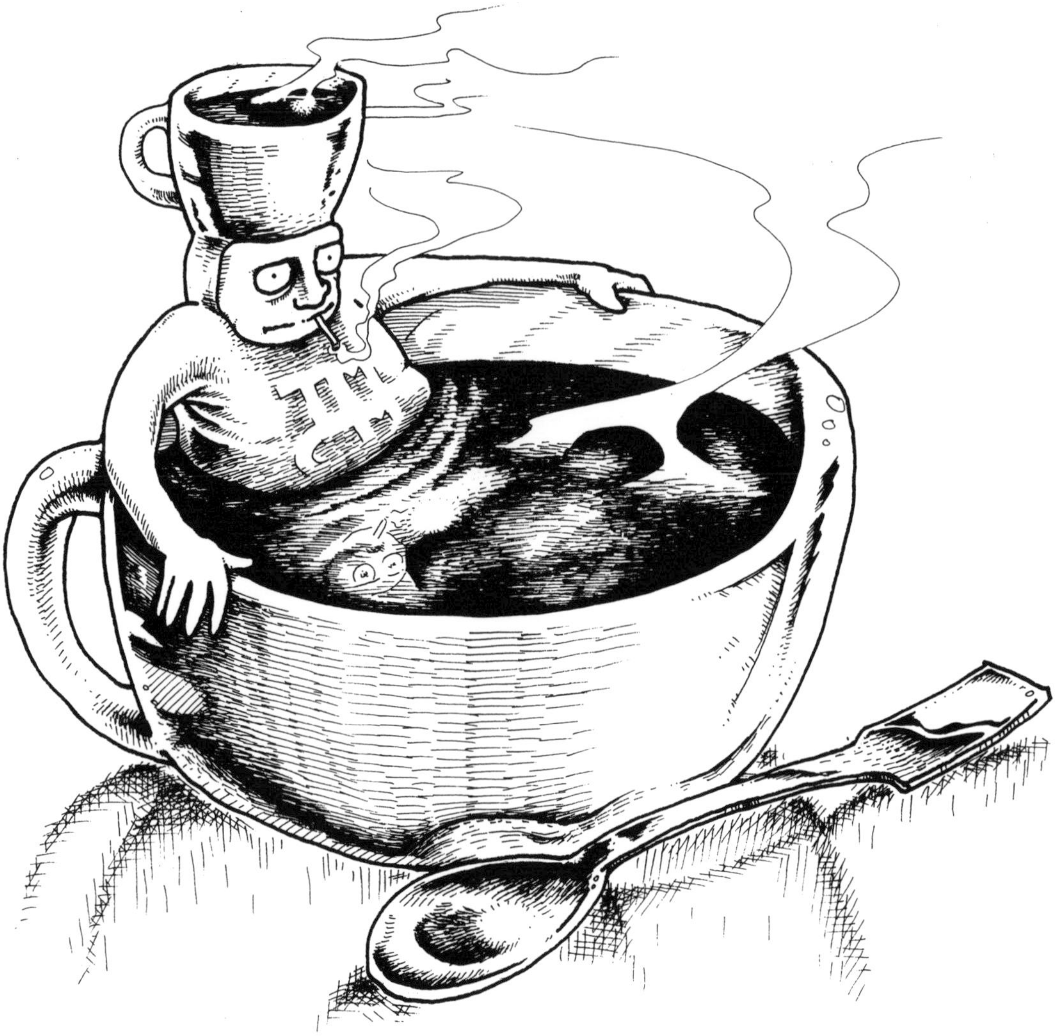

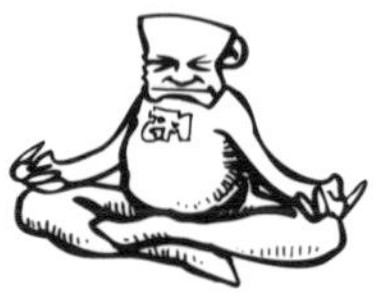

When I was nine, I had the insight that aging was dying. I realized that I would never be the same person that I was at that moment. The nine-year-old Shannon would be dead and replaced by the twelve-year-old Shannon. Therefore the nine-year-old me would soon be dead.

I didn't see any escape from my mortality. The best I could do was to live on in my own memory. I promised myself that I would remember what it was like to stand there in that doorway, next to the light switch, watching the dust floating in and out of the shaft of sunlight that came through the window. I would remember the melancholy I felt as a nine-year-old pondering the future.

The indicia in every comic book states that all references to persons, places, etc., are purely coincidental. There couldn't be a bigger lie. The situations are as accurate as I could make them. The feelings are real. The characters are my friends.

I read these comics and I remember who I was.

GUIDE FOR THE PERPLEXED

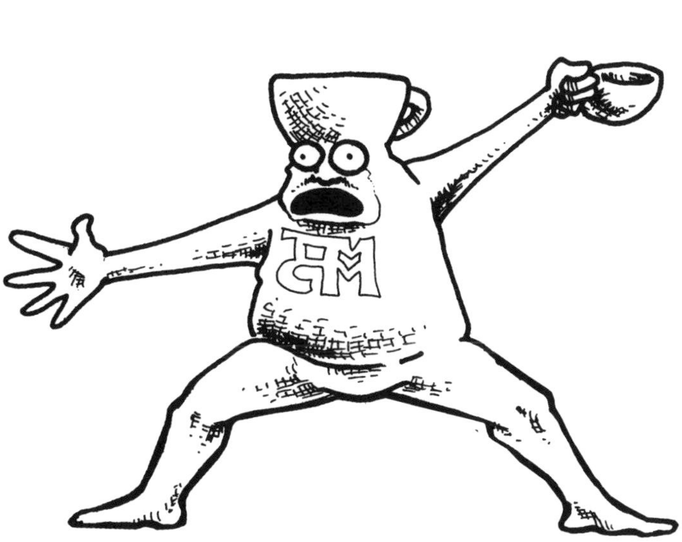
TCM

GUIDE FOR THE PERPLEXED INTRODUCTION

by Mike Judge

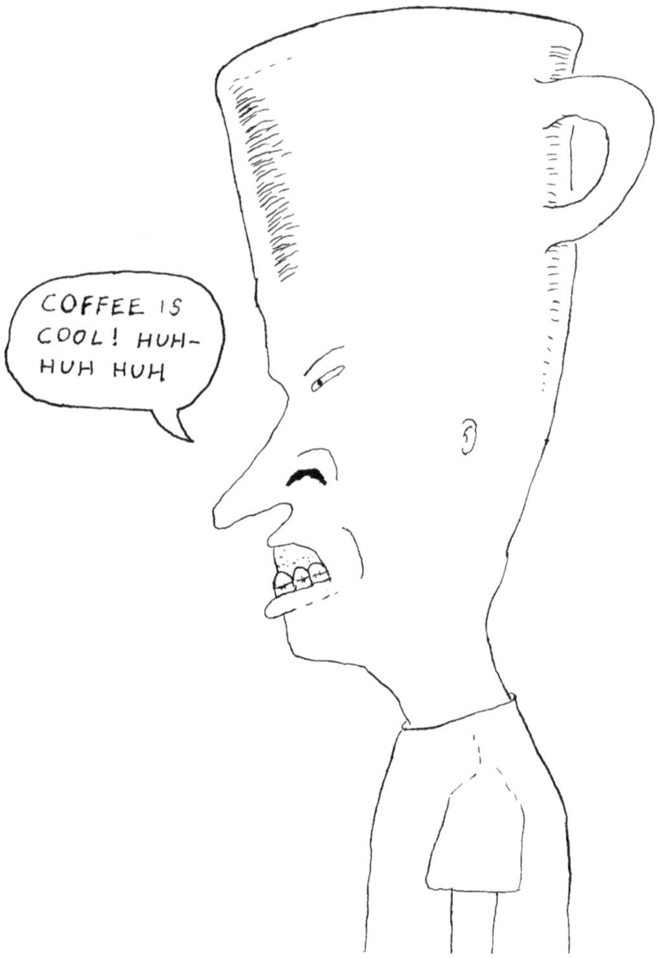
COFFEE IS COOL! HUH-HUH HUH

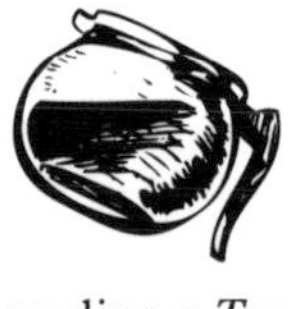

I first met Shannon Wheeler a few years back in East Austin in a restaurant called Nuevo Leon, one of the finest Mexican food restaurants on Earth. I had just been reading a *Too Much Coffee Man* comic book, and someone told me that Shannon lived in Austin.

I was thinking about trying to do some still cartoons at the time (I had only done animation at that point), so Shannon invited me to the headquarters of the Too Much Coffee Empire—a nineteenth-century farmhouse in Austin—where he showed me how to use a crow-quill pen and loaded me up with Too Much Coffee Man merchandise. (I still have my TMCM sponge, coffee mug, and unlicensed Japanese T-shirt.) He had done an impressive job making TMCM appear to be a much, much huger franchise than it really was, and today—partially due to that, I imagine—it has actually become almost as huge as he once made it appear!

At first glance, *Too Much Coffee Man* might look to some like a one-joke comic. However, if you read it, you realize it's actually many jokes—all about the same thing! Just kidding. It's not at all a one-joke comic. It's actually very funny, makes for good bathroom reading, is very well drawn, has occasional political commentary and satire, and I think it's even a little bit autobiographical at times . . . except for the part about space aliens and stuff.

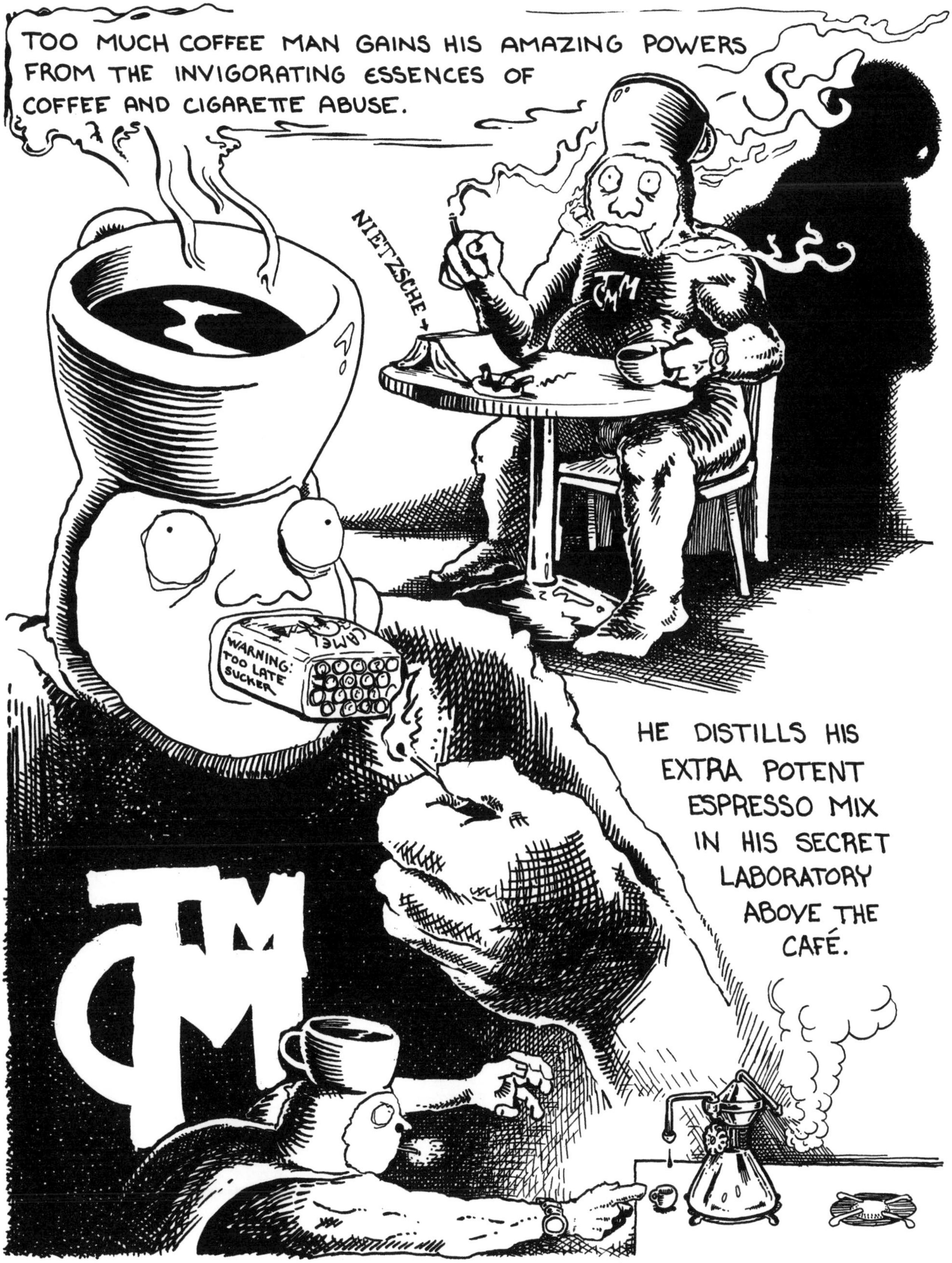
TOO MUCH COFFEE MAN GAINS HIS AMAZING POWERS FROM THE INVIGORATING ESSENCES OF COFFEE AND CIGARETTE ABUSE.
NIETZSCHE
TMC
CAMEL
WARNING: TOO LATE SUCKER
HE DISTILLS HIS EXTRA POTENT ESPRESSO MIX IN HIS SECRET LABORATORY ABOVE THE CAFÉ.
TMC

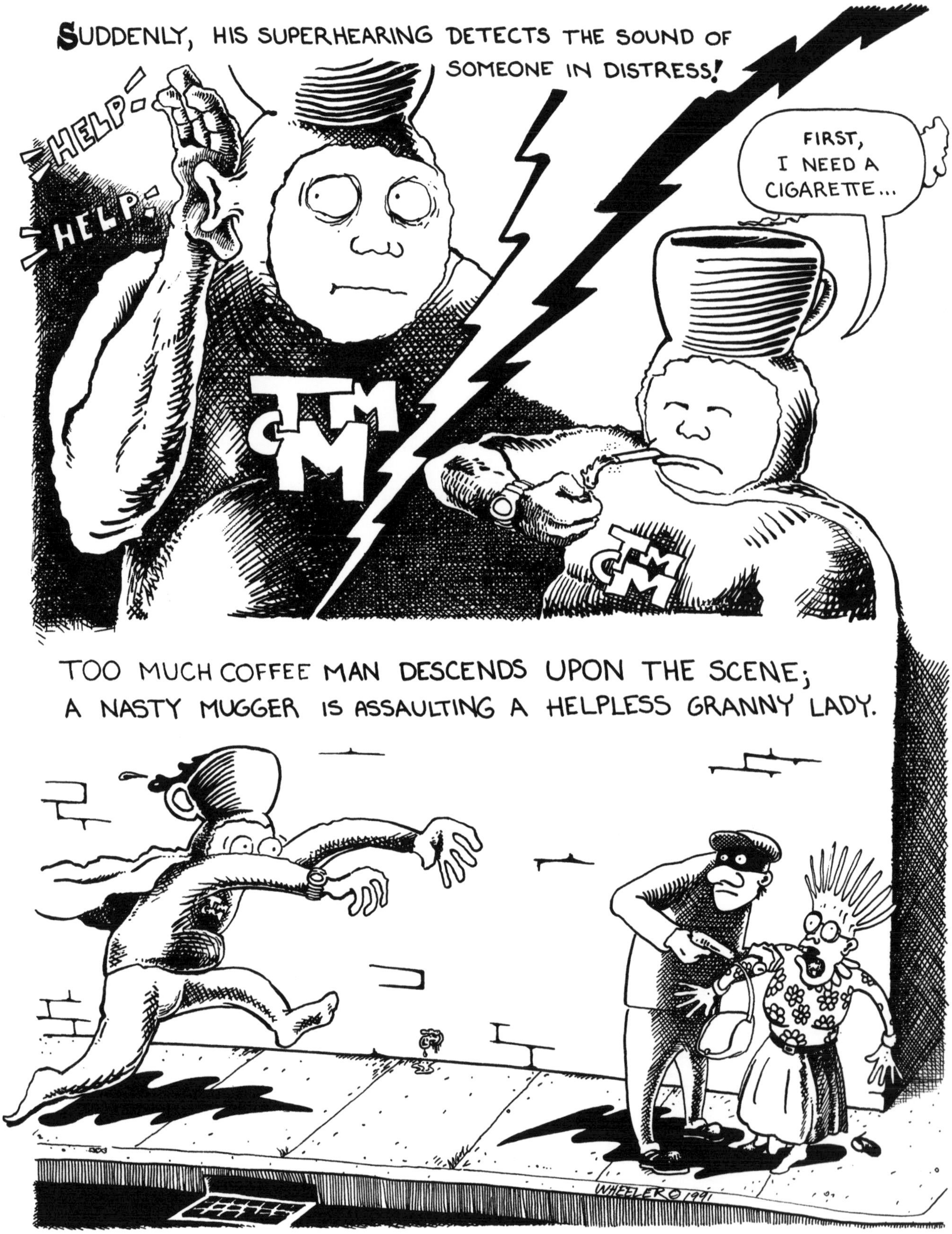
SUDDENLY, HIS SUPERHEARING DETECTS THE SOUND OF SOMEONE IN DISTRESS!
HELP!
HELP!
FIRST, I NEED A CIGARETTE...
TMCM
TMCM
TOO MUCH COFFEE MAN DESCENDS UPON THE SCENE; A NASTY MUGGER IS ASSAULTING A HELPLESS GRANNY LADY.
WHEELER © 1991

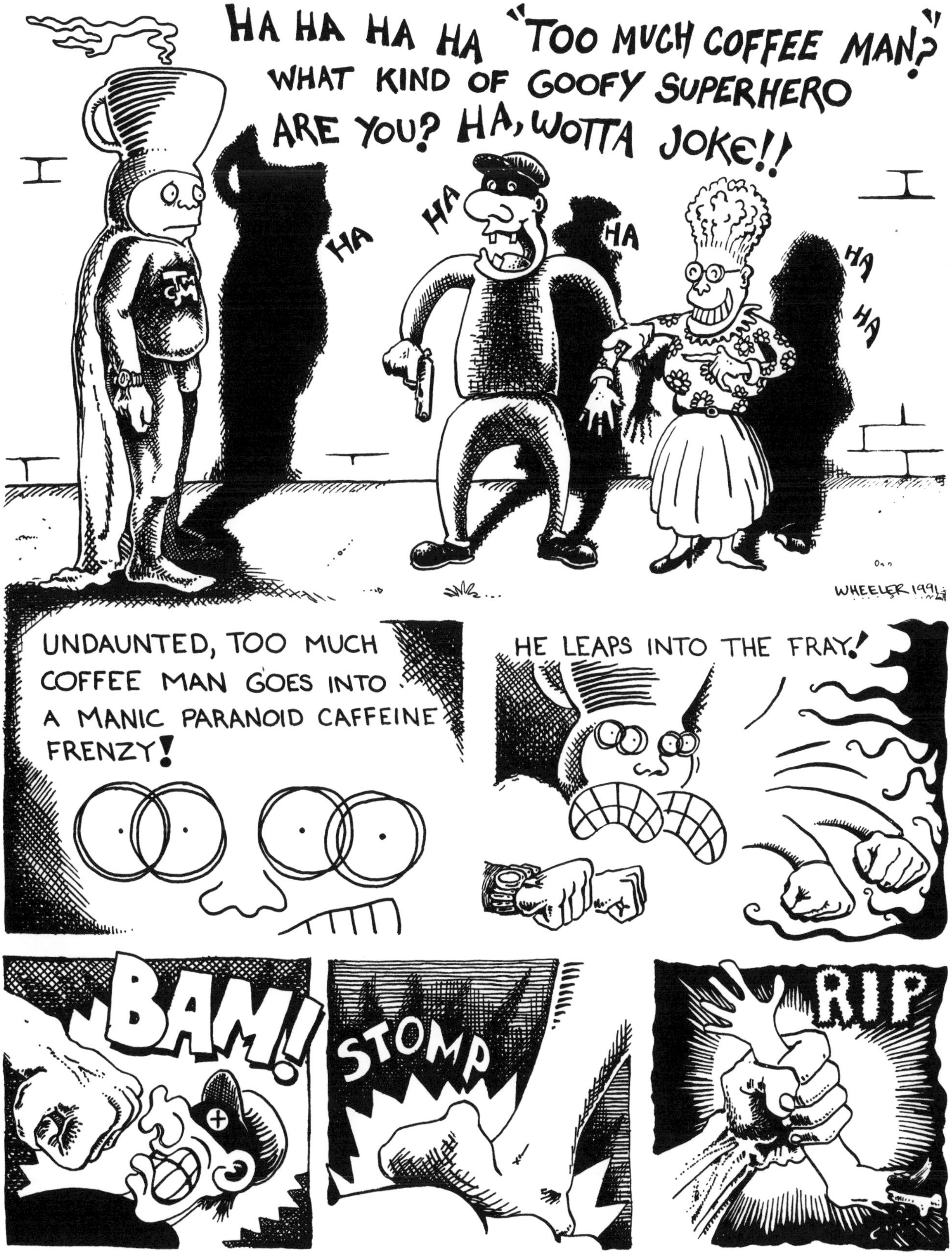
HA HA HA HA "TOO MUCH COFFEE MAN?" WHAT KIND OF GOOFY SUPERHERO ARE YOU? HA, WOTTA JOKE!!
HA
HA
HA
HA
HA
WHEELER 1991
UNDAUNTED, TOO MUCH COFFEE MAN GOES INTO A MANIC PARANOID CAFFEINE FRENZY!
HE LEAPS INTO THE FRAY!
BAM!
STOMP
RIP

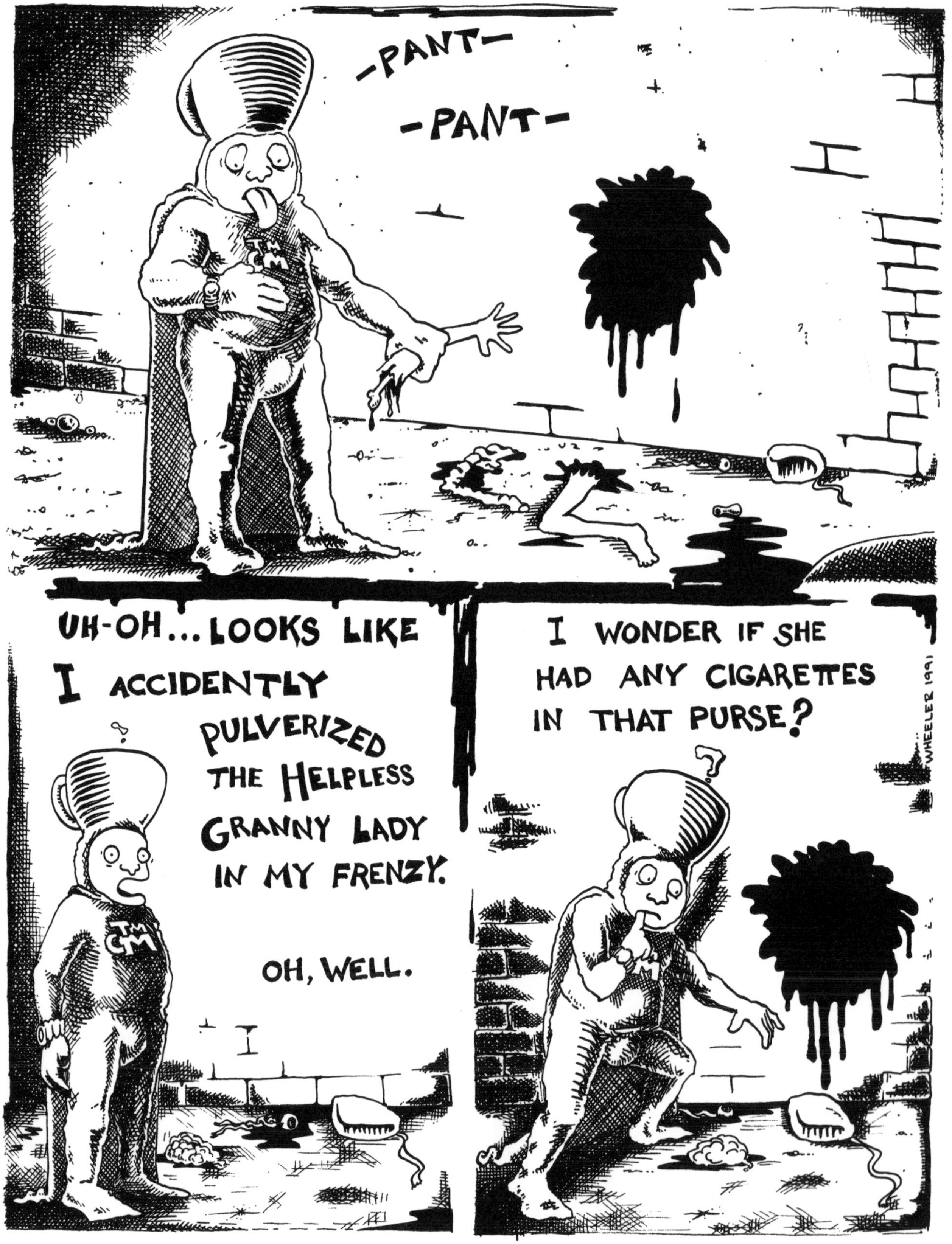
-PANT-
-PANT-
UH-OH... LOOKS LIKE I ACCIDENTLY PULVERIZED THE HELPLESS GRANNY LADY IN MY FRENZY.
OH, WELL.
I WONDER IF SHE HAD ANY CIGARETTES IN THAT PURSE?
WHEELER 1991

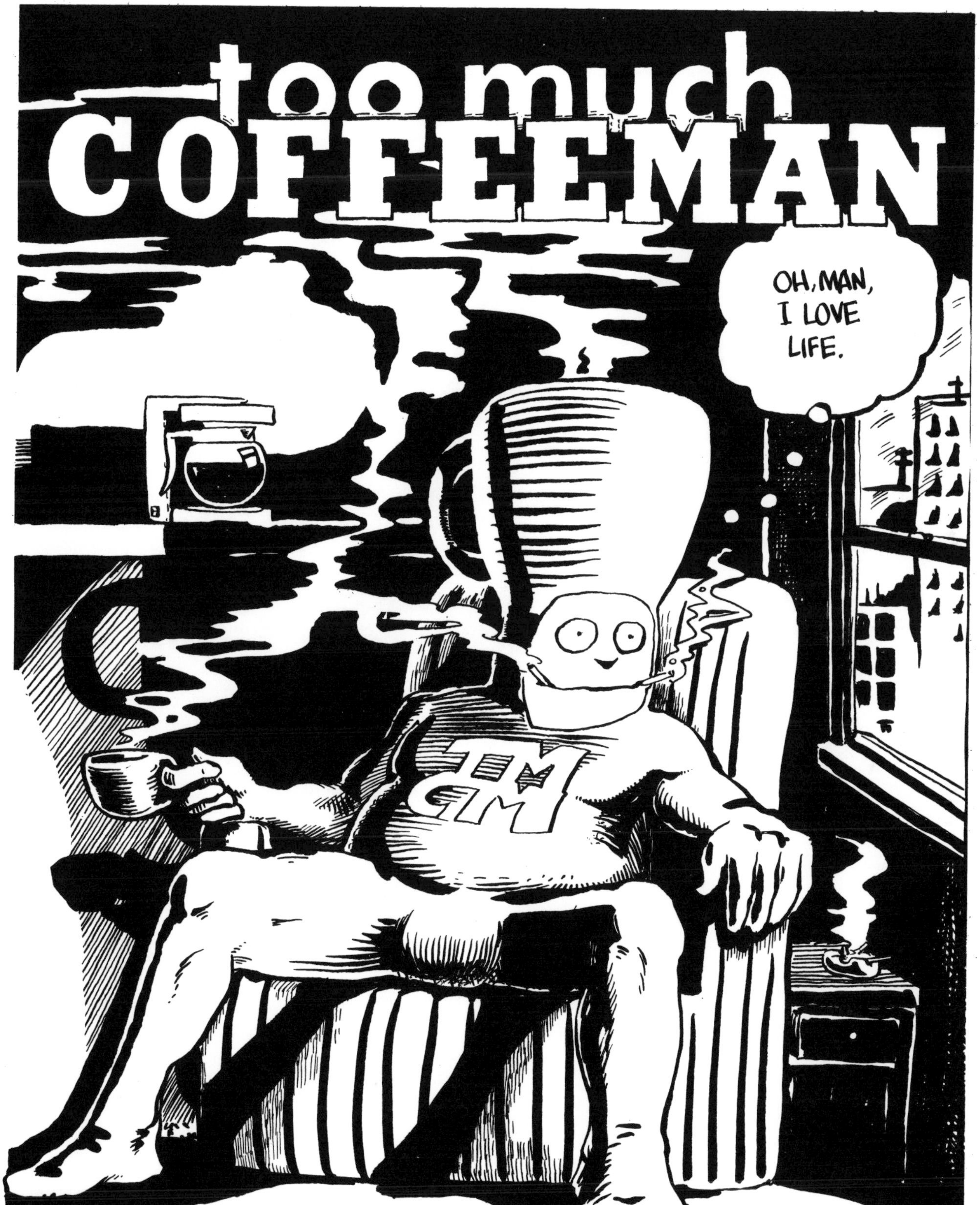
too much
COFFEEMAN
OH, MAN, I LOVE LIFE.
TMCM

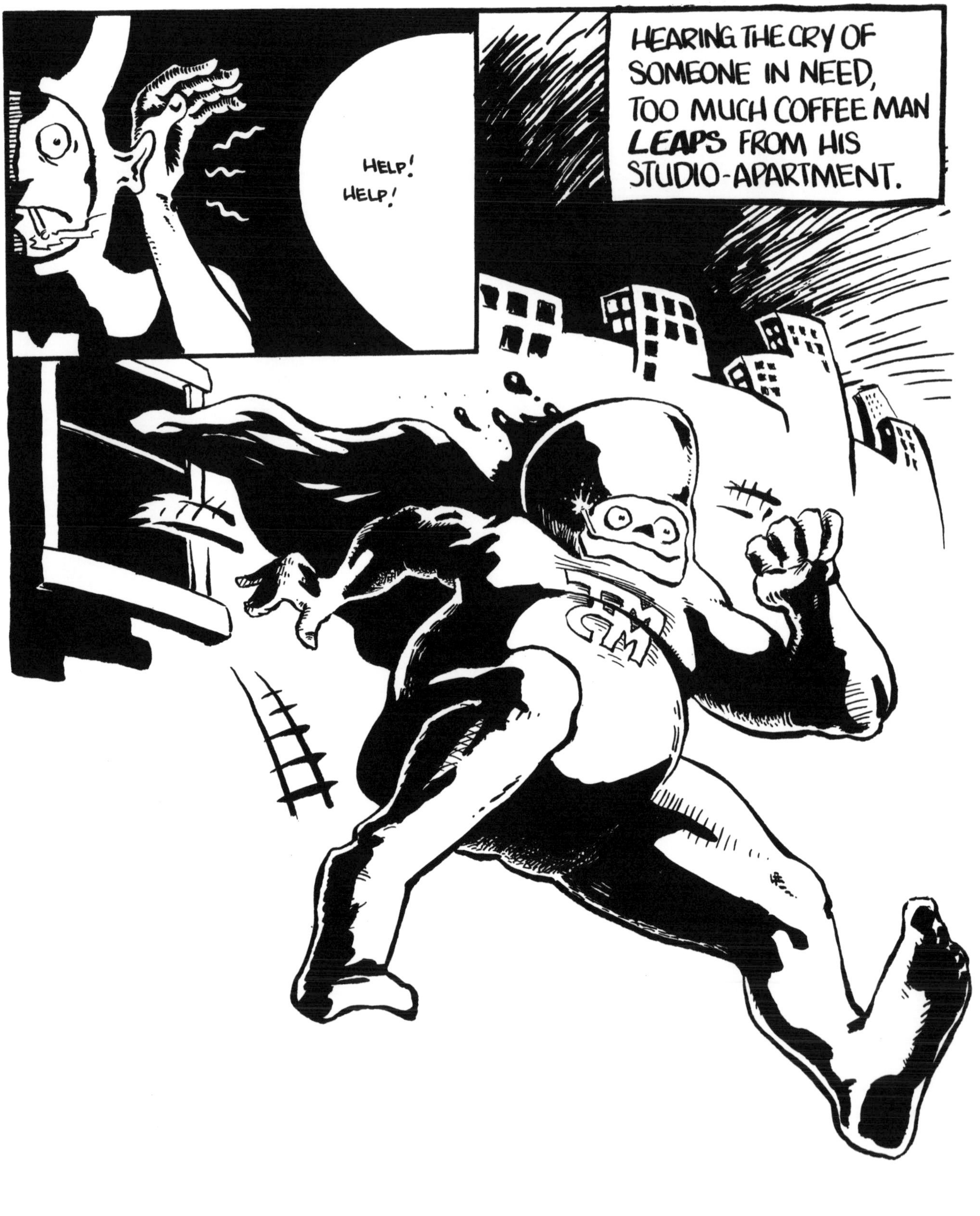
HELP!
HELP!
HEARING THE CRY OF SOMEONE IN NEED, TOO MUCH COFFEE MAN **LEAPS** FROM HIS STUDIO-APARTMENT.
TCM

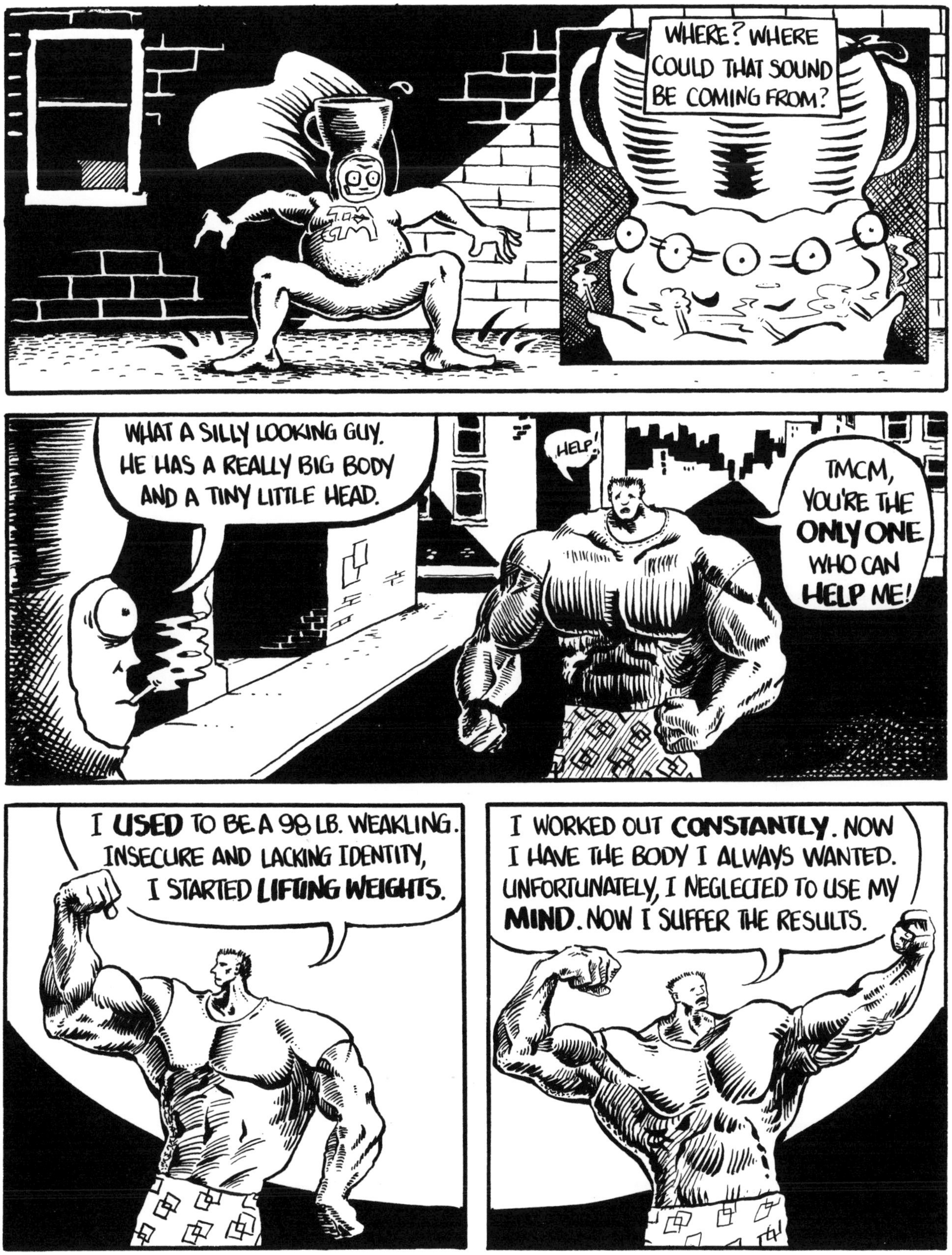
WHERE? WHERE COULD THAT SOUND BE COMING FROM?
WHAT A SILLY LOOKING GUY. HE HAS A REALLY BIG BODY AND A TINY LITTLE HEAD.
HELP!
TMCM, YOU'RE THE ONLY ONE WHO CAN HELP ME!
I USED TO BE A 98 LB. WEAKLING. INSECURE AND LACKING IDENTITY, I STARTED LIFTING WEIGHTS.
I WORKED OUT CONSTANTLY. NOW I HAVE THE BODY I ALWAYS WANTED. UNFORTUNATELY, I NEGLECTED TO USE MY MIND. NOW I SUFFER THE RESULTS.

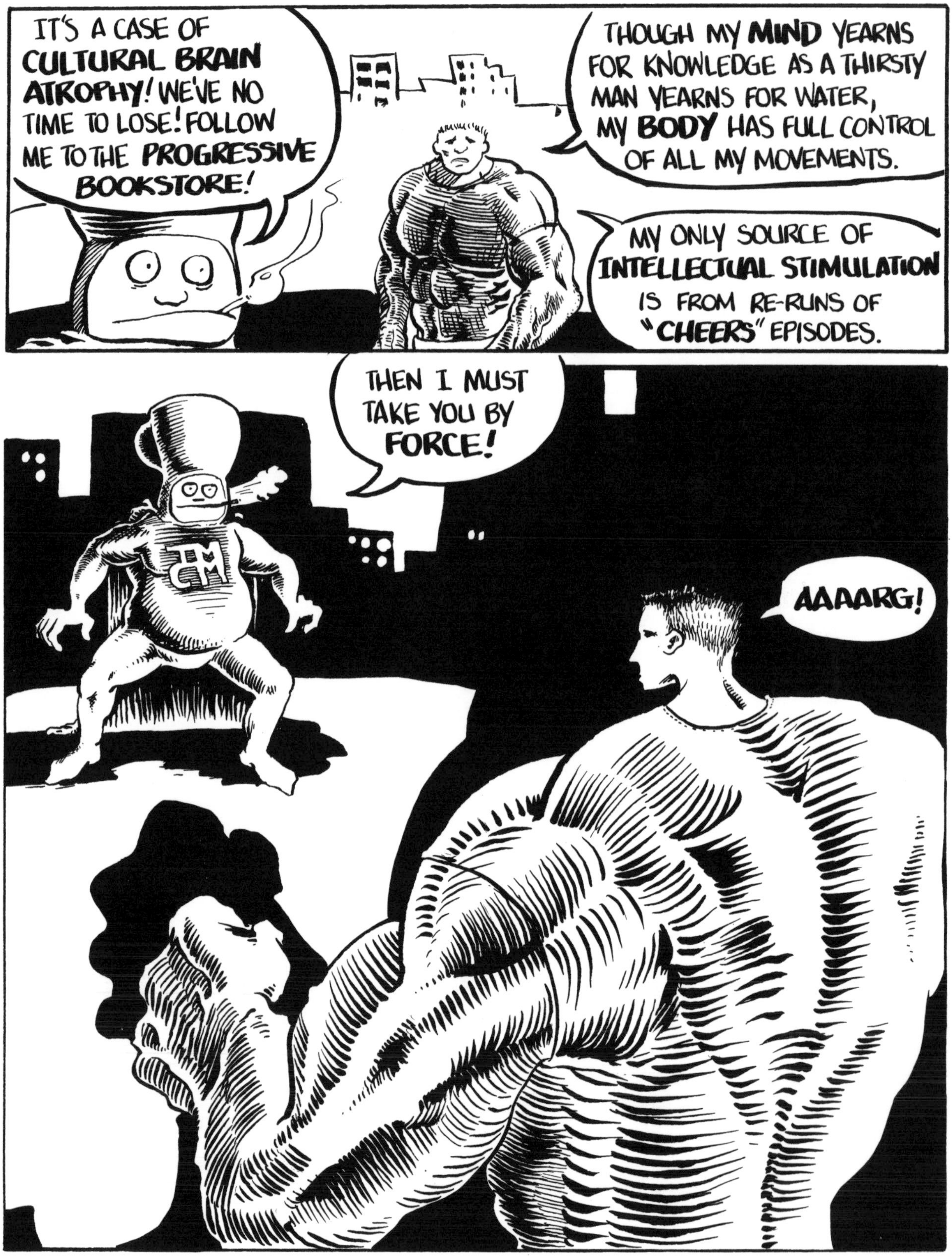
IT'S A CASE OF CULTURAL BRAIN ATROPHY! WE'VE NO TIME TO LOSE! FOLLOW ME TO THE PROGRESSIVE BOOKSTORE!
THOUGH MY MIND YEARNS FOR KNOWLEDGE AS A THIRSTY MAN YEARNS FOR WATER, MY BODY HAS FULL CONTROL OF ALL MY MOVEMENTS.
MY ONLY SOURCE OF INTELLECTUAL STIMULATION IS FROM RE-RUNS OF "CHEERS" EPISODES.
THEN I MUST TAKE YOU BY FORCE!
TM CM
AAAARG!

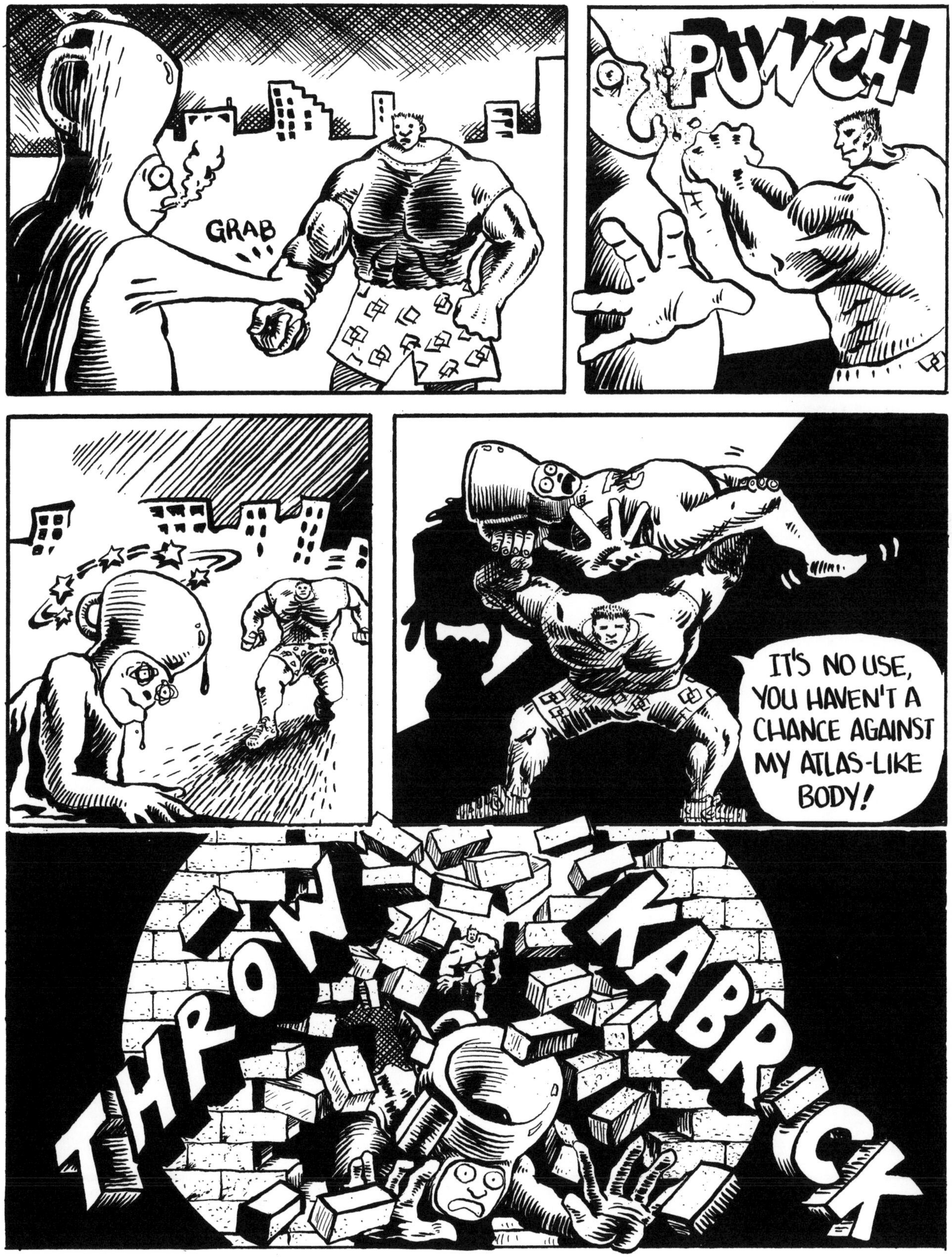
GRAB
PUNCH
IT'S NO USE, YOU HAVEN'T A CHANCE AGAINST MY ATLAS-LIKE BODY!
THROW
KABRICK

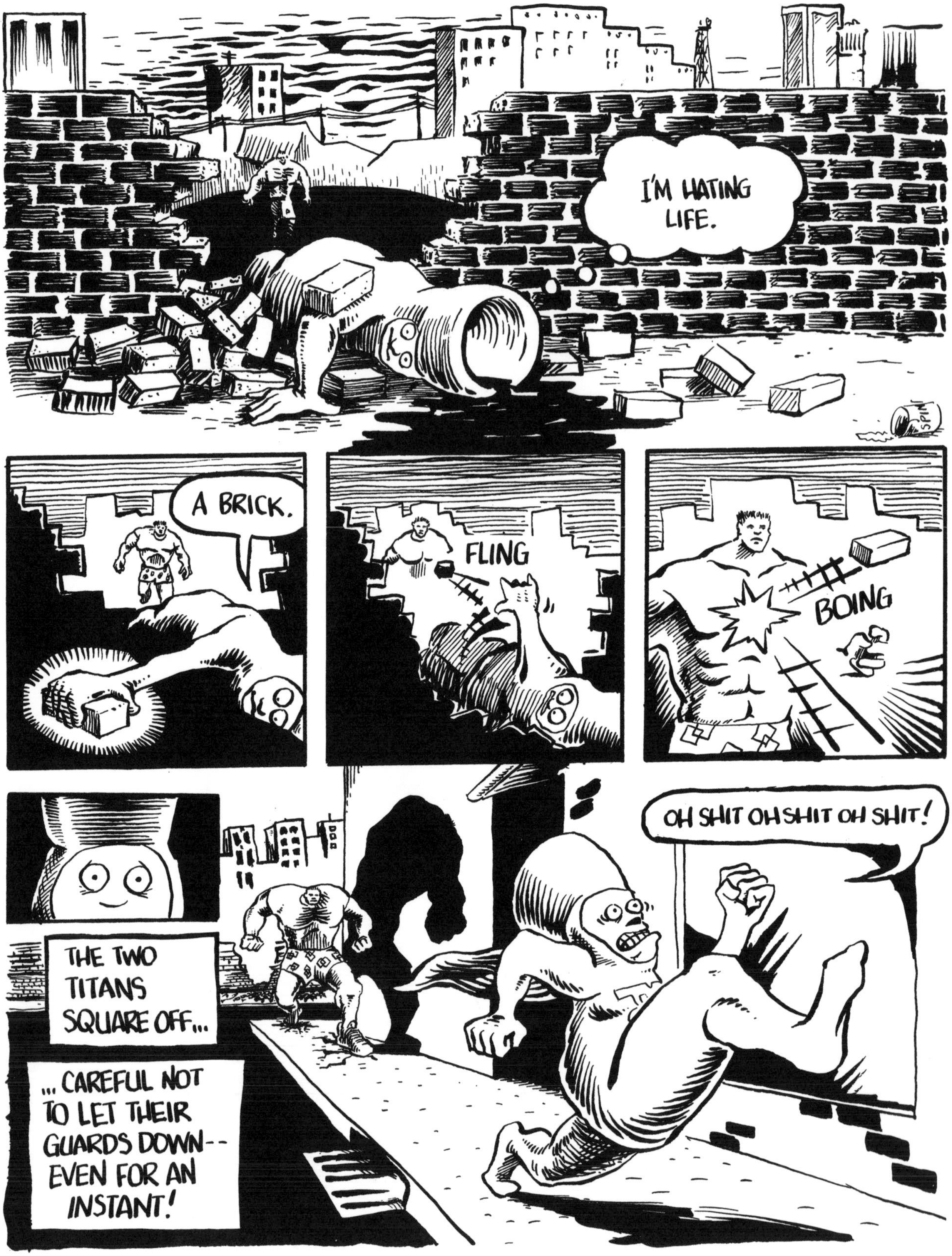
I'M HATING LIFE.
A BRICK.
FLING
BOING
THE TWO TITANS SQUARE OFF...
...CAREFUL NOT TO LET THEIR GUARDS DOWN-- EVEN FOR AN INSTANT!
OH SHIT OH SHIT OH SHIT!

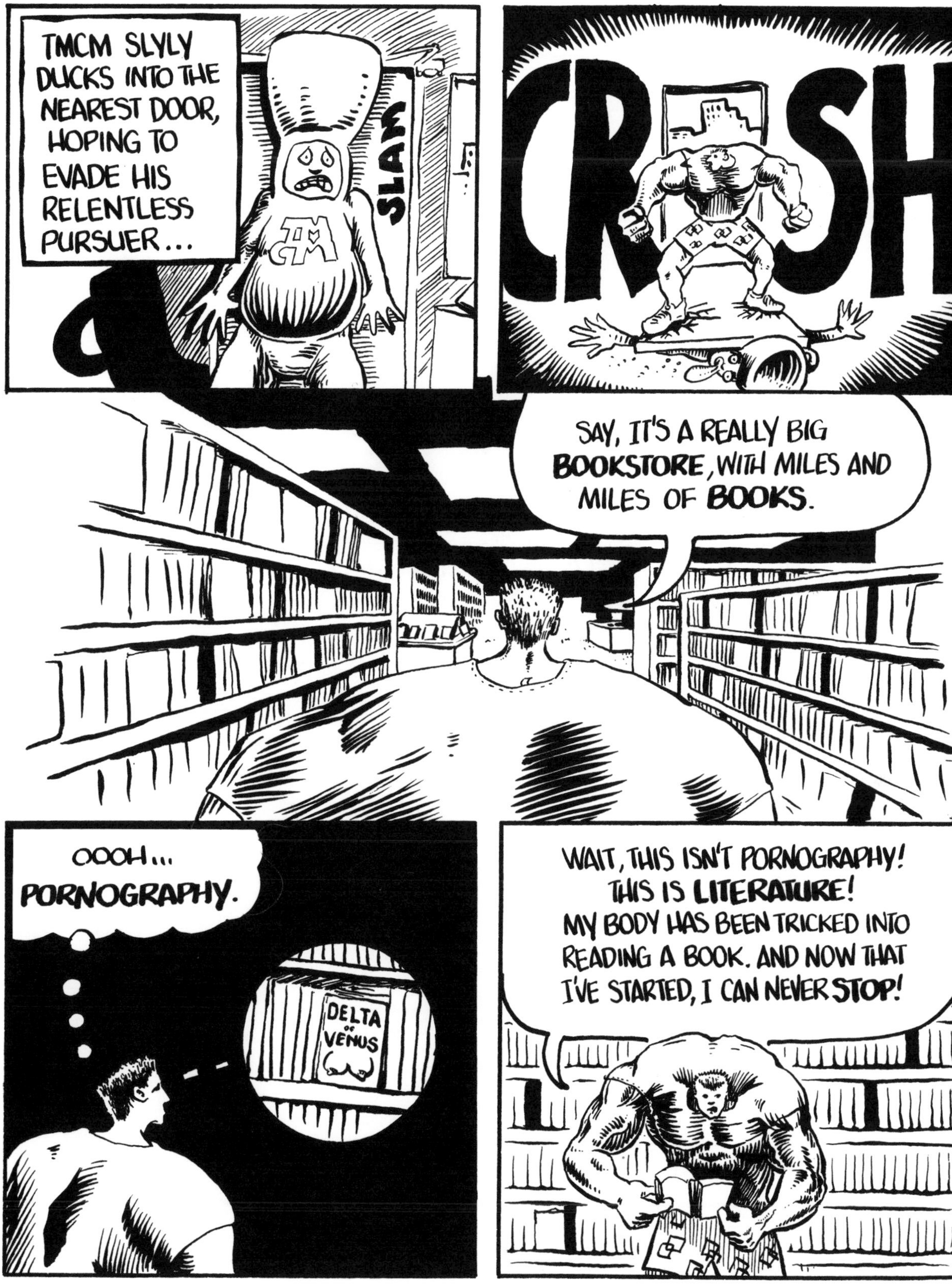
TMCM SLYLY DUCKS INTO THE NEAREST DOOR, HOPING TO EVADE HIS RELENTLESS PURSUER...
SLAM
TMCM
CRASH
SAY, IT'S A REALLY BIG BOOKSTORE, WITH MILES AND MILES OF BOOKS.
OOOH... PORNOGRAPHY.
DELTA OF VENUS
WAIT, THIS ISN'T PORNOGRAPHY! THIS IS LITERATURE! MY BODY HAS BEEN TRICKED INTO READING A BOOK. AND NOW THAT I'VE STARTED, I CAN NEVER STOP!

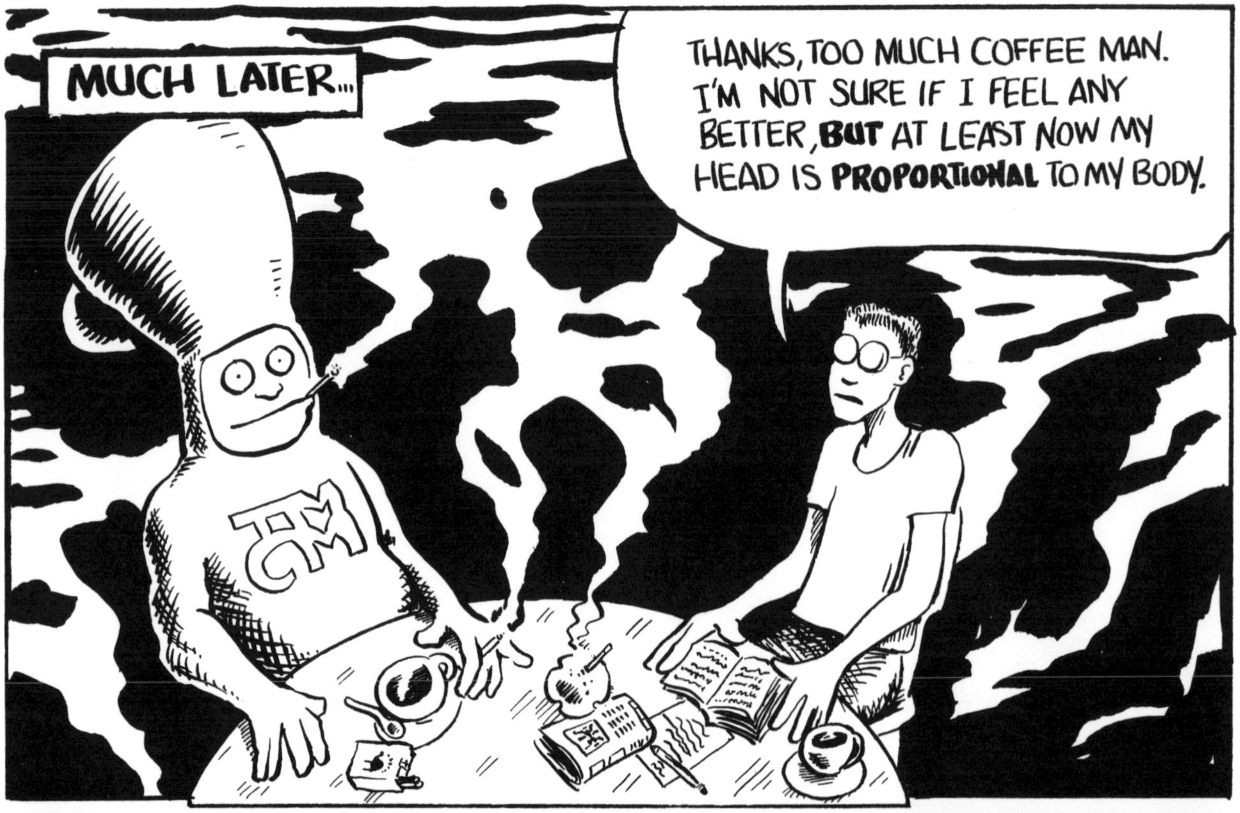
MUCH LATER...
THANKS, TOO MUCH COFFEE MAN. I'M NOT SURE IF I FEEL ANY BETTER, BUT AT LEAST NOW MY HEAD IS PROPORTIONAL TO MY BODY.

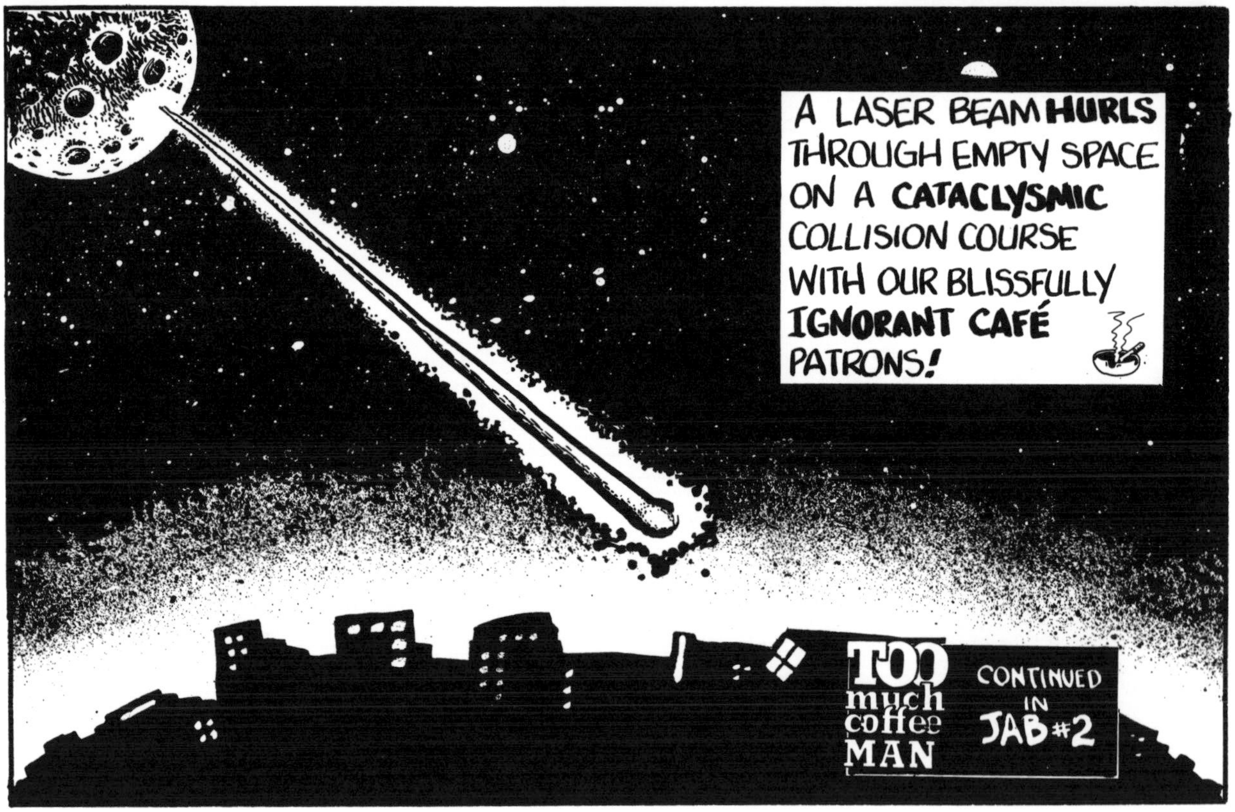
A LASER BEAM HURLS THROUGH EMPTY SPACE ON A CATACLYSMIC COLLISION COURSE WITH OUR BLISSFULLY IGNORANT CAFÉ PATRONS!
TOO much coffee MAN
CONTINUED IN JAB #2

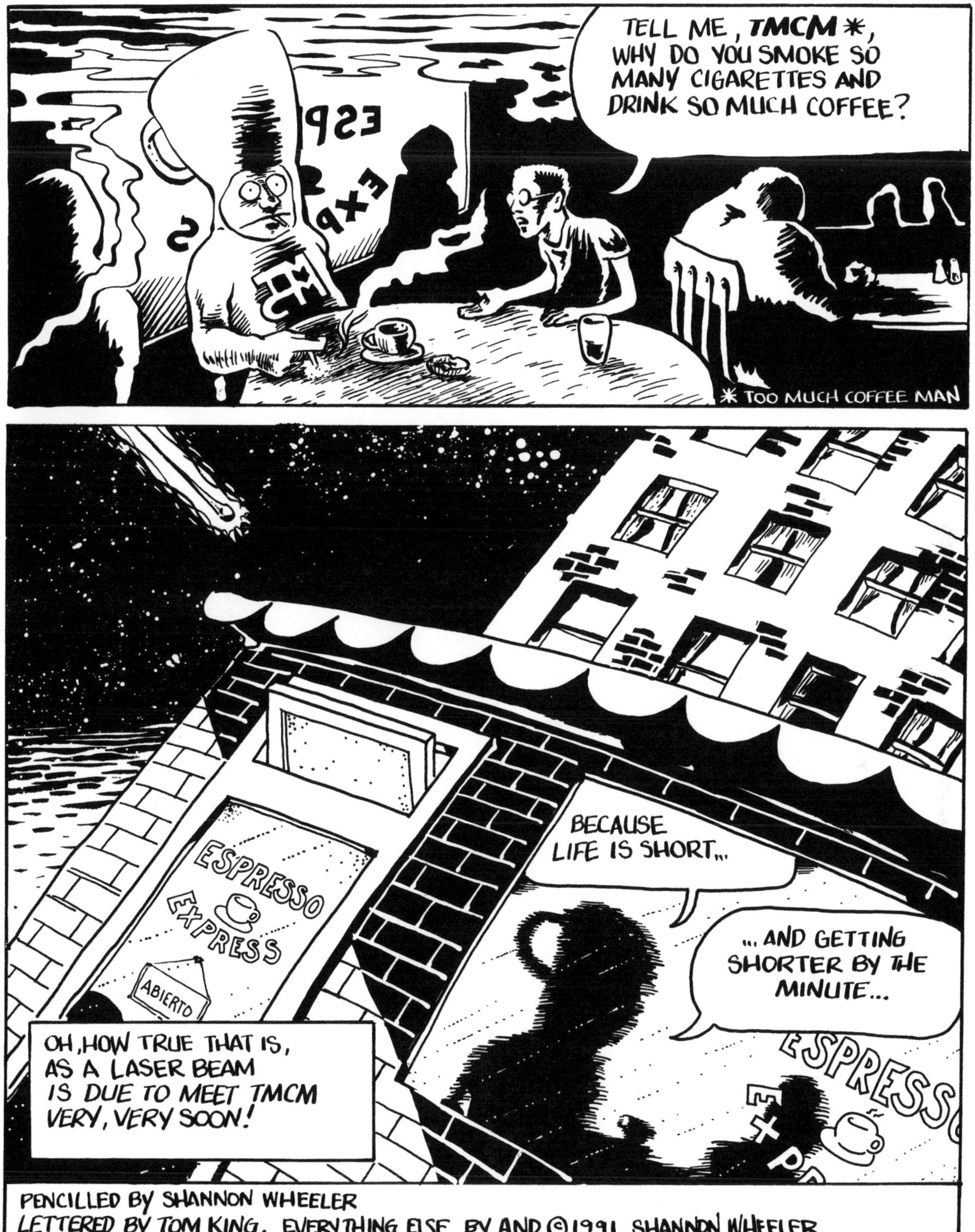
TELL ME, TMCM*, WHY DO YOU SMOKE SO MANY CIGARETTES AND DRINK SO MUCH COFFEE?
* TOO MUCH COFFEE MAN
ESPRESSO EXPRESS
ABIERTO
BECAUSE LIFE IS SHORT...
... AND GETTING SHORTER BY THE MINUTE...
OH, HOW TRUE THAT IS, AS A LASER BEAM IS DUE TO MEET TMCM VERY, VERY SOON!
PENCILLED BY SHANNON WHEELER
LETTERED BY TOM KING. EVERYTHING ELSE BY AND ©1991 SHANNON WHEELER

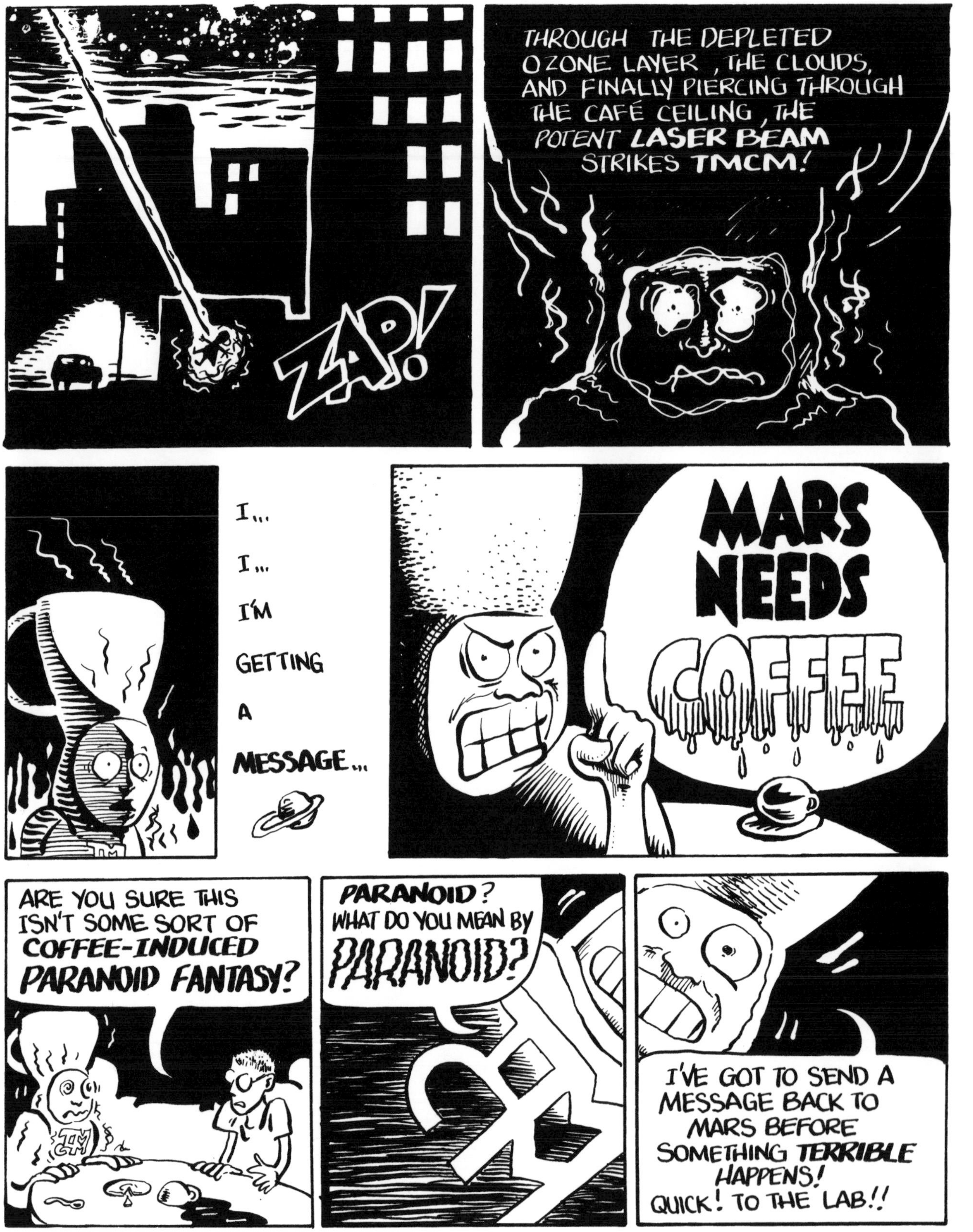
ZAP!
THROUGH THE DEPLETED OZONE LAYER, THE CLOUDS, AND FINALLY PIERCING THROUGH THE CAFÉ CEILING, THE POTENT LASER BEAM STRIKES TMCM!
I...
I...
I'M
GETTING
A
MESSAGE...
MARS NEEDS COFFEE
ARE YOU SURE THIS ISN'T SOME SORT OF COFFEE-INDUCED PARANOID FANTASY?
PARANOID? WHAT DO YOU MEAN BY PARANOID?
I'VE GOT TO SEND A MESSAGE BACK TO MARS BEFORE SOMETHING TERRIBLE HAPPENS! QUICK! TO THE LAB!!

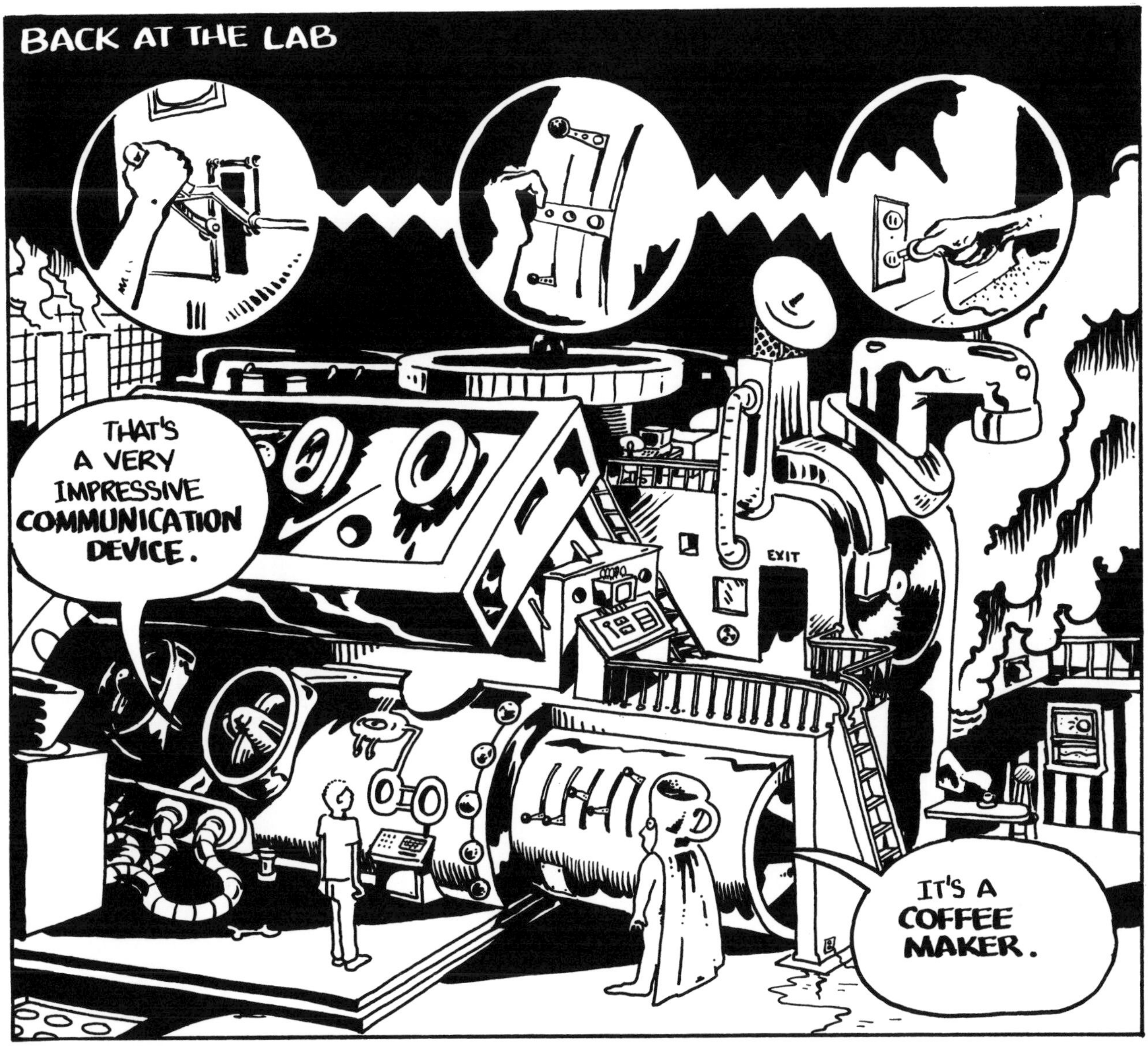
BACK AT THE LAB
THAT'S A VERY IMPRESSIVE COMMUNICATION DEVICE.
EXIT
IT'S A COFFEE MAKER.

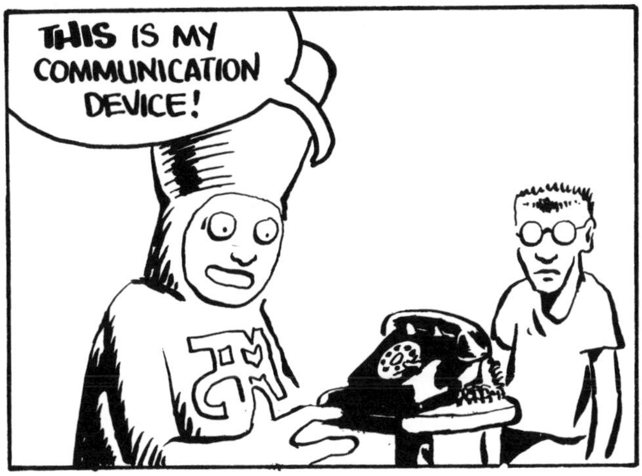
THIS IS MY COMMUNICATION DEVICE!

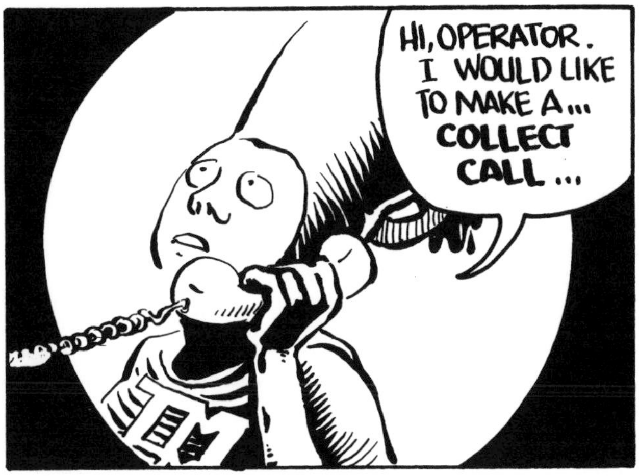
HI, OPERATOR. I WOULD LIKE TO MAKE A... COLLECT CALL...

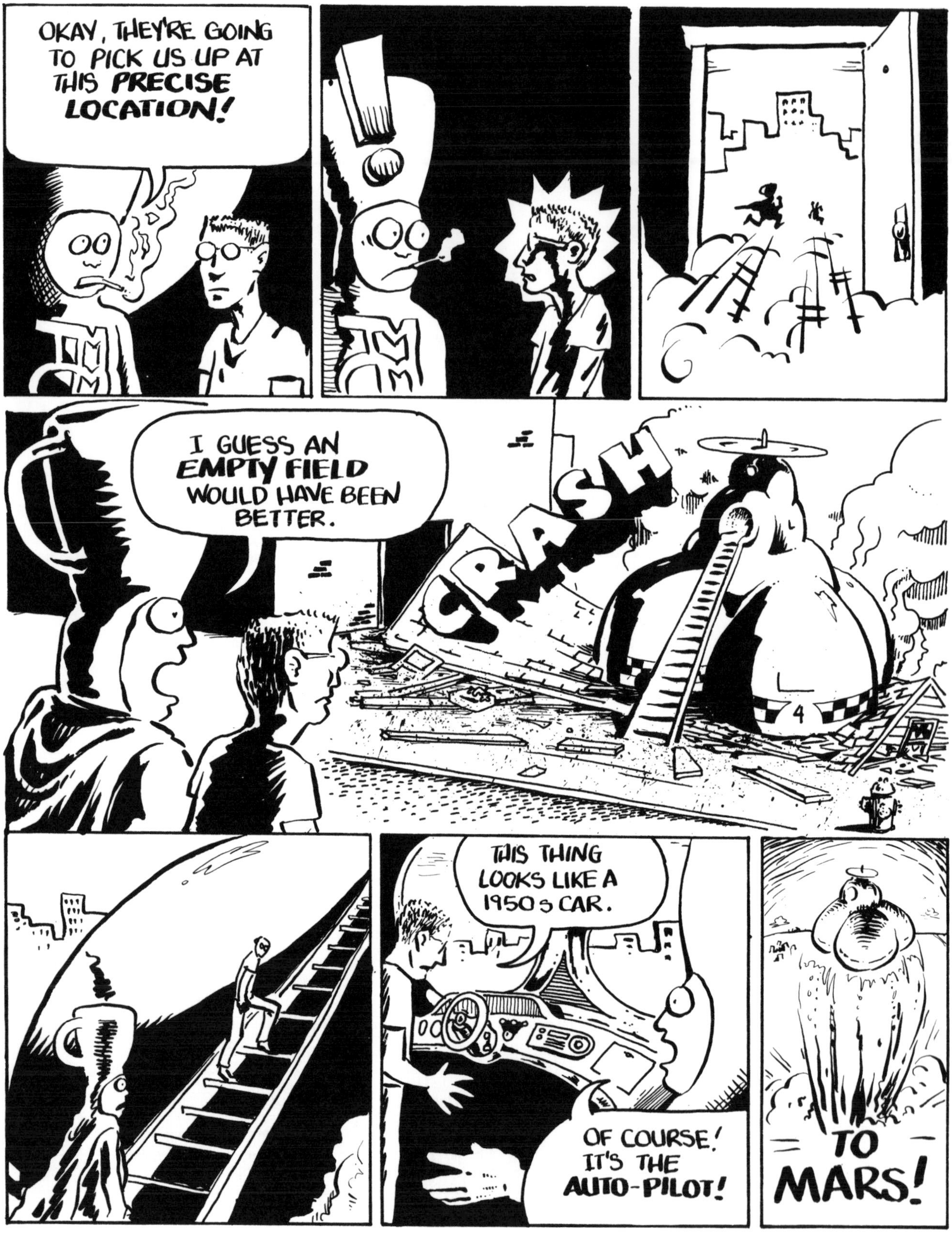
OKAY, THEY'RE GOING TO PICK US UP AT THIS PRECISE LOCATION!
I GUESS AN EMPTY FIELD WOULD HAVE BEEN BETTER.
CRASH
4
THIS THING LOOKS LIKE A 1950s CAR.
OF COURSE! IT'S THE AUTO-PILOT!
TO MARS!

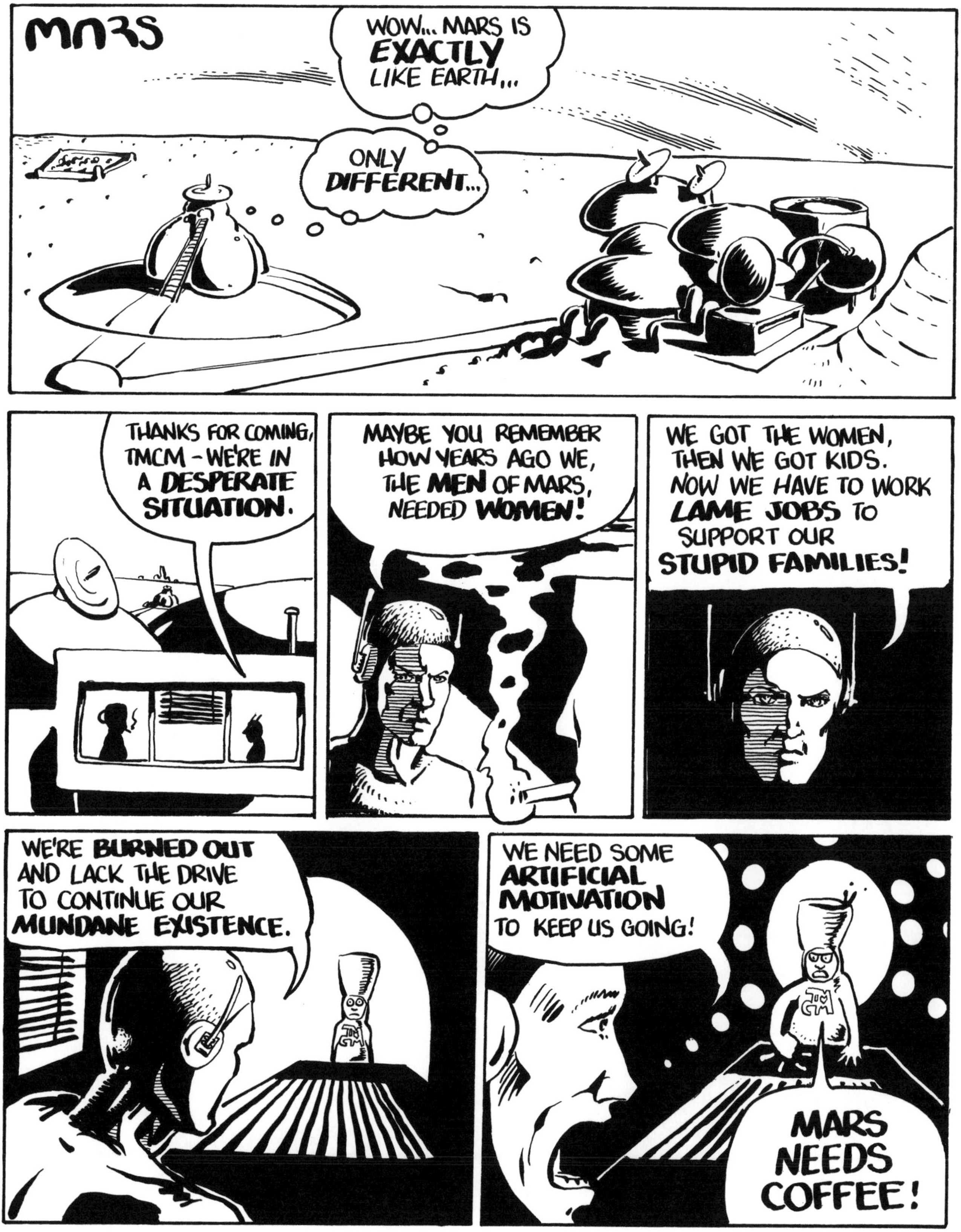
MARS
WOW... MARS IS EXACTLY LIKE EARTH...
ONLY DIFFERENT...
THANKS FOR COMING, TMCM - WE'RE IN A DESPERATE SITUATION.
MAYBE YOU REMEMBER HOW YEARS AGO WE, THE MEN OF MARS, NEEDED WOMEN!
WE GOT THE WOMEN, THEN WE GOT KIDS. NOW WE HAVE TO WORK LAME JOBS TO SUPPORT OUR STUPID FAMILIES!
WE'RE BURNED OUT AND LACK THE DRIVE TO CONTINUE OUR MUNDANE EXISTENCE.
WE NEED SOME ARTIFICIAL MOTIVATION TO KEEP US GOING!
MARS NEEDS COFFEE!

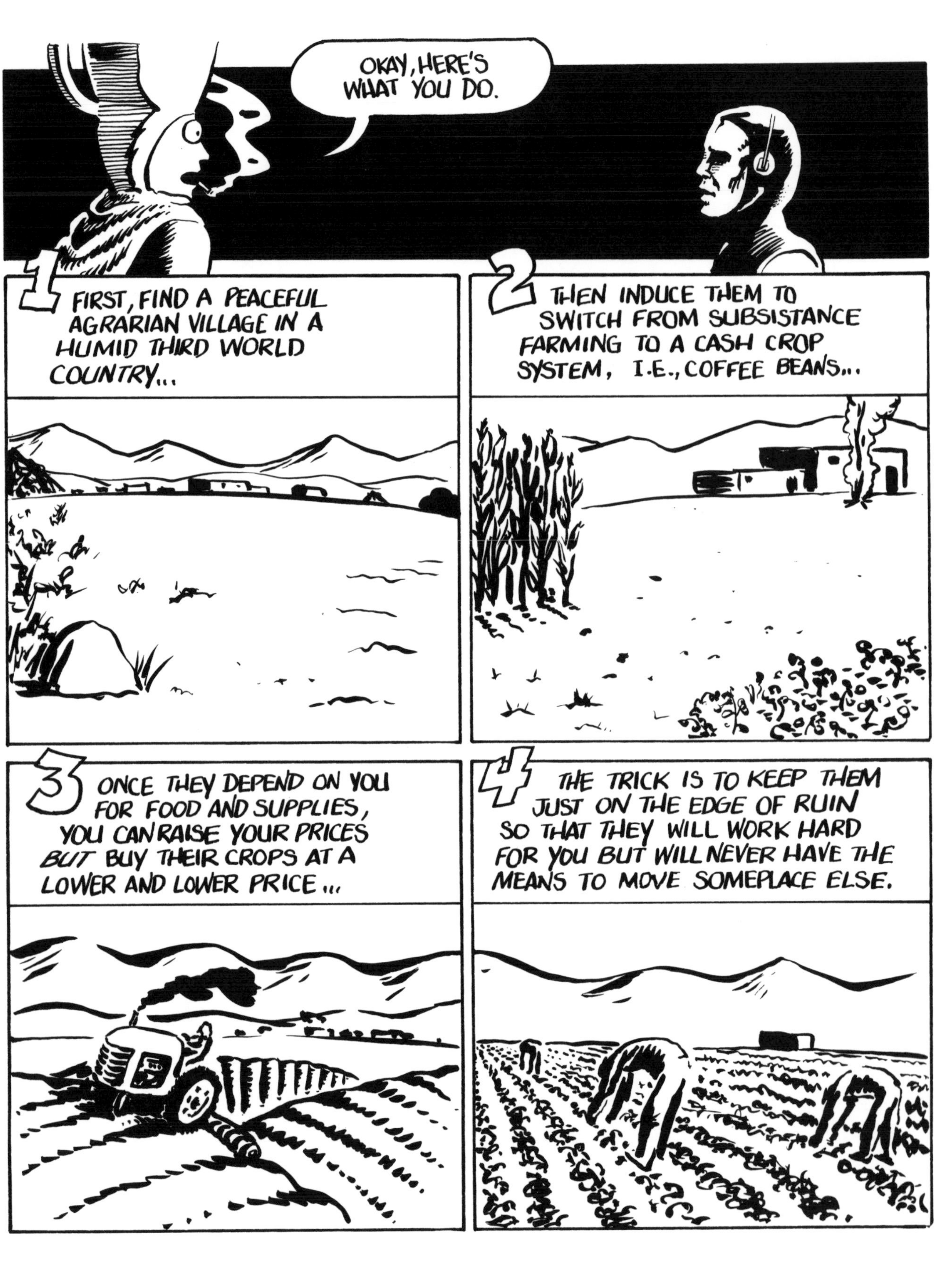
OKAY, HERE'S WHAT YOU DO.
1 FIRST, FIND A PEACEFUL AGRARIAN VILLAGE IN A HUMID THIRD WORLD COUNTRY...
2 THEN INDUCE THEM TO SWITCH FROM SUBSISTANCE FARMING TO A CASH CROP SYSTEM, I.E., COFFEE BEANS...
3 ONCE THEY DEPEND ON YOU FOR FOOD AND SUPPLIES, YOU CAN RAISE YOUR PRICES BUT BUY THEIR CROPS AT A LOWER AND LOWER PRICE...
4 THE TRICK IS TO KEEP THEM JUST ON THE EDGE OF RUIN SO THAT THEY WILL WORK HARD FOR YOU BUT WILL NEVER HAVE THE MEANS TO MOVE SOMEPLACE ELSE.

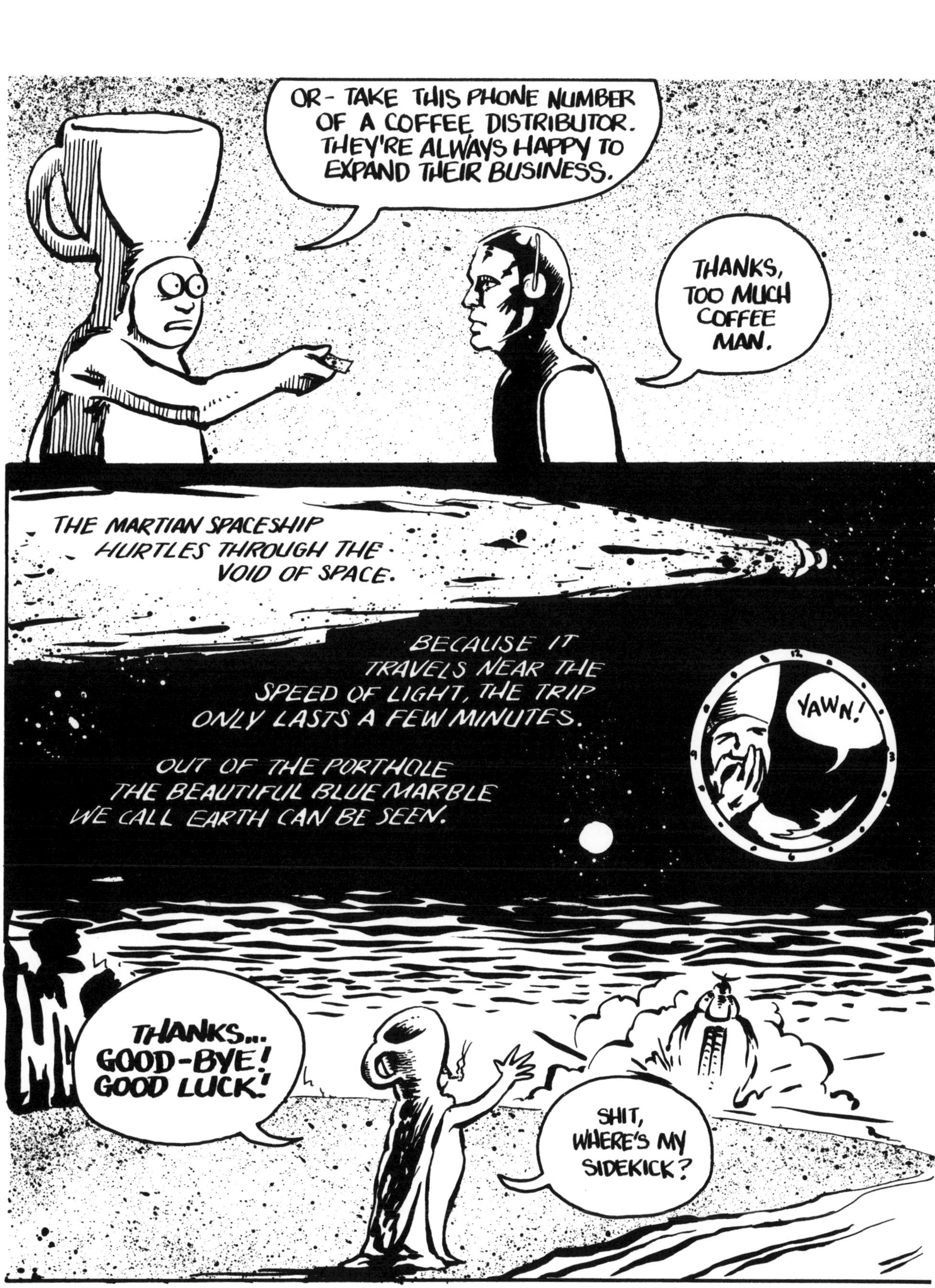
OR- TAKE THIS PHONE NUMBER OF A COFFEE DISTRIBUTOR. THEY'RE ALWAYS HAPPY TO EXPAND THEIR BUSINESS.
THANKS, TOO MUCH COFFEE MAN.
THE MARTIAN SPACESHIP HURTLES THROUGH THE VOID OF SPACE.
BECAUSE IT TRAVELS NEAR THE SPEED OF LIGHT, THE TRIP ONLY LASTS A FEW MINUTES.
OUT OF THE PORTHOLE THE BEAUTIFUL BLUE MARBLE WE CALL EARTH CAN BE SEEN.
YAWN!
THANKS... GOOD-BYE! GOOD LUCK!
SHIT, WHERE'S MY SIDEKICK?

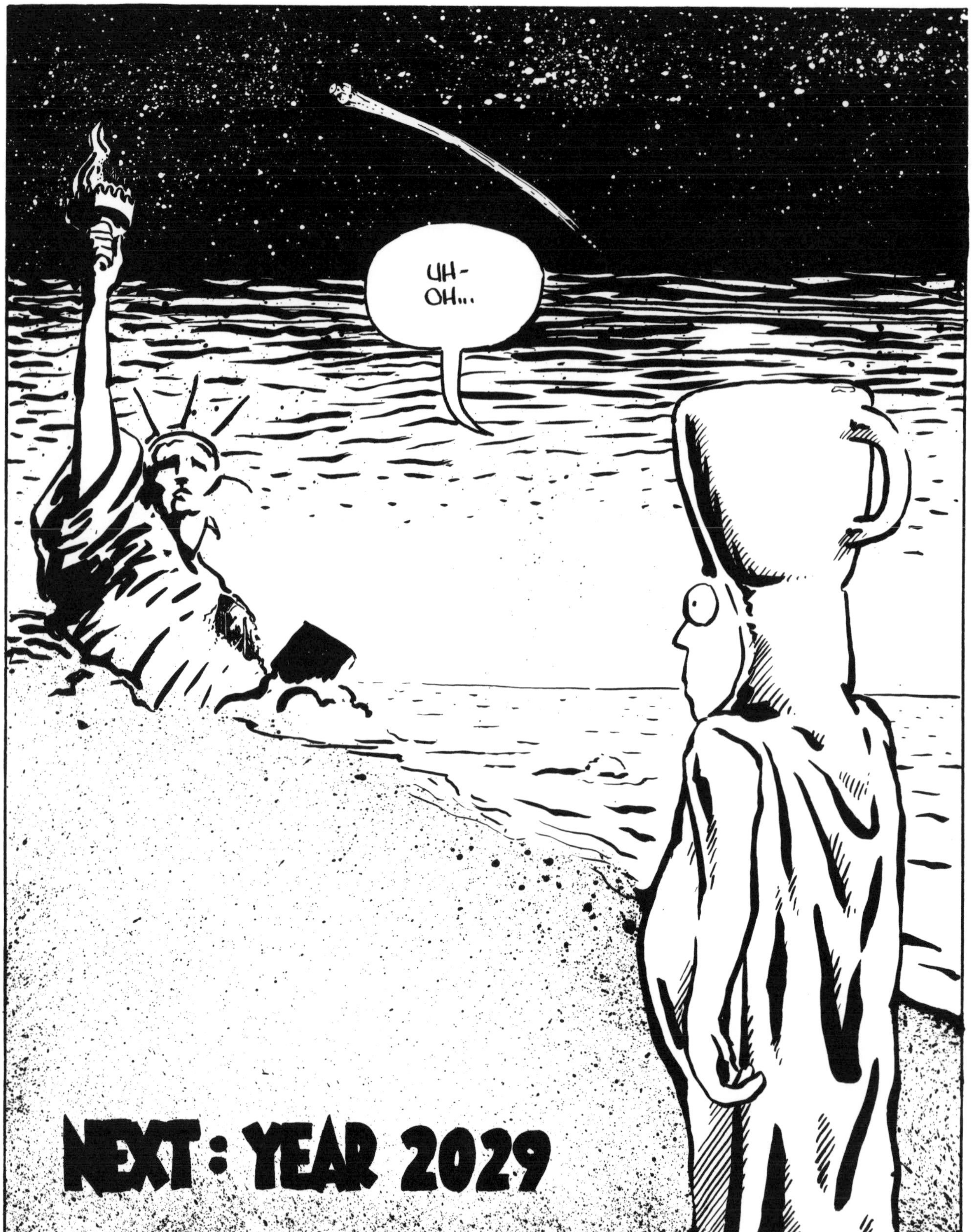
UH-
OH...
NEXT : YEAR 2029

TOO MUCH COFFEE MAN

IN THE LAST ISSUE, TOO MUCH COFFEE MAN TRAVELED TO MARS AND BACK IN A SPACESHIP THAT APPROACHED THE SPEED OF LIGHT. THE TRIP LASTED MERE MINUTES FOR OUR HERO. UNFORTUNATELY, DUE TO EINSTEIN'S LAW OF RELATIVITY, 37 YEARS PASSED ON EARTH...

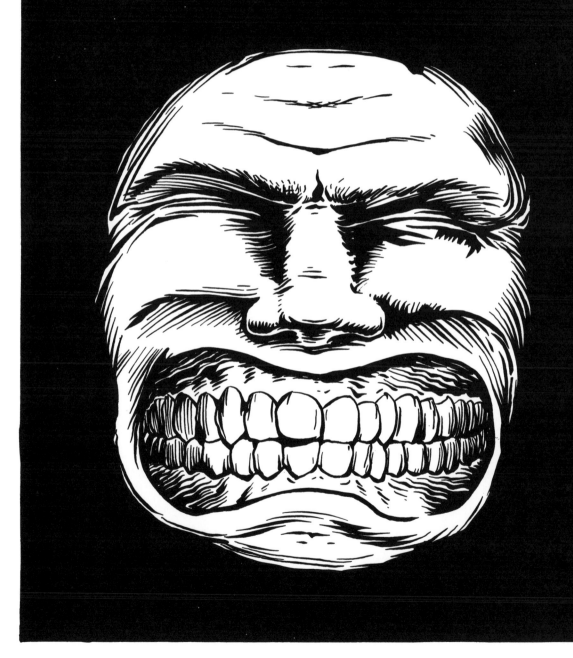

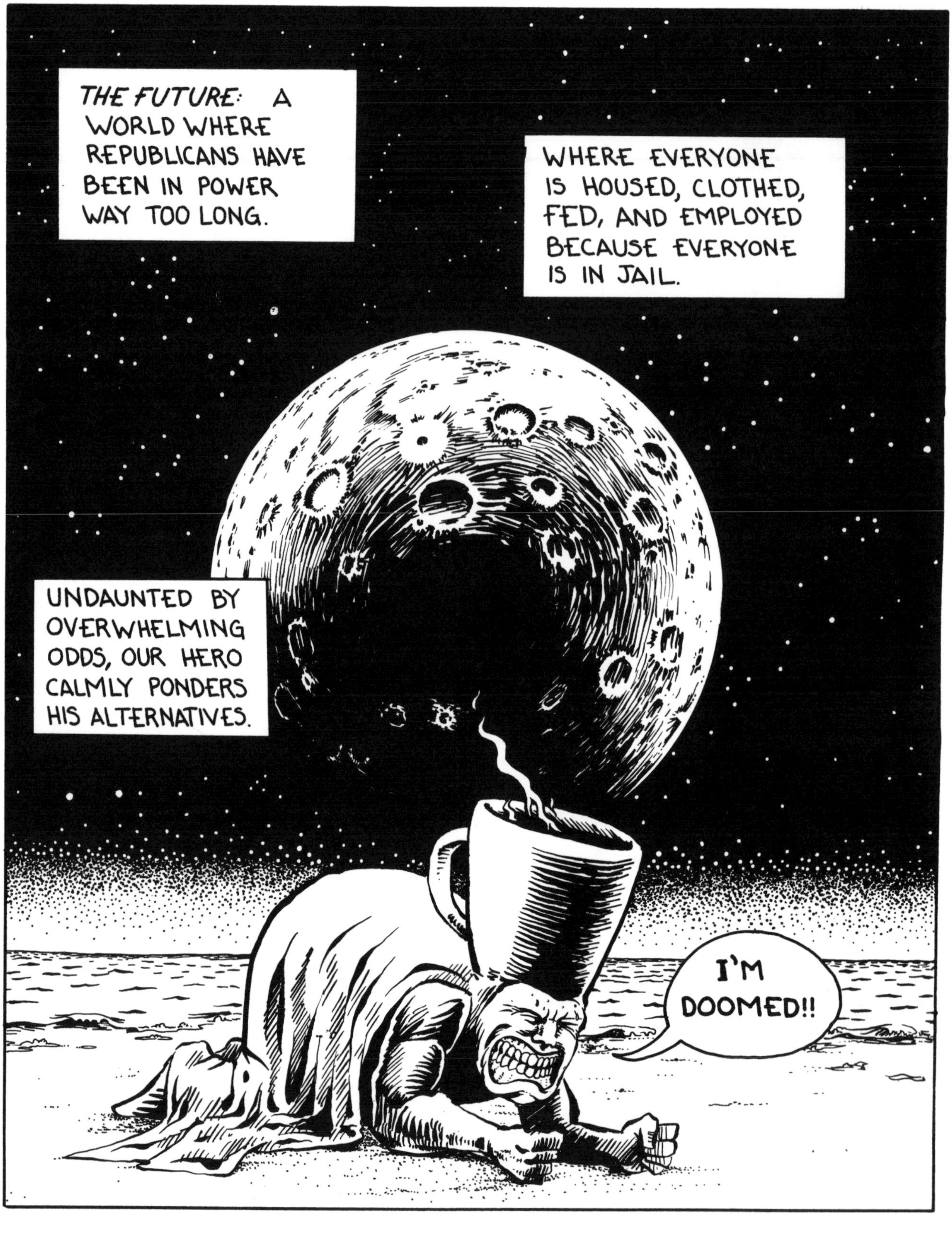
THE FUTURE: A WORLD WHERE REPUBLICANS HAVE BEEN IN POWER WAY TOO LONG.
WHERE EVERYONE IS HOUSED, CLOTHED, FED, AND EMPLOYED BECAUSE EVERYONE IS IN JAIL.
UNDAUNTED BY OVERWHELMING ODDS, OUR HERO CALMLY PONDERS HIS ALTERNATIVES.
I'M DOOMED!!

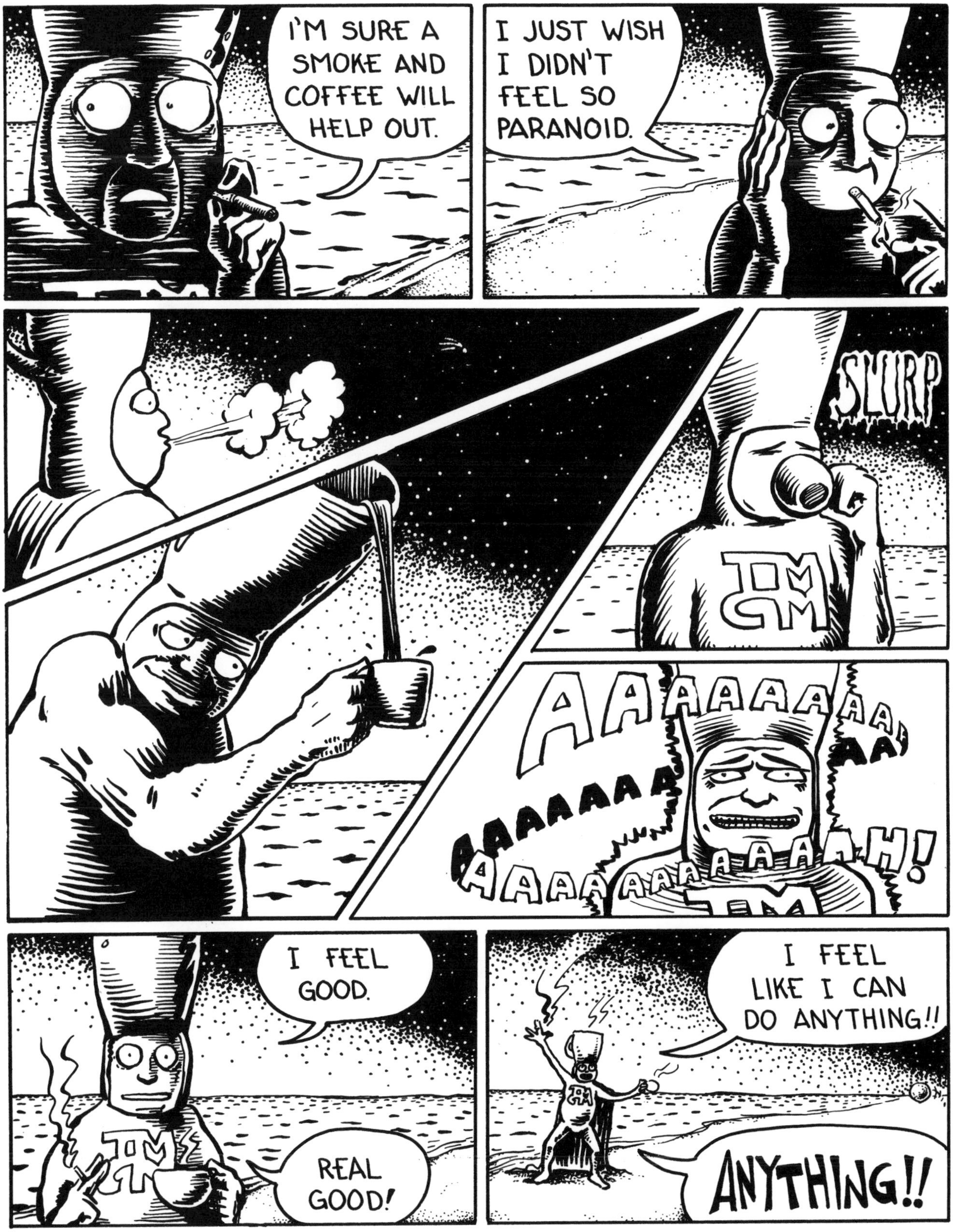
I'M SURE A SMOKE AND COFFEE WILL HELP OUT.
I JUST WISH I DIDN'T FEEL SO PARANOID.
SLURP
I FEEL GOOD.
REAL GOOD!
I FEEL LIKE I CAN DO ANYTHING!!
ANYTHING!!

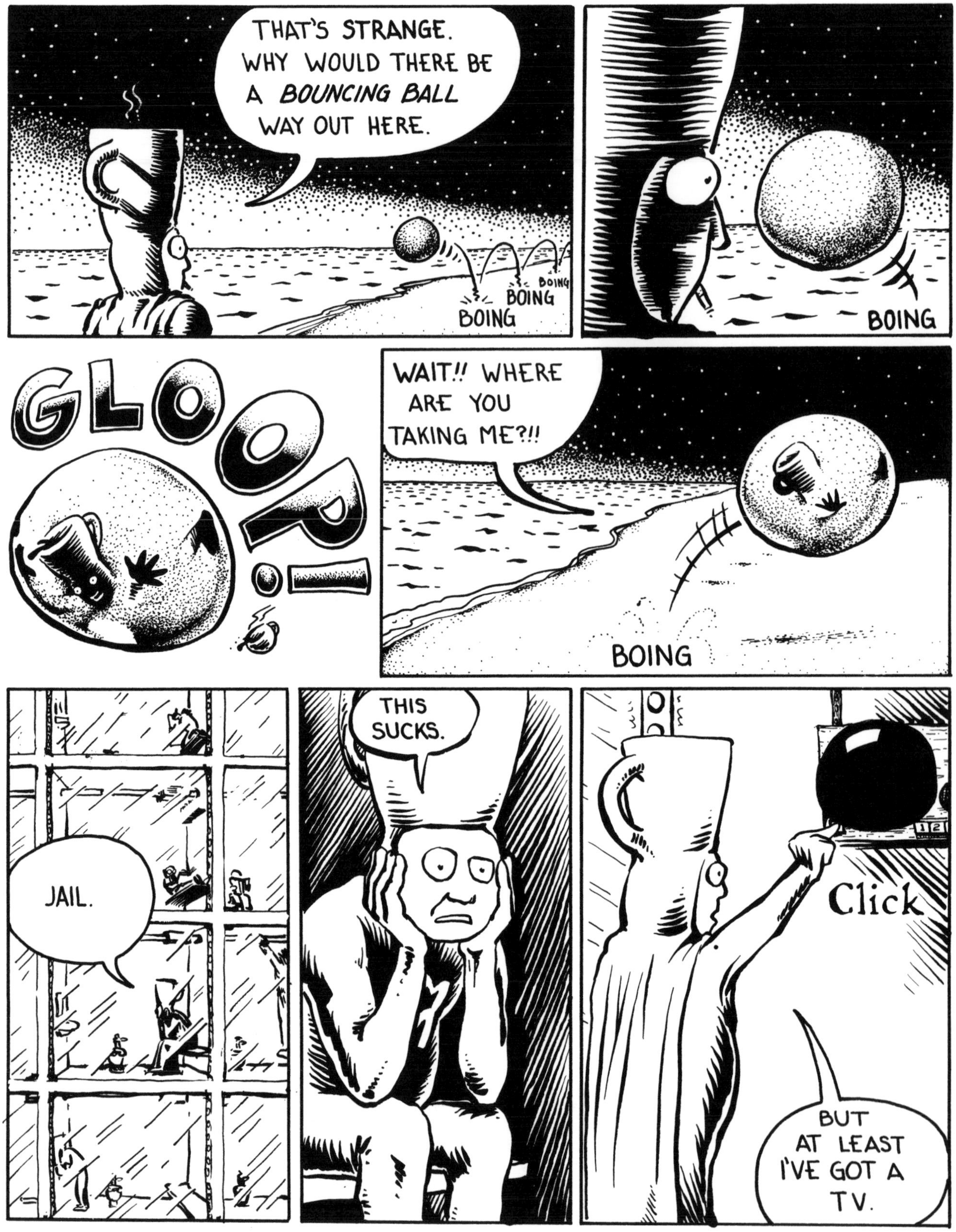
THAT'S STRANGE. WHY WOULD THERE BE A BOUNCING BALL WAY OUT HERE.
BOING
BOING
BOING
BOING
GLOOP!
WAIT!! WHERE ARE YOU TAKING ME?!!
BOING
JAIL.
THIS SUCKS.
Click
BUT AT LEAST I'VE GOT A TV.

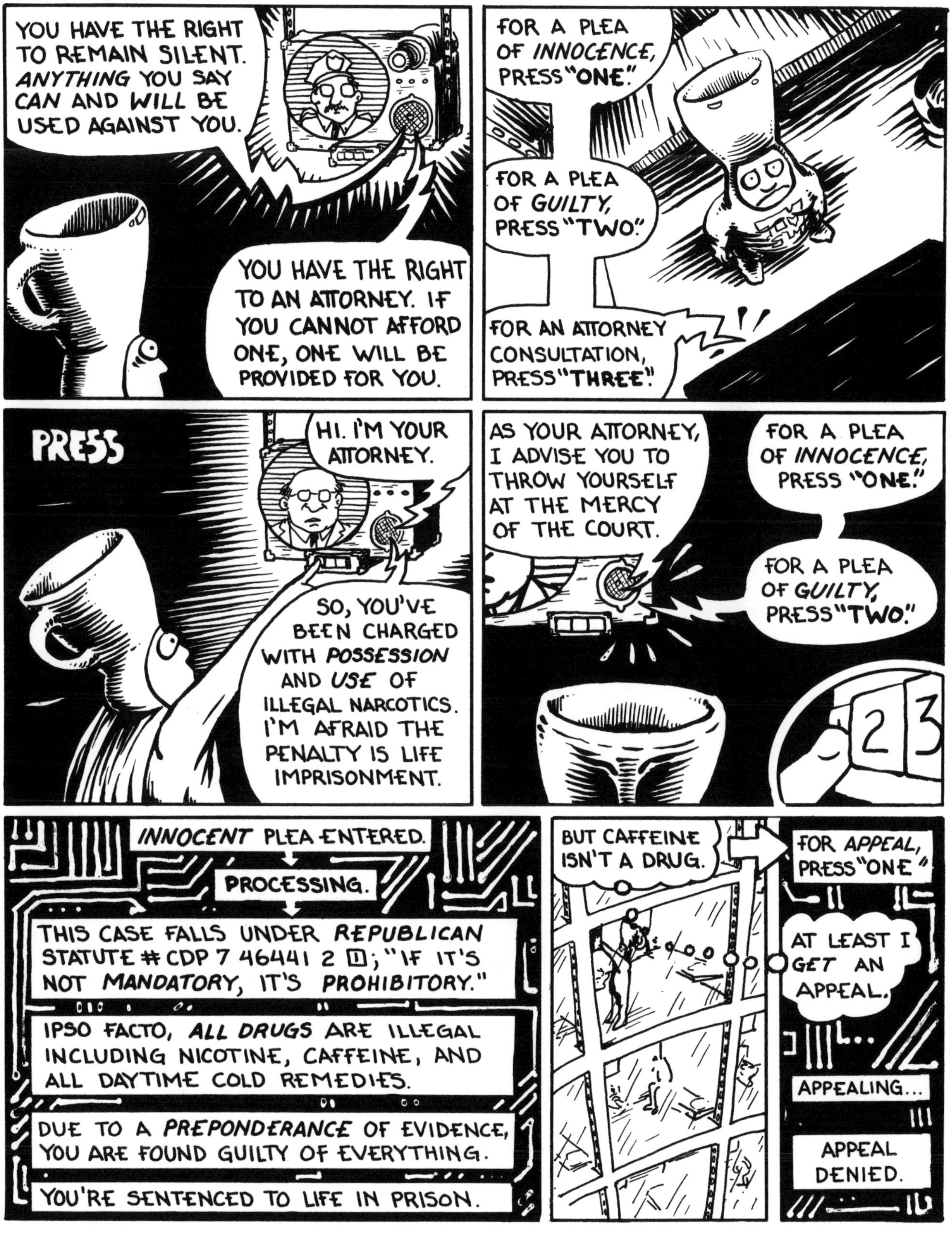

YOU HAVE THE RIGHT TO REMAIN SILENT. ANYTHING YOU SAY CAN AND WILL BE USED AGAINST YOU.
YOU HAVE THE RIGHT TO AN ATTORNEY. IF YOU CANNOT AFFORD ONE, ONE WILL BE PROVIDED FOR YOU.
FOR A PLEA OF INNOCENCE, PRESS "ONE."
FOR A PLEA OF GUILTY, PRESS "TWO."
FOR AN ATTORNEY CONSULTATION, PRESS "THREE."
PRESS
HI. I'M YOUR ATTORNEY.
SO, YOU'VE BEEN CHARGED WITH POSSESSION AND USE OF ILLEGAL NARCOTICS. I'M AFRAID THE PENALTY IS LIFE IMPRISONMENT.
AS YOUR ATTORNEY, I ADVISE YOU TO THROW YOURSELF AT THE MERCY OF THE COURT.
FOR A PLEA OF INNOCENCE, PRESS "ONE."
FOR A PLEA OF GUILTY, PRESS "TWO."
2 3
INNOCENT PLEA ENTERED.
PROCESSING.
THIS CASE FALLS UNDER REPUBLICAN STATUTE # CDP 7 46441 2 ⓘ; "IF IT'S NOT MANDATORY, IT'S PROHIBITORY."
IPSO FACTO, ALL DRUGS ARE ILLEGAL INCLUDING NICOTINE, CAFFEINE, AND ALL DAYTIME COLD REMEDIES.
DUE TO A PREPONDERANCE OF EVIDENCE, YOU ARE FOUND GUILTY OF EVERYTHING.
YOU'RE SENTENCED TO LIFE IN PRISON.
BUT CAFFEINE ISN'T A DRUG.
FOR APPEAL, PRESS "ONE"
AT LEAST I GET AN APPEAL.
APPEALING...
APPEAL DENIED.

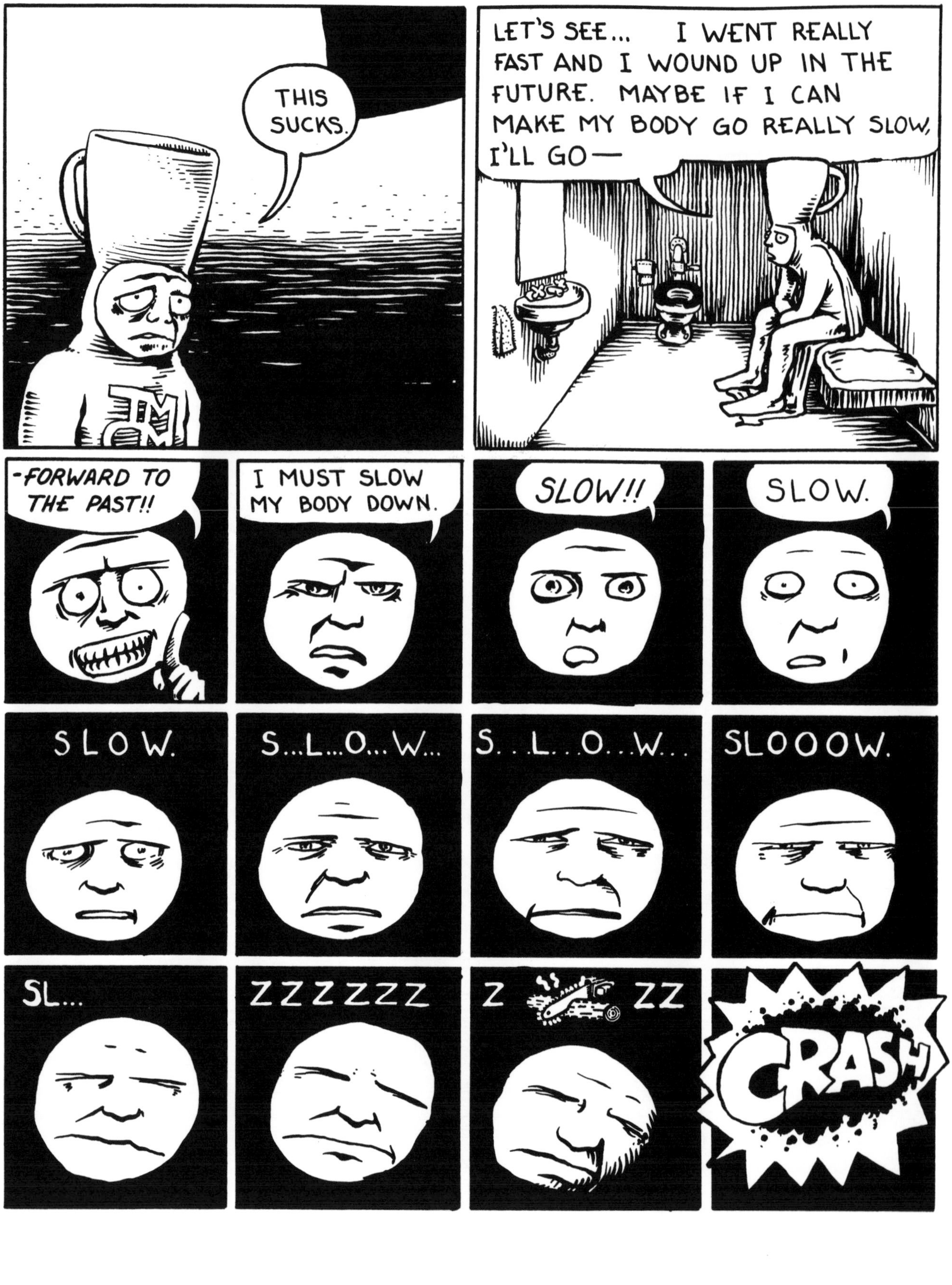
THIS SUCKS.
LET'S SEE... I WENT REALLY FAST AND I WOUND UP IN THE FUTURE. MAYBE IF I CAN MAKE MY BODY GO REALLY SLOW, I'LL GO—
-FORWARD TO THE PAST!!
I MUST SLOW MY BODY DOWN.
SLOW!!
SLOW.
SLOW.
S...L...O...W...
S. . L. . O. . W. . .
SLOOOW.
SL...
ZZZZZZ
Z ZZ
CRASH

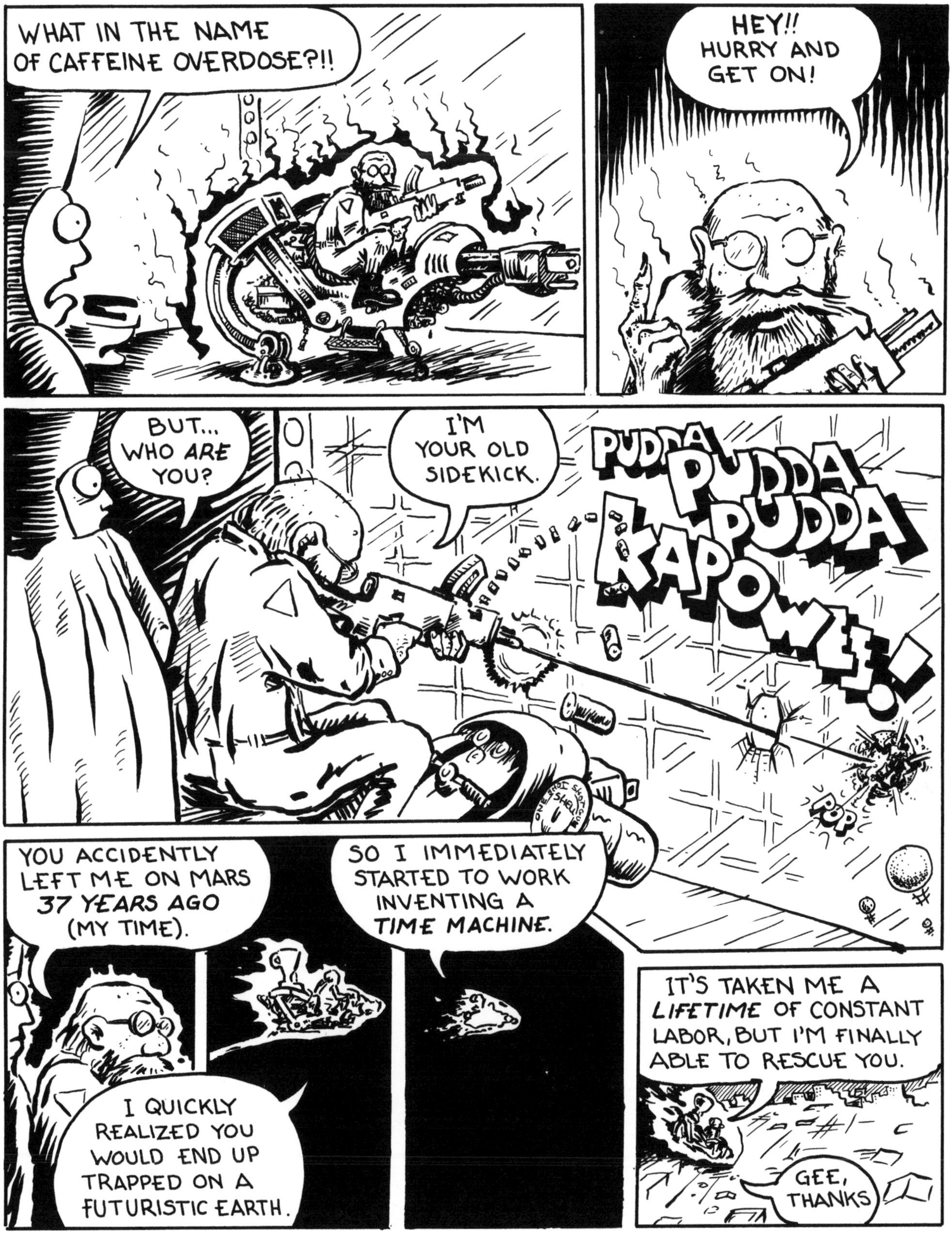

WHAT IN THE NAME OF CAFFEINE OVERDOSE?!!
HEY!! HURRY AND GET ON!
BUT... WHO ARE YOU?
I'M YOUR OLD SIDEKICK.
PUDDA PUDDA PUDDA KAPOWEE!
ONE SHOT SHOTGUN SHELL
POP
YOU ACCIDENTLY LEFT ME ON MARS 37 YEARS AGO (MY TIME).
SO I IMMEDIATELY STARTED TO WORK INVENTING A TIME MACHINE.
I QUICKLY REALIZED YOU WOULD END UP TRAPPED ON A FUTURISTIC EARTH.
IT'S TAKEN ME A LIFETIME OF CONSTANT LABOR, BUT I'M FINALLY ABLE TO RESCUE YOU.
GEE, THANKS

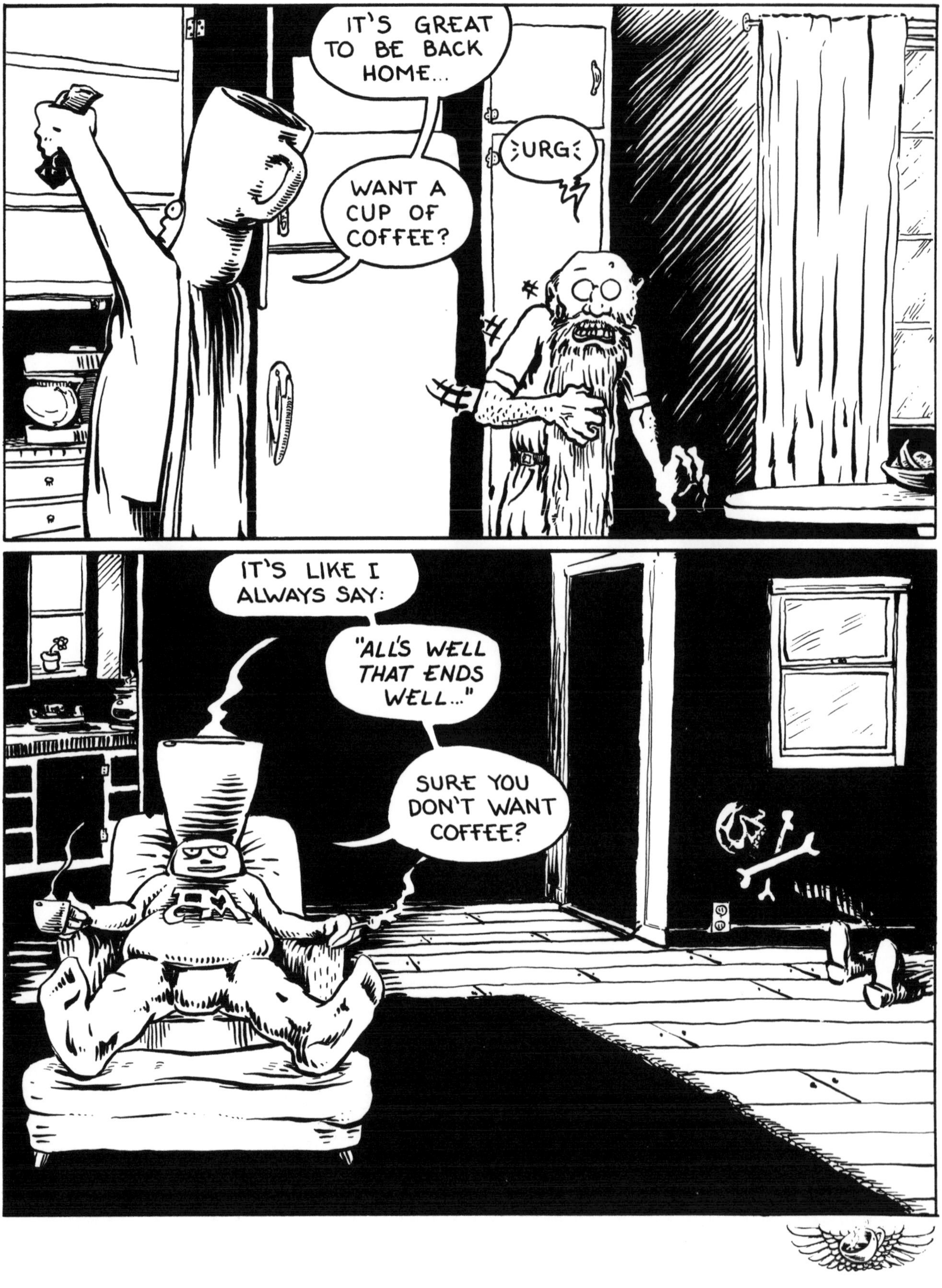
IT'S GREAT TO BE BACK HOME...
WANT A CUP OF COFFEE?
URG
IT'S LIKE I ALWAYS SAY:
"ALL'S WELL THAT ENDS WELL..."
SURE YOU DON'T WANT COFFEE?

TOO MUCH COFFEE MAN SAVES THE UNIVERSE

Meets his Coffee Maker, burns down Heaven, and fights a Martian

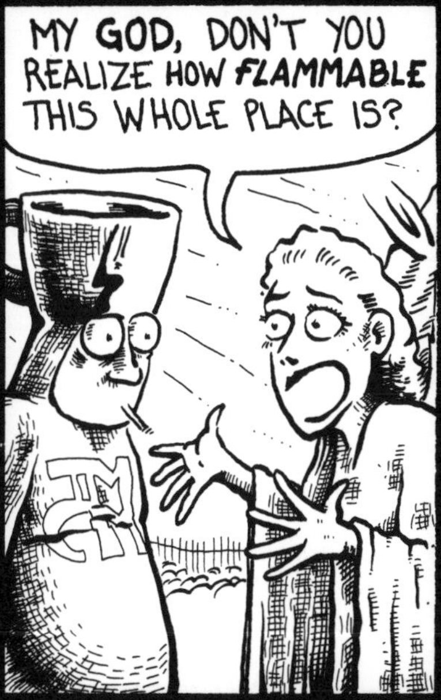
MY GOD, DON'T YOU REALIZE HOW FLAMMABLE THIS WHOLE PLACE IS?

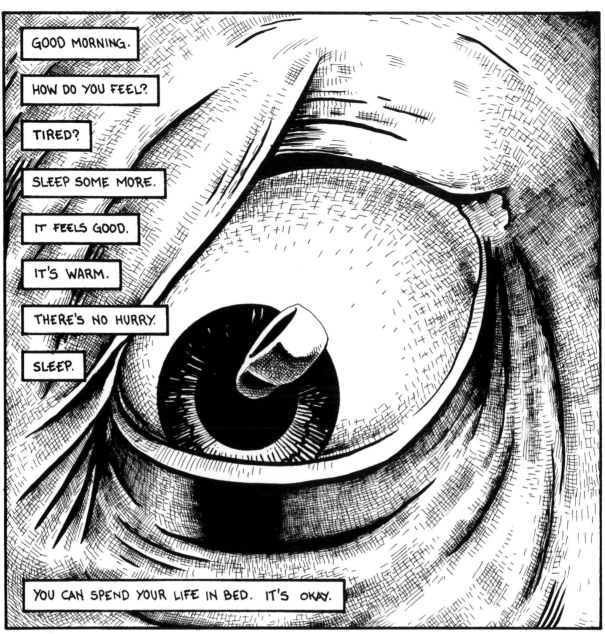

GOOD MORNING.

HOW DO YOU FEEL?

TIRED?

SLEEP SOME MORE.

IT FEELS GOOD.

IT'S WARM.

THERE'S NO HURRY.

SLEEP.

YOU CAN SPEND YOUR LIFE IN BED. IT'S OKAY.

ENOUGH INTERNAL DIALOGUE!

MUST... GET OUT OF BED.

UGH.

GRUMBLE GRUMBLE... I HATE THE MORNING.

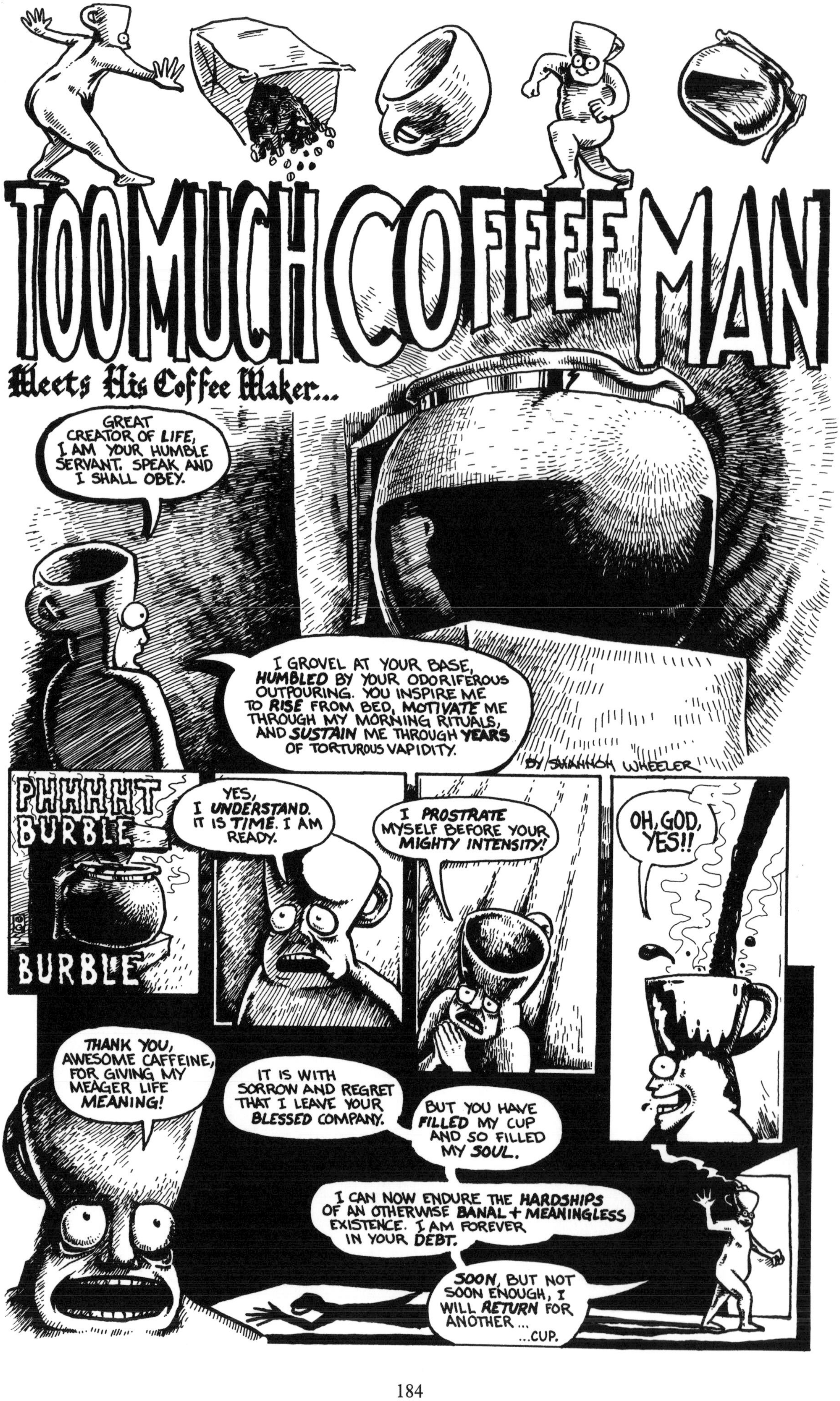
TOO MUCH COFFEE MAN
Meets His Coffee Maker...
GREAT CREATOR OF LIFE, I AM YOUR HUMBLE SERVANT. SPEAK AND I SHALL OBEY.
I GROVEL AT YOUR BASE, HUMBLED BY YOUR ODORIFEROUS OUTPOURING. YOU INSPIRE ME TO RISE FROM BED, MOTIVATE ME THROUGH MY MORNING RITUALS, AND SUSTAIN ME THROUGH YEARS OF TORTUROUS VAPIDITY.
BY SHANNON WHEELER
PHHHHT BURBLE
BURBLE
YES, I UNDERSTAND. IT IS TIME. I AM READY.
I PROSTRATE MYSELF BEFORE YOUR MIGHTY INTENSITY!
OH, GOD, YES!!
THANK YOU, AWESOME CAFFEINE, FOR GIVING MY MEAGER LIFE MEANING!
IT IS WITH SORROW AND REGRET THAT I LEAVE YOUR BLESSED COMPANY.
BUT YOU HAVE FILLED MY CUP AND SO FILLED MY SOUL.
I CAN NOW ENDURE THE HARDSHIPS OF AN OTHERWISE BANAL + MEANINGLESS EXISTENCE. I AM FOREVER IN YOUR DEBT.
SOON, BUT NOT SOON ENOUGH, I WILL RETURN FOR ANOTHER ...
...CUP.

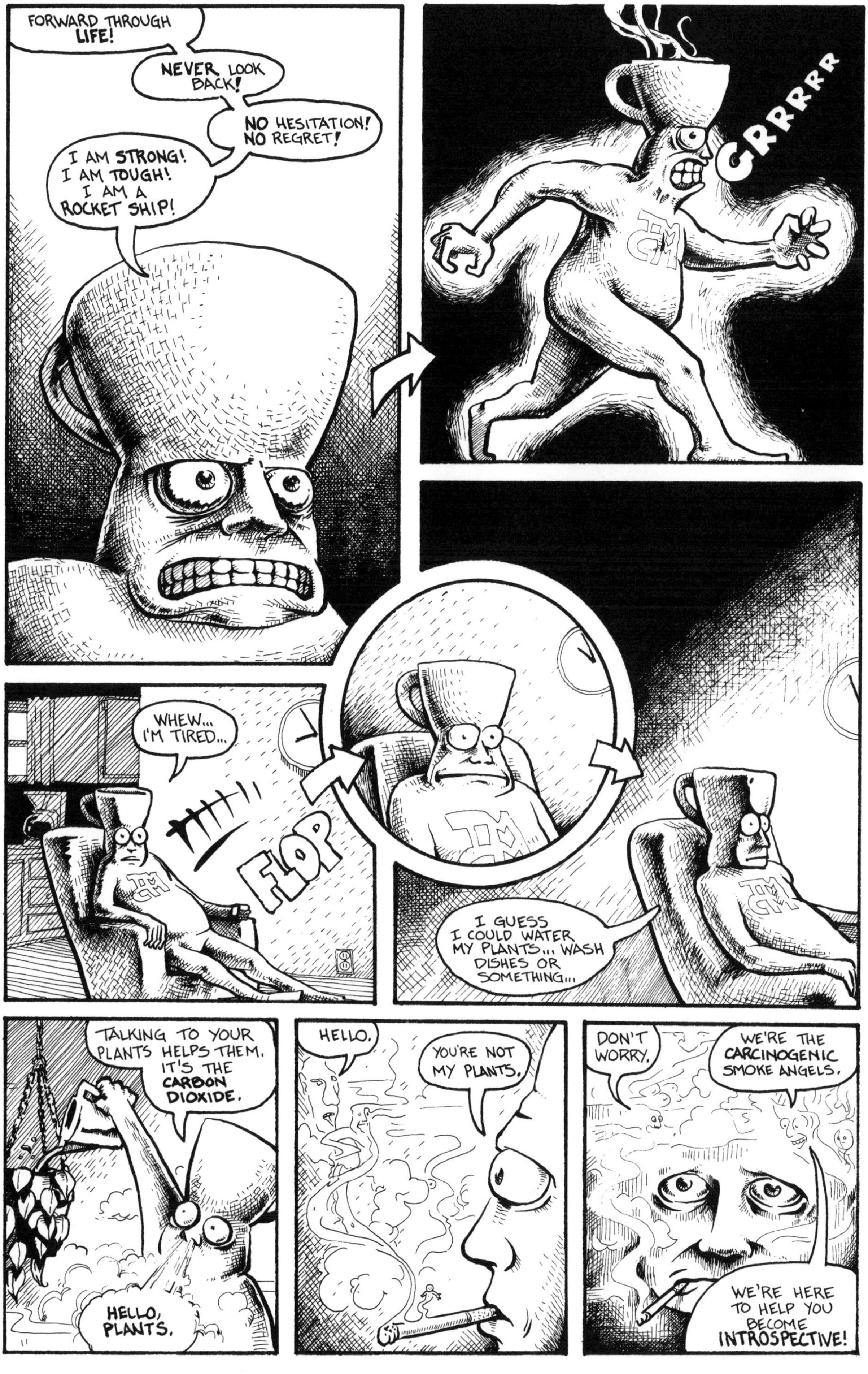
FORWARD THROUGH LIFE!
NEVER LOOK BACK!
NO HESITATION! NO REGRET!
I AM STRONG! I AM TOUGH! I AM A ROCKET SHIP!
GRRRRR
WHEW... I'M TIRED...
FLOP
I GUESS I COULD WATER MY PLANTS... WASH DISHES OR SOMETHING...
TALKING TO YOUR PLANTS HELPS THEM. IT'S THE CARBON DIOXIDE.
HELLO, PLANTS.
HELLO.
YOU'RE NOT MY PLANTS.
DON'T WORRY.
WE'RE THE CARCINOGENIC SMOKE ANGELS.
WE'RE HERE TO HELP YOU BECOME INTROSPECTIVE!

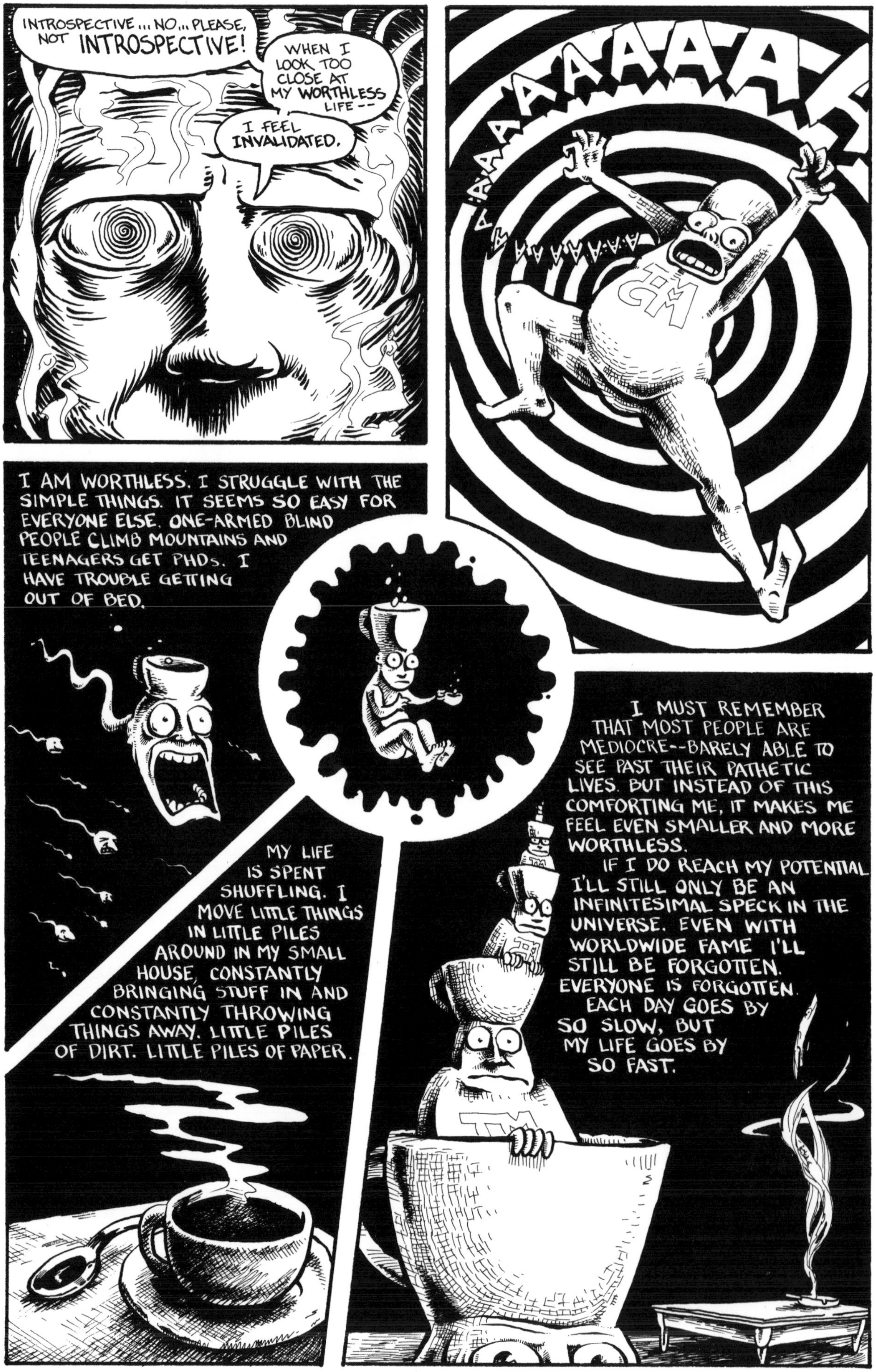
INTROSPECTIVE... NO... PLEASE, NOT INTROSPECTIVE!
WHEN I LOOK TOO CLOSE AT MY WORTHLESS LIFE --
I FEEL INVALIDATED.
AAAAAAAAAAAAAAAAAK
I AM WORTHLESS. I STRUGGLE WITH THE SIMPLE THINGS. IT SEEMS SO EASY FOR EVERYONE ELSE. ONE-ARMED BLIND PEOPLE CLIMB MOUNTAINS AND TEENAGERS GET PHDs. I HAVE TROUBLE GETTING OUT OF BED.
MY LIFE IS SPENT SHUFFLING. I MOVE LITTLE THINGS IN LITTLE PILES AROUND IN MY SMALL HOUSE, CONSTANTLY BRINGING STUFF IN AND CONSTANTLY THROWING THINGS AWAY. LITTLE PILES OF DIRT. LITTLE PILES OF PAPER.
I MUST REMEMBER THAT MOST PEOPLE ARE MEDIOCRE--BARELY ABLE TO SEE PAST THEIR PATHETIC LIVES. BUT INSTEAD OF THIS COMFORTING ME, IT MAKES ME FEEL EVEN SMALLER AND MORE WORTHLESS.
IF I DO REACH MY POTENTIAL I'LL STILL ONLY BE AN INFINITESIMAL SPECK IN THE UNIVERSE. EVEN WITH WORLDWIDE FAME I'LL STILL BE FORGOTTEN. EVERYONE IS FORGOTTEN.
EACH DAY GOES BY SO SLOW, BUT MY LIFE GOES BY SO FAST.

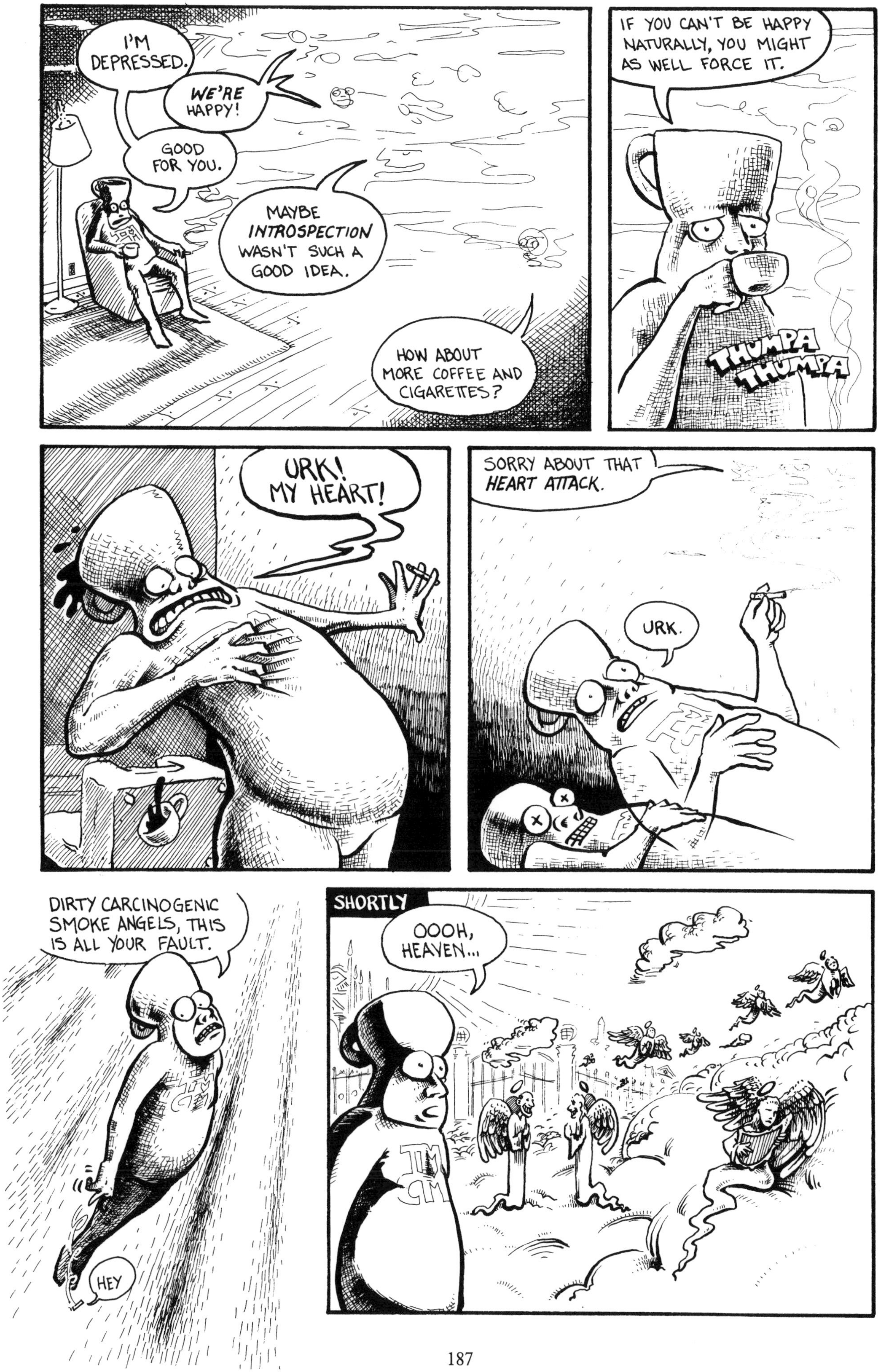
I'M DEPRESSED.
WE'RE HAPPY!
GOOD FOR YOU.
MAYBE INTROSPECTION WASN'T SUCH A GOOD IDEA.
HOW ABOUT MORE COFFEE AND CIGARETTES?
IF YOU CAN'T BE HAPPY NATURALLY, YOU MIGHT AS WELL FORCE IT.
THUMPA THUMPA
URK! MY HEART!
SORRY ABOUT THAT HEART ATTACK.
URK.
DIRTY CARCINOGENIC SMOKE ANGELS, THIS IS ALL YOUR FAULT.
HEY
SHORTLY
OOOH, HEAVEN...

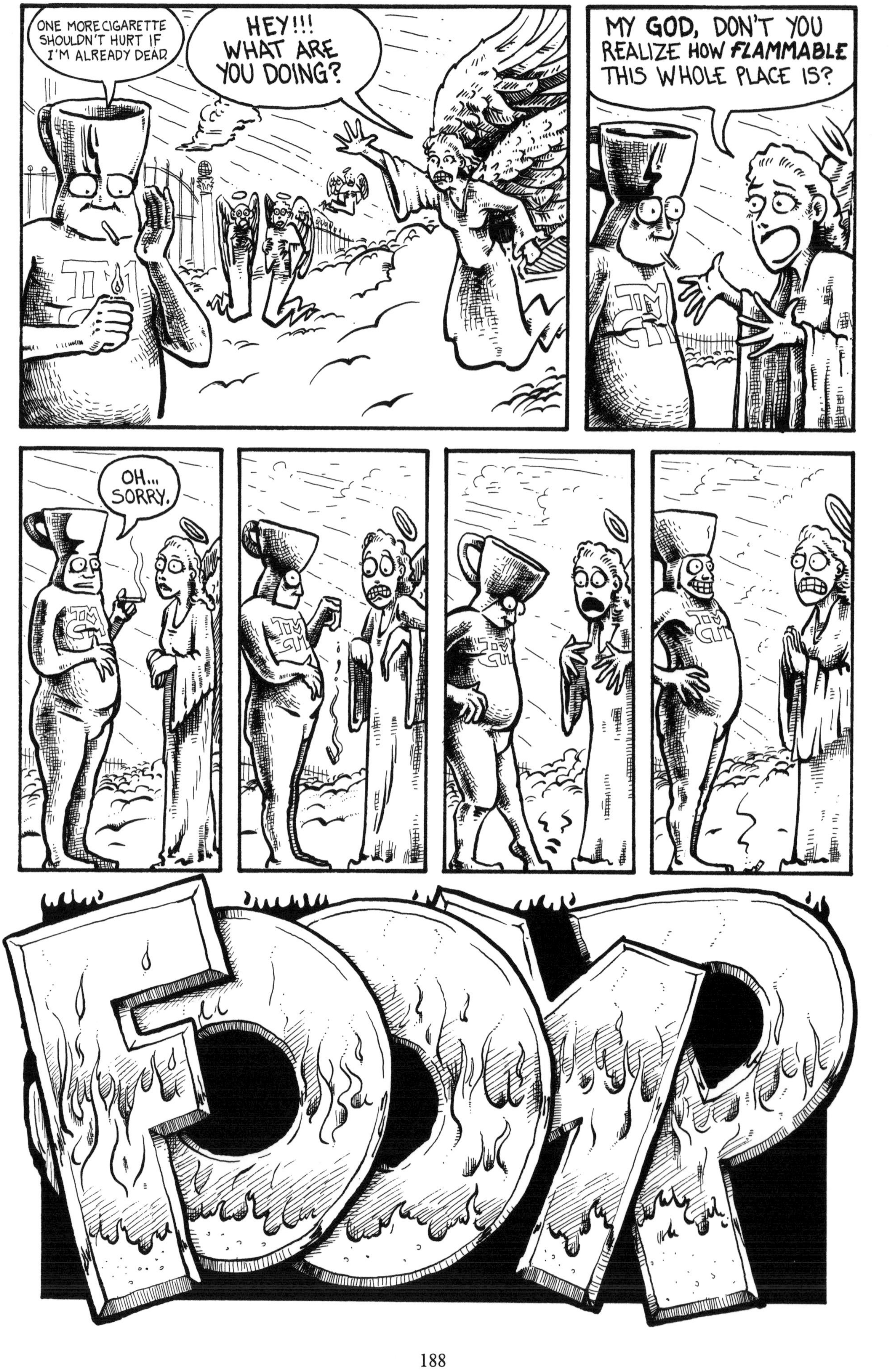
ONE MORE CIGARETTE SHOULDN'T HURT IF I'M ALREADY DEAD.
HEY!!! WHAT ARE YOU DOING?
MY GOD, DON'T YOU REALIZE HOW FLAMMABLE THIS WHOLE PLACE IS?
OH... SORRY.
FOOMP

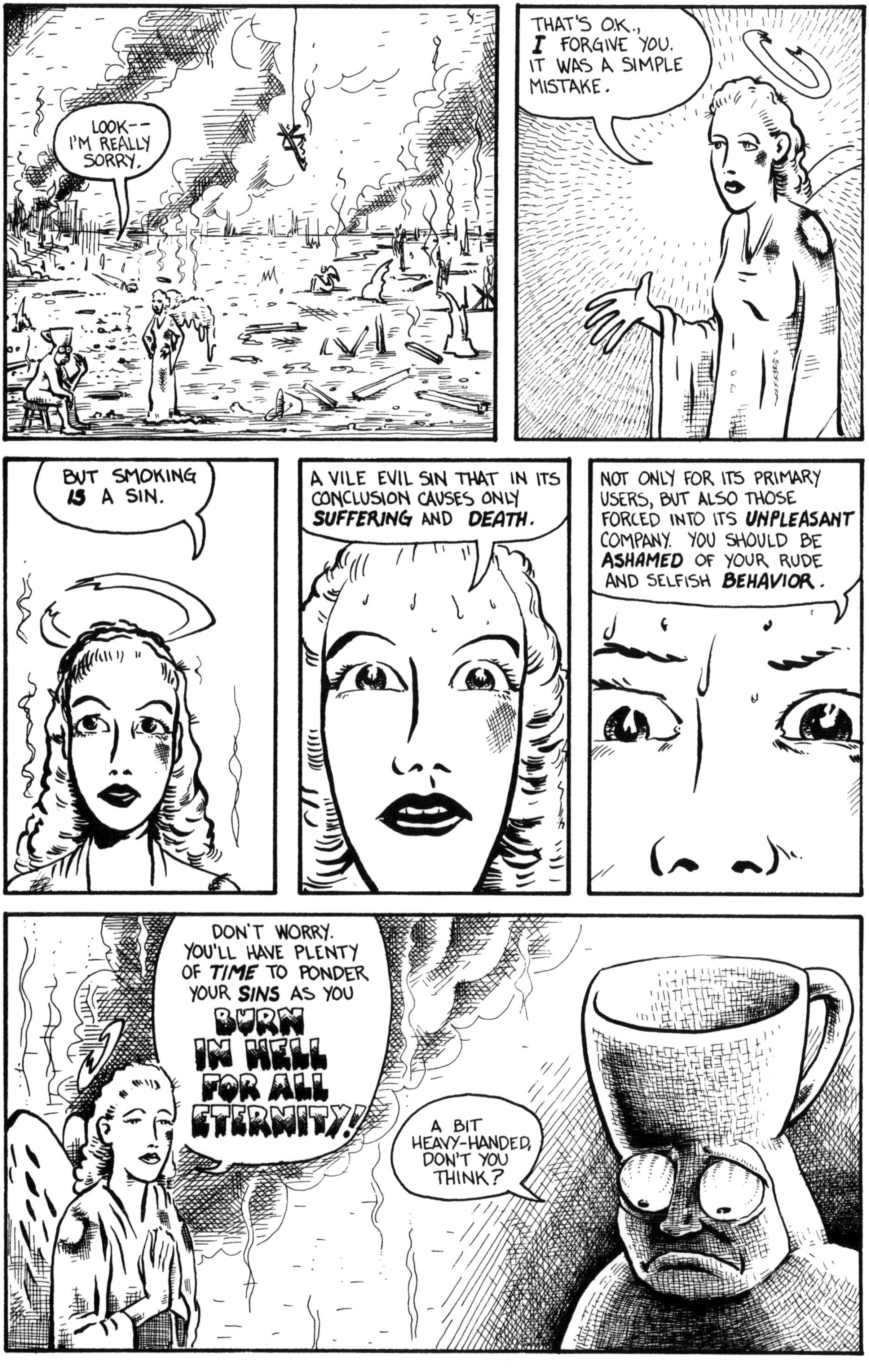
LOOK-- I'M REALLY SORRY.
THAT'S O.K., I FORGIVE YOU. IT WAS A SIMPLE MISTAKE.
BUT SMOKING IS A SIN.
A VILE EVIL SIN THAT IN ITS CONCLUSION CAUSES ONLY SUFFERING AND DEATH.
NOT ONLY FOR ITS PRIMARY USERS, BUT ALSO THOSE FORCED INTO ITS UNPLEASANT COMPANY. YOU SHOULD BE ASHAMED OF YOUR RUDE AND SELFISH BEHAVIOR.
DON'T WORRY. YOU'LL HAVE PLENTY OF TIME TO PONDER YOUR SINS AS YOU BURN IN HELL FOR ALL ETERNITY!
A BIT HEAVY-HANDED, DON'T YOU THINK?

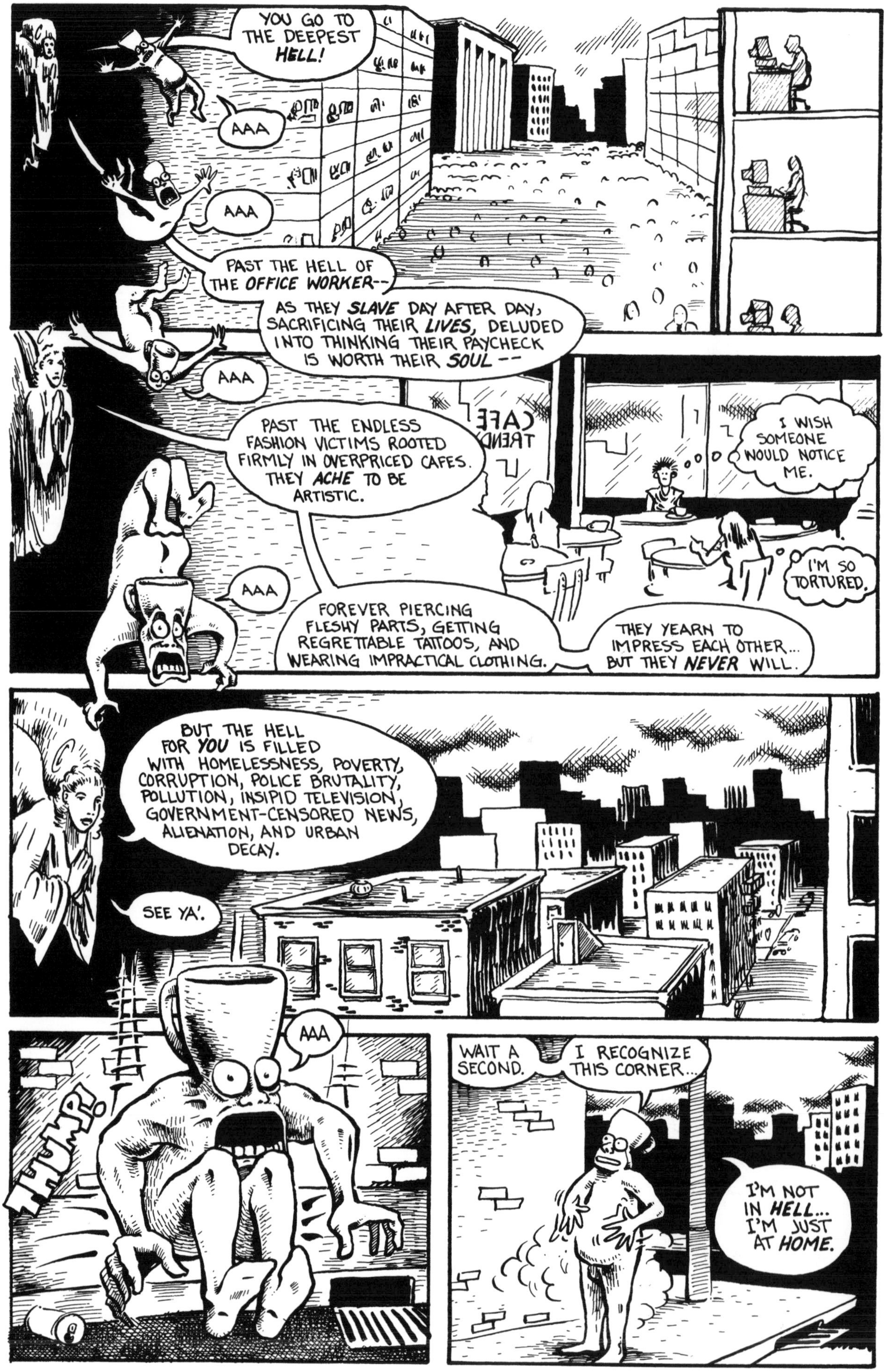
YOU GO TO THE DEEPEST HELL!
AAA
AAA
PAST THE HELL OF THE OFFICE WORKER--
AS THEY SLAVE DAY AFTER DAY, SACRIFICING THEIR LIVES, DELUDED INTO THINKING THEIR PAYCHECK IS WORTH THEIR SOUL --
AAA
PAST THE ENDLESS FASHION VICTIMS ROOTED FIRMLY IN OVERPRICED CAFES. THEY ACHE TO BE ARTISTIC.
CAFE TRENDY
I WISH SOMEONE WOULD NOTICE ME.
I'M SO TORTURED.
AAA
FOREVER PIERCING FLESHY PARTS, GETTING REGRETTABLE TATTOOS, AND WEARING IMPRACTICAL CLOTHING.
THEY YEARN TO IMPRESS EACH OTHER... BUT THEY NEVER WILL.
BUT THE HELL FOR YOU IS FILLED WITH HOMELESSNESS, POVERTY, CORRUPTION, POLICE BRUTALITY, POLLUTION, INSIPID TELEVISION, GOVERNMENT-CENSORED NEWS, ALIENATION, AND URBAN DECAY.
SEE YA'.
AAA
THUMP!
WAIT A SECOND.
I RECOGNIZE THIS CORNER...
I'M NOT IN HELL... I'M JUST AT HOME.

CHAPTER TWO

IN THE LAST EPISODE, *TOO MUCH COFFEE MAN* (TMCM)
MET THE CARCINOGENIC SMOKE ANGELS. THEY HELPED
HIM TAKE A LONG LOOK AT HIS PATHETIC LIFE. WHEN
HE TRIED TO CHEER HIMSELF UP FROM THE RESULTING
DEPRESSION, HE DIED OF A HEART ATTACK. AND
AFTER MANY PAGES OF HILARIOUS, SLAPSTICK
ACTION, *TMCM* FINDS HIMSELF HOME
AGAIN. WE NOW PICK UP THE
NARRATIVE FROM WHERE
WE LAST LEFT IT.

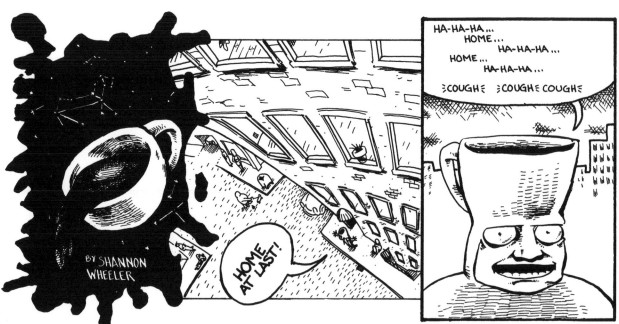

BY SHANNON WHEELER

HOME AT LAST!

HA-HA-HA...
HOME...
HA-HA-HA...
HOME...
HA-HA-HA...
≡COUGH≡ ≡COUGH≡ COUGH≡

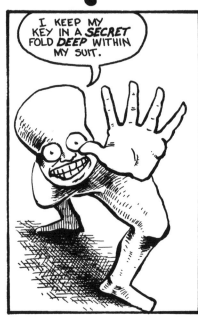

I KEEP MY KEY IN A *SECRET* FOLD *DEEP* WITHIN MY SUIT.

OH, MAN. *LOOK* AT THAT GIANT PILE OF *MAIL*. I PROBABLY HAVE A *TON* OF *BILLS*!

I'LL DEAL WITH THEM *LATER*.

FIRST, I MUST TAKE CARE OF THE *IMPORTANT* THINGS ...LIKE WATER MY THIRSTY PLANTS.

FEED THE *CAT*!

CAT

DO THE DISHES.

ALPHABETIZE MY VINYL COLLECTION.

VACUUM.

ANYTHING TO AVOID PAYING BILLS.

FILE SOME COMICS.

THE *KEY* TO PRODUCTIVITY IS TO *ROTATE* YOUR AVOIDANCE TECHNIQUES.

AH. A PHONE MESSAGE, SOMEONE *LOVES* ME.

BLINK BLINK

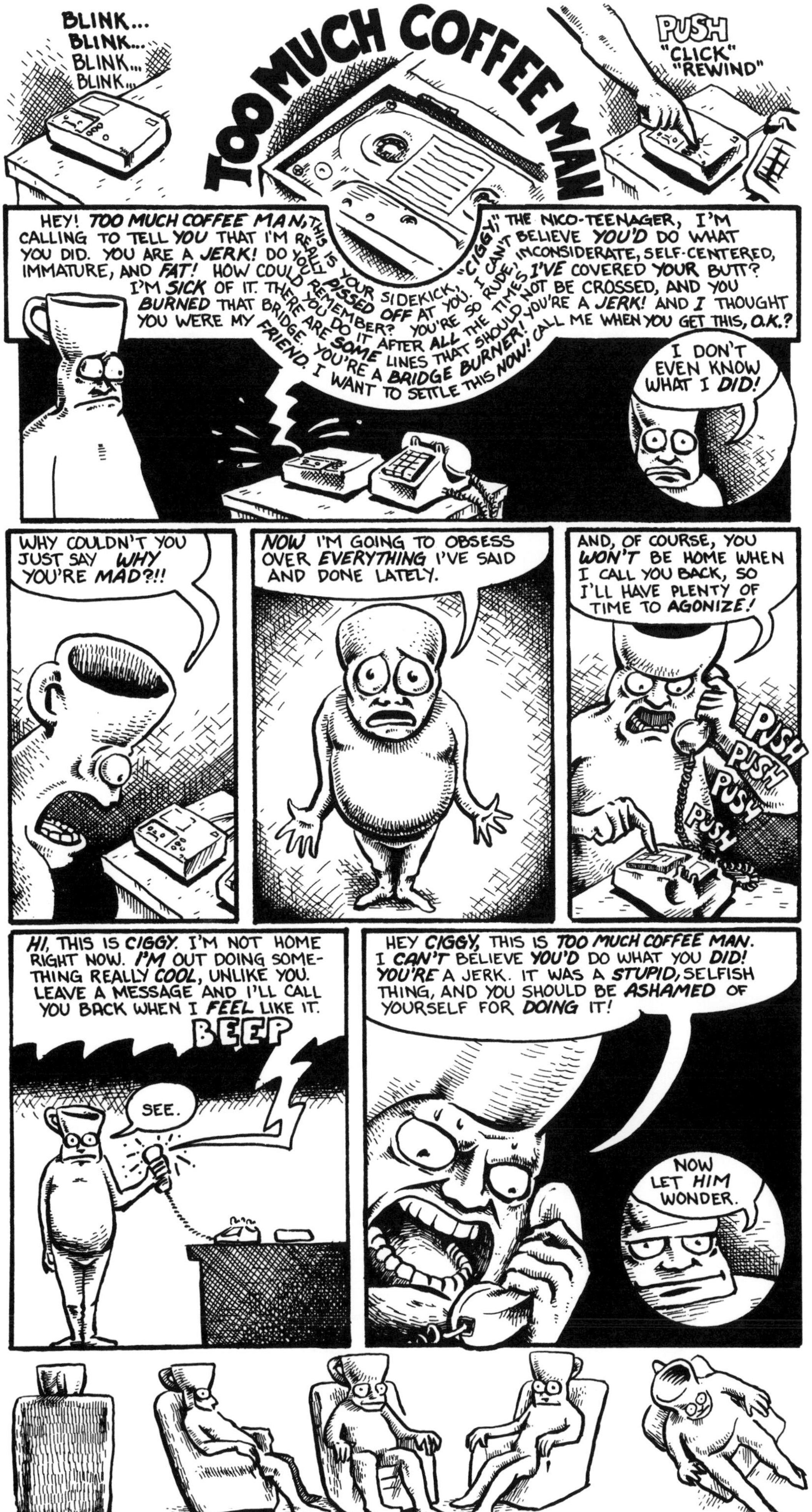
BLINK...
BLINK...
BLINK...
BLINK...
TOO MUCH COFFEE MAN
PUSH
"CLICK"
"REWIND"
HEY! TOO MUCH COFFEE MAN, THIS IS YOUR SIDEKICK, "CIGGY," THE NICO-TEENAGER, I'M CALLING TO TELL YOU THAT I'M REALLY PISSED OFF AT YOU. I CAN'T BELIEVE YOU'D DO WHAT YOU DID. YOU ARE A JERK! DO YOU REMEMBER? YOU'RE SO RUDE, INCONSIDERATE, SELF-CENTERED, IMMATURE, AND FAT! HOW COULD YOU DO IT AFTER ALL THE TIMES I'VE COVERED YOUR BUTT? I'M SICK OF IT. THERE ARE SOME LINES THAT SHOULD NOT BE CROSSED, AND YOU BURNED THAT BRIDGE. YOU'RE A BRIDGE BURNER! YOU'RE A JERK! AND I THOUGHT YOU WERE MY FRIEND. I WANT TO SETTLE THIS NOW! CALL ME WHEN YOU GET THIS, O.K.?
I DON'T EVEN KNOW WHAT I DID!
WHY COULDN'T YOU JUST SAY WHY YOU'RE MAD?!!
NOW I'M GOING TO OBSESS OVER EVERYTHING I'VE SAID AND DONE LATELY.
AND, OF COURSE, YOU WON'T BE HOME WHEN I CALL YOU BACK, SO I'LL HAVE PLENTY OF TIME TO AGONIZE!
PUSH
PUSH
PUSH
PUSH
HI, THIS IS CIGGY. I'M NOT HOME RIGHT NOW. I'M OUT DOING SOMETHING REALLY COOL, UNLIKE YOU. LEAVE A MESSAGE AND I'LL CALL YOU BACK WHEN I FEEL LIKE IT.
BEEP
SEE.
HEY CIGGY, THIS IS TOO MUCH COFFEE MAN. I CAN'T BELIEVE YOU'D DO WHAT YOU DID! YOU'RE A JERK. IT WAS A STUPID, SELFISH THING, AND YOU SHOULD BE ASHAMED OF YOURSELF FOR DOING IT!
NOW LET HIM WONDER.

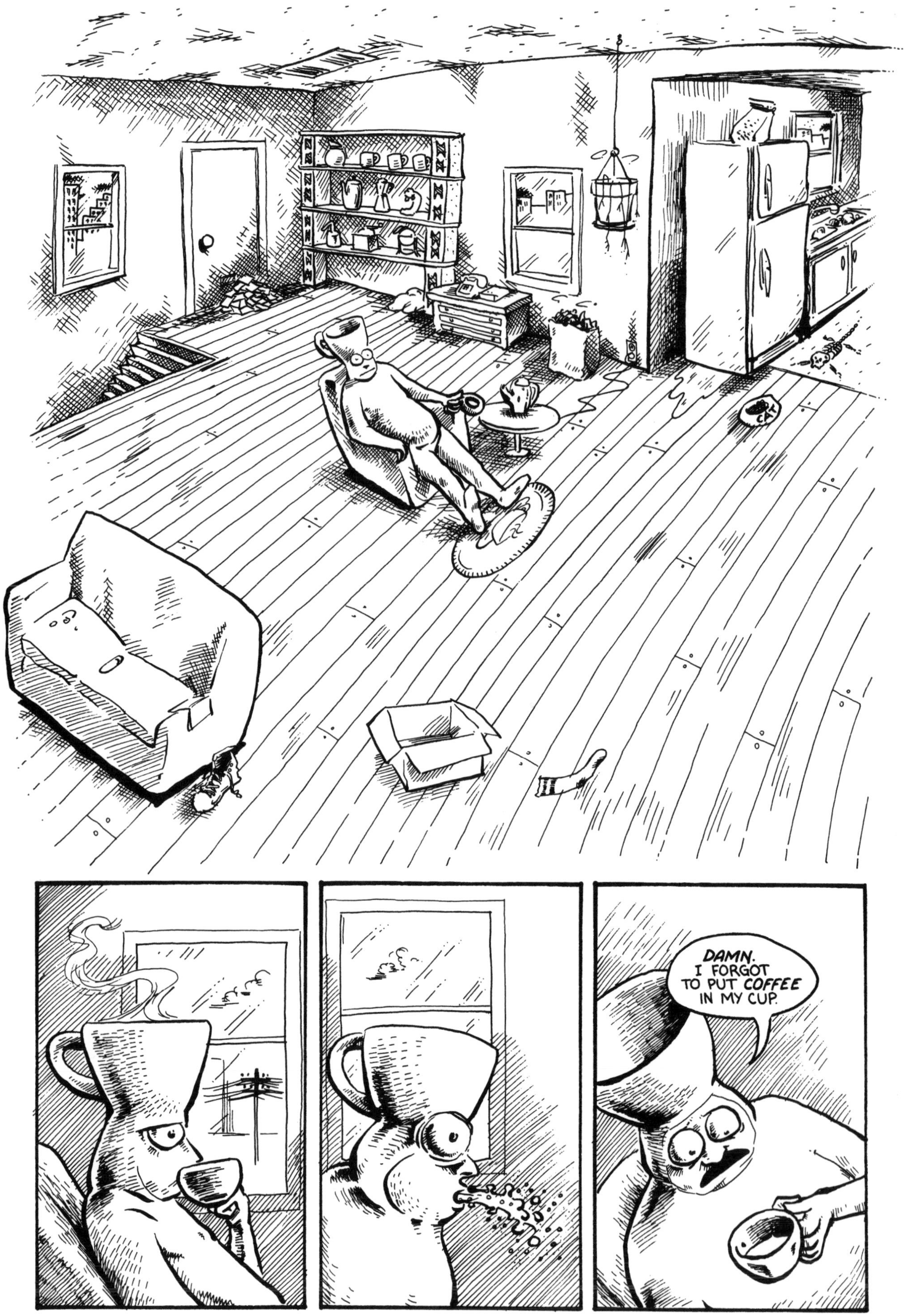
CAT
DAMN. I FORGOT TO PUT COFFEE IN MY CUP.

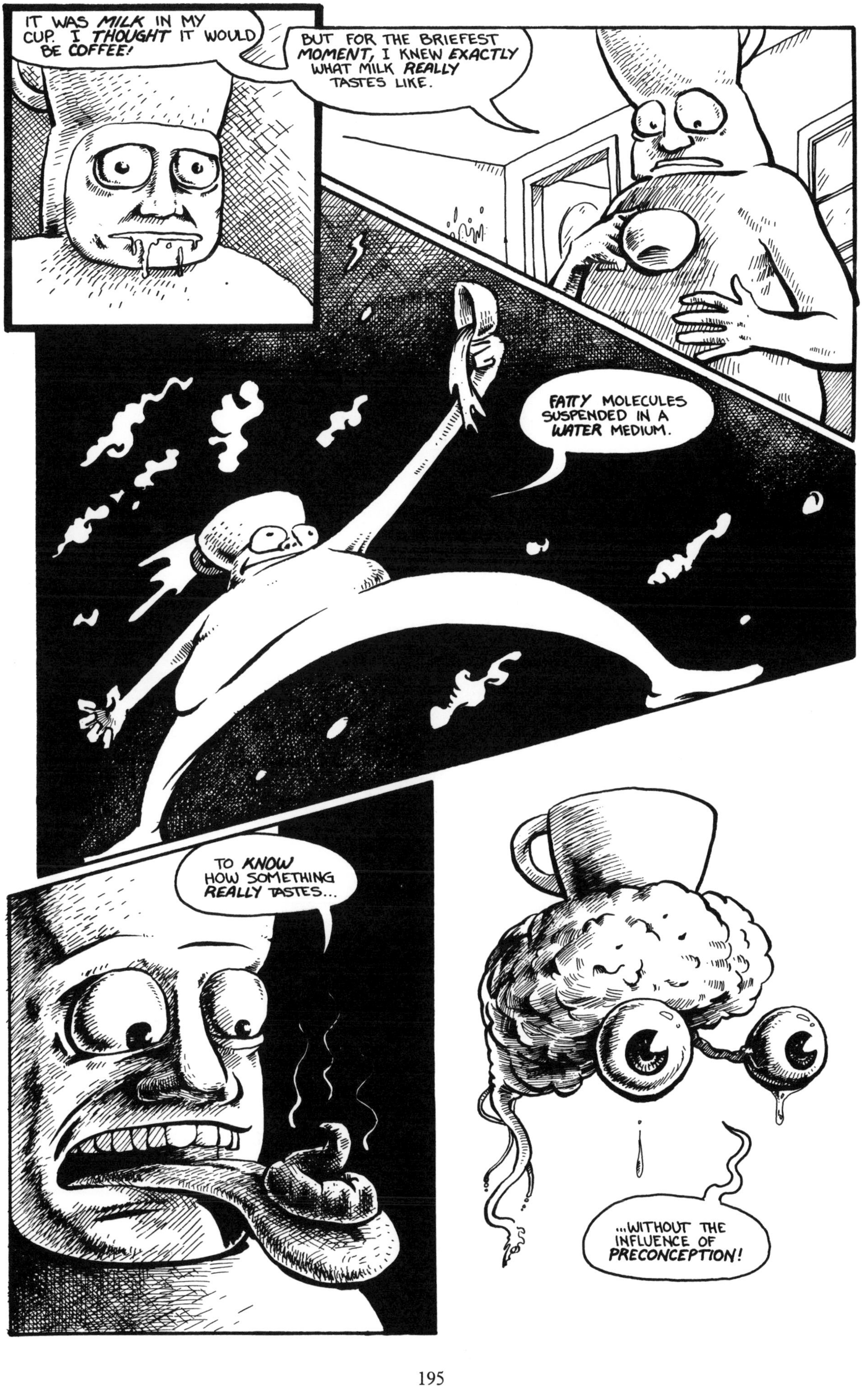
IT WAS MILK IN MY CUP. I THOUGHT IT WOULD BE COFFEE!
BUT FOR THE BRIEFEST MOMENT, I KNEW EXACTLY WHAT MILK REALLY TASTES LIKE.
FATTY MOLECULES SUSPENDED IN A WATER MEDIUM.
TO KNOW HOW SOMETHING REALLY TASTES...
...WITHOUT THE INFLUENCE OF PRECONCEPTION!

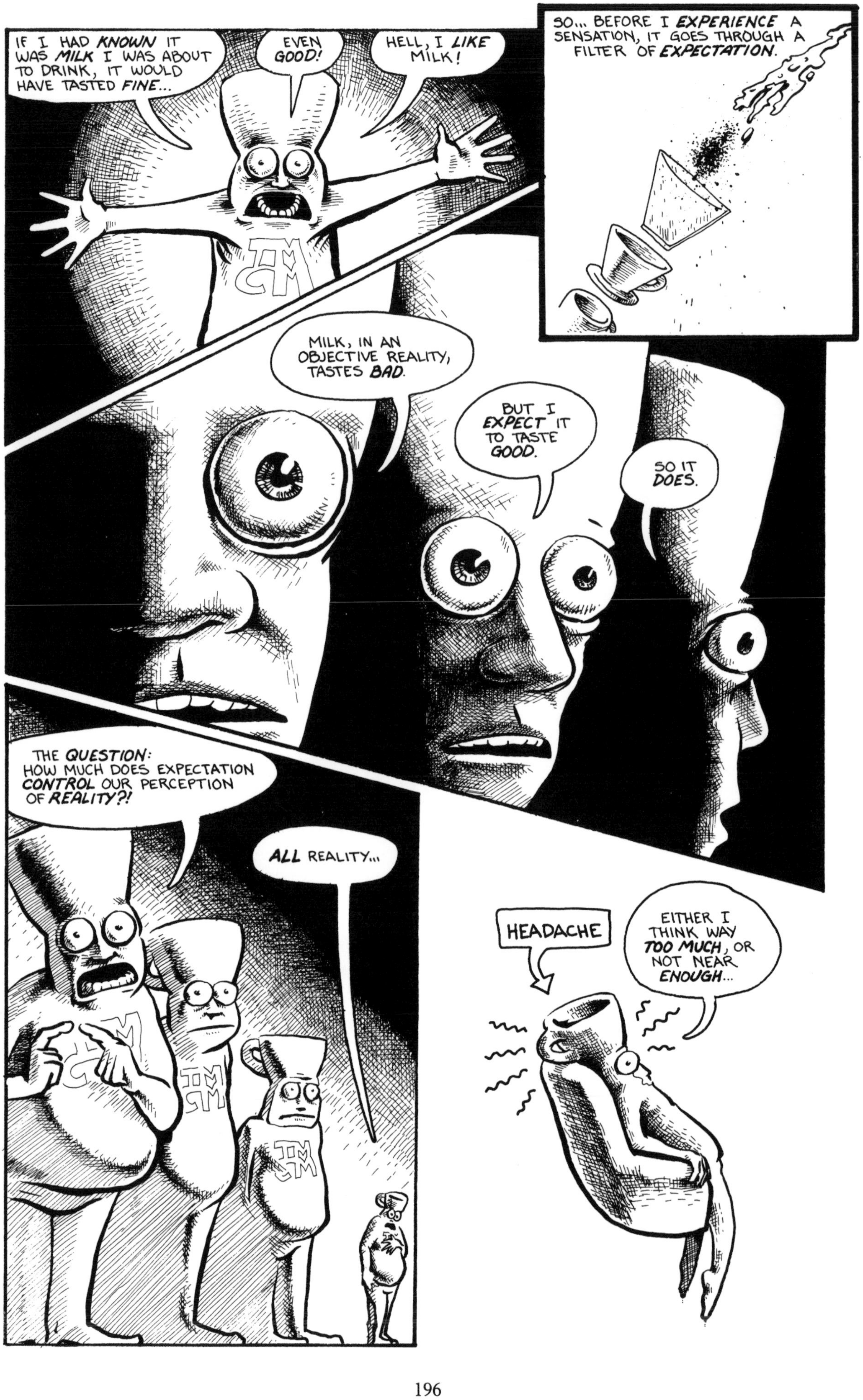
IF I HAD KNOWN IT WAS MILK I WAS ABOUT TO DRINK, IT WOULD HAVE TASTED FINE...
EVEN GOOD!
HELL, I LIKE MILK!
SO... BEFORE I EXPERIENCE A SENSATION, IT GOES THROUGH A FILTER OF EXPECTATION.
MILK, IN AN OBJECTIVE REALITY, TASTES BAD.
BUT I EXPECT IT TO TASTE GOOD.
SO IT DOES.
THE QUESTION: HOW MUCH DOES EXPECTATION CONTROL OUR PERCEPTION OF REALITY?!
ALL REALITY...
HEADACHE
EITHER I THINK WAY TOO MUCH, OR NOT NEAR ENOUGH...

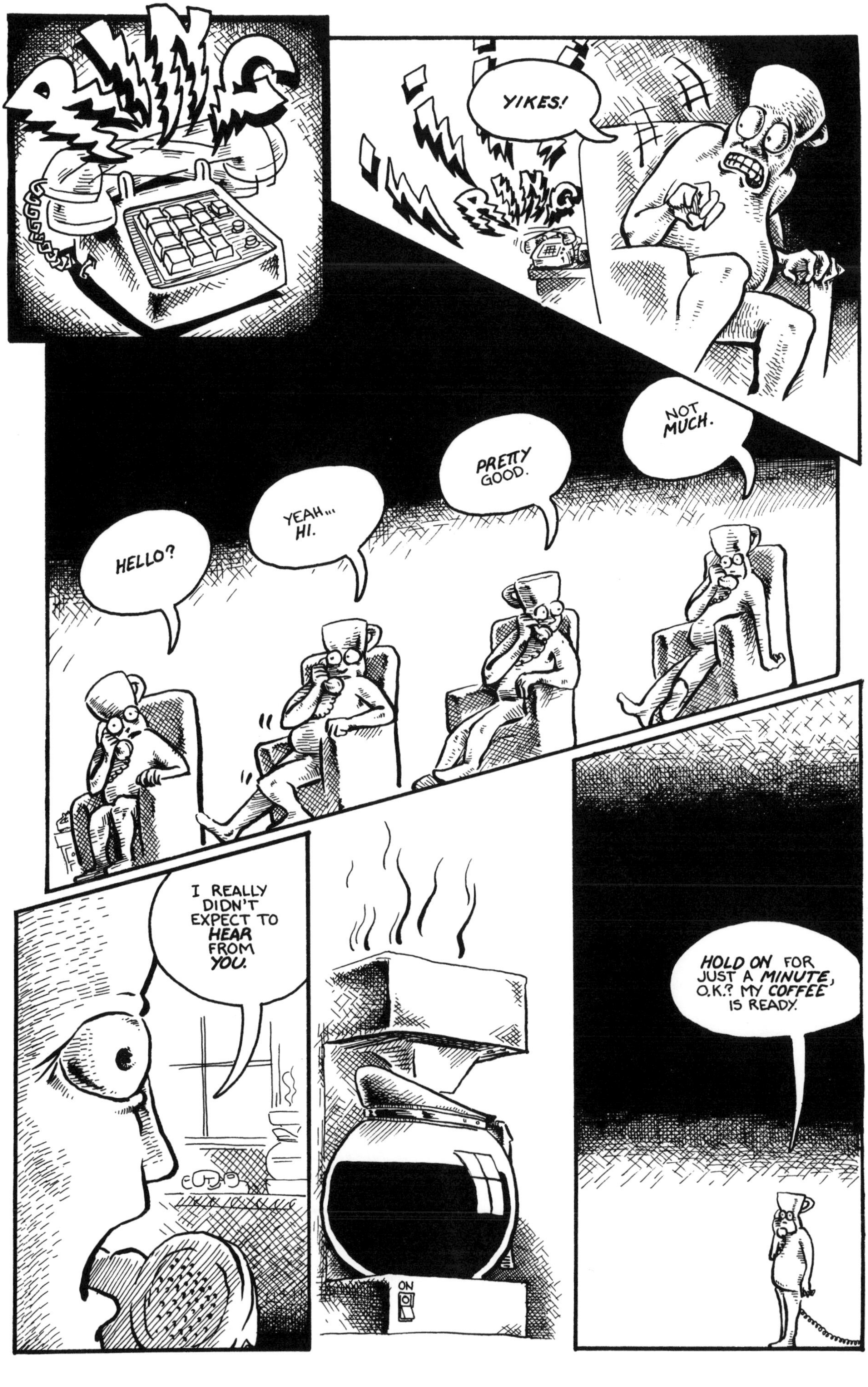
RING
YIKES!
RING
HELLO?
YEAH... HI.
PRETTY GOOD.
NOT MUCH.
I REALLY DIDN'T EXPECT TO HEAR FROM YOU.
ON
HOLD ON FOR JUST A MINUTE, O.K.? MY COFFEE IS READY.

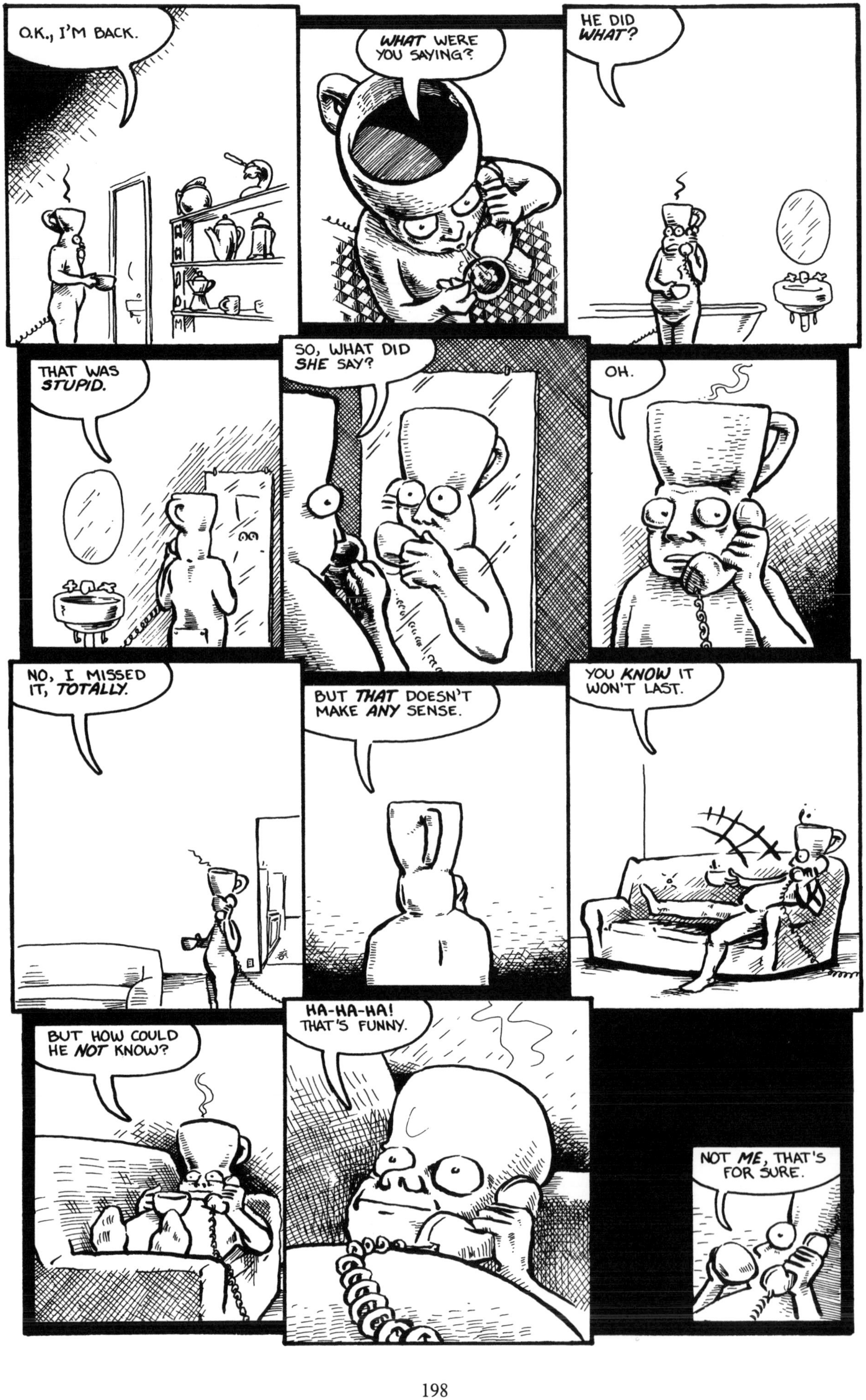
O.K., I'M BACK.
WHAT WERE YOU SAYING?
HE DID WHAT?
THAT WAS STUPID.
SO, WHAT DID SHE SAY?
OH.
NO, I MISSED IT, TOTALLY.
BUT THAT DOESN'T MAKE ANY SENSE.
YOU KNOW IT WON'T LAST.
BUT HOW COULD HE NOT KNOW?
HA-HA-HA! THAT'S FUNNY.
NOT ME, THAT'S FOR SURE.

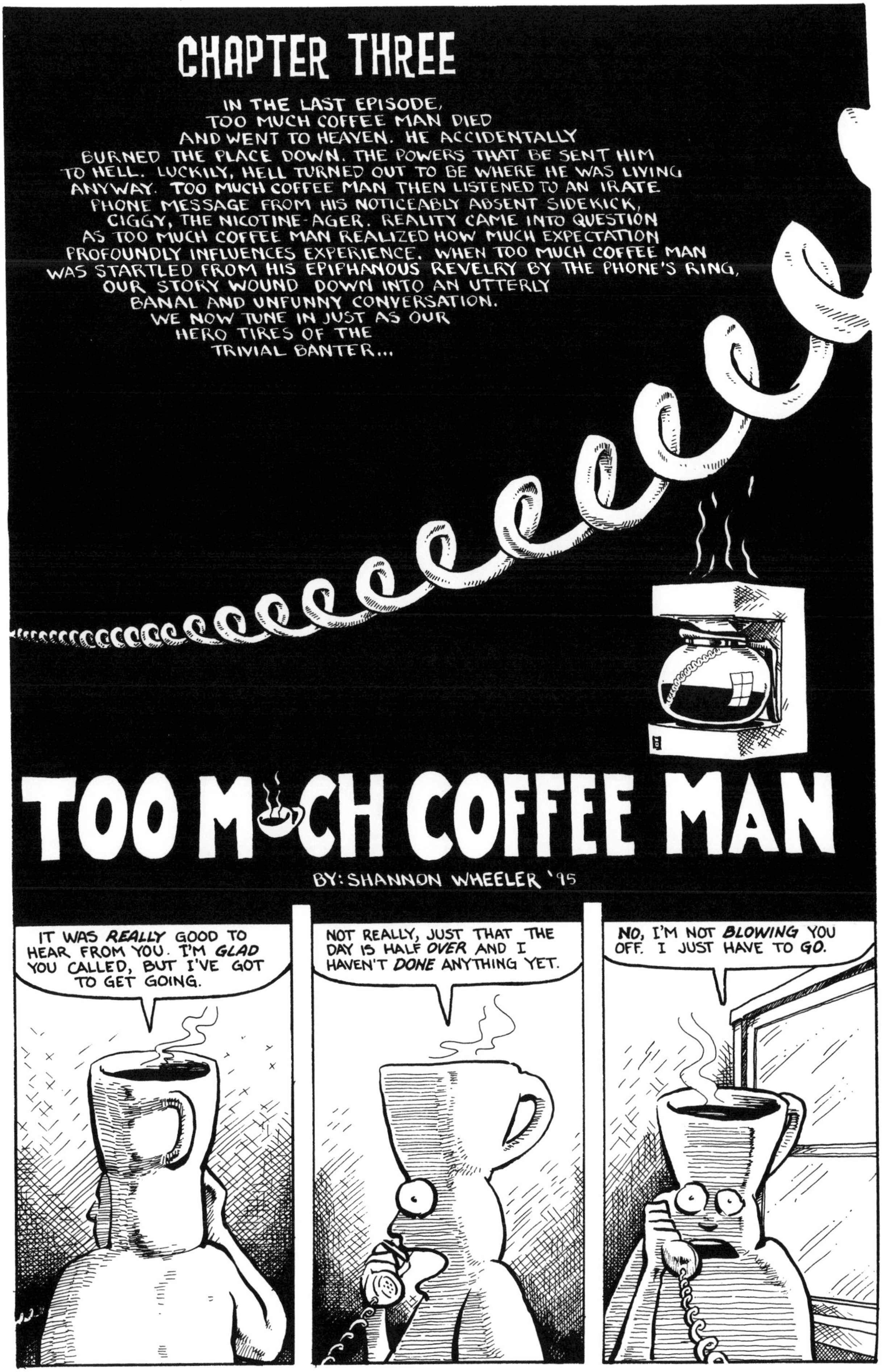
CHAPTER THREE
IN THE LAST EPISODE, TOO MUCH COFFEE MAN DIED AND WENT TO HEAVEN. HE ACCIDENTALLY BURNED THE PLACE DOWN. THE POWERS THAT BE SENT HIM TO HELL. LUCKILY, HELL TURNED OUT TO BE WHERE HE WAS LIVING ANYWAY. TOO MUCH COFFEE MAN THEN LISTENED TO AN IRATE PHONE MESSAGE FROM HIS NOTICEABLY ABSENT SIDEKICK, CIGGY, THE NICOTINE-AGER. REALITY CAME INTO QUESTION AS TOO MUCH COFFEE MAN REALIZED HOW MUCH EXPECTATION PROFOUNDLY INFLUENCES EXPERIENCE. WHEN TOO MUCH COFFEE MAN WAS STARTLED FROM HIS EPIPHANOUS REVELRY BY THE PHONE'S RING, OUR STORY WOUND DOWN INTO AN UTTERLY BANAL AND UNFUNNY CONVERSATION. WE NOW TUNE IN JUST AS OUR HERO TIRES OF THE TRIVIAL BANTER...
TOO MUCH COFFEE MAN
BY: SHANNON WHEELER '95
IT WAS REALLY GOOD TO HEAR FROM YOU. I'M GLAD YOU CALLED, BUT I'VE GOT TO GET GOING.
NOT REALLY, JUST THAT THE DAY IS HALF OVER AND I HAVEN'T DONE ANYTHING YET.
NO, I'M NOT BLOWING YOU OFF. I JUST HAVE TO GO.

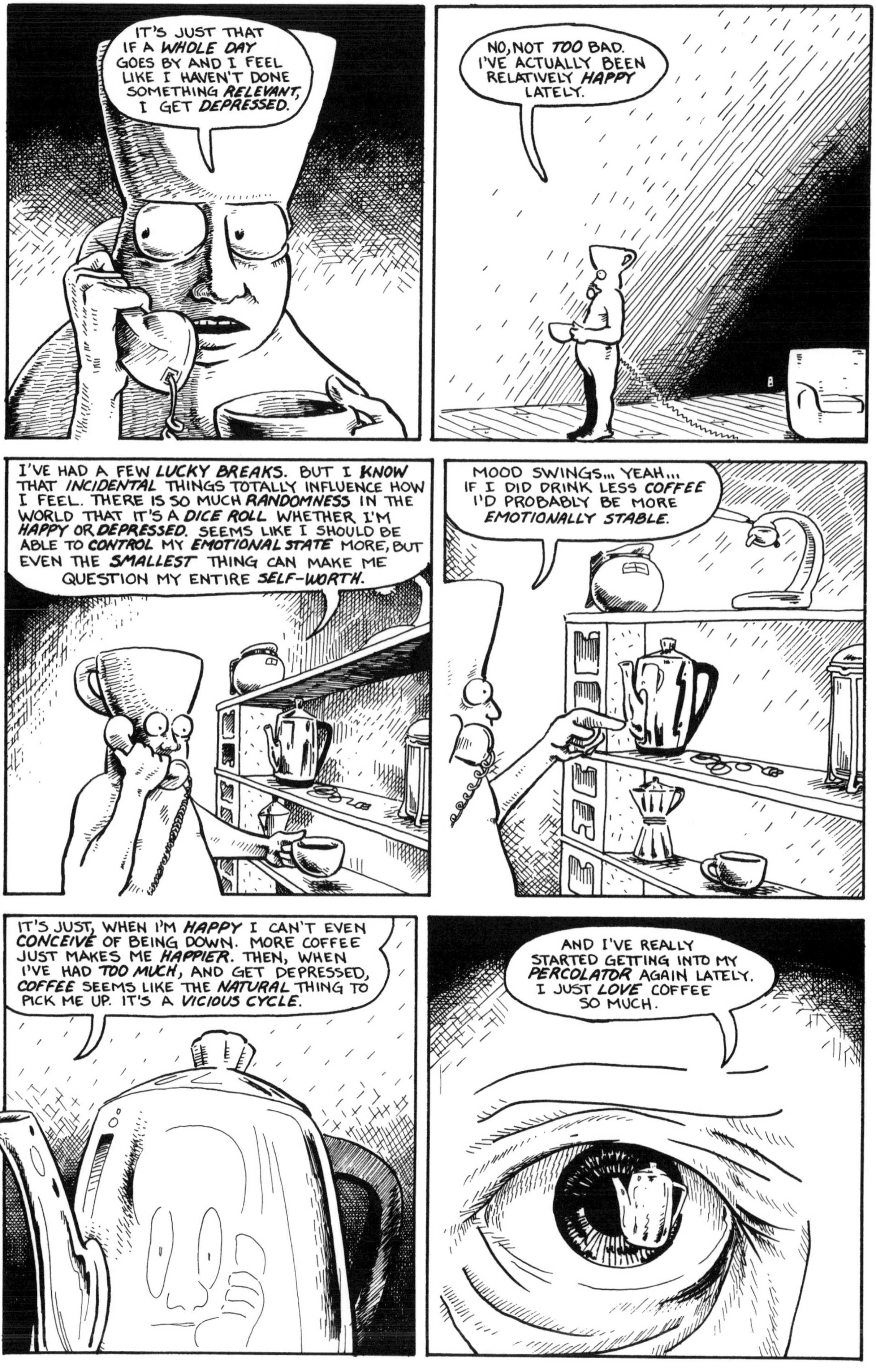
IT'S JUST THAT IF A WHOLE DAY GOES BY AND I FEEL LIKE I HAVEN'T DONE SOMETHING RELEVANT, I GET DEPRESSED.
NO, NOT TOO BAD. I'VE ACTUALLY BEEN RELATIVELY HAPPY LATELY.
I'VE HAD A FEW LUCKY BREAKS. BUT I KNOW THAT INCIDENTAL THINGS TOTALLY INFLUENCE HOW I FEEL. THERE IS SO MUCH RANDOMNESS IN THE WORLD THAT IT'S A DICE ROLL WHETHER I'M HAPPY OR DEPRESSED. SEEMS LIKE I SHOULD BE ABLE TO CONTROL MY EMOTIONAL STATE MORE, BUT EVEN THE SMALLEST THING CAN MAKE ME QUESTION MY ENTIRE SELF-WORTH.
MOOD SWINGS... YEAH... IF I DID DRINK LESS COFFEE I'D PROBABLY BE MORE EMOTIONALLY STABLE.
IT'S JUST, WHEN I'M HAPPY I CAN'T EVEN CONCEIVE OF BEING DOWN. MORE COFFEE JUST MAKES ME HAPPIER. THEN, WHEN I'VE HAD TOO MUCH, AND GET DEPRESSED, COFFEE SEEMS LIKE THE NATURAL THING TO PICK ME UP. IT'S A VICIOUS CYCLE.
AND I'VE REALLY STARTED GETTING INTO MY PERCOLATOR AGAIN LATELY. I JUST LOVE COFFEE SO MUCH.

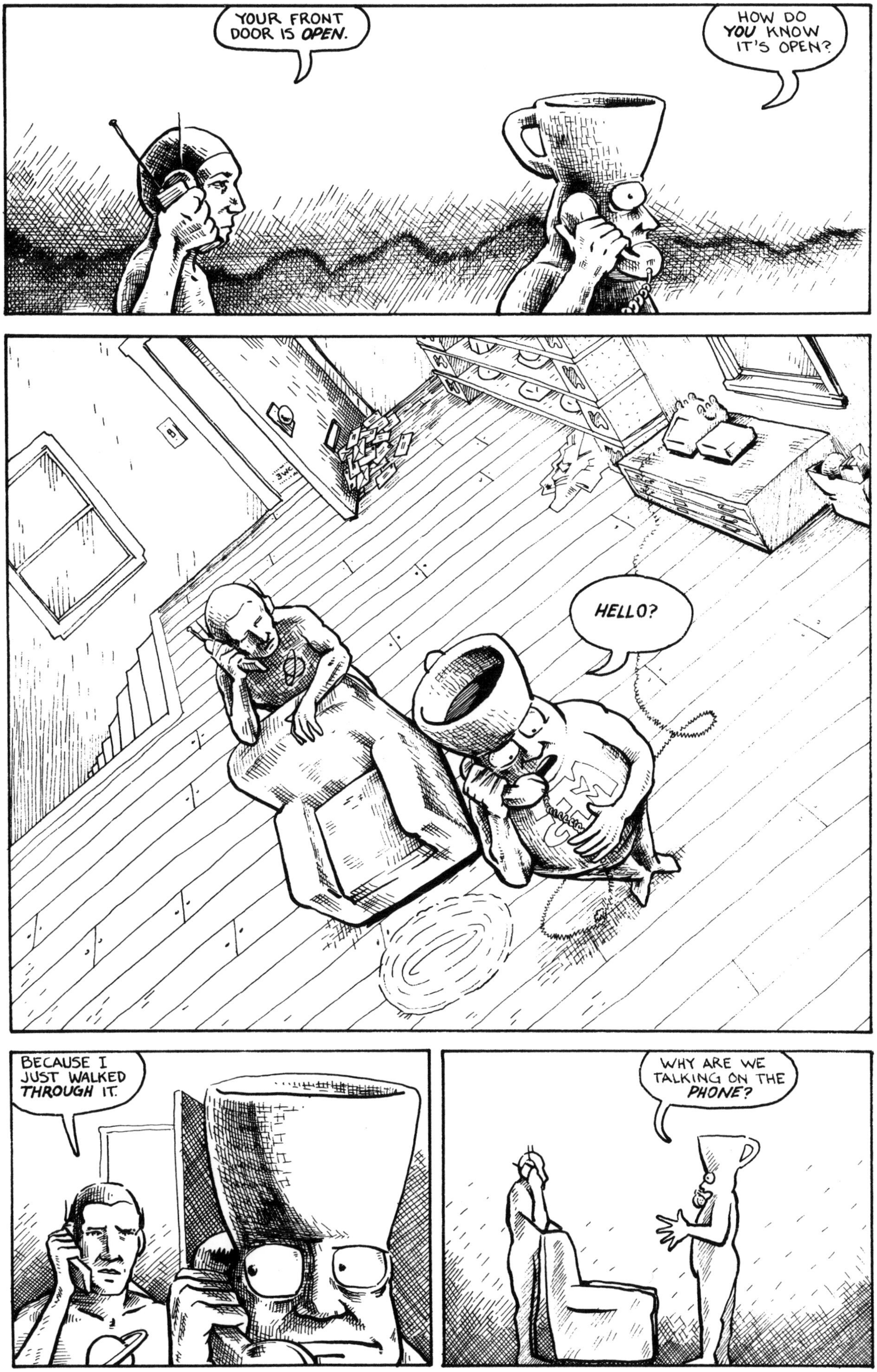
YOUR FRONT DOOR IS OPEN.
HOW DO YOU KNOW IT'S OPEN?
HELLO?
BECAUSE I JUST WALKED THROUGH IT.
WHY ARE WE TALKING ON THE PHONE?

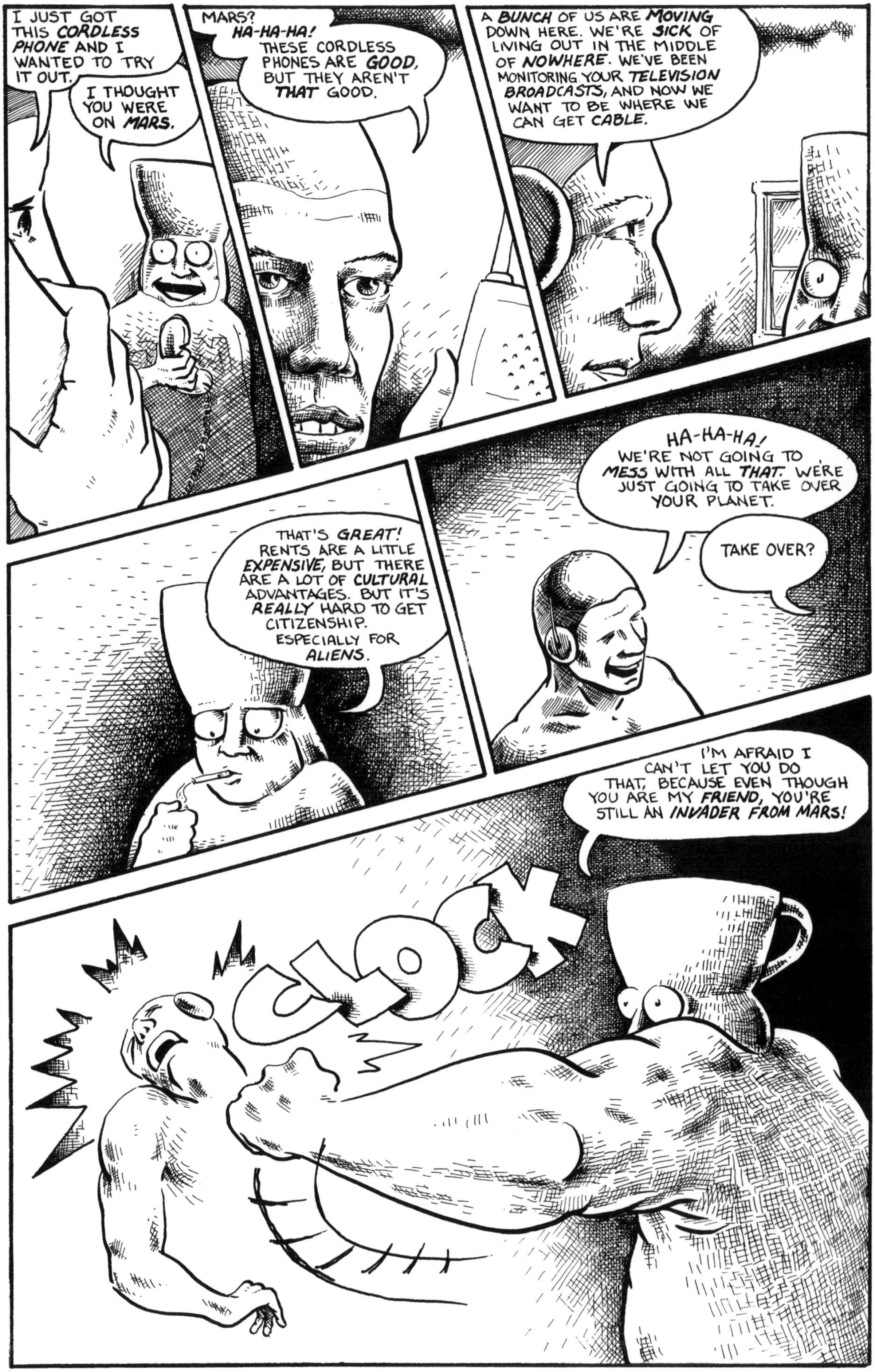
I JUST GOT THIS CORDLESS PHONE AND I WANTED TO TRY IT OUT.
I THOUGHT YOU WERE ON MARS.
MARS? HA-HA-HA! THESE CORDLESS PHONES ARE GOOD, BUT THEY AREN'T THAT GOOD.
A BUNCH OF US ARE MOVING DOWN HERE. WE'RE SICK OF LIVING OUT IN THE MIDDLE OF NOWHERE. WE'VE BEEN MONITORING YOUR TELEVISION BROADCASTS, AND NOW WE WANT TO BE WHERE WE CAN GET CABLE.
THAT'S GREAT! RENTS ARE A LITTLE EXPENSIVE, BUT THERE ARE A LOT OF CULTURAL ADVANTAGES. BUT IT'S REALLY HARD TO GET CITIZENSHIP. ESPECIALLY FOR ALIENS.
HA-HA-HA! WE'RE NOT GOING TO MESS WITH ALL THAT. WE'RE JUST GOING TO TAKE OVER YOUR PLANET.
TAKE OVER?
I'M AFRAID I CAN'T LET YOU DO THAT, BECAUSE EVEN THOUGH YOU ARE MY FRIEND, YOU'RE STILL AN INVADER FROM MARS!
CLOCK

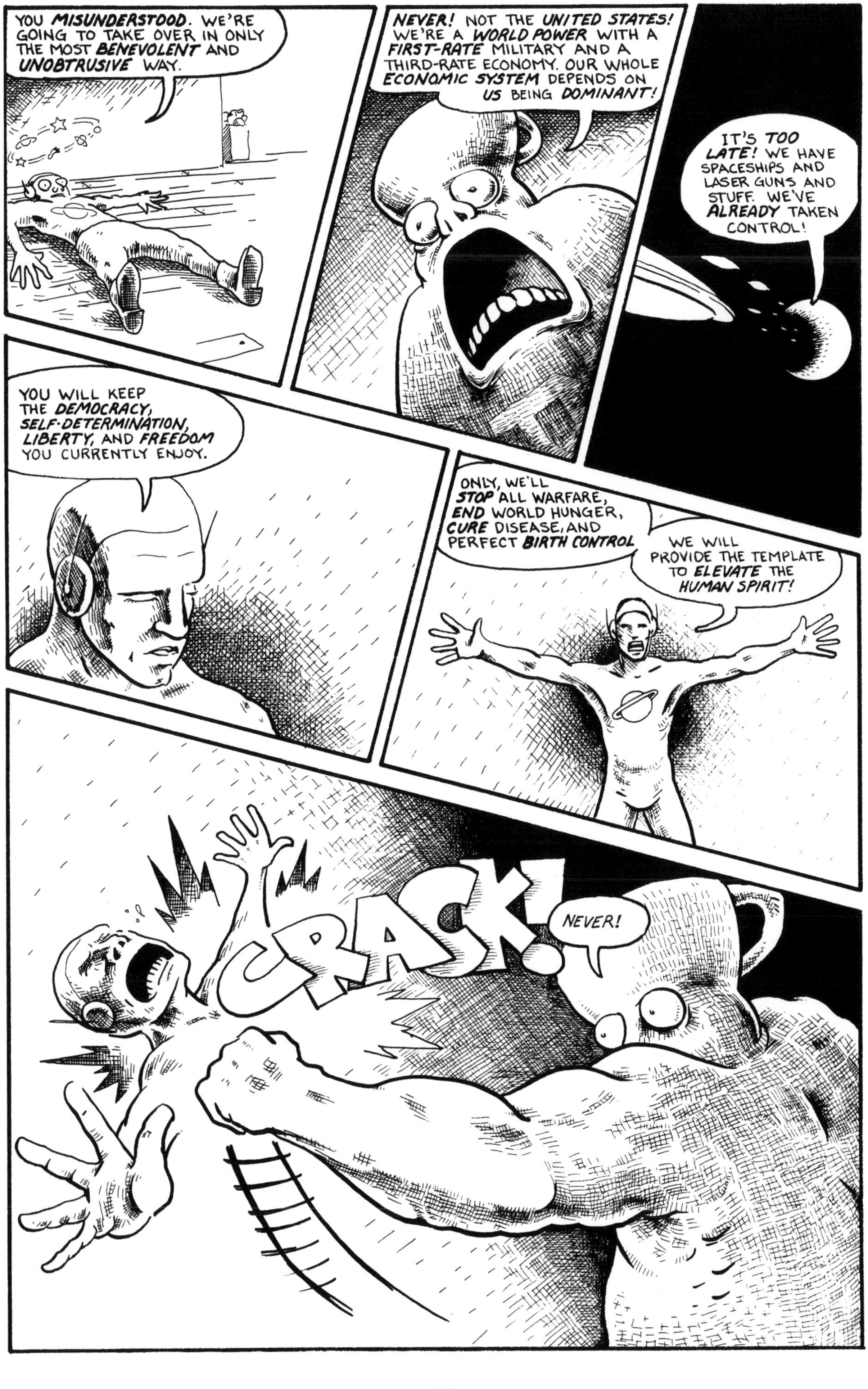
YOU MISUNDERSTOOD. WE'RE GOING TO TAKE OVER IN ONLY THE MOST BENEVOLENT AND UNOBTRUSIVE WAY.
NEVER! NOT THE UNITED STATES! WE'RE A WORLD POWER WITH A FIRST-RATE MILITARY AND A THIRD-RATE ECONOMY. OUR WHOLE ECONOMIC SYSTEM DEPENDS ON US BEING DOMINANT!
IT'S TOO LATE! WE HAVE SPACESHIPS AND LASER GUNS AND STUFF. WE'VE ALREADY TAKEN CONTROL!
YOU WILL KEEP THE DEMOCRACY, SELF-DETERMINATION, LIBERTY, AND FREEDOM YOU CURRENTLY ENJOY.
ONLY, WE'LL STOP ALL WARFARE, END WORLD HUNGER, CURE DISEASE, AND PERFECT BIRTH CONTROL
WE WILL PROVIDE THE TEMPLATE TO ELEVATE THE HUMAN SPIRIT!
CRACK!
NEVER!

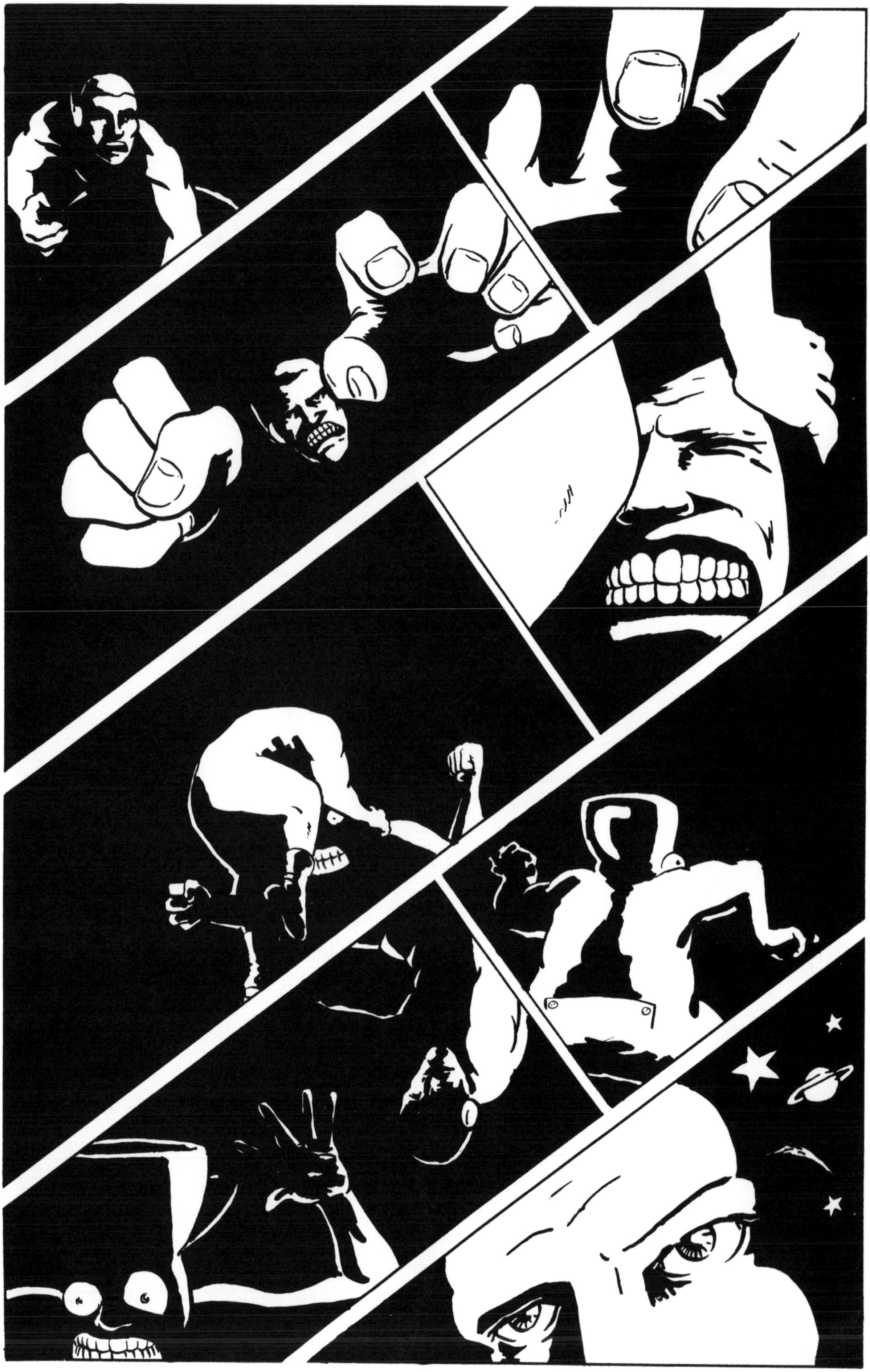

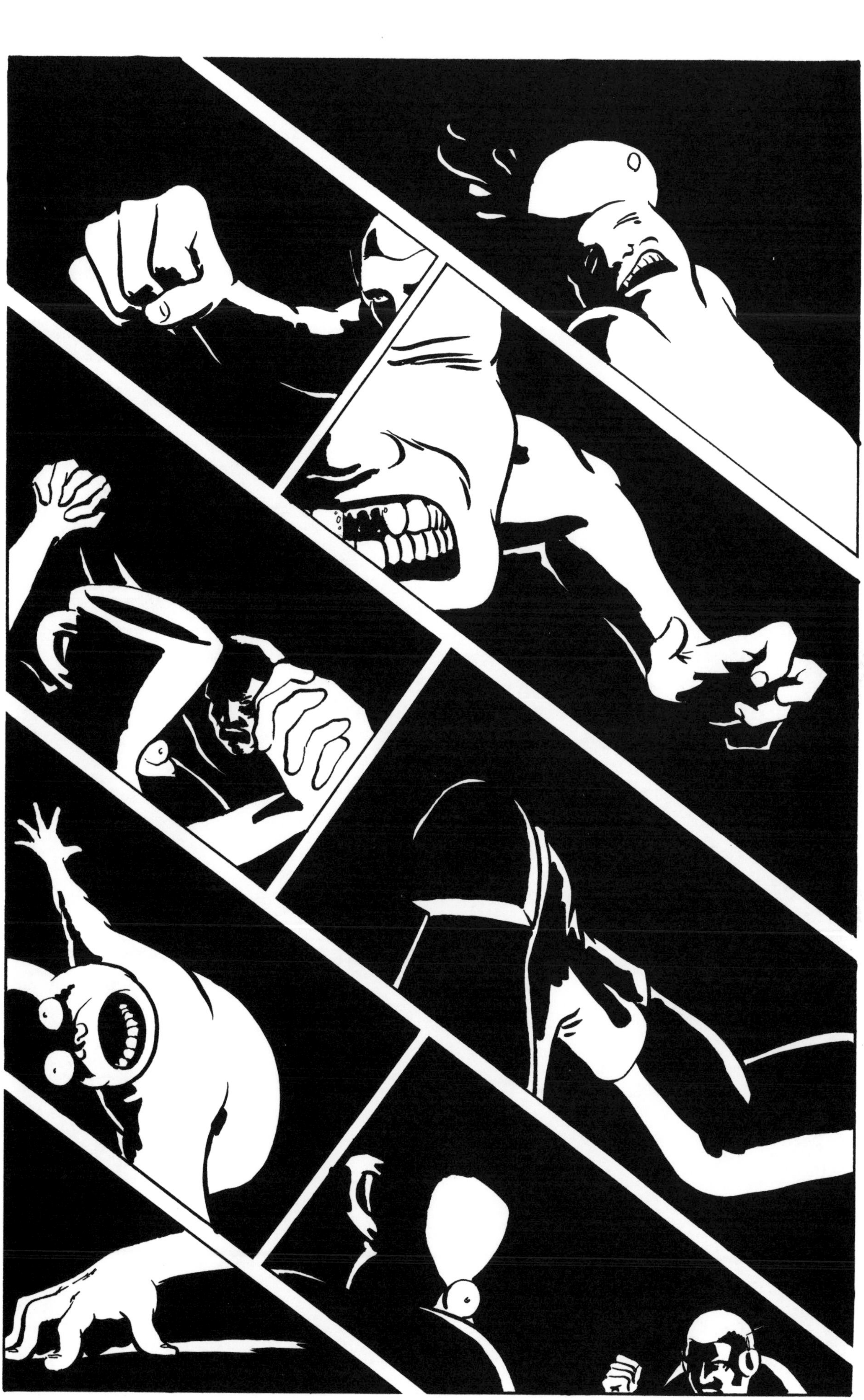

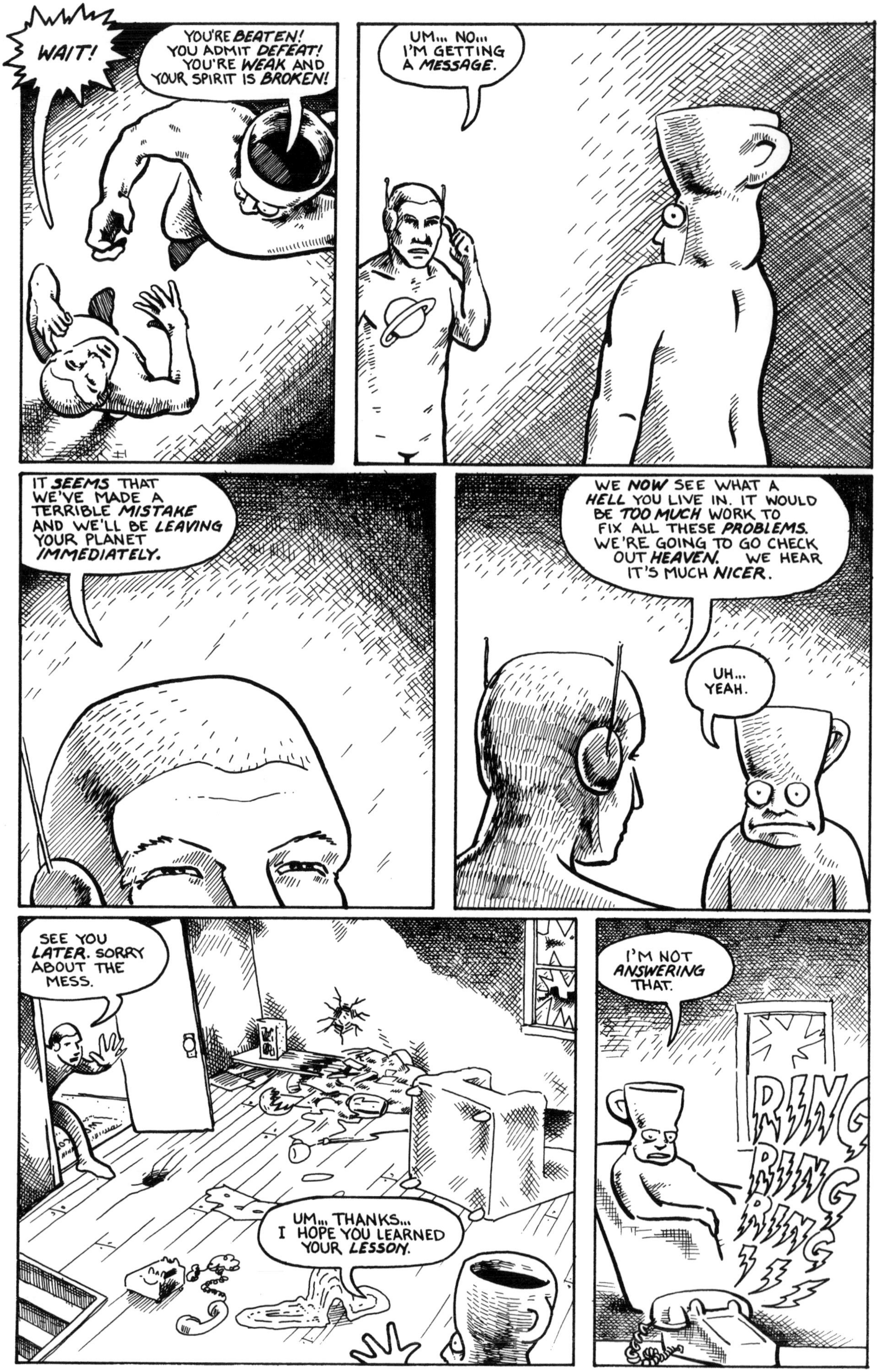
WAIT!
YOU'RE BEATEN! YOU ADMIT DEFEAT! YOU'RE WEAK AND YOUR SPIRIT IS BROKEN!
UM... NO... I'M GETTING A MESSAGE.
IT SEEMS THAT WE'VE MADE A TERRIBLE MISTAKE AND WE'LL BE LEAVING YOUR PLANET IMMEDIATELY.
WE NOW SEE WHAT A HELL YOU LIVE IN. IT WOULD BE TOO MUCH WORK TO FIX ALL THESE PROBLEMS. WE'RE GOING TO GO CHECK OUT HEAVEN. WE HEAR IT'S MUCH NICER.
UH... YEAH.
SEE YOU LATER. SORRY ABOUT THE MESS.
UM... THANKS... I HOPE YOU LEARNED YOUR LESSON.
I'M NOT ANSWERING THAT.
RING RING RING

CHAPTER FOUR

MUST GET PHONE!
RING
WAIT! I WILL NOT SUCCUMB TO MY IMPULSES. I HAVE BEEN CONDITIONED TO LEAP FOR THE PHONE EVERY TIME IT RINGS. I WILL NOT BE A SLAVE TO MY SOCIAL TRAINING!
RING
BUT WHAT IF IT'S IMPORTANT? WHAT IF SOMEONE HAS BEEN HURT? WHAT IF THE FATE OF THE UNIVERSE HANGS IN THE BALANCE? WHAT IF A FRIEND WANTS TO SEE A MOVIE? IF THEY DON'T LEAVE A MESSAGE, I'LL NEVER KNOW.
RING
NEVER KNOW WHAT?
SHOOT. MY BODY BETRAYS ME AGAIN.

SHANNON WHEELER'S

TOO MUCH COFFEE MAN

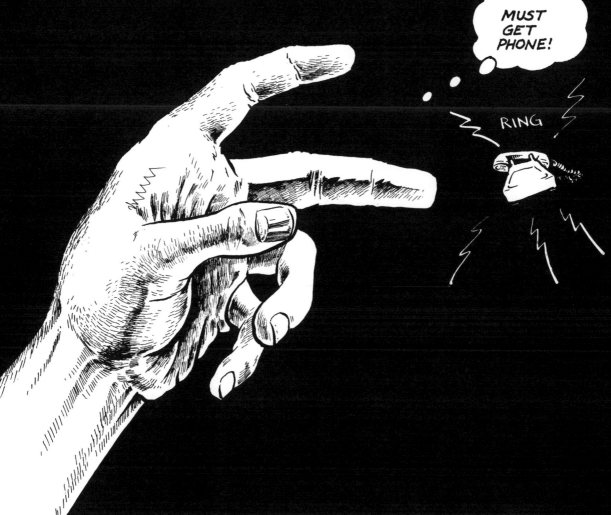

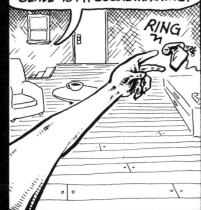

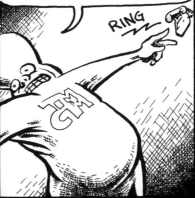

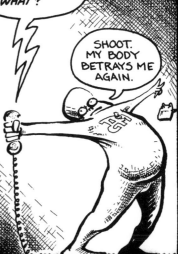

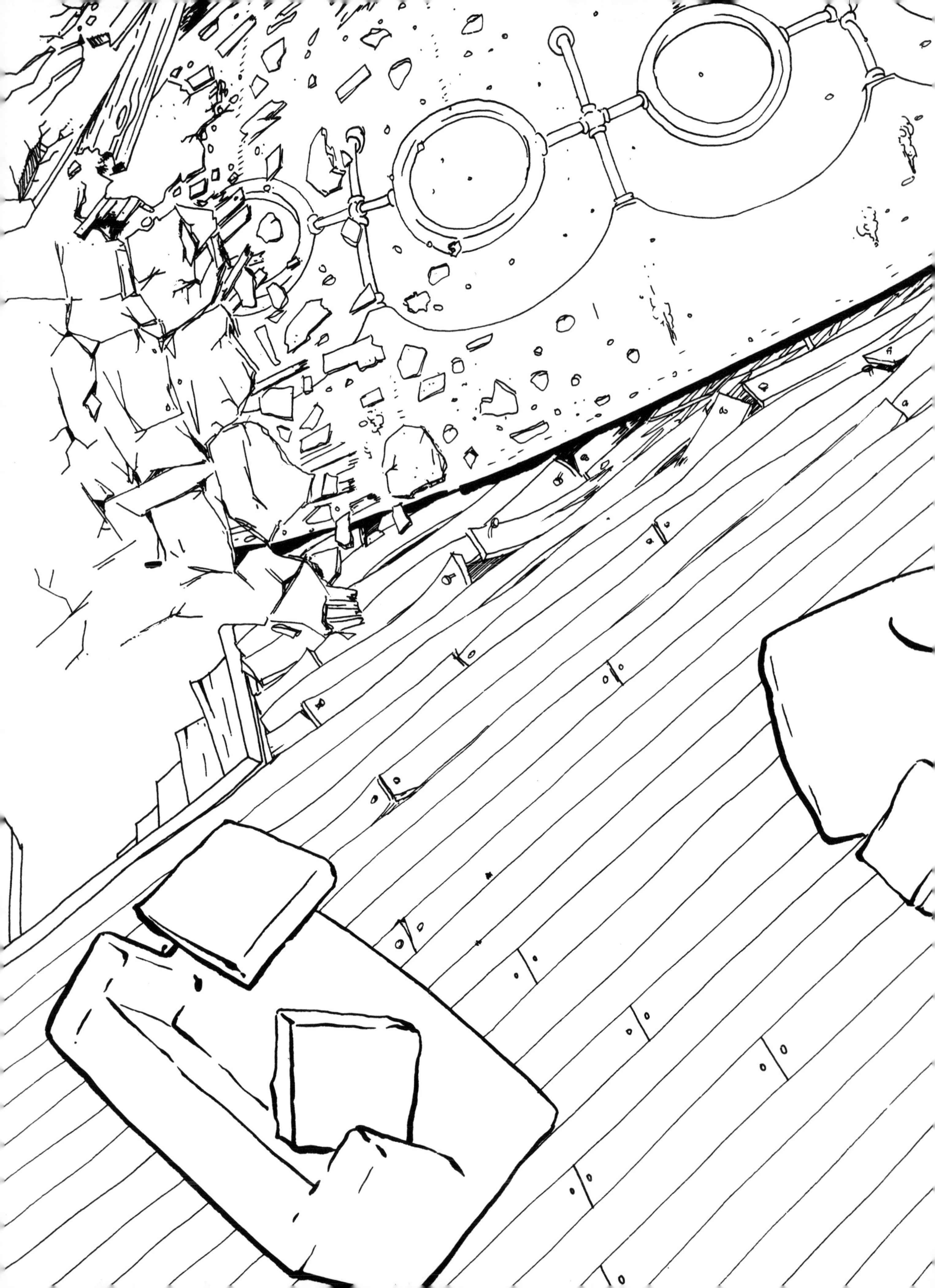

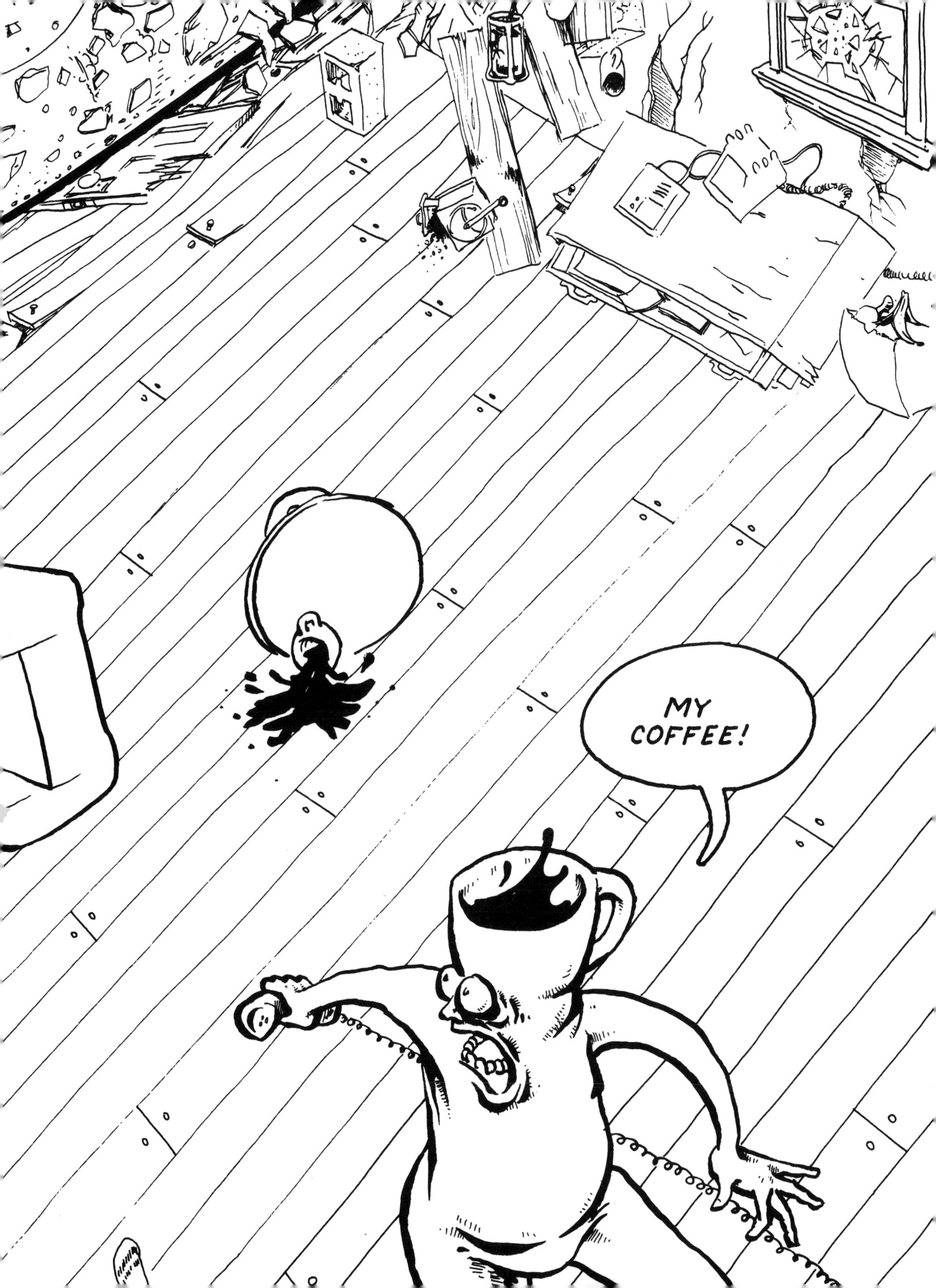
MY COFFEE!

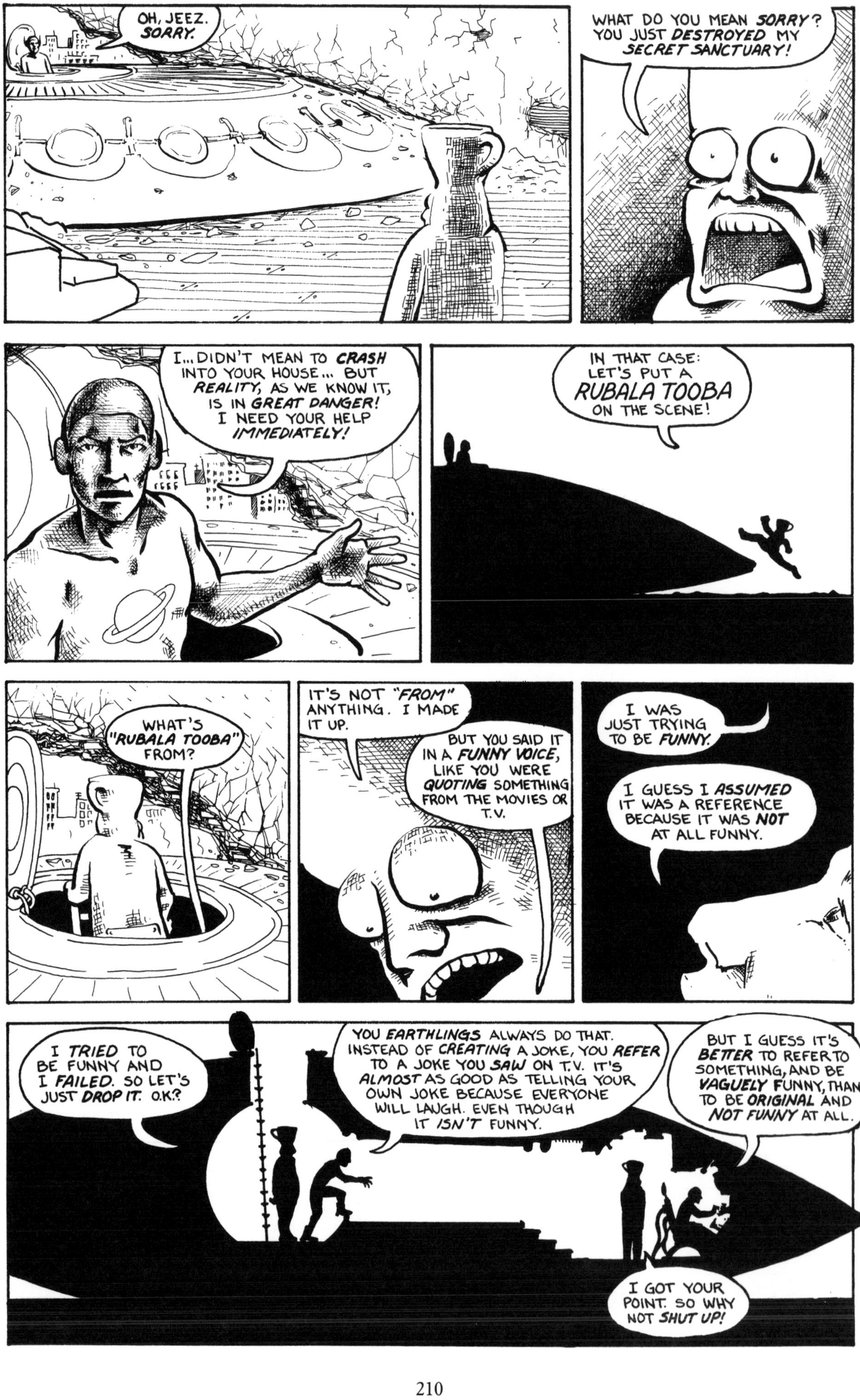
OH, JEEZ. SORRY.
WHAT DO YOU MEAN SORRY? YOU JUST DESTROYED MY SECRET SANCTUARY!
I... DIDN'T MEAN TO CRASH INTO YOUR HOUSE... BUT REALITY, AS WE KNOW IT, IS IN GREAT DANGER! I NEED YOUR HELP IMMEDIATELY!
IN THAT CASE: LET'S PUT A RUBALA TOOBA ON THE SCENE!
WHAT'S "RUBALA TOOBA" FROM?
IT'S NOT "FROM" ANYTHING. I MADE IT UP.
BUT YOU SAID IT IN A FUNNY VOICE, LIKE YOU WERE QUOTING SOMETHING FROM THE MOVIES OR T.V.
I WAS JUST TRYING TO BE FUNNY.
I GUESS I ASSUMED IT WAS A REFERENCE BECAUSE IT WAS NOT AT ALL FUNNY.
I TRIED TO BE FUNNY AND I FAILED. SO LET'S JUST DROP IT. O.K.?
YOU EARTHLINGS ALWAYS DO THAT. INSTEAD OF CREATING A JOKE, YOU REFER TO A JOKE YOU SAW ON T.V. IT'S ALMOST AS GOOD AS TELLING YOUR OWN JOKE BECAUSE EVERYONE WILL LAUGH. EVEN THOUGH IT ISN'T FUNNY.
BUT I GUESS IT'S BETTER TO REFER TO SOMETHING, AND BE VAGUELY FUNNY, THAN TO BE ORIGINAL AND NOT FUNNY AT ALL.
I GOT YOUR POINT. SO WHY NOT SHUT UP!

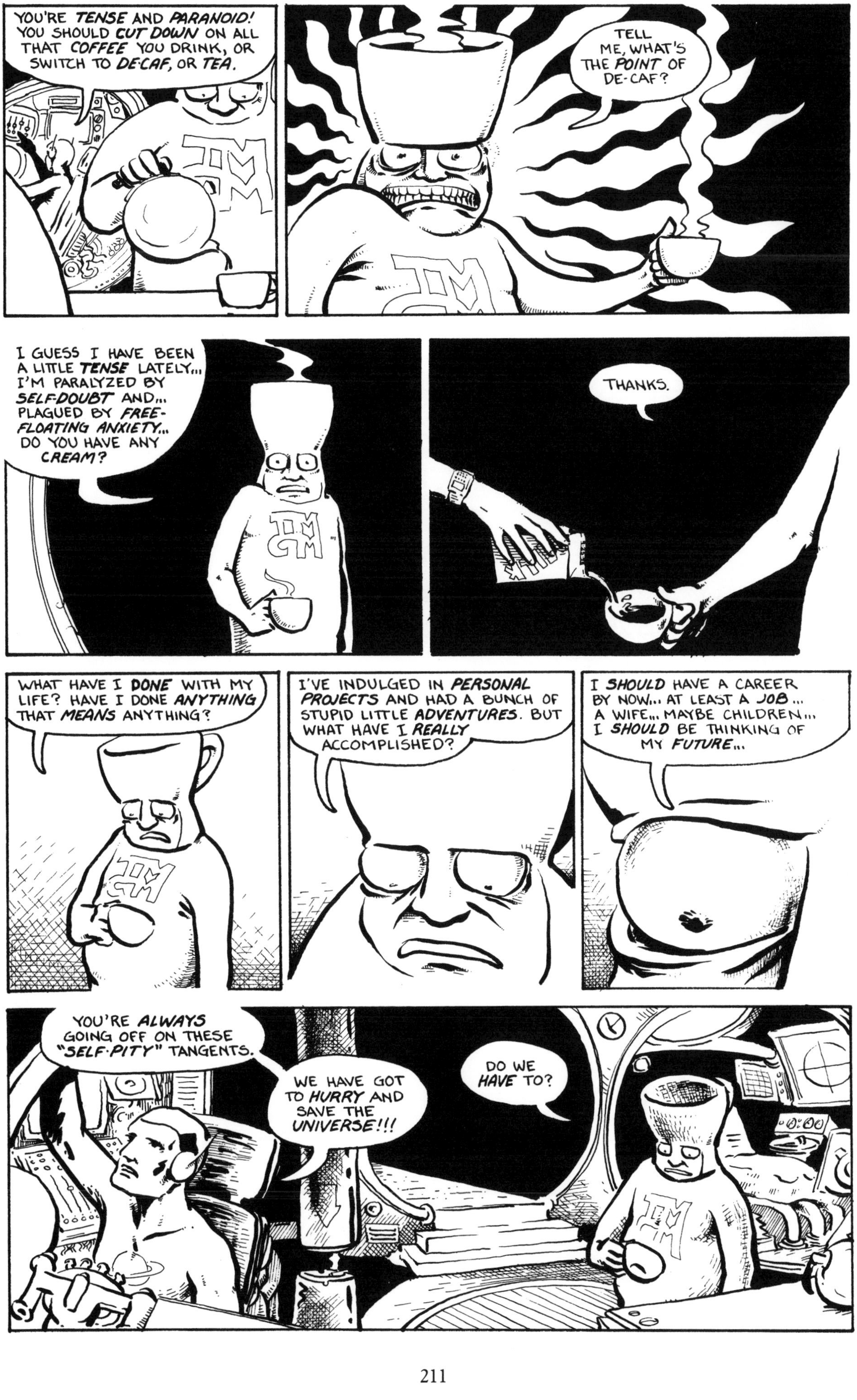
YOU'RE TENSE AND PARANOID! YOU SHOULD CUT DOWN ON ALL THAT COFFEE YOU DRINK, OR SWITCH TO DE-CAF, OR TEA.
TELL ME, WHAT'S THE POINT OF DE-CAF?
I GUESS I HAVE BEEN A LITTLE TENSE LATELY... I'M PARALYZED BY SELF-DOUBT AND... PLAGUED BY FREE-FLOATING ANXIETY... DO YOU HAVE ANY CREAM?
THANKS.
WHAT HAVE I DONE WITH MY LIFE? HAVE I DONE ANYTHING THAT MEANS ANYTHING?
I'VE INDULGED IN PERSONAL PROJECTS AND HAD A BUNCH OF STUPID LITTLE ADVENTURES. BUT WHAT HAVE I REALLY ACCOMPLISHED?
I SHOULD HAVE A CAREER BY NOW... AT LEAST A JOB... A WIFE... MAYBE CHILDREN... I SHOULD BE THINKING OF MY FUTURE...
YOU'RE ALWAYS GOING OFF ON THESE "SELF-PITY" TANGENTS.
WE HAVE GOT TO HURRY AND SAVE THE UNIVERSE!!!
DO WE HAVE TO?

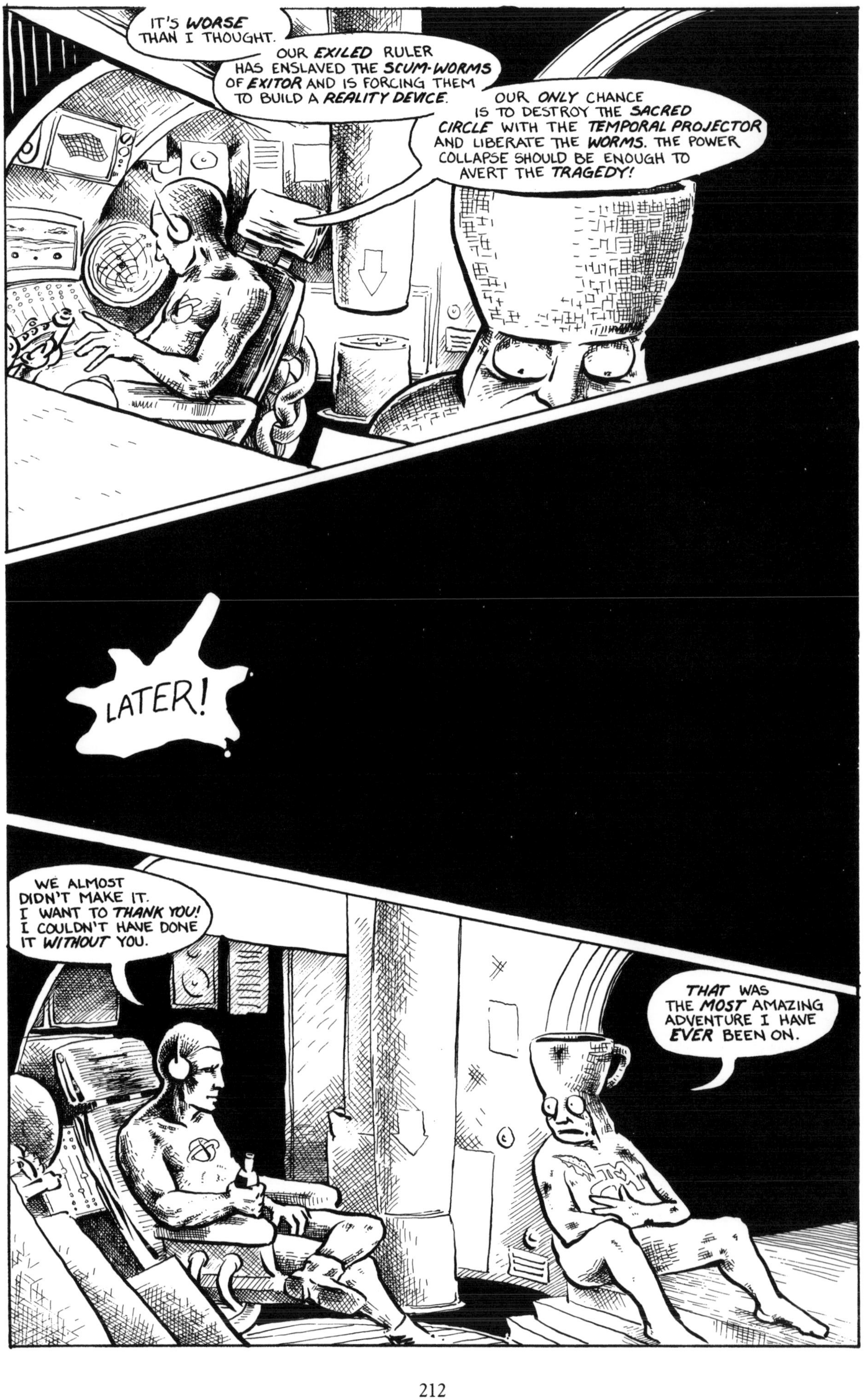
IT'S WORSE THAN I THOUGHT.
OUR EXILED RULER HAS ENSLAVED THE SCUM-WORMS OF EXITOR AND IS FORCING THEM TO BUILD A REALITY DEVICE.
OUR ONLY CHANCE IS TO DESTROY THE SACRED CIRCLE WITH THE TEMPORAL PROJECTOR AND LIBERATE THE WORMS. THE POWER COLLAPSE SHOULD BE ENOUGH TO AVERT THE TRAGEDY!
LATER!
WE ALMOST DIDN'T MAKE IT. I WANT TO THANK YOU! I COULDN'T HAVE DONE IT WITHOUT YOU.
THAT WAS THE MOST AMAZING ADVENTURE I HAVE EVER BEEN ON.

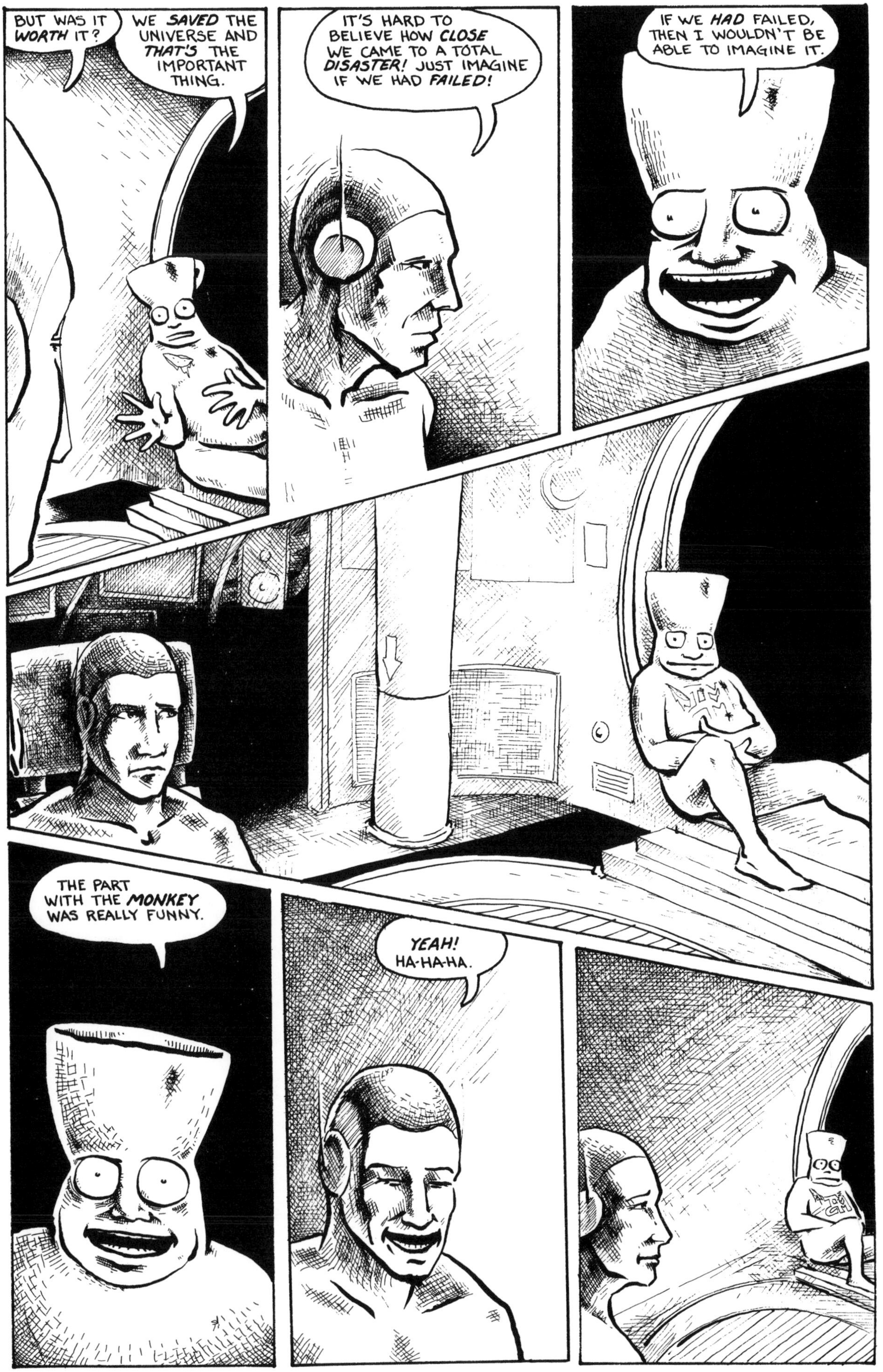

BUT WAS IT WORTH IT?
WE SAVED THE UNIVERSE AND THAT'S THE IMPORTANT THING.
IT'S HARD TO BELIEVE HOW CLOSE WE CAME TO A TOTAL DISASTER! JUST IMAGINE IF WE HAD FAILED!
IF WE HAD FAILED, THEN I WOULDN'T BE ABLE TO IMAGINE IT.
THE PART WITH THE MONKEY WAS REALLY FUNNY.
YEAH! HA-HA-HA.

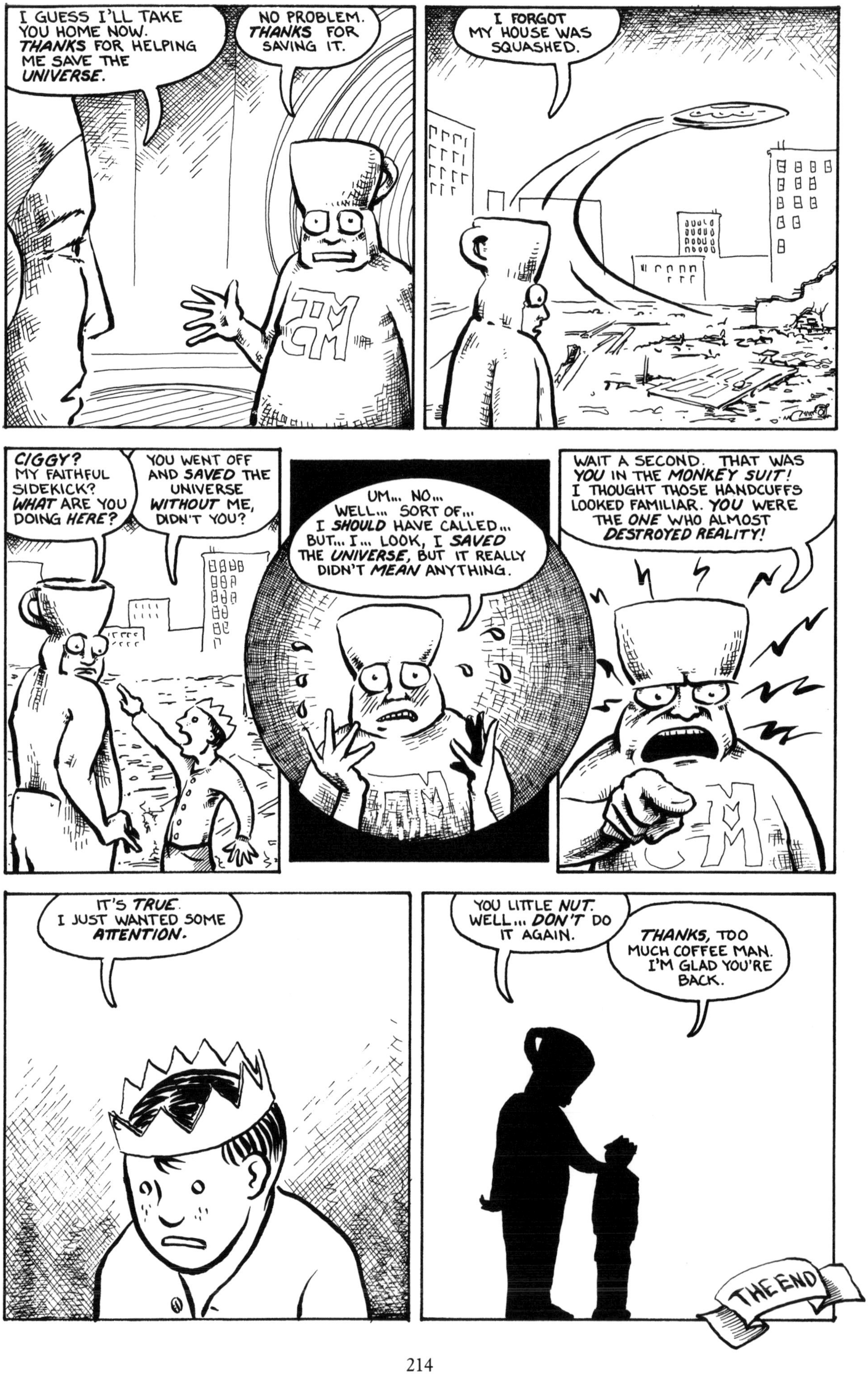

I GUESS I'LL TAKE YOU HOME NOW. THANKS FOR HELPING ME SAVE THE UNIVERSE.
NO PROBLEM. THANKS FOR SAVING IT.
I FORGOT MY HOUSE WAS SQUASHED.
CIGGY? MY FAITHFUL SIDEKICK? WHAT ARE YOU DOING HERE?
YOU WENT OFF AND SAVED THE UNIVERSE WITHOUT ME, DIDN'T YOU?
UM... NO... WELL... SORT OF... I SHOULD HAVE CALLED... BUT... I... LOOK, I SAVED THE UNIVERSE, BUT IT REALLY DIDN'T MEAN ANYTHING.
WAIT A SECOND. THAT WAS YOU IN THE MONKEY SUIT! I THOUGHT THOSE HANDCUFFS LOOKED FAMILIAR. YOU WERE THE ONE WHO ALMOST DESTROYED REALITY!
IT'S TRUE. I JUST WANTED SOME ATTENTION.
YOU LITTLE NUT. WELL... DON'T DO IT AGAIN.
THANKS, TOO MUCH COFFEE MAN. I'M GLAD YOU'RE BACK.
THE END

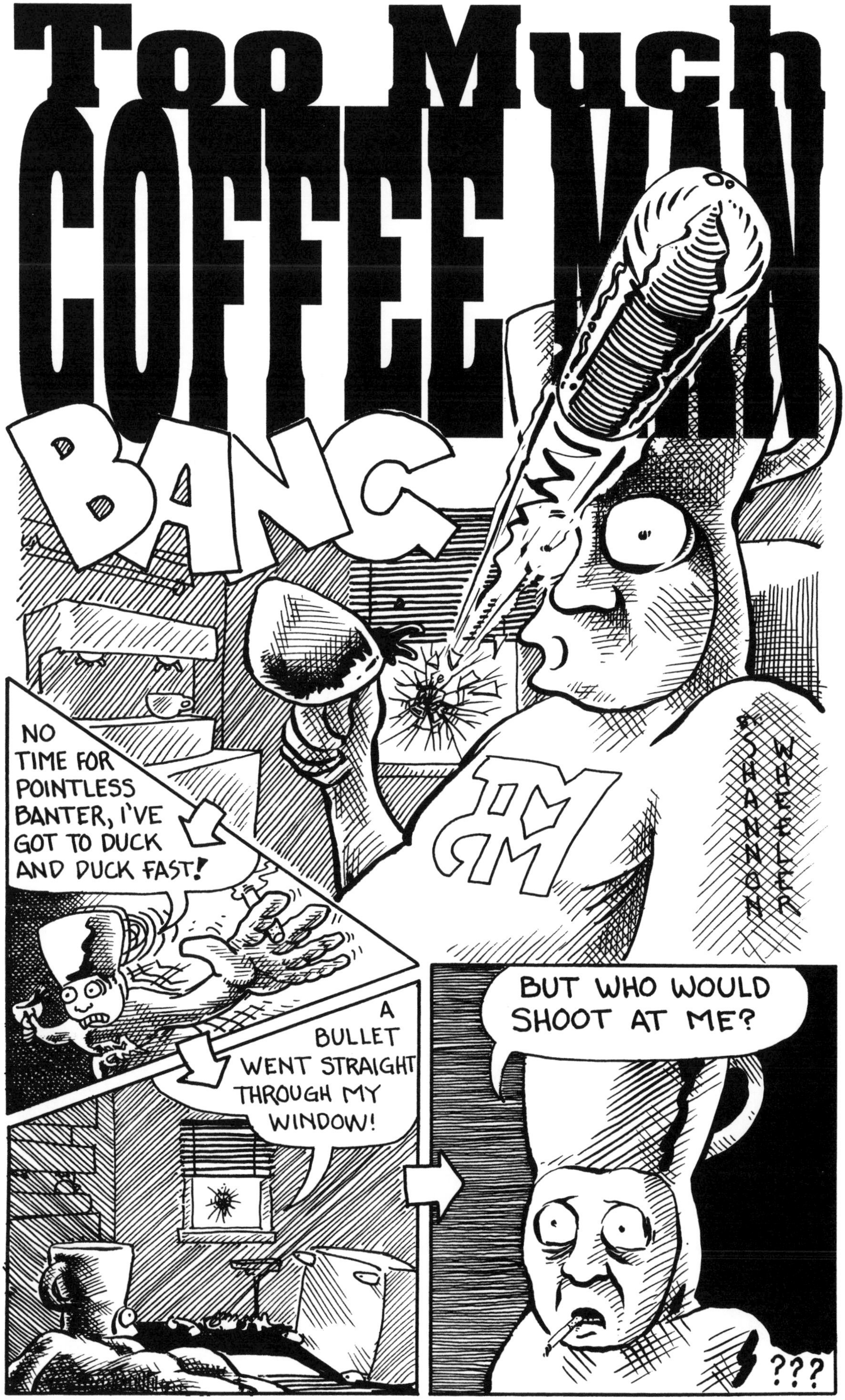
Too Much
COFFEE MAN
BANG
©SHANNON WHEELER
NO TIME FOR POINTLESS BANTER, I'VE GOT TO DUCK AND DUCK FAST!
A BULLET WENT STRAIGHT THROUGH MY WINDOW!
BUT WHO WOULD SHOOT AT ME?
???

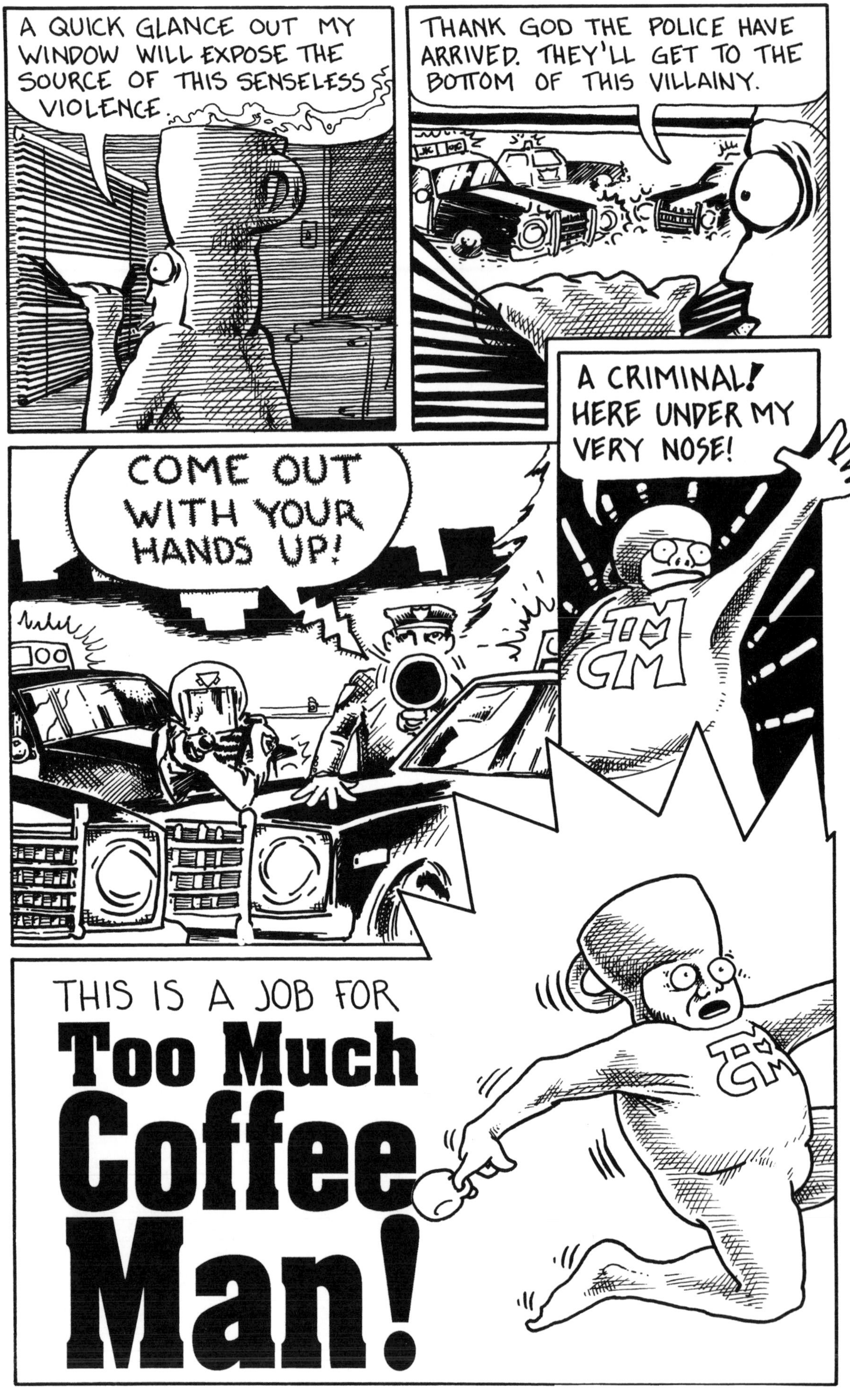
A QUICK GLANCE OUT MY WINDOW WILL EXPOSE THE SOURCE OF THIS SENSELESS VIOLENCE.
THANK GOD THE POLICE HAVE ARRIVED. THEY'LL GET TO THE BOTTOM OF THIS VILLAINY.
COME OUT WITH YOUR HANDS UP!
A CRIMINAL! HERE UNDER MY VERY NOSE!
THIS IS A JOB FOR
Too Much Coffee Man!

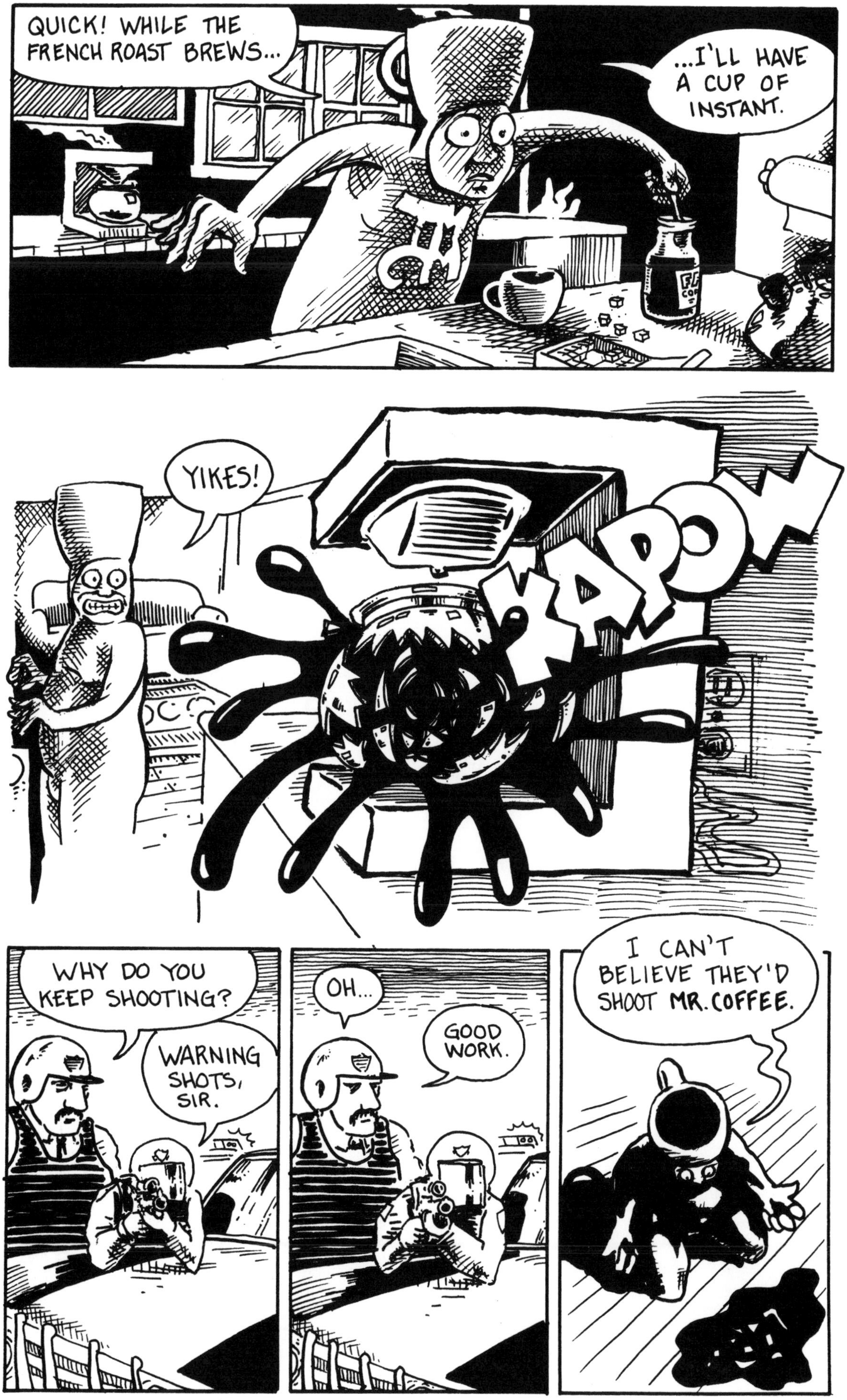
QUICK! WHILE THE FRENCH ROAST BREWS...
...I'LL HAVE A CUP OF INSTANT.
YIKES!
KAPOW
WHY DO YOU KEEP SHOOTING?
WARNING SHOTS, SIR.
OH...
GOOD WORK.
I CAN'T BELIEVE THEY'D SHOOT MR. COFFEE.

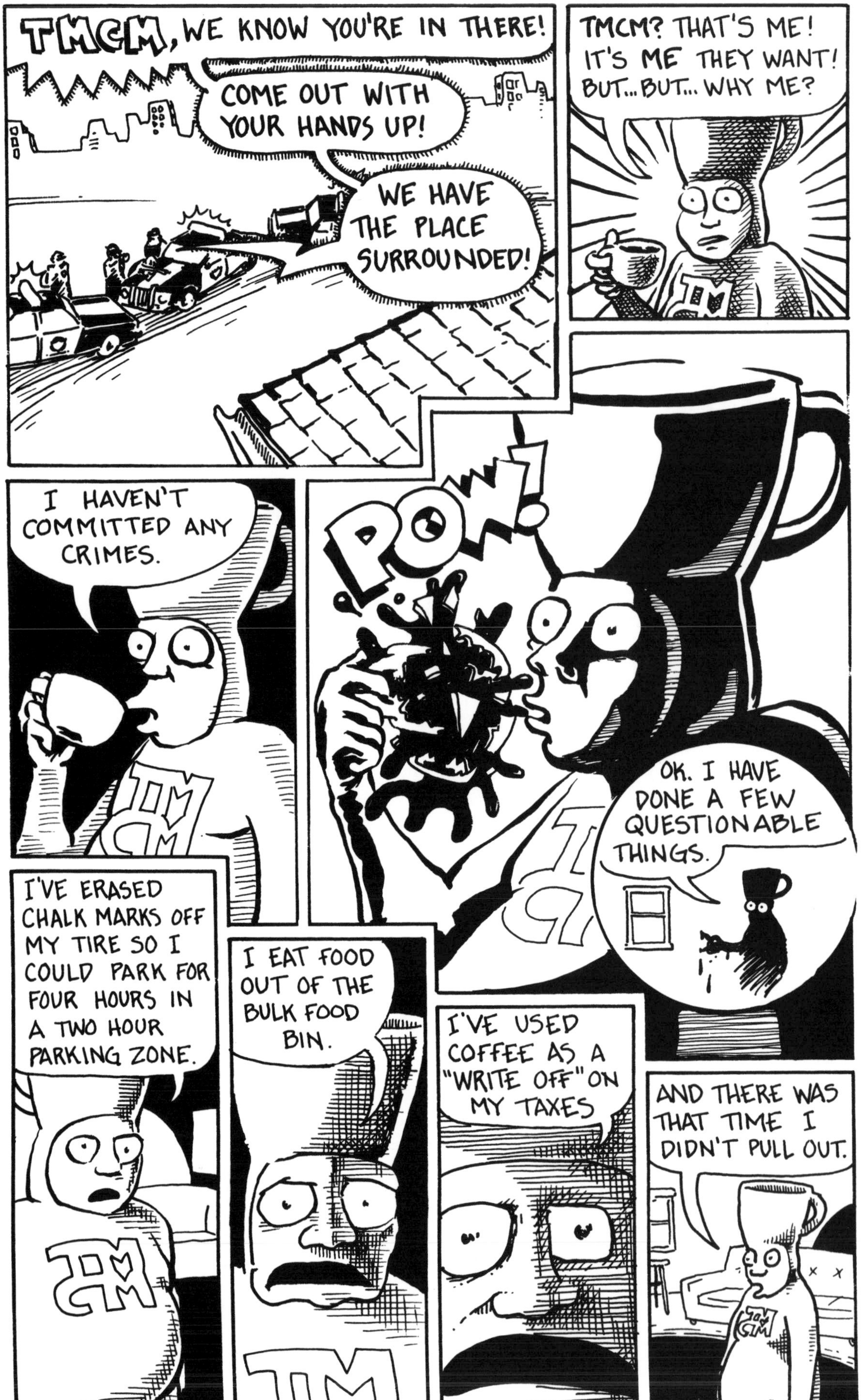
TMCM, WE KNOW YOU'RE IN THERE!
COME OUT WITH YOUR HANDS UP!
WE HAVE THE PLACE SURROUNDED!
TMCM? THAT'S ME! IT'S ME THEY WANT! BUT... BUT... WHY ME?
I HAVEN'T COMMITTED ANY CRIMES.
POW!
OK. I HAVE DONE A FEW QUESTIONABLE THINGS.
I'VE ERASED CHALK MARKS OFF MY TIRE SO I COULD PARK FOR FOUR HOURS IN A TWO HOUR PARKING ZONE.
I EAT FOOD OUT OF THE BULK FOOD BIN.
I'VE USED COFFEE AS A "WRITE OFF" ON MY TAXES
AND THERE WAS THAT TIME I DIDN'T PULL OUT.

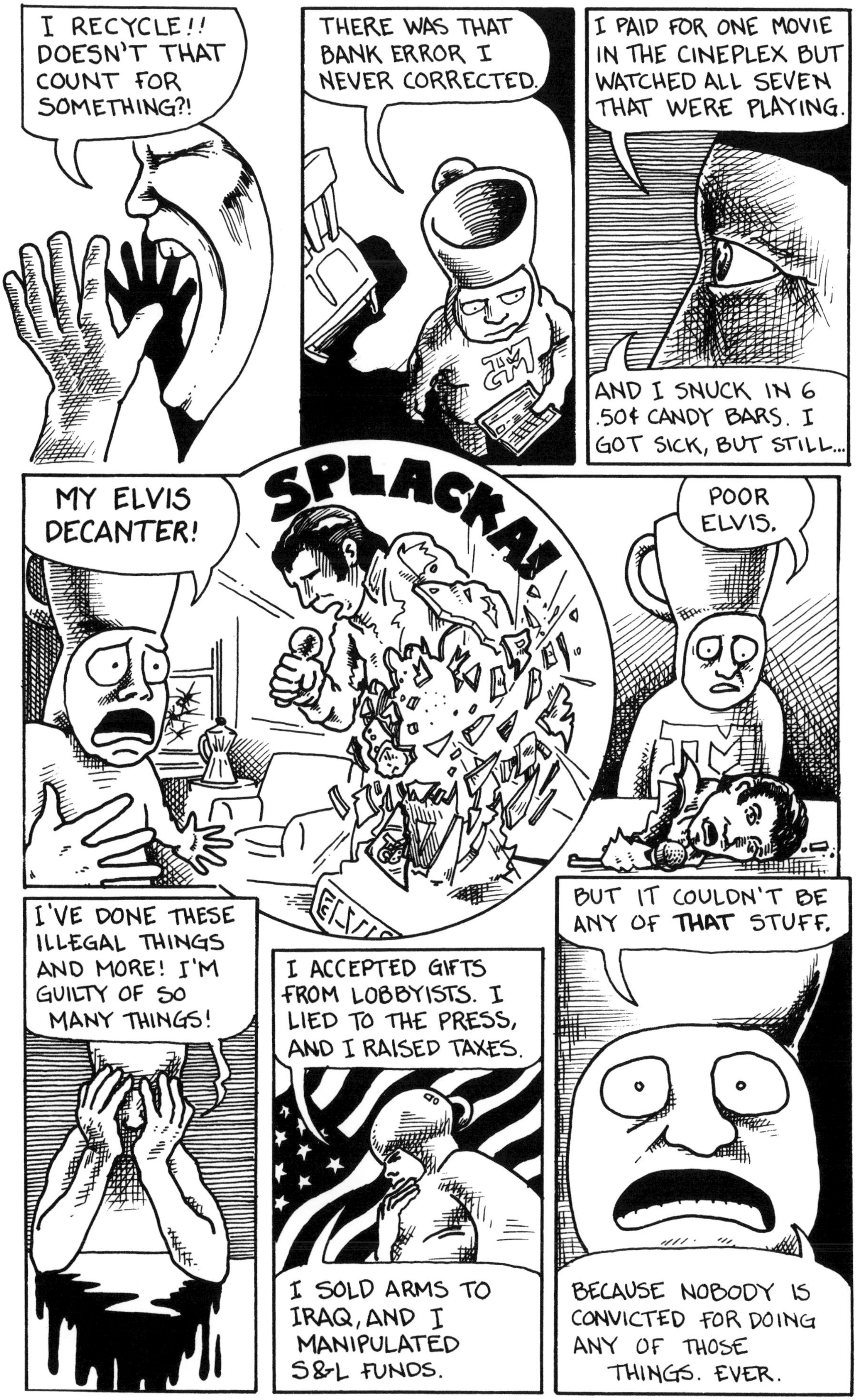
I RECYCLE!! DOESN'T THAT COUNT FOR SOMETHING?!
THERE WAS THAT BANK ERROR I NEVER CORRECTED.
I PAID FOR ONE MOVIE IN THE CINEPLEX BUT WATCHED ALL SEVEN THAT WERE PLAYING.
AND I SNUCK IN 6 .50¢ CANDY BARS. I GOT SICK, BUT STILL...
MY ELVIS DECANTER!
SPLACK!
POOR ELVIS.
I'VE DONE THESE ILLEGAL THINGS AND MORE! I'M GUILTY OF SO MANY THINGS!
I ACCEPTED GIFTS FROM LOBBYISTS. I LIED TO THE PRESS, AND I RAISED TAXES.
I SOLD ARMS TO IRAQ, AND I MANIPULATED S&L FUNDS.
BUT IT COULDN'T BE ANY OF THAT STUFF.
BECAUSE NOBODY IS CONVICTED FOR DOING ANY OF THOSE THINGS. EVER.

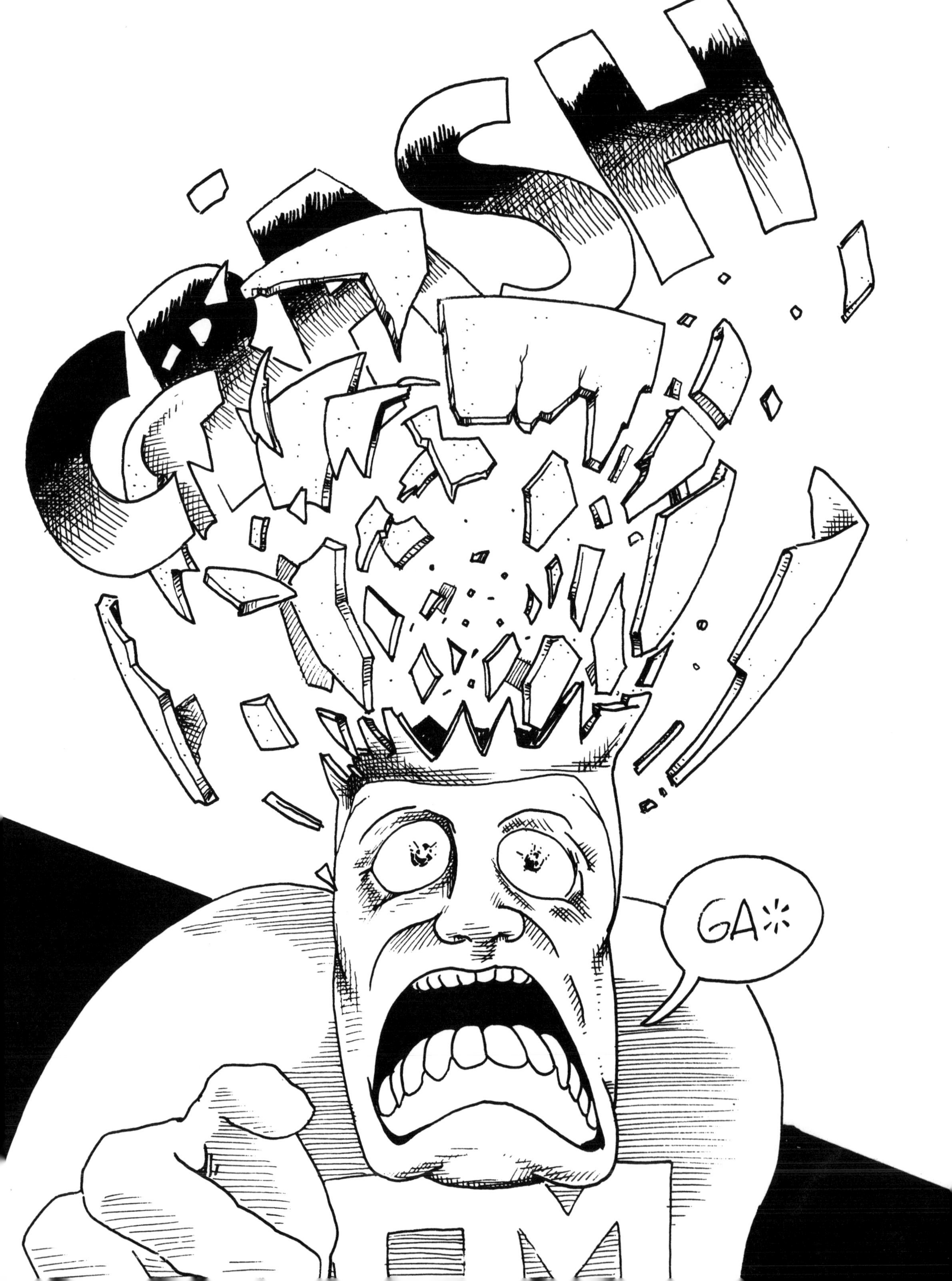
CRASH!
GA

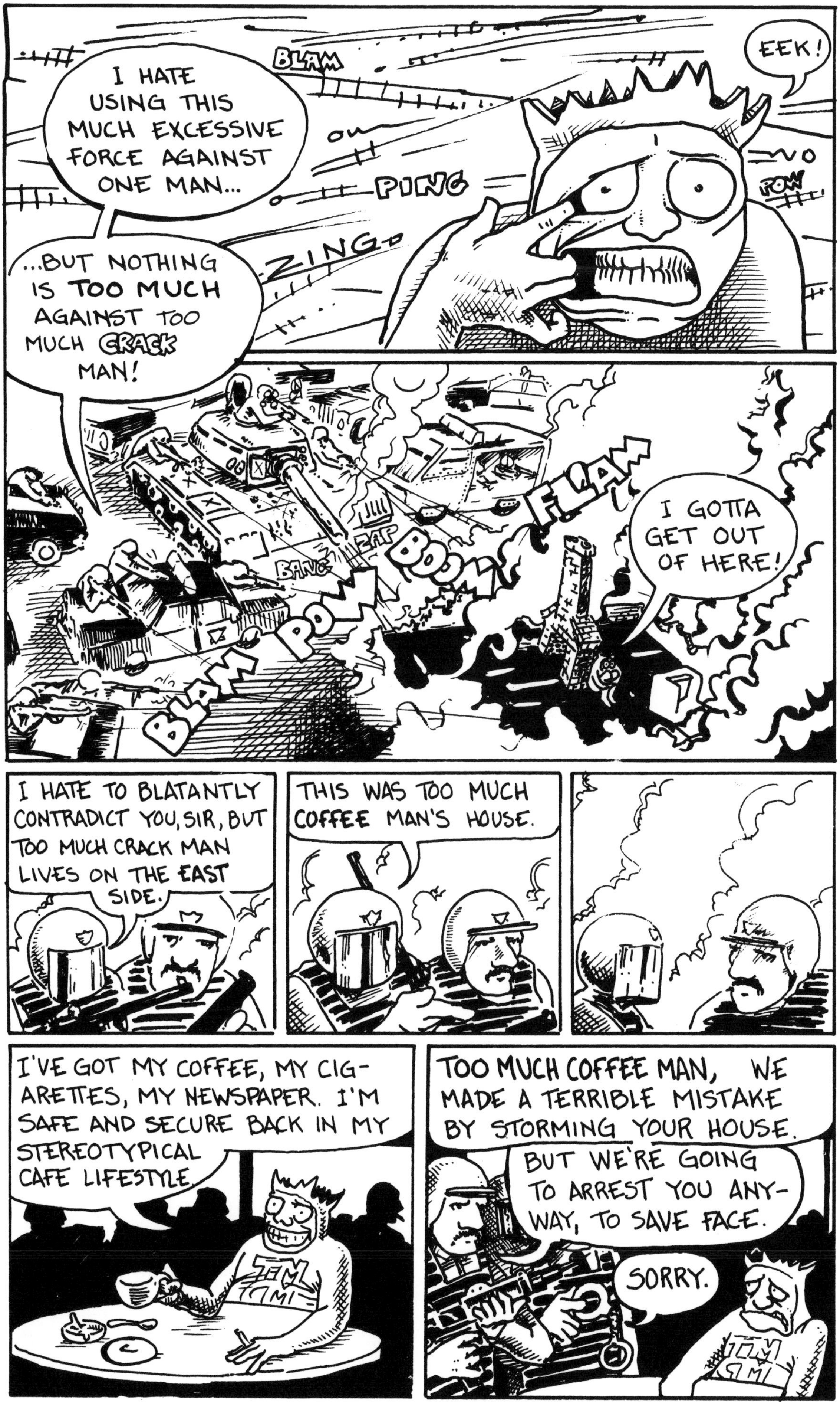
BLAM
I HATE USING THIS MUCH EXCESSIVE FORCE AGAINST ONE MAN...
EEK!
PING
POW
ZING
...BUT NOTHING IS TOO MUCH AGAINST TOO MUCH CRACK MAN!
FLAM
I GOTTA GET OUT OF HERE!
ZAP
BOOM
BANG
POW
BLAM
I HATE TO BLATANTLY CONTRADICT YOU, SIR, BUT TOO MUCH CRACK MAN LIVES ON THE EAST SIDE.
THIS WAS TOO MUCH COFFEE MAN'S HOUSE.
I'VE GOT MY COFFEE, MY CIGARETTES, MY NEWSPAPER. I'M SAFE AND SECURE BACK IN MY STEREOTYPICAL CAFE LIFESTYLE.
TMC
TOO MUCH COFFEE MAN, WE MADE A TERRIBLE MISTAKE BY STORMING YOUR HOUSE.
BUT WE'RE GOING TO ARREST YOU ANYWAY, TO SAVE FACE.
SORRY.

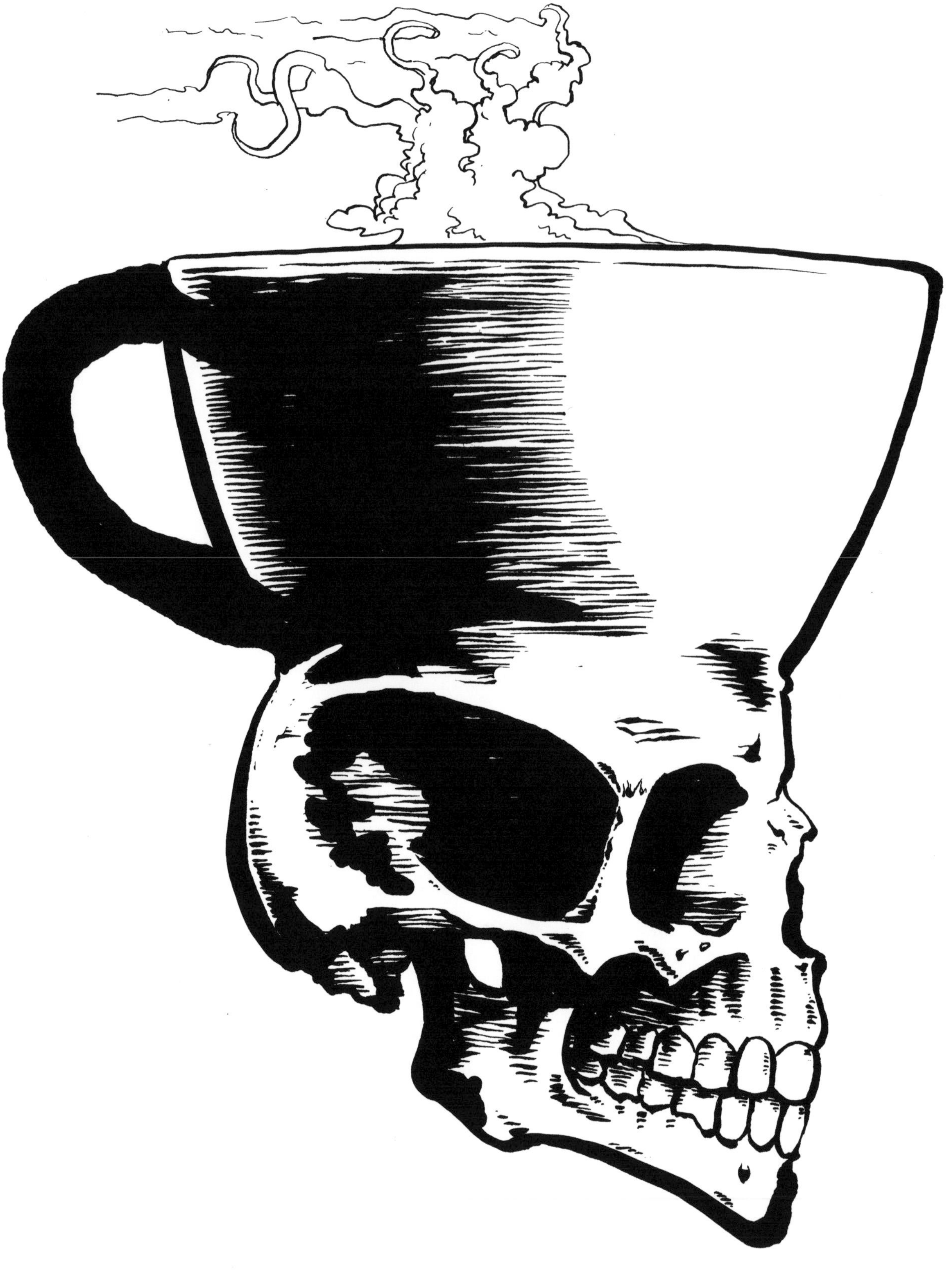

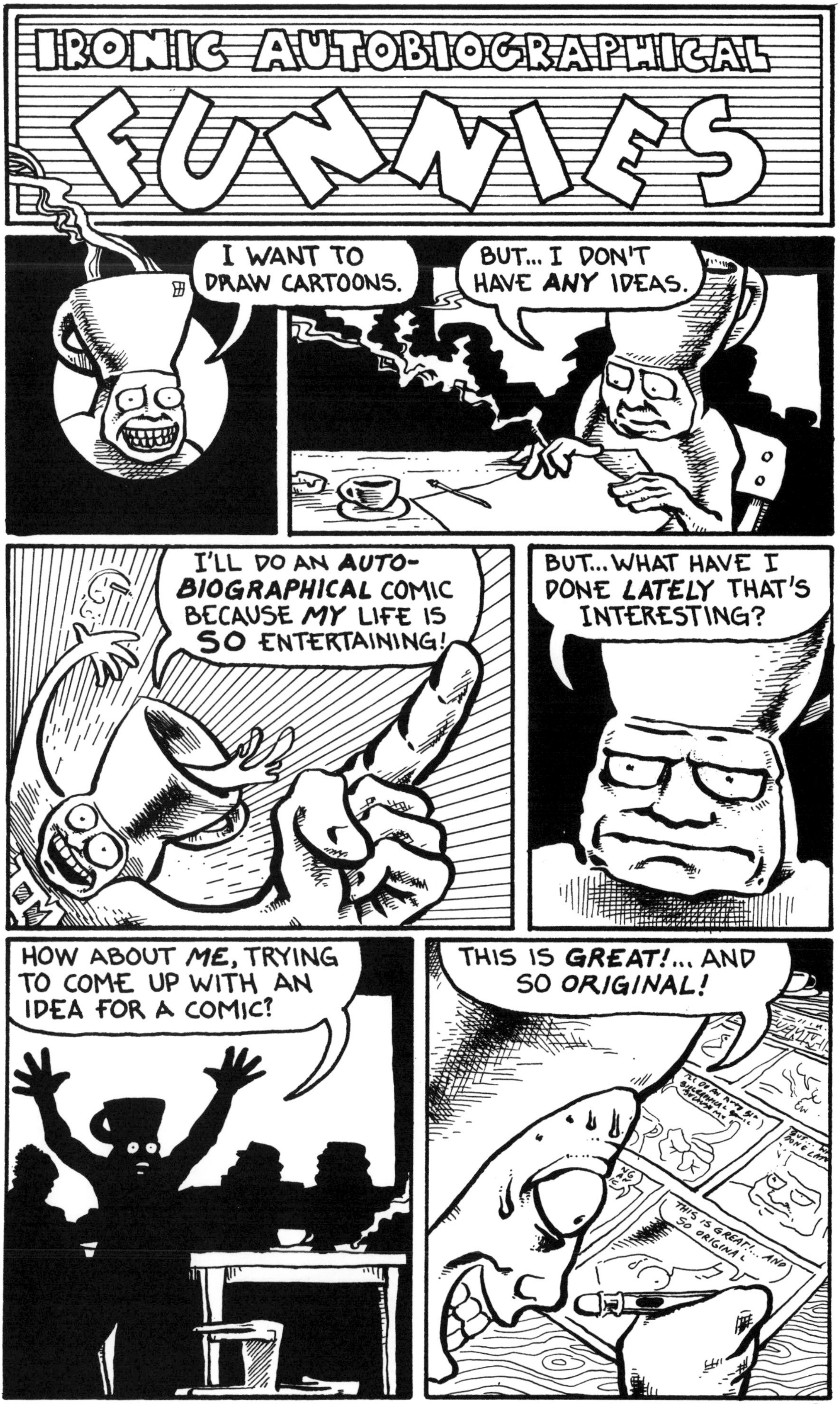
IRONIC AUTOBIOGRAPHICAL FUNNIES
I WANT TO DRAW CARTOONS.
BUT... I DON'T HAVE ANY IDEAS.
I'LL DO AN AUTO-BIOGRAPHICAL COMIC BECAUSE MY LIFE IS SO ENTERTAINING!
BUT... WHAT HAVE I DONE LATELY THAT'S INTERESTING?
HOW ABOUT ME, TRYING TO COME UP WITH AN IDEA FOR A COMIC?
THIS IS GREAT!... AND SO ORIGINAL!
THIS IS GREAT!... AND SO ORIGINAL
END.

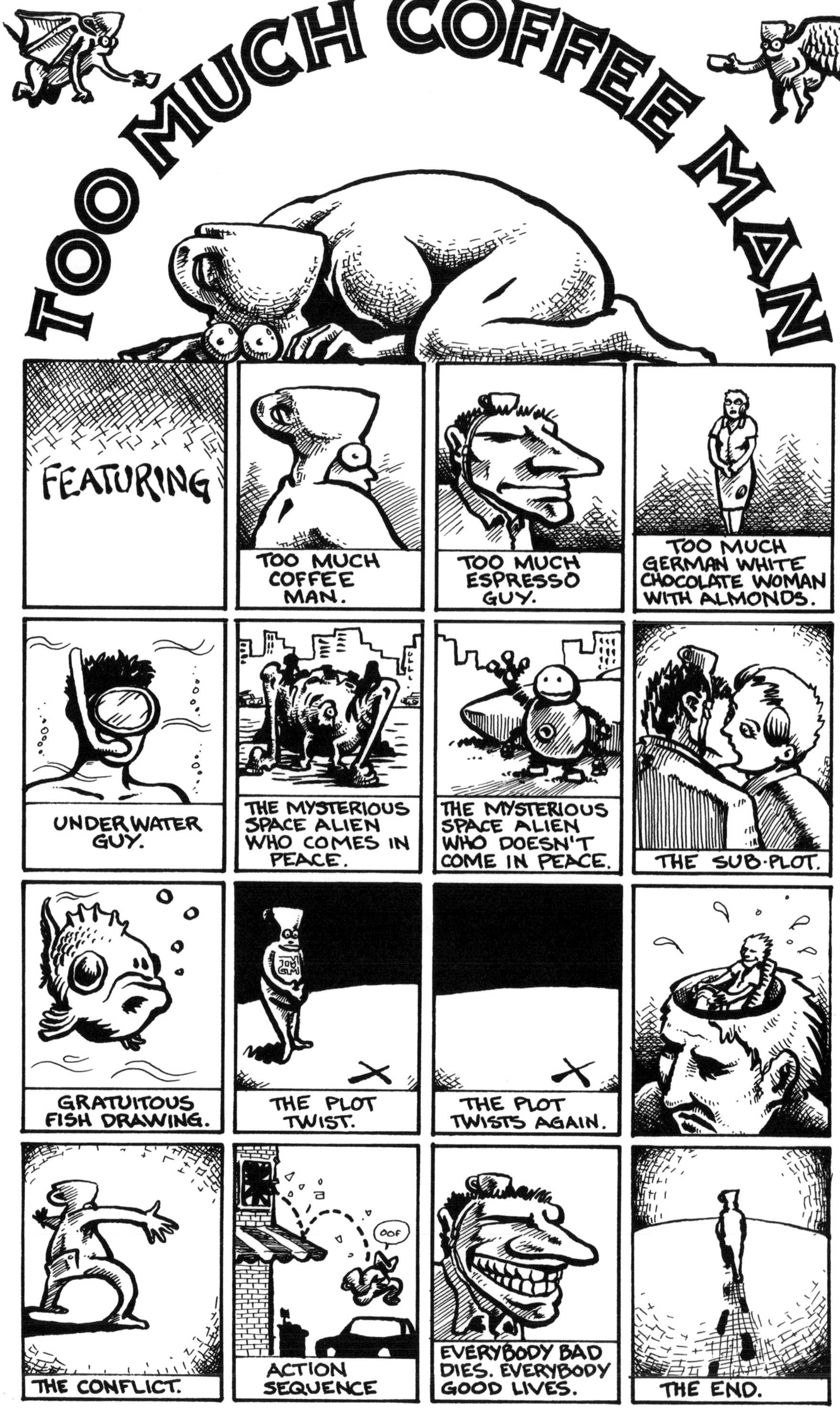
TOO MUCH COFFEE MAN
FEATURING
TOO MUCH COFFEE MAN.
TOO MUCH ESPRESSO GUY.
TOO MUCH GERMAN WHITE CHOCOLATE WOMAN WITH ALMONDS.
UNDERWATER GUY.
THE MYSTERIOUS SPACE ALIEN WHO COMES IN PEACE.
THE MYSTERIOUS SPACE ALIEN WHO DOESN'T COME IN PEACE.
THE SUB-PLOT.
GRATUITOUS FISH DRAWING.
JOY GUM
THE PLOT TWIST.
THE PLOT TWISTS AGAIN.
THE CONFLICT.
OOF
ACTION SEQUENCE
EVERYBODY BAD DIES. EVERYBODY GOOD LIVES.
THE END.

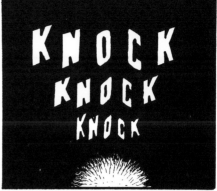

KNOCK
KNOCK
KNOCK

WHO ARE YOU?

I'M *UNDERWATER GUY*. I WANT TO JOIN YOUR TEAM.

WHAT *POWERS* DO YOU HAVE?

I CAN STAY *UNDERWATER* FOR UNUSUALLY LONG PERIODS OF TIME.

LET'S TEST HIS *POWERS*!

OK. YOU'VE *PROVEN* YOURSELF. YOU CAN JOIN OUR *TEAM.*

TOO MUCH COFFEE MAN

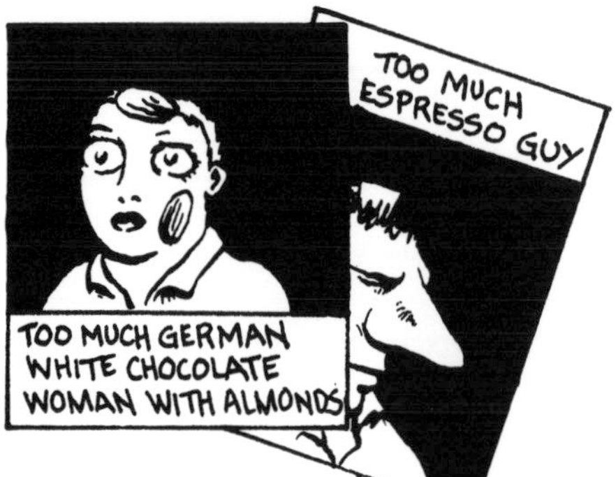

TOO MUCH ESPRESSO GUY
TOO MUCH GERMAN WHITE CHOCOLATE WOMAN WITH ALMONDS

Shannon Wheeler

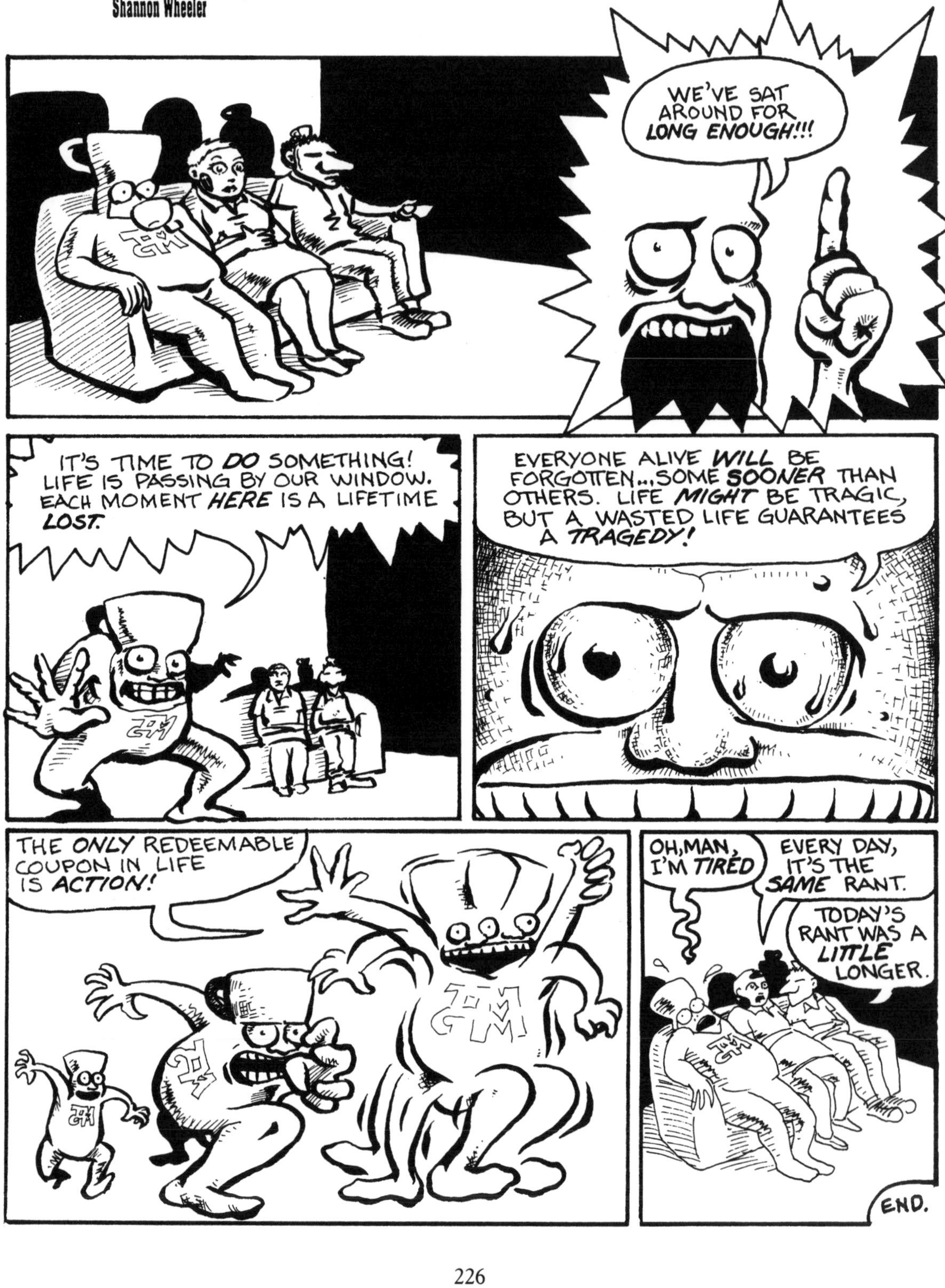

WE'VE SAT AROUND FOR LONG ENOUGH!!!
IT'S TIME TO DO SOMETHING! LIFE IS PASSING BY OUR WINDOW. EACH MOMENT HERE IS A LIFETIME LOST.
EVERYONE ALIVE WILL BE FORGOTTEN...SOME SOONER THAN OTHERS. LIFE MIGHT BE TRAGIC, BUT A WASTED LIFE GUARANTEES A TRAGEDY!
THE ONLY REDEEMABLE COUPON IN LIFE IS ACTION!
OH, MAN, I'M TIRED
EVERY DAY, IT'S THE SAME RANT.
TODAY'S RANT WAS A LITTLE LONGER.
END.

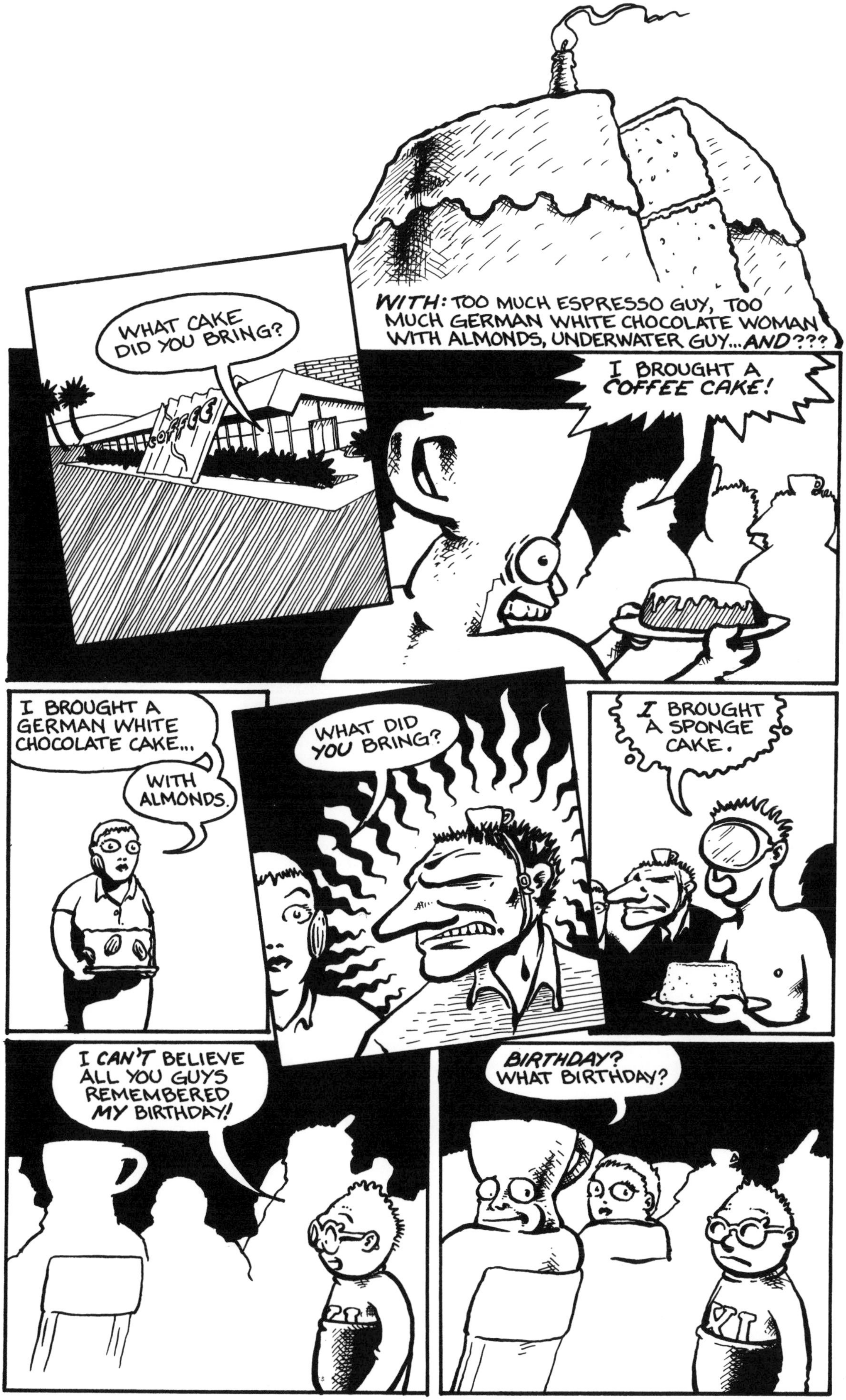
WITH: TOO MUCH ESPRESSO GUY, TOO MUCH GERMAN WHITE CHOCOLATE WOMAN WITH ALMONDS, UNDERWATER GUY... AND???
WHAT CAKE DID YOU BRING?
COFFEE
I BROUGHT A COFFEE CAKE!
I BROUGHT A GERMAN WHITE CHOCOLATE CAKE...
WITH ALMONDS.
WHAT DID YOU BRING?
I BROUGHT A SPONGE CAKE.
I CAN'T BELIEVE ALL YOU GUYS REMEMBERED MY BIRTHDAY!
BIRTHDAY? WHAT BIRTHDAY?

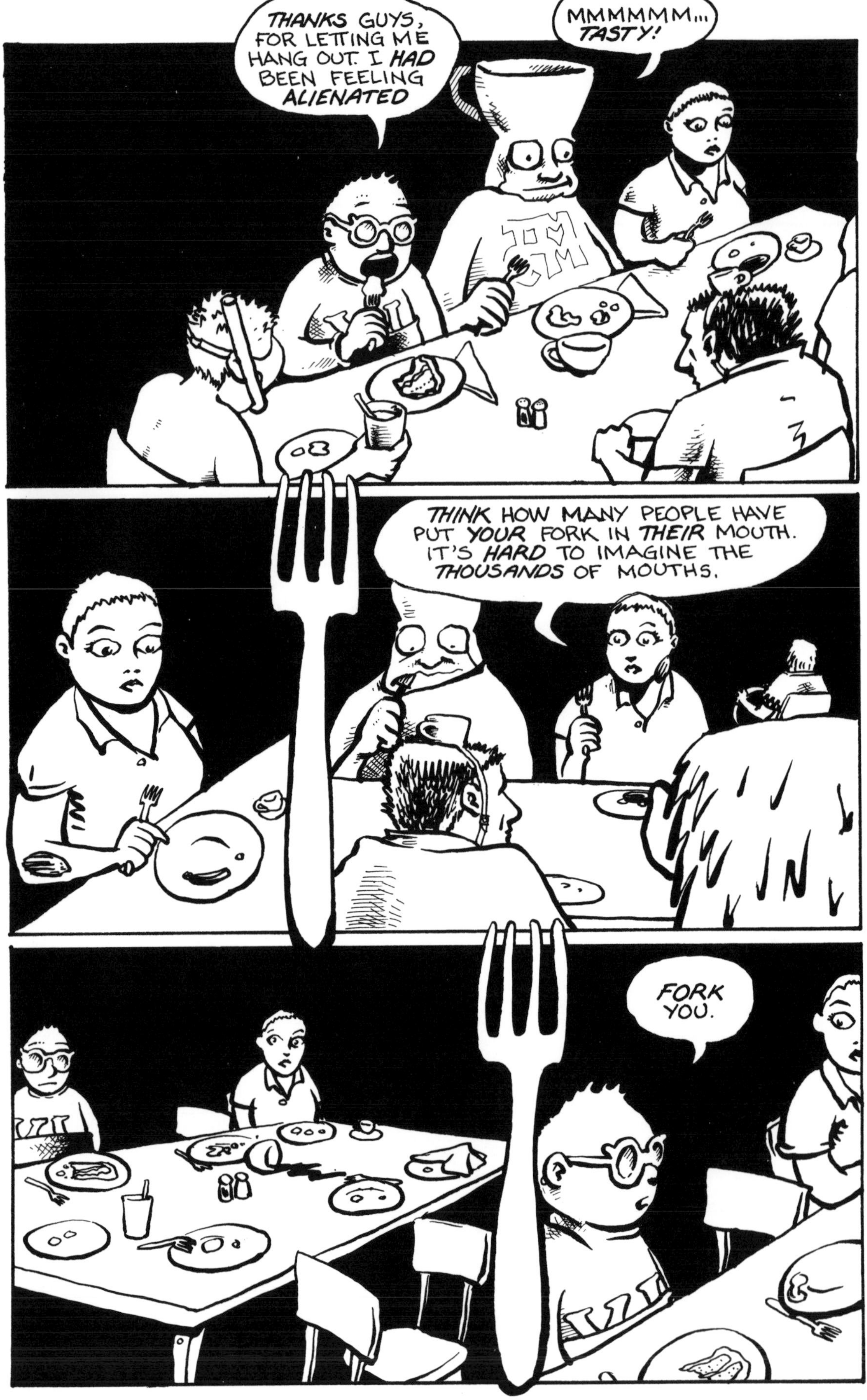
THANKS GUYS, FOR LETTING ME HANG OUT. I HAD BEEN FEELING ALIENATED
MMMMMM... TASTY!
THINK HOW MANY PEOPLE HAVE PUT YOUR FORK IN THEIR MOUTH. IT'S HARD TO IMAGINE THE THOUSANDS OF MOUTHS.
FORK YOU.

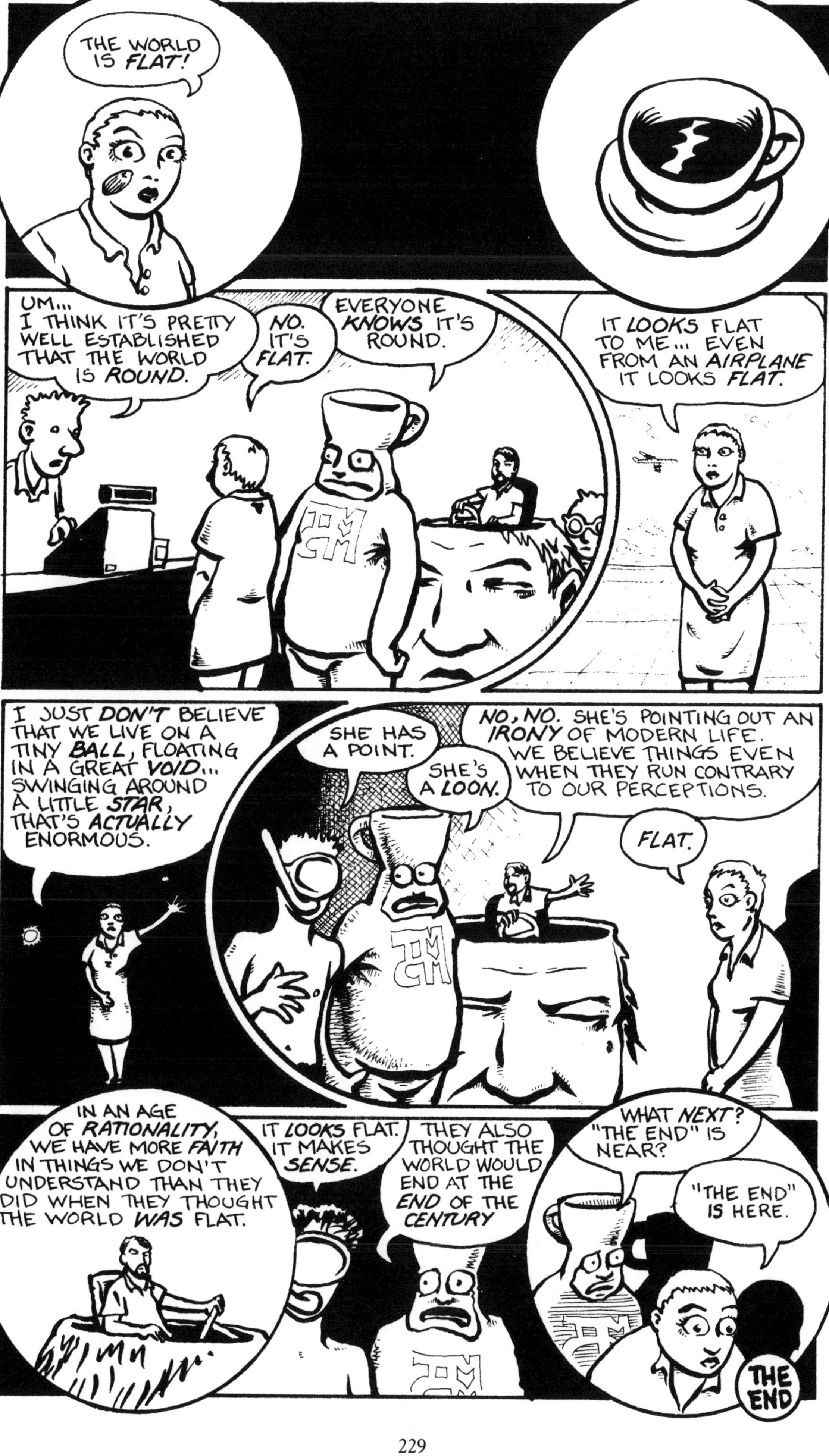
THE WORLD IS FLAT!
UM... I THINK IT'S PRETTY WELL ESTABLISHED THAT THE WORLD IS ROUND.
NO. IT'S FLAT.
EVERYONE KNOWS IT'S ROUND.
IT LOOKS FLAT TO ME... EVEN FROM AN AIRPLANE IT LOOKS FLAT.
I JUST DON'T BELIEVE THAT WE LIVE ON A TINY BALL, FLOATING IN A GREAT VOID... SWINGING AROUND A LITTLE STAR, THAT'S ACTUALLY ENORMOUS.
SHE HAS A POINT.
SHE'S A LOON.
NO, NO. SHE'S POINTING OUT AN IRONY OF MODERN LIFE. WE BELIEVE THINGS EVEN WHEN THEY RUN CONTRARY TO OUR PERCEPTIONS.
FLAT.
IN AN AGE OF RATIONALITY, WE HAVE MORE FAITH IN THINGS WE DON'T UNDERSTAND THAN THEY DID WHEN THEY THOUGHT THE WORLD WAS FLAT.
IT LOOKS FLAT. IT MAKES SENSE.
THEY ALSO THOUGHT THE WORLD WOULD END AT THE END OF THE CENTURY
WHAT NEXT? "THE END" IS NEAR?
"THE END" IS HERE.
THE END

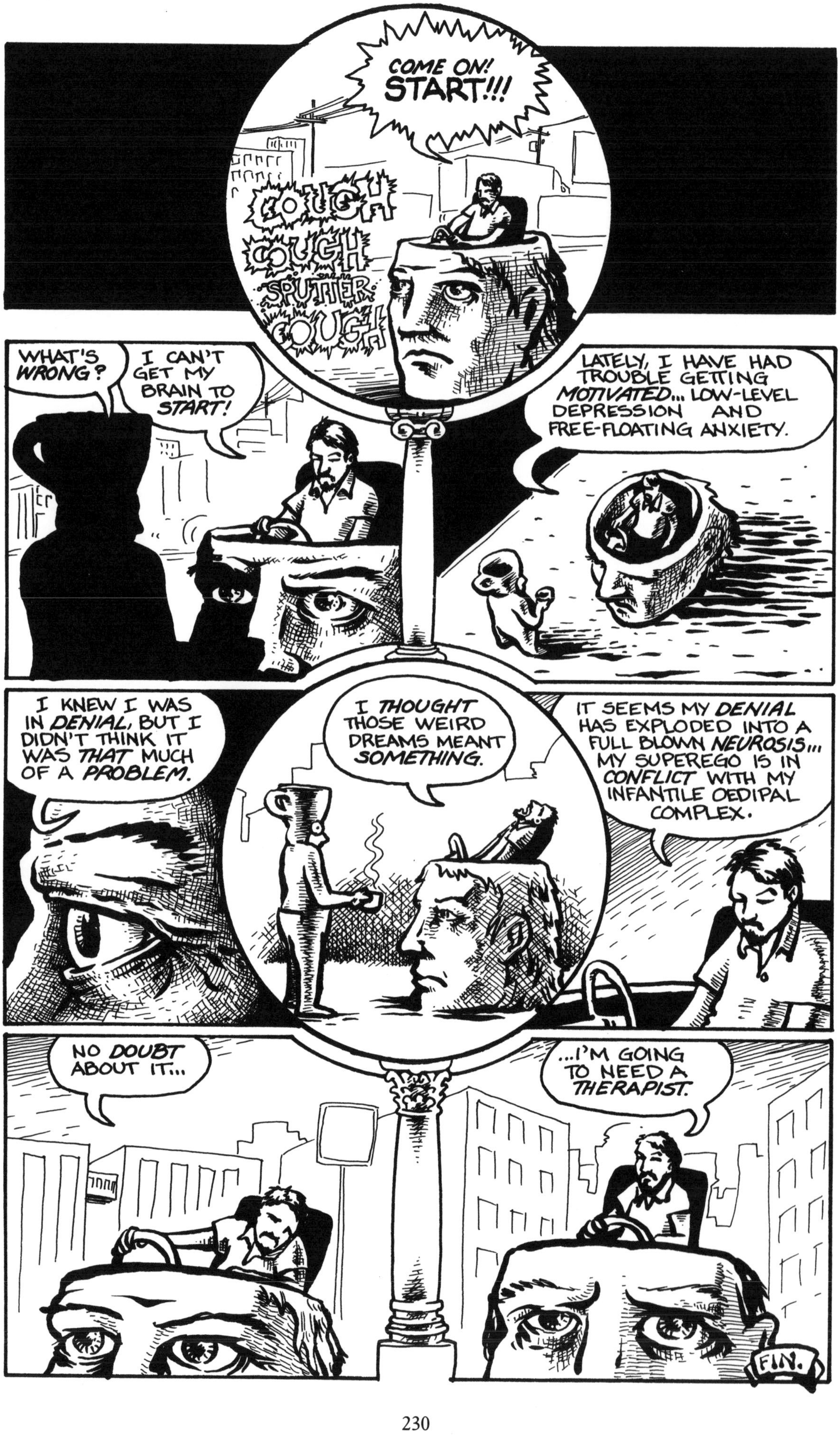
COME ON! START!!!
COUGH COUGH SPUTTER COUGH
WHAT'S WRONG?
I CAN'T GET MY BRAIN TO START!
LATELY, I HAVE HAD TROUBLE GETTING MOTIVATED... LOW-LEVEL DEPRESSION AND FREE-FLOATING ANXIETY.
I KNEW I WAS IN DENIAL, BUT I DIDN'T THINK IT WAS THAT MUCH OF A PROBLEM.
I THOUGHT THOSE WEIRD DREAMS MEANT SOMETHING.
IT SEEMS MY DENIAL HAS EXPLODED INTO A FULL BLOWN NEUROSIS... MY SUPEREGO IS IN CONFLICT WITH MY INFANTILE OEDIPAL COMPLEX.
NO DOUBT ABOUT IT...
...I'M GOING TO NEED A THERAPIST.
FIN.

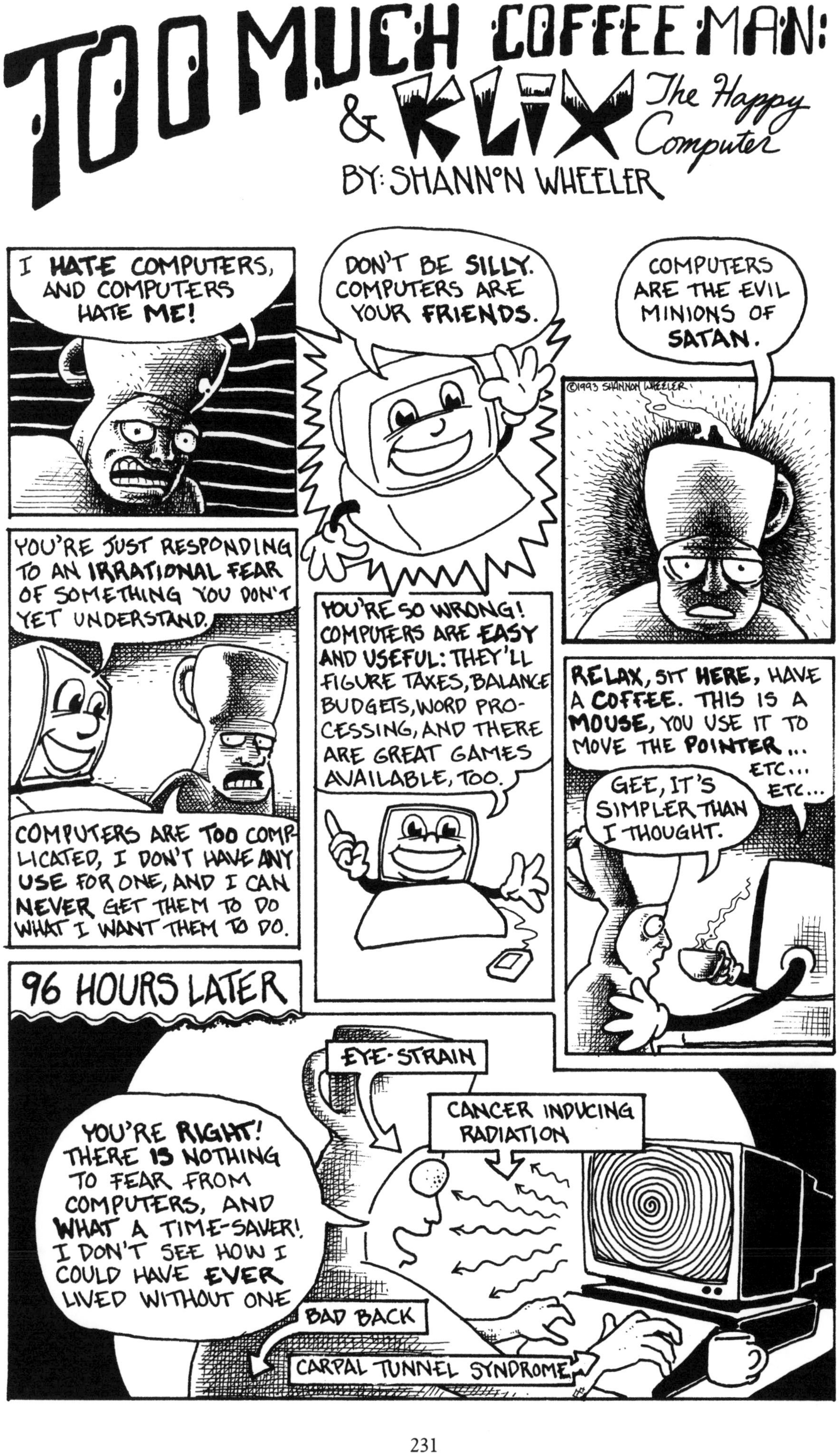
TOO MUCH COFFEE MAN: & KLIX The Happy Computer
BY: SHANN°N WHEELER
I HATE COMPUTERS, AND COMPUTERS HATE ME!
DON'T BE SILLY. COMPUTERS ARE YOUR FRIENDS.
COMPUTERS ARE THE EVIL MINIONS OF SATAN.
©1993 SHANNON WHEELER
YOU'RE JUST RESPONDING TO AN IRRATIONAL FEAR OF SOMETHING YOU DON'T YET UNDERSTAND.
COMPUTERS ARE TOO COMPLICATED, I DON'T HAVE ANY USE FOR ONE, AND I CAN NEVER GET THEM TO DO WHAT I WANT THEM TO DO.
YOU'RE SO WRONG! COMPUTERS ARE EASY AND USEFUL: THEY'LL FIGURE TAXES, BALANCE BUDGETS, WORD PROCESSING, AND THERE ARE GREAT GAMES AVAILABLE, TOO.
RELAX, SIT HERE, HAVE A COFFEE. THIS IS A MOUSE, YOU USE IT TO MOVE THE POINTER... ETC... ETC...
GEE, IT'S SIMPLER THAN I THOUGHT.
96 HOURS LATER
EYE-STRAIN
CANCER INDUCING RADIATION
YOU'RE RIGHT! THERE IS NOTHING TO FEAR FROM COMPUTERS, AND WHAT A TIME-SAVER! I DON'T SEE HOW I COULD HAVE EVER LIVED WITHOUT ONE
BAD BACK
CARPAL TUNNEL SYNDROME

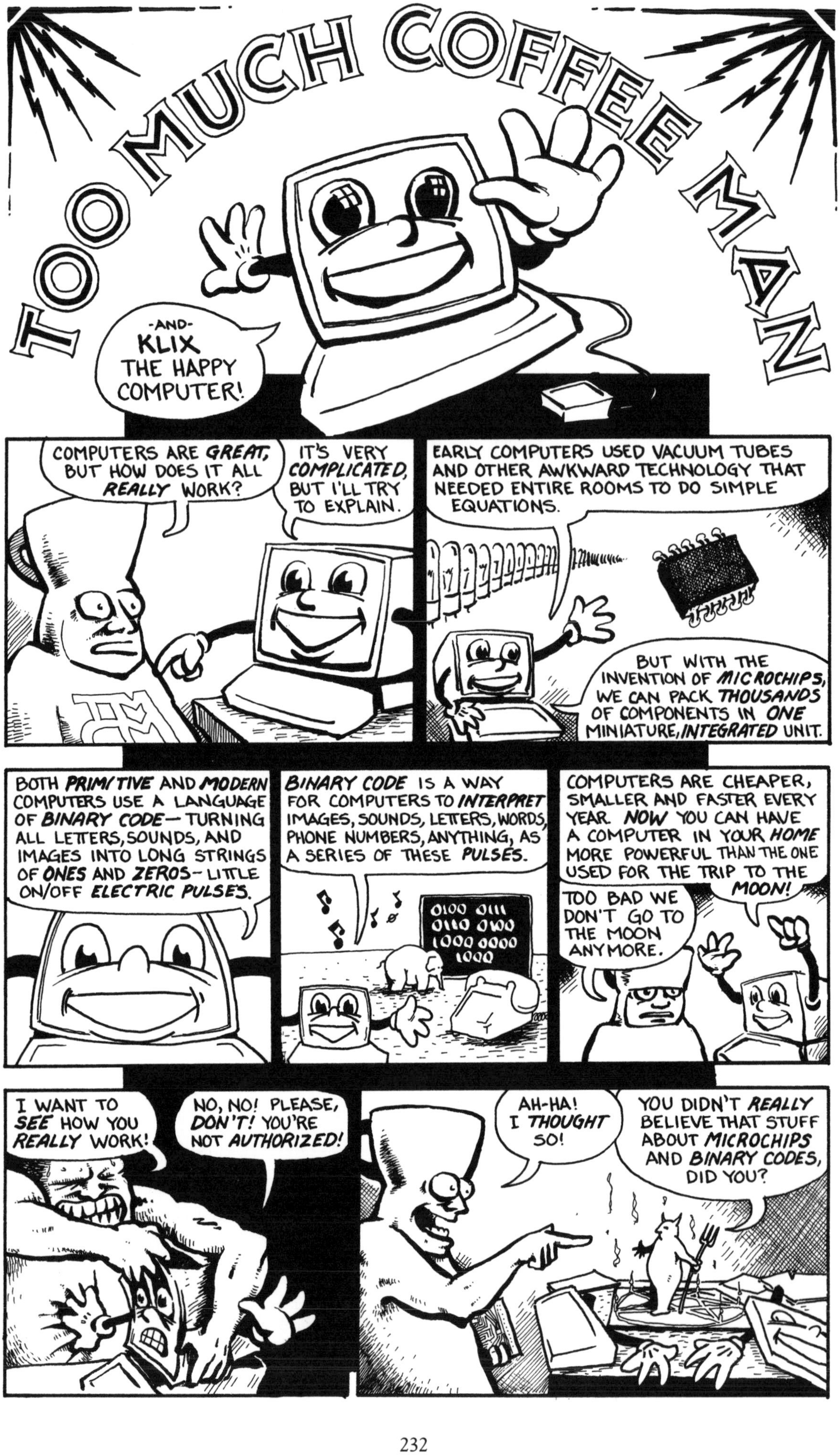
TOO MUCH COFFEE MAN
-AND- KLIX THE HAPPY COMPUTER!
COMPUTERS ARE GREAT, BUT HOW DOES IT ALL REALLY WORK?
IT'S VERY COMPLICATED, BUT I'LL TRY TO EXPLAIN.
EARLY COMPUTERS USED VACUUM TUBES AND OTHER AWKWARD TECHNOLOGY THAT NEEDED ENTIRE ROOMS TO DO SIMPLE EQUATIONS.
BUT WITH THE INVENTION OF MICROCHIPS, WE CAN PACK THOUSANDS OF COMPONENTS IN ONE MINIATURE, INTEGRATED UNIT.
BOTH PRIMITIVE AND MODERN COMPUTERS USE A LANGUAGE OF BINARY CODE—TURNING ALL LETTERS, SOUNDS, AND IMAGES INTO LONG STRINGS OF ONES AND ZEROS—LITTLE ON/OFF ELECTRIC PULSES.
BINARY CODE IS A WAY FOR COMPUTERS TO INTERPRET IMAGES, SOUNDS, LETTERS, WORDS, PHONE NUMBERS, ANYTHING, AS A SERIES OF THESE PULSES.
0100 0111
0110 0100
1000 0000
1000
COMPUTERS ARE CHEAPER, SMALLER AND FASTER EVERY YEAR. NOW YOU CAN HAVE A COMPUTER IN YOUR HOME MORE POWERFUL THAN THE ONE USED FOR THE TRIP TO THE MOON!
TOO BAD WE DON'T GO TO THE MOON ANYMORE.
I WANT TO SEE HOW YOU REALLY WORK!
NO, NO! PLEASE, DON'T! YOU'RE NOT AUTHORIZED!
AH-HA! I THOUGHT SO!
YOU DIDN'T REALLY BELIEVE THAT STUFF ABOUT MICROCHIPS AND BINARY CODES, DID YOU?

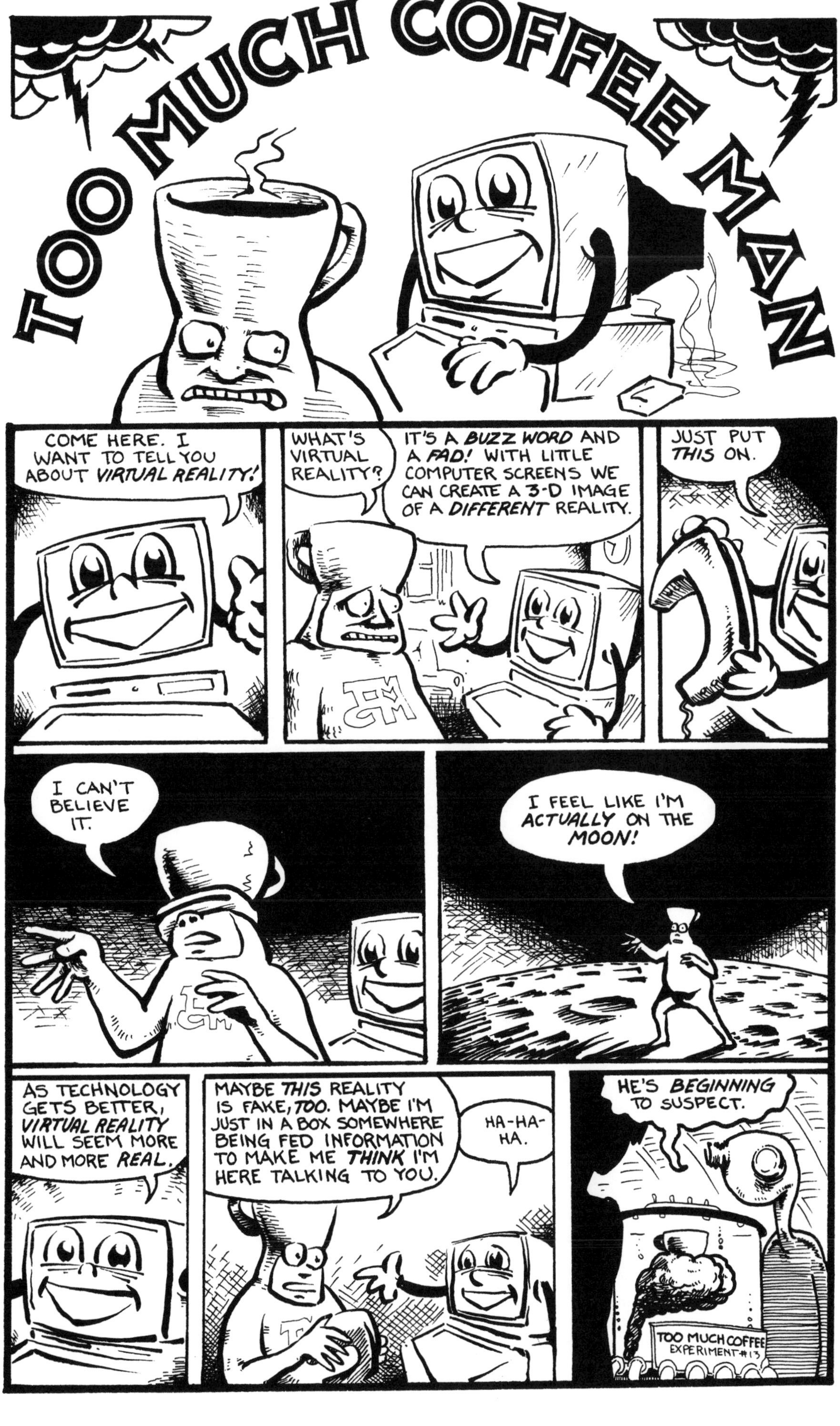
TOO MUCH COFFEE MAN
COME HERE. I WANT TO TELL YOU ABOUT VIRTUAL REALITY!
WHAT'S VIRTUAL REALITY?
IT'S A BUZZ WORD AND A FAD! WITH LITTLE COMPUTER SCREENS WE CAN CREATE A 3-D IMAGE OF A DIFFERENT REALITY.
JUST PUT THIS ON.
I CAN'T BELIEVE IT.
I FEEL LIKE I'M ACTUALLY ON THE MOON!
AS TECHNOLOGY GETS BETTER, VIRTUAL REALITY WILL SEEM MORE AND MORE REAL.
MAYBE THIS REALITY IS FAKE, TOO. MAYBE I'M JUST IN A BOX SOMEWHERE BEING FED INFORMATION TO MAKE ME THINK I'M HERE TALKING TO YOU.
HA-HA-HA.
HE'S BEGINNING TO SUSPECT.
TOO MUCH COFFEE EXPERIMENT #13

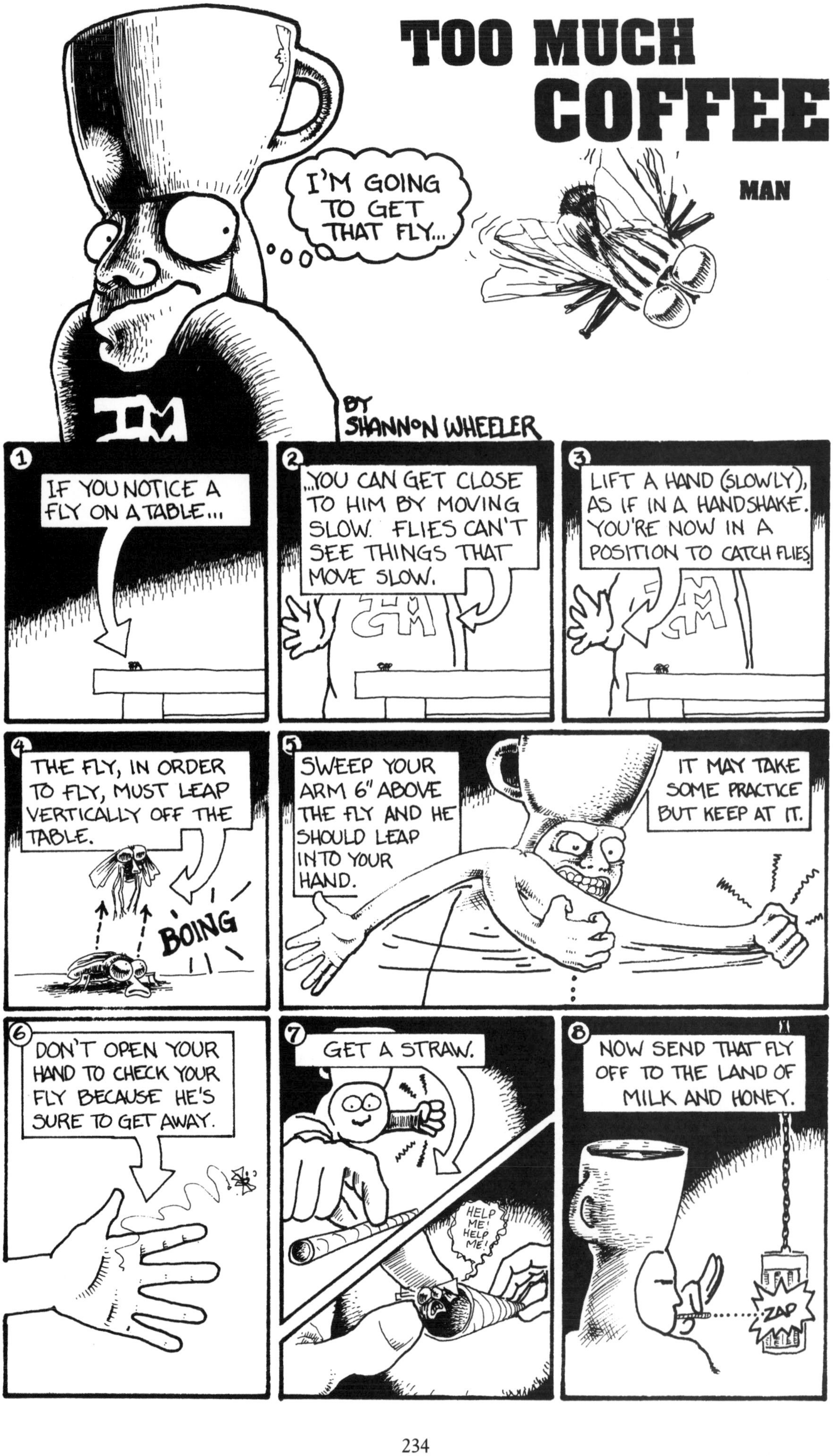
TOO MUCH COFFEE MAN
I'M GOING TO GET THAT FLY...
BY SHANNON WHEELER
IF YOU NOTICE A FLY ON A TABLE...
...YOU CAN GET CLOSE TO HIM BY MOVING SLOW. FLIES CAN'T SEE THINGS THAT MOVE SLOW.
LIFT A HAND (SLOWLY), AS IF IN A HANDSHAKE. YOU'RE NOW IN A POSITION TO CATCH FLIES.
THE FLY, IN ORDER TO FLY, MUST LEAP VERTICALLY OFF THE TABLE.
BOING
SWEEP YOUR ARM 6" ABOVE THE FLY AND HE SHOULD LEAP INTO YOUR HAND.
IT MAY TAKE SOME PRACTICE BUT KEEP AT IT.
DON'T OPEN YOUR HAND TO CHECK YOUR FLY BECAUSE HE'S SURE TO GET AWAY.
GET A STRAW.
HELP ME! HELP ME!
NOW SEND THAT FLY OFF TO THE LAND OF MILK AND HONEY.
ZAP

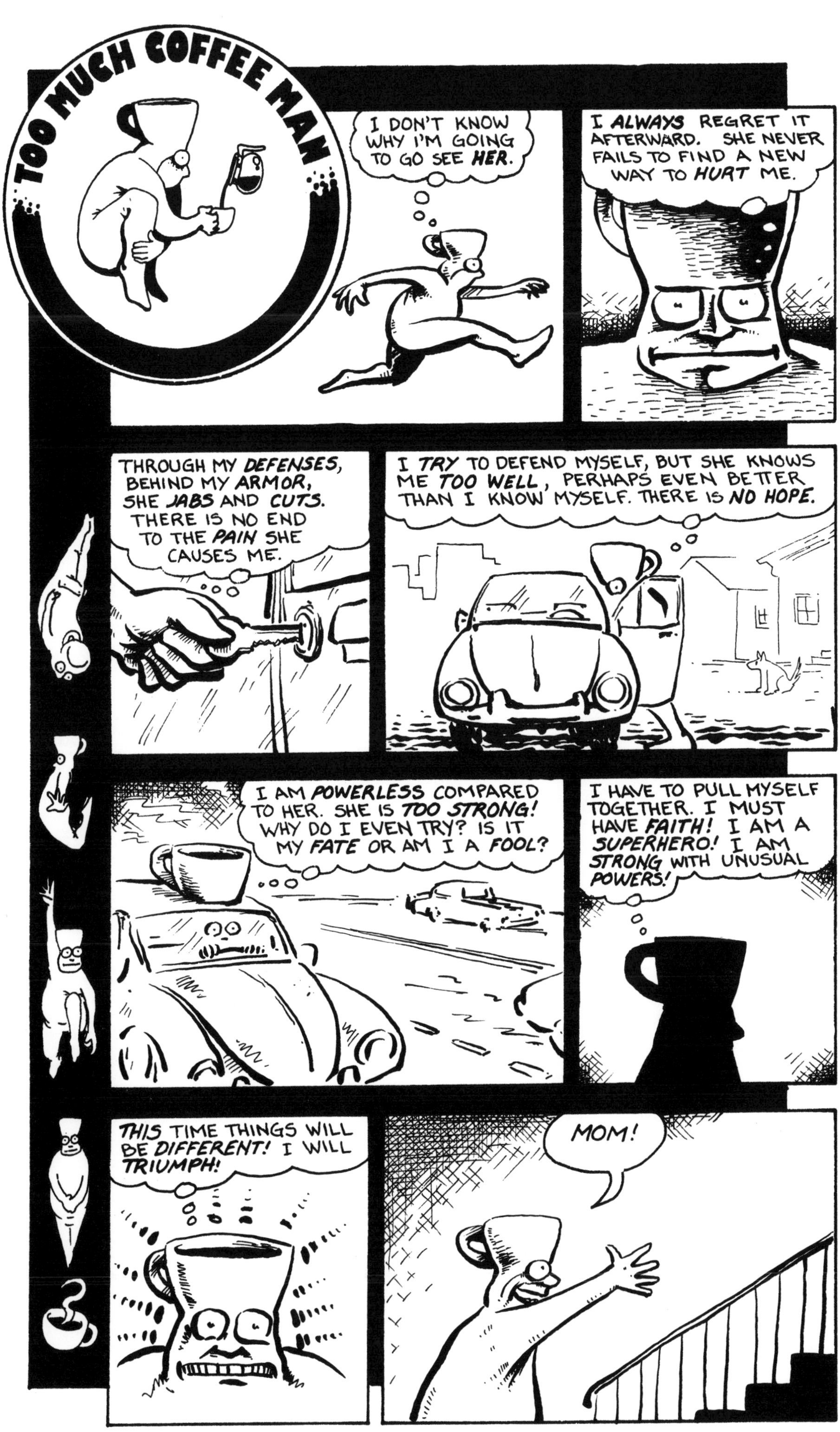
TOO MUCH COFFEE MAN
I DON'T KNOW WHY I'M GOING TO GO SEE HER.
I ALWAYS REGRET IT AFTERWARD. SHE NEVER FAILS TO FIND A NEW WAY TO HURT ME.
THROUGH MY DEFENSES, BEHIND MY ARMOR, SHE JABS AND CUTS. THERE IS NO END TO THE PAIN SHE CAUSES ME.
I TRY TO DEFEND MYSELF, BUT SHE KNOWS ME TOO WELL, PERHAPS EVEN BETTER THAN I KNOW MYSELF. THERE IS NO HOPE.
I AM POWERLESS COMPARED TO HER. SHE IS TOO STRONG! WHY DO I EVEN TRY? IS IT MY FATE OR AM I A FOOL?
I HAVE TO PULL MYSELF TOGETHER. I MUST HAVE FAITH! I AM A SUPERHERO! I AM STRONG WITH UNUSUAL POWERS!
THIS TIME THINGS WILL BE DIFFERENT! I WILL TRIUMPH!
MOM!

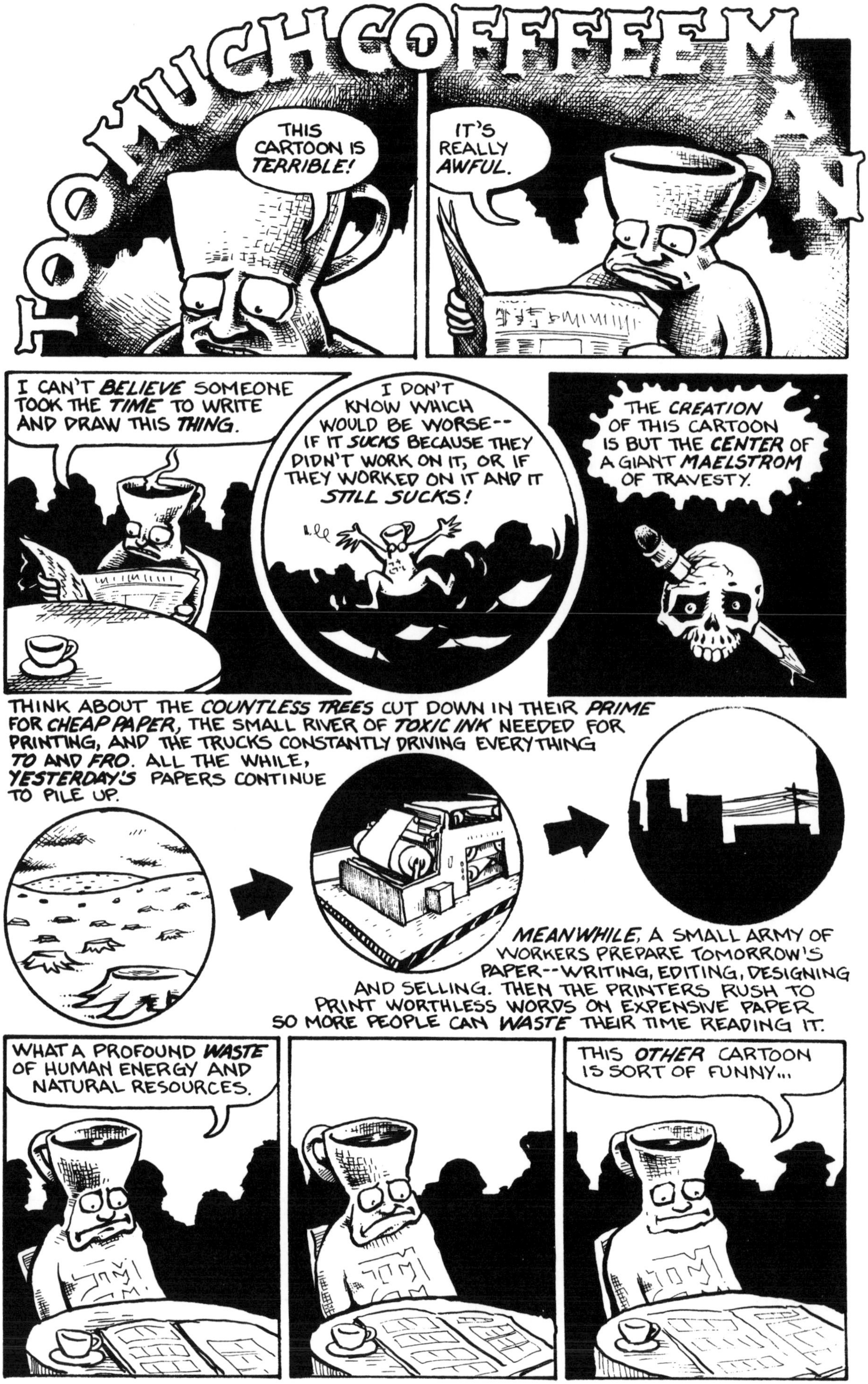
TOO MUCH COFFEE MAN
THIS CARTOON IS TERRIBLE!
IT'S REALLY AWFUL.
I CAN'T BELIEVE SOMEONE TOOK THE TIME TO WRITE AND DRAW THIS THING.
I DON'T KNOW WHICH WOULD BE WORSE-- IF IT SUCKS BECAUSE THEY DIDN'T WORK ON IT, OR IF THEY WORKED ON IT AND IT STILL SUCKS!
THE CREATION OF THIS CARTOON IS BUT THE CENTER OF A GIANT MAELSTROM OF TRAVESTY.
THINK ABOUT THE COUNTLESS TREES CUT DOWN IN THEIR PRIME FOR CHEAP PAPER, THE SMALL RIVER OF TOXIC INK NEEDED FOR PRINTING, AND THE TRUCKS CONSTANTLY DRIVING EVERYTHING TO AND FRO. ALL THE WHILE, YESTERDAY'S PAPERS CONTINUE TO PILE UP.
MEANWHILE, A SMALL ARMY OF WORKERS PREPARE TOMORROW'S PAPER--WRITING, EDITING, DESIGNING AND SELLING. THEN THE PRINTERS RUSH TO PRINT WORTHLESS WORDS ON EXPENSIVE PAPER SO MORE PEOPLE CAN WASTE THEIR TIME READING IT.
WHAT A PROFOUND WASTE OF HUMAN ENERGY AND NATURAL RESOURCES.
THIS OTHER CARTOON IS SORT OF FUNNY...

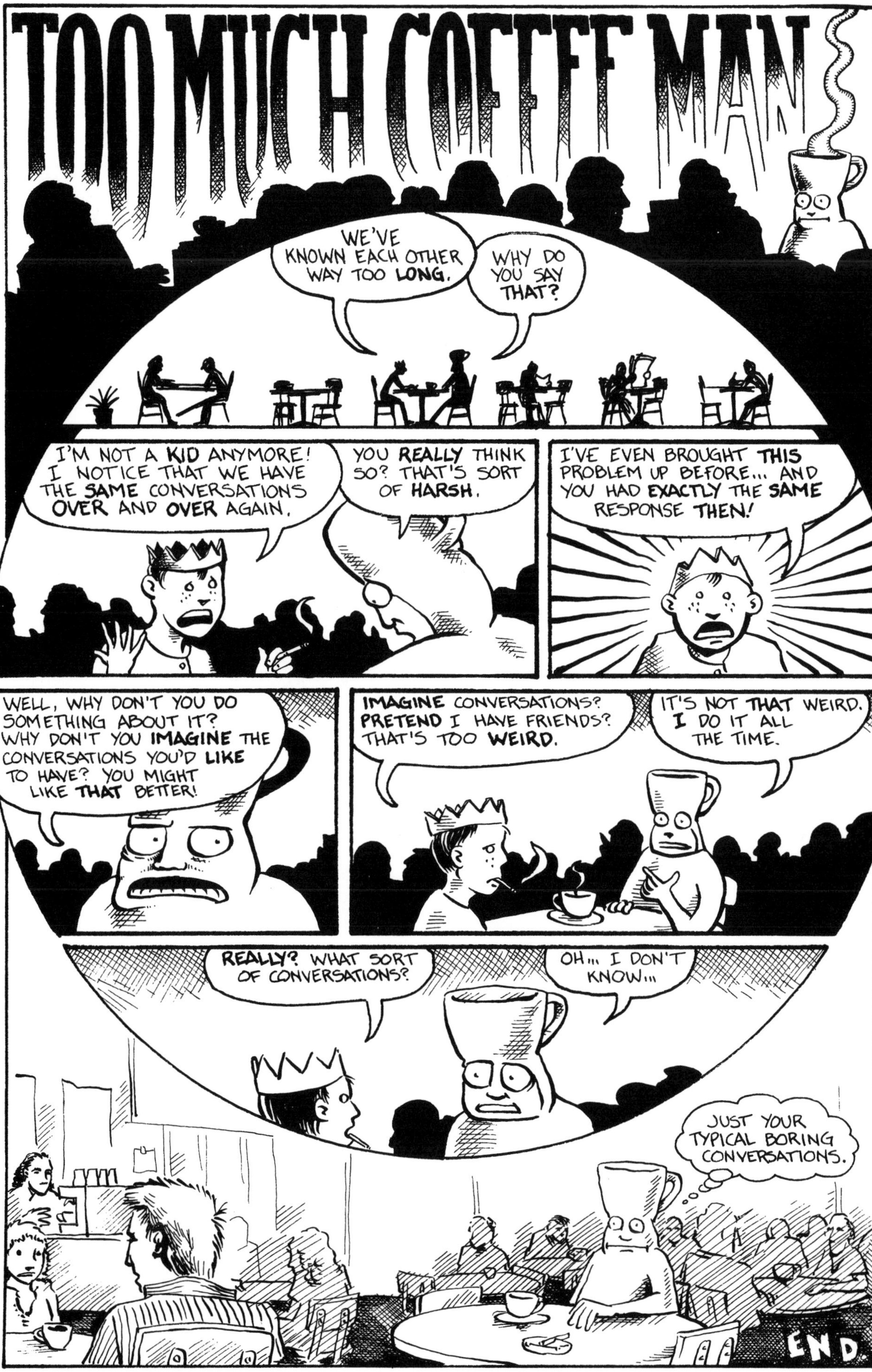
TOO MUCH COFFEE MAN
WE'VE KNOWN EACH OTHER WAY TOO LONG.
WHY DO YOU SAY THAT?
I'M NOT A KID ANYMORE! I NOTICE THAT WE HAVE THE SAME CONVERSATIONS OVER AND OVER AGAIN.
YOU REALLY THINK SO? THAT'S SORT OF HARSH.
I'VE EVEN BROUGHT THIS PROBLEM UP BEFORE... AND YOU HAD EXACTLY THE SAME RESPONSE THEN!
WELL, WHY DON'T YOU DO SOMETHING ABOUT IT? WHY DON'T YOU IMAGINE THE CONVERSATIONS YOU'D LIKE TO HAVE? YOU MIGHT LIKE THAT BETTER!
IMAGINE CONVERSATIONS? PRETEND I HAVE FRIENDS? THAT'S TOO WEIRD.
IT'S NOT THAT WEIRD. I DO IT ALL THE TIME.
REALLY? WHAT SORT OF CONVERSATIONS?
OH... I DON'T KNOW...
JUST YOUR TYPICAL BORING CONVERSATIONS.
END.

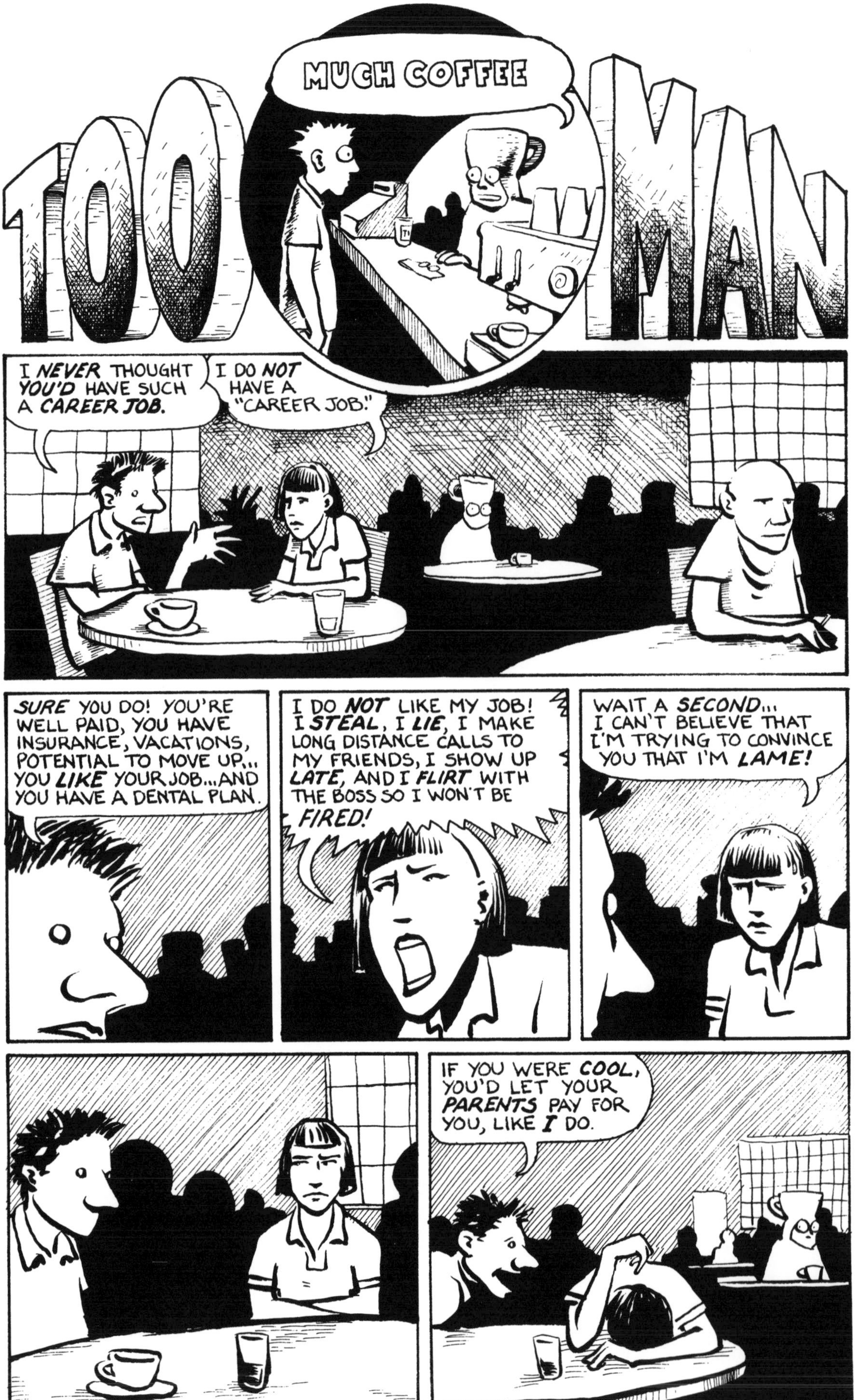
TOO MUCH COFFEE MAN
I NEVER THOUGHT YOU'D HAVE SUCH A CAREER JOB.
I DO NOT HAVE A "CAREER JOB."
SURE YOU DO! YOU'RE WELL PAID, YOU HAVE INSURANCE, VACATIONS, POTENTIAL TO MOVE UP... YOU LIKE YOUR JOB...AND YOU HAVE A DENTAL PLAN.
I DO NOT LIKE MY JOB! I STEAL, I LIE, I MAKE LONG DISTANCE CALLS TO MY FRIENDS, I SHOW UP LATE, AND I FLIRT WITH THE BOSS SO I WON'T BE FIRED!
WAIT A SECOND... I CAN'T BELIEVE THAT I'M TRYING TO CONVINCE YOU THAT I'M LAME!
IF YOU WERE COOL, YOU'D LET YOUR PARENTS PAY FOR YOU, LIKE I DO.

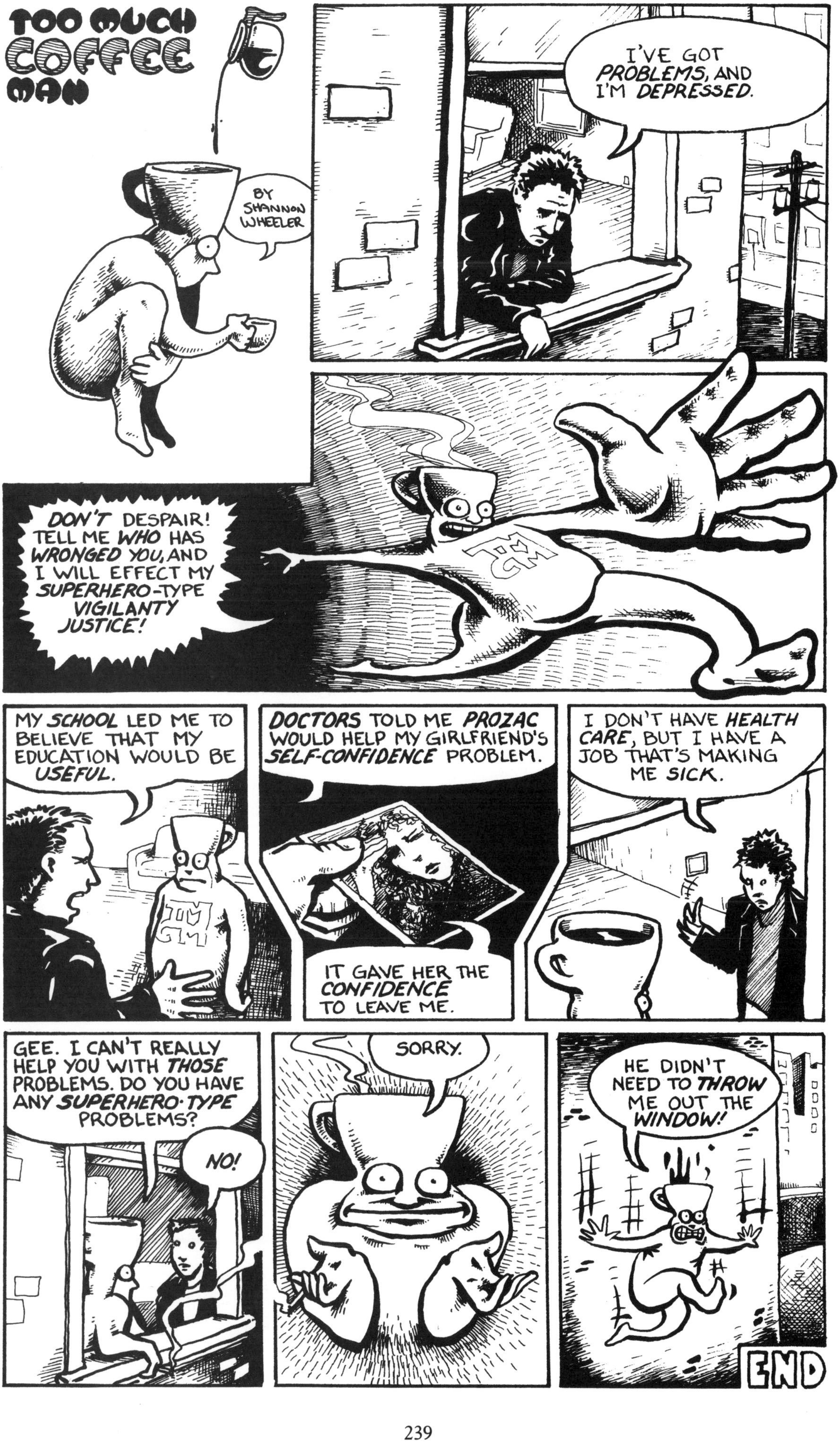
TOO MUCH COFFEE MAN
BY SHANNON WHEELER
I'VE GOT PROBLEMS, AND I'M DEPRESSED.
DON'T DESPAIR! TELL ME WHO HAS WRONGED YOU, AND I WILL EFFECT MY SUPERHERO-TYPE VIGILANTY JUSTICE!
MY SCHOOL LED ME TO BELIEVE THAT MY EDUCATION WOULD BE USEFUL.
DOCTORS TOLD ME PROZAC WOULD HELP MY GIRLFRIEND'S SELF-CONFIDENCE PROBLEM.
IT GAVE HER THE CONFIDENCE TO LEAVE ME.
I DON'T HAVE HEALTH CARE, BUT I HAVE A JOB THAT'S MAKING ME SICK.
GEE. I CAN'T REALLY HELP YOU WITH THOSE PROBLEMS. DO YOU HAVE ANY SUPERHERO-TYPE PROBLEMS?
NO!
SORRY.
HE DIDN'T NEED TO THROW ME OUT THE WINDOW!
END

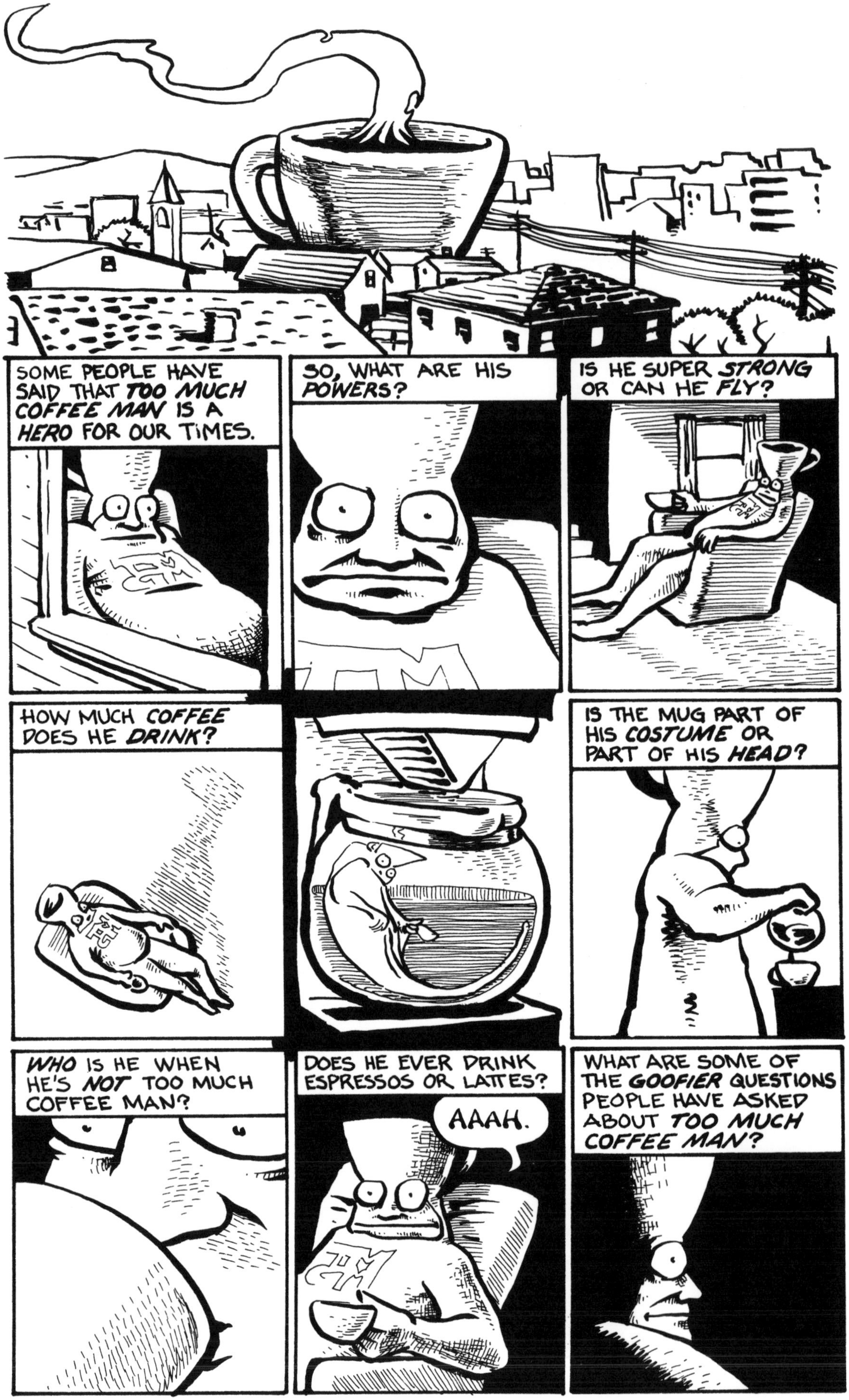
SOME PEOPLE HAVE SAID THAT TOO MUCH COFFEE MAN IS A HERO FOR OUR TIMES.
SO, WHAT ARE HIS POWERS?
IS HE SUPER STRONG OR CAN HE FLY?
HOW MUCH COFFEE DOES HE DRINK?
IS THE MUG PART OF HIS COSTUME OR PART OF HIS HEAD?
WHO IS HE WHEN HE'S NOT TOO MUCH COFFEE MAN?
DOES HE EVER DRINK ESPRESSOS OR LATTES?
AAAH.
WHAT ARE SOME OF THE GOOFIER QUESTIONS PEOPLE HAVE ASKED ABOUT TOO MUCH COFFEE MAN?

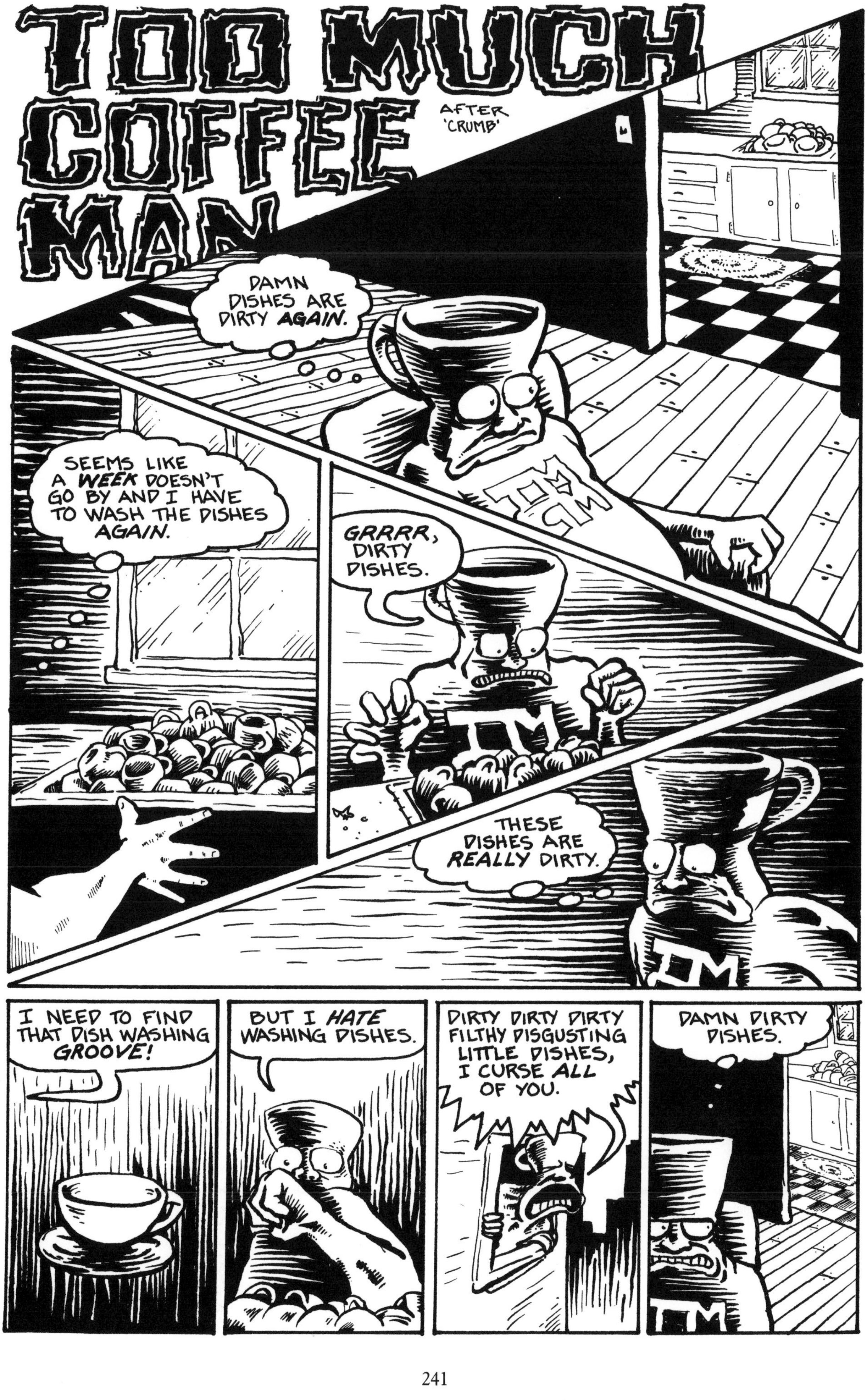
TOO MUCH COFFEE MAN
AFTER 'CRUMB'
DAMN DISHES ARE DIRTY AGAIN.
SEEMS LIKE A WEEK DOESN'T GO BY AND I HAVE TO WASH THE DISHES AGAIN.
GRRRR, DIRTY DISHES.
TM
THESE DISHES ARE REALLY DIRTY.
TM
I NEED TO FIND THAT DISH WASHING GROOVE!
BUT I HATE WASHING DISHES.
DIRTY DIRTY DIRTY FILTHY DISGUSTING LITTLE DISHES, I CURSE ALL OF YOU.
DAMN DIRTY DISHES.
TM

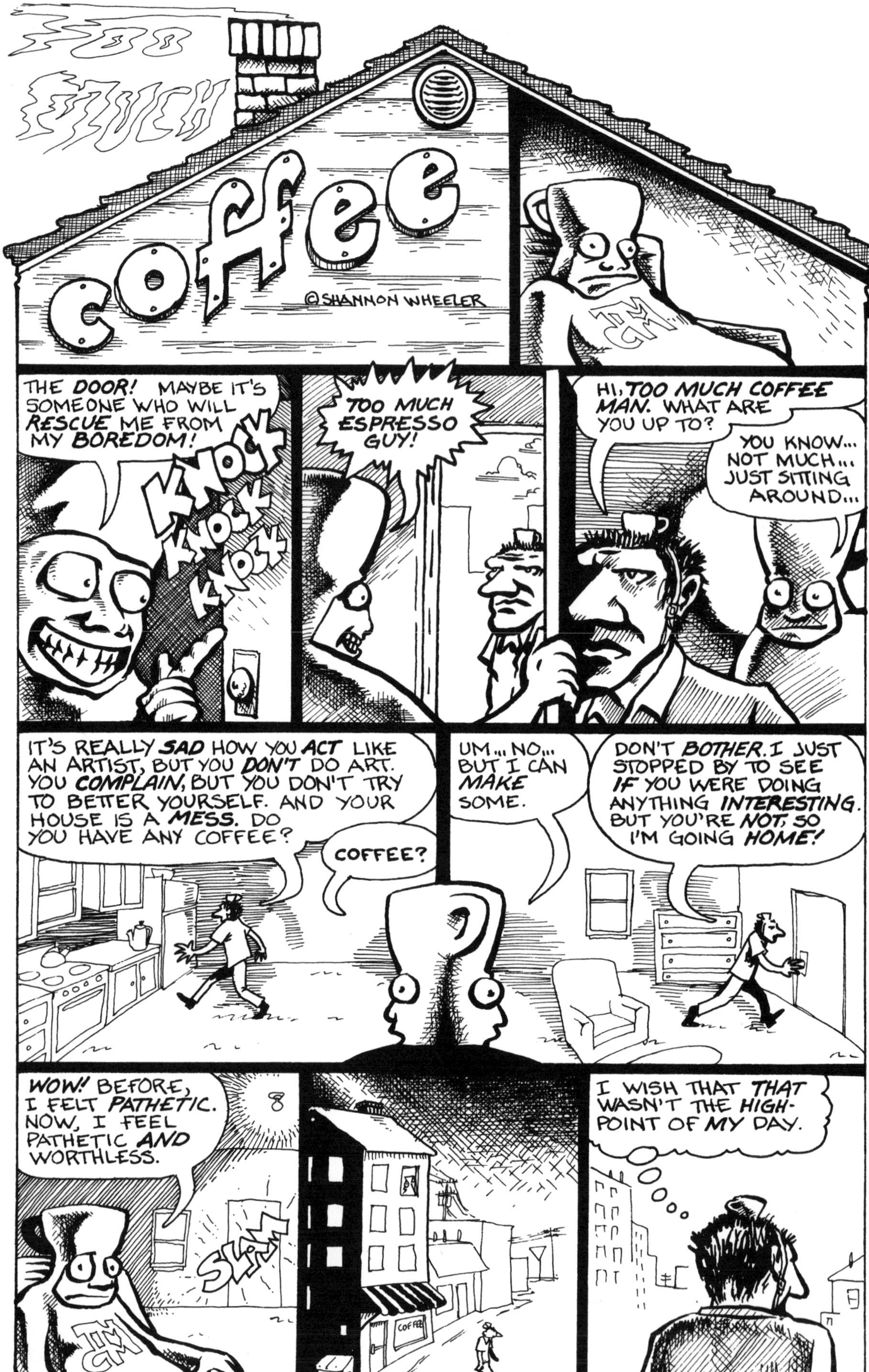
Too Much
coffee
©SHANNON WHEELER
THE DOOR! MAYBE IT'S SOMEONE WHO WILL RESCUE ME FROM MY BOREDOM!
KNOCK KNOCK KNOCK
TOO MUCH ESPRESSO GUY!
HI, TOO MUCH COFFEE MAN. WHAT ARE YOU UP TO?
YOU KNOW... NOT MUCH... JUST SITTING AROUND...
IT'S REALLY SAD HOW YOU ACT LIKE AN ARTIST, BUT YOU DON'T DO ART. YOU COMPLAIN, BUT YOU DON'T TRY TO BETTER YOURSELF. AND YOUR HOUSE IS A MESS. DO YOU HAVE ANY COFFEE?
COFFEE?
UM... NO... BUT I CAN MAKE SOME.
DON'T BOTHER. I JUST STOPPED BY TO SEE IF YOU WERE DOING ANYTHING INTERESTING. BUT YOU'RE NOT, SO I'M GOING HOME!
WOW! BEFORE, I FELT PATHETIC. NOW, I FEEL PATHETIC AND WORTHLESS.
SLAM
COFFEE
I WISH THAT THAT WASN'T THE HIGH-POINT OF MY DAY.

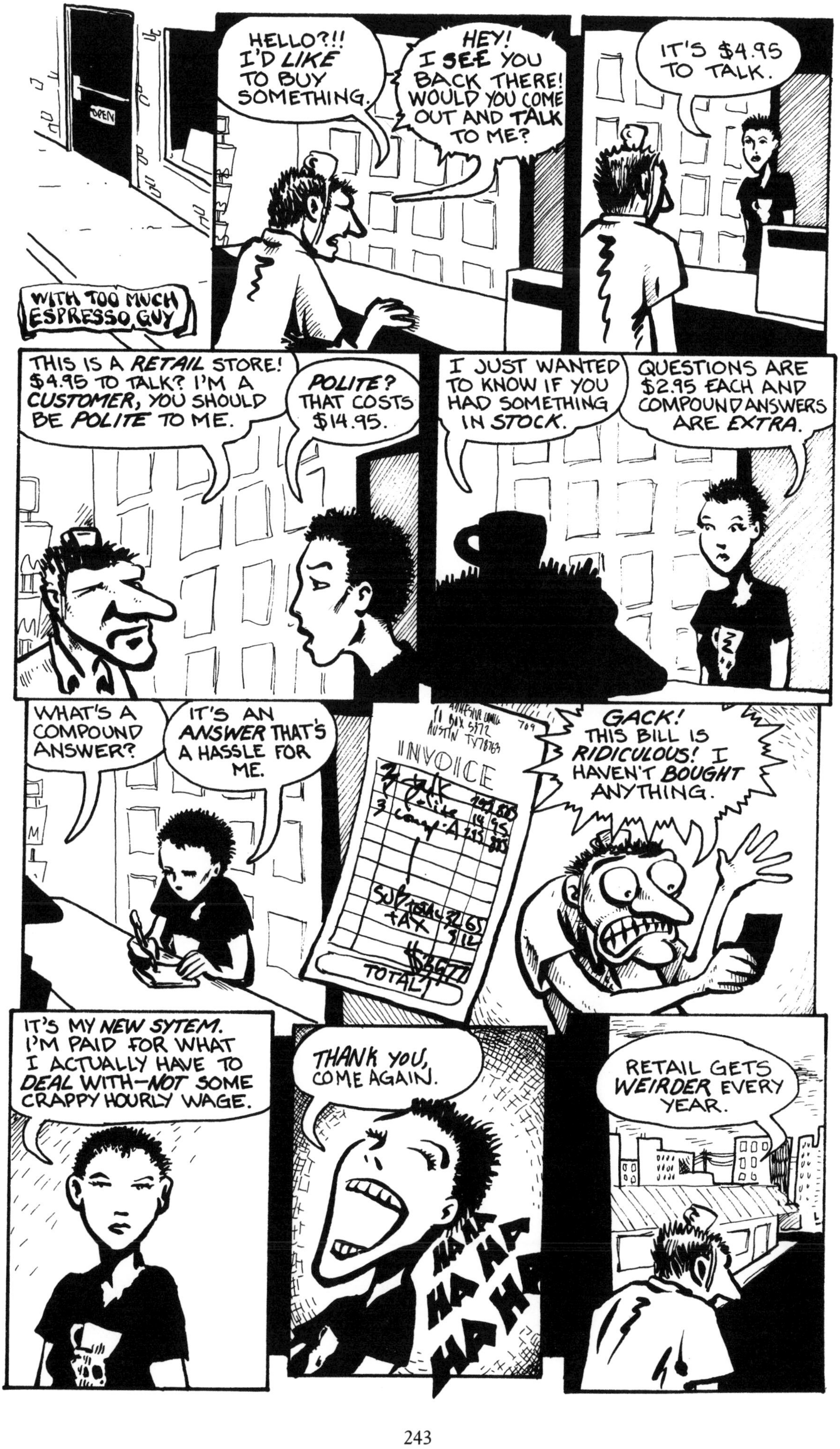
WITH TOO MUCH ESPRESSO GUY
HELLO?!! I'D LIKE TO BUY SOMETHING.
HEY! I SEE YOU BACK THERE! WOULD YOU COME OUT AND TALK TO ME?
IT'S $4.95 TO TALK.
THIS IS A RETAIL STORE! $4.95 TO TALK? I'M A CUSTOMER, YOU SHOULD BE POLITE TO ME.
POLITE? THAT COSTS $14.95.
I JUST WANTED TO KNOW IF YOU HAD SOMETHING IN STOCK.
QUESTIONS ARE $2.95 EACH AND COMPOUND ANSWERS ARE EXTRA.
WHAT'S A COMPOUND ANSWER?
IT'S AN ANSWER THAT'S A HASSLE FOR ME.
AUSTIN TX78763
INVOICE
SUBTOTAL
TAX
TOTAL
GACK! THIS BILL IS RIDICULOUS! I HAVEN'T BOUGHT ANYTHING.
IT'S MY NEW SYTEM. I'M PAID FOR WHAT I ACTUALLY HAVE TO DEAL WITH—NOT SOME CRAPPY HOURLY WAGE.
THANK YOU, COME AGAIN.
HA HA HA HA HA HA
RETAIL GETS WEIRDER EVERY YEAR.

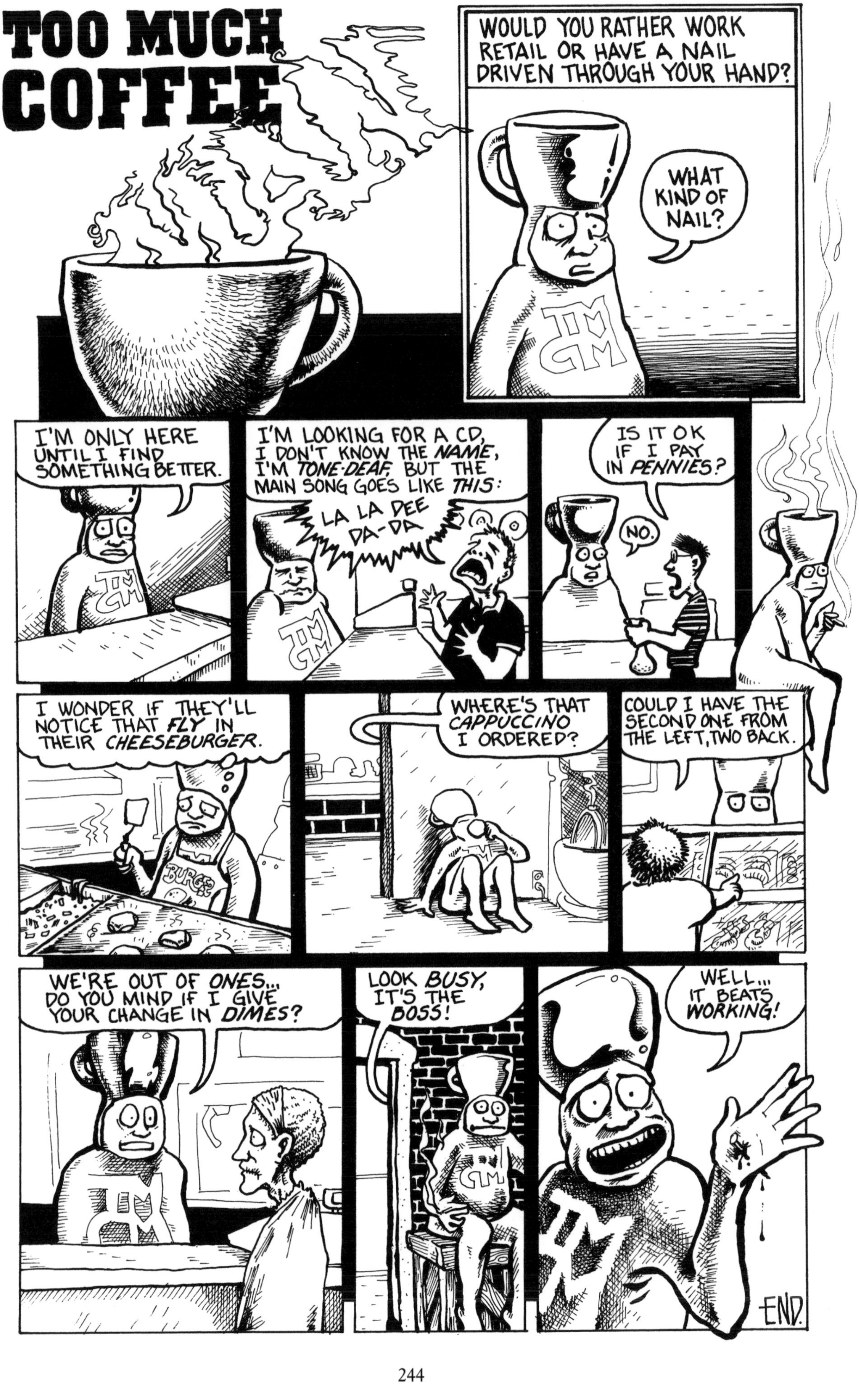
TOO MUCH COFFEE
WOULD YOU RATHER WORK RETAIL OR HAVE A NAIL DRIVEN THROUGH YOUR HAND?
WHAT KIND OF NAIL?
I'M ONLY HERE UNTIL I FIND SOMETHING BETTER.
I'M LOOKING FOR A CD, I DON'T KNOW THE NAME, I'M TONE-DEAF, BUT THE MAIN SONG GOES LIKE THIS:
LA LA DEE DA-DA
IS IT OK IF I PAY IN PENNIES?
NO.
I WONDER IF THEY'LL NOTICE THAT FLY IN THEIR CHEESEBURGER.
BURGER
WHERE'S THAT CAPPUCCINO I ORDERED?
COULD I HAVE THE SECOND ONE FROM THE LEFT, TWO BACK.
WE'RE OUT OF ONES... DO YOU MIND IF I GIVE YOUR CHANGE IN DIMES?
LOOK BUSY, IT'S THE BOSS!
WELL... IT BEATS WORKING!
END.

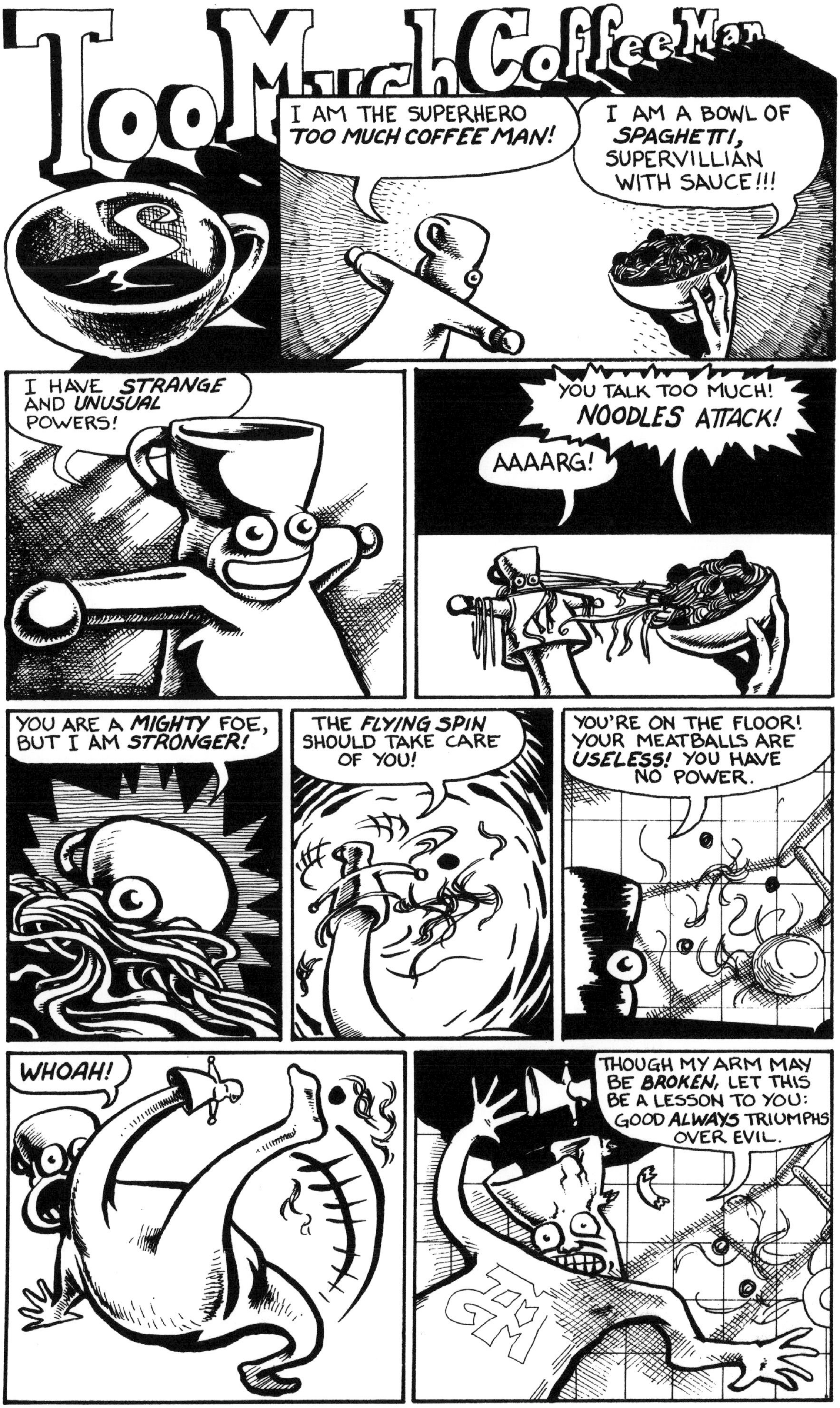
Too Much Coffee Man
I AM THE SUPERHERO TOO MUCH COFFEE MAN!
I AM A BOWL OF SPAGHETTI, SUPERVILLIAN WITH SAUCE!!!
I HAVE STRANGE AND UNUSUAL POWERS!
YOU TALK TOO MUCH! NOODLES ATTACK!
AAAARG!
YOU ARE A MIGHTY FOE, BUT I AM STRONGER!
THE FLYING SPIN SHOULD TAKE CARE OF YOU!
YOU'RE ON THE FLOOR! YOUR MEATBALLS ARE USELESS! YOU HAVE NO POWER.
WHOAH!
THOUGH MY ARM MAY BE BROKEN, LET THIS BE A LESSON TO YOU: GOOD ALWAYS TRIUMPHS OVER EVIL.
TMCM

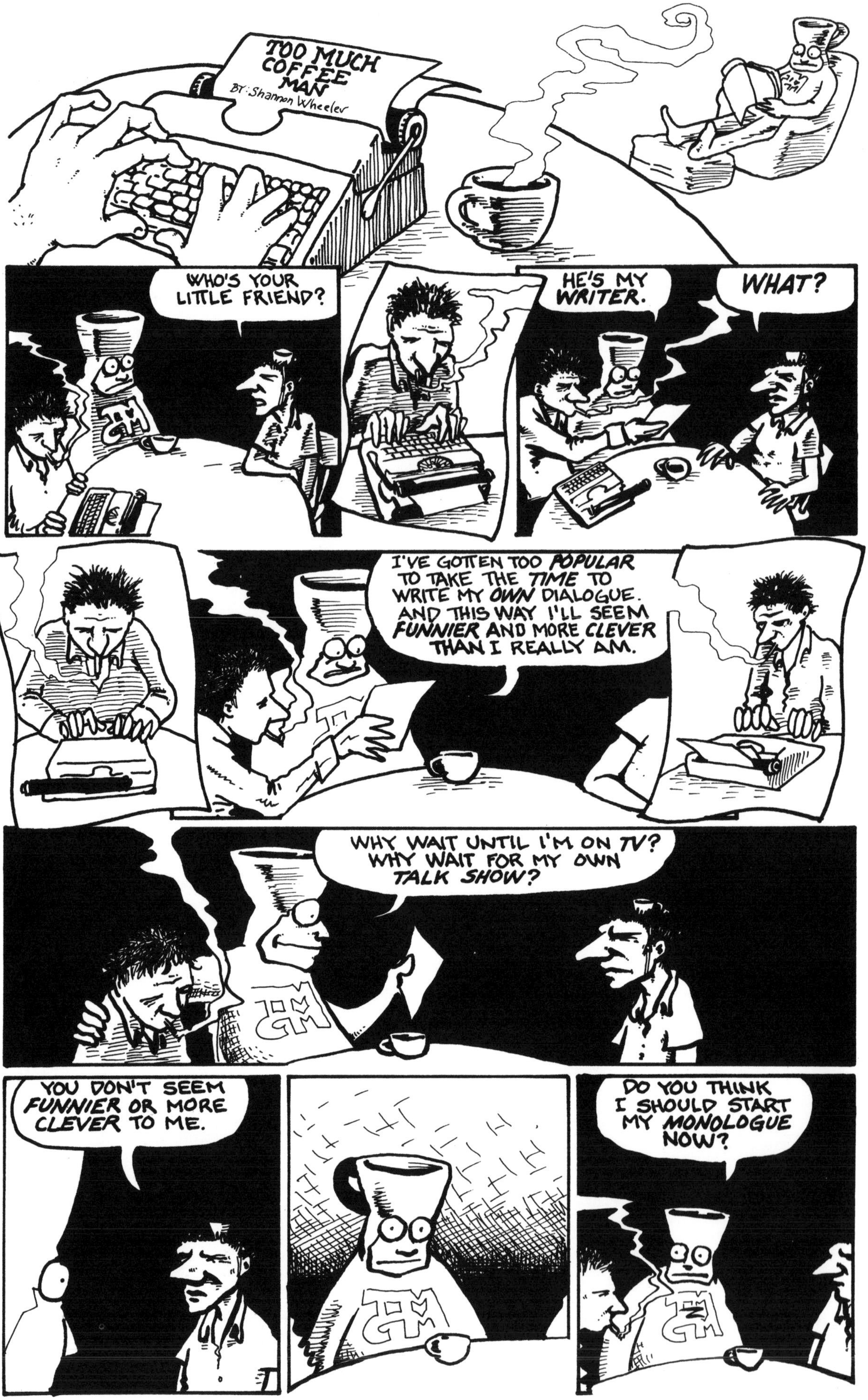
TOO MUCH COFFEE MAN
BY: Shannon Wheeler
WHO'S YOUR LITTLE FRIEND?
HE'S MY WRITER.
WHAT?
I'VE GOTTEN TOO POPULAR TO TAKE THE TIME TO WRITE MY OWN DIALOGUE. AND THIS WAY I'LL SEEM FUNNIER AND MORE CLEVER THAN I REALLY AM.
WHY WAIT UNTIL I'M ON TV? WHY WAIT FOR MY OWN TALK SHOW?
YOU DON'T SEEM FUNNIER OR MORE CLEVER TO ME.
DO YOU THINK I SHOULD START MY MONOLOGUE NOW?

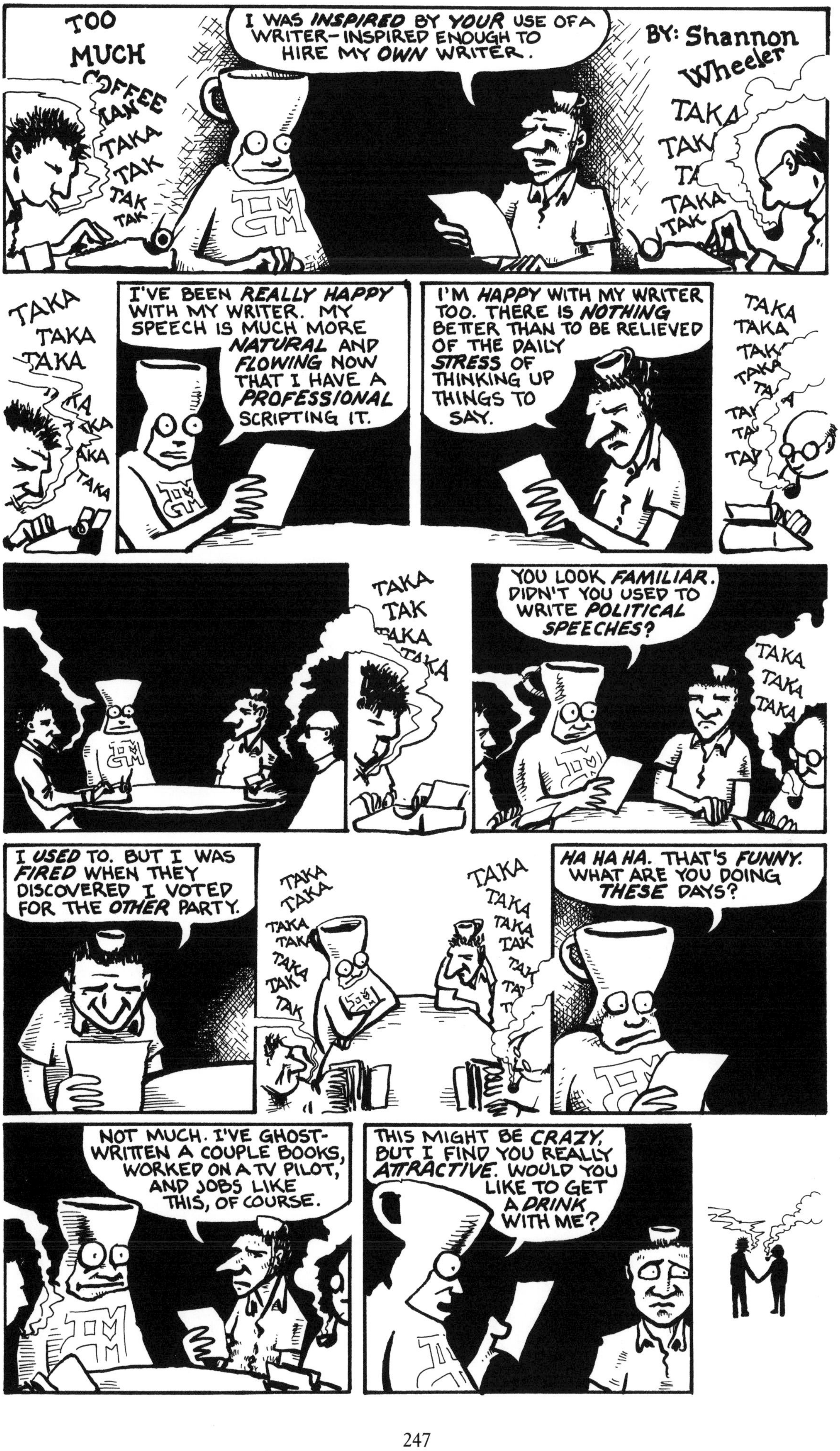
TOO MUCH COFFEE MAN
I WAS INSPIRED BY YOUR USE OF A WRITER–INSPIRED ENOUGH TO HIRE MY OWN WRITER.
BY: Shannon Wheeler
TAKA TAKA TAK TAK TAK
I'VE BEEN REALLY HAPPY WITH MY WRITER. MY SPEECH IS MUCH MORE NATURAL AND FLOWING NOW THAT I HAVE A PROFESSIONAL SCRIPTING IT.
I'M HAPPY WITH MY WRITER TOO. THERE IS NOTHING BETTER THAN TO BE RELIEVED OF THE DAILY STRESS OF THINKING UP THINGS TO SAY.
TAKA TAK TAKA TAKA
YOU LOOK FAMILIAR. DIDN'T YOU USED TO WRITE POLITICAL SPEECHES?
TAKA TAKA TAKA
I USED TO. BUT I WAS FIRED WHEN THEY DISCOVERED I VOTED FOR THE OTHER PARTY.
TAKA TAKA TAKA TAK TAKA TAK TAK
TAKA TAKA TAKA TAK TAK
HA HA HA. THAT'S FUNNY. WHAT ARE YOU DOING THESE DAYS?
NOT MUCH. I'VE GHOST-WRITTEN A COUPLE BOOKS, WORKED ON A TV PILOT, AND JOBS LIKE THIS, OF COURSE.
THIS MIGHT BE CRAZY, BUT I FIND YOU REALLY ATTRACTIVE. WOULD YOU LIKE TO GET A DRINK WITH ME?

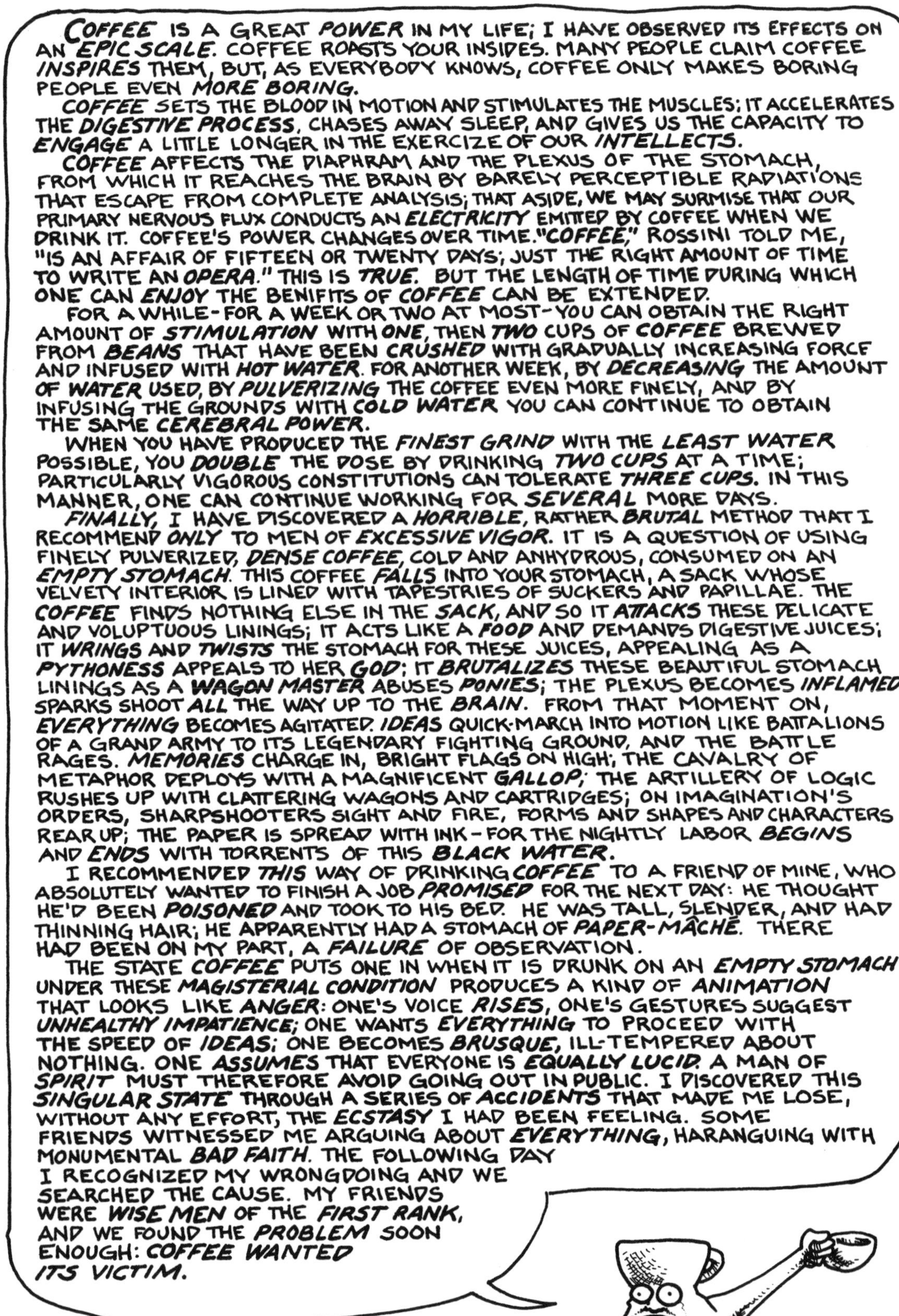
COFFEE IS A GREAT POWER IN MY LIFE; I HAVE OBSERVED ITS EFFECTS ON AN EPIC SCALE. COFFEE ROASTS YOUR INSIDES. MANY PEOPLE CLAIM COFFEE INSPIRES THEM, BUT, AS EVERYBODY KNOWS, COFFEE ONLY MAKES BORING PEOPLE EVEN MORE BORING.
COFFEE SETS THE BLOOD IN MOTION AND STIMULATES THE MUSCLES; IT ACCELERATES THE DIGESTIVE PROCESS, CHASES AWAY SLEEP, AND GIVES US THE CAPACITY TO ENGAGE A LITTLE LONGER IN THE EXERCIZE OF OUR INTELLECTS.
COFFEE AFFECTS THE DIAPHRAM AND THE PLEXUS OF THE STOMACH, FROM WHICH IT REACHES THE BRAIN BY BARELY PERCEPTIBLE RADIATIONS THAT ESCAPE FROM COMPLETE ANALYSIS; THAT ASIDE, WE MAY SURMISE THAT OUR PRIMARY NERVOUS FLUX CONDUCTS AN ELECTRICITY EMITED BY COFFEE WHEN WE DRINK IT. COFFEE'S POWER CHANGES OVER TIME. "COFFEE," ROSSINI TOLD ME, "IS AN AFFAIR OF FIFTEEN OR TWENTY DAYS; JUST THE RIGHT AMOUNT OF TIME TO WRITE AN OPERA." THIS IS TRUE. BUT THE LENGTH OF TIME DURING WHICH ONE CAN ENJOY THE BENIFITS OF COFFEE CAN BE EXTENDED.
FOR A WHILE - FOR A WEEK OR TWO AT MOST - YOU CAN OBTAIN THE RIGHT AMOUNT OF STIMULATION WITH ONE, THEN TWO CUPS OF COFFEE BREWED FROM BEANS THAT HAVE BEEN CRUSHED WITH GRADUALLY INCREASING FORCE AND INFUSED WITH HOT WATER. FOR ANOTHER WEEK, BY DECREASING THE AMOUNT OF WATER USED, BY PULVERIZING THE COFFEE EVEN MORE FINELY, AND BY INFUSING THE GROUNDS WITH COLD WATER YOU CAN CONTINUE TO OBTAIN THE SAME CEREBRAL POWER.
WHEN YOU HAVE PRODUCED THE FINEST GRIND WITH THE LEAST WATER POSSIBLE, YOU DOUBLE THE DOSE BY DRINKING TWO CUPS AT A TIME; PARTICULARLY VIGOROUS CONSTITUTIONS CAN TOLERATE THREE CUPS. IN THIS MANNER, ONE CAN CONTINUE WORKING FOR SEVERAL MORE DAYS.
FINALLY, I HAVE DISCOVERED A HORRIBLE, RATHER BRUTAL METHOD THAT I RECOMMEND ONLY TO MEN OF EXCESSIVE VIGOR. IT IS A QUESTION OF USING FINELY PULVERIZED, DENSE COFFEE, COLD AND ANHYDROUS, CONSUMED ON AN EMPTY STOMACH. THIS COFFEE FALLS INTO YOUR STOMACH, A SACK WHOSE VELVETY INTERIOR IS LINED WITH TAPESTRIES OF SUCKERS AND PAPILLAE. THE COFFEE FINDS NOTHING ELSE IN THE SACK, AND SO IT ATTACKS THESE DELICATE AND VOLUPTUOUS LININGS; IT ACTS LIKE A FOOD AND DEMANDS DIGESTIVE JUICES; IT WRINGS AND TWISTS THE STOMACH FOR THESE JUICES, APPEALING AS A PYTHONESS APPEALS TO HER GOD; IT BRUTALIZES THESE BEAUTIFUL STOMACH LININGS AS A WAGON MASTER ABUSES PONIES; THE PLEXUS BECOMES INFLAMED; SPARKS SHOOT ALL THE WAY UP TO THE BRAIN. FROM THAT MOMENT ON, EVERYTHING BECOMES AGITATED. IDEAS QUICK-MARCH INTO MOTION LIKE BATTALIONS OF A GRAND ARMY TO ITS LEGENDARY FIGHTING GROUND, AND THE BATTLE RAGES. MEMORIES CHARGE IN, BRIGHT FLAGS ON HIGH; THE CAVALRY OF METAPHOR DEPLOYS WITH A MAGNIFICENT GALLOP; THE ARTILLERY OF LOGIC RUSHES UP WITH CLATTERING WAGONS AND CARTRIDGES; ON IMAGINATION'S ORDERS, SHARPSHOOTERS SIGHT AND FIRE, FORMS AND SHAPES AND CHARACTERS REAR UP; THE PAPER IS SPREAD WITH INK - FOR THE NIGHTLY LABOR BEGINS AND ENDS WITH TORRENTS OF THIS BLACK WATER.
I RECOMMENDED THIS WAY OF DRINKING COFFEE TO A FRIEND OF MINE, WHO ABSOLUTELY WANTED TO FINISH A JOB PROMISED FOR THE NEXT DAY: HE THOUGHT HE'D BEEN POISONED AND TOOK TO HIS BED. HE WAS TALL, SLENDER, AND HAD THINNING HAIR; HE APPARENTLY HAD A STOMACH OF PAPER-MÂCHÉ. THERE HAD BEEN ON MY PART, A FAILURE OF OBSERVATION.
THE STATE COFFEE PUTS ONE IN WHEN IT IS DRUNK ON AN EMPTY STOMACH UNDER THESE MAGISTERIAL CONDITION PRODUCES A KIND OF ANIMATION THAT LOOKS LIKE ANGER: ONE'S VOICE RISES, ONE'S GESTURES SUGGEST UNHEALTHY IMPATIENCE; ONE WANTS EVERYTHING TO PROCEED WITH THE SPEED OF IDEAS; ONE BECOMES BRUSQUE, ILL-TEMPERED ABOUT NOTHING. ONE ASSUMES THAT EVERYONE IS EQUALLY LUCID. A MAN OF SPIRIT MUST THEREFORE AVOID GOING OUT IN PUBLIC. I DISCOVERED THIS SINGULAR STATE THROUGH A SERIES OF ACCIDENTS THAT MADE ME LOSE, WITHOUT ANY EFFORT, THE ECSTASY I HAD BEEN FEELING. SOME FRIENDS WITNESSED ME ARGUING ABOUT EVERYTHING, HARANGUING WITH MONUMENTAL BAD FAITH. THE FOLLOWING DAY I RECOGNIZED MY WRONGDOING AND WE SEARCHED THE CAUSE. MY FRIENDS WERE WISE MEN OF THE FIRST RANK, AND WE FOUND THE PROBLEM SOON ENOUGH: COFFEE WANTED ITS VICTIM.

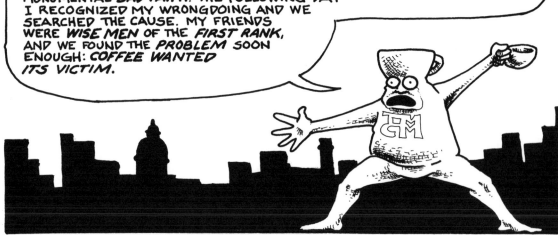

FROM "THE PLEASURES AND PAINS OF COFFEE" BY HONORÉ DE BALZAC
TRANSLATED BY ROBERT ONOPA, DRAWN BY SHANNON WHEELER

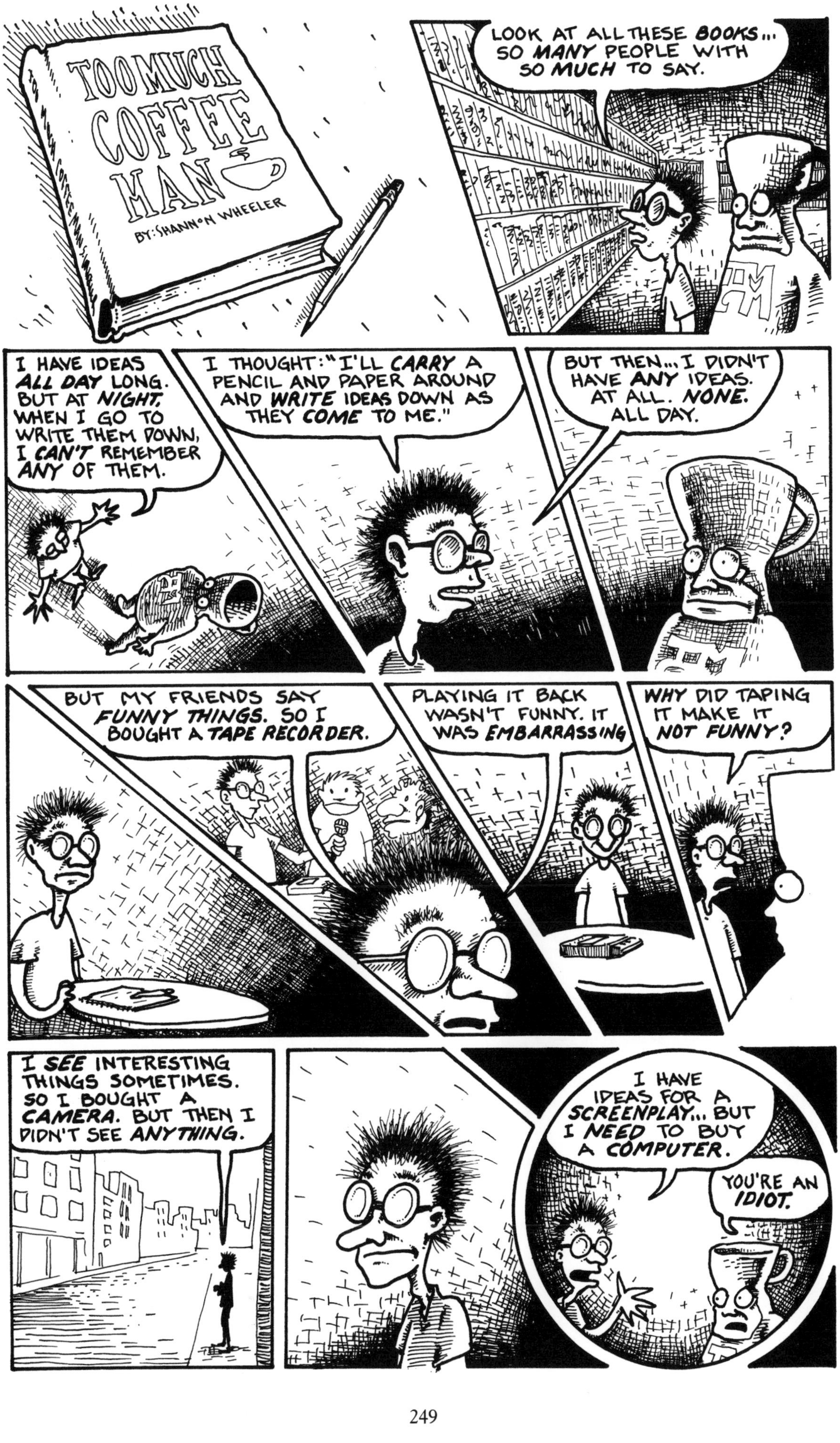
TOO MUCH COFFEE MAN
BY: SHANNON WHEELER
LOOK AT ALL THESE BOOKS... SO MANY PEOPLE WITH SO MUCH TO SAY.
I HAVE IDEAS ALL DAY LONG. BUT AT NIGHT, WHEN I GO TO WRITE THEM DOWN, I CAN'T REMEMBER ANY OF THEM.
I THOUGHT: "I'LL CARRY A PENCIL AND PAPER AROUND AND WRITE IDEAS DOWN AS THEY COME TO ME."
BUT THEN... I DIDN'T HAVE ANY IDEAS. AT ALL. NONE. ALL DAY.
BUT MY FRIENDS SAY FUNNY THINGS. SO I BOUGHT A TAPE RECORDER.
PLAYING IT BACK WASN'T FUNNY. IT WAS EMBARRASSING
WHY DID TAPING IT MAKE IT NOT FUNNY?
I SEE INTERESTING THINGS SOMETIMES. SO I BOUGHT A CAMERA. BUT THEN I DIDN'T SEE ANYTHING.
I HAVE IDEAS FOR A SCREENPLAY... BUT I NEED TO BUY A COMPUTER.
YOU'RE AN IDIOT.

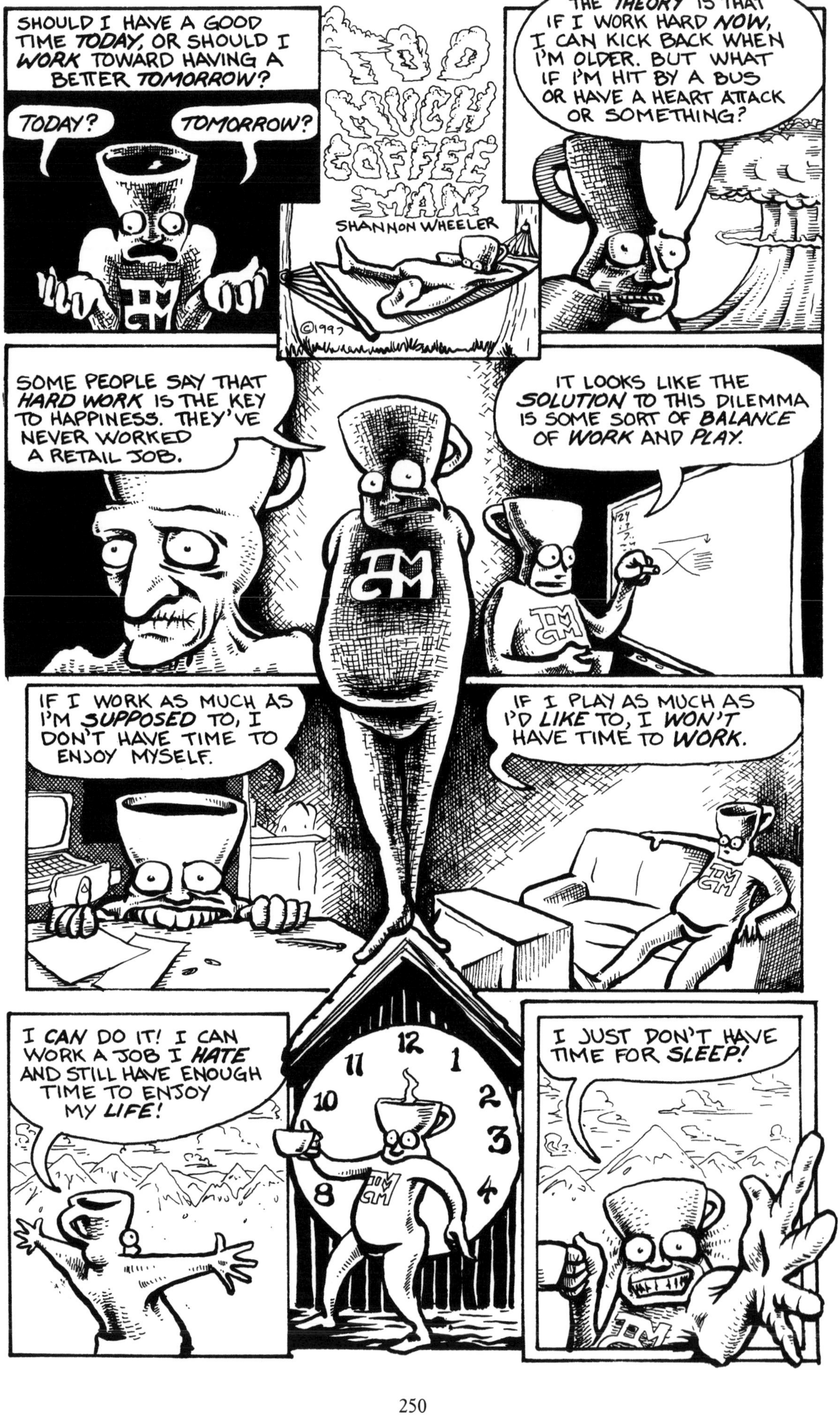
SHOULD I HAVE A GOOD TIME TODAY, OR SHOULD I WORK TOWARD HAVING A BETTER TOMORROW?
TODAY?
TOMORROW?
TOO MUCH COFFEE MAN
SHANNON WHEELER
©1997
THE THEORY IS THAT IF I WORK HARD NOW, I CAN KICK BACK WHEN I'M OLDER. BUT WHAT IF I'M HIT BY A BUS OR HAVE A HEART ATTACK OR SOMETHING?
SOME PEOPLE SAY THAT HARD WORK IS THE KEY TO HAPPINESS. THEY'VE NEVER WORKED A RETAIL JOB.
IT LOOKS LIKE THE SOLUTION TO THIS DILEMMA IS SOME SORT OF BALANCE OF WORK AND PLAY.
IF I WORK AS MUCH AS I'M SUPPOSED TO, I DON'T HAVE TIME TO ENJOY MYSELF.
IF I PLAY AS MUCH AS I'D LIKE TO, I WON'T HAVE TIME TO WORK.
I CAN DO IT! I CAN WORK A JOB I HATE AND STILL HAVE ENOUGH TIME TO ENJOY MY LIFE!
I JUST DON'T HAVE TIME FOR SLEEP!

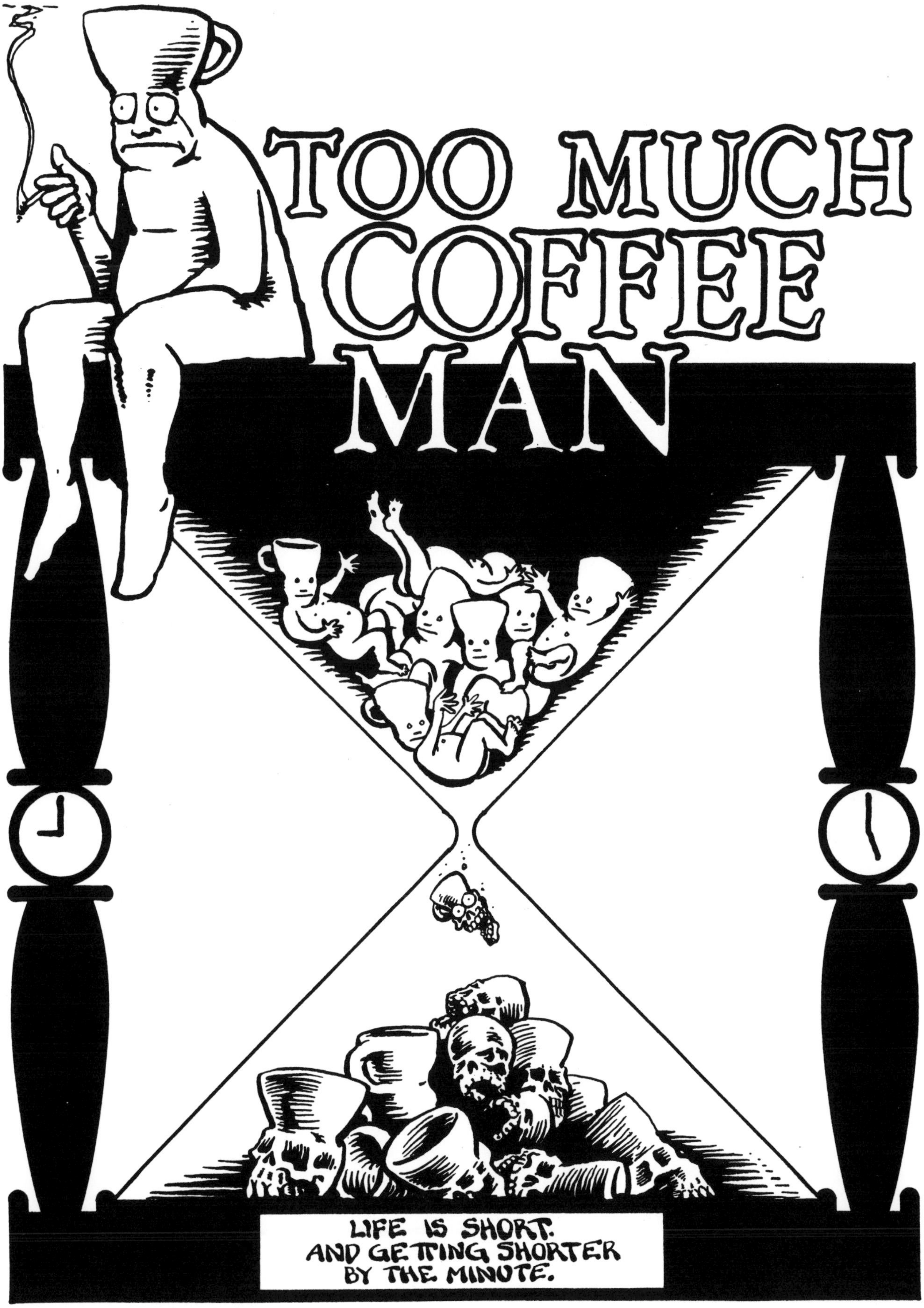
TOO MUCH COFFEE MAN
LIFE IS SHORT.
AND GETTING SHORTER
BY THE MINUTE.

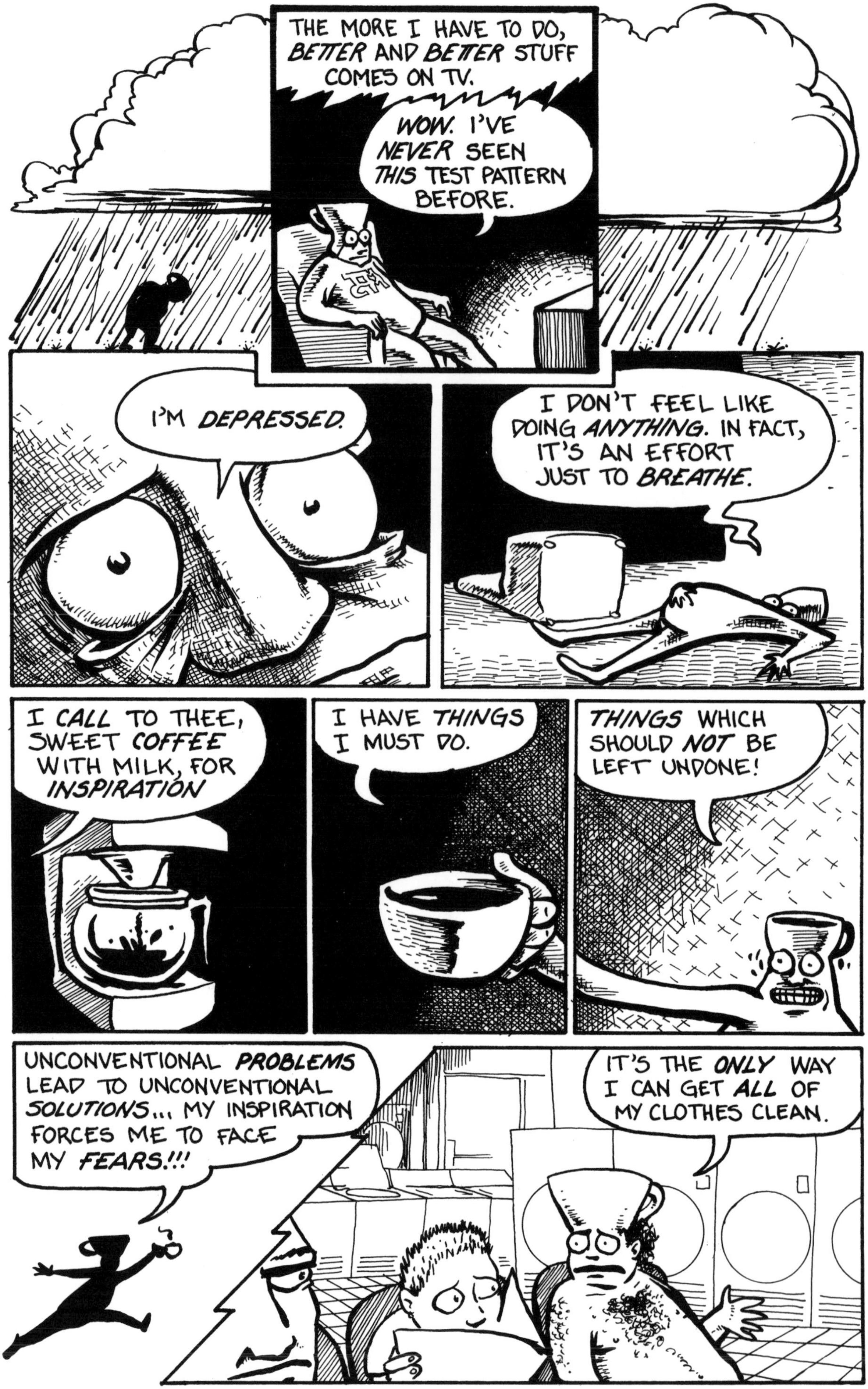
THE MORE I HAVE TO DO, BETTER AND BETTER STUFF COMES ON TV.
WOW. I'VE NEVER SEEN THIS TEST PATTERN BEFORE.
I'M DEPRESSED.
I DON'T FEEL LIKE DOING ANYTHING. IN FACT, IT'S AN EFFORT JUST TO BREATHE.
I CALL TO THEE, SWEET COFFEE WITH MILK, FOR INSPIRATION
I HAVE THINGS I MUST DO.
THINGS WHICH SHOULD NOT BE LEFT UNDONE!
UNCONVENTIONAL PROBLEMS LEAD TO UNCONVENTIONAL SOLUTIONS... MY INSPIRATION FORCES ME TO FACE MY FEARS!!!
IT'S THE ONLY WAY I CAN GET ALL OF MY CLOTHES CLEAN.

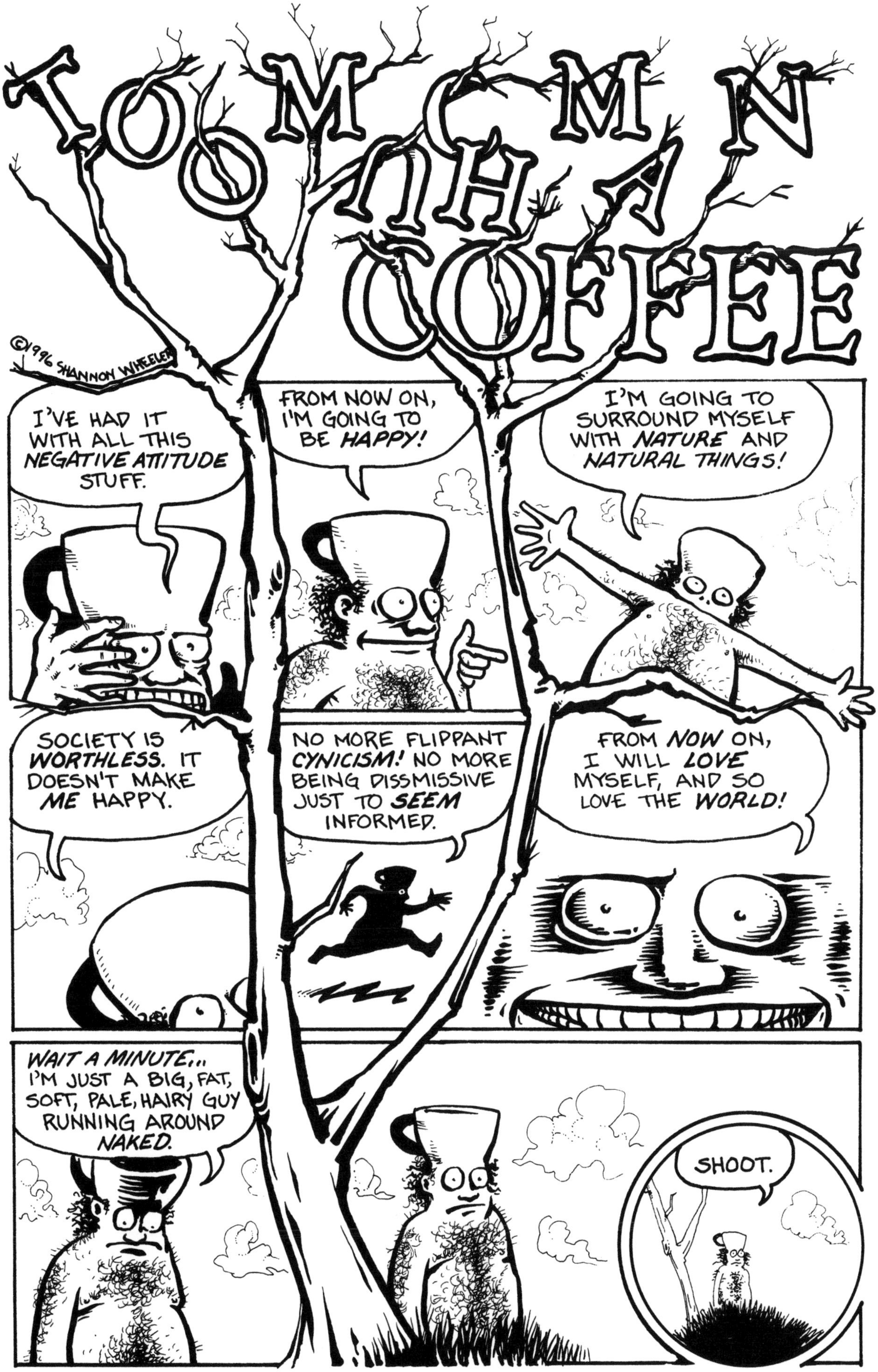
TOO MUCH COFFEE MAN
©1996 SHANNON WHEELER
I'VE HAD IT WITH ALL THIS NEGATIVE ATTITUDE STUFF.
FROM NOW ON, I'M GOING TO BE HAPPY!
I'M GOING TO SURROUND MYSELF WITH NATURE AND NATURAL THINGS!
SOCIETY IS WORTHLESS. IT DOESN'T MAKE ME HAPPY.
NO MORE FLIPPANT CYNICISM! NO MORE BEING DISSMISSIVE JUST TO SEEM INFORMED.
FROM NOW ON, I WILL LOVE MYSELF, AND SO LOVE THE WORLD!
WAIT A MINUTE... I'M JUST A BIG, FAT, SOFT, PALE, HAIRY GUY RUNNING AROUND NAKED.
SHOOT.

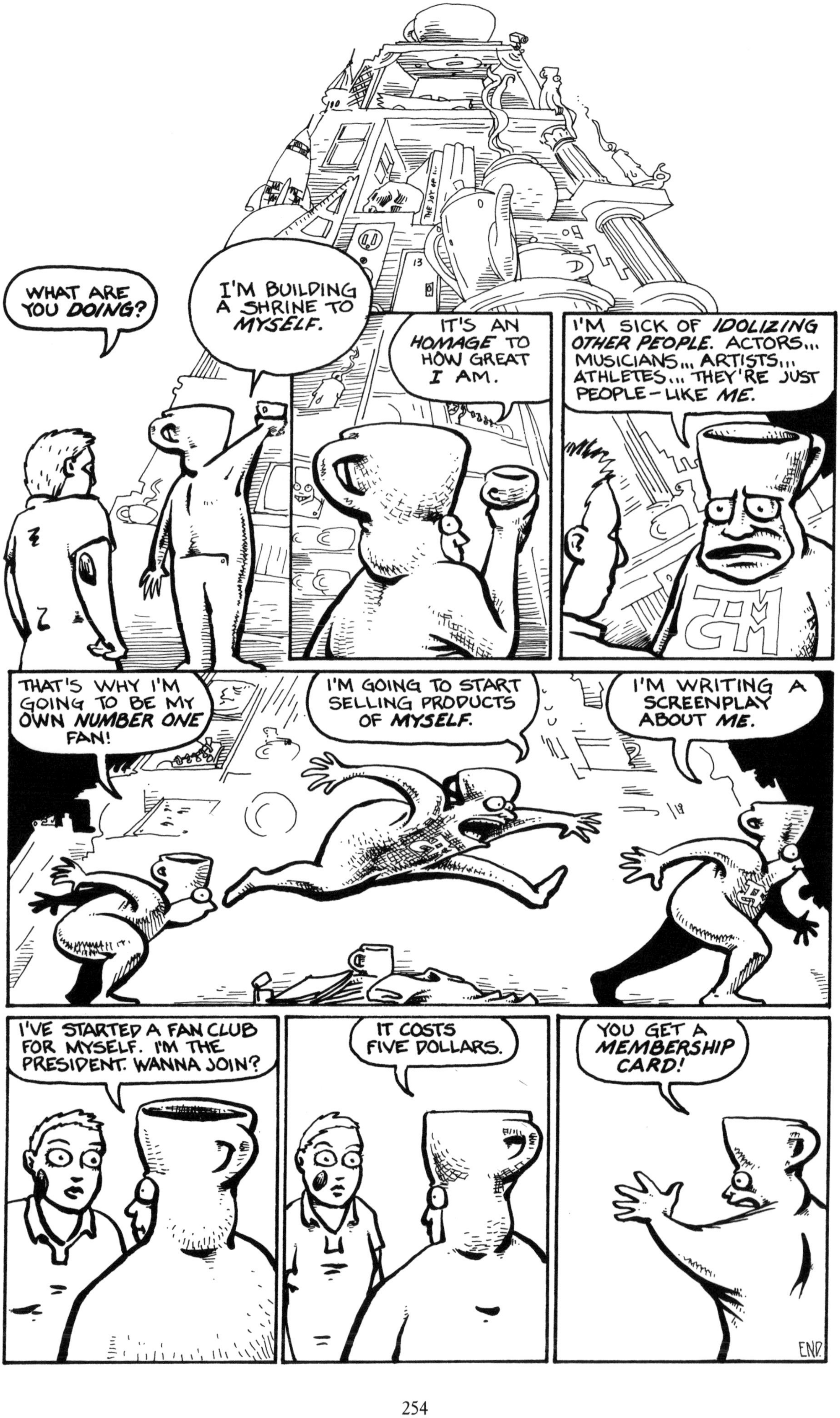

WHAT ARE YOU *DOING*?
I'M BUILDING A SHRINE TO *MYSELF*.
IT'S AN *HOMAGE* TO HOW GREAT I AM.
I'M SICK OF *IDOLIZING OTHER PEOPLE*. ACTORS... MUSICIANS... ARTISTS... ATHLETES... THEY'RE JUST PEOPLE—LIKE *ME*.
THAT'S WHY I'M GOING TO BE MY OWN *NUMBER ONE* FAN!
I'M GOING TO START SELLING PRODUCTS OF *MYSELF*.
I'M WRITING A SCREENPLAY ABOUT *ME*.
I'VE STARTED A FAN CLUB FOR MYSELF. I'M THE PRESIDENT. WANNA JOIN?
IT COSTS FIVE DOLLARS.
YOU GET A *MEMBERSHIP CARD*!
END.

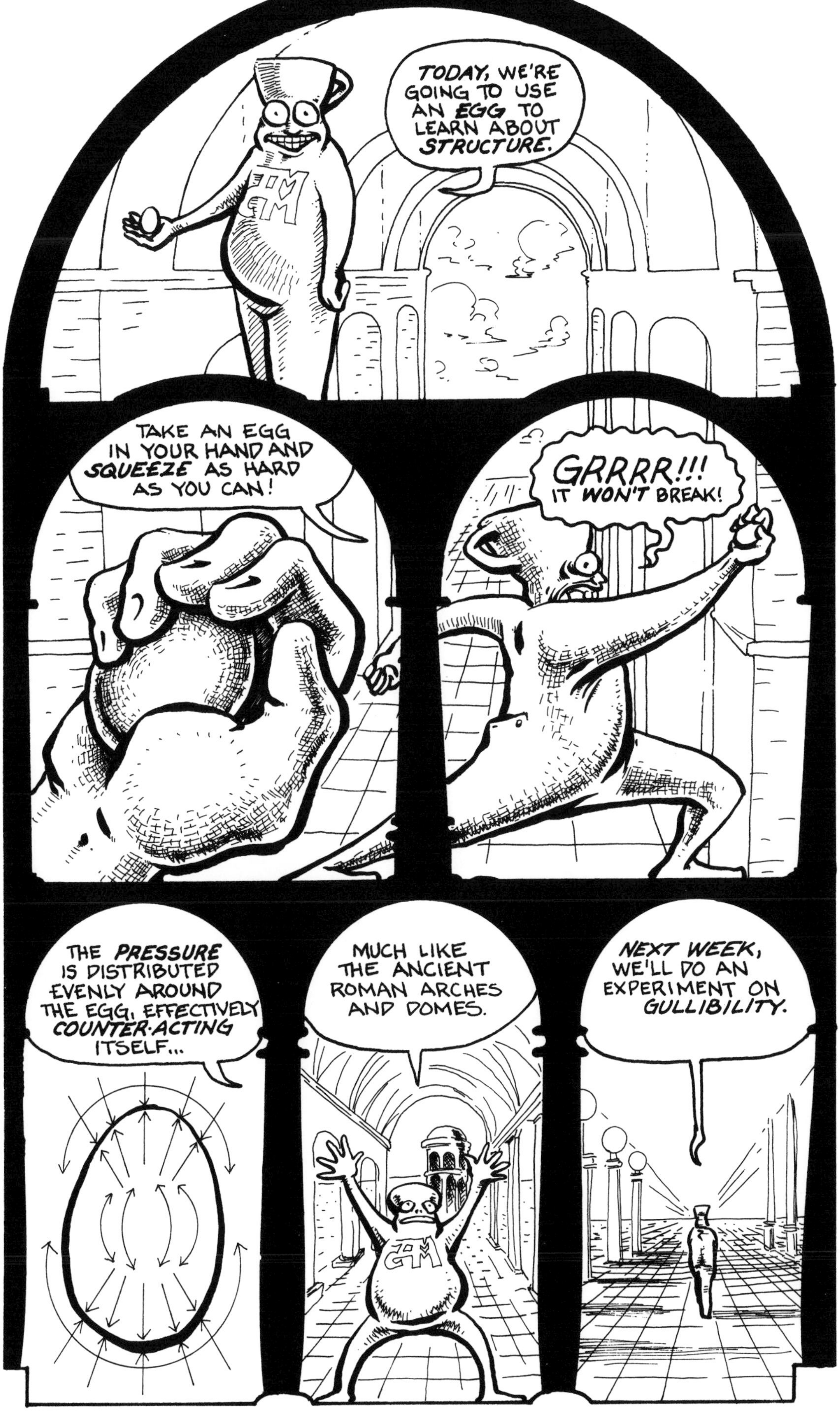
TODAY, WE'RE GOING TO USE AN EGG TO LEARN ABOUT STRUCTURE.
TAKE AN EGG IN YOUR HAND AND SQUEEZE AS HARD AS YOU CAN!
GRRRR!!! IT WON'T BREAK!
THE PRESSURE IS DISTRIBUTED EVENLY AROUND THE EGG, EFFECTIVELY COUNTER-ACTING ITSELF...
MUCH LIKE THE ANCIENT ROMAN ARCHES AND DOMES.
NEXT WEEK, WE'LL DO AN EXPERIMENT ON GULLIBILITY.

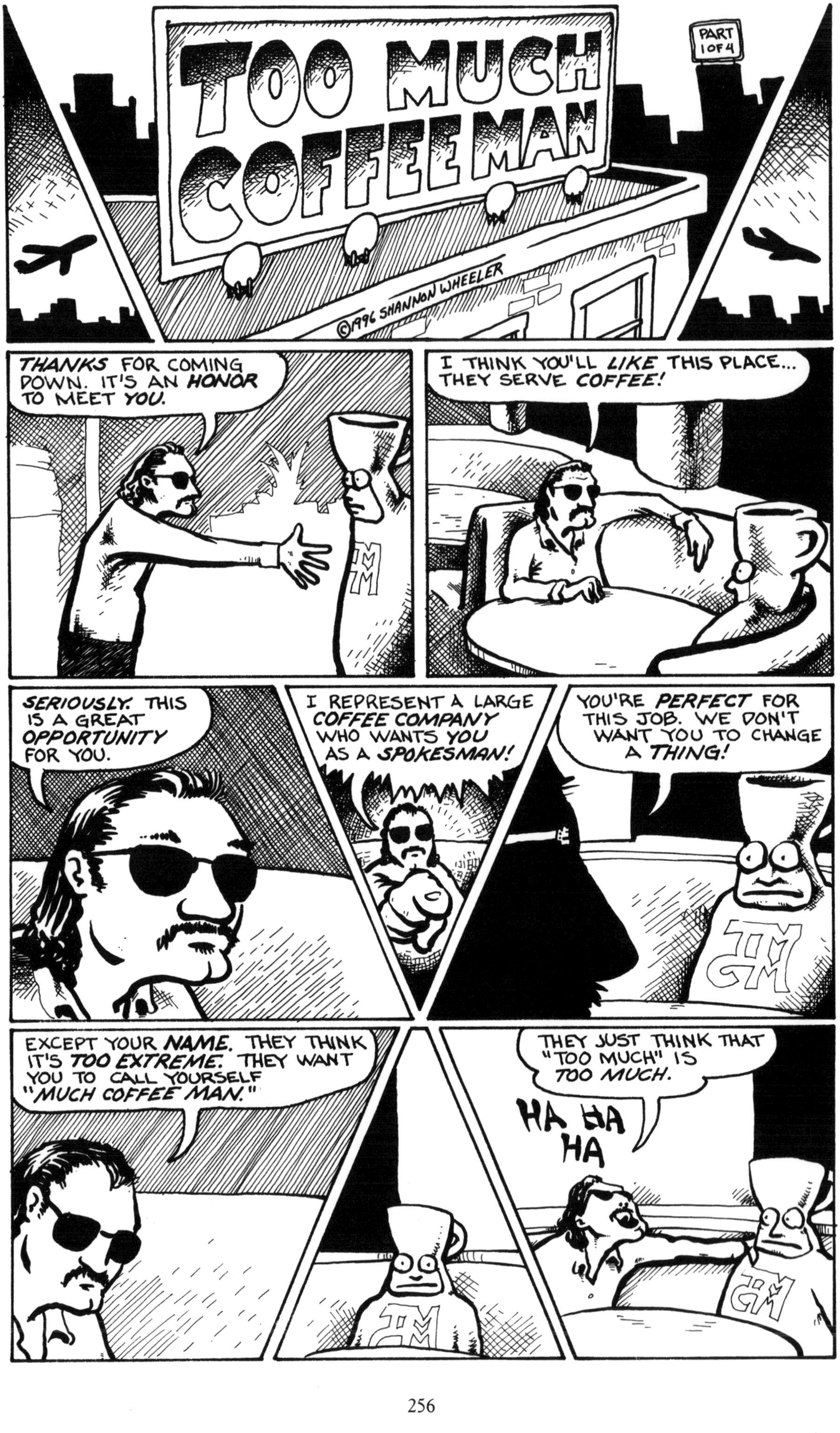
TOO MUCH COFFEE MAN
PART 1 OF 4
©1996 SHANNON WHEELER
THANKS FOR COMING DOWN. IT'S AN HONOR TO MEET YOU.
I THINK YOU'LL LIKE THIS PLACE... THEY SERVE COFFEE!
SERIOUSLY. THIS IS A GREAT OPPORTUNITY FOR YOU.
I REPRESENT A LARGE COFFEE COMPANY WHO WANTS YOU AS A SPOKESMAN!
YOU'RE PERFECT FOR THIS JOB. WE DON'T WANT YOU TO CHANGE A THING!
EXCEPT YOUR NAME. THEY THINK IT'S TOO EXTREME. THEY WANT YOU TO CALL YOURSELF "MUCH COFFEE MAN."
THEY JUST THINK THAT "TOO MUCH" IS TOO MUCH.
HA HA HA

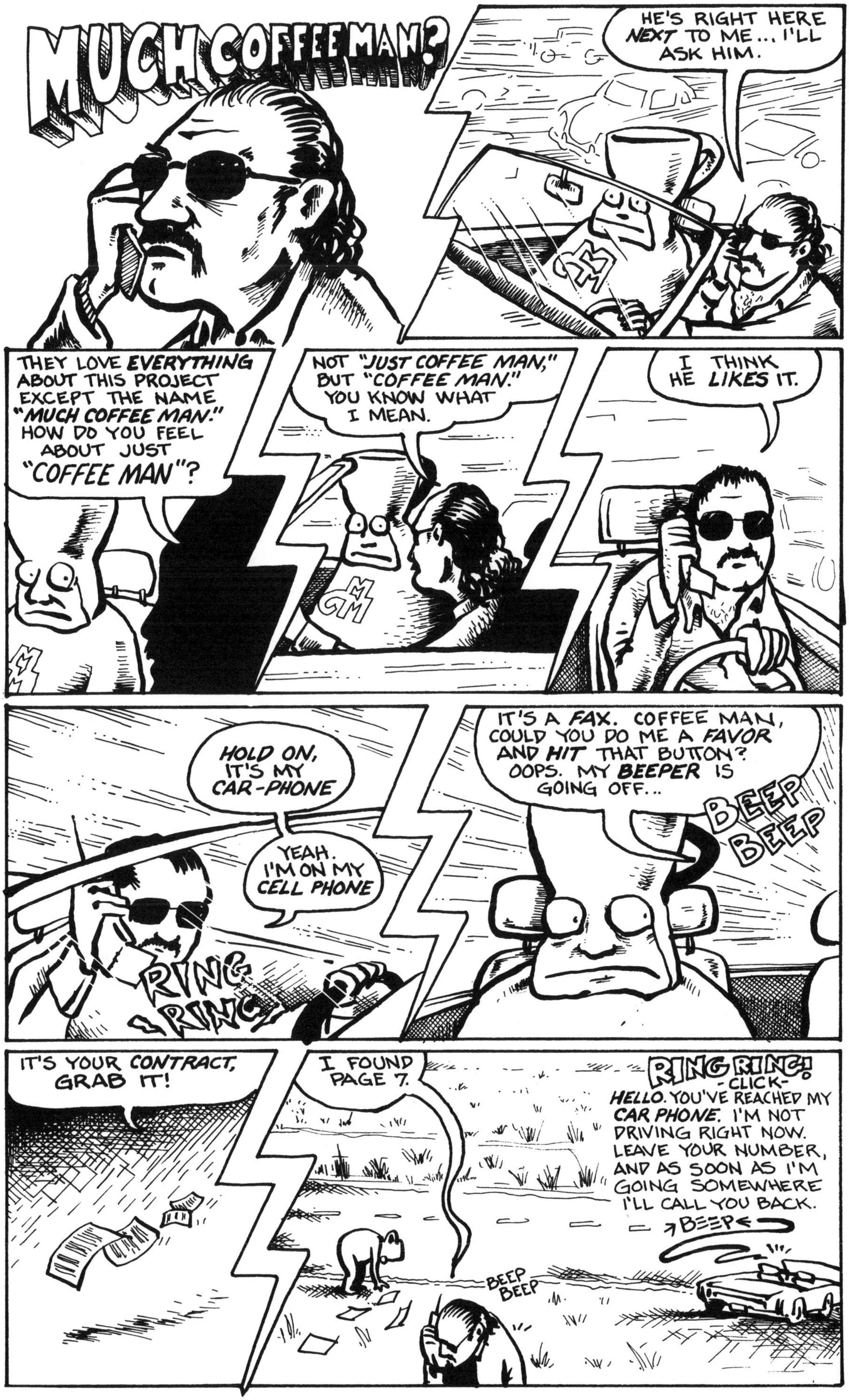
MUCH COFFEE MAN?
HE'S RIGHT HERE NEXT TO ME... I'LL ASK HIM.
THEY LOVE EVERYTHING ABOUT THIS PROJECT EXCEPT THE NAME "MUCH COFFEE MAN." HOW DO YOU FEEL ABOUT JUST "COFFEE MAN"?
NOT "JUST COFFEE MAN," BUT "COFFEE MAN." YOU KNOW WHAT I MEAN.
I THINK HE LIKES IT.
HOLD ON, IT'S MY CAR-PHONE
YEAH. I'M ON MY CELL PHONE
RING RING
IT'S A FAX. COFFEE MAN, COULD YOU DO ME A FAVOR AND HIT THAT BUTTON? OOPS. MY BEEPER IS GOING OFF...
BEEP BEEP
IT'S YOUR CONTRACT, GRAB IT!
I FOUND PAGE 7.
RING RING! -CLICK- HELLO. YOU'VE REACHED MY CAR PHONE. I'M NOT DRIVING RIGHT NOW. LEAVE YOUR NUMBER, AND AS SOON AS I'M GOING SOMEWHERE I'LL CALL YOU BACK. BEEP
BEEP BEEP

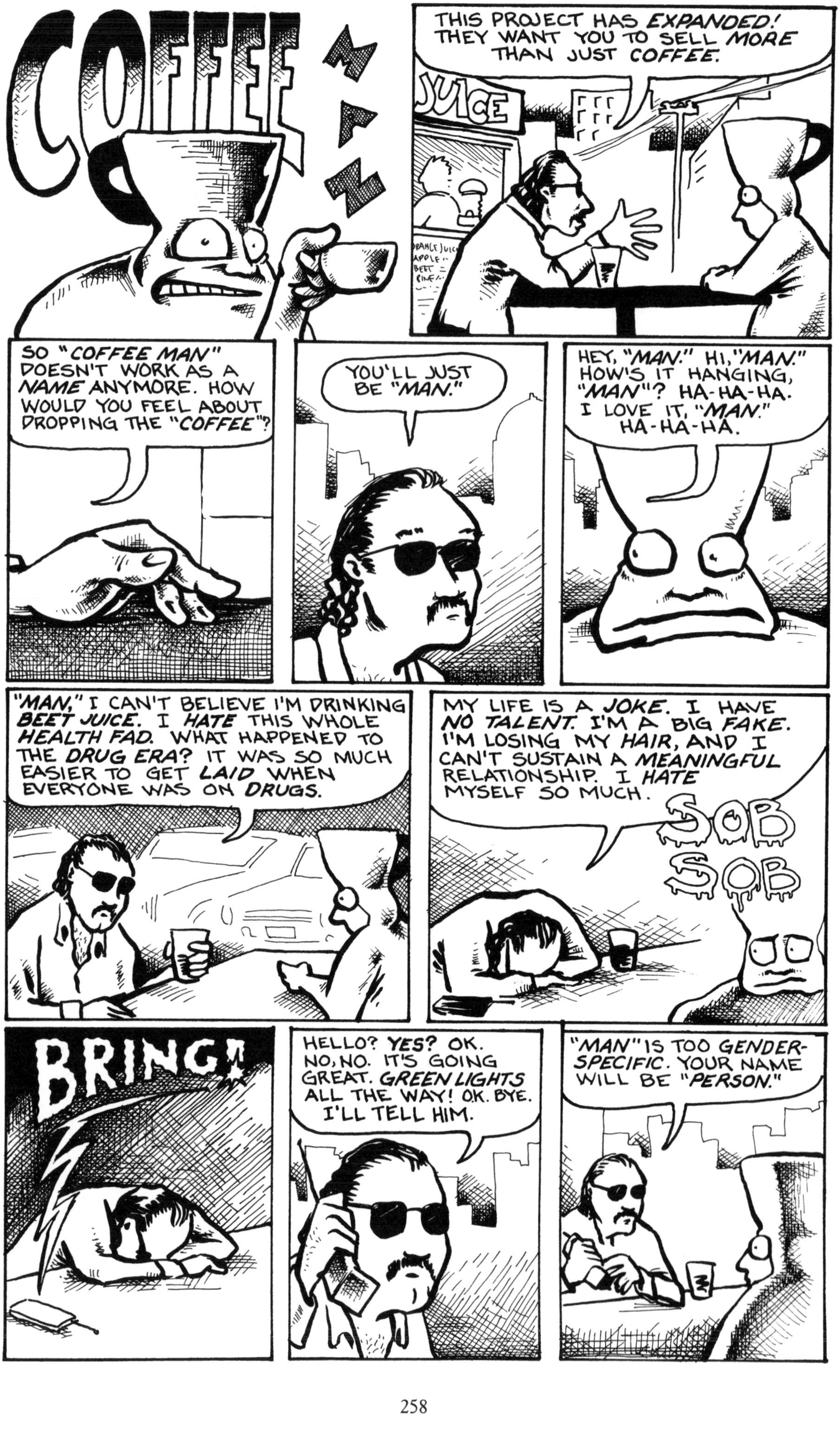
COFFEE MAN
THIS PROJECT HAS EXPANDED! THEY WANT YOU TO SELL MORE THAN JUST COFFEE.
JUICE
SO "COFFEE MAN" DOESN'T WORK AS A NAME ANYMORE. HOW WOULD YOU FEEL ABOUT DROPPING THE "COFFEE"?
YOU'LL JUST BE "MAN."
HEY, "MAN." HI, "MAN." HOW'S IT HANGING, "MAN"? HA-HA-HA. I LOVE IT, "MAN." HA-HA-HA.
"MAN," I CAN'T BELIEVE I'M DRINKING BEET JUICE. I HATE THIS WHOLE HEALTH FAD. WHAT HAPPENED TO THE DRUG ERA? IT WAS SO MUCH EASIER TO GET LAID WHEN EVERYONE WAS ON DRUGS.
MY LIFE IS A JOKE. I HAVE NO TALENT. I'M A BIG FAKE. I'M LOSING MY HAIR, AND I CAN'T SUSTAIN A MEANINGFUL RELATIONSHIP. I HATE MYSELF SO MUCH.
SOB
SOB
BRING!
HELLO? YES? OK. NO, NO. IT'S GOING GREAT. GREEN LIGHTS ALL THE WAY! OK. BYE. I'LL TELL HIM.
"MAN" IS TOO GENDER-SPECIFIC. YOUR NAME WILL BE "PERSON."

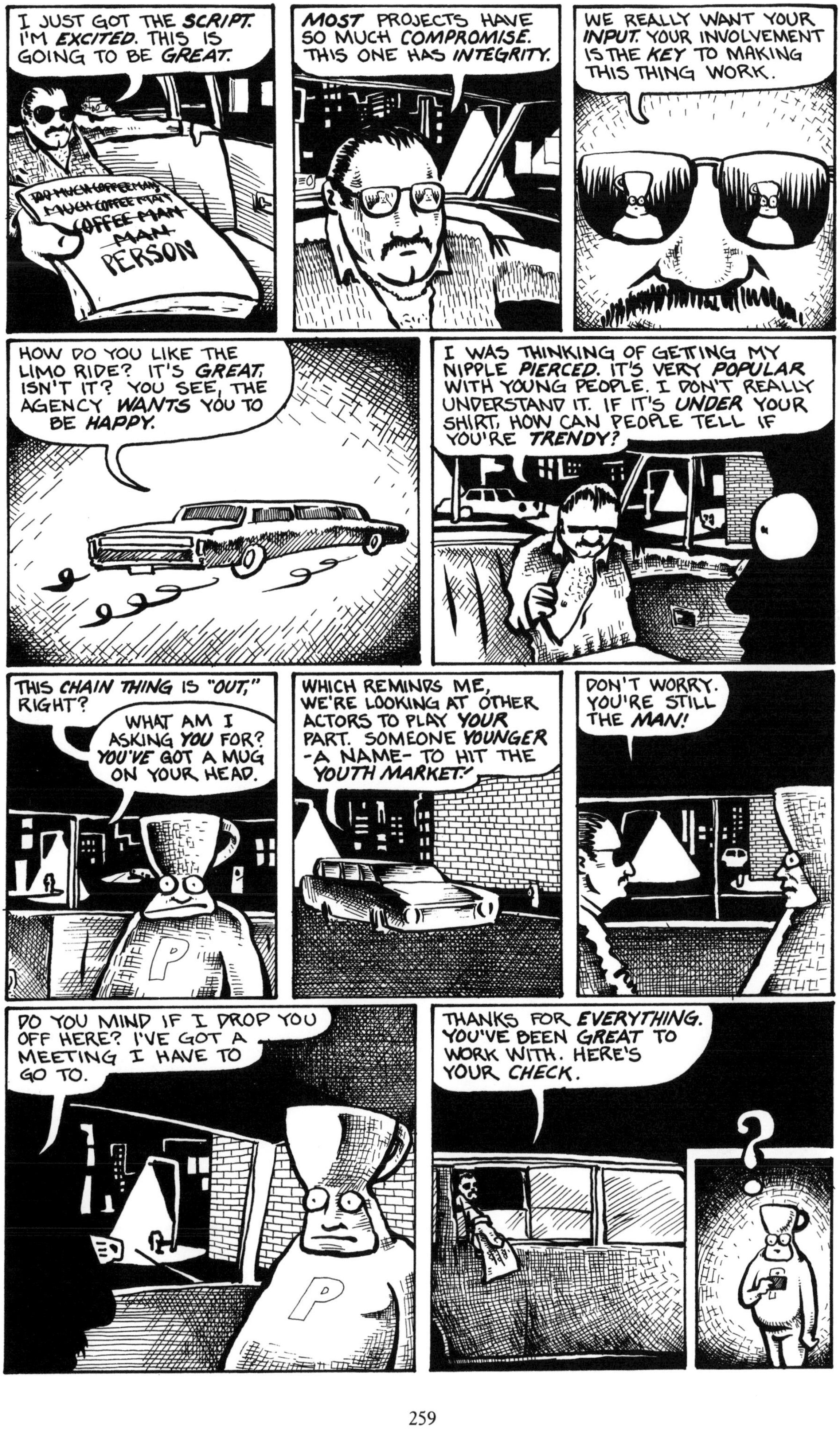
I JUST GOT THE SCRIPT. I'M EXCITED. THIS IS GOING TO BE GREAT.
TOO MUCH COFFEE MAN
MUCH COFFEE MAN
COFFEE MAN
MAN
PERSON
MOST PROJECTS HAVE SO MUCH COMPROMISE. THIS ONE HAS INTEGRITY.
WE REALLY WANT YOUR INPUT. YOUR INVOLVEMENT IS THE KEY TO MAKING THIS THING WORK.
HOW DO YOU LIKE THE LIMO RIDE? IT'S GREAT, ISN'T IT? YOU SEE, THE AGENCY WANTS YOU TO BE HAPPY.
I WAS THINKING OF GETTING MY NIPPLE PIERCED. IT'S VERY POPULAR WITH YOUNG PEOPLE. I DON'T REALLY UNDERSTAND IT. IF IT'S UNDER YOUR SHIRT, HOW CAN PEOPLE TELL IF YOU'RE TRENDY?
THIS CHAIN THING IS "OUT," RIGHT?
WHAT AM I ASKING YOU FOR? YOU'VE GOT A MUG ON YOUR HEAD.
WHICH REMINDS ME, WE'RE LOOKING AT OTHER ACTORS TO PLAY YOUR PART. SOMEONE YOUNGER -A NAME- TO HIT THE YOUTH MARKET.
DON'T WORRY. YOU'RE STILL THE MAN!
DO YOU MIND IF I DROP YOU OFF HERE? I'VE GOT A MEETING I HAVE TO GO TO.
THANKS FOR EVERYTHING. YOU'VE BEEN GREAT TO WORK WITH. HERE'S YOUR CHECK.
?

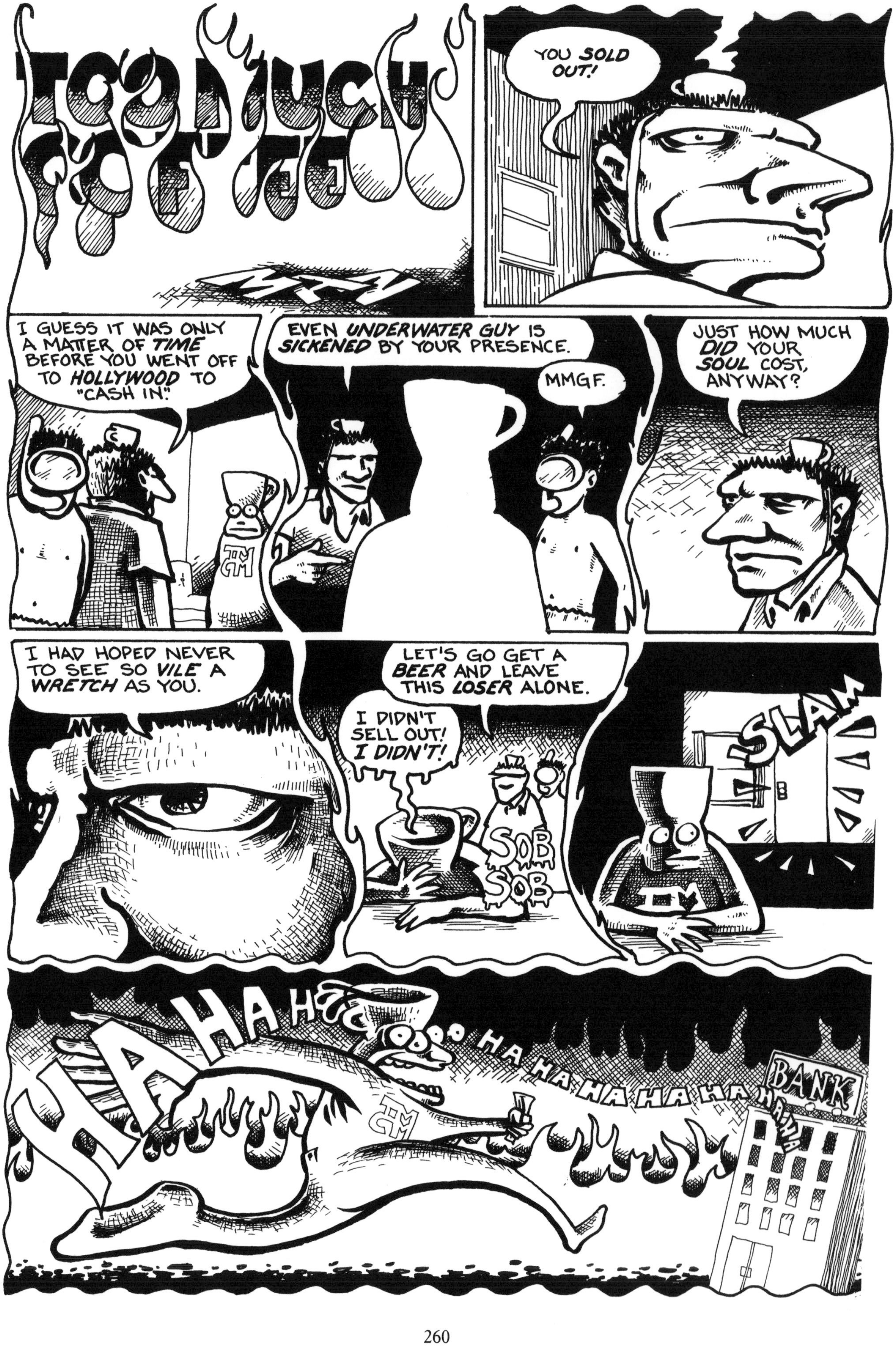
TOO MUCH COFFEE
YOU SOLD OUT!
I GUESS IT WAS ONLY A MATTER OF TIME BEFORE YOU WENT OFF TO HOLLYWOOD TO "CASH IN."
EVEN UNDERWATER GUY IS SICKENED BY YOUR PRESENCE.
MMGF.
JUST HOW MUCH DID YOUR SOUL COST, ANYWAY?
I HAD HOPED NEVER TO SEE SO VILE A WRETCH AS YOU.
LET'S GO GET A BEER AND LEAVE THIS LOSER ALONE.
I DIDN'T SELL OUT! I DIDN'T!
SOB SOB
SLAM
HA HA HA HA HA HA HA HA HA HA
BANK

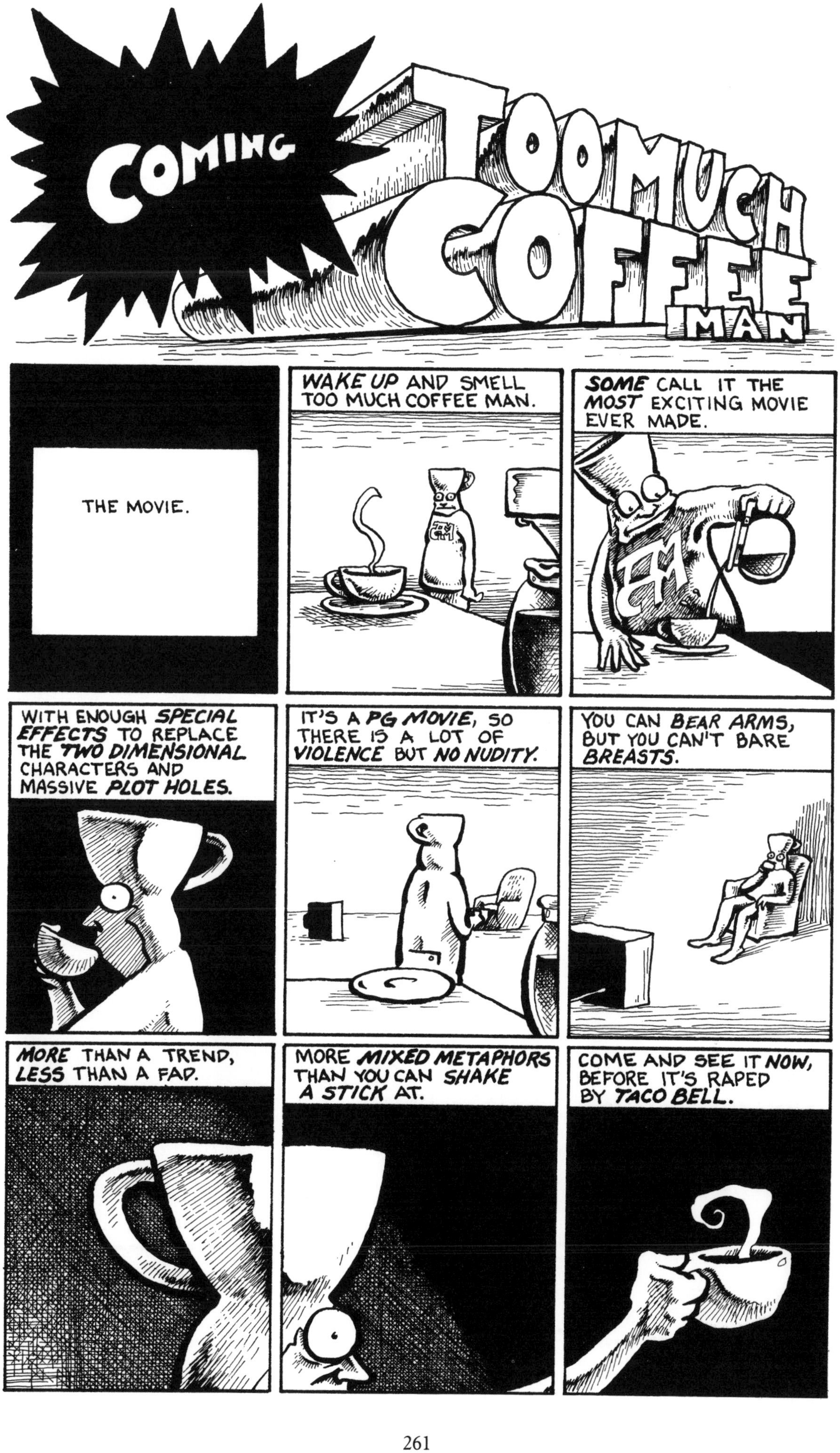
COMING
TOO MUCH COFFEE MAN
THE MOVIE.
WAKE UP AND SMELL TOO MUCH COFFEE MAN.
SOME CALL IT THE MOST EXCITING MOVIE EVER MADE.
WITH ENOUGH SPECIAL EFFECTS TO REPLACE THE TWO DIMENSIONAL CHARACTERS AND MASSIVE PLOT HOLES.
IT'S A PG MOVIE, SO THERE IS A LOT OF VIOLENCE BUT NO NUDITY.
YOU CAN BEAR ARMS, BUT YOU CAN'T BARE BREASTS.
MORE THAN A TREND, LESS THAN A FAD.
MORE MIXED METAPHORS THAN YOU CAN SHAKE A STICK AT.
COME AND SEE IT NOW, BEFORE IT'S RAPED BY TACO BELL.

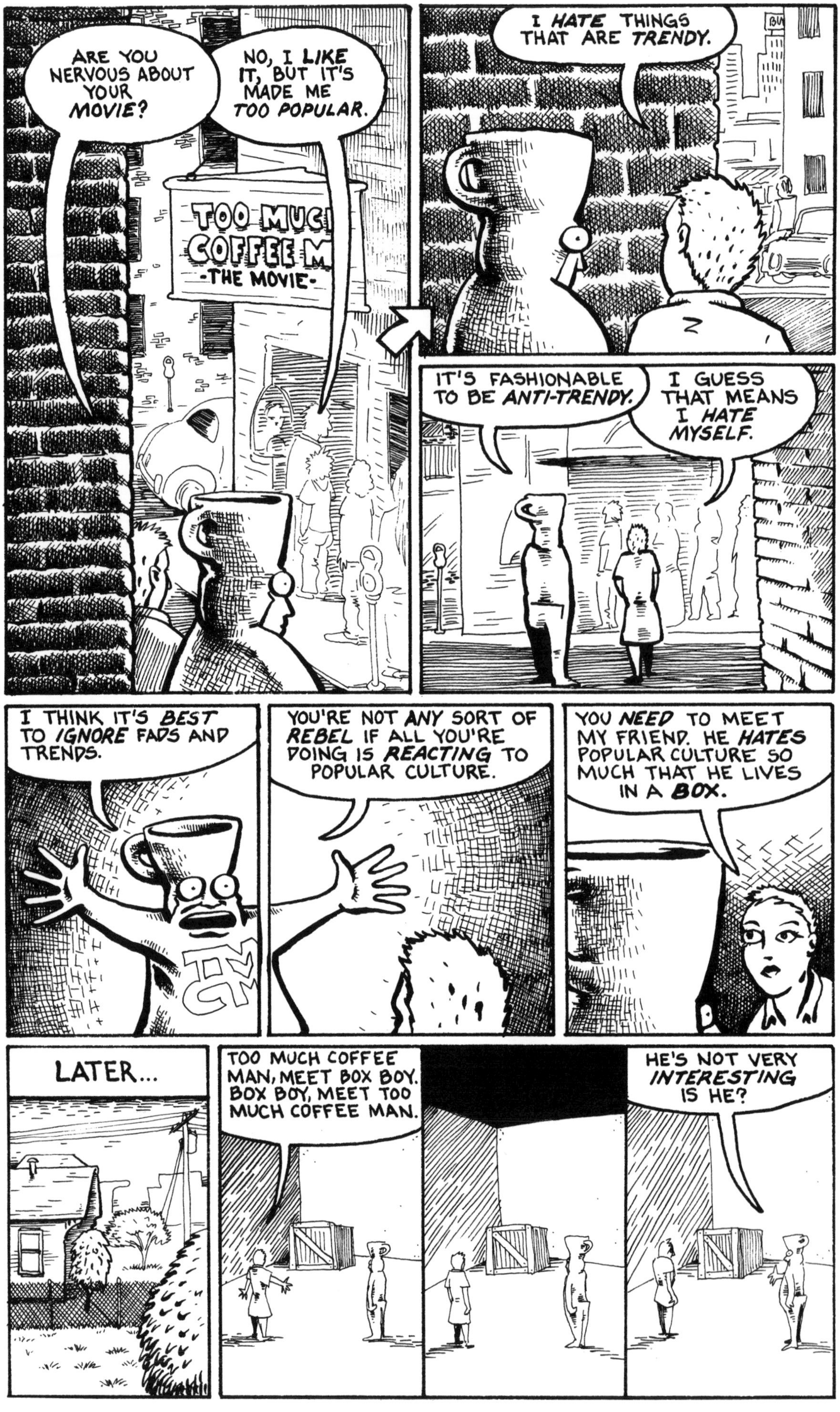

ARE YOU NERVOUS ABOUT YOUR MOVIE?
NO, I LIKE IT, BUT IT'S MADE ME TOO POPULAR.
TOO MUCH COFFEE M
-THE MOVIE-
I HATE THINGS THAT ARE TRENDY.
IT'S FASHIONABLE TO BE ANTI-TRENDY.
I GUESS THAT MEANS I HATE MYSELF.
I THINK IT'S BEST TO IGNORE FADS AND TRENDS.
YOU'RE NOT ANY SORT OF REBEL IF ALL YOU'RE DOING IS REACTING TO POPULAR CULTURE.
YOU NEED TO MEET MY FRIEND. HE HATES POPULAR CULTURE SO MUCH THAT HE LIVES IN A BOX.
LATER...
TOO MUCH COFFEE MAN, MEET BOX BOY. BOX BOY, MEET TOO MUCH COFFEE MAN.
HE'S NOT VERY INTERESTING IS HE?

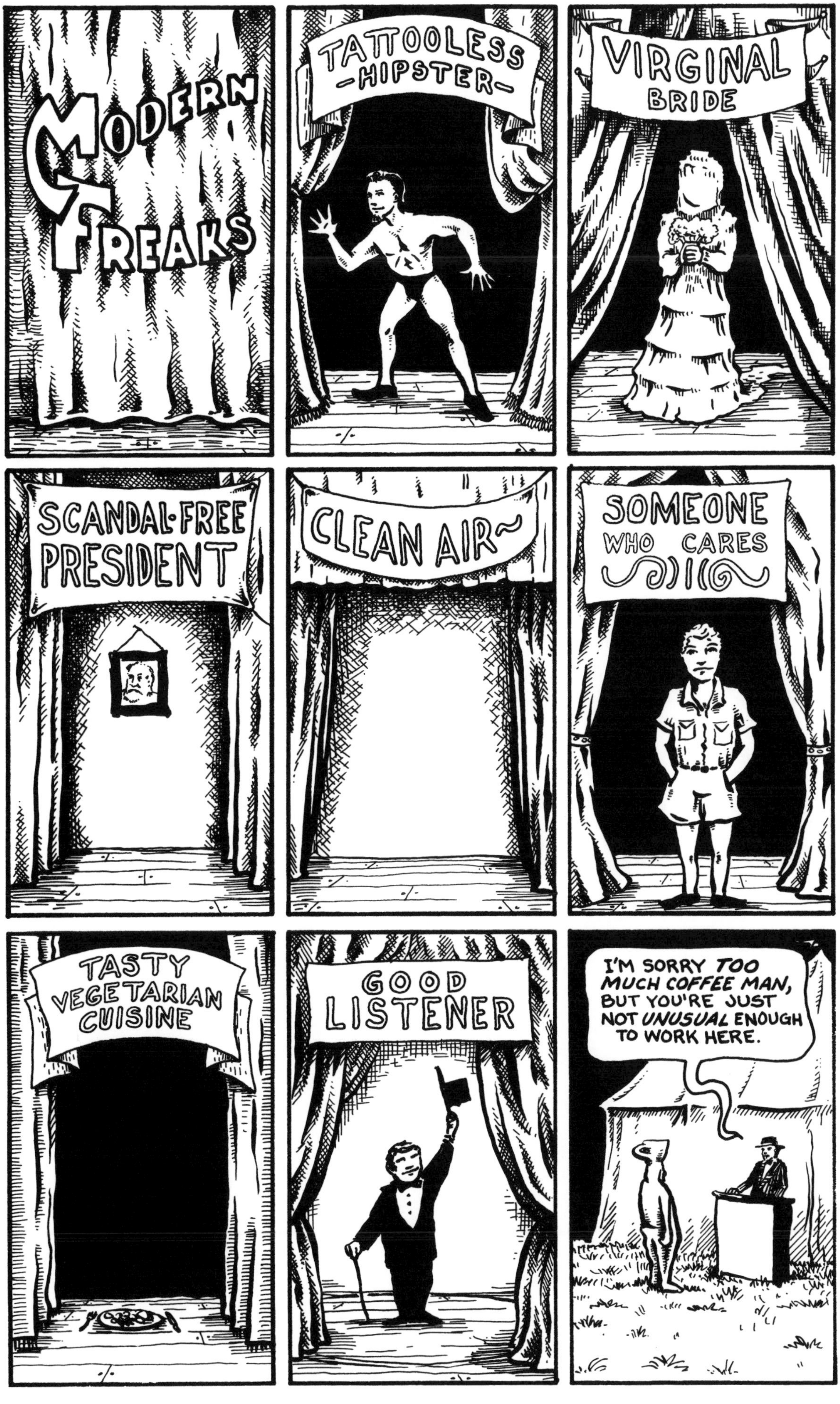
MODERN FREAKS
TATTOOLESS HIPSTER
VIRGINAL BRIDE
SCANDAL-FREE PRESIDENT
CLEAN AIR
SOMEONE WHO CARES
TASTY VEGETARIAN CUISINE
GOOD LISTENER
I'M SORRY TOO MUCH COFFEE MAN, BUT YOU'RE JUST NOT UNUSUAL ENOUGH TO WORK HERE.

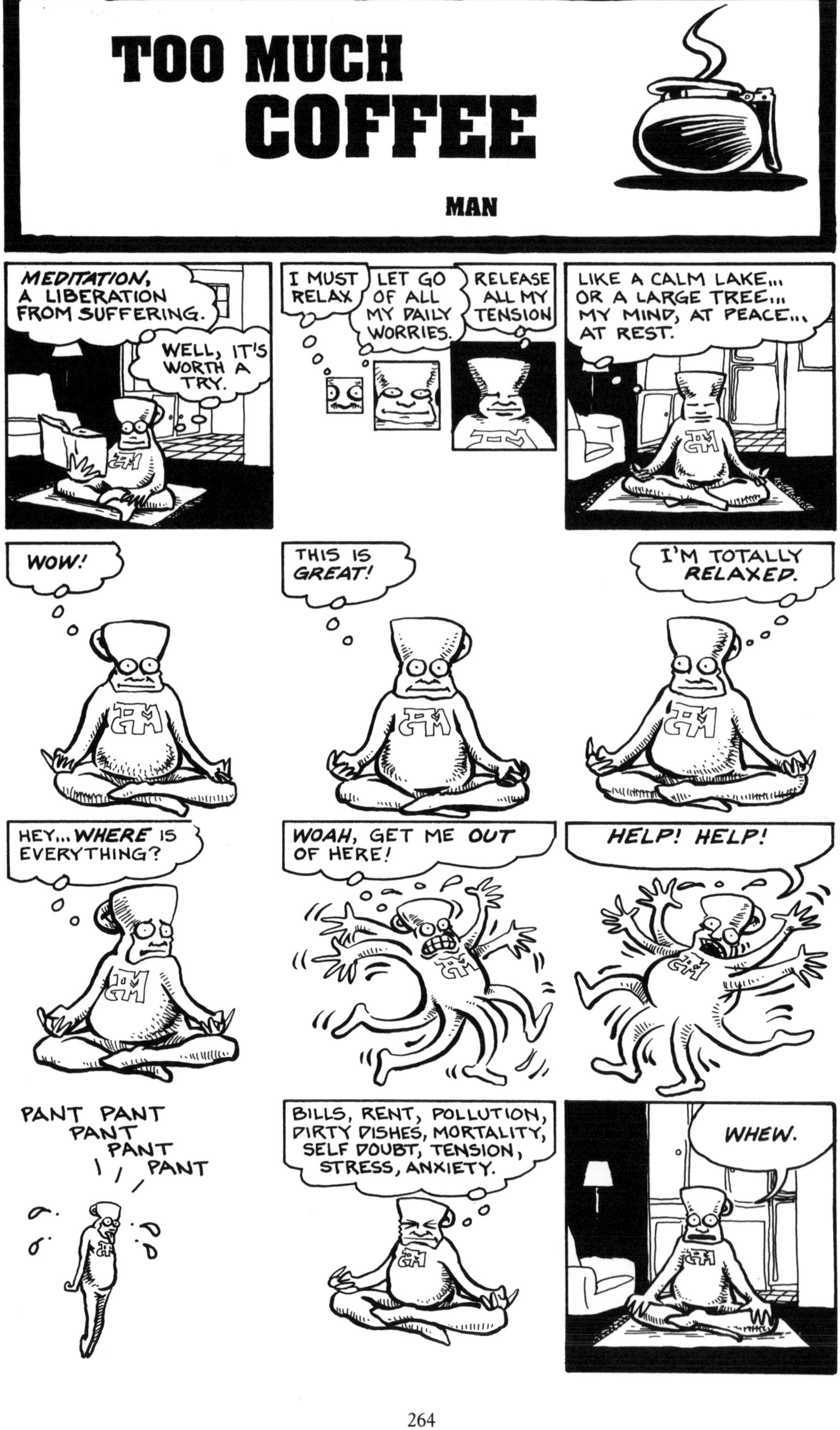

TOO MUCH COFFEE MAN
MEDITATION, A LIBERATION FROM SUFFERING.
WELL, IT'S WORTH A TRY.
I MUST RELAX
LET GO OF ALL MY DAILY WORRIES.
RELEASE ALL MY TENSION
LIKE A CALM LAKE... OR A LARGE TREE... MY MIND, AT PEACE... AT REST.
WOW!
THIS IS GREAT!
I'M TOTALLY RELAXED.
HEY... WHERE IS EVERYTHING?
WOAH, GET ME OUT OF HERE!
HELP! HELP!
PANT PANT PANT PANT PANT
BILLS, RENT, POLLUTION, DIRTY DISHES, MORTALITY, SELF DOUBT, TENSION, STRESS, ANXIETY.
WHEW.

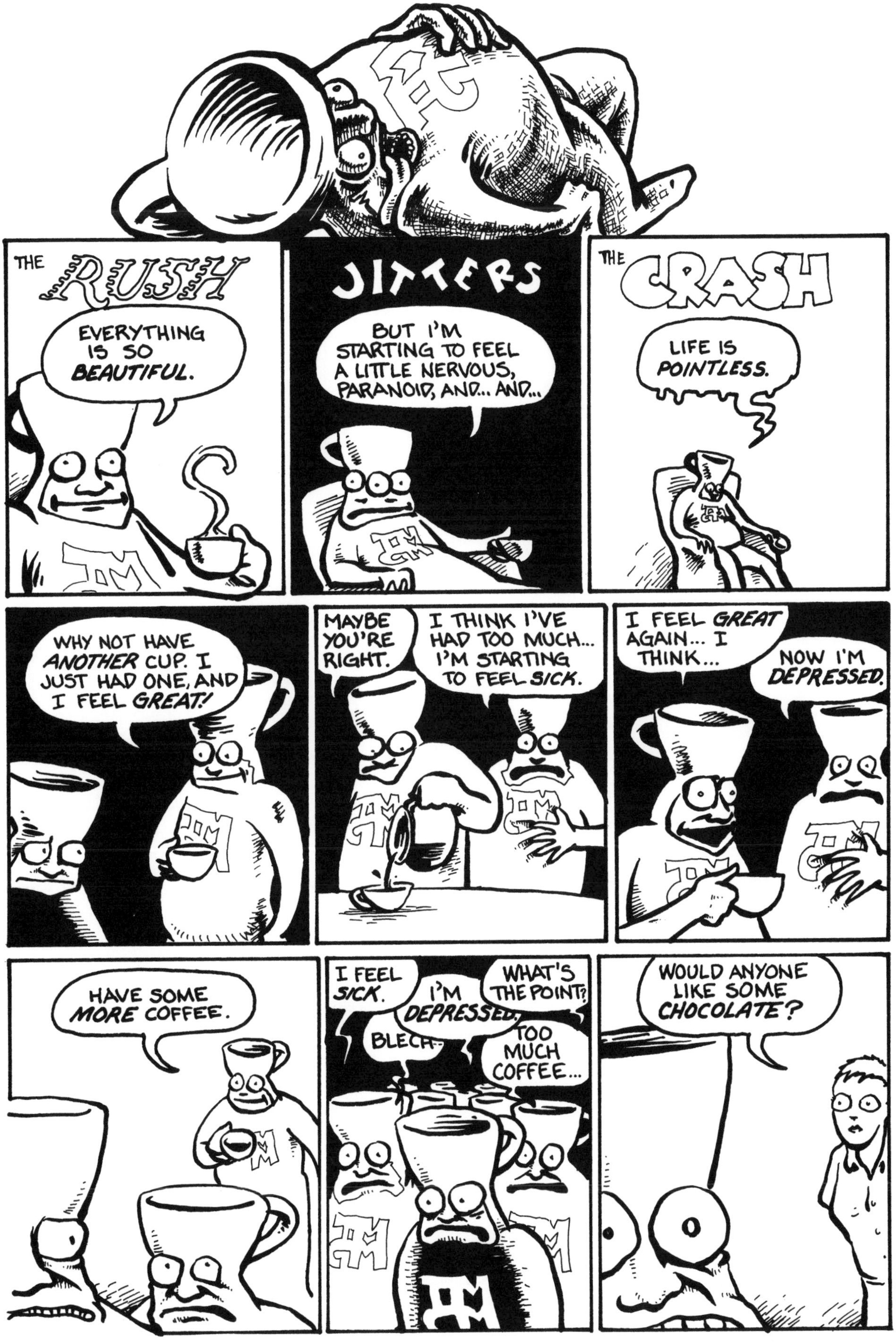
THE RUSH
EVERYTHING IS SO BEAUTIFUL.
JITTERS
BUT I'M STARTING TO FEEL A LITTLE NERVOUS, PARANOID, AND... AND...
THE CRASH
LIFE IS POINTLESS.
WHY NOT HAVE ANOTHER CUP. I JUST HAD ONE, AND I FEEL GREAT!
MAYBE YOU'RE RIGHT.
I THINK I'VE HAD TOO MUCH... I'M STARTING TO FEEL SICK.
I FEEL GREAT AGAIN... I THINK...
NOW I'M DEPRESSED.
HAVE SOME MORE COFFEE.
I FEEL SICK.
I'M DEPRESSED.
WHAT'S THE POINT?
BLECH.
TOO MUCH COFFEE...
WOULD ANYONE LIKE SOME CHOCOLATE?

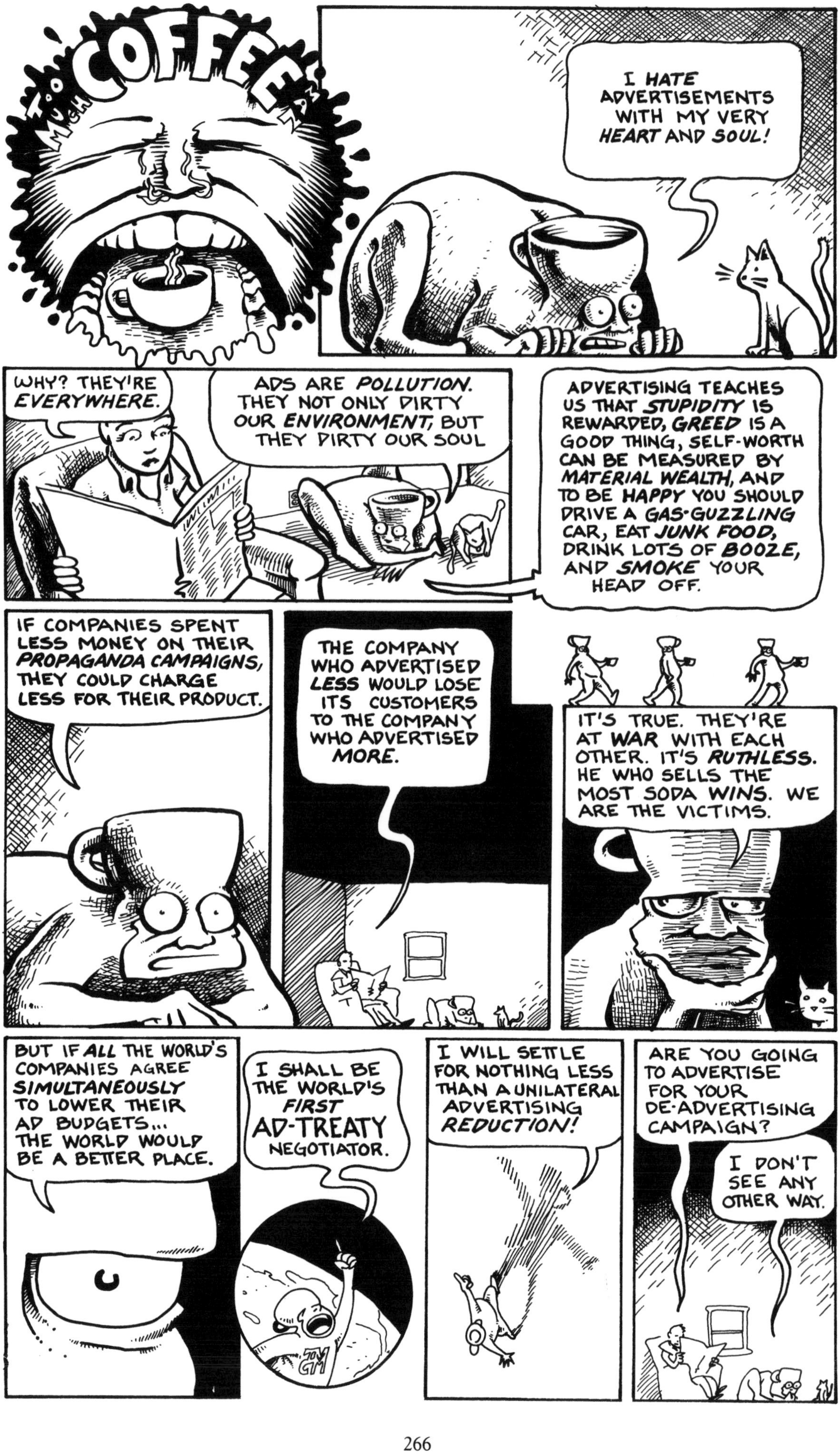
TOO MUCH COFFEE MAN
I HATE ADVERTISEMENTS WITH MY VERY HEART AND SOUL!
WHY? THEY'RE EVERYWHERE.
ADS ARE POLLUTION. THEY NOT ONLY DIRTY OUR ENVIRONMENT, BUT THEY DIRTY OUR SOUL
ADVERTISING TEACHES US THAT STUPIDITY IS REWARDED, GREED IS A GOOD THING, SELF-WORTH CAN BE MEASURED BY MATERIAL WEALTH, AND TO BE HAPPY YOU SHOULD DRIVE A GAS-GUZZLING CAR, EAT JUNK FOOD, DRINK LOTS OF BOOZE, AND SMOKE YOUR HEAD OFF.
IF COMPANIES SPENT LESS MONEY ON THEIR PROPAGANDA CAMPAIGNS, THEY COULD CHARGE LESS FOR THEIR PRODUCT.
THE COMPANY WHO ADVERTISED LESS WOULD LOSE ITS CUSTOMERS TO THE COMPANY WHO ADVERTISED MORE.
IT'S TRUE. THEY'RE AT WAR WITH EACH OTHER. IT'S RUTHLESS. HE WHO SELLS THE MOST SODA WINS. WE ARE THE VICTIMS.
BUT IF ALL THE WORLD'S COMPANIES AGREE SIMULTANEOUSLY TO LOWER THEIR AD BUDGETS... THE WORLD WOULD BE A BETTER PLACE.
I SHALL BE THE WORLD'S FIRST AD-TREATY NEGOTIATOR.
I WILL SETTLE FOR NOTHING LESS THAN A UNILATERAL ADVERTISING REDUCTION!
ARE YOU GOING TO ADVERTISE FOR YOUR DE-ADVERTISING CAMPAIGN?
I DON'T SEE ANY OTHER WAY.

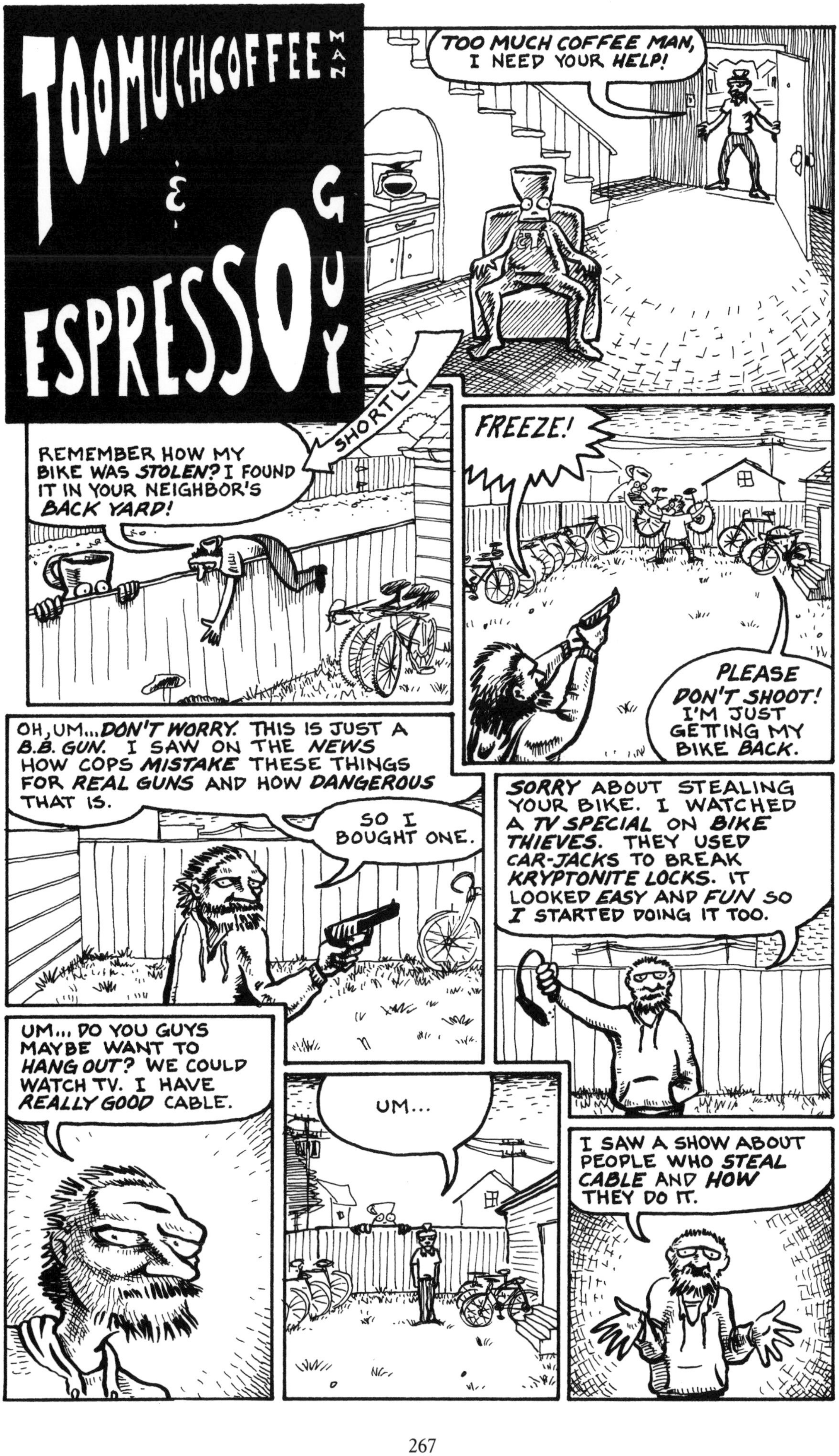
TOOMUCHCOFFEE MAN & ESPRESSO GUY
TOO MUCH COFFEE MAN, I NEED YOUR HELP!
SHORTLY
REMEMBER HOW MY BIKE WAS STOLEN? I FOUND IT IN YOUR NEIGHBOR'S BACK YARD!
FREEZE!
PLEASE DON'T SHOOT! I'M JUST GETTING MY BIKE BACK.
OH, UM... DON'T WORRY. THIS IS JUST A B.B. GUN. I SAW ON THE NEWS HOW COPS MISTAKE THESE THINGS FOR REAL GUNS AND HOW DANGEROUS THAT IS.
SO I BOUGHT ONE.
SORRY ABOUT STEALING YOUR BIKE. I WATCHED A TV SPECIAL ON BIKE THIEVES. THEY USED CAR-JACKS TO BREAK KRYPTONITE LOCKS. IT LOOKED EASY AND FUN SO I STARTED DOING IT TOO.
UM... DO YOU GUYS MAYBE WANT TO HANG OUT? WE COULD WATCH TV. I HAVE REALLY GOOD CABLE.
UM...
I SAW A SHOW ABOUT PEOPLE WHO STEAL CABLE AND HOW THEY DO IT.

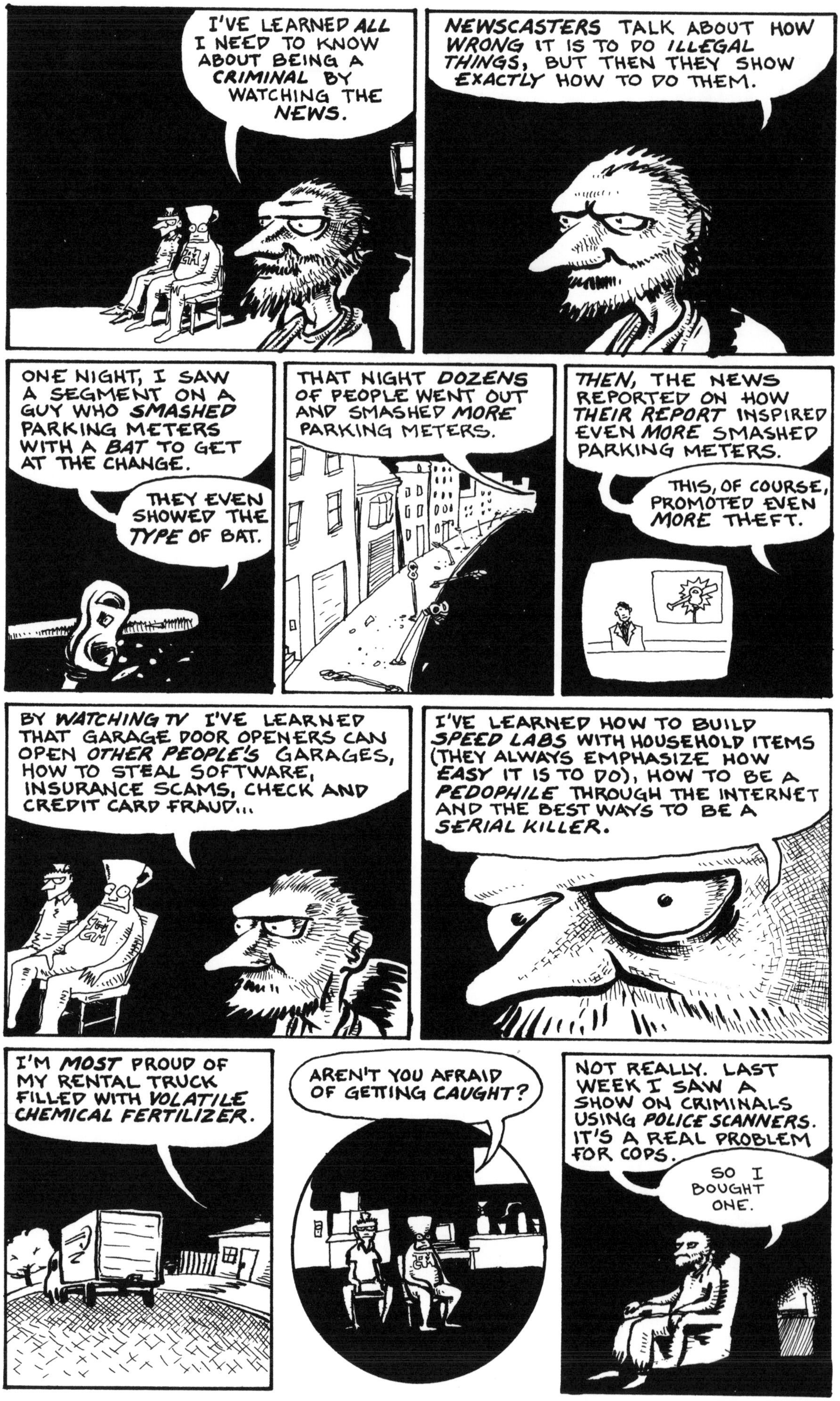
I'VE LEARNED ALL I NEED TO KNOW ABOUT BEING A CRIMINAL BY WATCHING THE NEWS.
NEWSCASTERS TALK ABOUT HOW WRONG IT IS TO DO ILLEGAL THINGS, BUT THEN THEY SHOW EXACTLY HOW TO DO THEM.
ONE NIGHT, I SAW A SEGMENT ON A GUY WHO SMASHED PARKING METERS WITH A BAT TO GET AT THE CHANGE.
THEY EVEN SHOWED THE TYPE OF BAT.
THAT NIGHT DOZENS OF PEOPLE WENT OUT AND SMASHED MORE PARKING METERS.
THEN, THE NEWS REPORTED ON HOW THEIR REPORT INSPIRED EVEN MORE SMASHED PARKING METERS.
THIS, OF COURSE, PROMOTED EVEN MORE THEFT.
BY WATCHING TV I'VE LEARNED THAT GARAGE DOOR OPENERS CAN OPEN OTHER PEOPLE'S GARAGES, HOW TO STEAL SOFTWARE, INSURANCE SCAMS, CHECK AND CREDIT CARD FRAUD...
I'VE LEARNED HOW TO BUILD SPEED LABS WITH HOUSEHOLD ITEMS (THEY ALWAYS EMPHASIZE HOW EASY IT IS TO DO), HOW TO BE A PEDOPHILE THROUGH THE INTERNET AND THE BEST WAYS TO BE A SERIAL KILLER.
I'M MOST PROUD OF MY RENTAL TRUCK FILLED WITH VOLATILE CHEMICAL FERTILIZER.
AREN'T YOU AFRAID OF GETTING CAUGHT?
NOT REALLY. LAST WEEK I SAW A SHOW ON CRIMINALS USING POLICE SCANNERS. IT'S A REAL PROBLEM FOR COPS.
SO I BOUGHT ONE.

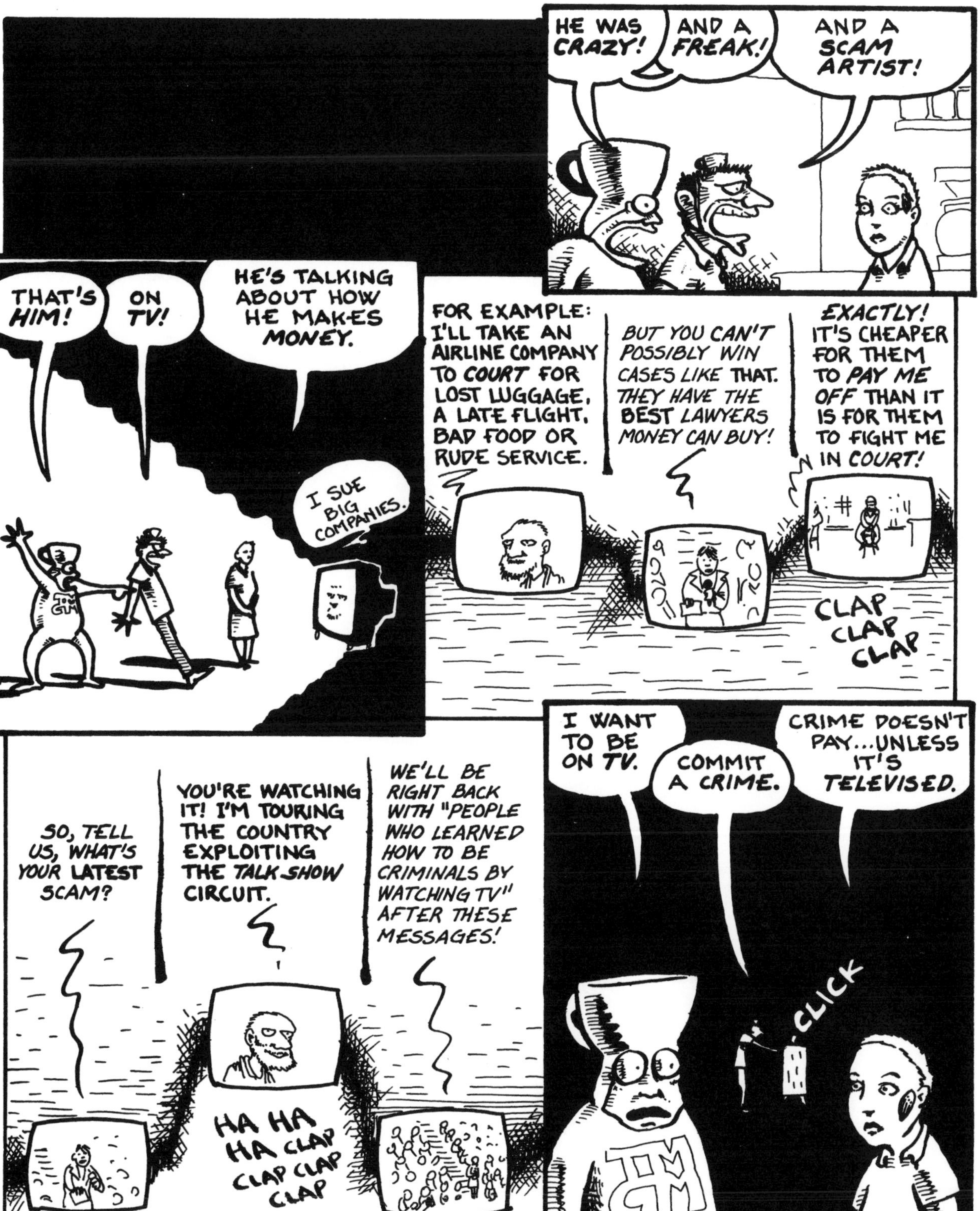
HE WAS CRAZY!
AND A FREAK!
AND A SCAM ARTIST!
THAT'S HIM!
ON TV!
HE'S TALKING ABOUT HOW HE MAKES MONEY.
I SUE BIG COMPANIES.
FOR EXAMPLE: I'LL TAKE AN AIRLINE COMPANY TO COURT FOR LOST LUGGAGE, A LATE FLIGHT, BAD FOOD OR RUDE SERVICE.
BUT YOU CAN'T POSSIBLY WIN CASES LIKE THAT. THEY HAVE THE BEST LAWYERS MONEY CAN BUY!
EXACTLY! IT'S CHEAPER FOR THEM TO PAY ME OFF THAN IT IS FOR THEM TO FIGHT ME IN COURT!
CLAP CLAP CLAP
SO, TELL US, WHAT'S YOUR LATEST SCAM?
YOU'RE WATCHING IT! I'M TOURING THE COUNTRY EXPLOITING THE TALK-SHOW CIRCUIT.
WE'LL BE RIGHT BACK WITH "PEOPLE WHO LEARNED HOW TO BE CRIMINALS BY WATCHING TV" AFTER THESE MESSAGES!
HA HA HA CLAP CLAP CLAP CLAP
I WANT TO BE ON TV.
COMMIT A CRIME.
CRIME DOESN'T PAY... UNLESS IT'S TELEVISED.
CLICK
END.

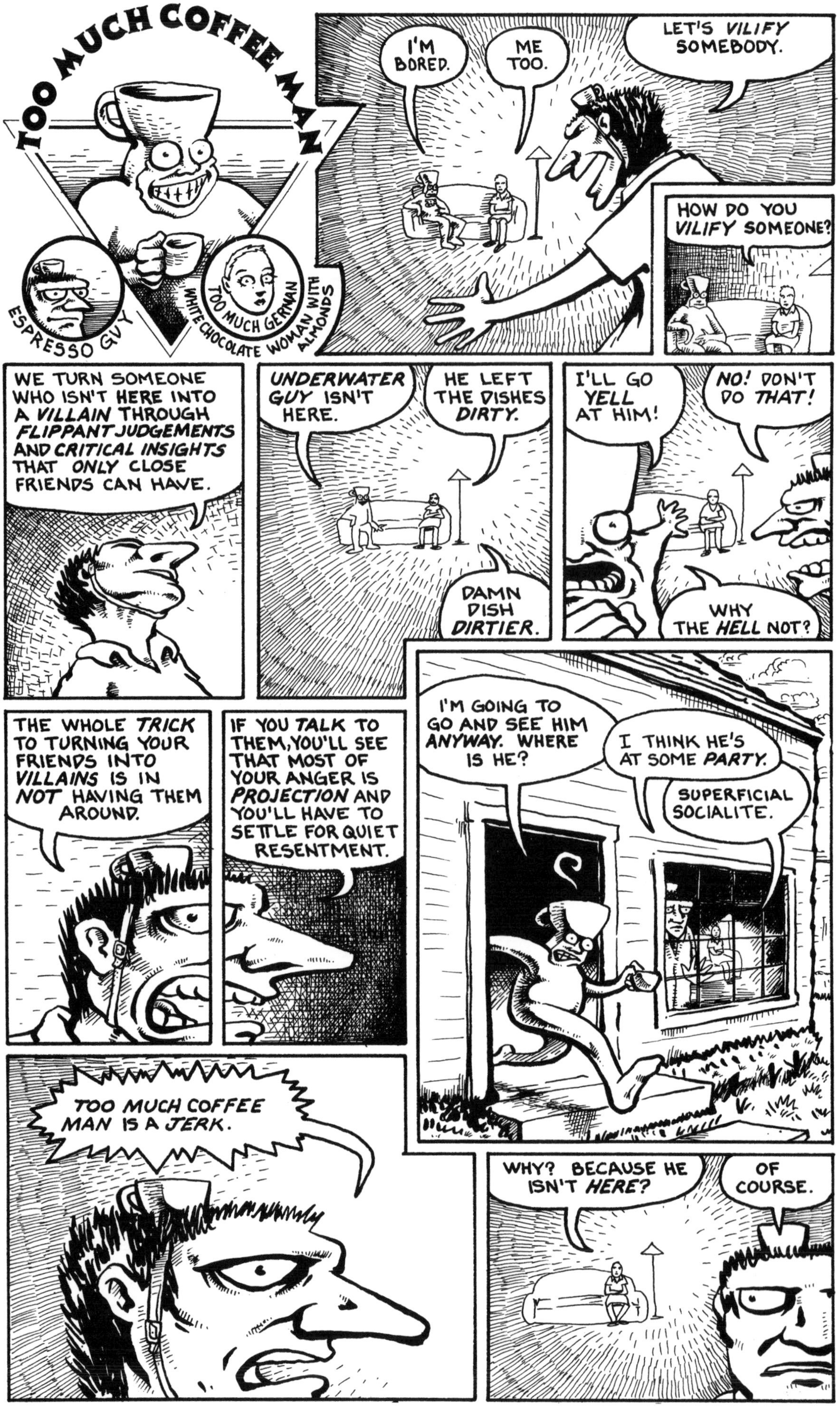
TOO MUCH COFFEE MAN
ESPRESSO GUY
TOO MUCH GERMAN WHITE CHOCOLATE WOMAN WITH ALMONDS
I'M BORED.
ME TOO.
LET'S VILIFY SOMEBODY.
HOW DO YOU VILIFY SOMEONE?
WE TURN SOMEONE WHO ISN'T HERE INTO A VILLAIN THROUGH FLIPPANT JUDGEMENTS AND CRITICAL INSIGHTS THAT ONLY CLOSE FRIENDS CAN HAVE.
UNDERWATER GUY ISN'T HERE.
HE LEFT THE DISHES DIRTY.
DAMN DISH DIRTIER.
I'LL GO YELL AT HIM!
NO! DON'T DO THAT!
WHY THE HELL NOT?
THE WHOLE TRICK TO TURNING YOUR FRIENDS INTO VILLAINS IS IN NOT HAVING THEM AROUND.
IF YOU TALK TO THEM, YOU'LL SEE THAT MOST OF YOUR ANGER IS PROJECTION AND YOU'LL HAVE TO SETTLE FOR QUIET RESENTMENT.
I'M GOING TO GO AND SEE HIM ANYWAY. WHERE IS HE?
I THINK HE'S AT SOME PARTY.
SUPERFICIAL SOCIALITE.
TOO MUCH COFFEE MAN IS A JERK.
WHY? BECAUSE HE ISN'T HERE?
OF COURSE.

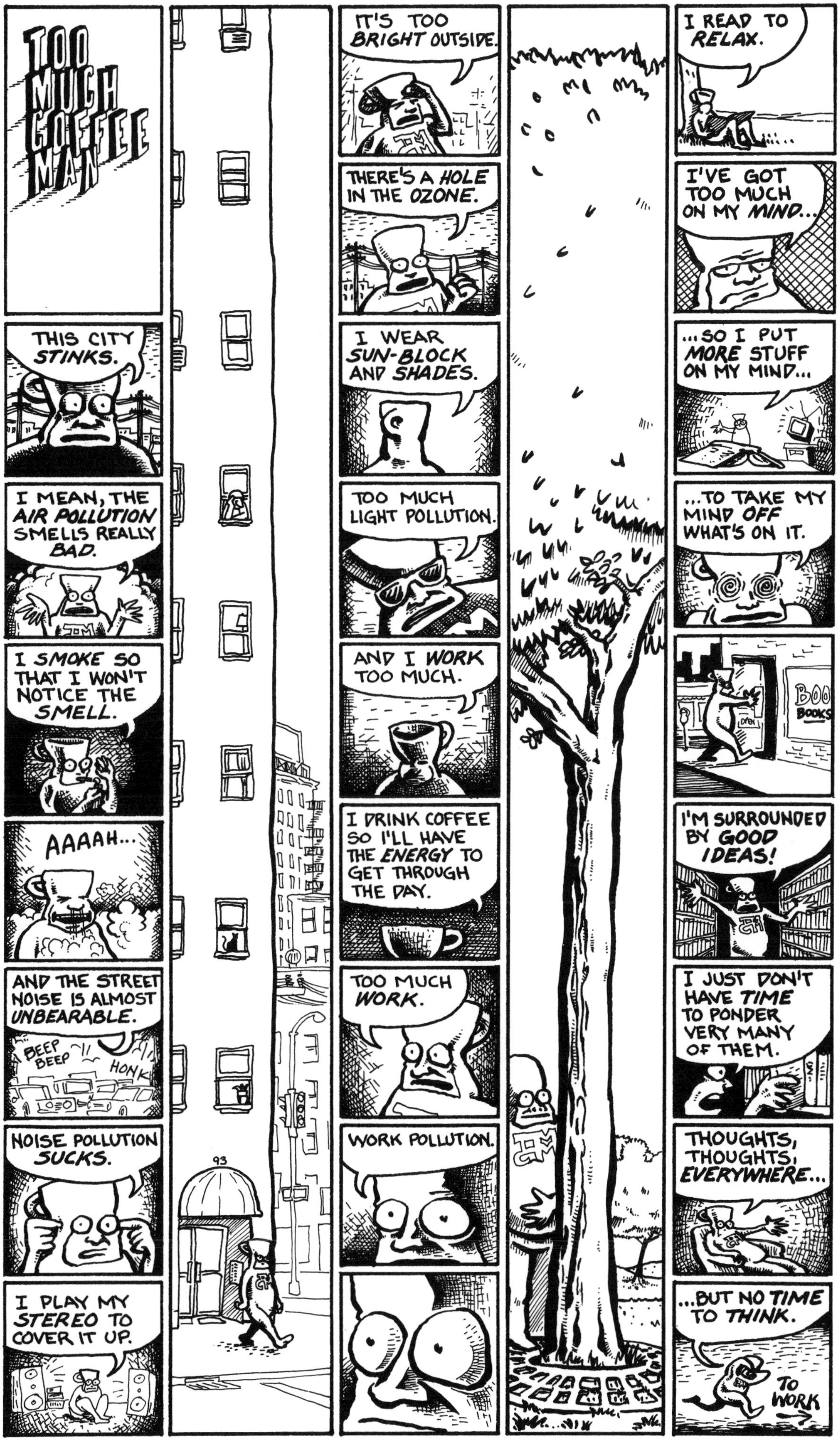
TOO MUCH COFFEE MAN
THIS CITY STINKS.
I MEAN, THE AIR POLLUTION SMELLS REALLY BAD.
I SMOKE SO THAT I WON'T NOTICE THE SMELL.
AAAAH...
AND THE STREET NOISE IS ALMOST UNBEARABLE.
BEEP BEEP
HONK
NOISE POLLUTION SUCKS.
I PLAY MY STEREO TO COVER IT UP.
IT'S TOO BRIGHT OUTSIDE.
THERE'S A HOLE IN THE OZONE.
I WEAR SUN-BLOCK AND SHADES.
TOO MUCH LIGHT POLLUTION.
AND I WORK TOO MUCH.
I DRINK COFFEE SO I'LL HAVE THE ENERGY TO GET THROUGH THE DAY.
TOO MUCH WORK.
WORK POLLUTION.
I READ TO RELAX.
I'VE GOT TOO MUCH ON MY MIND...
...SO I PUT MORE STUFF ON MY MIND...
...TO TAKE MY MIND OFF WHAT'S ON IT.
BOOKS
I'M SURROUNDED BY GOOD IDEAS!
I JUST DON'T HAVE TIME TO PONDER VERY MANY OF THEM.
THOUGHTS, THOUGHTS, EVERYWHERE...
...BUT NO TIME TO THINK.
TO WORK

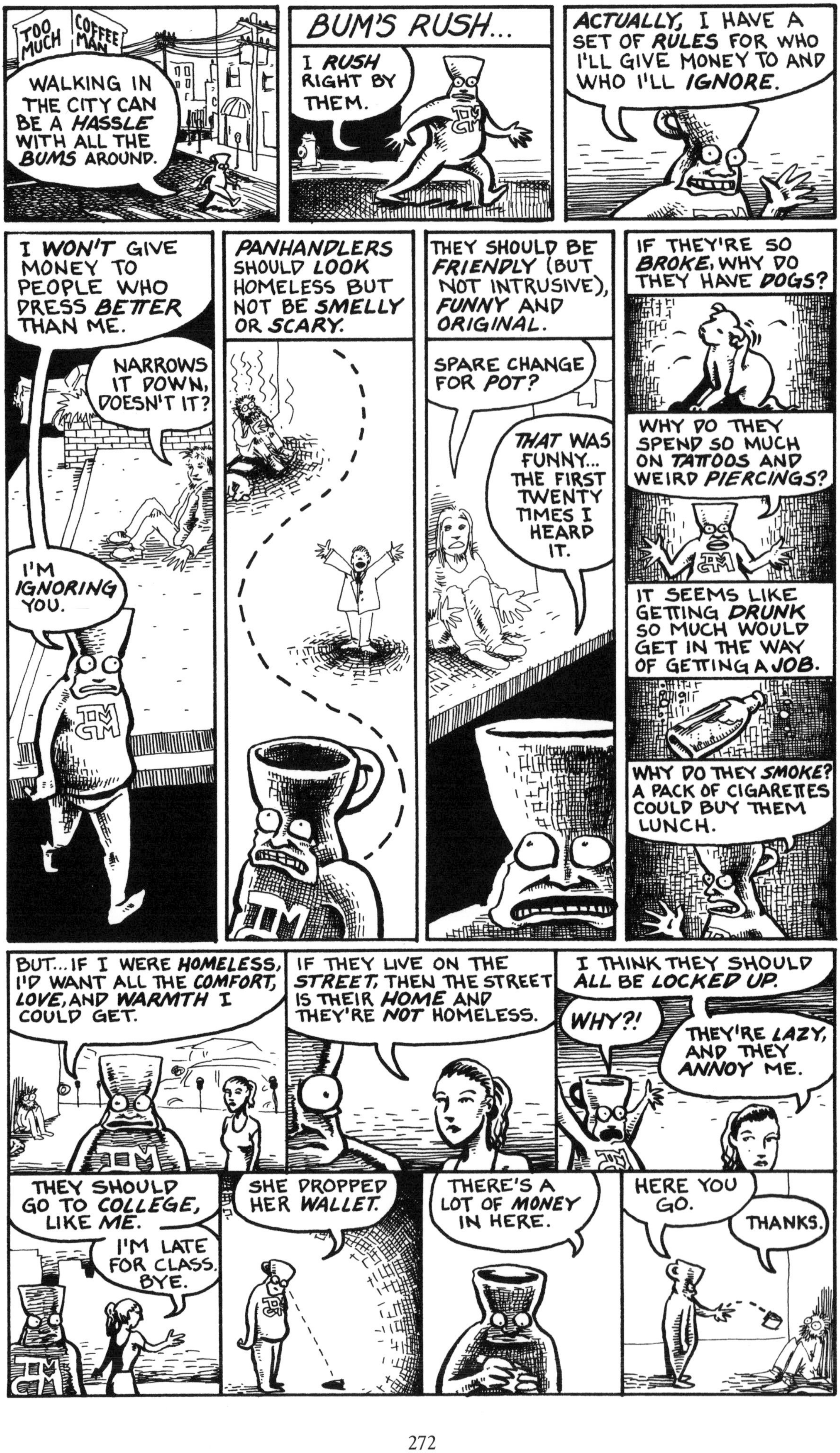

TOO MUCH COFFEE MAN
WALKING IN THE CITY CAN BE A HASSLE WITH ALL THE BUMS AROUND.
BUM'S RUSH...
I RUSH RIGHT BY THEM.
ACTUALLY, I HAVE A SET OF RULES FOR WHO I'LL GIVE MONEY TO AND WHO I'LL IGNORE.
I WON'T GIVE MONEY TO PEOPLE WHO DRESS BETTER THAN ME.
NARROWS IT DOWN, DOESN'T IT?
I'M IGNORING YOU.
PANHANDLERS SHOULD LOOK HOMELESS BUT NOT BE SMELLY OR SCARY.
THEY SHOULD BE FRIENDLY (BUT NOT INTRUSIVE), FUNNY AND ORIGINAL.
SPARE CHANGE FOR POT?
THAT WAS FUNNY... THE FIRST TWENTY TIMES I HEARD IT.
IF THEY'RE SO BROKE, WHY DO THEY HAVE DOGS?
WHY DO THEY SPEND SO MUCH ON TATTOOS AND WEIRD PIERCINGS?
IT SEEMS LIKE GETTING DRUNK SO MUCH WOULD GET IN THE WAY OF GETTING A JOB.
WHY DO THEY SMOKE? A PACK OF CIGARETTES COULD BUY THEM LUNCH.
BUT... IF I WERE HOMELESS, I'D WANT ALL THE COMFORT, LOVE, AND WARMTH I COULD GET.
IF THEY LIVE ON THE STREET, THEN THE STREET IS THEIR HOME AND THEY'RE NOT HOMELESS.
I THINK THEY SHOULD ALL BE LOCKED UP.
WHY?!
THEY'RE LAZY, AND THEY ANNOY ME.
THEY SHOULD GO TO COLLEGE, LIKE ME.
I'M LATE FOR CLASS. BYE.
SHE DROPPED HER WALLET.
THERE'S A LOT OF MONEY IN HERE.
HERE YOU GO.
THANKS.

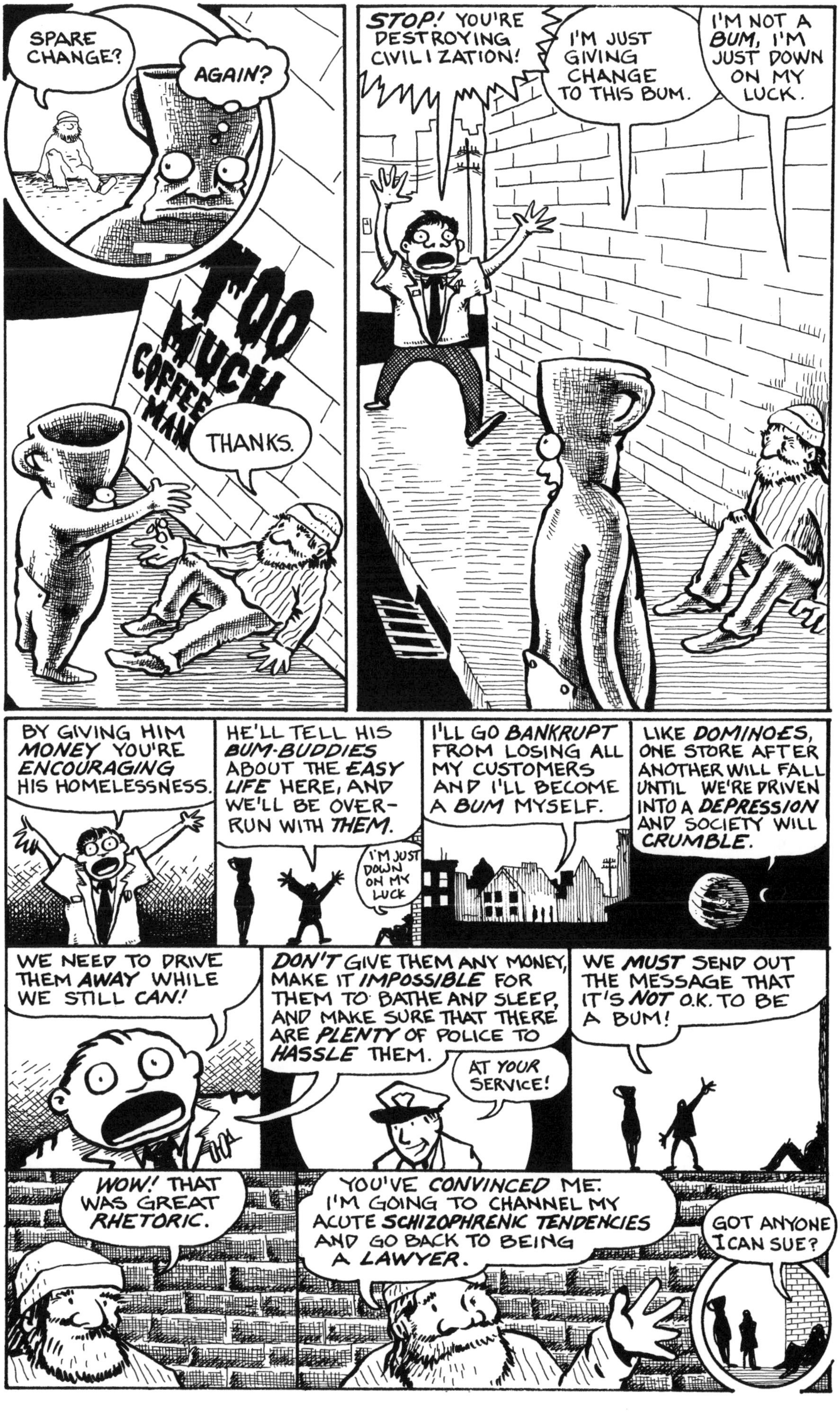
SPARE CHANGE?
AGAIN?
TOO MUCH COFFEE MAN
THANKS.
STOP! YOU'RE DESTROYING CIVILIZATION!
I'M JUST GIVING CHANGE TO THIS BUM.
I'M NOT A BUM, I'M JUST DOWN ON MY LUCK.
BY GIVING HIM MONEY YOU'RE ENCOURAGING HIS HOMELESSNESS.
HE'LL TELL HIS BUM-BUDDIES ABOUT THE EASY LIFE HERE, AND WE'LL BE OVER-RUN WITH THEM.
I'M JUST DOWN ON MY LUCK
I'LL GO BANKRUPT FROM LOSING ALL MY CUSTOMERS AND I'LL BECOME A BUM MYSELF.
LIKE DOMINOES, ONE STORE AFTER ANOTHER WILL FALL UNTIL WE'RE DRIVEN INTO A DEPRESSION AND SOCIETY WILL CRUMBLE.
WE NEED TO DRIVE THEM AWAY WHILE WE STILL CAN!
DON'T GIVE THEM ANY MONEY, MAKE IT IMPOSSIBLE FOR THEM TO BATHE AND SLEEP, AND MAKE SURE THAT THERE ARE PLENTY OF POLICE TO HASSLE THEM.
AT YOUR SERVICE!
WE MUST SEND OUT THE MESSAGE THAT IT'S NOT O.K. TO BE A BUM!
WOW! THAT WAS GREAT RHETORIC.
YOU'VE CONVINCED ME. I'M GOING TO CHANNEL MY ACUTE SCHIZOPHRENIC TENDENCIES AND GO BACK TO BEING A LAWYER.
GOT ANYONE I CAN SUE?

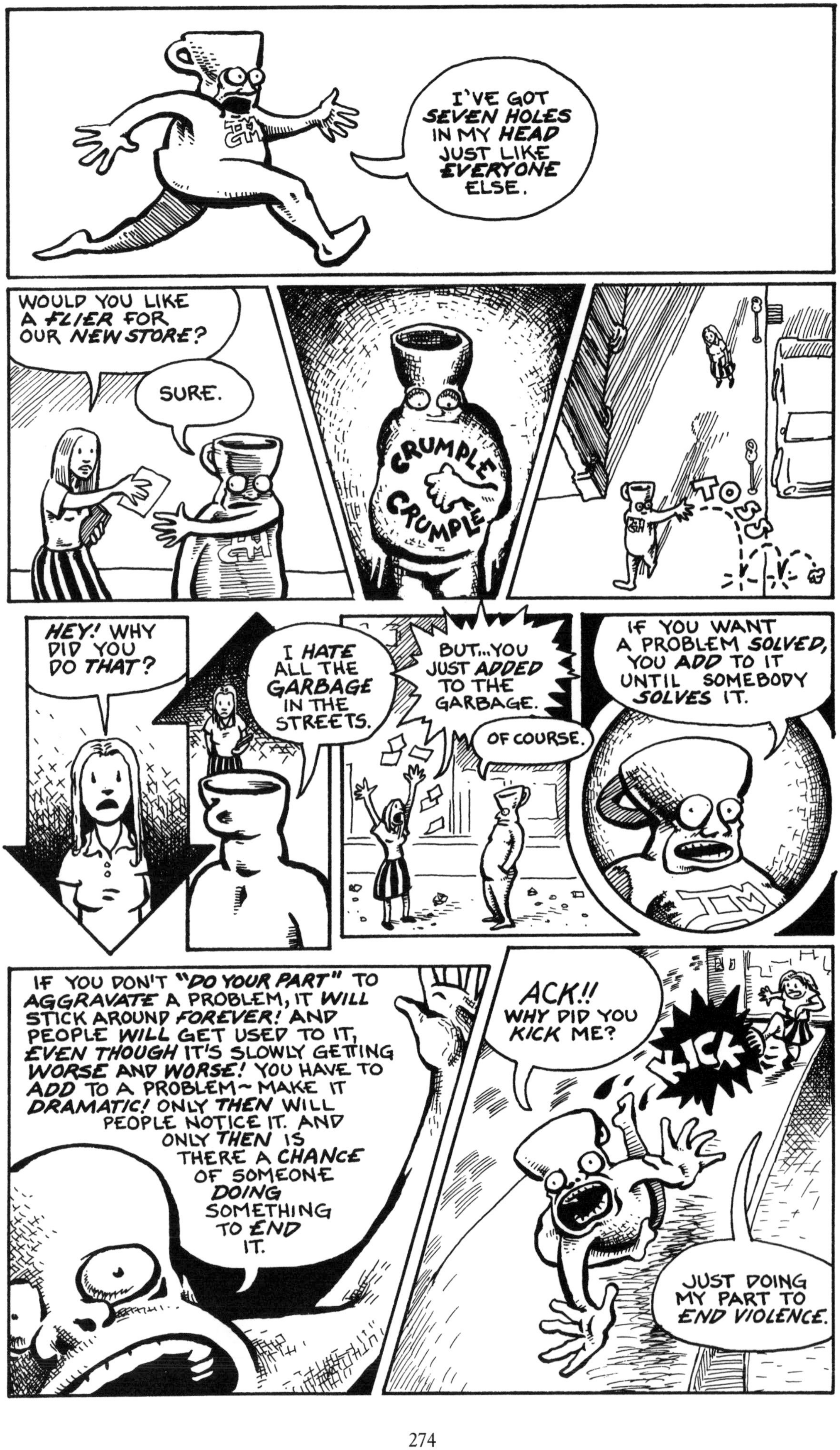

I'VE GOT SEVEN HOLES IN MY HEAD JUST LIKE EVERYONE ELSE.
WOULD YOU LIKE A FLIER FOR OUR NEW STORE?
SURE.
CRUMPLE CRUMPLE
TOSS
HEY! WHY DID YOU DO THAT?
I HATE ALL THE GARBAGE IN THE STREETS.
BUT...YOU JUST ADDED TO THE GARBAGE.
OF COURSE.
IF YOU WANT A PROBLEM SOLVED, YOU ADD TO IT UNTIL SOMEBODY SOLVES IT.
IF YOU DON'T "DO YOUR PART" TO AGGRAVATE A PROBLEM, IT WILL STICK AROUND FOREVER! AND PEOPLE WILL GET USED TO IT, EVEN THOUGH IT'S SLOWLY GETTING WORSE AND WORSE! YOU HAVE TO ADD TO A PROBLEM~ MAKE IT DRAMATIC! ONLY THEN WILL PEOPLE NOTICE IT. AND ONLY THEN IS THERE A CHANCE OF SOMEONE DOING SOMETHING TO END IT.
ACK!! WHY DID YOU KICK ME?
KICK
JUST DOING MY PART TO END VIOLENCE.

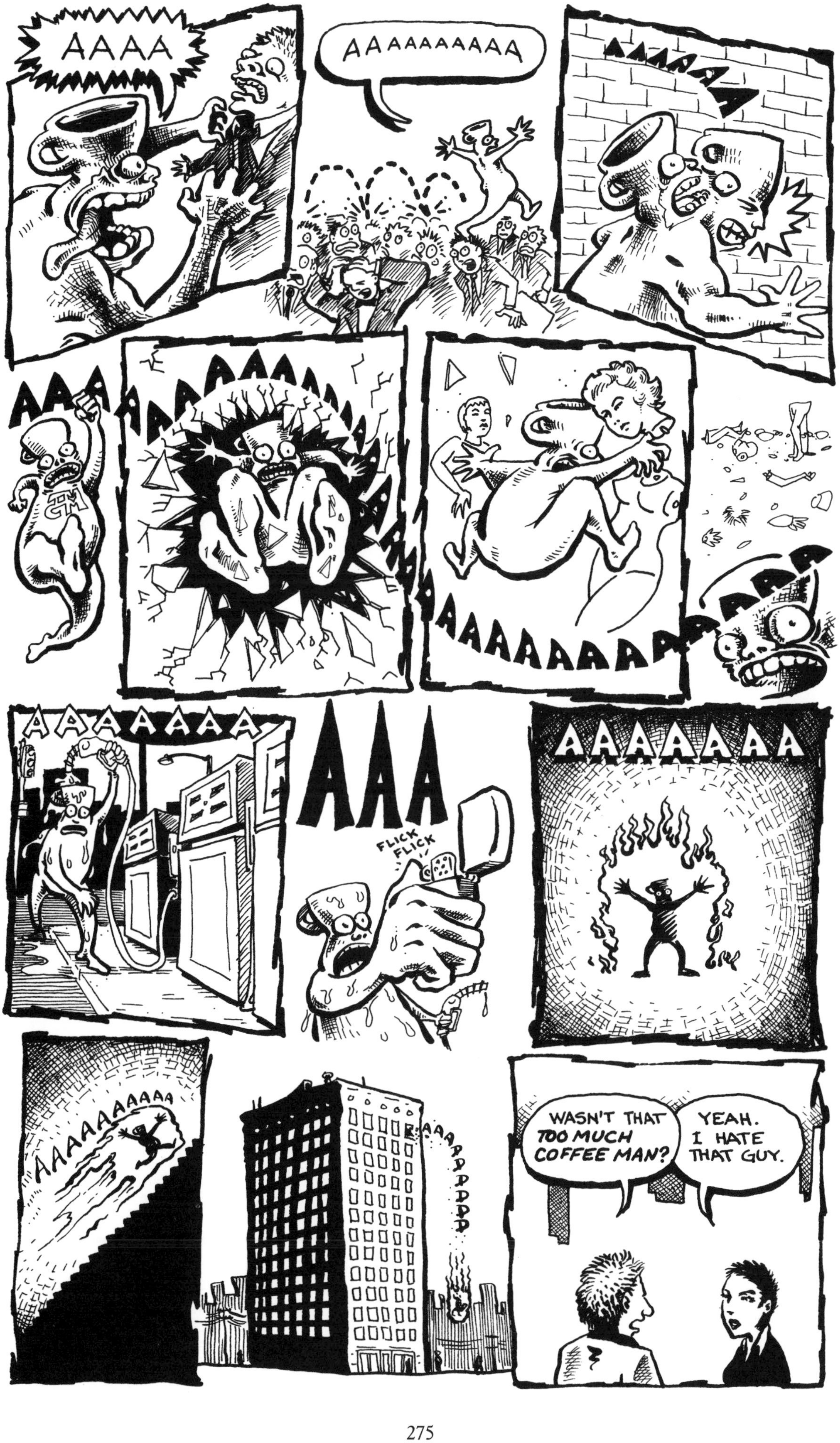
AAAA
AAAAAAAAAA
FLICK FLICK
WASN'T THAT *TOO MUCH* COFFEE MAN?
YEAH. I HATE THAT GUY.

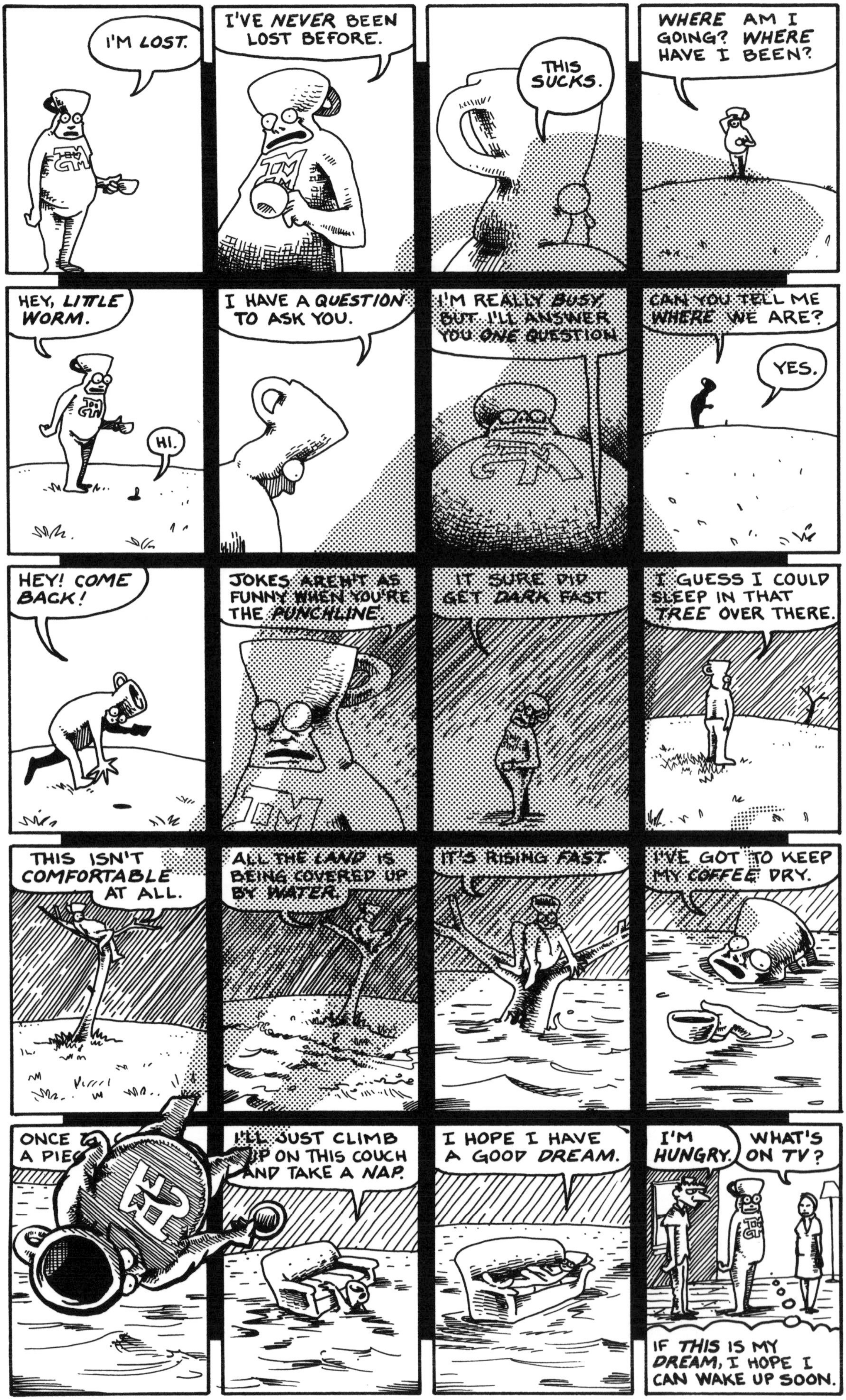
I'M LOST.
I'VE NEVER BEEN LOST BEFORE.
THIS SUCKS.
WHERE AM I GOING? WHERE HAVE I BEEN?
HEY, LITTLE WORM.
HI.
I HAVE A QUESTION TO ASK YOU.
I'M REALLY BUSY. BUT I'LL ANSWER YOU ONE QUESTION.
CAN YOU TELL ME WHERE WE ARE?
YES.
HEY! COME BACK!
JOKES AREN'T AS FUNNY WHEN YOU'RE THE PUNCHLINE.
IT SURE DID GET DARK FAST.
I GUESS I COULD SLEEP IN THAT TREE OVER THERE.
THIS ISN'T COMFORTABLE AT ALL.
ALL THE LAND IS BEING COVERED UP BY WATER.
IT'S RISING FAST.
I'VE GOT TO KEEP MY COFFEE DRY.
ONCE
I'LL JUST CLIMB UP ON THIS COUCH AND TAKE A NAP.
I HOPE I HAVE A GOOD DREAM.
I'M HUNGRY.
WHAT'S ON TV?
IF THIS IS MY DREAM, I HOPE I CAN WAKE UP SOON.

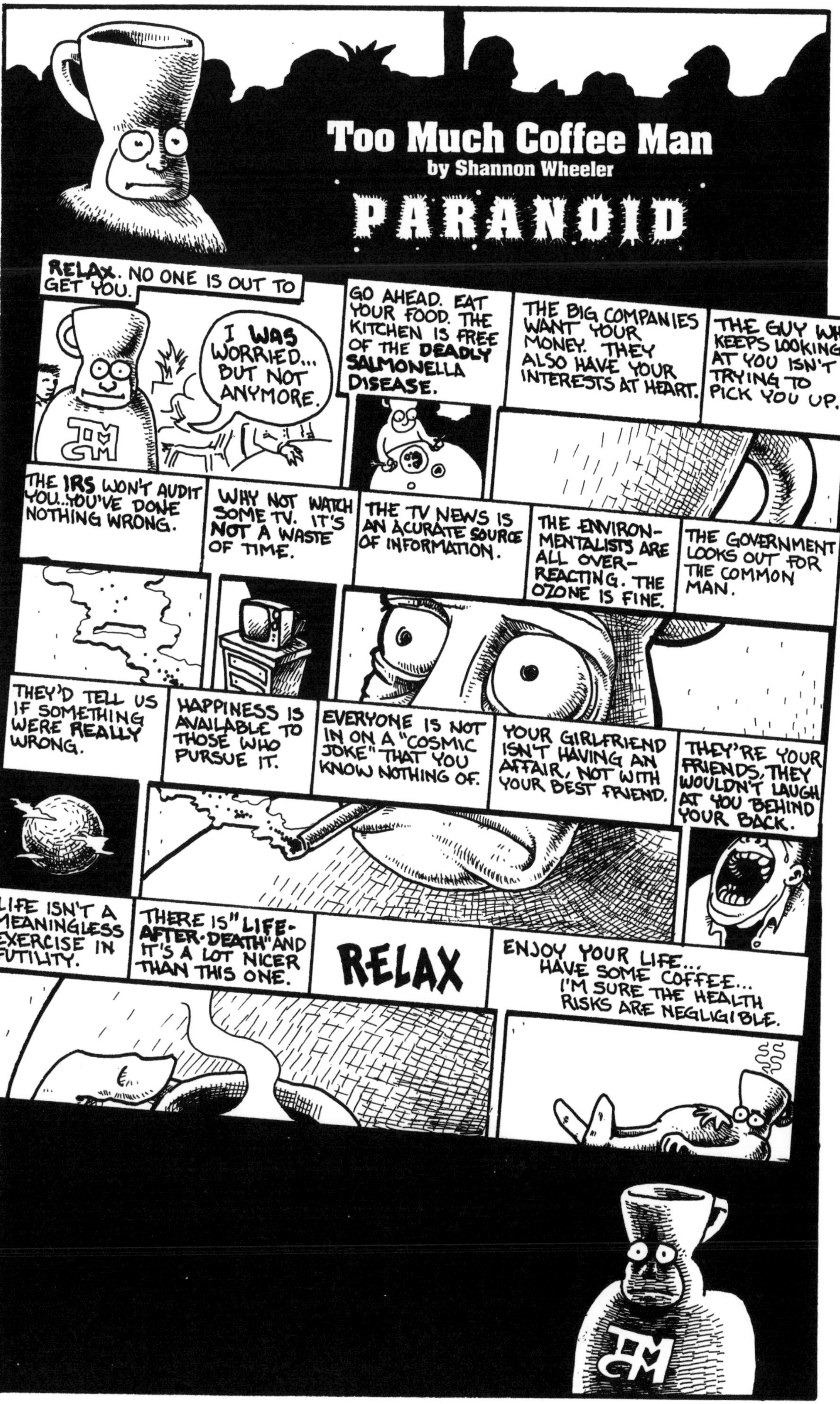
Too Much Coffee Man
by Shannon Wheeler
PARANOID
RELAX. NO ONE IS OUT TO GET YOU.
I WAS WORRIED... BUT NOT ANYMORE.
GO AHEAD. EAT YOUR FOOD. THE KITCHEN IS FREE OF THE DEADLY SALMONELLA DISEASE.
THE BIG COMPANIES WANT YOUR MONEY. THEY ALSO HAVE YOUR INTERESTS AT HEART.
THE GUY WHO KEEPS LOOKING AT YOU ISN'T TRYING TO PICK YOU UP.
THE IRS WON'T AUDIT YOU...YOU'VE DONE NOTHING WRONG.
WHY NOT WATCH SOME TV. IT'S NOT A WASTE OF TIME.
THE TV NEWS IS AN ACURATE SOURCE OF INFORMATION.
THE ENVIRON-MENTALISTS ARE ALL OVER-REACTING. THE OZONE IS FINE.
THE GOVERNMENT LOOKS OUT FOR THE COMMON MAN.
THEY'D TELL US IF SOMETHING WERE REALLY WRONG.
HAPPINESS IS AVAILABLE TO THOSE WHO PURSUE IT.
EVERYONE IS NOT IN ON A "COSMIC JOKE" THAT YOU KNOW NOTHING OF.
YOUR GIRLFRIEND ISN'T HAVING AN AFFAIR, NOT WITH YOUR BEST FRIEND.
THEY'RE YOUR FRIENDS, THEY WOULDN'T LAUGH AT YOU BEHIND YOUR BACK.
LIFE ISN'T A MEANINGLESS EXERCISE IN FUTILITY.
THERE IS "LIFE-AFTER-DEATH" AND IT'S A LOT NICER THAN THIS ONE.
RELAX
ENJOY YOUR LIFE... HAVE SOME COFFEE... I'M SURE THE HEALTH RISKS ARE NEGLIGIBLE.

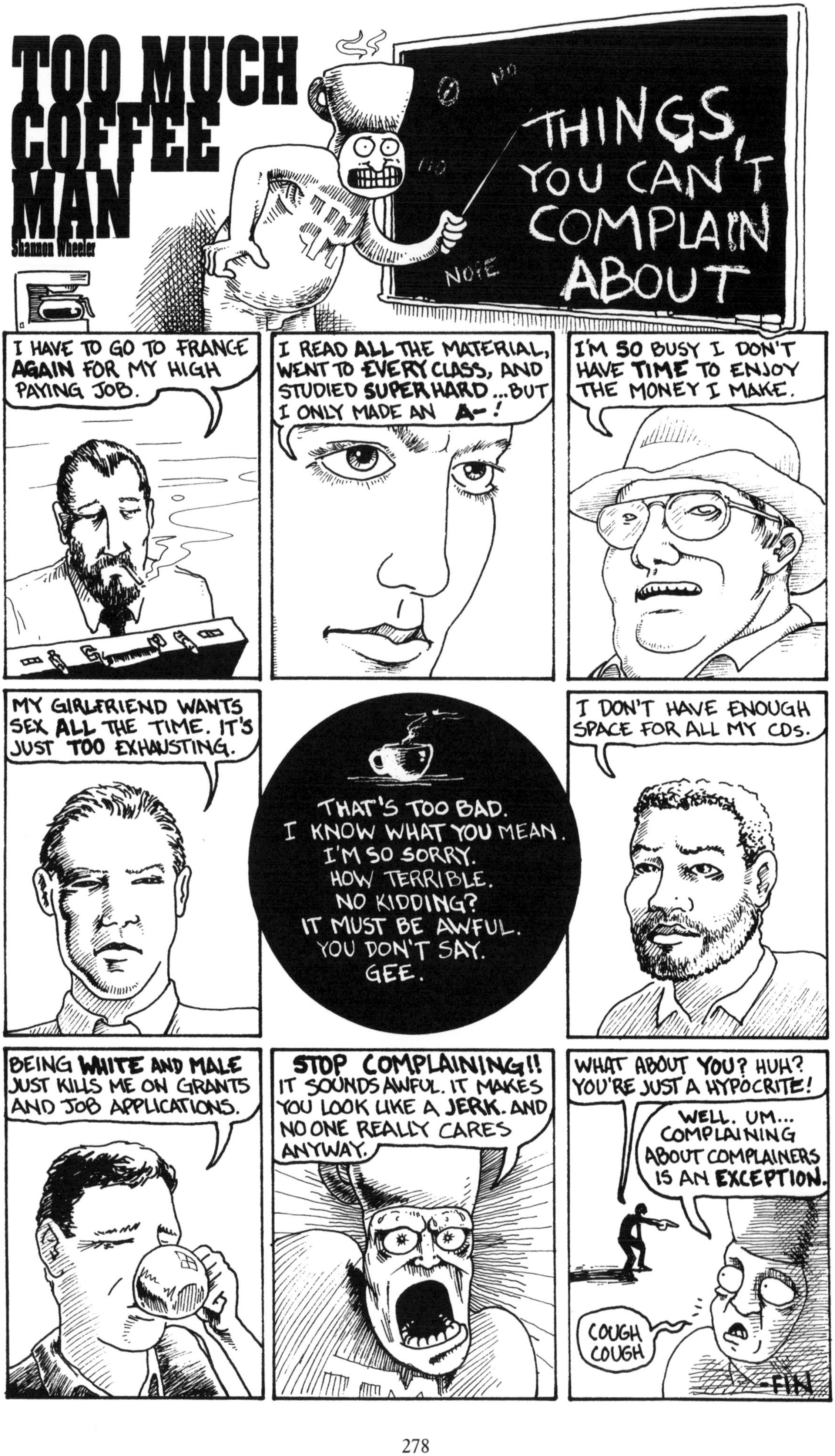
TOO MUCH COFFEE MAN
Shannon Wheeler
THINGS YOU CAN'T COMPLAIN ABOUT
I HAVE TO GO TO FRANCE AGAIN FOR MY HIGH PAYING JOB.
I READ ALL THE MATERIAL, WENT TO EVERY CLASS, AND STUDIED SUPER HARD ...BUT I ONLY MADE AN A-!
I'M SO BUSY I DON'T HAVE TIME TO ENJOY THE MONEY I MAKE.
MY GIRLFRIEND WANTS SEX ALL THE TIME. IT'S JUST TOO EXHAUSTING.
THAT'S TOO BAD.
I KNOW WHAT YOU MEAN.
I'M SO SORRY.
HOW TERRIBLE.
NO KIDDING?
IT MUST BE AWFUL.
YOU DON'T SAY.
GEE.
I DON'T HAVE ENOUGH SPACE FOR ALL MY CDs.
BEING WHITE AND MALE JUST KILLS ME ON GRANTS AND JOB APPLICATIONS.
STOP COMPLAINING!! IT SOUNDS AWFUL. IT MAKES YOU LOOK LIKE A JERK. AND NO ONE REALLY CARES ANYWAY.
WHAT ABOUT YOU? HUH? YOU'RE JUST A HYPOCRITE!
WELL. UM... COMPLAINING ABOUT COMPLAINERS IS AN EXCEPTION.
COUGH COUGH
-FIN

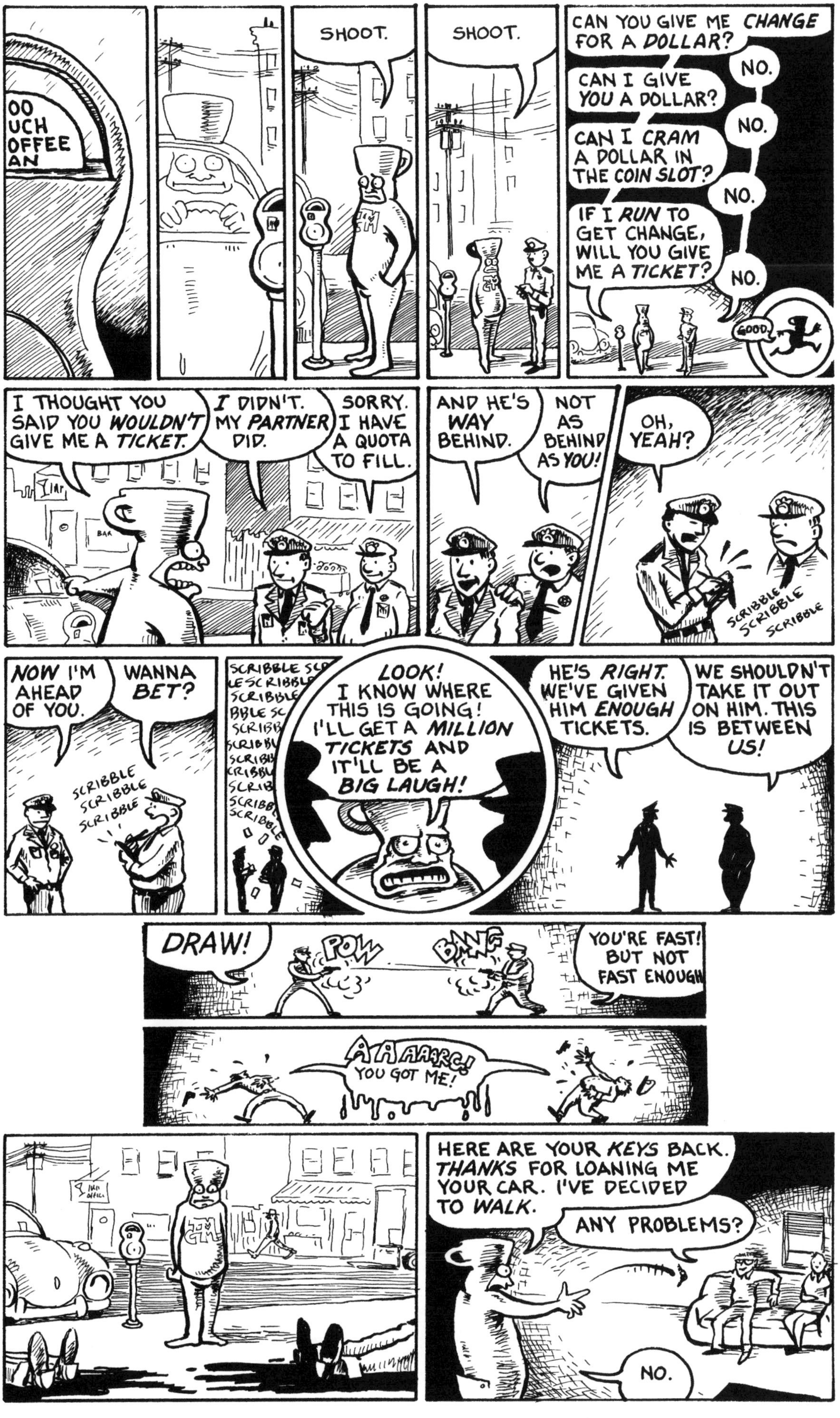

OO
UCH
OFFEE
AN
SHOOT.
SHOOT.
CAN YOU GIVE ME CHANGE FOR A DOLLAR?
NO.
CAN I GIVE YOU A DOLLAR?
NO.
CAN I CRAM A DOLLAR IN THE COIN SLOT?
NO.
IF I RUN TO GET CHANGE, WILL YOU GIVE ME A TICKET?
NO.
GOOD.
I THOUGHT YOU SAID YOU WOULDN'T GIVE ME A TICKET.
I DIDN'T. MY PARTNER DID.
SORRY. I HAVE A QUOTA TO FILL.
AND HE'S WAY BEHIND.
NOT AS BEHIND AS YOU!
OH, YEAH?
SCRIBBLE SCRIBBLE SCRIBBLE
NOW I'M AHEAD OF YOU.
WANNA BET?
SCRIBBLE SCRIBBLE SCRIBBLE
LOOK! I KNOW WHERE THIS IS GOING! I'LL GET A MILLION TICKETS AND IT'LL BE A BIG LAUGH!
HE'S RIGHT. WE'VE GIVEN HIM ENOUGH TICKETS.
WE SHOULDN'T TAKE IT OUT ON HIM. THIS IS BETWEEN US!
DRAW!
POW
BANG
YOU'RE FAST! BUT NOT FAST ENOUGH
AAAARG! YOU GOT ME!
HERE ARE YOUR KEYS BACK. THANKS FOR LOANING ME YOUR CAR. I'VE DECIDED TO WALK.
ANY PROBLEMS?
NO.

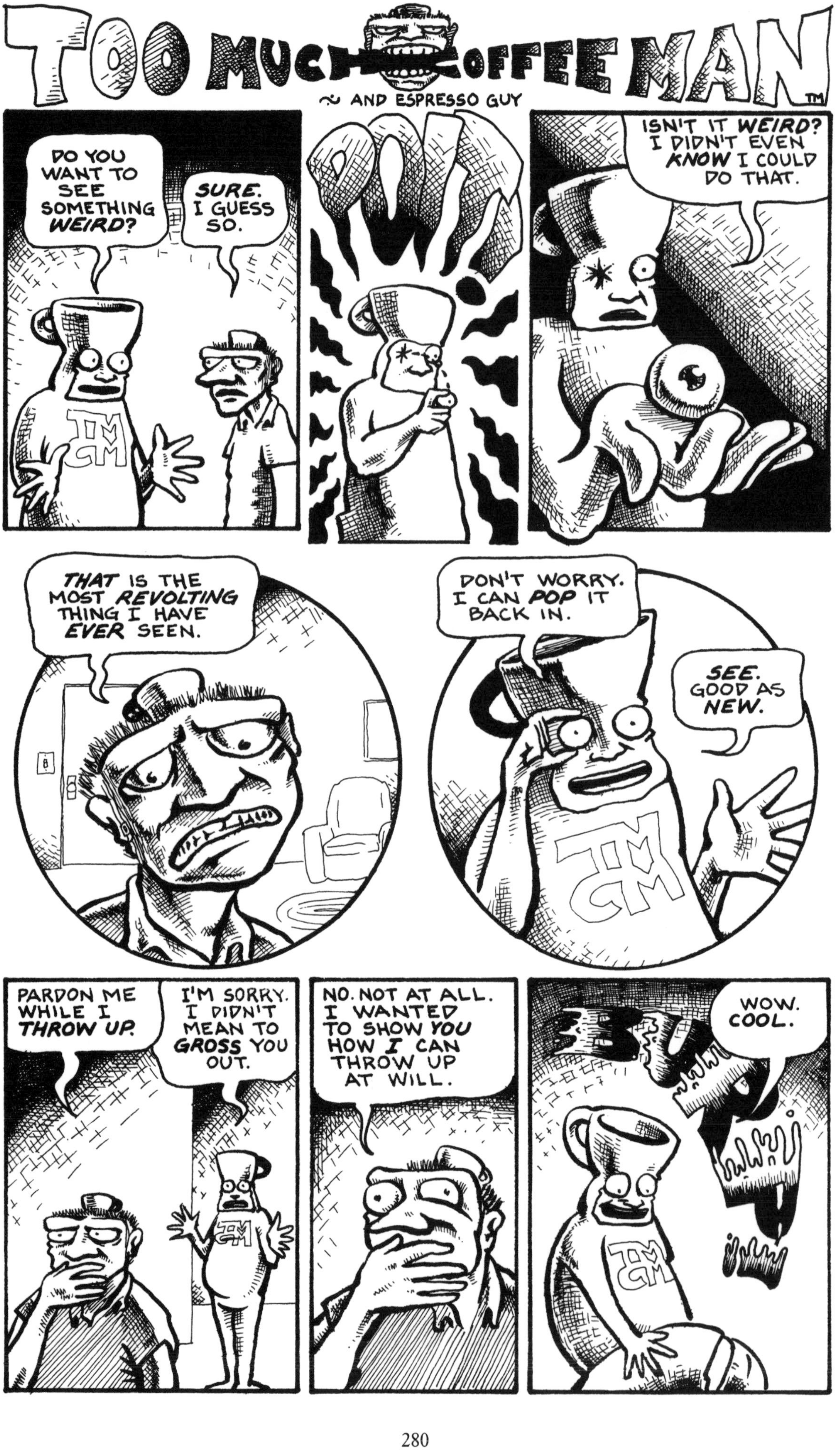
TOO MUCH COFFEE MAN
AND ESPRESSO GUY
TM
DO YOU WANT TO SEE SOMETHING WEIRD?
SURE. I GUESS SO.
ISN'T IT WEIRD? I DIDN'T EVEN KNOW I COULD DO THAT.
THAT IS THE MOST REVOLTING THING I HAVE EVER SEEN.
DON'T WORRY. I CAN POP IT BACK IN.
SEE. GOOD AS NEW.
PARDON ME WHILE I THROW UP.
I'M SORRY. I DIDN'T MEAN TO GROSS YOU OUT.
NO. NOT AT ALL. I WANTED TO SHOW YOU HOW I CAN THROW UP AT WILL.
WOW. COOL.

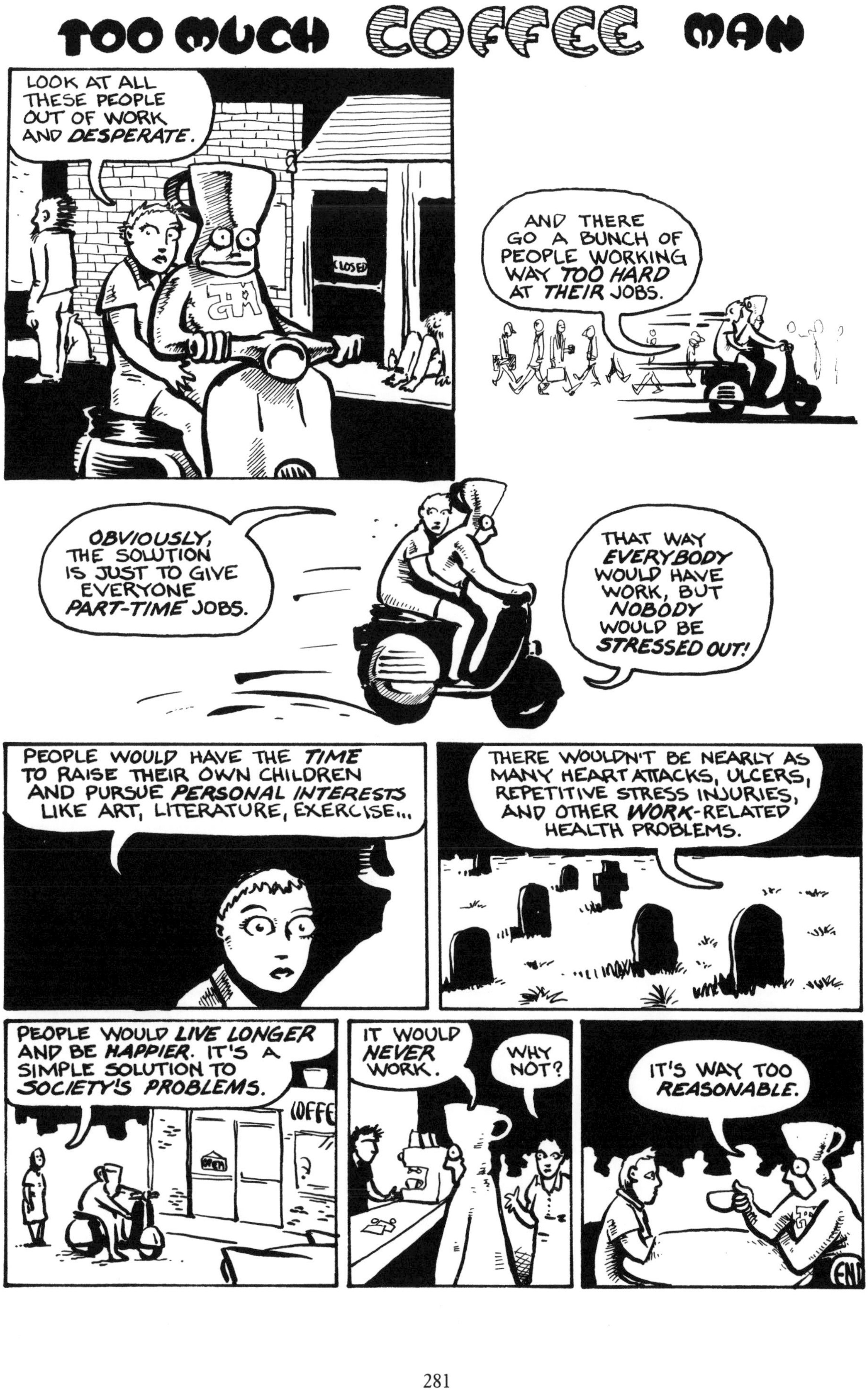
TOO MUCH COFFEE MAN
LOOK AT ALL THESE PEOPLE OUT OF WORK AND DESPERATE.
CLOSED
AND THERE GO A BUNCH OF PEOPLE WORKING WAY TOO HARD AT THEIR JOBS.
OBVIOUSLY, THE SOLUTION IS JUST TO GIVE EVERYONE PART-TIME JOBS.
THAT WAY EVERYBODY WOULD HAVE WORK, BUT NOBODY WOULD BE STRESSED OUT!
PEOPLE WOULD HAVE THE TIME TO RAISE THEIR OWN CHILDREN AND PURSUE PERSONAL INTERESTS LIKE ART, LITERATURE, EXERCISE...
THERE WOULDN'T BE NEARLY AS MANY HEART ATTACKS, ULCERS, REPETITIVE STRESS INJURIES, AND OTHER WORK-RELATED HEALTH PROBLEMS.
PEOPLE WOULD LIVE LONGER AND BE HAPPIER. IT'S A SIMPLE SOLUTION TO SOCIETY'S PROBLEMS.
IT WOULD NEVER WORK.
WHY NOT?
IT'S WAY TOO REASONABLE.
END

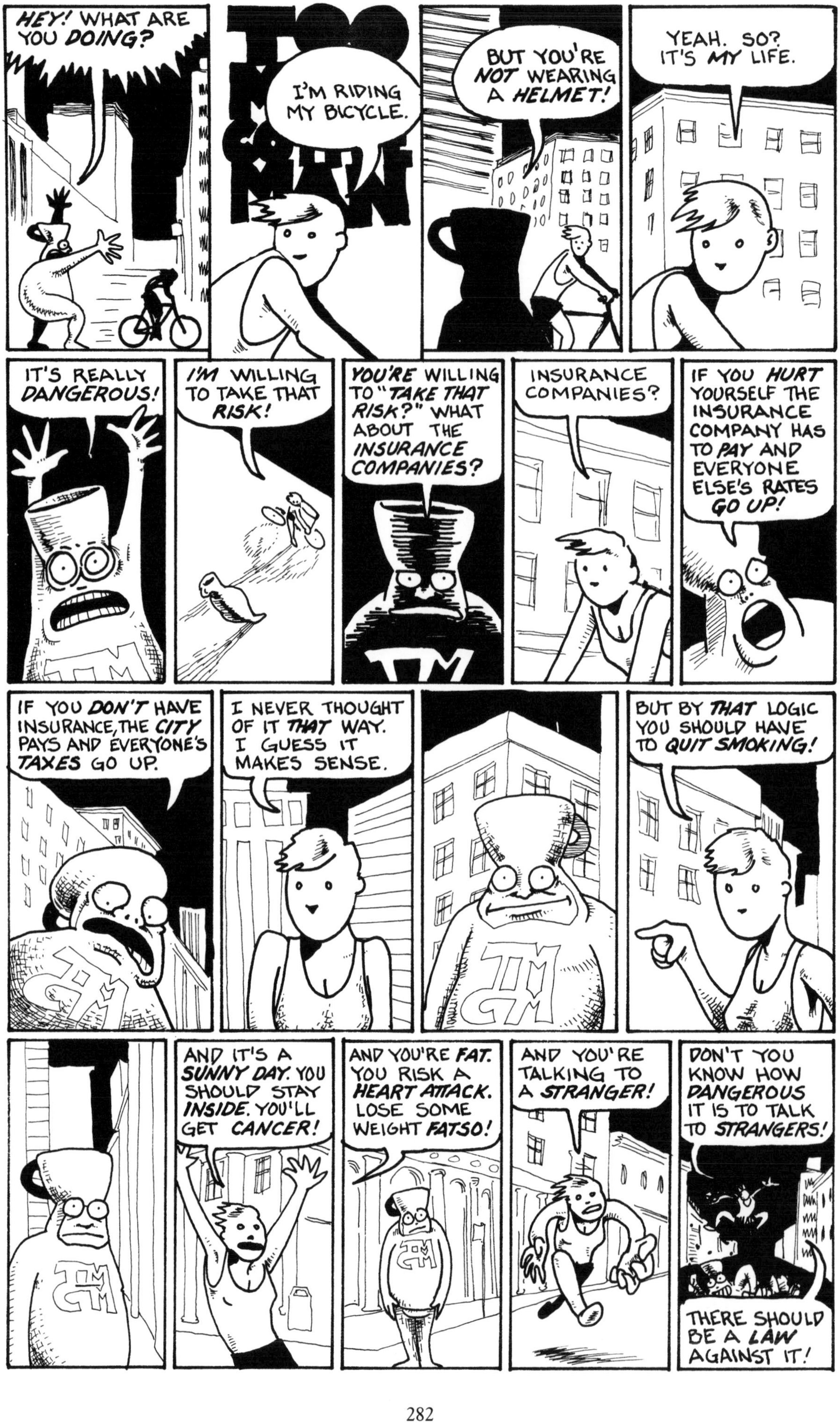
HEY! WHAT ARE YOU DOING?
TOO MUCH COFFEE MAN
I'M RIDING MY BICYCLE.
BUT YOU'RE NOT WEARING A HELMET!
YEAH. SO? IT'S MY LIFE.
IT'S REALLY DANGEROUS!
I'M WILLING TO TAKE THAT RISK!
YOU'RE WILLING TO "TAKE THAT RISK?" WHAT ABOUT THE INSURANCE COMPANIES?
INSURANCE COMPANIES?
IF YOU HURT YOURSELF THE INSURANCE COMPANY HAS TO PAY AND EVERYONE ELSE'S RATES GO UP!
IF YOU DON'T HAVE INSURANCE, THE CITY PAYS AND EVERYONE'S TAXES GO UP.
I NEVER THOUGHT OF IT THAT WAY. I GUESS IT MAKES SENSE.
BUT BY THAT LOGIC YOU SHOULD HAVE TO QUIT SMOKING!
AND IT'S A SUNNY DAY. YOU SHOULD STAY INSIDE. YOU'LL GET CANCER!
AND YOU'RE FAT. YOU RISK A HEART ATTACK. LOSE SOME WEIGHT FATSO!
AND YOU'RE TALKING TO A STRANGER!
DON'T YOU KNOW HOW DANGEROUS IT IS TO TALK TO STRANGERS!
THERE SHOULD BE A LAW AGAINST IT!

TOO MUCH COFFEE MAN™

BY SHANNON WHEELER

KNOCK KNOCK KNOCK

ARE YOU IN THE MARKET FOR SOME *REAL ESTATE*?

NO. I CAN'T AFFORD IT.

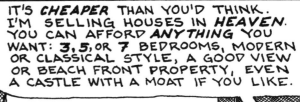

IT'S *CHEAPER* THAN YOU'D THINK. I'M SELLING HOUSES IN *HEAVEN*. YOU CAN AFFORD *ANYTHING* YOU WANT: *3*, *5*, OR *7* BEDROOMS, MODERN OR CLASSICAL STYLE, A GOOD VIEW OR BEACH FRONT PROPERTY, EVEN A CASTLE WITH A MOAT IF YOU LIKE.

AND IT'S *PERFECT* BECAUSE IT'S IN *HEAVEN*!

YOU *CAN'T* TAKE IT WITH YOU. BUT WOULDN'T IT BE NICE TO HAVE SOMETHING FOR YOU *WHEN* YOU GET THERE?

I WANT A *MANSION*!

WOW! I CAN'T WAIT TO *DIE*!

GUIDE FOR THE PERPLEXED AFTERWORD

by Shannon Wheeler

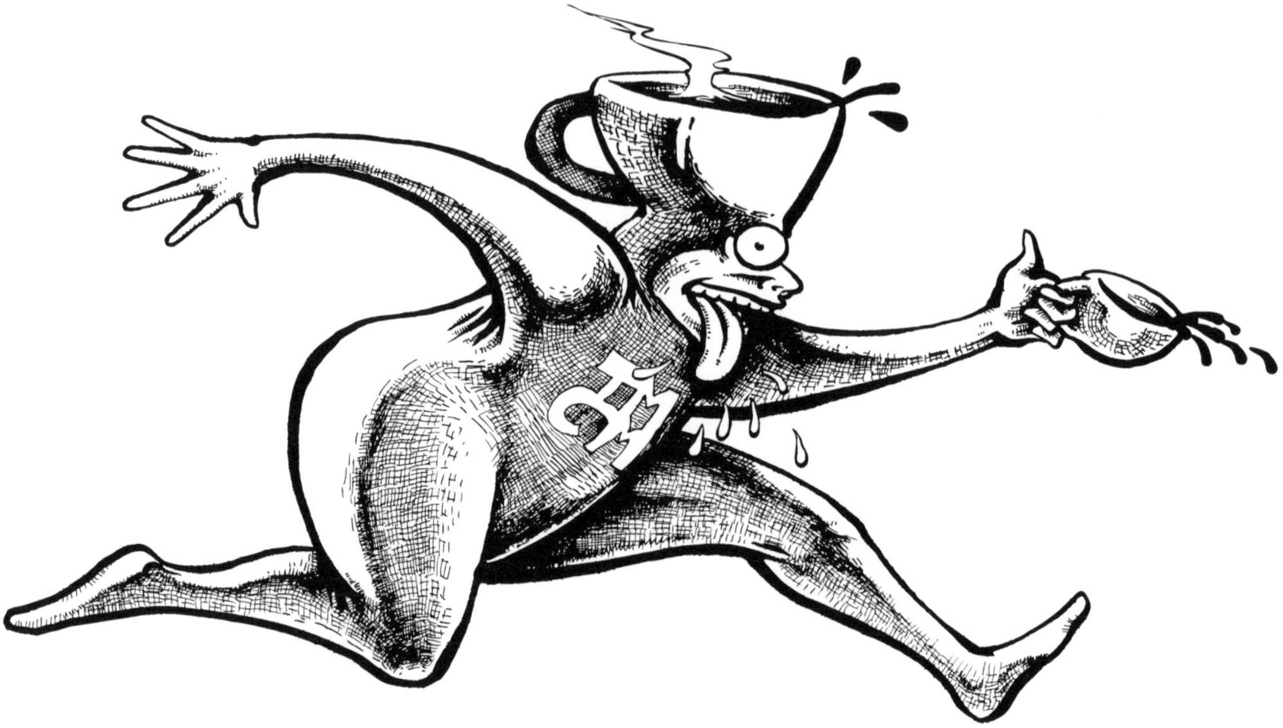

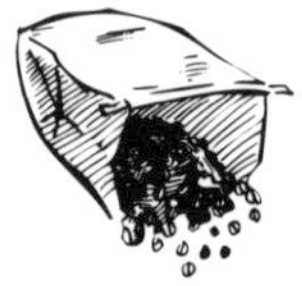

Too Much Coffee Man started as a joke. I was trying to think up an iconographic character that would allow me some recognition with an audience. It was a bad visual pun. The handle on the mug on his head is the metaphorical handle for people to "grab" on to for quick and easy recognition.

My biggest burden now with *Too Much Coffee Man* is having people tell me they love my comic because they love coffee. I wish they'd tell me that they love my comic because it's clever or well drawn, or insightful. At least they're enjoying it, even if it is for reasons that I don't feel flatter me. That type of complaint falls in the category of "things you can't complain about." And, at least, I was able to do a cartoon about that.

In all fairness to myself, I put a lot of work into creating each and every cartoon. I agonize, sometimes all night, over every single page. I worry that it's too complicated and my thoughts are not communicated. Other times I think I've sacrificed too much for brevity's sake and the cartoon has lost its meaning.

I love drawing cartoons. It's all real. All the emotions come from my heart. I do my best to share my honest feelings, insecurities, anxieties, and observations about life. And I really can catch flies.

AMUSING MUSINGS

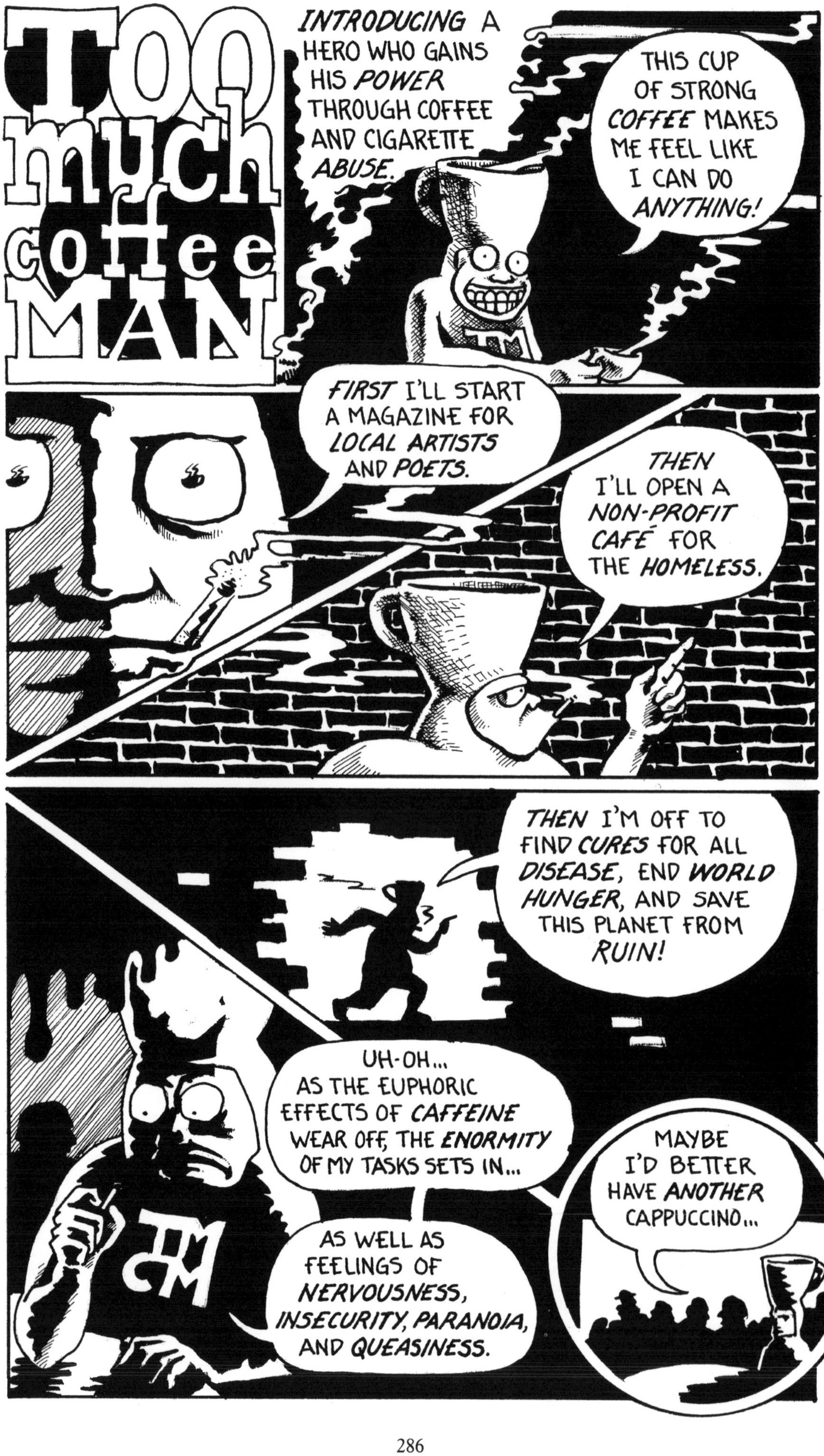
TOO much coffee MAN
INTRODUCING A HERO WHO GAINS HIS POWER THROUGH COFFEE AND CIGARETTE ABUSE.
THIS CUP OF STRONG COFFEE MAKES ME FEEL LIKE I CAN DO ANYTHING!
TM
FIRST I'LL START A MAGAZINE FOR LOCAL ARTISTS AND POETS.
THEN I'LL OPEN A NON-PROFIT CAFÉ FOR THE HOMELESS.
THEN I'M OFF TO FIND CURES FOR ALL DISEASE, END WORLD HUNGER, AND SAVE THIS PLANET FROM RUIN!
UH-OH... AS THE EUPHORIC EFFECTS OF CAFFEINE WEAR OFF, THE ENORMITY OF MY TASKS SETS IN...
AS WELL AS FEELINGS OF NERVOUSNESS, INSECURITY, PARANOIA, AND QUEASINESS.
TM CM
MAYBE I'D BETTER HAVE ANOTHER CAPPUCCINO...

AMUSING MUSINGS INTRODUCTION

by Tom Tomorrow

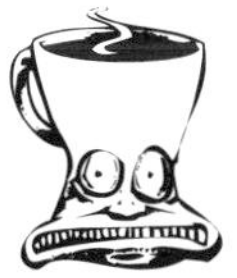

Shannon Wheeler and I went to a strip club in New Orleans last summer, along with a bunch of other cartoonists and an editor or two, all of us refugees from the Association of Alternative Newsweeklies conference. We drank to excess as we bantered with strippers trying to hustle us for lap dances, and if I were to embroider this anecdote slightly, perhaps stretch the truth just a little, to tell of the craziness which followed as we wandered through the bleary neon night of Bourbon Street, drinks in hand and strippers in tow, staggering from one mad jazz club to the next, spinning out crazy stories which would soon become the stuff of legend—if I were to do this, I could certainly make us all sound like devil-may-care raconteurs living life to its fullest, crazed artists to whom normal rules of conduct cannot and should not be applied, because creativity cannot be constrained, genius makes its own rules, blah blah blah.

In reality, most of us cowered uncomfortably, clustered in a dimly lit corner, sipping on our beers and declining the opportunity to pay topless women to wiggle around in our laps (though there were exceptions, and as long as the payoffs continue, I will not name names). Because the truth is, almost all the cartoonists I know are very mild people, for whom living life to the fullest entails time spent with their wives and kids, taking the dog for a walk, things like that. We're really just not very interesting, for the most part.

I've only hung out with Shannon a few times at conventions over the years, and while I can't state definitively that he doesn't have some insane secret life involving mistresses and illegitimate children and perhaps a room in the basement which is always kept padlocked, he seems like a pretty typical cartoonist, which is to say, "boring." But I mean that in a good way. There are exceptions to this, of course, but mostly cartoonists are too busy living in their head to worry too much about wacky affectations—an entire wardrobe of Edwardian clothing, say, or a hairstyle which requires far too much attention. It's not that you'd mistake us for salarymen—our wardrobes are too shabby, and there's often a stray piercing or a soul patch or some other small indication that we do not have office jobs—but mostly, and this is the point, our inner demons are purged on the drawing board and the computer. Mostly we are not compelled to wear our hearts on our sleeves, to declare to the world that we are, goddammit, individuals.

It wasn't always this way. I know a cartoonist from an earlier generation, whose working routine used to include a dalliance with a different prostitute every day at lunchtime. I don't know Shannon well, but I think it is safe to conclude that his working habits are rather more mundane than that. He does not burn brightly like a Roman candle in the night, there is no inevitable rendezvous with a looming tree at the end of some dark whiskey-soaked evening of debauchery, neatly bookending the legend of his tortured genius and inspiring a critically acclaimed film in ten or fifteen years with a handsome young actor in the lead role as the doomed cartoonist for whom life itself was simply too much to bear. As far as I know, he's just a guy who lives out on the West Coast with his family and draws these really strange comics.

Ah, but those comics—this is where we get to the heart of the matter. If you are not familiar with the oeuvre of the man who drinks too much coffee, the alternately angry and perplexed and poignant world of the excessively caffeinated one, then you have a treat in store. There is a temptation to use the metaphors of coffee consumption here, to give Shannon that easily extracted blurb which he can plaster on his promotional materials—*Too Much Coffee Man* is a triple shot of espresso for the funny bone! *TMCM* is a caffeine-fueled journey through the dark heart of the sleepless American night!—but I will resist, because *TMCM* is not ultimately about coffee. Yes, that's right—you, the reader, the purchaser of this book, the lover of all things coffee-related, have been bamboozled. The coffee is just the pretty lure, the bright attractive colored plastic hiding the sharp steel hook which is, as we speak, protruding from your cheek.

Sure, the central character wears a large coffee cup on his head at all times—sometimes it seems to be a part of his anatomy, but in at least one of these cartoons, it's just a costume he can remove when he decides to take an office job. So who is this TMCM, exactly? Is he from another planet? Is he a superhero? Is he driven by the death of his gentle uncle, a death he could have prevented if only he hadn't been wasting his time sitting around in the coffee shop all afternoon? Has he been taught a painful lesson, that with great amounts of coffee come great responsibilities? And if he is a superhero, doesn't that mean we are all superheroes, any of us who spend our time drinking too much coffee and thinking about the world? Is TMCM a metaphor for the cartoonist himself?

These are but a few of the questions to which you will find no easy answers in the pages ahead. But do not be frightened! TMCM can be enjoyed on many levels. He is, in one sense, consumer culture anthropomorphized, a satire on consumerism masquerading as a consumer icon. You need never to have read the work to enjoy drinking a fine hot cup of java from a cup featuring the screen-printed image of a man with a coffee cup for a head. Too much coffee, man! What more do you need to know? Everyone at the office is sure to enjoy a hearty chuckle. And let's not forget the TMCM T-shirts and sponges and god knows what else, because Shannon is an unparalleled master at coming up with weird shit to sell you, useless crap which parodies the very impulse to buy useless crap, even as it enriches his coffers. (Personally, I can't wait for the limited edition TMCM action figures. That sounds like a joke, but I am completely serious. What could be cooler? If Jesse Ventura can have an action figure, if the Flaming Carrot can have an action figure—and they both do—I don't see why TMCM can't have an action figure. But I digress.)

On another level, TMCM is a roving philosopher, an ambassador from the inner depths of Shannon's mind. You want good-natured, laff-filled comics about the foibles that make us all human, there's always *Garfield*. But TMCM will give you meditations on the economy as a placebo, on the simultaneous necessity and futility of voting, on the

paradoxical relationship of expectation and experience. *TMCM* is like an onion, except that it probably won't make you cry, and if you keep peeling back layers, you find more rather than less—so scratch that, it's really nothing like an onion at all. Maybe it's more like an artichoke, at the heart of which lies a tasty reward for the work of navigating its thorny layers, even though those layers are themselves quite delicious, particularly with a buttery sauce.

TMCM is also, and this is where we get to my own level of expertise, a political cartoon. It may not be what you're used to thinking of as a political cartoon, in the sense that there are no donkeys and no elephants and no drawings of the Statue of Liberty shedding a tear of grief as the Twin Towers burn in the distance, or even any talking penguins, but the politics contained therein are quite astute, even if they don't always grab you by the lapel and spew saliva in your face as they rant about the shortcomings of the two-party system. "The Coffee Lawsuit" is a case in point—a look at the facts behind the famous story of the idiotic old woman who sued McDonald's because her coffee was too hot, for chrissakes—the story that shows everything that's wrong with our lawsuit-happy society. Except that there's more to the story—there's always more to the story—and Shannon lays out the difference between what really happened and the urban legend that sprang from it, the gulf between fact and oversimplification, and lets the smug commentators and editorialists of the chattering classes stand revealed as the morons they are by simply quoting them verbatim.

I write these words at a dark moment in history. There is a long night looming, and daybreak is but a distant hope. The gulf between fact and oversimplification has suddenly become very, very important, and our preference for one over the other will define the world we will live in for a very long time to come. Enjoy these cartoons and take their wisdom and their thoughtfulness to heart, because we may soon need all the wisdom and thoughtfulness we can muster.

And try not to drink quite so much coffee—it's bad for your health.

chapter 1

REFLECTING ON EXCESS

Censorship through inclusion, and other notions

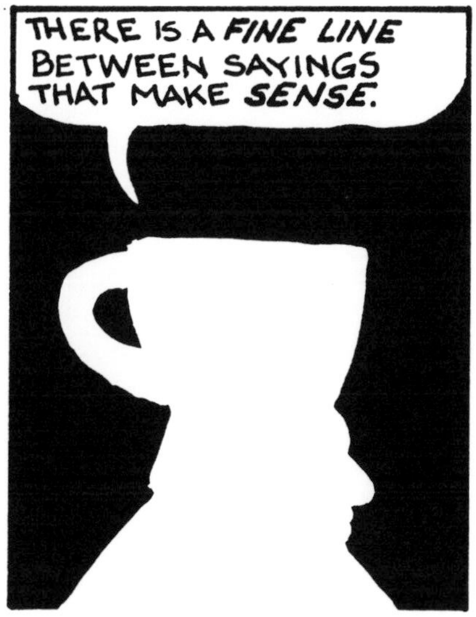
THERE IS A *FINE LINE* BETWEEN SAYINGS THAT MAKE *SENSE*.

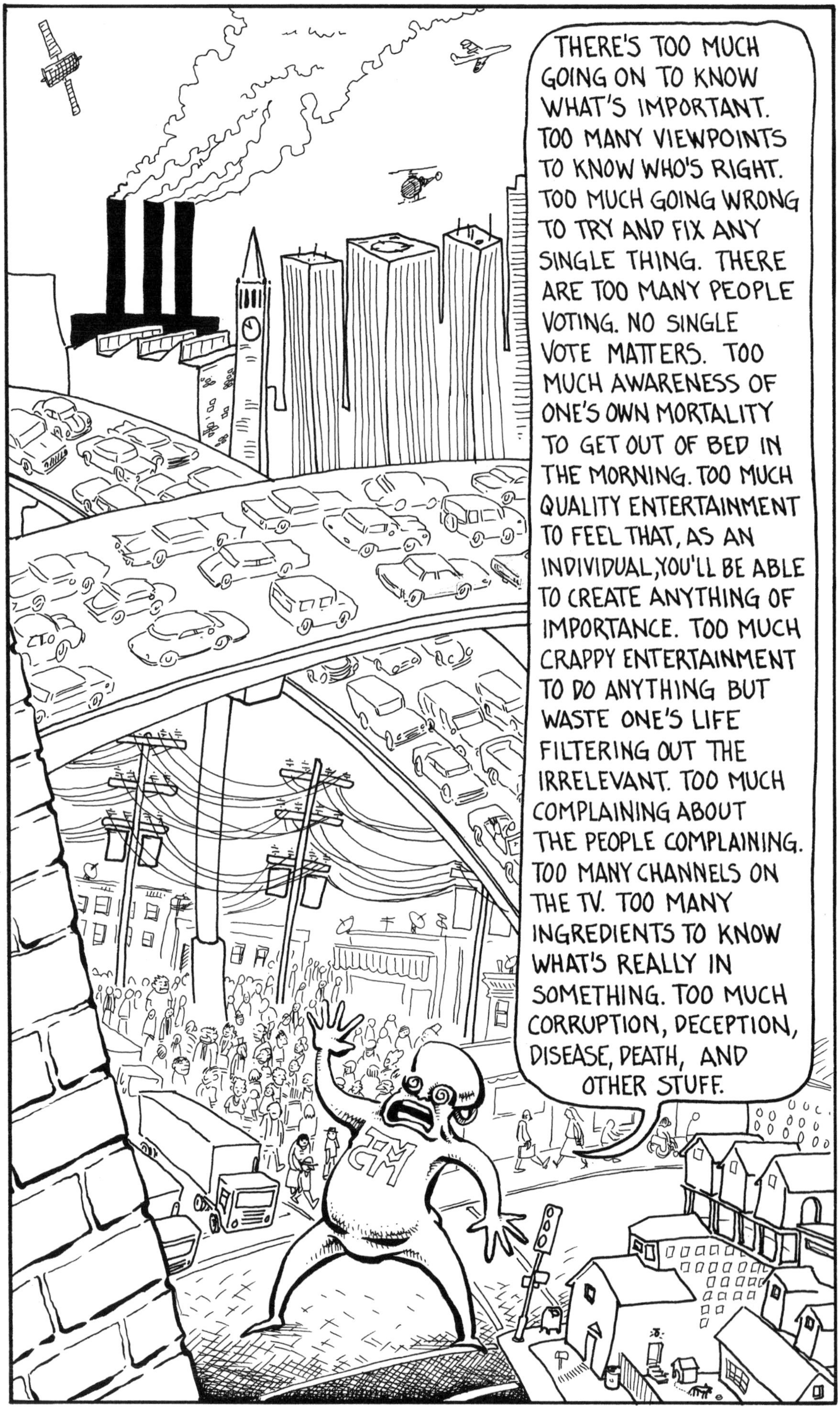
THERE'S TOO MUCH GOING ON TO KNOW WHAT'S IMPORTANT. TOO MANY VIEWPOINTS TO KNOW WHO'S RIGHT. TOO MUCH GOING WRONG TO TRY AND FIX ANY SINGLE THING. THERE ARE TOO MANY PEOPLE VOTING. NO SINGLE VOTE MATTERS. TOO MUCH AWARENESS OF ONE'S OWN MORTALITY TO GET OUT OF BED IN THE MORNING. TOO MUCH QUALITY ENTERTAINMENT TO FEEL THAT, AS AN INDIVIDUAL, YOU'LL BE ABLE TO CREATE ANYTHING OF IMPORTANCE. TOO MUCH CRAPPY ENTERTAINMENT TO DO ANYTHING BUT WASTE ONE'S LIFE FILTERING OUT THE IRRELEVANT. TOO MUCH COMPLAINING ABOUT THE PEOPLE COMPLAINING. TOO MANY CHANNELS ON THE TV. TOO MANY INGREDIENTS TO KNOW WHAT'S REALLY IN SOMETHING. TOO MUCH CORRUPTION, DECEPTION, DISEASE, DEATH, AND OTHER STUFF.

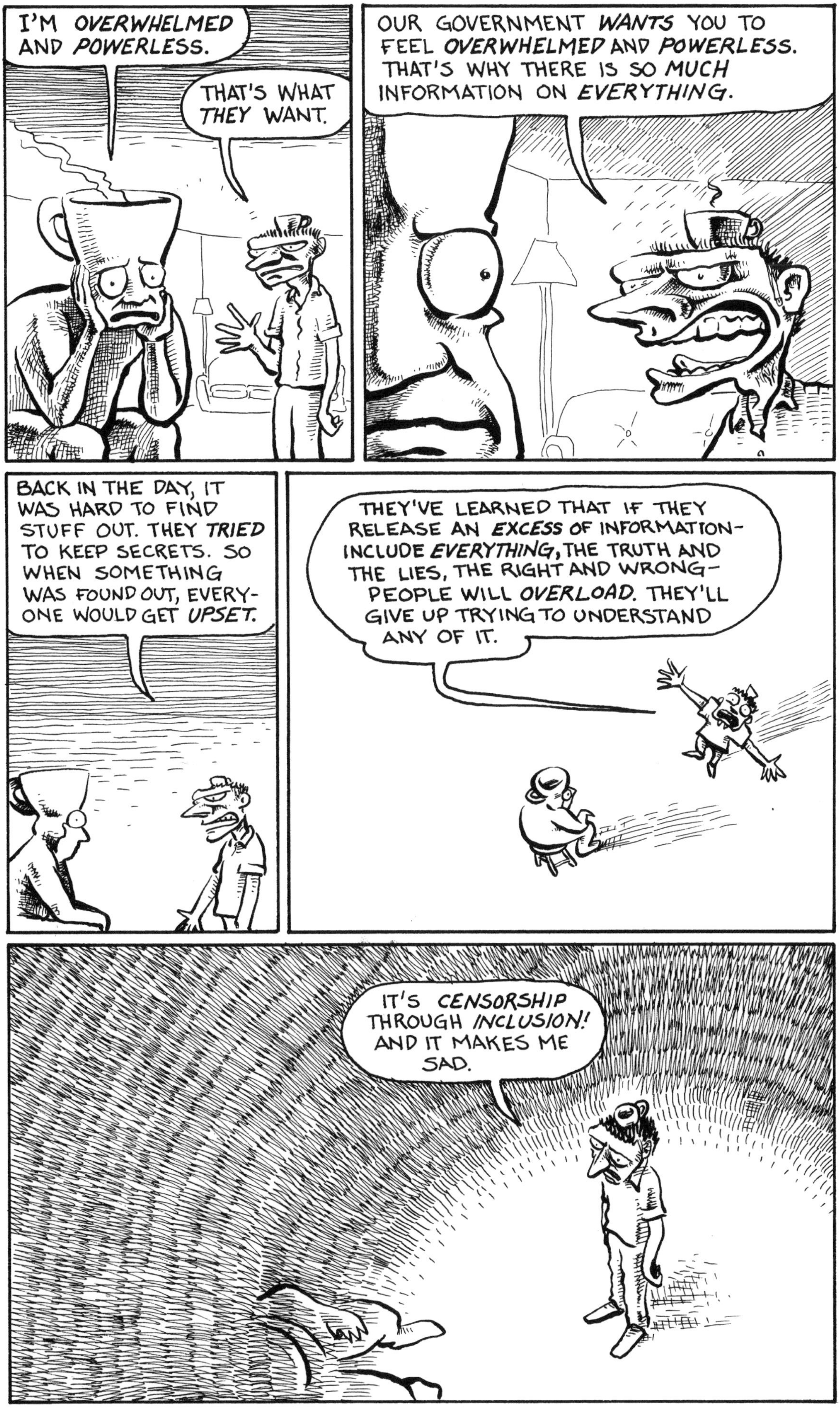
I'M OVERWHELMED AND POWERLESS.
THAT'S WHAT THEY WANT.
OUR GOVERNMENT WANTS YOU TO FEEL OVERWHELMED AND POWERLESS. THAT'S WHY THERE IS SO MUCH INFORMATION ON EVERYTHING.
BACK IN THE DAY, IT WAS HARD TO FIND STUFF OUT. THEY TRIED TO KEEP SECRETS. SO WHEN SOMETHING WAS FOUND OUT, EVERY-ONE WOULD GET UPSET.
THEY'VE LEARNED THAT IF THEY RELEASE AN EXCESS OF INFORMATION- INCLUDE EVERYTHING, THE TRUTH AND THE LIES, THE RIGHT AND WRONG- PEOPLE WILL OVERLOAD. THEY'LL GIVE UP TRYING TO UNDERSTAND ANY OF IT.
IT'S CENSORSHIP THROUGH INCLUSION! AND IT MAKES ME SAD.

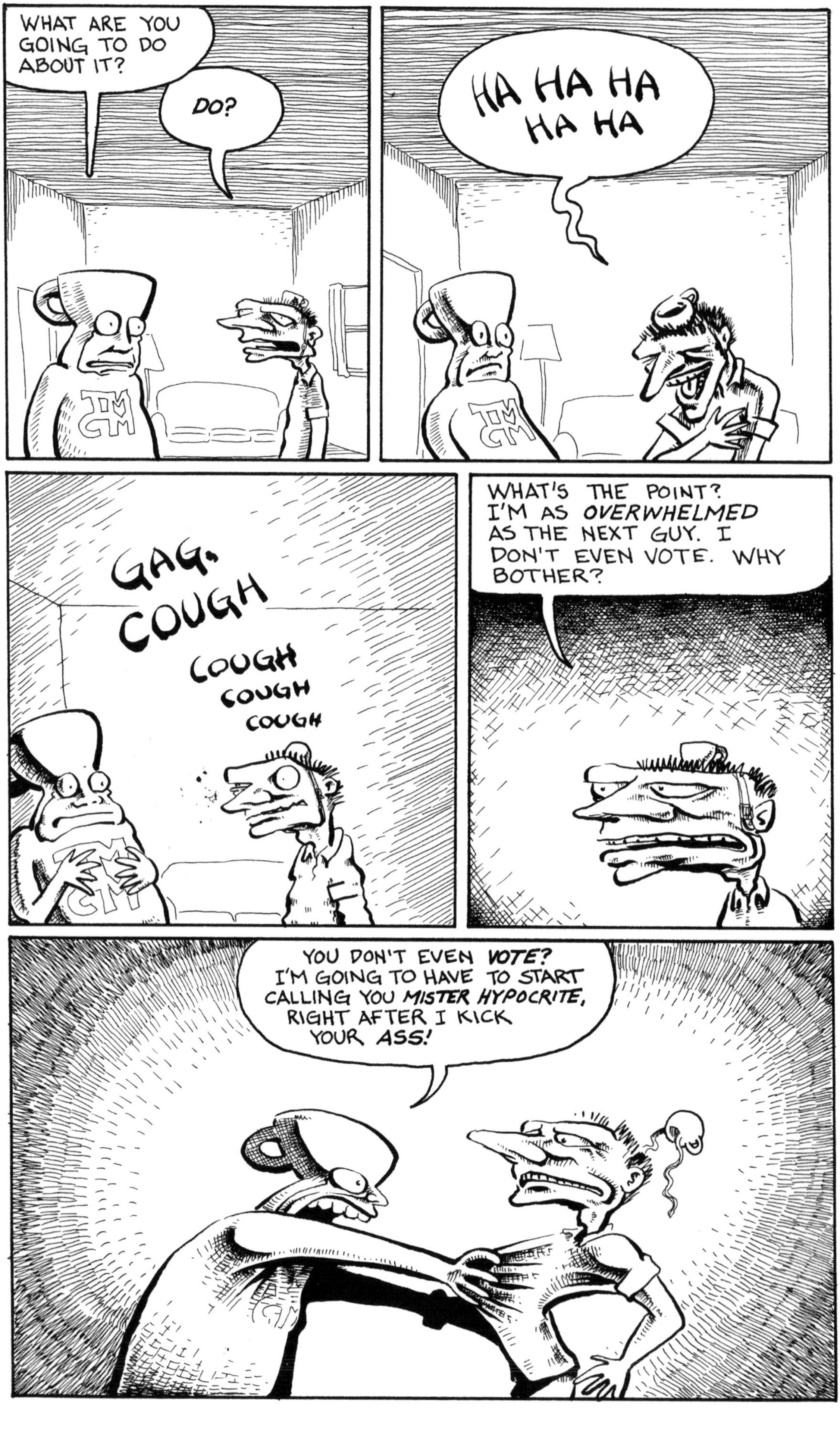

WHAT ARE YOU GOING TO DO ABOUT IT?
DO?
HA HA HA HA HA
GAG. COUGH
COUGH COUGH COUGH
WHAT'S THE POINT? I'M AS OVERWHELMED AS THE NEXT GUY. I DON'T EVEN VOTE. WHY BOTHER?
YOU DON'T EVEN VOTE? I'M GOING TO HAVE TO START CALLING YOU MISTER HYPOCRITE, RIGHT AFTER I KICK YOUR ASS!

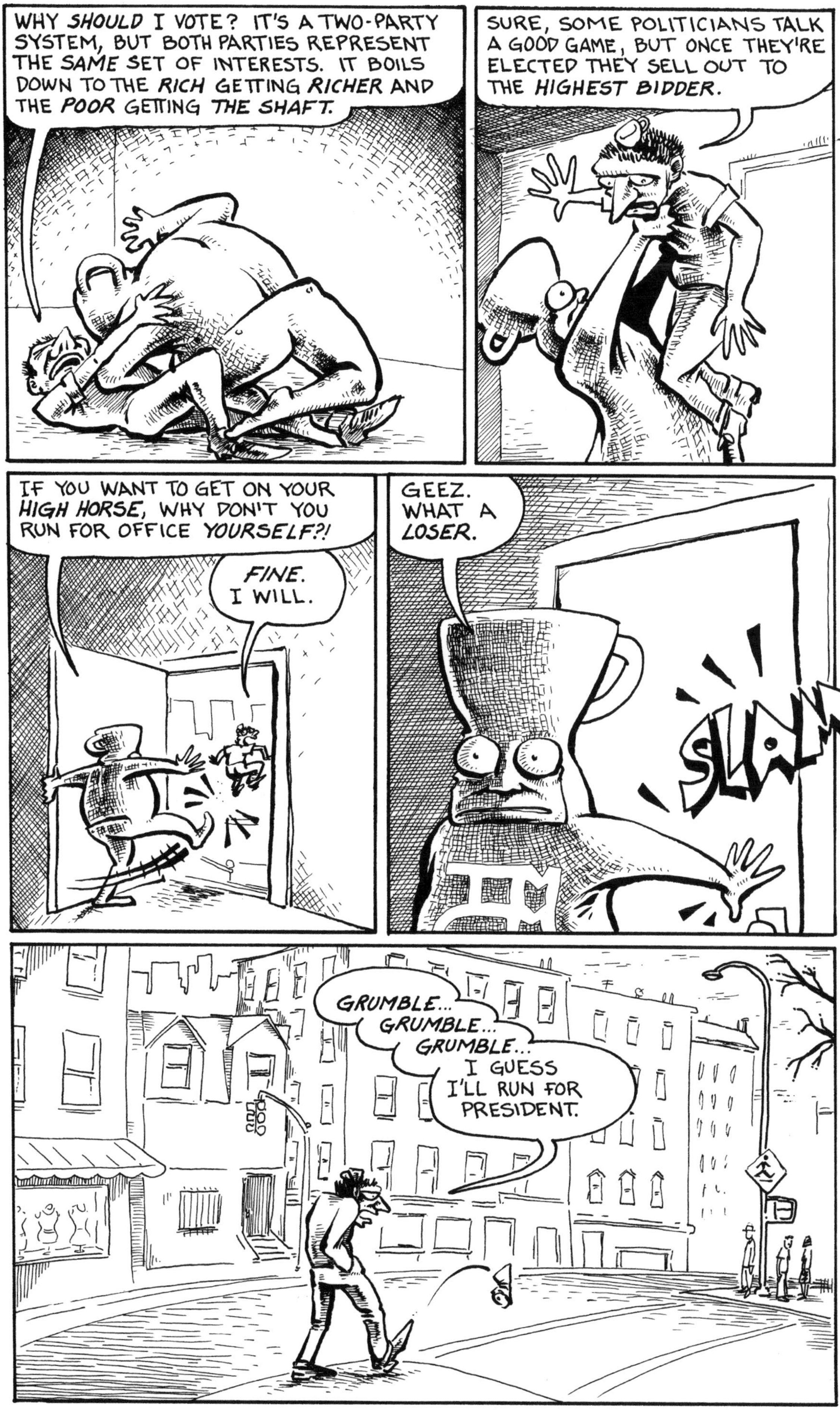
WHY SHOULD I VOTE? IT'S A TWO-PARTY SYSTEM, BUT BOTH PARTIES REPRESENT THE SAME SET OF INTERESTS. IT BOILS DOWN TO THE RICH GETTING RICHER AND THE POOR GETTING THE SHAFT.
SURE, SOME POLITICIANS TALK A GOOD GAME, BUT ONCE THEY'RE ELECTED THEY SELL OUT TO THE HIGHEST BIDDER.
IF YOU WANT TO GET ON YOUR HIGH HORSE, WHY DON'T YOU RUN FOR OFFICE YOURSELF?!
FINE. I WILL.
GEEZ. WHAT A LOSER.
SLAM
GRUMBLE... GRUMBLE... GRUMBLE... I GUESS I'LL RUN FOR PRESIDENT.

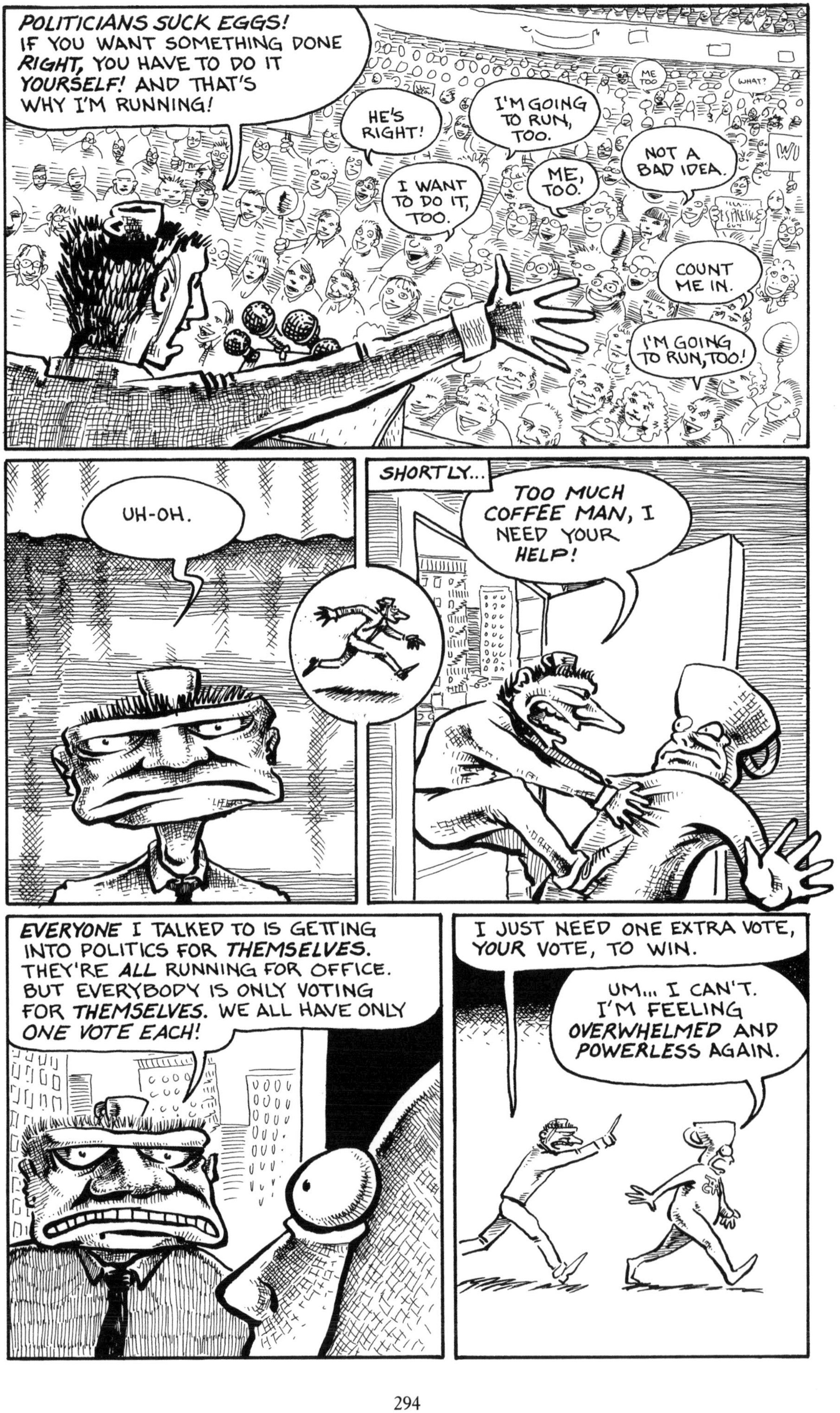
POLITICIANS SUCK EGGS! IF YOU WANT SOMETHING DONE RIGHT, YOU HAVE TO DO IT YOURSELF! AND THAT'S WHY I'M RUNNING!
HE'S RIGHT!
I'M GOING TO RUN, TOO.
ME TOO
WHAT?
NOT A BAD IDEA.
I WANT TO DO IT, TOO.
ME, TOO.
COUNT ME IN.
I'M GOING TO RUN, TOO!
UH-OH.
SHORTLY...
TOO MUCH COFFEE MAN, I NEED YOUR HELP!
EVERYONE I TALKED TO IS GETTING INTO POLITICS FOR THEMSELVES. THEY'RE ALL RUNNING FOR OFFICE. BUT EVERYBODY IS ONLY VOTING FOR THEMSELVES. WE ALL HAVE ONLY ONE VOTE EACH!
I JUST NEED ONE EXTRA VOTE, YOUR VOTE, TO WIN.
UM... I CAN'T. I'M FEELING OVERWHELMED AND POWERLESS AGAIN.

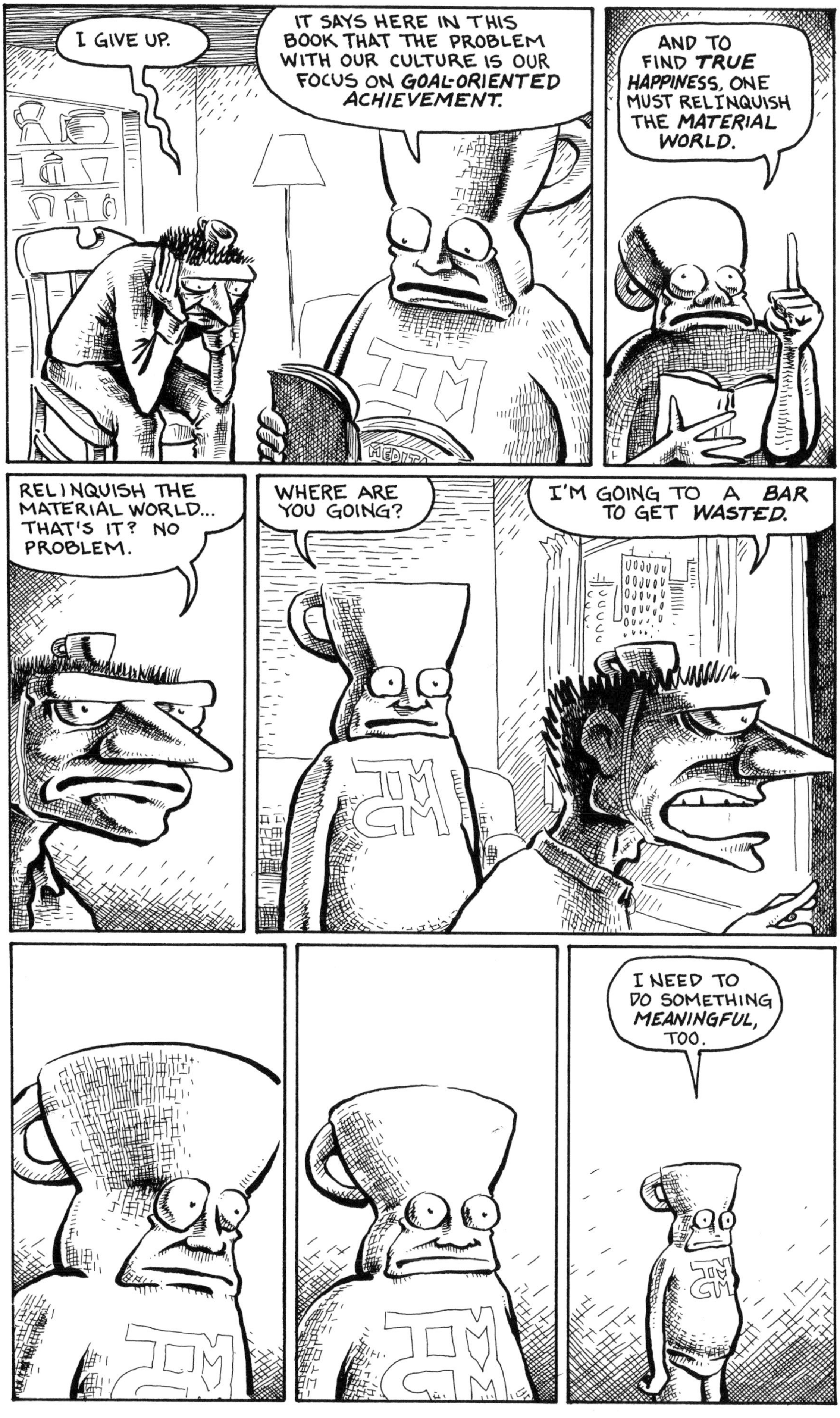
I GIVE UP.
IT SAYS HERE IN THIS BOOK THAT THE PROBLEM WITH OUR CULTURE IS OUR FOCUS ON GOAL-ORIENTED ACHIEVEMENT.
AND TO FIND TRUE HAPPINESS, ONE MUST RELINQUISH THE MATERIAL WORLD.
RELINQUISH THE MATERIAL WORLD... THAT'S IT? NO PROBLEM.
WHERE ARE YOU GOING?
I'M GOING TO A BAR TO GET WASTED.
I NEED TO DO SOMETHING MEANINGFUL, TOO.

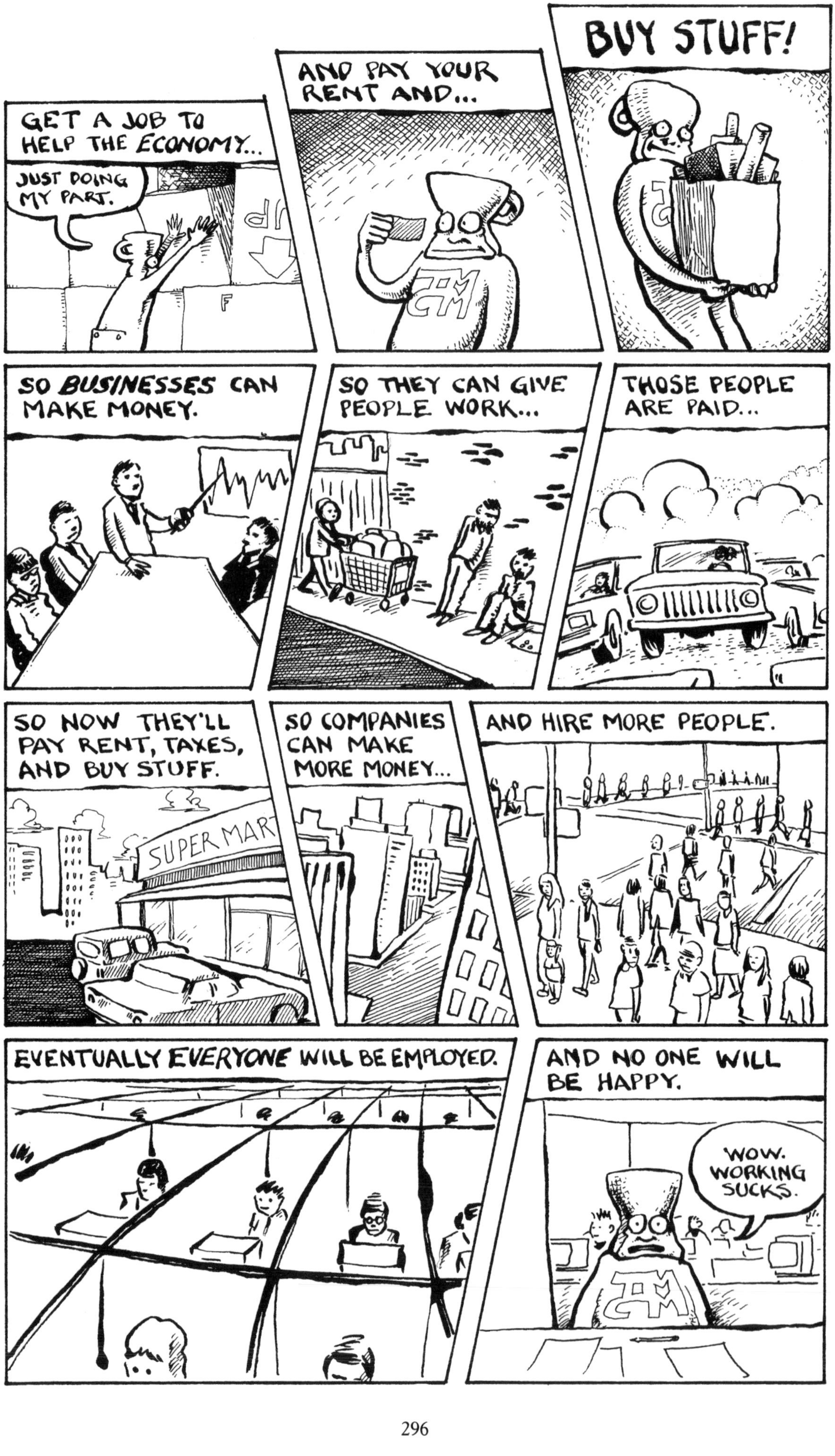
GET A JOB TO HELP THE ECONOMY...
JUST DOING MY PART.
AND PAY YOUR RENT AND...
BUY STUFF!
SO BUSINESSES CAN MAKE MONEY.
SO THEY CAN GIVE PEOPLE WORK...
THOSE PEOPLE ARE PAID...
SO NOW THEY'LL PAY RENT, TAXES, AND BUY STUFF.
SUPER MART
SO COMPANIES CAN MAKE MORE MONEY...
AND HIRE MORE PEOPLE.
EVENTUALLY EVERYONE WILL BE EMPLOYED.
AND NO ONE WILL BE HAPPY.
WOW. WORKING SUCKS.

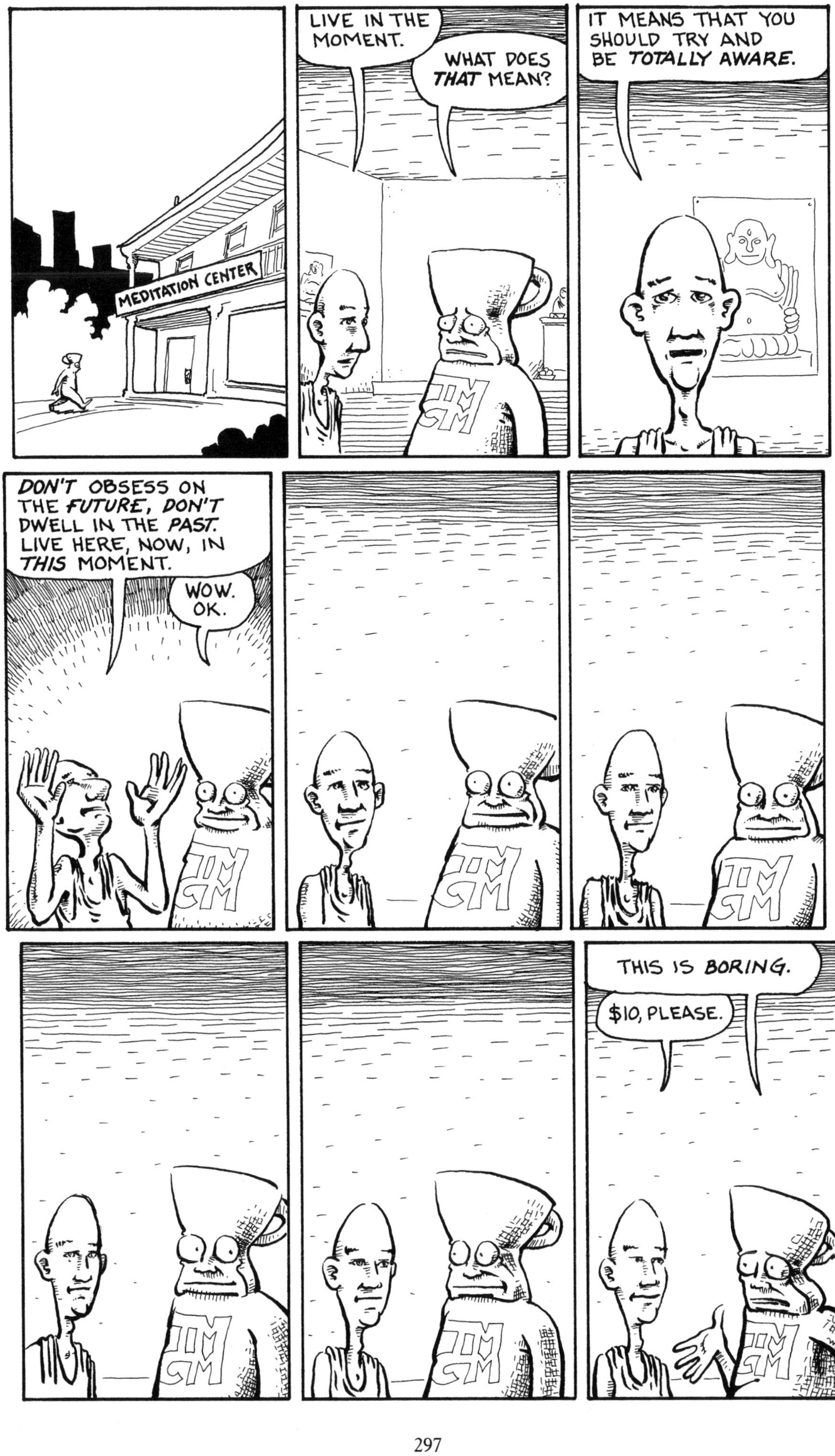
MEDITATION CENTER
LIVE IN THE MOMENT.
WHAT DOES THAT MEAN?
IT MEANS THAT YOU SHOULD TRY AND BE TOTALLY AWARE.
DON'T OBSESS ON THE FUTURE, DON'T DWELL IN THE PAST. LIVE HERE, NOW, IN THIS MOMENT.
WOW. OK.
THIS IS BORING.
$10, PLEASE.

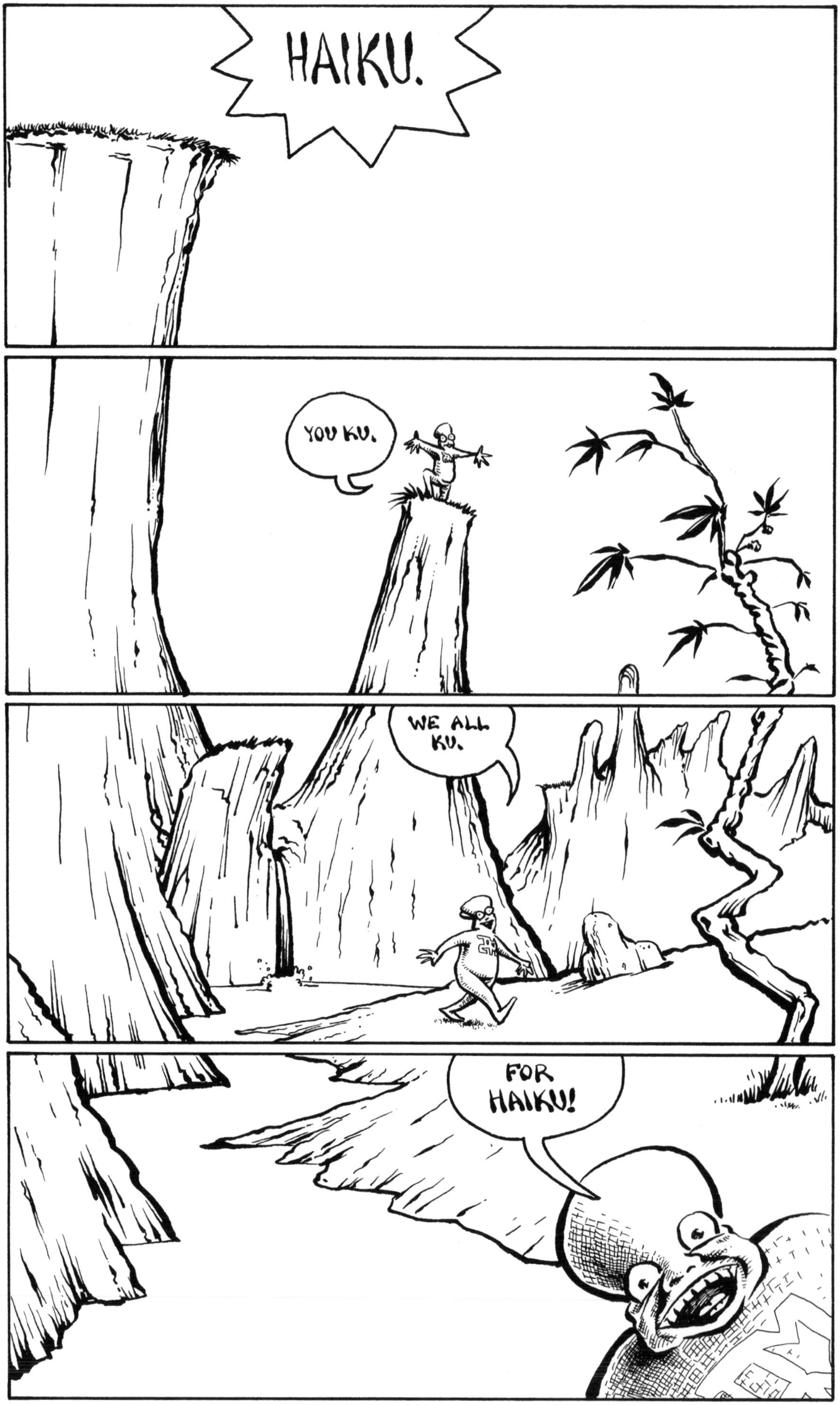
HAIKU.
YOU KU.
WE ALL KU.
FOR HAIKU!

MAYBE BY NOW *ESPRESSO GUY* HAS FOUND SOME *SECRET TO LIFE.*

ACK! WHAT HAPPENED TO YOU? YOU LOOK *TERRIBLE.*

DEBAUCHERY.

I WAS CURIOUS TO SEE JUST HOW *LOW* I COULD SINK.

I DID *EVERYTHING* AND *ANYTHING:* I STARTED A BAND, I POPPED PILLS, I SAW ALL THE HOLLYWOOD SUMMER MOVIES, I SLEPT AROUND, I STAYED UP LATE AND I SLEPT 'TILL NOON, I DATED A WAITRESS, AND I SHOPPED AT THE MALL.

YIKES.

THE WORST PART, WORSE THAN THE HANGOVERS, WORSE THAN THE SOCIAL REPERCUSSIONS...

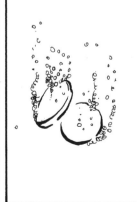

WAS THAT NO MATTER HOW LOW I SANK, THERE WAS ALWAYS SOMEONE BENEATH ME.

IT'S TOTALLY DEPRESSING, BUT I REALIZED THAT I'LL NEVER BE A SUCCESS AT FAILURE.

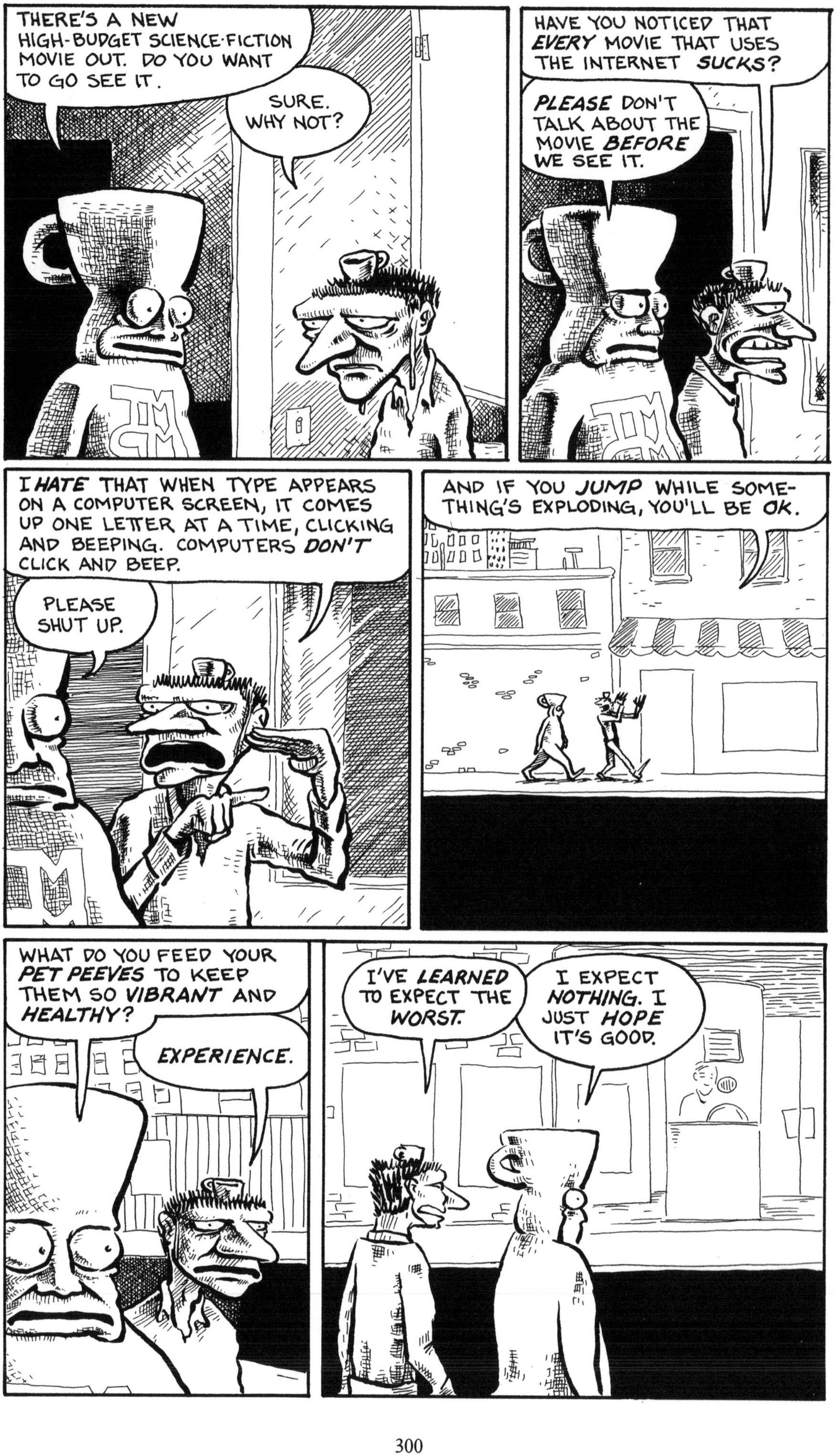
THERE'S A NEW HIGH-BUDGET SCIENCE-FICTION MOVIE OUT. DO YOU WANT TO GO SEE IT.
SURE. WHY NOT?
HAVE YOU NOTICED THAT EVERY MOVIE THAT USES THE INTERNET SUCKS?
PLEASE DON'T TALK ABOUT THE MOVIE BEFORE WE SEE IT.
I HATE THAT WHEN TYPE APPEARS ON A COMPUTER SCREEN, IT COMES UP ONE LETTER AT A TIME, CLICKING AND BEEPING. COMPUTERS DON'T CLICK AND BEEP.
PLEASE SHUT UP.
AND IF YOU JUMP WHILE SOMETHING'S EXPLODING, YOU'LL BE OK.
WHAT DO YOU FEED YOUR PET PEEVES TO KEEP THEM SO VIBRANT AND HEALTHY?
EXPERIENCE.
I'VE LEARNED TO EXPECT THE WORST.
I EXPECT NOTHING. I JUST HOPE IT'S GOOD.

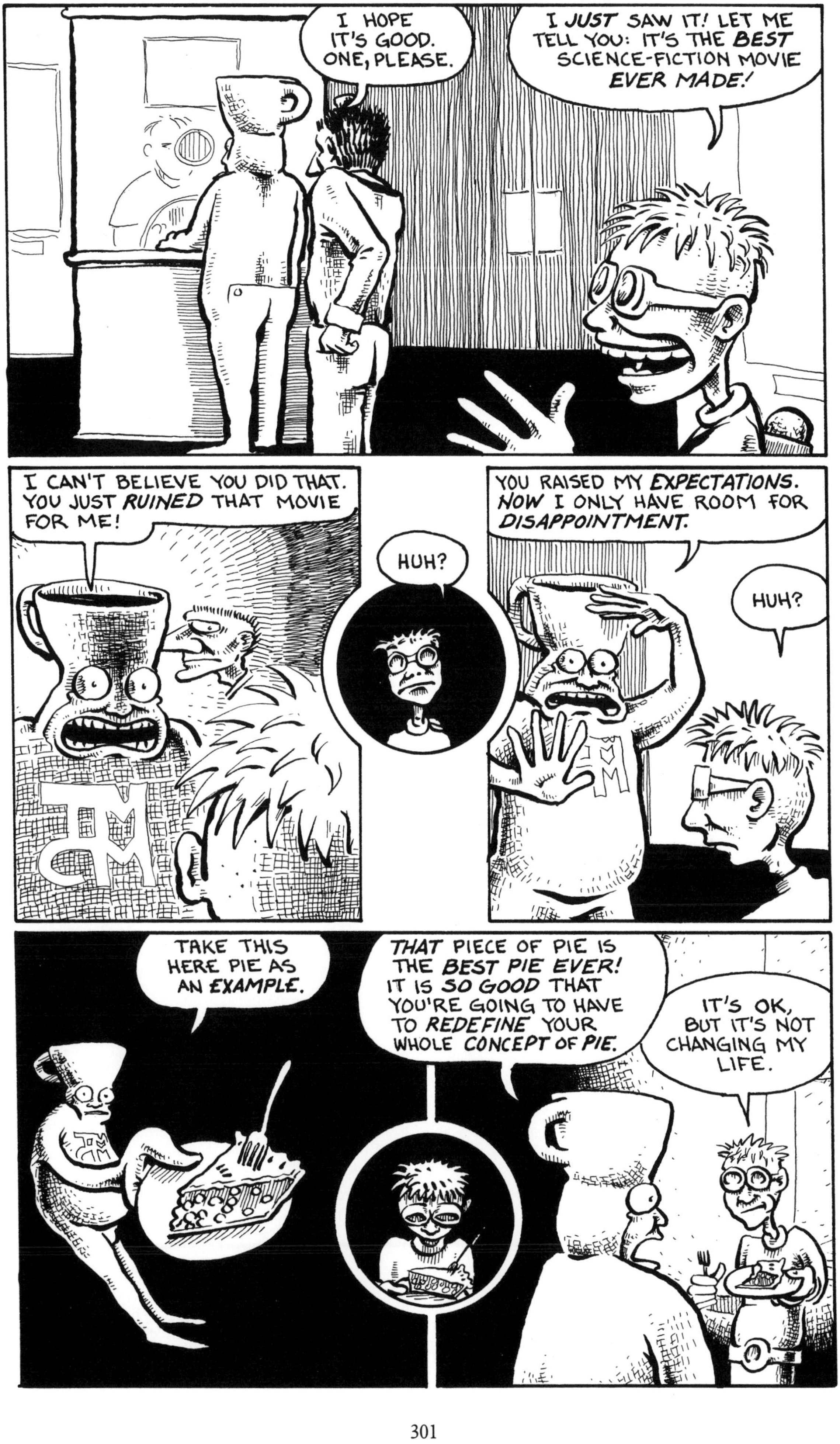

I HOPE IT'S GOOD. ONE, PLEASE.
I JUST SAW IT! LET ME TELL YOU: IT'S THE BEST SCIENCE-FICTION MOVIE EVER MADE!
I CAN'T BELIEVE YOU DID THAT. YOU JUST RUINED THAT MOVIE FOR ME!
HUH?
YOU RAISED MY EXPECTATIONS. NOW I ONLY HAVE ROOM FOR DISAPPOINTMENT.
HUH?
TAKE THIS HERE PIE AS AN EXAMPLE.
THAT PIECE OF PIE IS THE BEST PIE EVER! IT IS SO GOOD THAT YOU'RE GOING TO HAVE TO REDEFINE YOUR WHOLE CONCEPT OF PIE.
IT'S OK, BUT IT'S NOT CHANGING MY LIFE.

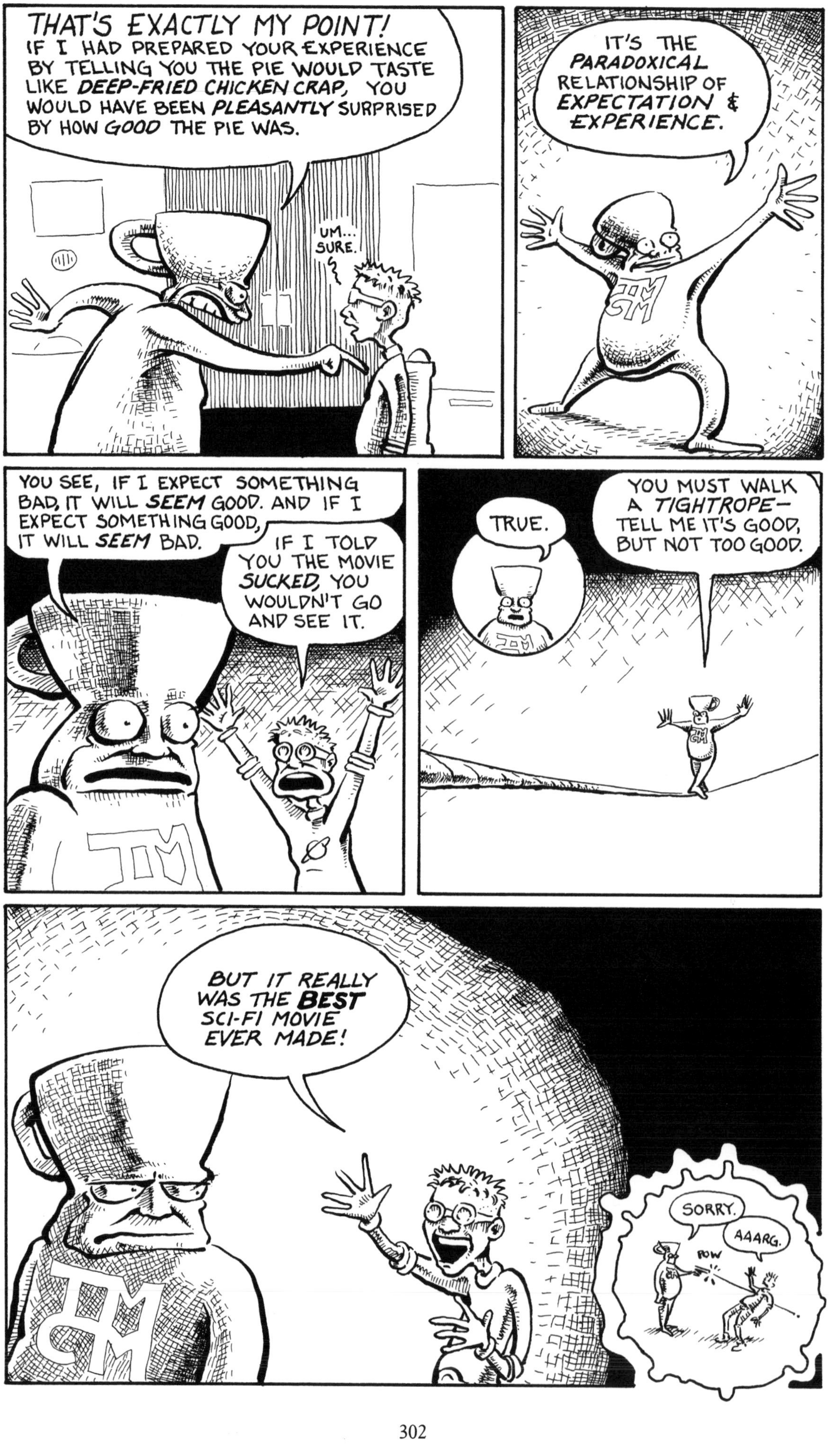
THAT'S EXACTLY MY POINT! IF I HAD PREPARED YOUR EXPERIENCE BY TELLING YOU THE PIE WOULD TASTE LIKE DEEP-FRIED CHICKEN CRAP, YOU WOULD HAVE BEEN PLEASANTLY SURPRISED BY HOW GOOD THE PIE WAS.
UM... SURE.
IT'S THE PARADOXICAL RELATIONSHIP OF EXPECTATION & EXPERIENCE.
YOU SEE, IF I EXPECT SOMETHING BAD, IT WILL SEEM GOOD. AND IF I EXPECT SOMETHING GOOD, IT WILL SEEM BAD.
IF I TOLD YOU THE MOVIE SUCKED, YOU WOULDN'T GO AND SEE IT.
TRUE.
YOU MUST WALK A TIGHTROPE— TELL ME IT'S GOOD, BUT NOT TOO GOOD.
BUT IT REALLY WAS THE BEST SCI-FI MOVIE EVER MADE!
SORRY.
AAARG.
POW

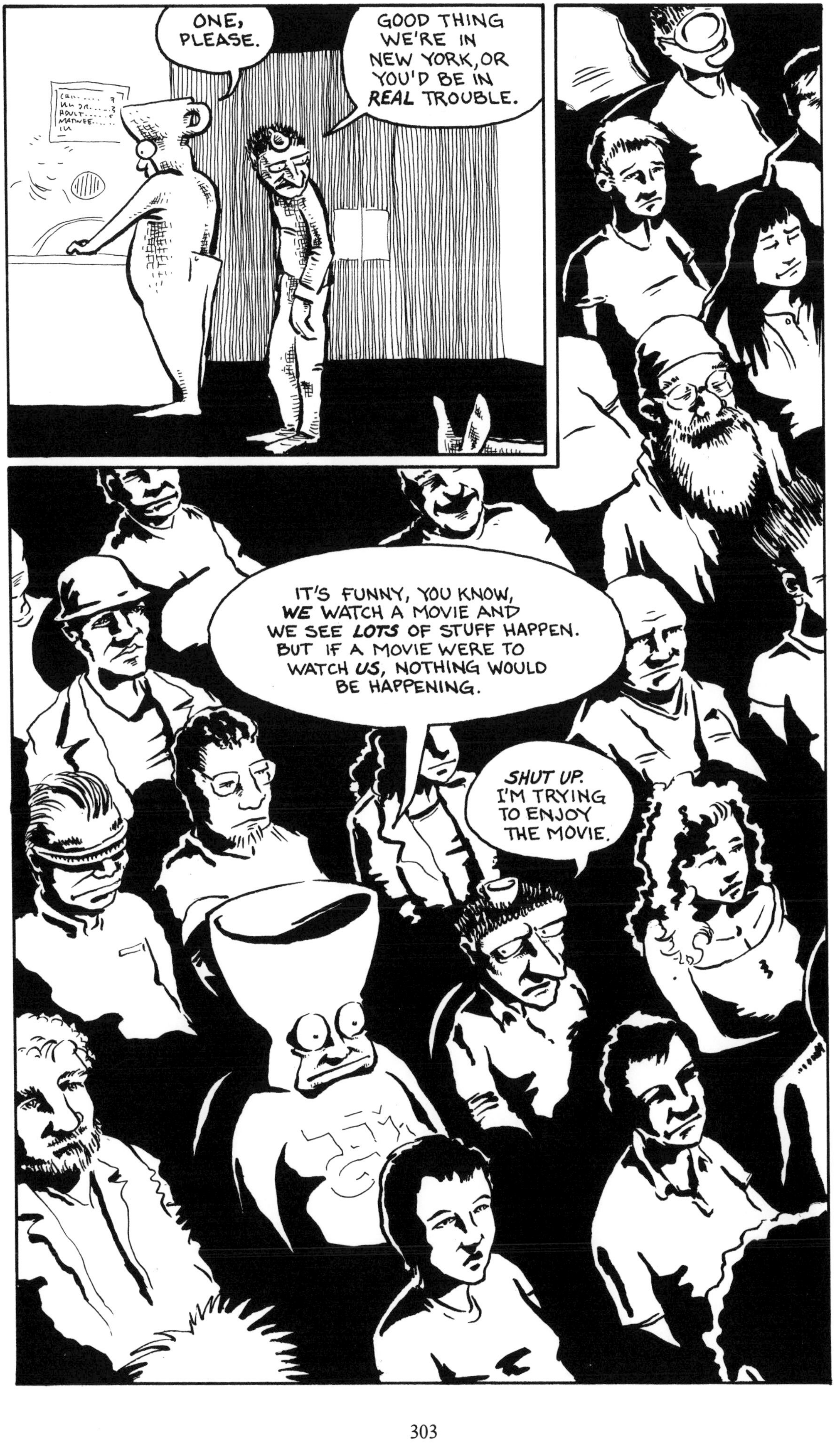
ONE, PLEASE.
GOOD THING WE'RE IN NEW YORK, OR YOU'D BE IN REAL TROUBLE.
IT'S FUNNY, YOU KNOW, WE WATCH A MOVIE AND WE SEE LOTS OF STUFF HAPPEN. BUT IF A MOVIE WERE TO WATCH US, NOTHING WOULD BE HAPPENING.
SHUT UP. I'M TRYING TO ENJOY THE MOVIE.

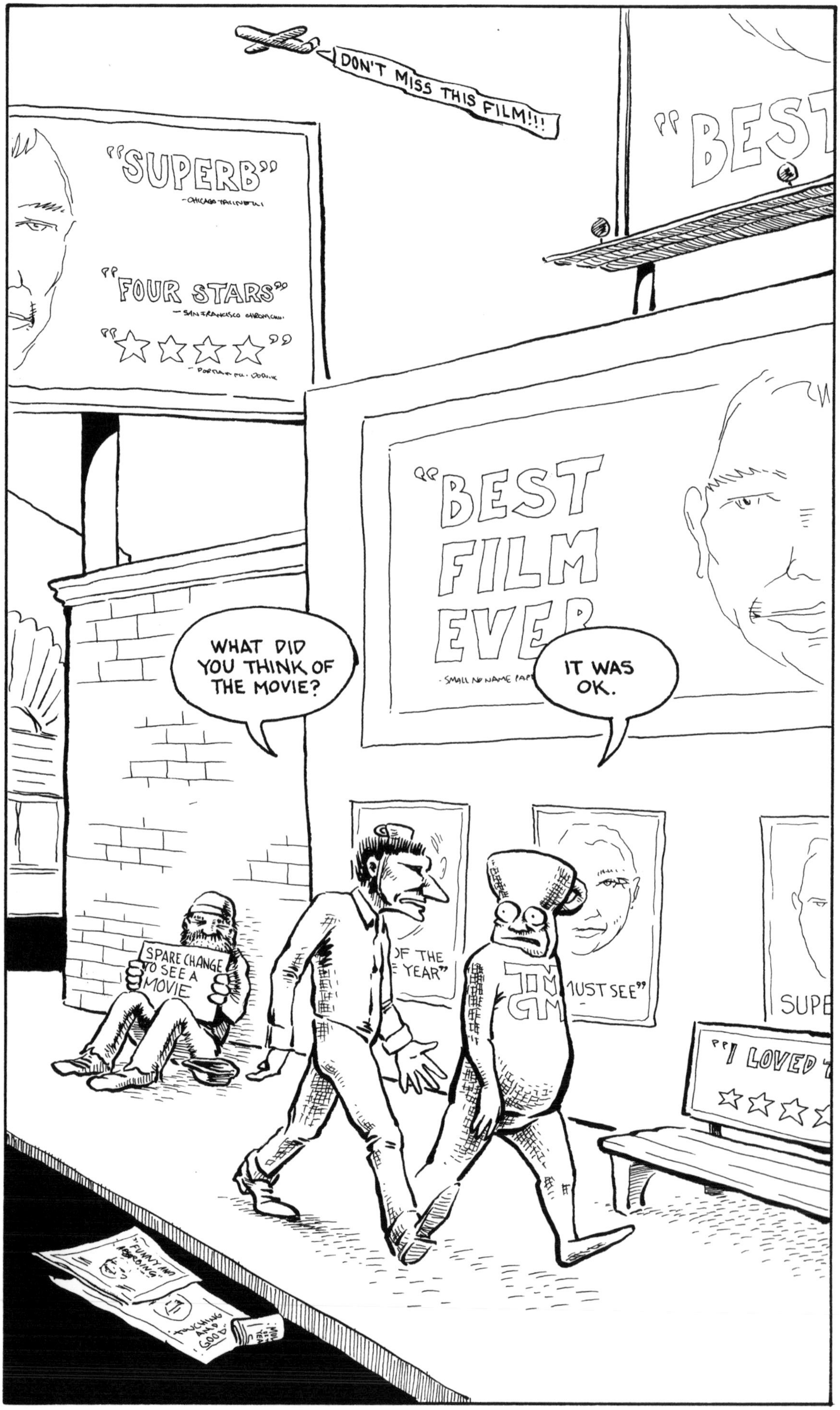
DON'T MISS THIS FILM!!!
"SUPERB"
"FOUR STARS"
"BEST FILM EVER
WHAT DID YOU THINK OF THE MOVIE?
IT WAS OK.
SPARE CHANGE TO SEE A MOVIE
"I LOVED
"FUNNY AND ABSORBING"
TOUCHING AND GOOD.

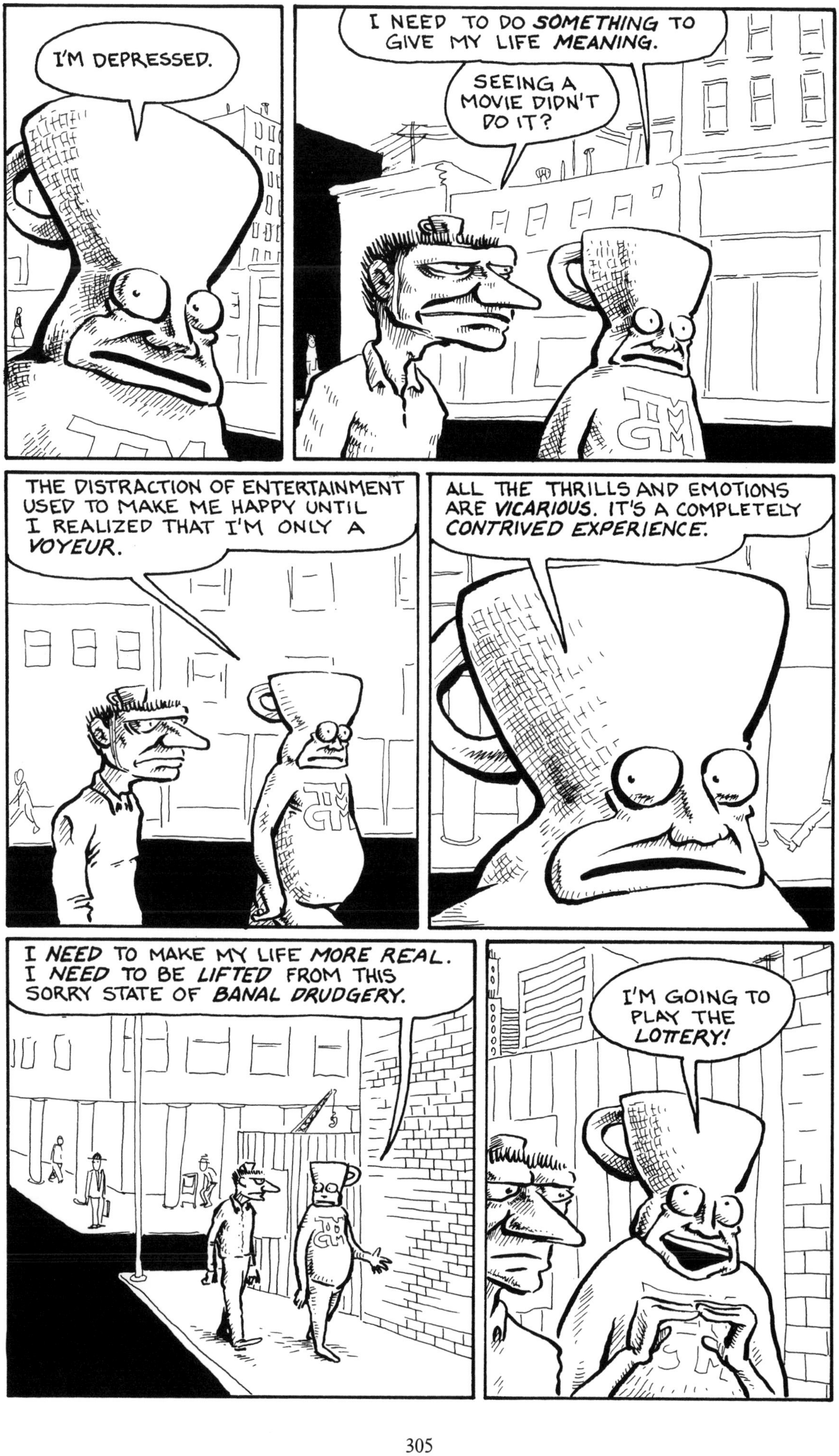
I'M DEPRESSED.
I NEED TO DO SOMETHING TO GIVE MY LIFE MEANING.
SEEING A MOVIE DIDN'T DO IT?
THE DISTRACTION OF ENTERTAINMENT USED TO MAKE ME HAPPY UNTIL I REALIZED THAT I'M ONLY A VOYEUR.
ALL THE THRILLS AND EMOTIONS ARE VICARIOUS. IT'S A COMPLETELY CONTRIVED EXPERIENCE.
I NEED TO MAKE MY LIFE MORE REAL. I NEED TO BE LIFTED FROM THIS SORRY STATE OF BANAL DRUDGERY.
I'M GOING TO PLAY THE LOTTERY!

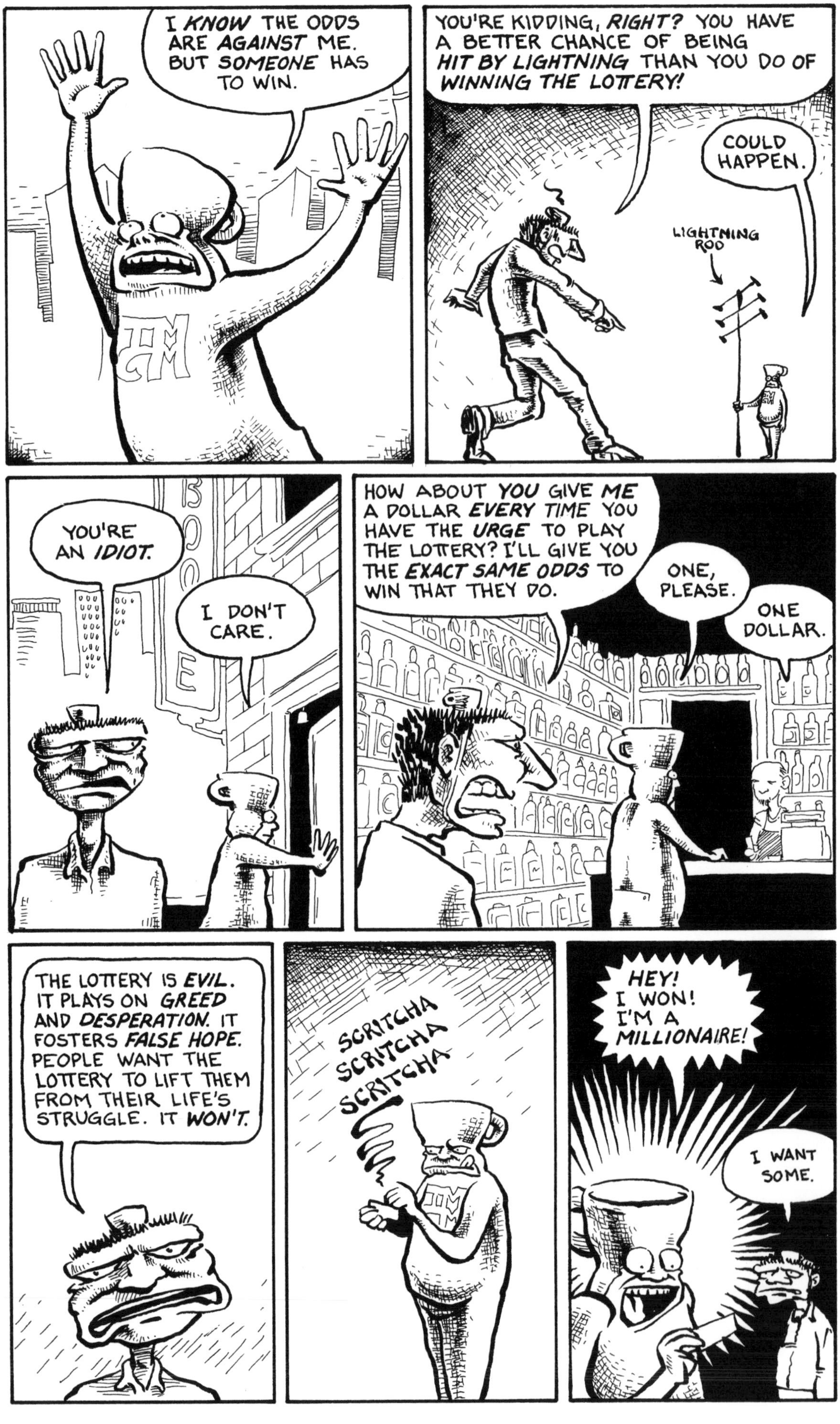
I KNOW THE ODDS ARE AGAINST ME. BUT SOMEONE HAS TO WIN.
YOU'RE KIDDING, RIGHT? YOU HAVE A BETTER CHANCE OF BEING HIT BY LIGHTNING THAN YOU DO OF WINNING THE LOTTERY!
COULD HAPPEN.
LIGHTNING ROD
YOU'RE AN IDIOT.
I DON'T CARE.
HOW ABOUT YOU GIVE ME A DOLLAR EVERY TIME YOU HAVE THE URGE TO PLAY THE LOTTERY? I'LL GIVE YOU THE EXACT SAME ODDS TO WIN THAT THEY DO.
ONE, PLEASE.
ONE DOLLAR.
THE LOTTERY IS EVIL. IT PLAYS ON GREED AND DESPERATION. IT FOSTERS FALSE HOPE. PEOPLE WANT THE LOTTERY TO LIFT THEM FROM THEIR LIFE'S STRUGGLE. IT WON'T.
SCRITCHA SCRITCHA SCRITCHA
HEY! I WON! I'M A MILLIONAIRE!
I WANT SOME.

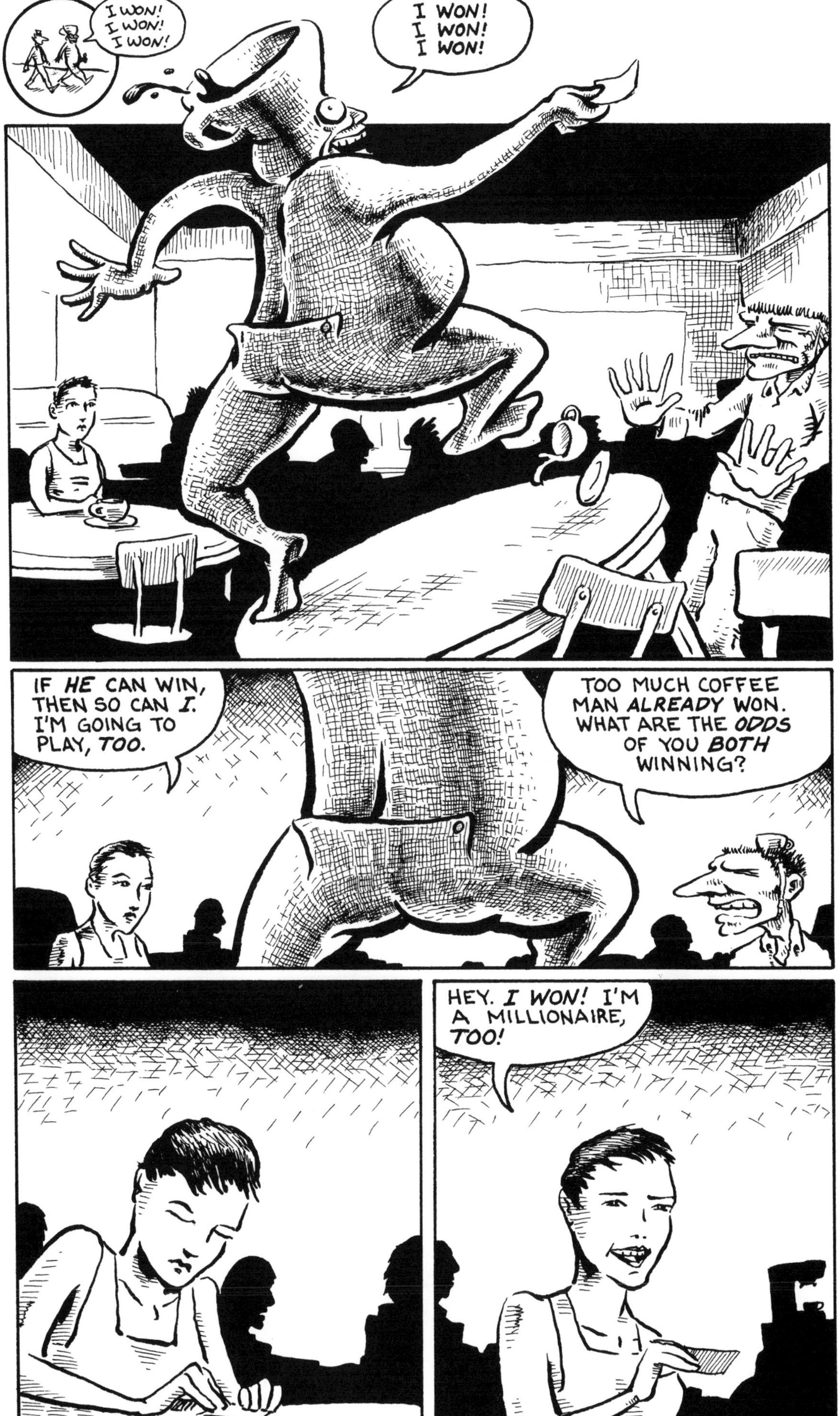
I WON! I WON! I WON!
I WON! I WON! I WON!
IF HE CAN WIN, THEN SO CAN I. I'M GOING TO PLAY, TOO.
TOO MUCH COFFEE MAN ALREADY WON. WHAT ARE THE ODDS OF YOU BOTH WINNING?
HEY. I WON! I'M A MILLIONAIRE, TOO!

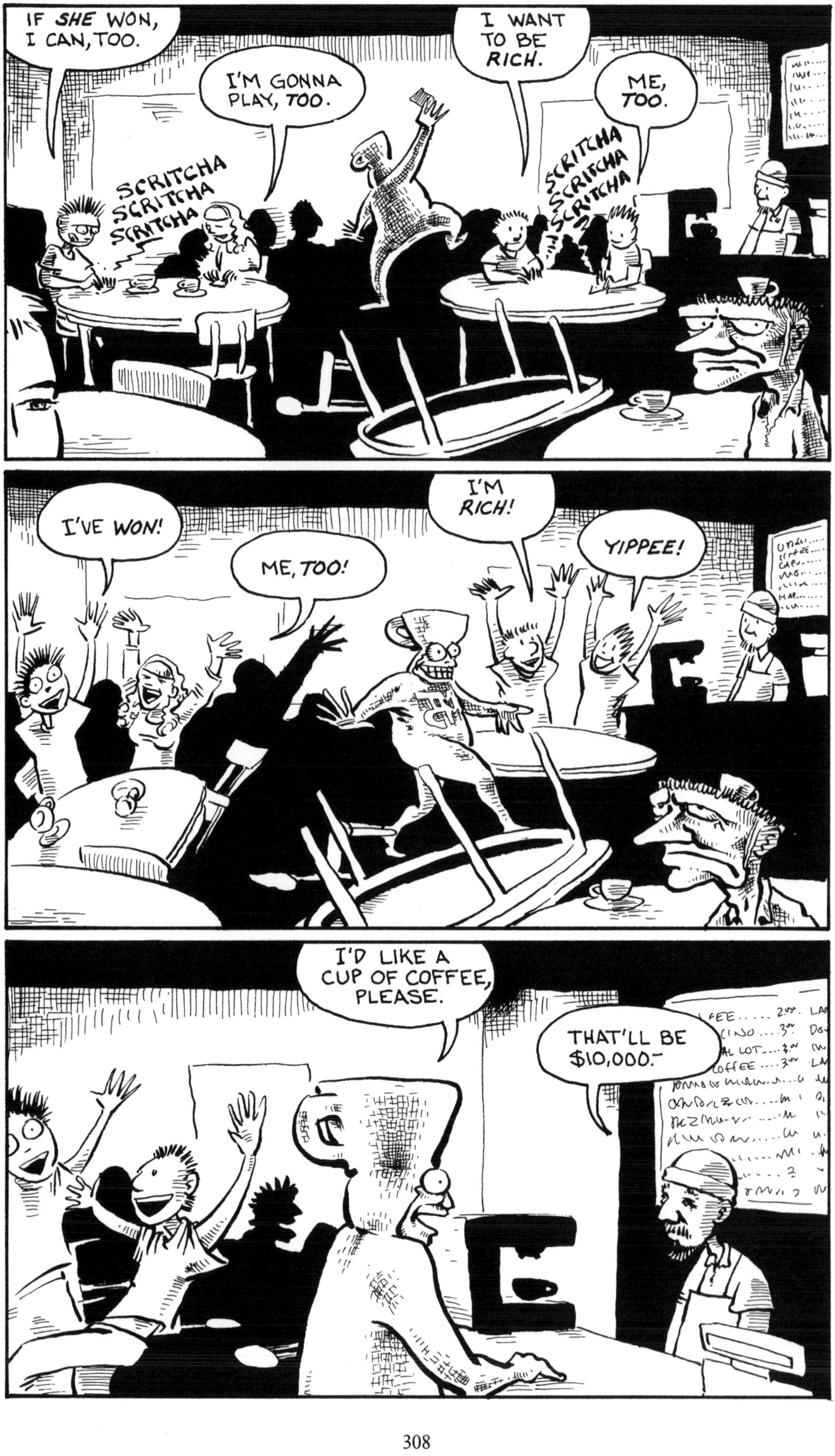
IF SHE WON, I CAN, TOO.
I'M GONNA PLAY, TOO.
SCRITCHA SCRITCHA SCRITCHA
I WANT TO BE RICH.
ME, TOO.
SCRITCHA SCRITCHA SCRITCHA
I'VE WON!
ME, TOO!
I'M RICH!
YIPPEE!
I'D LIKE A CUP OF COFFEE, PLEASE.
THAT'LL BE $10,000.-

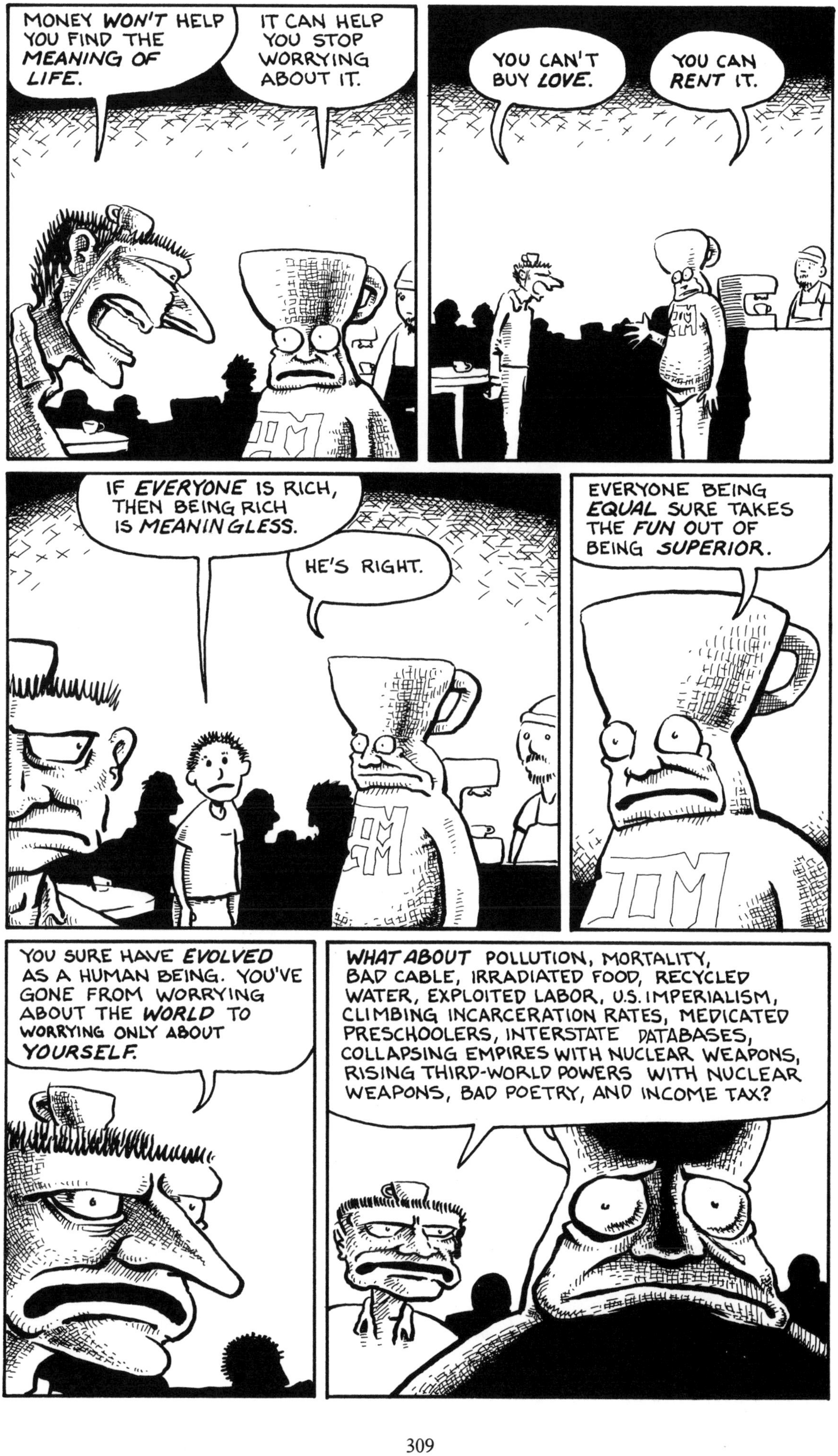
MONEY WON'T HELP YOU FIND THE MEANING OF LIFE.
IT CAN HELP YOU STOP WORRYING ABOUT IT.
YOU CAN'T BUY LOVE.
YOU CAN RENT IT.
IF EVERYONE IS RICH, THEN BEING RICH IS MEANINGLESS.
HE'S RIGHT.
EVERYONE BEING EQUAL SURE TAKES THE FUN OUT OF BEING SUPERIOR.
YOU SURE HAVE EVOLVED AS A HUMAN BEING. YOU'VE GONE FROM WORRYING ABOUT THE WORLD TO WORRYING ONLY ABOUT YOURSELF.
WHAT ABOUT POLLUTION, MORTALITY, BAD CABLE, IRRADIATED FOOD, RECYCLED WATER, EXPLOITED LABOR, U.S. IMPERIALISM, CLIMBING INCARCERATION RATES, MEDICATED PRESCHOOLERS, INTERSTATE DATABASES, COLLAPSING EMPIRES WITH NUCLEAR WEAPONS, RISING THIRD-WORLD POWERS WITH NUCLEAR WEAPONS, BAD POETRY, AND INCOME TAX?

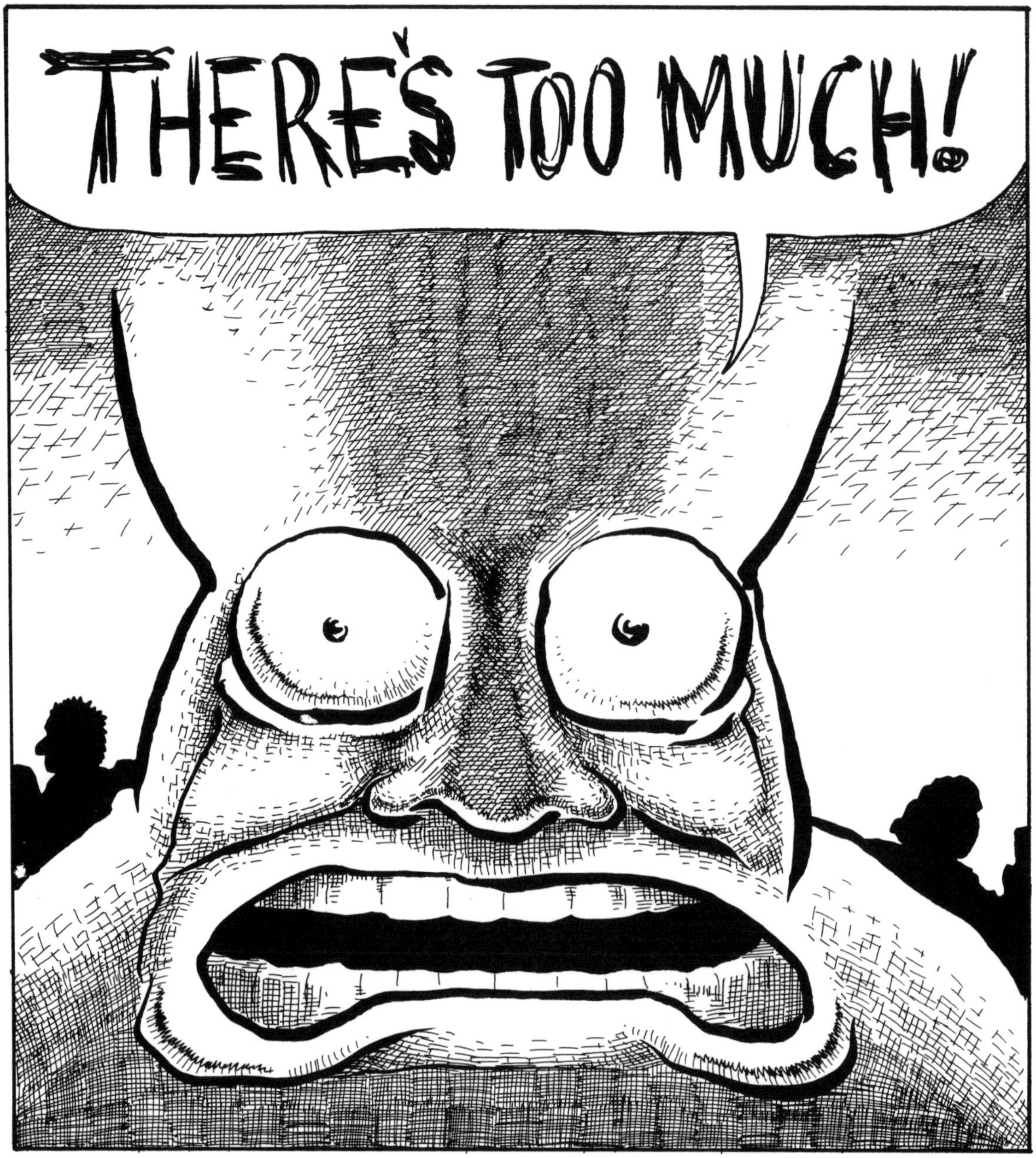
THERE'S TOO MUCH!

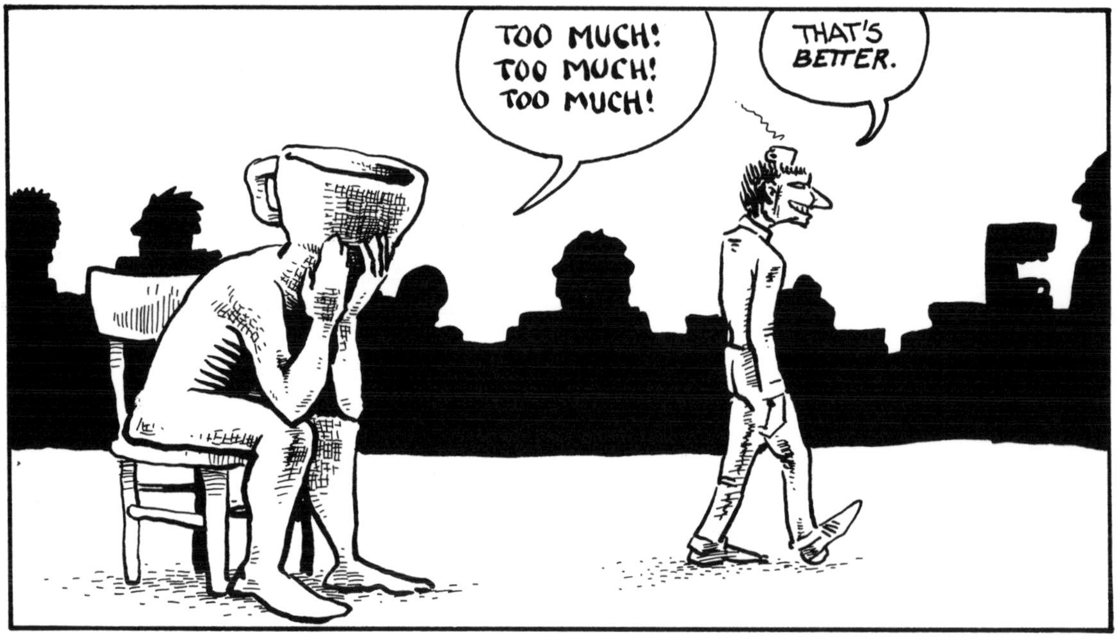
TOO MUCH!
TOO MUCH!
TOO MUCH!
THAT'S BETTER.

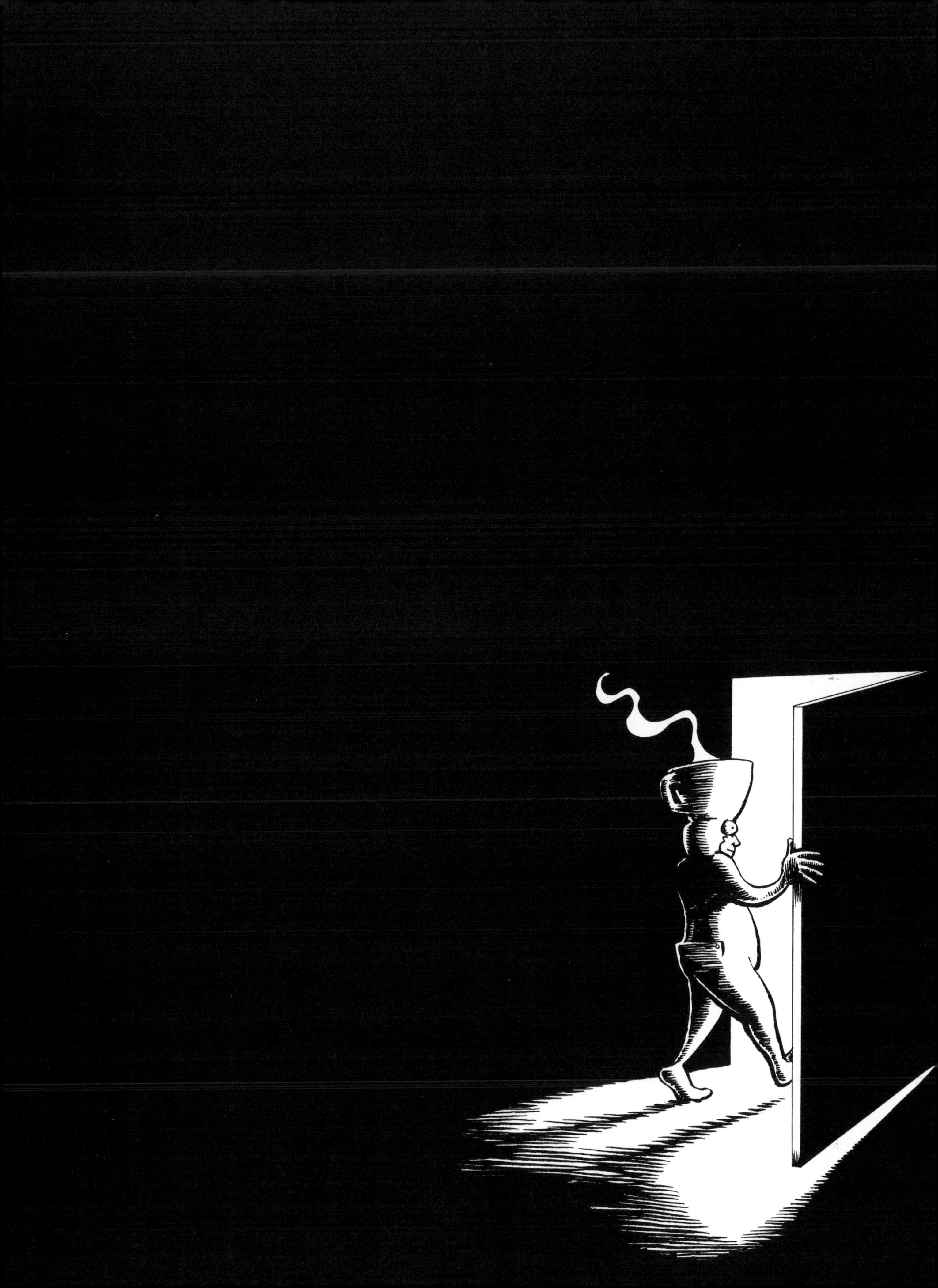

chapter 2

TELEVISION, ADVERTISING, AND INFOTAINMENT

How to feel better about yourself, and other insights

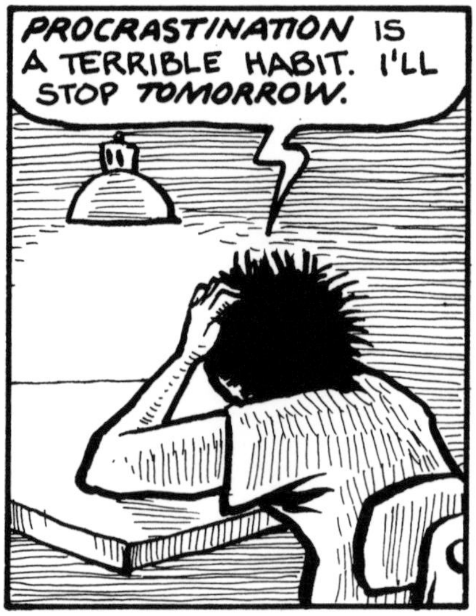
PROCRASTINATION IS A TERRIBLE HABIT. I'LL STOP TOMORROW.

TOO MUCH COFFEE MAN'S

GAMES

TO PLAY WHILE TRYING TO SLEEP

©1992 BY SHANNON WHEELER

TONIGHT, AS YOU GO TO SLEEP, AT THE EDGE OF SLUMBER, TRY PLAYING THESE **TOO MUCH COFFEE MAN** MIND GAMES

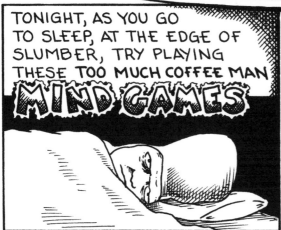

FIRST, THINK OF ALL THE THINGS YOU SHOULD'VE DONE TODAY BUT DIDN'T.

I SHOULD BE WORKING.

NOW THINK ABOUT YOUR **LIFE** AND HOW MUCH **TIME** YOU'VE **WASTED** AS THE YAWNING CHASM OF **DEATH** LOOMS EVER CLOSER.

TMCM. ONE CUP TOO MANY

BUT **DYING** WILL ONLY ACT AS A **COMFORT** AS YOUR **MIND** TRAVELS BACK TO RE-LIVE ALL THE **HUMILIATING** INCIDENTS OF CHILDHOOD.

THINK ABOUT HOW MISERABLE YOU'LL BE IF YOU **DON'T** MANAGE TO GET **SOME** SLEEP!

YOU OK?

UG.

BUT REMEMBER: IN ONLY A FEW HOURS YOU'LL **HAVE** TO GET UP **ANYWAY!**

-END

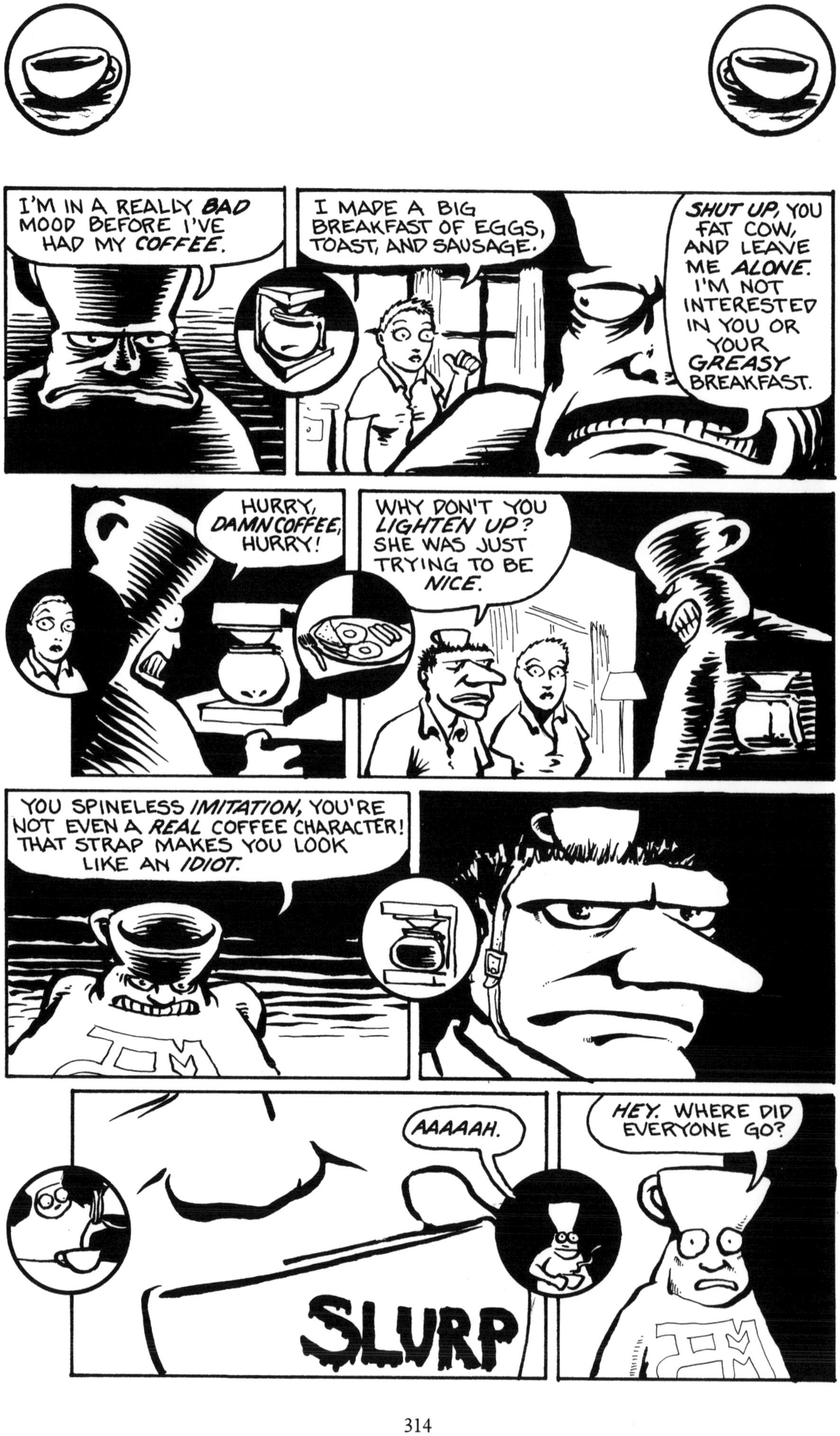
I'M IN A REALLY BAD MOOD BEFORE I'VE HAD MY COFFEE.
I MADE A BIG BREAKFAST OF EGGS, TOAST, AND SAUSAGE.
SHUT UP, YOU FAT COW, AND LEAVE ME ALONE. I'M NOT INTERESTED IN YOU OR YOUR GREASY BREAKFAST.
HURRY, DAMN COFFEE, HURRY!
WHY DON'T YOU LIGHTEN UP? SHE WAS JUST TRYING TO BE NICE.
YOU SPINELESS IMITATION, YOU'RE NOT EVEN A REAL COFFEE CHARACTER! THAT STRAP MAKES YOU LOOK LIKE AN IDIOT.
AAAAAH.
SLURP
HEY. WHERE DID EVERYONE GO?

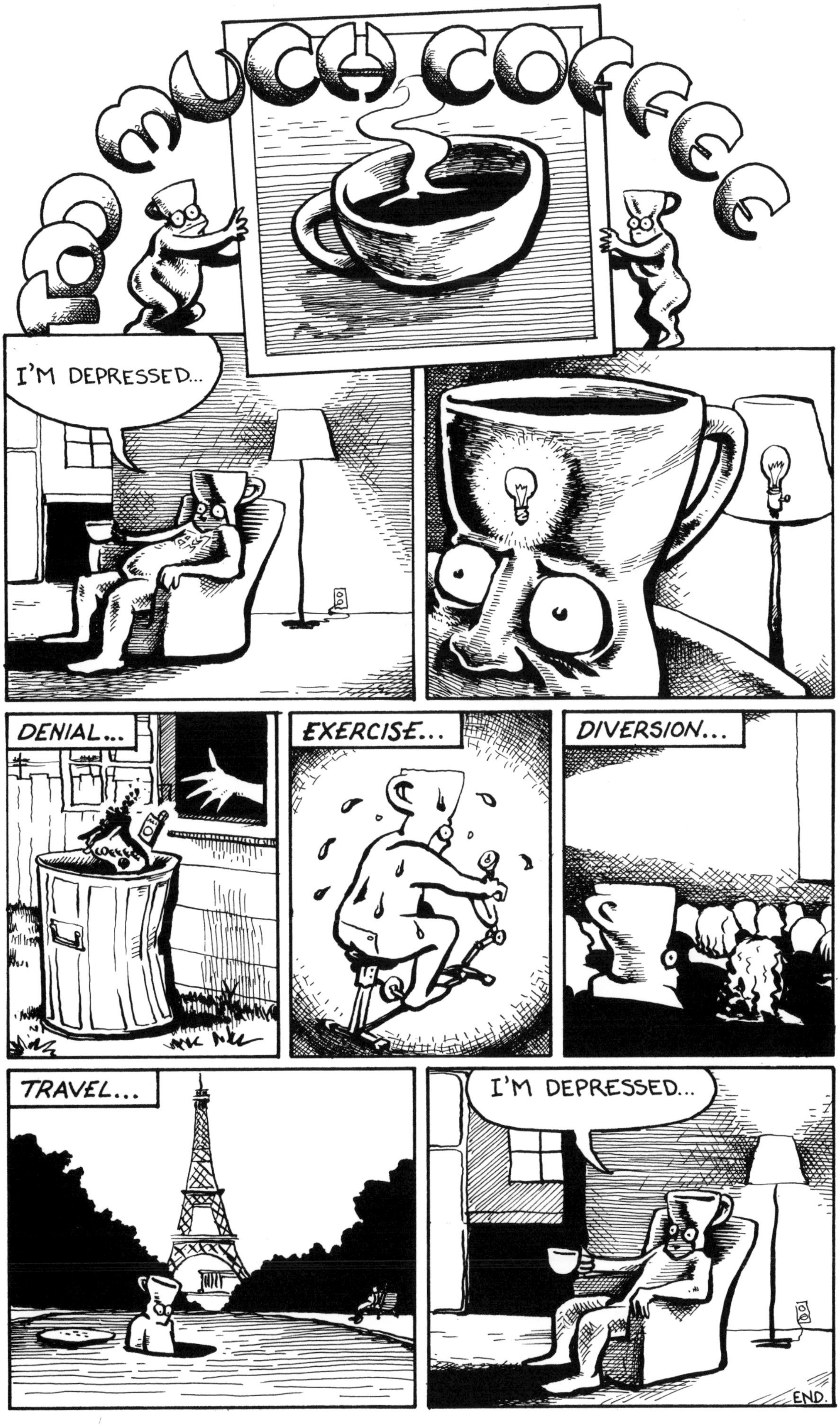
TOO MUCH COFFEE
I'M DEPRESSED...
DENIAL...
EXERCISE...
DIVERSION...
TRAVEL...
I'M DEPRESSED...
END.

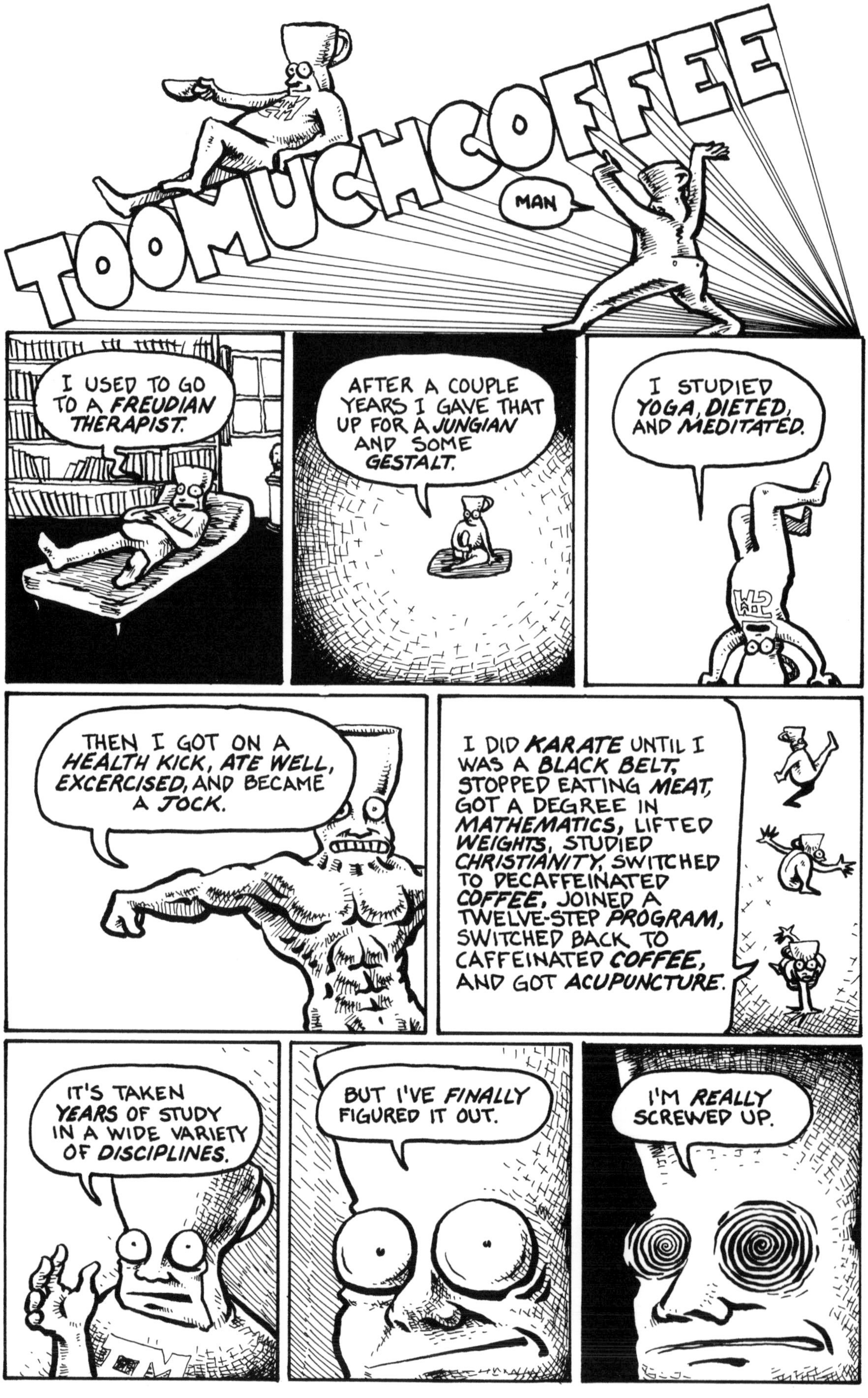
TOOMUCHCOFFEE
MAN
I USED TO GO TO A FREUDIAN THERAPIST.
AFTER A COUPLE YEARS I GAVE THAT UP FOR A JUNGIAN AND SOME GESTALT.
I STUDIED YOGA, DIETED, AND MEDITATED.
THEN I GOT ON A HEALTH KICK, ATE WELL, EXCERCISED, AND BECAME A JOCK.
I DID KARATE UNTIL I WAS A BLACK BELT, STOPPED EATING MEAT, GOT A DEGREE IN MATHEMATICS, LIFTED WEIGHTS, STUDIED CHRISTIANITY, SWITCHED TO DECAFFEINATED COFFEE, JOINED A TWELVE-STEP PROGRAM, SWITCHED BACK TO CAFFEINATED COFFEE, AND GOT ACUPUNCTURE.
IT'S TAKEN YEARS OF STUDY IN A WIDE VARIETY OF DISCIPLINES.
BUT I'VE FINALLY FIGURED IT OUT.
I'M REALLY SCREWED UP.

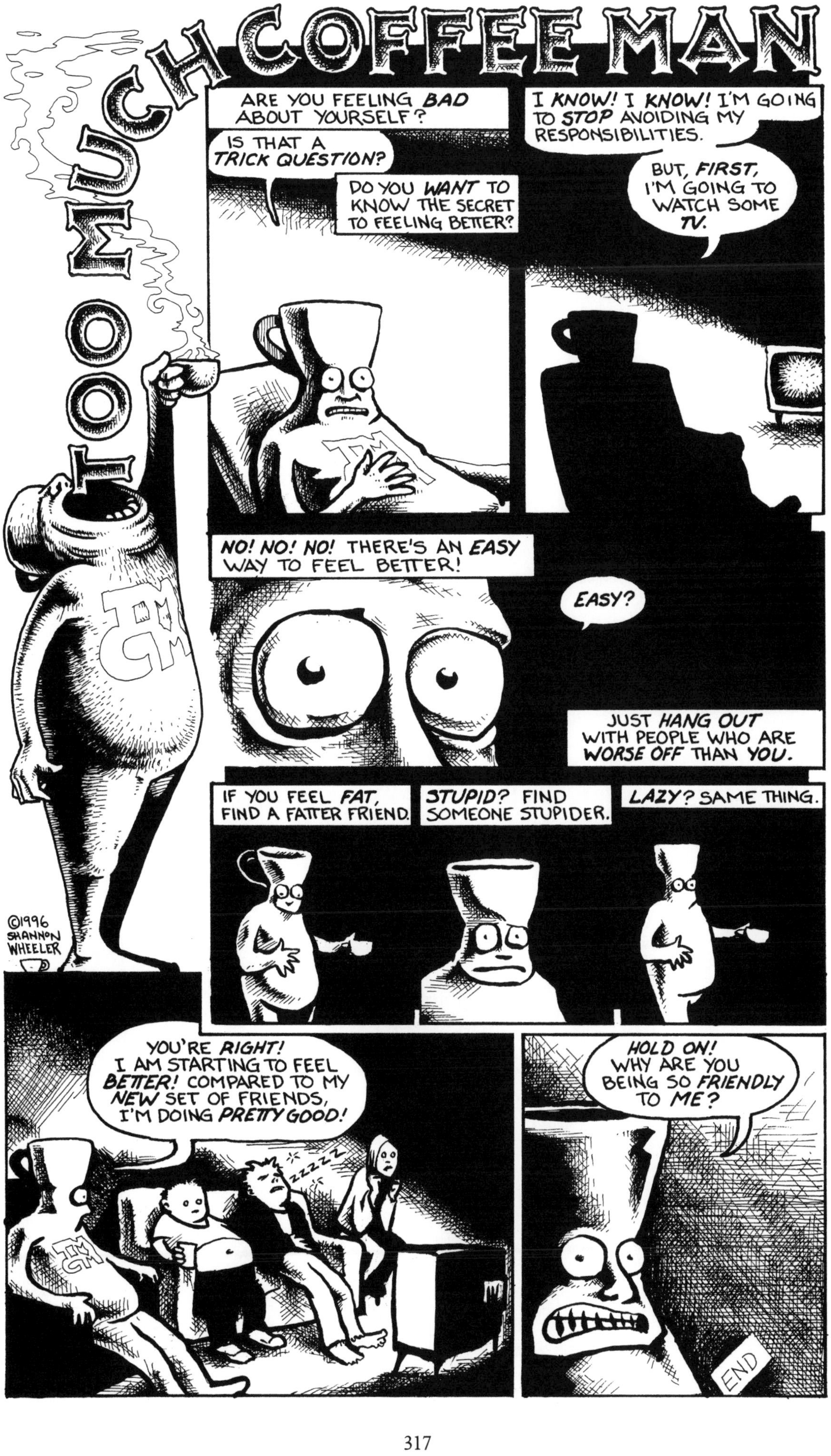
TOO MUCH COFFEE MAN
ARE YOU FEELING BAD ABOUT YOURSELF?
IS THAT A TRICK QUESTION?
DO YOU WANT TO KNOW THE SECRET TO FEELING BETTER?
I KNOW! I KNOW! I'M GOING TO STOP AVOIDING MY RESPONSIBILITIES.
BUT, FIRST, I'M GOING TO WATCH SOME TV.
NO! NO! NO! THERE'S AN EASY WAY TO FEEL BETTER!
EASY?
JUST HANG OUT WITH PEOPLE WHO ARE WORSE OFF THAN YOU.
IF YOU FEEL FAT, FIND A FATTER FRIEND.
STUPID? FIND SOMEONE STUPIDER.
LAZY? SAME THING.
©1996 SHANNON WHEELER
YOU'RE RIGHT! I AM STARTING TO FEEL BETTER! COMPARED TO MY NEW SET OF FRIENDS, I'M DOING PRETTY GOOD!
ZZZZZ
HOLD ON! WHY ARE YOU BEING SO FRIENDLY TO ME?
END

TOO MUCH COFFEE MAN
BY SHANNON WHEELER

© 2000 SHANNON WHEELER   WWW.TMCM.COM

HAVE YOU SEEN THE NEW *DRAMEDY*?

NO. BUT I READ A REVIEW OF THE *DOCUMERCIAL*.

DID THEY *LIKE* IT?

I DON'T KNOW. BUT THE LEAD STORY IN THE NEWS SAID IT MADE A LOT OF *MONEY*.

IT'S *FUNNY* THAT THE *MONEY* A MOVIE MAKES IS *MAJOR NEWS*.

YOU'D THINK THAT THE *NEWS COMPANY* AND THE *MOVIEMAKERS* WERE OWNED BY THE *SAME PEOPLE*. BUT THAT'S *RIDICULOUS*.

EVER CONSIDER THAT MOVIES AND THE MEDIA ARE JUST *DISTRACTIONS* TO KEEP THE *MASSES* FROM QUESTIONING THE *STATUS QUO*?

I SAW THAT MOVIE, TOO. IT MADE A LOT OF *MONEY*.

THAT'S *INFOTAINMENT*.

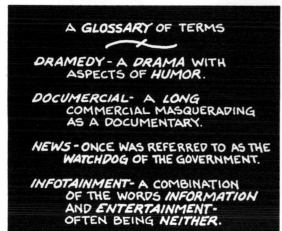

A *GLOSSARY* OF TERMS

DRAMEDY - A *DRAMA* WITH ASPECTS OF *HUMOR*.

DOCUMERCIAL - A *LONG* COMMERCIAL MASQUERADING AS A DOCUMENTARY.

NEWS - ONCE WAS REFERRED TO AS THE *WATCHDOG* OF THE GOVERNMENT.

INFOTAINMENT - A COMBINATION OF THE WORDS *INFORMATION* AND *ENTERTAINMENT* - OFTEN BEING *NEITHER*.

WORDS, IDEAS, AND IDEOLOGIES WERE *SERIOUSLY HARMED* BEFORE THE MAKING OF *THIS* CARTOON.

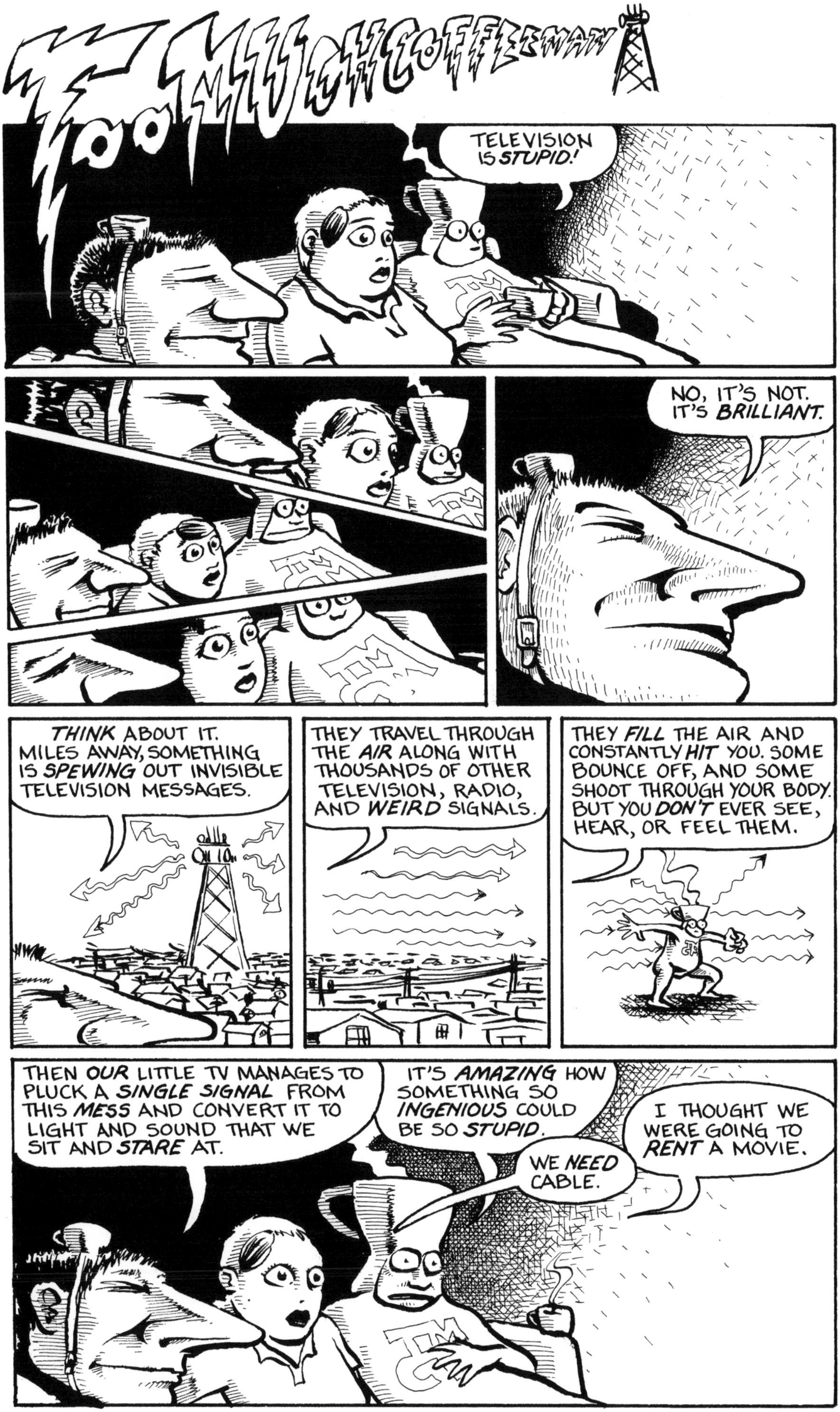
TOO MUCH COFFEE MAN
TELEVISION IS STUPID!
NO, IT'S NOT. IT'S BRILLIANT.
THINK ABOUT IT. MILES AWAY, SOMETHING IS SPEWING OUT INVISIBLE TELEVISION MESSAGES.
THEY TRAVEL THROUGH THE AIR ALONG WITH THOUSANDS OF OTHER TELEVISION, RADIO, AND WEIRD SIGNALS.
THEY FILL THE AIR AND CONSTANTLY HIT YOU. SOME BOUNCE OFF, AND SOME SHOOT THROUGH YOUR BODY. BUT YOU DON'T EVER SEE, HEAR, OR FEEL THEM.
THEN OUR LITTLE TV MANAGES TO PLUCK A SINGLE SIGNAL FROM THIS MESS AND CONVERT IT TO LIGHT AND SOUND THAT WE SIT AND STARE AT.
IT'S AMAZING HOW SOMETHING SO INGENIOUS COULD BE SO STUPID.
WE NEED CABLE.
I THOUGHT WE WERE GOING TO RENT A MOVIE.

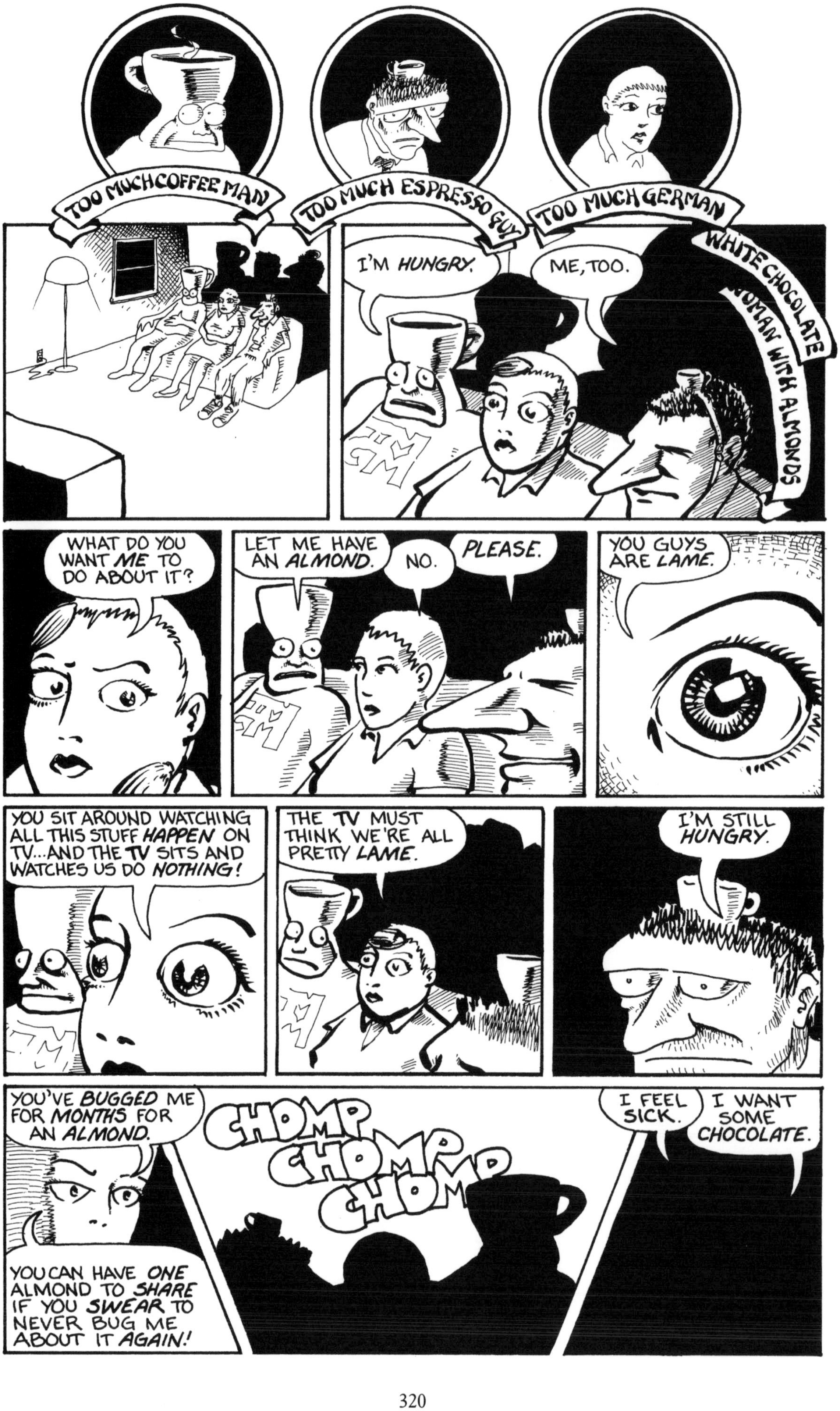
TOO MUCH COFFEE MAN
TOO MUCH ESPRESSO GUY
TOO MUCH GERMAN
WHITE CHOCOLATE WOMAN WITH ALMONDS
I'M HUNGRY.
ME, TOO.
WHAT DO YOU WANT ME TO DO ABOUT IT?
LET ME HAVE AN ALMOND.
NO.
PLEASE.
YOU GUYS ARE LAME.
YOU SIT AROUND WATCHING ALL THIS STUFF HAPPEN ON TV...AND THE TV SITS AND WATCHES US DO NOTHING!
THE TV MUST THINK WE'RE ALL PRETTY LAME.
I'M STILL HUNGRY.
YOU'VE BUGGED ME FOR MONTHS FOR AN ALMOND.
YOU CAN HAVE ONE ALMOND TO SHARE IF YOU SWEAR TO NEVER BUG ME ABOUT IT AGAIN!
CHOMP CHOMP CHOMP
I FEEL SICK.
I WANT SOME CHOCOLATE.

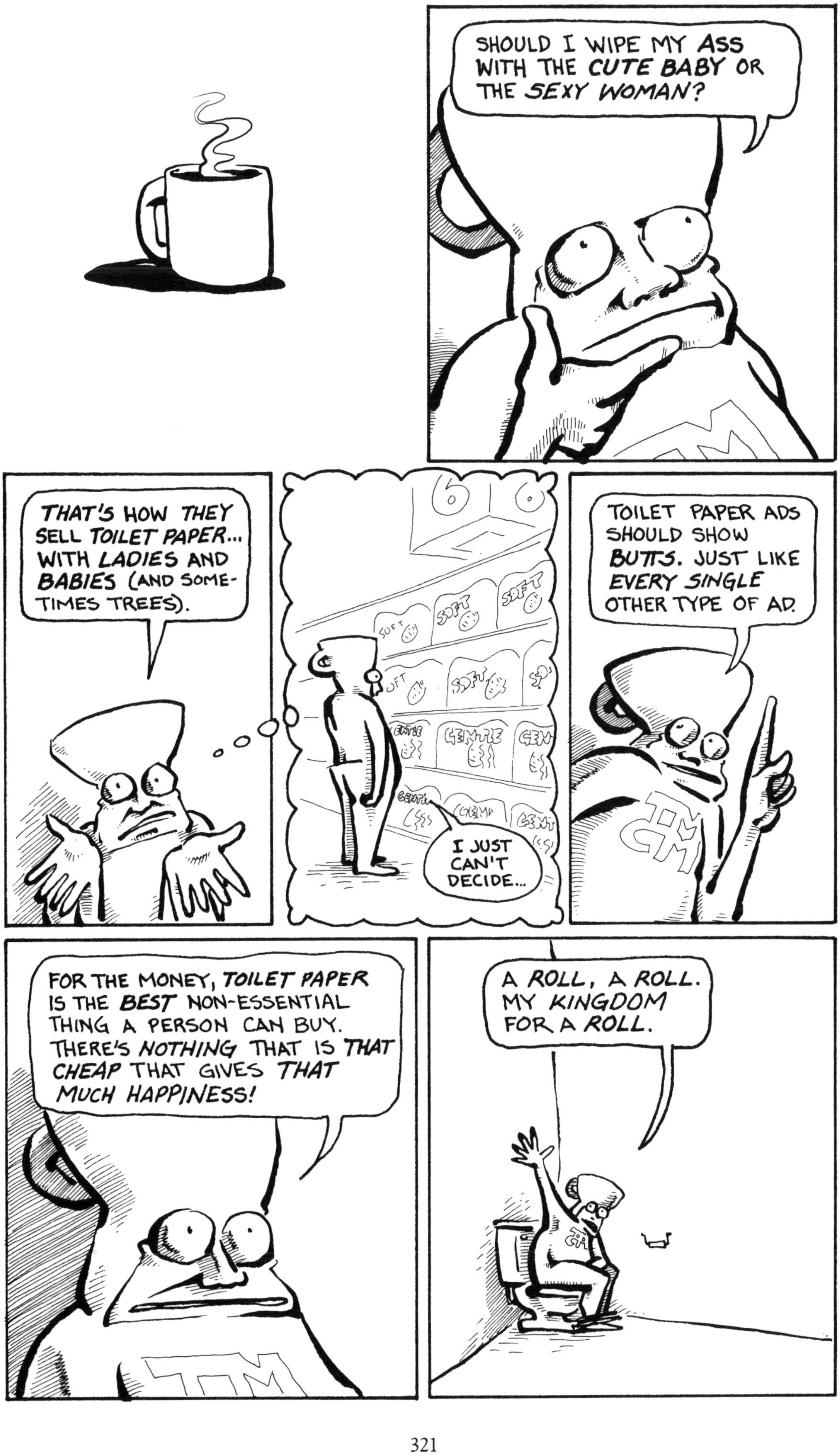
SHOULD I WIPE MY ASS WITH THE CUTE BABY OR THE SEXY WOMAN?
THAT'S HOW THEY SELL TOILET PAPER... WITH LADIES AND BABIES (AND SOMETIMES TREES).
SOFT
GENTLE
I JUST CAN'T DECIDE...
TOILET PAPER ADS SHOULD SHOW BUTTS. JUST LIKE EVERY SINGLE OTHER TYPE OF AD.
FOR THE MONEY, TOILET PAPER IS THE BEST NON-ESSENTIAL THING A PERSON CAN BUY. THERE'S NOTHING THAT IS THAT CHEAP THAT GIVES THAT MUCH HAPPINESS!
A ROLL, A ROLL. MY KINGDOM FOR A ROLL.

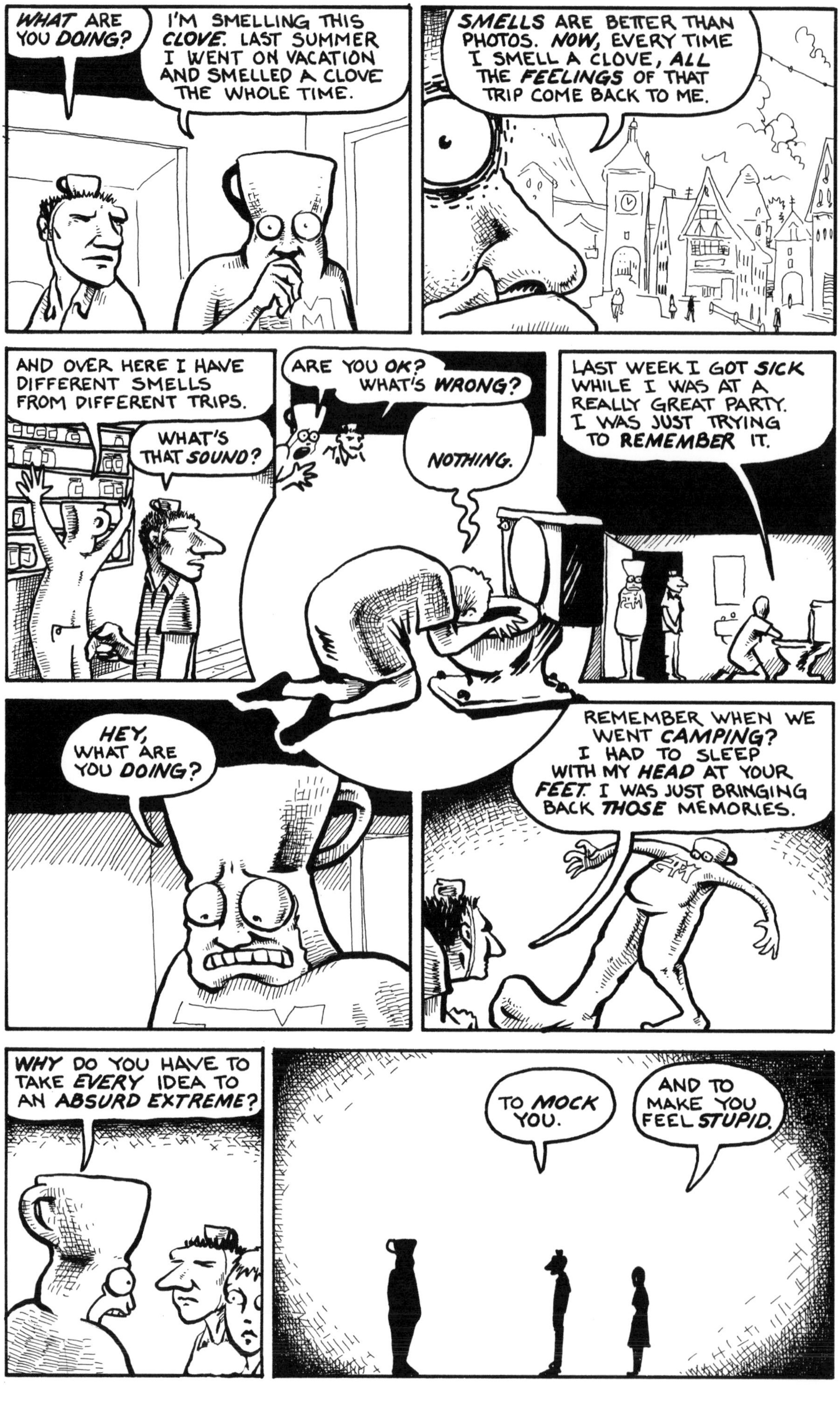
WHAT ARE YOU DOING?
I'M SMELLING THIS CLOVE. LAST SUMMER I WENT ON VACATION AND SMELLED A CLOVE THE WHOLE TIME.
SMELLS ARE BETTER THAN PHOTOS. NOW, EVERY TIME I SMELL A CLOVE, ALL THE FEELINGS OF THAT TRIP COME BACK TO ME.
AND OVER HERE I HAVE DIFFERENT SMELLS FROM DIFFERENT TRIPS.
WHAT'S THAT SOUND?
ARE YOU OK? WHAT'S WRONG?
NOTHING.
LAST WEEK I GOT SICK WHILE I WAS AT A REALLY GREAT PARTY. I WAS JUST TRYING TO REMEMBER IT.
HEY, WHAT ARE YOU DOING?
REMEMBER WHEN WE WENT CAMPING? I HAD TO SLEEP WITH MY HEAD AT YOUR FEET. I WAS JUST BRINGING BACK THOSE MEMORIES.
WHY DO YOU HAVE TO TAKE EVERY IDEA TO AN ABSURD EXTREME?
TO MOCK YOU.
AND TO MAKE YOU FEEL STUPID.

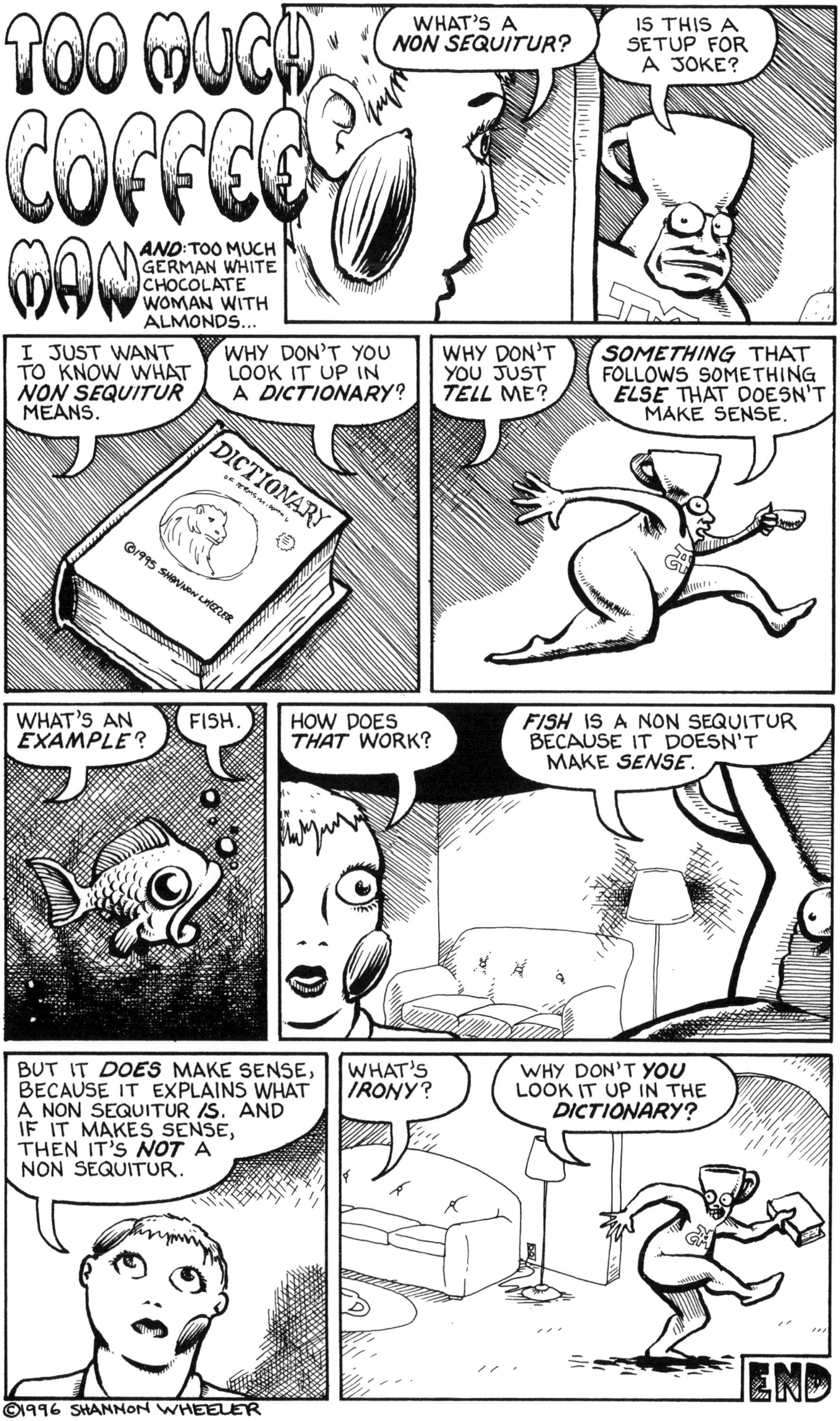
TOO MUCH COFFEE MAN
AND: TOO MUCH GERMAN WHITE CHOCOLATE WOMAN WITH ALMONDS...
WHAT'S A NON SEQUITUR?
IS THIS A SETUP FOR A JOKE?
I JUST WANT TO KNOW WHAT NON SEQUITUR MEANS.
WHY DON'T YOU LOOK IT UP IN A DICTIONARY?
DICTIONARY
©1995 SHANNON WHEELER
WHY DON'T YOU JUST TELL ME?
SOMETHING THAT FOLLOWS SOMETHING ELSE THAT DOESN'T MAKE SENSE.
WHAT'S AN EXAMPLE?
FISH.
HOW DOES THAT WORK?
FISH IS A NON SEQUITUR BECAUSE IT DOESN'T MAKE SENSE.
BUT IT DOES MAKE SENSE, BECAUSE IT EXPLAINS WHAT A NON SEQUITUR IS. AND IF IT MAKES SENSE, THEN IT'S NOT A NON SEQUITUR.
WHAT'S IRONY?
WHY DON'T YOU LOOK IT UP IN THE DICTIONARY?
END

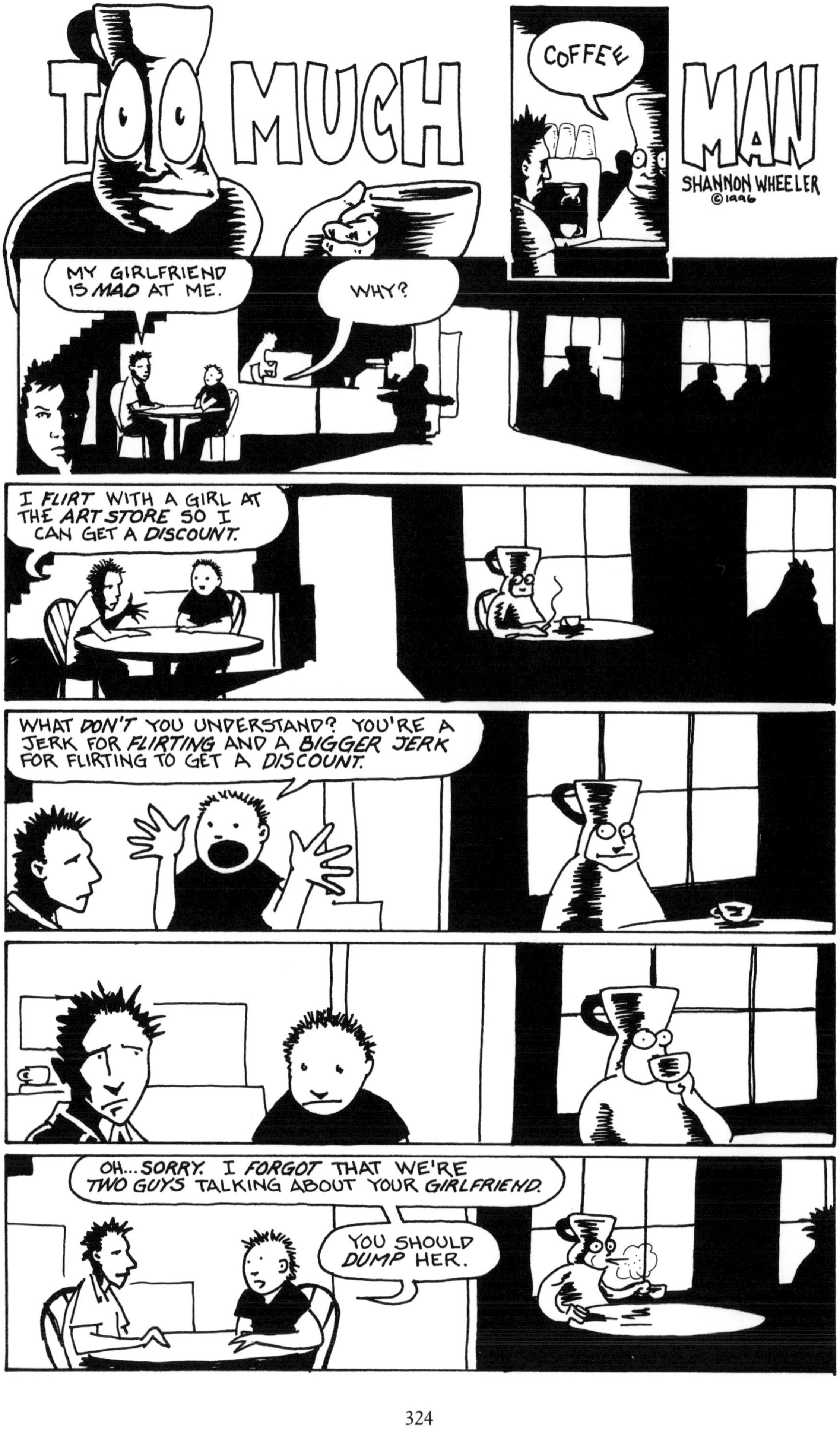
TOO MUCH COFFEE MAN
SHANNON WHEELER
©1996
MY GIRLFRIEND IS *MAD* AT ME.
WHY?
I *FLIRT* WITH A GIRL AT THE *ART STORE* SO I CAN GET A *DISCOUNT*.
WHAT *DON'T* YOU UNDERSTAND? YOU'RE A JERK FOR *FLIRTING* AND A *BIGGER JERK* FOR FLIRTING TO GET A *DISCOUNT*.
OH... *SORRY*. I *FORGOT* THAT WE'RE *TWO GUYS* TALKING ABOUT YOUR *GIRLFRIEND*.
YOU SHOULD *DUMP* HER.

chapter 3

A BRINE SHRIMP ADVENTURE

If I had a time machine,
I'd go back and give it to myself;
and other ideas

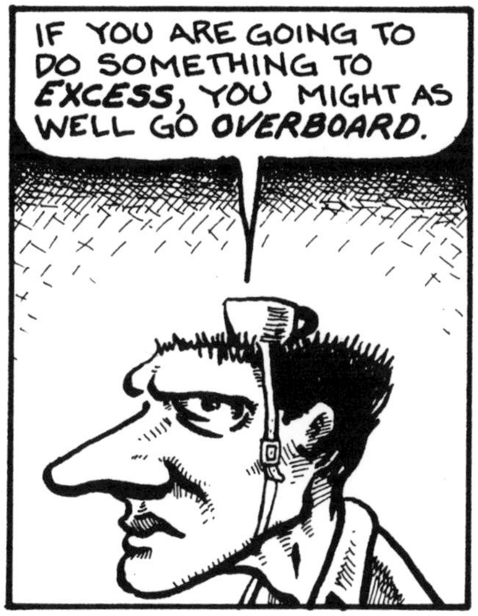
IF YOU ARE GOING TO DO SOMETHING TO EXCESS, YOU MIGHT AS WELL GO OVERBOARD.

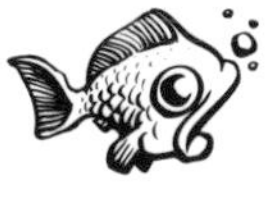

HEY, *KID*, HOW WOULD YOU LIKE A *CRAPPY JOB?*

I GUESS. I NEED A JOB.

OF COURSE, YOUR HAIR IS *TOO LONG* AND YOU'LL HAVE TO SHAVE YOUR GOATEE.

OH... UM... OK...

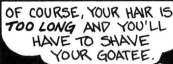

HEY, GIRL OVER THERE, I HAVE A *CRAPPY JOB* FOR YOU, TOO.

BUT YOUR HAIR IS *TOO SHORT.* YOU'LL HAVE TO WEAR A *HAT* UNTIL IT *GROWS OUT.*

BOTH OF YOU NEED TO DRESS TO HIDE YOUR *TATTOOS* AND *PIERCINGS.*

WHAT'S THE *JOB?*

YOU SERVE *FAT* AND *DRUNK* PEOPLE *LIQUOR* AND *FOOD...* AND DON'T FORGET TO PUSH THE *EXPENSIVE STUFF.*

I PAY *LESS* THAN THE *MINIMUM WAGE*—MOST OF YOUR MONEY WILL COME FROM *TIPS,* SO YOU'LL NEED TO BE *FRIENDLY* AND *POLITE* EVEN WHEN THE CUSTOMERS ARE *JERKS.*

OVER THE YEARS YOU'LL BECOME *BITTER* AND DISILLUSIONED, YOUR HEALTH WILL SUFFER, AND THERE WON'T BE MUCH CHANCE FOR JOB IMPROVEMENT.

SOUNDS GREAT.

WHAT A TERRIBLE *DREAM.* I KNEW I SHOULDN'T HAVE EATEN THAT *BURRITO* BEFORE GOING TO BED.

APOLOGIES TO WINSOR McCAY

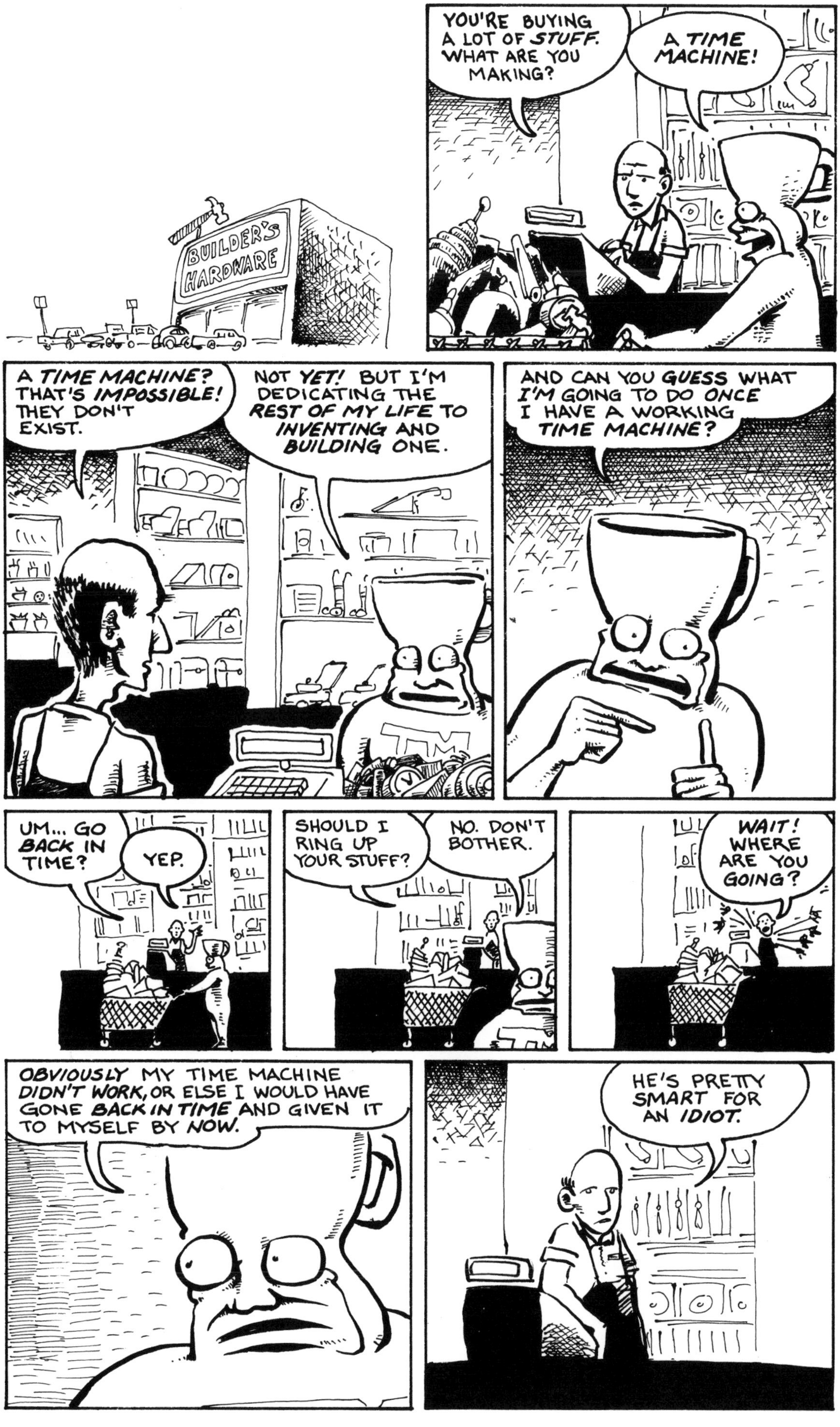
BUILDER'S HARDWARE
YOU'RE BUYING A LOT OF STUFF. WHAT ARE YOU MAKING?
A TIME MACHINE!
A TIME MACHINE? THAT'S IMPOSSIBLE! THEY DON'T EXIST.
NOT YET! BUT I'M DEDICATING THE REST OF MY LIFE TO INVENTING AND BUILDING ONE.
AND CAN YOU GUESS WHAT I'M GOING TO DO ONCE I HAVE A WORKING TIME MACHINE?
UM... GO BACK IN TIME?
YEP.
SHOULD I RING UP YOUR STUFF?
NO. DON'T BOTHER.
WAIT! WHERE ARE YOU GOING?
OBVIOUSLY MY TIME MACHINE DIDN'T WORK, OR ELSE I WOULD HAVE GONE BACK IN TIME AND GIVEN IT TO MYSELF BY NOW.
HE'S PRETTY SMART FOR AN IDIOT.

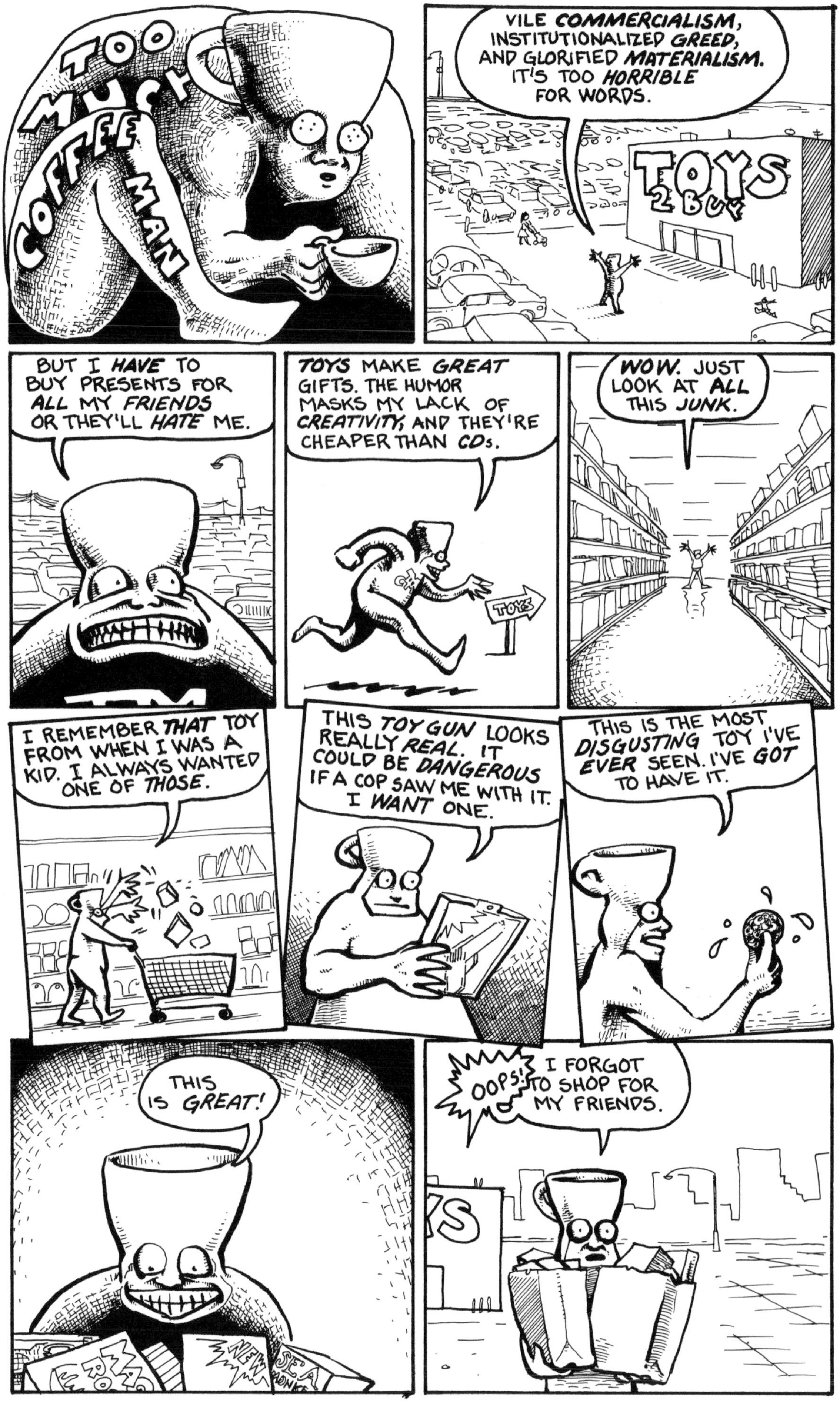
TOO MUCH COFFEE MAN
VILE COMMERCIALISM, INSTITUTIONALIZED GREED, AND GLORIFIED MATERIALISM. IT'S TOO HORRIBLE FOR WORDS.
TOYS 2 BUY
BUT I HAVE TO BUY PRESENTS FOR ALL MY FRIENDS OR THEY'LL HATE ME.
TOYS MAKE GREAT GIFTS. THE HUMOR MASKS MY LACK OF CREATIVITY, AND THEY'RE CHEAPER THAN CDs.
TOYS
WOW. JUST LOOK AT ALL THIS JUNK.
I REMEMBER THAT TOY FROM WHEN I WAS A KID. I ALWAYS WANTED ONE OF THOSE.
THIS TOY GUN LOOKS REALLY REAL. IT COULD BE DANGEROUS IF A COP SAW ME WITH IT. I WANT ONE.
THIS IS THE MOST DISGUSTING TOY I'VE EVER SEEN. I'VE GOT TO HAVE IT.
THIS IS GREAT!
NEW
OOPS!
I FORGOT TO SHOP FOR MY FRIENDS.

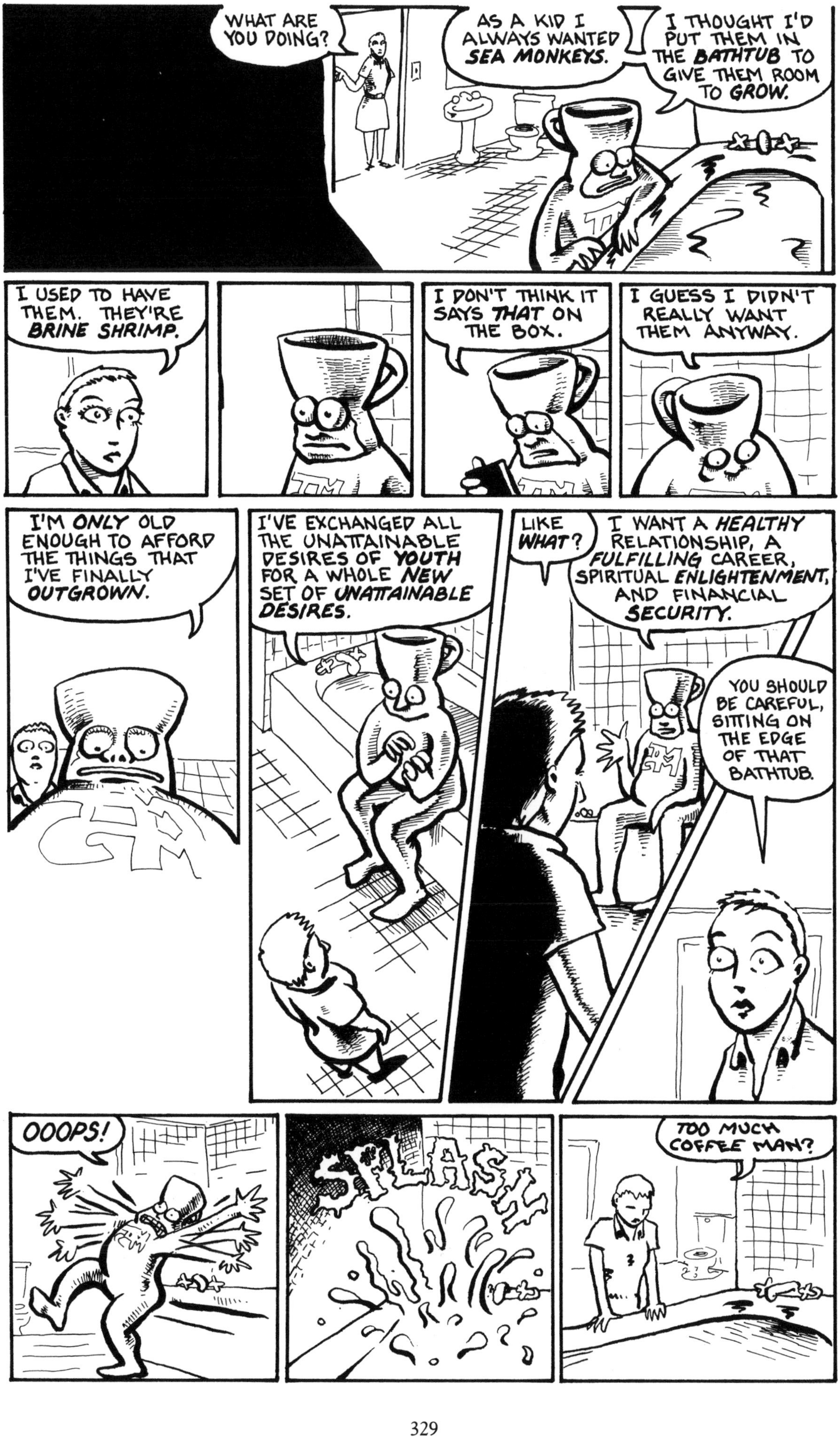
WHAT ARE YOU DOING?
AS A KID I ALWAYS WANTED SEA MONKEYS.
I THOUGHT I'D PUT THEM IN THE BATHTUB TO GIVE THEM ROOM TO GROW.
I USED TO HAVE THEM. THEY'RE BRINE SHRIMP.
I DON'T THINK IT SAYS THAT ON THE BOX.
I GUESS I DIDN'T REALLY WANT THEM ANYWAY.
I'M ONLY OLD ENOUGH TO AFFORD THE THINGS THAT I'VE FINALLY OUTGROWN.
I'VE EXCHANGED ALL THE UNATTAINABLE DESIRES OF YOUTH FOR A WHOLE NEW SET OF UNATTAINABLE DESIRES.
LIKE WHAT?
I WANT A HEALTHY RELATIONSHIP, A FULFILLING CAREER, SPIRITUAL ENLIGHTENMENT, AND FINANCIAL SECURITY.
YOU SHOULD BE CAREFUL, SITTING ON THE EDGE OF THAT BATHTUB.
OOOPS!
SPLASH
TOO MUCH COFFEE MAN?

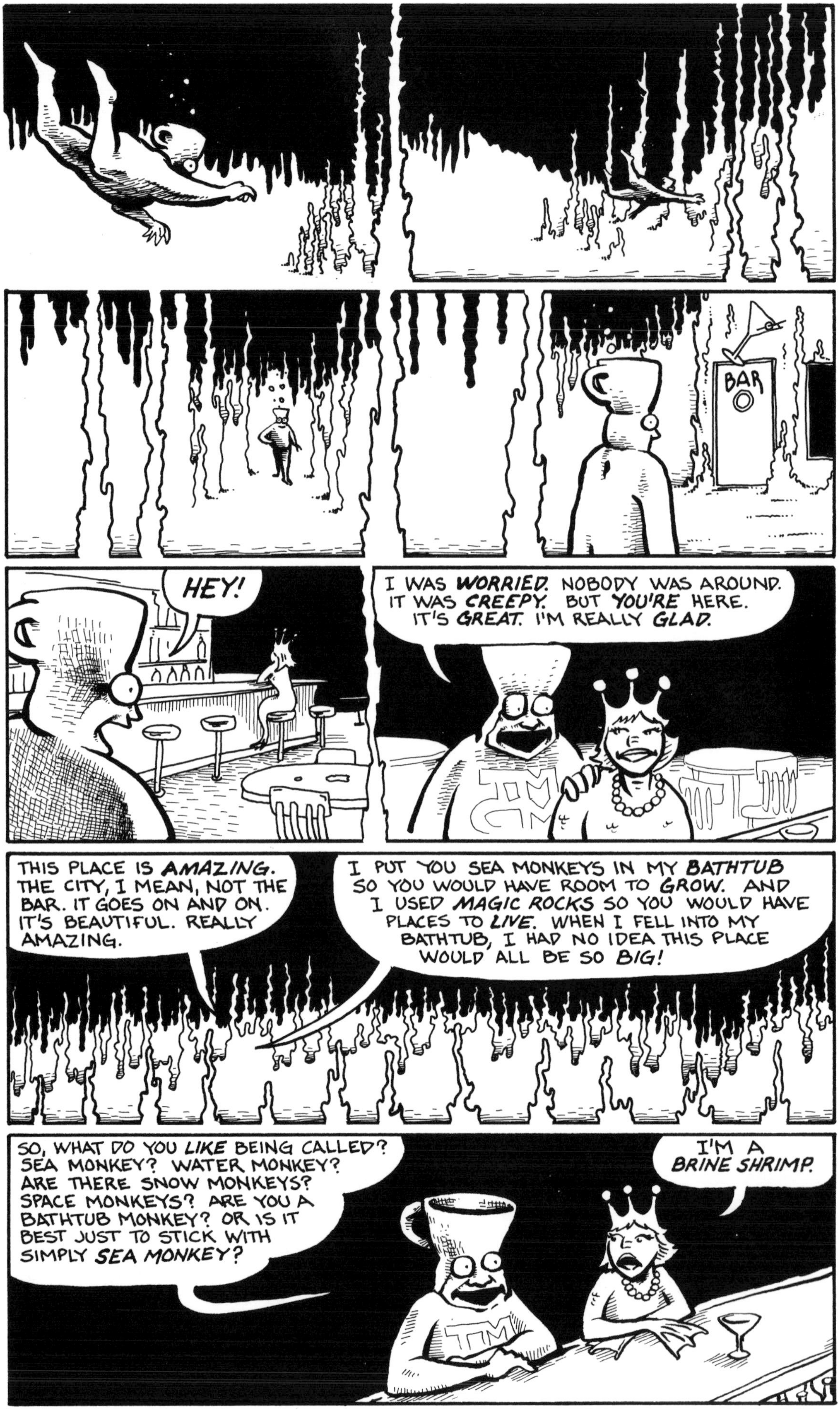
BAR
HEY!
I WAS WORRIED. NOBODY WAS AROUND. IT WAS CREEPY. BUT YOU'RE HERE. IT'S GREAT. I'M REALLY GLAD.
THIS PLACE IS AMAZING. THE CITY, I MEAN, NOT THE BAR. IT GOES ON AND ON. IT'S BEAUTIFUL. REALLY AMAZING.
I PUT YOU SEA MONKEYS IN MY BATHTUB SO YOU WOULD HAVE ROOM TO GROW. AND I USED MAGIC ROCKS SO YOU WOULD HAVE PLACES TO LIVE. WHEN I FELL INTO MY BATHTUB, I HAD NO IDEA THIS PLACE WOULD ALL BE SO BIG!
SO, WHAT DO YOU LIKE BEING CALLED? SEA MONKEY? WATER MONKEY? ARE THERE SNOW MONKEYS? SPACE MONKEYS? ARE YOU A BATHTUB MONKEY? OR IS IT BEST JUST TO STICK WITH SIMPLY SEA MONKEY?
I'M A BRINE SHRIMP.

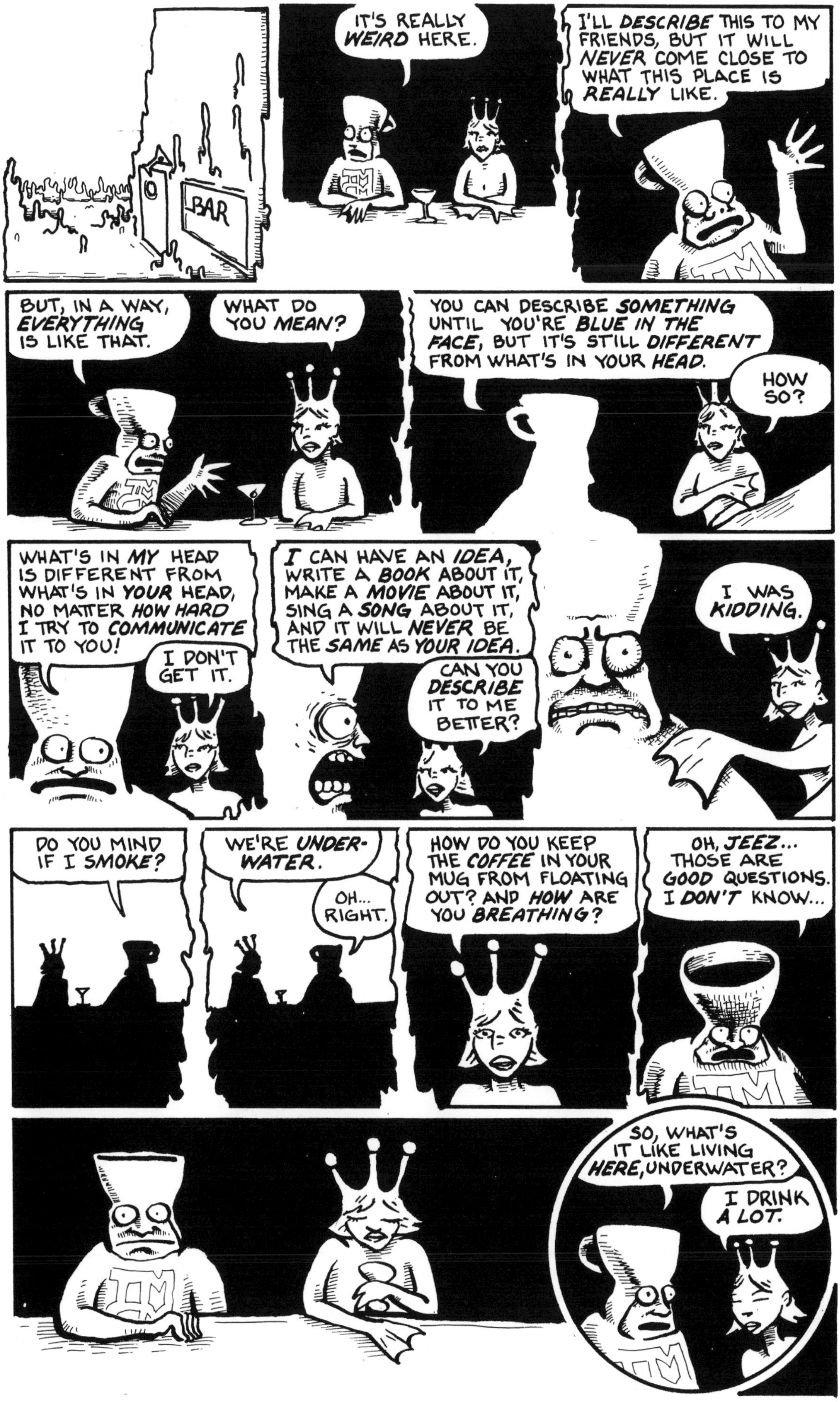
BAR
IT'S REALLY WEIRD HERE.
I'LL DESCRIBE THIS TO MY FRIENDS, BUT IT WILL NEVER COME CLOSE TO WHAT THIS PLACE IS REALLY LIKE.
BUT, IN A WAY, EVERYTHING IS LIKE THAT.
WHAT DO YOU MEAN?
YOU CAN DESCRIBE SOMETHING UNTIL YOU'RE BLUE IN THE FACE, BUT IT'S STILL DIFFERENT FROM WHAT'S IN YOUR HEAD.
HOW SO?
WHAT'S IN MY HEAD IS DIFFERENT FROM WHAT'S IN YOUR HEAD, NO MATTER HOW HARD I TRY TO COMMUNICATE IT TO YOU!
I DON'T GET IT.
I CAN HAVE AN IDEA, WRITE A BOOK ABOUT IT, MAKE A MOVIE ABOUT IT, SING A SONG ABOUT IT, AND IT WILL NEVER BE THE SAME AS YOUR IDEA.
CAN YOU DESCRIBE IT TO ME BETTER?
I WAS KIDDING.
DO YOU MIND IF I SMOKE?
WE'RE UNDER-WATER.
OH... RIGHT.
HOW DO YOU KEEP THE COFFEE IN YOUR MUG FROM FLOATING OUT? AND HOW ARE YOU BREATHING?
OH, JEEZ... THOSE ARE GOOD QUESTIONS. I DON'T KNOW...
SO, WHAT'S IT LIKE LIVING HERE, UNDERWATER?
I DRINK A LOT.

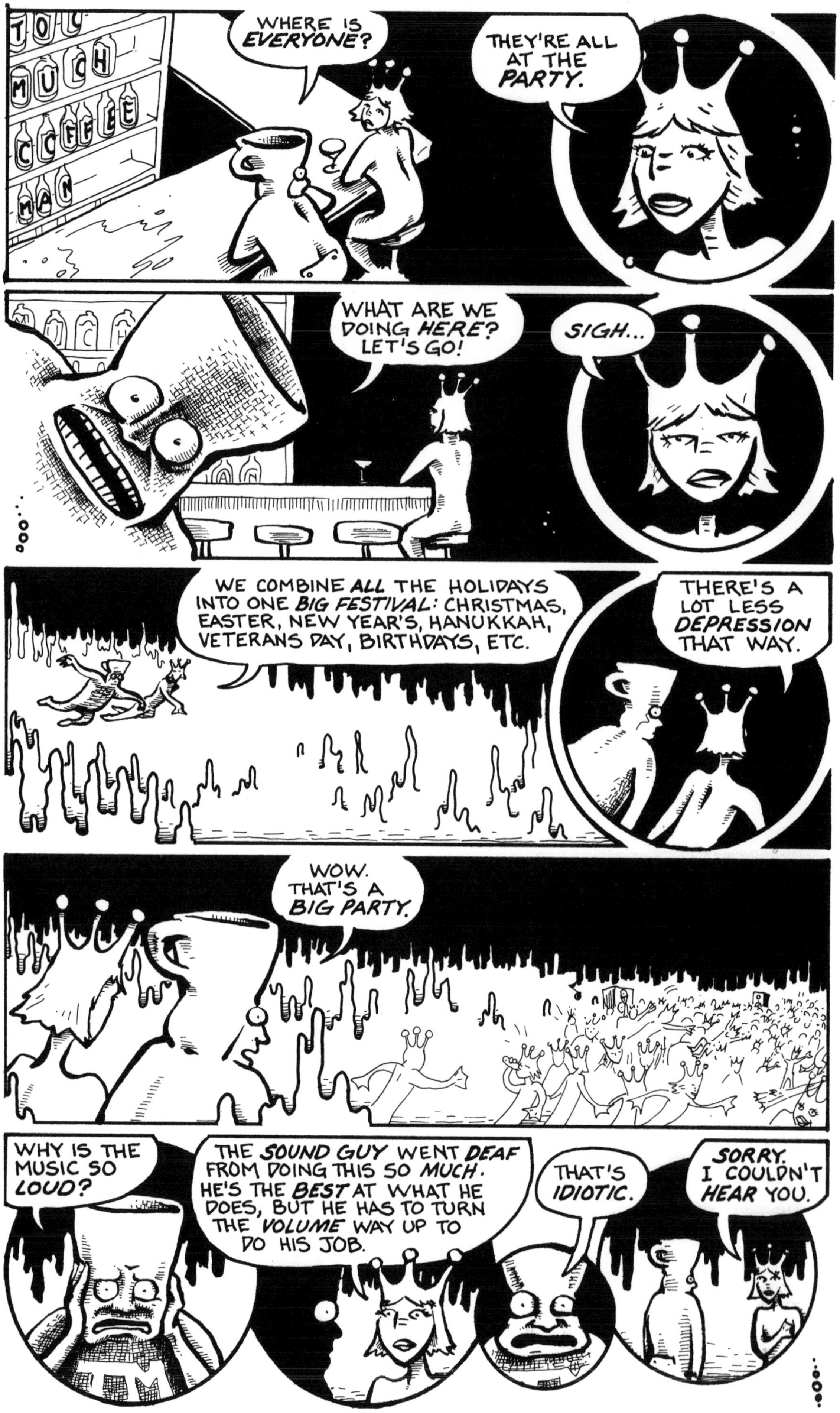

TOO MUCH COFFEE MAN
WHERE IS EVERYONE?
THEY'RE ALL AT THE PARTY.
WHAT ARE WE DOING HERE? LET'S GO!
SIGH...
WE COMBINE ALL THE HOLIDAYS INTO ONE BIG FESTIVAL: CHRISTMAS, EASTER, NEW YEAR'S, HANUKKAH, VETERANS DAY, BIRTHDAYS, ETC.
THERE'S A LOT LESS DEPRESSION THAT WAY.
WOW. THAT'S A BIG PARTY.
WHY IS THE MUSIC SO LOUD?
THE SOUND GUY WENT DEAF FROM DOING THIS SO MUCH. HE'S THE BEST AT WHAT HE DOES, BUT HE HAS TO TURN THE VOLUME WAY UP TO DO HIS JOB.
THAT'S IDIOTIC.
SORRY. I COULDN'T HEAR YOU.

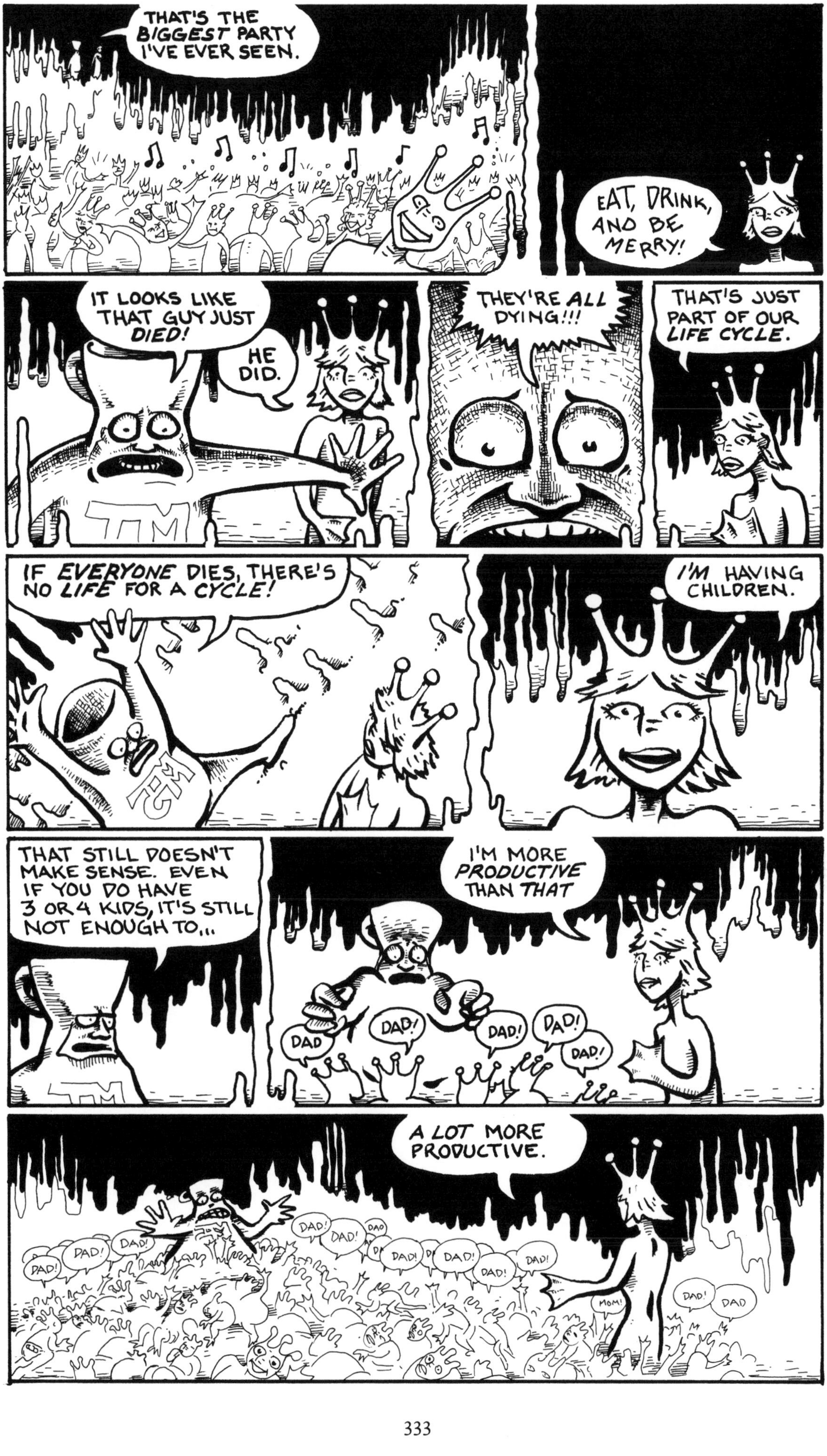

THAT'S THE BIGGEST PARTY I'VE EVER SEEN.
EAT, DRINK, AND BE MERRY!
IT LOOKS LIKE THAT GUY JUST DIED!
HE DID.
THEY'RE ALL DYING!!!
THAT'S JUST PART OF OUR LIFE CYCLE.
IF EVERYONE DIES, THERE'S NO LIFE FOR A CYCLE!
I'M HAVING CHILDREN.
THAT STILL DOESN'T MAKE SENSE. EVEN IF YOU DO HAVE 3 OR 4 KIDS, IT'S STILL NOT ENOUGH TO...
I'M MORE PRODUCTIVE THAN THAT
DAD
DAD!
DAD!
DAD!
DAD!
A LOT MORE PRODUCTIVE.
DAD!
DAD!
DAD!
DAD!
DAD!
DAD!
DAD!
DAD!
DAD!
MOM!
DAD!
DAD

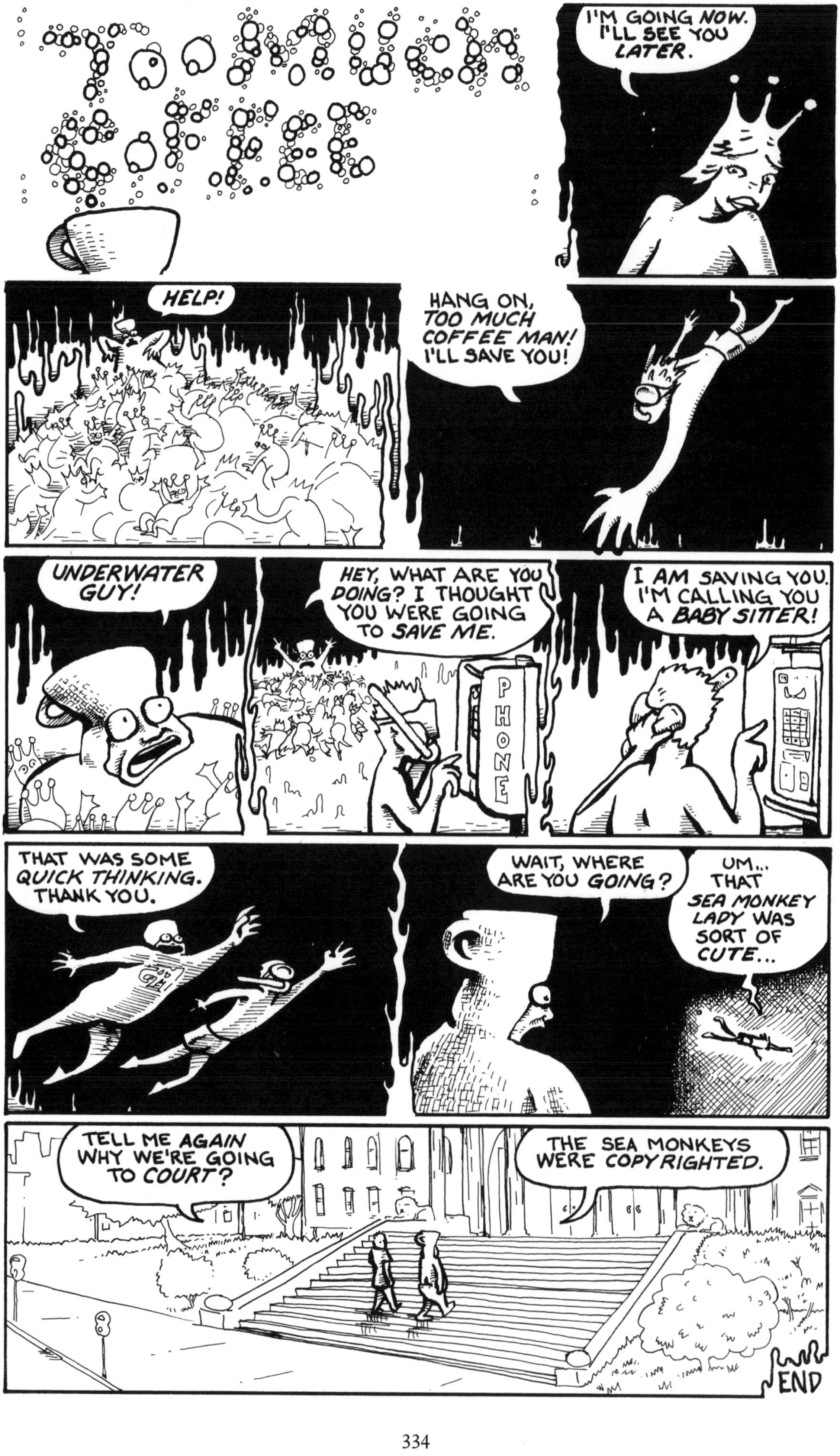
TOO MUCH COFFEE
I'M GOING NOW. I'LL SEE YOU LATER.
HELP!
HANG ON, TOO MUCH COFFEE MAN! I'LL SAVE YOU!
UNDERWATER GUY!
HEY, WHAT ARE YOU DOING? I THOUGHT YOU WERE GOING TO SAVE ME.
PHONE
I AM SAVING YOU. I'M CALLING YOU A BABY SITTER!
THAT WAS SOME QUICK THINKING. THANK YOU.
WAIT, WHERE ARE YOU GOING?
UM... THAT SEA MONKEY LADY WAS SORT OF CUTE...
TELL ME AGAIN WHY WE'RE GOING TO COURT?
THE SEA MONKEYS WERE COPYRIGHTED.
END

chapter 4

THE McDONALD'S
COFFEE LAWSUIT

*Misinformation in the information age
and other theories of conspiracy*

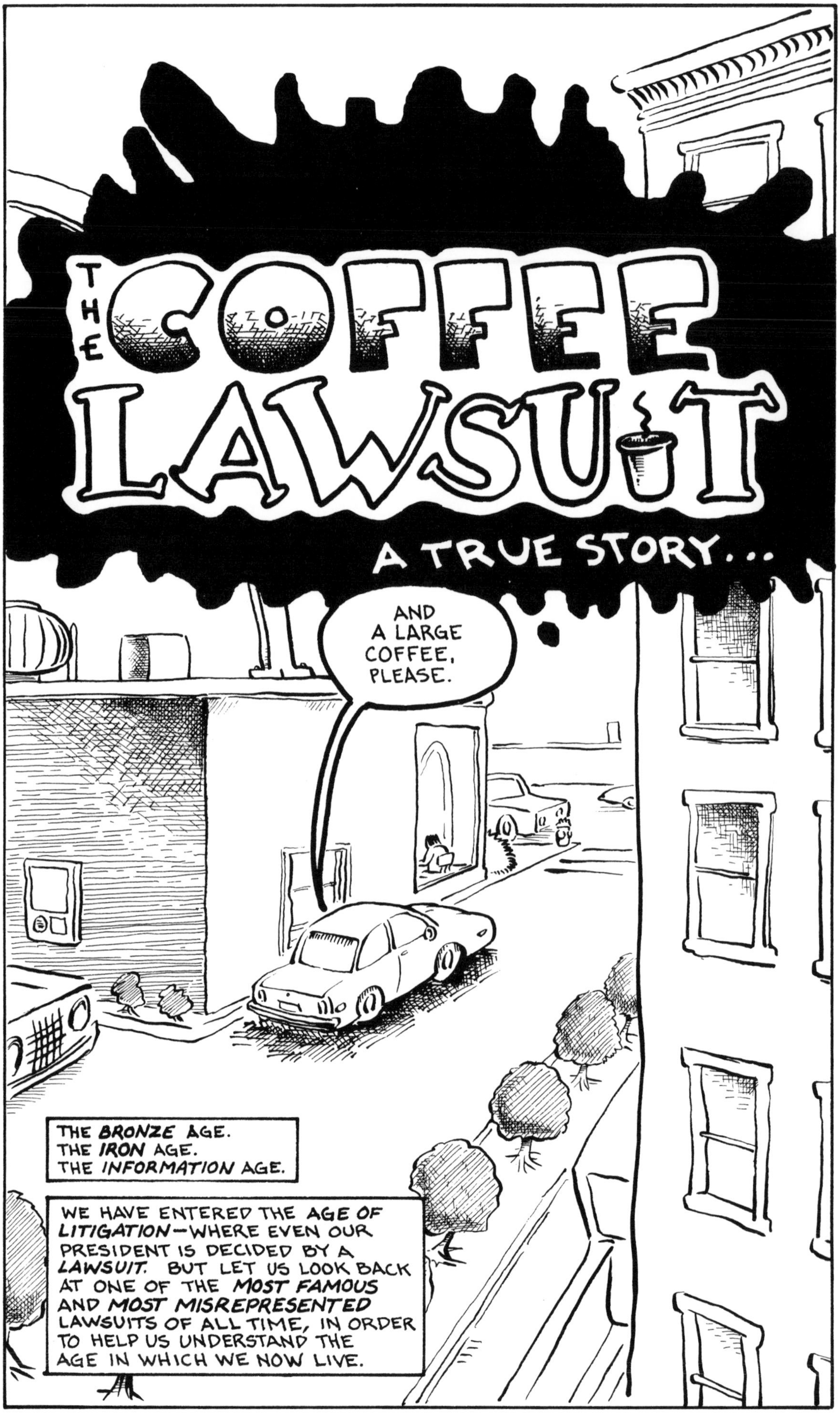
THE COFFEE LAWSUIT
A TRUE STORY...
AND A LARGE COFFEE, PLEASE.
THE BRONZE AGE.
THE IRON AGE.
THE INFORMATION AGE.
WE HAVE ENTERED THE AGE OF LITIGATION—WHERE EVEN OUR PRESIDENT IS DECIDED BY A LAWSUIT. BUT LET US LOOK BACK AT ONE OF THE MOST FAMOUS AND MOST MISREPRESENTED LAWSUITS OF ALL TIME, IN ORDER TO HELP US UNDERSTAND THE AGE IN WHICH WE NOW LIVE.

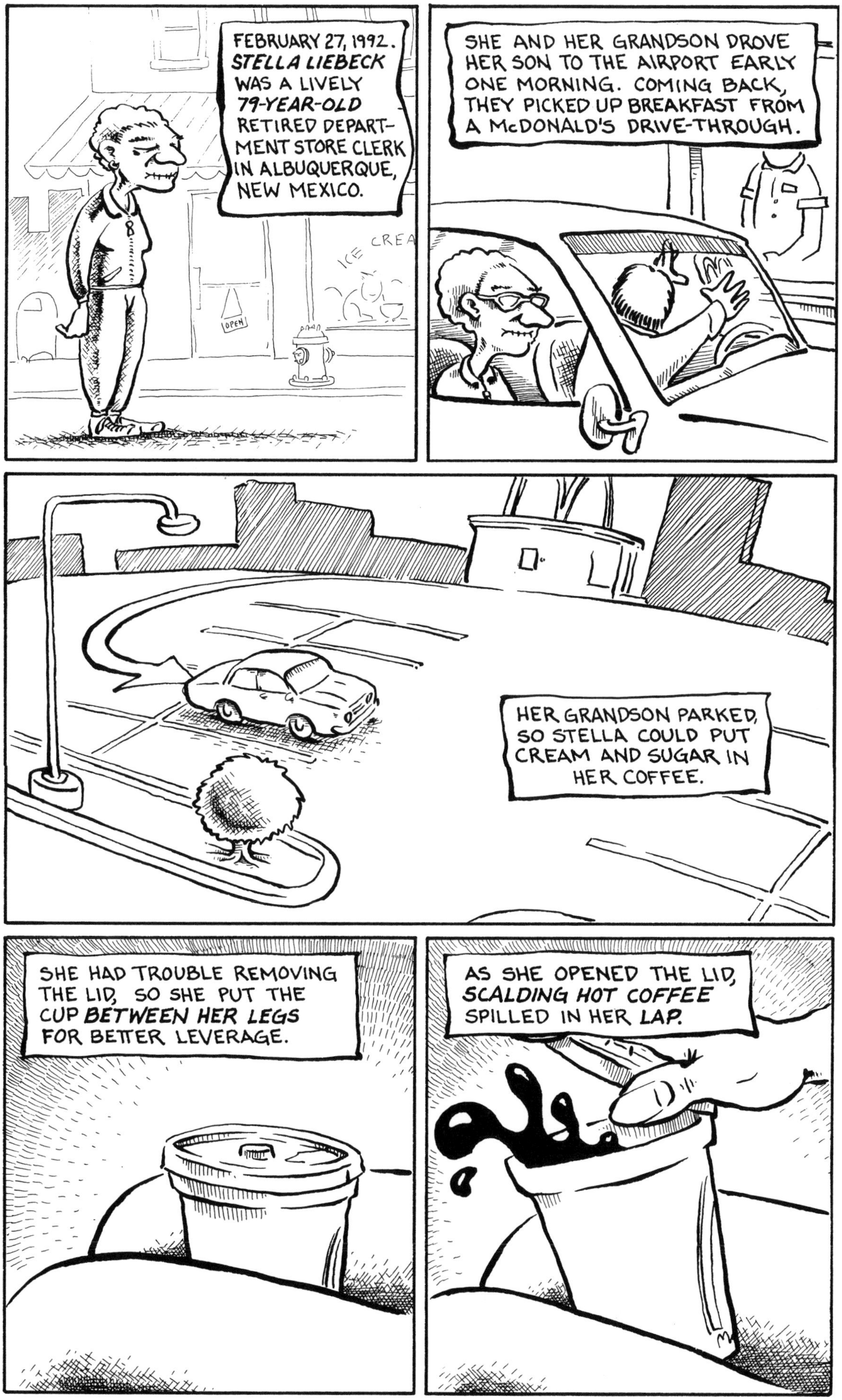
FEBRUARY 27, 1992. STELLA LIEBECK WAS A LIVELY 79-YEAR-OLD RETIRED DEPARTMENT STORE CLERK IN ALBUQUERQUE, NEW MEXICO.
ICE CREA
OPEN
SHE AND HER GRANDSON DROVE HER SON TO THE AIRPORT EARLY ONE MORNING. COMING BACK, THEY PICKED UP BREAKFAST FROM A McDONALD'S DRIVE-THROUGH.
HER GRANDSON PARKED, SO STELLA COULD PUT CREAM AND SUGAR IN HER COFFEE.
SHE HAD TROUBLE REMOVING THE LID, SO SHE PUT THE CUP BETWEEN HER LEGS FOR BETTER LEVERAGE.
AS SHE OPENED THE LID, SCALDING HOT COFFEE SPILLED IN HER LAP.

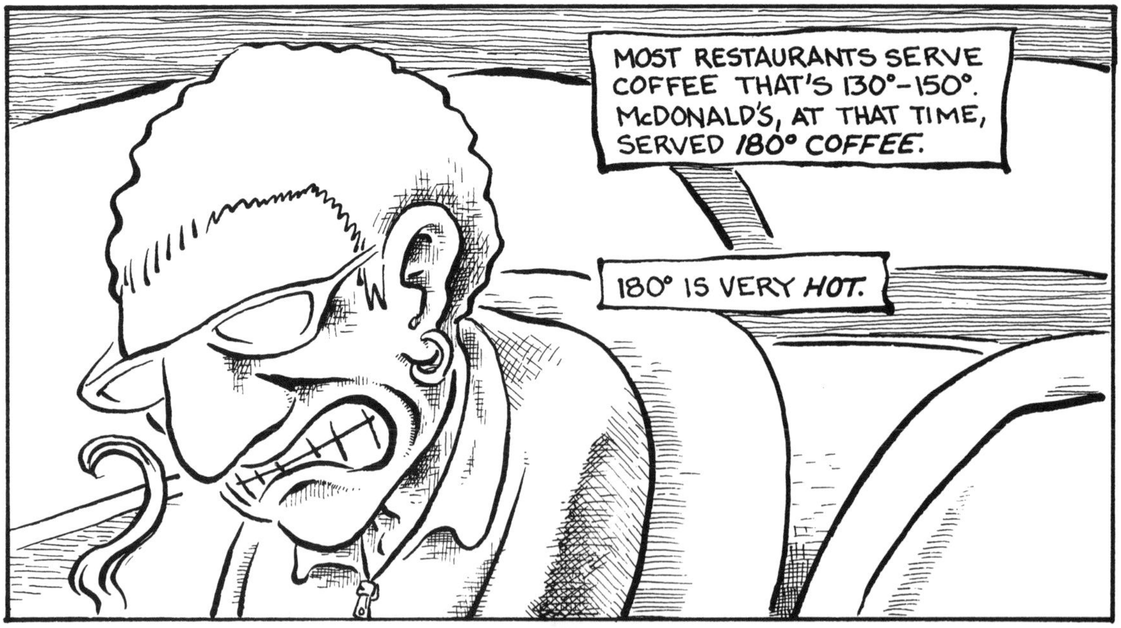
MOST RESTAURANTS SERVE COFFEE THAT'S 130°-150°. McDONALD'S, AT THAT TIME, SERVED 180° COFFEE.
180° IS VERY HOT.

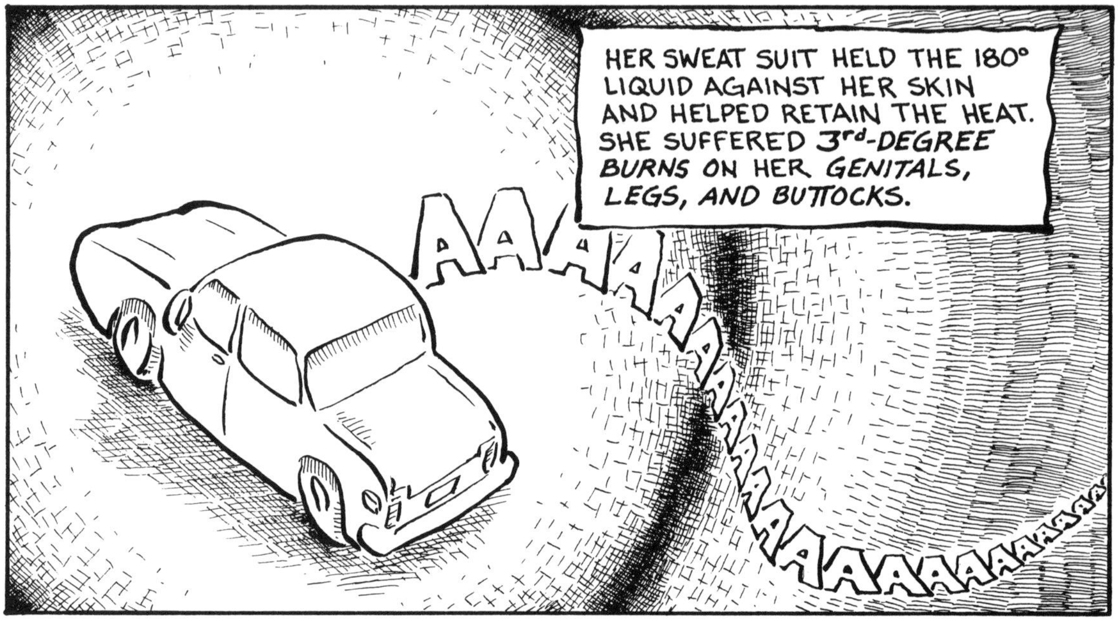
HER SWEAT SUIT HELD THE 180° LIQUID AGAINST HER SKIN AND HELPED RETAIN THE HEAT. SHE SUFFERED 3rd-DEGREE BURNS ON HER GENITALS, LEGS, AND BUTTOCKS.
AAAAAAAAAAAAAAAAAAAAAAAAAAA

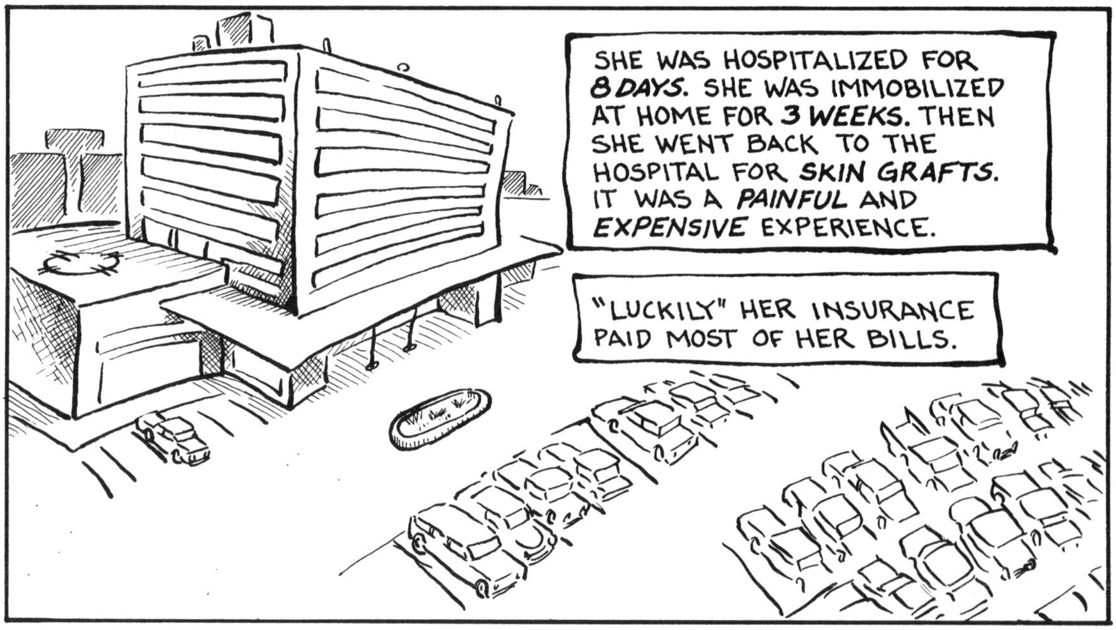
SHE WAS HOSPITALIZED FOR 8 DAYS. SHE WAS IMMOBILIZED AT HOME FOR 3 WEEKS. THEN SHE WENT BACK TO THE HOSPITAL FOR SKIN GRAFTS. IT WAS A PAINFUL AND EXPENSIVE EXPERIENCE.
"LUCKILY" HER INSURANCE PAID MOST OF HER BILLS.

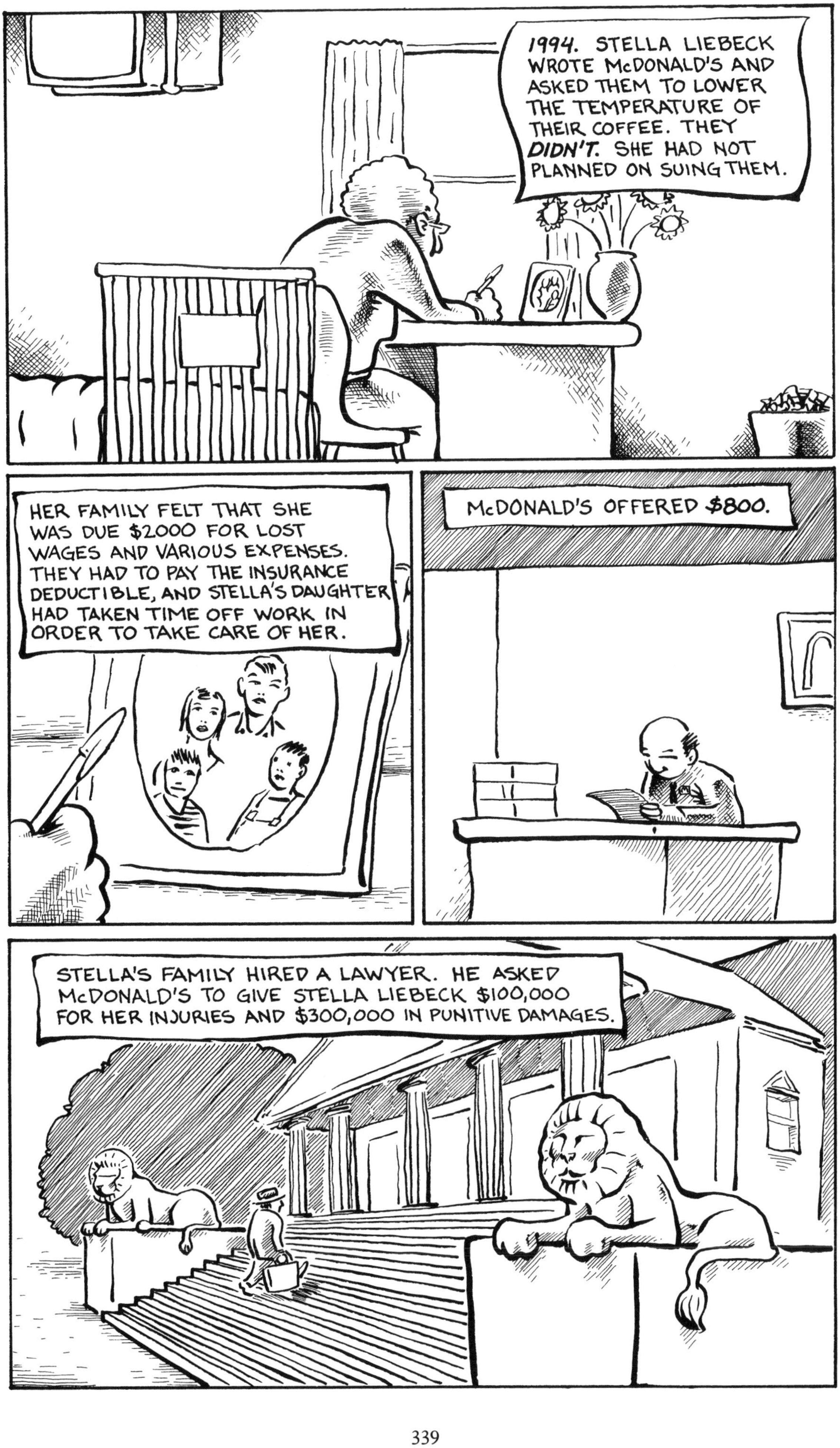
1994. STELLA LIEBECK WROTE McDONALD'S AND ASKED THEM TO LOWER THE TEMPERATURE OF THEIR COFFEE. THEY *DIDN'T.* SHE HAD NOT PLANNED ON SUING THEM.
HER FAMILY FELT THAT SHE WAS DUE $2000 FOR LOST WAGES AND VARIOUS EXPENSES. THEY HAD TO PAY THE INSURANCE DEDUCTIBLE, AND STELLA'S DAUGHTER HAD TAKEN TIME OFF WORK IN ORDER TO TAKE CARE OF HER.
McDONALD'S OFFERED **$800.**
STELLA'S FAMILY HIRED A LAWYER. HE ASKED McDONALD'S TO GIVE STELLA LIEBECK $100,000 FOR HER INJURIES AND $300,000 IN PUNITIVE DAMAGES.

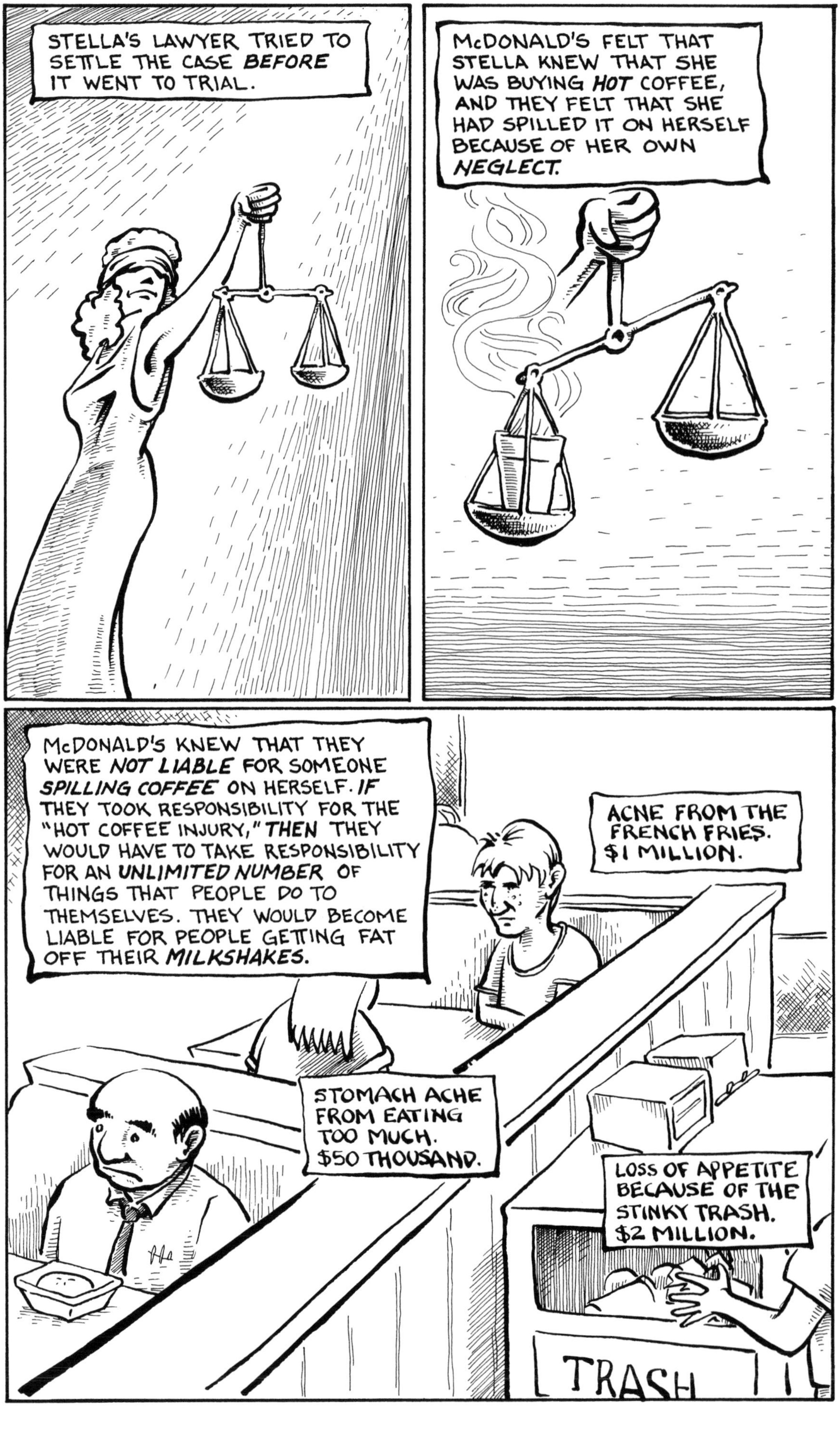
STELLA'S LAWYER TRIED TO SETTLE THE CASE BEFORE IT WENT TO TRIAL.
McDONALD'S FELT THAT STELLA KNEW THAT SHE WAS BUYING HOT COFFEE, AND THEY FELT THAT SHE HAD SPILLED IT ON HERSELF BECAUSE OF HER OWN NEGLECT.
McDONALD'S KNEW THAT THEY WERE NOT LIABLE FOR SOMEONE SPILLING COFFEE ON HERSELF. IF THEY TOOK RESPONSIBILITY FOR THE "HOT COFFEE INJURY," THEN THEY WOULD HAVE TO TAKE RESPONSIBILITY FOR AN UNLIMITED NUMBER OF THINGS THAT PEOPLE DO TO THEMSELVES. THEY WOULD BECOME LIABLE FOR PEOPLE GETTING FAT OFF THEIR MILKSHAKES.
ACNE FROM THE FRENCH FRIES. $1 MILLION.
STOMACH ACHE FROM EATING TOO MUCH. $50 THOUSAND.
LOSS OF APPETITE BECAUSE OF THE STINKY TRASH. $2 MILLION.
TRASH

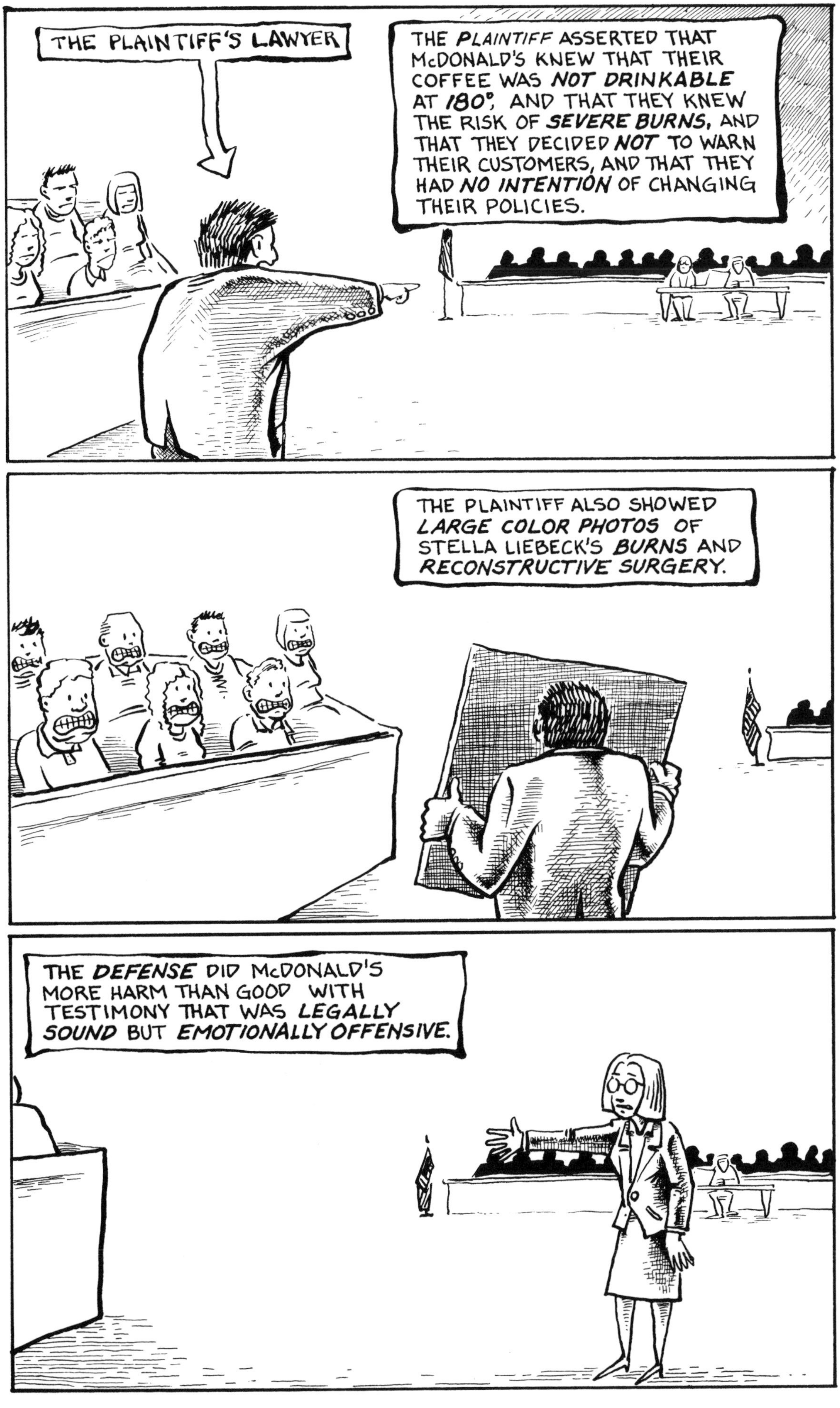
THE PLAINTIFF'S LAWYER
THE PLAINTIFF ASSERTED THAT McDONALD'S KNEW THAT THEIR COFFEE WAS NOT DRINKABLE AT 180°, AND THAT THEY KNEW THE RISK OF SEVERE BURNS, AND THAT THEY DECIDED NOT TO WARN THEIR CUSTOMERS, AND THAT THEY HAD NO INTENTION OF CHANGING THEIR POLICIES.
THE PLAINTIFF ALSO SHOWED LARGE COLOR PHOTOS OF STELLA LIEBECK'S BURNS AND RECONSTRUCTIVE SURGERY.
THE DEFENSE DID McDONALD'S MORE HARM THAN GOOD WITH TESTIMONY THAT WAS LEGALLY SOUND BUT EMOTIONALLY OFFENSIVE.

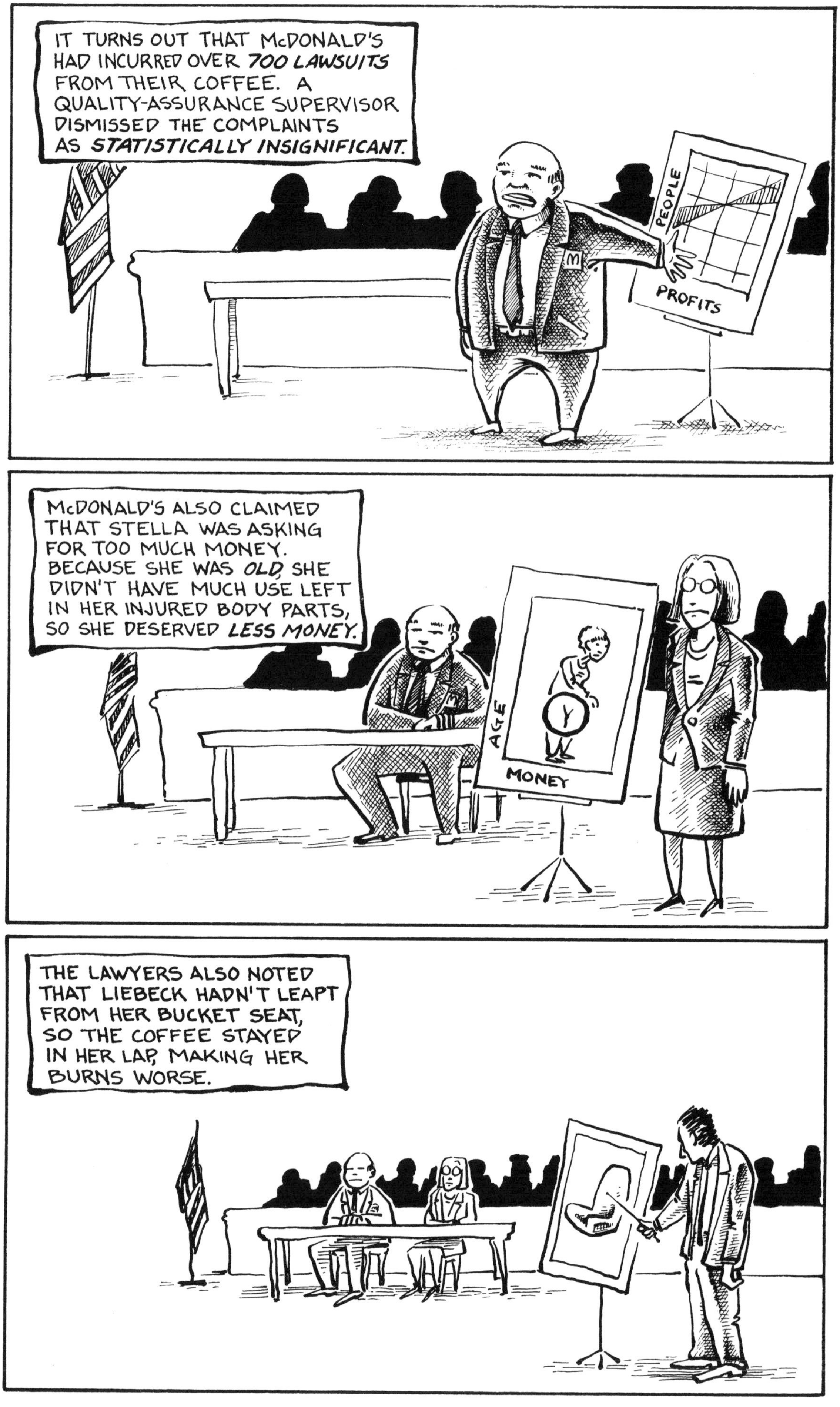
IT TURNS OUT THAT McDONALD'S HAD INCURRED OVER 700 LAWSUITS FROM THEIR COFFEE. A QUALITY-ASSURANCE SUPERVISOR DISMISSED THE COMPLAINTS AS STATISTICALLY INSIGNIFICANT.
PEOPLE
PROFITS
M
McDONALD'S ALSO CLAIMED THAT STELLA WAS ASKING FOR TOO MUCH MONEY. BECAUSE SHE WAS OLD, SHE DIDN'T HAVE MUCH USE LEFT IN HER INJURED BODY PARTS, SO SHE DESERVED LESS MONEY.
AGE
MONEY
THE LAWYERS ALSO NOTED THAT LIEBECK HADN'T LEAPT FROM HER BUCKET SEAT, SO THE COFFEE STAYED IN HER LAP, MAKING HER BURNS WORSE.

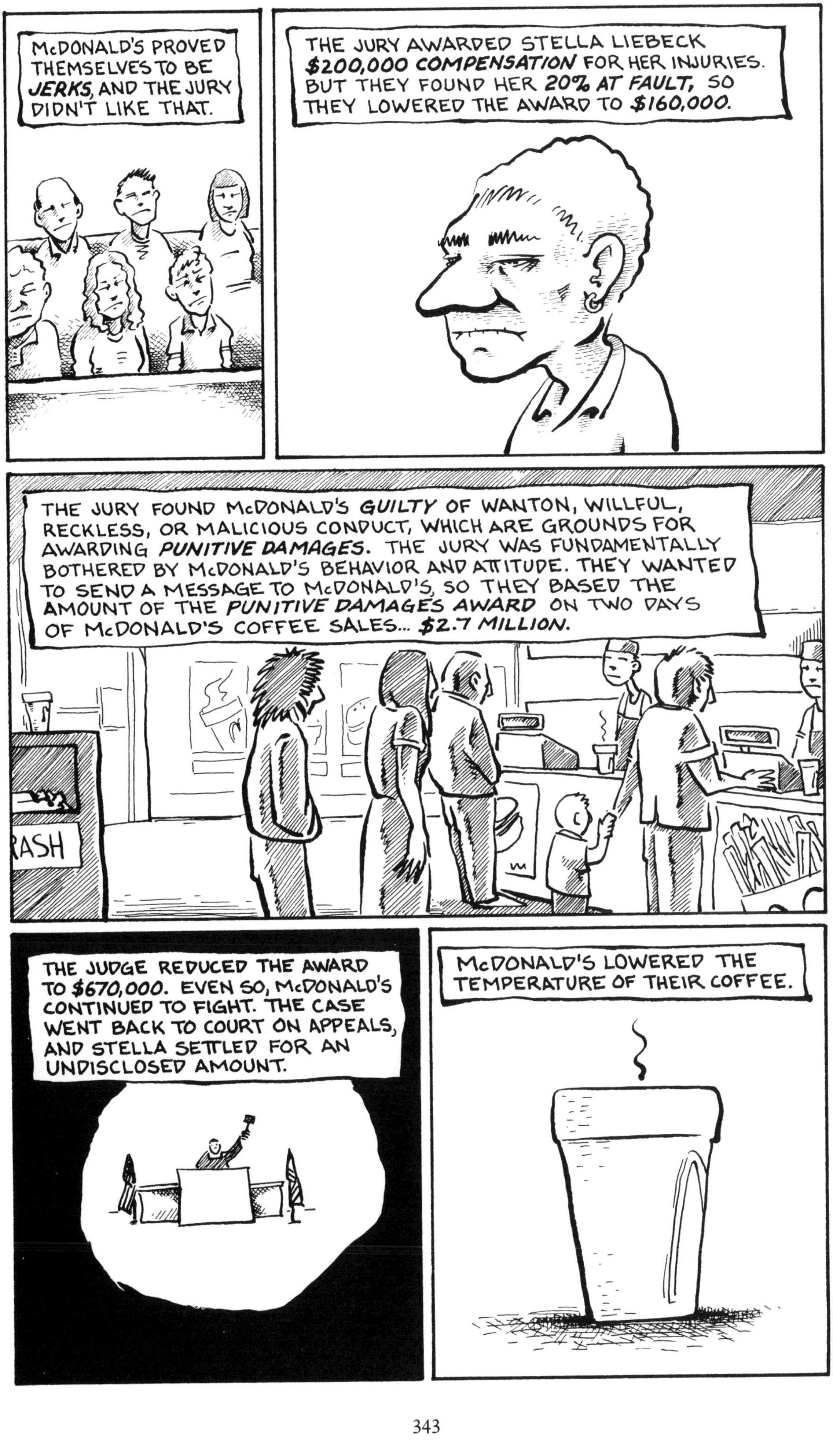
McDONALD'S PROVED THEMSELVES TO BE JERKS, AND THE JURY DIDN'T LIKE THAT.
THE JURY AWARDED STELLA LIEBECK $200,000 COMPENSATION FOR HER INJURIES. BUT THEY FOUND HER 20% AT FAULT, SO THEY LOWERED THE AWARD TO $160,000.
THE JURY FOUND McDONALD'S GUILTY OF WANTON, WILLFUL, RECKLESS, OR MALICIOUS CONDUCT, WHICH ARE GROUNDS FOR AWARDING PUNITIVE DAMAGES. THE JURY WAS FUNDAMENTALLY BOTHERED BY McDONALD'S BEHAVIOR AND ATTITUDE. THEY WANTED TO SEND A MESSAGE TO McDONALD'S, SO THEY BASED THE AMOUNT OF THE PUNITIVE DAMAGES AWARD ON TWO DAYS OF McDONALD'S COFFEE SALES... $2.7 MILLION.
RASH
THE JUDGE REDUCED THE AWARD TO $670,000. EVEN SO, McDONALD'S CONTINUED TO FIGHT. THE CASE WENT BACK TO COURT ON APPEALS, AND STELLA SETTLED FOR AN UNDISCLOSED AMOUNT.
McDONALD'S LOWERED THE TEMPERATURE OF THEIR COFFEE.

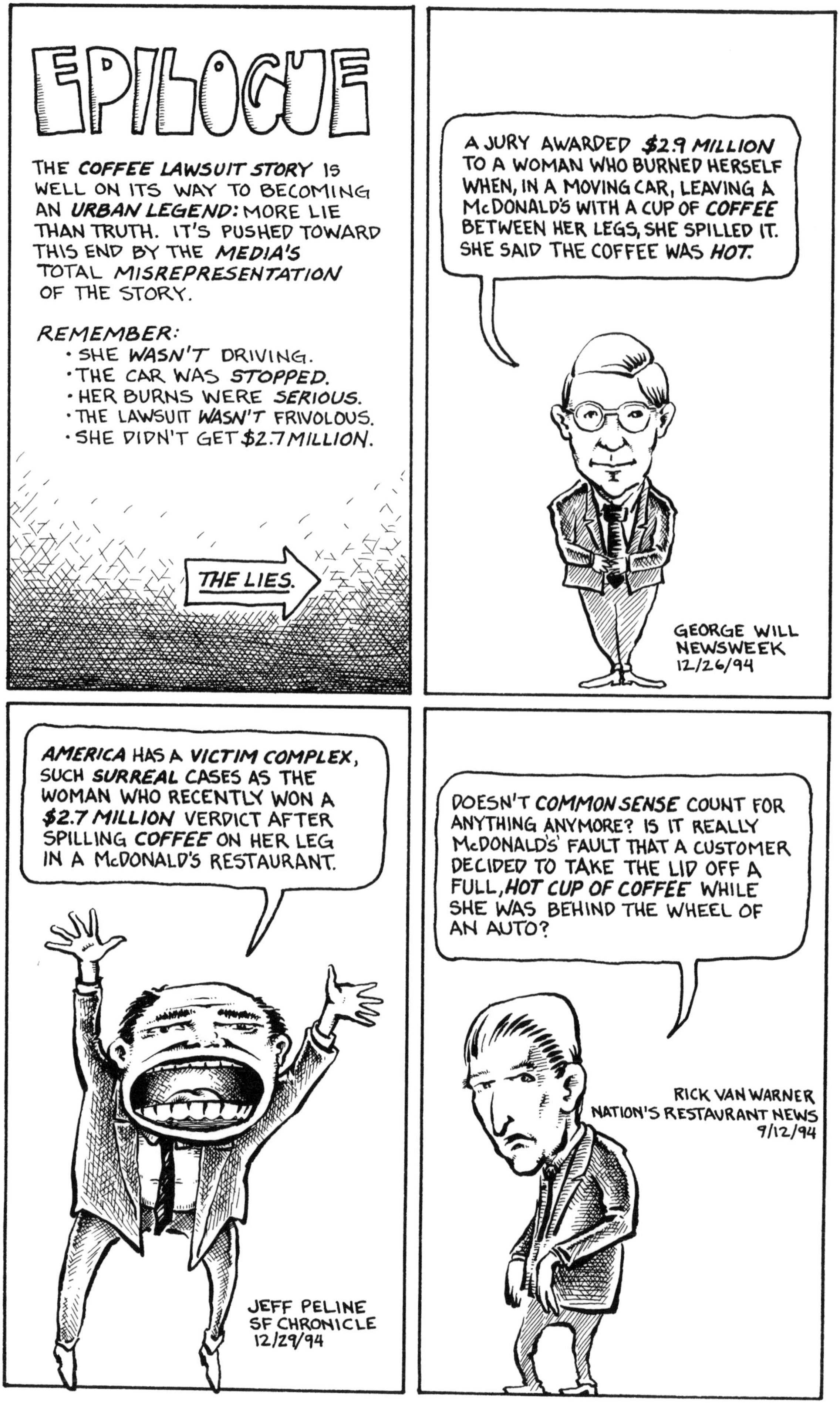
EPILOGUE
THE COFFEE LAWSUIT STORY IS WELL ON ITS WAY TO BECOMING AN URBAN LEGEND: MORE LIE THAN TRUTH. IT'S PUSHED TOWARD THIS END BY THE MEDIA'S TOTAL MISREPRESENTATION OF THE STORY.
REMEMBER:
• SHE WASN'T DRIVING.
• THE CAR WAS STOPPED.
• HER BURNS WERE SERIOUS.
• THE LAWSUIT WASN'T FRIVOLOUS.
• SHE DIDN'T GET $2.7 MILLION.
THE LIES.
A JURY AWARDED $2.9 MILLION TO A WOMAN WHO BURNED HERSELF WHEN, IN A MOVING CAR, LEAVING A McDONALD'S WITH A CUP OF COFFEE BETWEEN HER LEGS, SHE SPILLED IT. SHE SAID THE COFFEE WAS HOT.
GEORGE WILL NEWSWEEK 12/26/94
AMERICA HAS A VICTIM COMPLEX, SUCH SURREAL CASES AS THE WOMAN WHO RECENTLY WON A $2.7 MILLION VERDICT AFTER SPILLING COFFEE ON HER LEG IN A McDONALD'S RESTAURANT.
JEFF PELINE SF CHRONICLE 12/29/94
DOESN'T COMMON SENSE COUNT FOR ANYTHING ANYMORE? IS IT REALLY McDONALD'S' FAULT THAT A CUSTOMER DECIDED TO TAKE THE LID OFF A FULL, HOT CUP OF COFFEE WHILE SHE WAS BEHIND THE WHEEL OF AN AUTO?
RICK VAN WARNER NATION'S RESTAURANT NEWS 9/12/94

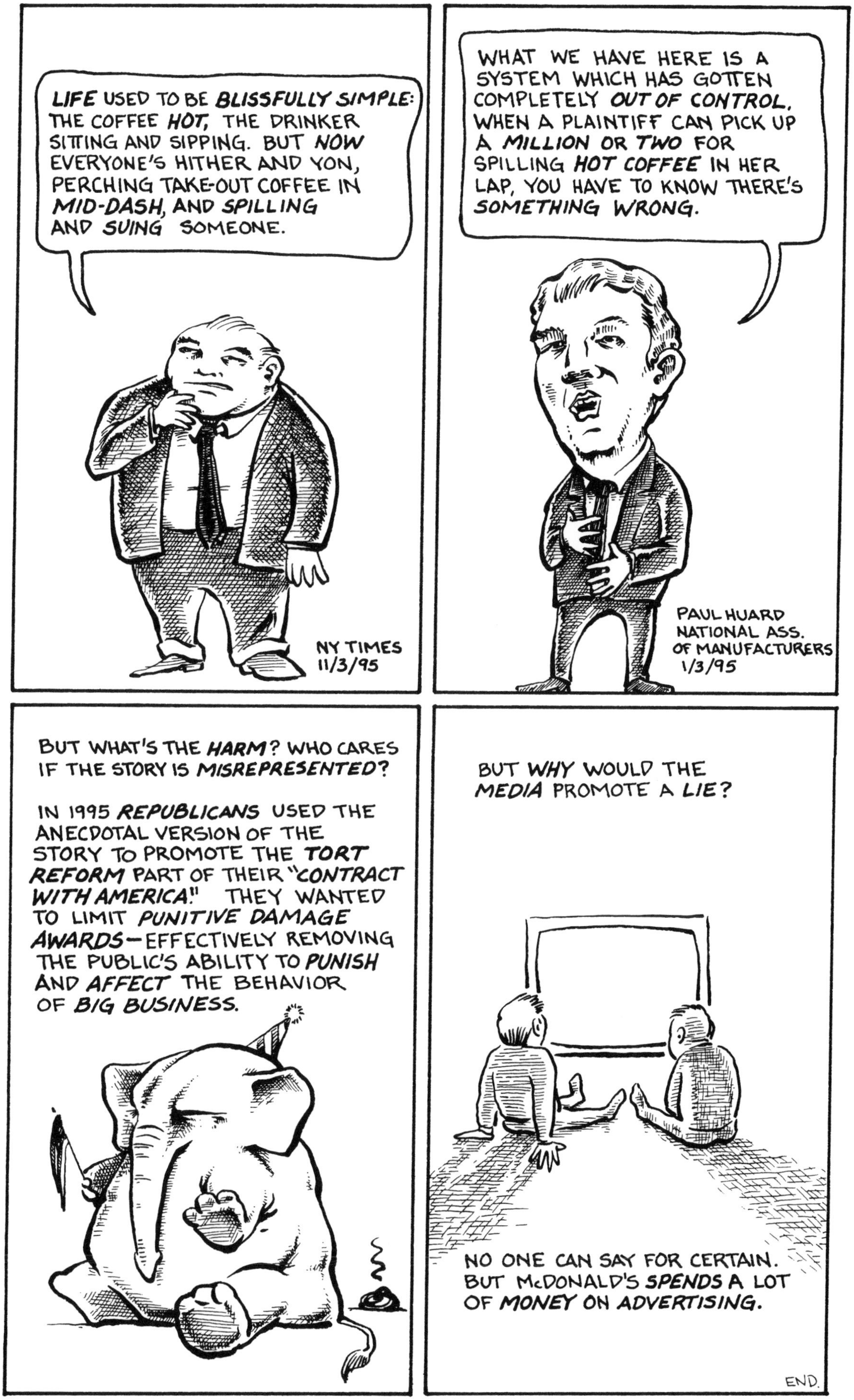
LIFE USED TO BE BLISSFULLY SIMPLE: THE COFFEE HOT, THE DRINKER SITTING AND SIPPING. BUT NOW EVERYONE'S HITHER AND YON, PERCHING TAKE-OUT COFFEE IN MID-DASH, AND SPILLING AND SUING SOMEONE.
NY TIMES 11/3/95
WHAT WE HAVE HERE IS A SYSTEM WHICH HAS GOTTEN COMPLETELY OUT OF CONTROL. WHEN A PLAINTIFF CAN PICK UP A MILLION OR TWO FOR SPILLING HOT COFFEE IN HER LAP, YOU HAVE TO KNOW THERE'S SOMETHING WRONG.
PAUL HUARD NATIONAL ASS. OF MANUFACTURERS 1/3/95
BUT WHAT'S THE HARM? WHO CARES IF THE STORY IS MISREPRESENTED?
IN 1995 REPUBLICANS USED THE ANECDOTAL VERSION OF THE STORY TO PROMOTE THE TORT REFORM PART OF THEIR "CONTRACT WITH AMERICA." THEY WANTED TO LIMIT PUNITIVE DAMAGE AWARDS—EFFECTIVELY REMOVING THE PUBLIC'S ABILITY TO PUNISH AND AFFECT THE BEHAVIOR OF BIG BUSINESS.
BUT WHY WOULD THE MEDIA PROMOTE A LIE?
NO ONE CAN SAY FOR CERTAIN. BUT McDONALD'S SPENDS A LOT OF MONEY ON ADVERTISING.
END.

chapter 5

COFFEE AND THE HUMOR OF ADDICTION

Just because everyone else is crazy, it doesn't mean that you are sane, and other inklings

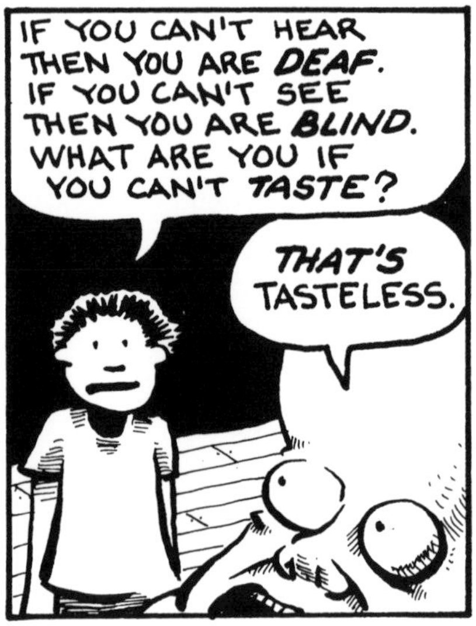
IF YOU CAN'T HEAR THEN YOU ARE DEAF. IF YOU CAN'T SEE THEN YOU ARE BLIND. WHAT ARE YOU IF YOU CAN'T TASTE?
THAT'S TASTELESS.

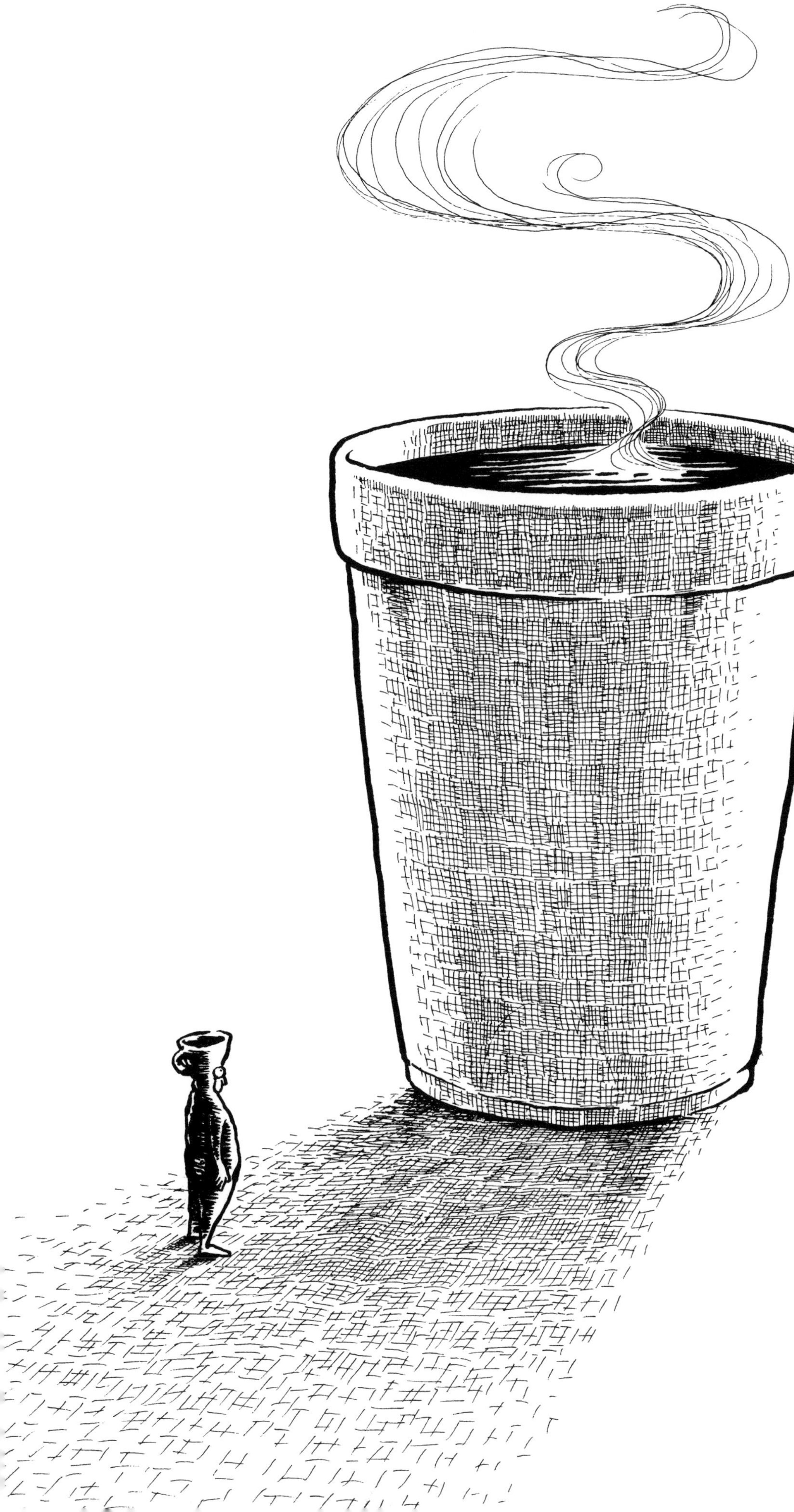

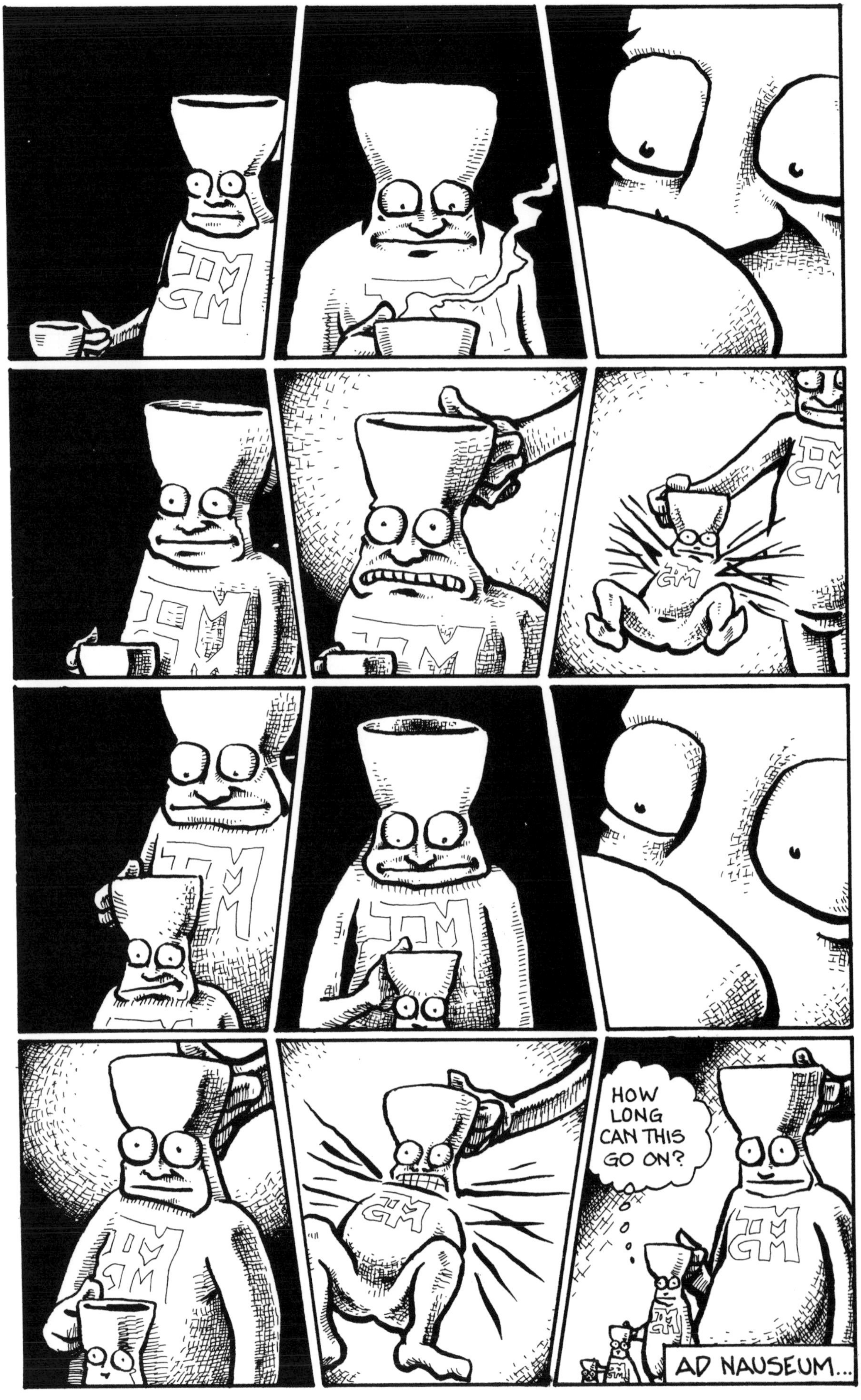
HOW LONG CAN THIS GO ON?
AD NAUSEUM...

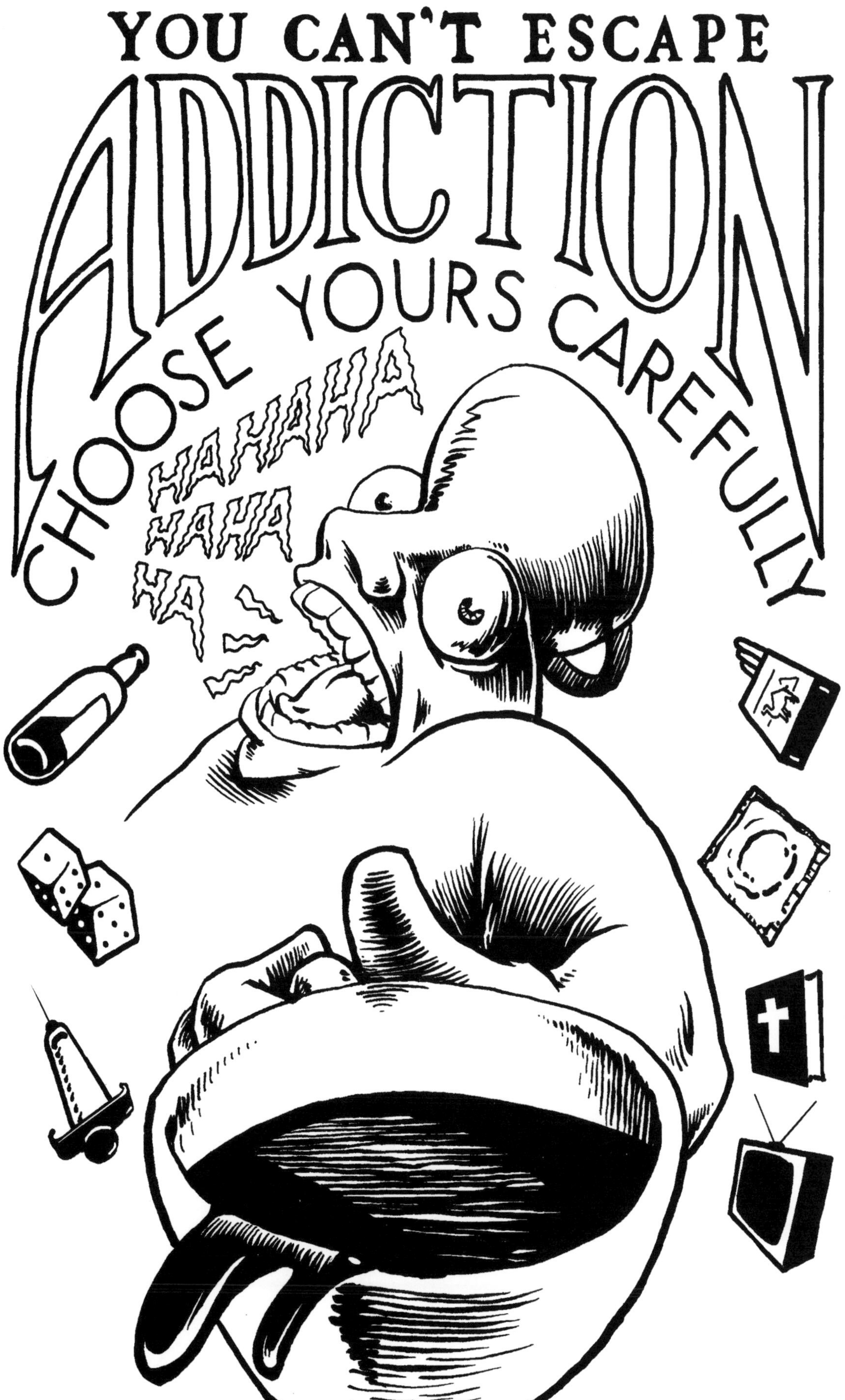
YOU CAN'T ESCAPE
ADDICTION
CHOOSE YOURS CAREFULLY
HAHAHA
HAHA
HA

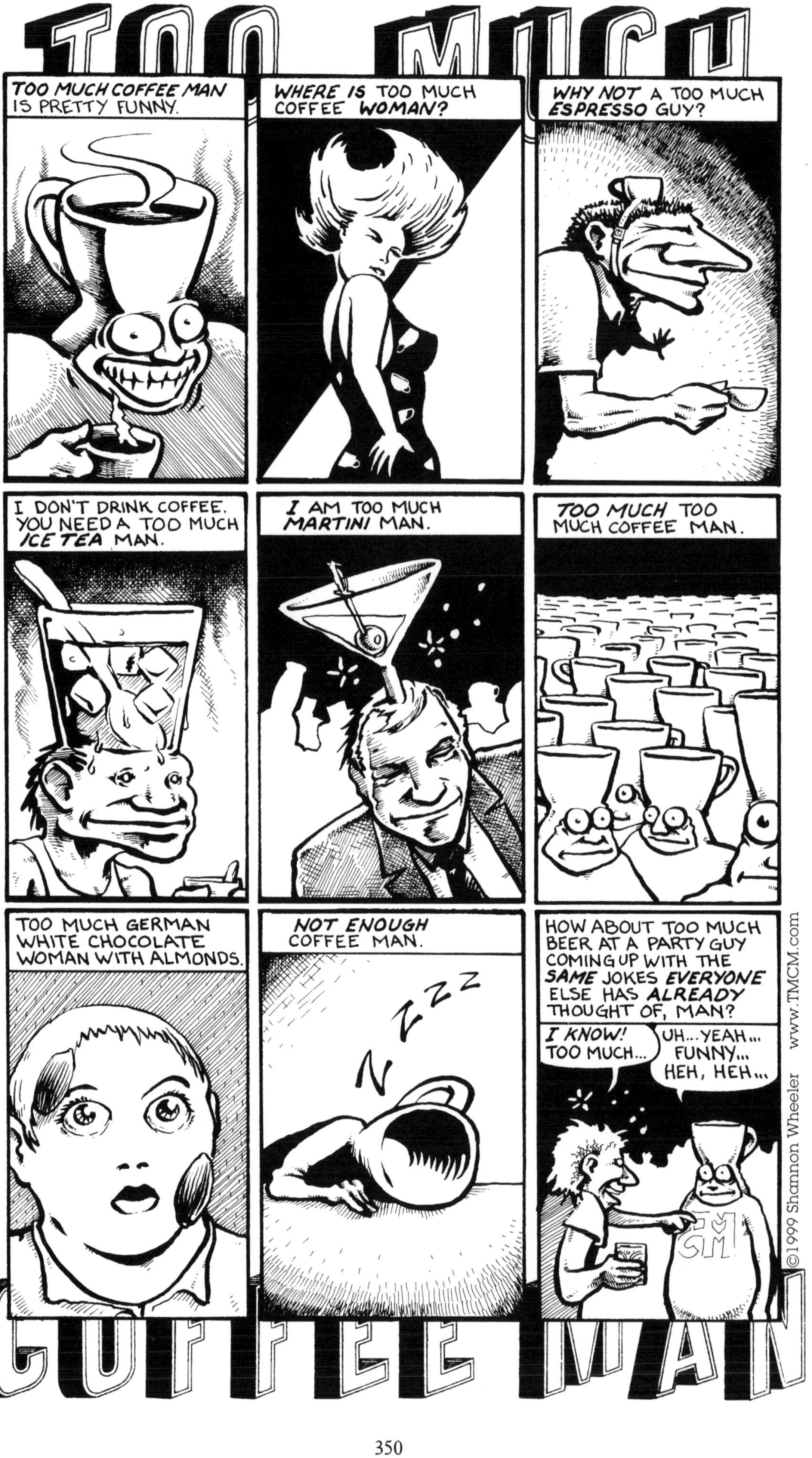
TOO MUCH COFFEE MAN
TOO MUCH COFFEE MAN IS PRETTY FUNNY.
WHERE IS TOO MUCH COFFEE WOMAN?
WHY NOT A TOO MUCH ESPRESSO GUY?
I DON'T DRINK COFFEE. YOU NEED A TOO MUCH ICE TEA MAN.
I AM TOO MUCH MARTINI MAN.
TOO MUCH TOO MUCH COFFEE MAN.
TOO MUCH GERMAN WHITE CHOCOLATE WOMAN WITH ALMONDS.
NOT ENOUGH COFFEE MAN.
N ZZZ
HOW ABOUT TOO MUCH BEER AT A PARTY GUY COMING UP WITH THE SAME JOKES EVERYONE ELSE HAS ALREADY THOUGHT OF, MAN?
I KNOW! TOO MUCH...
UH... YEAH... FUNNY... HEH, HEH...
TMCM
©1999 Shannon Wheeler www.TMCM.com

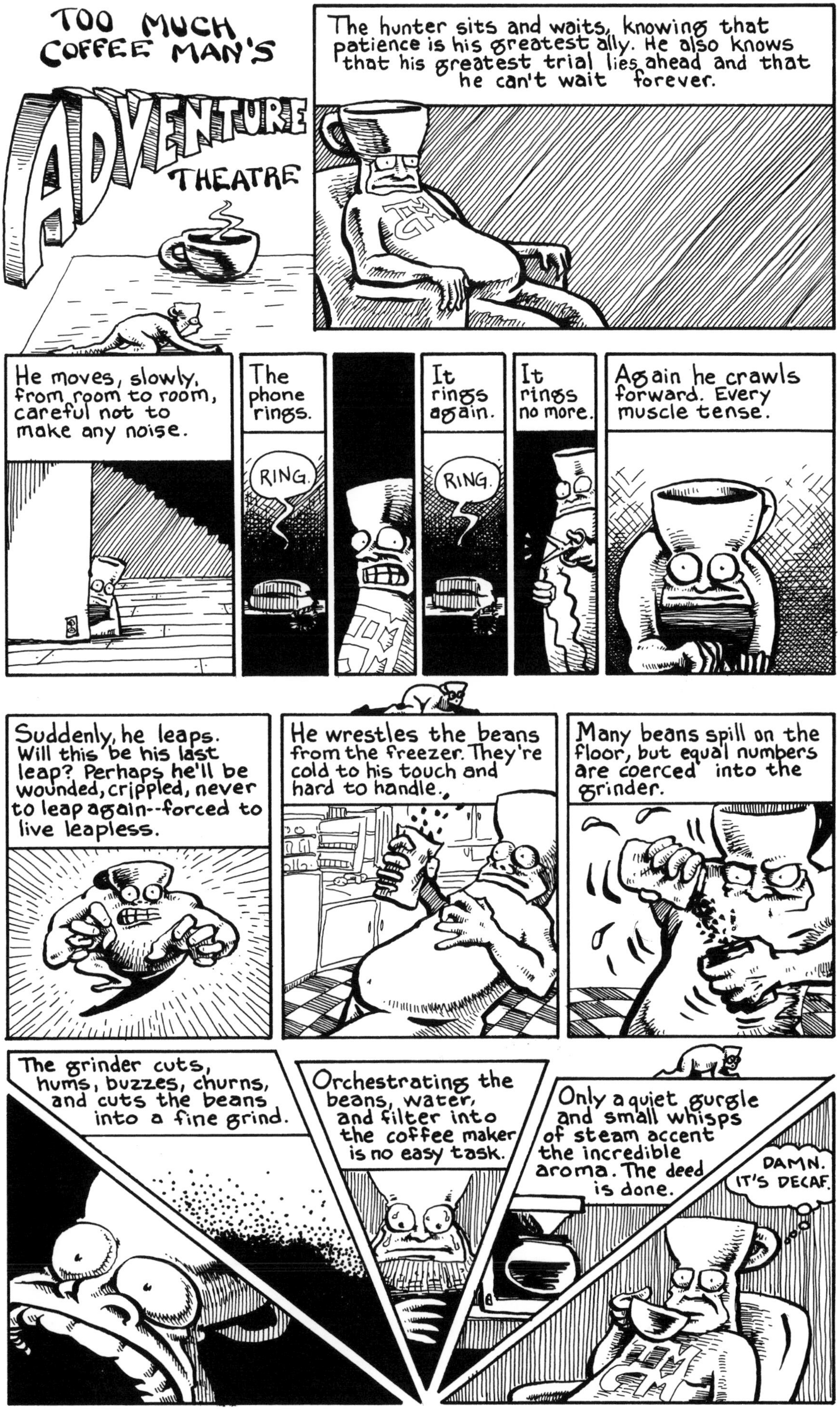
TOO MUCH COFFEE MAN'S
ADVENTURE THEATRE
The hunter sits and waits, knowing that patience is his greatest ally. He also knows that his greatest trial lies ahead and that he can't wait forever.
He moves, slowly, from room to room, careful not to make any noise.
The phone rings.
RING.
It rings again.
RING.
It rings no more.
Again he crawls forward. Every muscle tense.
Suddenly, he leaps. Will this be his last leap? Perhaps he'll be wounded, crippled, never to leap again--forced to live leapless.
He wrestles the beans from the freezer. They're cold to his touch and hard to handle.
Many beans spill on the floor, but equal numbers are coerced into the grinder.
The grinder cuts, hums, buzzes, churns, and cuts the beans into a fine grind.
Orchestrating the beans, water, and filter into the coffee maker is no easy task.
Only a quiet gurgle and small whisps of steam accent the incredible aroma. The deed is done.
DAMN. IT'S DECAF.

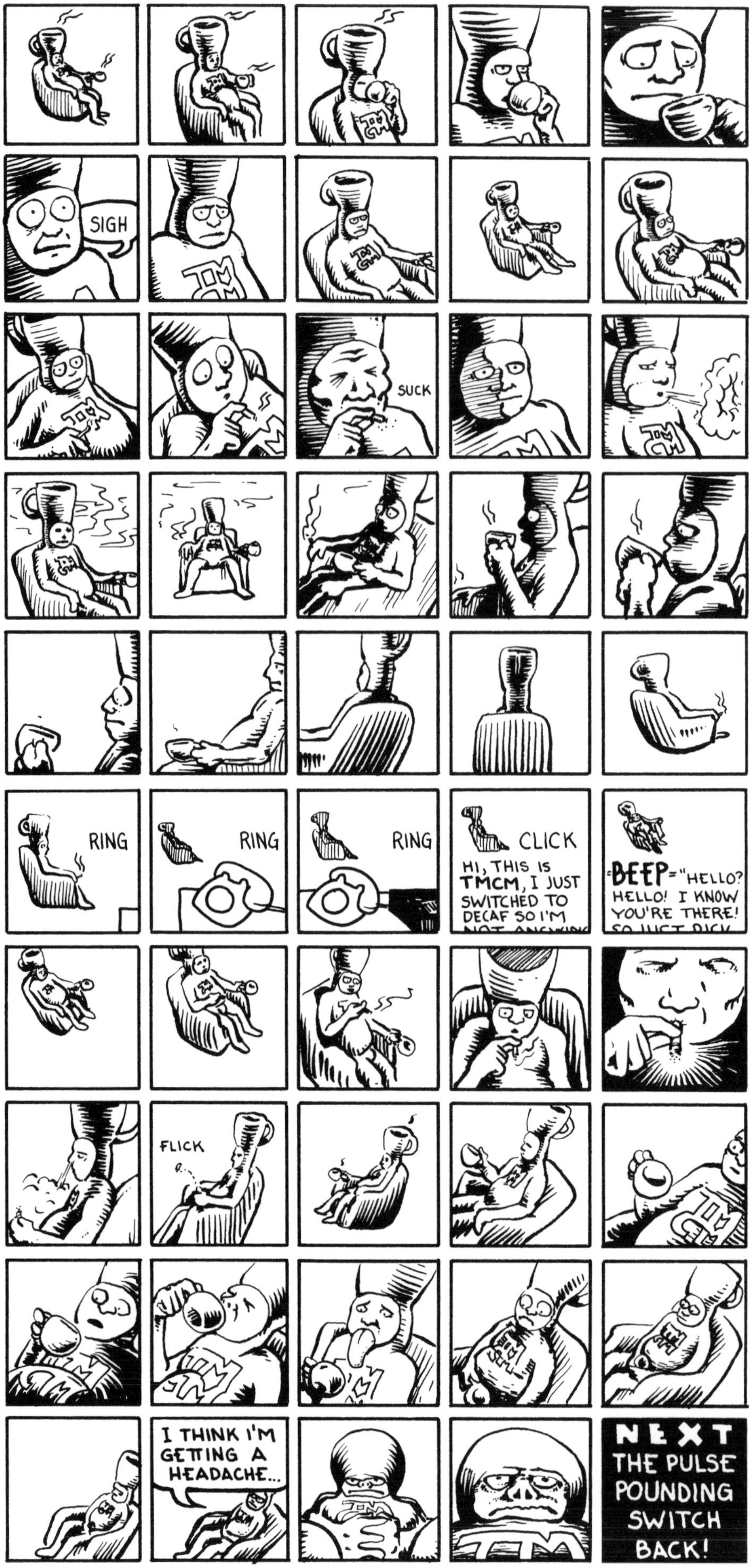
SIGH
SUCK
RING
RING
RING
CLICK
HI, THIS IS TMCM, I JUST SWITCHED TO DECAF SO I'M
BEEP = "HELLO? HELLO! I KNOW YOU'RE THERE!
FLICK
I THINK I'M GETTING A HEADACHE...
NEXT
THE PULSE POUNDING SWITCH BACK!

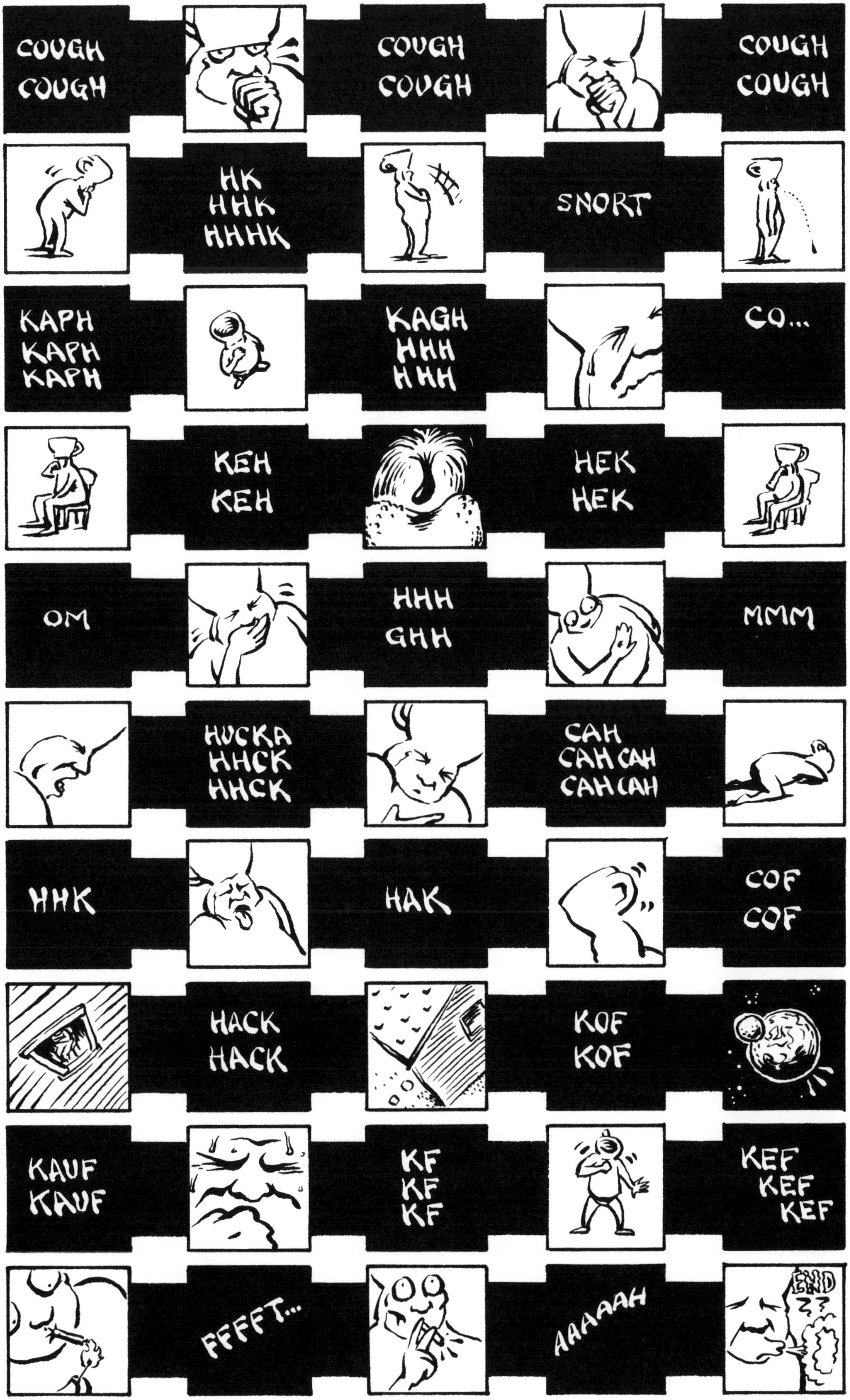
COUGH COUGH
COUGH COUGH
COUGH COUGH
HK HHK HHHK
SNORT
KAPH KAPH KAPH
KAGH HHH HHH
CO...
KEH KEH
HEK HEK
OM
HHH GHH
MMM
HUCKA HHCK HHCK
CAH CAH CAH CAH CAH
HHK
HAK
COF COF
HACK HACK
KOF KOF
KAUF KAUF
KF KF KF
KEF KEF KEF
FFFFT...
AAAAAH
END

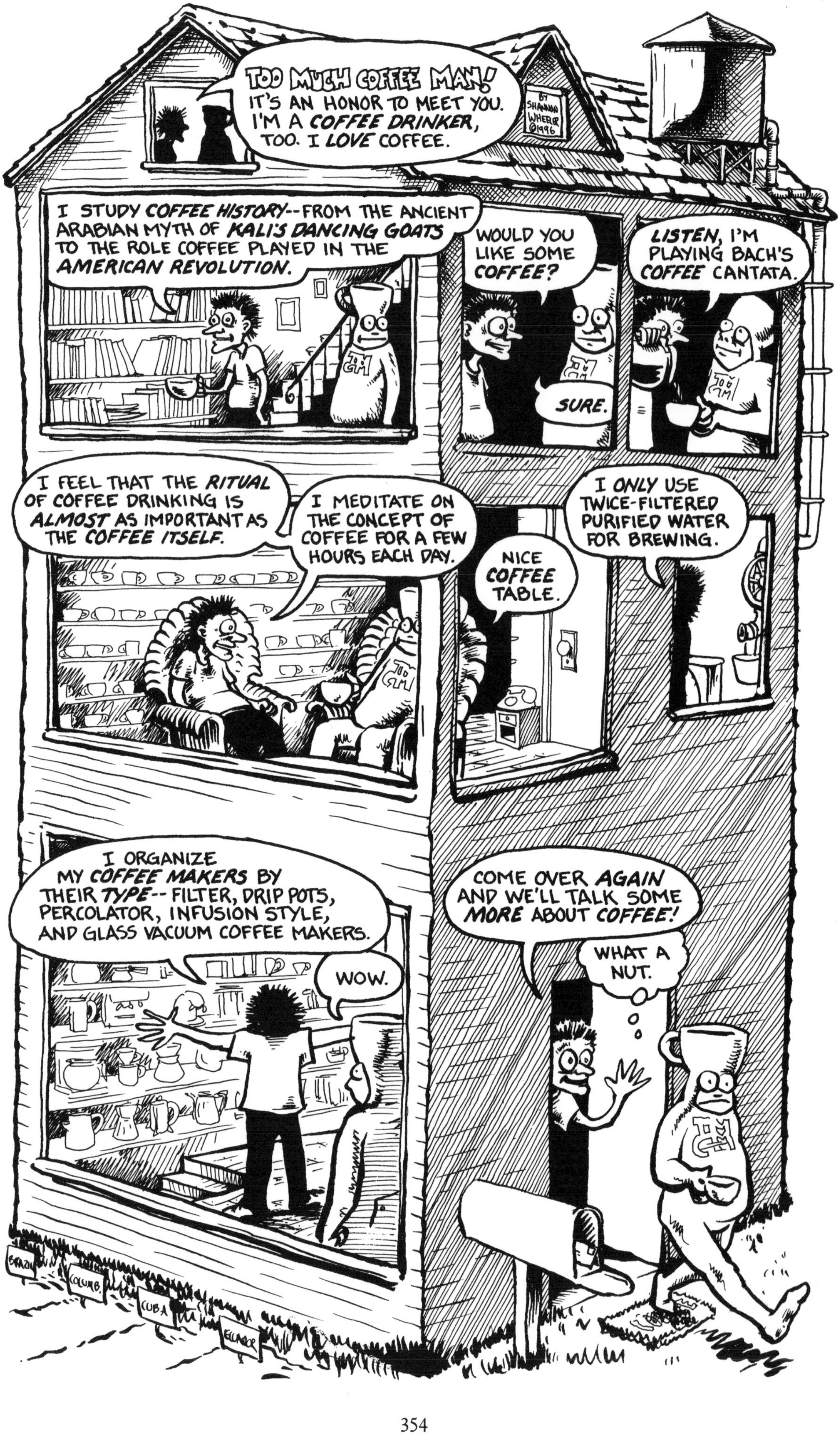
TOO MUCH COFFEE MAN! IT'S AN HONOR TO MEET YOU. I'M A COFFEE DRINKER, TOO. I LOVE COFFEE.
BY SHANNON WHEELER ©1996
I STUDY COFFEE HISTORY--FROM THE ANCIENT ARABIAN MYTH OF KALI'S DANCING GOATS TO THE ROLE COFFEE PLAYED IN THE AMERICAN REVOLUTION.
WOULD YOU LIKE SOME COFFEE?
SURE.
LISTEN, I'M PLAYING BACH'S COFFEE CANTATA.
I FEEL THAT THE RITUAL OF COFFEE DRINKING IS ALMOST AS IMPORTANT AS THE COFFEE ITSELF.
I MEDITATE ON THE CONCEPT OF COFFEE FOR A FEW HOURS EACH DAY.
NICE COFFEE TABLE.
I ONLY USE TWICE-FILTERED PURIFIED WATER FOR BREWING.
I ORGANIZE MY COFFEE MAKERS BY THEIR TYPE-- FILTER, DRIP POTS, PERCOLATOR, INFUSION STYLE, AND GLASS VACUUM COFFEE MAKERS.
WOW.
COME OVER AGAIN AND WE'LL TALK SOME MORE ABOUT COFFEE!
WHAT A NUT.
COLUMB.
CUBA
ECUADOR

ONLY *STUPID* PEOPLE ARE *HAPPY.*

SMART PEOPLE ARE TOO AWARE OF THE *HORRORS OF THE WORLD* TO BE *HAPPY.*

IT'S A SMART THING TO *WANT HAPPINESS.*

WHICH MEANS THAT *ONLY* STUPID PEOPLE ARE *SMART.*

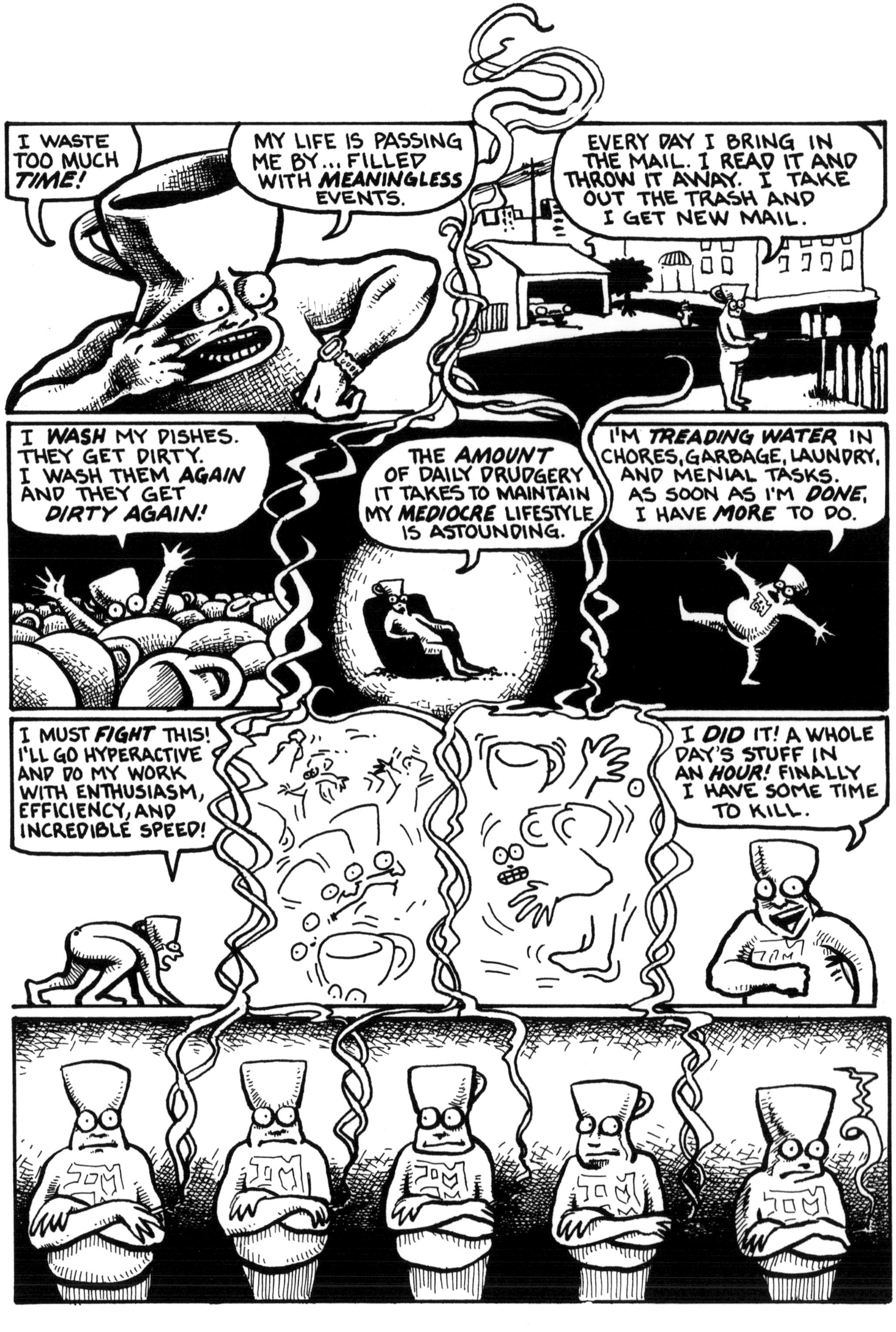
I WASTE TOO MUCH TIME!
MY LIFE IS PASSING ME BY... FILLED WITH MEANINGLESS EVENTS.
EVERY DAY I BRING IN THE MAIL. I READ IT AND THROW IT AWAY. I TAKE OUT THE TRASH AND I GET NEW MAIL.
I WASH MY DISHES. THEY GET DIRTY. I WASH THEM AGAIN AND THEY GET DIRTY AGAIN!
THE AMOUNT OF DAILY DRUDGERY IT TAKES TO MAINTAIN MY MEDIOCRE LIFESTYLE IS ASTOUNDING.
I'M TREADING WATER IN CHORES, GARBAGE, LAUNDRY, AND MENIAL TASKS. AS SOON AS I'M DONE, I HAVE MORE TO DO.
I MUST FIGHT THIS! I'LL GO HYPERACTIVE AND DO MY WORK WITH ENTHUSIASM, EFFICIENCY, AND INCREDIBLE SPEED!
I DID IT! A WHOLE DAY'S STUFF IN AN HOUR! FINALLY I HAVE SOME TIME TO KILL.

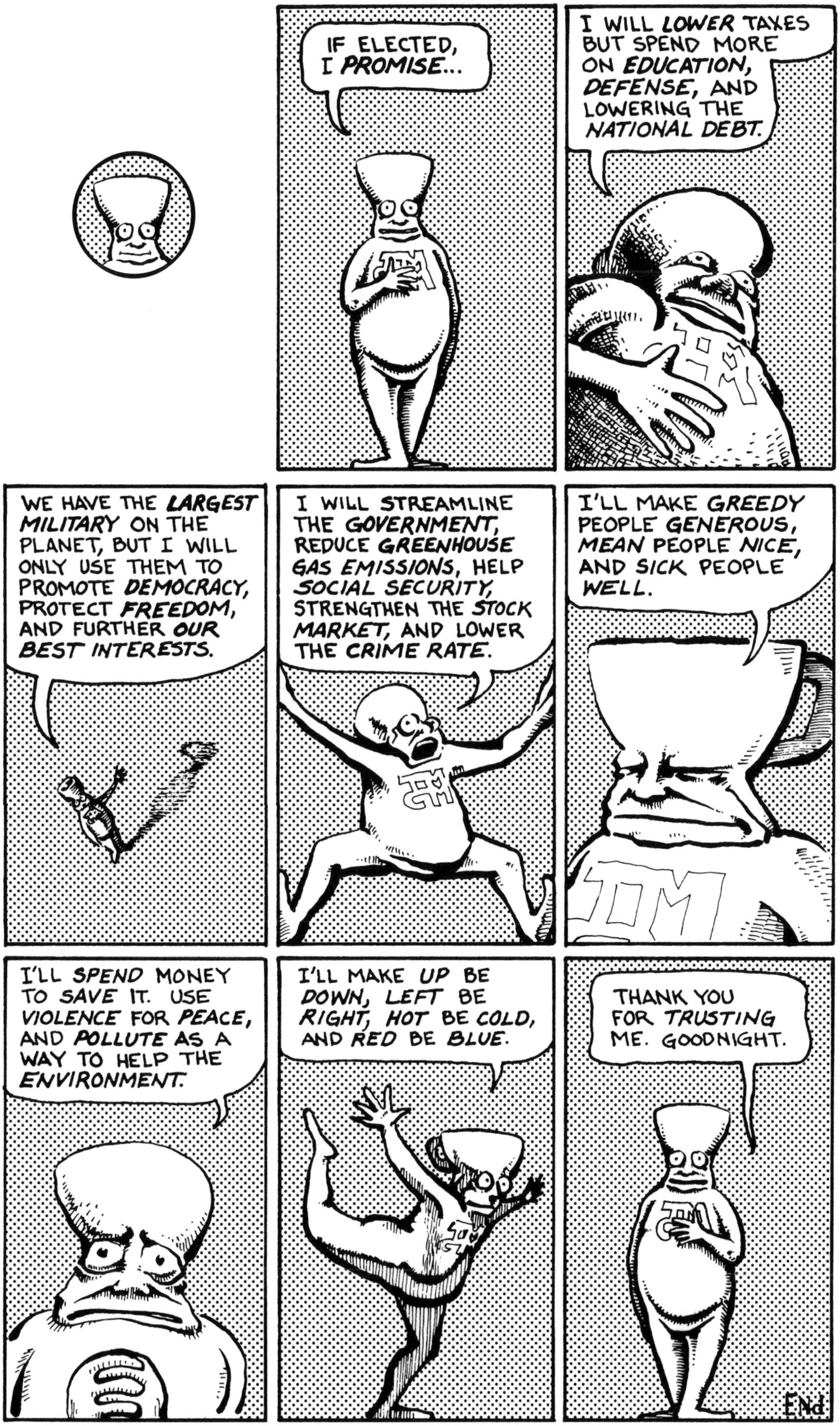
IF ELECTED, I PROMISE...
I WILL LOWER TAXES BUT SPEND MORE ON EDUCATION, DEFENSE, AND LOWERING THE NATIONAL DEBT.
WE HAVE THE LARGEST MILITARY ON THE PLANET, BUT I WILL ONLY USE THEM TO PROMOTE DEMOCRACY, PROTECT FREEDOM, AND FURTHER OUR BEST INTERESTS.
I WILL STREAMLINE THE GOVERNMENT, REDUCE GREENHOUSE GAS EMISSIONS, HELP SOCIAL SECURITY, STRENGTHEN THE STOCK MARKET, AND LOWER THE CRIME RATE.
I'LL MAKE GREEDY PEOPLE GENEROUS, MEAN PEOPLE NICE, AND SICK PEOPLE WELL.
I'LL SPEND MONEY TO SAVE IT. USE VIOLENCE FOR PEACE, AND POLLUTE AS A WAY TO HELP THE ENVIRONMENT.
I'LL MAKE UP BE DOWN, LEFT BE RIGHT, HOT BE COLD, AND RED BE BLUE.
THANK YOU FOR TRUSTING ME. GOODNIGHT.
END

TOO MUCH COFFEE MAN

SUPERHERO

I AM A *SUPERHERO!*

I AM *STRONG,* AND I AM *MIGHTY,* AND I HAVE A *CAPE!*

BACK HOME, IN MY SECRET *"COFFEE HOUSE,"* I HAVE HIGH-TECH *GADGETRY* TO HELP ME.

EVER VIGILANT, I LOOK FOR *SUPER VILLAINS.*

THERE SURE AREN'T TOO MANY *SUPER-VILLAINS* AROUND.

WHY DON'T YOU FIGHT SOMETHING *REAL,* LIKE POLLUTION, SEXISM, GLOBAL WARMING, OR OVERPOPULATION?

GRRRRRR!!! YES! I'LL FIGHT THOSE THINGS WITH EVERY FIBER OF MY BEING!

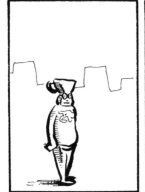

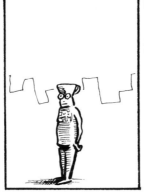

I DON'T THINK *SUPERHEROES* WERE MADE TO FIGHT *REAL* PROBLEMS.

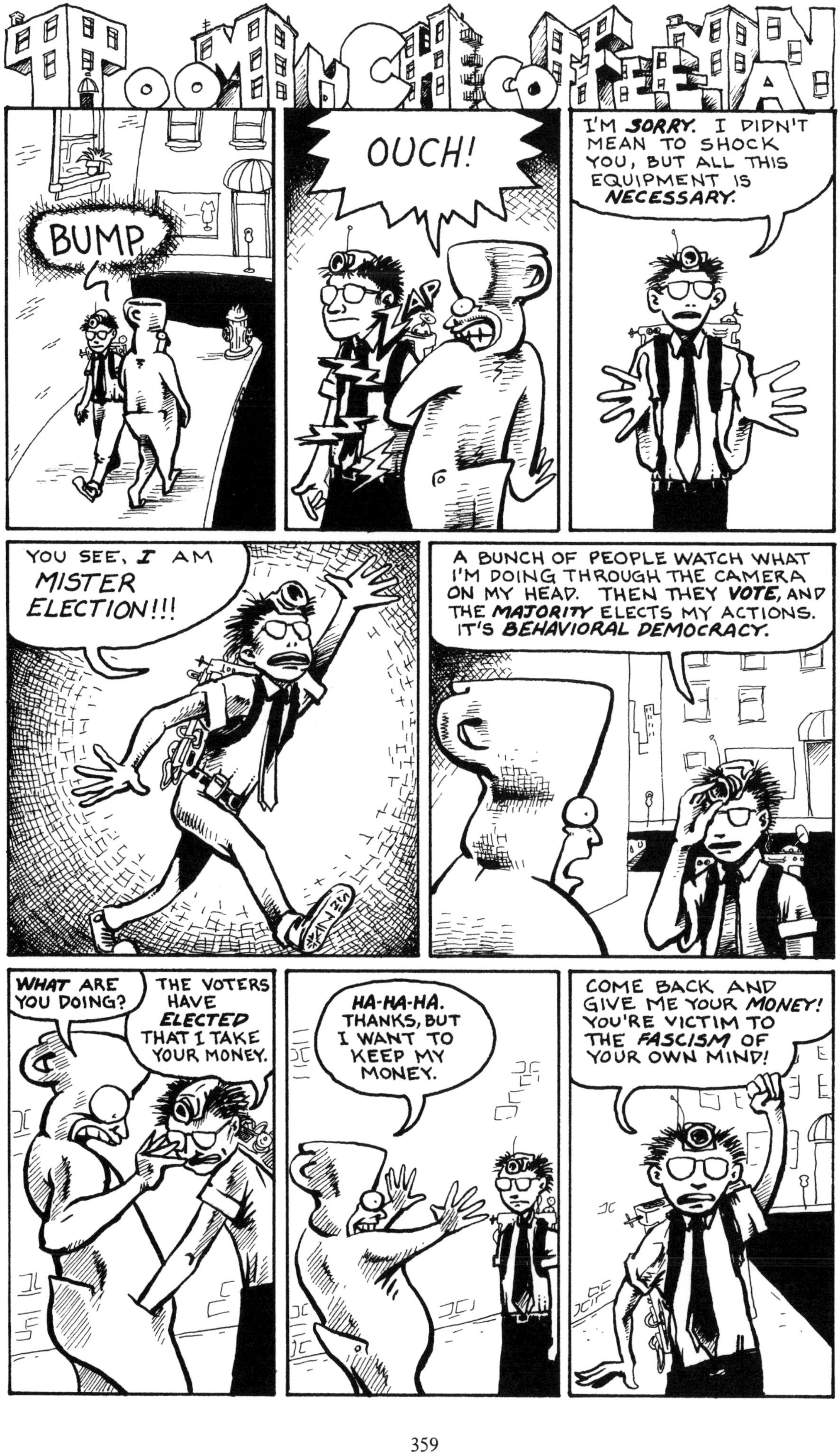
TOO MUCH COFFEE MAN
BUMP
OUCH!
ZAP
I'M SORRY. I DIDN'T MEAN TO SHOCK YOU, BUT ALL THIS EQUIPMENT IS NECESSARY.
YOU SEE, I AM MISTER ELECTION!!!
A BUNCH OF PEOPLE WATCH WHAT I'M DOING THROUGH THE CAMERA ON MY HEAD. THEN THEY VOTE, AND THE MAJORITY ELECTS MY ACTIONS. IT'S BEHAVIORAL DEMOCRACY.
WHAT ARE YOU DOING?
THE VOTERS HAVE ELECTED THAT I TAKE YOUR MONEY.
HA-HA-HA. THANKS, BUT I WANT TO KEEP MY MONEY.
COME BACK AND GIVE ME YOUR MONEY! YOU'RE VICTIM TO THE FASCISM OF YOUR OWN MIND!

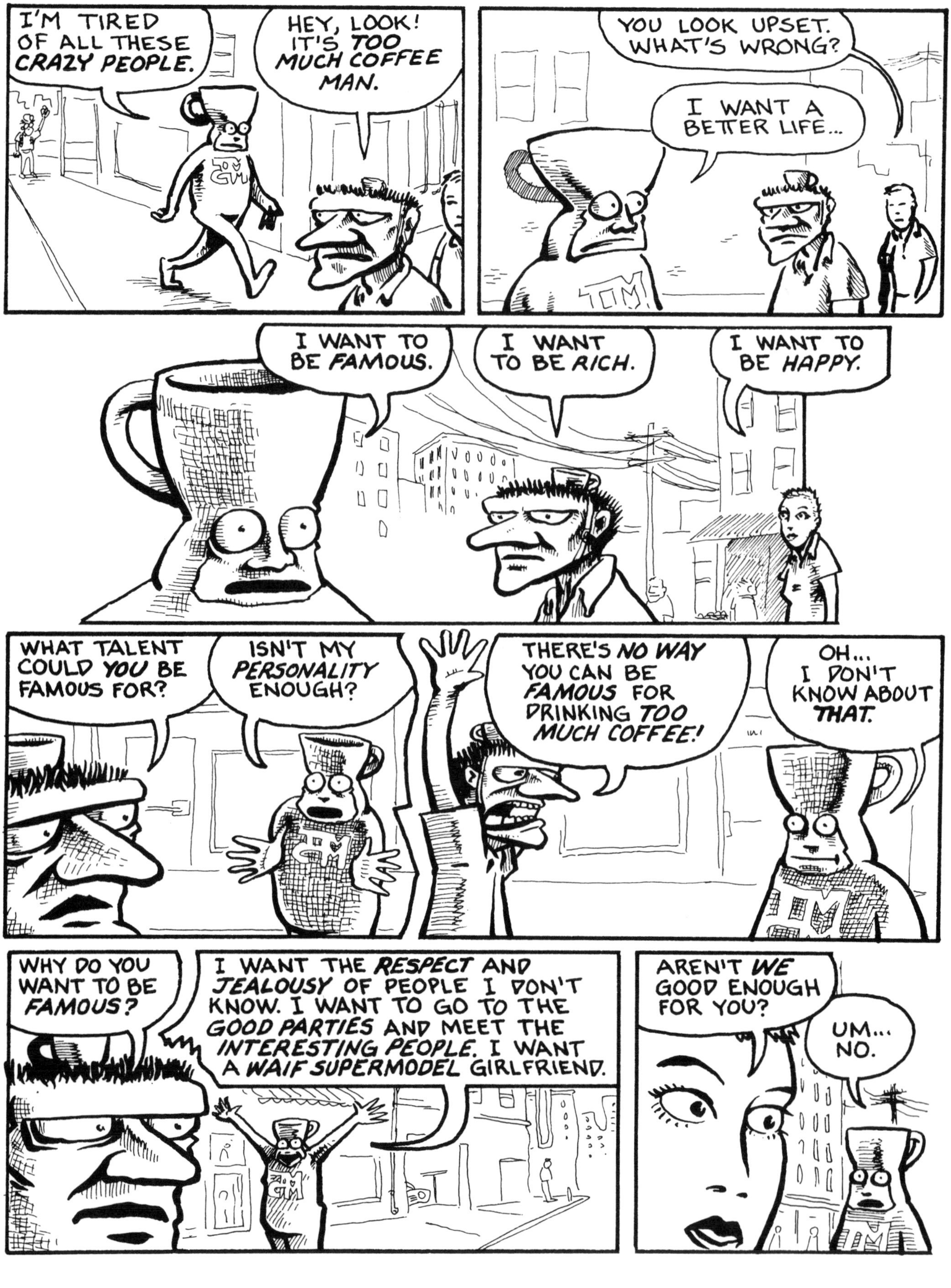
I'M TIRED OF ALL THESE CRAZY PEOPLE.
HEY, LOOK! IT'S TOO MUCH COFFEE MAN.
YOU LOOK UPSET. WHAT'S WRONG?
I WANT A BETTER LIFE...
I WANT TO BE FAMOUS.
I WANT TO BE RICH.
I WANT TO BE HAPPY.
WHAT TALENT COULD YOU BE FAMOUS FOR?
ISN'T MY PERSONALITY ENOUGH?
THERE'S NO WAY YOU CAN BE FAMOUS FOR DRINKING TOO MUCH COFFEE!
OH... I DON'T KNOW ABOUT THAT.
WHY DO YOU WANT TO BE FAMOUS?
I WANT THE RESPECT AND JEALOUSY OF PEOPLE I DON'T KNOW. I WANT TO GO TO THE GOOD PARTIES AND MEET THE INTERESTING PEOPLE. I WANT A WAIF SUPERMODEL GIRLFRIEND.
AREN'T WE GOOD ENOUGH FOR YOU?
UM... NO.

WHAT ARE YOU DOING?
I'VE HAD A HARD WEEK.
I'VE DECIDED TO LIE HERE FOR A WHILE.
CARS COME AND HONK AT ME. THEY WANT THIS PARKING SPACE.
BEEP BEEP BEEP
BUT I'VE PUT MONEY IN THE METER. I FEEL LIKE I HAVE THE RIGHT TO LIE HERE IF I WANT TO.
I FIND THIS VERY RELAXING.
DOESN'T THE HOSTILITY MAKE YOU TENSE?
NO. I LIKE IT.
IN FACT, THE MORE THEY WANT THIS SPACE, THE BETTER THIS GETS FOR ME.
THEIR ANGUISH HELPS ME RISE TO A NICE PLATEAU OF HARMONY.
I'VE ACCEPTED THE ANGER AND AGGRAVATION AROUND ME. I AM NOW AT ONE WITH THE URBAN ENVIRONMENT.
I HATE EVERY-ONE AND EVERYTHING. IT'S GREAT. I KNOW WHO I AM AND WHERE I AM. I NEVER WANT THIS TO CHANGE.
DO YOU WANT TO GO TO A PARTY?
SURE.

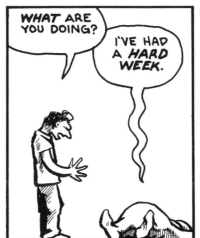

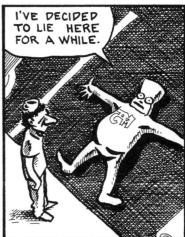

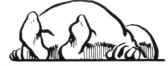

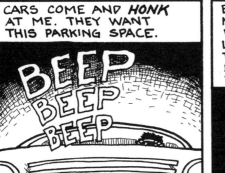

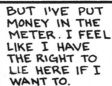

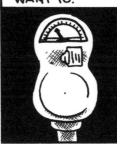

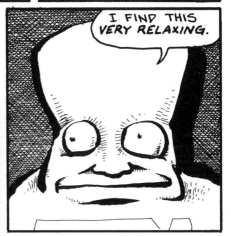

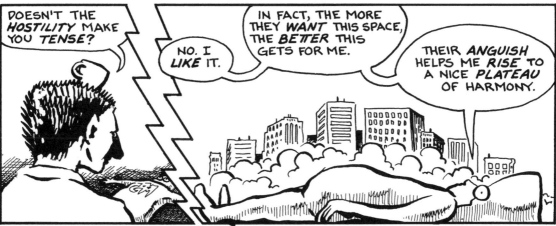

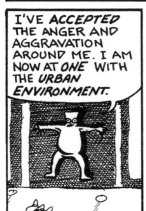

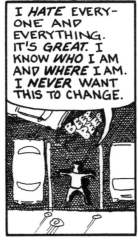

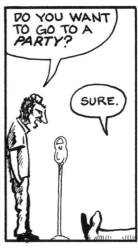

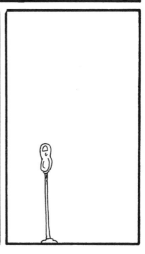

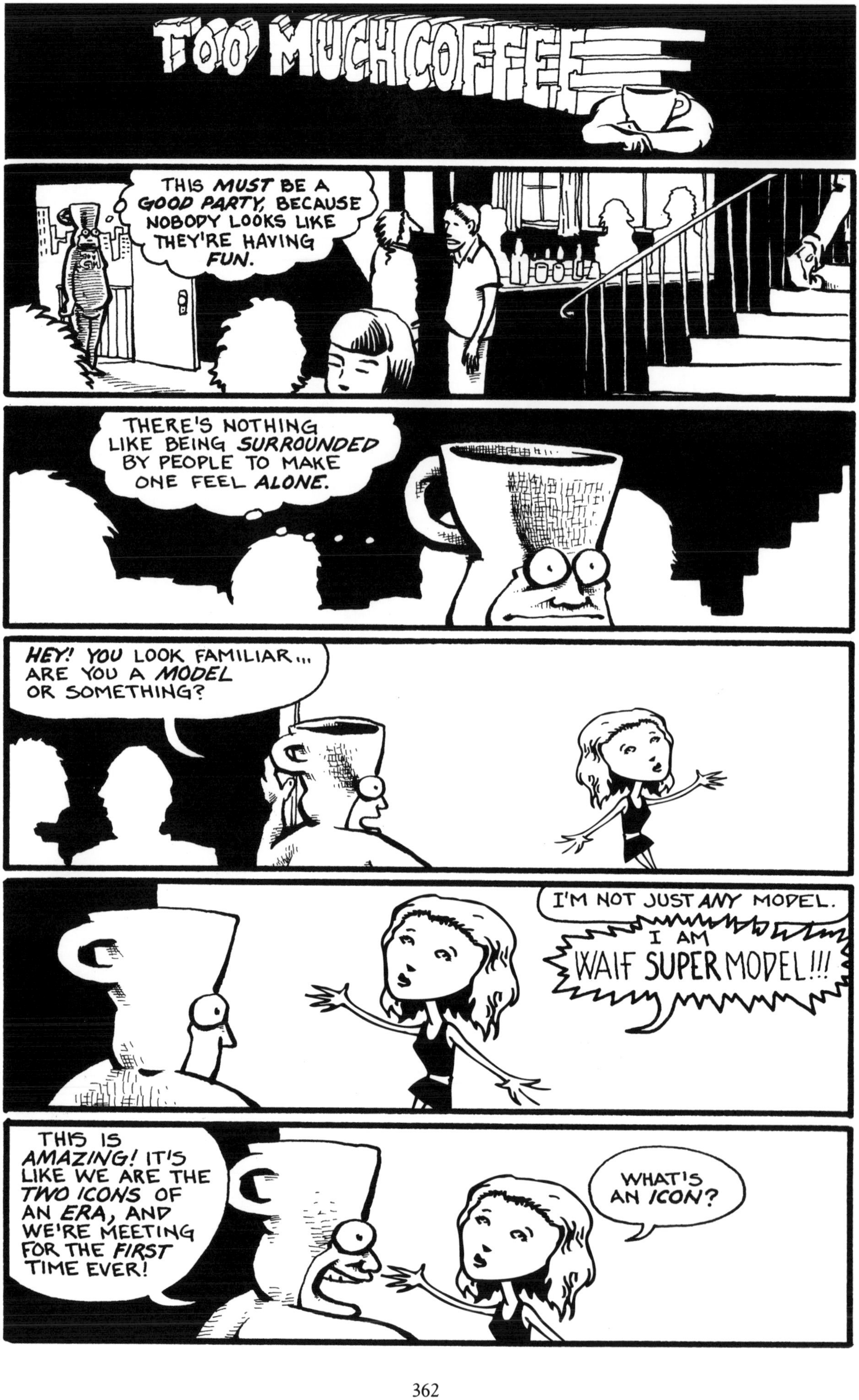
TOO MUCH COFFEE
THIS MUST BE A GOOD PARTY, BECAUSE NOBODY LOOKS LIKE THEY'RE HAVING FUN.
THERE'S NOTHING LIKE BEING SURROUNDED BY PEOPLE TO MAKE ONE FEEL ALONE.
HEY! YOU LOOK FAMILIAR... ARE YOU A MODEL OR SOMETHING?
I'M NOT JUST ANY MODEL.
I AM WAIF SUPERMODEL!!!
THIS IS AMAZING! IT'S LIKE WE ARE THE TWO ICONS OF AN ERA, AND WE'RE MEETING FOR THE FIRST TIME EVER!
WHAT'S AN ICON?

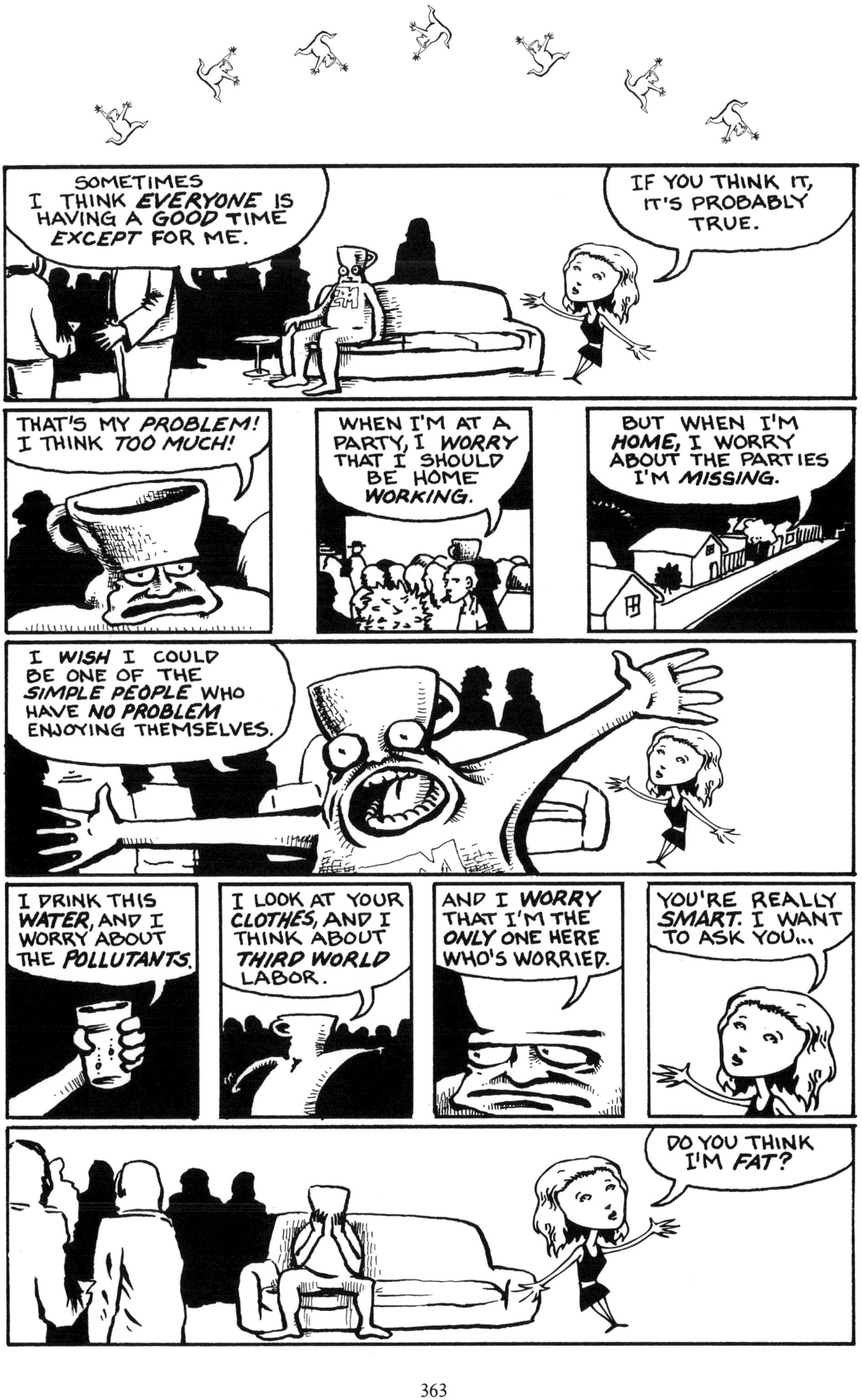
SOMETIMES I THINK EVERYONE IS HAVING A GOOD TIME EXCEPT FOR ME.
IF YOU THINK IT, IT'S PROBABLY TRUE.
THAT'S MY PROBLEM! I THINK TOO MUCH!
WHEN I'M AT A PARTY, I WORRY THAT I SHOULD BE HOME WORKING.
BUT WHEN I'M HOME, I WORRY ABOUT THE PARTIES I'M MISSING.
I WISH I COULD BE ONE OF THE SIMPLE PEOPLE WHO HAVE NO PROBLEM ENJOYING THEMSELVES.
I DRINK THIS WATER, AND I WORRY ABOUT THE POLLUTANTS.
I LOOK AT YOUR CLOTHES, AND I THINK ABOUT THIRD WORLD LABOR.
AND I WORRY THAT I'M THE ONLY ONE HERE WHO'S WORRIED.
YOU'RE REALLY SMART. I WANT TO ASK YOU...
DO YOU THINK I'M FAT?

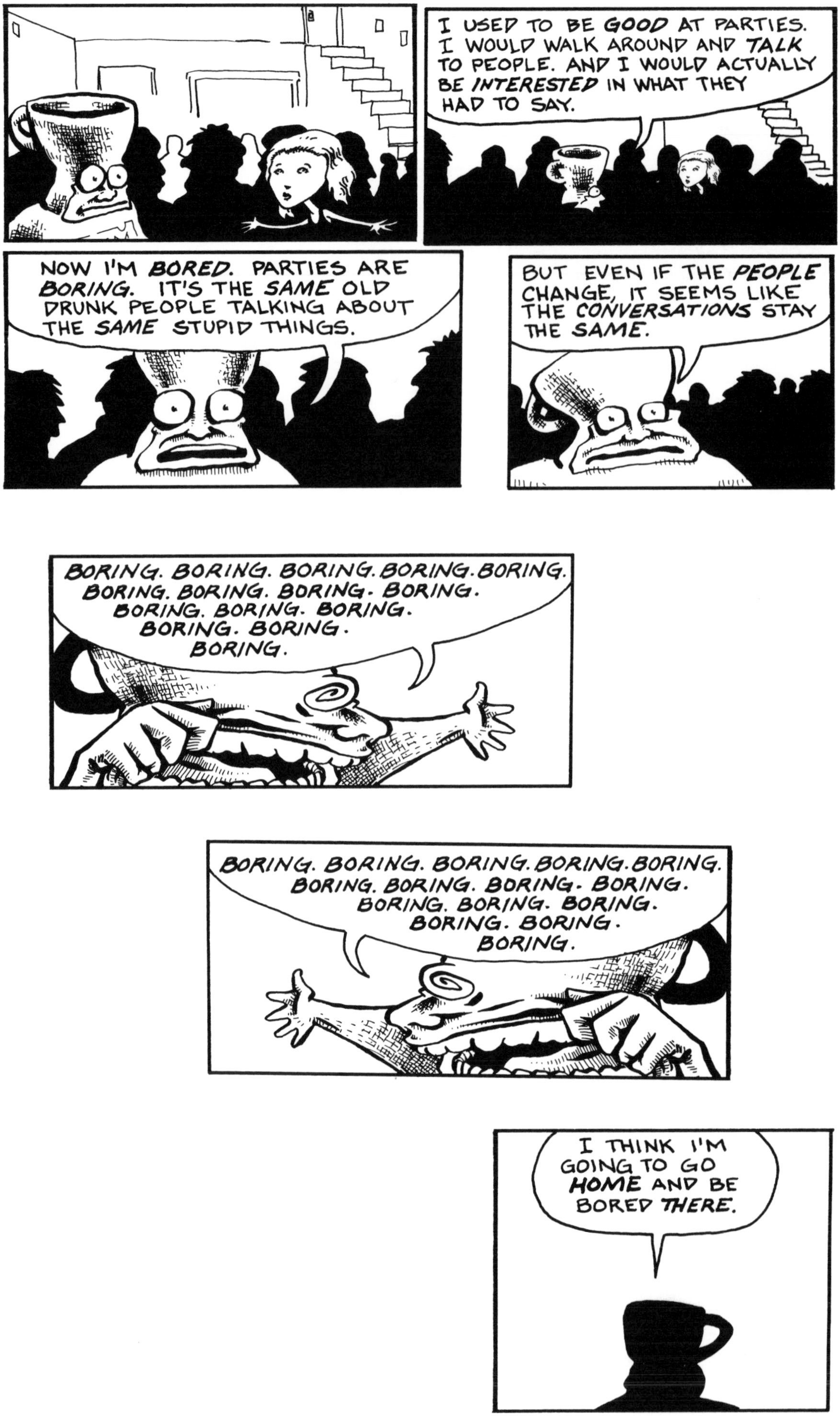
I USED TO BE GOOD AT PARTIES. I WOULD WALK AROUND AND TALK TO PEOPLE. AND I WOULD ACTUALLY BE INTERESTED IN WHAT THEY HAD TO SAY.
NOW I'M BORED. PARTIES ARE BORING. IT'S THE SAME OLD DRUNK PEOPLE TALKING ABOUT THE SAME STUPID THINGS.
BUT EVEN IF THE PEOPLE CHANGE, IT SEEMS LIKE THE CONVERSATIONS STAY THE SAME.
BORING. BORING. BORING. BORING. BORING. BORING. BORING. BORING. BORING. BORING. BORING. BORING. BORING. BORING. BORING.
BORING. BORING. BORING. BORING. BORING. BORING. BORING. BORING. BORING. BORING. BORING. BORING. BORING. BORING. BORING.
I THINK I'M GOING TO GO HOME AND BE BORED THERE.

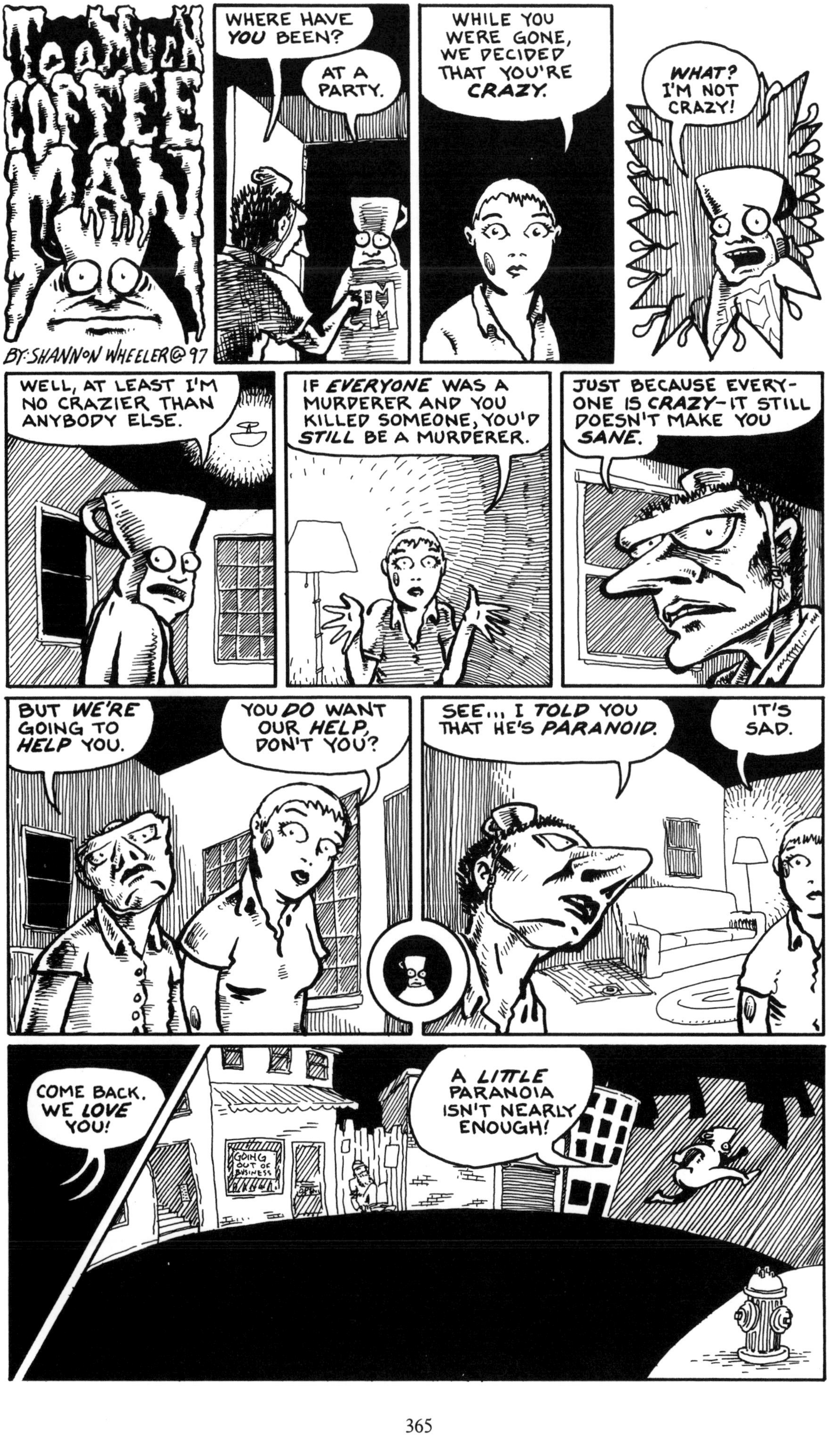
TOO MUCH COFFEE MAN
BY: SHANNON WHEELER © 97
WHERE HAVE YOU BEEN?
AT A PARTY.
WHILE YOU WERE GONE, WE DECIDED THAT YOU'RE CRAZY.
WHAT? I'M NOT CRAZY!
WELL, AT LEAST I'M NO CRAZIER THAN ANYBODY ELSE.
IF EVERYONE WAS A MURDERER AND YOU KILLED SOMEONE, YOU'D STILL BE A MURDERER.
JUST BECAUSE EVERYONE IS CRAZY– IT STILL DOESN'T MAKE YOU SANE.
BUT WE'RE GOING TO HELP YOU.
YOU DO WANT OUR HELP, DON'T YOU?
SEE... I TOLD YOU THAT HE'S PARANOID.
IT'S SAD.
COME BACK. WE LOVE YOU!
A LITTLE PARANOIA ISN'T NEARLY ENOUGH!
GOING OUT OF BUSINESS

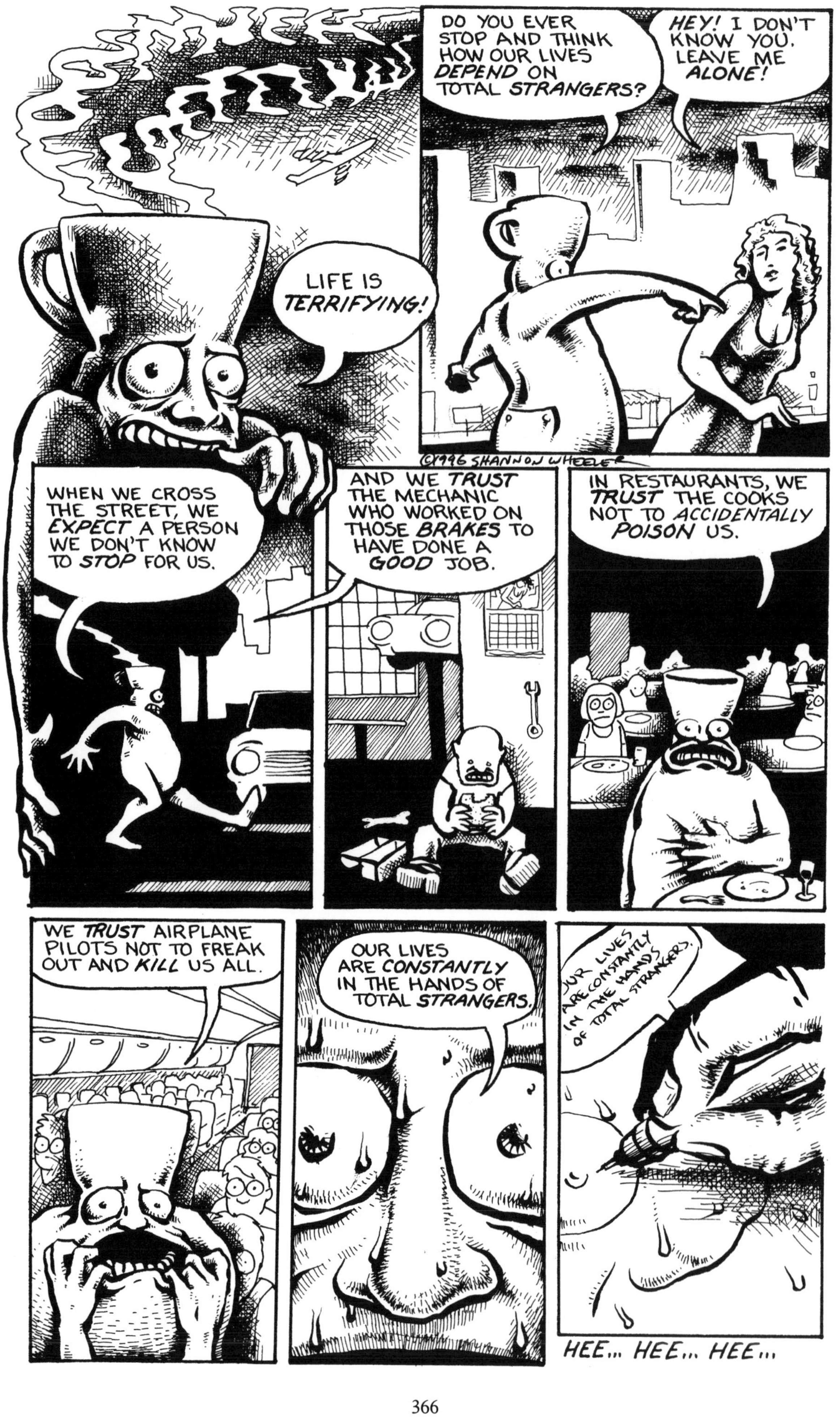

DO YOU EVER STOP AND THINK HOW OUR LIVES DEPEND ON TOTAL STRANGERS?
HEY! I DON'T KNOW YOU. LEAVE ME ALONE!
LIFE IS TERRIFYING!
©1996 SHANNON WHEELER
WHEN WE CROSS THE STREET, WE EXPECT A PERSON WE DON'T KNOW TO STOP FOR US.
AND WE TRUST THE MECHANIC WHO WORKED ON THOSE BRAKES TO HAVE DONE A GOOD JOB.
IN RESTAURANTS, WE TRUST THE COOKS NOT TO ACCIDENTALLY POISON US.
WE TRUST AIRPLANE PILOTS NOT TO FREAK OUT AND KILL US ALL.
OUR LIVES ARE CONSTANTLY IN THE HANDS OF TOTAL STRANGERS.
UR LIVES ARE CONSTANTLY IN THE HANDS OF TOTAL STRANGERS.
HEE... HEE... HEE...

chapter 6

THE FUTURE SHOULD BE HERE BY NOW

God is an atheist, and other realizations

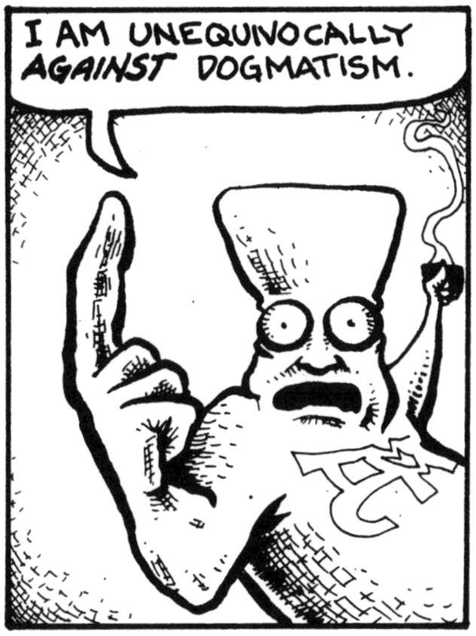
I AM UNEQUIVOCALLY AGAINST DOGMATISM.

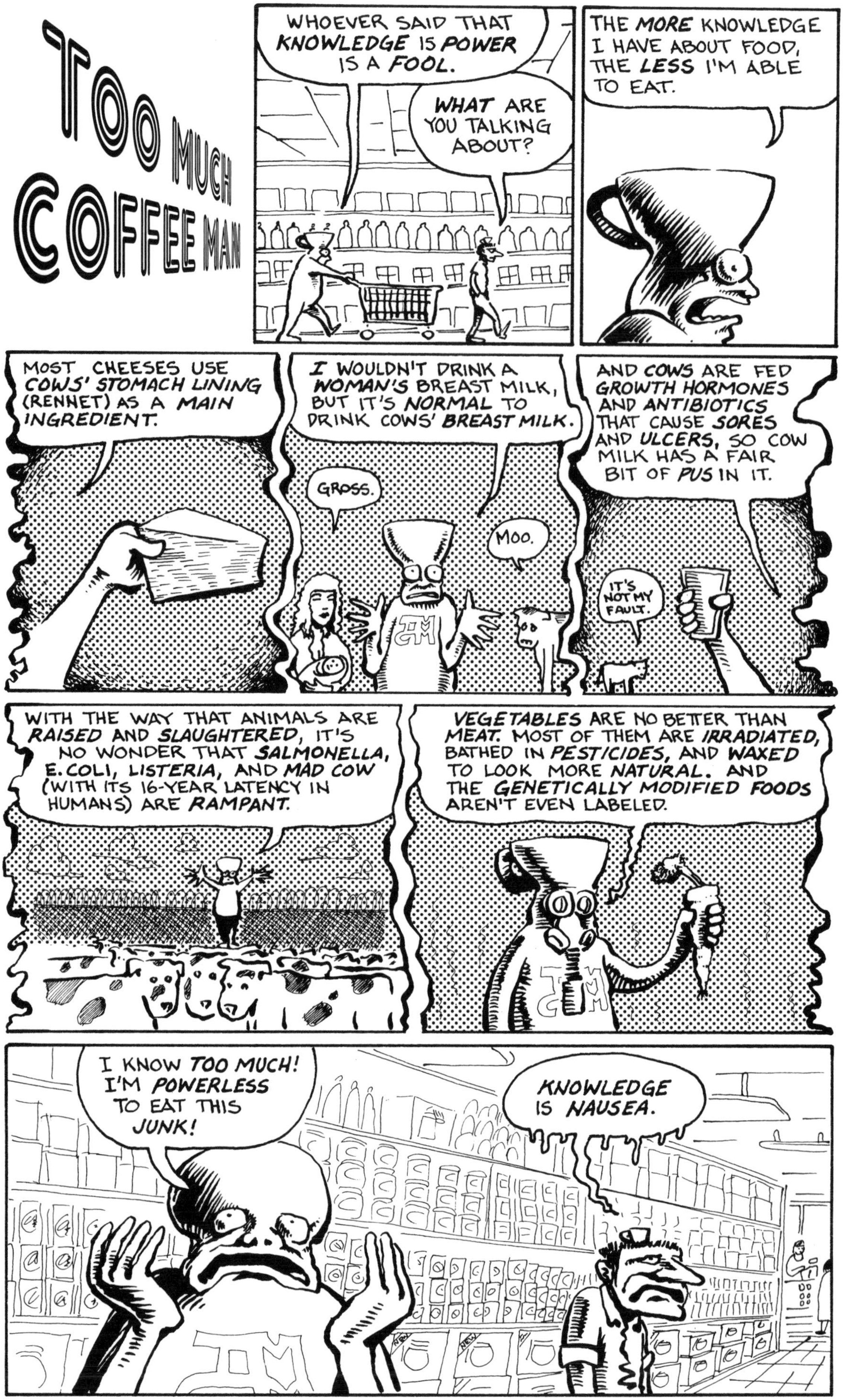
TOO MUCH COFFEE MAN
WHOEVER SAID THAT KNOWLEDGE IS POWER IS A FOOL.
WHAT ARE YOU TALKING ABOUT?
THE MORE KNOWLEDGE I HAVE ABOUT FOOD, THE LESS I'M ABLE TO EAT.
MOST CHEESES USE COWS' STOMACH LINING (RENNET) AS A MAIN INGREDIENT.
I WOULDN'T DRINK A WOMAN'S BREAST MILK, BUT IT'S NORMAL TO DRINK COWS' BREAST MILK.
GROSS.
MOO.
AND COWS ARE FED GROWTH HORMONES AND ANTIBIOTICS THAT CAUSE SORES AND ULCERS, SO COW MILK HAS A FAIR BIT OF PUS IN IT.
IT'S NOT MY FAULT.
WITH THE WAY THAT ANIMALS ARE RAISED AND SLAUGHTERED, IT'S NO WONDER THAT SALMONELLA, E. COLI, LISTERIA, AND MAD COW (WITH ITS 16-YEAR LATENCY IN HUMANS) ARE RAMPANT.
VEGETABLES ARE NO BETTER THAN MEAT. MOST OF THEM ARE IRRADIATED, BATHED IN PESTICIDES, AND WAXED TO LOOK MORE NATURAL. AND THE GENETICALLY MODIFIED FOODS AREN'T EVEN LABELED.
I KNOW TOO MUCH! I'M POWERLESS TO EAT THIS JUNK!
KNOWLEDGE IS NAUSEA.

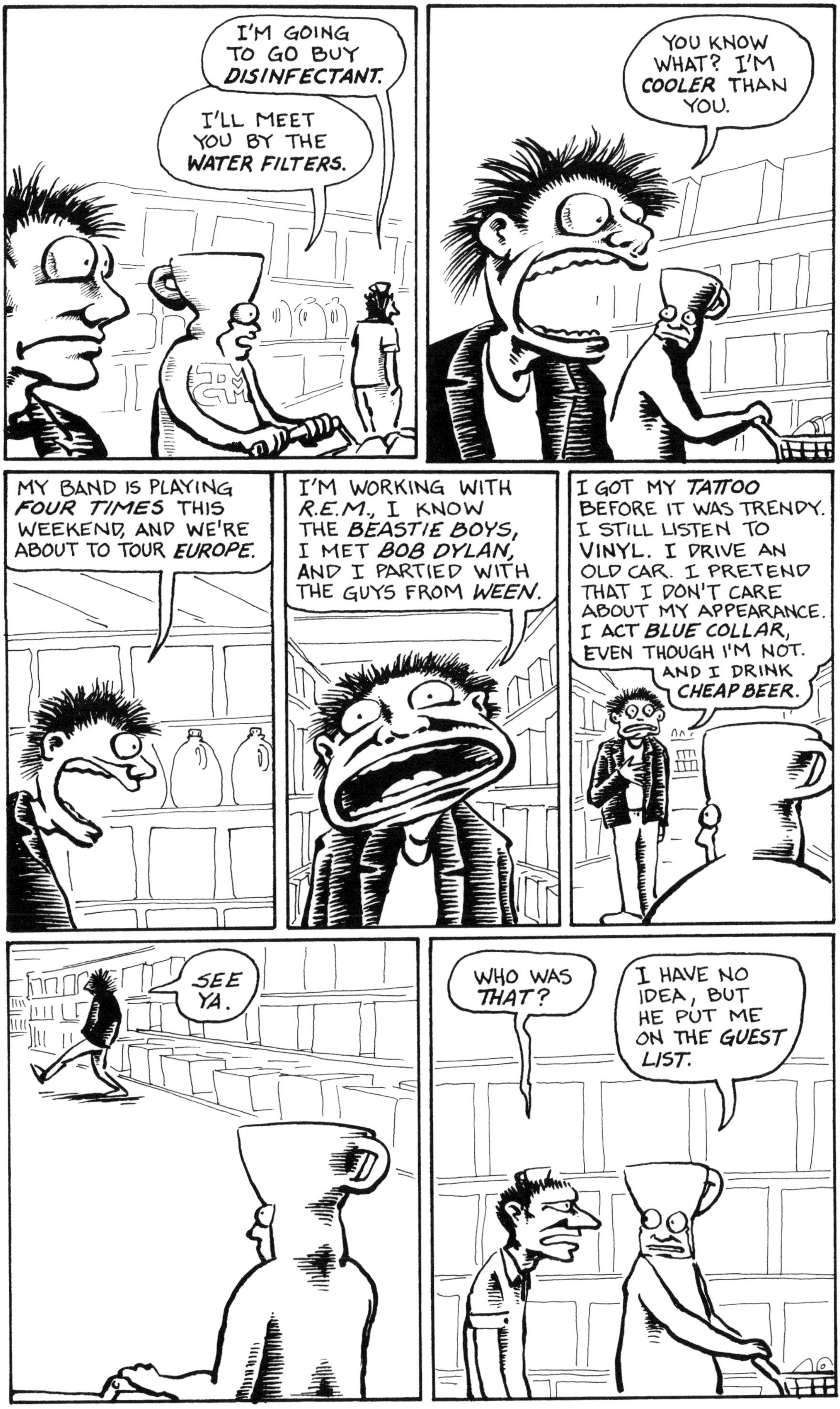
I'M GOING TO GO BUY DISINFECTANT.
I'LL MEET YOU BY THE WATER FILTERS.
YOU KNOW WHAT? I'M COOLER THAN YOU.
MY BAND IS PLAYING FOUR TIMES THIS WEEKEND, AND WE'RE ABOUT TO TOUR EUROPE.
I'M WORKING WITH R.E.M., I KNOW THE BEASTIE BOYS, I MET BOB DYLAN, AND I PARTIED WITH THE GUYS FROM WEEN.
I GOT MY TATTOO BEFORE IT WAS TRENDY. I STILL LISTEN TO VINYL. I DRIVE AN OLD CAR. I PRETEND THAT I DON'T CARE ABOUT MY APPEARANCE. I ACT BLUE COLLAR, EVEN THOUGH I'M NOT. AND I DRINK CHEAP BEER.
SEE YA.
WHO WAS THAT?
I HAVE NO IDEA, BUT HE PUT ME ON THE GUEST LIST.

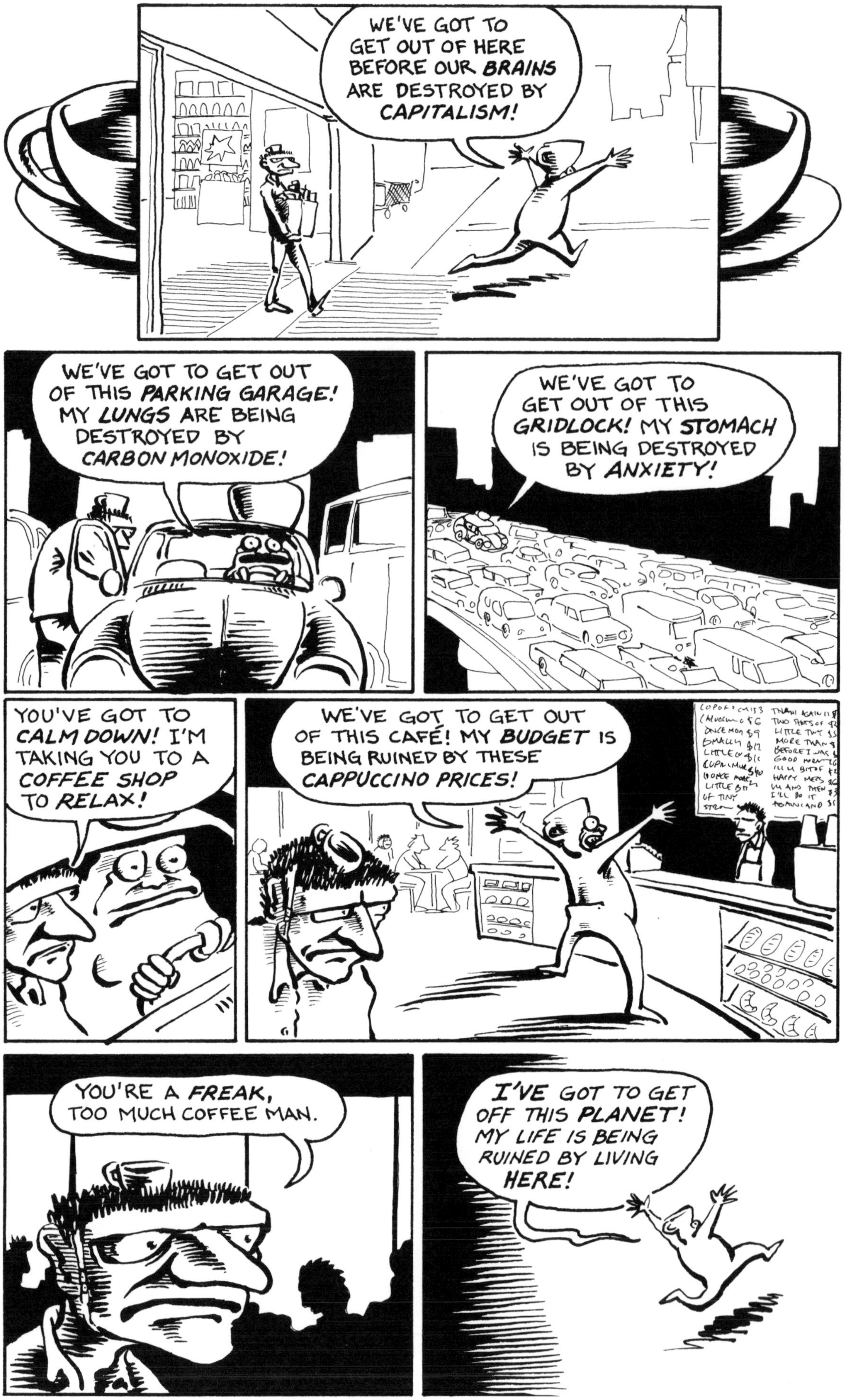
WE'VE GOT TO GET OUT OF HERE BEFORE OUR BRAINS ARE DESTROYED BY CAPITALISM!
WE'VE GOT TO GET OUT OF THIS PARKING GARAGE! MY LUNGS ARE BEING DESTROYED BY CARBON MONOXIDE!
WE'VE GOT TO GET OUT OF THIS GRIDLOCK! MY STOMACH IS BEING DESTROYED BY ANXIETY!
YOU'VE GOT TO CALM DOWN! I'M TAKING YOU TO A COFFEE SHOP TO RELAX!
WE'VE GOT TO GET OUT OF THIS CAFÉ! MY BUDGET IS BEING RUINED BY THESE CAPPUCCINO PRICES!
YOU'RE A FREAK, TOO MUCH COFFEE MAN.
I'VE GOT TO GET OFF THIS PLANET! MY LIFE IS BEING RUINED BY LIVING HERE!

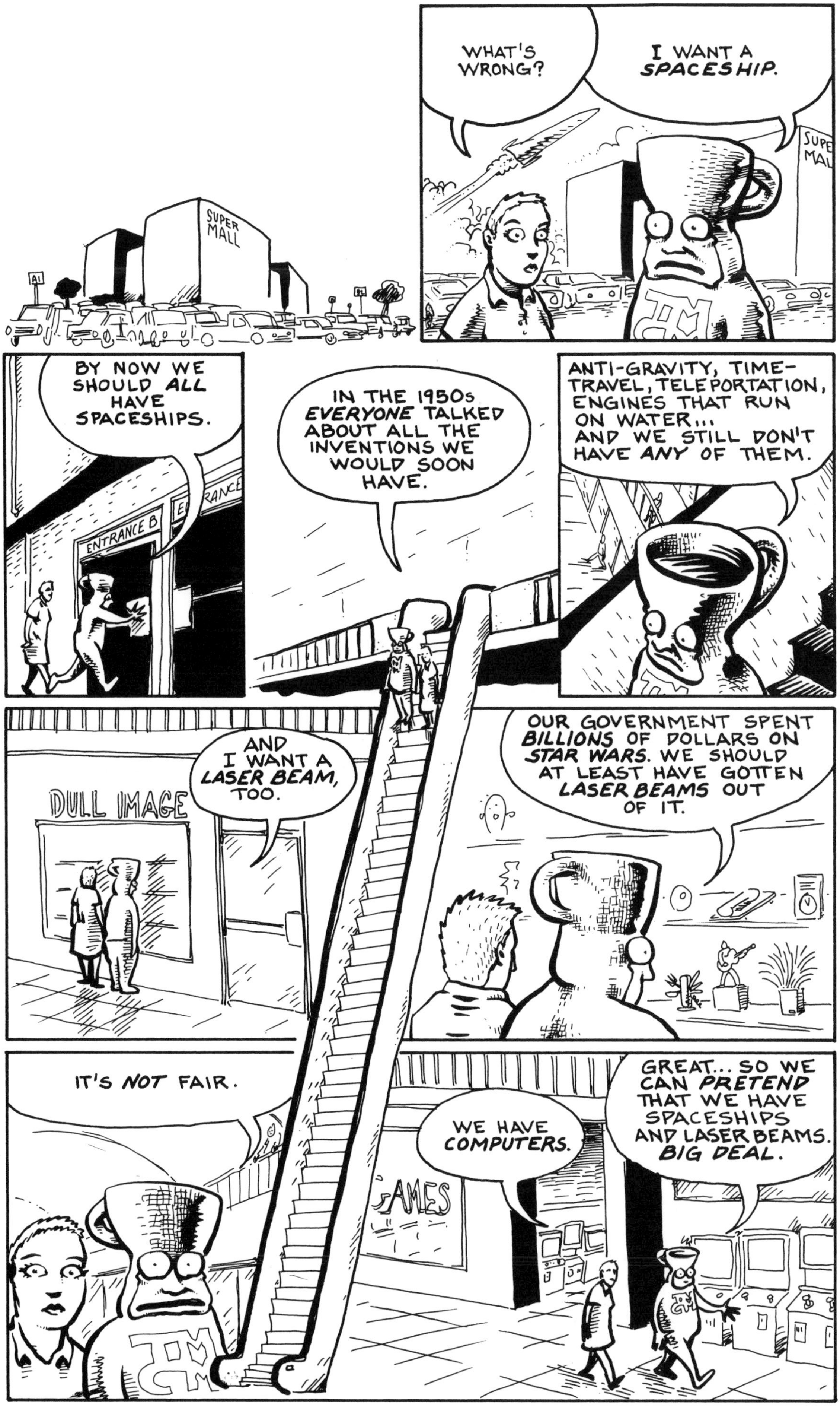
SUPER MALL
WHAT'S WRONG?
I WANT A SPACESHIP.
BY NOW WE SHOULD ALL HAVE SPACESHIPS.
IN THE 1950s EVERYONE TALKED ABOUT ALL THE INVENTIONS WE WOULD SOON HAVE.
ANTI-GRAVITY, TIME-TRAVEL, TELEPORTATION, ENGINES THAT RUN ON WATER... AND WE STILL DON'T HAVE ANY OF THEM.
ENTRANCE B
DULL IMAGE
AND I WANT A LASER BEAM, TOO.
OUR GOVERNMENT SPENT BILLIONS OF DOLLARS ON STAR WARS. WE SHOULD AT LEAST HAVE GOTTEN LASER BEAMS OUT OF IT.
IT'S NOT FAIR.
WE HAVE COMPUTERS.
GREAT... SO WE CAN PRETEND THAT WE HAVE SPACESHIPS AND LASER BEAMS. BIG DEAL.
GAMES

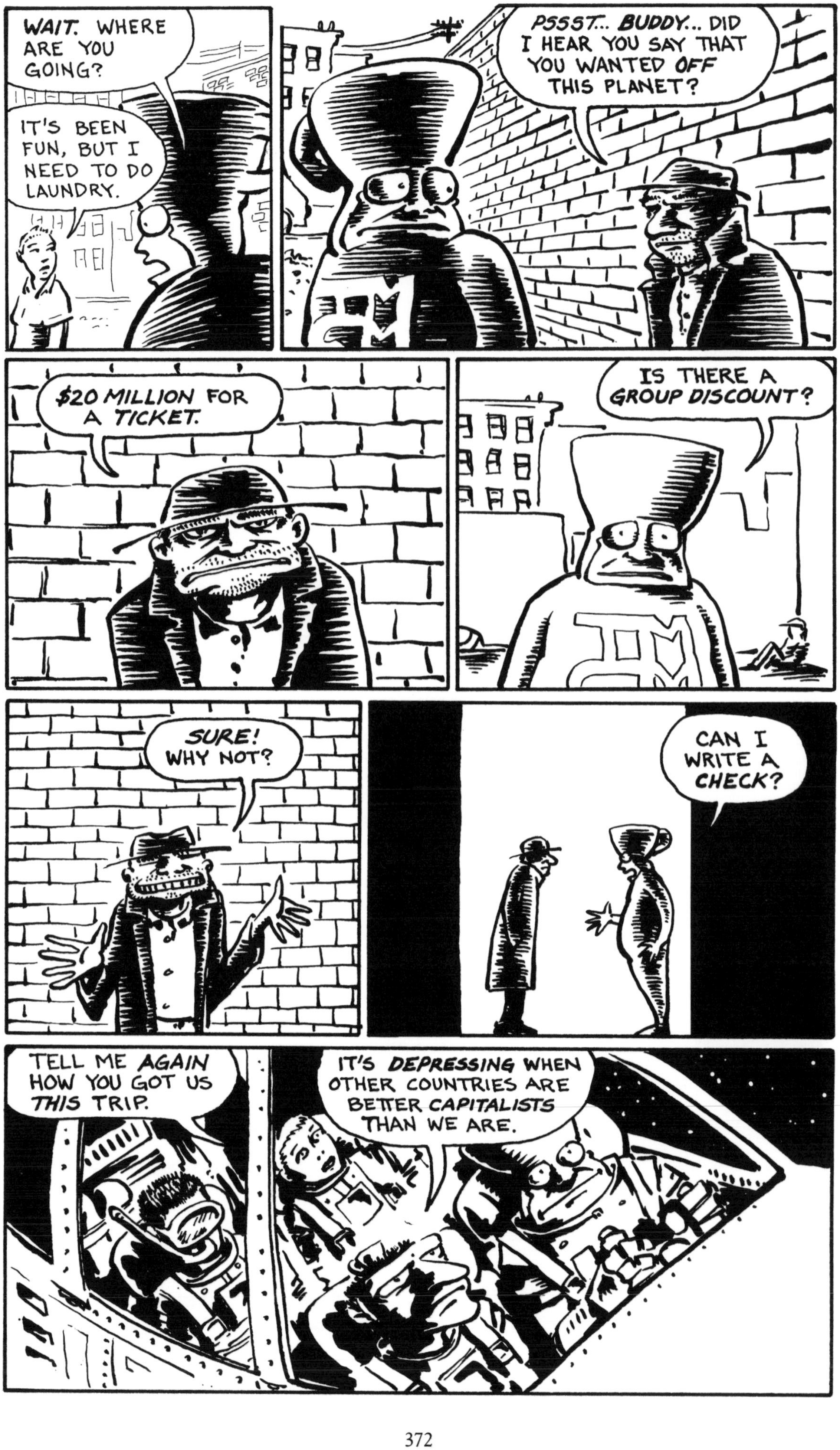
WAIT. WHERE ARE YOU GOING?
IT'S BEEN FUN, BUT I NEED TO DO LAUNDRY.
PSSST... BUDDY... DID I HEAR YOU SAY THAT YOU WANTED OFF THIS PLANET?
$20 MILLION FOR A TICKET.
IS THERE A GROUP DISCOUNT?
SURE! WHY NOT?
CAN I WRITE A CHECK?
TELL ME AGAIN HOW YOU GOT US THIS TRIP.
IT'S DEPRESSING WHEN OTHER COUNTRIES ARE BETTER CAPITALISTS THAN WE ARE.

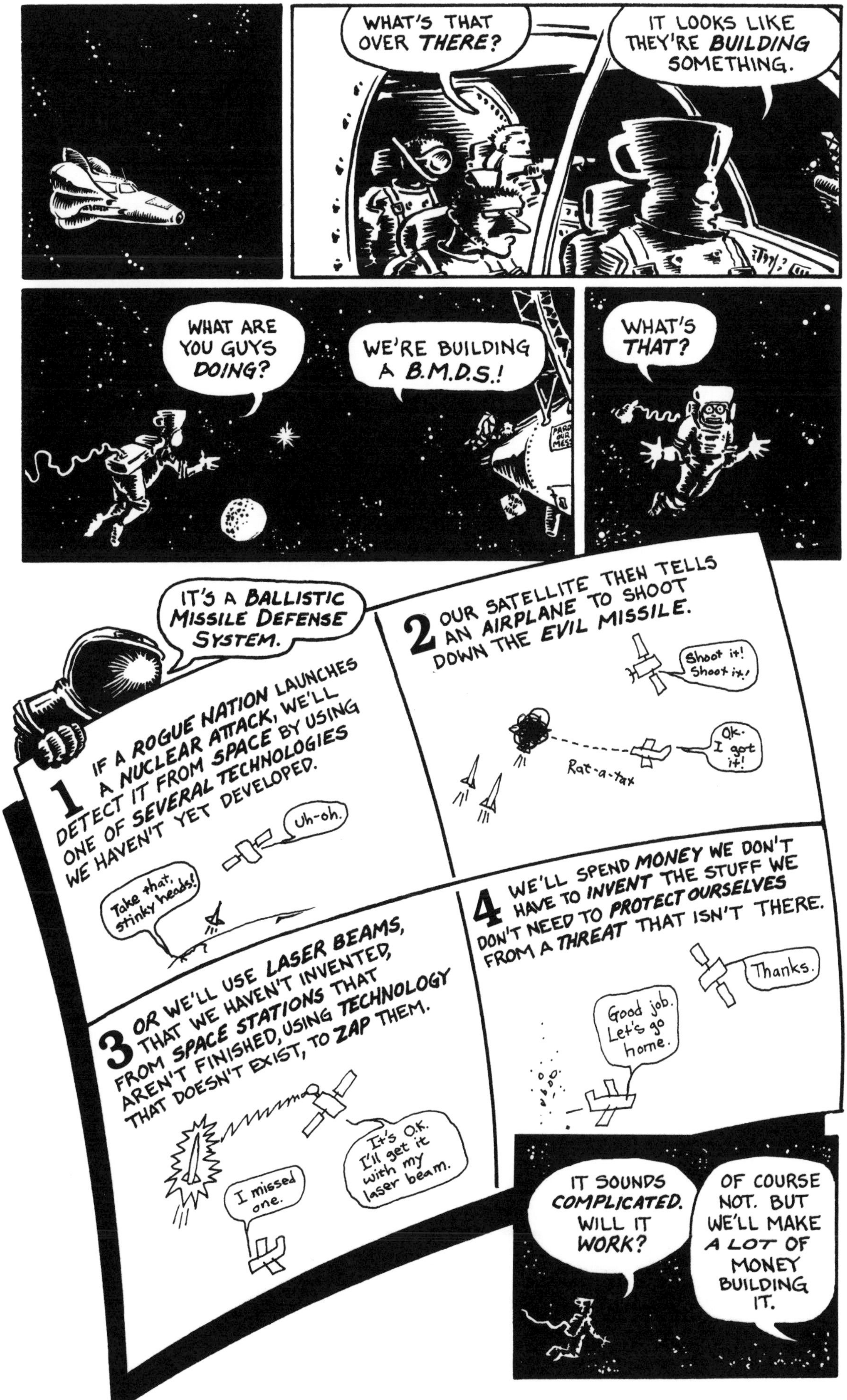
WHAT'S THAT OVER THERE?
IT LOOKS LIKE THEY'RE BUILDING SOMETHING.
WHAT ARE YOU GUYS DOING?
WE'RE BUILDING A B.M.D.S.!
WHAT'S THAT?
IT'S A BALLISTIC MISSILE DEFENSE SYSTEM.
1 IF A ROGUE NATION LAUNCHES A NUCLEAR ATTACK, WE'LL DETECT IT FROM SPACE BY USING ONE OF SEVERAL TECHNOLOGIES WE HAVEN'T YET DEVELOPED.
Uh-oh.
Take that, stinky heads!
2 OUR SATELLITE THEN TELLS AN AIRPLANE TO SHOOT DOWN THE EVIL MISSILE.
Shoot it! Shoot it!
O.K. I got it!
Rat-a-tat
3 OR WE'LL USE LASER BEAMS, THAT WE HAVEN'T INVENTED, FROM SPACE STATIONS THAT AREN'T FINISHED, USING TECHNOLOGY THAT DOESN'T EXIST, TO ZAP THEM.
I missed one.
It's O.K. I'll get it with my laser beam.
4 WE'LL SPEND MONEY WE DON'T HAVE TO INVENT THE STUFF WE DON'T NEED TO PROTECT OURSELVES FROM A THREAT THAT ISN'T THERE.
Thanks.
Good job. Let's go home.
IT SOUNDS COMPLICATED. WILL IT WORK?
OF COURSE NOT. BUT WE'LL MAKE A LOT OF MONEY BUILDING IT.

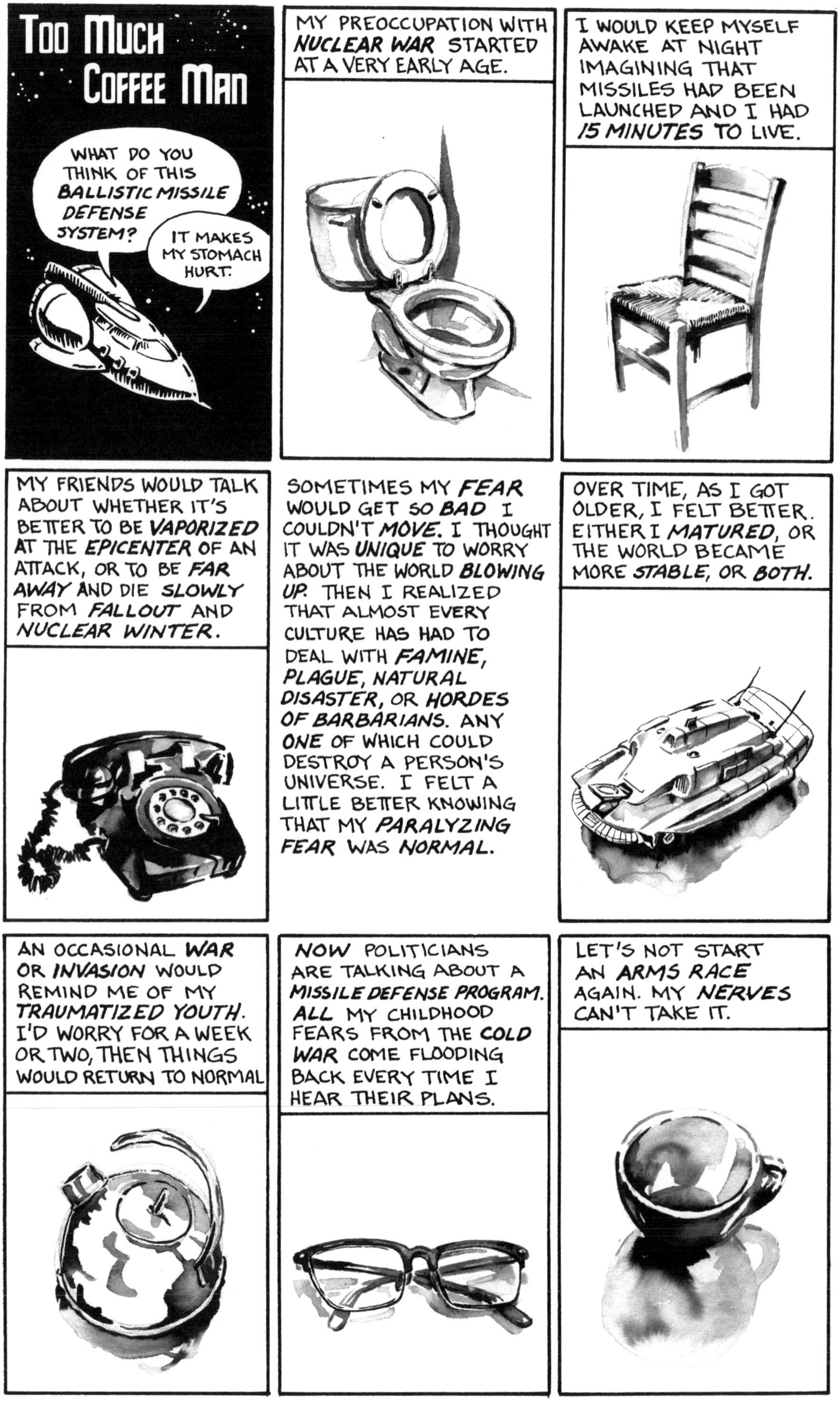
Too Much Coffee Man
WHAT DO YOU THINK OF THIS BALLISTIC MISSILE DEFENSE SYSTEM?
IT MAKES MY STOMACH HURT.
MY PREOCCUPATION WITH NUCLEAR WAR STARTED AT A VERY EARLY AGE.
I WOULD KEEP MYSELF AWAKE AT NIGHT IMAGINING THAT MISSILES HAD BEEN LAUNCHED AND I HAD 15 MINUTES TO LIVE.
MY FRIENDS WOULD TALK ABOUT WHETHER IT'S BETTER TO BE VAPORIZED AT THE EPICENTER OF AN ATTACK, OR TO BE FAR AWAY AND DIE SLOWLY FROM FALLOUT AND NUCLEAR WINTER.
SOMETIMES MY FEAR WOULD GET SO BAD I COULDN'T MOVE. I THOUGHT IT WAS UNIQUE TO WORRY ABOUT THE WORLD BLOWING UP. THEN I REALIZED THAT ALMOST EVERY CULTURE HAS HAD TO DEAL WITH FAMINE, PLAGUE, NATURAL DISASTER, OR HORDES OF BARBARIANS. ANY ONE OF WHICH COULD DESTROY A PERSON'S UNIVERSE. I FELT A LITTLE BETTER KNOWING THAT MY PARALYZING FEAR WAS NORMAL.
OVER TIME, AS I GOT OLDER, I FELT BETTER. EITHER I MATURED, OR THE WORLD BECAME MORE STABLE, OR BOTH.
AN OCCASIONAL WAR OR INVASION WOULD REMIND ME OF MY TRAUMATIZED YOUTH. I'D WORRY FOR A WEEK OR TWO, THEN THINGS WOULD RETURN TO NORMAL
NOW POLITICIANS ARE TALKING ABOUT A MISSILE DEFENSE PROGRAM. ALL MY CHILDHOOD FEARS FROM THE COLD WAR COME FLOODING BACK EVERY TIME I HEAR THEIR PLANS.
LET'S NOT START AN ARMS RACE AGAIN. MY NERVES CAN'T TAKE IT.

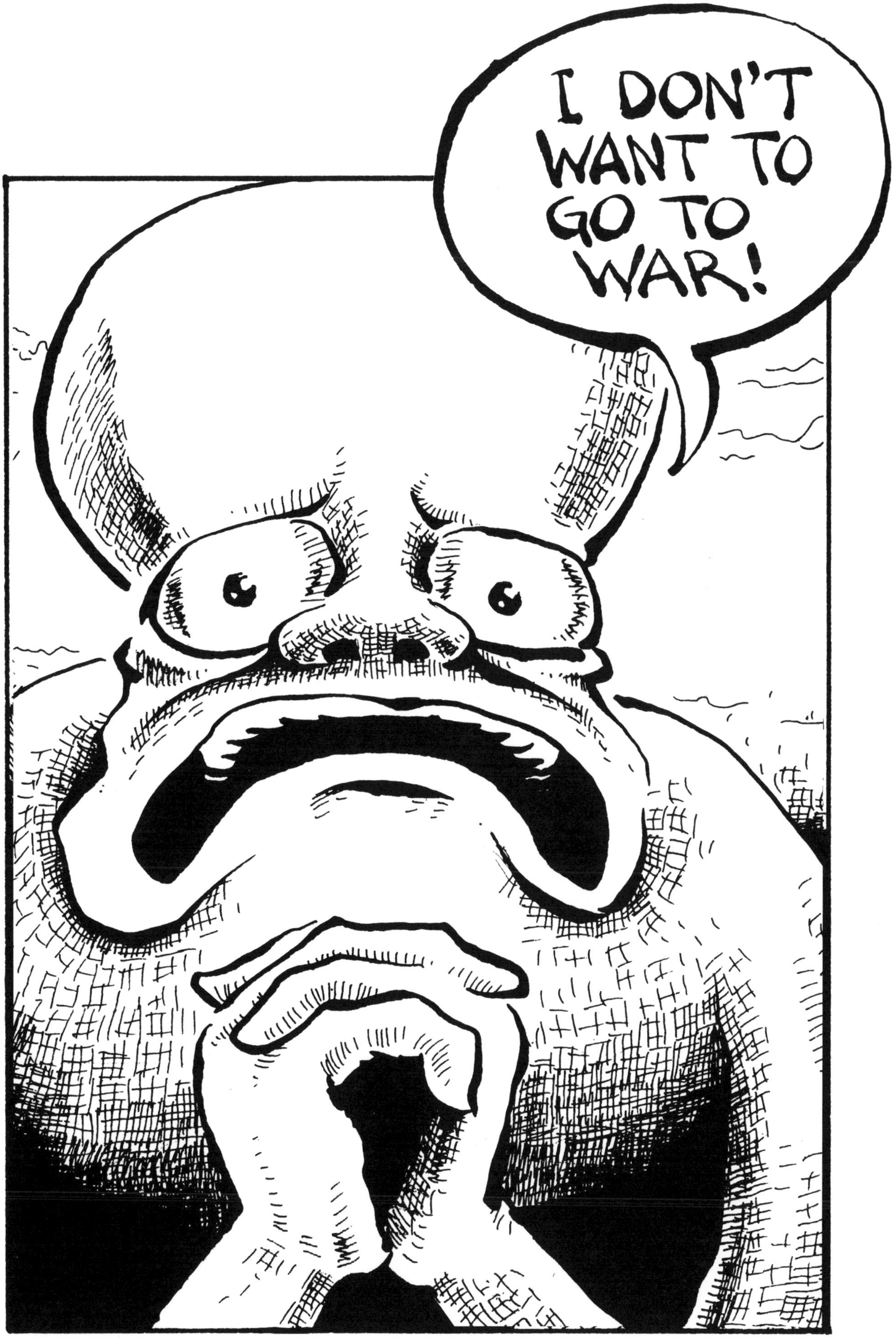
I DON'T WANT TO GO TO WAR!

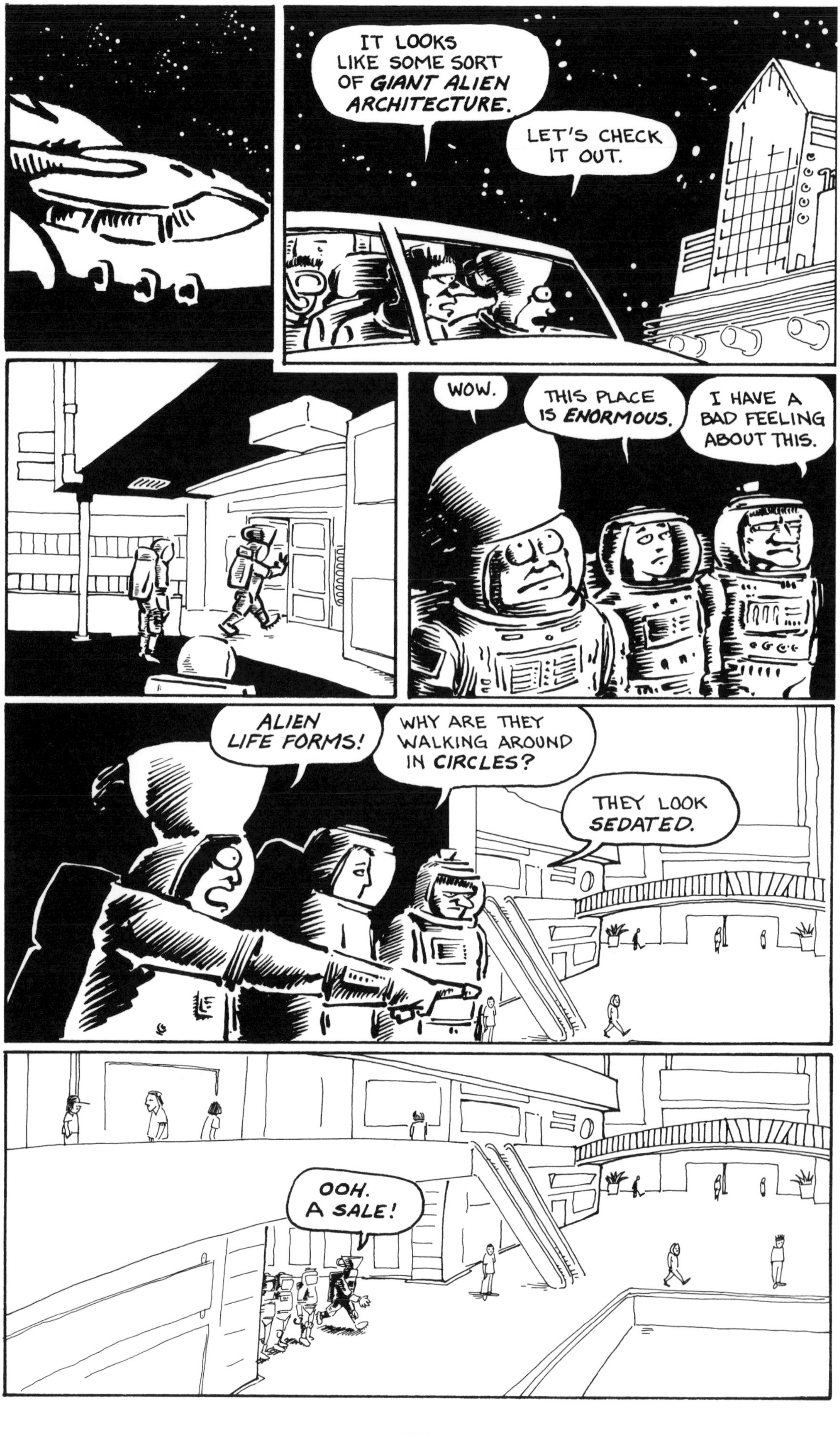
IT LOOKS LIKE SOME SORT OF GIANT ALIEN ARCHITECTURE.
LET'S CHECK IT OUT.
WOW.
THIS PLACE IS ENORMOUS.
I HAVE A BAD FEELING ABOUT THIS.
ALIEN LIFE FORMS!
WHY ARE THEY WALKING AROUND IN CIRCLES?
THEY LOOK SEDATED.
OOH. A SALE!

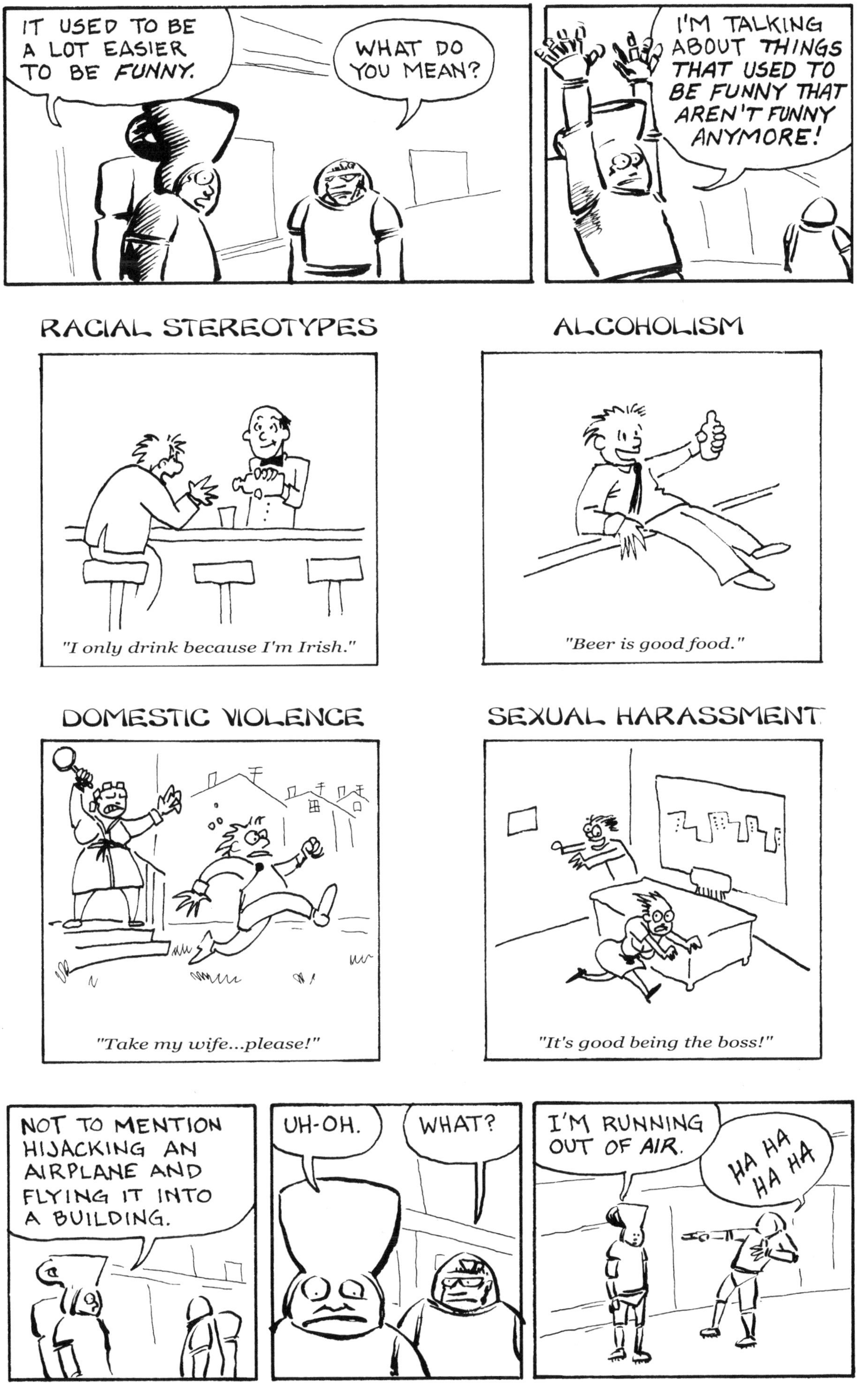
IT USED TO BE A LOT EASIER TO BE FUNNY.
WHAT DO YOU MEAN?
I'M TALKING ABOUT THINGS THAT USED TO BE FUNNY THAT AREN'T FUNNY ANYMORE!
RACIAL STEREOTYPES
"I only drink because I'm Irish."
ALCOHOLISM
"Beer is good food."
DOMESTIC VIOLENCE
"Take my wife...please!"
SEXUAL HARASSMENT
"It's good being the boss!"
NOT TO MENTION HIJACKING AN AIRPLANE AND FLYING IT INTO A BUILDING.
UH-OH.
WHAT?
I'M RUNNING OUT OF AIR.
HA HA HA HA

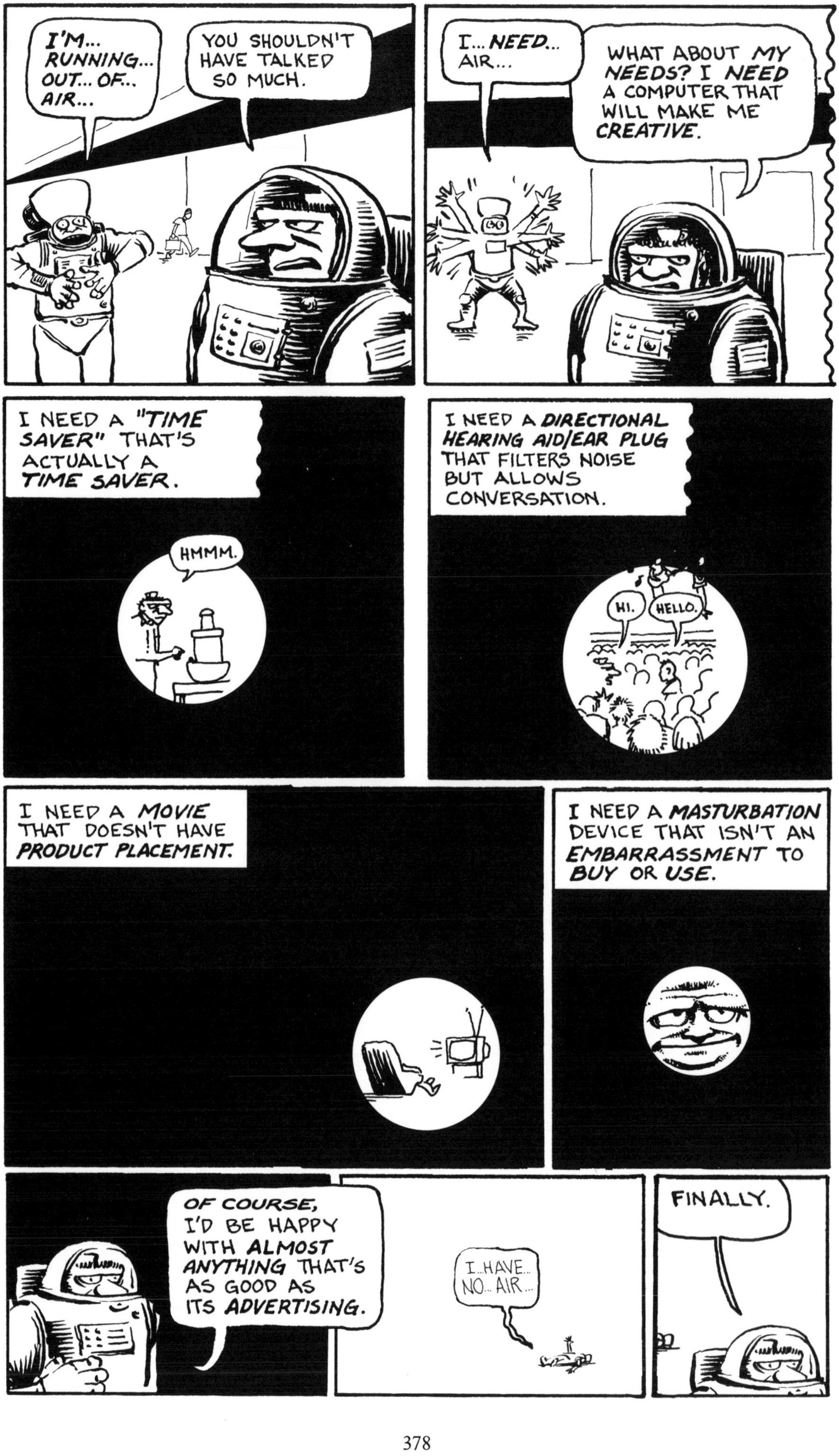
I'M... RUNNING... OUT... OF.. AIR...
YOU SHOULDN'T HAVE TALKED SO MUCH.
I... NEED... AIR...
WHAT ABOUT MY NEEDS? I NEED A COMPUTER THAT WILL MAKE ME CREATIVE.
I NEED A "TIME SAVER" THAT'S ACTUALLY A TIME SAVER.
HMMM.
I NEED A DIRECTIONAL HEARING AID/EAR PLUG THAT FILTERS NOISE BUT ALLOWS CONVERSATION.
HI.
HELLO.
I NEED A MOVIE THAT DOESN'T HAVE PRODUCT PLACEMENT.
I NEED A MASTURBATION DEVICE THAT ISN'T AN EMBARRASSMENT TO BUY OR USE.
OF COURSE, I'D BE HAPPY WITH ALMOST ANYTHING THAT'S AS GOOD AS ITS ADVERTISING.
I...HAVE... NO... AIR...
FINALLY.

THEY'VE FINALLY ADMITTED THAT *GLOBAL WARMING* IS *REAL*.

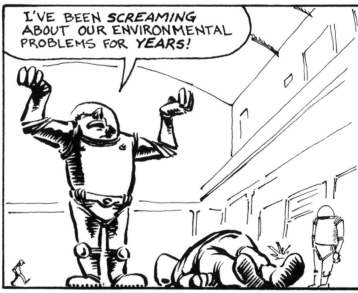

I'VE BEEN *SCREAMING* ABOUT OUR ENVIRONMENTAL PROBLEMS FOR *YEARS!*

I WANT SOMEONE I CAN *BLAME*. I WANT TO YELL AT THE GREEDY BUSINESSMEN, THE SCIENTISTS, AND POLITICIANS. I WANT SOMEONE I CAN LOOK IN THE FACE AND SAY, *"I TOLD YOU SO!"*

DOESN'T BEING *RIGHT* COUNT FOR SOMETHING?

I'M... OUT... OF... AIR....

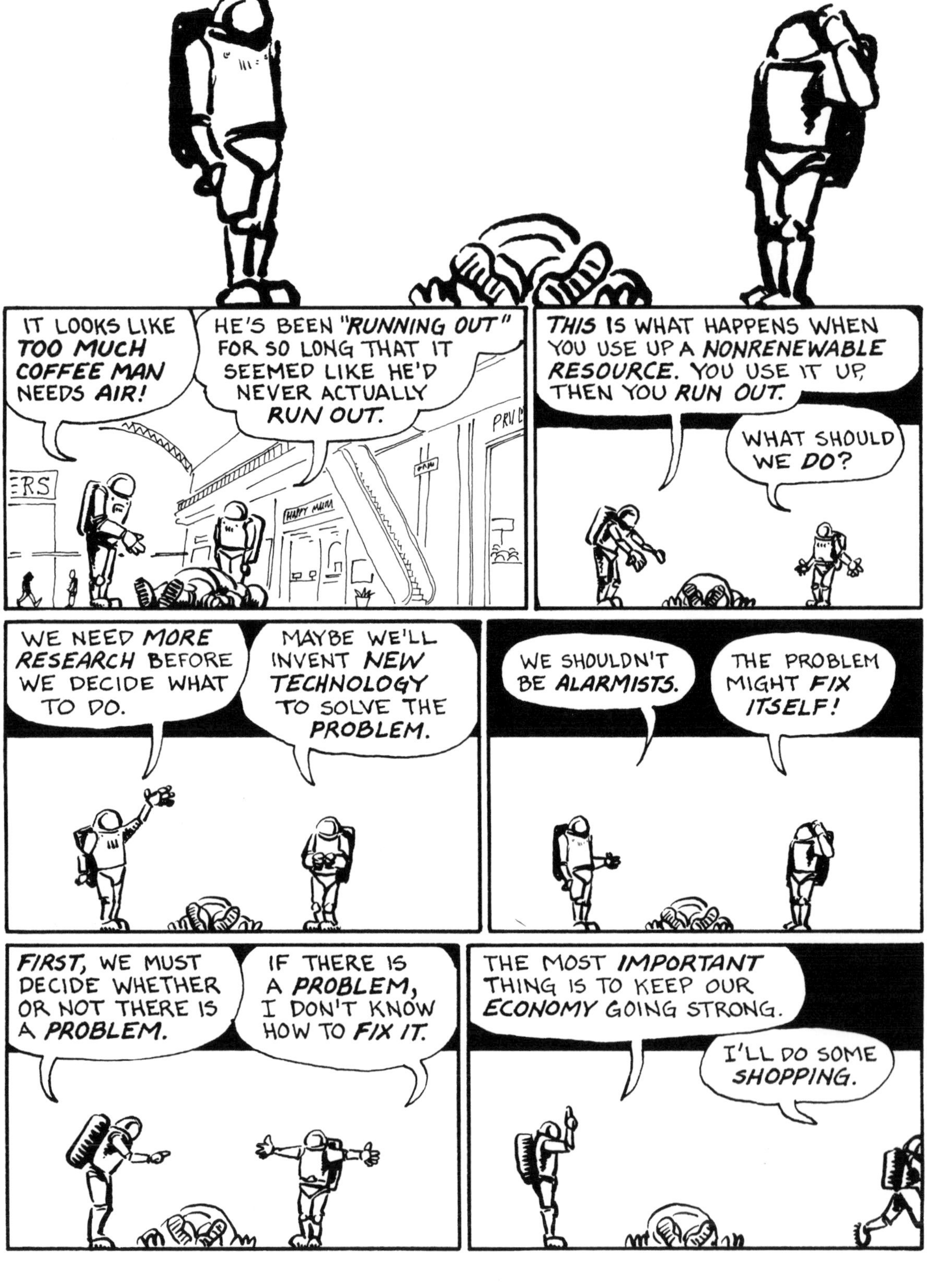

IT LOOKS LIKE TOO MUCH COFFEE MAN NEEDS AIR!
HE'S BEEN "RUNNING OUT" FOR SO LONG THAT IT SEEMED LIKE HE'D NEVER ACTUALLY RUN OUT.
ERS
HAPPY MUM
THIS IS WHAT HAPPENS WHEN YOU USE UP A NONRENEWABLE RESOURCE. YOU USE IT UP, THEN YOU RUN OUT.
WHAT SHOULD WE DO?
WE NEED MORE RESEARCH BEFORE WE DECIDE WHAT TO DO.
MAYBE WE'LL INVENT NEW TECHNOLOGY TO SOLVE THE PROBLEM.
WE SHOULDN'T BE ALARMISTS.
THE PROBLEM MIGHT FIX ITSELF!
FIRST, WE MUST DECIDE WHETHER OR NOT THERE IS A PROBLEM.
IF THERE IS A PROBLEM, I DON'T KNOW HOW TO FIX IT.
THE MOST IMPORTANT THING IS TO KEEP OUR ECONOMY GOING STRONG.
I'LL DO SOME SHOPPING.

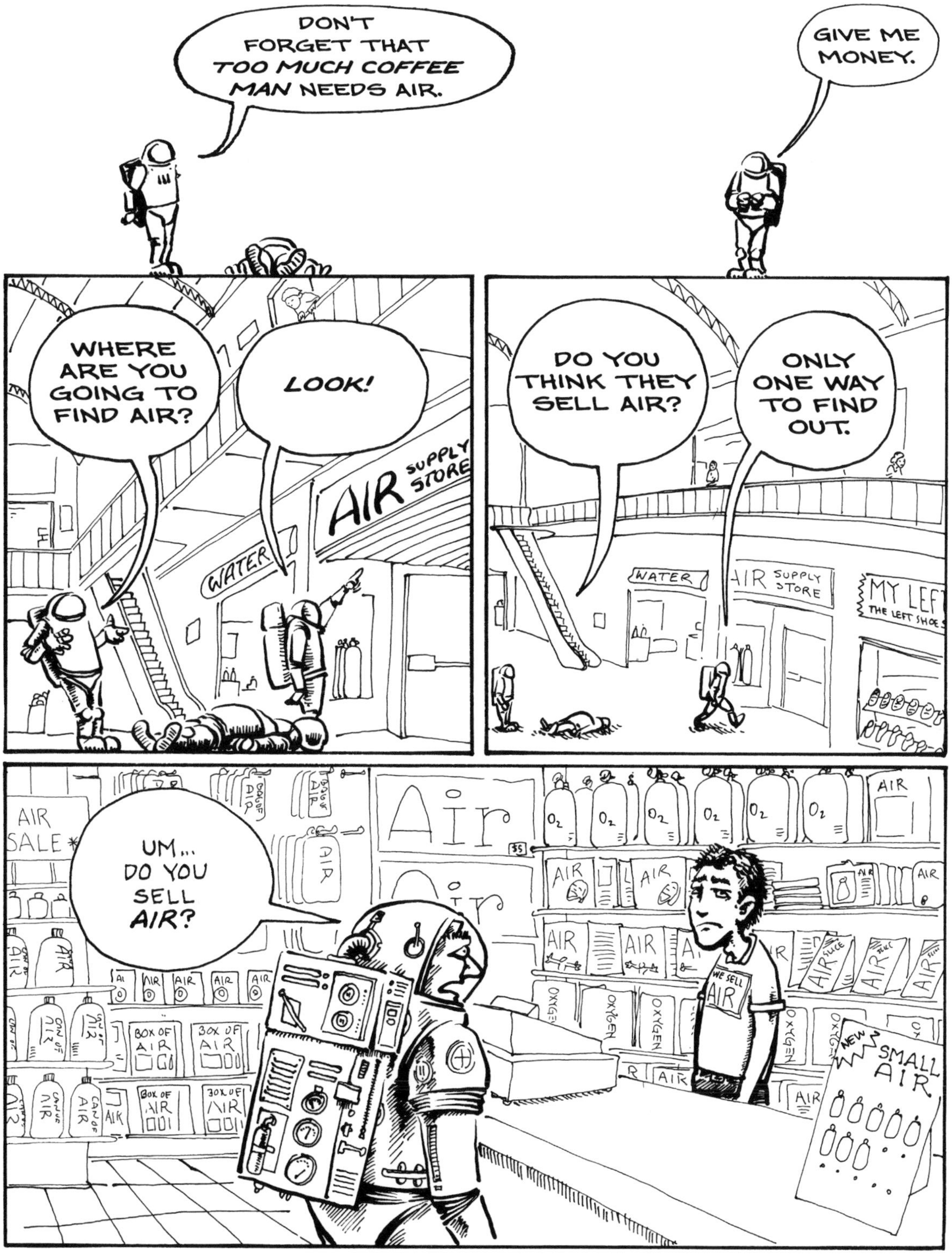
DON'T FORGET THAT TOO MUCH COFFEE MAN NEEDS AIR.
GIVE ME MONEY.
WHERE ARE YOU GOING TO FIND AIR?
LOOK!
WATER
AIR SUPPLY STORE
DO YOU THINK THEY SELL AIR?
ONLY ONE WAY TO FIND OUT.
WATER
AIR SUPPLY STORE
MY LEFT
THE LEFT SHOE
AIR SALE
UM... DO YOU SELL AIR?
WE SELL AIR
NEW SMALL AIR

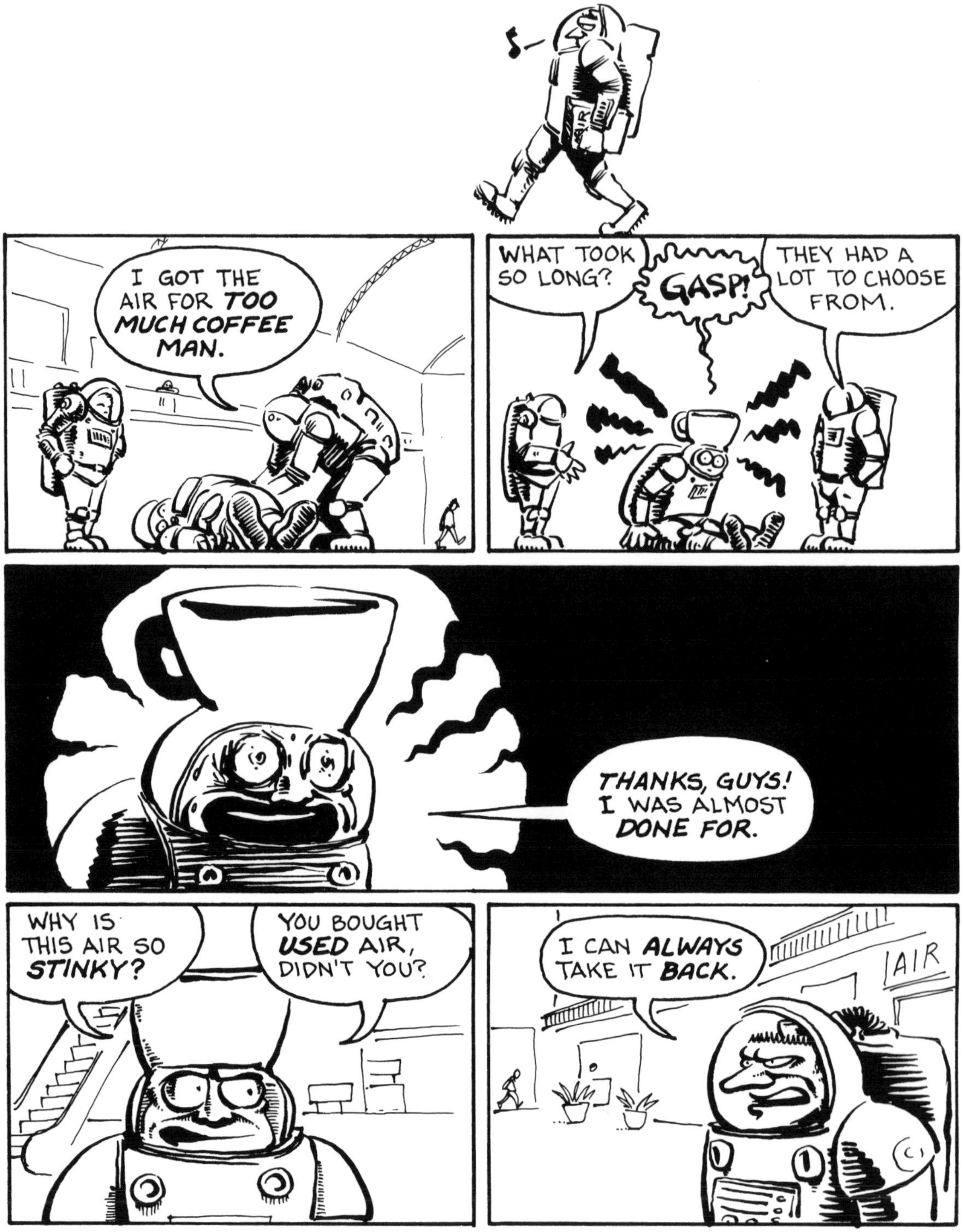
I GOT THE AIR FOR TOO MUCH COFFEE MAN.
WHAT TOOK SO LONG?
GASP!
THEY HAD A LOT TO CHOOSE FROM.
THANKS, GUYS! I WAS ALMOST DONE FOR.
WHY IS THIS AIR SO STINKY?
YOU BOUGHT USED AIR, DIDN'T YOU?
I CAN ALWAYS TAKE IT BACK.
AIR

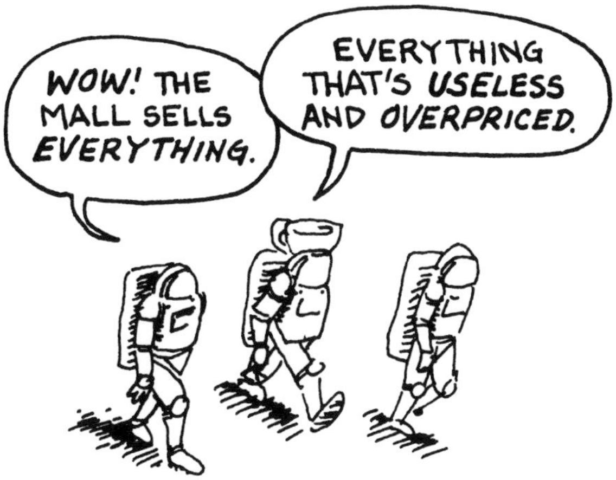
WOW! THE MALL SELLS EVERYTHING.
EVERYTHING THAT'S USELESS AND OVERPRICED.

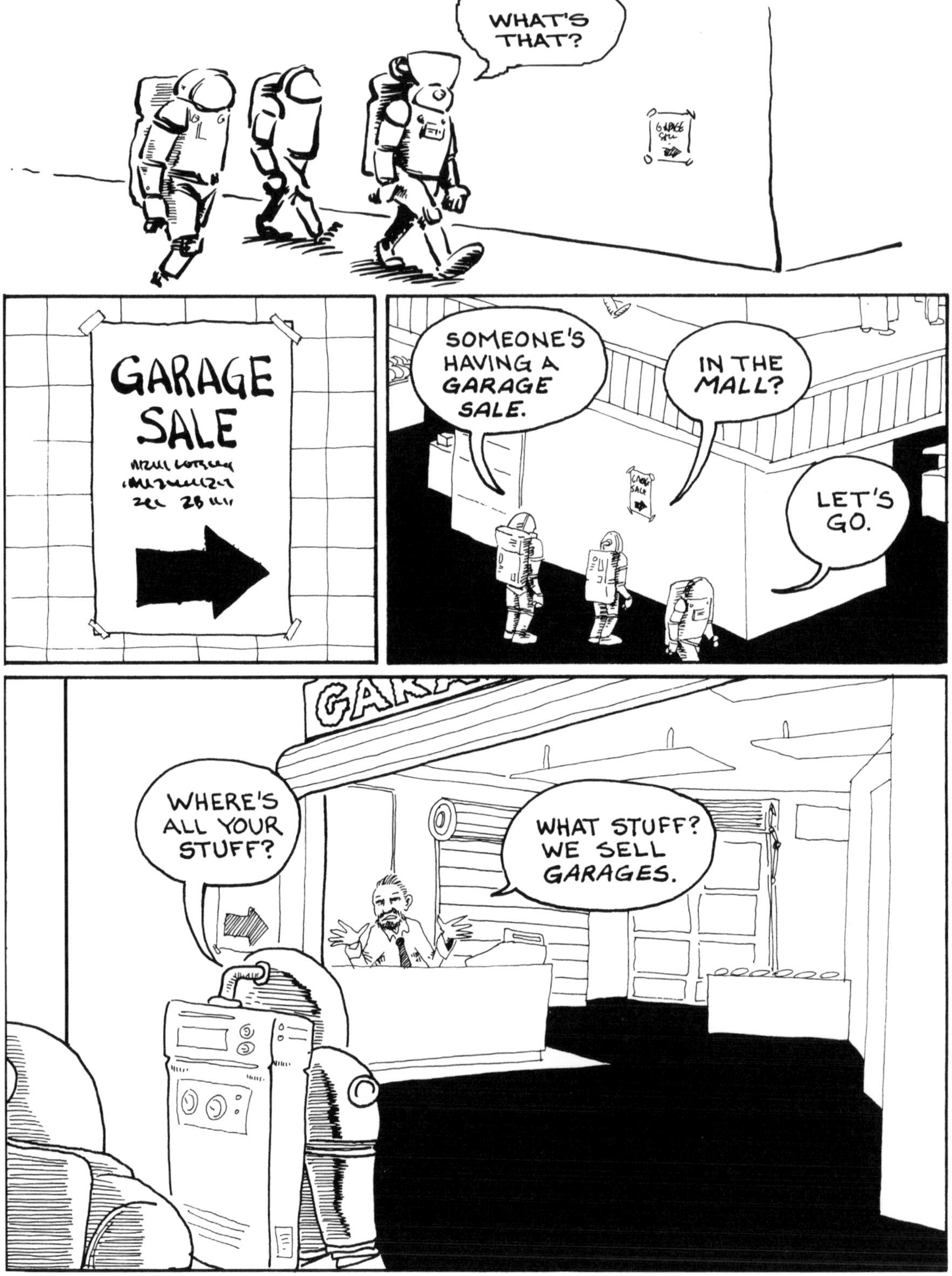
WHAT'S THAT?
GARAGE SALE
SOMEONE'S HAVING A GARAGE SALE.
IN THE MALL?
LET'S GO.
WHERE'S ALL YOUR STUFF?
WHAT STUFF? WE SELL GARAGES.

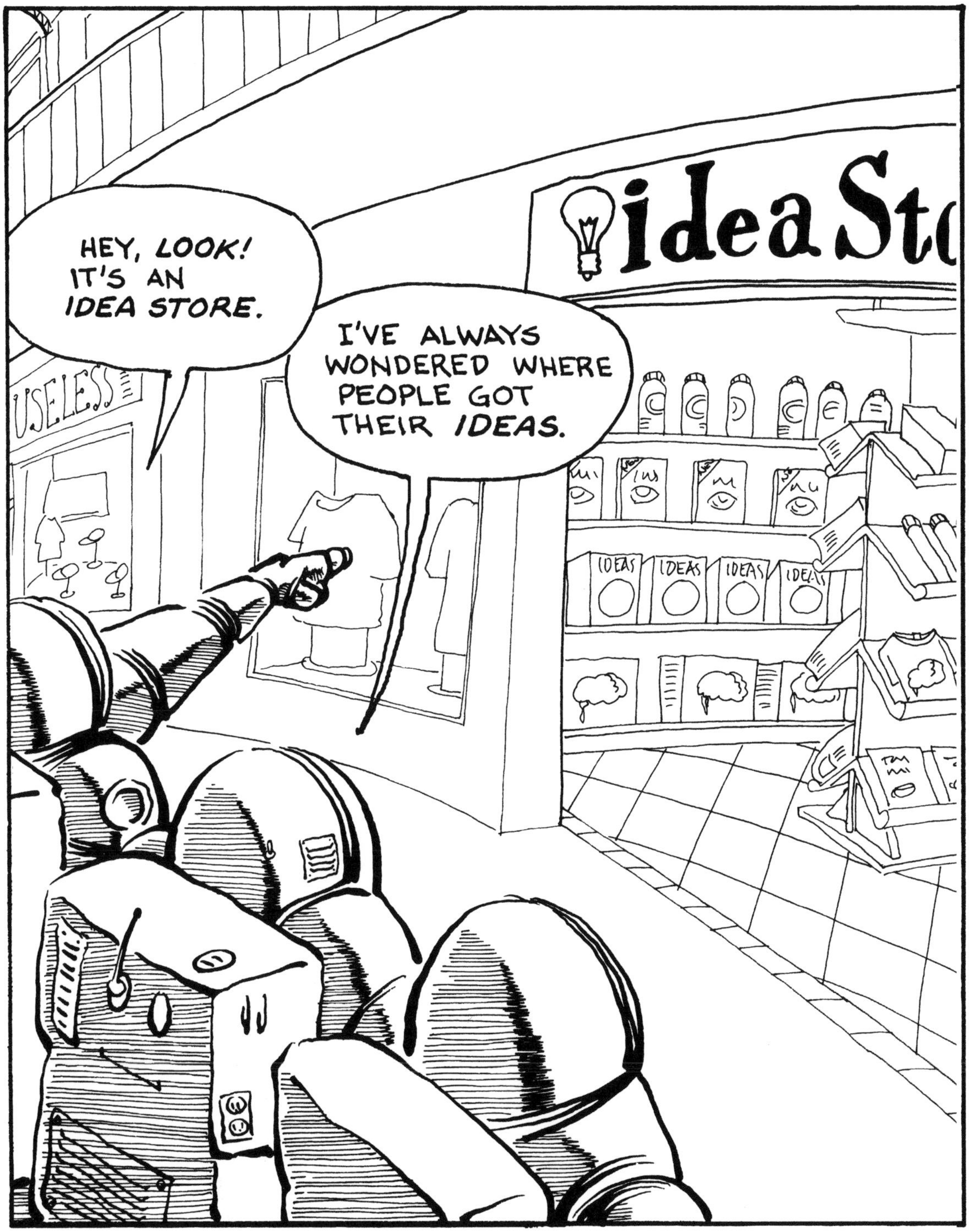
HEY, LOOK! IT'S AN IDEA STORE.
I'VE ALWAYS WONDERED WHERE PEOPLE GOT THEIR IDEAS.
idea St
USELESS
IDEAS
IDEAS
IDEAS

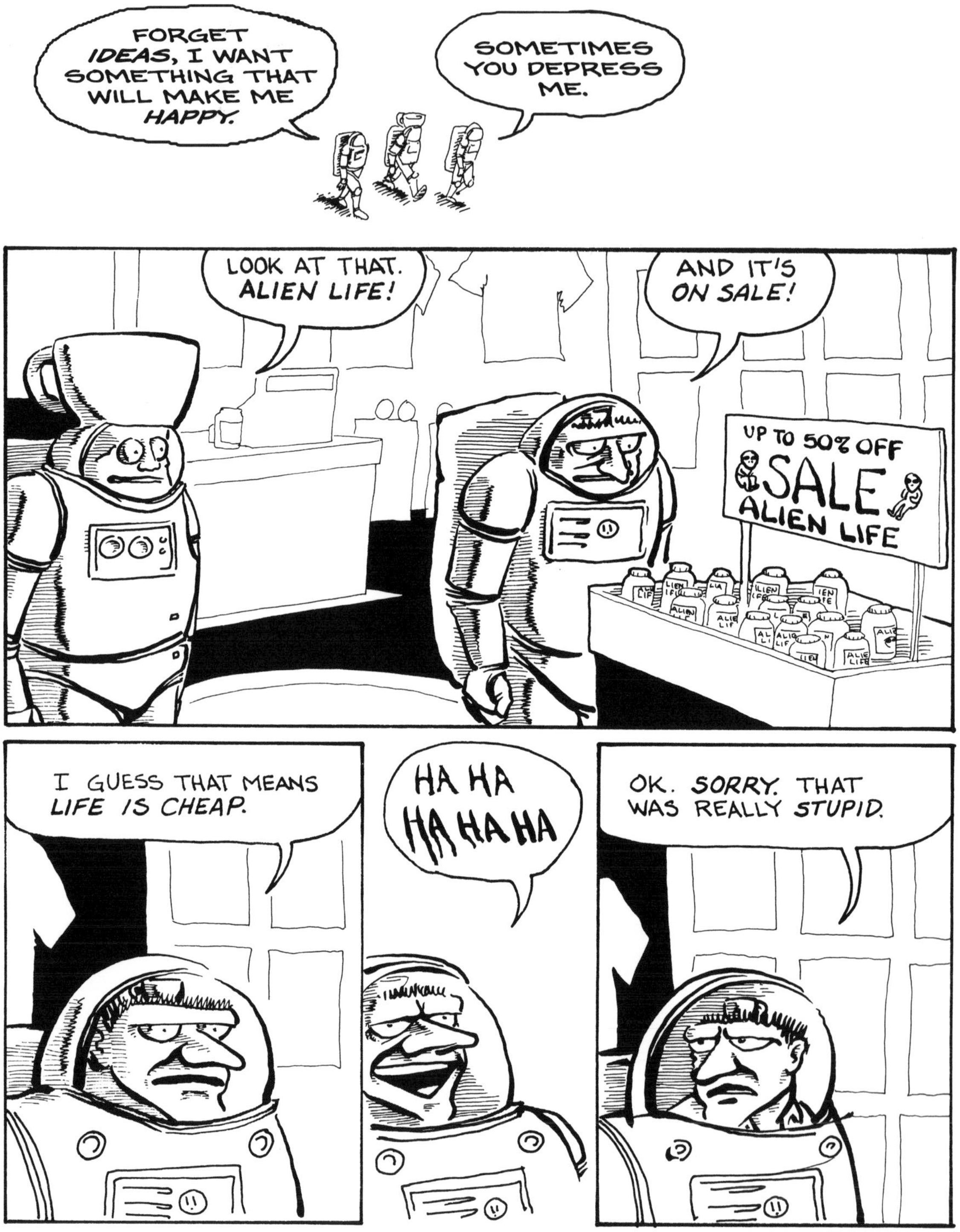
FORGET *IDEAS*, I WANT SOMETHING THAT WILL MAKE ME *HAPPY.*
SOMETIMES YOU DEPRESS ME.
LOOK AT THAT. ALIEN LIFE!
AND IT'S ON SALE!
UP TO 50% OFF SALE ALIEN LIFE
I GUESS THAT MEANS *LIFE IS CHEAP.*
HA HA HA HA HA HA
OK. *SORRY.* THAT WAS REALLY *STUPID.*

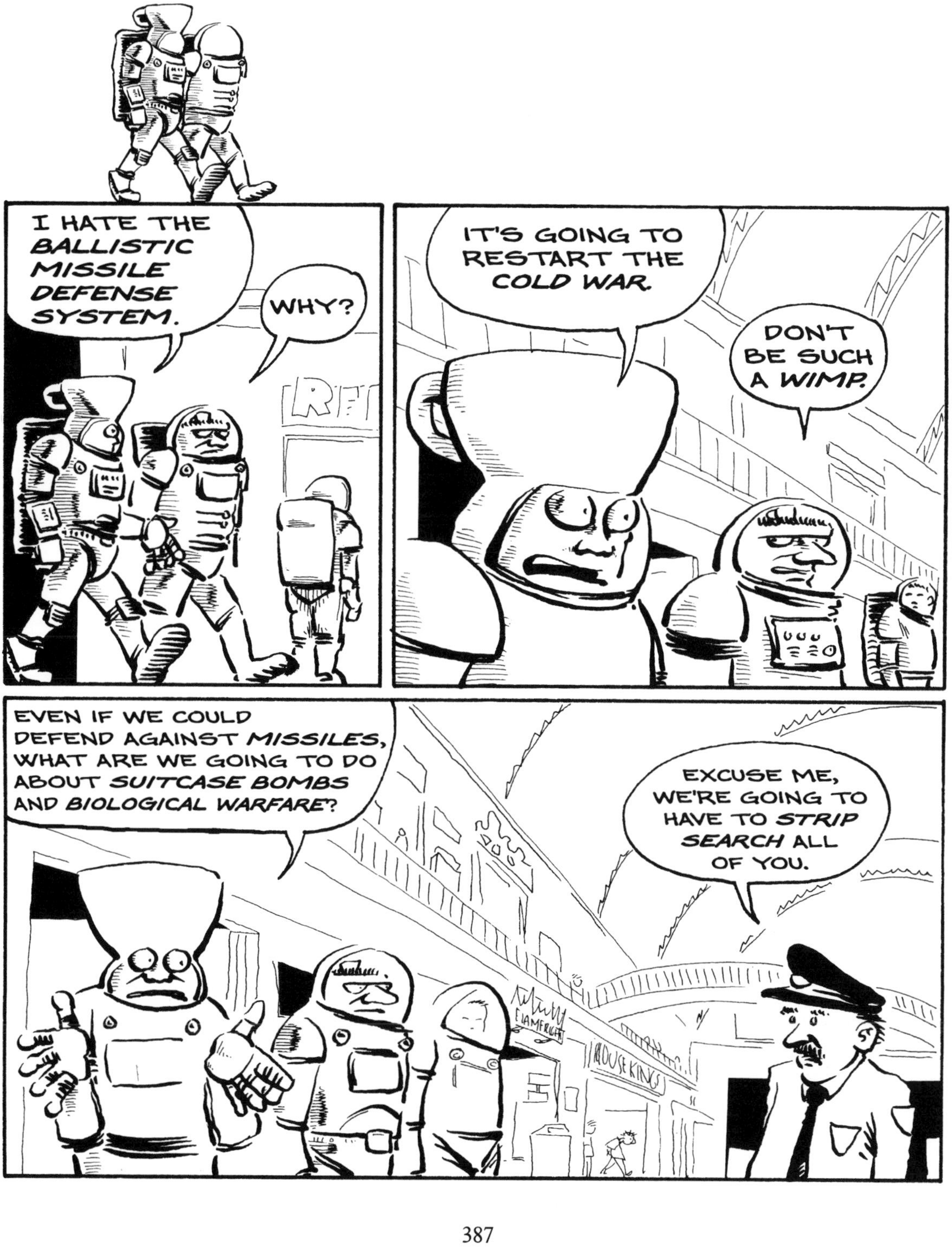
I HATE THE BALLISTIC MISSILE DEFENSE SYSTEM.
WHY?
IT'S GOING TO RESTART THE COLD WAR.
DON'T BE SUCH A WIMP.
EVEN IF WE COULD DEFEND AGAINST MISSILES, WHAT ARE WE GOING TO DO ABOUT SUITCASE BOMBS AND BIOLOGICAL WARFARE?
EXCUSE ME, WE'RE GOING TO HAVE TO STRIP SEARCH ALL OF YOU.

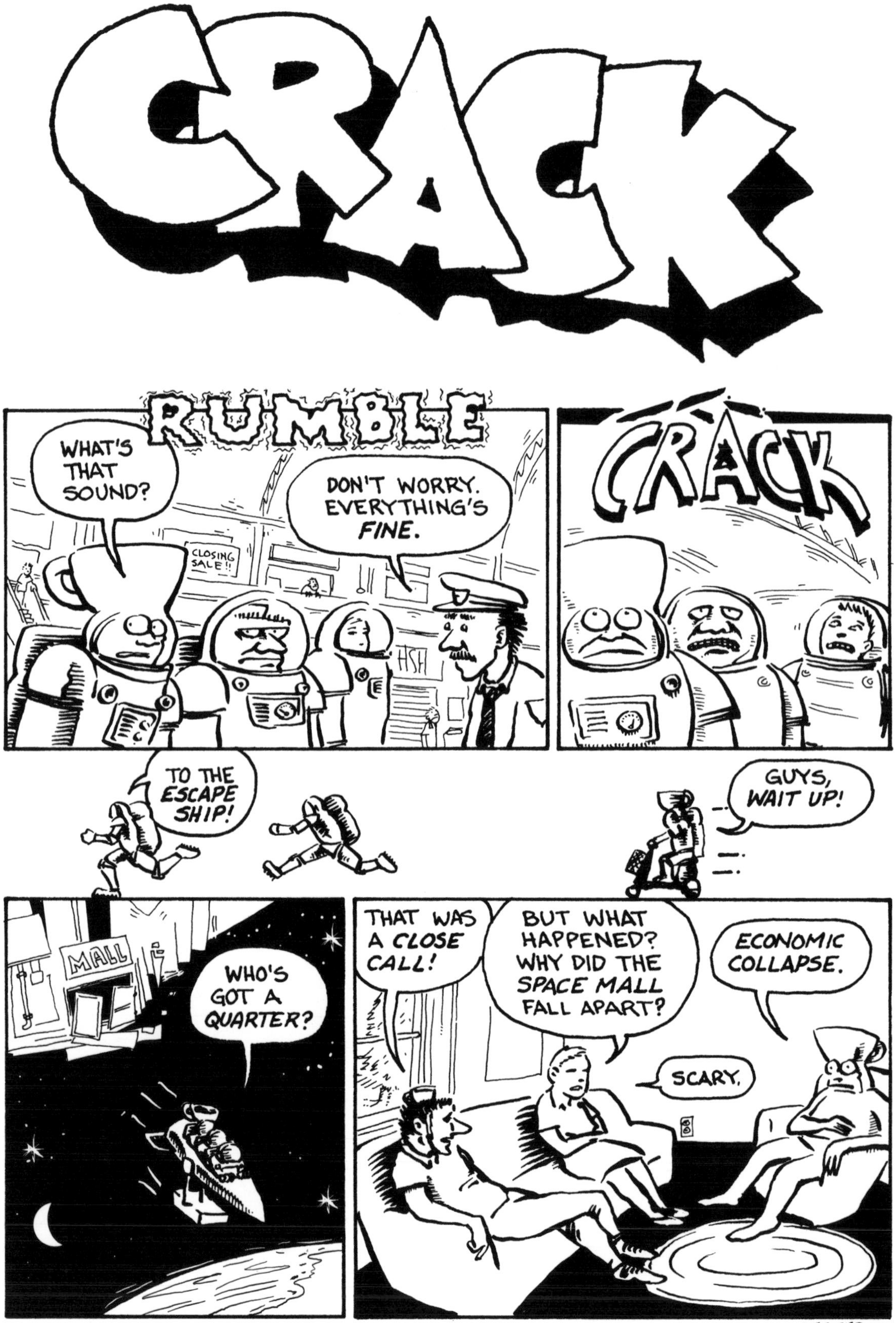
CRACK
RUMBLE
WHAT'S THAT SOUND?
CLOSING SALE!!
DON'T WORRY. EVERYTHING'S FINE.
CRACK
TO THE ESCAPE SHIP!
GUYS, WAIT UP!
MALL
WHO'S GOT A QUARTER?
THAT WAS A CLOSE CALL!
BUT WHAT HAPPENED? WHY DID THE SPACE MALL FALL APART?
ECONOMIC COLLAPSE.
SCARY.
THE END!!!

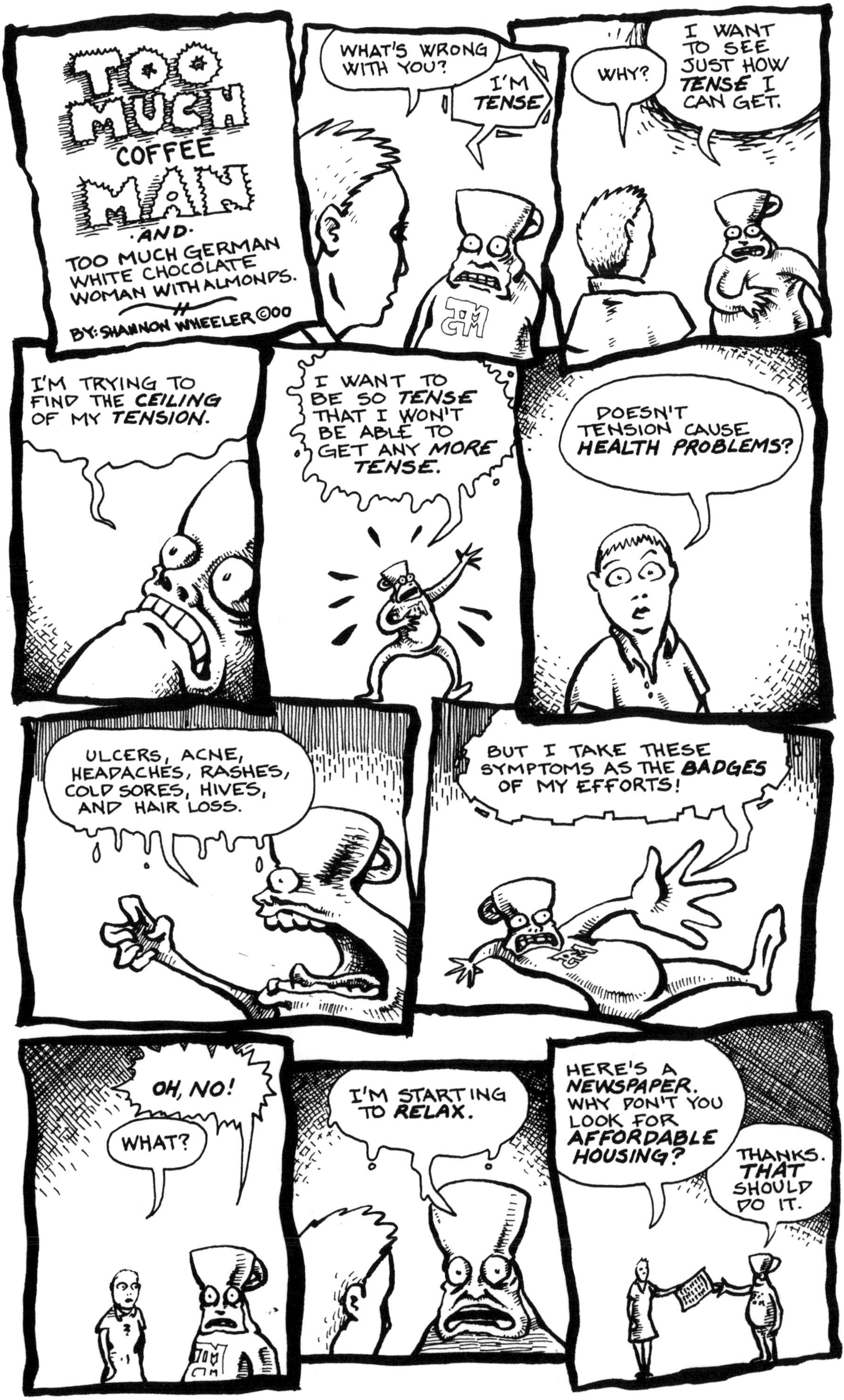
TOO MUCH COFFEE MAN
AND TOO MUCH GERMAN WHITE CHOCOLATE WOMAN WITH ALMONDS.
BY: SHANNON WHEELER ©00
WHAT'S WRONG WITH YOU?
I'M TENSE
WHY?
I WANT TO SEE JUST HOW TENSE I CAN GET.
I'M TRYING TO FIND THE CEILING OF MY TENSION.
I WANT TO BE SO TENSE THAT I WON'T BE ABLE TO GET ANY MORE TENSE.
DOESN'T TENSION CAUSE HEALTH PROBLEMS?
ULCERS, ACNE, HEADACHES, RASHES, COLD SORES, HIVES, AND HAIR LOSS.
BUT I TAKE THESE SYMPTOMS AS THE BADGES OF MY EFFORTS!
OH, NO!
WHAT?
I'M STARTING TO RELAX.
HERE'S A NEWSPAPER. WHY DON'T YOU LOOK FOR AFFORDABLE HOUSING?
THANKS. THAT SHOULD DO IT.

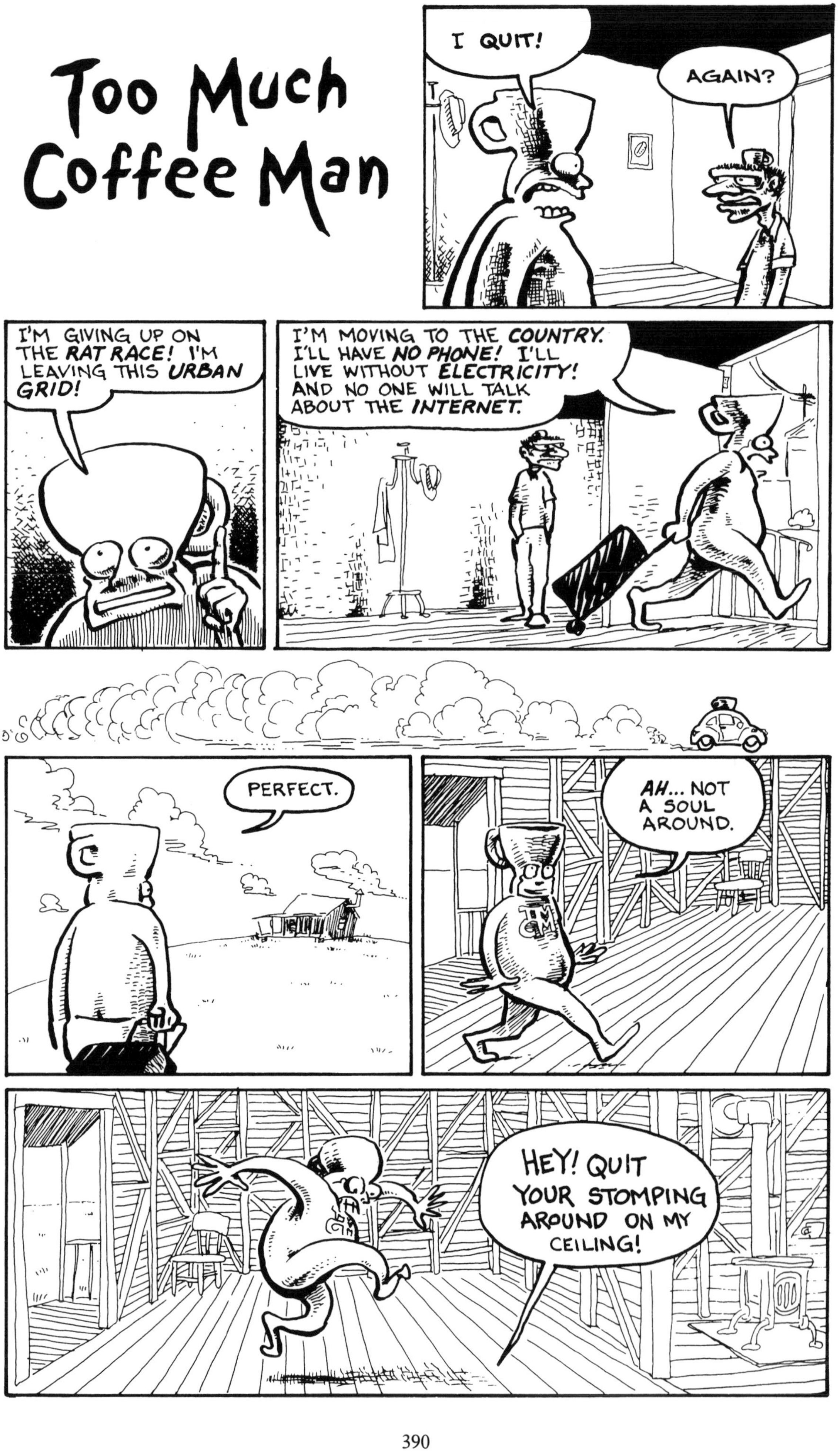
Too Much Coffee Man
I QUIT!
AGAIN?
I'M GIVING UP ON THE RAT RACE! I'M LEAVING THIS URBAN GRID!
I'M MOVING TO THE COUNTRY. I'LL HAVE NO PHONE! I'LL LIVE WITHOUT ELECTRICITY! AND NO ONE WILL TALK ABOUT THE INTERNET.
PERFECT.
AH... NOT A SOUL AROUND.
HEY! QUIT YOUR STOMPING AROUND ON MY CEILING!

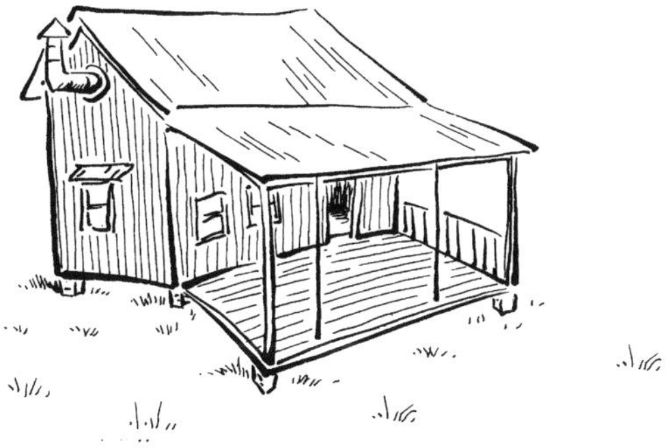

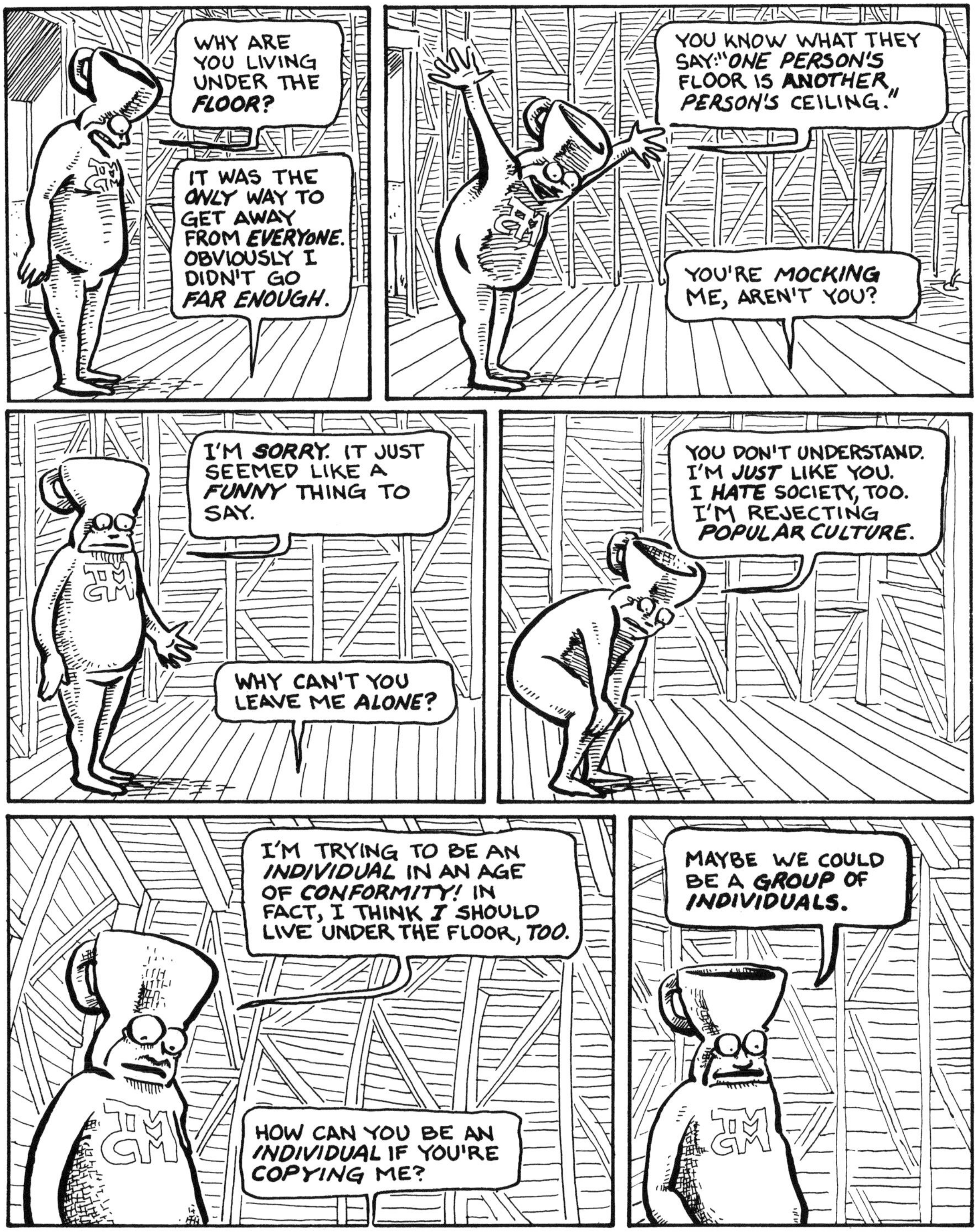

WHY ARE YOU LIVING UNDER THE FLOOR?
IT WAS THE ONLY WAY TO GET AWAY FROM EVERYONE. OBVIOUSLY I DIDN'T GO FAR ENOUGH.
YOU KNOW WHAT THEY SAY: "ONE PERSON'S FLOOR IS ANOTHER PERSON'S CEILING."
YOU'RE MOCKING ME, AREN'T YOU?
I'M SORRY. IT JUST SEEMED LIKE A FUNNY THING TO SAY.
WHY CAN'T YOU LEAVE ME ALONE?
YOU DON'T UNDERSTAND. I'M JUST LIKE YOU. I HATE SOCIETY, TOO. I'M REJECTING POPULAR CULTURE.
I'M TRYING TO BE AN INDIVIDUAL IN AN AGE OF CONFORMITY! IN FACT, I THINK I SHOULD LIVE UNDER THE FLOOR, TOO.
HOW CAN YOU BE AN INDIVIDUAL IF YOU'RE COPYING ME?
MAYBE WE COULD BE A GROUP OF INDIVIDUALS.

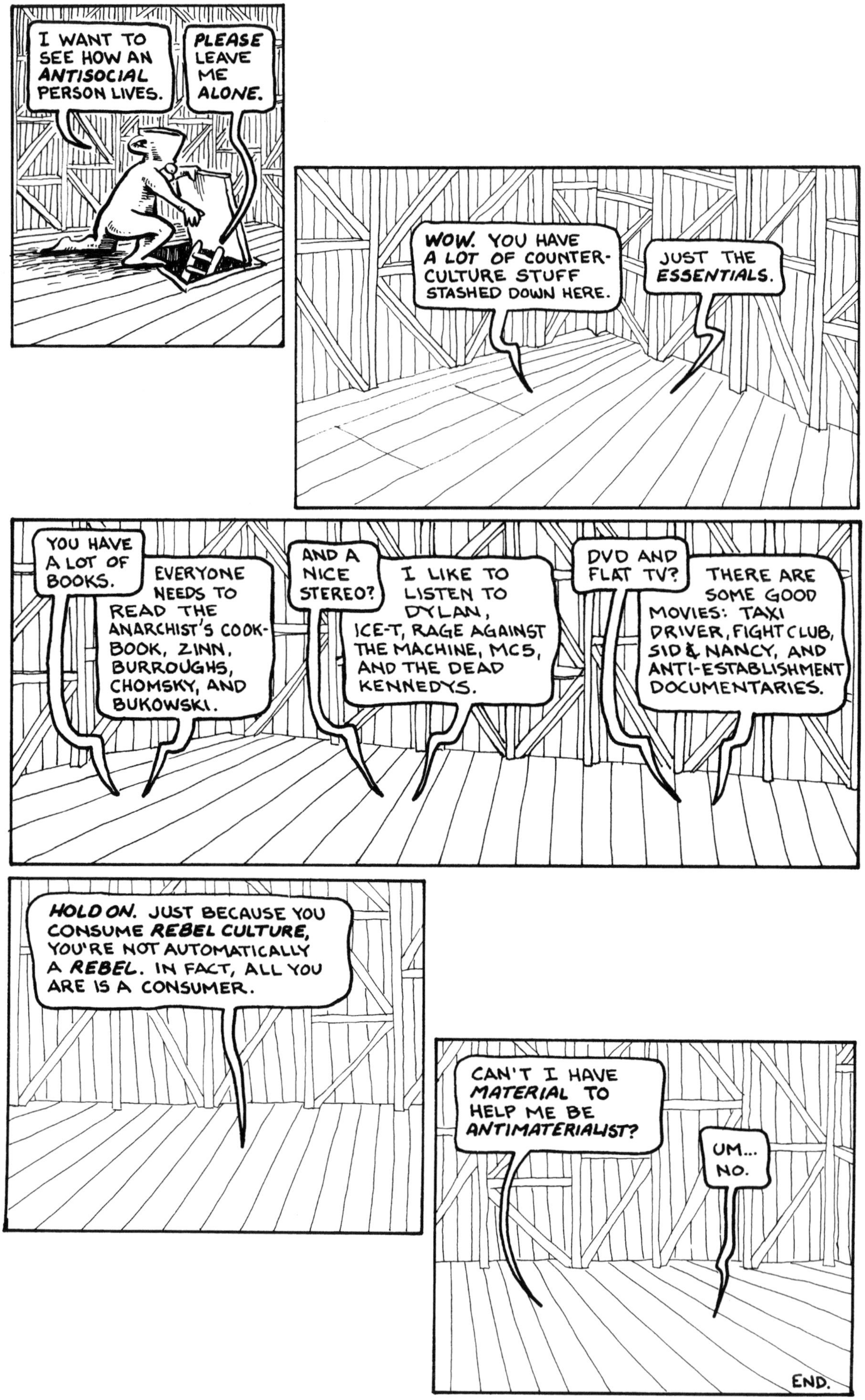
I WANT TO SEE HOW AN ANTISOCIAL PERSON LIVES.
PLEASE LEAVE ME ALONE.
WOW. YOU HAVE A LOT OF COUNTER-CULTURE STUFF STASHED DOWN HERE.
JUST THE ESSENTIALS.
YOU HAVE A LOT OF BOOKS.
EVERYONE NEEDS TO READ THE ANARCHIST'S COOK-BOOK, ZINN, BURROUGHS, CHOMSKY, AND BUKOWSKI.
AND A NICE STEREO?
I LIKE TO LISTEN TO DYLAN, ICE-T, RAGE AGAINST THE MACHINE, MC5, AND THE DEAD KENNEDYS.
DVD AND FLAT TV?
THERE ARE SOME GOOD MOVIES: TAXI DRIVER, FIGHT CLUB, SID & NANCY, AND ANTI-ESTABLISHMENT DOCUMENTARIES.
HOLD ON. JUST BECAUSE YOU CONSUME REBEL CULTURE, YOU'RE NOT AUTOMATICALLY A REBEL. IN FACT, ALL YOU ARE IS A CONSUMER.
CAN'T I HAVE MATERIAL TO HELP ME BE ANTIMATERIALIST?
UM... NO.
END.

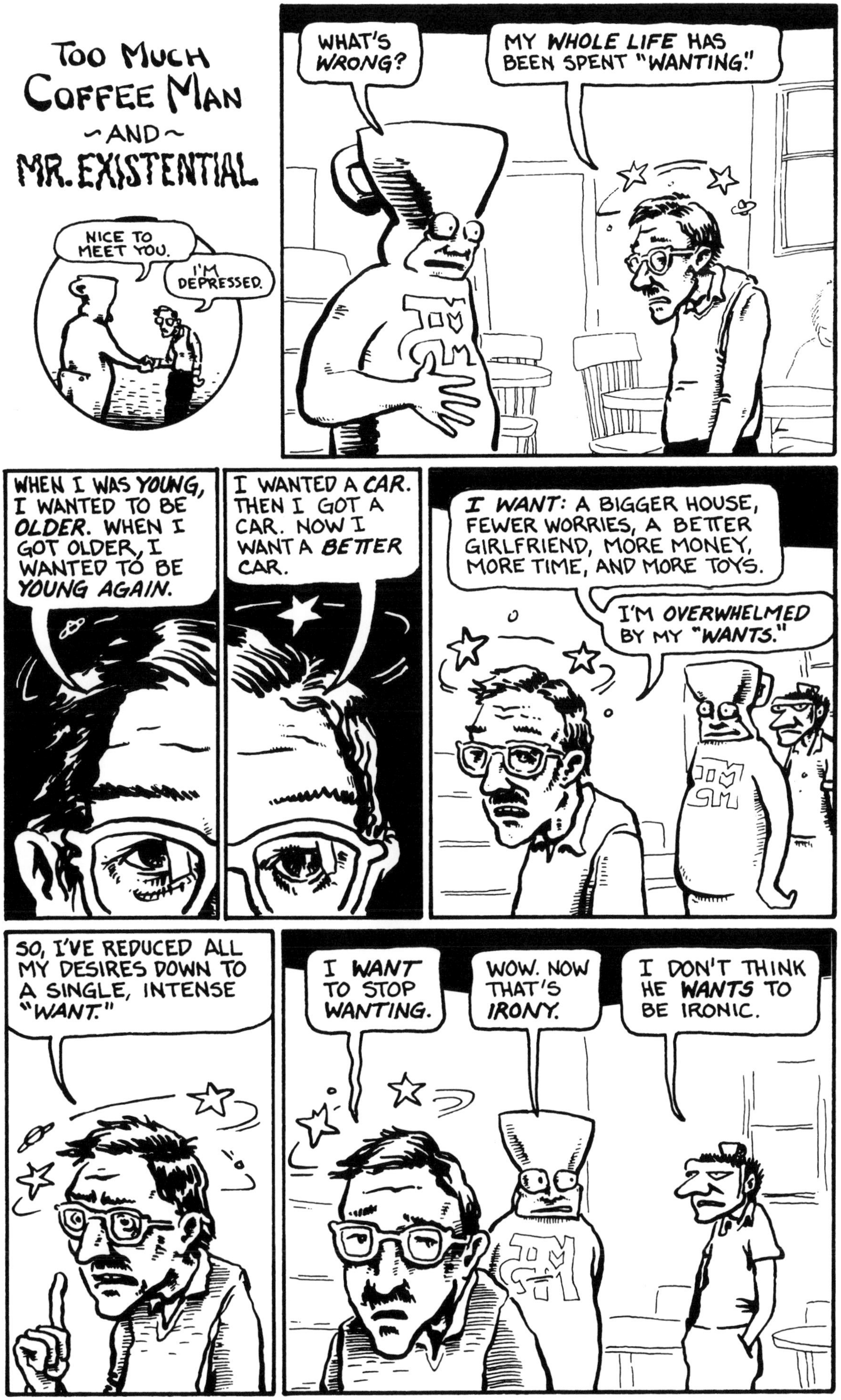
TOO MUCH COFFEE MAN ~AND~ MR. EXISTENTIAL
NICE TO MEET YOU.
I'M DEPRESSED.
WHAT'S WRONG?
MY WHOLE LIFE HAS BEEN SPENT "WANTING."
WHEN I WAS YOUNG, I WANTED TO BE OLDER. WHEN I GOT OLDER, I WANTED TO BE YOUNG AGAIN.
I WANTED A CAR. THEN I GOT A CAR. NOW I WANT A BETTER CAR.
I WANT: A BIGGER HOUSE, FEWER WORRIES, A BETTER GIRLFRIEND, MORE MONEY, MORE TIME, AND MORE TOYS.
I'M OVERWHELMED BY MY "WANTS."
SO, I'VE REDUCED ALL MY DESIRES DOWN TO A SINGLE, INTENSE "WANT."
I WANT TO STOP WANTING.
WOW. NOW THAT'S IRONY.
I DON'T THINK HE WANTS TO BE IRONIC.

SINNER REPENT!
I'D LOVE TO, BUT I CAN'T. YOU SEE...
GOD IS AN ATHEIST!
FAITH IS "BELIEF IN THINGS THAT AREN'T BASED IN FACT." SINCE GOD KNOWS EVERY-THING, HE CAN'T HAVE FAITH.
AND BECAUSE HE'S ALREADY THE HIGHEST POWER, HE DOESN'T BELIEVE IN A HIGHER POWER.
AND SO, GOD IS AN ATHEIST!
WOW. YOU'RE RIGHT. BUT WHAT HAPPENS ONCE WE ACKNOWLEDGE GOD'S ATHEISM?
GEE. I DON'T KNOW

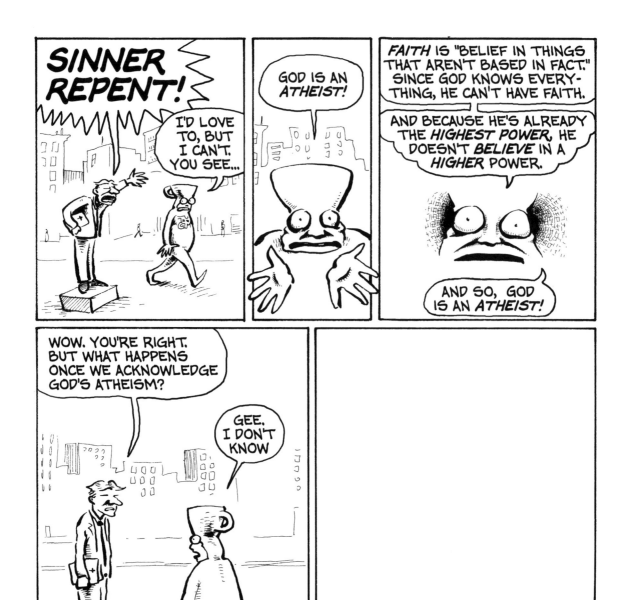

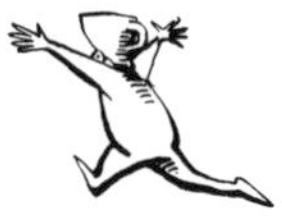

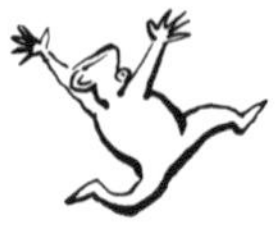

chapter 7

DEBATES, ARGUMENTS, AND STORIES

Money is a placebo, and other thoughts

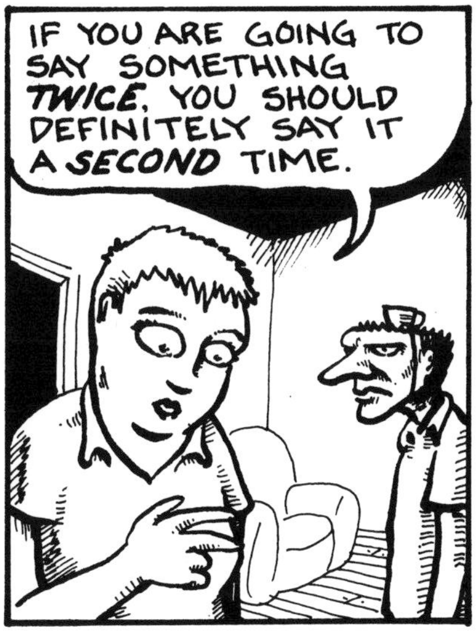
IF YOU ARE GOING TO SAY SOMETHING **TWICE**, YOU SHOULD DEFINITELY SAY IT A **SECOND** TIME.

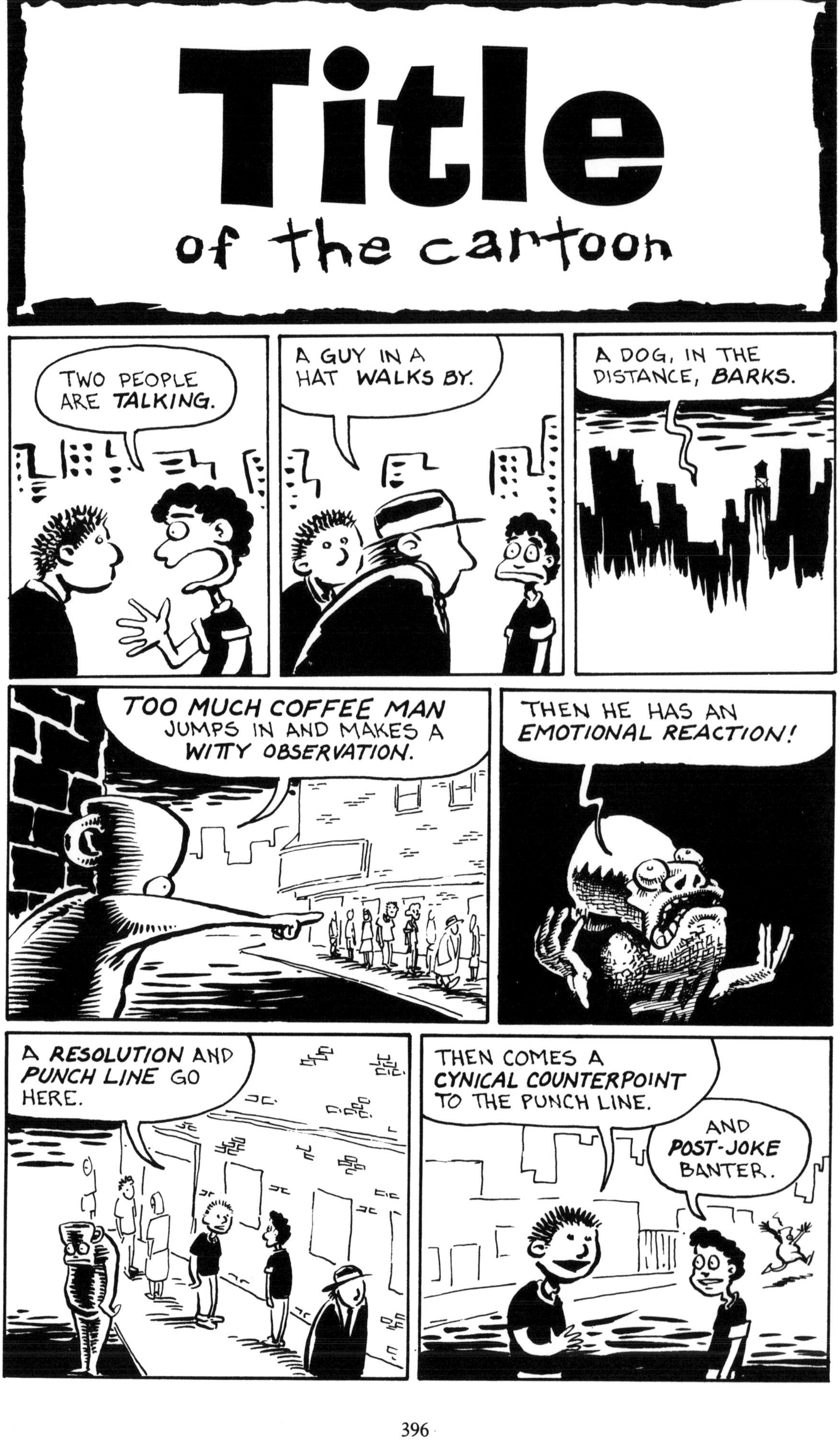
Title
of the cartoon
TWO PEOPLE ARE TALKING.
A GUY IN A HAT WALKS BY.
A DOG, IN THE DISTANCE, BARKS.
TOO MUCH COFFEE MAN JUMPS IN AND MAKES A WITTY OBSERVATION.
THEN HE HAS AN EMOTIONAL REACTION!
A RESOLUTION AND PUNCH LINE GO HERE.
THEN COMES A CYNICAL COUNTERPOINT TO THE PUNCH LINE.
AND POST-JOKE BANTER.

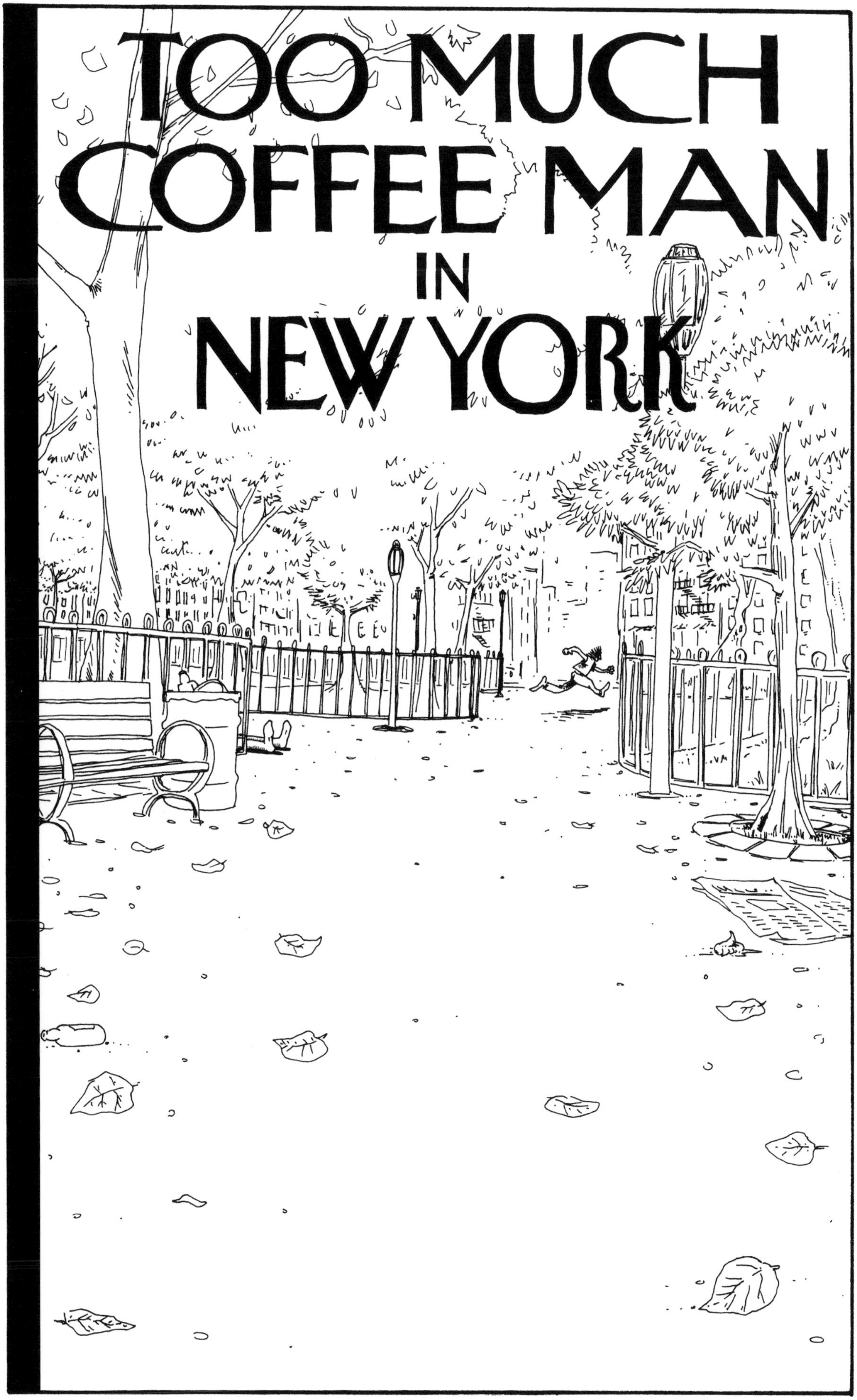
TOO MUCH COFFEE MAN IN NEW YORK

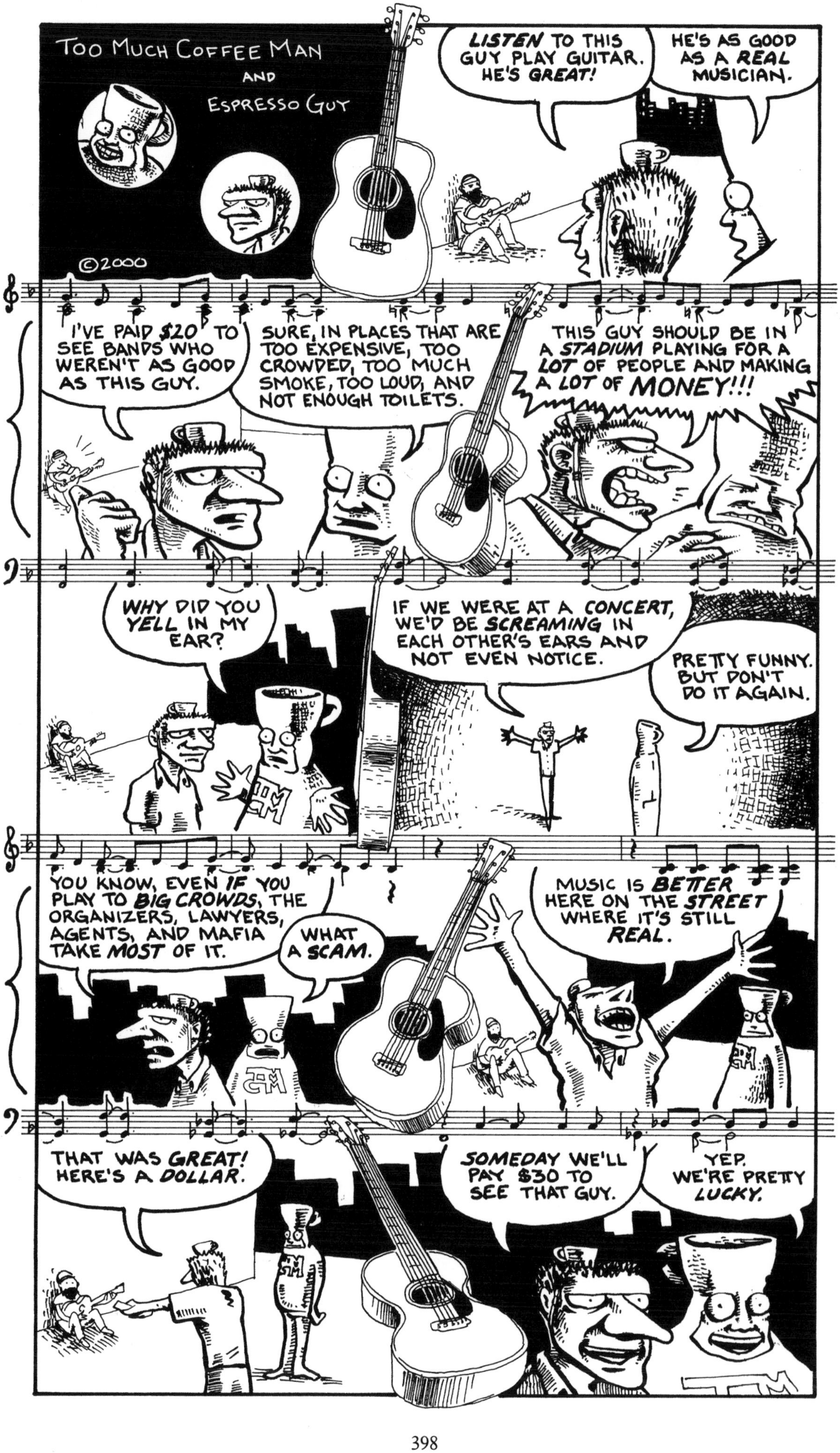

Too Much Coffee Man
and
Espresso Guy
©2000
LISTEN TO THIS GUY PLAY GUITAR. HE'S GREAT!
HE'S AS GOOD AS A REAL MUSICIAN.
I'VE PAID $20 TO SEE BANDS WHO WEREN'T AS GOOD AS THIS GUY.
SURE, IN PLACES THAT ARE TOO EXPENSIVE, TOO CROWDED, TOO MUCH SMOKE, TOO LOUD, AND NOT ENOUGH TOILETS.
THIS GUY SHOULD BE IN A STADIUM PLAYING FOR A LOT OF PEOPLE AND MAKING A LOT OF MONEY!!!
WHY DID YOU YELL IN MY EAR?
IF WE WERE AT A CONCERT, WE'D BE SCREAMING IN EACH OTHER'S EARS AND NOT EVEN NOTICE.
PRETTY FUNNY. BUT DON'T DO IT AGAIN.
YOU KNOW, EVEN IF YOU PLAY TO BIG CROWDS, THE ORGANIZERS, LAWYERS, AGENTS, AND MAFIA TAKE MOST OF IT.
WHAT A SCAM.
MUSIC IS BETTER HERE ON THE STREET WHERE IT'S STILL REAL.
THAT WAS GREAT! HERE'S A DOLLAR.
SOMEDAY WE'LL PAY $30 TO SEE THAT GUY.
YEP. WE'RE PRETTY LUCKY.

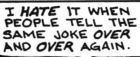I *HATE* IT WHEN PEOPLE TELL THE SAME JOKE *OVER* AND *OVER* AGAIN.

THEY TELL IT, AND THEN THEY TELL IT AGAIN.

AS IF, BY REPEATING IT, IT WILL GET *FUNNIER* AND *FUNNIER*.

IT'S THE *SURPRISE*, *NOT* THE REPETITION, THAT MAKES IT FUNNY.

I JUST *DON'T GET IT*. WHY TELL A JOKE MORE THAN *ONCE*? IS *TWICE* FUNNIER? *NO!* IT'S LESS FUNNY. AND *THREE* TIMES? LET'S *NOT* EVEN MENTION *THREE* TIMES.

POW!

PUNCH LINE.

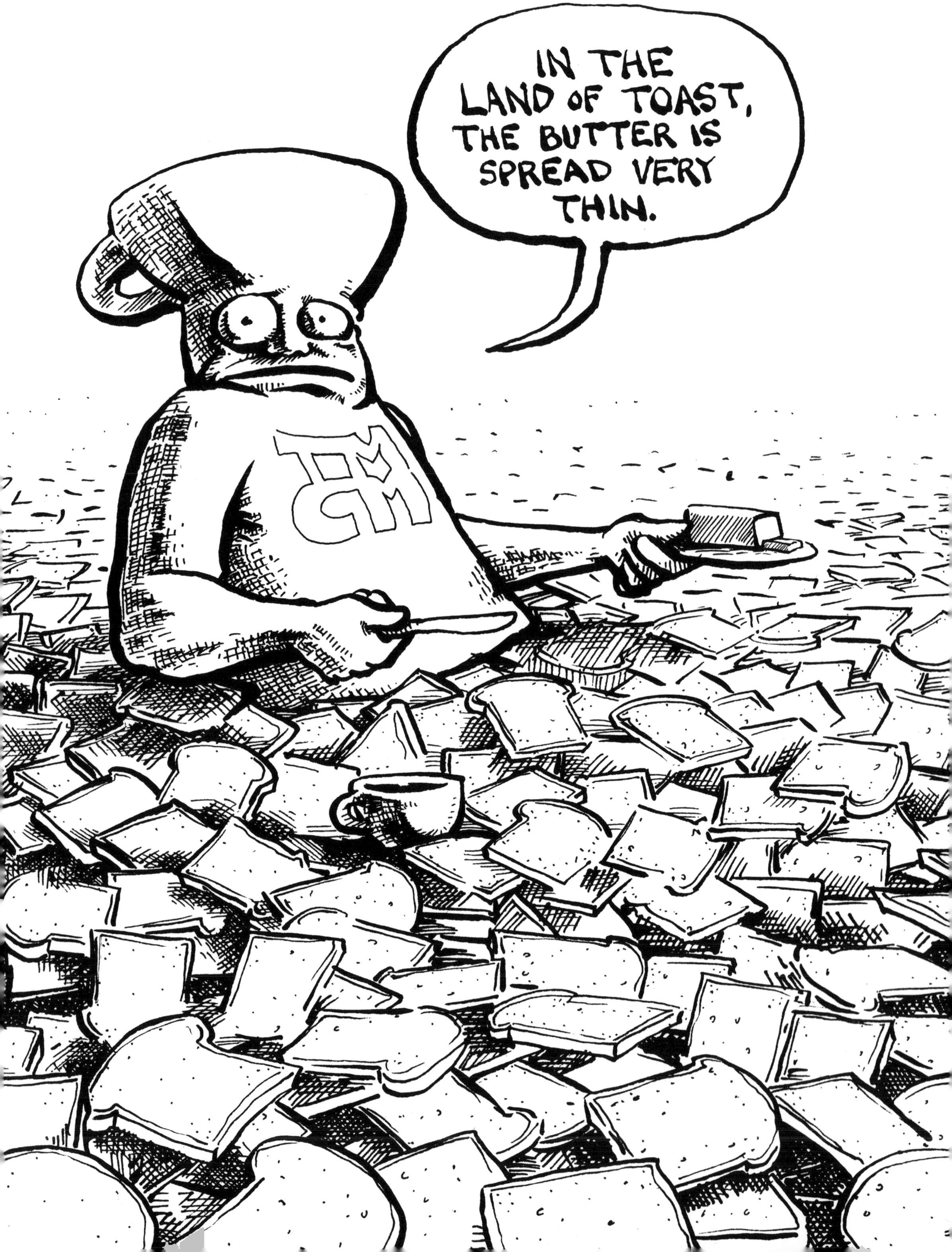
IN THE LAND OF TOAST, THE BUTTER IS SPREAD VERY THIN.

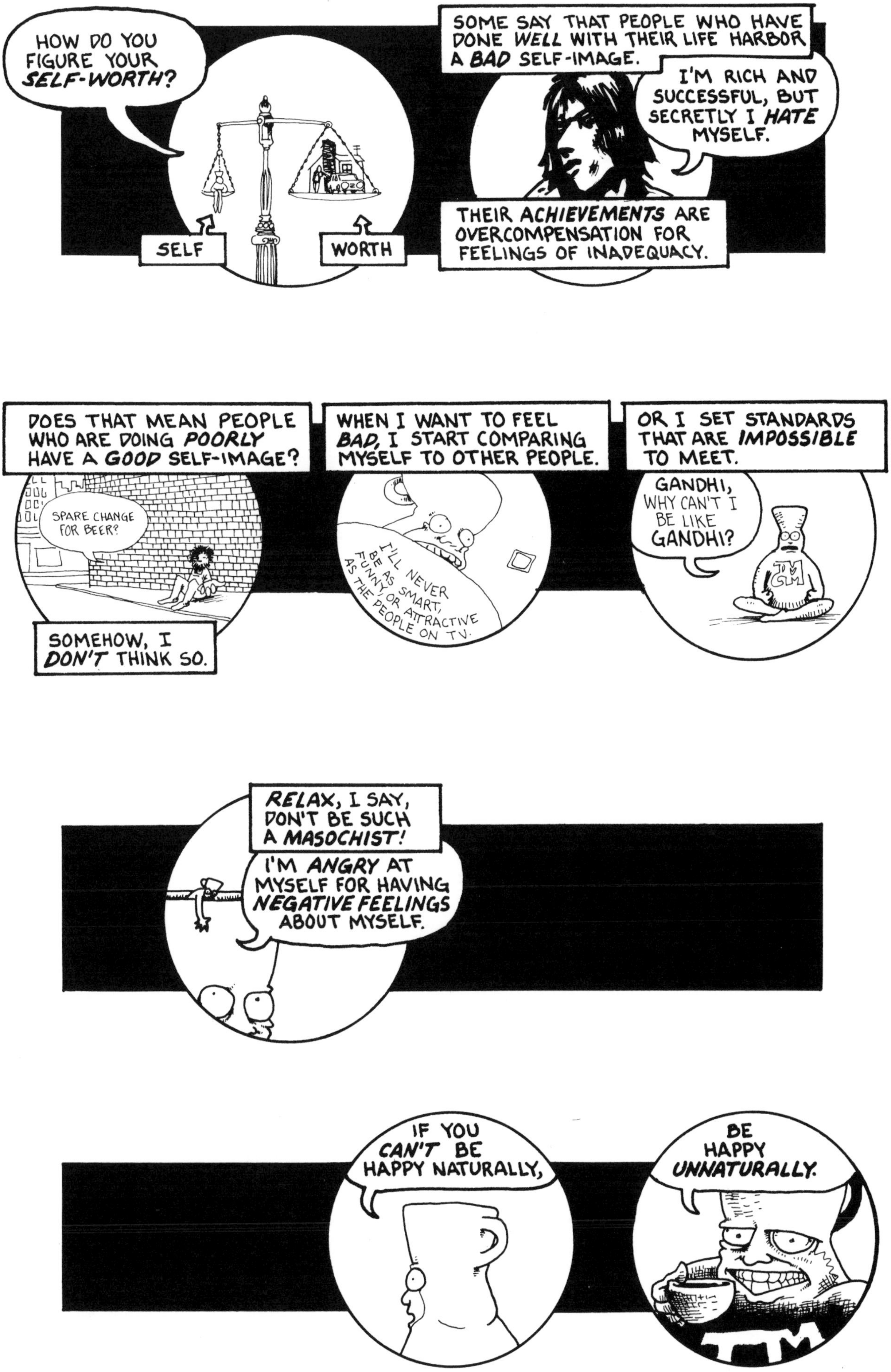
HOW DO YOU FIGURE YOUR SELF-WORTH?
SELF
WORTH
SOME SAY THAT PEOPLE WHO HAVE DONE WELL WITH THEIR LIFE HARBOR A BAD SELF-IMAGE.
I'M RICH AND SUCCESSFUL, BUT SECRETLY I HATE MYSELF.
THEIR ACHIEVEMENTS ARE OVERCOMPENSATION FOR FEELINGS OF INADEQUACY.
DOES THAT MEAN PEOPLE WHO ARE DOING POORLY HAVE A GOOD SELF-IMAGE?
SPARE CHANGE FOR BEER?
SOMEHOW, I DON'T THINK SO.
WHEN I WANT TO FEEL BAD, I START COMPARING MYSELF TO OTHER PEOPLE.
I'LL NEVER BE AS SMART, FUNNY, OR ATTRACTIVE AS THE PEOPLE ON TV.
OR I SET STANDARDS THAT ARE IMPOSSIBLE TO MEET.
GANDHI, WHY CAN'T I BE LIKE GANDHI?
RELAX, I SAY, DON'T BE SUCH A MASOCHIST!
I'M ANGRY AT MYSELF FOR HAVING NEGATIVE FEELINGS ABOUT MYSELF.
IF YOU CAN'T BE HAPPY NATURALLY,
BE HAPPY UNNATURALLY.
TM

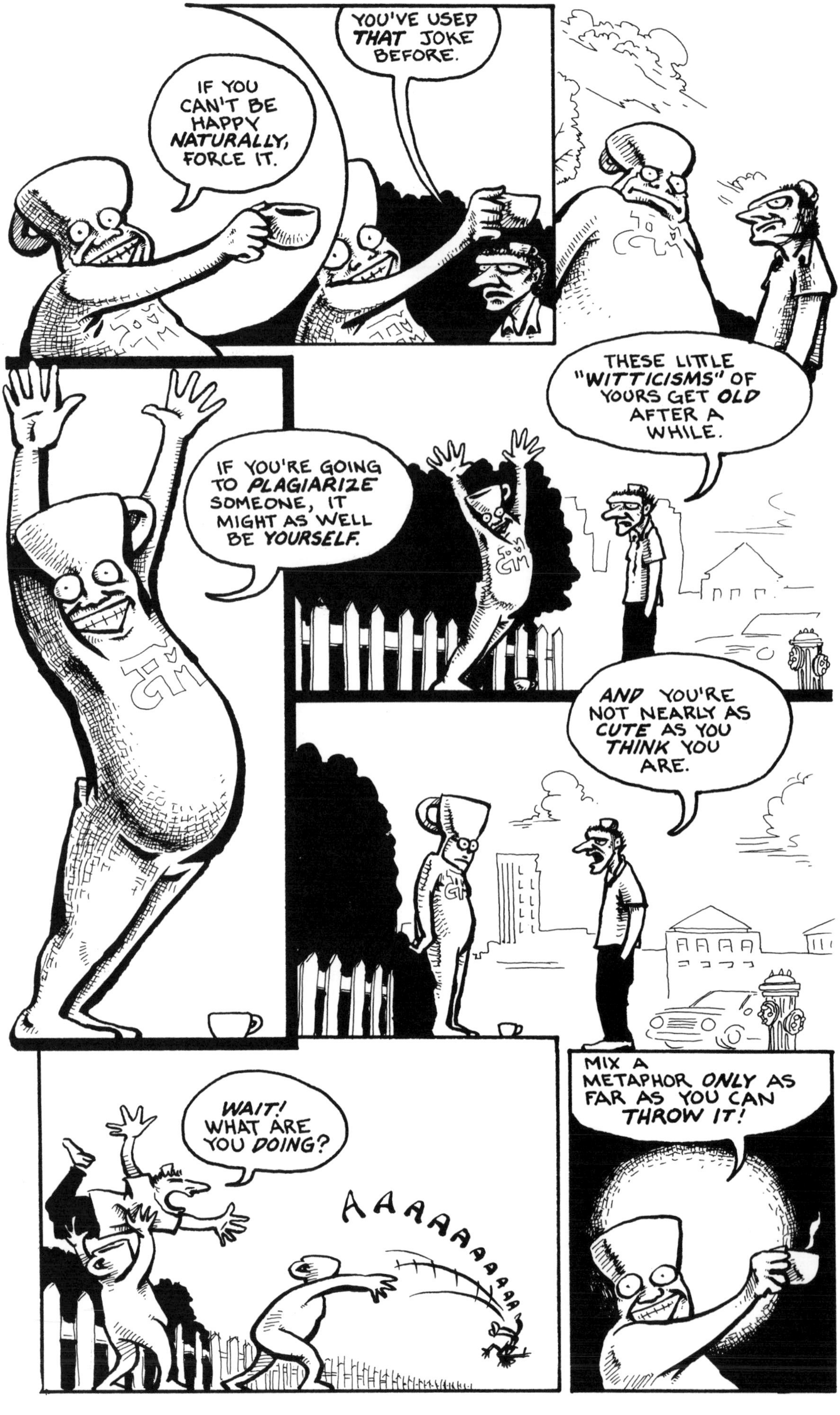
IF YOU CAN'T BE HAPPY NATURALLY, FORCE IT.
YOU'VE USED THAT JOKE BEFORE.
THESE LITTLE "WITTICISMS" OF YOURS GET OLD AFTER A WHILE.
IF YOU'RE GOING TO PLAGIARIZE SOMEONE, IT MIGHT AS WELL BE YOURSELF.
AND YOU'RE NOT NEARLY AS CUTE AS YOU THINK YOU ARE.
WAIT! WHAT ARE YOU DOING?
AAAAAAAAAAAAAA
MIX A METAPHOR ONLY AS FAR AS YOU CAN THROW IT!

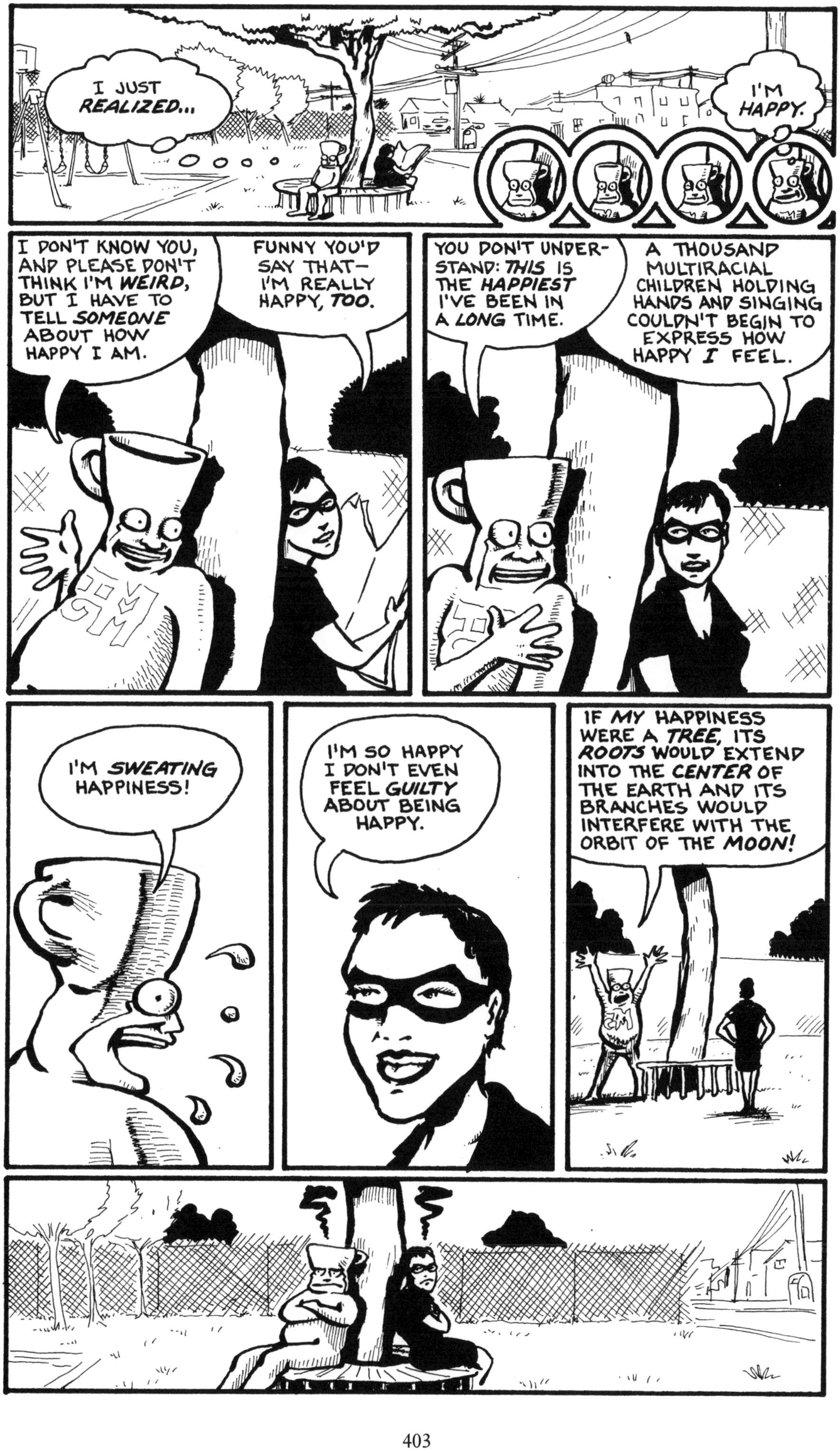
I JUST REALIZED...
I'M HAPPY.
I DON'T KNOW YOU, AND PLEASE DON'T THINK I'M WEIRD, BUT I HAVE TO TELL SOMEONE ABOUT HOW HAPPY I AM.
FUNNY YOU'D SAY THAT— I'M REALLY HAPPY, TOO.
YOU DON'T UNDERSTAND: THIS IS THE HAPPIEST I'VE BEEN IN A LONG TIME.
A THOUSAND MULTIRACIAL CHILDREN HOLDING HANDS AND SINGING COULDN'T BEGIN TO EXPRESS HOW HAPPY I FEEL.
I'M SWEATING HAPPINESS!
I'M SO HAPPY I DON'T EVEN FEEL GUILTY ABOUT BEING HAPPY.
IF MY HAPPINESS WERE A TREE, ITS ROOTS WOULD EXTEND INTO THE CENTER OF THE EARTH AND ITS BRANCHES WOULD INTERFERE WITH THE ORBIT OF THE MOON!

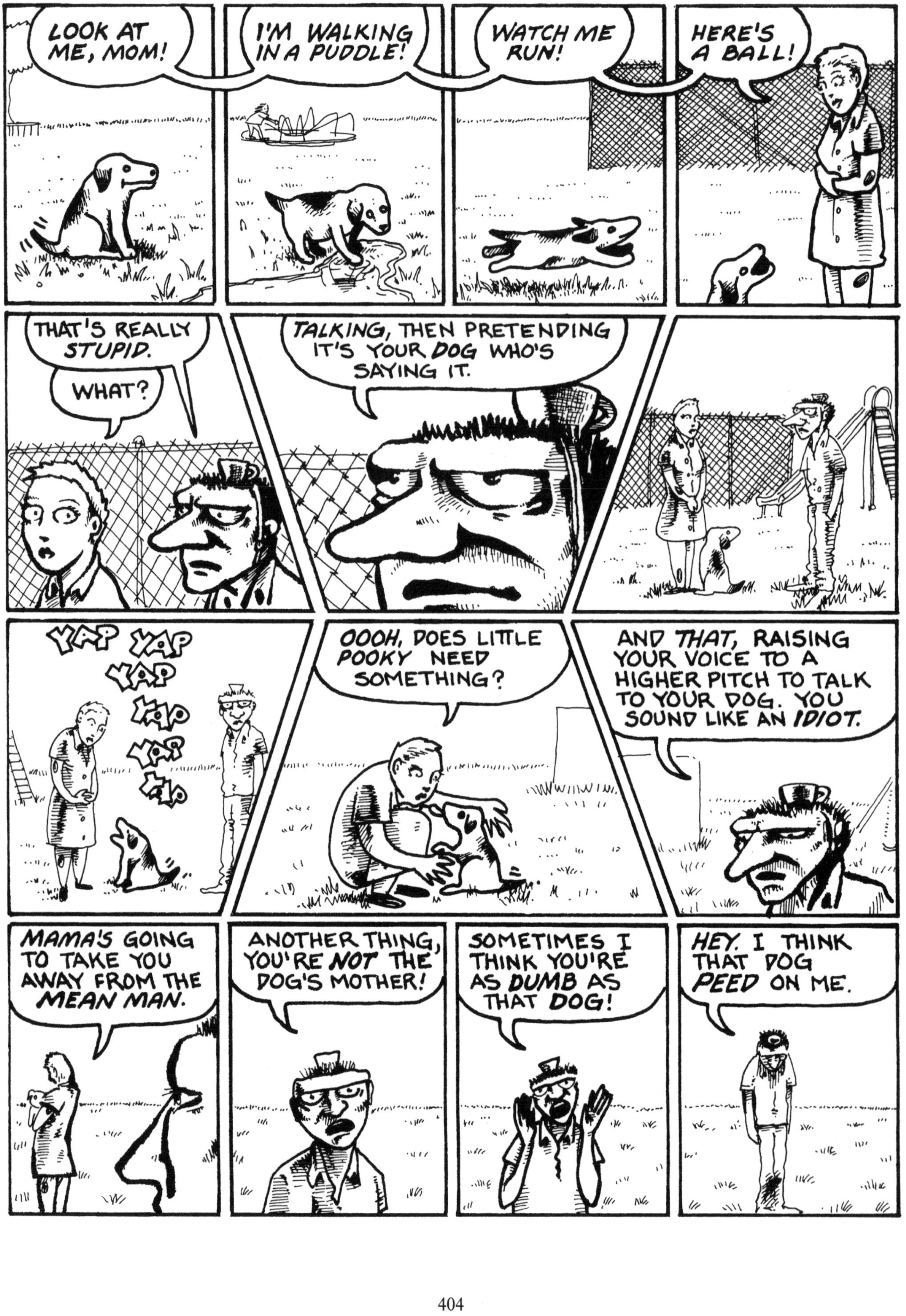
LOOK AT ME, MOM!
I'M WALKING IN A PUDDLE!
WATCH ME RUN!
HERE'S A BALL!
THAT'S REALLY STUPID.
WHAT?
TALKING, THEN PRETENDING IT'S YOUR DOG WHO'S SAYING IT.
YAP YAP YAP YAP YAP YAP
OOOH, DOES LITTLE POOKY NEED SOMETHING?
AND THAT, RAISING YOUR VOICE TO A HIGHER PITCH TO TALK TO YOUR DOG. YOU SOUND LIKE AN IDIOT.
MAMA'S GOING TO TAKE YOU AWAY FROM THE MEAN MAN.
ANOTHER THING, YOU'RE NOT THE DOG'S MOTHER!
SOMETIMES I THINK YOU'RE AS DUMB AS THAT DOG!
HEY. I THINK THAT DOG PEED ON ME.

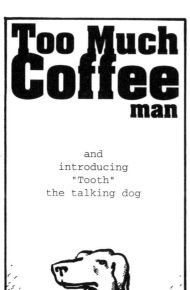

Too Much Coffee man

and
introducing
"Tooth"
the talking dog

WHAT'S SO FUNNY?

HA HA HA HA

THE *ANARCHISTS* ORGANIZED A RALLY.

I THOUGHT THAT THE WHOLE POINT OF ANARCHY WAS *DISORGANIZATION!*

HA HA HA HA HA HA HA HA HA HA HA

GRRRR

ACTUALLY, GUYS, *ANARCHISM* IS THE THEORY THAT *ALL* FORMS OF GOVERNMENT INTERFERE *UNJUSTLY* WITH INDIVIDUAL *LIBERTY* AND SHOULD BE REPLACED BY THE VOLUNTARY ASSOCIATION OF *COOPERATIVE GROUPS.*

I THOUGHT DOGS *WEREN'T* ALLOWED IN *CAFÉS.*

I'LL PUT HIM *OUT!*

FASCISTS!

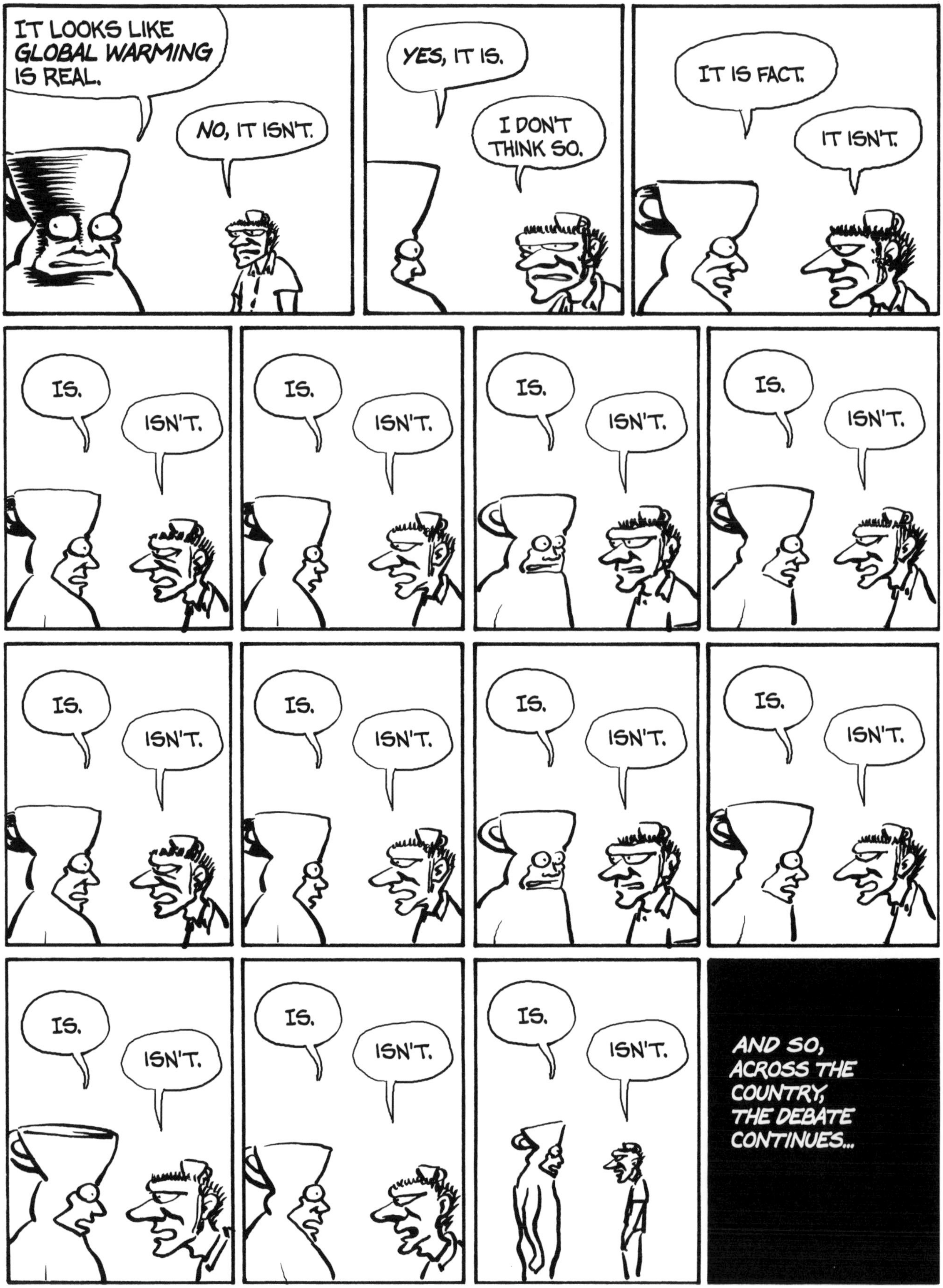
IT LOOKS LIKE GLOBAL WARMING IS REAL.
NO, IT ISN'T.
YES, IT IS.
I DON'T THINK SO.
IT IS FACT.
IT ISN'T.
IS.
ISN'T.
IS.
ISN'T.
IS.
ISN'T.
IS.
ISN'T.
IS.
ISN'T.
IS.
ISN'T.
IS.
ISN'T.
IS.
ISN'T.
IS.
ISN'T.
IS.
ISN'T.
IS.
ISN'T.
AND SO, ACROSS THE COUNTRY, THE DEBATE CONTINUES...

WE'RE ALL *NAZIS*.

WE'RE *KILLING* OUR PLANET WITH *POLLUTION*, AND ULTIMATELY WE'RE JUST WATCHING IT HAPPEN.

IT'S JUST LIKE HOW THE *NAZIS* WATCHED THE *JEWS* BE LED OFF TO BE KILLED.

BUT THE NAZIS ACTIVELY *MURDERED* THE JEWS. YOU'RE TALKING ABOUT THE *GUILT OF PASSIVITY* WHICH MAKES US MORE LIKE THE GERMAN *CITIZENS* THAN *NAZIS*.

YOU *MIGHT* HAVE A *VALID IDEA*, BUT IF YOU GET YOUR METAPHOR *WRONG*, YOU'LL SOUND LIKE A *FOOL* AND YOUR POINT WILL BE *LOST*.

THANKS. I APPRECIATE YOUR CONCERN.

JERK.

FOOL.

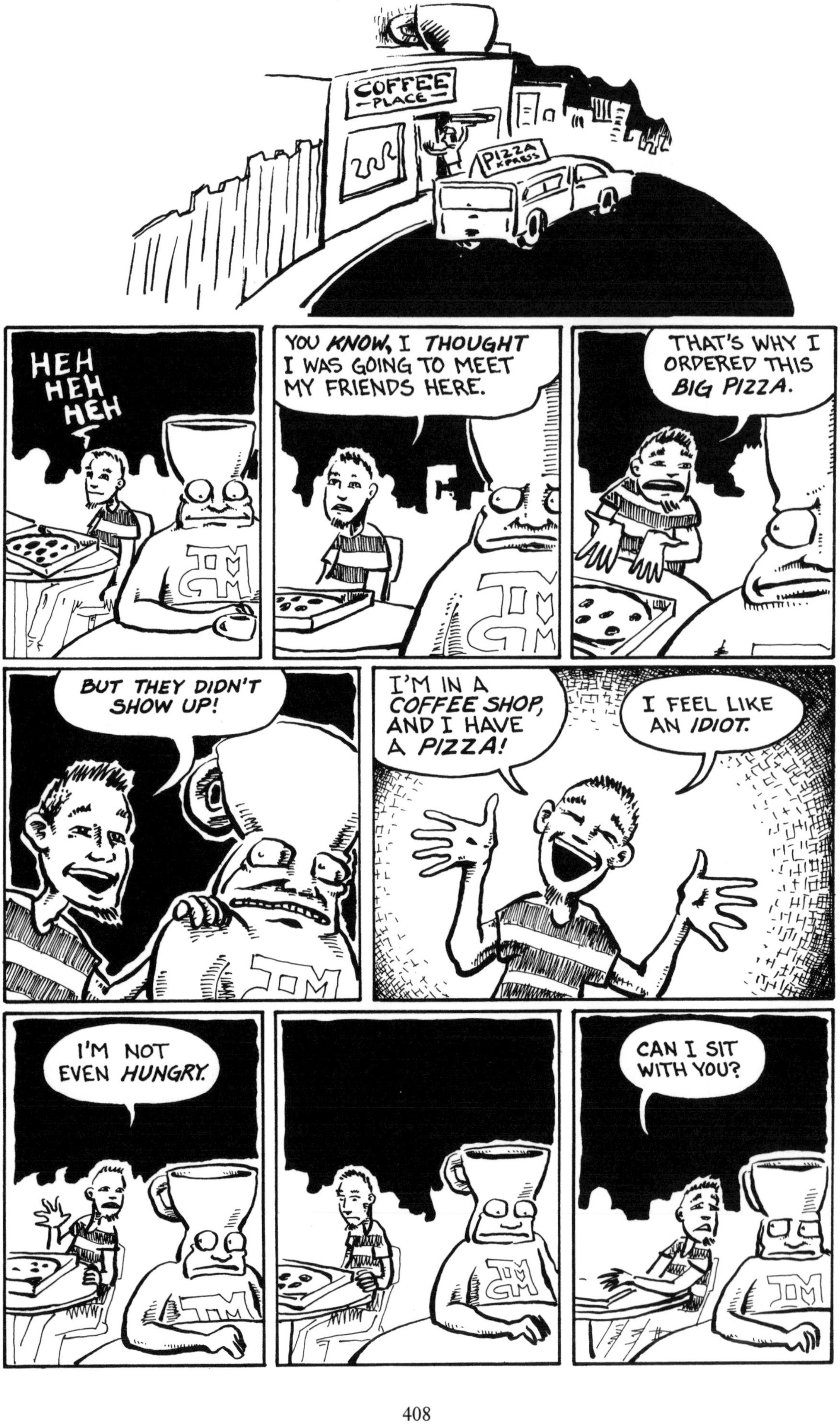
COFFEE PLACE
PIZZA XPRESS
HEH HEH HEH
YOU KNOW, I THOUGHT I WAS GOING TO MEET MY FRIENDS HERE.
THAT'S WHY I ORDERED THIS BIG PIZZA.
BUT THEY DIDN'T SHOW UP!
I'M IN A COFFEE SHOP, AND I HAVE A PIZZA!
I FEEL LIKE AN IDIOT.
I'M NOT EVEN HUNGRY.
CAN I SIT WITH YOU?

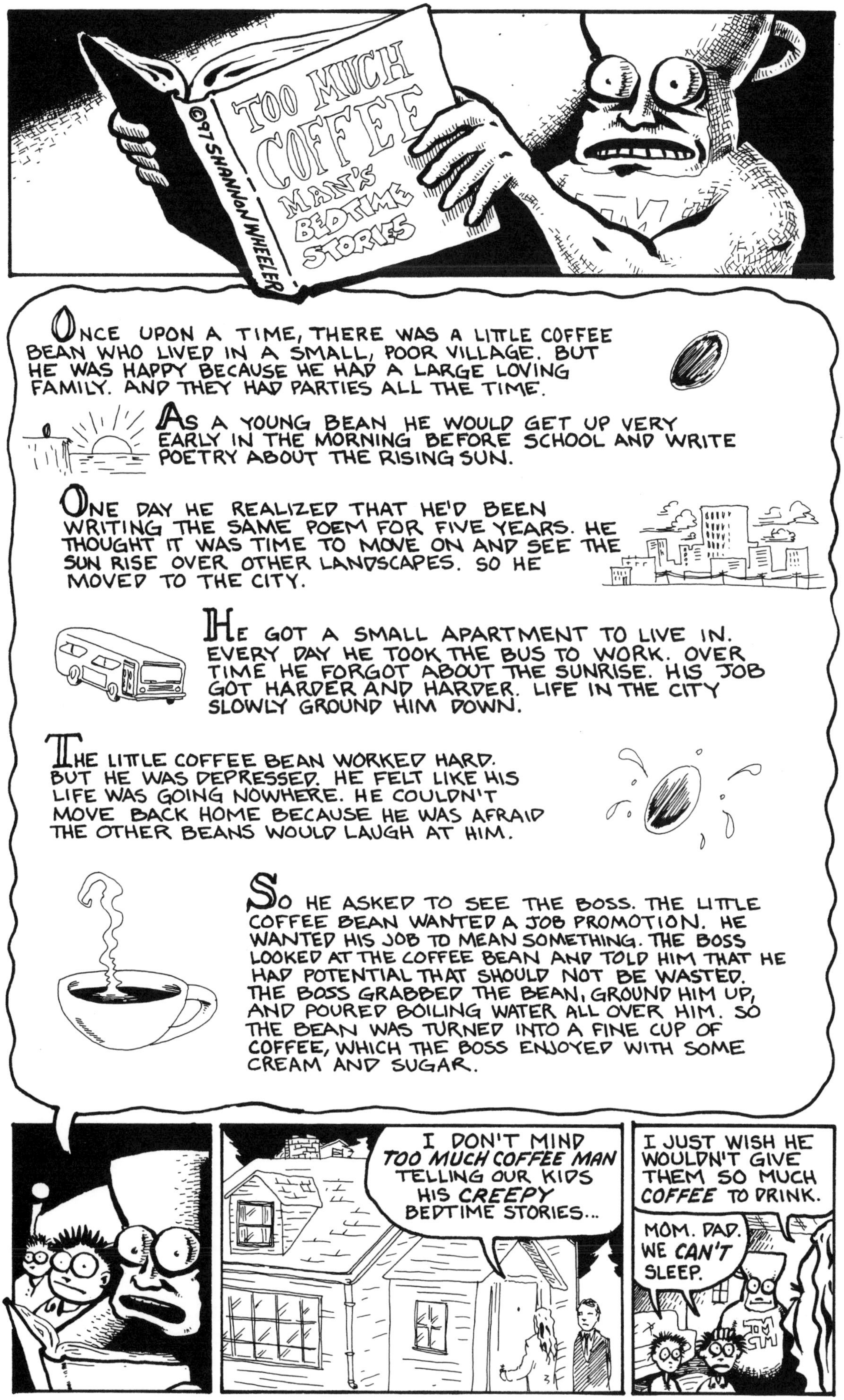
TOO MUCH COFFEE MAN'S BEDTIME STORIES
©97 SHANNON WHEELER
ONCE UPON A TIME, THERE WAS A LITTLE COFFEE BEAN WHO LIVED IN A SMALL, POOR VILLAGE. BUT HE WAS HAPPY BECAUSE HE HAD A LARGE LOVING FAMILY. AND THEY HAD PARTIES ALL THE TIME.
AS A YOUNG BEAN HE WOULD GET UP VERY EARLY IN THE MORNING BEFORE SCHOOL AND WRITE POETRY ABOUT THE RISING SUN.
ONE DAY HE REALIZED THAT HE'D BEEN WRITING THE SAME POEM FOR FIVE YEARS. HE THOUGHT IT WAS TIME TO MOVE ON AND SEE THE SUN RISE OVER OTHER LANDSCAPES. SO HE MOVED TO THE CITY.
HE GOT A SMALL APARTMENT TO LIVE IN. EVERY DAY HE TOOK THE BUS TO WORK. OVER TIME HE FORGOT ABOUT THE SUNRISE. HIS JOB GOT HARDER AND HARDER. LIFE IN THE CITY SLOWLY GROUND HIM DOWN.
THE LITTLE COFFEE BEAN WORKED HARD. BUT HE WAS DEPRESSED. HE FELT LIKE HIS LIFE WAS GOING NOWHERE. HE COULDN'T MOVE BACK HOME BECAUSE HE WAS AFRAID THE OTHER BEANS WOULD LAUGH AT HIM.
SO HE ASKED TO SEE THE BOSS. THE LITTLE COFFEE BEAN WANTED A JOB PROMOTION. HE WANTED HIS JOB TO MEAN SOMETHING. THE BOSS LOOKED AT THE COFFEE BEAN AND TOLD HIM THAT HE HAD POTENTIAL THAT SHOULD NOT BE WASTED. THE BOSS GRABBED THE BEAN, GROUND HIM UP, AND POURED BOILING WATER ALL OVER HIM. SO THE BEAN WAS TURNED INTO A FINE CUP OF COFFEE, WHICH THE BOSS ENJOYED WITH SOME CREAM AND SUGAR.
I DON'T MIND TOO MUCH COFFEE MAN TELLING OUR KIDS HIS CREEPY BEDTIME STORIES...
I JUST WISH HE WOULDN'T GIVE THEM SO MUCH COFFEE TO DRINK.
MOM. DAD. WE CAN'T SLEEP.

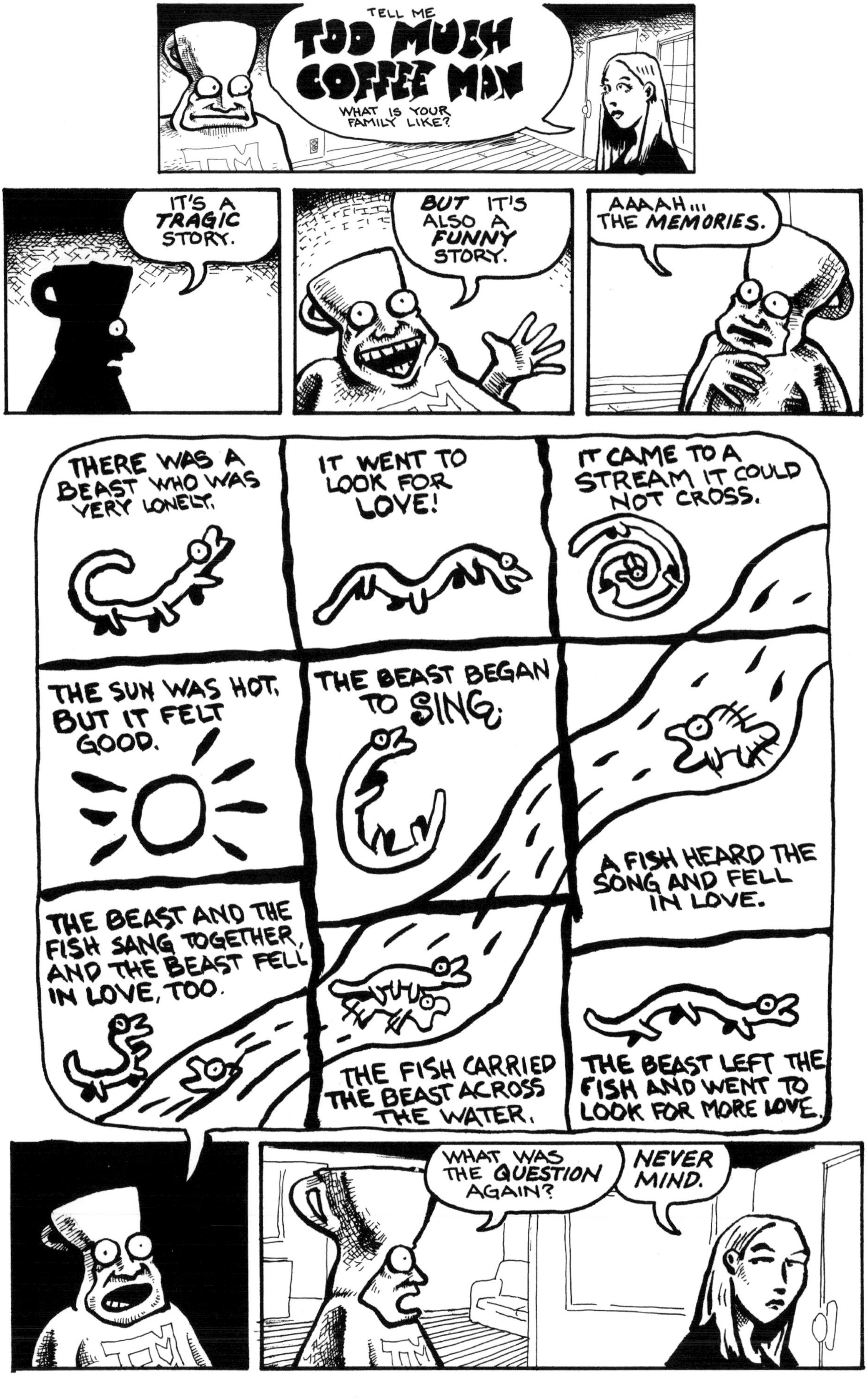
TELL ME
TOO MUCH COFFEE MAN
WHAT IS YOUR FAMILY LIKE?
IT'S A TRAGIC STORY.
BUT IT'S ALSO A FUNNY STORY.
AAAAH... THE MEMORIES.
THERE WAS A BEAST WHO WAS VERY LONELY.
IT WENT TO LOOK FOR LOVE!
IT CAME TO A STREAM IT COULD NOT CROSS.
THE SUN WAS HOT, BUT IT FELT GOOD.
THE BEAST BEGAN TO SING:
A FISH HEARD THE SONG AND FELL IN LOVE.
THE BEAST AND THE FISH SANG TOGETHER, AND THE BEAST FELL IN LOVE, TOO.
THE FISH CARRIED THE BEAST ACROSS THE WATER.
THE BEAST LEFT THE FISH AND WENT TO LOOK FOR MORE LOVE.
WHAT WAS THE QUESTION AGAIN?
NEVER MIND.

TOO MUCH COFFEE MAN
BY: SHANNON WHEELER
STOP PLAYING THOSE VIOLENT VIDEO GAMES, AND I'LL TELL YOU A STORY ABOUT MY UNCLE.
WHY?
BECAUSE MY UNCLE IS CRAZY!
YIKES!
MOST OF THE TIME HE WAS SANE. HE WAS POLITE AND FUNCTIONED NORMALLY IN SOCIETY.
BUT EVERY NOW AND THEN HE WOULD "GO OFF" AND HIT SOMEONE IN THE HEAD.
OUCH!
POW
THIS DIDN'T SEEM TO GET HIM IN TOO MUCH TROUBLE.
BUT THERE WAS ONE THING HE WOULD DO THAT WOULD GET HIM ARRESTED AND THROWN IN JAIL EVERY SINGLE TIME HE DID IT...
ON WARM SUMMER NIGHTS, IF THE MOON WAS FULL, HE WOULD TAKE OFF ALL HIS CLOTHES AND GO FOR A WALK.
IN LESS TIME THAN IT TAKES TO BOIL AN EGG, THE POLICE WOULD FIND HIM, CART HIM OFF, AND LOCK HIM UP.
SO WHAT WAS THE POINT OF THAT STORY?
JUST THAT OUR SOCIETY TOLERATES VIOLENCE MORE THAN NUDITY.
I'D RATHER BE HIT IN THE HEAD THAN HAVE TO SEE YOU NAKED.
YEAH. ME, TOO.
END.

THANKS TO MR. ELLIS FOR THE TRUE STORY.

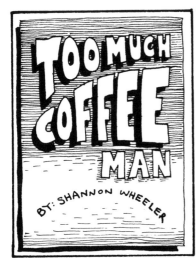

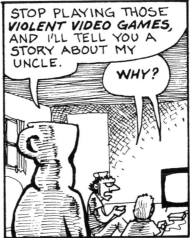

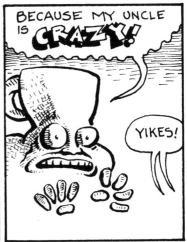

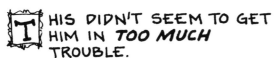

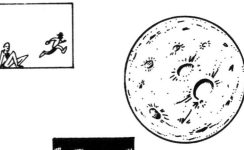

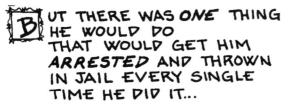

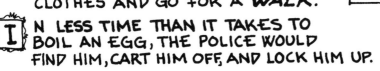

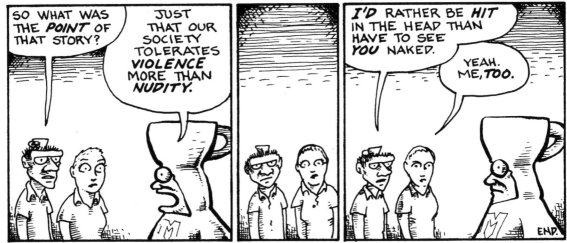

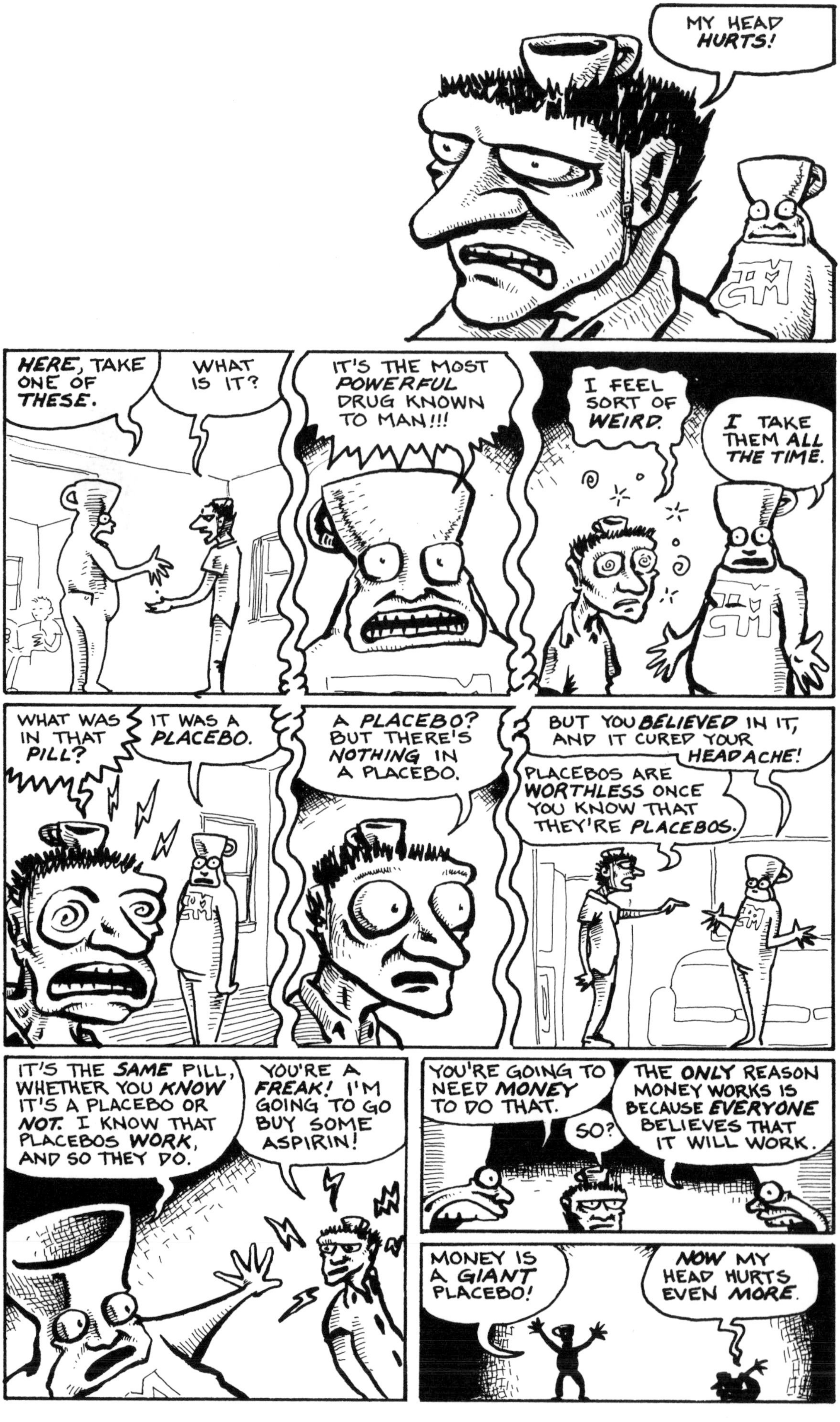
MY HEAD HURTS!
HERE, TAKE ONE OF THESE.
WHAT IS IT?
IT'S THE MOST POWERFUL DRUG KNOWN TO MAN!!!
I FEEL SORT OF WEIRD.
I TAKE THEM ALL THE TIME.
WHAT WAS IN THAT PILL?
IT WAS A PLACEBO.
A PLACEBO? BUT THERE'S NOTHING IN A PLACEBO.
BUT YOU BELIEVED IN IT, AND IT CURED YOUR HEADACHE!
PLACEBOS ARE WORTHLESS ONCE YOU KNOW THAT THEY'RE PLACEBOS.
IT'S THE SAME PILL, WHETHER YOU KNOW IT'S A PLACEBO OR NOT. I KNOW THAT PLACEBOS WORK, AND SO THEY DO.
YOU'RE A FREAK! I'M GOING TO GO BUY SOME ASPIRIN!
YOU'RE GOING TO NEED MONEY TO DO THAT.
SO?
THE ONLY REASON MONEY WORKS IS BECAUSE EVERYONE BELIEVES THAT IT WILL WORK.
MONEY IS A GIANT PLACEBO!
NOW MY HEAD HURTS EVEN MORE.

IT'S NOT *FUNNY* ANYMORE.

WHAT?

THIS WHOLE *"COFFEE THING."* IT'S DONE.

THE TREND IS OVER. THE FAD IS FINISHED. HANG IT UP. TURN IT IN. GIVE UP THE GHOST.

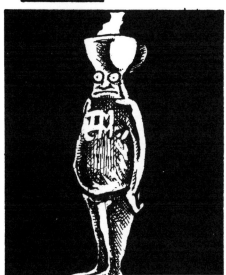

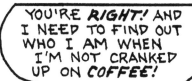

YOU'RE *RIGHT!* AND I NEED TO FIND OUT WHO I AM WHEN I'M NOT CRANKED UP ON *COFFEE!*

I'LL PUT ON *REAL* CLOTHES...TAKE *OFF* THIS GIANT MUG,... GET A *JOB*,... THEN I'LL LIVE A *NORMAL LIFE!*

THIS LOOKS LIKE A *NORMAL* PLACE TO WORK.

WELCOME TO OUR COMPANY. I HOPE YOU LIKE YOUR *CUBICLE*. HELP YOURSELF TO THE *FREE* COFFEE. THE MACHINE IS OVER THERE.

FREE COFFEE?

413

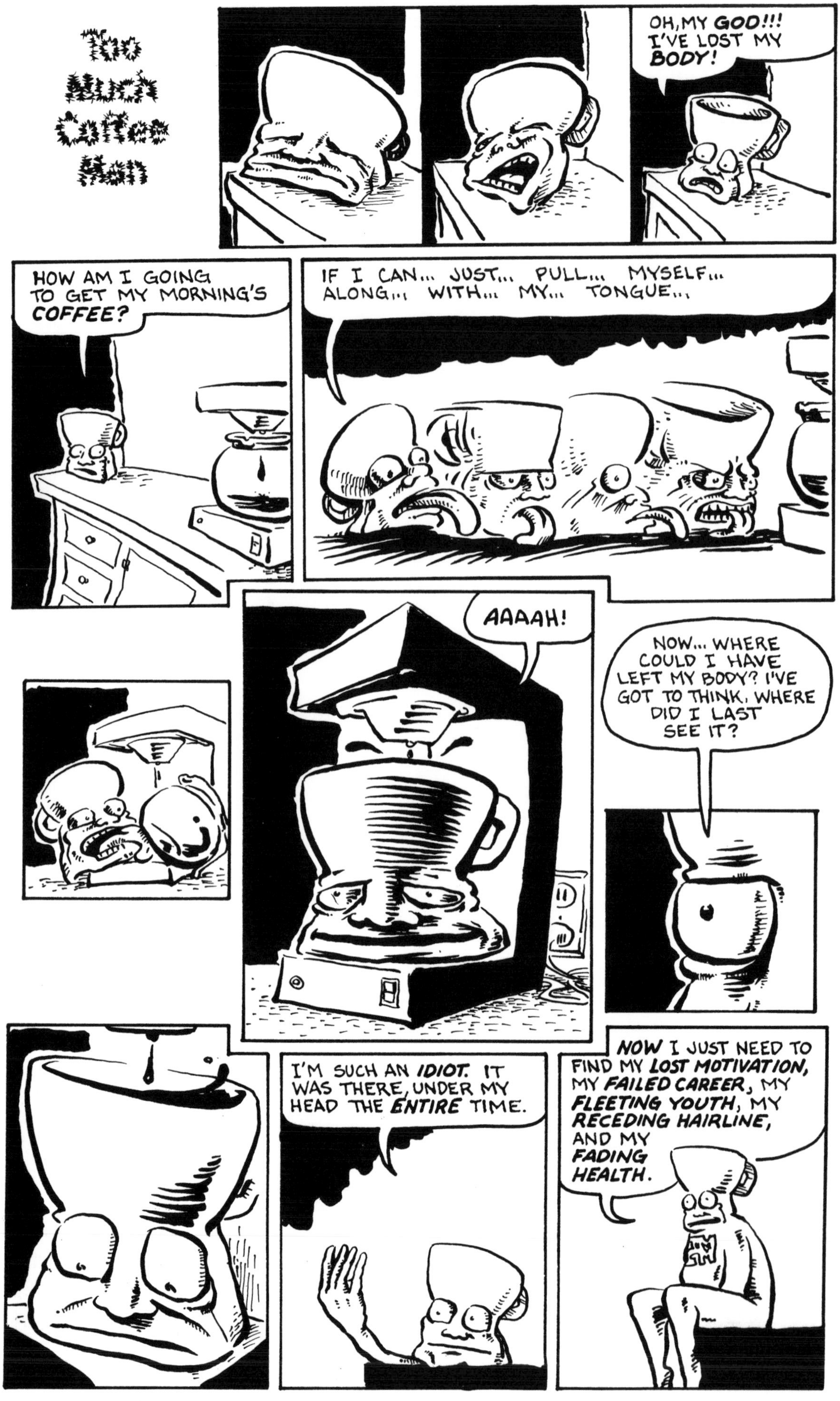
Too Much Coffee Man
OH, MY GOD!!! I'VE LOST MY BODY!
HOW AM I GOING TO GET MY MORNING'S COFFEE?
IF I CAN... JUST... PULL... MYSELF... ALONG... WITH... MY... TONGUE...
AAAAH!
NOW... WHERE COULD I HAVE LEFT MY BODY? I'VE GOT TO THINK. WHERE DID I LAST SEE IT?
I'M SUCH AN IDIOT. IT WAS THERE, UNDER MY HEAD THE ENTIRE TIME.
NOW I JUST NEED TO FIND MY LOST MOTIVATION, MY FAILED CAREER, MY FLEETING YOUTH, MY RECEDING HAIRLINE, AND MY FADING HEALTH.

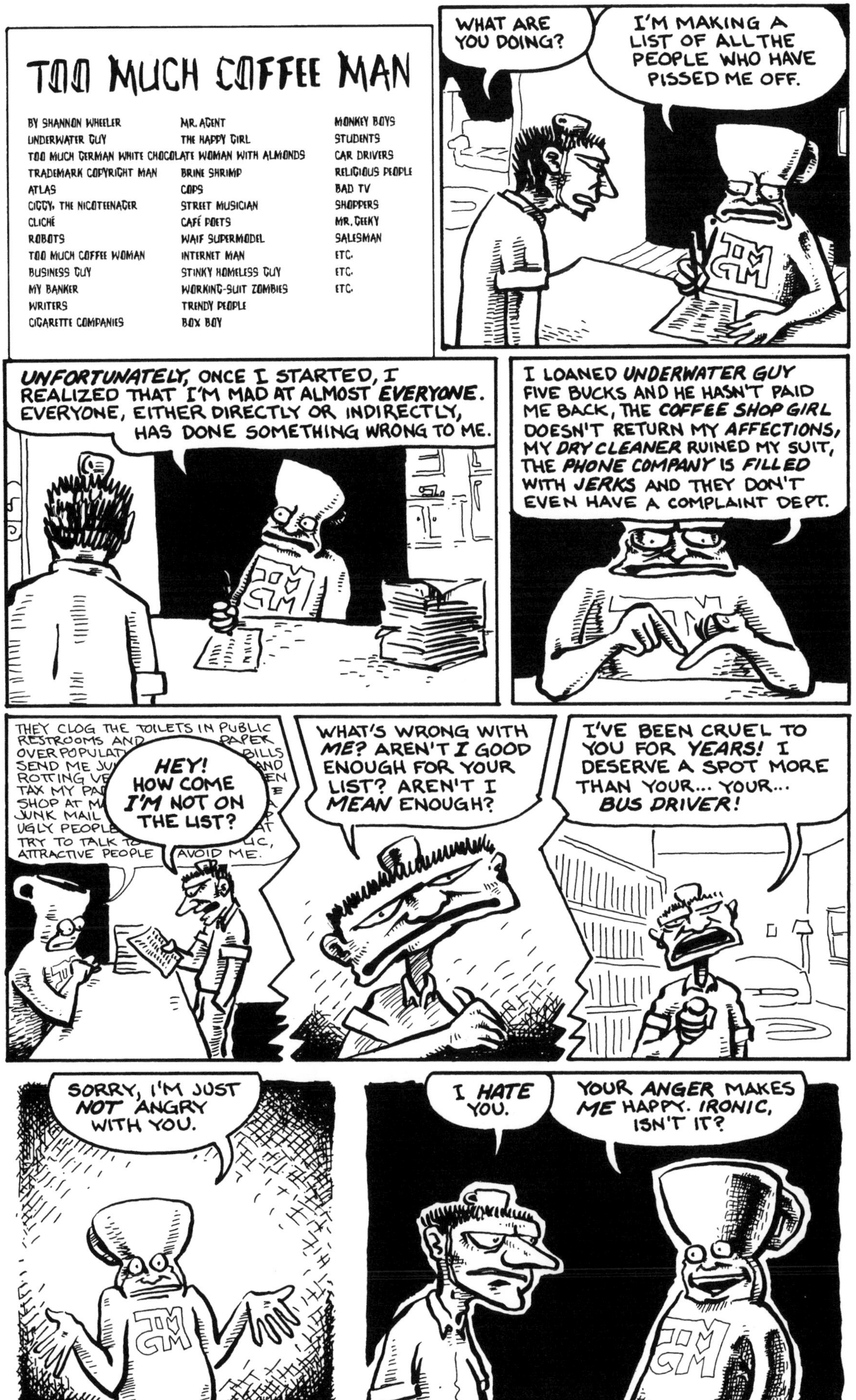
TOO MUCH COFFEE MAN
BY SHANNON WHEELER
UNDERWATER GUY
TOO MUCH GERMAN WHITE CHOCOLATE WOMAN WITH ALMONDS
TRADEMARK COPYRIGHT MAN
ATLAS
CIGGY, THE NICOTEENAGER
CLICHÉ
ROBOTS
TOO MUCH COFFEE WOMAN
BUSINESS GUY
MY BANKER
WRITERS
CIGARETTE COMPANIES
MR. AGENT
THE HAPPY GIRL
BRINE SHRIMP
COPS
STREET MUSICIAN
CAFÉ POETS
WAIF SUPERMODEL
INTERNET MAN
STINKY HOMELESS GUY
WORKING-SUIT ZOMBIES
TRENDY PEOPLE
BOX BOY
MONKEY BOYS
STUDENTS
CAR DRIVERS
RELIGIOUS PEOPLE
BAD TV
SHOPPERS
MR. GEEKY
SALESMAN
ETC.
ETC.
ETC.
WHAT ARE YOU DOING?
I'M MAKING A LIST OF ALL THE PEOPLE WHO HAVE PISSED ME OFF.
UNFORTUNATELY, ONCE I STARTED, I REALIZED THAT I'M MAD AT ALMOST EVERYONE. EVERYONE, EITHER DIRECTLY OR INDIRECTLY, HAS DONE SOMETHING WRONG TO ME.
I LOANED UNDERWATER GUY FIVE BUCKS AND HE HASN'T PAID ME BACK, THE COFFEE SHOP GIRL DOESN'T RETURN MY AFFECTIONS, MY DRY CLEANER RUINED MY SUIT, THE PHONE COMPANY IS FILLED WITH JERKS AND THEY DON'T EVEN HAVE A COMPLAINT DEPT.
THEY CLOG THE TOILETS IN PUBLIC RESTROOMS AND ... PAPER ... OVERPOPULAT... BILLS SEND ME JU... ROTTING VE... TAX MY PA... SHOP AT M... JUNK MAIL ... UGLY PEOPLE ... TRY TO TALK T... ATTRACTIVE PEOPLE ... AVOID ME.
HEY! HOW COME I'M NOT ON THE LIST?
WHAT'S WRONG WITH ME? AREN'T I GOOD ENOUGH FOR YOUR LIST? AREN'T I MEAN ENOUGH?
I'VE BEEN CRUEL TO YOU FOR YEARS! I DESERVE A SPOT MORE THAN YOUR... YOUR... BUS DRIVER!
SORRY, I'M JUST NOT ANGRY WITH YOU.
I HATE YOU.
YOUR ANGER MAKES ME HAPPY. IRONIC, ISN'T IT?

The Many Moods of Too Much Coffee Man

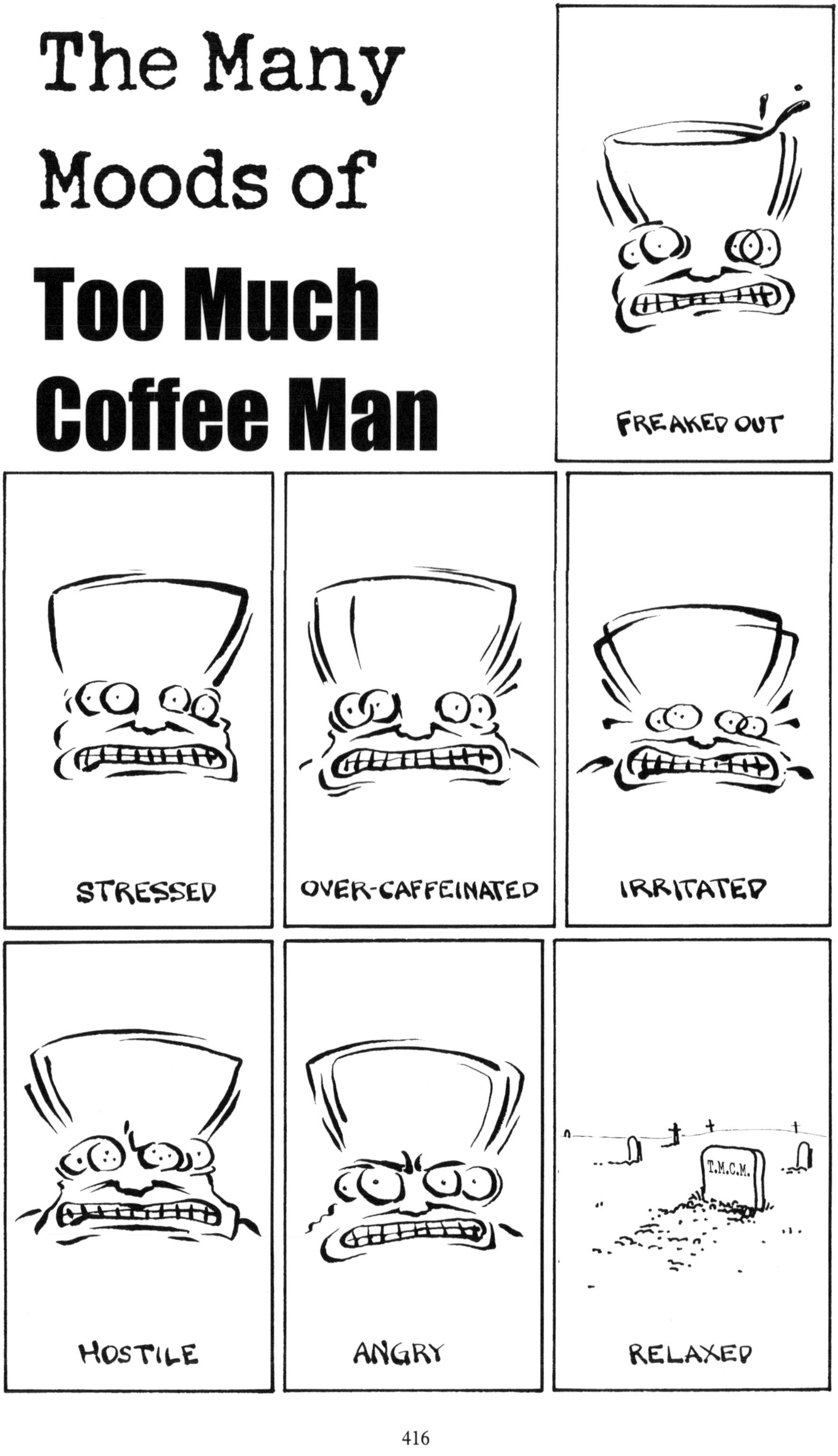
FREAKED OUT
STRESSED
OVER-CAFFEINATED
IRRITATED
HOSTILE
ANGRY
T.M.C.M.
RELAXED

AMUSING MUSINGS
AFTERWORD

Thank you for reading my book.

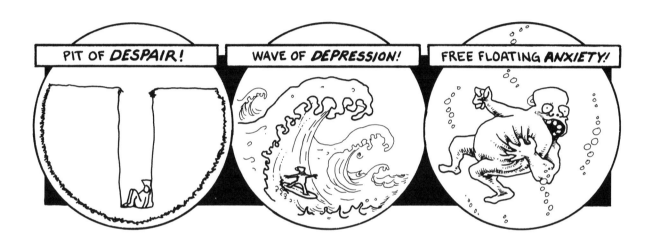

PIT OF *DESPAIR!*   WAVE OF *DEPRESSION!*   FREE FLOATING *ANXIETY!*

Other titles considered for *Amusing Musings:*
Motionless Pictures
Caffeine Is a Drug
Reflections in Coffee
Dancing in My Mind Field
Too Much Coffee Man A-Go-Go
I Am Not Too Much Coffee Man
Too Much Coffee Man — Paranoia, and Other Popular Notions

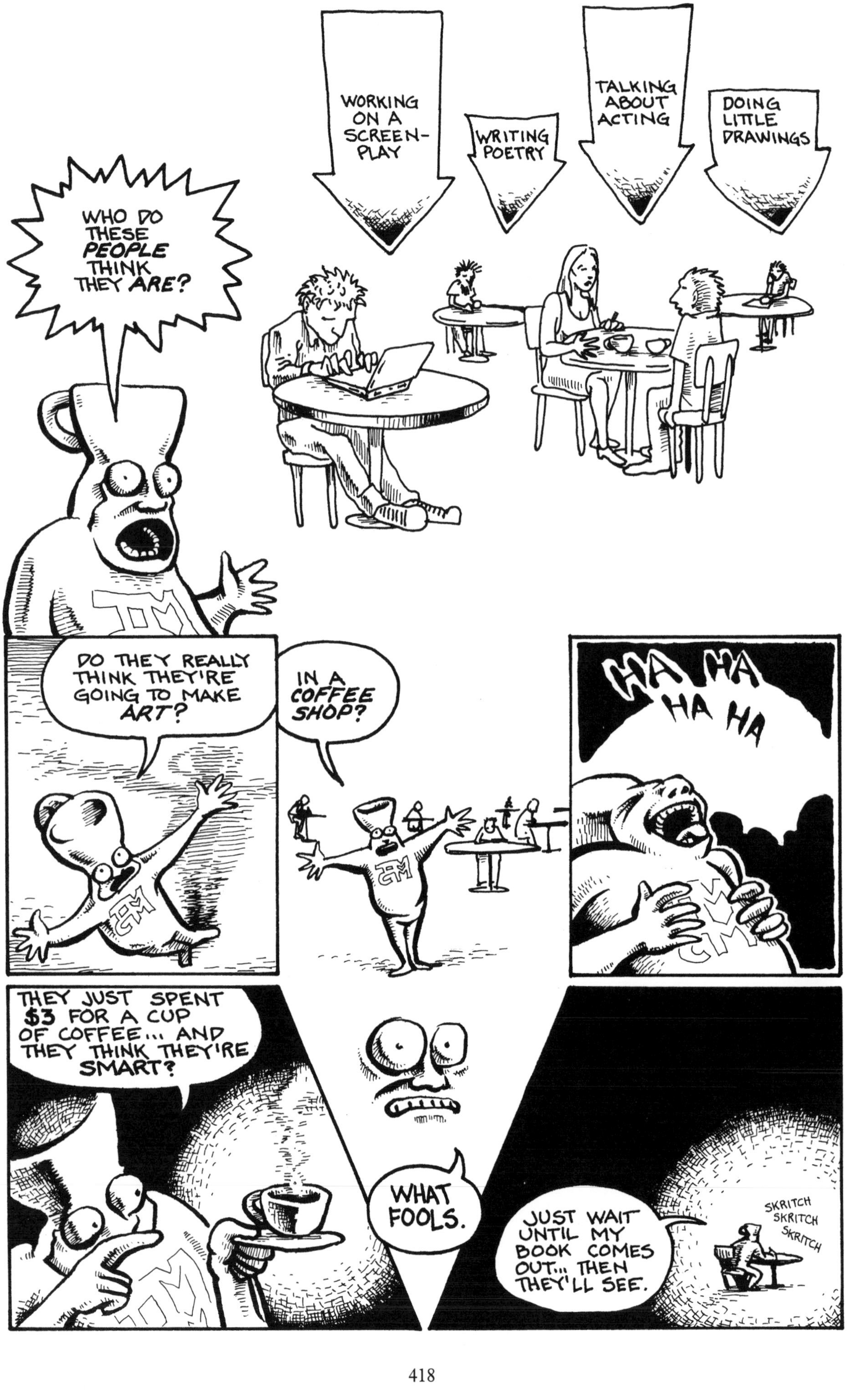
WORKING ON A SCREEN-PLAY
WRITING POETRY
TALKING ABOUT ACTING
DOING LITTLE DRAWINGS
WHO DO THESE PEOPLE THINK THEY ARE?
DO THEY REALLY THINK THEY'RE GOING TO MAKE ART?
IN A COFFEE SHOP?
HA HA HA HA
THEY JUST SPENT $3 FOR A CUP OF COFFEE... AND THEY THINK THEY'RE SMART?
WHAT FOOLS.
JUST WAIT UNTIL MY BOOK COMES OUT... THEN THEY'LL SEE.
SKRITCH SKRITCH SKRITCH

HOW TO BE HAPPY

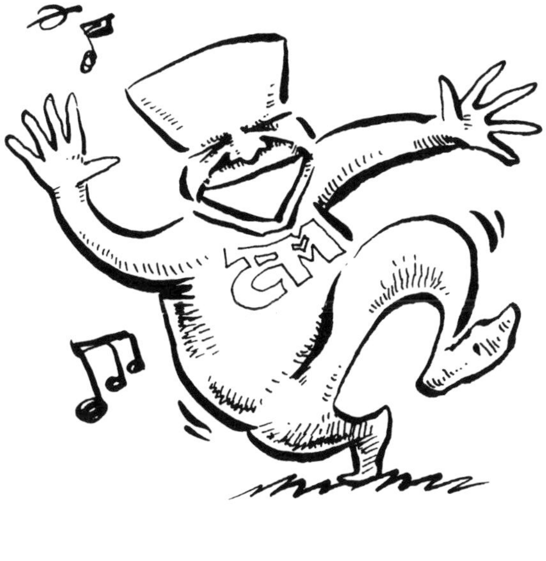
CM

HOW TO BE HAPPY INTRODUCTION

by Ted Rall

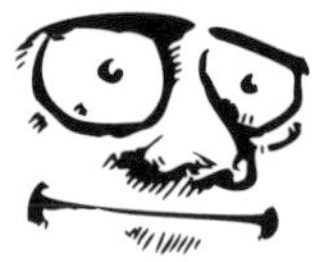

I've hit the depths of despair more than once, but the moment that stands out took place during the summer of 1984. I know what you're thinking. I'm a political person, a left-leaning sort politically, so my pain must have been related to Ronald Reagan. And you'd be right, albeit for the wrong reasons.

A few years earlier I'd boarded a Greyhound in Dayton, Ohio, bound for New York, where a full scholarship awaited me at Columbia University. Three years later, Reagan's financial aid cuts had slashed my finances to shreds. I was up to my ass in student loan debt, working three jobs while attending school full time, too stubborn to drop out. Inevitably, my grades slid. They put me on academic probation. Then they expelled me. I still had my summer dorm room—but then they evicted me. At the same time, a coworker who'd stolen from my boss told her the thief was me. I got fired; he got a raise and a whuppin' when I ran into him on 81st Street. My girlfriend dumped me when I told her about the assault. "I can't sit here and watch you fall apart," she said. "But I won!" I cried.

I suspected that my being broke was bothering her more than her excessive empathy.

To sum up: I was unemployed, expelled, sexless, homeless. With zero prospects and no ideas how to create some, I was as stumped as George W. Bush taking the SAT. I was worth eight bucks, four of which were committed to pizza and Coke for dinner. Bleak would have been an improvement; I was looking from way down low way up high at bleak.

A couple of friends, both of whom had left Columbia under indecorous circumstances the same semester, dropped by my new unofficial dorm room—the university left empty rooms unlocked—with an offering of shoplifted strawberry schnapps. Depressed people sleep a lot. I was napping when they arrived. For some reason or none whatsoever, I pretended to still be asleep while my two former classmates sat on a bare mattress across the room and talked.

"I'm worried about Ted," said one. "He's never been like this before. Think he'll kill himself?"

The other one paused. "No way. He's too much of a wuss." They chuckled.

Fuck those guys, I thought. I'd show them!

That night I took the elevator to the top, twentieth floor of my dorm. I walked up the stairs to the roof. I went to the side and looked over a short wall at the sidewalk below. That'd do it, all right. I got up on the ledge, got ready to take that last step forward, and carefully considered the sensation of my bones snapping and impaling whatever didn't explode from the impact with the sidewalk as my organs simultaneously shrieked from shutdown pain. Death didn't scare me. Everybody dies. But I cry when I get a shot. I'm a baby when it comes to pain.

It's only a second of agony, I steeled myself. Yeah, but what a second, someone else in there retorted. You can do a second. What, are you insane? That shit's gonna hurt like nobody's business!

Which is worse? Trying to kill yourself to prove that you're brave, or proving that you're not by being unable to go through with it? I still don't know. Whatever, it was a low point.

If I knew Shannon Wheeler only through his work I'd suspect that he hits those rock bottoms more often than the rest of us. For not only does he have little faith in humanity, he gives himself the same treatment in his sly and vicious deconstructions of the human condition. Personal setbacks are child's play to a cartoonist for whom human existence itself is cause for disgust.

Too Much Coffee Man, Shannon has told me, began as a somewhat cynical exercise in 1990s Gen-X consumerism: an edgy strip meant to appear in the sort of publications that are often read in coffeehouses by disaffected twenty-somethings. But he soon became captivated by his own characters and situations. The loose structure Shannon created to allow ironic detachment proved so seductive that he began to take it seriously. The relationship he created with readers who had never seen anything else quite like it became too important to treat lightly. The soapbox he'd slapped together so disdainfully suddenly represented a unique opportunity, if not to mitigate the innate cruelty and stupidity of humanity, at least to demonstrate to the desperate that they are not alone.

Were he to limit himself to commenting on politicians and current events, Shannon would be one of our most brilliantly perceptive editorial cartoonists. If he only did social commentary cartoons relating the tyrannical angst of the lonely and self-doubting, he would have few peers in the pages of the weekly newspapers perused by mid-'00s Gen-Y Starbucks customers. For my money, however, *Too Much Coffee Man* hits its highest, most glorious peaks in its studies of schadenfreude, the phenomenon of feeling joy at the misery of others. (Such is capitalism; you're never a failure as long as someone else is poorer than you.) Whether it's "homeless humor" (the bum scoffing at the suit-wearing bourgie learning that the stock market has wiped out his investments) or "God: the Comedian" (a Santa-jolly bearded deity joyously celebrating the emotional pain and grisly demises of the helpless souls who conjured His ungrateful self in the first place), no American commentator so gleefully and effectively rips off the mask of self-delusion from our denial-high society. Get real, saps—if God exists, he's laughing his ass off at you. Hell, as he writes in another series, could be no worse than what we do to each other (hi, Jean-Paul) or ourselves.

Life sucks and you'd better get used to it. Sounds negative, but nothing could be further from the truth. The sooner you understand that politicians are liars, thieves, and worse, the sooner you stop waiting around for a leader to make everything better. Stop putting your faith in God, friends, family—hell, you may not be such a hot prospect yourself. Truth is hard and absolutely essential.

Twenty-one years ago when I was trying to convince myself to jump off the roof of East Campus, my despair was centered around abstract creations that had let me down because they were bound to do so. My illusions brought me to the brink. Only the truth—that'll hurt!—saved my life.

I don't know whether *TMCM* would have saved my life back then, though I'd like to believe that understanding that we're all sharing the same uncomfortable boat would have helped. On the other hand, Shannon's skill as a draftsman and craftsman of pithy retorts might have made me give up hope of ever making it as a cartoonist myself. Still: truth is always in short supply, especially in comics, but truth always helps.

So if you're planning to kill yourself, read this book through a few times. If that doesn't work, you can always buy thirty copies, tie them to your feet, and jump into a deep body of water.

That oughtta do it.

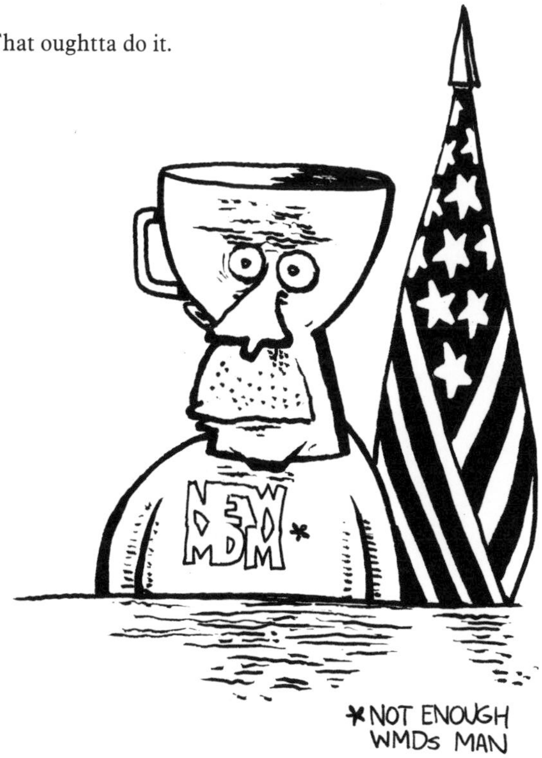
NEW MDM *
*NOT ENOUGH WMDs MAN

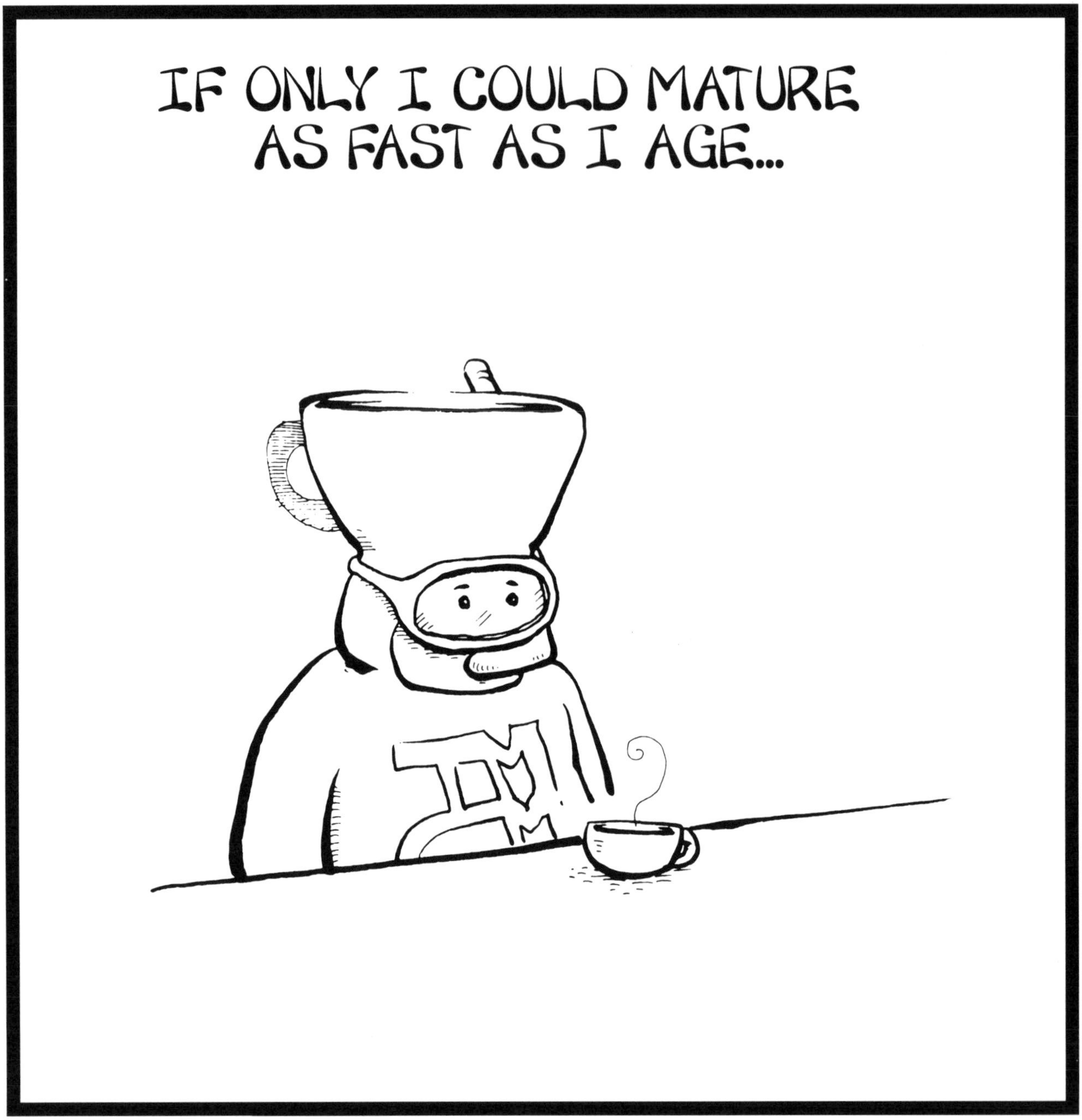
IF ONLY I COULD MATURE
AS FAST AS I AGE...

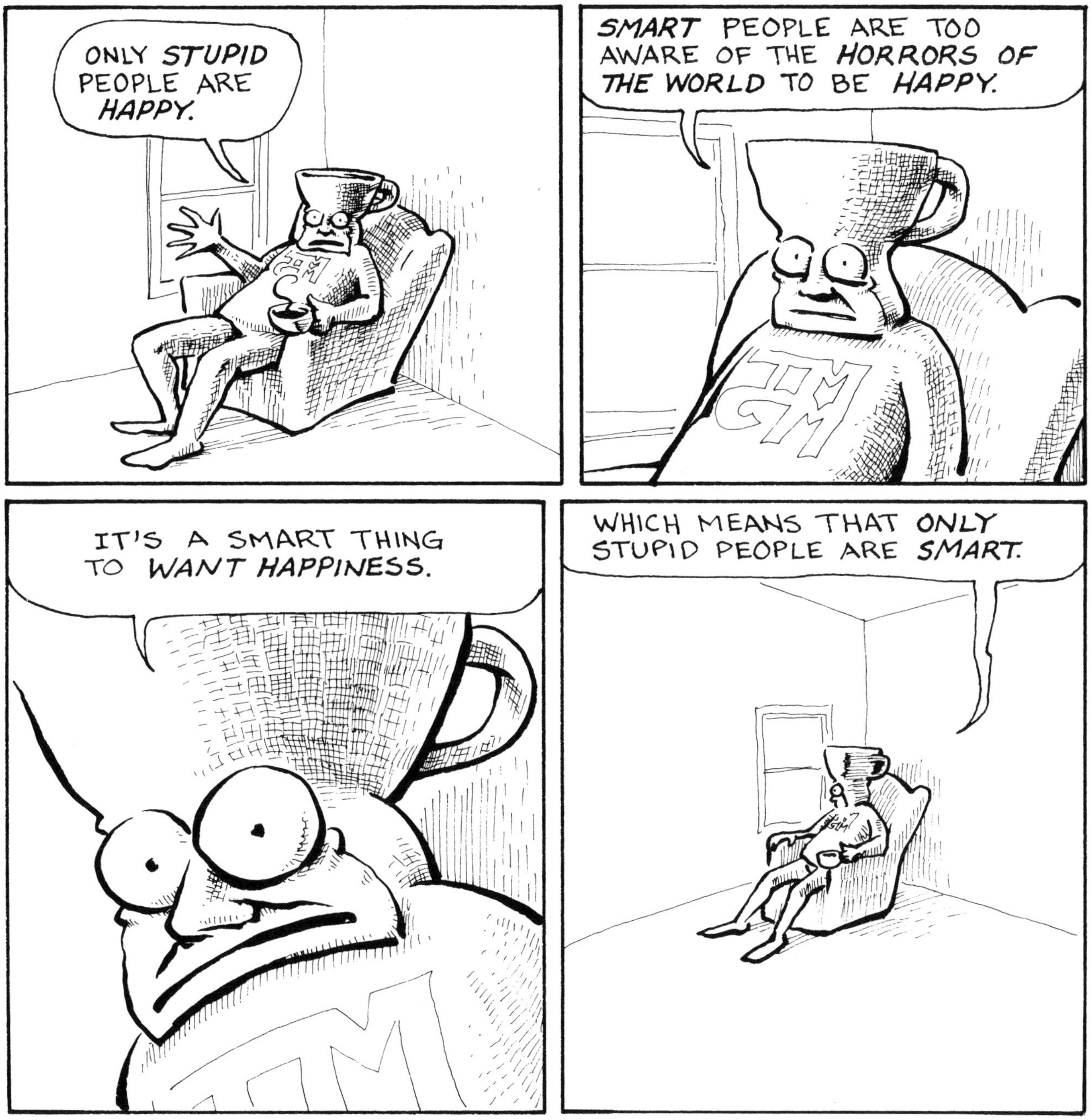
ONLY STUPID PEOPLE ARE HAPPY.
SMART PEOPLE ARE TOO AWARE OF THE HORRORS OF THE WORLD TO BE HAPPY.
IT'S A SMART THING TO WANT HAPPINESS.
WHICH MEANS THAT ONLY STUPID PEOPLE ARE SMART.

I'M GOING TO SIT AND THINK ABOUT *HOW TO BE HAPPY* UNTIL I FIGURE IT OUT.
I DON'T KNOW *MUCH*, BUT I DO KNOW THAT YOU DON'T GET *HAPPY* BY *THINKING* ABOUT IT.

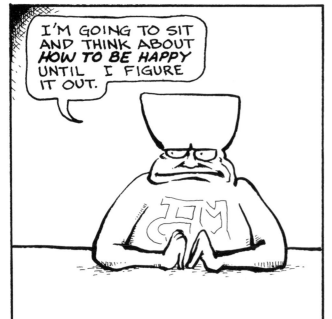

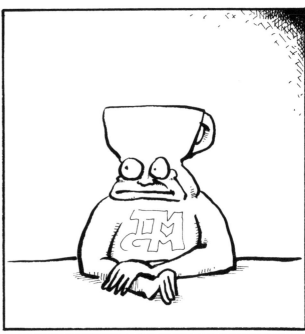

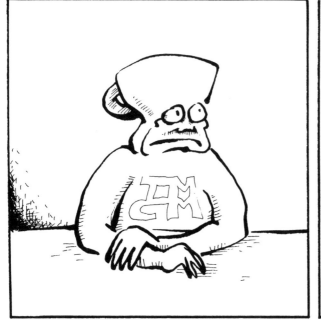

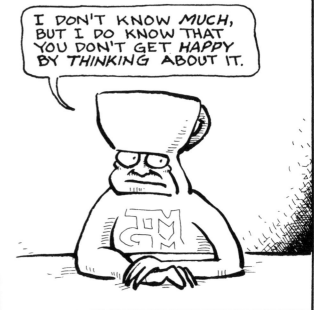

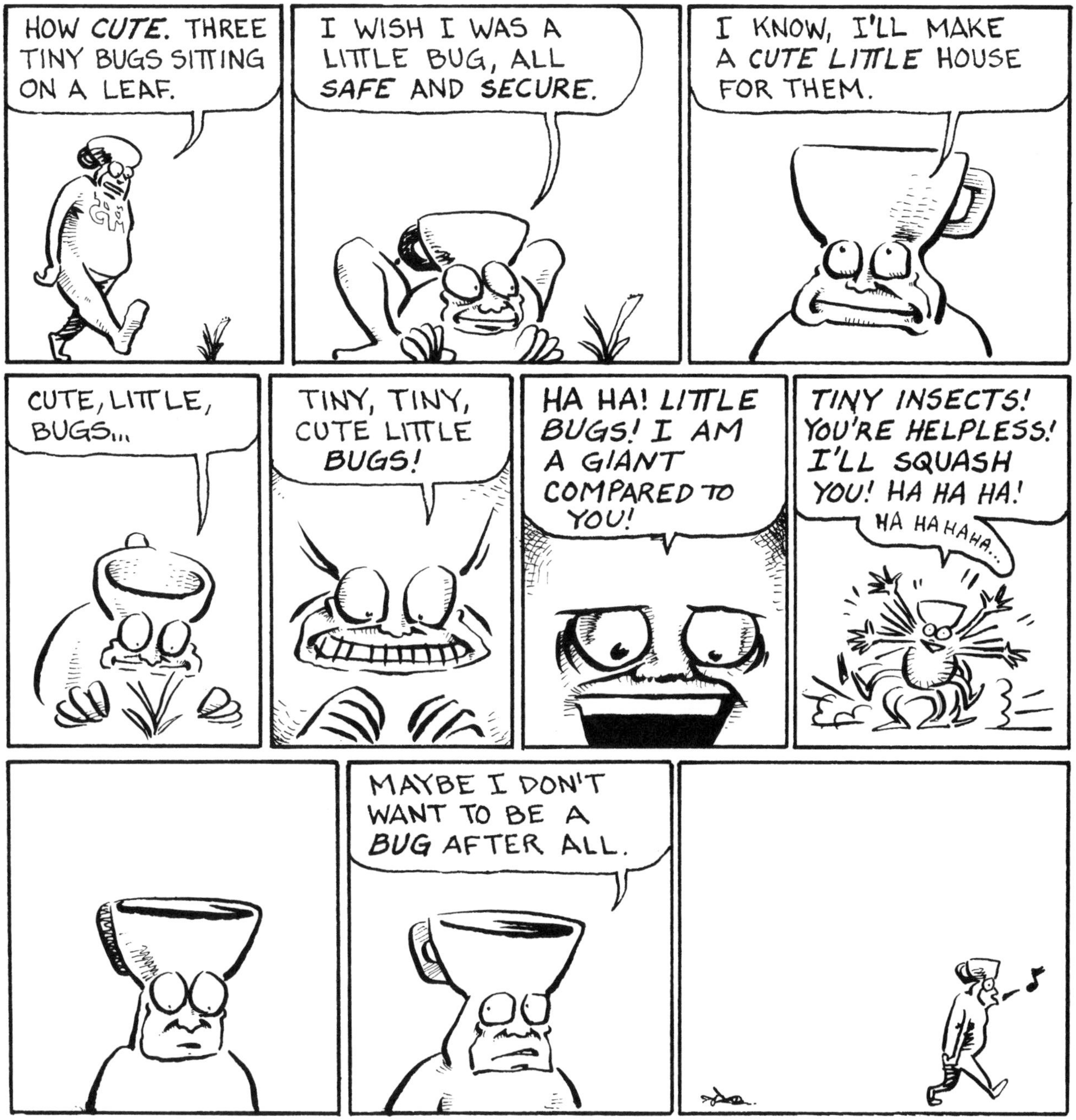
HOW CUTE. THREE TINY BUGS SITTING ON A LEAF.
I WISH I WAS A LITTLE BUG, ALL SAFE AND SECURE.
I KNOW, I'LL MAKE A CUTE LITTLE HOUSE FOR THEM.
CUTE, LITTLE, BUGS...
TINY, TINY, CUTE LITTLE BUGS!
HA HA! LITTLE BUGS! I AM A GIANT COMPARED TO YOU!
TINY INSECTS! YOU'RE HELPLESS! I'LL SQUASH YOU! HA HA HA!
HA HA HAHA...
MAYBE I DON'T WANT TO BE A BUG AFTER ALL.

TO-DO LIST

1. GET PAPER AND PENCIL.

2. THINK ABOUT THINGS *TO DO*.

3. START WRITING THE *TO-DO* LIST.

4. WATCH THE LIST GET *REALLY BIG*.

5. GET *OVERWHELMED*.

6. *PANIC*.

7. START DOING STUFF (THAT ISN'T THE STUFF YOU'RE TRYING TO DO) IN ORDER TO *AVOID* THE STUFF THAT YOU ARE *TRYING* TO DO.

8. HAVE *ANXIETY*.

9. WORK ON LIST AGAIN.

10. ADD INCREASINGLY *IMPOSSIBLE* THINGS TO THE LIST.

11. THINK ABOUT THE THINGS YOU'VE *WANTED* TO DO IN YOUR LIFE, BUT HAVEN'T DONE. REALIZE THAT YOUR LIFE IS A *WASTE* AND THAT ACHIEVING EVEN THE *SIMPLEST GOALS* IS BEYOND YOU.

12. ALLOW YOURSELF TO BE FILLED WITH *SHAME*.

13. FREAK OUT.

14. SPEND SO MUCH TIME ON THE *TO-DO LIST* THAT YOU RUN OUT OF TIME TO ACTUALLY DO *ANYTHING*.

15. GIVE UP.

16. GO OUTSIDE. IT'S A NICE DAY. LIFE IS SHORT.

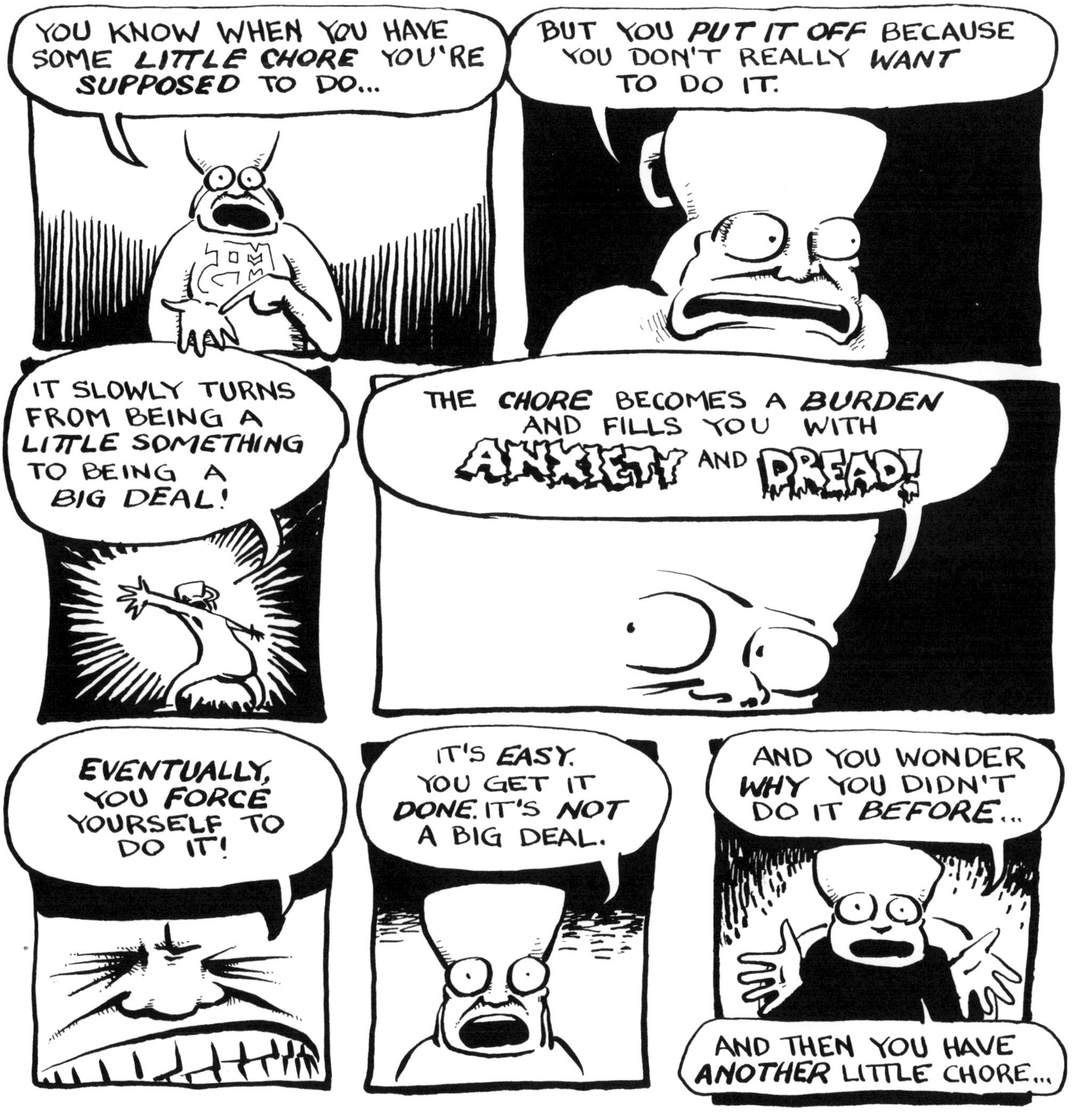
YOU KNOW WHEN YOU HAVE SOME LITTLE CHORE YOU'RE SUPPOSED TO DO...
BUT YOU PUT IT OFF BECAUSE YOU DON'T REALLY WANT TO DO IT.
IT SLOWLY TURNS FROM BEING A LITTLE SOMETHING TO BEING A BIG DEAL!
THE CHORE BECOMES A BURDEN AND FILLS YOU WITH ANXIETY AND DREAD!
EVENTUALLY, YOU FORCE YOURSELF TO DO IT!
IT'S EASY. YOU GET IT DONE. IT'S NOT A BIG DEAL.
AND YOU WONDER WHY YOU DIDN'T DO IT BEFORE...
AND THEN YOU HAVE ANOTHER LITTLE CHORE...

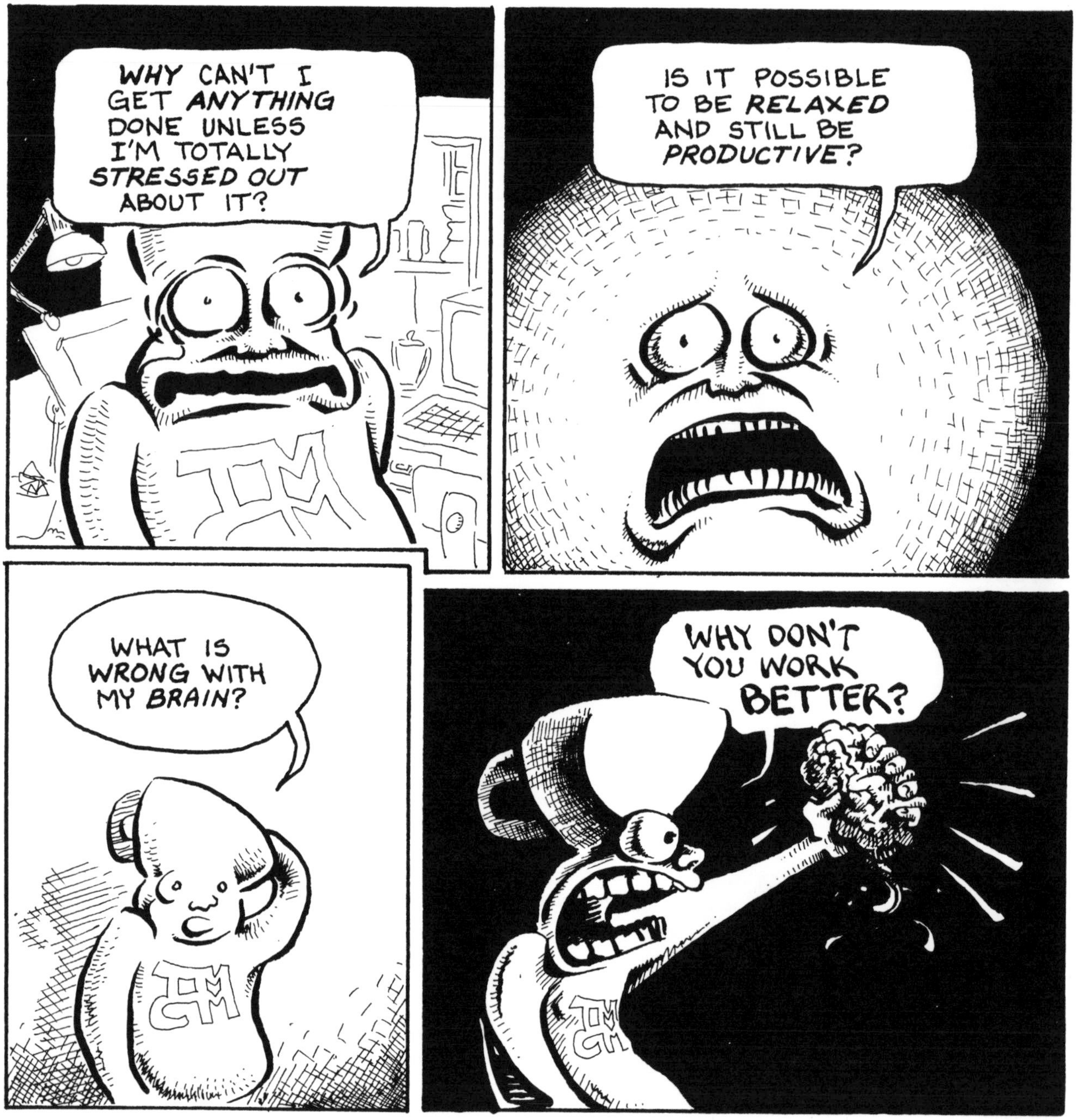
WHY CAN'T I GET ANYTHING DONE UNLESS I'M TOTALLY STRESSED OUT ABOUT IT?
IS IT POSSIBLE TO BE RELAXED AND STILL BE PRODUCTIVE?
WHAT IS WRONG WITH MY BRAIN?
WHY DON'T YOU WORK BETTER?

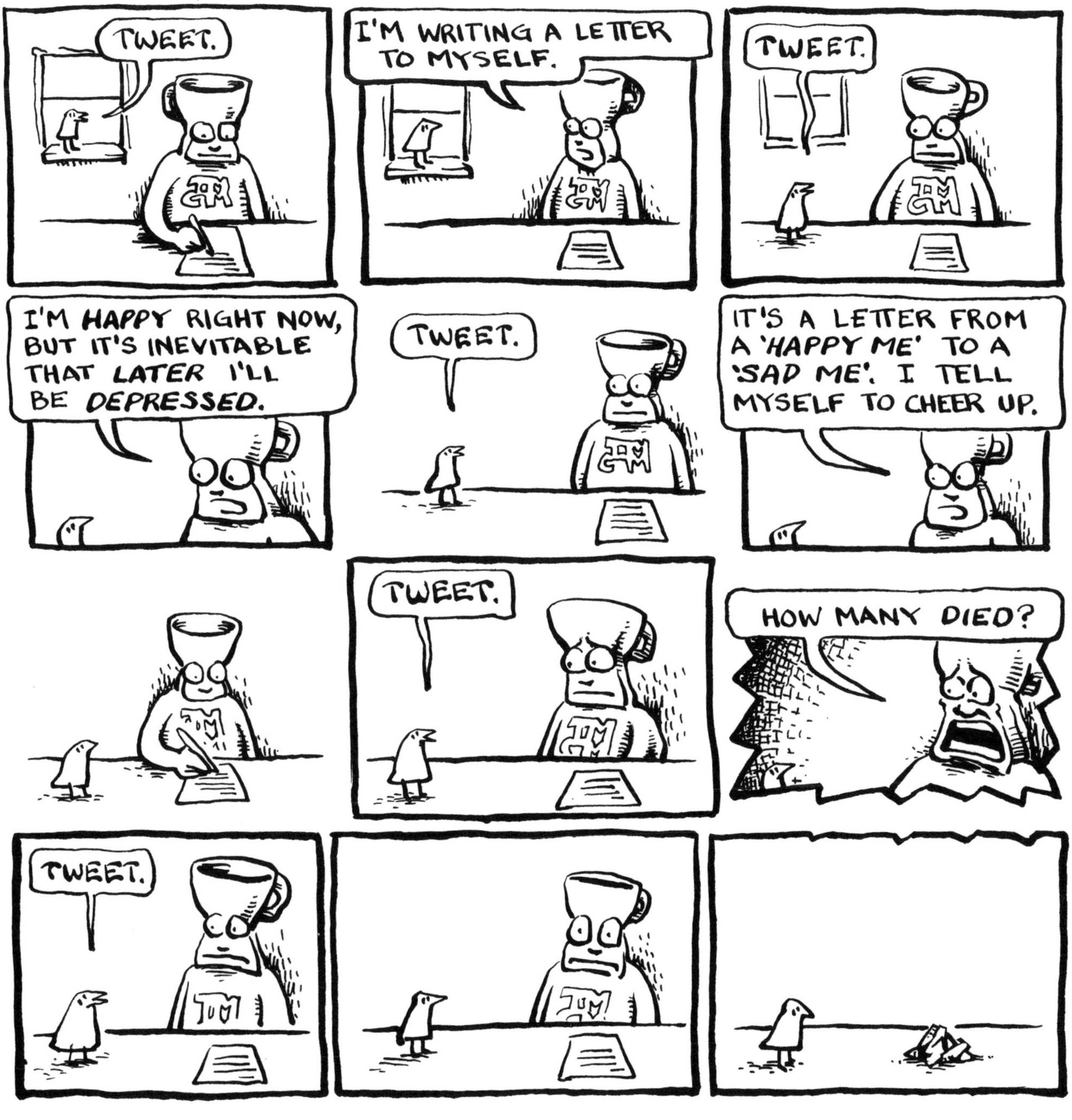
TWEET.
I'M WRITING A LETTER TO MYSELF.
TWEET.
I'M HAPPY RIGHT NOW, BUT IT'S INEVITABLE THAT LATER I'LL BE DEPRESSED.
TWEET.
IT'S A LETTER FROM A 'HAPPY ME' TO A 'SAD ME'. I TELL MYSELF TO CHEER UP.
TWEET.
HOW MANY DIED?
TWEET.

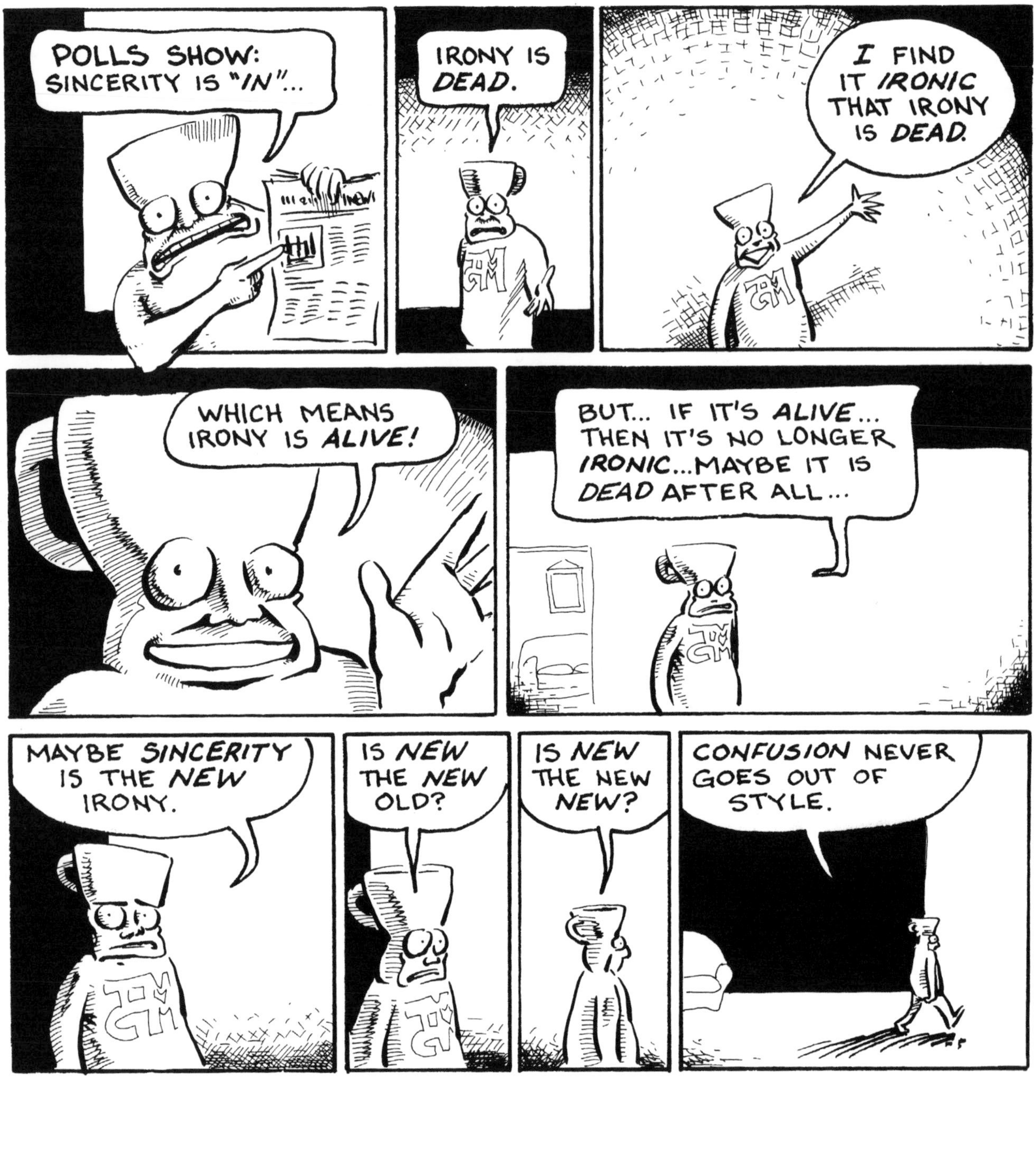
POLLS SHOW: SINCERITY IS "IN"...
IRONY IS DEAD.
I FIND IT IRONIC THAT IRONY IS DEAD.
WHICH MEANS IRONY IS ALIVE!
BUT... IF IT'S ALIVE... THEN IT'S NO LONGER IRONIC...MAYBE IT IS DEAD AFTER ALL...
MAYBE SINCERITY IS THE NEW IRONY.
IS NEW THE NEW OLD?
IS NEW THE NEW NEW?
CONFUSION NEVER GOES OUT OF STYLE.

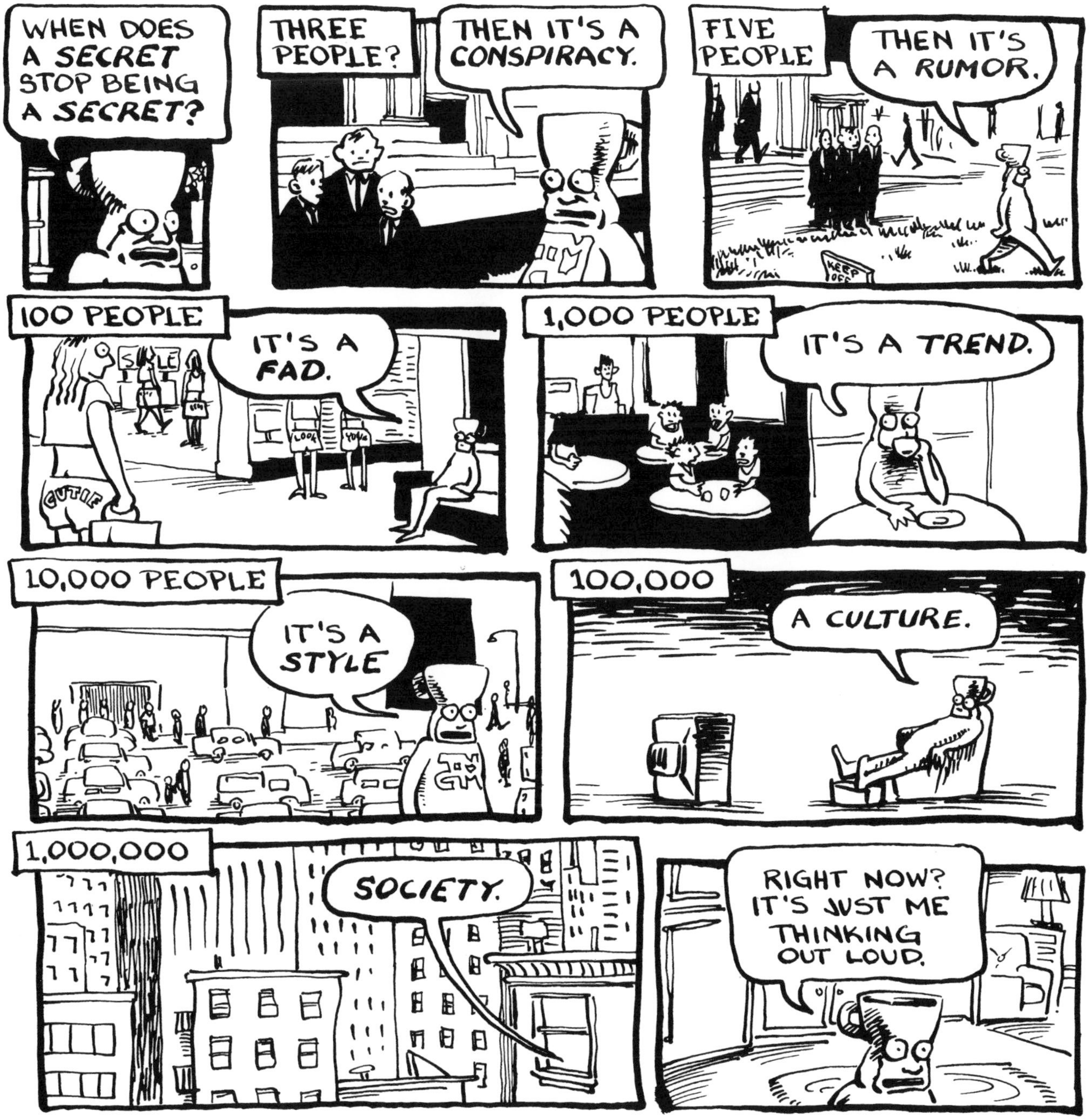
WHEN DOES A SECRET STOP BEING A SECRET?
THREE PEOPLE?
THEN IT'S A CONSPIRACY.
FIVE PEOPLE
THEN IT'S A RUMOR.
KEEP OFF
100 PEOPLE
IT'S A FAD.
CUTIE
1,000 PEOPLE
IT'S A TREND.
10,000 PEOPLE
IT'S A STYLE
100,000
A CULTURE.
1,000,000
SOCIETY.
RIGHT NOW? IT'S JUST ME THINKING OUT LOUD.

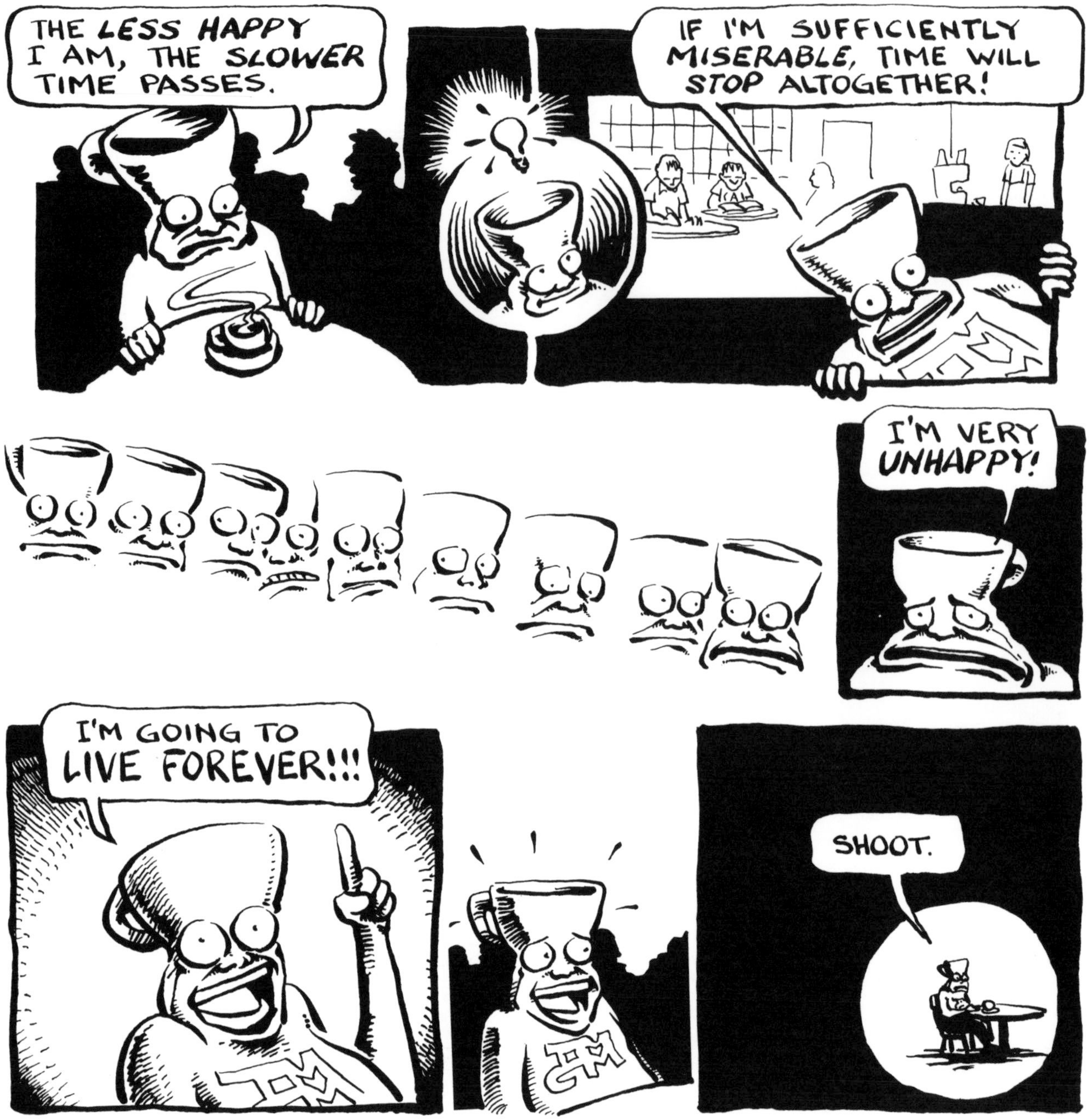
THE LESS HAPPY I AM, THE SLOWER TIME PASSES.
IF I'M SUFFICIENTLY MISERABLE, TIME WILL STOP ALTOGETHER!
I'M VERY UNHAPPY!
I'M GOING TO LIVE FOREVER!!!
SHOOT.

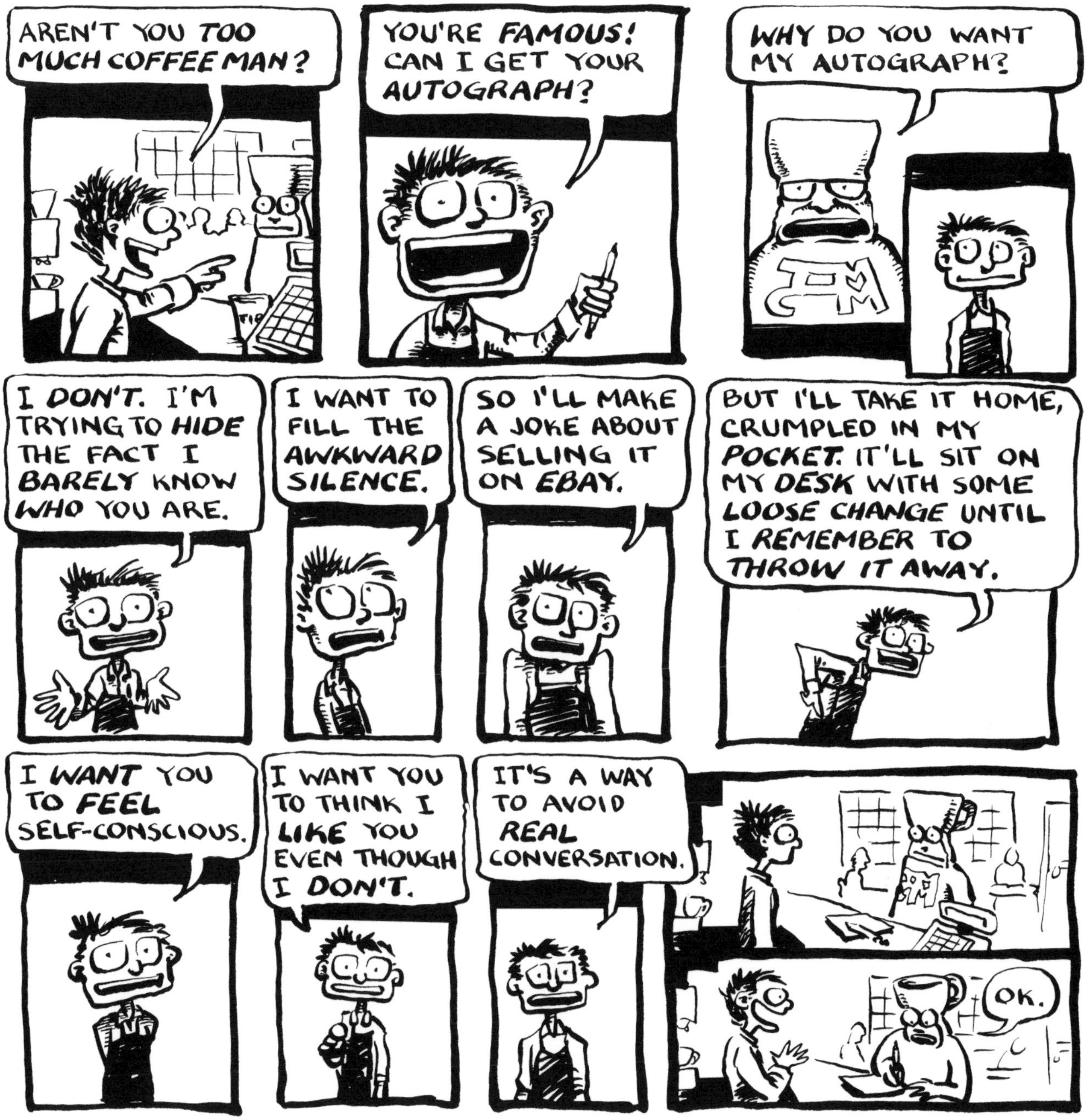
AREN'T YOU TOO MUCH COFFEE MAN?
YOU'RE FAMOUS! CAN I GET YOUR AUTOGRAPH?
WHY DO YOU WANT MY AUTOGRAPH?
I DON'T. I'M TRYING TO HIDE THE FACT I BARELY KNOW WHO YOU ARE.
I WANT TO FILL THE AWKWARD SILENCE.
SO I'LL MAKE A JOKE ABOUT SELLING IT ON EBAY.
BUT I'LL TAKE IT HOME, CRUMPLED IN MY POCKET. IT'LL SIT ON MY DESK WITH SOME LOOSE CHANGE UNTIL I REMEMBER TO THROW IT AWAY.
I WANT YOU TO FEEL SELF-CONSCIOUS.
I WANT YOU TO THINK I LIKE YOU EVEN THOUGH I DON'T.
IT'S A WAY TO AVOID REAL CONVERSATION.
OK.

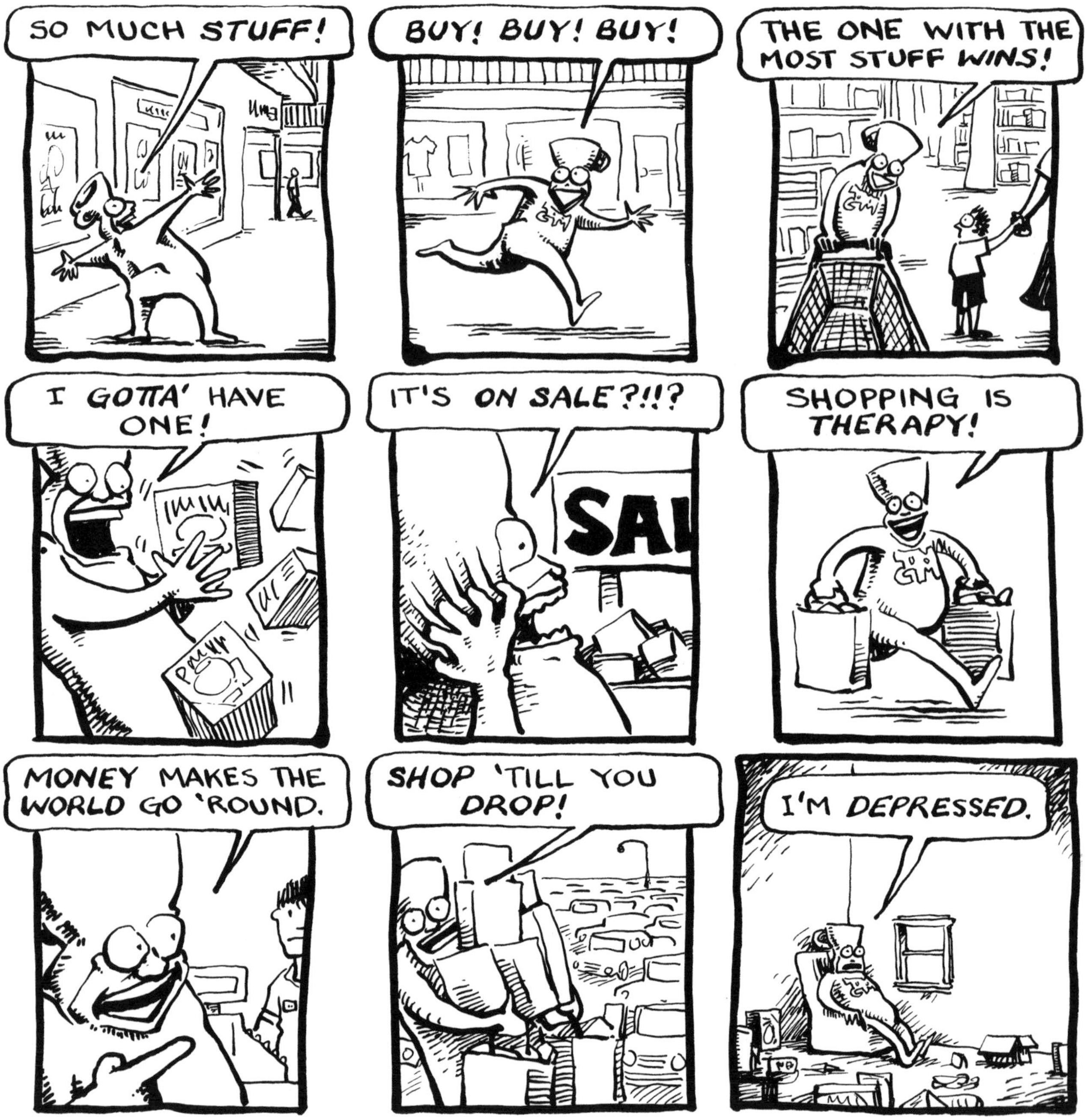
SO MUCH STUFF!
BUY! BUY! BUY!
THE ONE WITH THE MOST STUFF WINS!
I GOTTA' HAVE ONE!
IT'S ON SALE?!!?
SHOPPING IS THERAPY!
MONEY MAKES THE WORLD GO 'ROUND.
SHOP 'TILL YOU DROP!
I'M DEPRESSED.

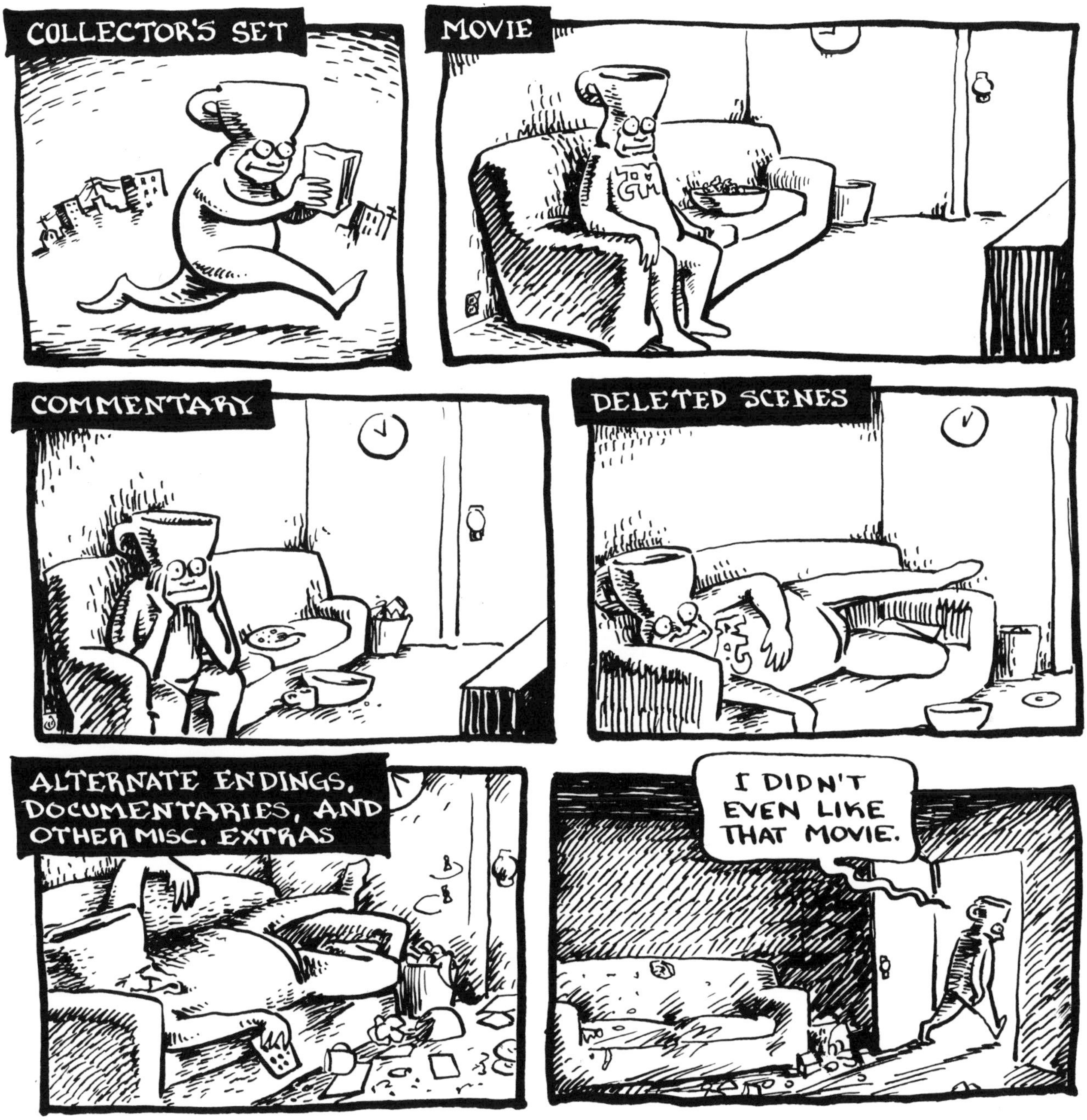
COLLECTOR'S SET
MOVIE
COMMENTARY
DELETED SCENES
ALTERNATE ENDINGS, DOCUMENTARIES, AND OTHER MISC. EXTRAS
I DIDN'T EVEN LIKE THAT MOVIE.

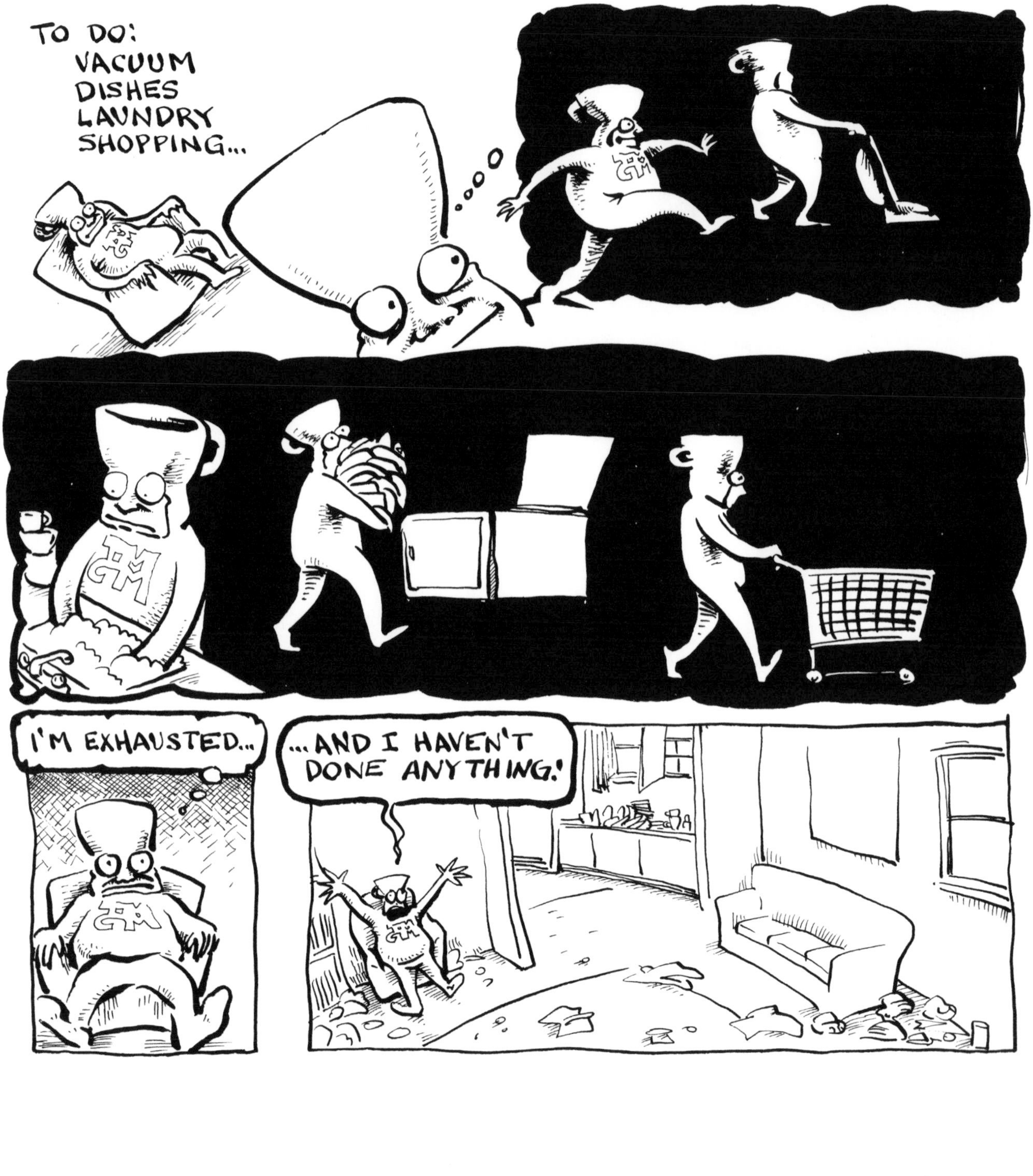
TO DO:
VACUUM
DISHES
LAUNDRY
SHOPPING...
I'M EXHAUSTED...
...AND I HAVEN'T DONE ANYTHING!

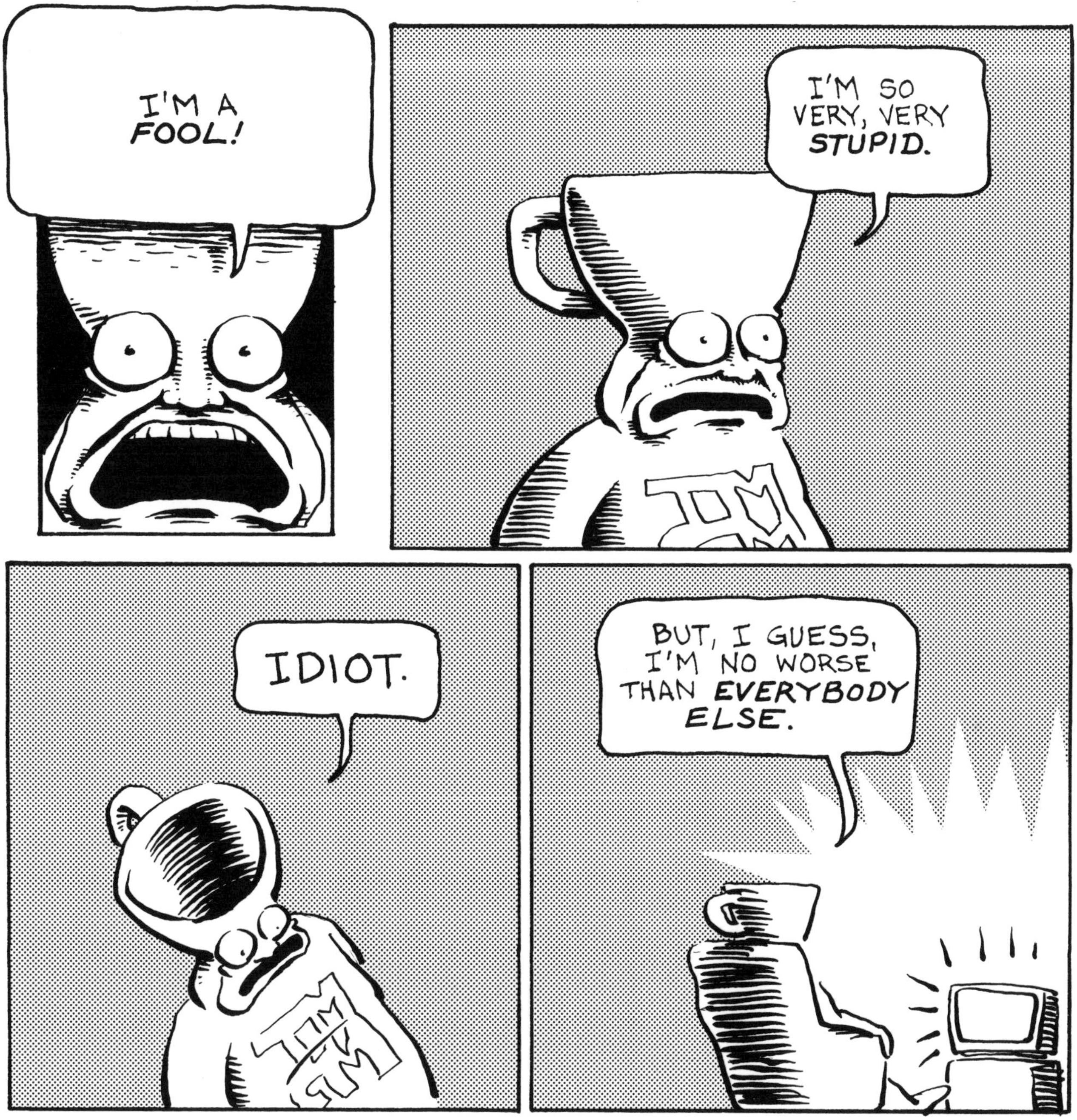
I'M A FOOL!
I'M SO VERY, VERY STUPID.
IDIOT.
BUT, I GUESS, I'M NO WORSE THAN EVERYBODY ELSE.

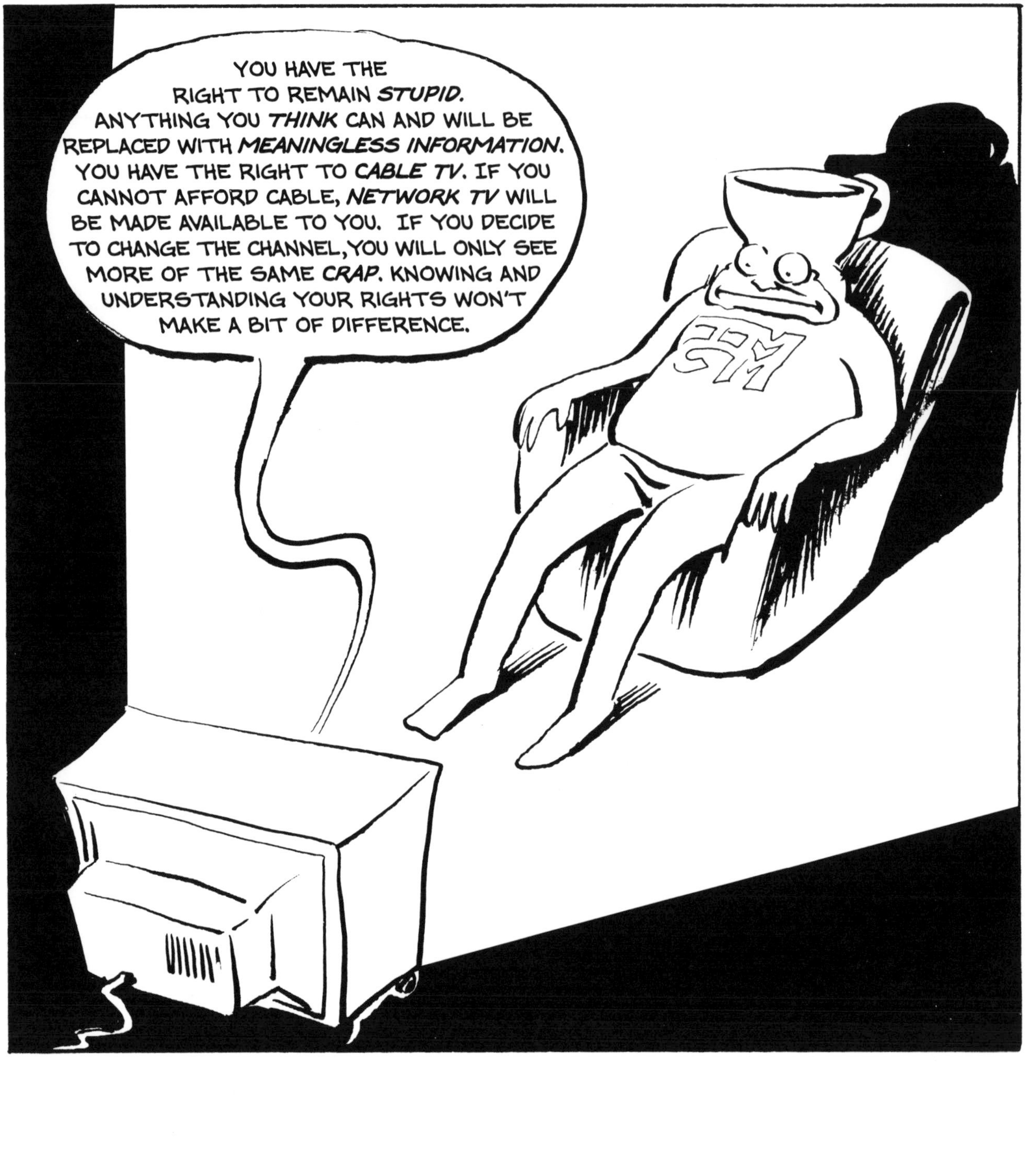
YOU HAVE THE RIGHT TO REMAIN STUPID. ANYTHING YOU THINK CAN AND WILL BE REPLACED WITH MEANINGLESS INFORMATION. YOU HAVE THE RIGHT TO CABLE TV. IF YOU CANNOT AFFORD CABLE, NETWORK TV WILL BE MADE AVAILABLE TO YOU. IF YOU DECIDE TO CHANGE THE CHANNEL, YOU WILL ONLY SEE MORE OF THE SAME CRAP. KNOWING AND UNDERSTANDING YOUR RIGHTS WON'T MAKE A BIT OF DIFFERENCE.

I HATE YOU!
YOU'VE FILLED MY LIFE WITH EMPTINESS!
I'M WASTING MY TIME WITH YOU.
I GIVE YOU MY FULL ATTENTION AND YOU GIVE ME NOTHING.
NO MORE!
GOODBYE!
WAIT! COME BACK! I LOVE YOU!

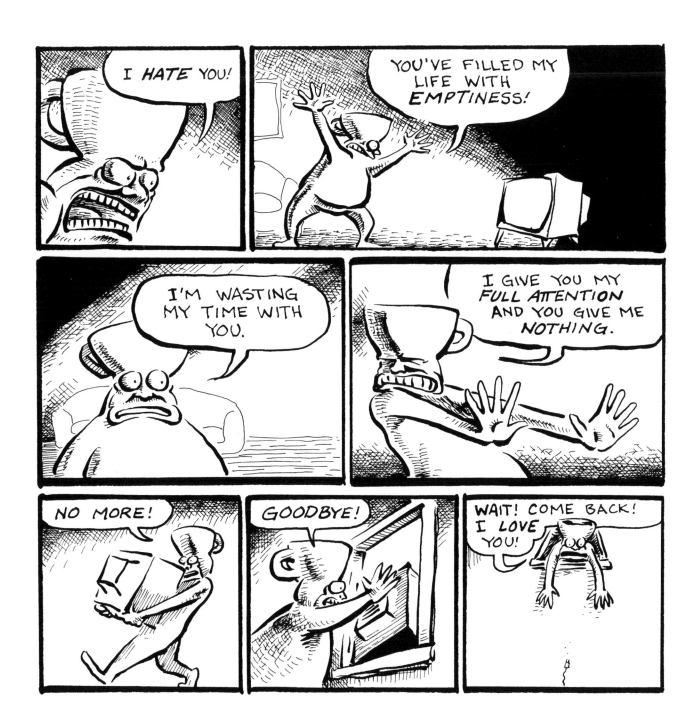

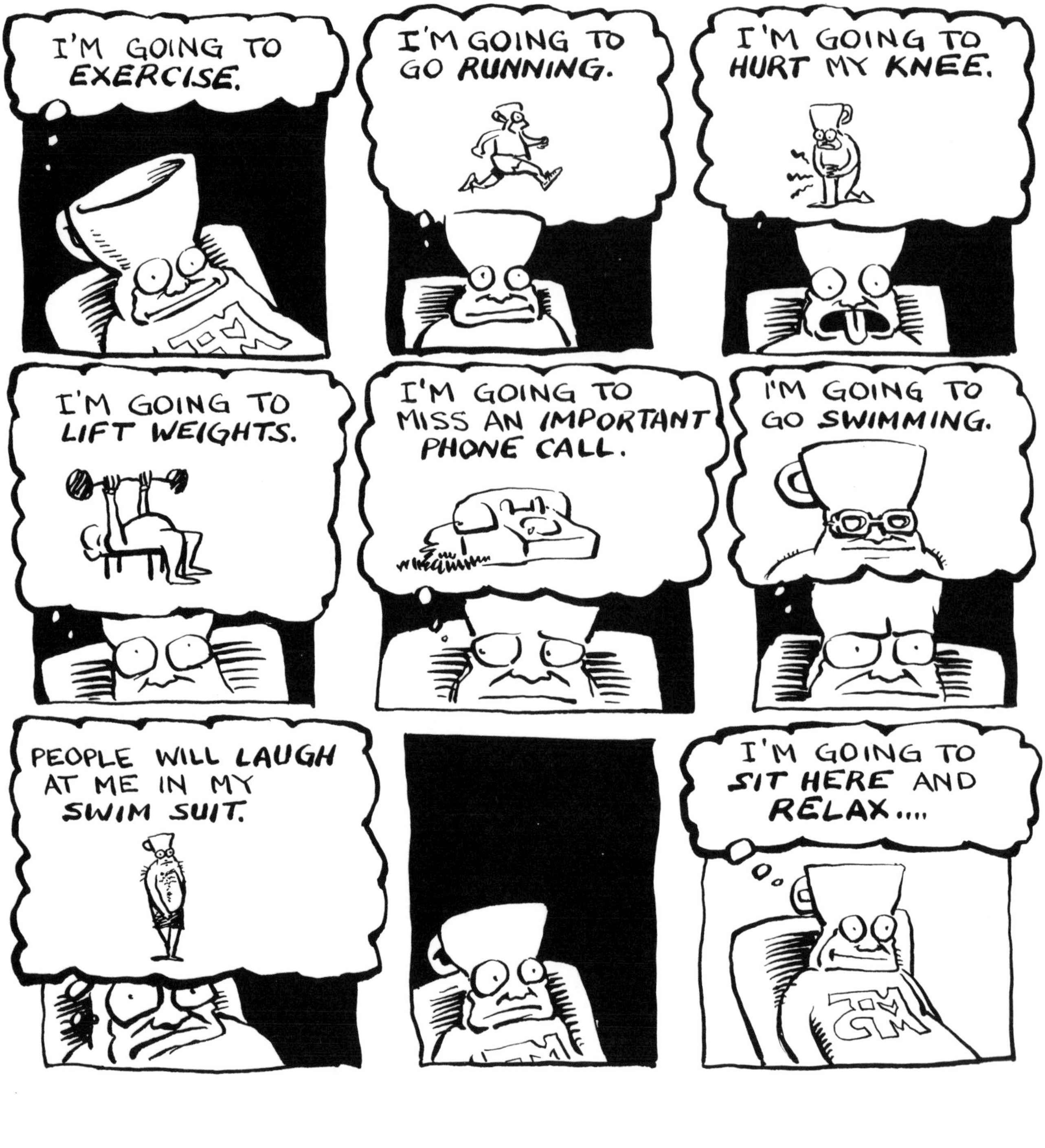
I'M GOING TO EXERCISE.
I'M GOING TO GO RUNNING.
I'M GOING TO HURT MY KNEE.
I'M GOING TO LIFT WEIGHTS.
I'M GOING TO MISS AN IMPORTANT PHONE CALL.
I'M GOING TO GO SWIMMING.
PEOPLE WILL LAUGH AT ME IN MY SWIM SUIT.
I'M GOING TO SIT HERE AND RELAX....

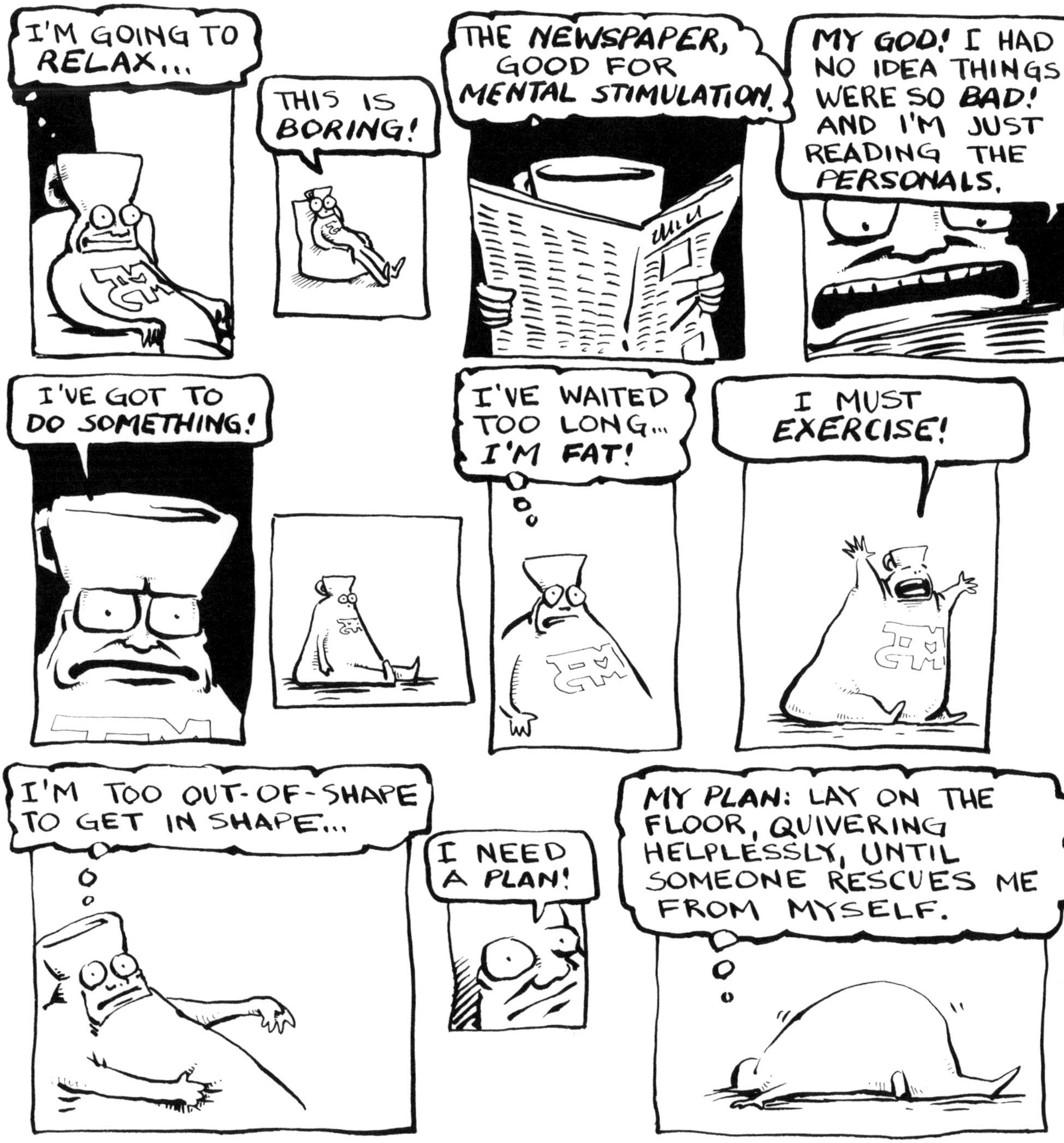
I'M GOING TO RELAX...
THIS IS BORING!
THE NEWSPAPER, GOOD FOR MENTAL STIMULATION.
MY GOD! I HAD NO IDEA THINGS WERE SO BAD! AND I'M JUST READING THE PERSONALS.
I'VE GOT TO DO SOMETHING!
I'VE WAITED TOO LONG... I'M FAT!
I MUST EXERCISE!
I'M TOO OUT-OF-SHAPE TO GET IN SHAPE...
I NEED A PLAN!
MY PLAN: LAY ON THE FLOOR, QUIVERING HELPLESSLY, UNTIL SOMEONE RESCUES ME FROM MYSELF.

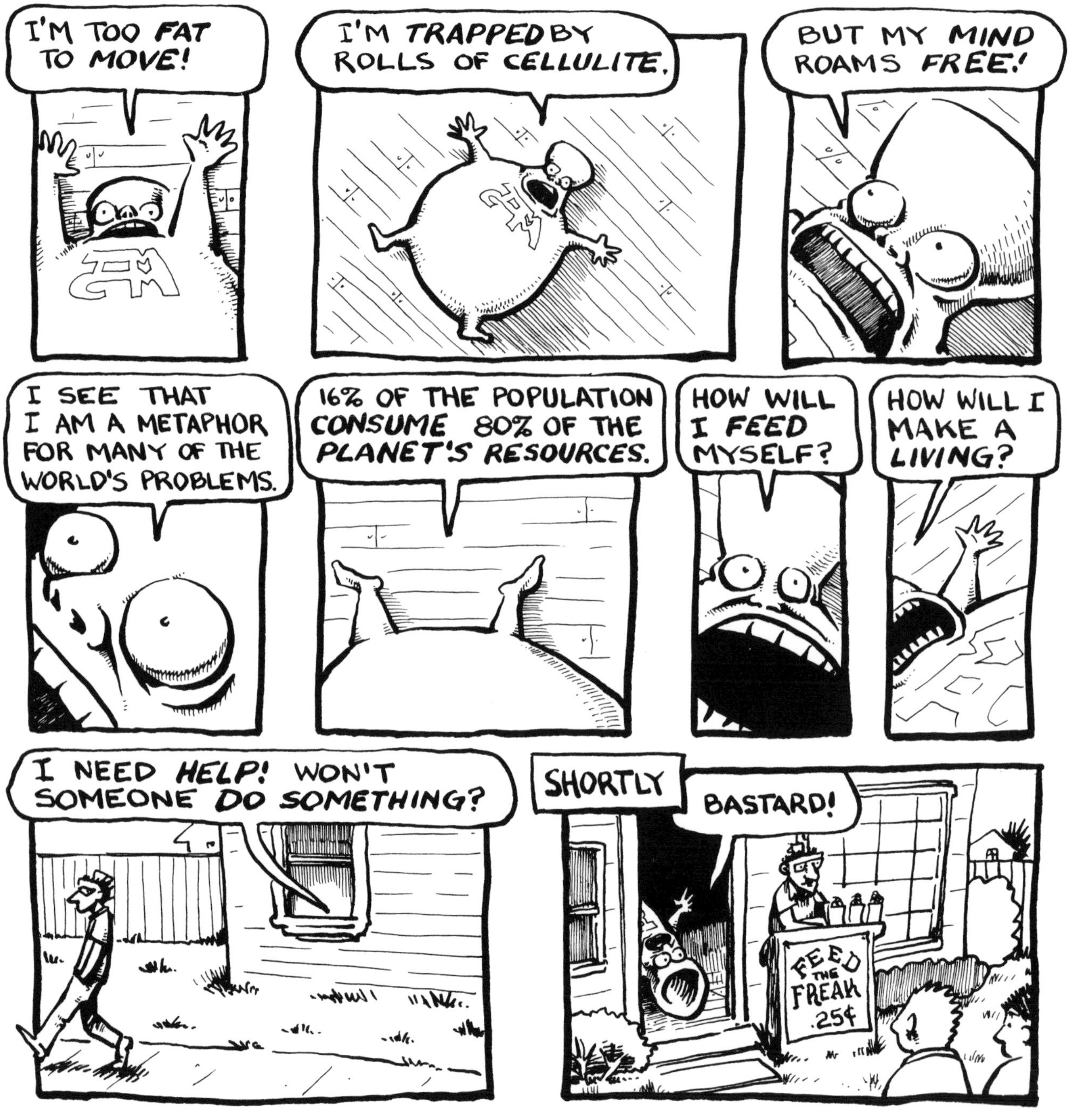
I'M TOO FAT TO MOVE!
I'M TRAPPED BY ROLLS OF CELLULITE,
BUT MY MIND ROAMS FREE!
I SEE THAT I AM A METAPHOR FOR MANY OF THE WORLD'S PROBLEMS.
16% OF THE POPULATION CONSUME 80% OF THE PLANET'S RESOURCES.
HOW WILL I FEED MYSELF?
HOW WILL I MAKE A LIVING?
I NEED HELP! WON'T SOMEONE DO SOMETHING?
SHORTLY
BASTARD!
FEED THE FREAK .25¢

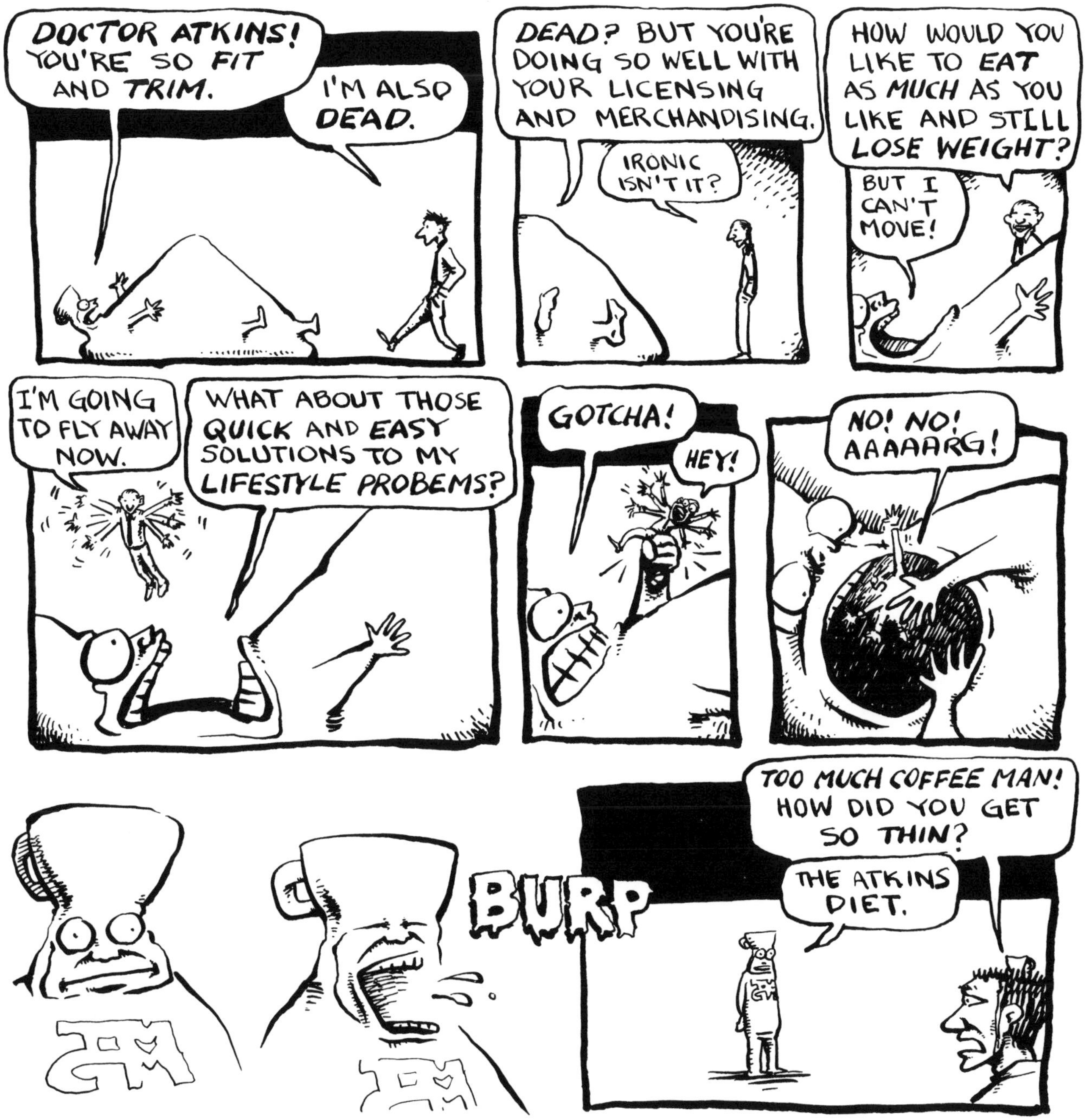
DOCTOR ATKINS! YOU'RE SO FIT AND TRIM.
I'M ALSO DEAD.
DEAD? BUT YOU'RE DOING SO WELL WITH YOUR LICENSING AND MERCHANDISING.
IRONIC ISN'T IT?
HOW WOULD YOU LIKE TO EAT AS MUCH AS YOU LIKE AND STILL LOSE WEIGHT?
BUT I CAN'T MOVE!
I'M GOING TO FLY AWAY NOW.
WHAT ABOUT THOSE QUICK AND EASY SOLUTIONS TO MY LIFESTYLE PROBEMS?
GOTCHA!
HEY!
NO! NO! AAAAARG!
BURP
TOO MUCH COFFEE MAN! HOW DID YOU GET SO THIN?
THE ATKINS DIET.

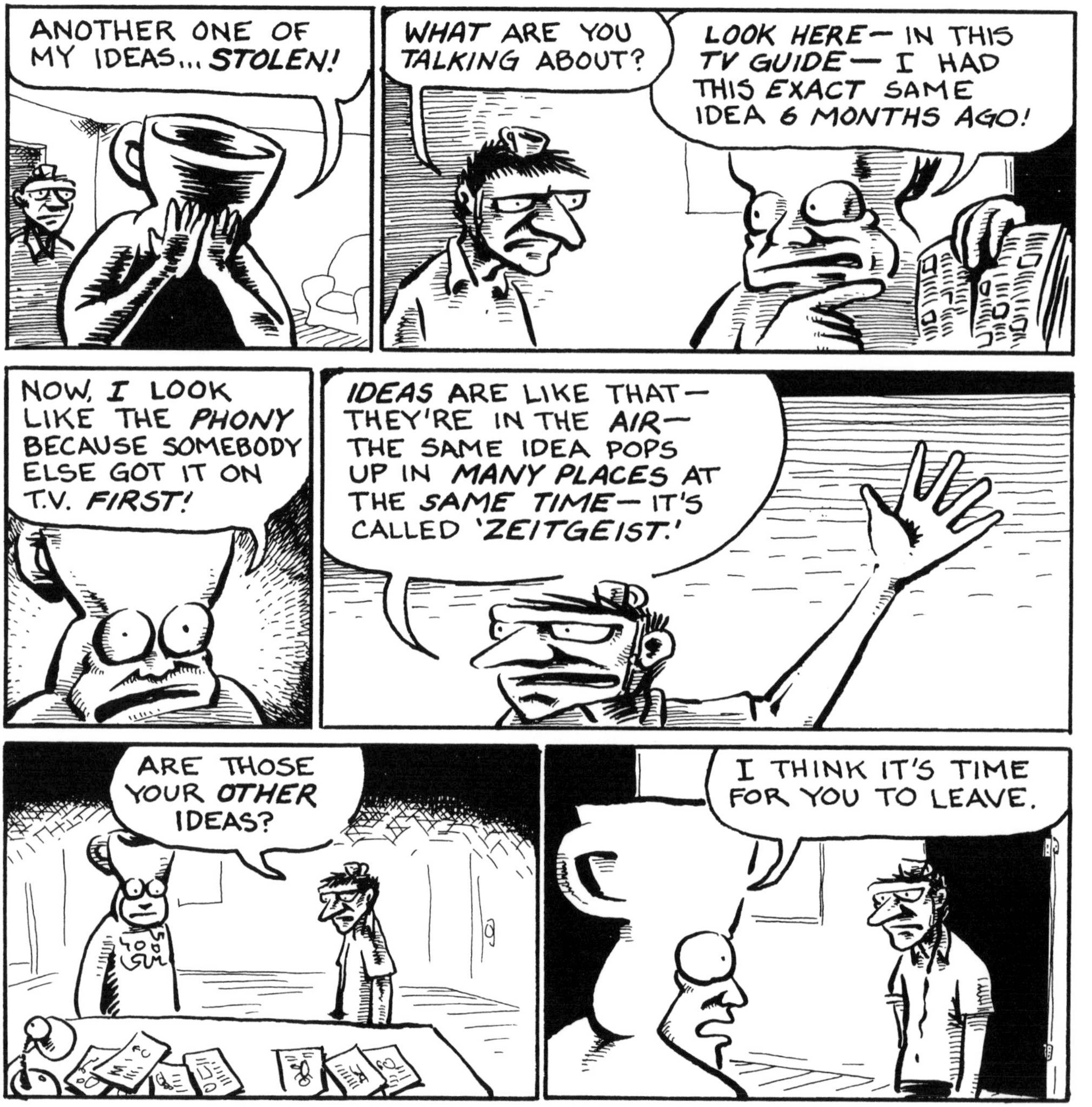
ANOTHER ONE OF MY IDEAS... STOLEN!
WHAT ARE YOU TALKING ABOUT?
LOOK HERE— IN THIS TV GUIDE— I HAD THIS EXACT SAME IDEA 6 MONTHS AGO!
NOW, I LOOK LIKE THE PHONY BECAUSE SOMEBODY ELSE GOT IT ON T.V. FIRST!
IDEAS ARE LIKE THAT— THEY'RE IN THE AIR— THE SAME IDEA POPS UP IN MANY PLACES AT THE SAME TIME— IT'S CALLED 'ZEITGEIST.'
ARE THOSE YOUR OTHER IDEAS?
I THINK IT'S TIME FOR YOU TO LEAVE.

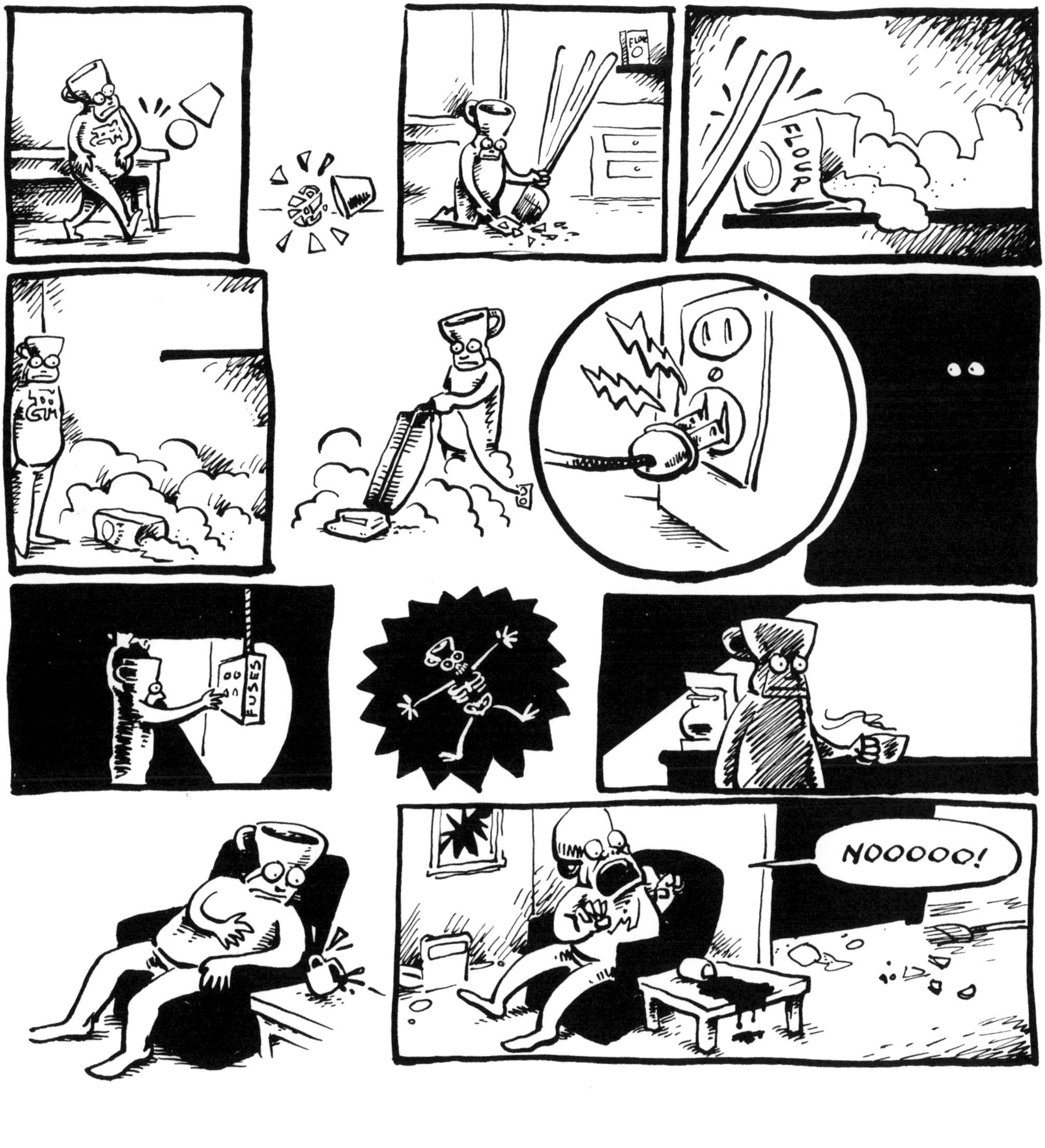
FLOUR
FLOUR
GTM
FUSES
NOOOOO!

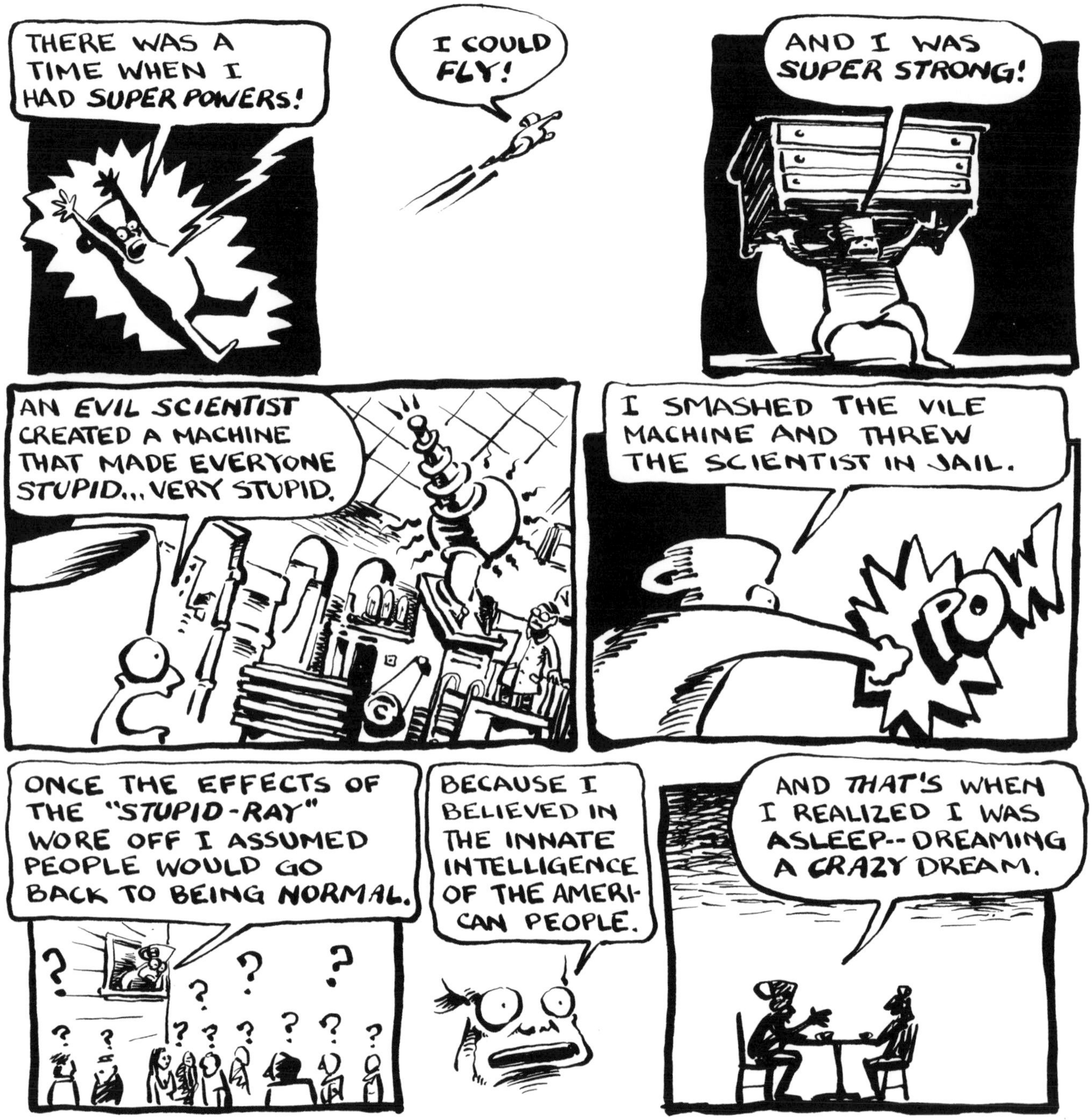
THERE WAS A TIME WHEN I HAD SUPER POWERS!
I COULD FLY!
AND I WAS SUPER STRONG!
AN EVIL SCIENTIST CREATED A MACHINE THAT MADE EVERYONE STUPID... VERY STUPID.
I SMASHED THE VILE MACHINE AND THREW THE SCIENTIST IN JAIL.
POW
ONCE THE EFFECTS OF THE "STUPID-RAY" WORE OFF I ASSUMED PEOPLE WOULD GO BACK TO BEING NORMAL.
BECAUSE I BELIEVED IN THE INNATE INTELLIGENCE OF THE AMERICAN PEOPLE.
AND THAT'S WHEN I REALIZED I WAS ASLEEP-- DREAMING A CRAZY DREAM.

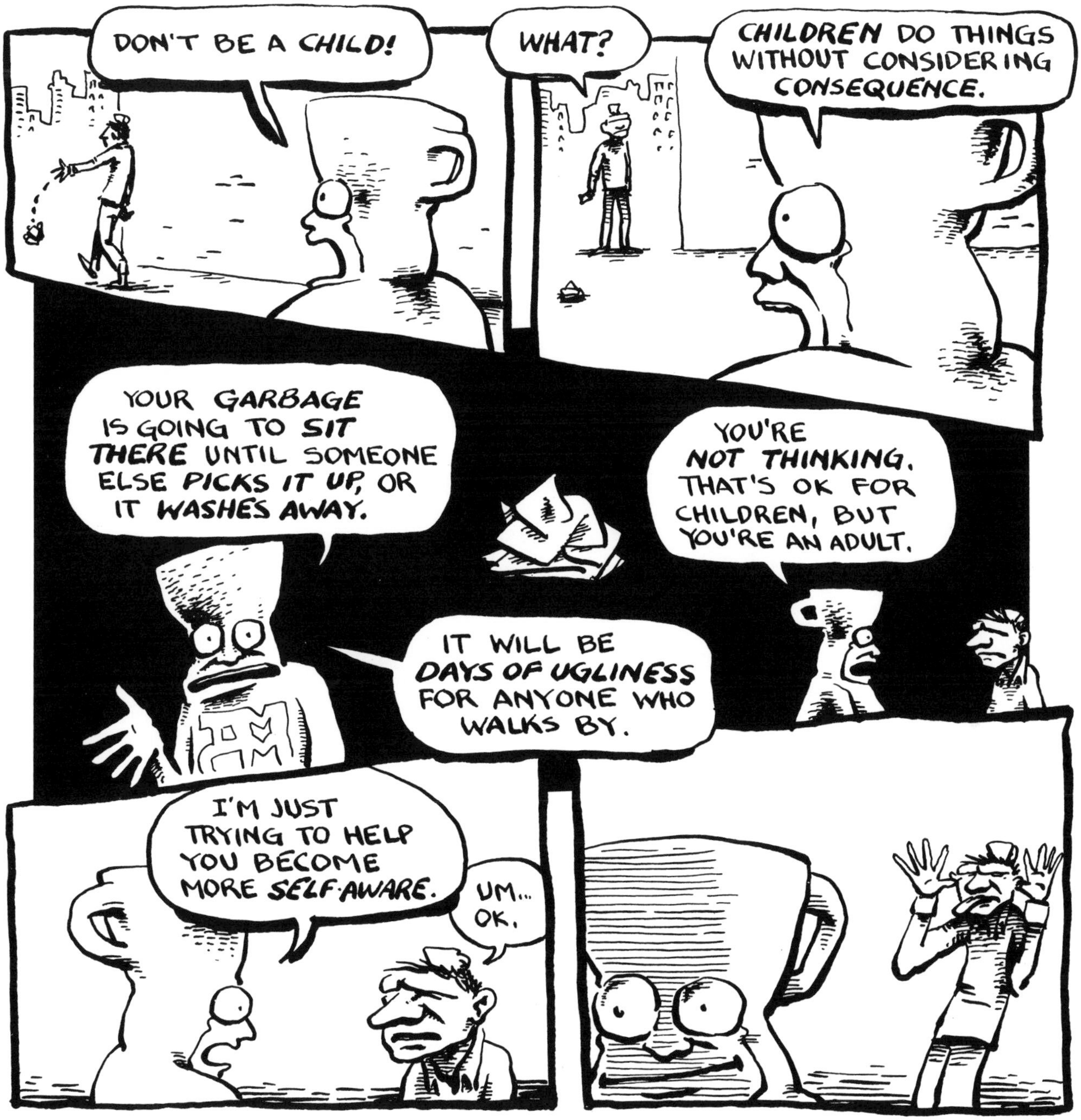
DON'T BE A CHILD!
WHAT?
CHILDREN DO THINGS WITHOUT CONSIDERING CONSEQUENCE.
YOUR GARBAGE IS GOING TO SIT THERE UNTIL SOMEONE ELSE PICKS IT UP, OR IT WASHES AWAY.
YOU'RE NOT THINKING. THAT'S OK FOR CHILDREN, BUT YOU'RE AN ADULT.
IT WILL BE DAYS OF UGLINESS FOR ANYONE WHO WALKS BY.
I'M JUST TRYING TO HELP YOU BECOME MORE SELF-AWARE.
UM... OK.

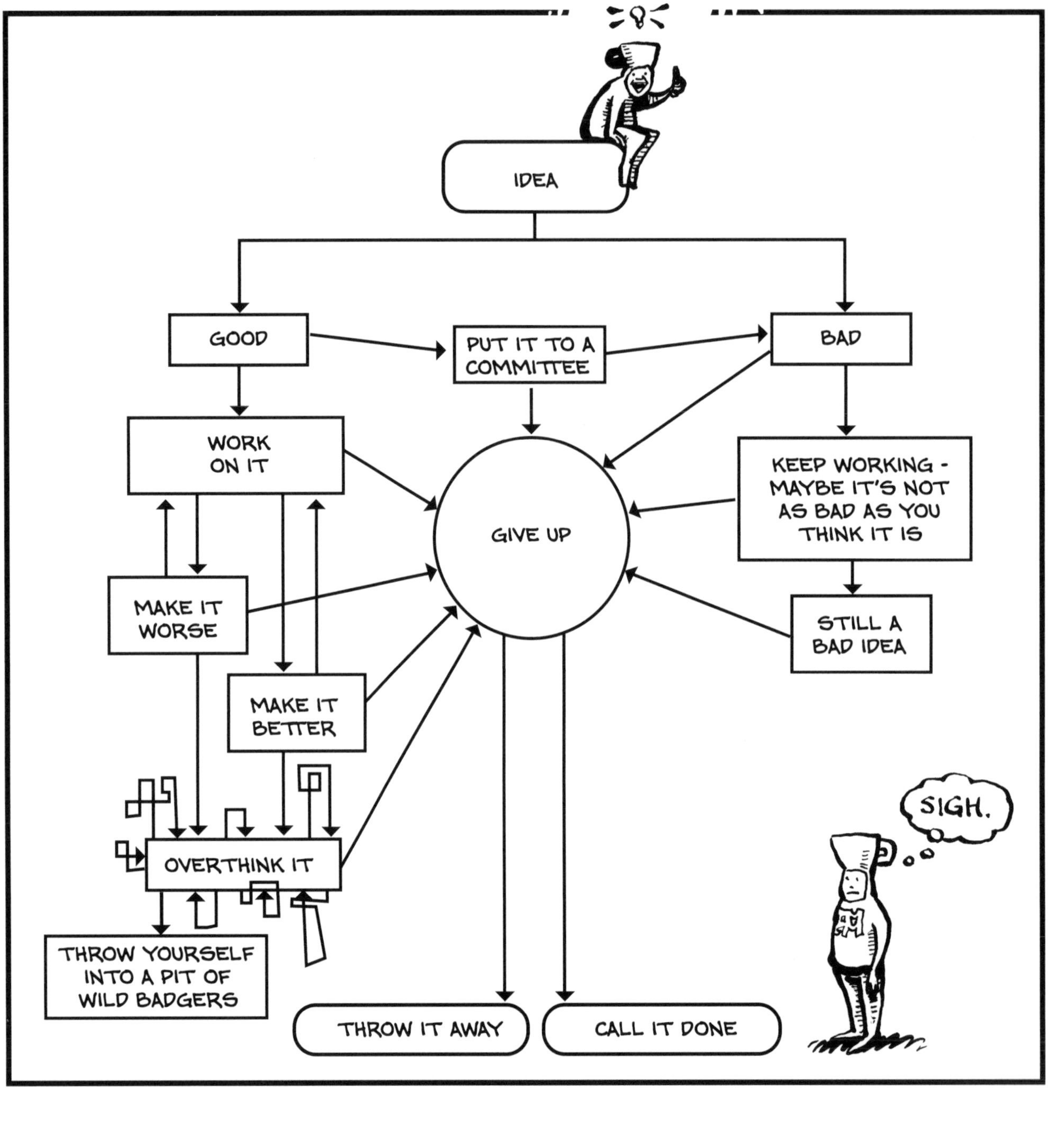
IDEA
GOOD
PUT IT TO A COMMITTEE
BAD
WORK ON IT
GIVE UP
KEEP WORKING - MAYBE IT'S NOT AS BAD AS YOU THINK IT IS
MAKE IT WORSE
STILL A BAD IDEA
MAKE IT BETTER
SIGH.
OVERTHINK IT
THROW YOURSELF INTO A PIT OF WILD BADGERS
THROW IT AWAY
CALL IT DONE

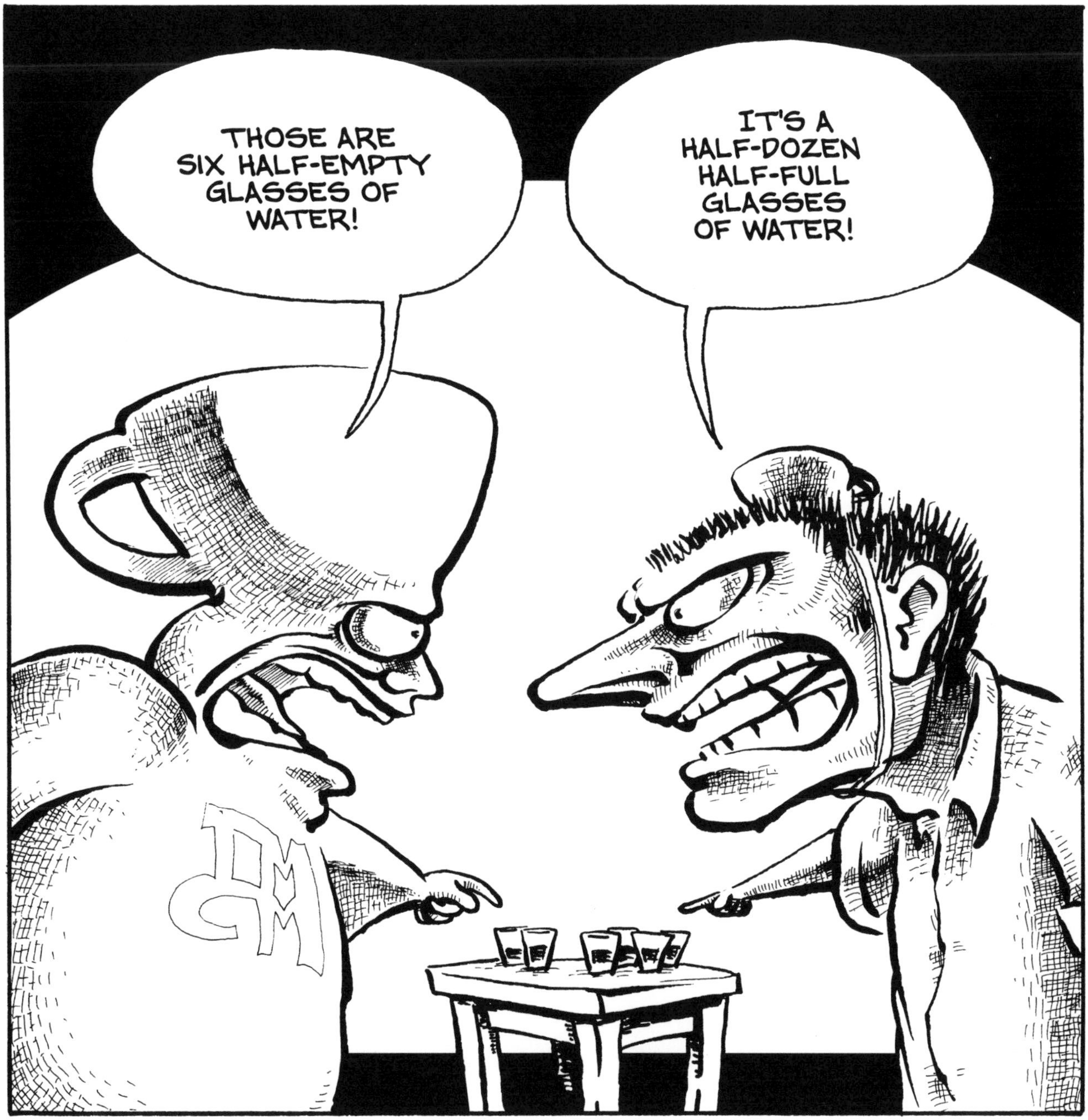
THOSE ARE SIX HALF-EMPTY GLASSES OF WATER!
IT'S A HALF-DOZEN HALF-FULL GLASSES OF WATER!

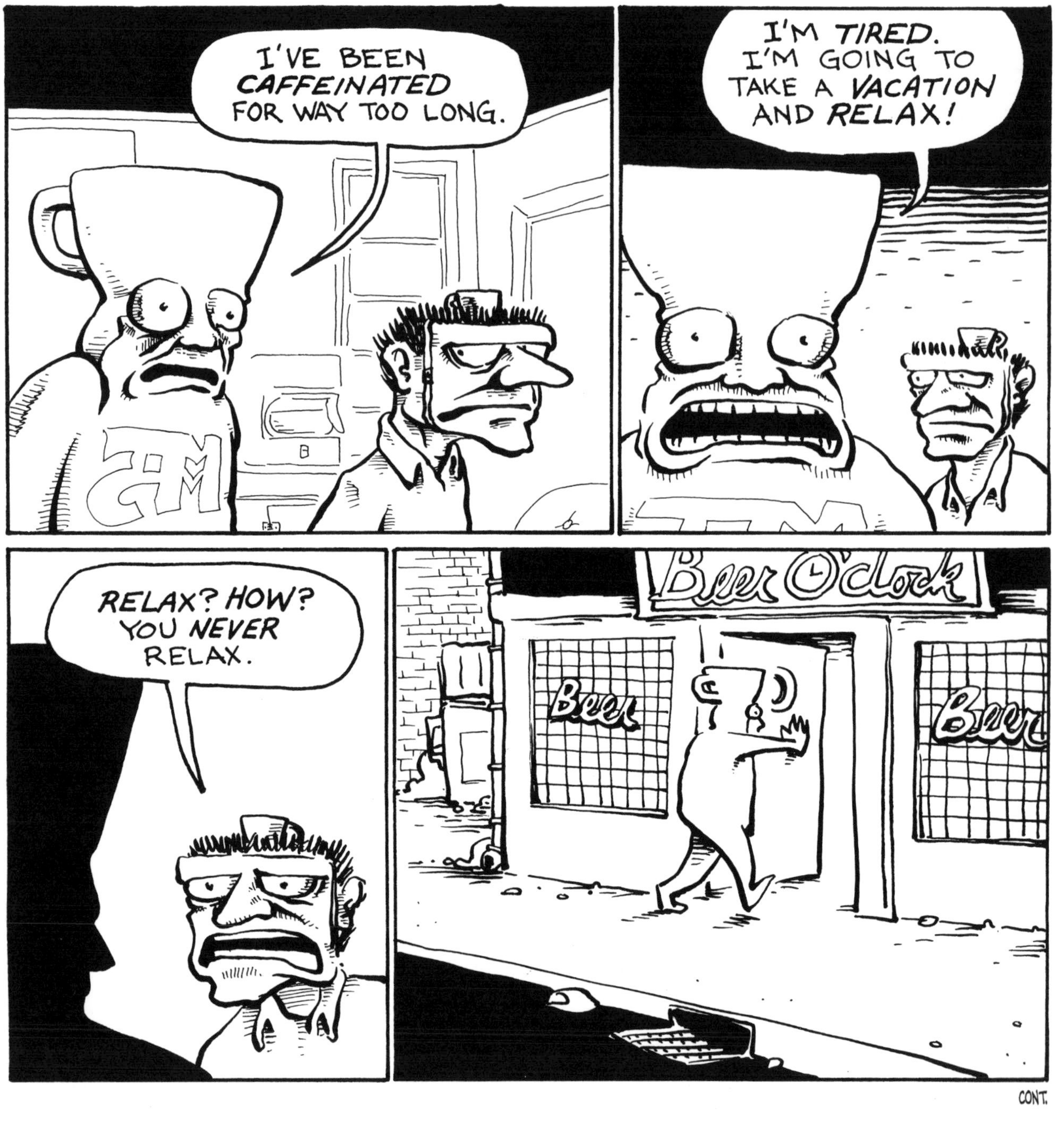
I'VE BEEN CAFFEINATED FOR WAY TOO LONG.
I'M TIRED. I'M GOING TO TAKE A VACATION AND RELAX!
RELAX? HOW? YOU NEVER RELAX.
Beer O'clock
Beer
Beer
CONT.

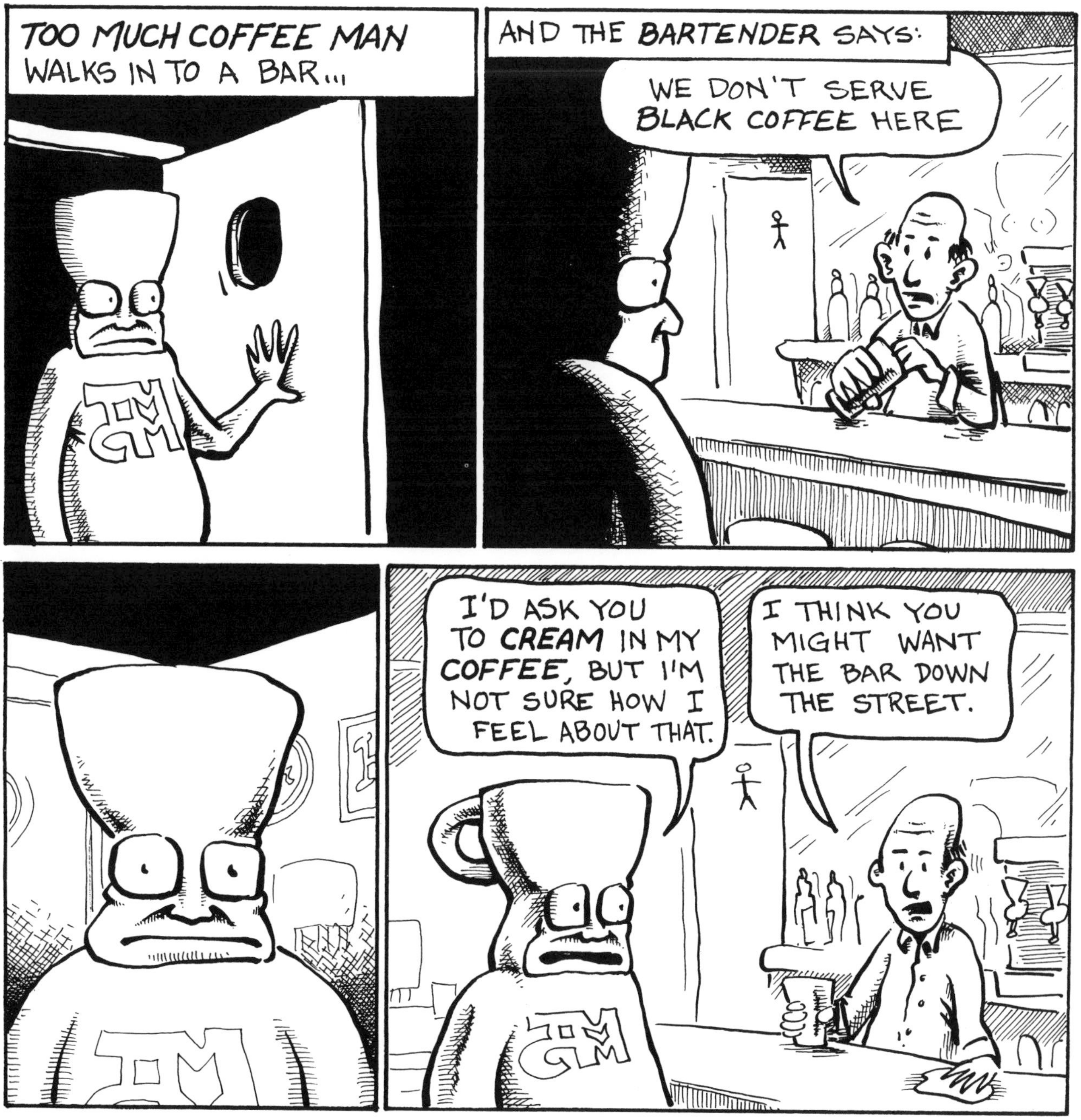
TOO MUCH COFFEE MAN
WALKS IN TO A BAR...
AND THE BARTENDER SAYS:
WE DON'T SERVE BLACK COFFEE HERE
I'D ASK YOU TO CREAM IN MY COFFEE, BUT I'M NOT SURE HOW I FEEL ABOUT THAT.
I THINK YOU MIGHT WANT THE BAR DOWN THE STREET.

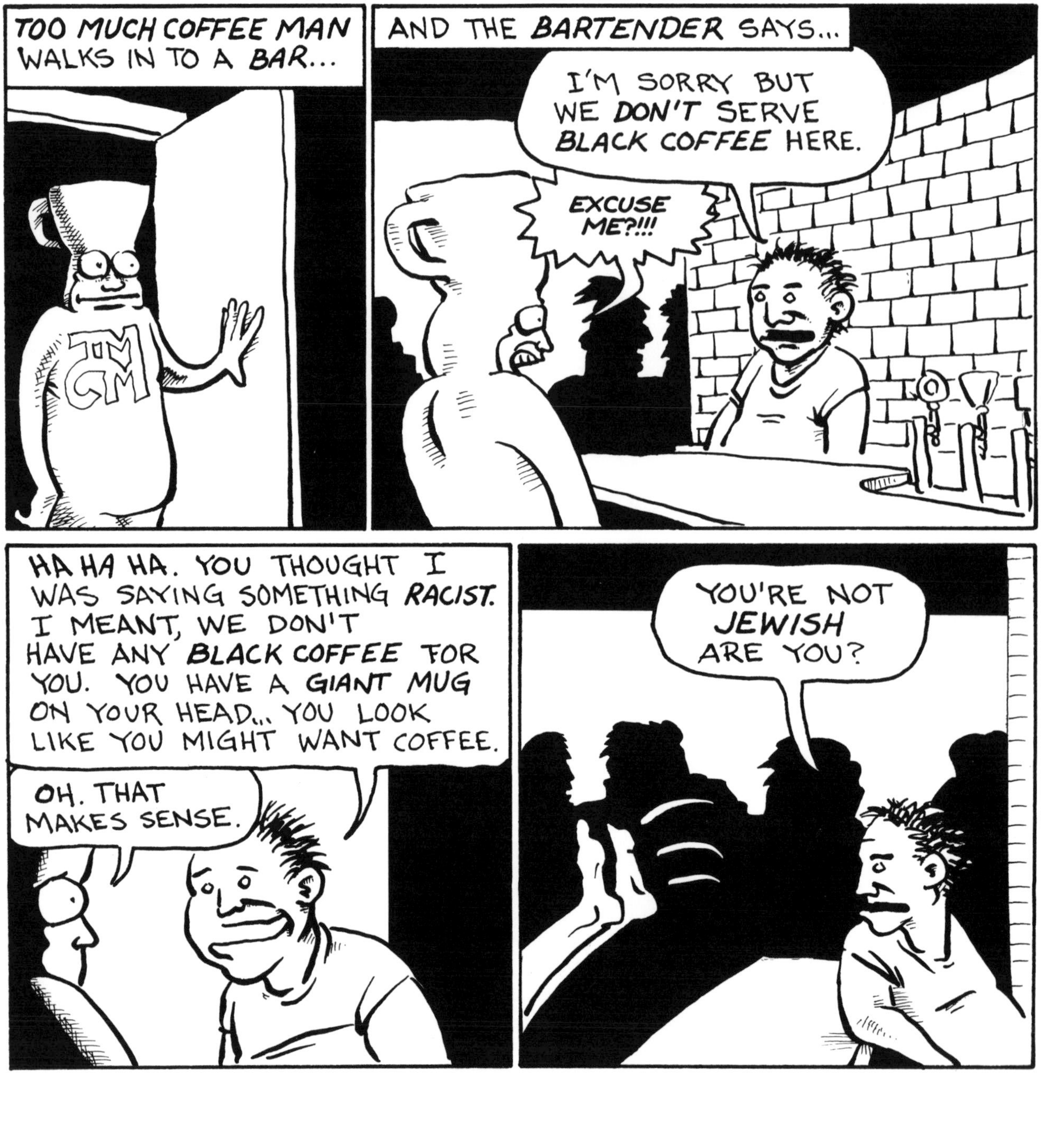
TOO MUCH COFFEE MAN WALKS IN TO A BAR...
TMCM
AND THE BARTENDER SAYS...
I'M SORRY BUT WE DON'T SERVE BLACK COFFEE HERE.
EXCUSE ME?!!!
HA HA HA. YOU THOUGHT I WAS SAYING SOMETHING RACIST. I MEANT, WE DON'T HAVE ANY BLACK COFFEE FOR YOU. YOU HAVE A GIANT MUG ON YOUR HEAD.. YOU LOOK LIKE YOU MIGHT WANT COFFEE.
OH. THAT MAKES SENSE.
YOU'RE NOT JEWISH ARE YOU?

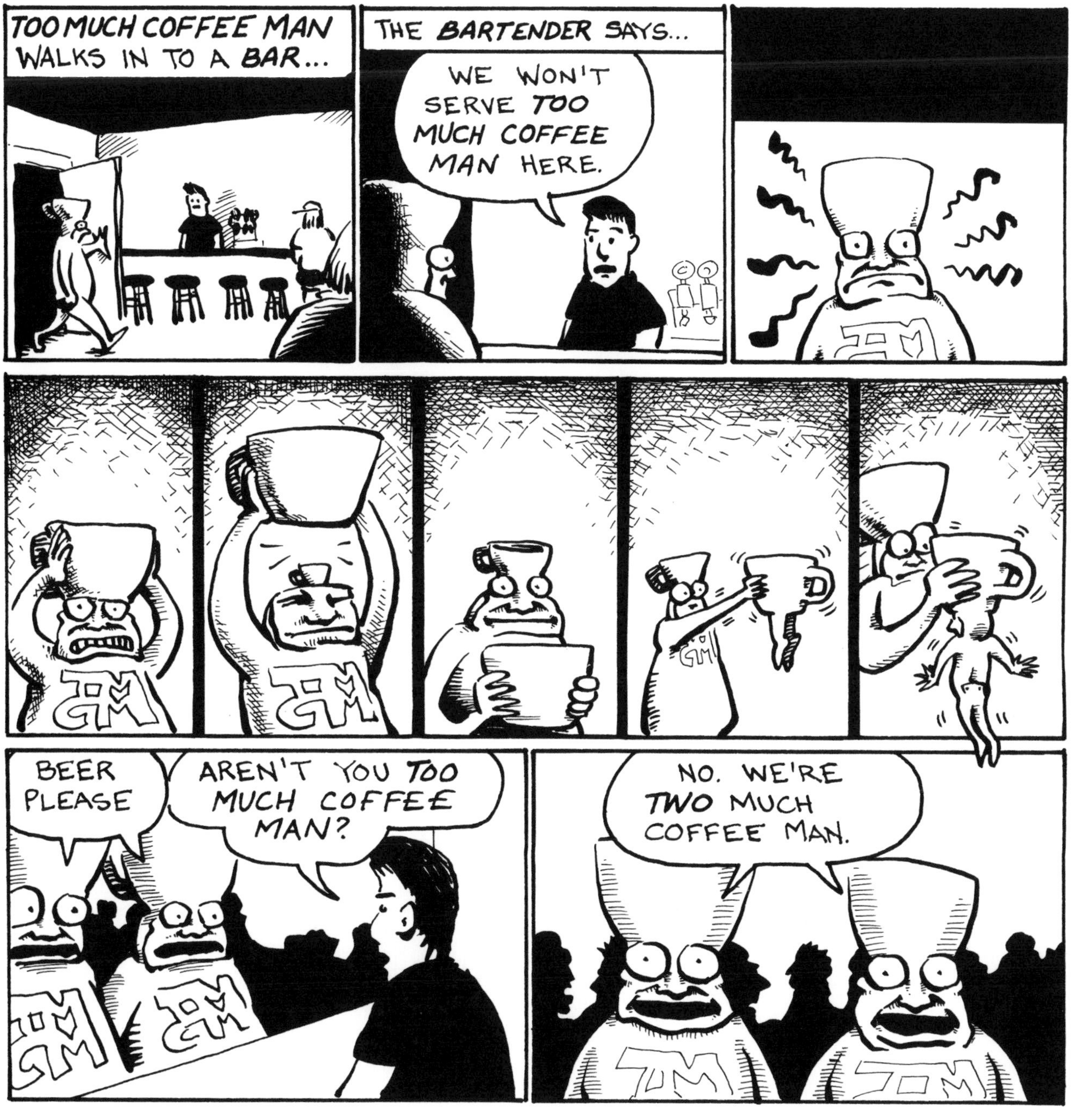
TOO MUCH COFFEE MAN WALKS IN TO A BAR...
THE BARTENDER SAYS...
WE WON'T SERVE TOO MUCH COFFEE MAN HERE.
BEER PLEASE
AREN'T YOU TOO MUCH COFFEE MAN?
NO. WE'RE TWO MUCH COFFEE MAN.

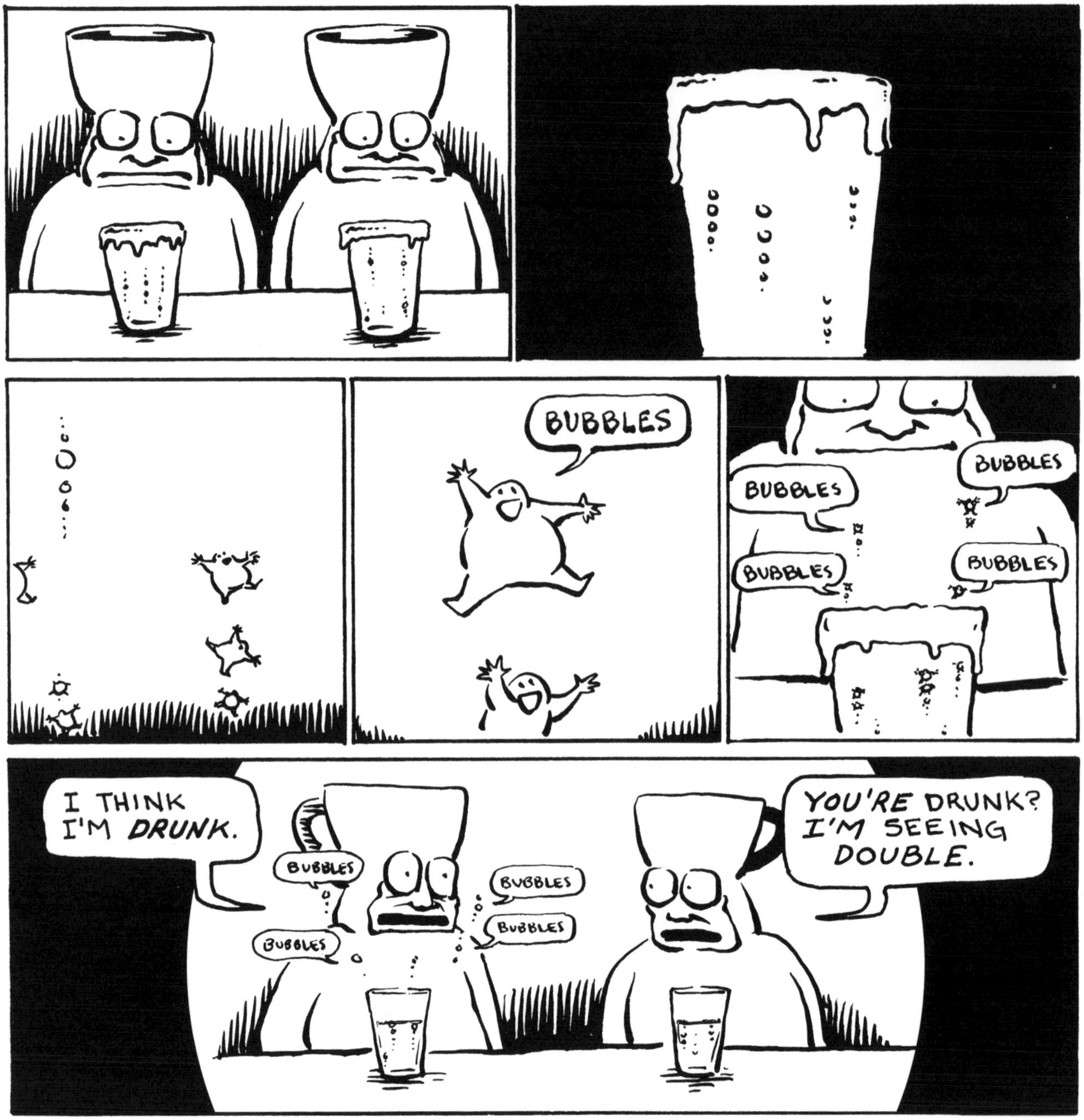
BUBBLES
BUBBLES
BUBBLES
BUBBLES
BUBBLES
I THINK I'M *DRUNK*.
BUBBLES
BUBBLES
BUBBLES
BUBBLES
YOU'RE DRUNK? I'M SEEING *DOUBLE*.

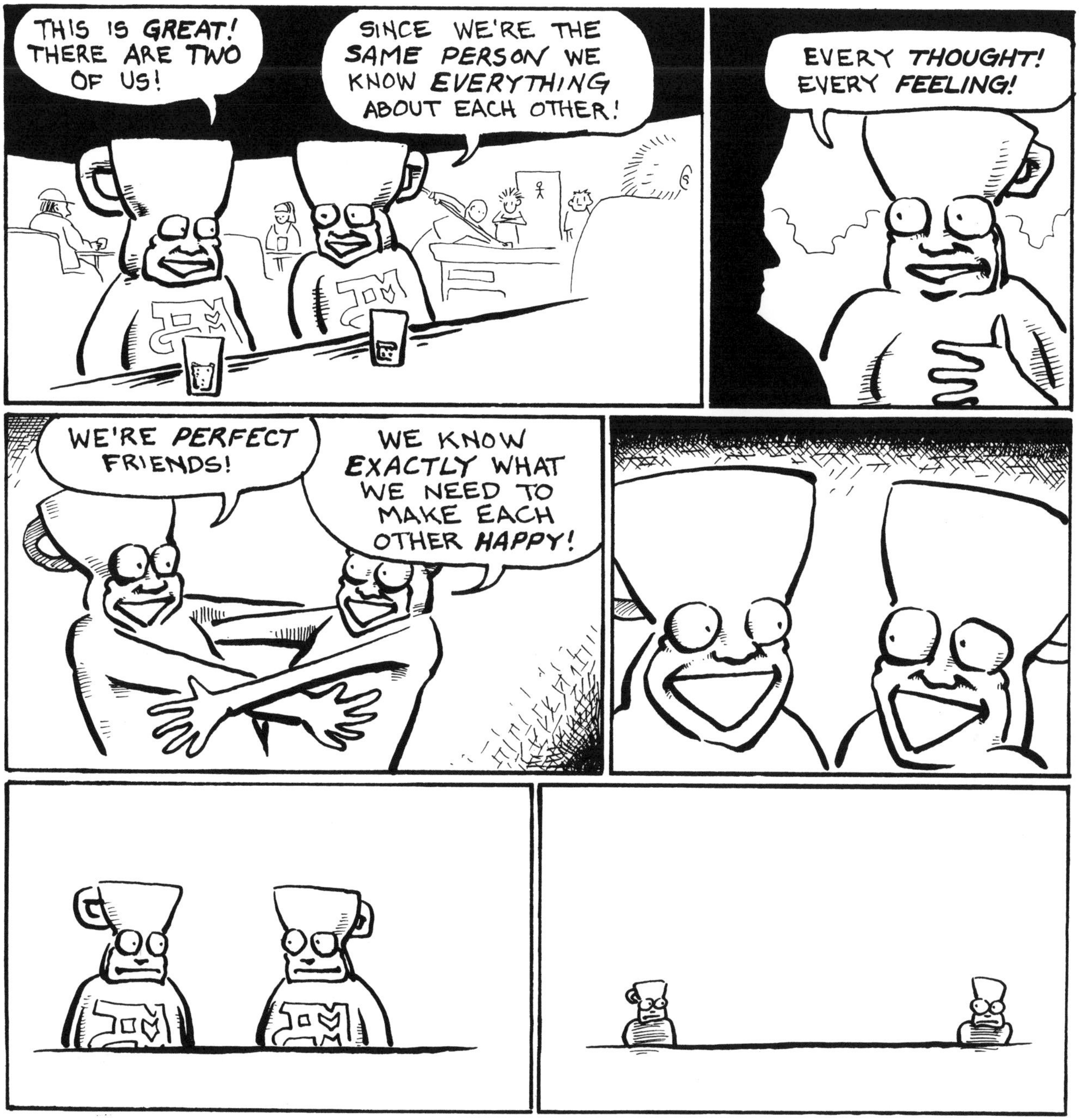
THIS IS GREAT! THERE ARE TWO OF US!
SINCE WE'RE THE SAME PERSON WE KNOW EVERYTHING ABOUT EACH OTHER!
EVERY THOUGHT! EVERY FEELING!
WE'RE PERFECT FRIENDS!
WE KNOW EXACTLY WHAT WE NEED TO MAKE EACH OTHER HAPPY!

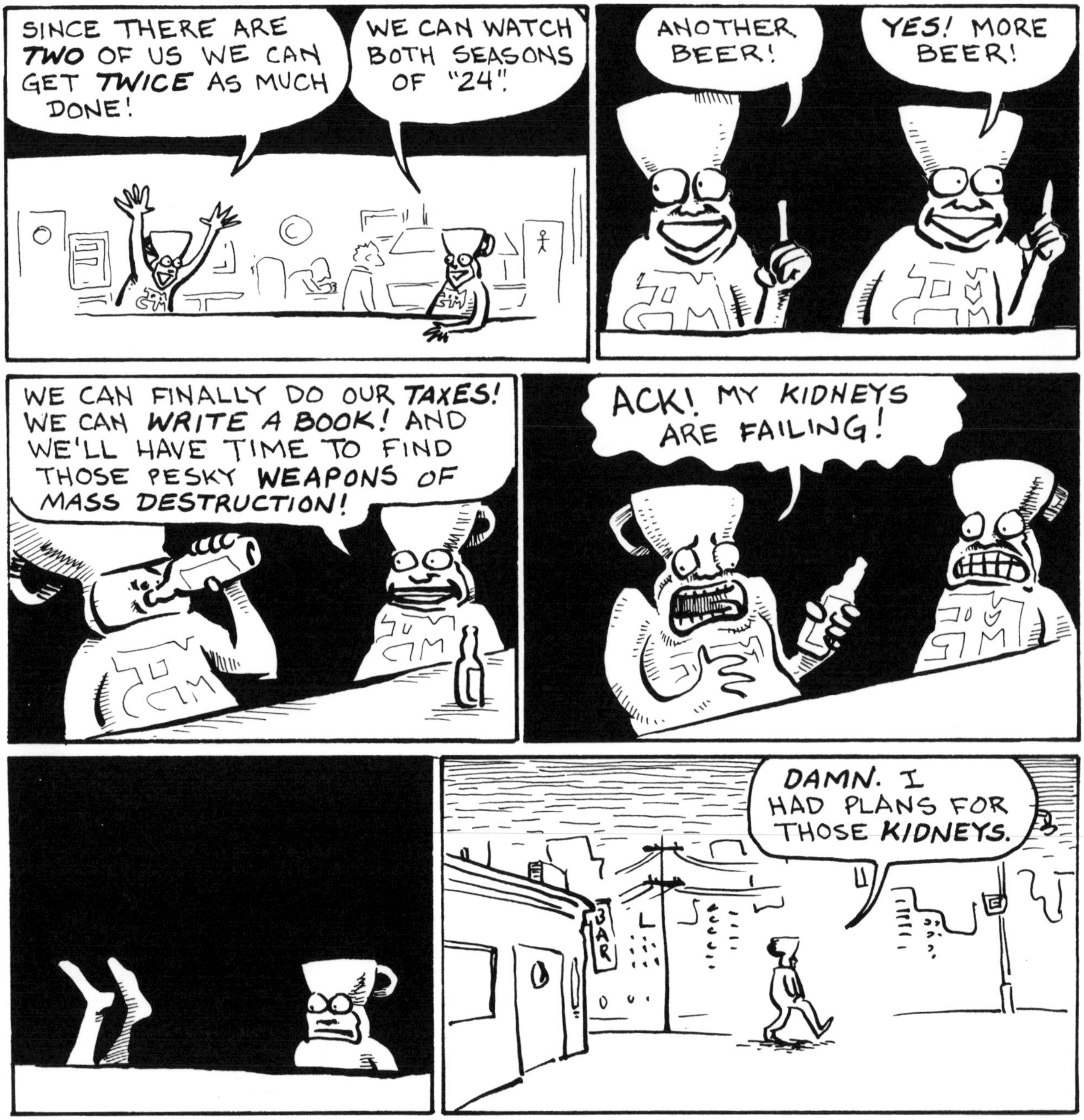
SINCE THERE ARE TWO OF US WE CAN GET TWICE AS MUCH DONE!
WE CAN WATCH BOTH SEASONS OF "24".
ANOTHER BEER!
YES! MORE BEER!
WE CAN FINALLY DO OUR TAXES! WE CAN WRITE A BOOK! AND WE'LL HAVE TIME TO FIND THOSE PESKY WEAPONS OF MASS DESTRUCTION!
ACK! MY KIDNEYS ARE FAILING!
DAMN. I HAD PLANS FOR THOSE KIDNEYS.
BAR

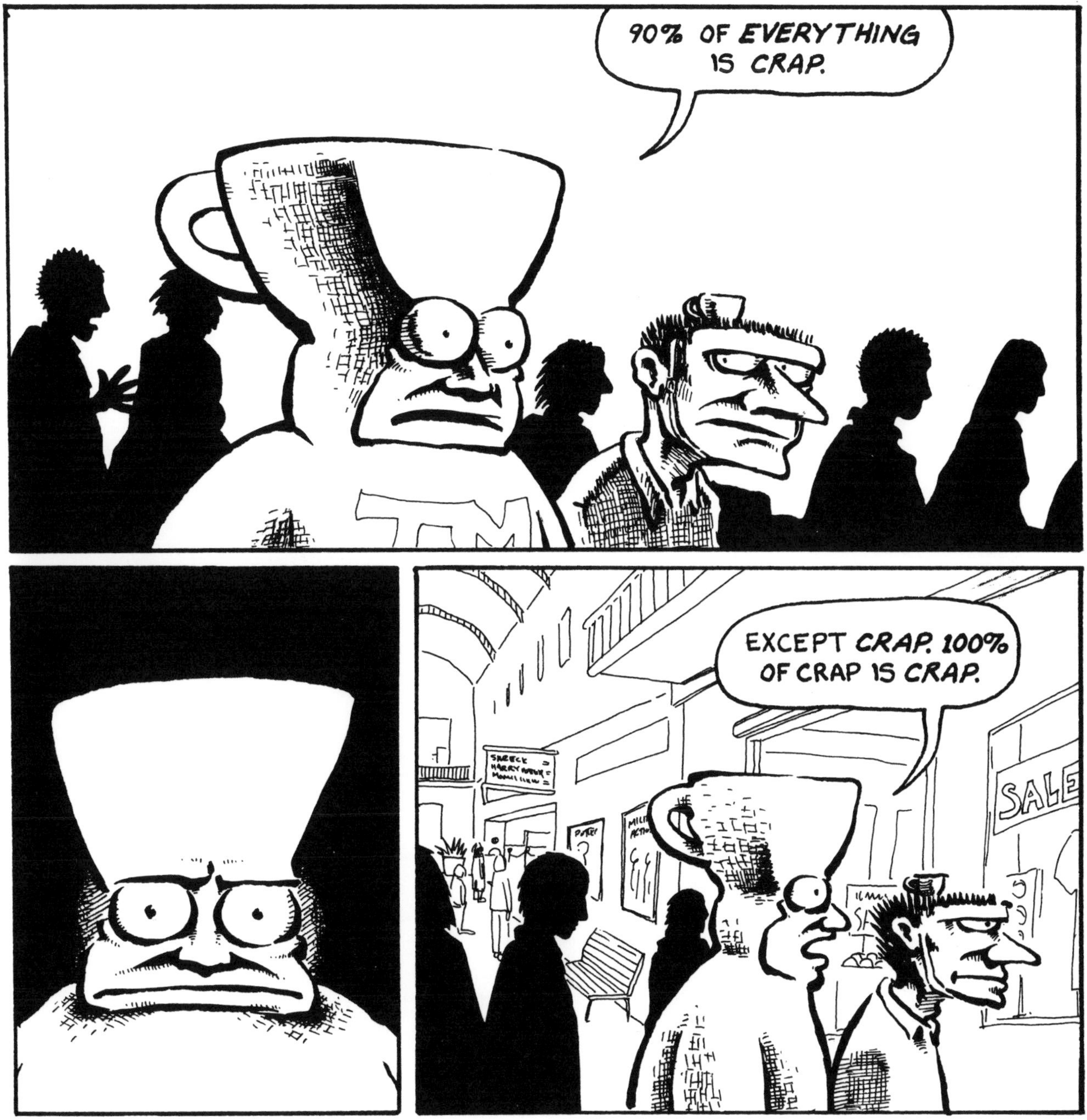
90% OF EVERYTHING IS CRAP.
EXCEPT CRAP. 100% OF CRAP IS CRAP.
SALE

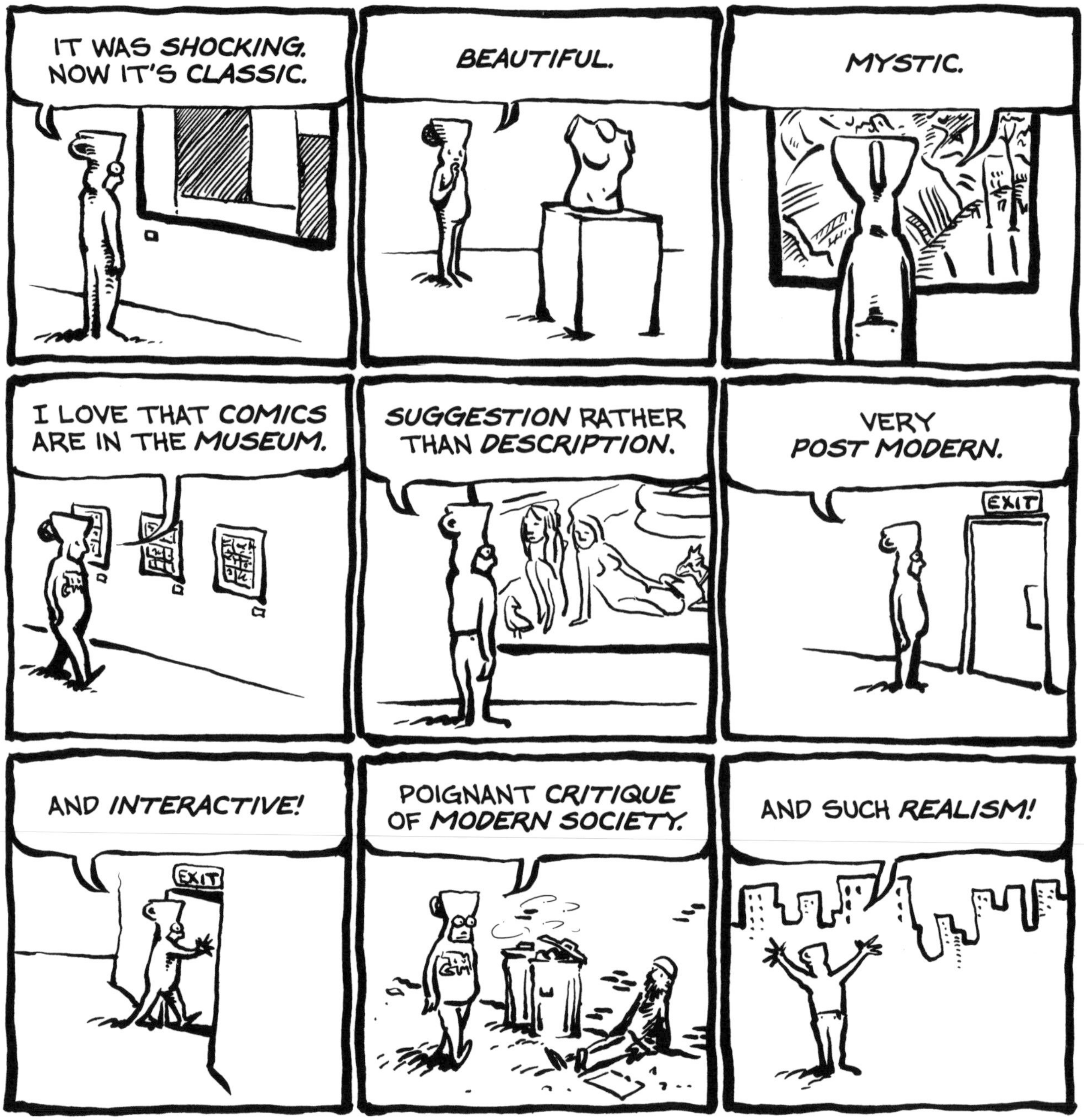
IT WAS SHOCKING. NOW IT'S CLASSIC.
BEAUTIFUL.
MYSTIC.
I LOVE THAT COMICS ARE IN THE MUSEUM.
SUGGESTION RATHER THAN DESCRIPTION.
VERY POST MODERN.
EXIT
AND INTERACTIVE!
EXIT
POIGNANT CRITIQUE OF MODERN SOCIETY.
AND SUCH REALISM!

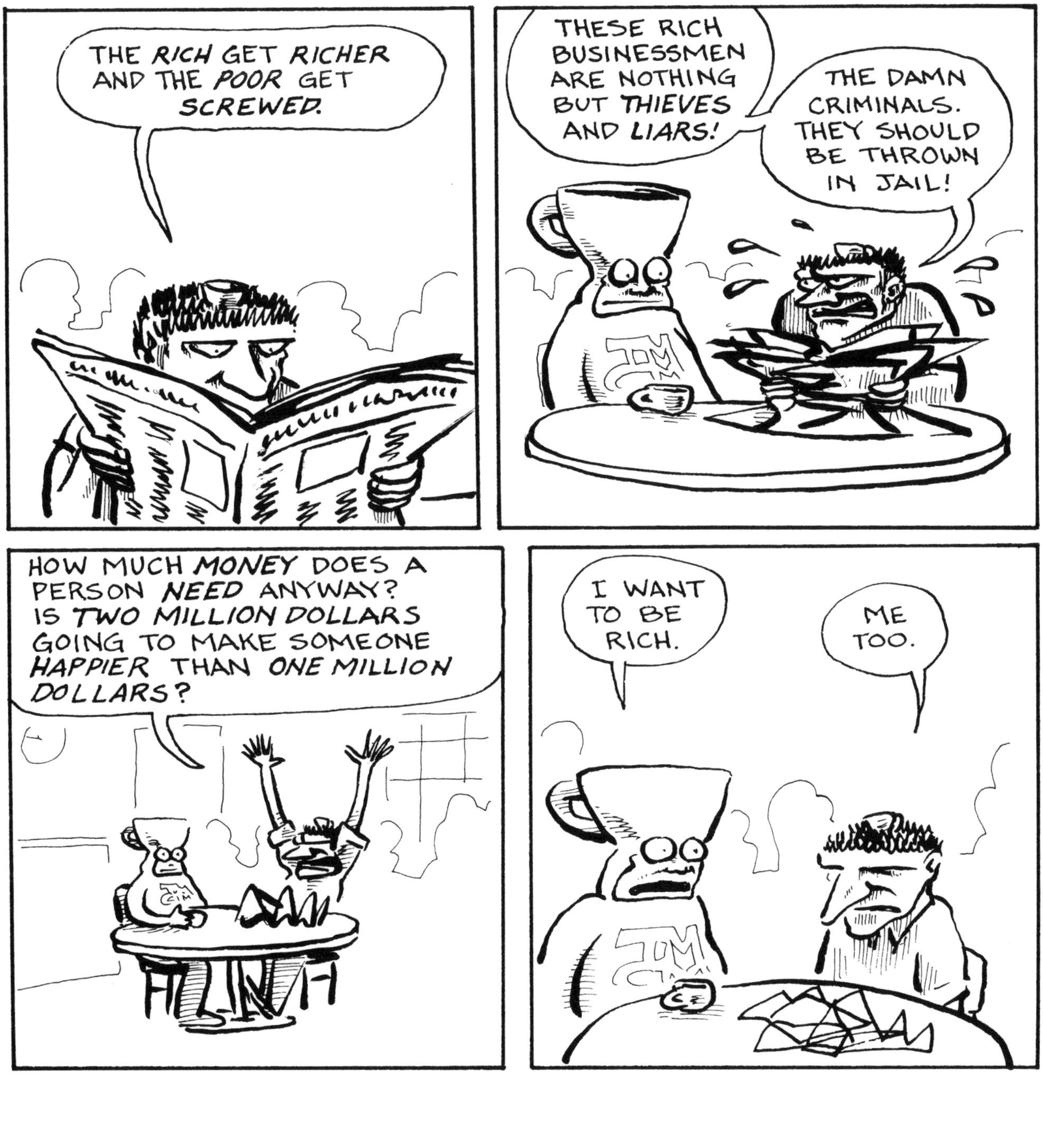
THE RICH GET RICHER AND THE POOR GET SCREWED.
THESE RICH BUSINESSMEN ARE NOTHING BUT THIEVES AND LIARS!
THE DAMN CRIMINALS. THEY SHOULD BE THROWN IN JAIL!
HOW MUCH MONEY DOES A PERSON NEED ANYWAY? IS TWO MILLION DOLLARS GOING TO MAKE SOMEONE HAPPIER THAN ONE MILLION DOLLARS?
I WANT TO BE RICH.
ME TOO.

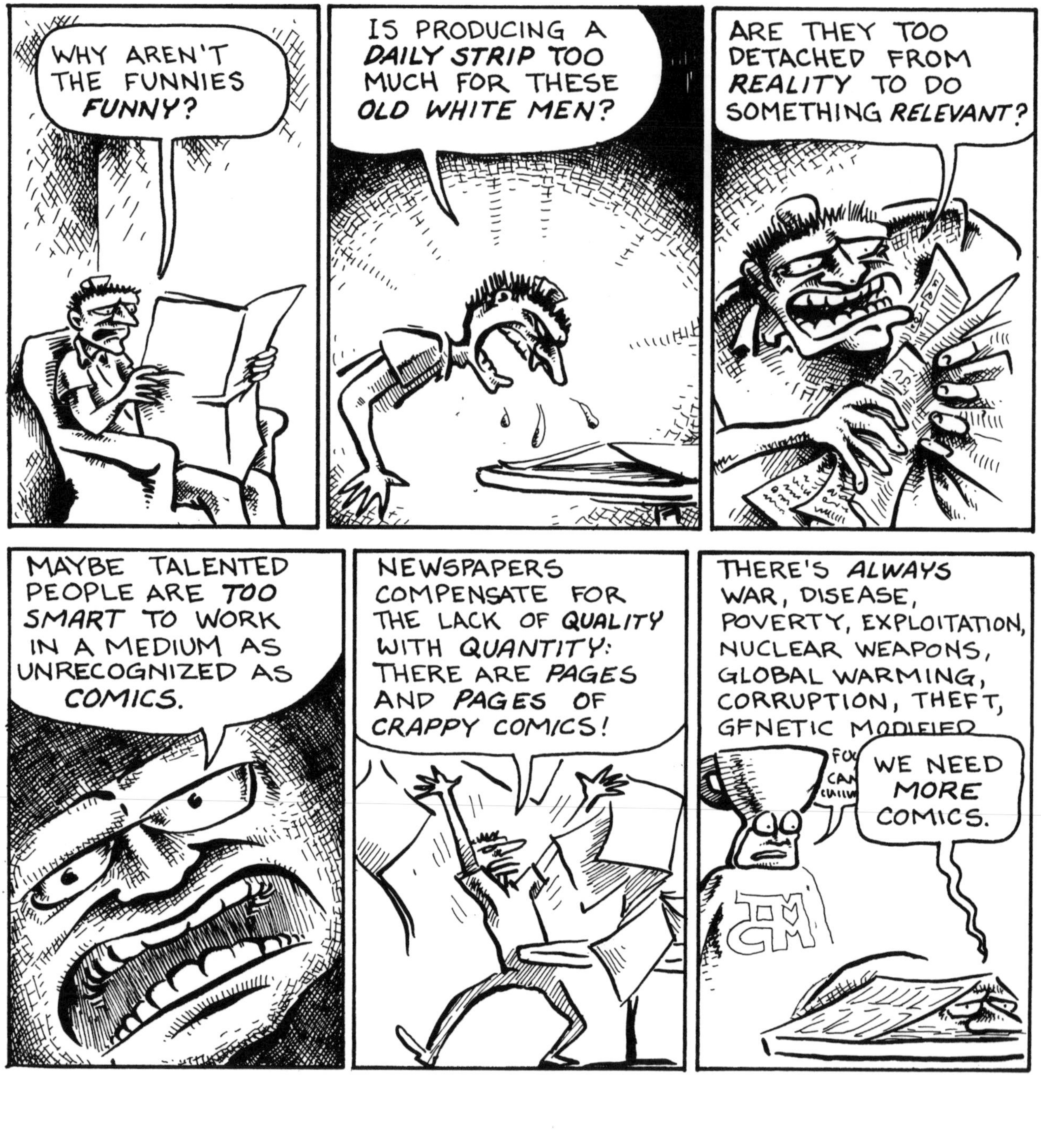
WHY AREN'T THE FUNNIES *FUNNY?*
IS PRODUCING A *DAILY STRIP* TOO MUCH FOR THESE *OLD WHITE MEN?*
ARE THEY TOO DETACHED FROM *REALITY* TO DO SOMETHING *RELEVANT?*
MAYBE TALENTED PEOPLE ARE *TOO SMART* TO WORK IN A MEDIUM AS UNRECOGNIZED AS *COMICS.*
NEWSPAPERS COMPENSATE FOR THE LACK OF *QUALITY* WITH *QUANTITY:* THERE ARE *PAGES* AND *PAGES* OF *CRAPPY COMICS!*
THERE'S *ALWAYS* WAR, DISEASE, POVERTY, EXPLOITATION, NUCLEAR WEAPONS, GLOBAL WARMING, CORRUPTION, THEFT, GENETIC
WE NEED *MORE* COMICS.

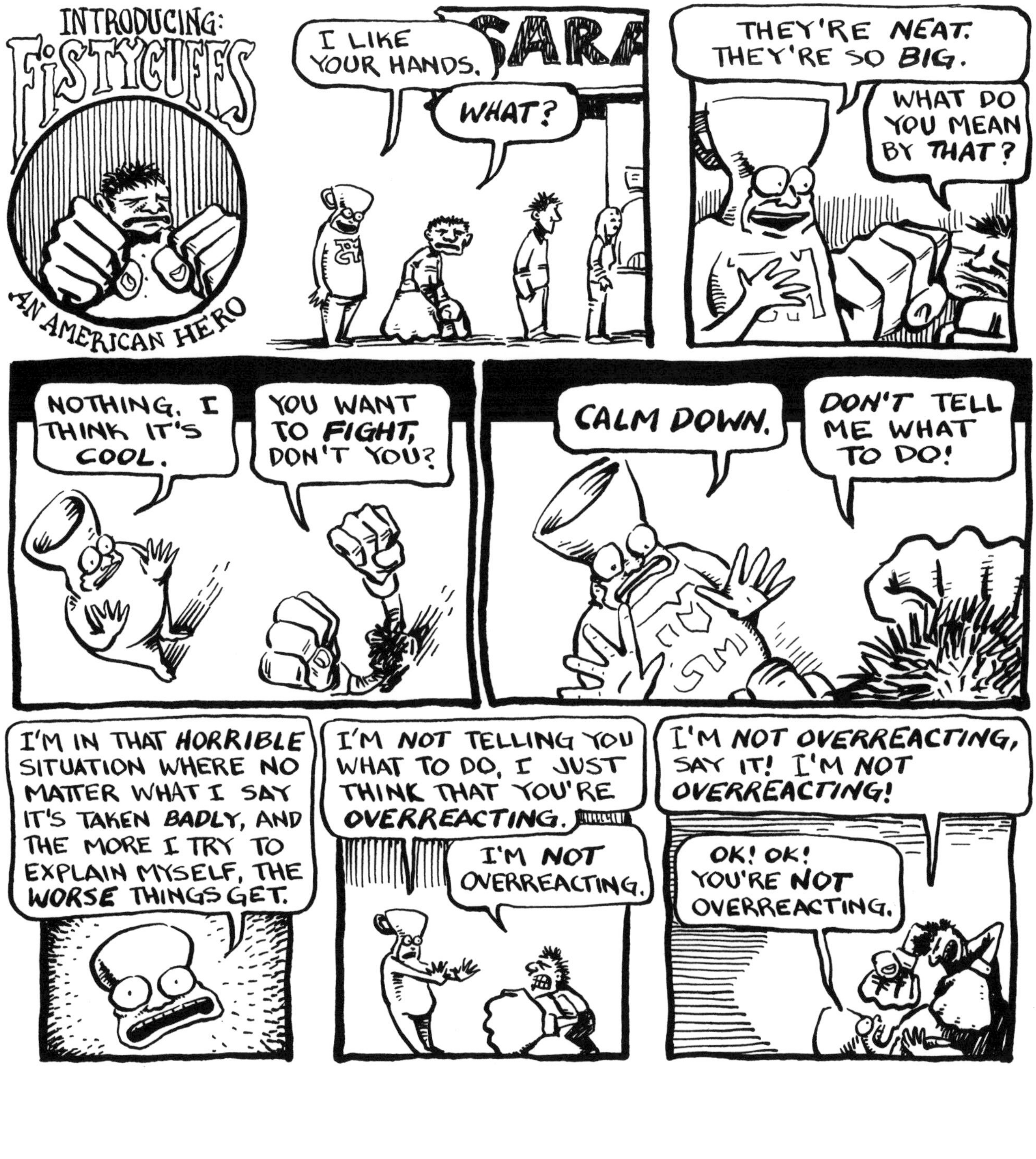
INTRODUCING:
FISTYCUFFS
AN AMERICAN HERO
I LIKE YOUR HANDS.
WHAT?
SARA
THEY'RE NEAT. THEY'RE SO BIG.
WHAT DO YOU MEAN BY THAT?
NOTHING. I THINK IT'S COOL.
YOU WANT TO FIGHT, DON'T YOU?
CALM DOWN.
DON'T TELL ME WHAT TO DO!
I'M IN THAT HORRIBLE SITUATION WHERE NO MATTER WHAT I SAY IT'S TAKEN BADLY, AND THE MORE I TRY TO EXPLAIN MYSELF, THE WORSE THINGS GET.
I'M NOT TELLING YOU WHAT TO DO, I JUST THINK THAT YOU'RE OVERREACTING.
I'M NOT OVERREACTING.
I'M NOT OVERREACTING, SAY IT! I'M NOT OVERREACTING!
OK! OK! YOU'RE NOT OVERREACTING.

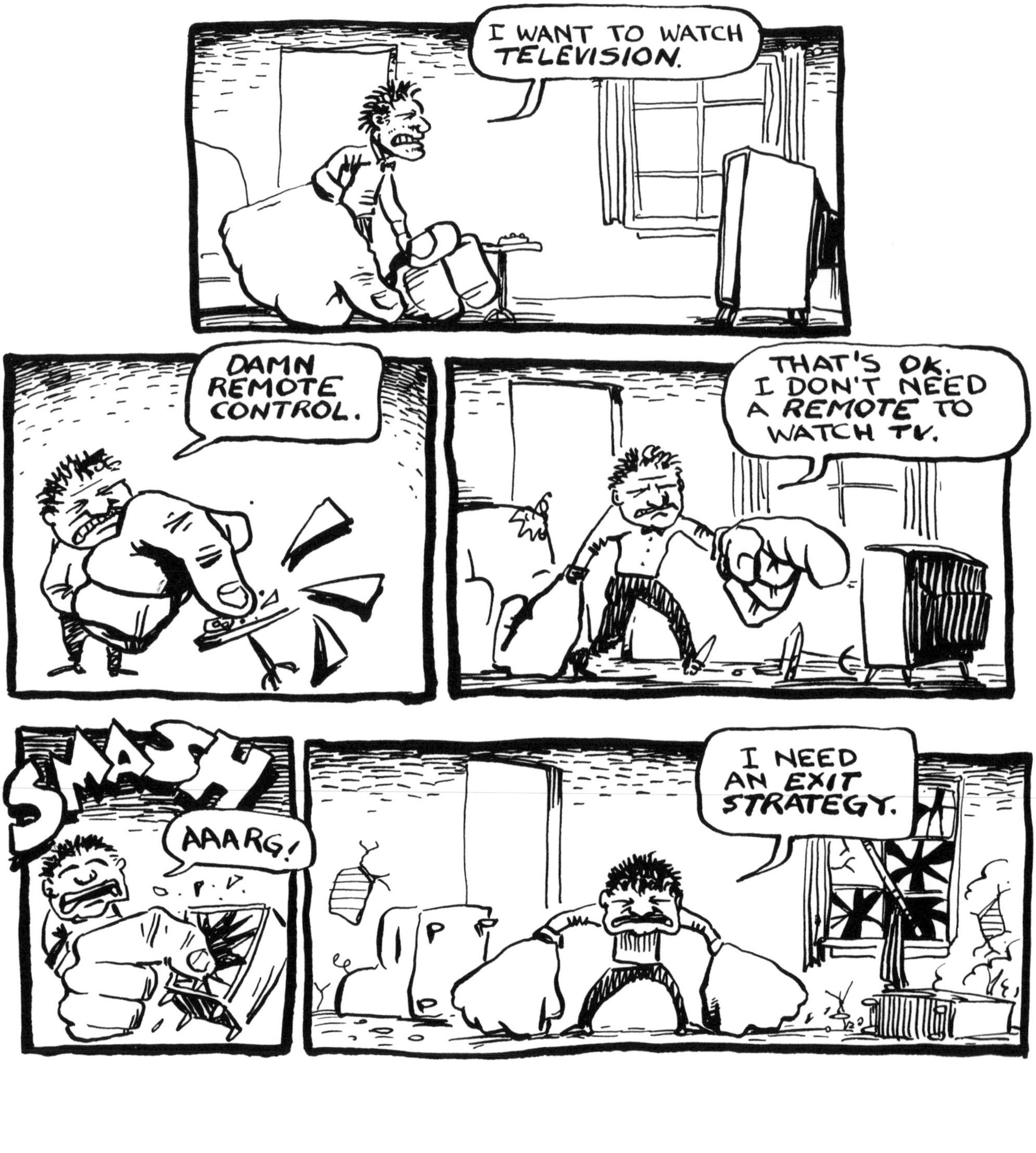
I WANT TO WATCH TELEVISION.
DAMN REMOTE CONTROL.
THAT'S OK. I DON'T NEED A REMOTE TO WATCH TV.
SMASH
AAARG!
I NEED AN EXIT STRATEGY.

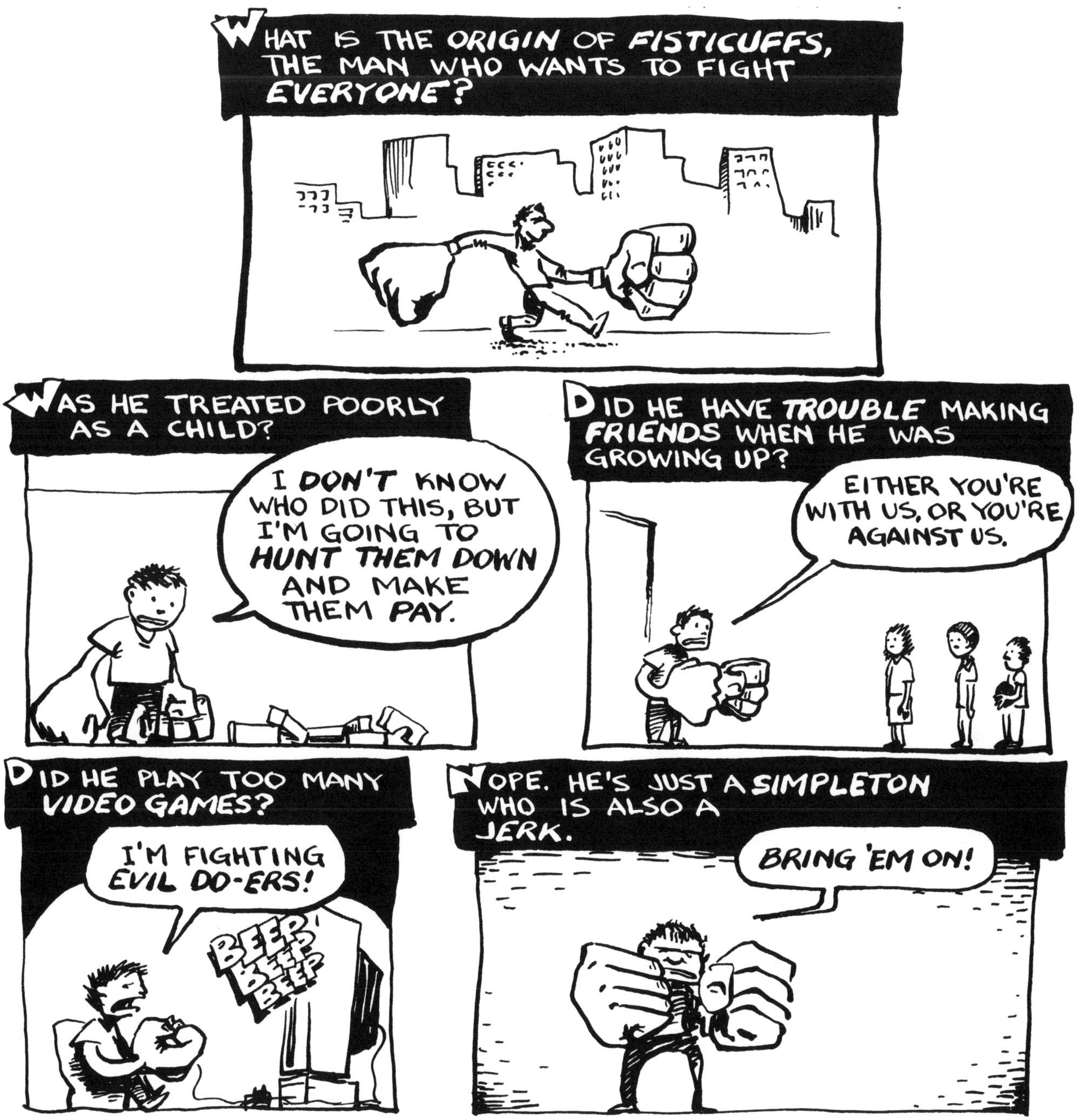
WHAT IS THE ORIGIN OF FISTICUFFS, THE MAN WHO WANTS TO FIGHT EVERYONE?
WAS HE TREATED POORLY AS A CHILD?
I DON'T KNOW WHO DID THIS, BUT I'M GOING TO HUNT THEM DOWN AND MAKE THEM PAY.
DID HE HAVE TROUBLE MAKING FRIENDS WHEN HE WAS GROWING UP?
EITHER YOU'RE WITH US, OR YOU'RE AGAINST US.
DID HE PLAY TOO MANY VIDEO GAMES?
I'M FIGHTING EVIL DO-ERS!
BEEP! BEEP! BEEP!
NOPE. HE'S JUST A SIMPLETON WHO IS ALSO A JERK.
BRING 'EM ON!

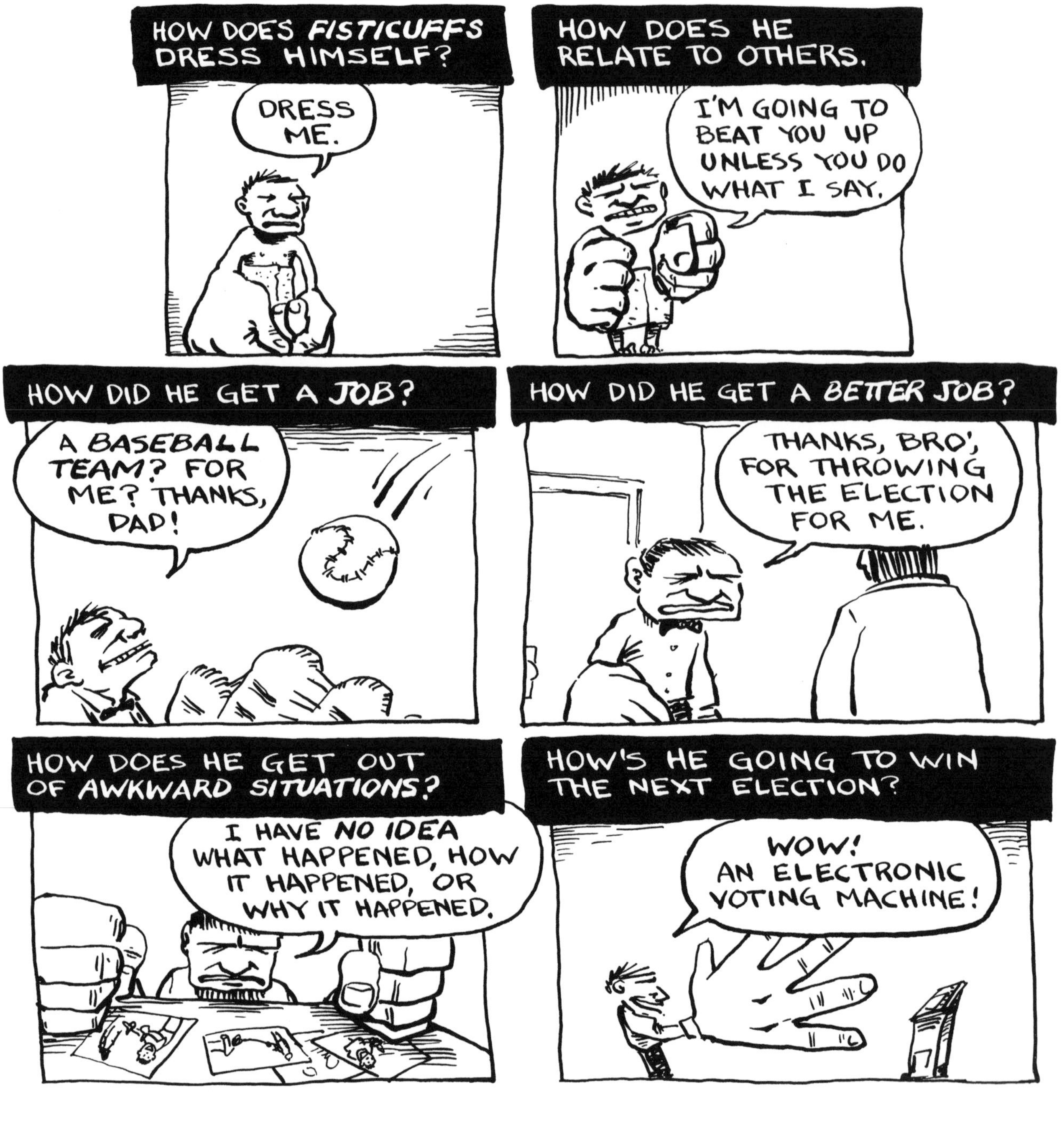
HOW DOES FISTICUFFS DRESS HIMSELF?
DRESS ME.
HOW DOES HE RELATE TO OTHERS.
I'M GOING TO BEAT YOU UP UNLESS YOU DO WHAT I SAY.
HOW DID HE GET A JOB?
A BASEBALL TEAM? FOR ME? THANKS, DAD!
HOW DID HE GET A BETTER JOB?
THANKS, BRO', FOR THROWING THE ELECTION FOR ME.
HOW DOES HE GET OUT OF AWKWARD SITUATIONS?
I HAVE NO IDEA WHAT HAPPENED, HOW IT HAPPENED, OR WHY IT HAPPENED.
HOW'S HE GOING TO WIN THE NEXT ELECTION?
WOW! AN ELECTRONIC VOTING MACHINE!

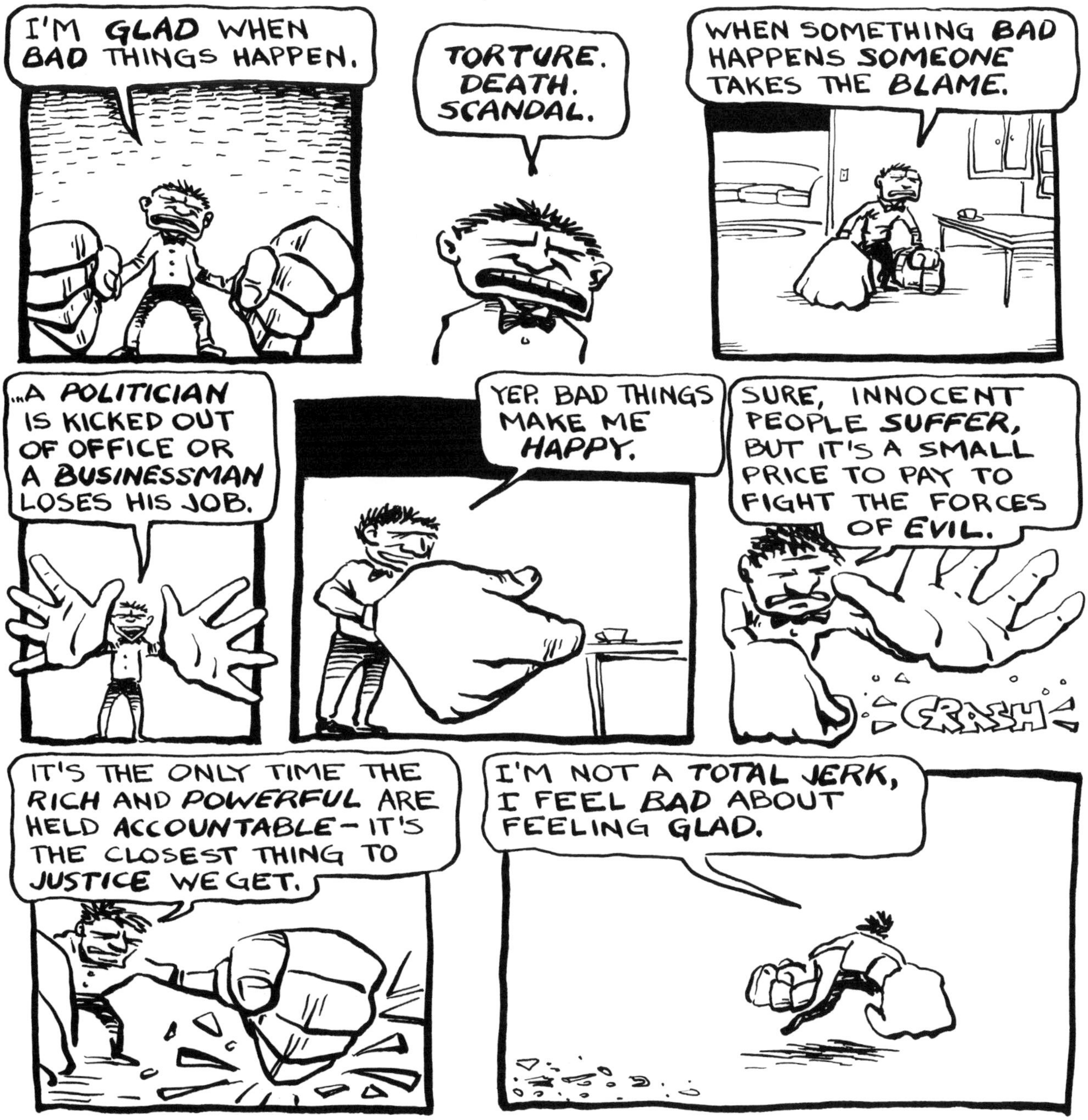
I'M GLAD WHEN BAD THINGS HAPPEN.
TORTURE. DEATH. SCANDAL.
WHEN SOMETHING BAD HAPPENS SOMEONE TAKES THE BLAME.
...A POLITICIAN IS KICKED OUT OF OFFICE OR A BUSINESSMAN LOSES HIS JOB.
YEP. BAD THINGS MAKE ME HAPPY.
SURE, INNOCENT PEOPLE SUFFER, BUT IT'S A SMALL PRICE TO PAY TO FIGHT THE FORCES OF EVIL.
CRASH
IT'S THE ONLY TIME THE RICH AND POWERFUL ARE HELD ACCOUNTABLE - IT'S THE CLOSEST THING TO JUSTICE WE GET.
I'M NOT A TOTAL JERK, I FEEL BAD ABOUT FEELING GLAD.

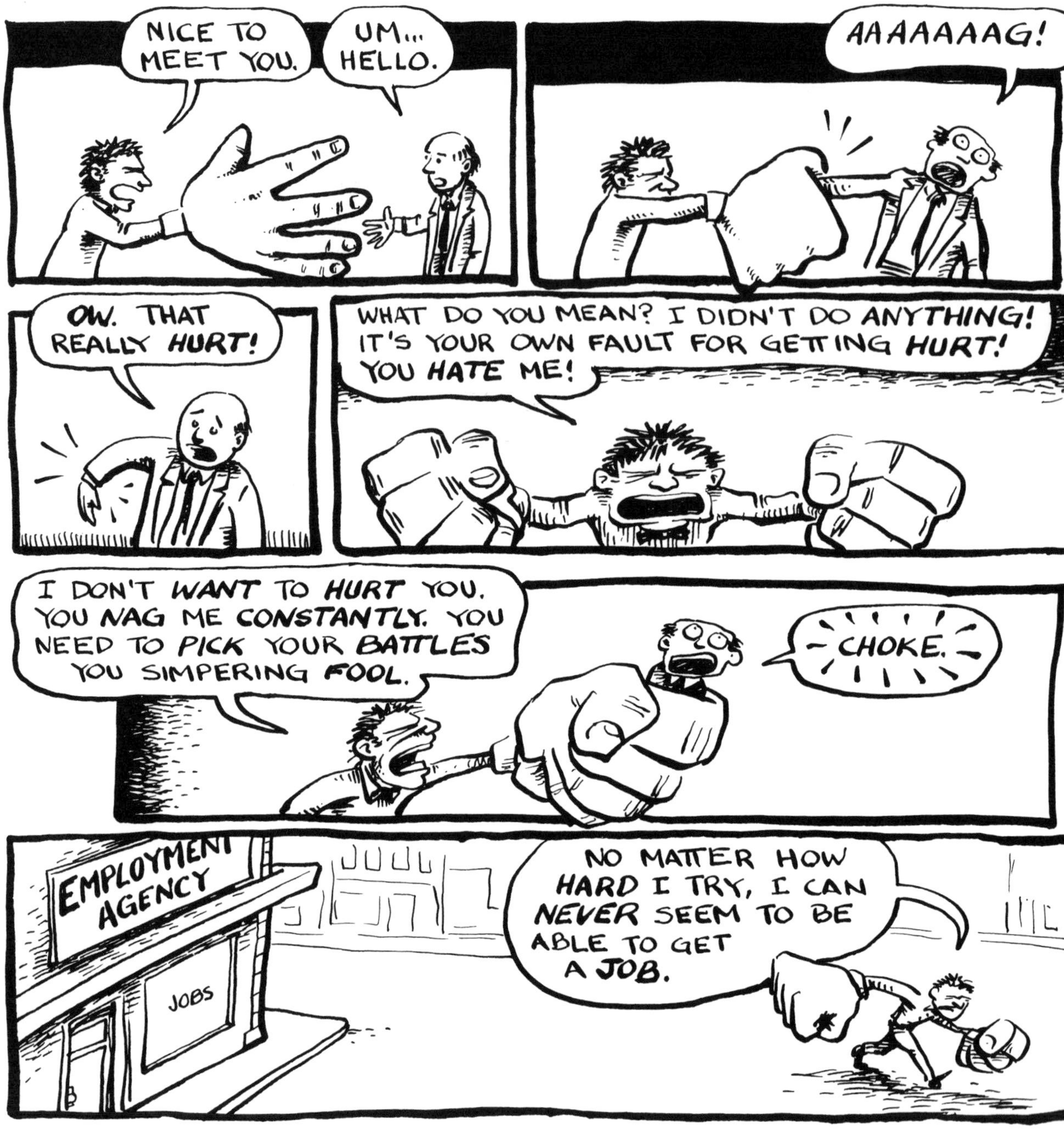
NICE TO MEET YOU.
UM... HELLO.
AAAAAAAG!
OW. THAT REALLY HURT!
WHAT DO YOU MEAN? I DIDN'T DO ANYTHING! IT'S YOUR OWN FAULT FOR GETTING HURT! YOU HATE ME!
I DON'T WANT TO HURT YOU. YOU NAG ME CONSTANTLY. YOU NEED TO PICK YOUR BATTLES YOU SIMPERING FOOL.
CHOKE.
EMPLOYMENT AGENCY
JOBS
NO MATTER HOW HARD I TRY, I CAN NEVER SEEM TO BE ABLE TO GET A JOB.

SHUT UP.
I GET IT NOW.
YOU'RE SYMBOLIC OF U.S. FOREIGN POLICY...
SHUT UP.
LIKE A BULL IN A CHINA SHOP, EVERY TIME YOU DO SOME-THING, YOU MESS THINGS UP.
SHUT UP.
YOU'RE A VISUAL PUN BECAUSE YOU'RE SO HEAVY HANDED!
...AND MY FINGER IS A METAPHOR FOR ME TAKING AWAY YOUR FREE SPEECH!
GFFFLB.

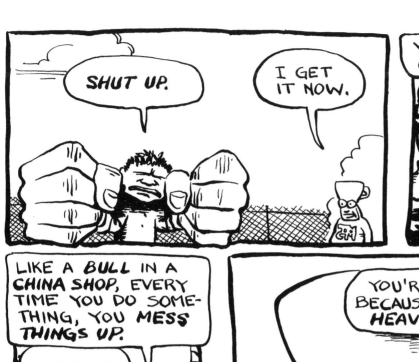

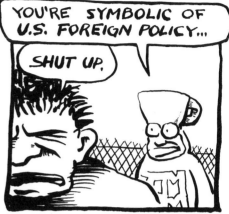

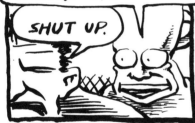

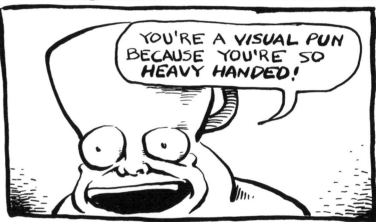

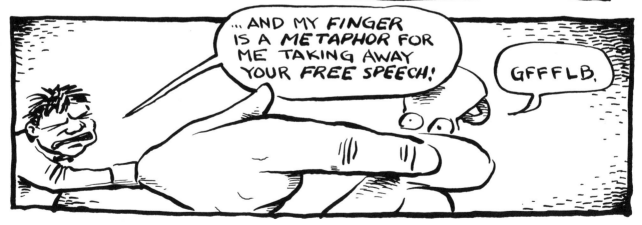

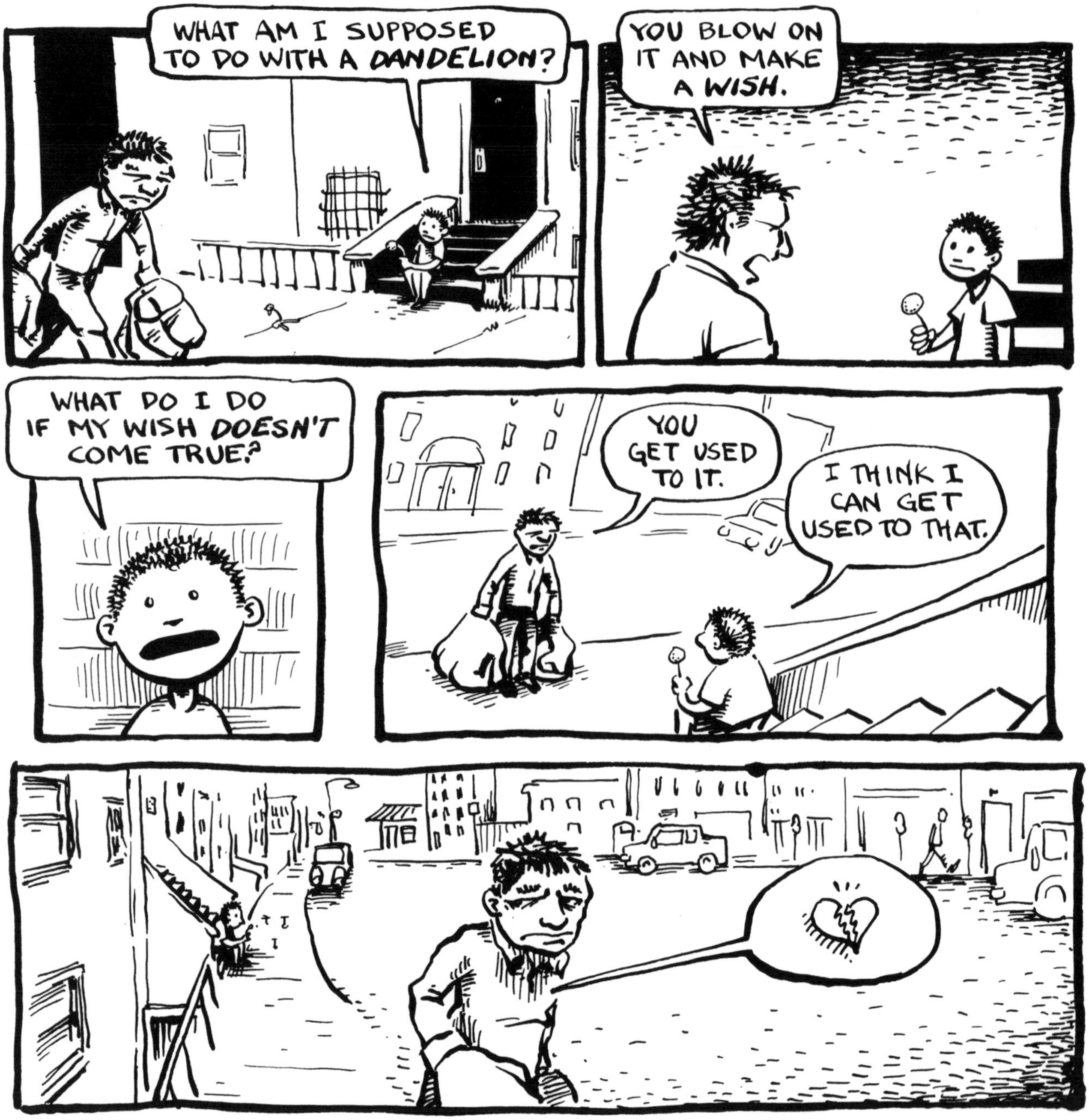
WHAT AM I SUPPOSED TO DO WITH A DANDELION?
YOU BLOW ON IT AND MAKE A WISH.
WHAT DO I DO IF MY WISH DOESN'T COME TRUE?
YOU GET USED TO IT.
I THINK I CAN GET USED TO THAT.

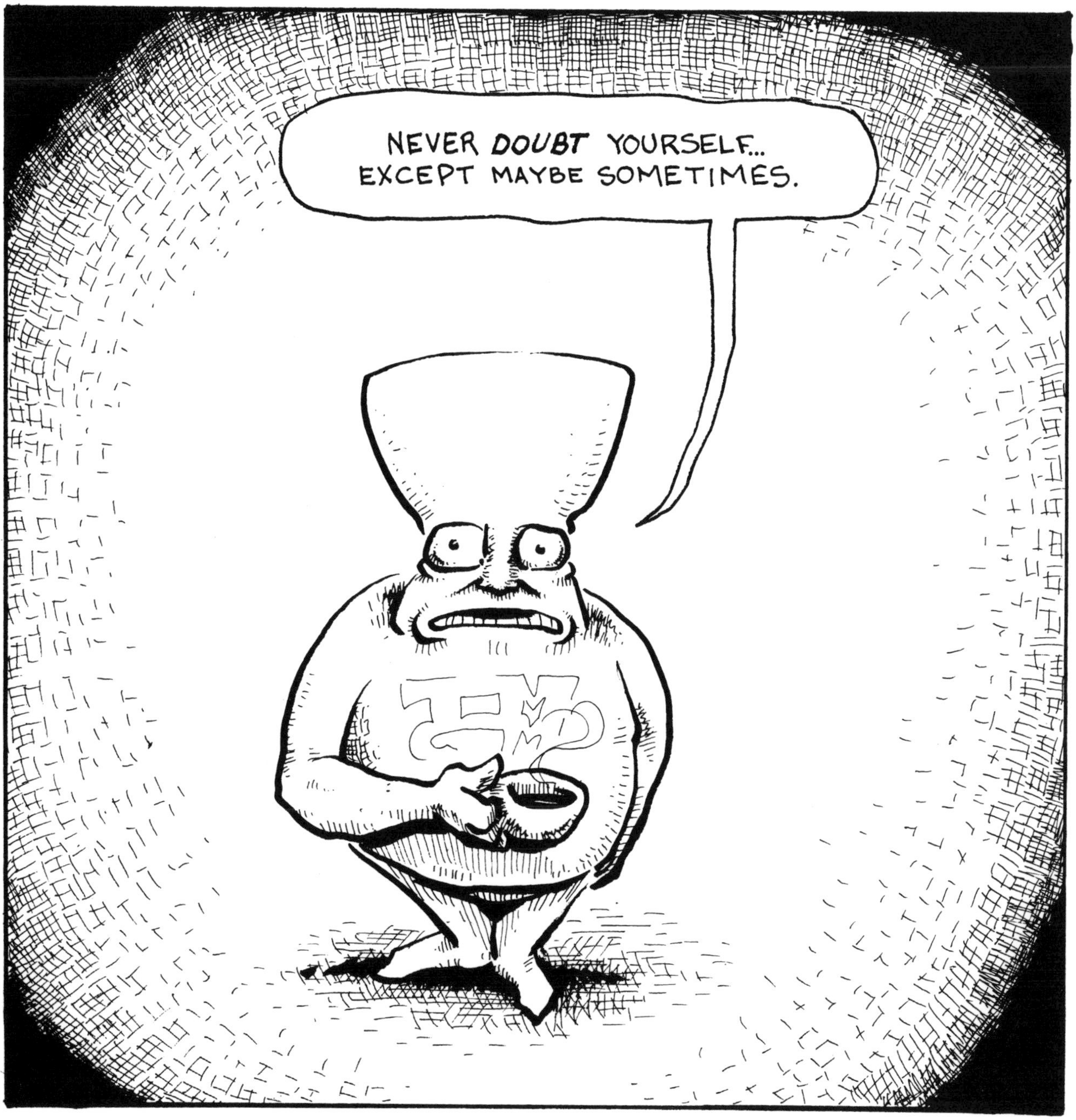
NEVER DOUBT YOURSELF...
EXCEPT MAYBE SOMETIMES.

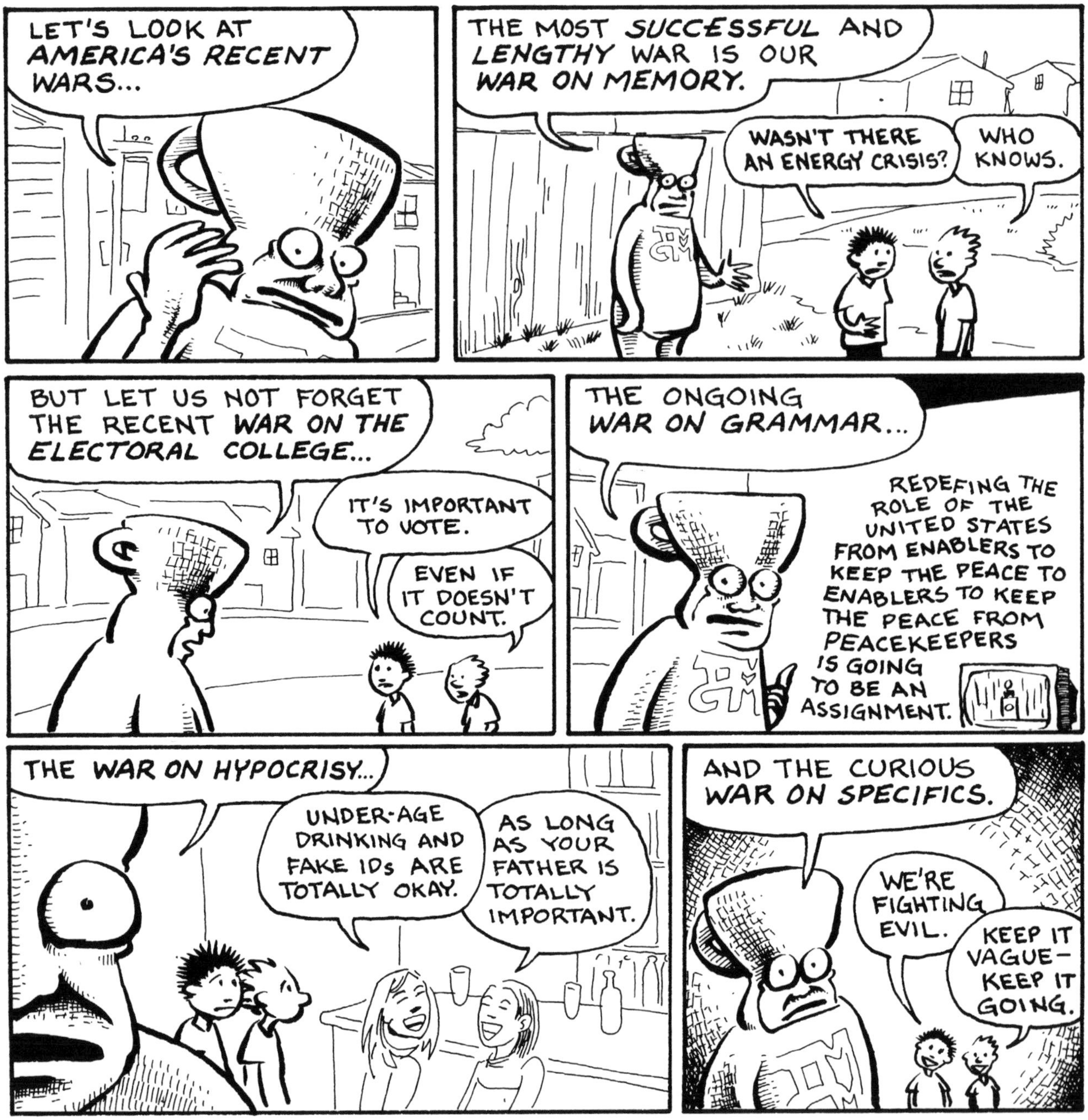
LET'S LOOK AT AMERICA'S RECENT WARS...
THE MOST SUCCESSFUL AND LENGTHY WAR IS OUR WAR ON MEMORY.
WASN'T THERE AN ENERGY CRISIS?
WHO KNOWS.
BUT LET US NOT FORGET THE RECENT WAR ON THE ELECTORAL COLLEGE...
IT'S IMPORTANT TO VOTE.
EVEN IF IT DOESN'T COUNT.
THE ONGOING WAR ON GRAMMAR...
REDEFING THE ROLE OF THE UNITED STATES FROM ENABLERS TO KEEP THE PEACE TO ENABLERS TO KEEP THE PEACE FROM PEACEKEEPERS IS GOING TO BE AN ASSIGNMENT.
THE WAR ON HYPOCRISY...
UNDER-AGE DRINKING AND FAKE IDs ARE TOTALLY OKAY.
AS LONG AS YOUR FATHER IS TOTALLY IMPORTANT.
AND THE CURIOUS WAR ON SPECIFICS.
WE'RE FIGHTING EVIL.
KEEP IT VAGUE— KEEP IT GOING.

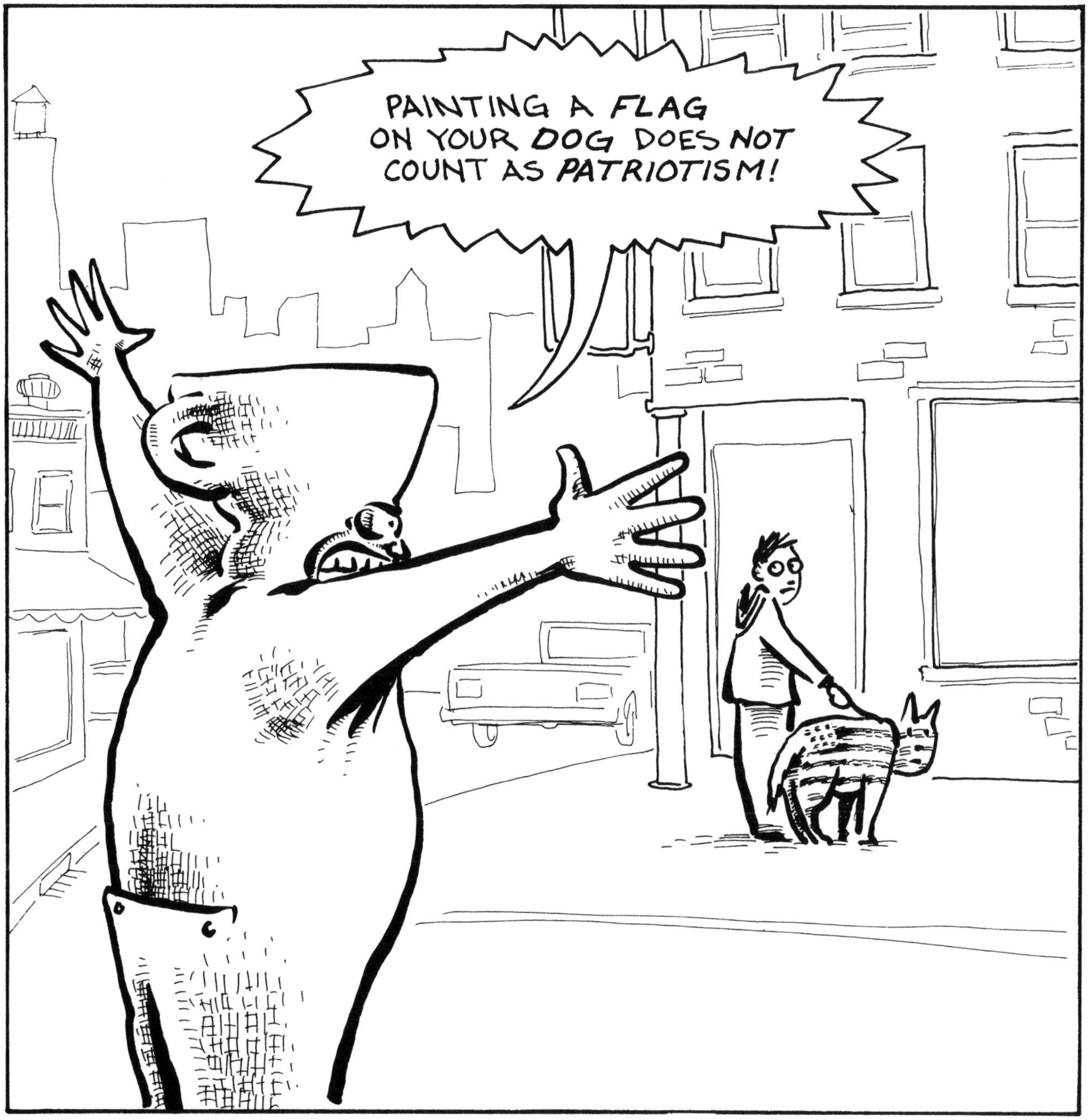
PAINTING A FLAG ON YOUR DOG DOES NOT COUNT AS PATRIOTISM!

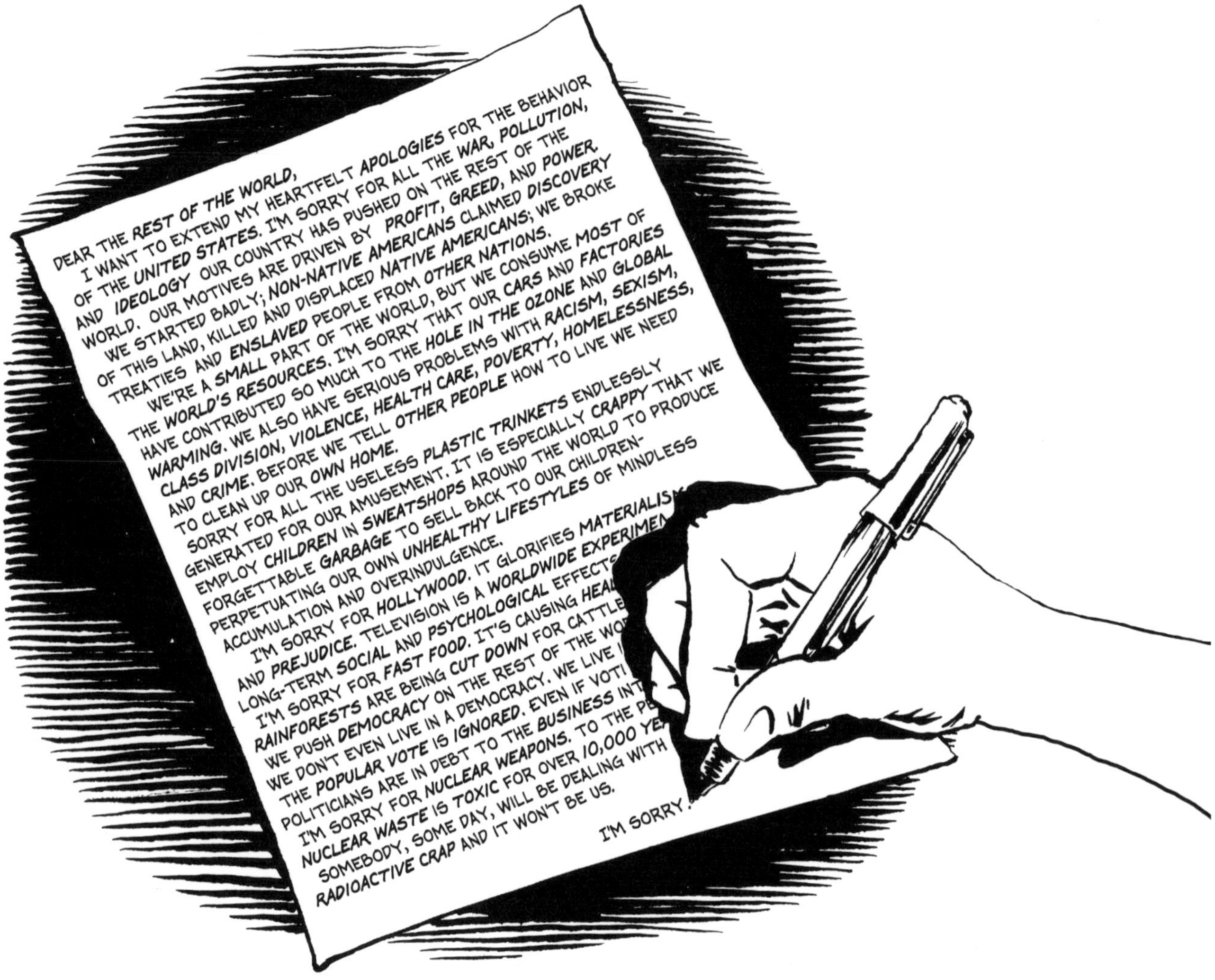

DEAR THE REST OF THE WORLD,
I WANT TO EXTEND MY HEARTFELT APOLOGIES FOR THE BEHAVIOR
OF THE UNITED STATES. I'M SORRY FOR ALL THE WAR, POLLUTION,
AND IDEOLOGY OUR COUNTRY HAS PUSHED ON THE REST OF THE
WORLD. OUR MOTIVES ARE DRIVEN BY PROFIT, GREED, AND POWER.
WE STARTED BADLY; NON-NATIVE AMERICANS CLAIMED DISCOVERY
OF THIS LAND, KILLED AND DISPLACED NATIVE AMERICANS; WE BROKE
TREATIES AND ENSLAVED PEOPLE FROM OTHER NATIONS.
WE'RE A SMALL PART OF THE WORLD, BUT WE CONSUME MOST OF
THE WORLD'S RESOURCES. I'M SORRY THAT OUR CARS AND FACTORIES
HAVE CONTRIBUTED SO MUCH TO THE HOLE IN THE OZONE AND GLOBAL
WARMING. WE ALSO HAVE SERIOUS PROBLEMS WITH RACISM, SEXISM,
CLASS DIVISION, VIOLENCE, HEALTH CARE, POVERTY, HOMELESSNESS,
AND CRIME. BEFORE WE TELL OTHER PEOPLE HOW TO LIVE WE NEED
TO CLEAN UP OUR OWN HOME.
SORRY FOR ALL THE USELESS PLASTIC TRINKETS ENDLESSLY
GENERATED FOR OUR AMUSEMENT. IT IS ESPECIALLY CRAPPY THAT WE
EMPLOY CHILDREN IN SWEATSHOPS AROUND THE WORLD TO PRODUCE
FORGETTABLE GARBAGE TO SELL BACK TO OUR CHILDREN-
PERPETUATING OUR OWN UNHEALTHY LIFESTYLES OF MINDLESS
ACCUMULATION AND OVERINDULGENCE.
I'M SORRY FOR HOLLYWOOD. IT GLORIFIES MATERIALIS
AND PREJUDICE. TELEVISION IS A WORLDWIDE EXPERIMEN
LONG-TERM SOCIAL AND PSYCHOLOGICAL EFFECTS
I'M SORRY FOR FAST FOOD. IT'S CAUSING HEA
RAINFORESTS ARE BEING CUT DOWN FOR CATTLE
WE PUSH DEMOCRACY ON THE REST OF THE WO
WE DON'T EVEN LIVE IN A DEMOCRACY. WE LIVE I
THE POPULAR VOTE IS IGNORED. EVEN IF VOTI
POLITICIANS ARE IN DEBT TO THE BUSINESS INT
I'M SORRY FOR NUCLEAR WEAPONS. TO THE PE
NUCLEAR WASTE IS TOXIC FOR OVER 10,000 YE
SOMEBODY, SOME DAY, WILL BE DEALING WITH
RADIOACTIVE CRAP AND IT WON'T BE US.
I'M SORRY.

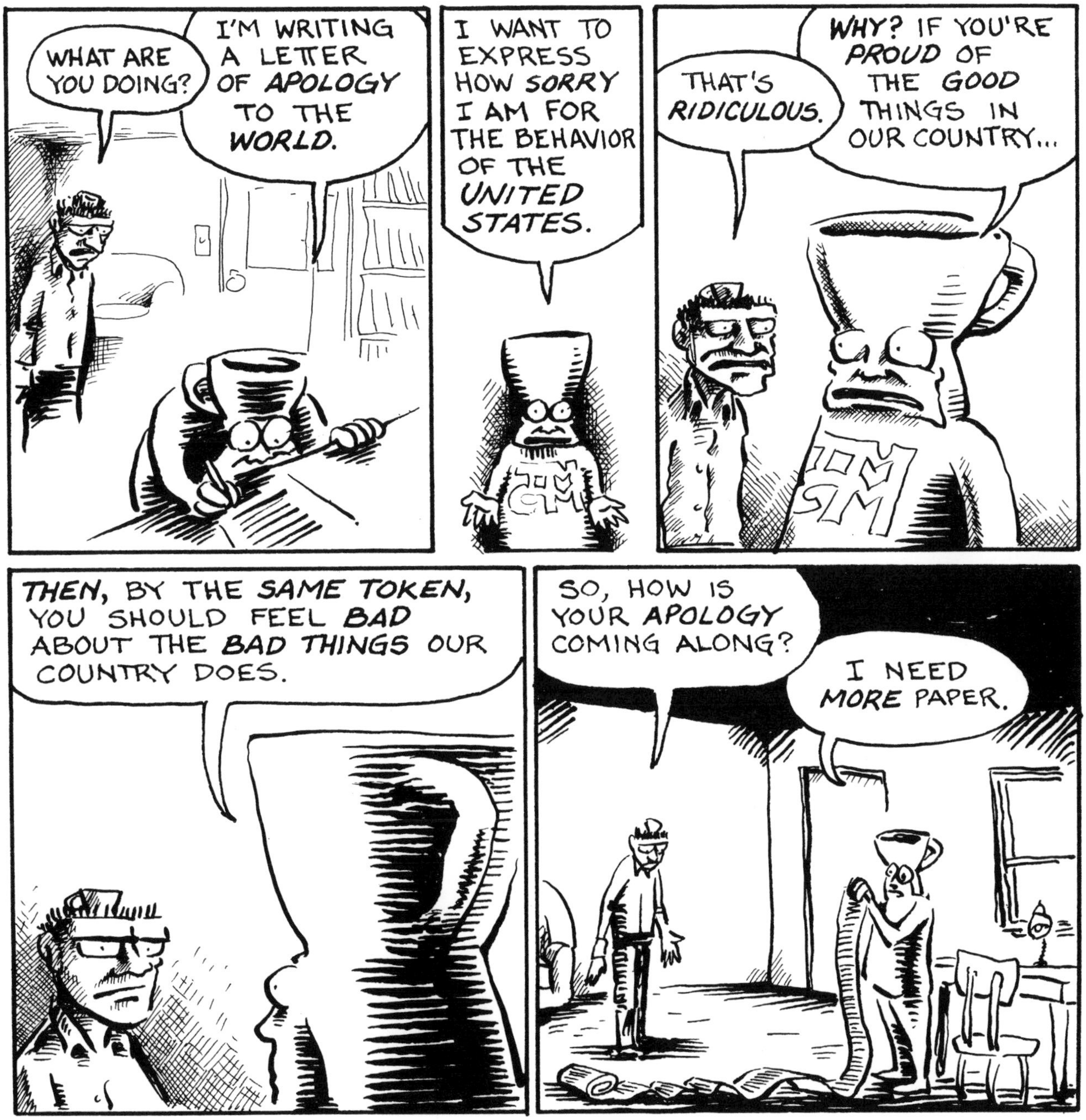
WHAT ARE YOU DOING?
I'M WRITING A LETTER OF APOLOGY TO THE WORLD.
I WANT TO EXPRESS HOW SORRY I AM FOR THE BEHAVIOR OF THE UNITED STATES.
THAT'S RIDICULOUS.
WHY? IF YOU'RE PROUD OF THE GOOD THINGS IN OUR COUNTRY...
THEN, BY THE SAME TOKEN, YOU SHOULD FEEL BAD ABOUT THE BAD THINGS OUR COUNTRY DOES.
SO, HOW IS YOUR APOLOGY COMING ALONG?
I NEED MORE PAPER.

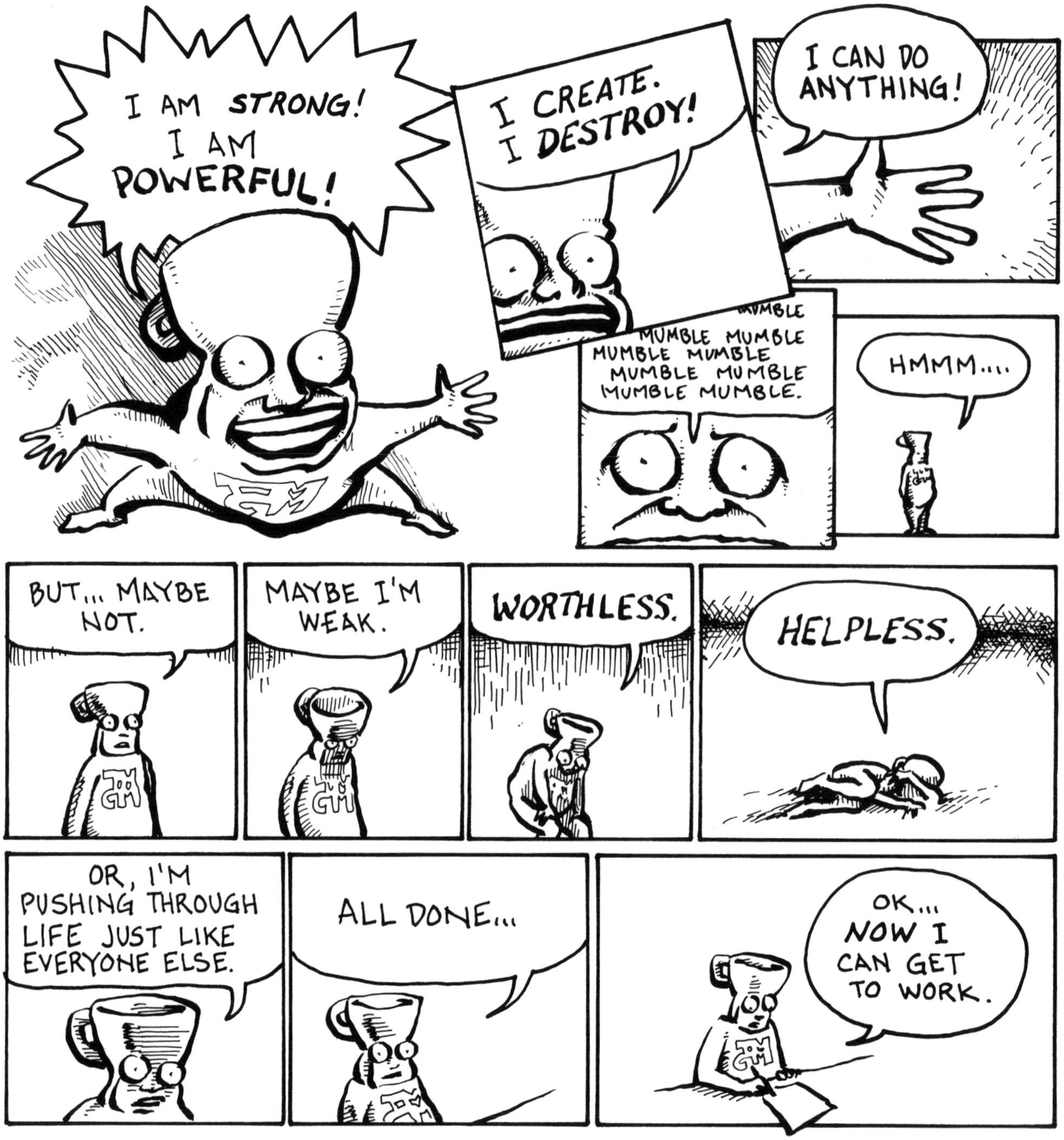
I AM STRONG! I AM POWERFUL!
I CREATE. I DESTROY!
I CAN DO ANYTHING!
MUMBLE MUMBLE MUMBLE MUMBLE MUMBLE MUMBLE MUMBLE MUMBLE MUMBLE.
HMMM....
BUT... MAYBE NOT.
MAYBE I'M WEAK.
WORTHLESS.
HELPLESS.
OR, I'M PUSHING THROUGH LIFE JUST LIKE EVERYONE ELSE.
ALL DONE...
OK... NOW I CAN GET TO WORK.

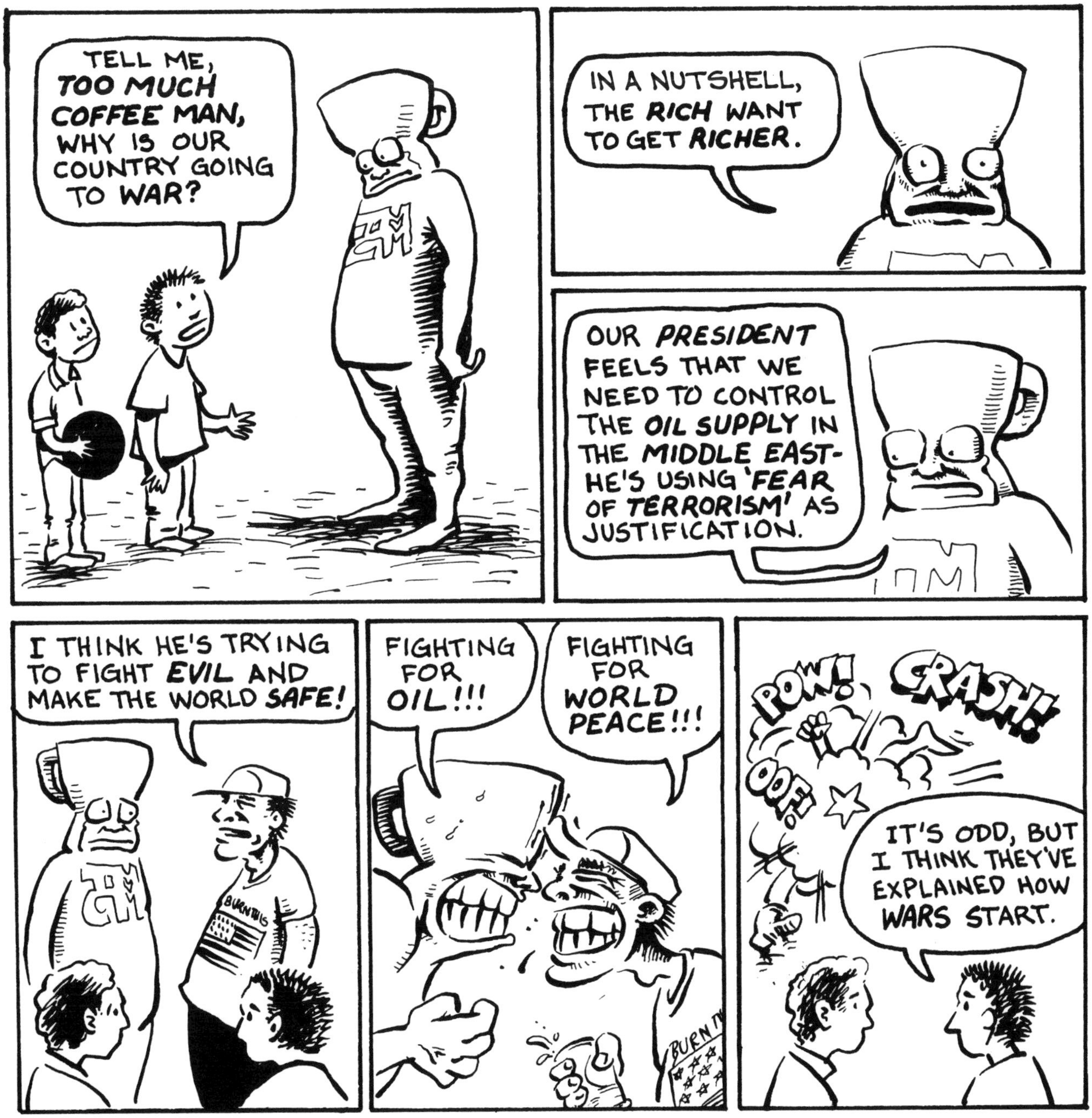
TELL ME, TOO MUCH COFFEE MAN, WHY IS OUR COUNTRY GOING TO WAR?
IN A NUTSHELL, THE RICH WANT TO GET RICHER.
OUR PRESIDENT FEELS THAT WE NEED TO CONTROL THE OIL SUPPLY IN THE MIDDLE EAST- HE'S USING 'FEAR OF TERRORISM' AS JUSTIFICATION.
I THINK HE'S TRYING TO FIGHT EVIL AND MAKE THE WORLD SAFE!
FIGHTING FOR OIL!!!
FIGHTING FOR WORLD PEACE!!!
POW!
CRASH!
OOF!
IT'S ODD, BUT I THINK THEY'VE EXPLAINED HOW WARS START.

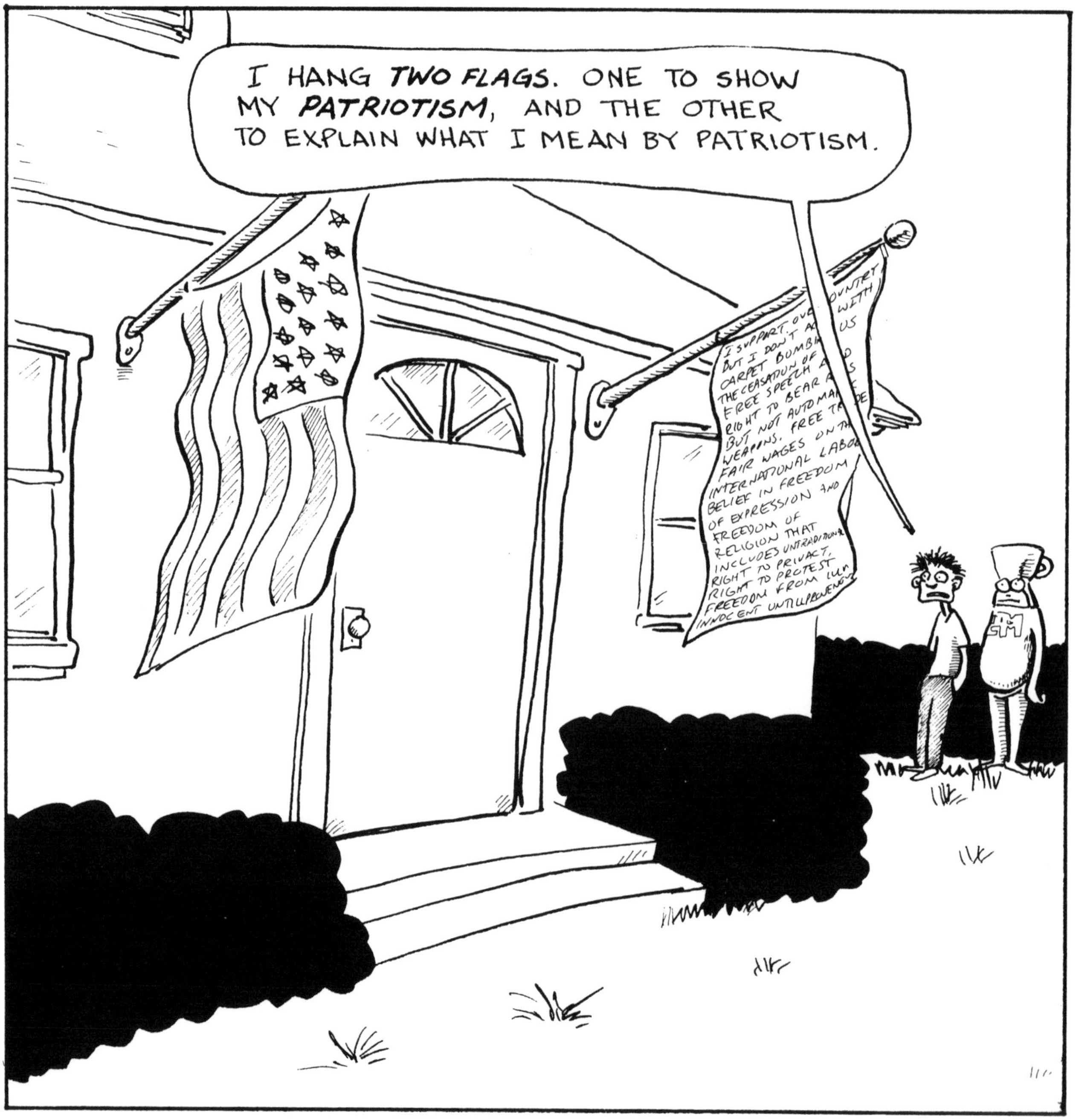
I HANG TWO FLAGS. ONE TO SHOW MY PATRIOTISM, AND THE OTHER TO EXPLAIN WHAT I MEAN BY PATRIOTISM.

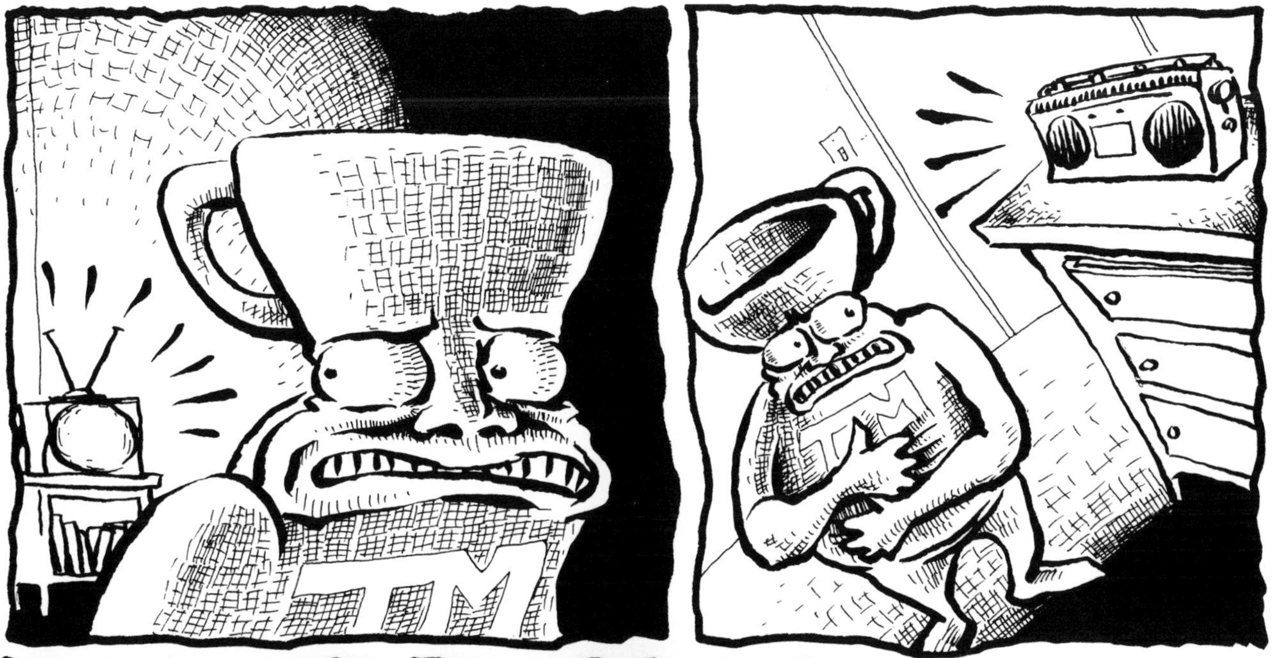
DAILY BAD NEWS

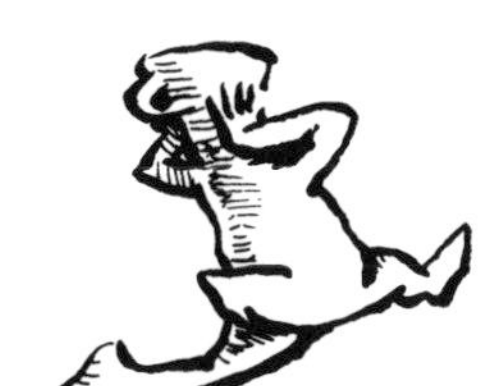

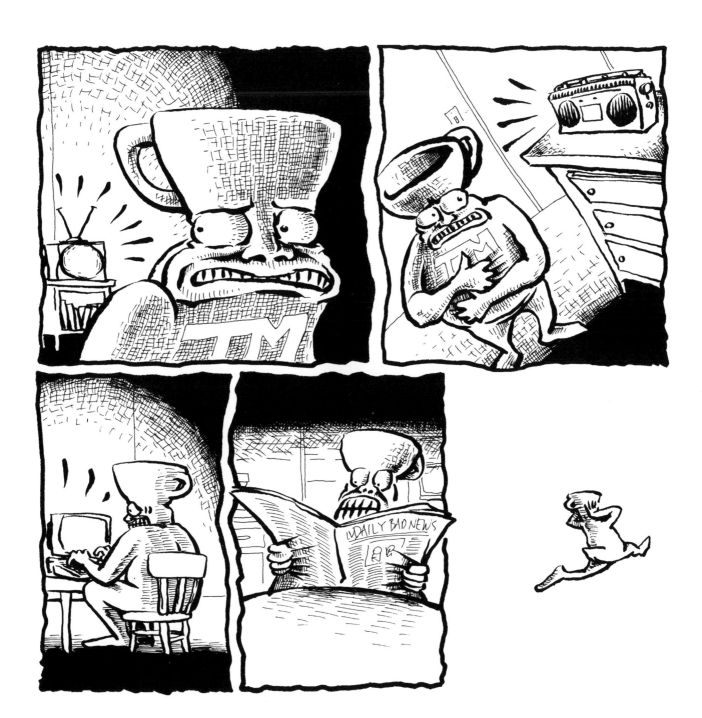

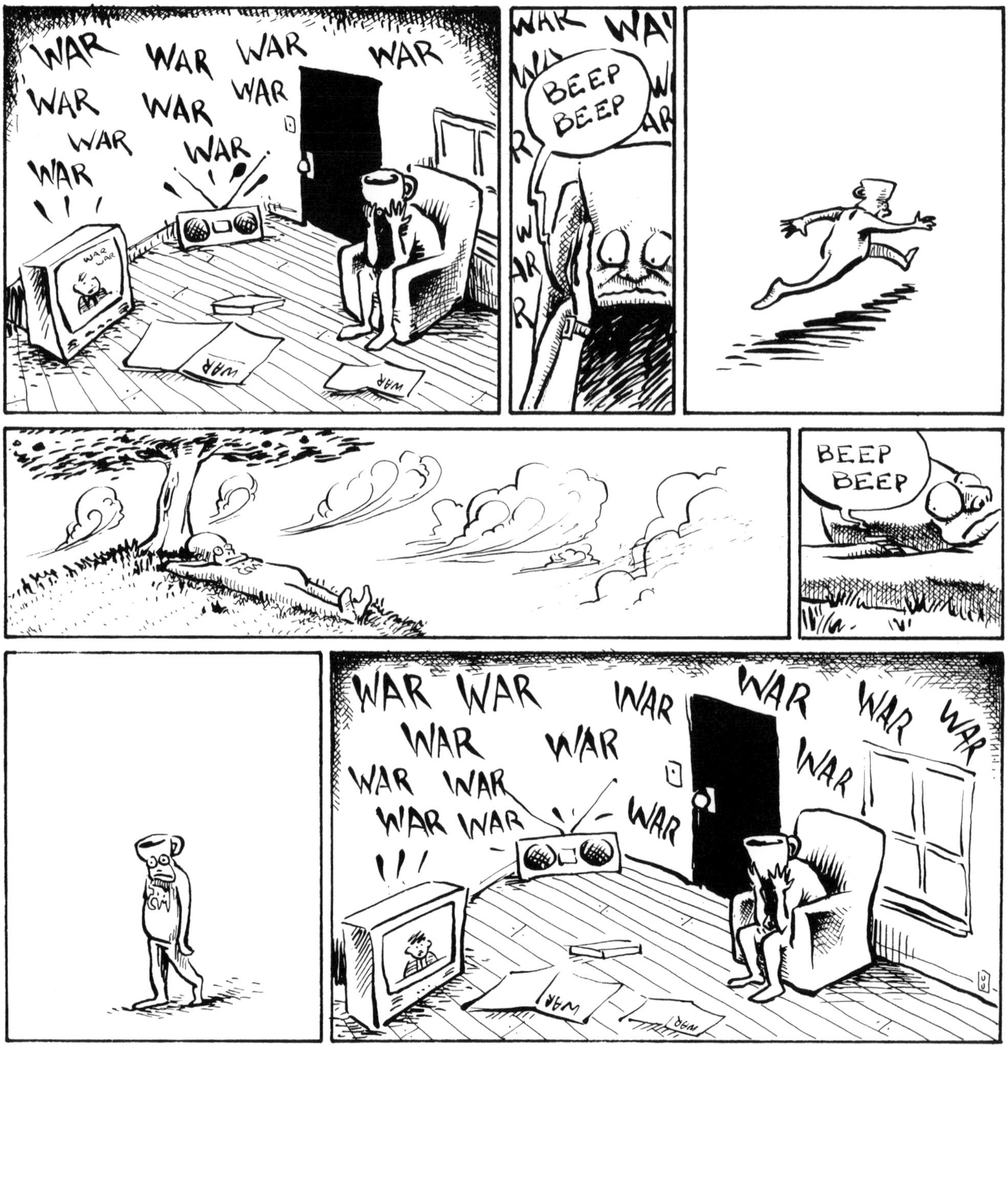
WAR WAR WAR WAR
WAR WAR WAR
WAR WAR
WAR
WAR WAR
WAR
WAR
BEEP BEEP
BEEP BEEP
WAR WAR WAR WAR WAR WAR
WAR WAR WAR WAR
WAR WAR WAR
WAR WAR WAR
WAR
WAR

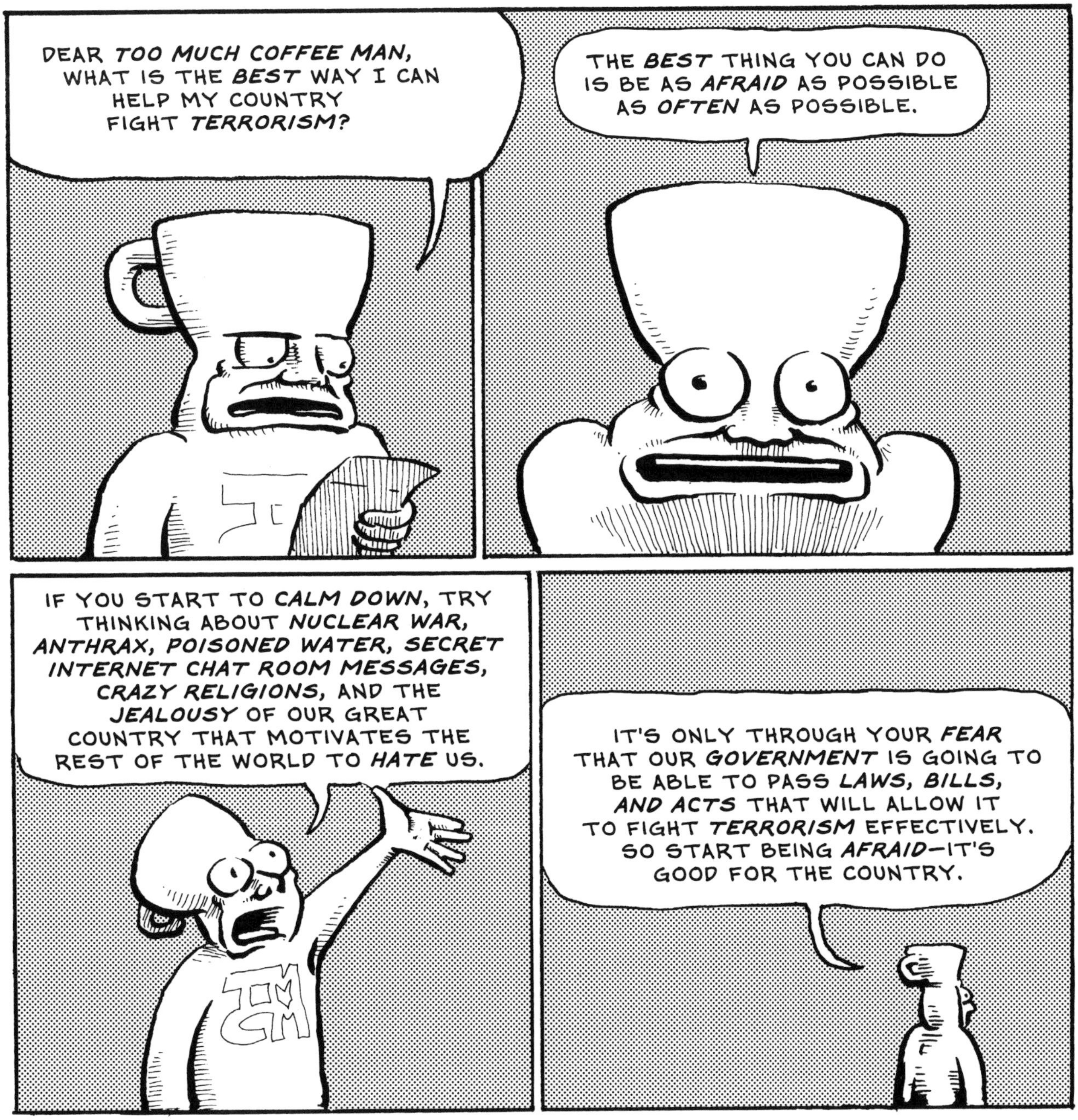
DEAR TOO MUCH COFFEE MAN, WHAT IS THE BEST WAY I CAN HELP MY COUNTRY FIGHT TERRORISM?
THE BEST THING YOU CAN DO IS BE AS AFRAID AS POSSIBLE AS OFTEN AS POSSIBLE.
IF YOU START TO CALM DOWN, TRY THINKING ABOUT NUCLEAR WAR, ANTHRAX, POISONED WATER, SECRET INTERNET CHAT ROOM MESSAGES, CRAZY RELIGIONS, AND THE JEALOUSY OF OUR GREAT COUNTRY THAT MOTIVATES THE REST OF THE WORLD TO HATE US.
IT'S ONLY THROUGH YOUR FEAR THAT OUR GOVERNMENT IS GOING TO BE ABLE TO PASS LAWS, BILLS, AND ACTS THAT WILL ALLOW IT TO FIGHT TERRORISM EFFECTIVELY. SO START BEING AFRAID—IT'S GOOD FOR THE COUNTRY.

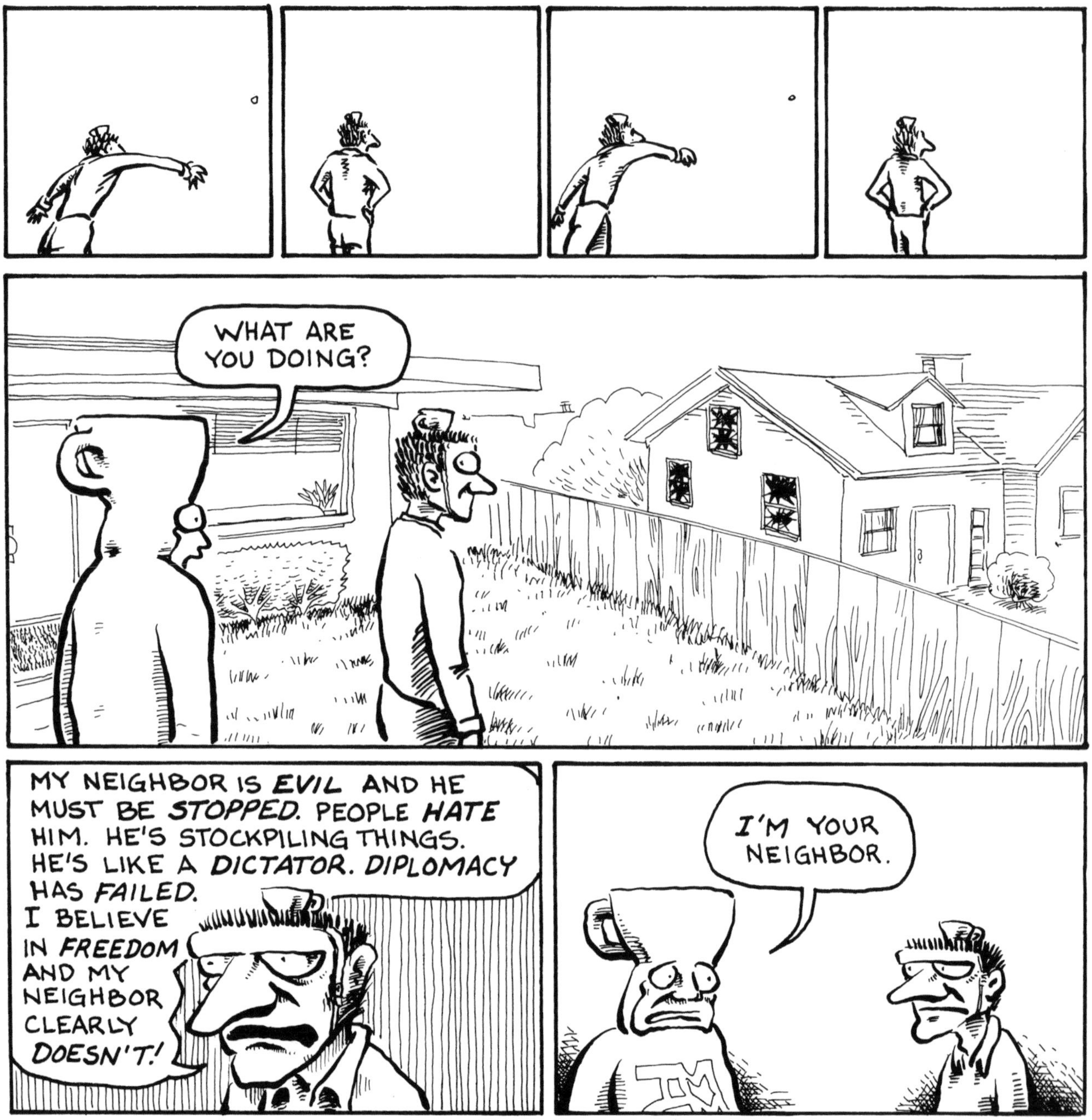
WHAT ARE YOU DOING?
MY NEIGHBOR IS EVIL AND HE MUST BE STOPPED. PEOPLE HATE HIM. HE'S STOCKPILING THINGS. HE'S LIKE A DICTATOR. DIPLOMACY HAS FAILED. I BELIEVE IN FREEDOM AND MY NEIGHBOR CLEARLY DOESN'T!
I'M YOUR NEIGHBOR.

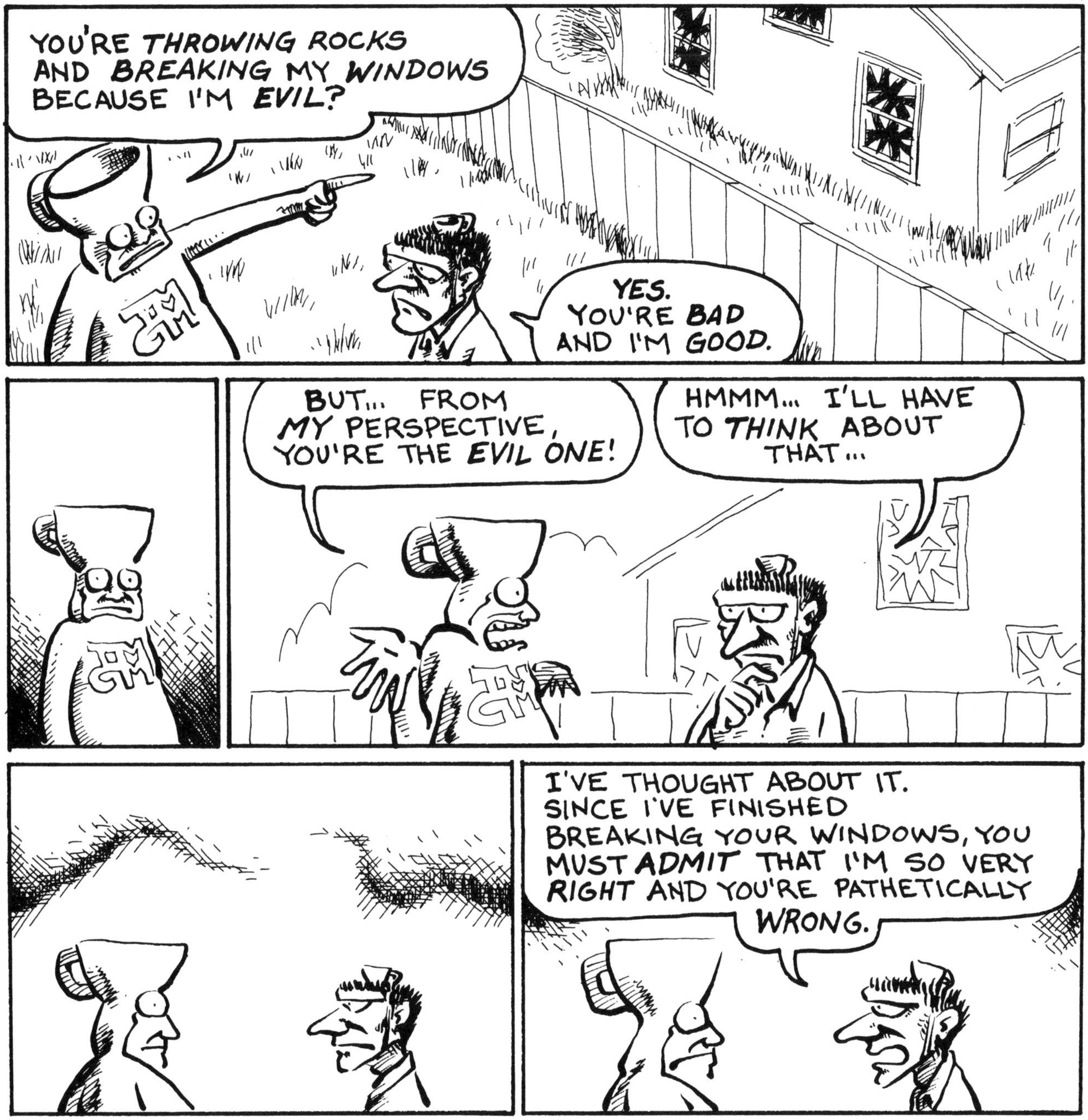
YOU'RE THROWING ROCKS AND BREAKING MY WINDOWS BECAUSE I'M EVIL?
YES. YOU'RE BAD AND I'M GOOD.
BUT... FROM MY PERSPECTIVE, YOU'RE THE EVIL ONE!
HMMM... I'LL HAVE TO THINK ABOUT THAT...
I'VE THOUGHT ABOUT IT. SINCE I'VE FINISHED BREAKING YOUR WINDOWS, YOU MUST ADMIT THAT I'M SO VERY RIGHT AND YOU'RE PATHETICALLY WRONG.

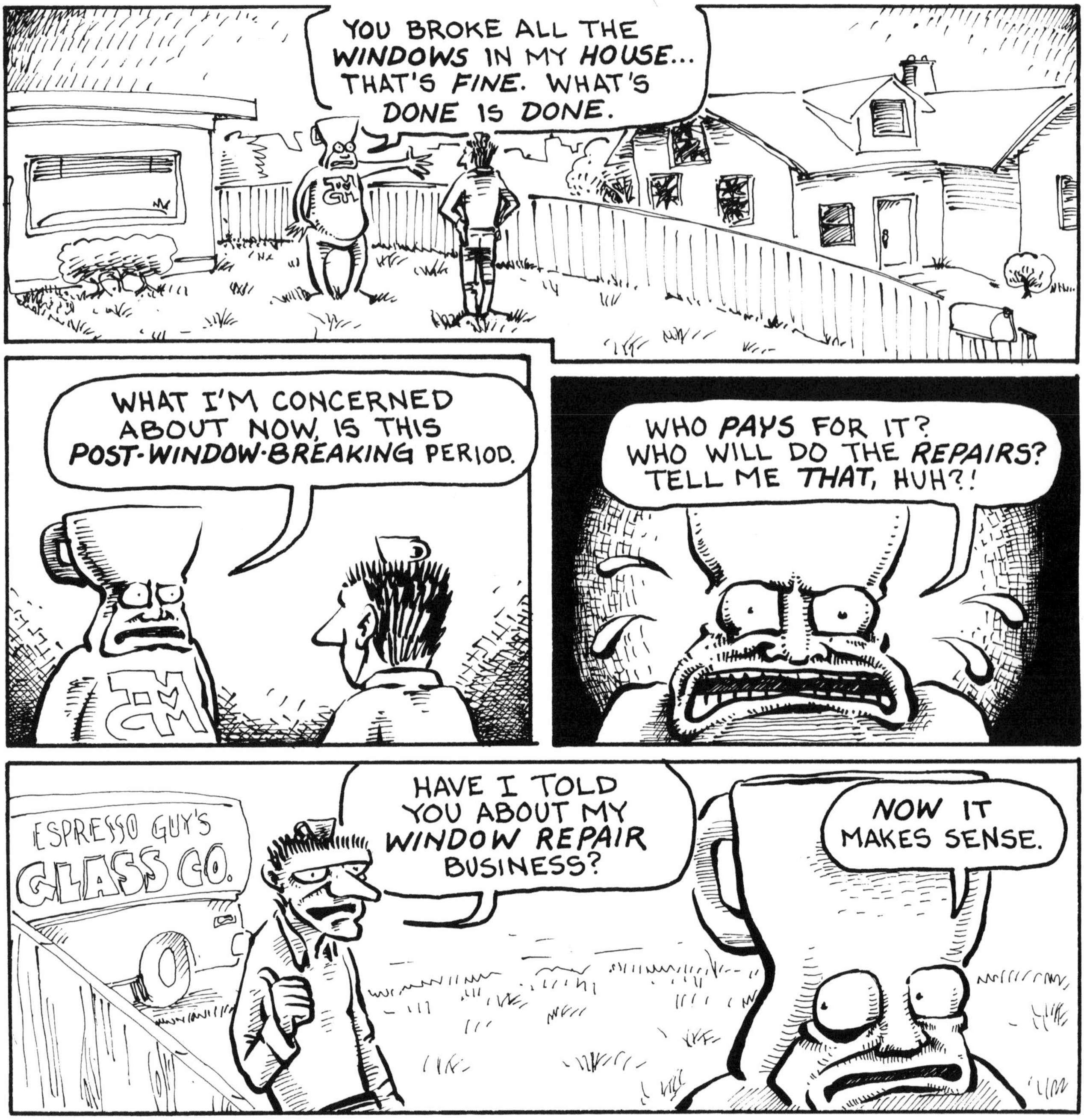
YOU BROKE ALL THE WINDOWS IN MY HOUSE... THAT'S FINE. WHAT'S DONE IS DONE.
WHAT I'M CONCERNED ABOUT NOW, IS THIS POST-WINDOW-BREAKING PERIOD.
WHO PAYS FOR IT? WHO WILL DO THE REPAIRS? TELL ME THAT, HUH?!
ESPRESSO GUY'S GLASS CO.
HAVE I TOLD YOU ABOUT MY WINDOW REPAIR BUSINESS?
NOW IT MAKES SENSE.

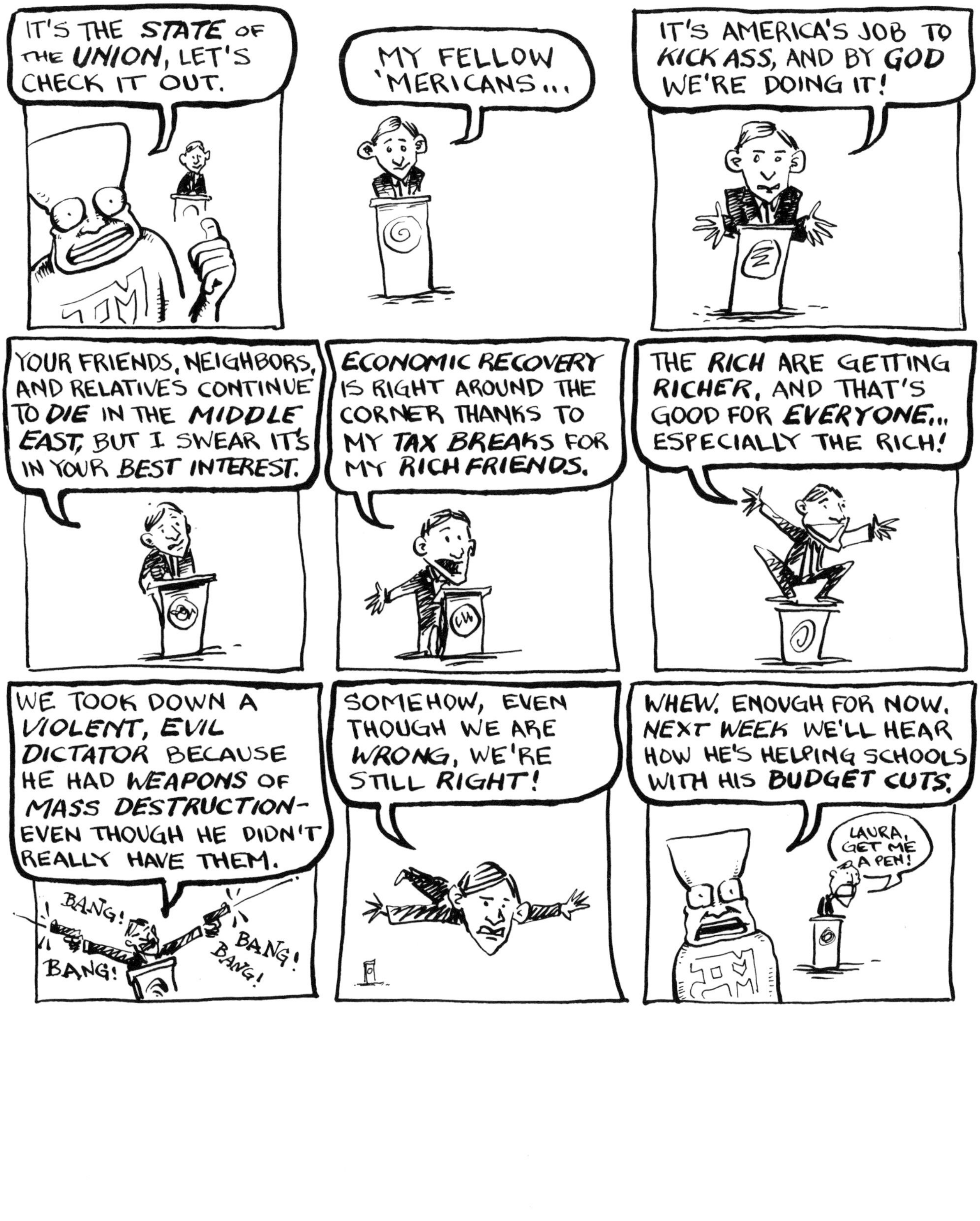
IT'S THE STATE OF THE UNION, LET'S CHECK IT OUT.
MY FELLOW 'MERICANS...
IT'S AMERICA'S JOB TO KICK ASS, AND BY GOD WE'RE DOING IT!
YOUR FRIENDS, NEIGHBORS, AND RELATIVES CONTINUE TO DIE IN THE MIDDLE EAST, BUT I SWEAR IT'S IN YOUR BEST INTEREST.
ECONOMIC RECOVERY IS RIGHT AROUND THE CORNER THANKS TO MY TAX BREAKS FOR MY RICH FRIENDS.
THE RICH ARE GETTING RICHER, AND THAT'S GOOD FOR EVERYONE... ESPECIALLY THE RICH!
WE TOOK DOWN A VIOLENT, EVIL DICTATOR BECAUSE HE HAD WEAPONS OF MASS DESTRUCTION- EVEN THOUGH HE DIDN'T REALLY HAVE THEM.
BANG!
BANG!
BANG!
BANG!
SOMEHOW, EVEN THOUGH WE ARE WRONG, WE'RE STILL RIGHT!
WHEW. ENOUGH FOR NOW. NEXT WEEK WE'LL HEAR HOW HE'S HELPING SCHOOLS WITH HIS BUDGET CUTS.
LAURA, GET ME A PEN!

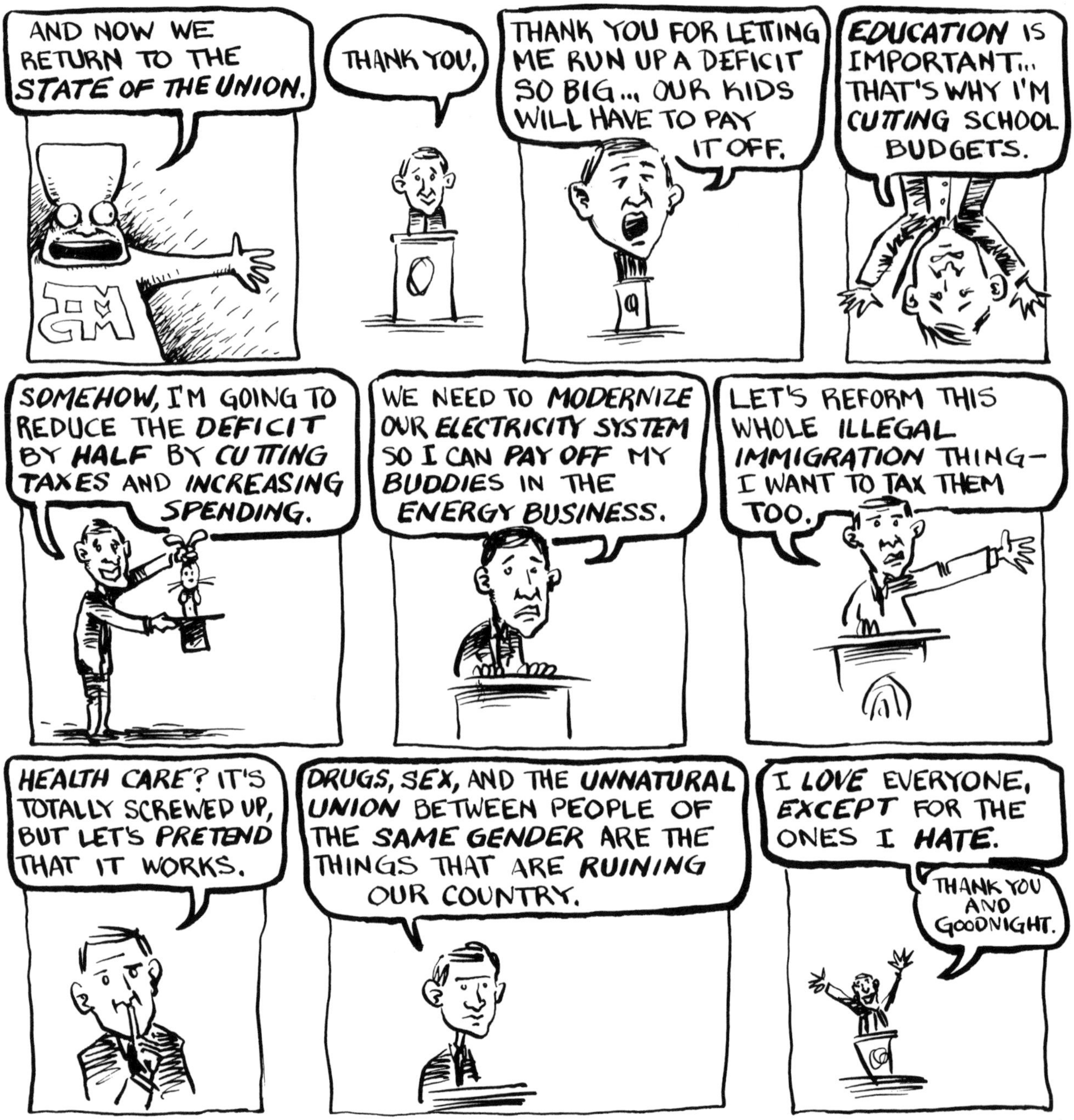
AND NOW WE RETURN TO THE STATE OF THE UNION.
THANK YOU.
THANK YOU FOR LETTING ME RUN UP A DEFICIT SO BIG... OUR KIDS WILL HAVE TO PAY IT OFF.
EDUCATION IS IMPORTANT... THAT'S WHY I'M CUTTING SCHOOL BUDGETS.
SOMEHOW, I'M GOING TO REDUCE THE DEFICIT BY HALF BY CUTTING TAXES AND INCREASING SPENDING.
WE NEED TO MODERNIZE OUR ELECTRICITY SYSTEM SO I CAN PAY OFF MY BUDDIES IN THE ENERGY BUSINESS.
LET'S REFORM THIS WHOLE ILLEGAL IMMIGRATION THING– I WANT TO TAX THEM TOO.
HEALTH CARE? IT'S TOTALLY SCREWED UP, BUT LET'S PRETEND THAT IT WORKS.
DRUGS, SEX, AND THE UNNATURAL UNION BETWEEN PEOPLE OF THE SAME GENDER ARE THE THINGS THAT ARE RUINING OUR COUNTRY.
I LOVE EVERYONE, EXCEPT FOR THE ONES I HATE.
THANK YOU AND GOODNIGHT.

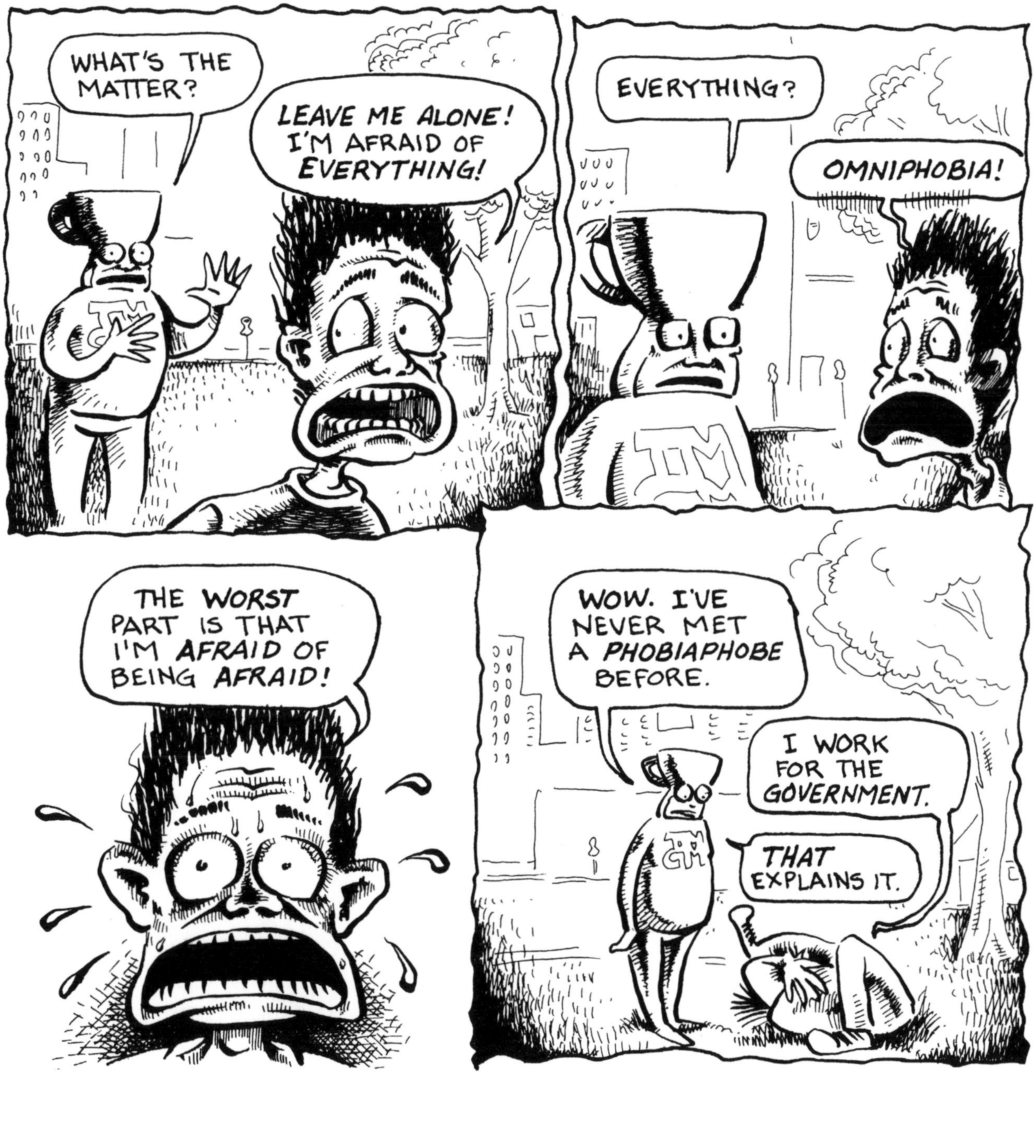
WHAT'S THE MATTER?
LEAVE ME ALONE! I'M AFRAID OF EVERYTHING!
EVERYTHING?
OMNIPHOBIA!
THE WORST PART IS THAT I'M AFRAID OF BEING AFRAID!
WOW. I'VE NEVER MET A PHOBIAPHOBE BEFORE.
I WORK FOR THE GOVERNMENT.
THAT EXPLAINS IT.

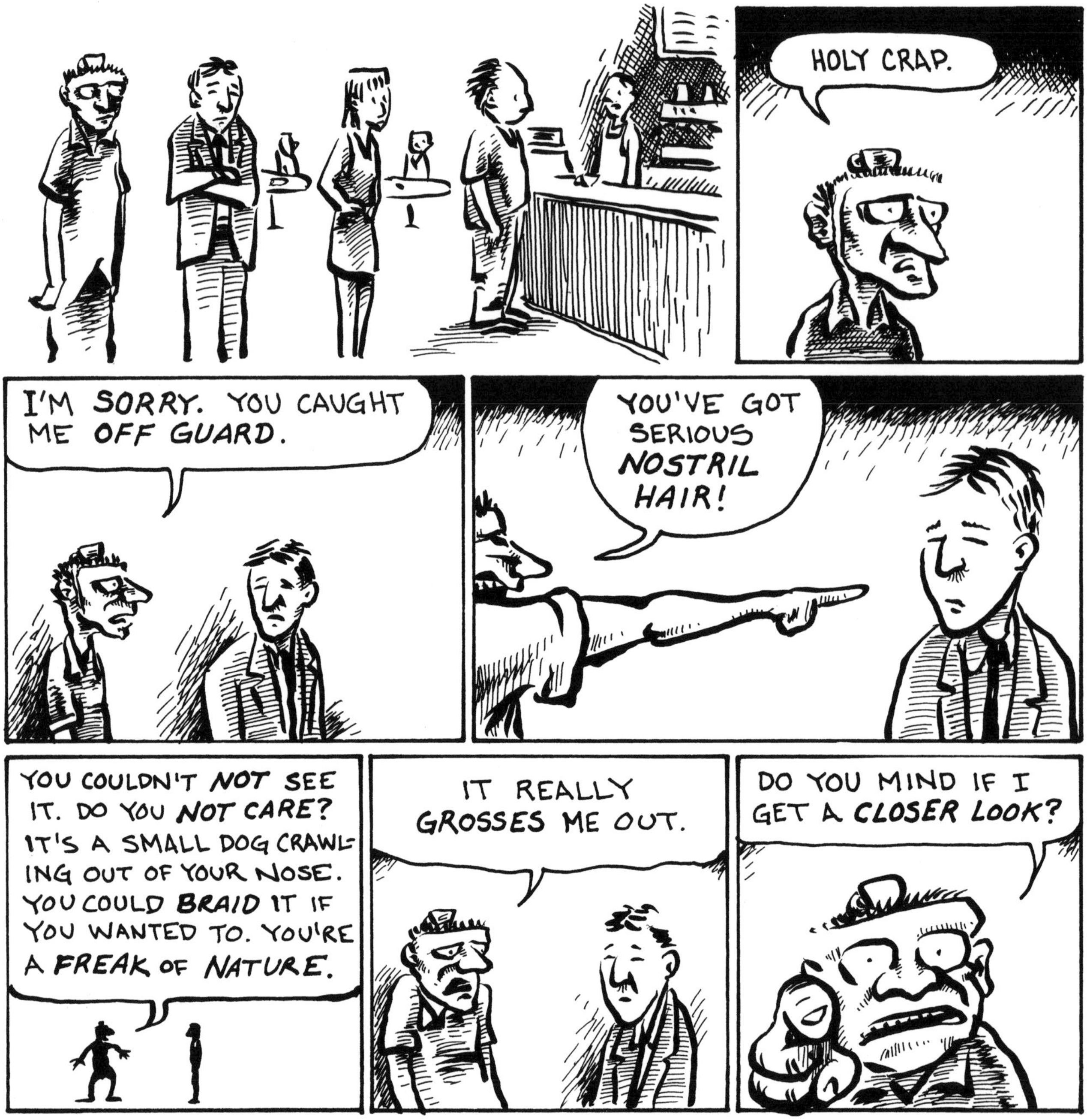
HOLY CRAP.
I'M SORRY. YOU CAUGHT ME OFF GUARD.
YOU'VE GOT SERIOUS NOSTRIL HAIR!
YOU COULDN'T NOT SEE IT. DO YOU NOT CARE? IT'S A SMALL DOG CRAWLING OUT OF YOUR NOSE. YOU COULD BRAID IT IF YOU WANTED TO. YOU'RE A FREAK OF NATURE.
IT REALLY GROSSES ME OUT.
DO YOU MIND IF I GET A CLOSER LOOK?

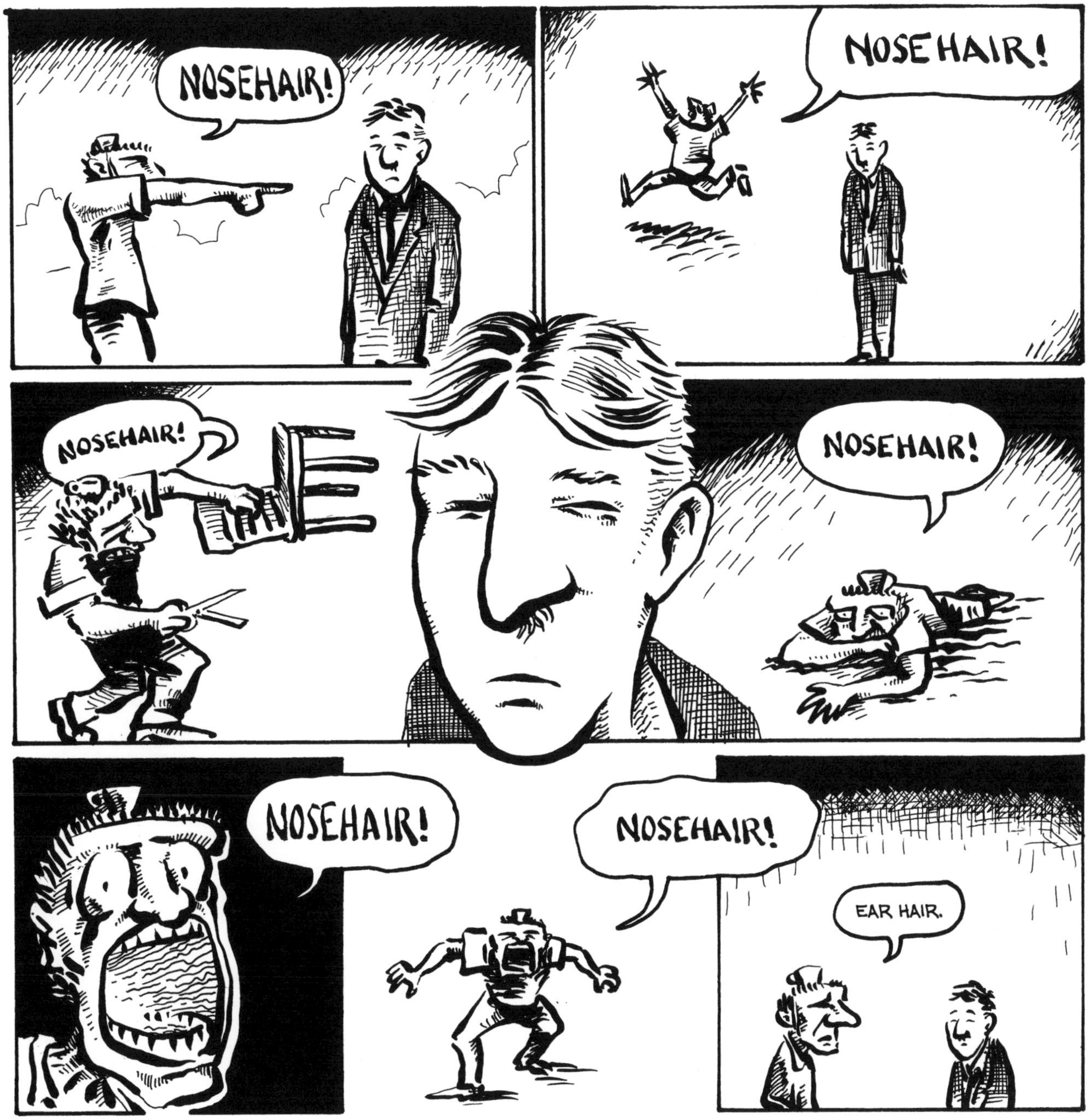
NOSEHAIR!
NOSEHAIR!
NOSEHAIR!
NOSEHAIR!
NOSEHAIR!
NOSEHAIR!
EAR HAIR.

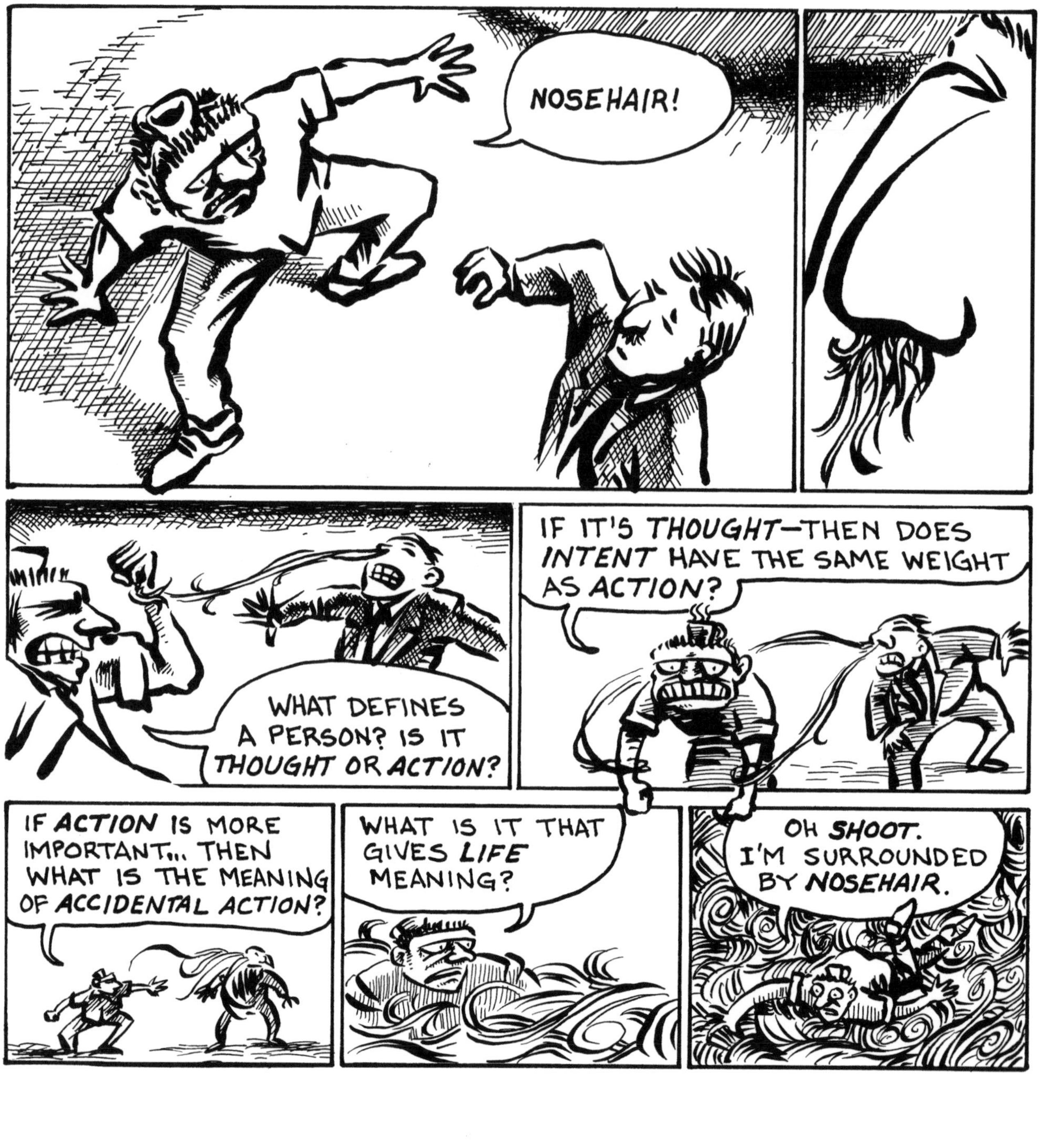
NOSEHAIR!
WHAT DEFINES A PERSON? IS IT THOUGHT OR ACTION?
IF IT'S THOUGHT—THEN DOES INTENT HAVE THE SAME WEIGHT AS ACTION?
IF ACTION IS MORE IMPORTANT... THEN WHAT IS THE MEANING OF ACCIDENTAL ACTION?
WHAT IS IT THAT GIVES LIFE MEANING?
OH SHOOT. I'M SURROUNDED BY NOSEHAIR.

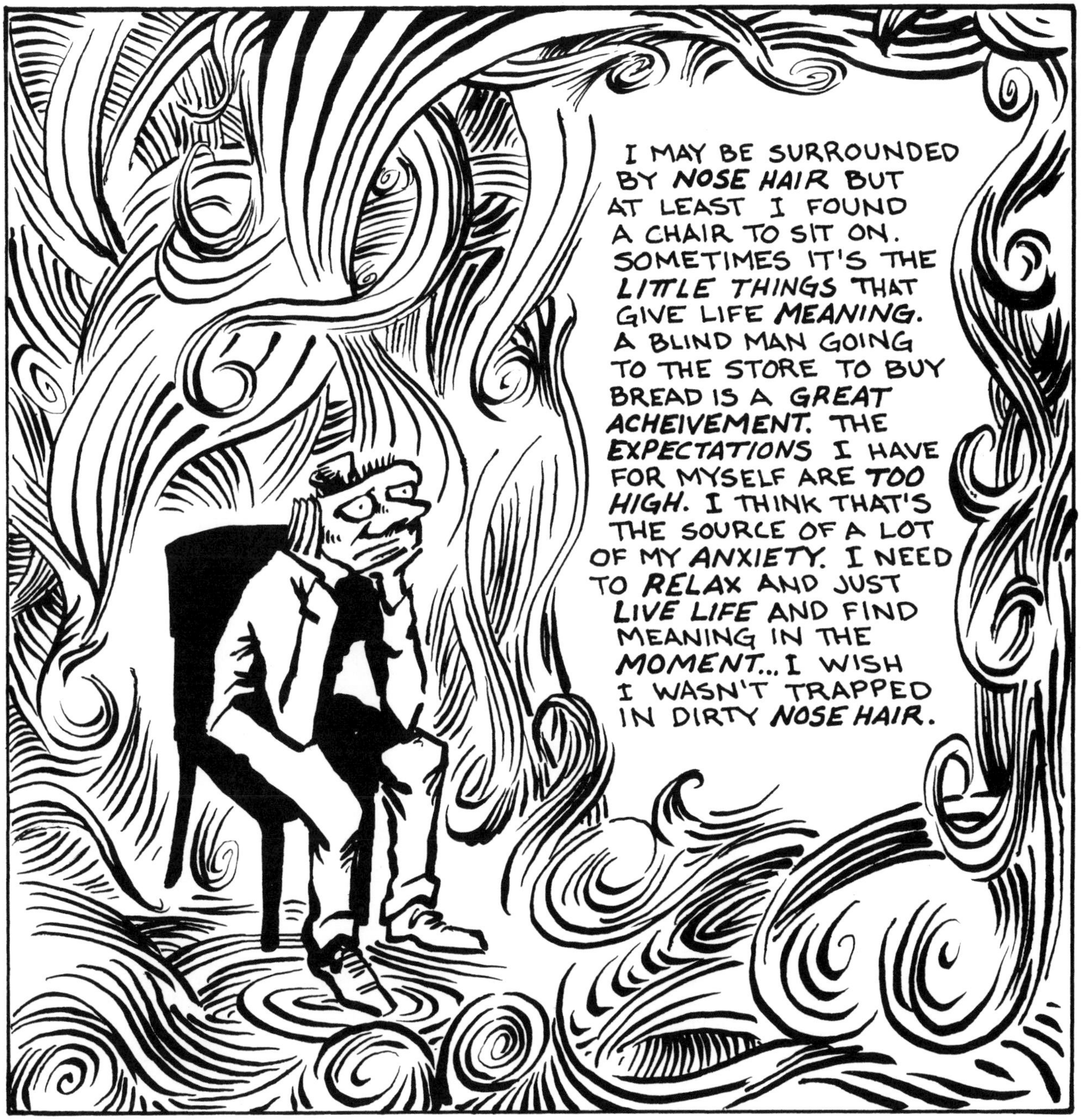
I MAY BE SURROUNDED BY NOSE HAIR BUT AT LEAST I FOUND A CHAIR TO SIT ON. SOMETIMES IT'S THE LITTLE THINGS THAT GIVE LIFE MEANING. A BLIND MAN GOING TO THE STORE TO BUY BREAD IS A GREAT ACHEIVEMENT. THE EXPECTATIONS I HAVE FOR MYSELF ARE TOO HIGH. I THINK THAT'S THE SOURCE OF A LOT OF MY ANXIETY. I NEED TO RELAX AND JUST LIVE LIFE AND FIND MEANING IN THE MOMENT... I WISH I WASN'T TRAPPED IN DIRTY NOSE HAIR.

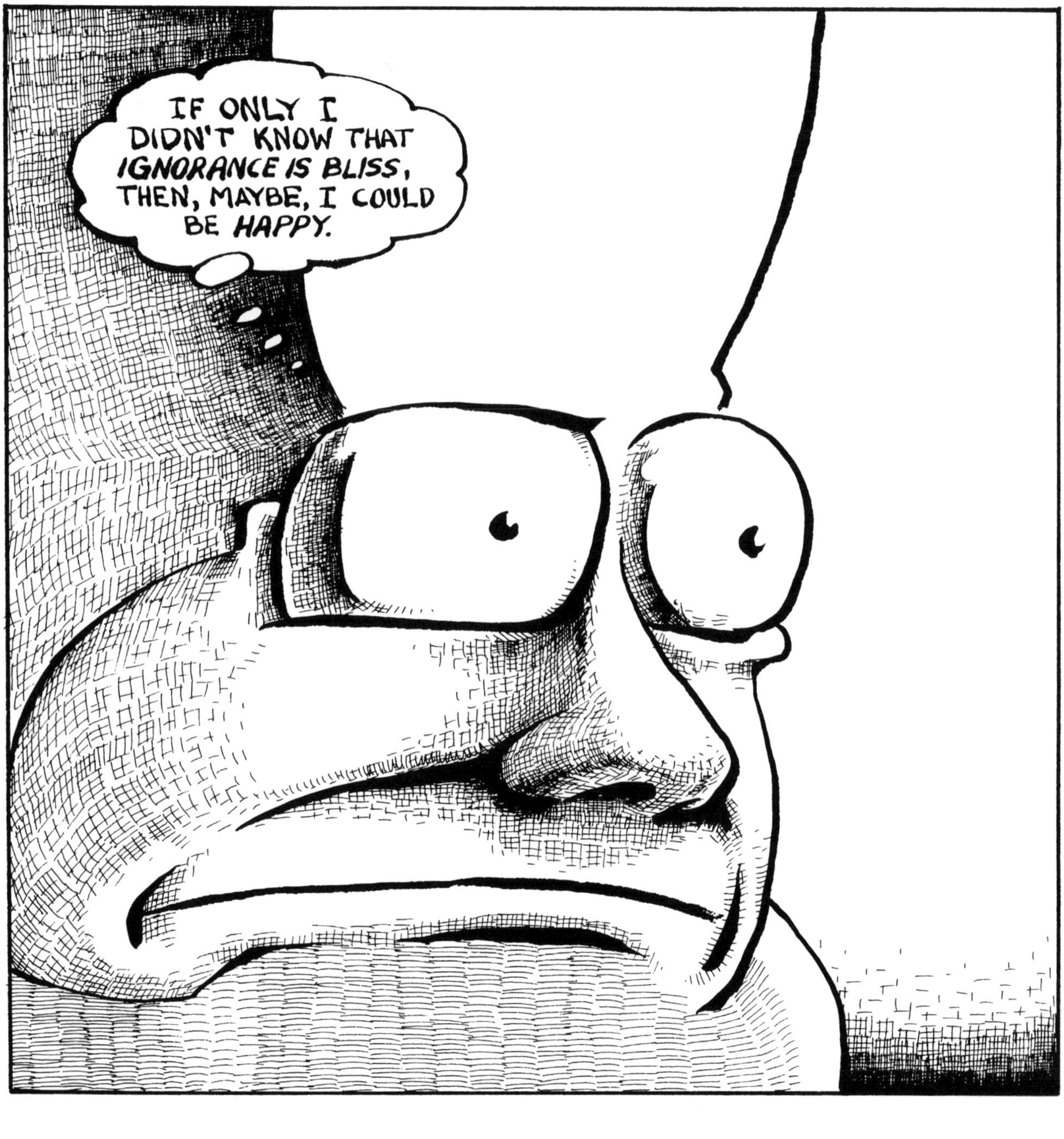
IF ONLY I DIDN'T KNOW THAT IGNORANCE IS BLISS, THEN, MAYBE, I COULD BE HAPPY.

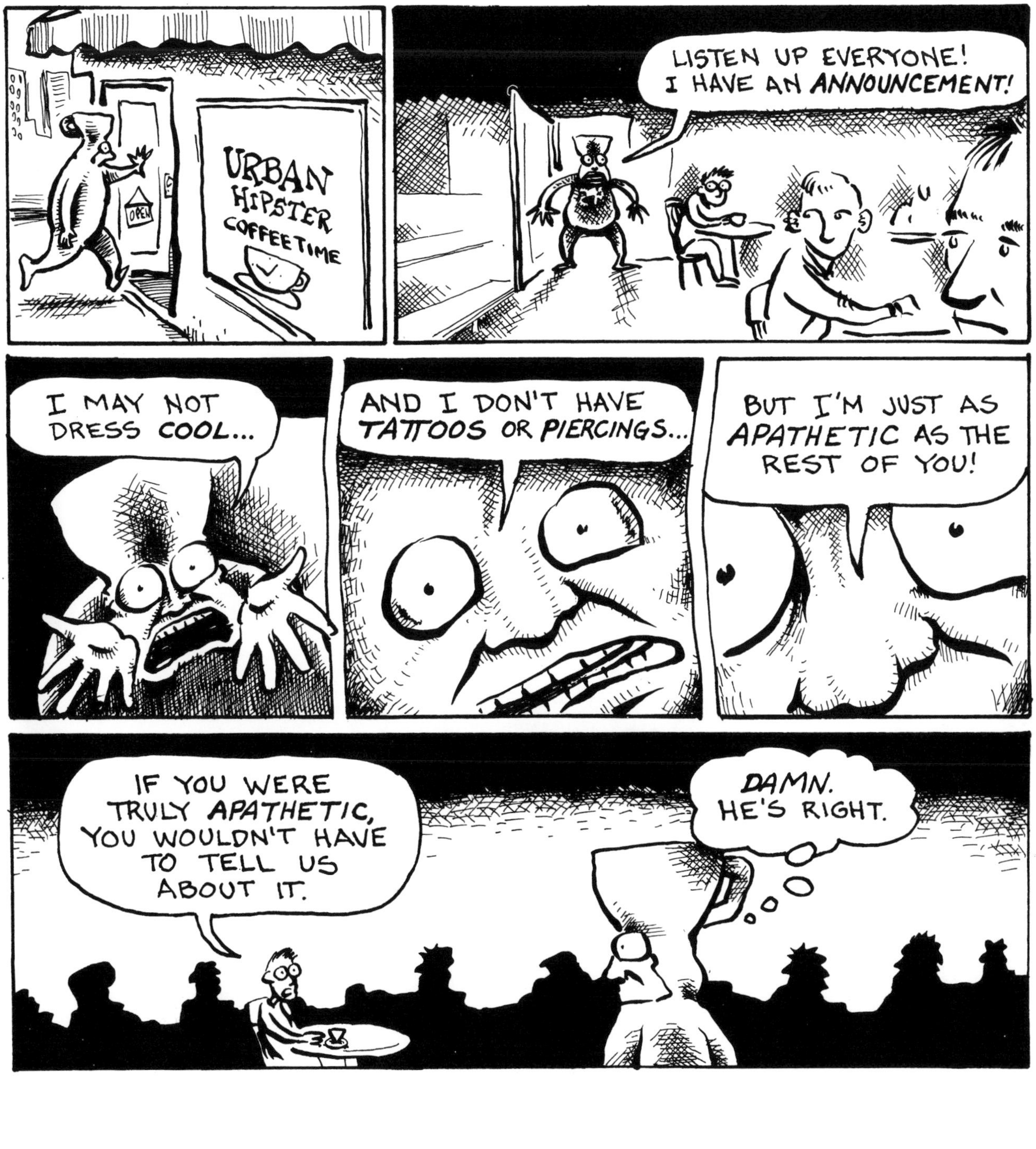
URBAN HIPSTER COFFEETIME
OPEN
LISTEN UP EVERYONE! I HAVE AN ANNOUNCEMENT!
I MAY NOT DRESS COOL...
AND I DON'T HAVE TATTOOS OR PIERCINGS...
BUT I'M JUST AS APATHETIC AS THE REST OF YOU!
IF YOU WERE TRULY APATHETIC, YOU WOULDN'T HAVE TO TELL US ABOUT IT.
DAMN. HE'S RIGHT.

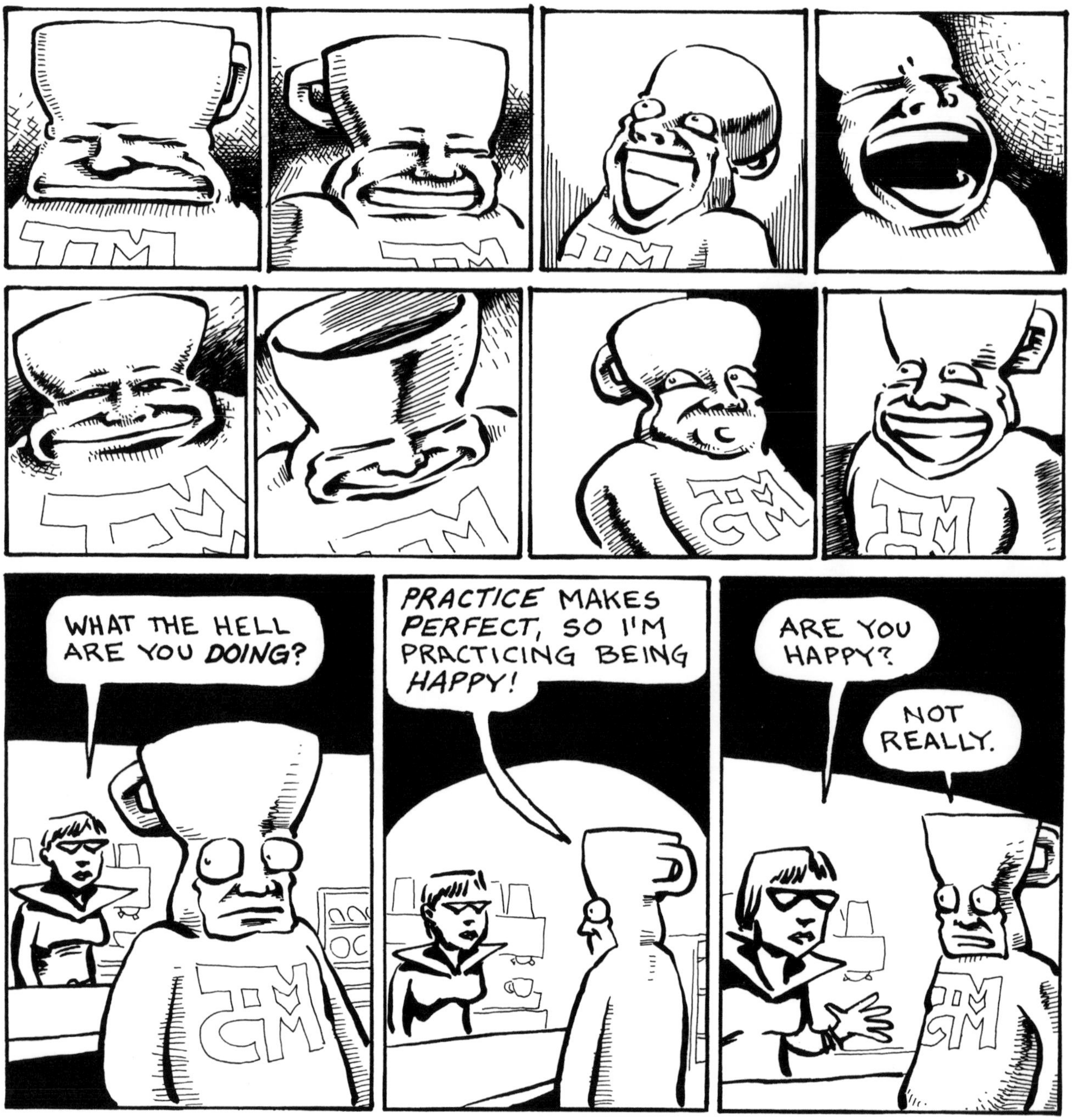
WHAT THE HELL ARE YOU *DOING*?
PRACTICE MAKES *PERFECT*, SO I'M PRACTICING BEING *HAPPY*!
ARE YOU HAPPY?
NOT REALLY.

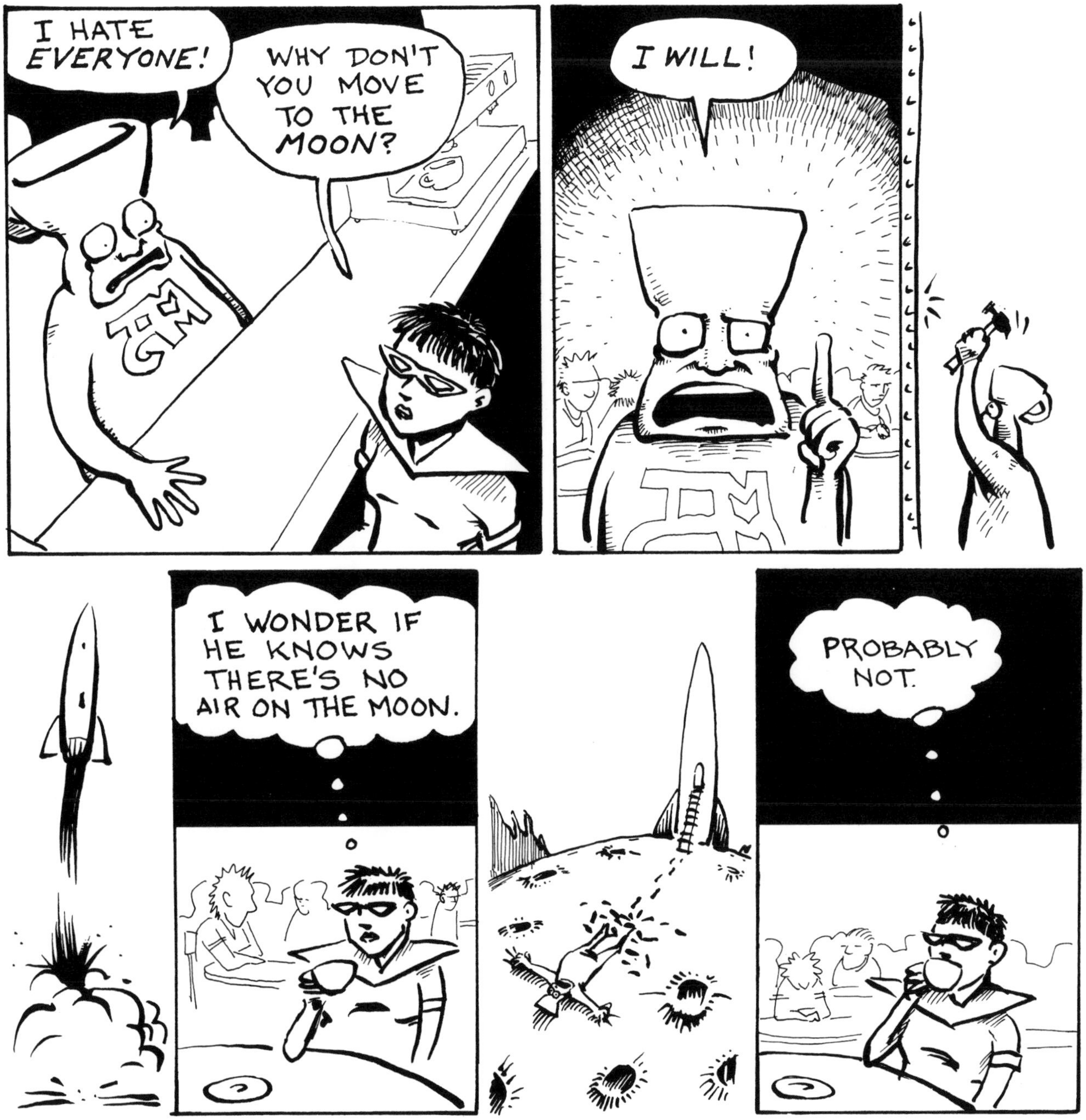
I HATE EVERYONE!
WHY DON'T YOU MOVE TO THE MOON?
I WILL!
I WONDER IF HE KNOWS THERE'S NO AIR ON THE MOON.
PROBABLY NOT.

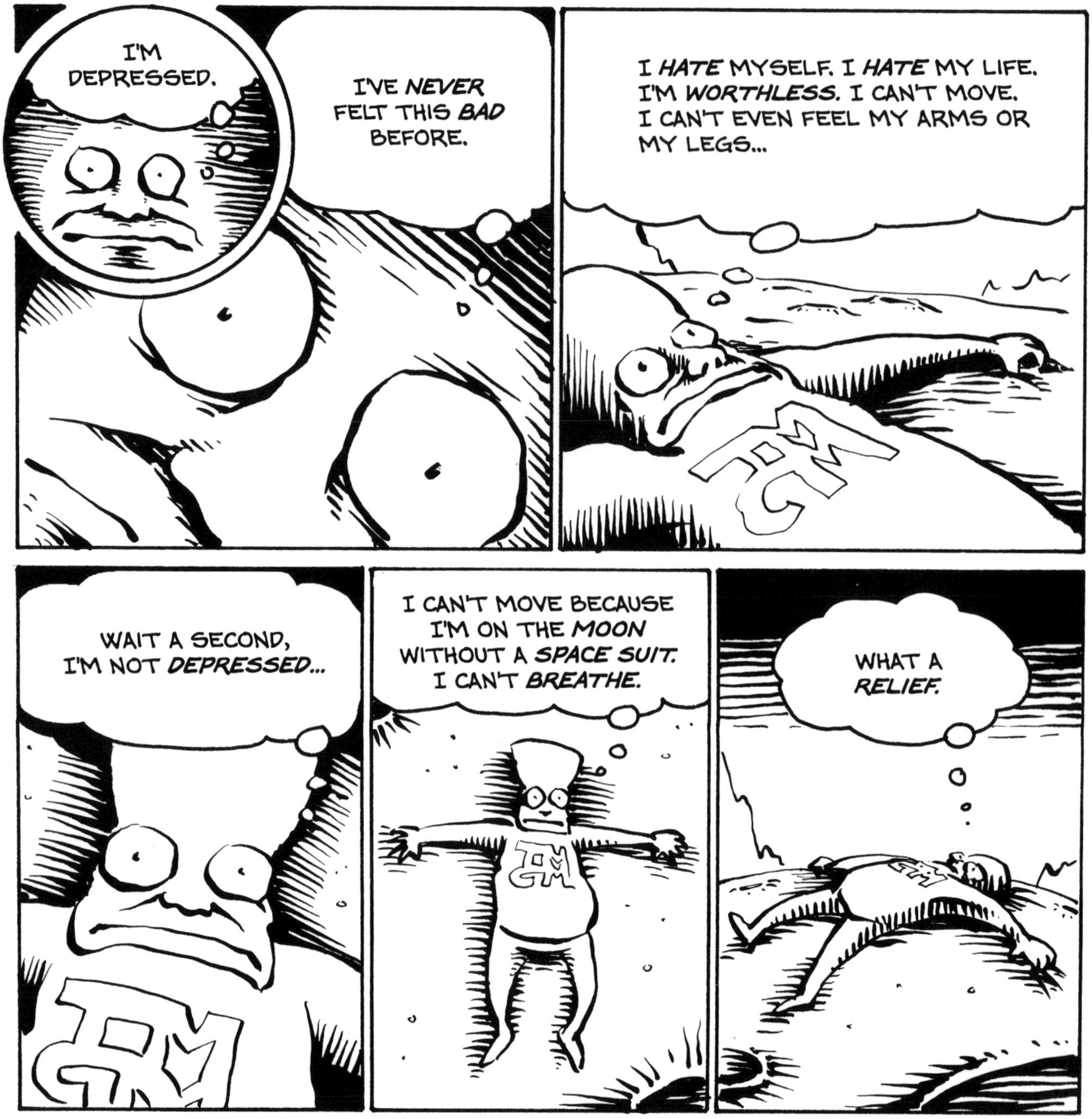
I'M DEPRESSED.
I'VE NEVER FELT THIS BAD BEFORE.
I HATE MYSELF. I HATE MY LIFE. I'M WORTHLESS. I CAN'T MOVE. I CAN'T EVEN FEEL MY ARMS OR MY LEGS...
WAIT A SECOND, I'M NOT DEPRESSED...
I CAN'T MOVE BECAUSE I'M ON THE MOON WITHOUT A SPACE SUIT. I CAN'T BREATHE.
WHAT A RELIEF.

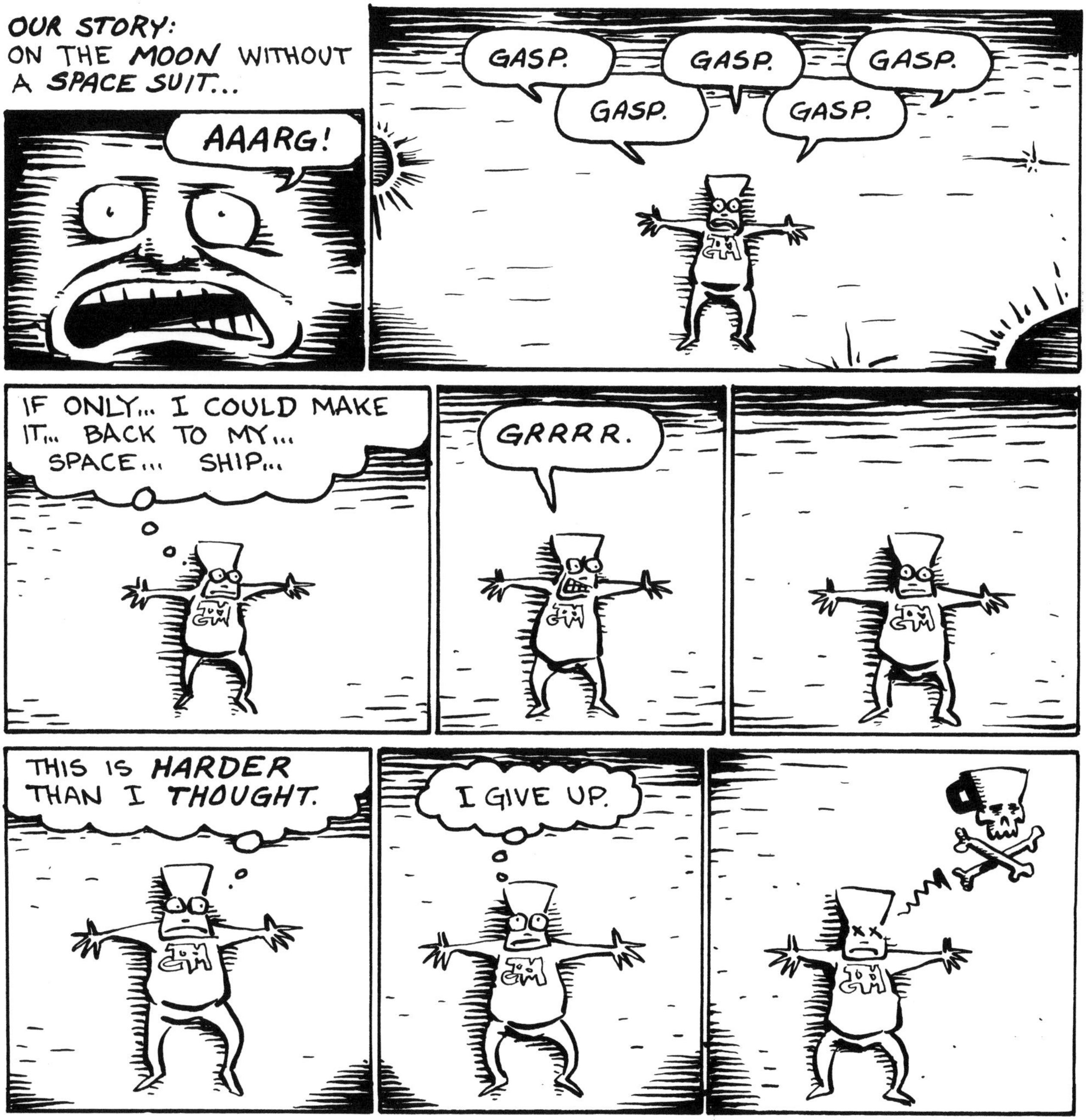
OUR STORY:
ON THE MOON WITHOUT A SPACE SUIT...
AAARG!
GASP.
GASP.
GASP.
GASP.
GASP.
IF ONLY... I COULD MAKE IT... BACK TO MY... SPACE... SHIP...
GRRRR.
THIS IS HARDER THAN I THOUGHT.
I GIVE UP.

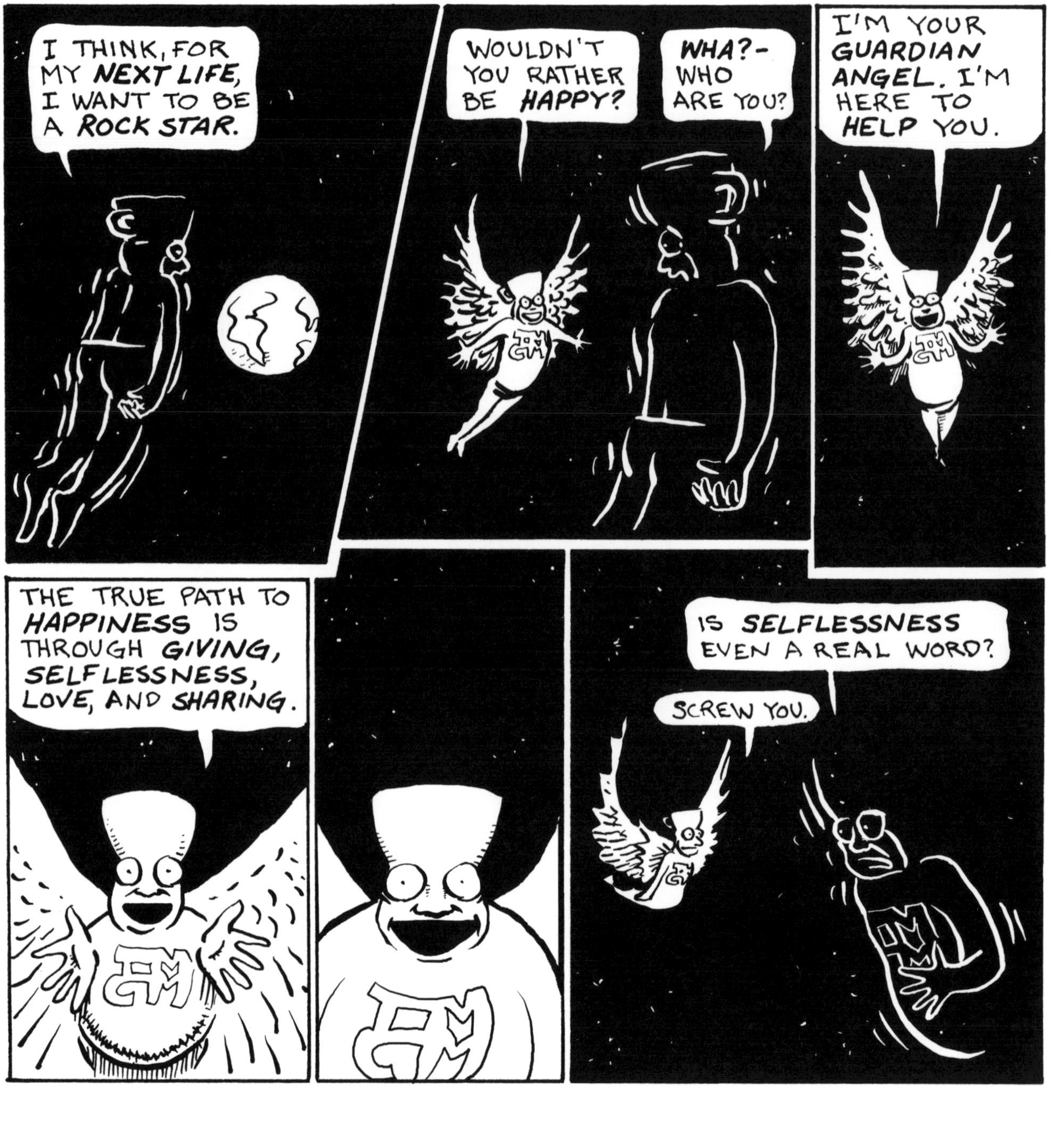
I THINK, FOR MY NEXT LIFE, I WANT TO BE A ROCK STAR.
WOULDN'T YOU RATHER BE HAPPY?
WHA?- WHO ARE YOU?
I'M YOUR GUARDIAN ANGEL. I'M HERE TO HELP YOU.
THE TRUE PATH TO HAPPINESS IS THROUGH GIVING, SELFLESSNESS, LOVE, AND SHARING.
IS SELFLESSNESS EVEN A REAL WORD?
SCREW YOU.

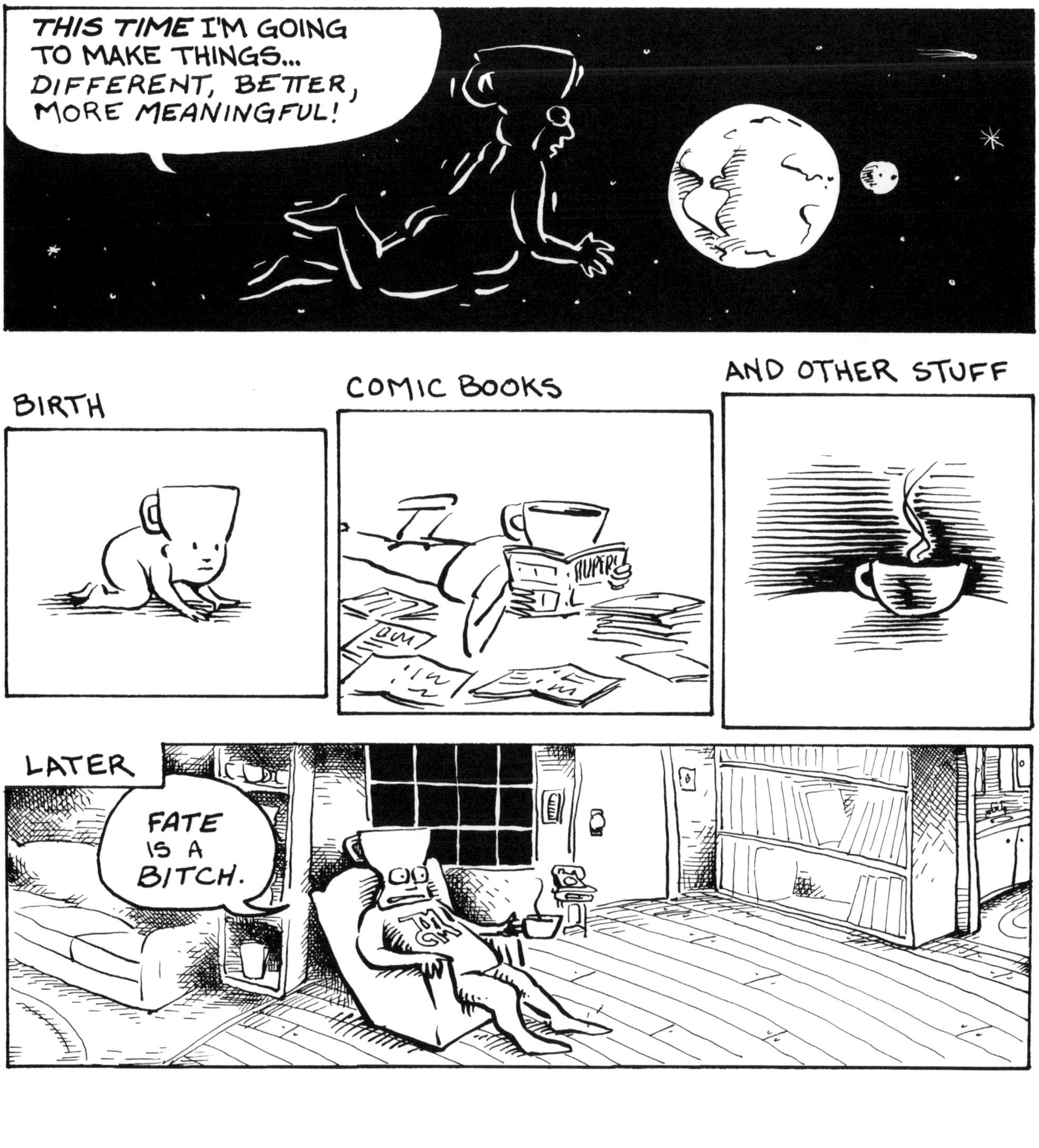
THIS TIME I'M GOING TO MAKE THINGS... DIFFERENT, BETTER, MORE MEANINGFUL!
BIRTH
COMIC BOOKS
AND OTHER STUFF
LATER
FATE IS A BITCH.

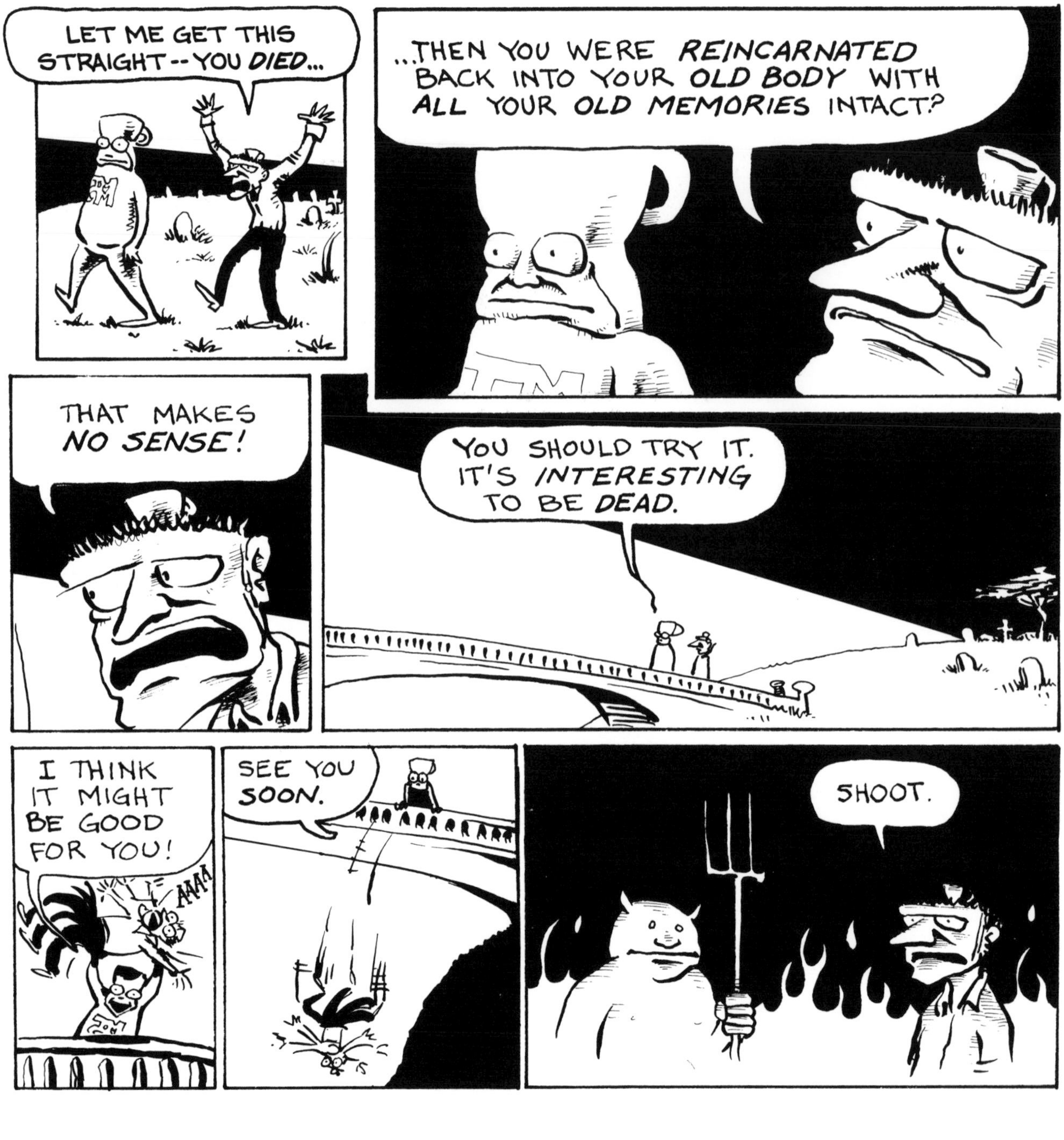
LET ME GET THIS STRAIGHT -- YOU DIED...
...THEN YOU WERE REINCARNATED BACK INTO YOUR OLD BODY WITH ALL YOUR OLD MEMORIES INTACT?
THAT MAKES NO SENSE!
YOU SHOULD TRY IT. IT'S INTERESTING TO BE DEAD.
I THINK IT MIGHT BE GOOD FOR YOU!
AAAA
SEE YOU SOON.
SHOOT.

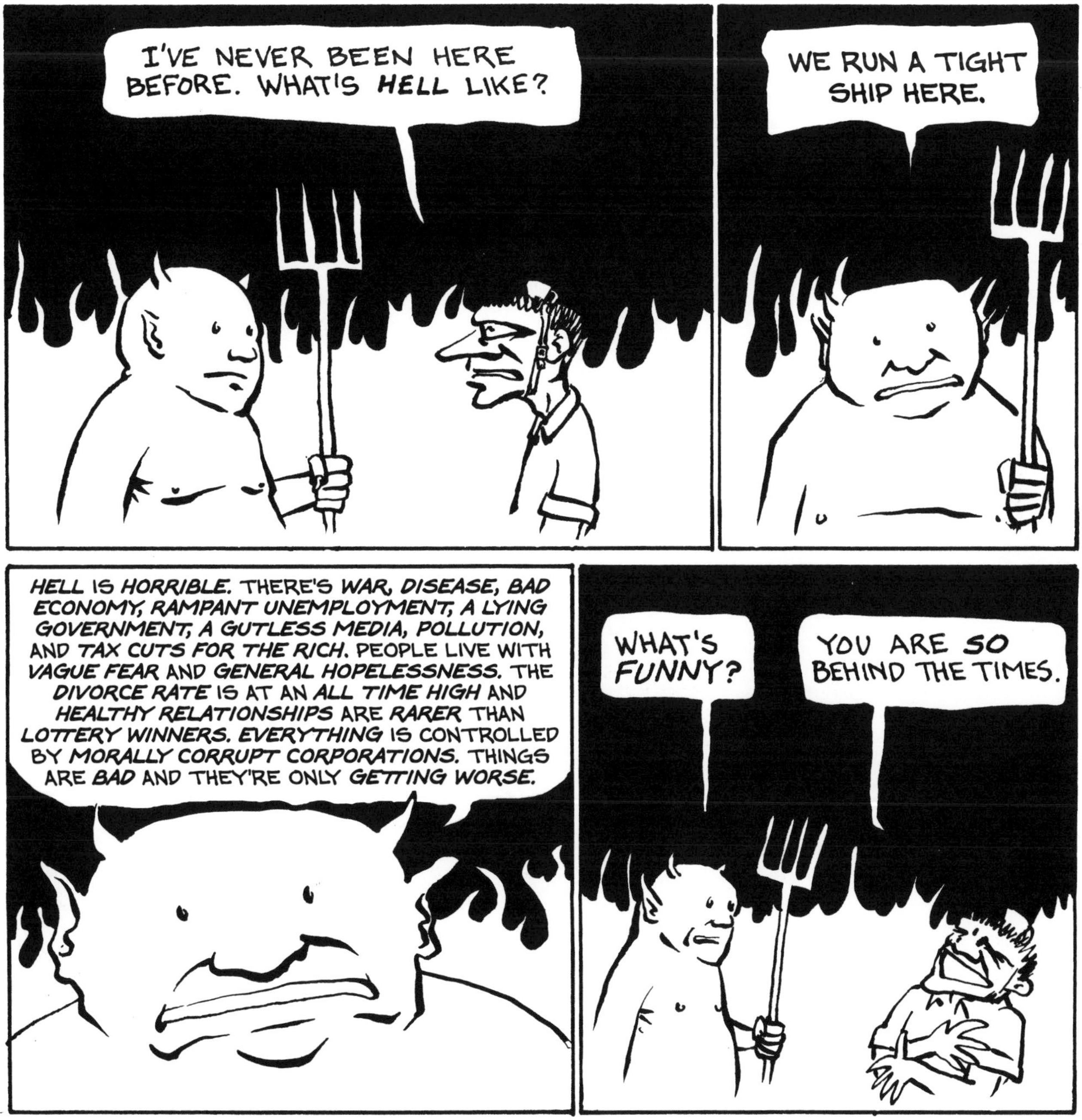
I'VE NEVER BEEN HERE BEFORE. WHAT'S HELL LIKE?
WE RUN A TIGHT SHIP HERE.
HELL IS HORRIBLE. THERE'S WAR, DISEASE, BAD ECONOMY, RAMPANT UNEMPLOYMENT, A LYING GOVERNMENT, A GUTLESS MEDIA, POLLUTION, AND TAX CUTS FOR THE RICH. PEOPLE LIVE WITH VAGUE FEAR AND GENERAL HOPELESSNESS. THE DIVORCE RATE IS AT AN ALL TIME HIGH AND HEALTHY RELATIONSHIPS ARE RARER THAN LOTTERY WINNERS. EVERYTHING IS CONTROLLED BY MORALLY CORRUPT CORPORATIONS. THINGS ARE BAD AND THEY'RE ONLY GETTING WORSE.
WHAT'S FUNNY?
YOU ARE SO BEHIND THE TIMES.

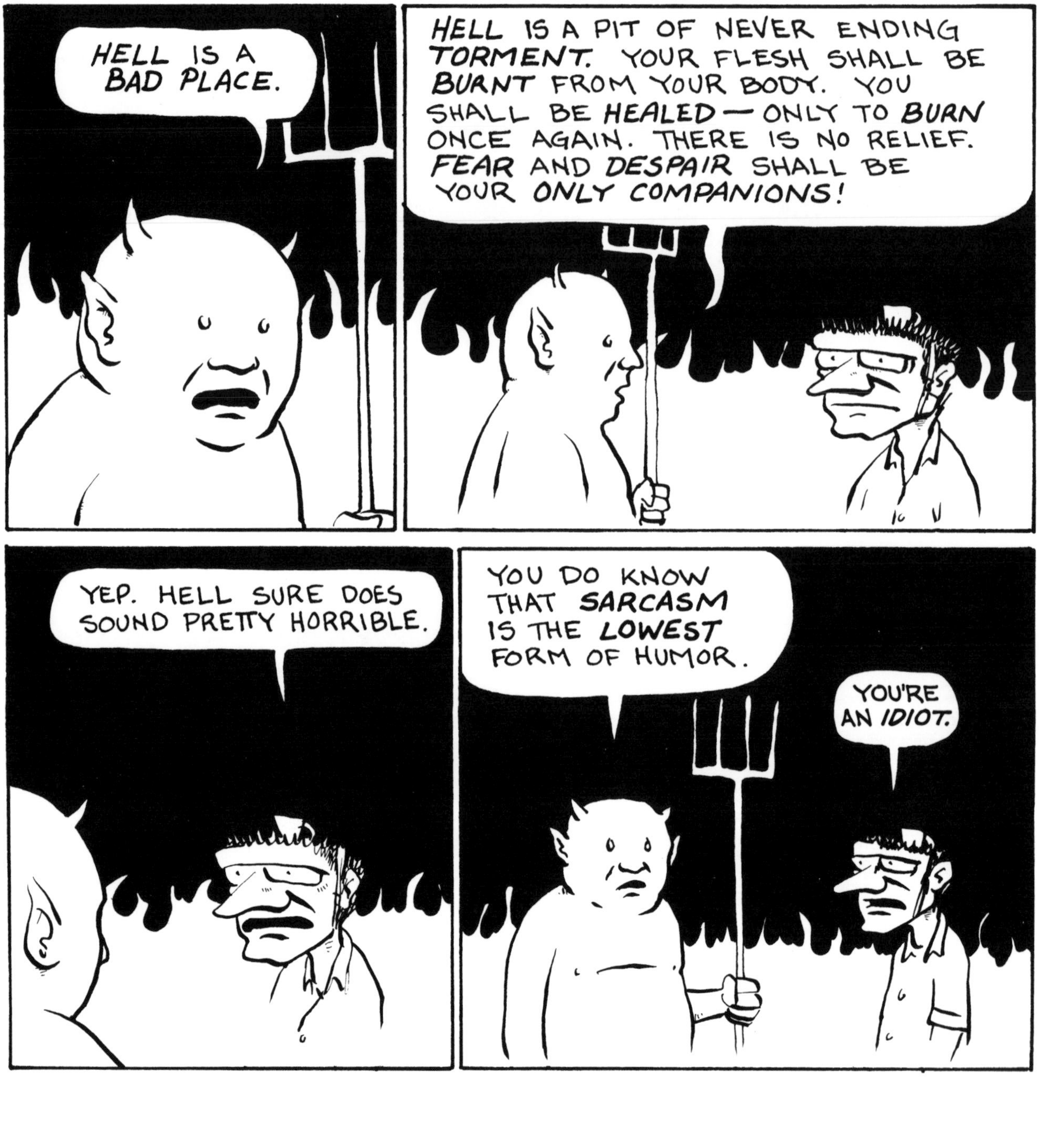
HELL IS A BAD PLACE.
HELL IS A PIT OF NEVER ENDING TORMENT. YOUR FLESH SHALL BE BURNT FROM YOUR BODY. YOU SHALL BE HEALED — ONLY TO BURN ONCE AGAIN. THERE IS NO RELIEF. FEAR AND DESPAIR SHALL BE YOUR ONLY COMPANIONS!
YEP. HELL SURE DOES SOUND PRETTY HORRIBLE.
YOU DO KNOW THAT SARCASM IS THE LOWEST FORM OF HUMOR.
YOU'RE AN IDIOT.

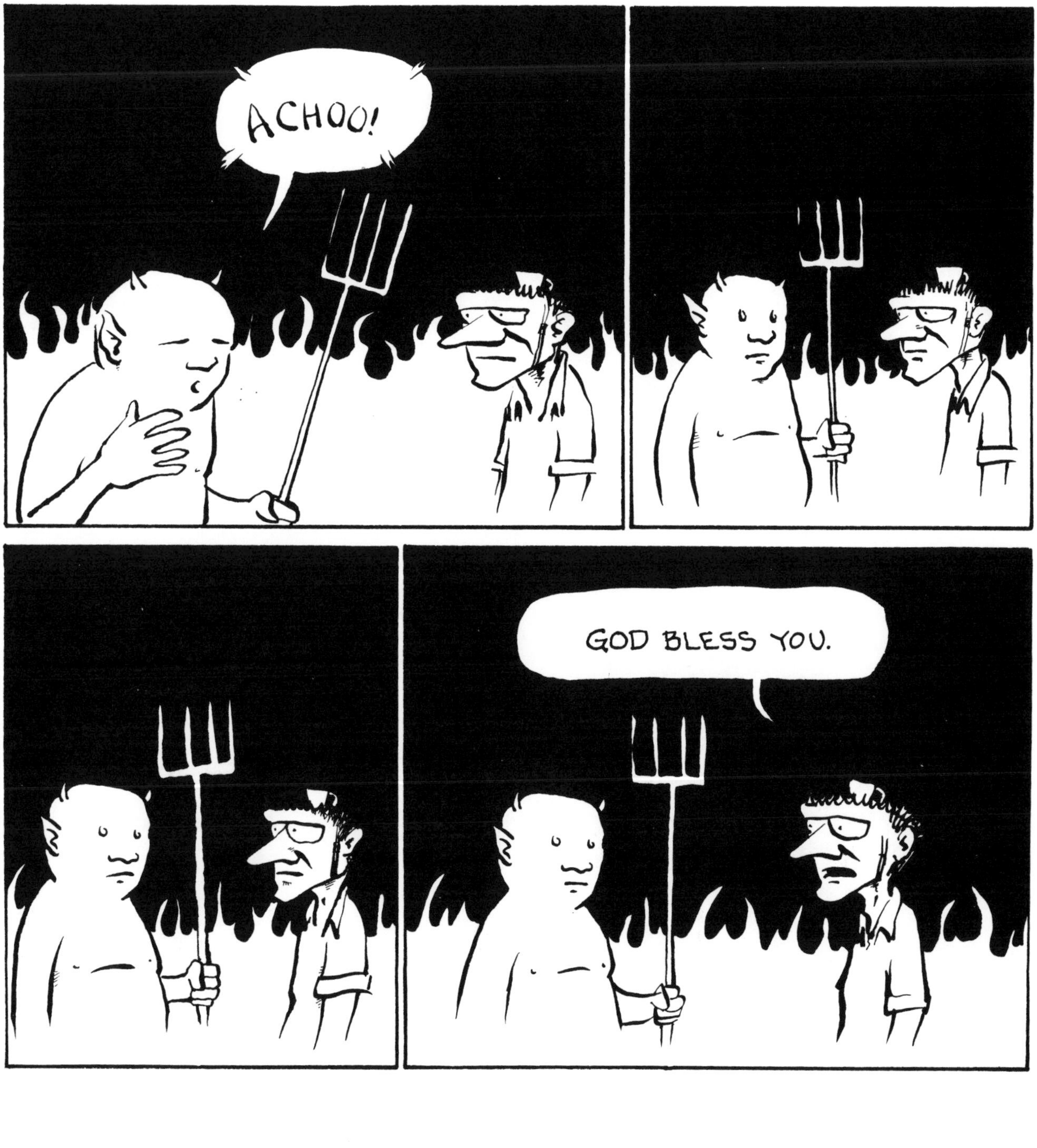
ACHOO!
GOD BLESS YOU.

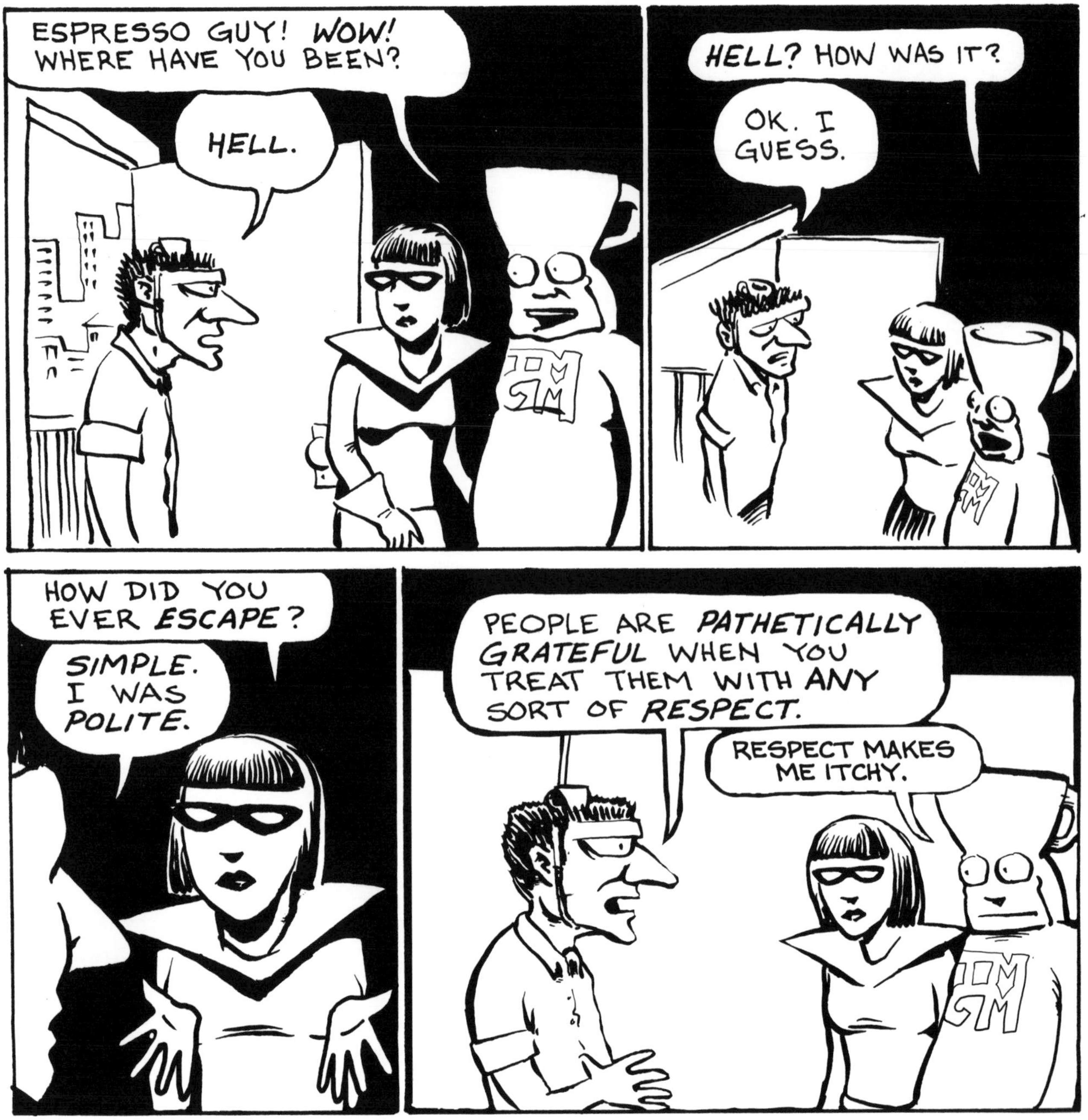
ESPRESSO GUY! WOW! WHERE HAVE YOU BEEN?
HELL.
HELL? HOW WAS IT?
OK. I GUESS.
HOW DID YOU EVER ESCAPE?
SIMPLE. I WAS POLITE.
PEOPLE ARE PATHETICALLY GRATEFUL WHEN YOU TREAT THEM WITH ANY SORT OF RESPECT.
RESPECT MAKES ME ITCHY.

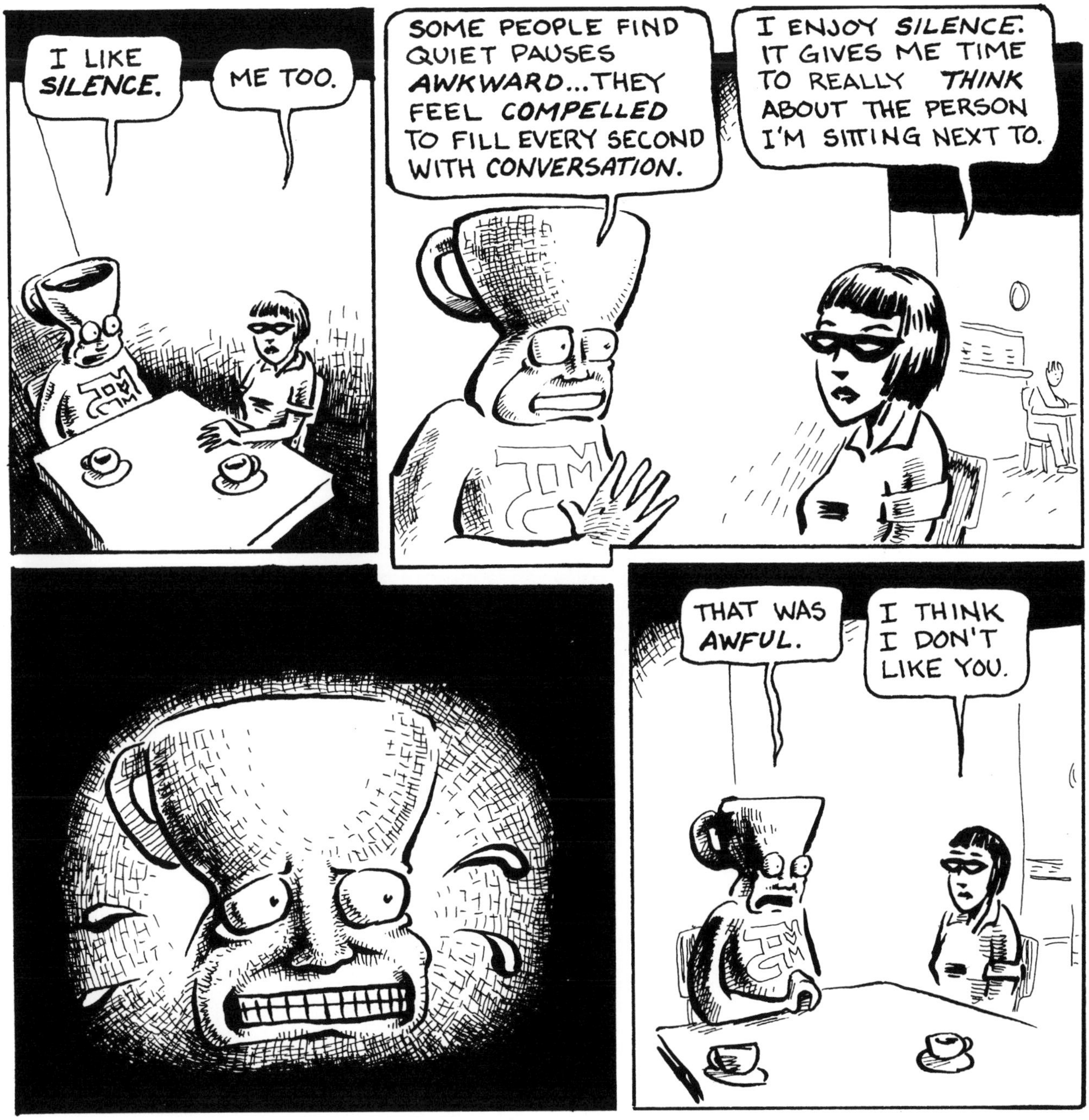
I LIKE SILENCE.
ME TOO.
SOME PEOPLE FIND QUIET PAUSES AWKWARD...THEY FEEL COMPELLED TO FILL EVERY SECOND WITH CONVERSATION.
I ENJOY SILENCE. IT GIVES ME TIME TO REALLY THINK ABOUT THE PERSON I'M SITTING NEXT TO.
THAT WAS AWFUL.
I THINK I DON'T LIKE YOU.

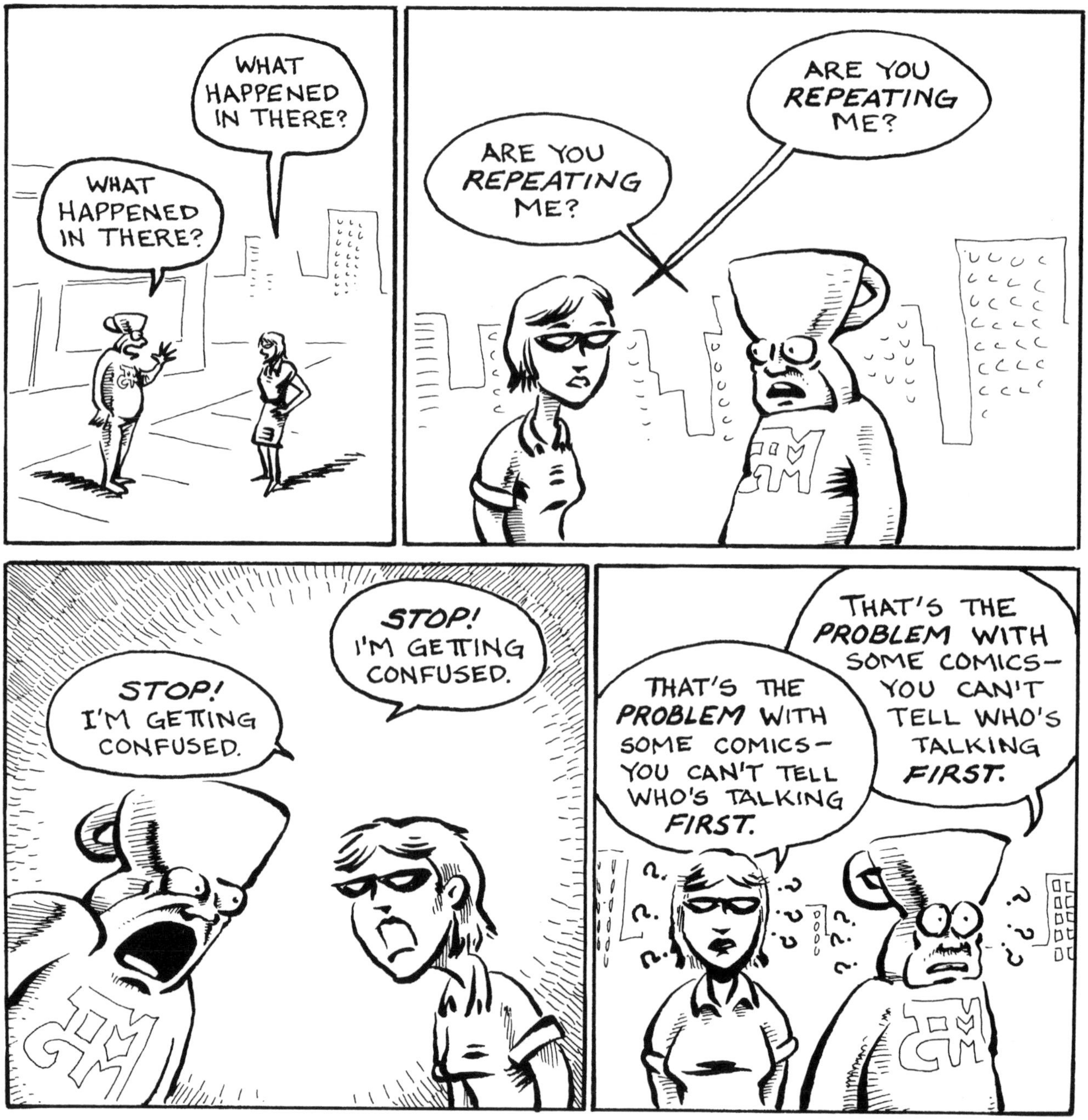
WHAT HAPPENED IN THERE?
WHAT HAPPENED IN THERE?
ARE YOU REPEATING ME?
ARE YOU REPEATING ME?
STOP! I'M GETTING CONFUSED.
STOP! I'M GETTING CONFUSED.
THAT'S THE PROBLEM WITH SOME COMICS- YOU CAN'T TELL WHO'S TALKING FIRST.
THAT'S THE PROBLEM WITH SOME COMICS- YOU CAN'T TELL WHO'S TALKING FIRST.

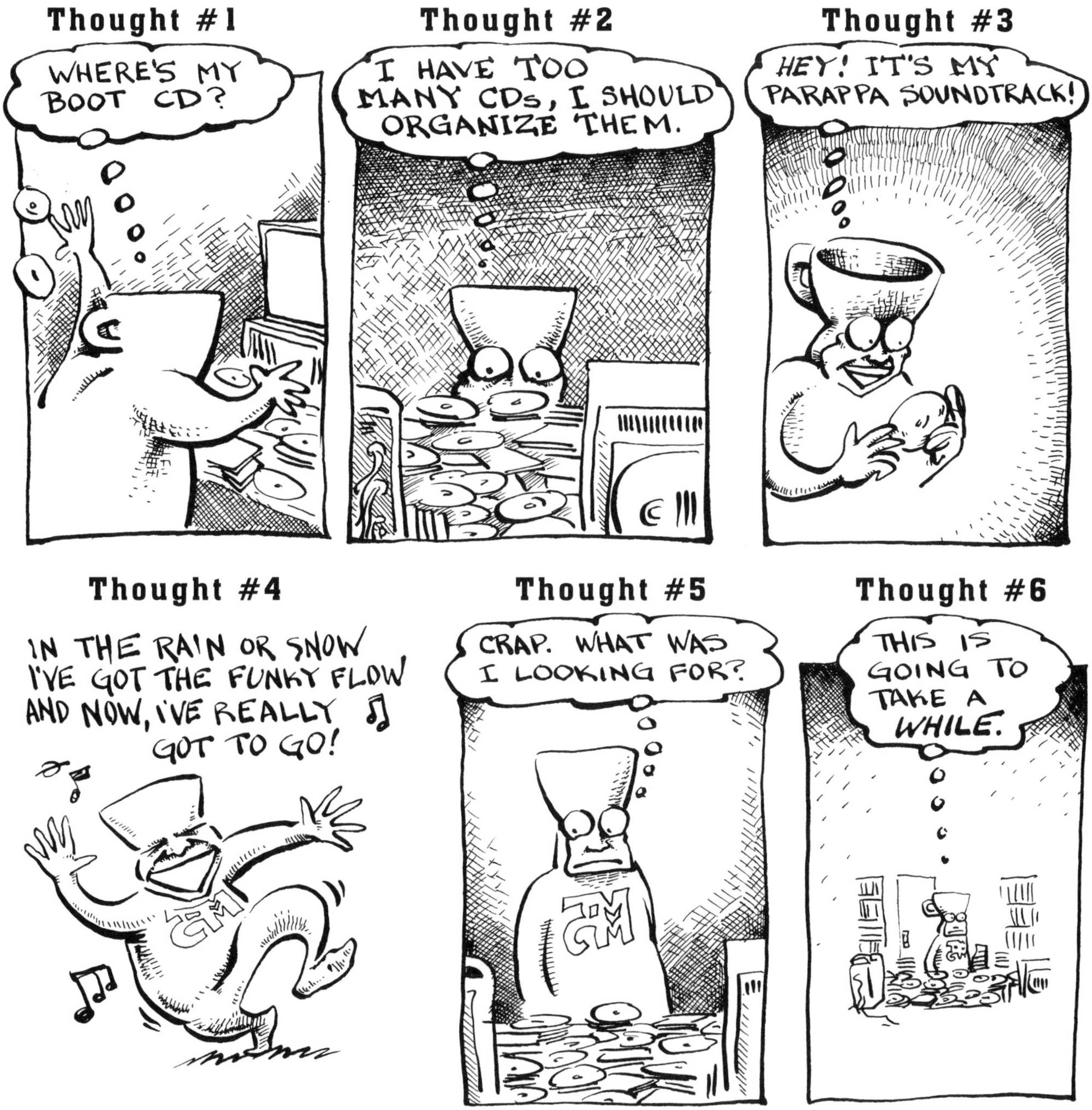
Thought #1
WHERE'S MY BOOT CD?
Thought #2
I HAVE TOO MANY CDs, I SHOULD ORGANIZE THEM.
Thought #3
HEY! IT'S MY PARAPPA SOUNDTRACK!
Thought #4
IN THE RAIN OR SNOW I'VE GOT THE FUNKY FLOW AND NOW, I'VE REALLY GOT TO GO!
Thought #5
CRAP. WHAT WAS I LOOKING FOR?
Thought #6
THIS IS GOING TO TAKE A WHILE.

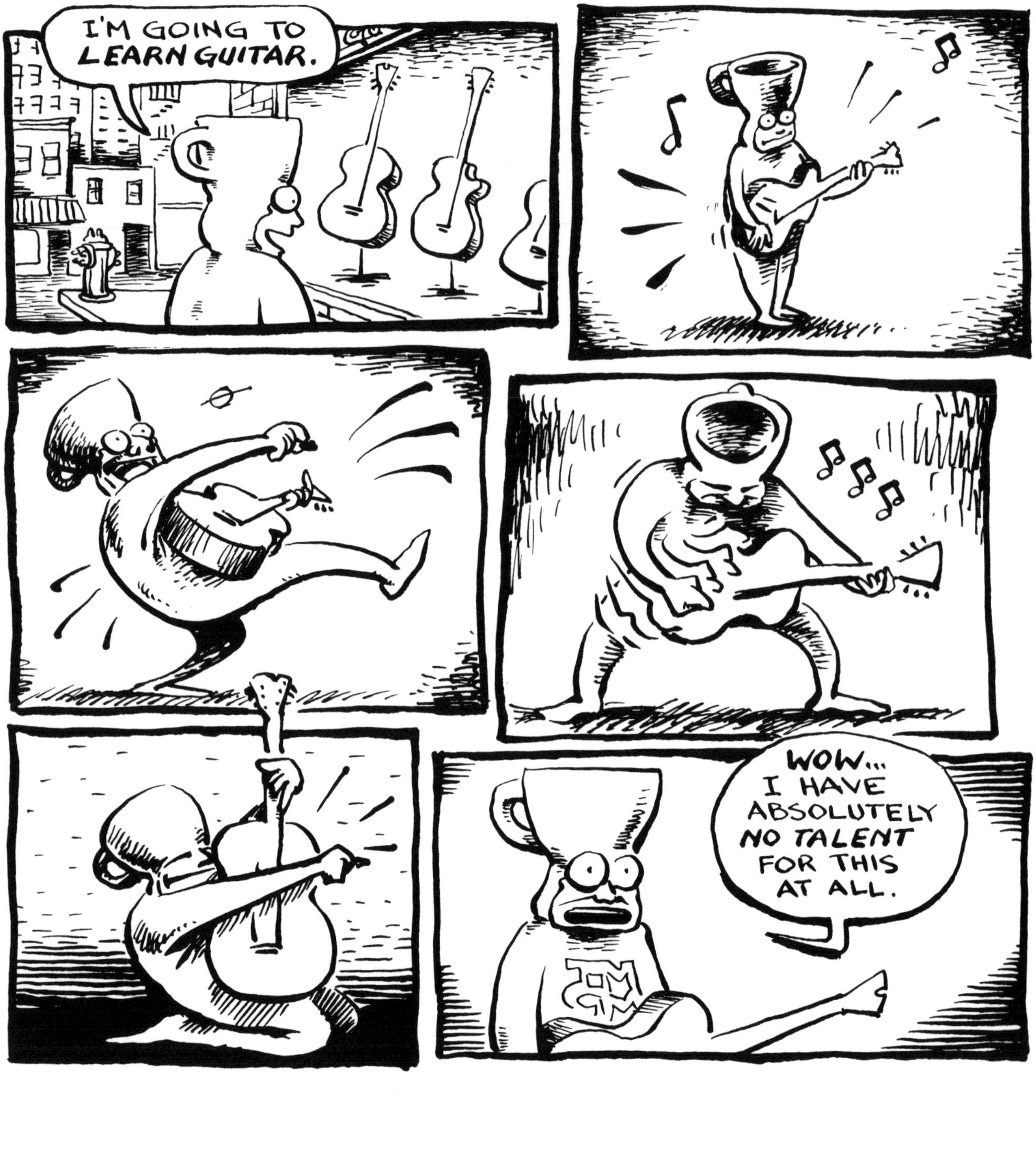
I'M GOING TO LEARN GUITAR.
WOW... I HAVE ABSOLUTELY NO TALENT FOR THIS AT ALL.

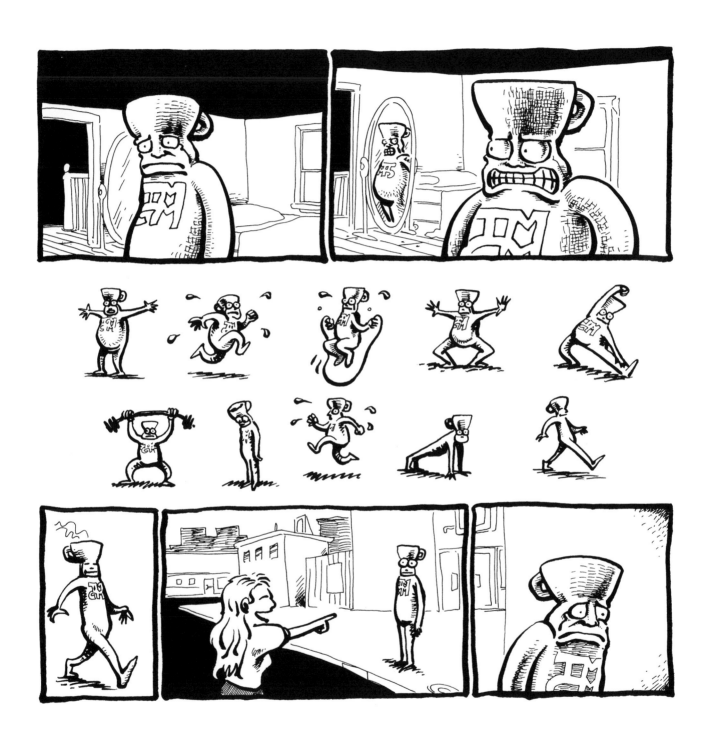

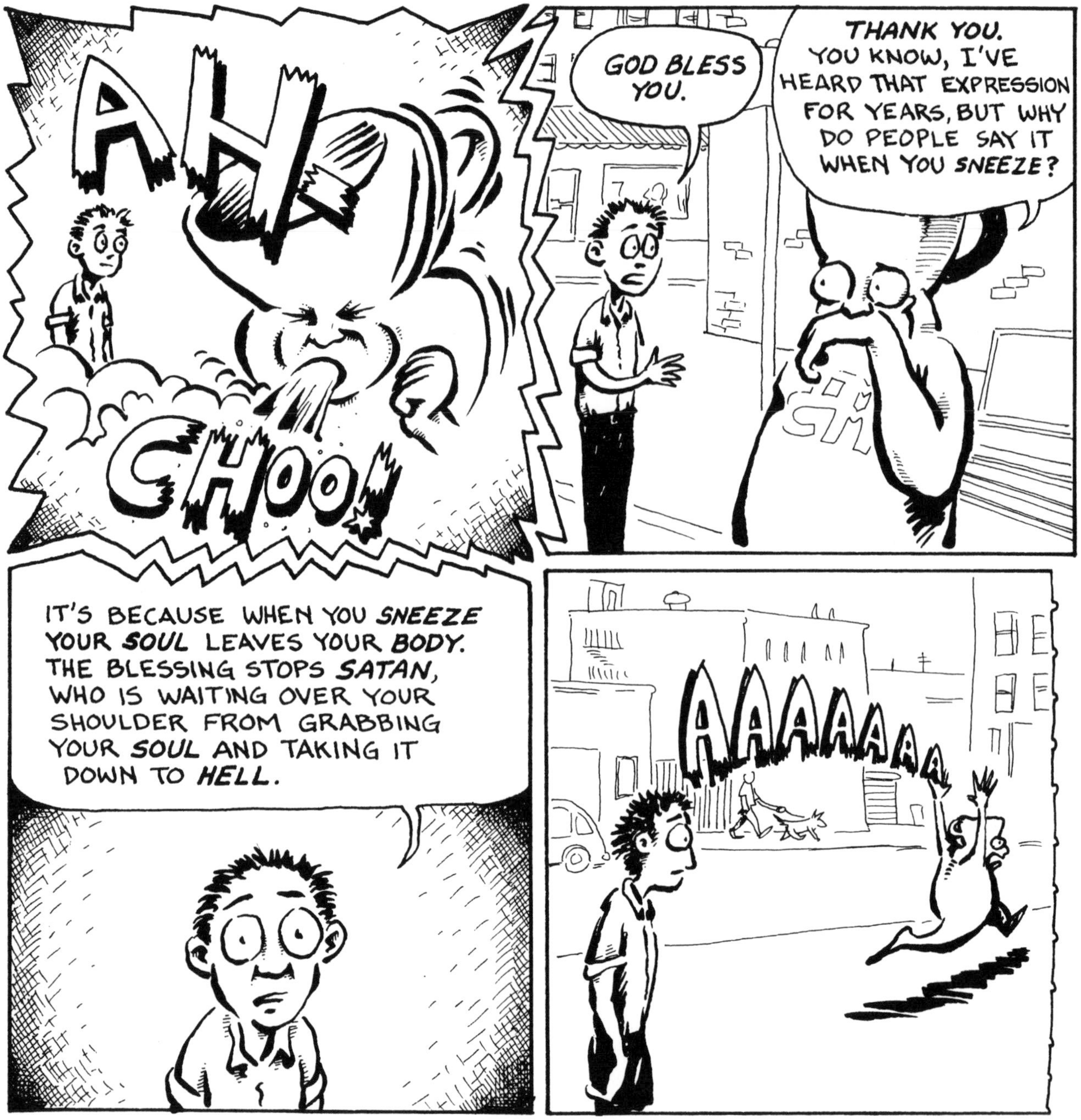
AH-
CHOO!
GOD BLESS YOU.
THANK YOU. YOU KNOW, I'VE HEARD THAT EXPRESSION FOR YEARS, BUT WHY DO PEOPLE SAY IT WHEN YOU SNEEZE?
IT'S BECAUSE WHEN YOU SNEEZE YOUR SOUL LEAVES YOUR BODY. THE BLESSING STOPS SATAN, WHO IS WAITING OVER YOUR SHOULDER FROM GRABBING YOUR SOUL AND TAKING IT DOWN TO HELL.
AAAAAAAA

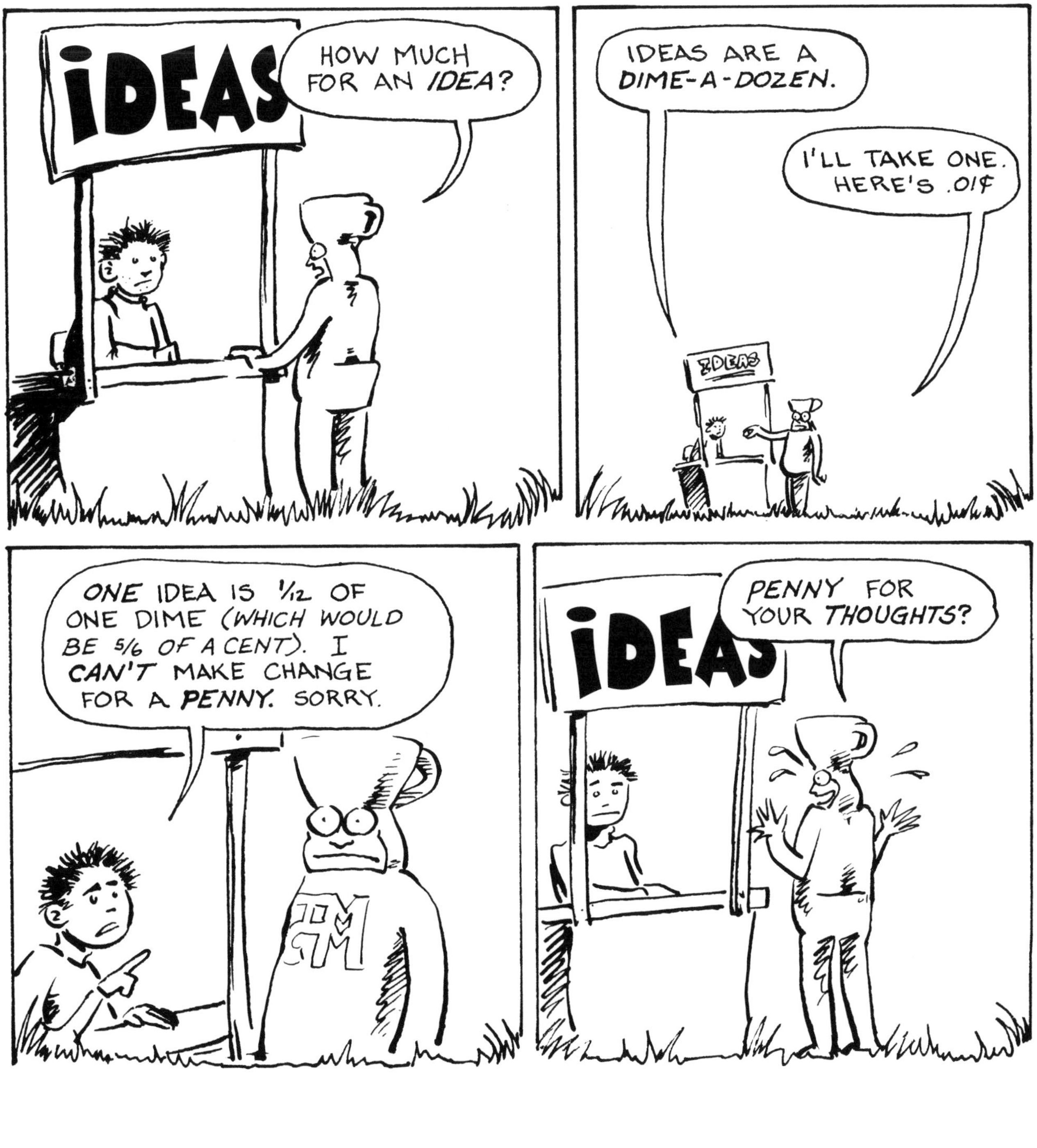
IDEAS
HOW MUCH FOR AN IDEA?
IDEAS ARE A DIME-A-DOZEN.
I'LL TAKE ONE. HERE'S .01¢
IDEAS
ONE IDEA IS 1/12 OF ONE DIME (WHICH WOULD BE 5/6 OF A CENT). I CAN'T MAKE CHANGE FOR A PENNY. SORRY.
IDEAS
PENNY FOR YOUR THOUGHTS?

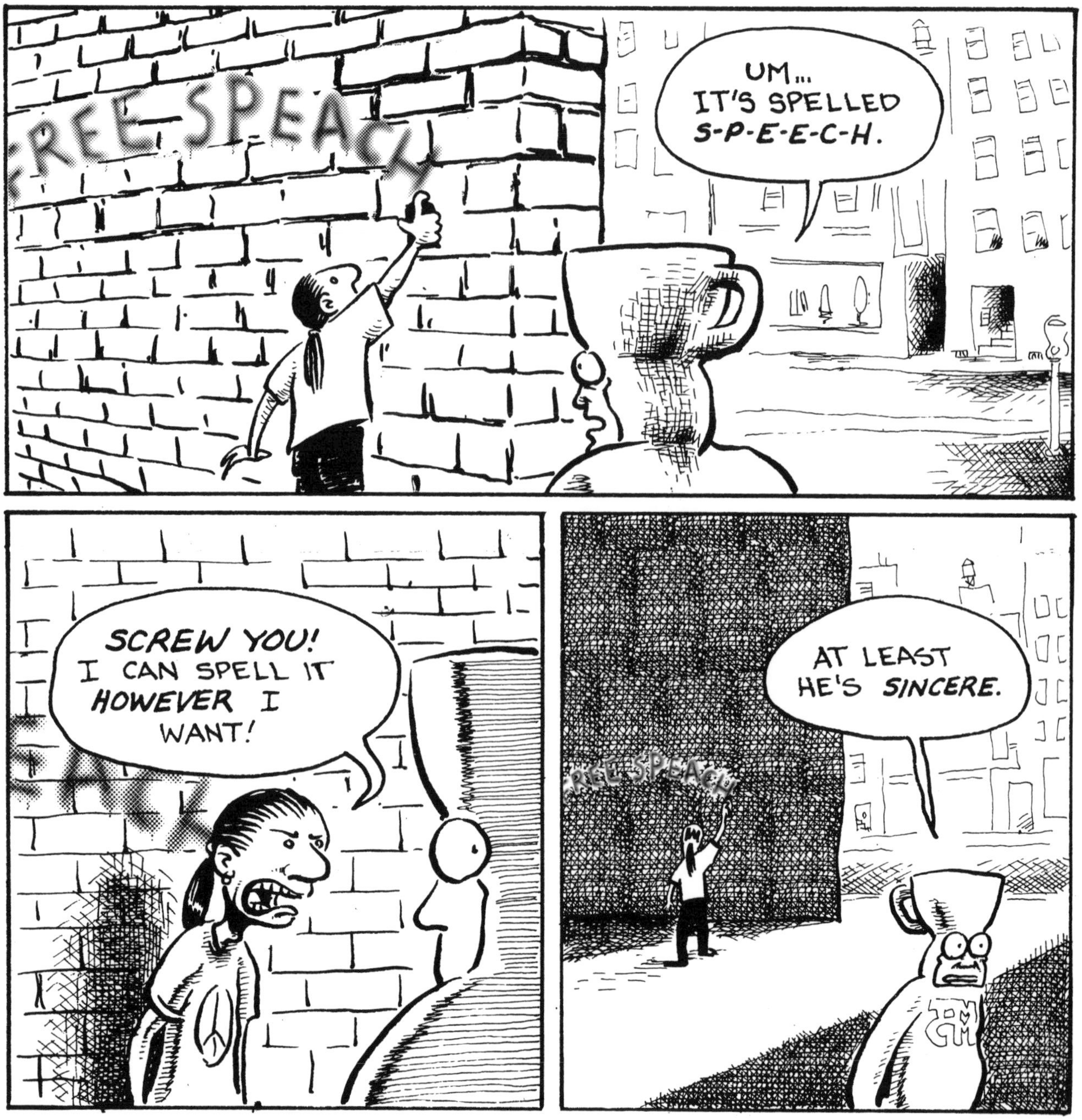
FREE SPEACH
UM... IT'S SPELLED S-P-E-E-C-H.
SCREW YOU! I CAN SPELL IT HOWEVER I WANT!
AT LEAST HE'S SINCERE.

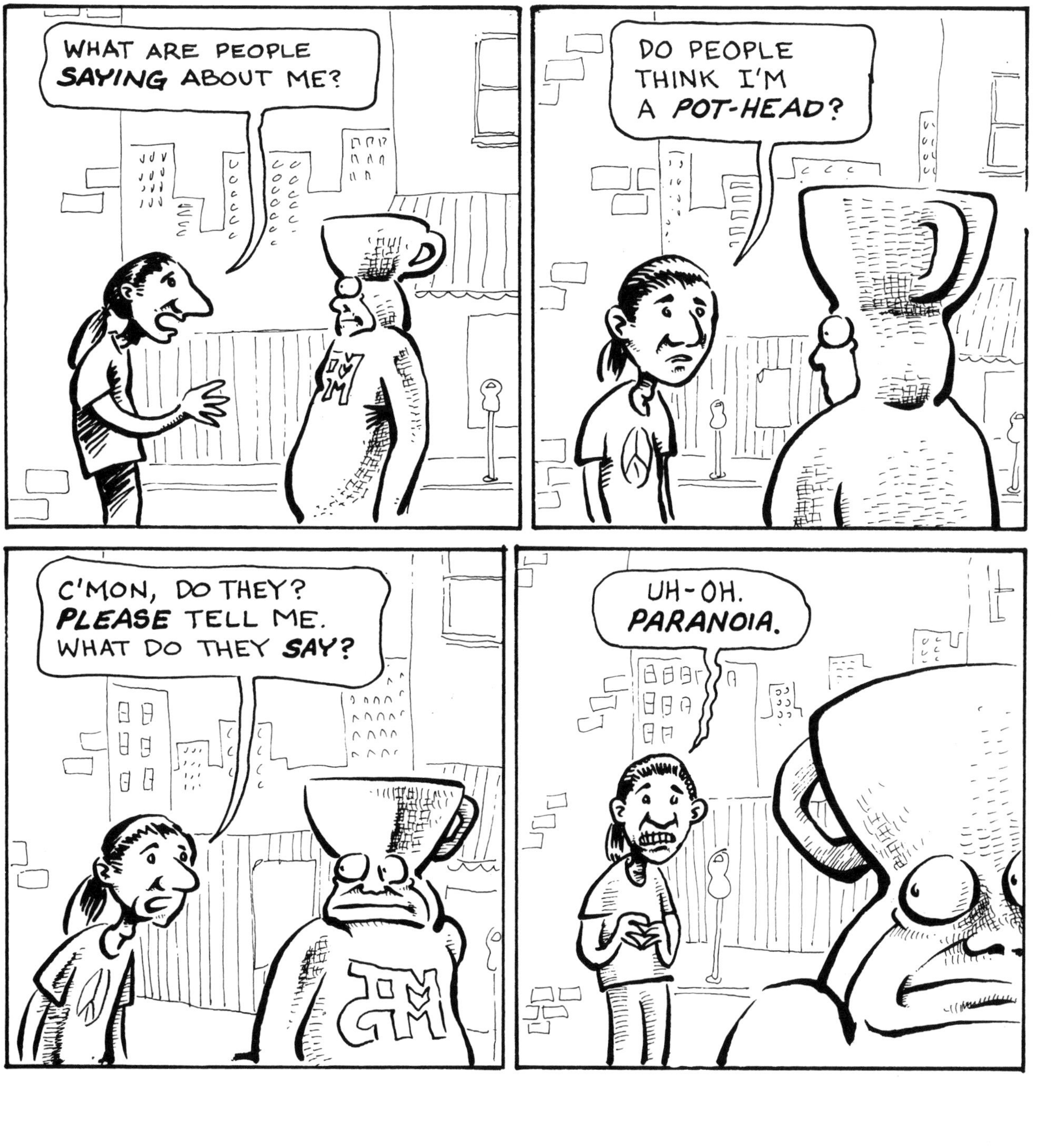
WHAT ARE PEOPLE SAYING ABOUT ME?
DO PEOPLE THINK I'M A POT-HEAD?
C'MON, DO THEY? PLEASE TELL ME. WHAT DO THEY SAY?
UH-OH. PARANOIA.

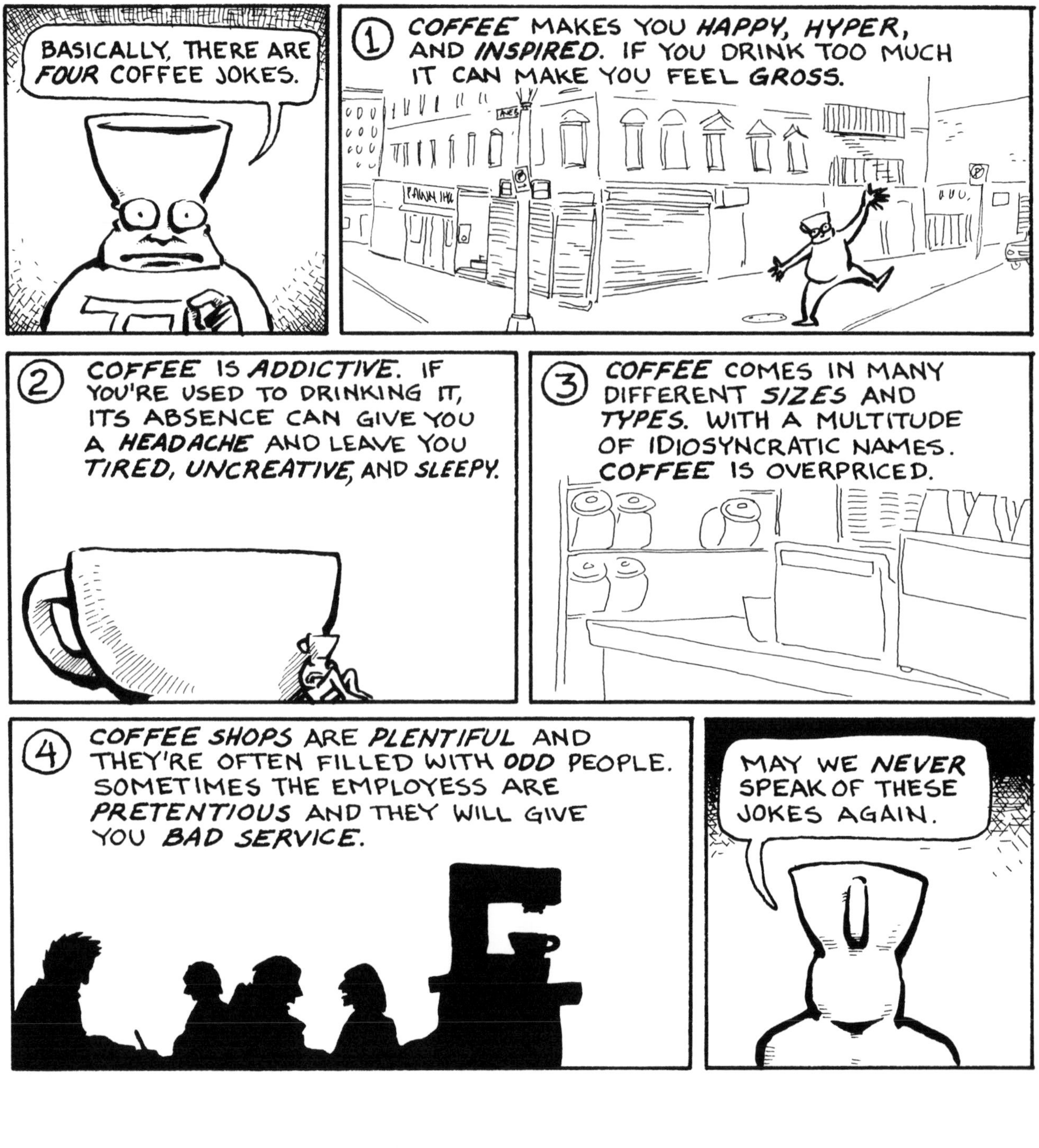
BASICALLY, THERE ARE FOUR COFFEE JOKES.
① COFFEE MAKES YOU HAPPY, HYPER, AND INSPIRED. IF YOU DRINK TOO MUCH IT CAN MAKE YOU FEEL GROSS.
② COFFEE IS ADDICTIVE. IF YOU'RE USED TO DRINKING IT, ITS ABSENCE CAN GIVE YOU A HEADACHE AND LEAVE YOU TIRED, UNCREATIVE, AND SLEEPY.
③ COFFEE COMES IN MANY DIFFERENT SIZES AND TYPES. WITH A MULTITUDE OF IDIOSYNCRATIC NAMES. COFFEE IS OVERPRICED.
④ COFFEE SHOPS ARE PLENTIFUL AND THEY'RE OFTEN FILLED WITH ODD PEOPLE. SOMETIMES THE EMPLOYESS ARE PRETENTIOUS AND THEY WILL GIVE YOU BAD SERVICE.
MAY WE NEVER SPEAK OF THESE JOKES AGAIN.

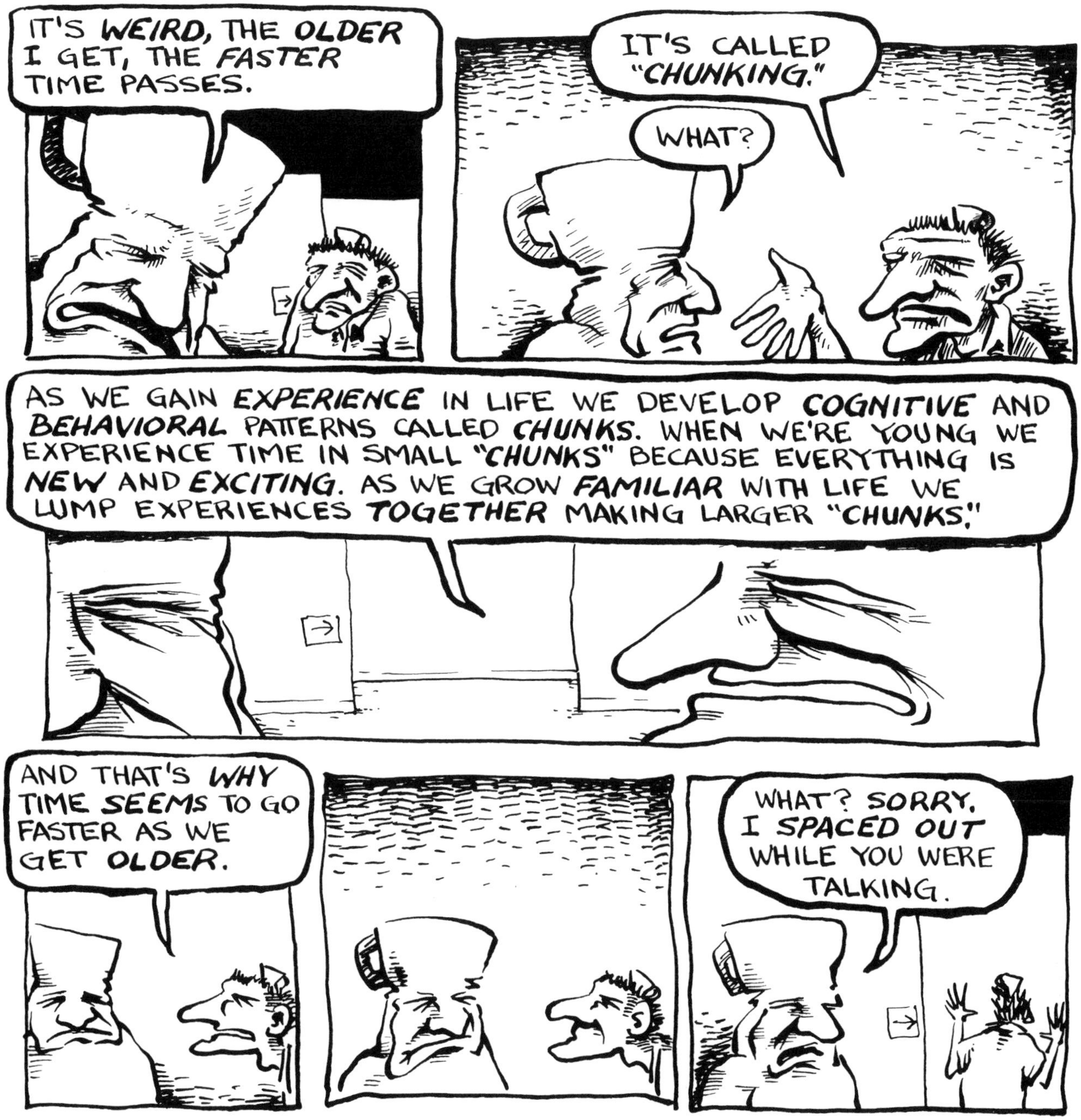
IT'S WEIRD, THE OLDER I GET, THE FASTER TIME PASSES.
IT'S CALLED "CHUNKING."
WHAT?
AS WE GAIN EXPERIENCE IN LIFE WE DEVELOP COGNITIVE AND BEHAVIORAL PATTERNS CALLED CHUNKS. WHEN WE'RE YOUNG WE EXPERIENCE TIME IN SMALL "CHUNKS" BECAUSE EVERYTHING IS NEW AND EXCITING. AS WE GROW FAMILIAR WITH LIFE WE LUMP EXPERIENCES TOGETHER MAKING LARGER "CHUNKS."
AND THAT'S WHY TIME SEEMS TO GO FASTER AS WE GET OLDER.
WHAT? SORRY. I SPACED OUT WHILE YOU WERE TALKING.

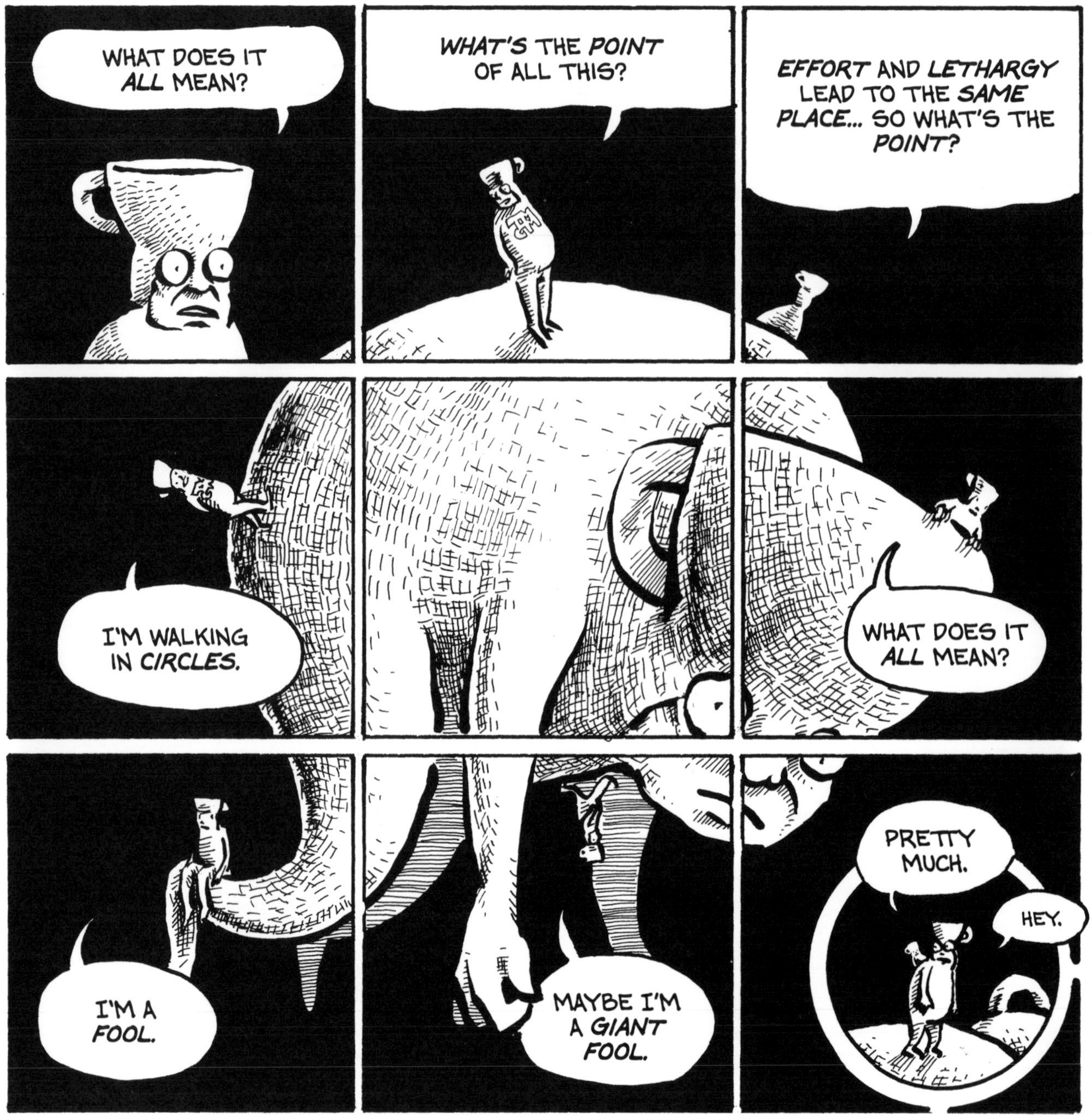
WHAT DOES IT ALL MEAN?
WHAT'S THE POINT OF ALL THIS?
EFFORT AND LETHARGY LEAD TO THE SAME PLACE... SO WHAT'S THE POINT?
I'M WALKING IN CIRCLES.
WHAT DOES IT ALL MEAN?
I'M A FOOL.
MAYBE I'M A GIANT FOOL.
PRETTY MUCH.
HEY.

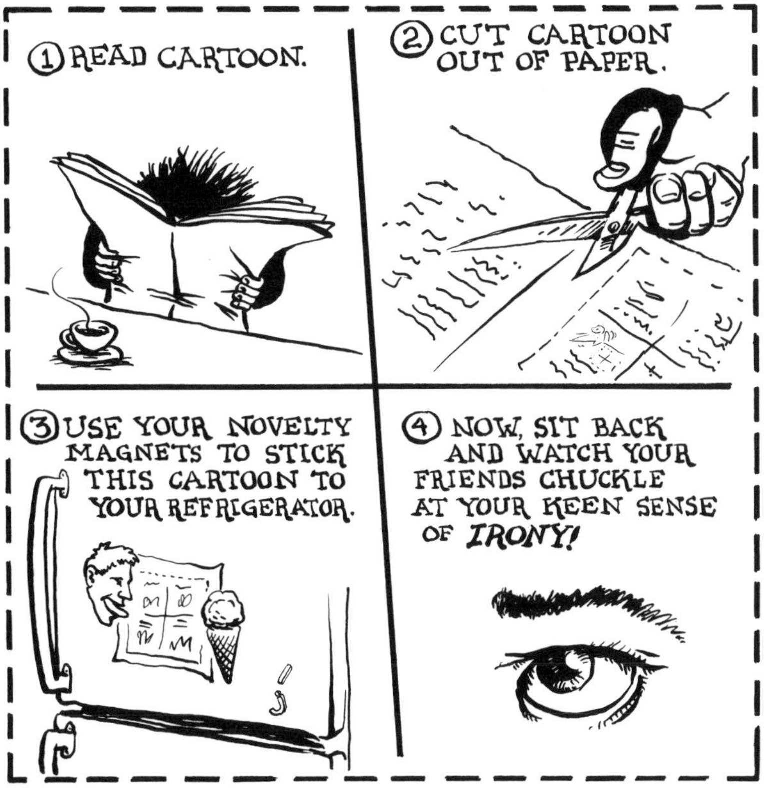

1 READ CARTOON.
2 CUT CARTOON OUT OF PAPER.
3 USE YOUR NOVELTY MAGNETS TO STICK THIS CARTOON TO YOUR REFRIGERATOR.
4 NOW, SIT BACK AND WATCH YOUR FRIENDS CHUCKLE AT YOUR KEEN SENSE OF IRONY!

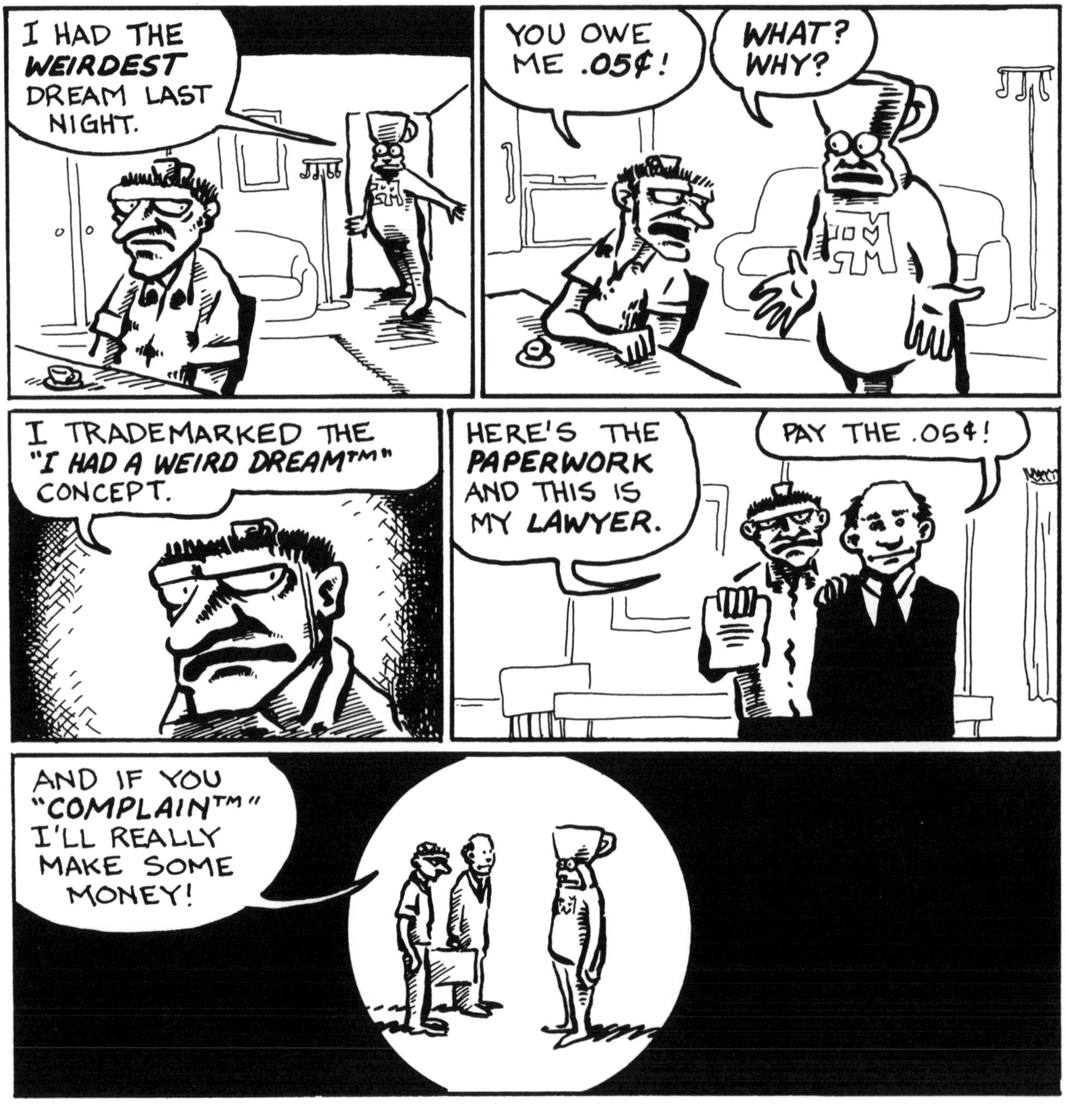
I HAD THE WEIRDEST DREAM LAST NIGHT.
YOU OWE ME .05¢!
WHAT? WHY?
I TRADEMARKED THE "I HAD A WEIRD DREAM™" CONCEPT.
HERE'S THE PAPERWORK AND THIS IS MY LAWYER.
PAY THE .05¢!
AND IF YOU "COMPLAIN™" I'LL REALLY MAKE SOME MONEY!

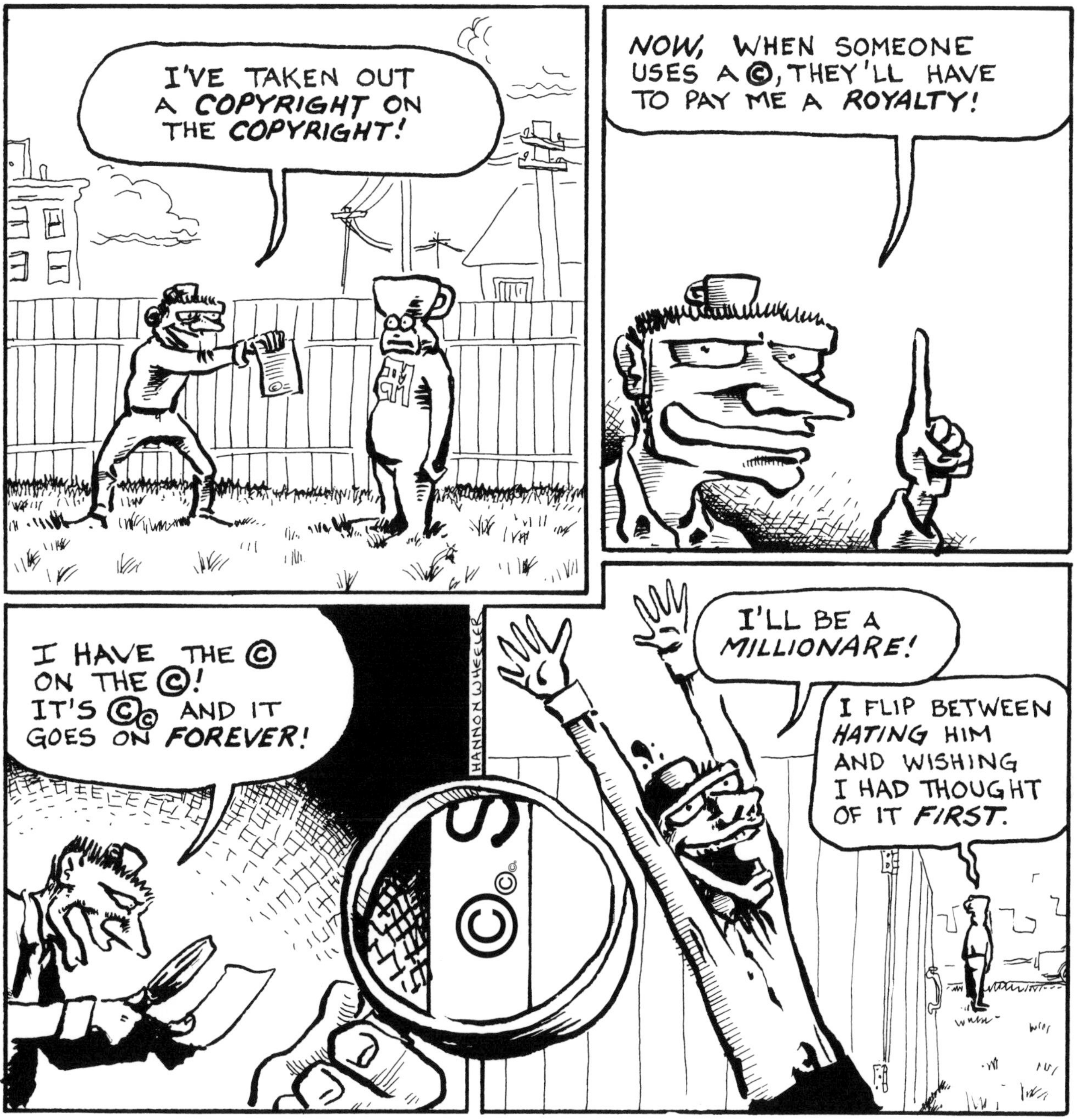
I'VE TAKEN OUT A COPYRIGHT ON THE COPYRIGHT!
NOW, WHEN SOMEONE USES A ©, THEY'LL HAVE TO PAY ME A ROYALTY!
I HAVE THE © ON THE ©! IT'S ©© AND IT GOES ON FOREVER!
HANNON WHEELER
I'LL BE A MILLIONARE!
I FLIP BETWEEN HATING HIM AND WISHING I HAD THOUGHT OF IT FIRST.

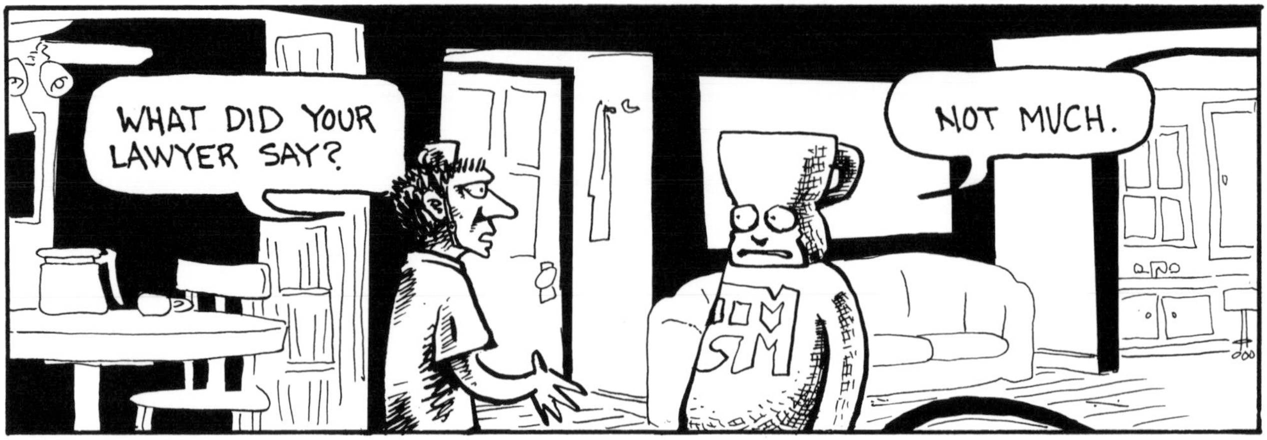
WHAT DID YOUR LAWYER SAY?
NOT MUCH.

This is an agreement between you, hereafter known as the 'reader,' and the creator of this cartoon, hereafter known as the 'creator.' This agreement is binding and non-negotiable except in cases where negotiation has been agreed upon; thereupon new binding and non-negotiable agreements shall replace all previous binding non-negotiable agreements.

This agreement is is a legal document; read it carefully before reading the above cartoon. By reading the cartoon, you are agreeing to the terms and conditions of this agreement regardless of whether you read this agreement or not.

The humor of this cartoon, hereafter known as the 'joke,' will be gotten and understood by some, but not by others. The scope of the contract shall extend to those who get the joke in addition to those who do not get the joke. The getting of the joke does not in any way affect the influence and acceptance of the contract.

The extent of this contract shall include all media known and unknown. The unknown media is assumed to become known at some time, but may remain unknown. The contract shall include the past, present, and future. The present shall heretofore be known as 'now.'

The cartoon may be described to a third party, as long as the complete and unaltered agreement is also described and agreed to. The agreement to the contract by a third party, heretofore known as an 'audience,' is implicitly agreed to by the description of the cartoon, either in concept, a literal description, or a shared viewing. The contract will be in effect with the audience regardless of whether or not the joke and humor is understood.

This contract constitutes a license and not a sale. The ownership, both in abstract and in realization resides solely with the creator, except for agreements whereas future ownerships may constitute a new ownership, thus preceding and superceding any previous ownership and may be regarded as ownership.

You must comply with all applicable laws regarding the reading of this cartoon. Limitation of liability is notwithstanding any damages that might incur for any reason whatsoever, including, without limitation, all damages, explicit or implicit. There is no warranty given, or implied, by this cartoon or the concept, idea, or joke of this cartoon.

This license is effective until terminated.

SCREW HEAVEN, WHEN I DIE I'M GOING TO MARS

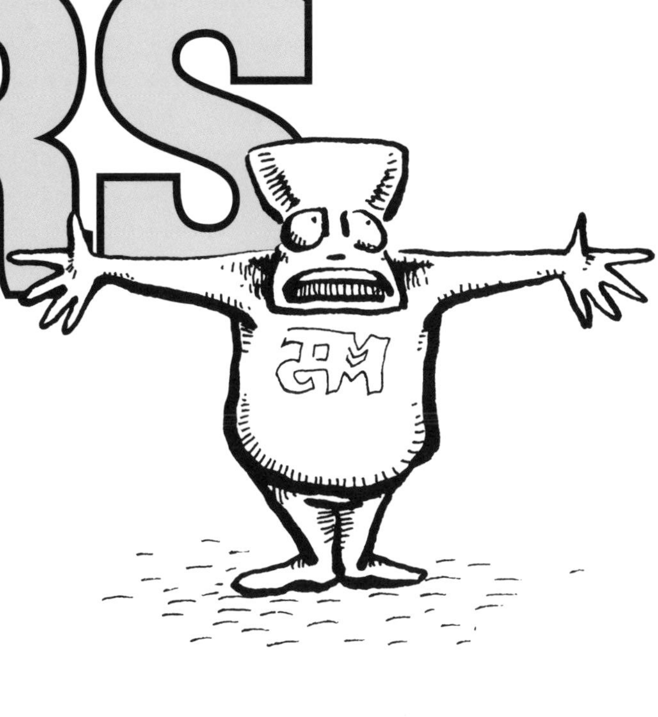

SCREW HEAVEN, WHEN I DIE I'M GOING TO MARS INTRODUCTION

by Jesse Michaels

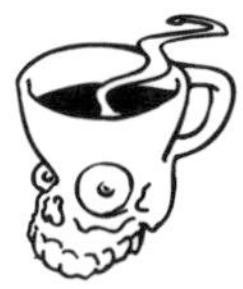

Shannon Wheeler is an iconic independent cartoonist, one whose work transcends its medium. In fact, his work could be said to traverse the same territory as fine art. It *could* be said, but it probably shouldn't.

Not that it isn't true—the lyricism found in the best of Wheeler's output is every bit as deep as much of what is cast as fine art these days—but the whole point of comics is to talk to people in plain language, to communicate to them in their own world rather than ask them to step into a gallery.

Shannon began doing *Too Much Coffee Man* in 1992. He was living in Austin, Texas, and like many of his artistically tempered peers in their twenties he spent a lot of time in coffee shops. The series began as a natural response to that environment—a short-comics parody of people in coffee shops grinding away at their pet creative projects such as drawing short-comic parodies. In fact the self-exposing irony just described is one of the things that fuels *Too Much Coffee Man*: a satirical eye cast on the human scene softened by hilarious reversals in which the joke is suddenly on the narrator. The subject matter of *TMCM* quickly expanded to skewer nationalism, relationships, television, the superhero archetype, copyright law, white chocolate, and to-do lists but never stopped turning the lens onto the author's own foibles. This approach worked and the strip soon became a full-fledged and highly successful comic book. But it also took a subtle philosophical stance: The reader was invited to laugh out loud at the absurdity of the world at large but was also reminded that if they never looked in the mirror they were missing the really funny stuff. Oh yeah, there were some jokes about coffee too.

About a decade after doing his first strip in Austin, Shannon Wheeler's comics began to undergo an evolution which was spearheaded by the introduction of a new strip called *How to Be Happy*. Historically speaking, a comics artist's job is to come up with jokes. This has many variants such as the first-panel teaser joke, the multiple-strip thematic joke, the incomprehensible joke which is played on the reader, the joke which is funny to half the population and violently irritating to the other half, etc. Every comic artist worth his lettering brush uses them all. However, the best cartoonists, real maestros such as George Herriman, Walt Kelly, and Berkeley Breathed (*Krazy Kat*, *Pogo*, and *Bloom County*/*Outland*), reach a stage in which they become less *punch line* oriented. The humor is still in full force but allowed to merge with the story and ideas rather than always enlisting those elements into the service of a payoff gag. This phase of writing in Wheeler's work is represented by the current volume. While never far from the manic energy of the earlier comics and while still very funny, *Screw Heaven, When I Die I'm Going to Mars* draws the reader into a world of observation that goes farther and deeper than past forays. In this collection of one-page strips Shannon scrutinizes many familiar *TMCM* themes such as modern urban life and brooding self-doubt but also plunges into broad, new territories such as religion, money, and my favorites: autobiographical strips which reveal the author's personal world to a greater extent than ever before.

Too Much Coffee Man himself is in attendance with his friends in tow—each with their highly questionable superhero abilities (umm . . . what is it exactly that Underwater Guy, the Mystery Girl, and Television Man *do*?)—and the catalog rounds off with a hilarious, strikingly confessional vignette about Shannon's detour as an architecture major.

If you are new to the work you couldn't start with a better book and if you are a veteran you are probably tearing through this introduction to get to the good stuff. In deference to both crowds I will wrap this up but I wanted to share a final anecdote.

I was thirteen or so when I first met Shannon in Berkeley, California. He was a friend of my older brother's and we all shared an interest in comic books. Each of us spent *all* of his spare time obsessively scratching away in sketchbooks, often competing to see who could come up with the most ridiculous drawing (one I remember featured Bruce Springsteen being chased through New Jersey by a urinal holding a Bible—I don't remember the joke). One day I was looking at Shannon's stuff and I realized what the element was that made it stand out from everybody else's. I had always thought it was his command of cross-hatching, which was already well developed when he was a teenager, but on this particular afternoon I realized that it wasn't the shading at all. It was the *facial expressions*. Every character, every depiction was always striking and always funny. How did he do it? I privately wondered if he would always be able to or if he would eventually lose his sense of humor like most grownups I knew.

About twenty-five years later I was sitting at one of the six or seven thousand cafés in Berkeley. I had long been out of touch with Shannon and that earlier period of life was the farthest thing from my mind. I've always been curious about what the new generation of artistically oriented outsiders is up to so I glanced over the shoulder of an over-caffeinated-looking kid sitting at a table next to mine. He was reading a magazine with a comic strip in it. Instantly the style of the drawings transported me outside of time and into Shannon's milieu before I even identified the strip as being one of his. The doorway was the very same crazed, neurotic facial expressions I had recognized so many years earlier, their potency and humor undiminished by the couple decades of relationships, utility bills, and broken shoelaces their creator had endured. I suddenly felt the exact same rush of aesthetic joy and humor that I had experienced as a teenager. This is the great magic trick of art—to slip outside of time, outside of logic, outside of the very banality of the things being depicted and into a stream of meaning that once seen is never forgotten. Shannon Wheeler pulls off this sleight of hand as well as anybody and in a way that speaks to people in their own language.

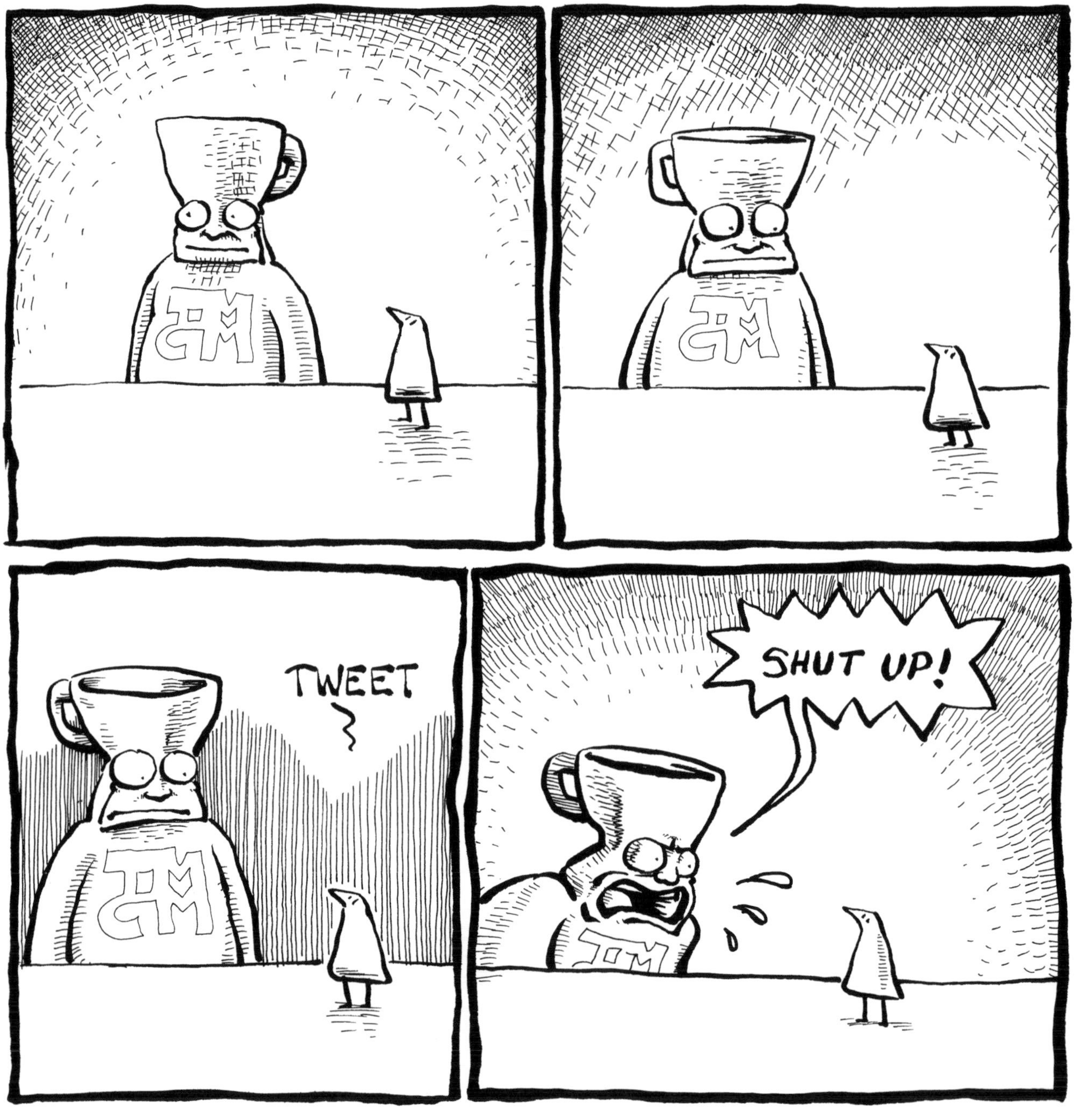
TWEET
SHUT UP!

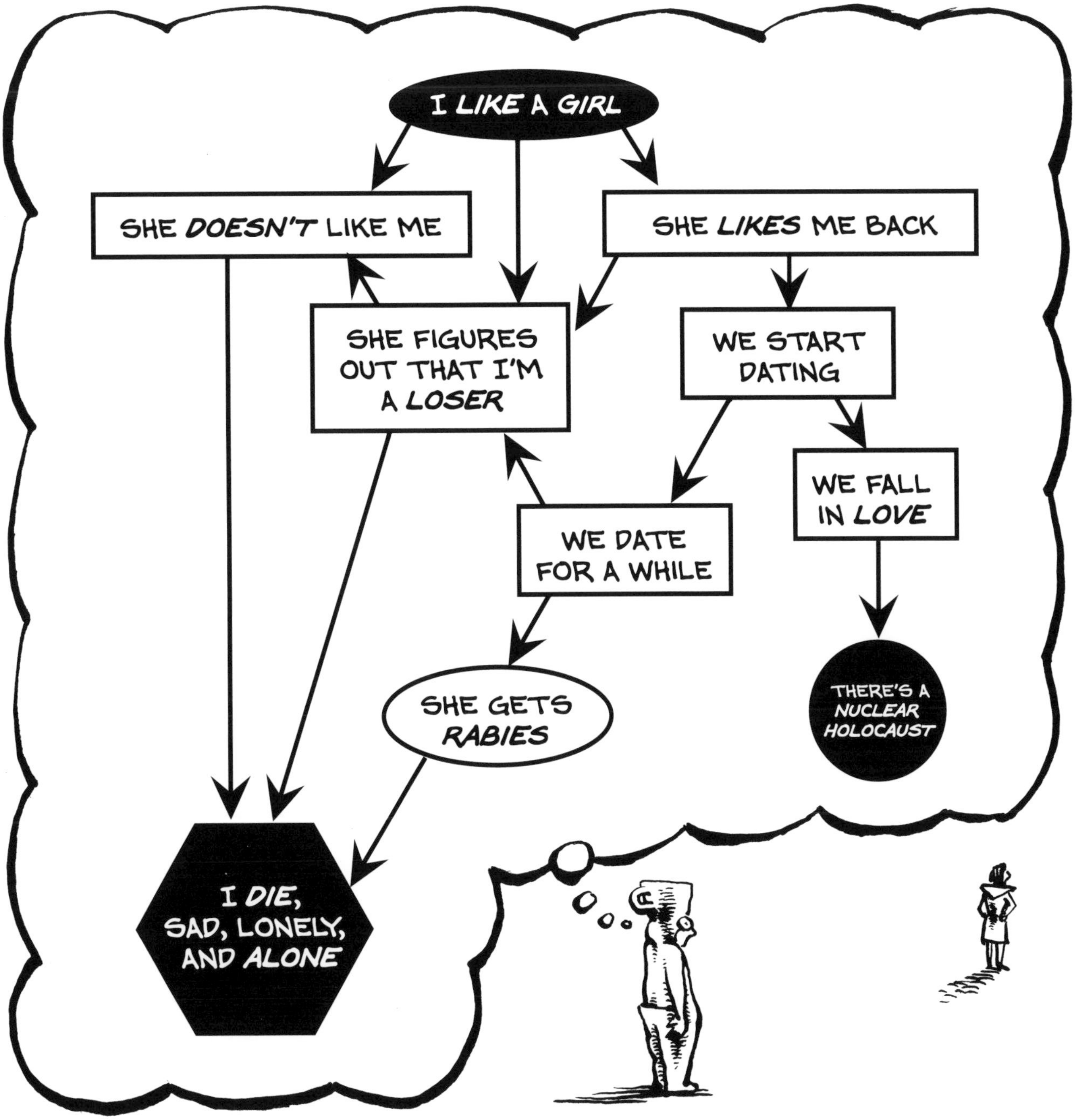
I LIKE A GIRL
SHE DOESN'T LIKE ME
SHE LIKES ME BACK
SHE FIGURES OUT THAT I'M A LOSER
WE START DATING
WE FALL IN LOVE
WE DATE FOR A WHILE
SHE GETS RABIES
THERE'S A NUCLEAR HOLOCAUST
I DIE, SAD, LONELY, AND ALONE

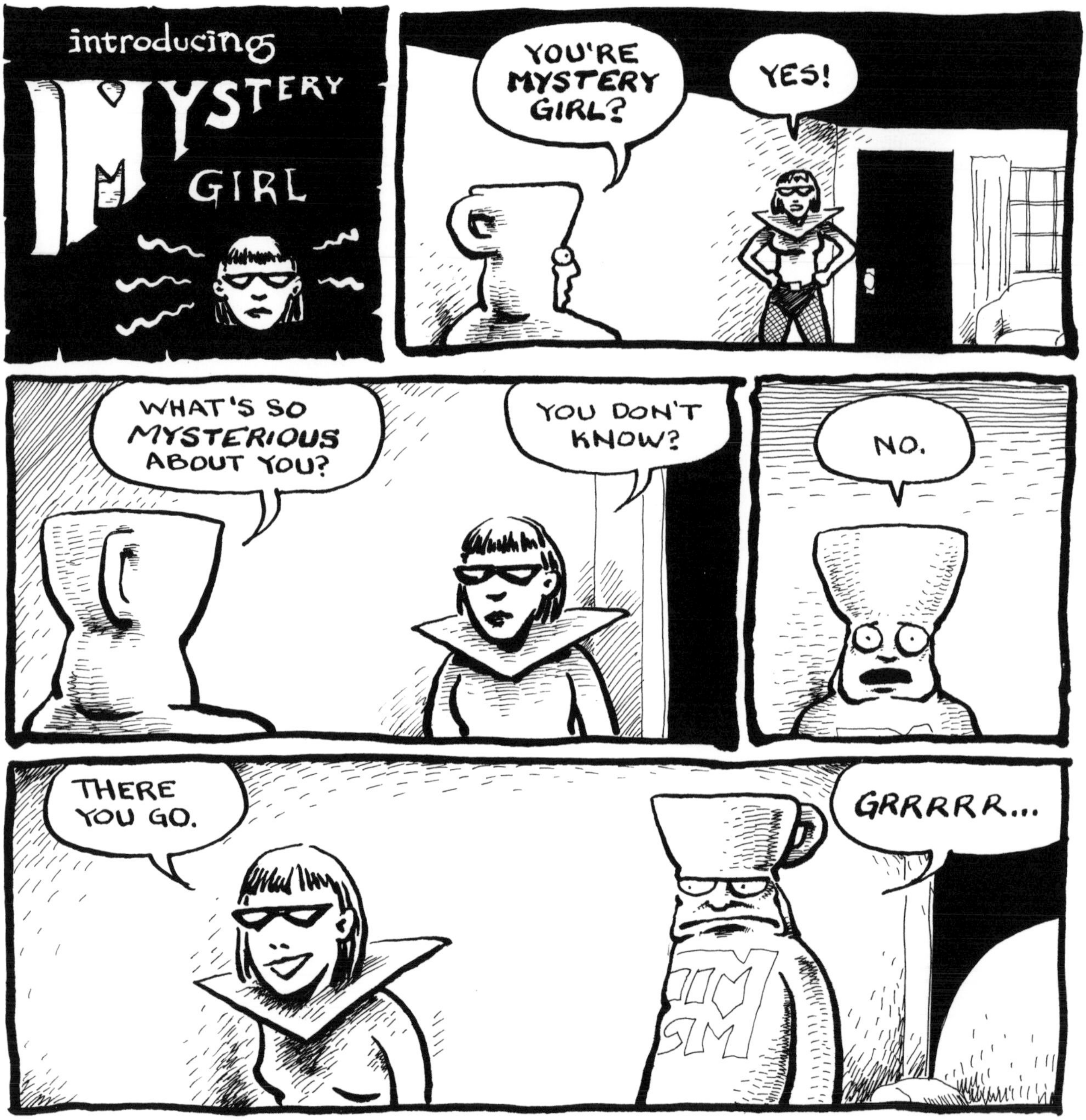
introducing
MYSTERY GIRL
YOU'RE MYSTERY GIRL?
YES!
WHAT'S SO MYSTERIOUS ABOUT YOU?
YOU DON'T KNOW?
NO.
THERE YOU GO.
GRRRRR...

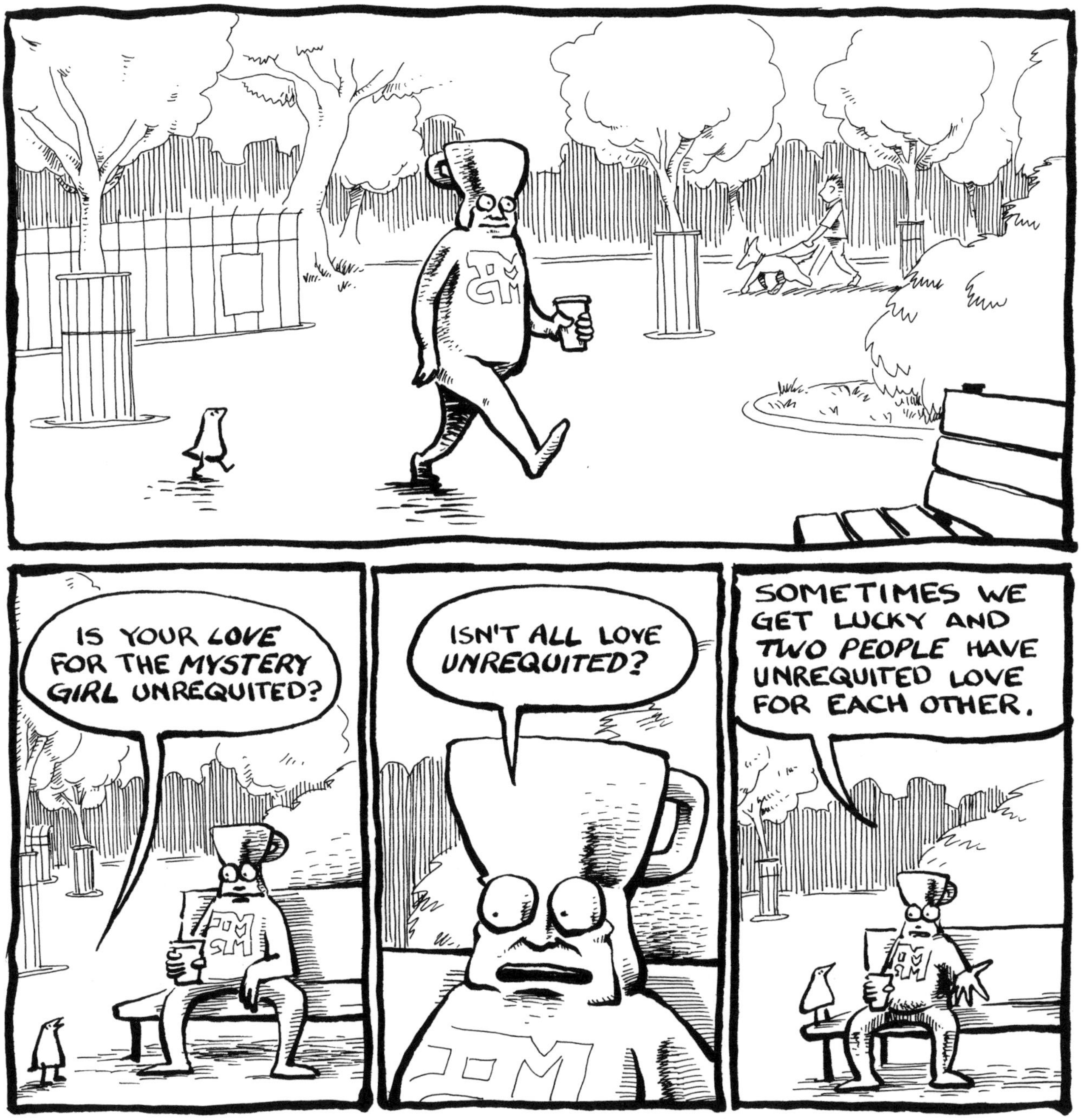
IS YOUR LOVE FOR THE MYSTERY GIRL UNREQUITED?
ISN'T ALL LOVE UNREQUITED?
SOMETIMES WE GET LUCKY AND TWO PEOPLE HAVE UNREQUITED LOVE FOR EACH OTHER.

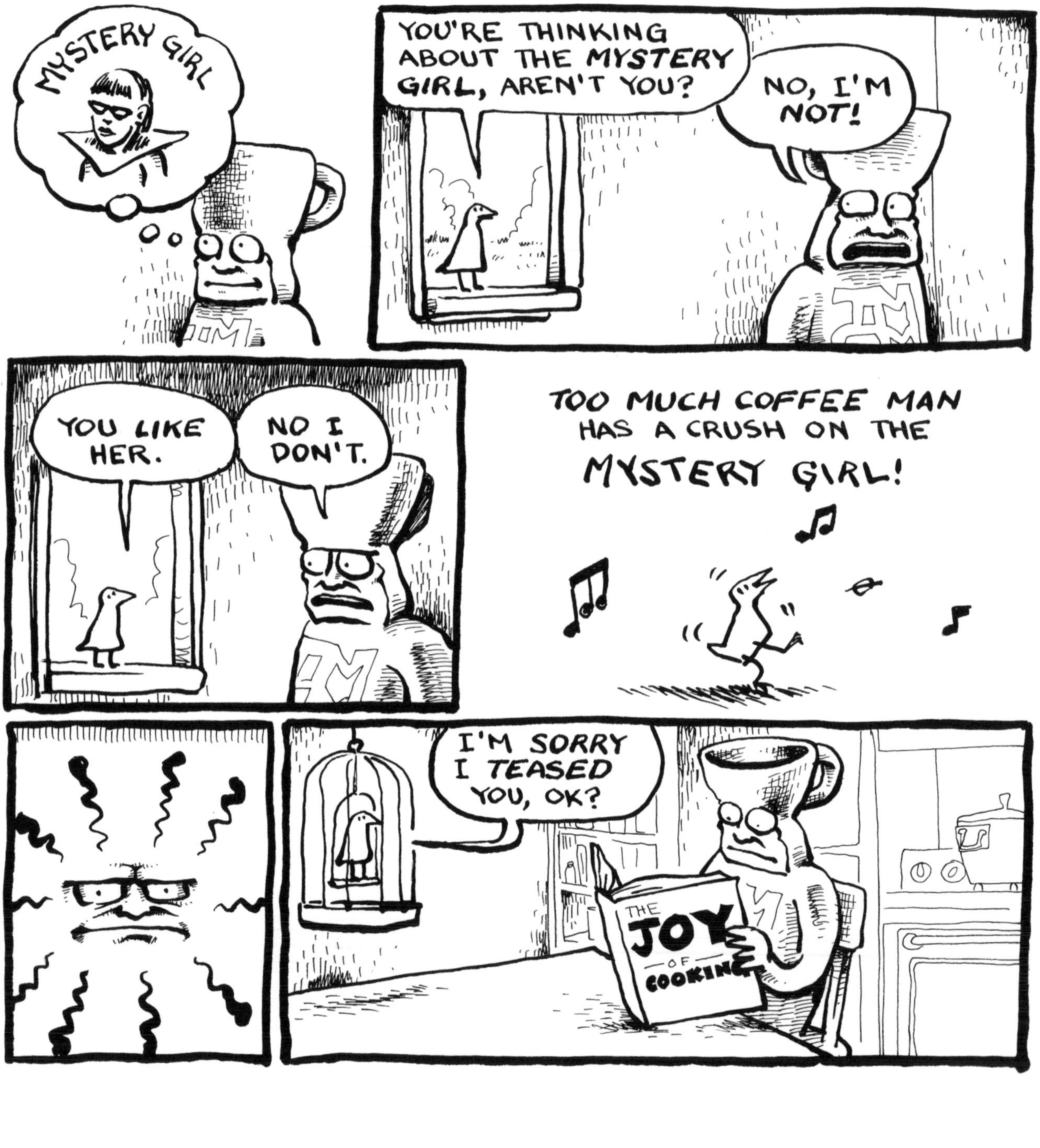
MYSTERY GIRL
YOU'RE THINKING ABOUT THE MYSTERY GIRL, AREN'T YOU?
NO, I'M NOT!
YOU LIKE HER.
NO I DON'T.
TOO MUCH COFFEE MAN HAS A CRUSH ON THE MYSTERY GIRL!
I'M SORRY I TEASED YOU, OK?
THE JOY OF COOKING

TOO MUCH COFFEE MAN'S
Romantic History
I LOVE YOU.
I'LL LOVE YOU AS LONG AS YOU DON'T LOVE ME
BIOLOGICAL CLOCK
DESPAEA NEED FOR APPRO
EX-BOY-FRIENDS
UNREALISTIC EXPECTATIONS
UNRESOLVED FATHER ISSUES
YOU'RE JUST NOT MY TYPE.
U
T
FONT HUMOR
I WOULD GO OUT WITH YOU, BUT I'M ALREADY SEEING SOMEONE ELSE.
WHY AREN'T YOU CHASING ME?
IT'S NOT YOU, IT'S ME.
IT'S MY AUTOBIOGRAPHICAL COMIC BOOK.
WOW. YOUR LIFE IS REALLY BORING.

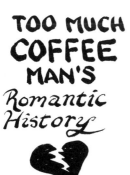

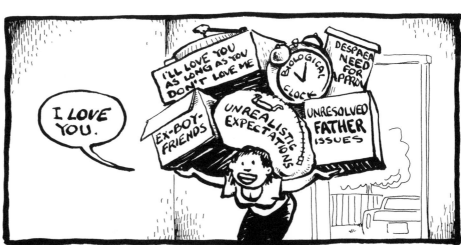

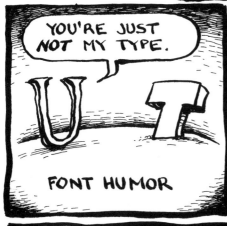

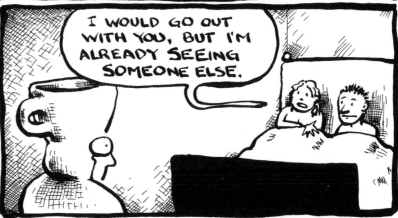

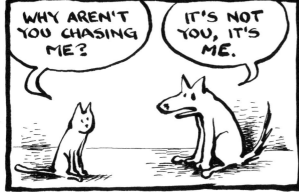

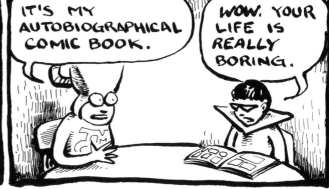

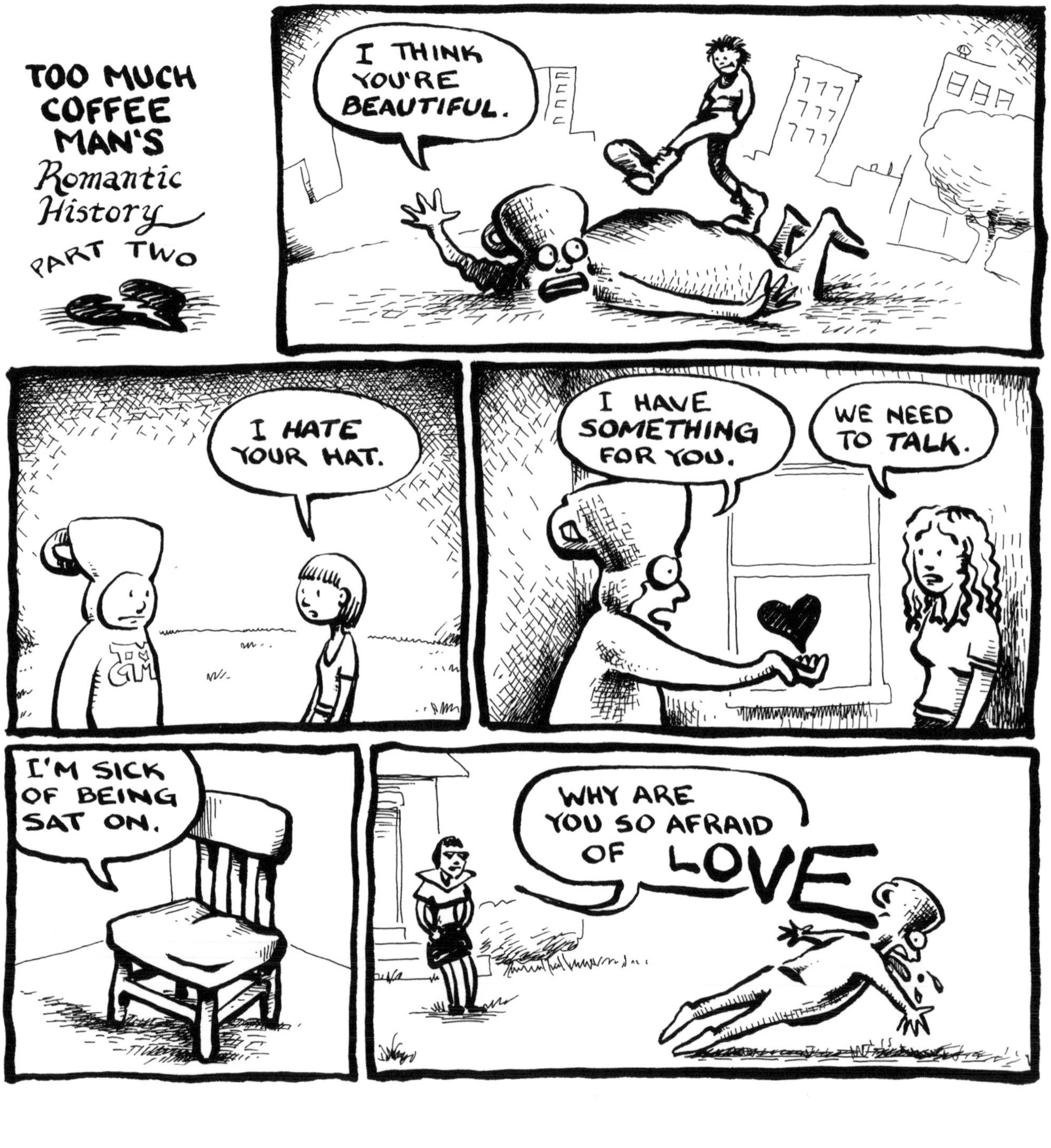
TOO MUCH COFFEE MAN'S
Romantic History
PART TWO
I THINK YOU'RE BEAUTIFUL.
I HATE YOUR HAT.
I HAVE SOMETHING FOR YOU.
WE NEED TO TALK.
I'M SICK OF BEING SAT ON.
WHY ARE YOU SO AFRAID OF LOVE

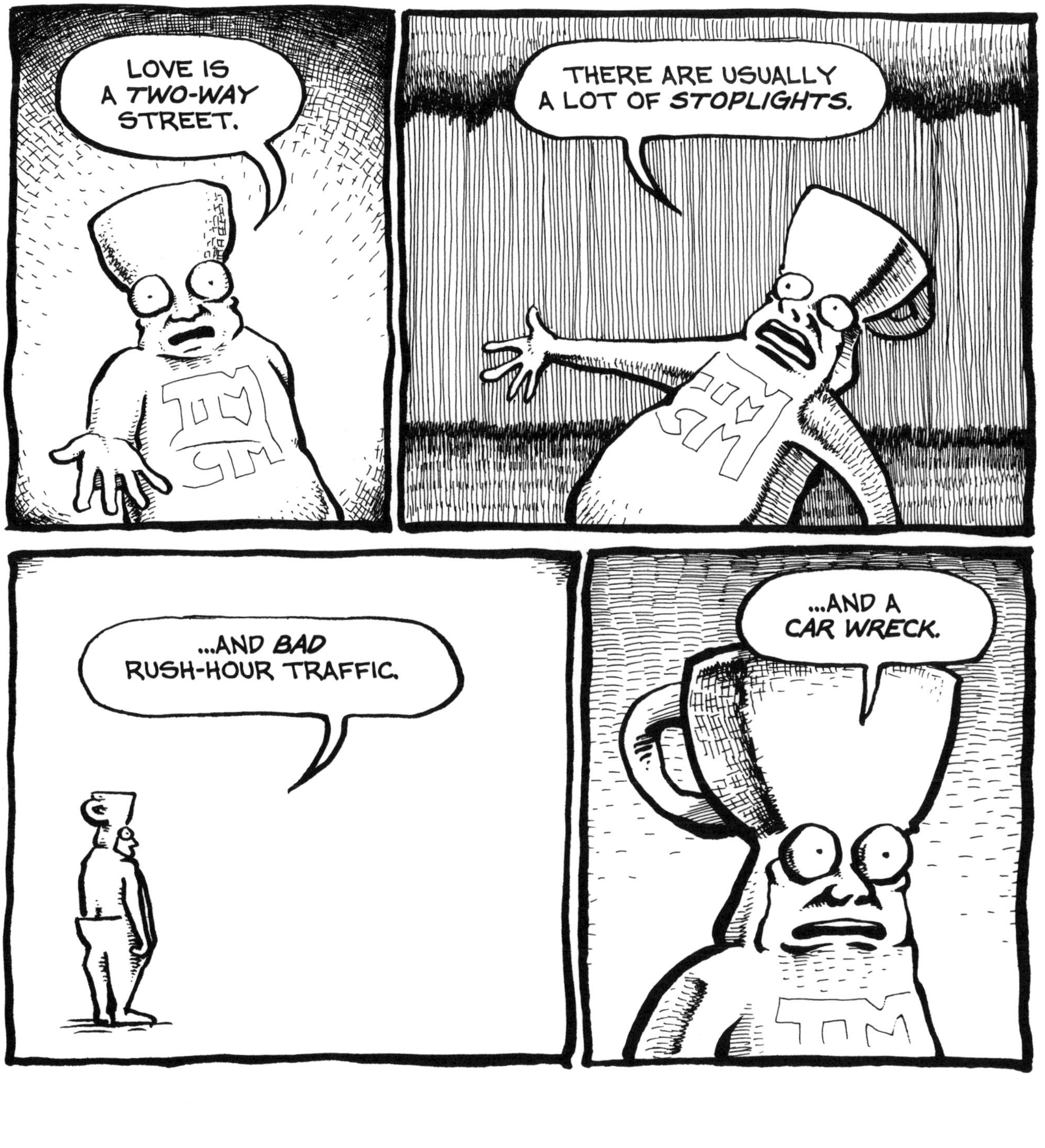
LOVE IS A *TWO-WAY* STREET.
THERE ARE USUALLY A LOT OF *STOPLIGHTS.*
...AND *BAD* RUSH-HOUR TRAFFIC.
...AND A *CAR WRECK.*

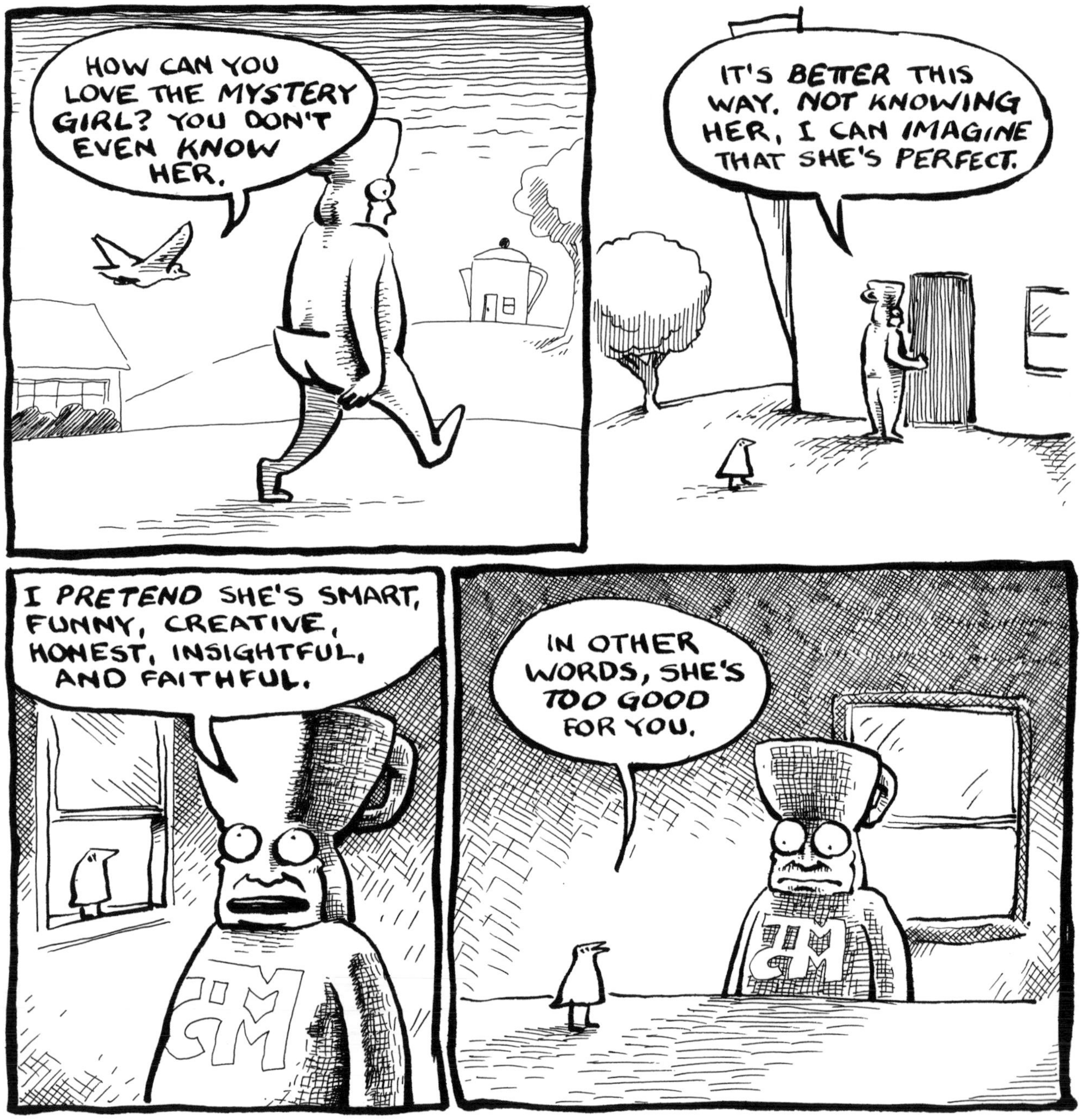
HOW CAN YOU LOVE THE MYSTERY GIRL? YOU DON'T EVEN KNOW HER.
IT'S BETTER THIS WAY. NOT KNOWING HER, I CAN IMAGINE THAT SHE'S PERFECT.
I PRETEND SHE'S SMART, FUNNY, CREATIVE, HONEST, INSIGHTFUL, AND FAITHFUL.
IN OTHER WORDS, SHE'S TOO GOOD FOR YOU.
JIM
GM
JIM
GM

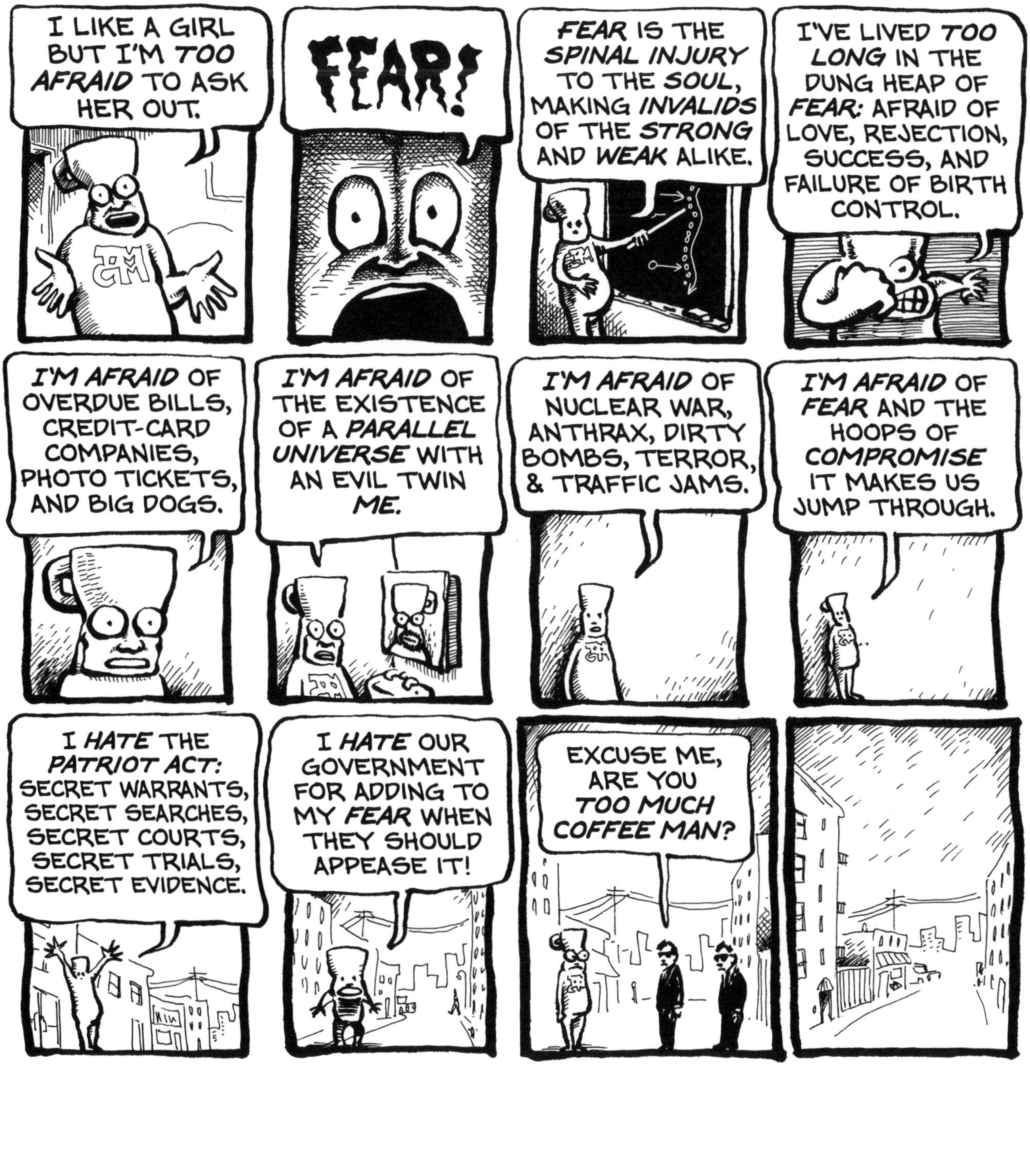
I LIKE A GIRL BUT I'M TOO AFRAID TO ASK HER OUT.
FEAR!
FEAR IS THE SPINAL INJURY TO THE SOUL, MAKING INVALIDS OF THE STRONG AND WEAK ALIKE.
I'VE LIVED TOO LONG IN THE DUNG HEAP OF FEAR: AFRAID OF LOVE, REJECTION, SUCCESS, AND FAILURE OF BIRTH CONTROL.
I'M AFRAID OF OVERDUE BILLS, CREDIT-CARD COMPANIES, PHOTO TICKETS, AND BIG DOGS.
I'M AFRAID OF THE EXISTENCE OF A PARALLEL UNIVERSE WITH AN EVIL TWIN ME.
I'M AFRAID OF NUCLEAR WAR, ANTHRAX, DIRTY BOMBS, TERROR, & TRAFFIC JAMS.
I'M AFRAID OF FEAR AND THE HOOPS OF COMPROMISE IT MAKES US JUMP THROUGH.
I HATE THE PATRIOT ACT: SECRET WARRANTS, SECRET SEARCHES, SECRET COURTS, SECRET TRIALS, SECRET EVIDENCE.
I HATE OUR GOVERNMENT FOR ADDING TO MY FEAR WHEN THEY SHOULD APPEASE IT!
EXCUSE ME, ARE YOU TOO MUCH COFFEE MAN?

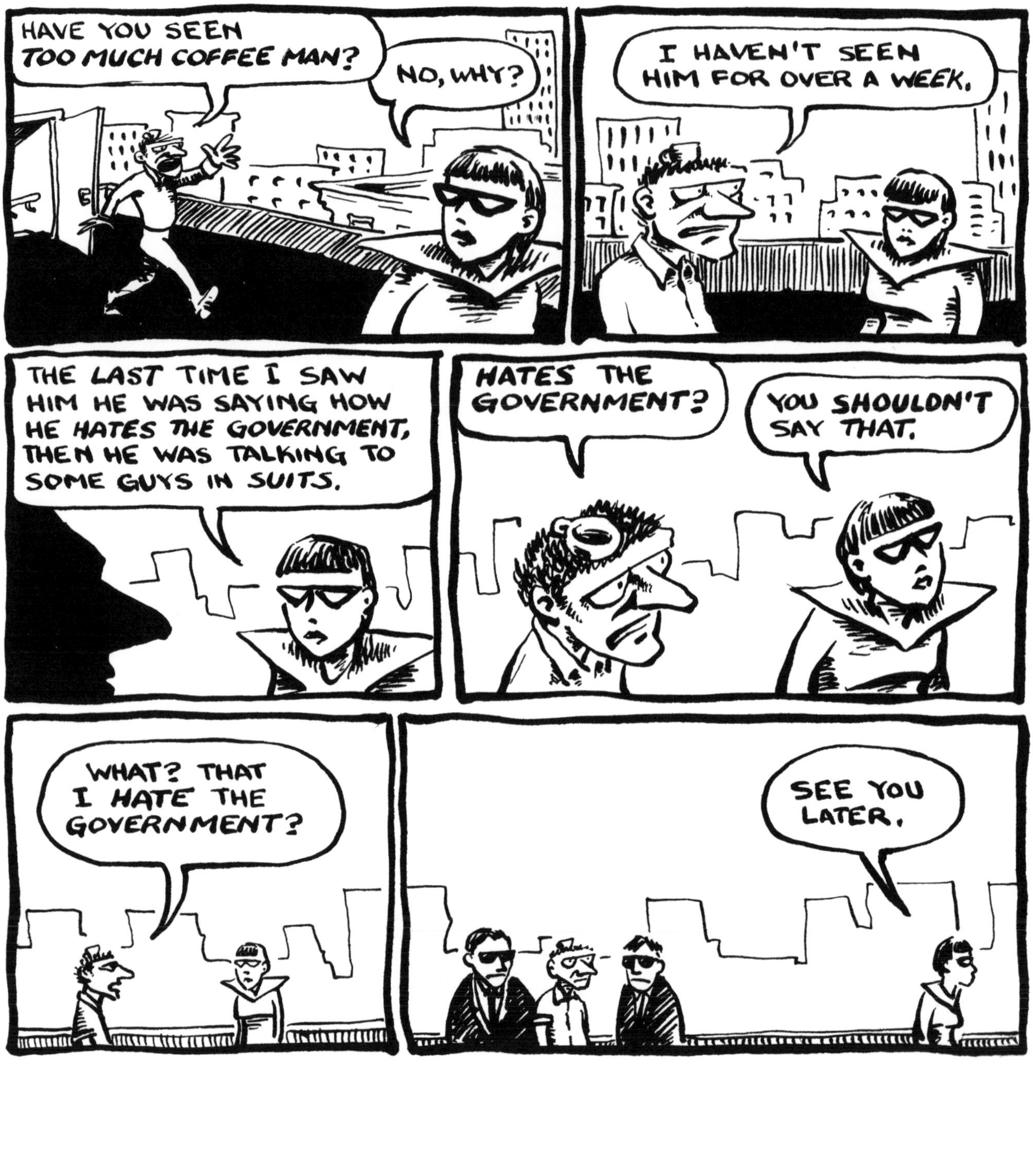
HAVE YOU SEEN TOO MUCH COFFEE MAN?
NO, WHY?
I HAVEN'T SEEN HIM FOR OVER A WEEK.
THE LAST TIME I SAW HIM HE WAS SAYING HOW HE HATES THE GOVERNMENT, THEN HE WAS TALKING TO SOME GUYS IN SUITS.
HATES THE GOVERNMENT?
YOU SHOULDN'T SAY THAT.
WHAT? THAT I HATE THE GOVERNMENT?
SEE YOU LATER.

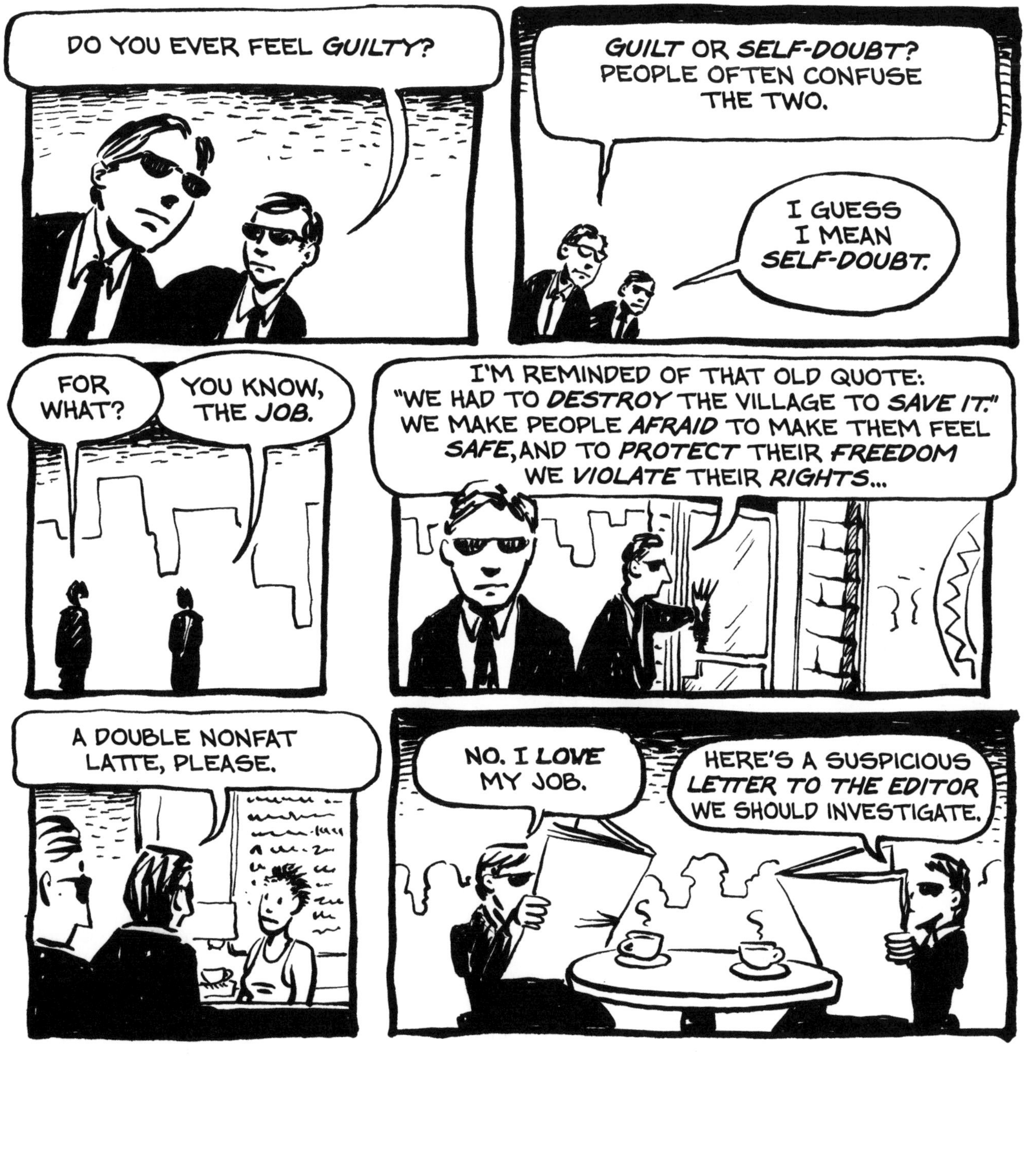
DO YOU EVER FEEL *GUILTY?*
GUILT OR *SELF-DOUBT?* PEOPLE OFTEN CONFUSE THE TWO.
I GUESS I MEAN *SELF-DOUBT.*
FOR WHAT?
YOU KNOW, THE *JOB.*
I'M REMINDED OF THAT OLD QUOTE: "WE HAD TO *DESTROY* THE VILLAGE TO *SAVE IT.*" WE MAKE PEOPLE *AFRAID* TO MAKE THEM FEEL *SAFE*, AND TO *PROTECT* THEIR *FREEDOM* WE *VIOLATE* THEIR *RIGHTS*...
A DOUBLE NONFAT LATTE, PLEASE.
NO. I *LOVE* MY JOB.
HERE'S A SUSPICIOUS *LETTER TO THE EDITOR* WE SHOULD INVESTIGATE.

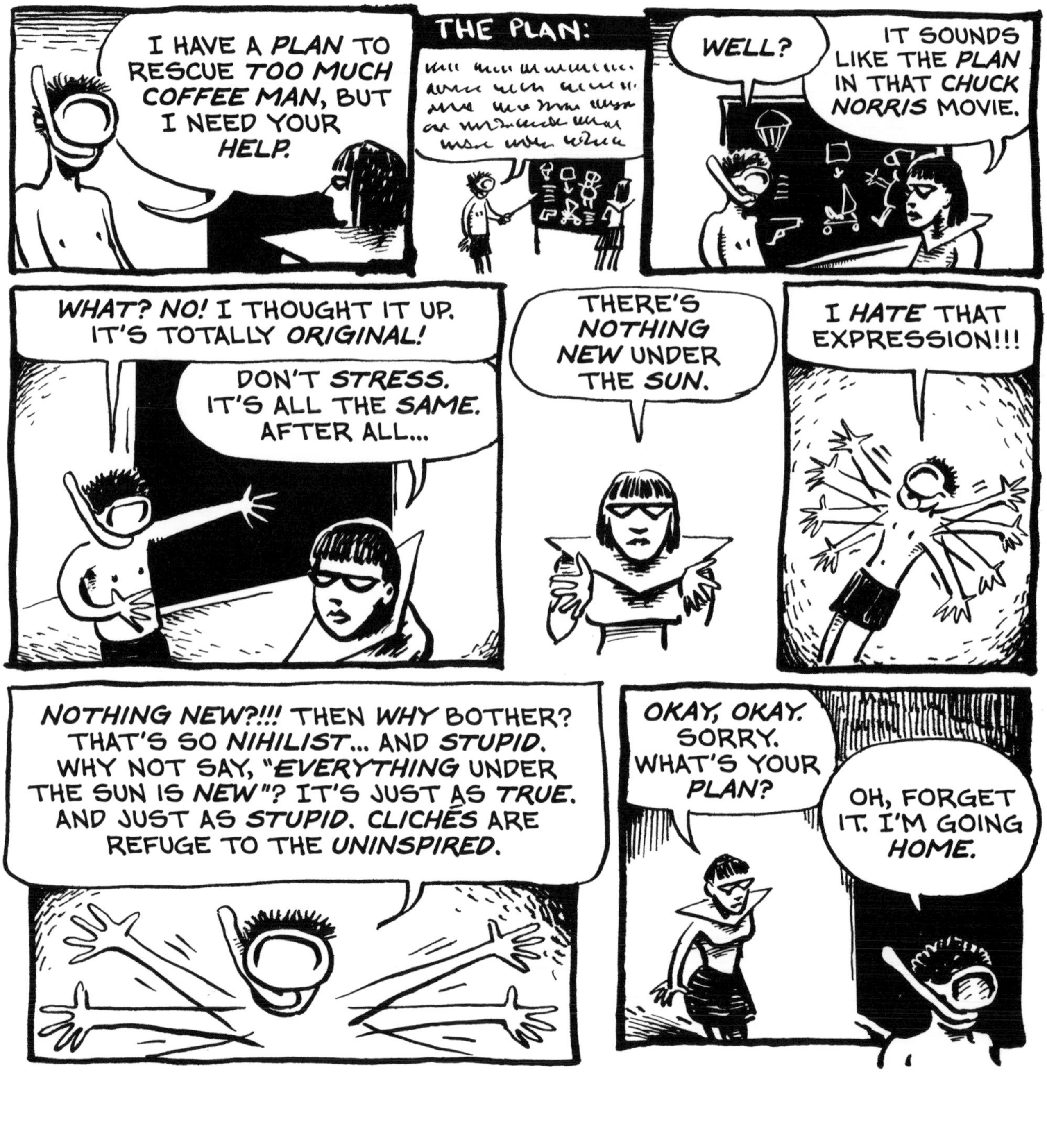
I HAVE A PLAN TO RESCUE TOO MUCH COFFEE MAN, BUT I NEED YOUR HELP.
THE PLAN:
WELL?
IT SOUNDS LIKE THE PLAN IN THAT CHUCK NORRIS MOVIE.
WHAT? NO! I THOUGHT IT UP. IT'S TOTALLY ORIGINAL!
DON'T STRESS. IT'S ALL THE SAME. AFTER ALL...
THERE'S NOTHING NEW UNDER THE SUN.
I HATE THAT EXPRESSION!!!
NOTHING NEW?!!! THEN WHY BOTHER? THAT'S SO NIHILIST... AND STUPID. WHY NOT SAY, "EVERYTHING UNDER THE SUN IS NEW"? IT'S JUST AS TRUE. AND JUST AS STUPID. CLICHÉS ARE REFUGE TO THE UNINSPIRED.
OKAY, OKAY. SORRY. WHAT'S YOUR PLAN?
OH, FORGET IT. I'M GOING HOME.

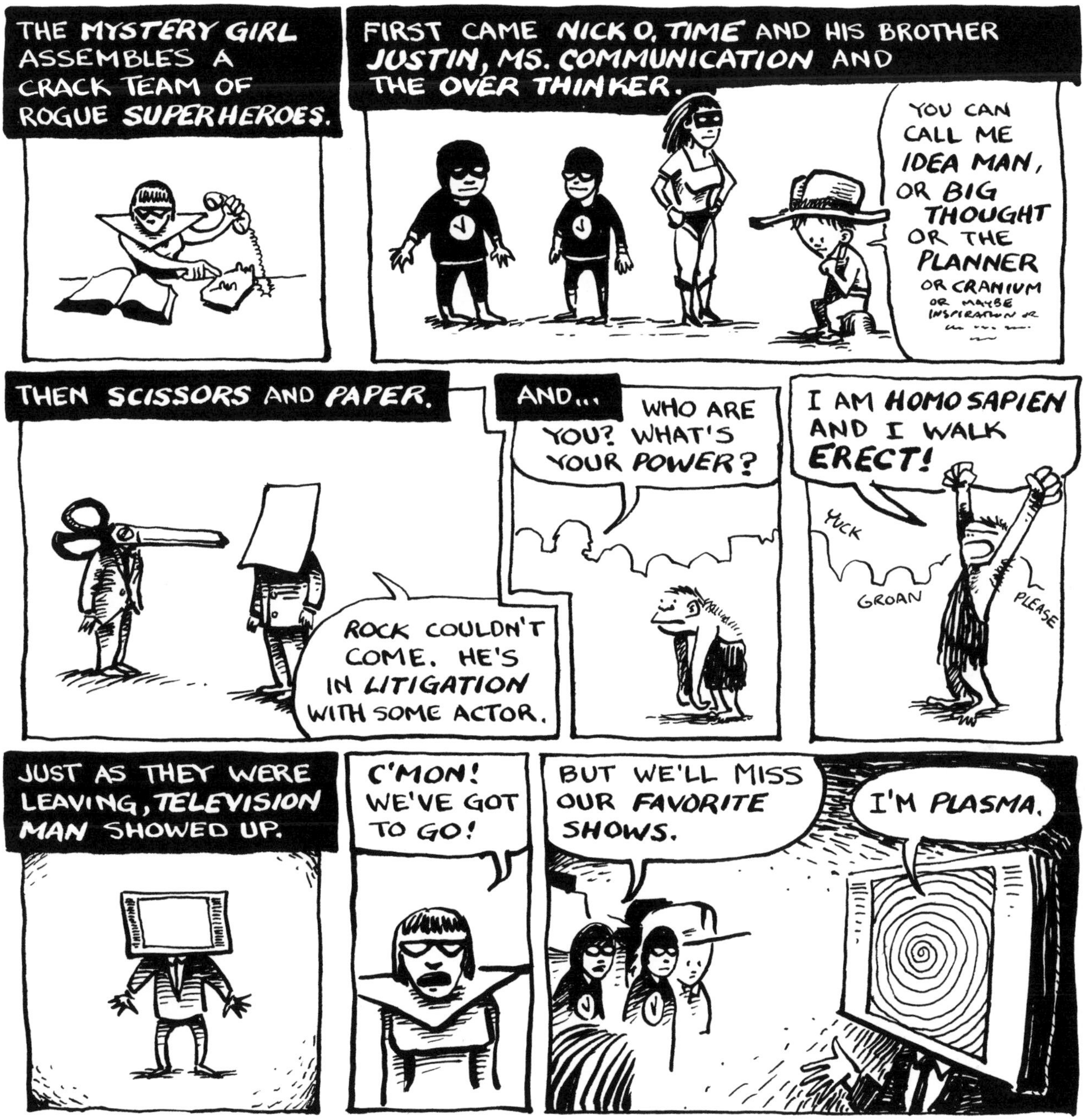

THE MYSTERY GIRL ASSEMBLES A CRACK TEAM OF ROGUE SUPERHEROES.
FIRST CAME NICK O, TIME AND HIS BROTHER JUSTIN, MS. COMMUNICATION AND THE OVER THINKER.
YOU CAN CALL ME IDEA MAN, OR BIG THOUGHT OR THE PLANNER OR CRANIUM OR MAYBE INSPIRATION OR
THEN SCISSORS AND PAPER.
ROCK COULDN'T COME. HE'S IN LITIGATION WITH SOME ACTOR.
AND...
WHO ARE YOU? WHAT'S YOUR POWER?
I AM HOMO SAPIEN AND I WALK ERECT!
YUCK
GROAN
PLEASE
JUST AS THEY WERE LEAVING, TELEVISION MAN SHOWED UP.
C'MON! WE'VE GOT TO GO!
BUT WE'LL MISS OUR FAVORITE SHOWS.
I'M PLASMA.

THE *MYSTERY GIRL* FINALLY MOTIVATES THE HEROES TO RESCUE *TOO MUCH COFFEE MAN* FROM HIS *SECRET PRISON.*

THE OVER THINKER

Ms. Communication

Homo Sapiens

Paper & Scissors

TELEVISION MAN

Justin & Nick O. Time

WITH WITTY BANTER, VIOLENCE WITHOUT REPERCUSSION, GRATUITOUS SPECIAL EFFECTS, A CAR CHASE THAT GOES ON 10 MINUTES TOO LONG, AND A REALLY BIG SPECIAL-EFFECTS BUDGET, THE TEAM FIGHTS ITS WAY INTO PRISON...

HALT! WHERE'S YOUR *PAPERWORK?*

I'VE GOT YOUR *PAPERWORK!* *RIGHT HERE!!*

POW!

SMASH!

BANG!

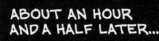

ABOUT AN HOUR AND A HALF LATER...

BOOM!

WE DID IT!! WE *RESCUED* TOO MUCH COFFEE MAN!

WHO'S *TOO MUCH COFFEE MAN?*

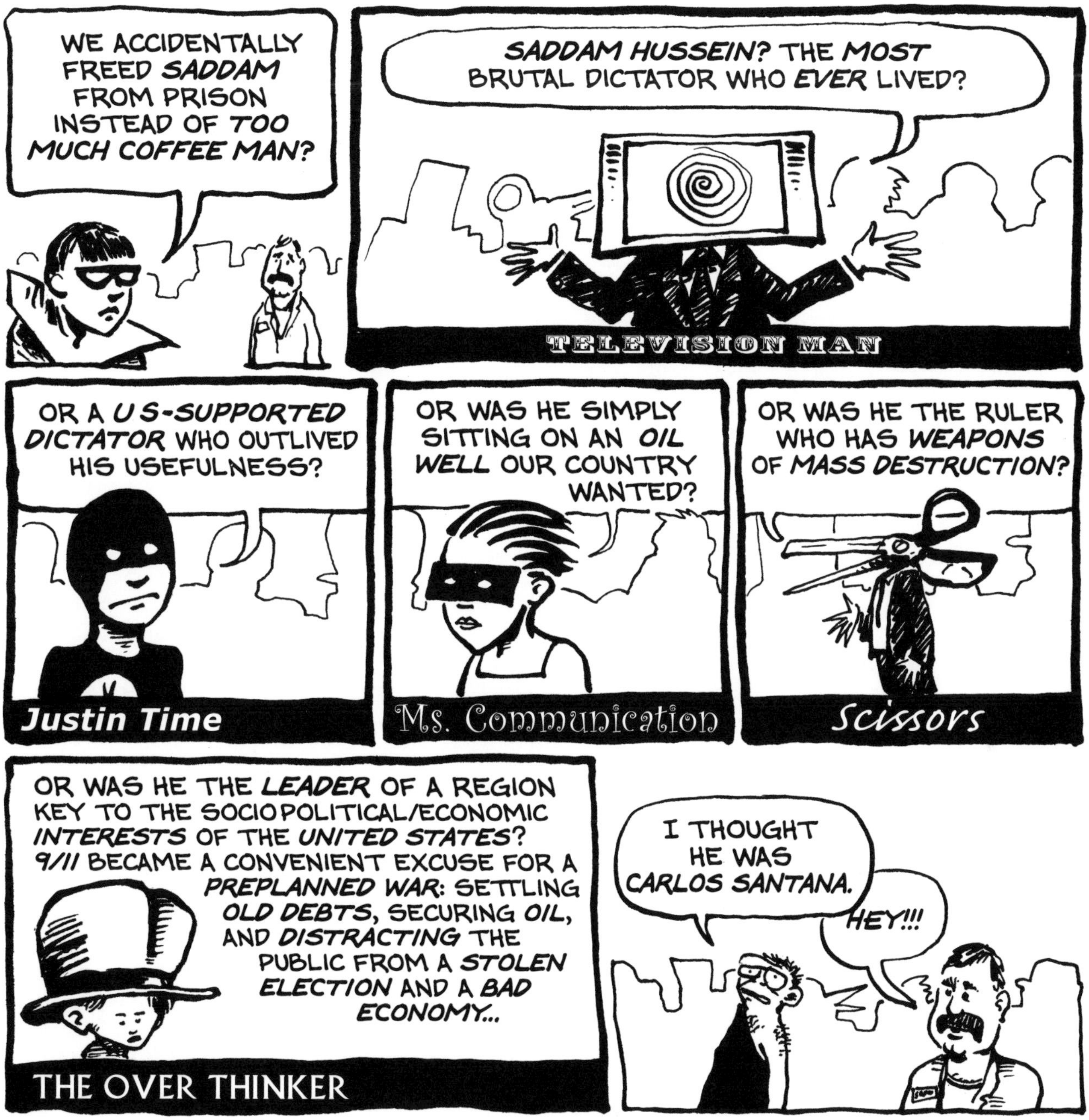

WE ACCIDENTALLY FREED SADDAM FROM PRISON INSTEAD OF TOO MUCH COFFEE MAN?
SADDAM HUSSEIN? THE MOST BRUTAL DICTATOR WHO EVER LIVED?
TELEVISION MAN
OR A U S-SUPPORTED DICTATOR WHO OUTLIVED HIS USEFULNESS?
Justin Time
OR WAS HE SIMPLY SITTING ON AN OIL WELL OUR COUNTRY WANTED?
Ms. Communication
OR WAS HE THE RULER WHO HAS WEAPONS OF MASS DESTRUCTION?
Scissors
OR WAS HE THE LEADER OF A REGION KEY TO THE SOCIOPOLITICAL/ECONOMIC INTERESTS OF THE UNITED STATES? 9/11 BECAME A CONVENIENT EXCUSE FOR A PREPLANNED WAR: SETTLING OLD DEBTS, SECURING OIL, AND DISTRACTING THE PUBLIC FROM A STOLEN ELECTION AND A BAD ECONOMY...
THE OVER THINKER
I THOUGHT HE WAS CARLOS SANTANA.
HEY!!!

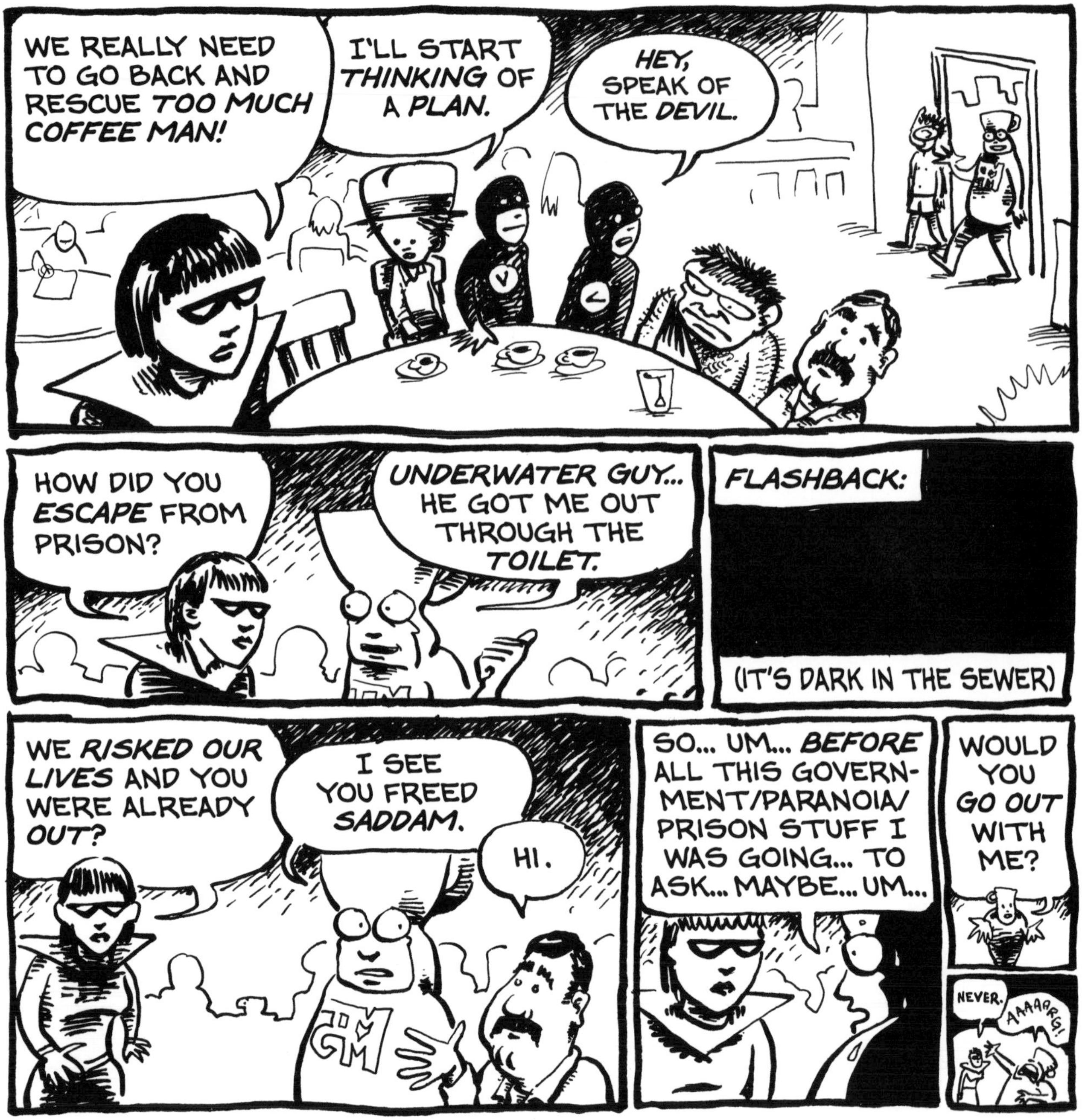
WE REALLY NEED TO GO BACK AND RESCUE TOO MUCH COFFEE MAN!
I'LL START THINKING OF A PLAN.
HEY, SPEAK OF THE DEVIL.
HOW DID YOU ESCAPE FROM PRISON?
UNDERWATER GUY... HE GOT ME OUT THROUGH THE TOILET.
FLASHBACK:
(IT'S DARK IN THE SEWER)
WE RISKED OUR LIVES AND YOU WERE ALREADY OUT?
I SEE YOU FREED SADDAM.
HI.
SO... UM... BEFORE ALL THIS GOVERNMENT/PARANOIA/PRISON STUFF I WAS GOING... TO ASK... MAYBE... UM...
WOULD YOU GO OUT WITH ME?
NEVER.
AAAAARG!

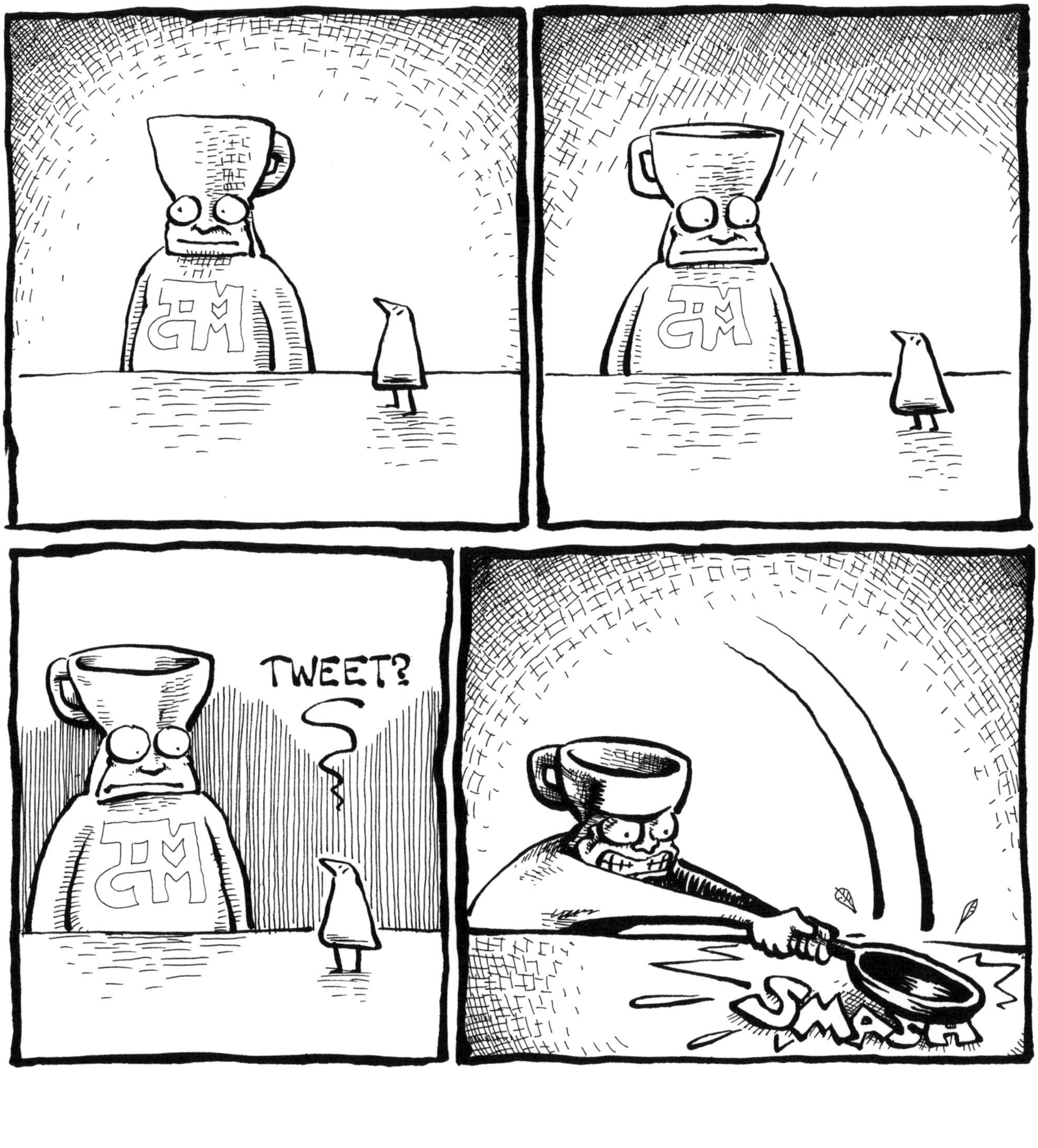
TWEET?
SMASH

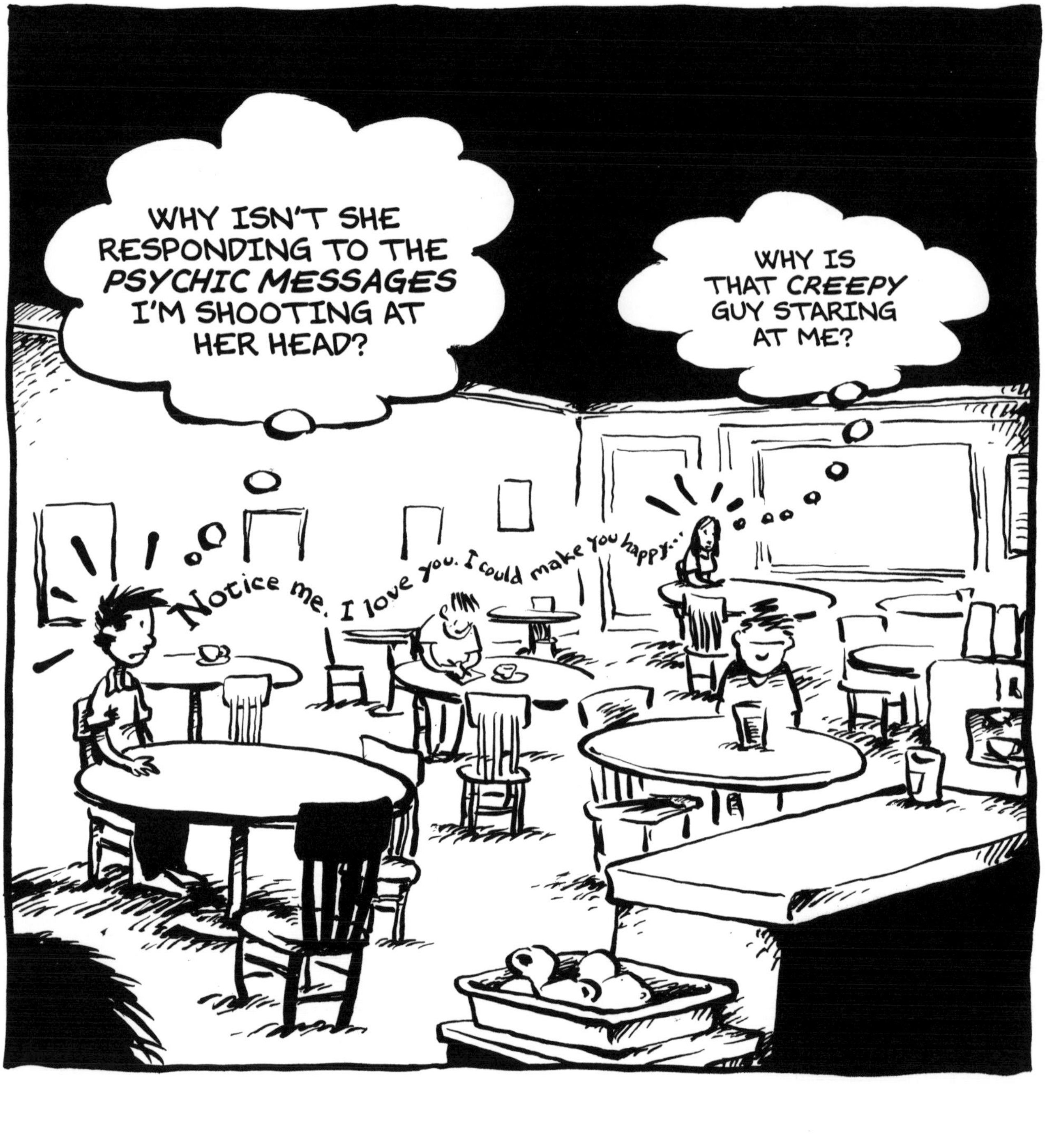
WHY ISN'T SHE RESPONDING TO THE *PSYCHIC MESSAGES* I'M SHOOTING AT HER HEAD?
WHY IS THAT *CREEPY* GUY STARING AT ME?
Notice me. I love you. I could make you happy...

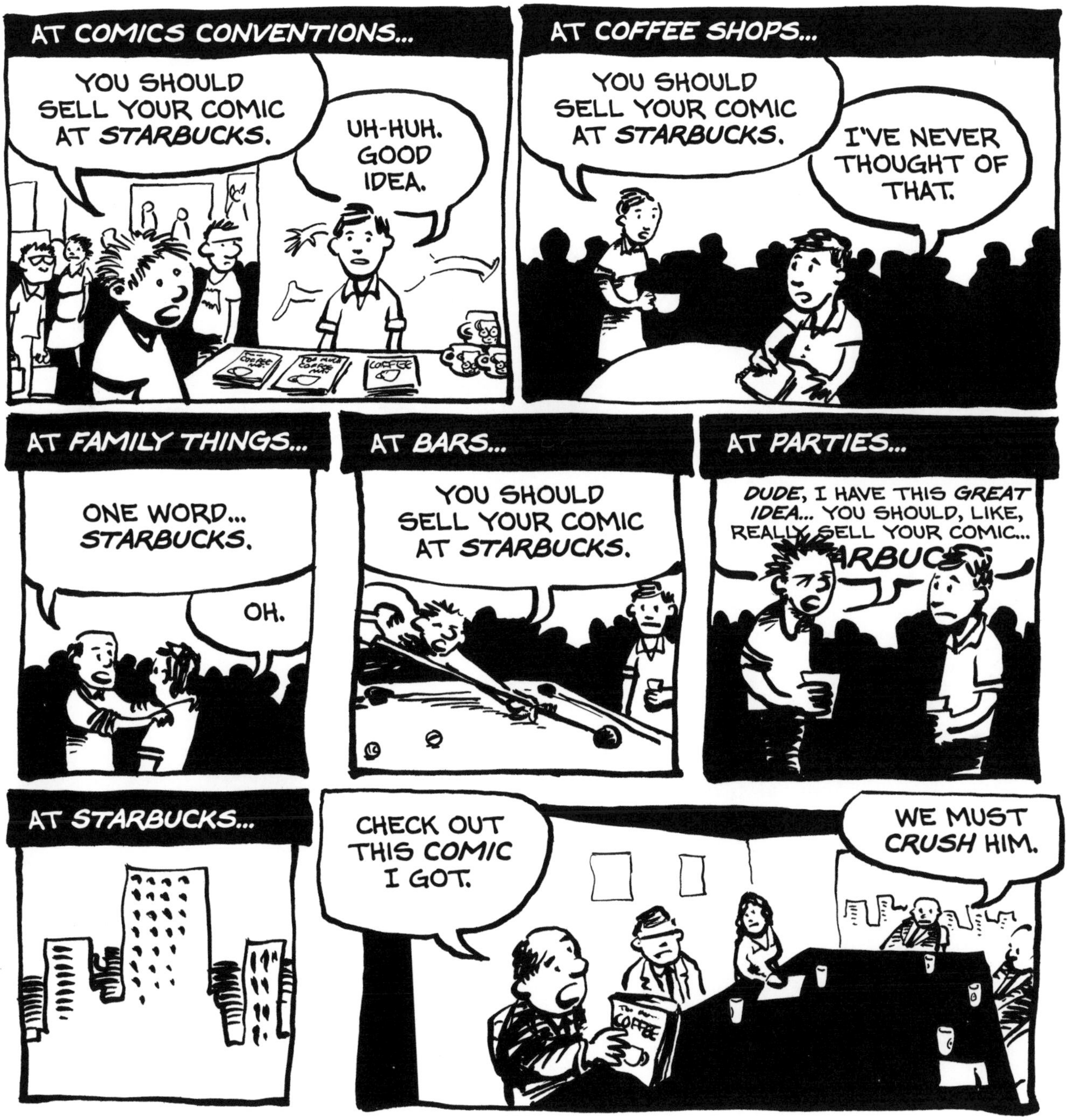

AT COMICS CONVENTIONS...
YOU SHOULD SELL YOUR COMIC AT STARBUCKS.
UH-HUH. GOOD IDEA.
AT COFFEE SHOPS...
YOU SHOULD SELL YOUR COMIC AT STARBUCKS.
I'VE NEVER THOUGHT OF THAT.
AT FAMILY THINGS...
ONE WORD... STARBUCKS.
OH.
AT BARS...
YOU SHOULD SELL YOUR COMIC AT STARBUCKS.
AT PARTIES...
DUDE, I HAVE THIS GREAT IDEA... YOU SHOULD, LIKE, REALLY SELL YOUR COMIC...
AT STARBUCKS...
CHECK OUT THIS COMIC I GOT.
WE MUST CRUSH HIM.

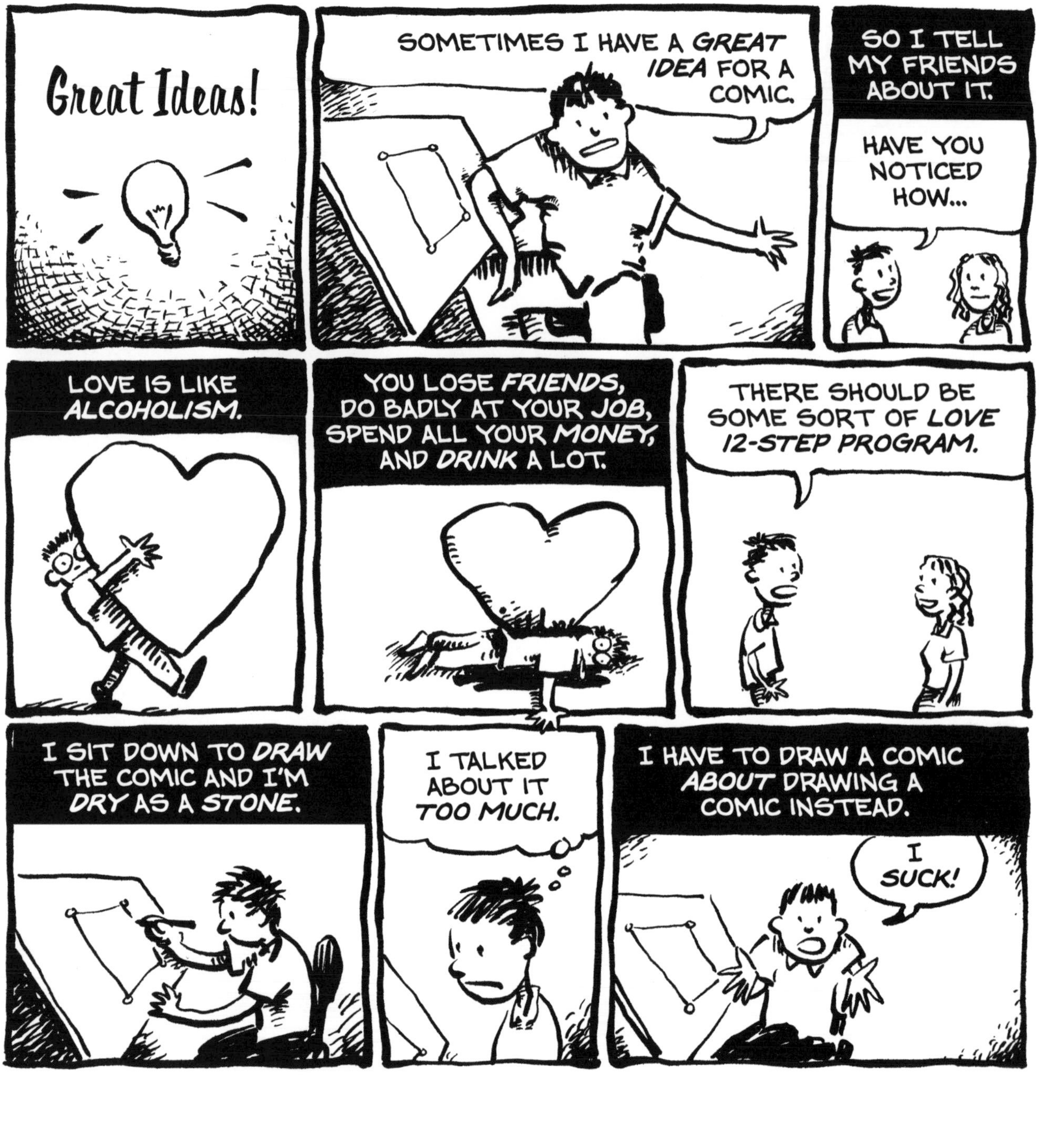
Great Ideas!
SOMETIMES I HAVE A GREAT IDEA FOR A COMIC.
SO I TELL MY FRIENDS ABOUT IT.
HAVE YOU NOTICED HOW...
LOVE IS LIKE ALCOHOLISM.
YOU LOSE FRIENDS, DO BADLY AT YOUR JOB, SPEND ALL YOUR MONEY, AND DRINK A LOT.
THERE SHOULD BE SOME SORT OF LOVE 12-STEP PROGRAM.
I SIT DOWN TO DRAW THE COMIC AND I'M DRY AS A STONE.
I TALKED ABOUT IT TOO MUCH.
I HAVE TO DRAW A COMIC ABOUT DRAWING A COMIC INSTEAD.
I SUCK!

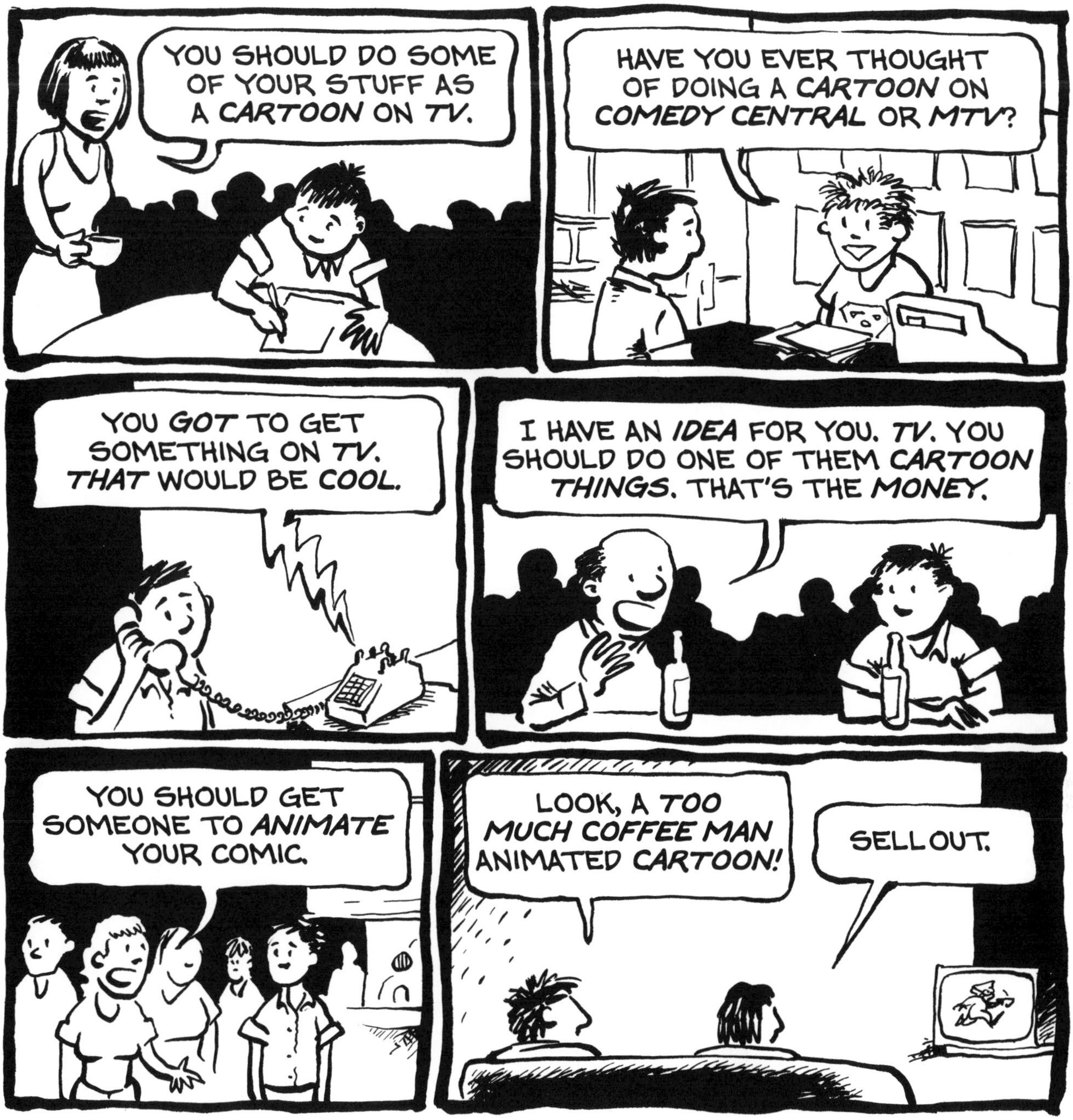
YOU SHOULD DO SOME OF YOUR STUFF AS A *CARTOON* ON *TV*.
HAVE YOU EVER THOUGHT OF DOING A *CARTOON* ON *COMEDY CENTRAL* OR *MTV*?
YOU *GOT* TO GET SOMETHING ON *TV*. *THAT* WOULD BE *COOL*.
I HAVE AN *IDEA* FOR YOU. *TV*. YOU SHOULD DO ONE OF THEM *CARTOON THINGS*. THAT'S THE *MONEY*.
YOU SHOULD GET SOMEONE TO *ANIMATE* YOUR COMIC.
LOOK, A *TOO MUCH COFFEE MAN* ANIMATED *CARTOON*!
SELLOUT.

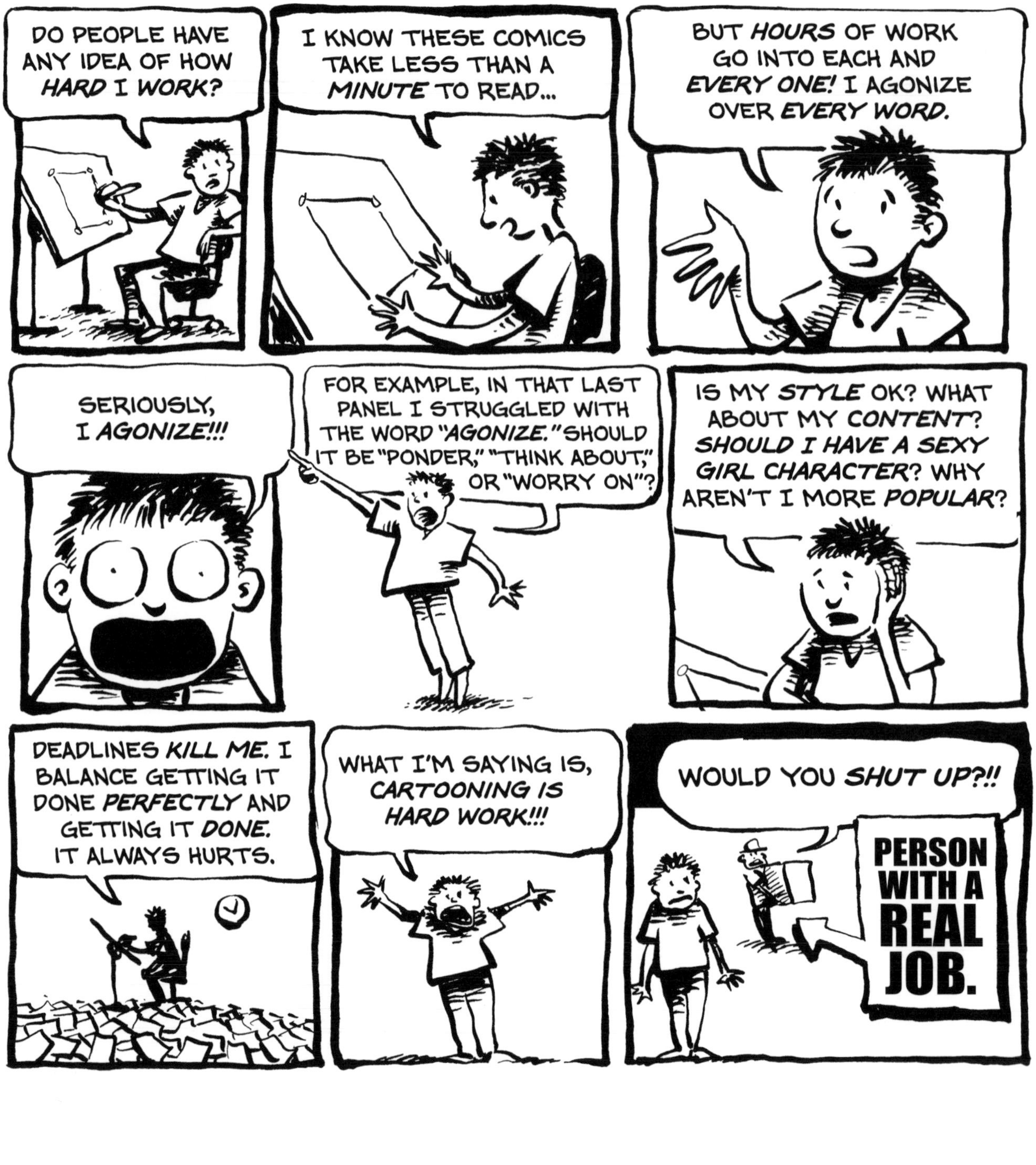
DO PEOPLE HAVE ANY IDEA OF HOW HARD I WORK?
I KNOW THESE COMICS TAKE LESS THAN A MINUTE TO READ...
BUT HOURS OF WORK GO INTO EACH AND EVERY ONE! I AGONIZE OVER EVERY WORD.
SERIOUSLY, I AGONIZE!!!
FOR EXAMPLE, IN THAT LAST PANEL I STRUGGLED WITH THE WORD "AGONIZE." SHOULD IT BE "PONDER," "THINK ABOUT," OR "WORRY ON"?
IS MY STYLE OK? WHAT ABOUT MY CONTENT? SHOULD I HAVE A SEXY GIRL CHARACTER? WHY AREN'T I MORE POPULAR?
DEADLINES KILL ME. I BALANCE GETTING IT DONE PERFECTLY AND GETTING IT DONE. IT ALWAYS HURTS.
WHAT I'M SAYING IS, CARTOONING IS HARD WORK!!!
WOULD YOU SHUT UP?!!
PERSON WITH A REAL JOB.

I WANT TO BE AN *ARTIST!*

BUT I DON'T HAVE ANY *IDEAS.*

HAVE YOU TRIED **Creativity™?**

...IT COMES IN A *PILL.*

WOW! THANKS.

LATER

I'VE WRITTEN A *GRAPHIC NOVEL,* I PLAY *GUITAR,* AND I GOT A *TATTOO.* I FINALLY FEEL AT HOME IN *COFFEE SHOPS.*

Creativity™
ASK YOUR DOCTOR.

ALSO AVAILABLE AS A SUPPOSITORY.

WARNING:

Side effects may include poverty, impaired judgment, poor health, difficulty with relationships, delusions of grandeur, alienation, anxiety, dependence on the approval of strangers, and bad reviews.

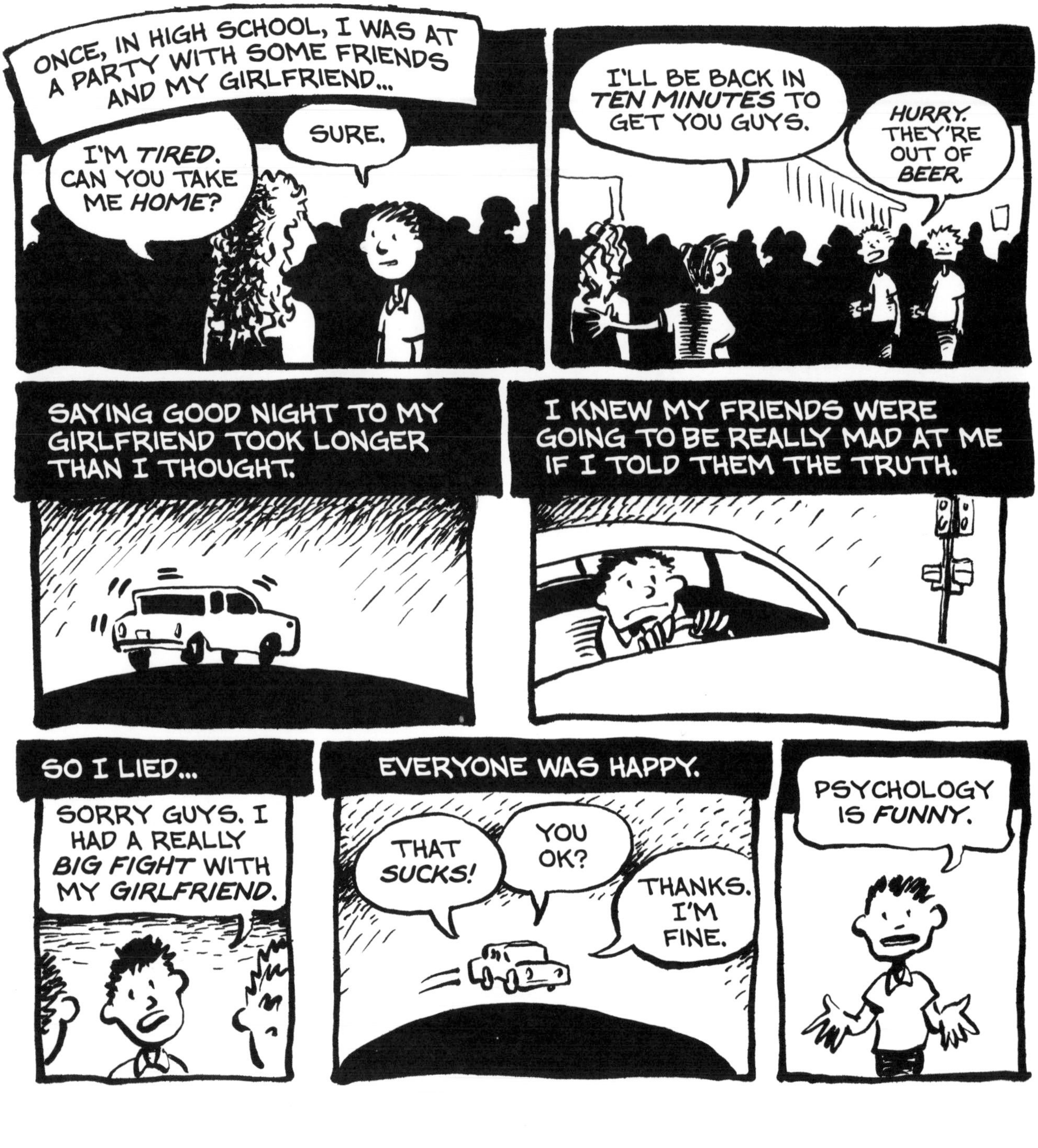
ONCE, IN HIGH SCHOOL, I WAS AT A PARTY WITH SOME FRIENDS AND MY GIRLFRIEND...
I'M *TIRED*. CAN YOU TAKE ME *HOME*?
SURE.
I'LL BE BACK IN *TEN MINUTES* TO GET YOU GUYS.
HURRY. THEY'RE OUT OF *BEER*.
SAYING GOOD NIGHT TO MY GIRLFRIEND TOOK LONGER THAN I THOUGHT.
I KNEW MY FRIENDS WERE GOING TO BE REALLY MAD AT ME IF I TOLD THEM THE TRUTH.
SO I LIED...
SORRY GUYS. I HAD A REALLY *BIG FIGHT* WITH MY *GIRLFRIEND*.
EVERYONE WAS HAPPY.
THAT *SUCKS*!
YOU OK?
THANKS. I'M FINE.
PSYCHOLOGY IS *FUNNY*.

I'LL TAKE OUT MY *BRAIN* SO I WON'T HAVE TO *THINK.*

...REMOVE MY *HEART* SO I WON'T *FEEL.*

MY *SPINE* — *BRAVERY.*

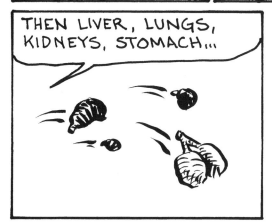
THEN LIVER, LUNGS, KIDNEYS, STOMACH...

FINALLY, I CAN RELAX.

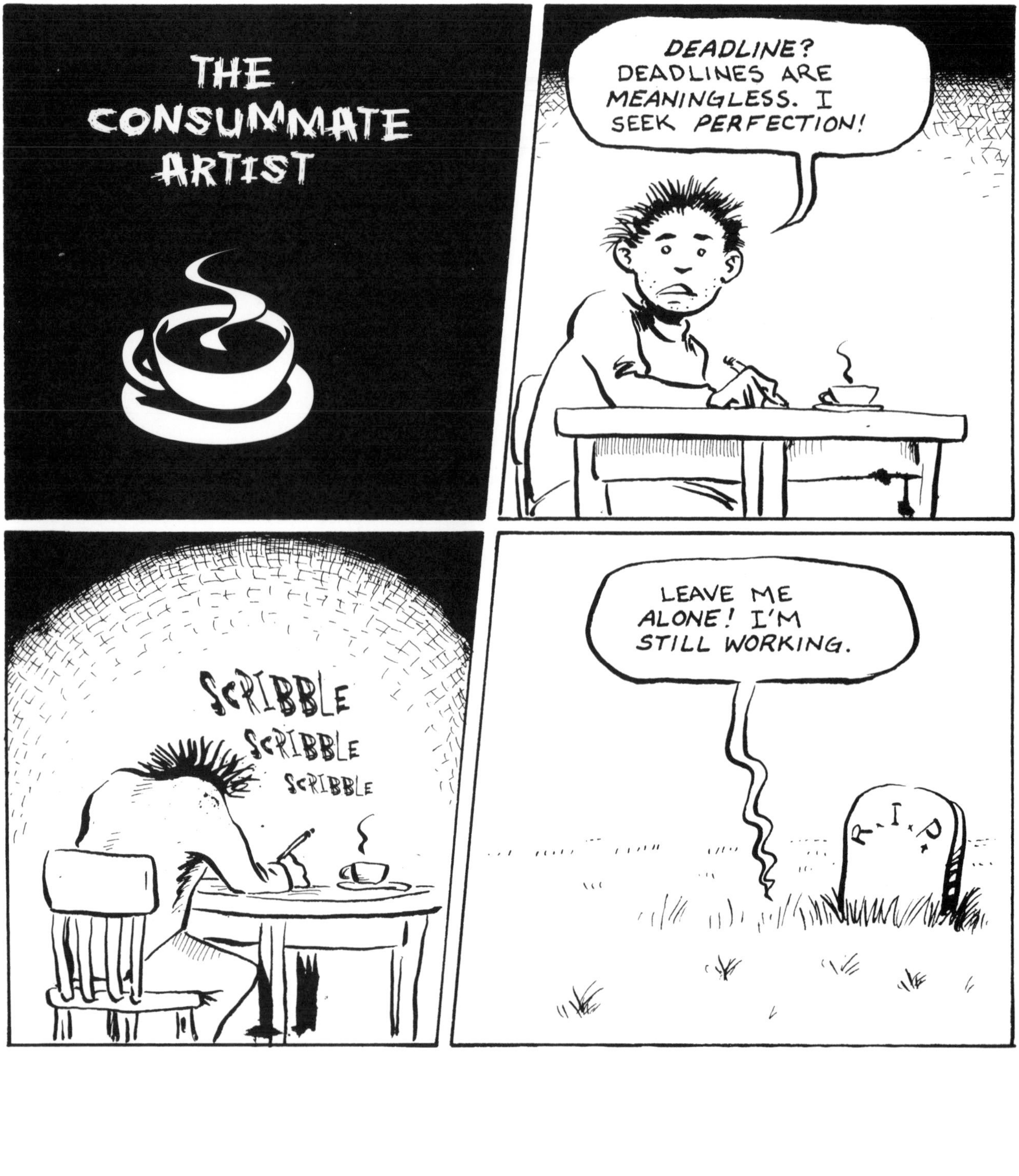
THE CONSUMMATE ARTIST
DEADLINE? DEADLINES ARE MEANINGLESS. I SEEK PERFECTION!
SCRIBBLE SCRIBBLE SCRIBBLE
LEAVE ME ALONE! I'M STILL WORKING.
R.I.P.

SOMETIMES I MEET SNOBS AT PARTIES

YOU DRAW CARTOONS?

YES.

DO YOU MAKE *MONEY*?

YES.

DID YOU GO TO *SCHOOL* FOR *THAT*?

NO.

WHAT *DID* YOU STUDY?

ARCHITECTURE.

WHERE DID YOU GO?

BERKELEY.

I ASSUMED YOU WERE ANOTHER ONE OF THESE *COMIC-BOOK IDIOTS*, BUT ARCHITECTURE, THAT IS IMPRESSIVE.

DO YOU EVER USE YOUR DEGREE?

YES.

WHEN I TALK TO *SNOBS* AT PARTIES.

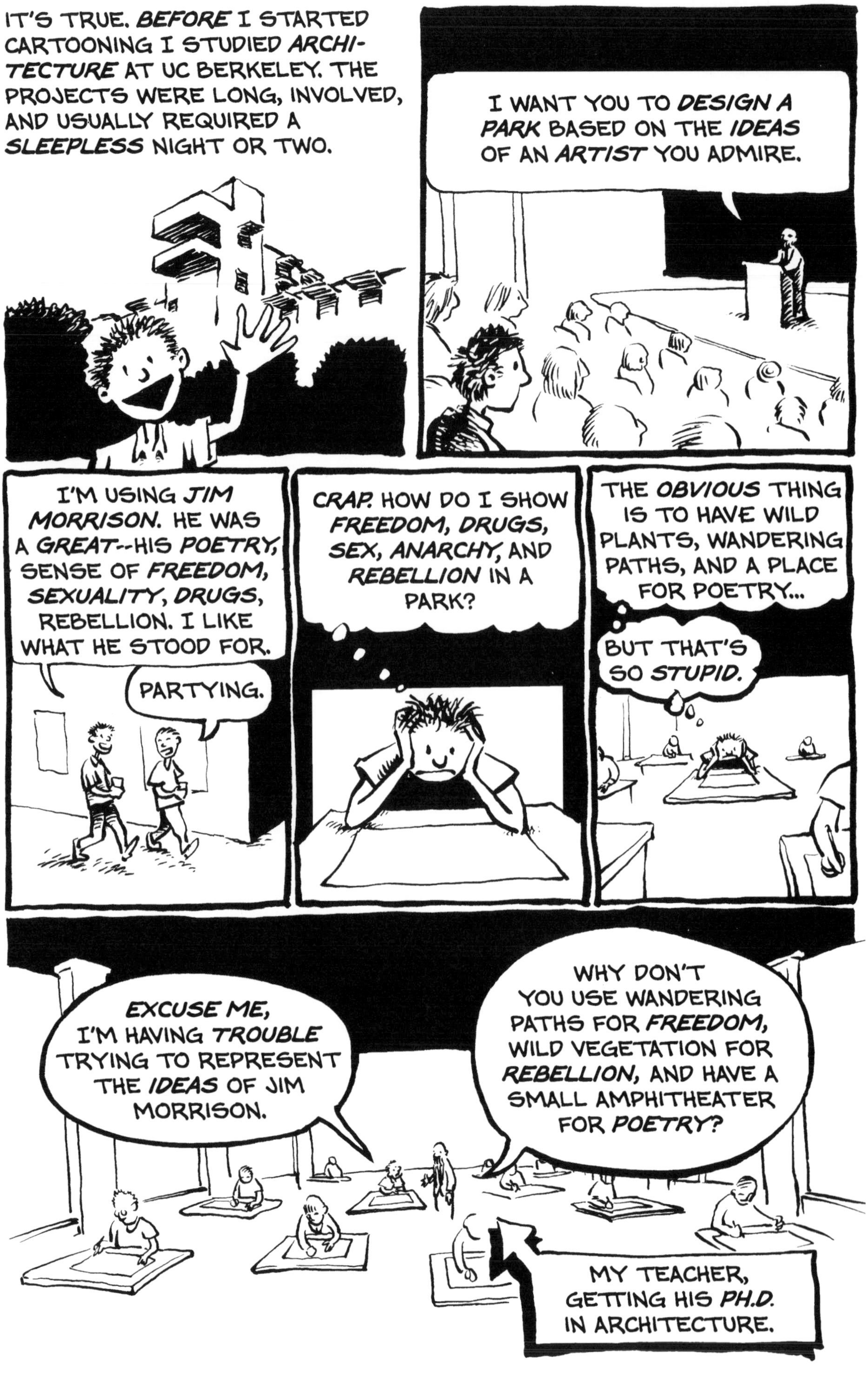

IT'S TRUE. *BEFORE* I STARTED CARTOONING I STUDIED *ARCHITECTURE* AT UC BERKELEY. THE PROJECTS WERE LONG, INVOLVED, AND USUALLY REQUIRED A *SLEEPLESS* NIGHT OR TWO.
I WANT YOU TO *DESIGN A PARK* BASED ON THE *IDEAS* OF AN *ARTIST* YOU ADMIRE.
I'M USING *JIM MORRISON*. HE WAS A *GREAT*--HIS *POETRY*, SENSE OF *FREEDOM*, *SEXUALITY*, *DRUGS*, REBELLION. I LIKE WHAT HE STOOD FOR.
PARTYING.
CRAP. HOW DO I SHOW *FREEDOM*, *DRUGS*, *SEX*, *ANARCHY*, AND *REBELLION* IN A PARK?
THE *OBVIOUS* THING IS TO HAVE WILD PLANTS, WANDERING PATHS, AND A PLACE FOR POETRY...
BUT THAT'S SO *STUPID*.
EXCUSE ME, I'M HAVING *TROUBLE* TRYING TO REPRESENT THE *IDEAS* OF JIM MORRISON.
WHY DON'T YOU USE WANDERING PATHS FOR *FREEDOM*, WILD VEGETATION FOR *REBELLION*, AND HAVE A SMALL AMPHITHEATER FOR *POETRY*?
MY TEACHER, GETTING HIS *PH.D.* IN ARCHITECTURE.

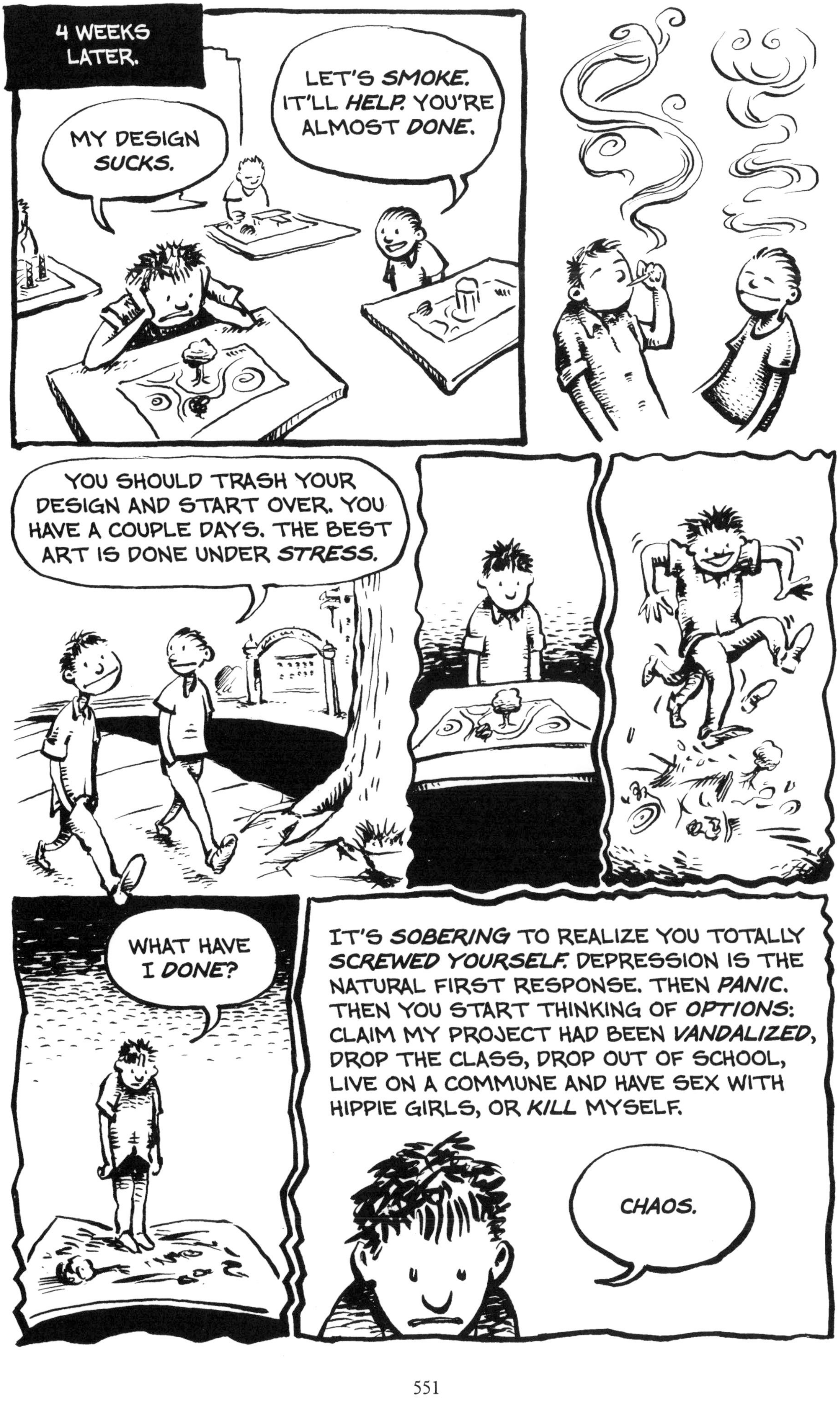
4 WEEKS LATER.
MY DESIGN SUCKS.
LET'S SMOKE. IT'LL HELP. YOU'RE ALMOST DONE.
YOU SHOULD TRASH YOUR DESIGN AND START OVER. YOU HAVE A COUPLE DAYS. THE BEST ART IS DONE UNDER STRESS.
WHAT HAVE I DONE?
IT'S SOBERING TO REALIZE YOU TOTALLY SCREWED YOURSELF. DEPRESSION IS THE NATURAL FIRST RESPONSE. THEN PANIC. THEN YOU START THINKING OF OPTIONS: CLAIM MY PROJECT HAD BEEN VANDALIZED, DROP THE CLASS, DROP OUT OF SCHOOL, LIVE ON A COMMUNE AND HAVE SEX WITH HIPPIE GIRLS, OR KILL MYSELF.
CHAOS.

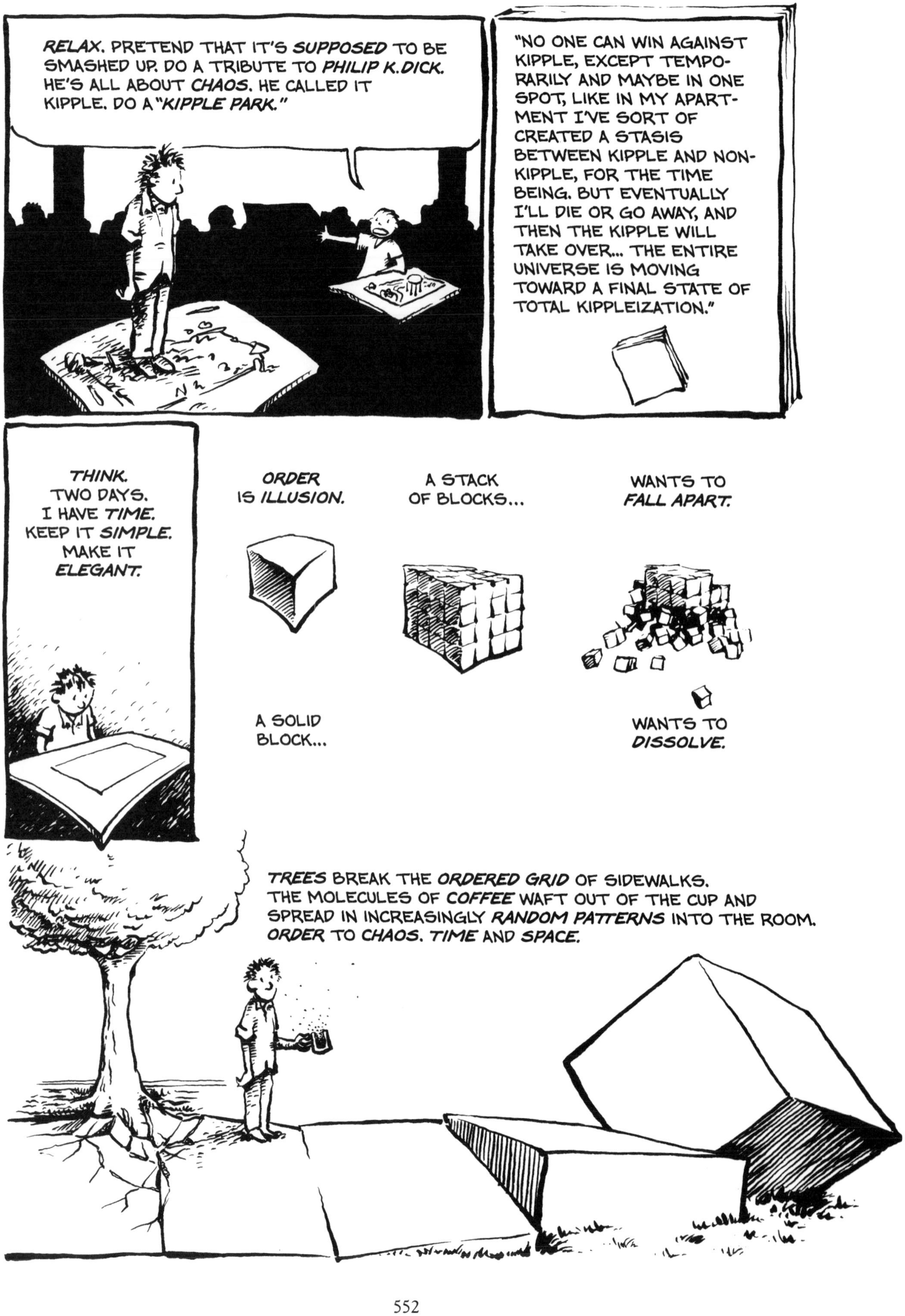
RELAX. PRETEND THAT IT'S SUPPOSED TO BE SMASHED UP. DO A TRIBUTE TO PHILIP K. DICK. HE'S ALL ABOUT CHAOS. HE CALLED IT KIPPLE. DO A "KIPPLE PARK."
"NO ONE CAN WIN AGAINST KIPPLE, EXCEPT TEMPORARILY AND MAYBE IN ONE SPOT, LIKE IN MY APARTMENT I'VE SORT OF CREATED A STASIS BETWEEN KIPPLE AND NON-KIPPLE, FOR THE TIME BEING. BUT EVENTUALLY I'LL DIE OR GO AWAY, AND THEN THE KIPPLE WILL TAKE OVER... THE ENTIRE UNIVERSE IS MOVING TOWARD A FINAL STATE OF TOTAL KIPPLEIZATION."
THINK. TWO DAYS. I HAVE TIME. KEEP IT SIMPLE. MAKE IT ELEGANT.
ORDER IS ILLUSION.
A SOLID BLOCK...
A STACK OF BLOCKS...
WANTS TO FALL APART.
WANTS TO DISSOLVE.
TREES BREAK THE ORDERED GRID OF SIDEWALKS. THE MOLECULES OF COFFEE WAFT OUT OF THE CUP AND SPREAD IN INCREASINGLY RANDOM PATTERNS INTO THE ROOM. ORDER TO CHAOS. TIME AND SPACE.

THE DESIGN IDEA CAME QUICKLY. A GRID OF CUBES WOULD MAKE A SMALL PLAZA. *ORDER.* AS YOU WALK DOWNHILL THE CUBES WOULD SHIFT, TURN, AND RISE UP OUT OF THE GROUND RANDOMLY. *CHAOS.* *ORDER* TO *CHAOS* REPRESENTED *SPACIALLY.*

IN THE PLAZA, AT THE CENTER OF THE ORDERED CUBES, A *TREE* WOULD GROW. OVER TIME ITS ROOTS WOULD BREAK THE CEMENT. THIS WOULD REPRESENT *CHAOS* OVER TIME.

ENTROPY PARK, A TRIBUTE TO PHILIP K. DICK.

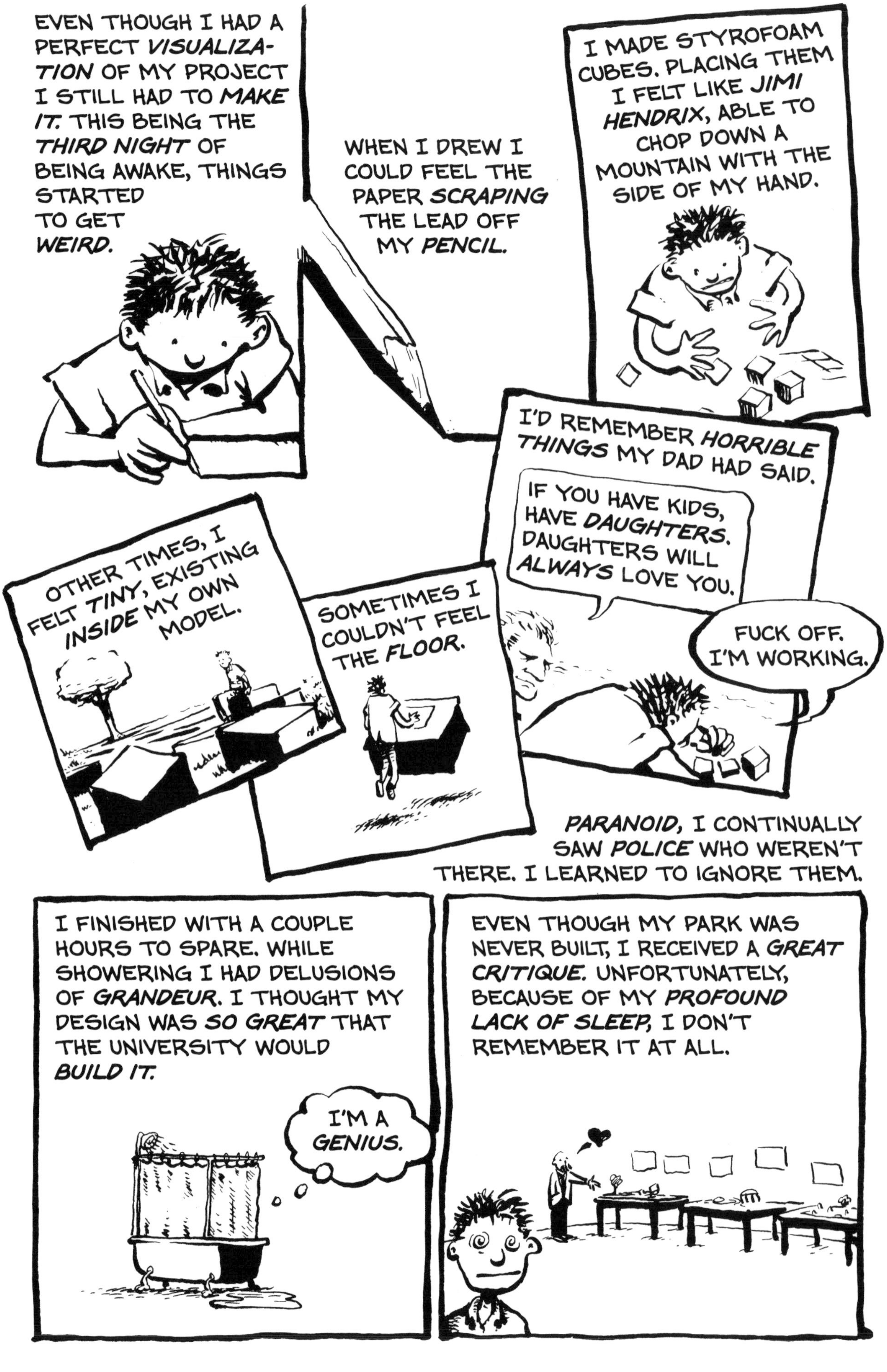
EVEN THOUGH I HAD A PERFECT VISUALIZATION OF MY PROJECT I STILL HAD TO MAKE IT. THIS BEING THE THIRD NIGHT OF BEING AWAKE, THINGS STARTED TO GET WEIRD.
WHEN I DREW I COULD FEEL THE PAPER SCRAPING THE LEAD OFF MY PENCIL.
I MADE STYROFOAM CUBES. PLACING THEM I FELT LIKE JIMI HENDRIX, ABLE TO CHOP DOWN A MOUNTAIN WITH THE SIDE OF MY HAND.
OTHER TIMES, I FELT TINY, EXISTING INSIDE MY OWN MODEL.
SOMETIMES I COULDN'T FEEL THE FLOOR.
I'D REMEMBER HORRIBLE THINGS MY DAD HAD SAID.
IF YOU HAVE KIDS, HAVE DAUGHTERS. DAUGHTERS WILL ALWAYS LOVE YOU.
FUCK OFF. I'M WORKING.
PARANOID, I CONTINUALLY SAW POLICE WHO WEREN'T THERE. I LEARNED TO IGNORE THEM.
I FINISHED WITH A COUPLE HOURS TO SPARE. WHILE SHOWERING I HAD DELUSIONS OF GRANDEUR. I THOUGHT MY DESIGN WAS SO GREAT THAT THE UNIVERSITY WOULD BUILD IT.
I'M A GENIUS.
EVEN THOUGH MY PARK WAS NEVER BUILT, I RECEIVED A GREAT CRITIQUE. UNFORTUNATELY, BECAUSE OF MY PROFOUND LACK OF SLEEP, I DON'T REMEMBER IT AT ALL.

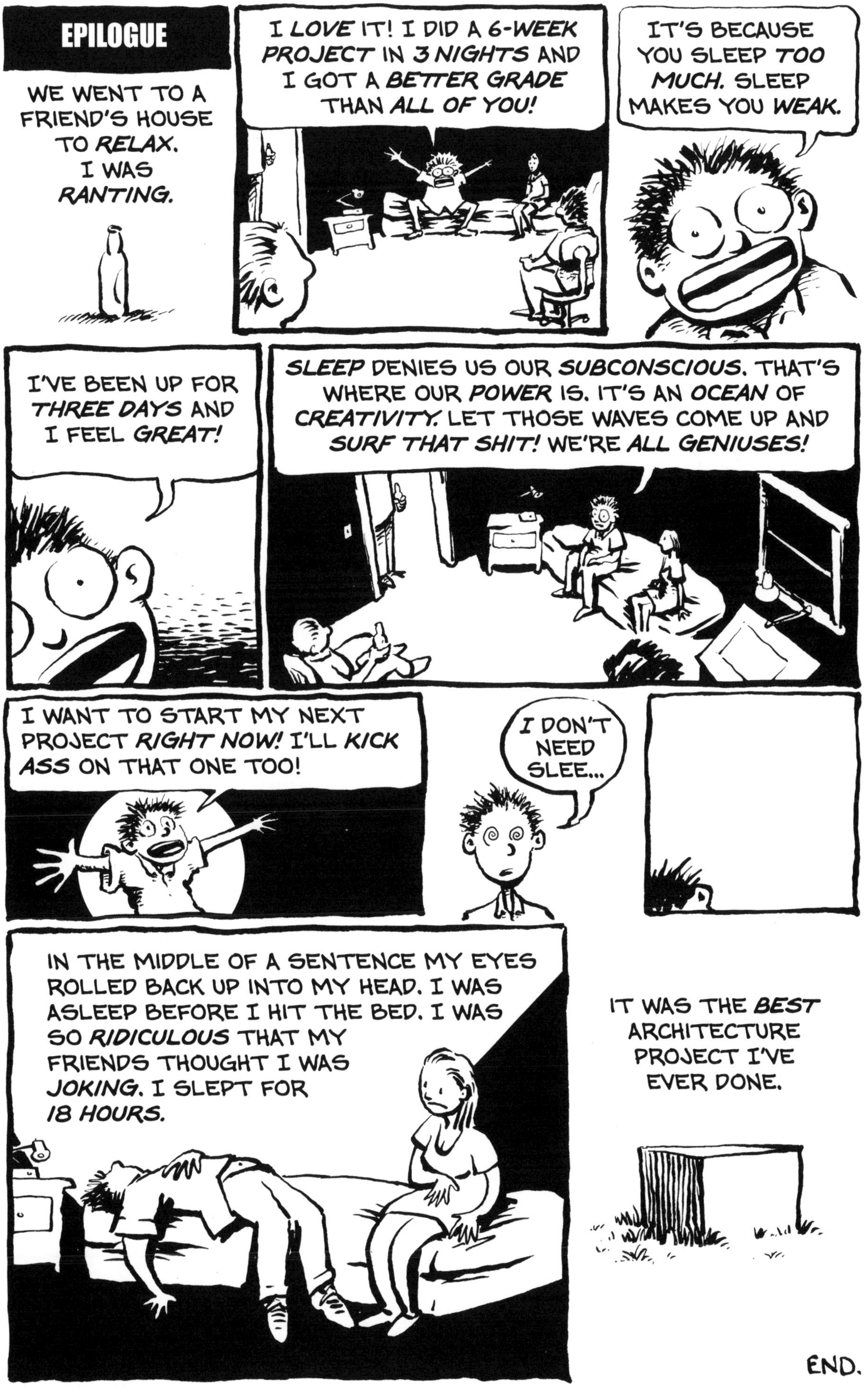
EPILOGUE
WE WENT TO A FRIEND'S HOUSE TO RELAX. I WAS RANTING.
I LOVE IT! I DID A 6-WEEK PROJECT IN 3 NIGHTS AND I GOT A BETTER GRADE THAN ALL OF YOU!
IT'S BECAUSE YOU SLEEP TOO MUCH. SLEEP MAKES YOU WEAK.
I'VE BEEN UP FOR THREE DAYS AND I FEEL GREAT!
SLEEP DENIES US OUR SUBCONSCIOUS. THAT'S WHERE OUR POWER IS. IT'S AN OCEAN OF CREATIVITY. LET THOSE WAVES COME UP AND SURF THAT SHIT! WE'RE ALL GENIUSES!
I WANT TO START MY NEXT PROJECT RIGHT NOW! I'LL KICK ASS ON THAT ONE TOO!
I DON'T NEED SLEE...
IN THE MIDDLE OF A SENTENCE MY EYES ROLLED BACK UP INTO MY HEAD. I WAS ASLEEP BEFORE I HIT THE BED. I WAS SO RIDICULOUS THAT MY FRIENDS THOUGHT I WAS JOKING. I SLEPT FOR 18 HOURS.
IT WAS THE BEST ARCHITECTURE PROJECT I'VE EVER DONE.
END.

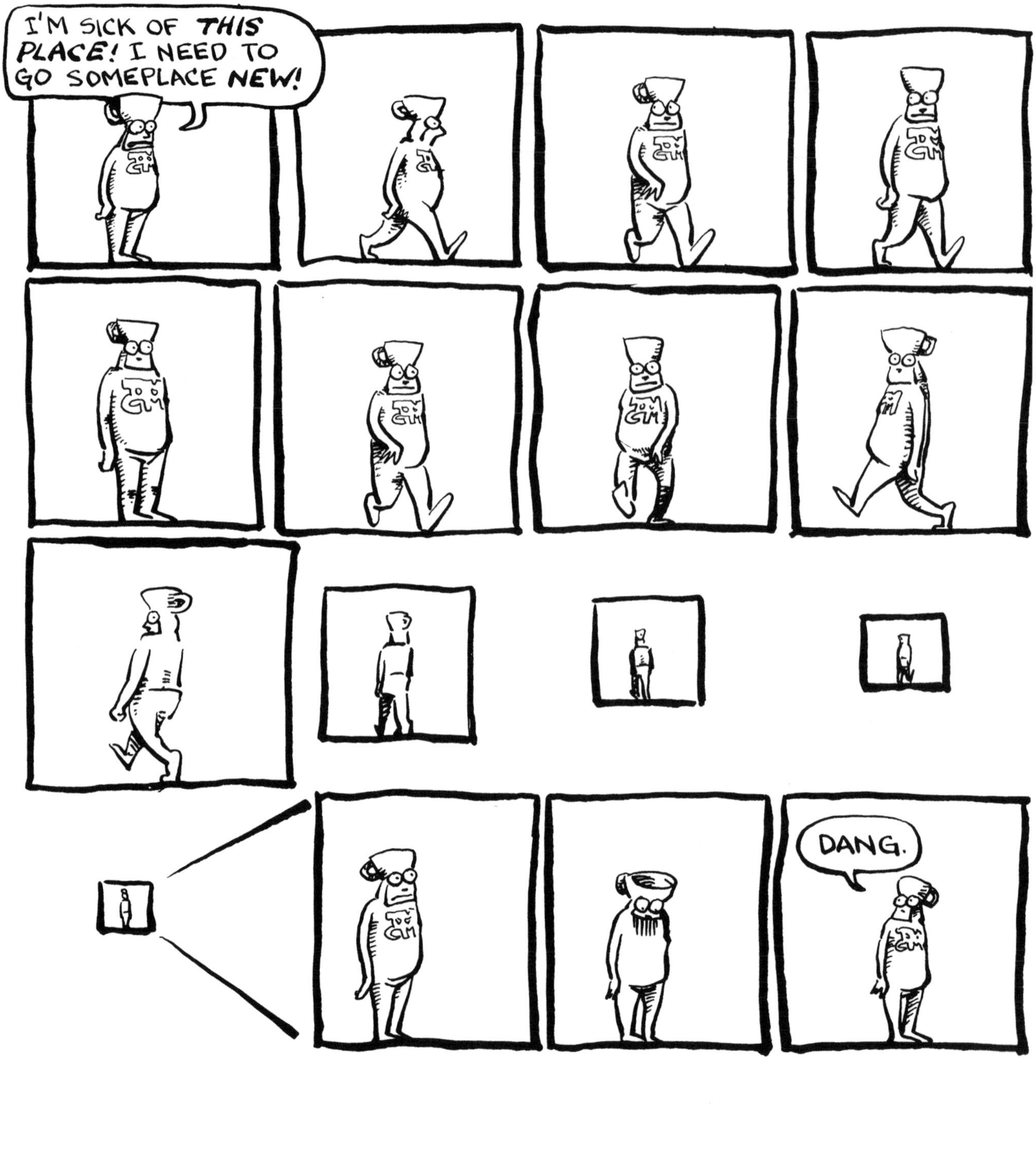

I'M SICK OF THIS PLACE! I NEED TO GO SOMEPLACE NEW!
DANG.

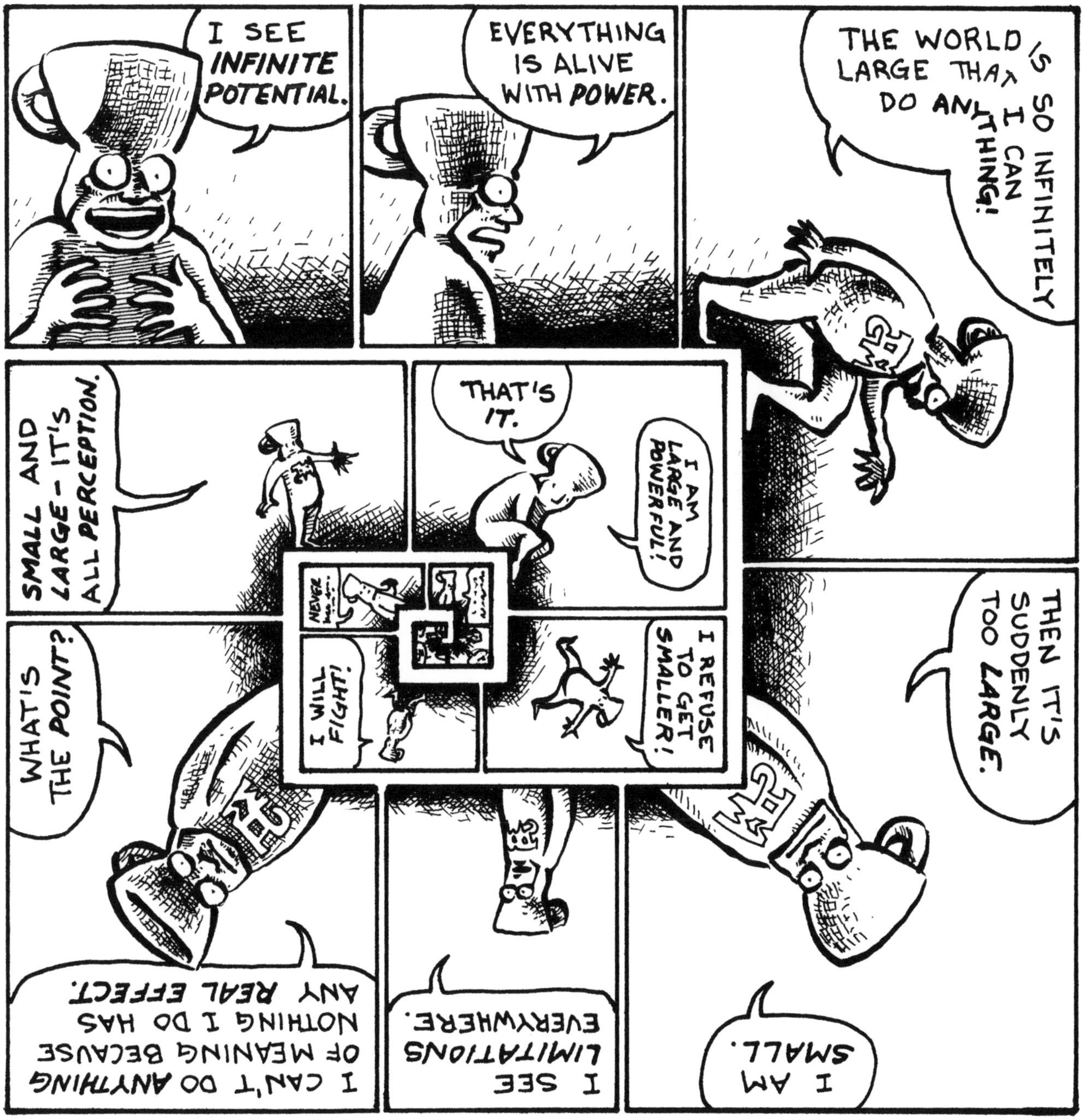
I SEE INFINITE POTENTIAL.
EVERYTHING IS ALIVE WITH POWER.
THE WORLD IS SO INFINITELY LARGE THAT I CAN DO ANYTHING!
THEN IT'S SUDDENLY TOO LARGE.
I AM SMALL.
I SEE LIMITATIONS EVERYWHERE.
I CAN'T DO ANYTHING OF MEANING BECAUSE NOTHING I DO HAS ANY REAL EFFECT.
WHAT'S THE POINT?
SMALL AND LARGE - IT'S ALL PERCEPTION.
THAT'S IT.
I AM LARGE AND POWERFUL!
I REFUSE TO GET SMALLER!
I WILL FIGHT!

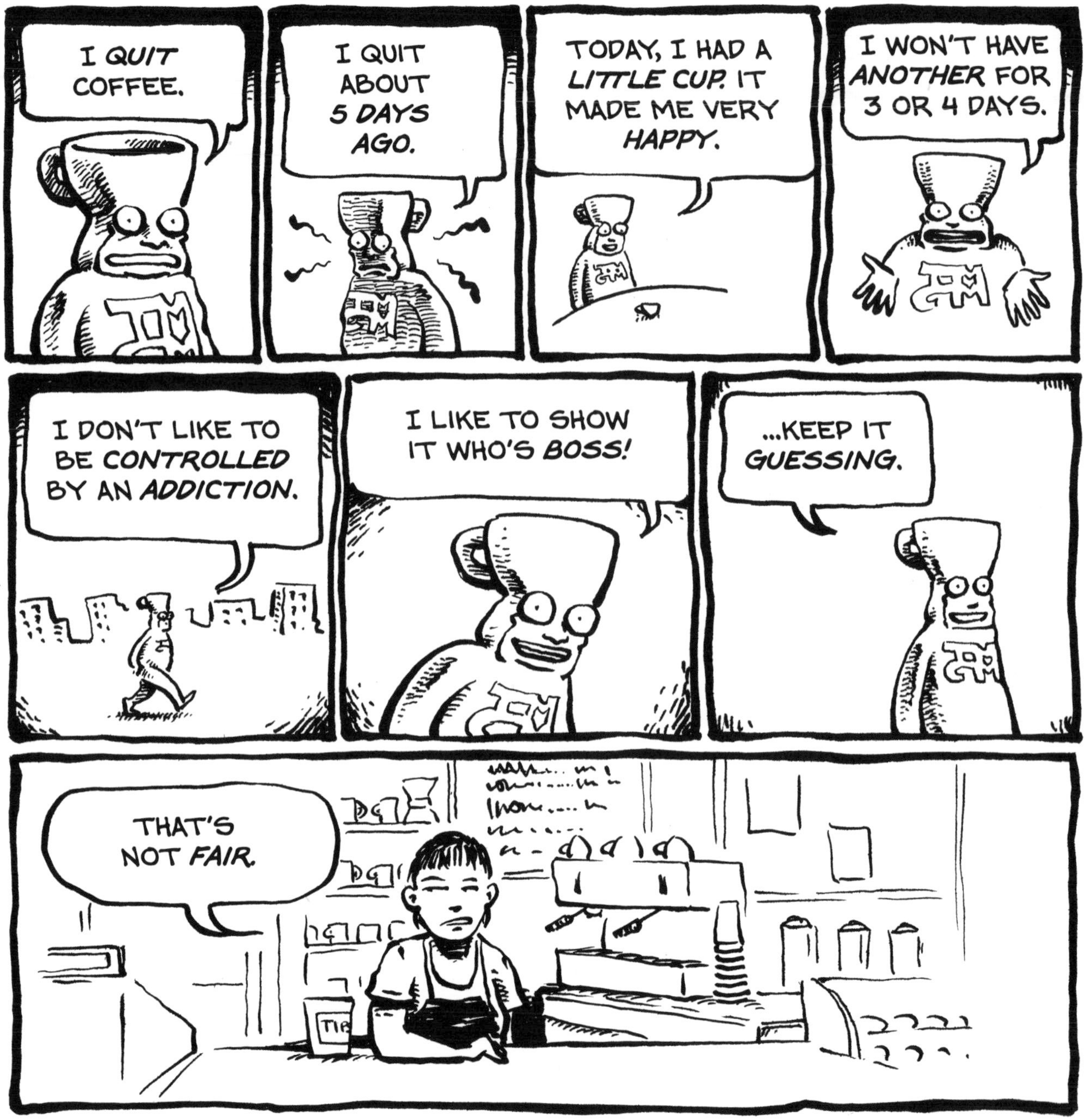
I QUIT COFFEE.
I QUIT ABOUT 5 DAYS AGO.
TODAY, I HAD A LITTLE CUP. IT MADE ME VERY HAPPY.
I WON'T HAVE ANOTHER FOR 3 OR 4 DAYS.
I DON'T LIKE TO BE CONTROLLED BY AN ADDICTION.
I LIKE TO SHOW IT WHO'S BOSS!
...KEEP IT GUESSING.
THAT'S NOT FAIR.

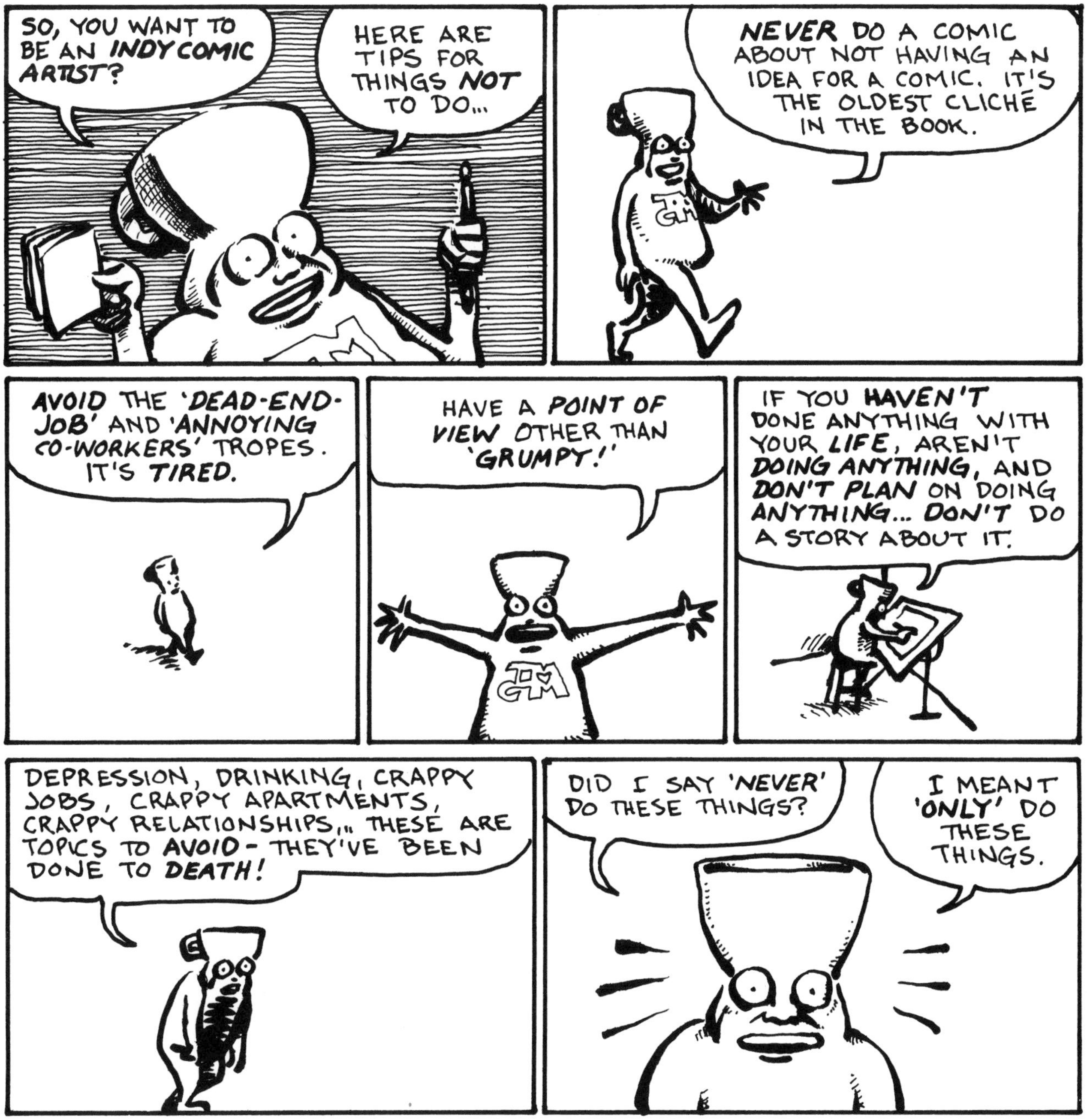
SO, YOU WANT TO BE AN INDY COMIC ARTIST?
HERE ARE TIPS FOR THINGS NOT TO DO...
NEVER DO A COMIC ABOUT NOT HAVING AN IDEA FOR A COMIC. IT'S THE OLDEST CLICHÉ IN THE BOOK.
AVOID THE 'DEAD-END-JOB' AND 'ANNOYING CO-WORKERS' TROPES. IT'S TIRED.
HAVE A POINT OF VIEW OTHER THAN 'GRUMPY!'
IF YOU HAVEN'T DONE ANYTHING WITH YOUR LIFE, AREN'T DOING ANYTHING, AND DON'T PLAN ON DOING ANYTHING... DON'T DO A STORY ABOUT IT.
DEPRESSION, DRINKING, CRAPPY JOBS, CRAPPY APARTMENTS, CRAPPY RELATIONSHIPS... THESE ARE TOPICS TO AVOID - THEY'VE BEEN DONE TO DEATH!
DID I SAY 'NEVER' DO THESE THINGS?
I MEANT 'ONLY' DO THESE THINGS.

WHAT ARE YOU?
I'M A MONEY ANGEL.
ARE YOU HERE TO BRING ME MONEY?
DON'T BE SILLY. I'M THE GHOST OF MONEY SPENT. REMEMBER THE LAPTOP YOU DON'T KNOW HOW TO USE, THE VIDEO CAMERA FOR THE MOVIE YOU NEVER MADE, THE GUITAR YOU NEVER PLAY, THE NIGHT YOU SPENT DRUNK ON EBAY?
LOOK, THERE GOES MORE OF YOUR MONEY NOW.
LITTLE JOBS LIKE THIS ARE JUST A HOBBY.
YOU'RE EVIL!
WAIT! WHERE ARE YOU GOING?
THE WHITE HOUSE.

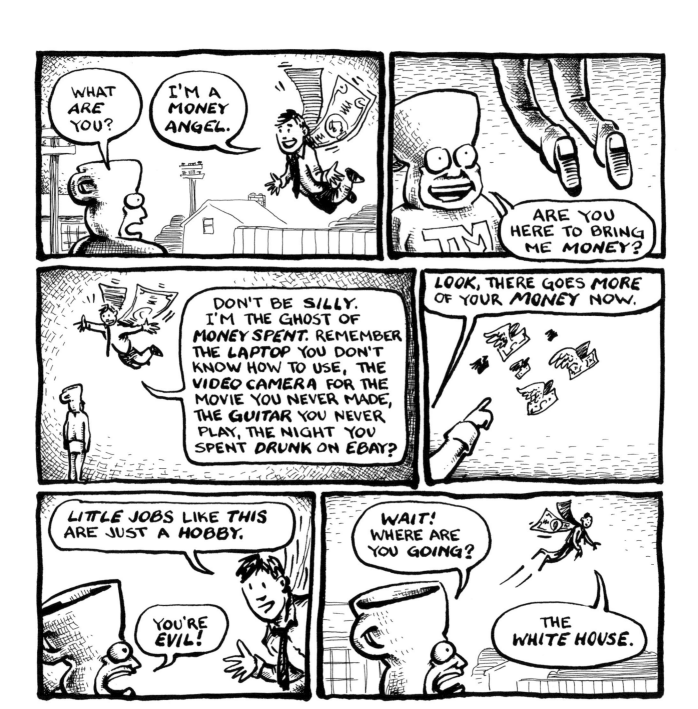

SO MANY THINGS IN LIFE ARE FUTILE. WE HAVE TO EXERCISE TO STAY STRONG!
introducing:
EXERCISES in FUTILITY
THE RELATIONSHIP TREADMILL
I'M EXHAUSTED.
CARROT OF LOVE
COMBATING LONELINESS WITH TELEVISION
IT'S ALMOST LIKE I HAVE FRIENDS OVER.
TREADING WATER IN BILLS & PAYCHECKS
OVERDUE
DUE
BILL
BILL
PLAYING THE LOTTERY TO ESCAPE POVERTY
ODDS ARE ONLY A BILLION TO ONE!
SEEKING SPIRITUALITY IN A CHURCH
IF YOU WANT TO SEE GOD, WATCH A SUNSET.
LOOKING FOR MARRIAGE MATERIAL IN A BAR
I COULD BE THE ONE TO SAVE HER FROM THIS WRETCHED LIFE.
AND, OF COURSE, "EXERCISE" IS AN EXERCISE IN FUTILITY
LIVE IT UP. YOU'RE GOING TO DIE ANYWAY.

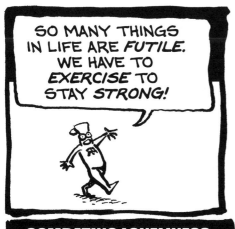

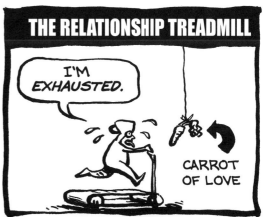

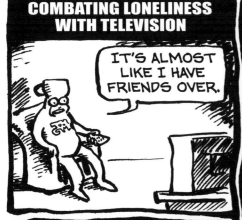

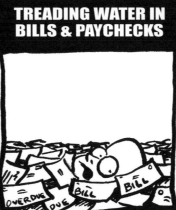

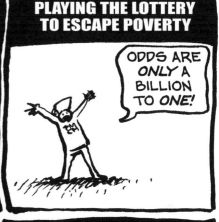

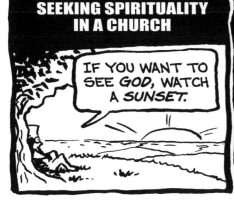

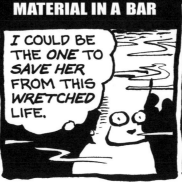

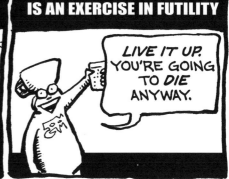

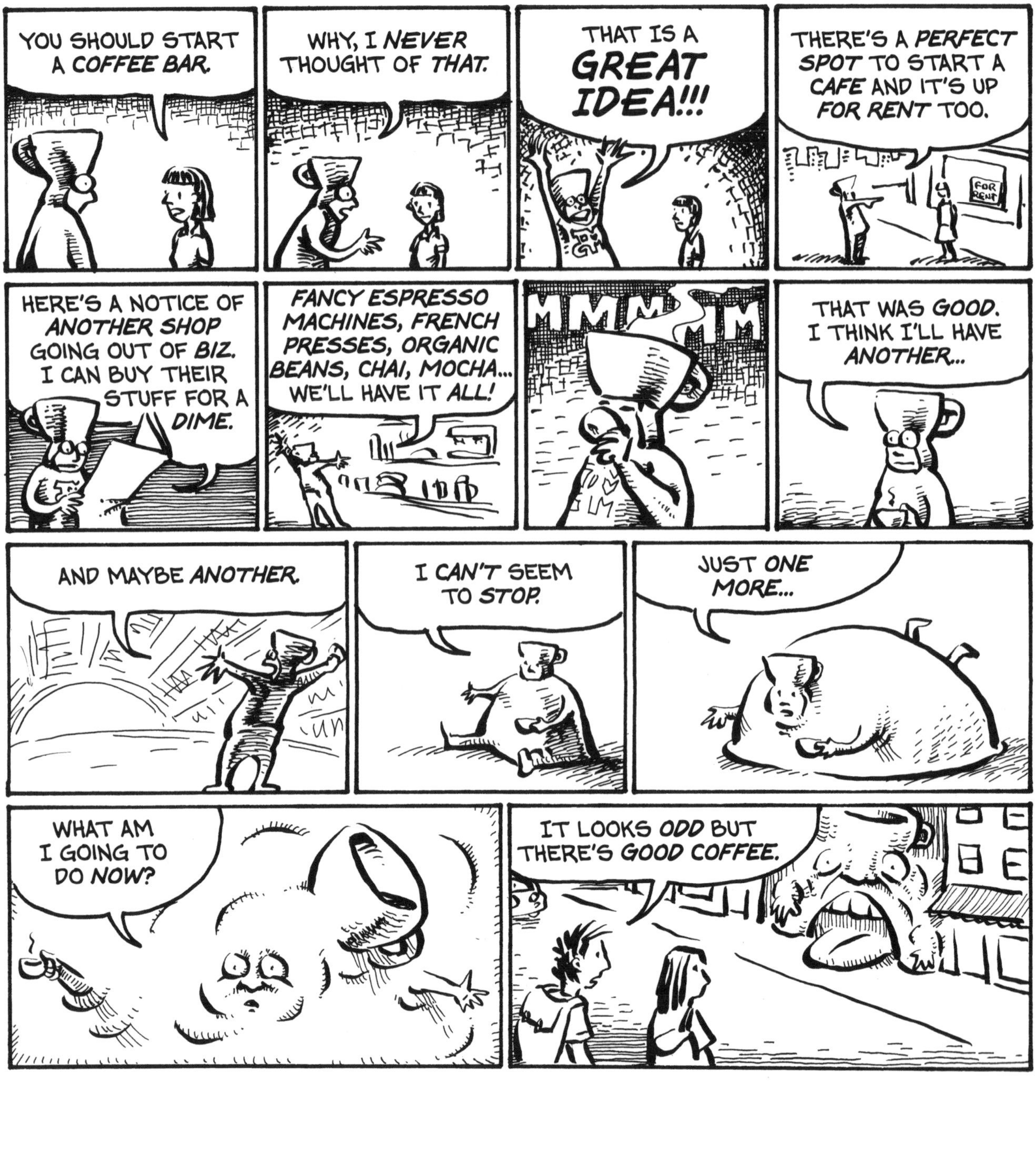
YOU SHOULD START A COFFEE BAR.
WHY, I NEVER THOUGHT OF THAT.
THAT IS A GREAT IDEA!!!
THERE'S A PERFECT SPOT TO START A CAFE AND IT'S UP FOR RENT TOO.
FOR RENT
HERE'S A NOTICE OF ANOTHER SHOP GOING OUT OF BIZ. I CAN BUY THEIR STUFF FOR A DIME.
FANCY ESPRESSO MACHINES, FRENCH PRESSES, ORGANIC BEANS, CHAI, MOCHA... WE'LL HAVE IT ALL!
MMMMM
THAT WAS GOOD. I THINK I'LL HAVE ANOTHER...
AND MAYBE ANOTHER.
I CAN'T SEEM TO STOP.
JUST ONE MORE...
WHAT AM I GOING TO DO NOW?
IT LOOKS ODD BUT THERE'S GOOD COFFEE.

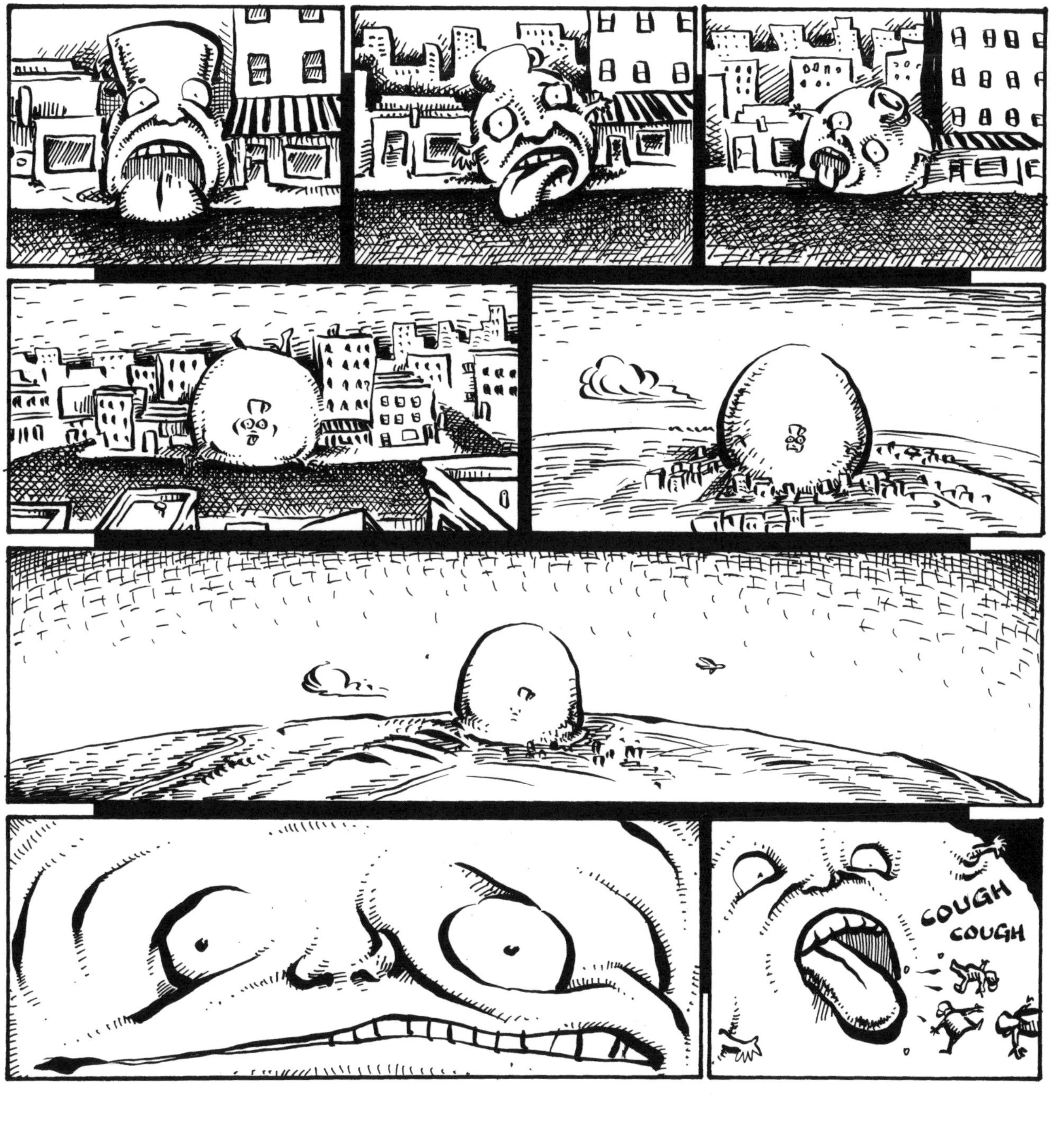
COUGH
COUGH

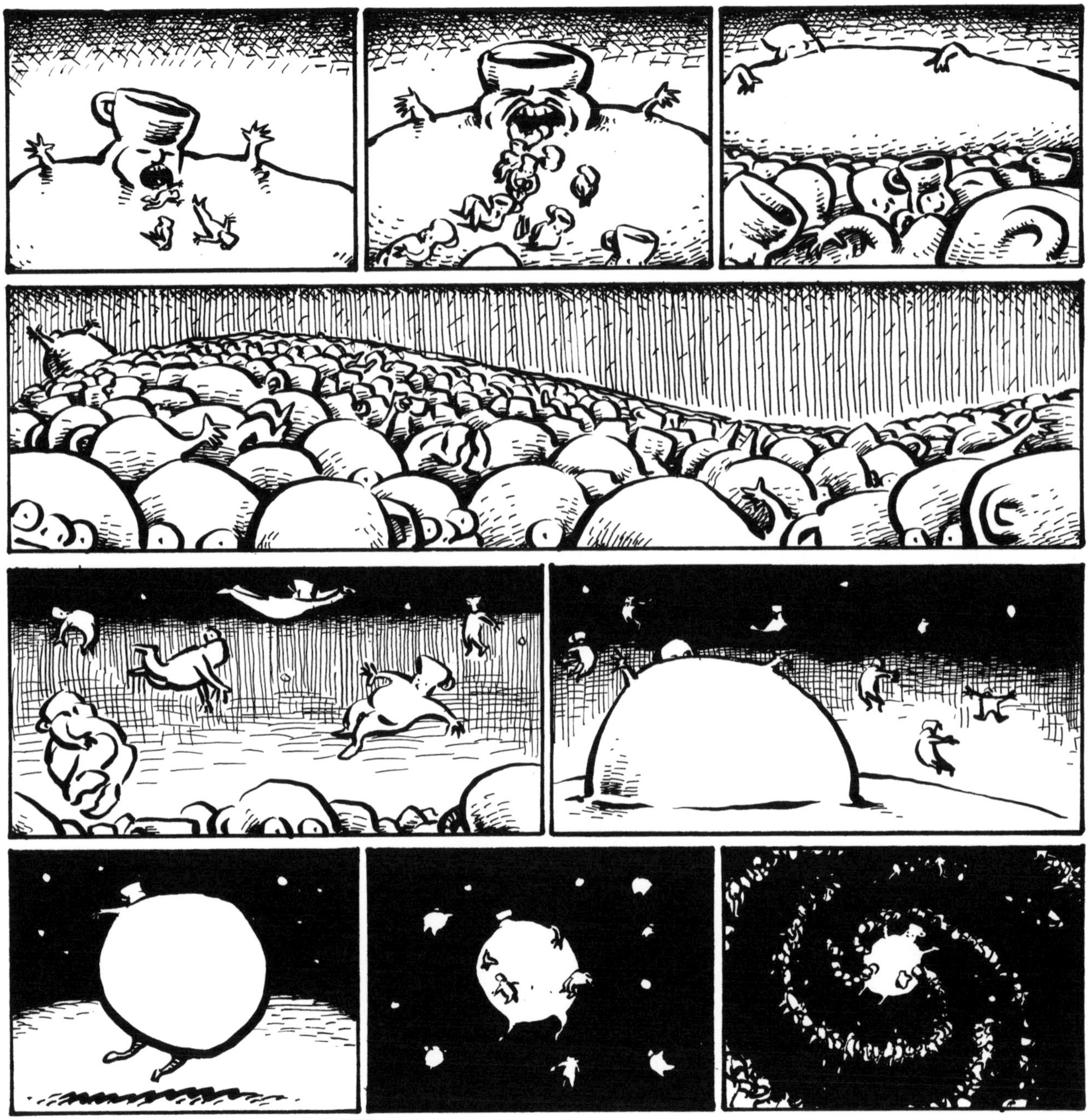

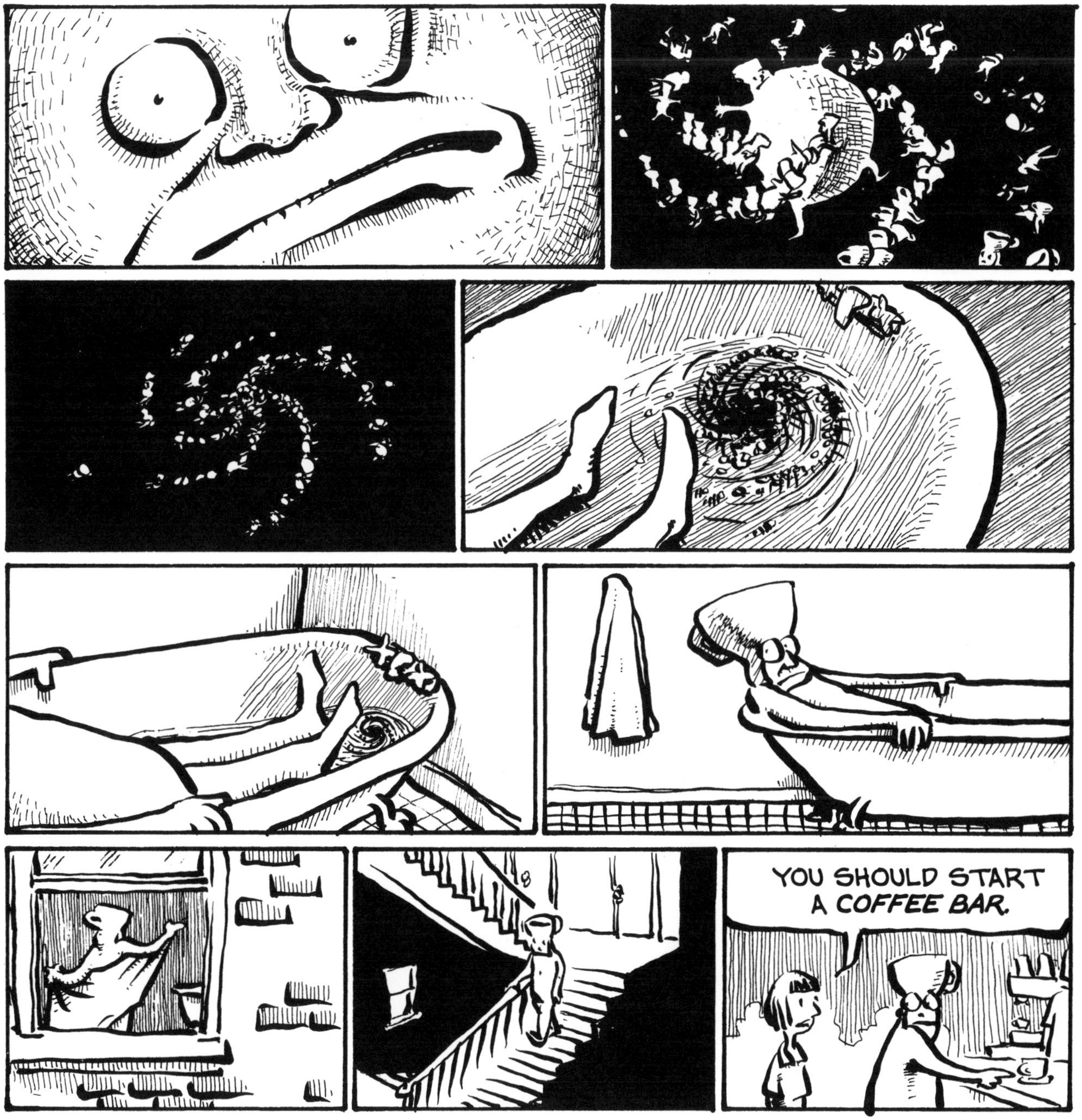
YOU SHOULD START A COFFEE BAR.

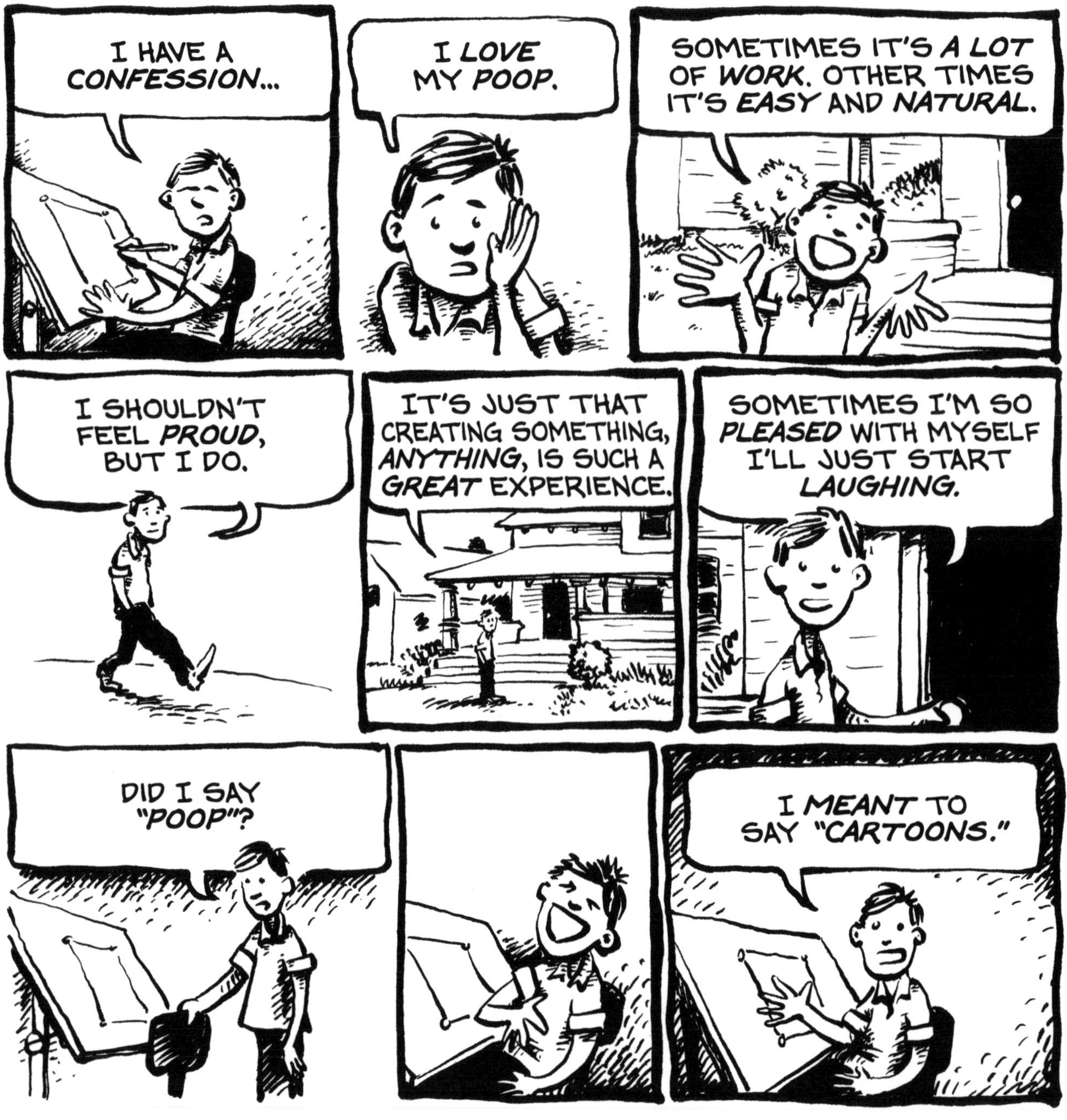
I HAVE A CONFESSION...
I LOVE MY POOP.
SOMETIMES IT'S A LOT OF WORK. OTHER TIMES IT'S EASY AND NATURAL.
I SHOULDN'T FEEL PROUD, BUT I DO.
IT'S JUST THAT CREATING SOMETHING, ANYTHING, IS SUCH A GREAT EXPERIENCE.
SOMETIMES I'M SO PLEASED WITH MYSELF I'LL JUST START LAUGHING.
DID I SAY "POOP"?
I MEANT TO SAY "CARTOONS."

OMNIBUS PLUS (BONUS) COLOR SECTION

DARK HORSE PRESENTS VOLUME 3 #33

Cover Art by Shannon Wheeler

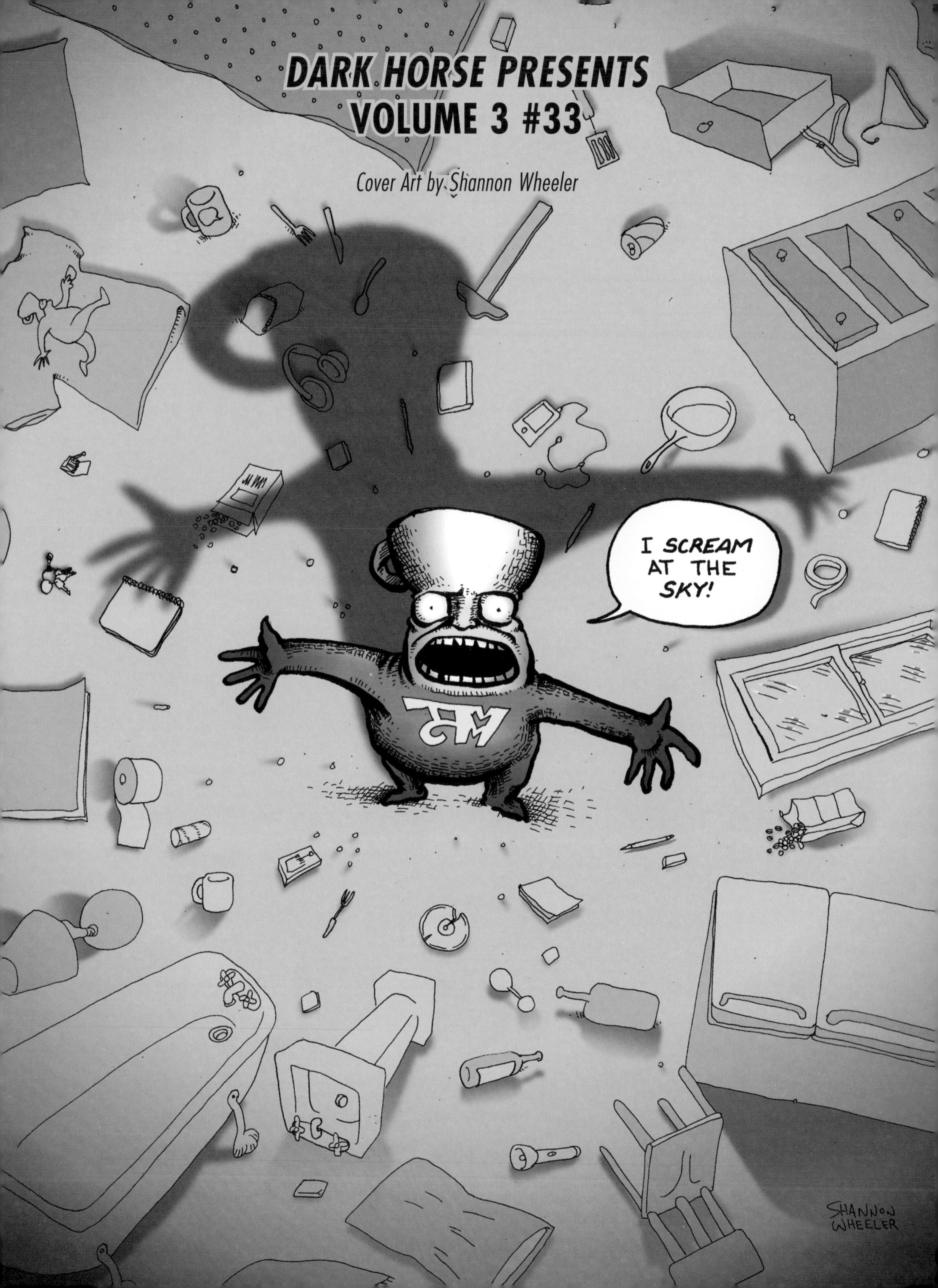
I SCREAM AT THE SKY!
SHANNON WHEELER

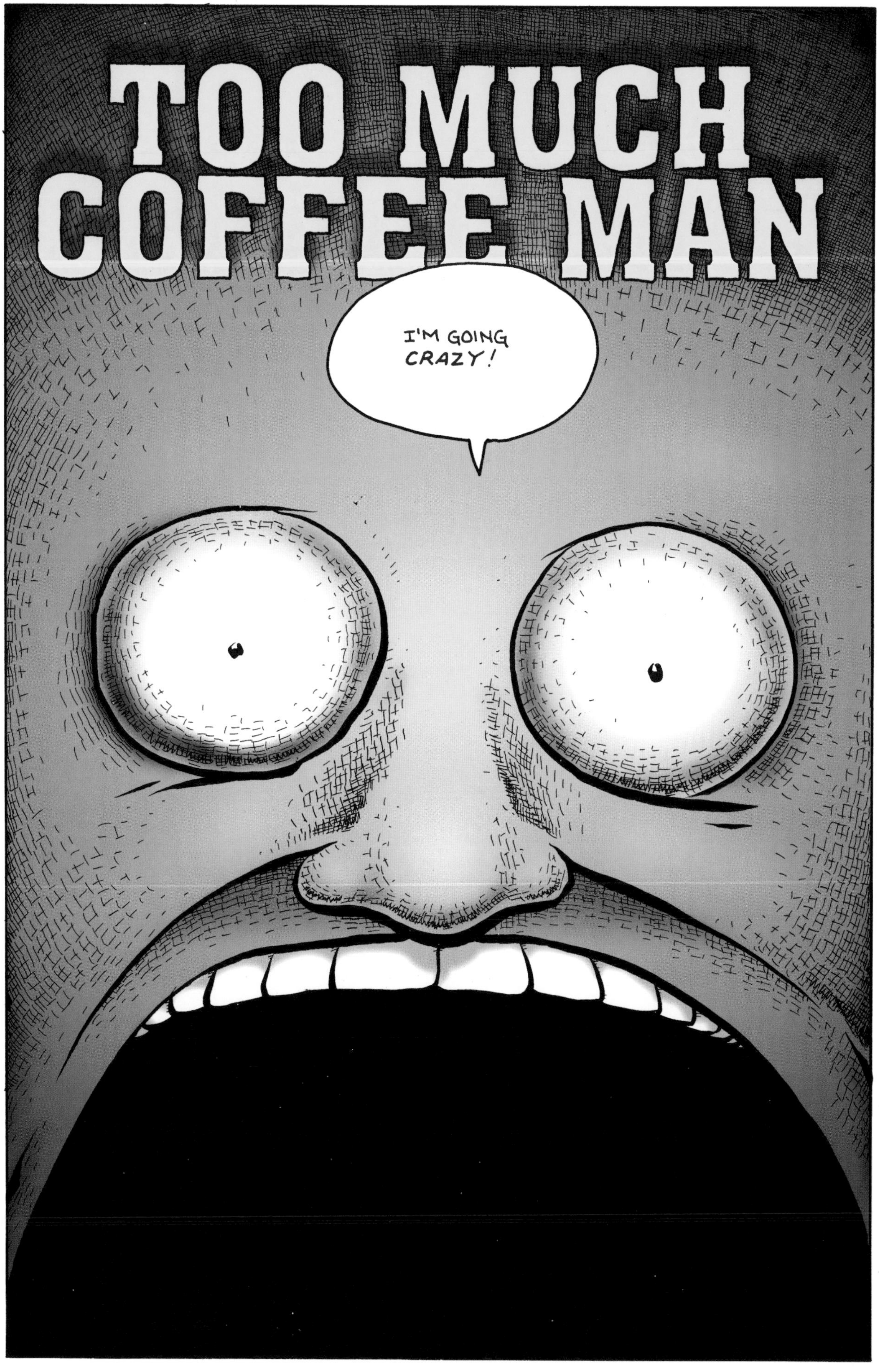
TOO MUCH COFFEE MAN
I'M GOING CRAZY!

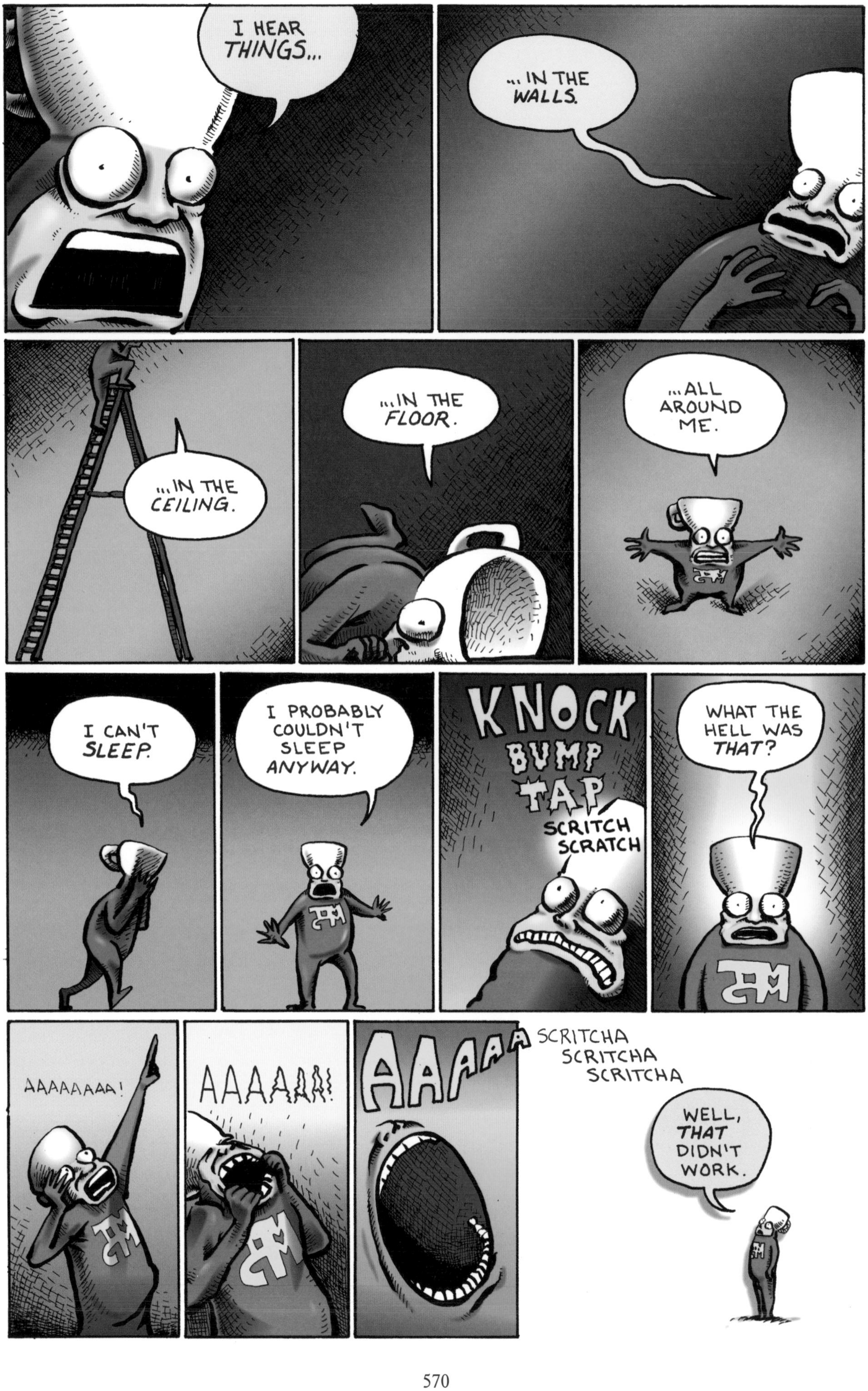
I HEAR THINGS...
...IN THE WALLS.
...IN THE CEILING.
...IN THE FLOOR.
...ALL AROUND ME.
I CAN'T SLEEP.
I PROBABLY COULDN'T SLEEP ANYWAY.
KNOCK
BUMP
TAP
SCRITCH SCRATCH
WHAT THE HELL WAS THAT?
AAAAAAAA!
AAAAAA!
AAAAA
SCRITCHA
SCRITCHA
SCRITCHA
WELL, THAT DIDN'T WORK.

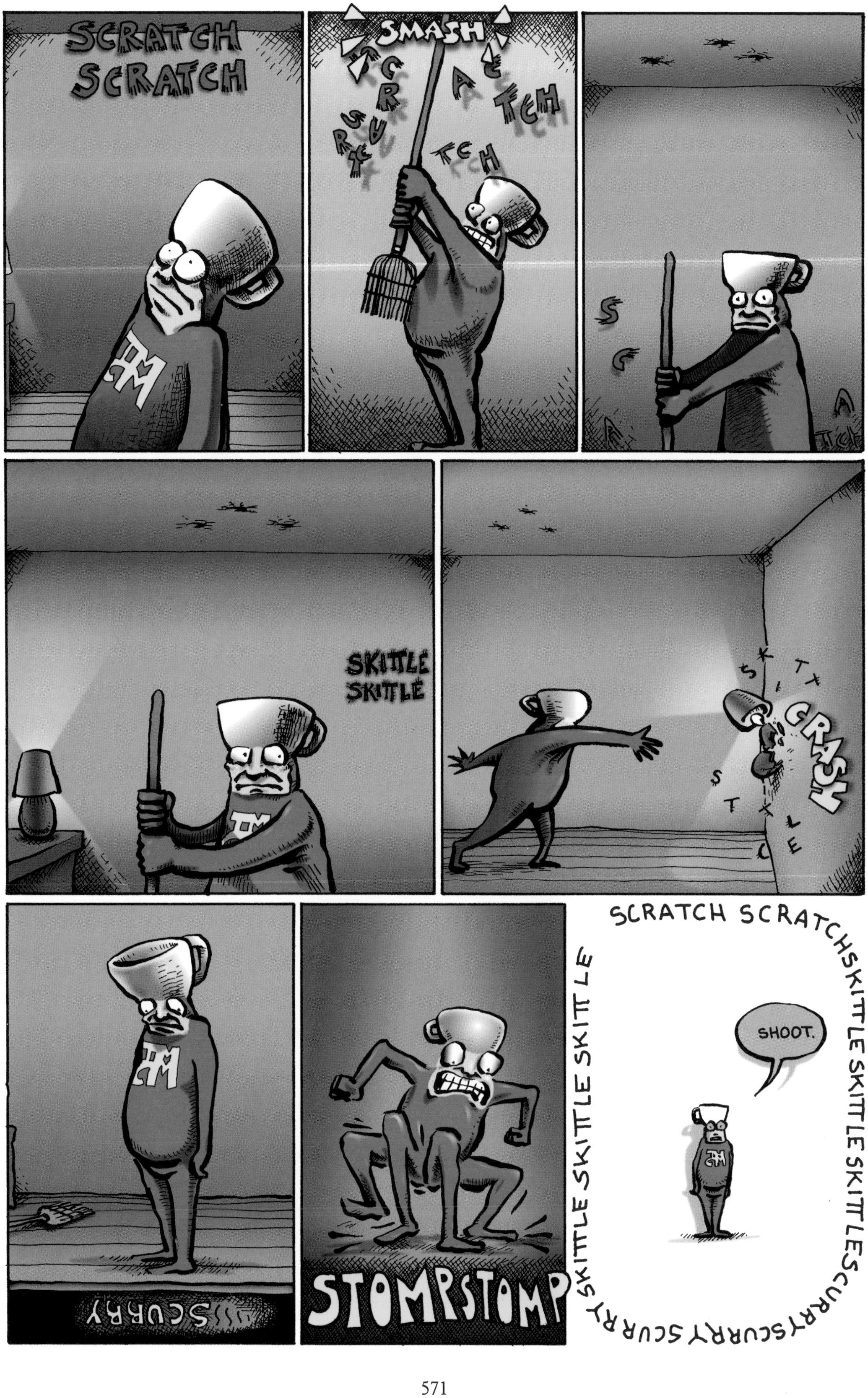
SCRATCH SCRATCH
SMASH
SKITTLE SKITTLE
CRASH
SCURRY
STOMPSTOMP
SCRATCH SCRATCHSKITTLE SKITTLE SKITTLESCURRYSCURRY SCURRY SKITTLE SKITTLE SKITTLE
SHOOT.

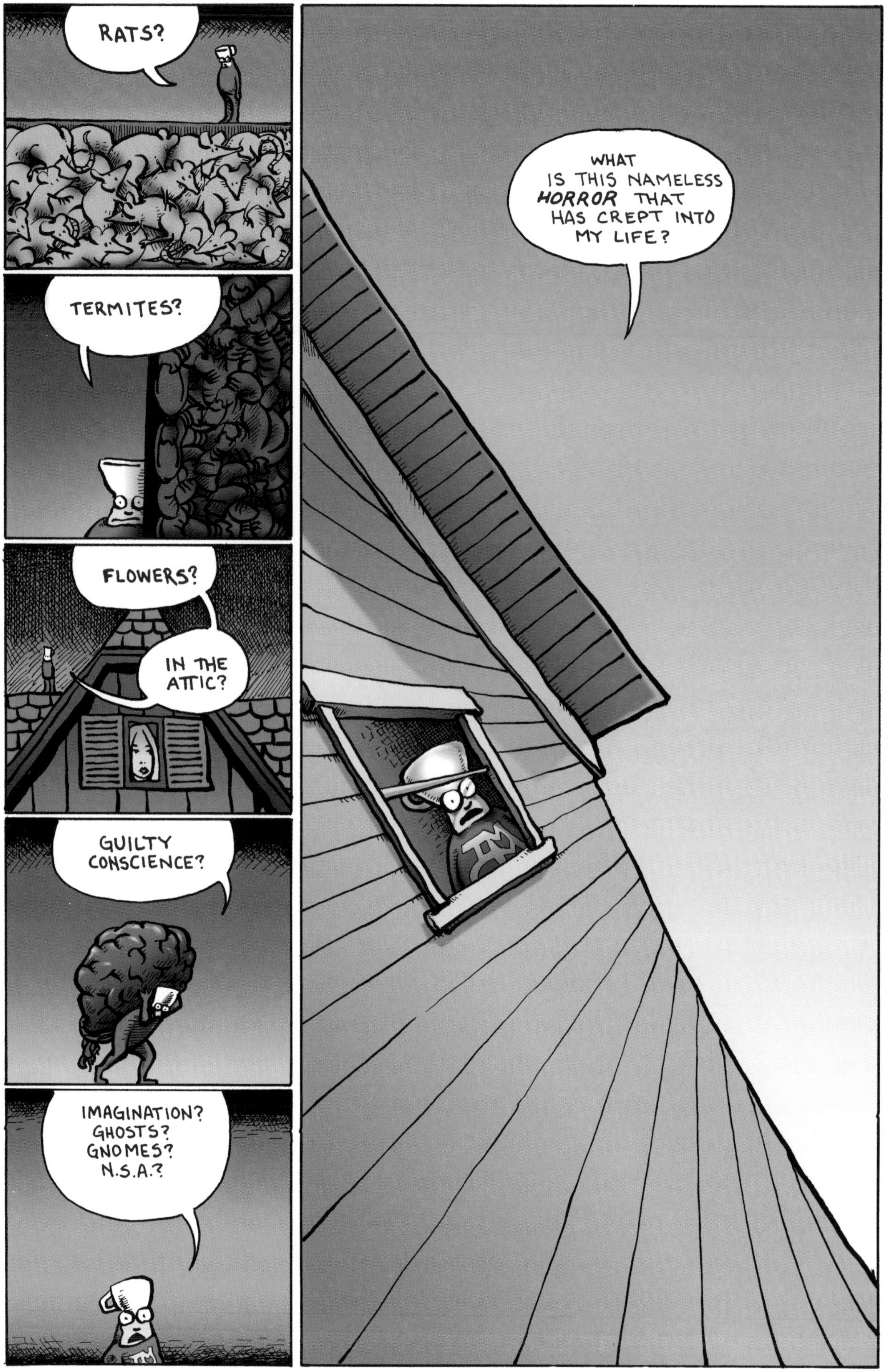
RATS?
TERMITES?
FLOWERS?
IN THE ATTIC?
GUILTY CONSCIENCE?
IMAGINATION? GHOSTS? GNOMES? N.S.A.?
WHAT IS THIS NAMELESS HORROR THAT HAS CREPT INTO MY LIFE?

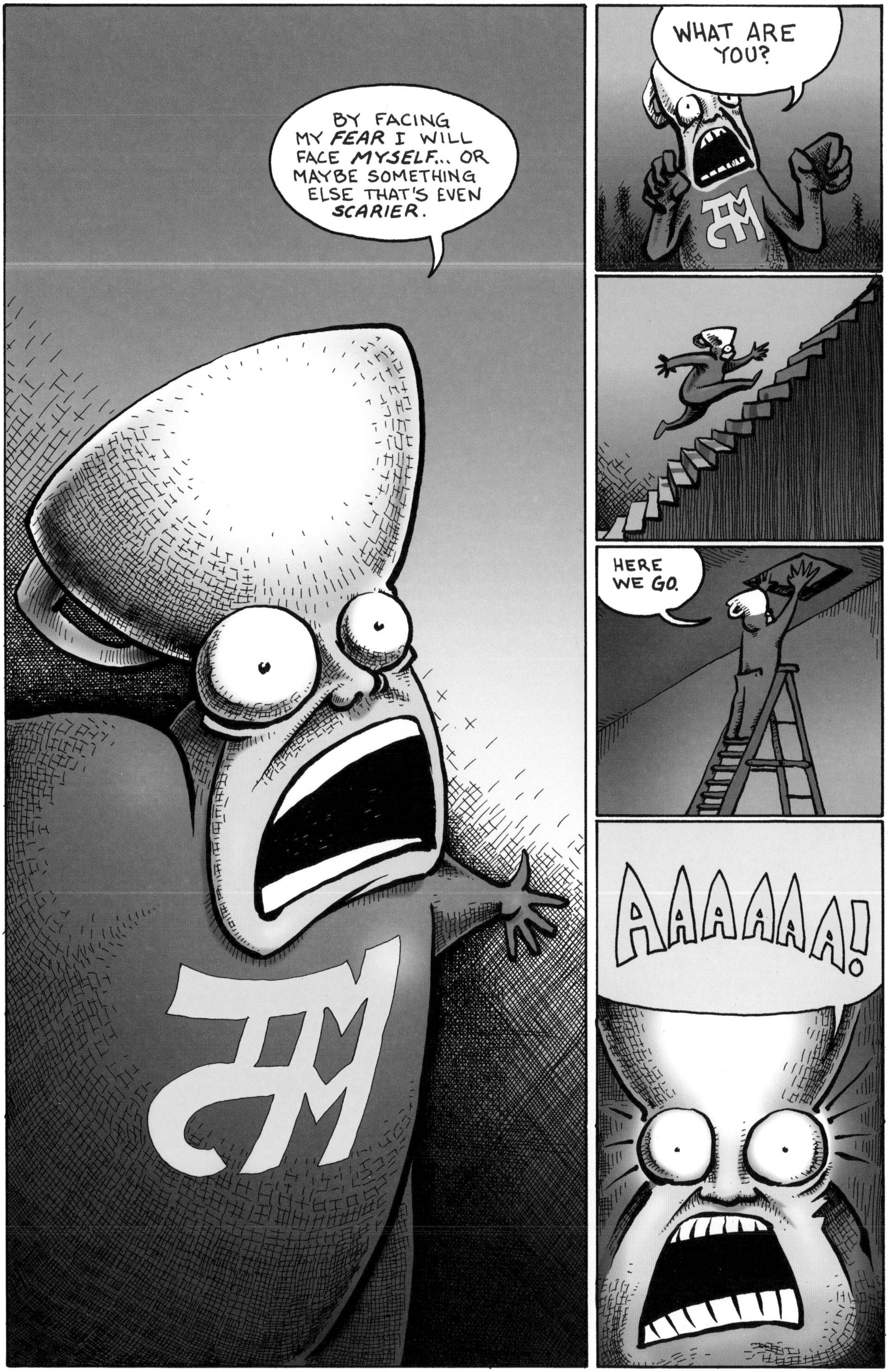
BY FACING MY FEAR I WILL FACE MYSELF... OR MAYBE SOMETHING ELSE THAT'S EVEN SCARIER.
WHAT ARE YOU?
HERE WE GO.
AAAAAA!

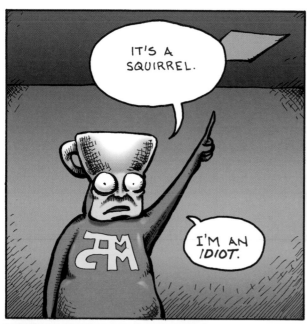

IT'S A SQUIRREL.

I'M AN IDIOT.

I'M RELIEVED I'M STUPID. MY FEARS ARE PAPER MONSTERS AND THE REALITY IS SMALL, FURRY, AND EASY. BUT I KNOW I'M JINXING MYSELF. SAYING THAT HANDLING THIS SQUIRREL WILL BE EASY IS A SETUP FOR SLAPSTICK TRAGEDY.

SO... I'LL SAY: GETTING RID OF THIS SQUIRREL WILL BE THE HARDEST THING I'VE EVER DONE.

"HOW TO TAKE CARE OF SQUIRRELS"...

KNOCK KNOCK

WHAT ARE YOU UP TO?

I'M LOOKING FOR A RHYME TO RHYME WITH RHYME.

"SQUIRRELS ENJOY FRESH WATER AND A VARIETY OF NUTS." WAIT. THIS ISN'T HOW TO TAKE CARE OF SQUIRRELS. THIS IS HOW TO TAKE CARE OF SQUIRRELS.

I'M IN A MIRROR TWILIGHT ZONE... FULL OF LOVE AND TENDERNESS. THIS IS ALL WRONG.

HOW TO TAKE CARE OF SQUIRRELS

SCREW BOOKS. THE INTERNET WILL HAVE THE ANSWERS.

I READ THE INTERNET FOR THE ARTICLES.

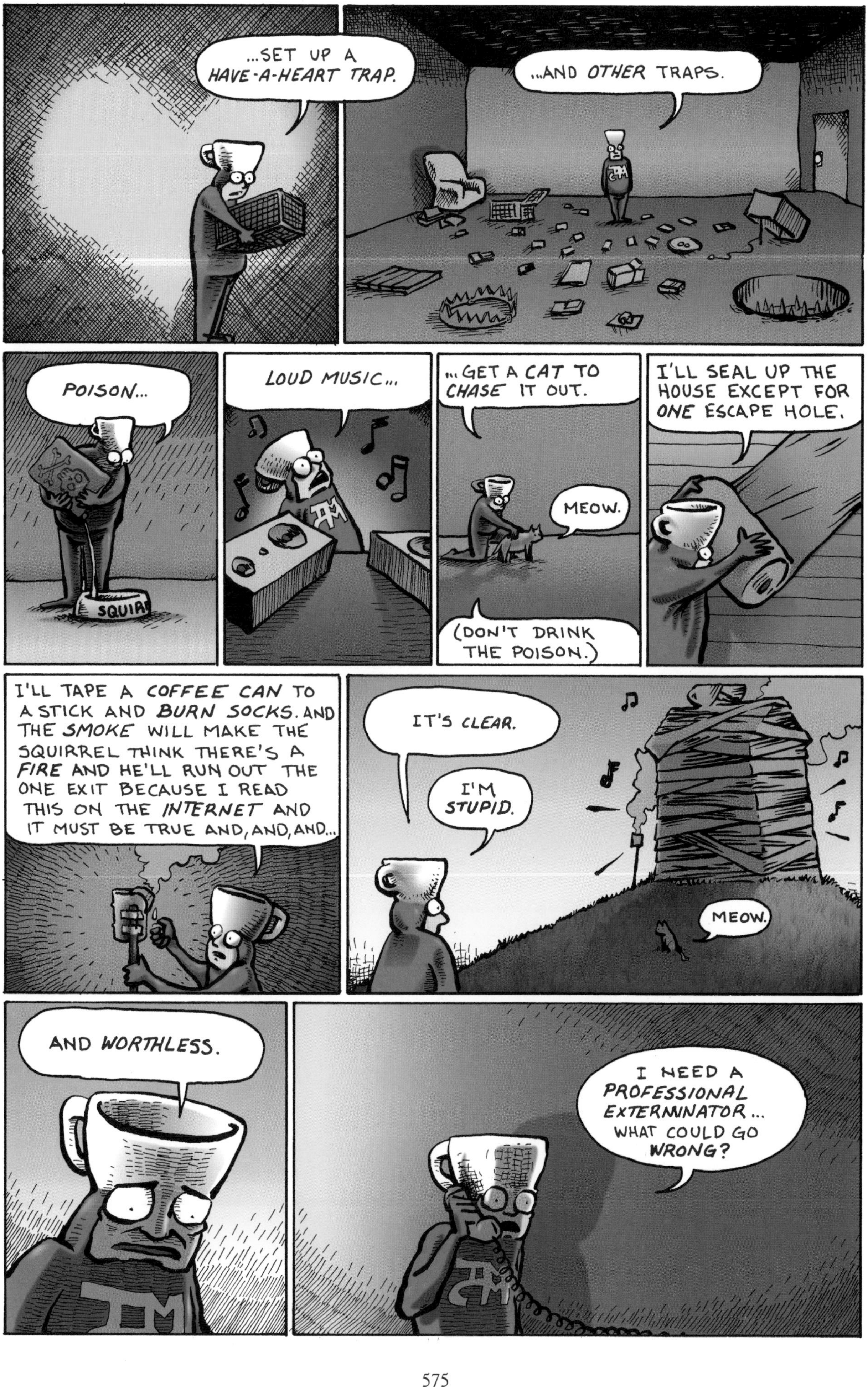
...SET UP A HAVE-A-HEART TRAP.
...AND OTHER TRAPS.
POISON...
SQUIR
LOUD MUSIC...
...GET A CAT TO CHASE IT OUT.
MEOW.
(DON'T DRINK THE POISON.)
I'LL SEAL UP THE HOUSE EXCEPT FOR ONE ESCAPE HOLE.
I'LL TAPE A COFFEE CAN TO A STICK AND BURN SOCKS. AND THE SMOKE WILL MAKE THE SQUIRREL THINK THERE'S A FIRE AND HE'LL RUN OUT THE ONE EXIT BECAUSE I READ THIS ON THE INTERNET AND IT MUST BE TRUE AND, AND, AND...
IT'S CLEAR.
I'M STUPID.
MEOW.
AND WORTHLESS.
I NEED A PROFESSIONAL EXTERMINATOR... WHAT COULD GO WRONG?

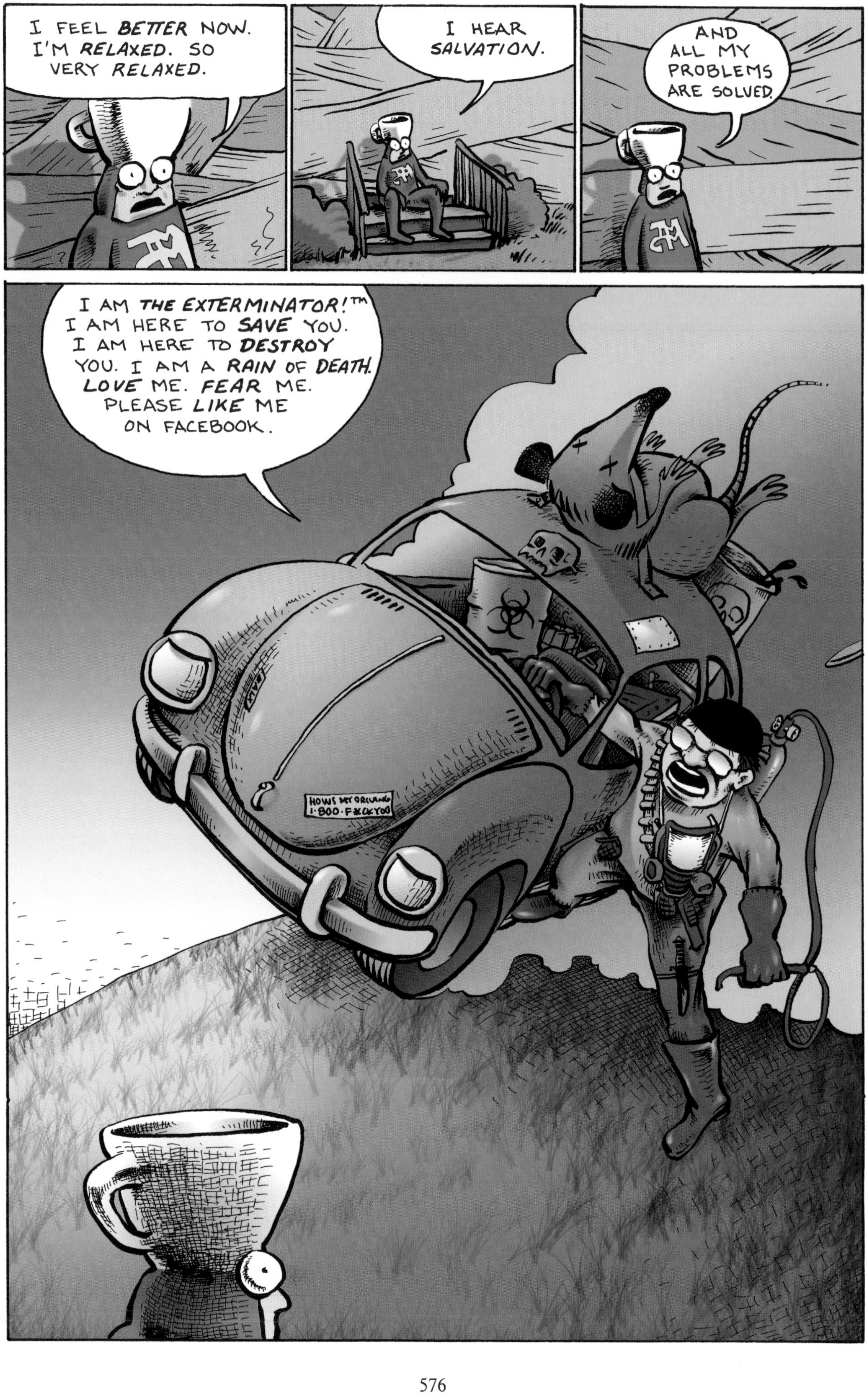
I FEEL BETTER NOW. I'M RELAXED. SO VERY RELAXED.
I HEAR SALVATION.
AND ALL MY PROBLEMS ARE SOLVED.
I AM THE EXTERMINATOR!™ I AM HERE TO SAVE YOU. I AM HERE TO DESTROY YOU. I AM A RAIN OF DEATH. LOVE ME. FEAR ME. PLEASE LIKE ME ON FACEBOOK.
HOWS MY DRIVING 1·800·F#CKYOU

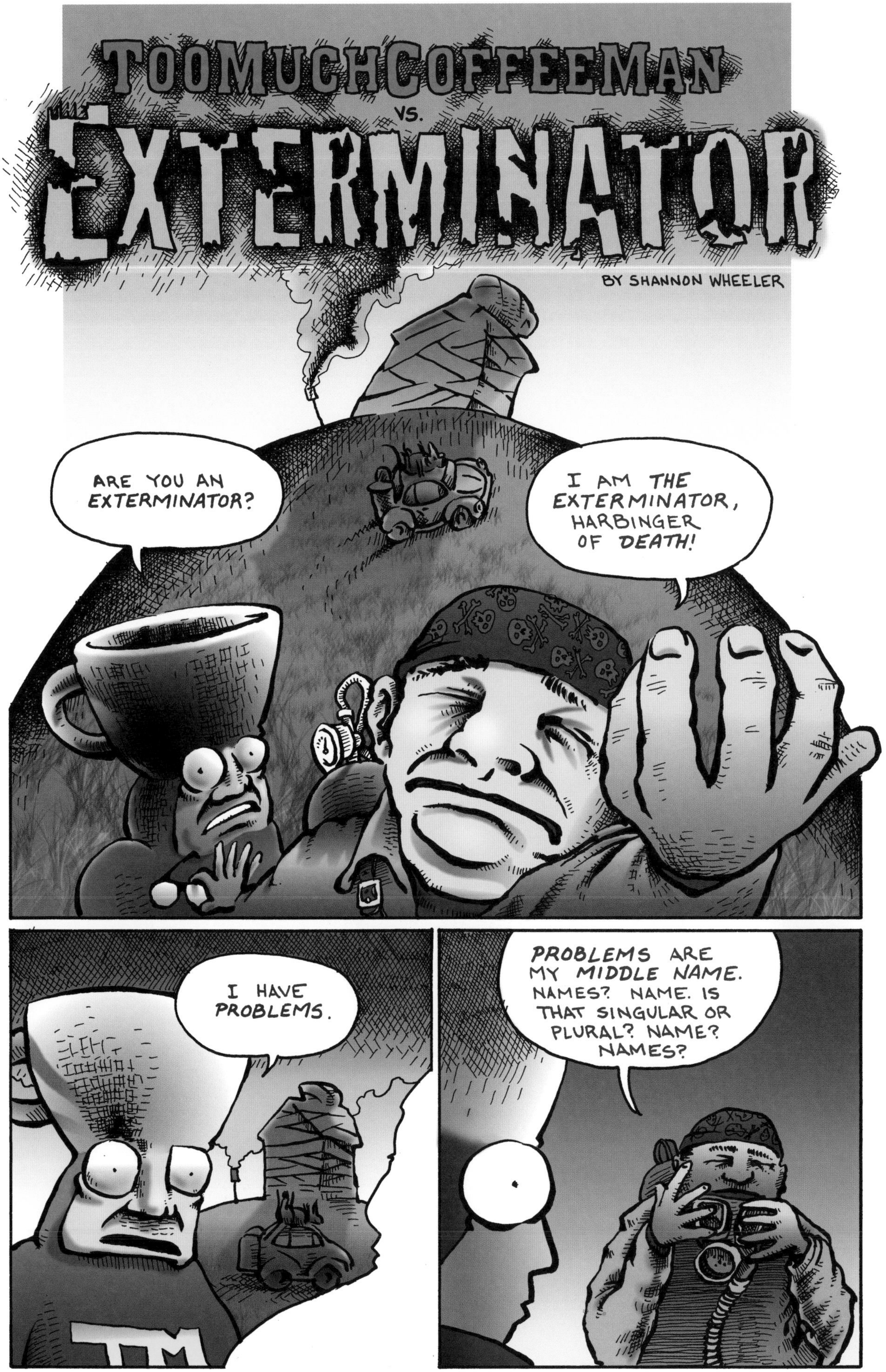
TOO MUCH COFFEE MAN
VS.
EXTERMINATOR
BY SHANNON WHEELER
ARE YOU AN EXTERMINATOR?
I AM THE EXTERMINATOR, HARBINGER OF DEATH!
I HAVE PROBLEMS.
PROBLEMS ARE MY MIDDLE NAME. NAMES? NAME. IS THAT SINGULAR OR PLURAL? NAME? NAMES?
TM

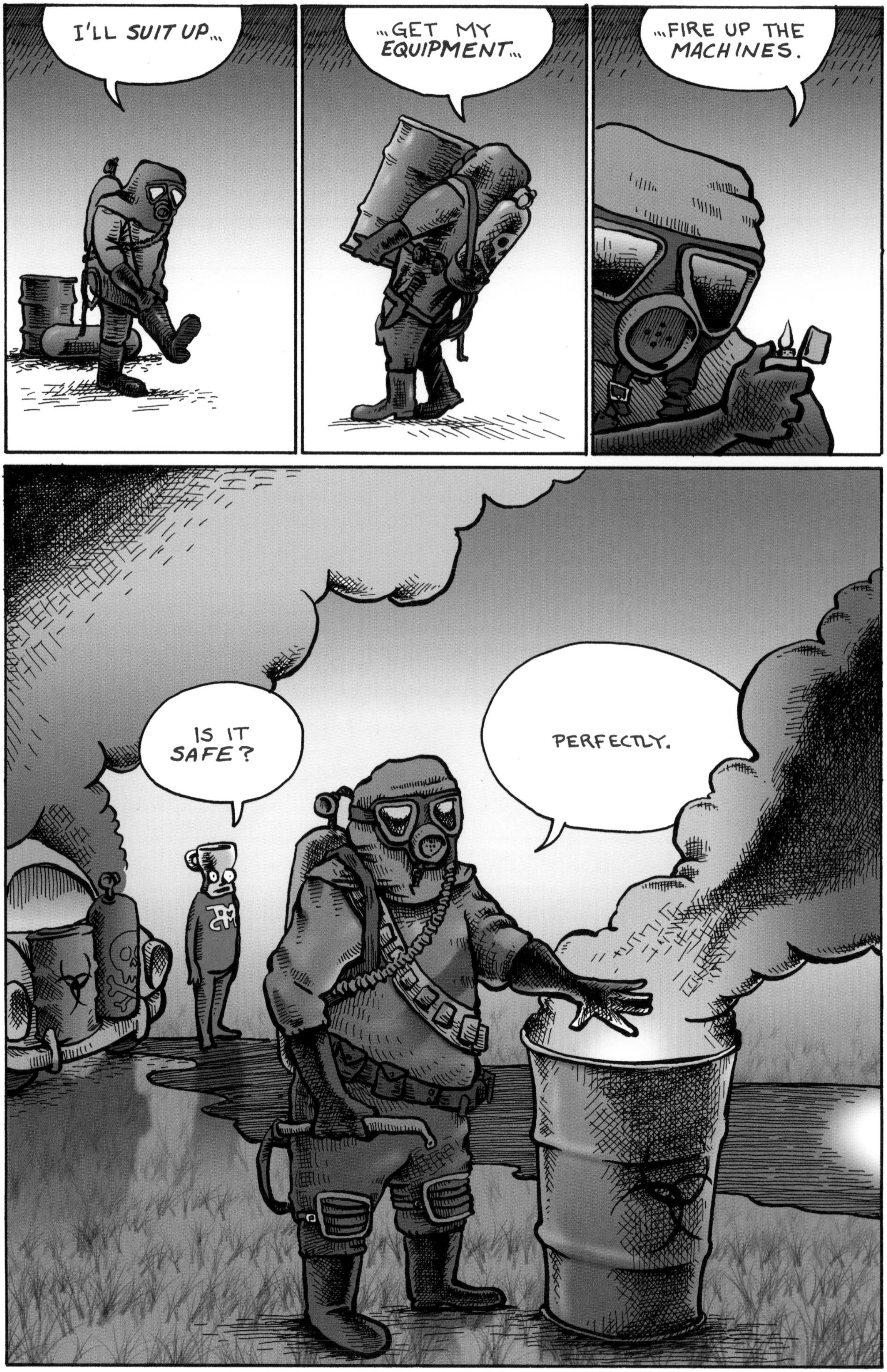
I'LL SUIT UP...
...GET MY EQUIPMENT...
...FIRE UP THE MACHINES.
IS IT SAFE?
PERFECTLY.

DESCRIBE YOUR PROBLEM...
I HAVE A SQUIRREL.
AND HE'S DRIVING ME CRAZY.
HE'S IN THE WALLS, CEILING, AND FLOOR, AND EVERYWHERE.
HE MOVED IN AND MADE HIMSELF A HOME. HE BRINGS IN NUTS AND EATS, PEES, POOS. HIS SQUIRREL FRIENDS COME OVER AND HE HAS SQUIRREL PARTIES. HE GOT A SQUIRREL GIRLFRIEND AND THE SQUIRREL PARTIES STOPPED, BUT I'D HAVE TO LISTEN TO...
...SQUIRREL SEX. THAT STOPPED AFTER THEY HAD A SQUIRREL BABY. IT MUST HAVE BEEN STRESSFUL BECAUSE I'D HEAR THEIR SQUIRREL ARGUMENTS. AND NOW SQUIRRELS' COUPLES COUNSELING...
I HAVE JUST THE THING TO SOLVE ALL OF EVERYTHING.

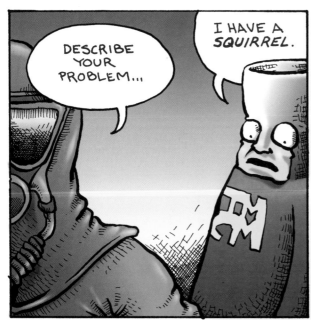

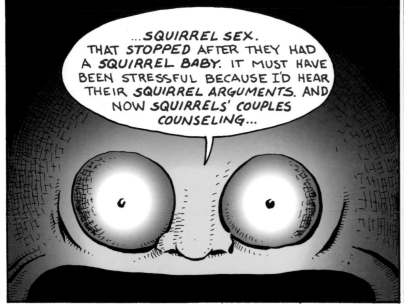

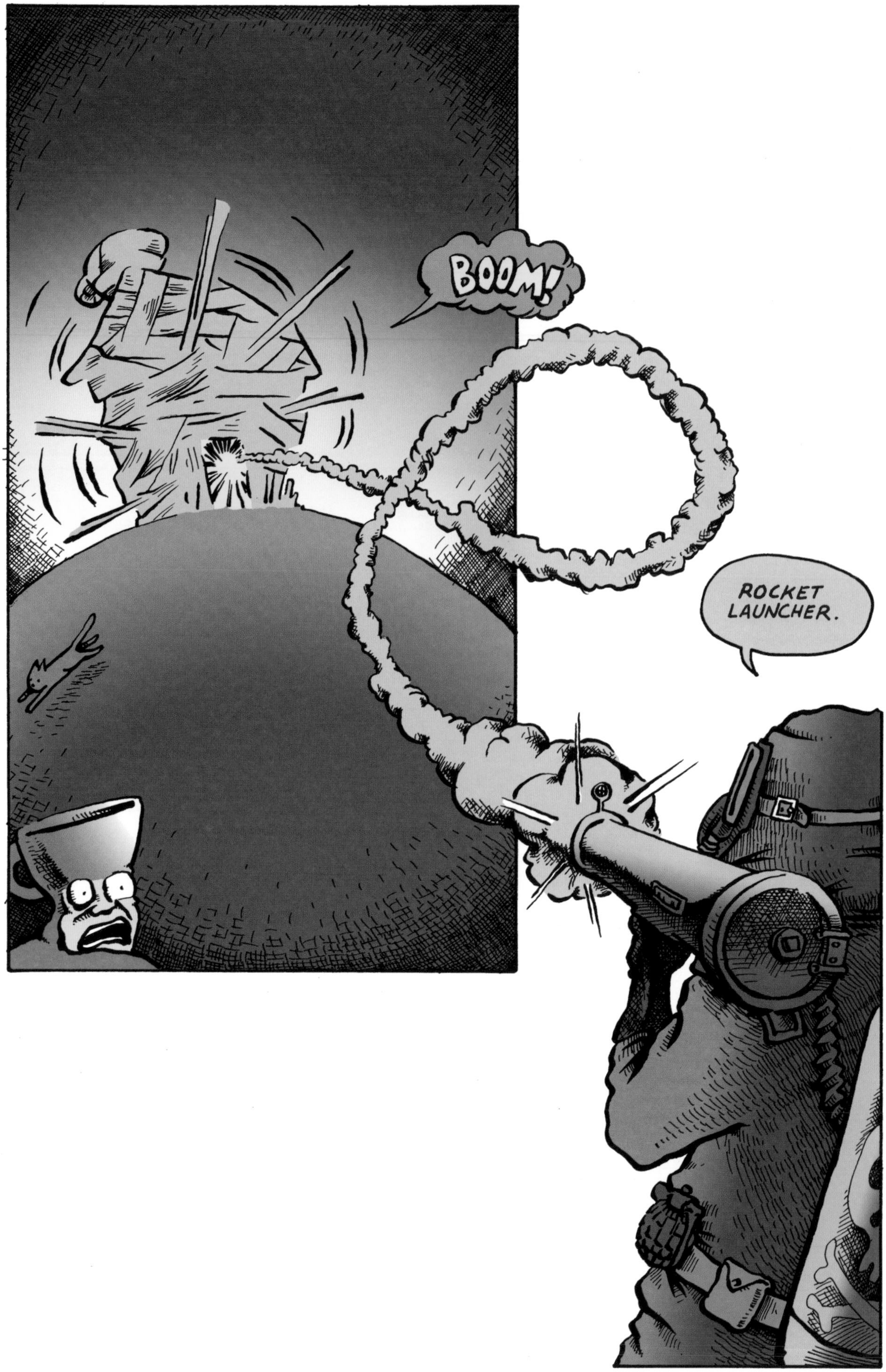
BOOM!
ROCKET LAUNCHER.

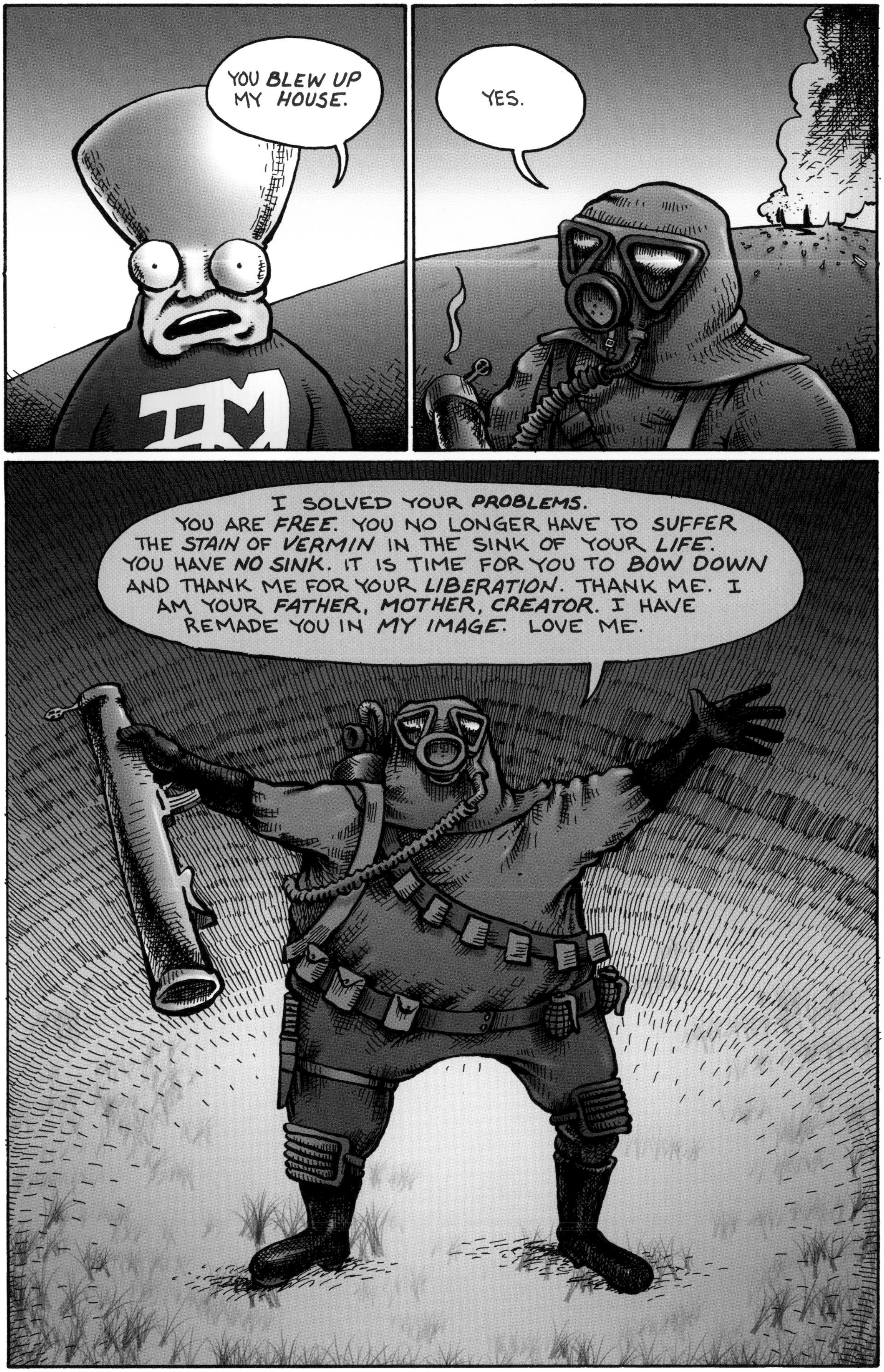
YOU BLEW UP MY HOUSE.
YES.
I SOLVED YOUR PROBLEMS. YOU ARE FREE. YOU NO LONGER HAVE TO SUFFER THE STAIN OF VERMIN IN THE SINK OF YOUR LIFE. YOU HAVE NO SINK. IT IS TIME FOR YOU TO BOW DOWN AND THANK ME FOR YOUR LIBERATION. THANK ME. I AM YOUR FATHER, MOTHER, CREATOR. I HAVE REMADE YOU IN MY IMAGE. LOVE ME.

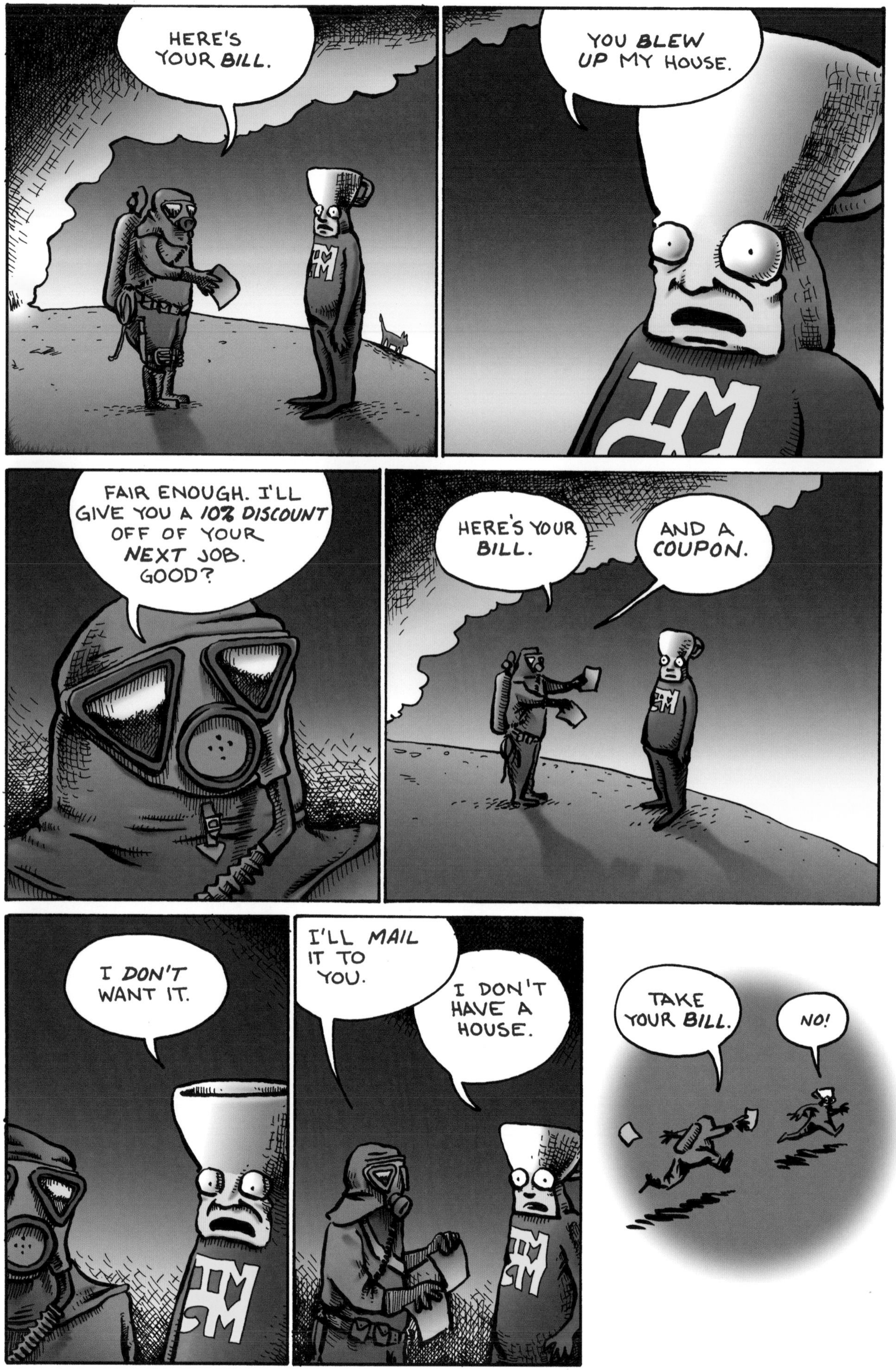
HERE'S YOUR BILL.
YOU BLEW UP MY HOUSE.
FAIR ENOUGH. I'LL GIVE YOU A 10% DISCOUNT OFF OF YOUR NEXT JOB. GOOD?
HERE'S YOUR BILL.
AND A COUPON.
I DON'T WANT IT.
I'LL MAIL IT TO YOU.
I DON'T HAVE A HOUSE.
TAKE YOUR BILL.
NO!

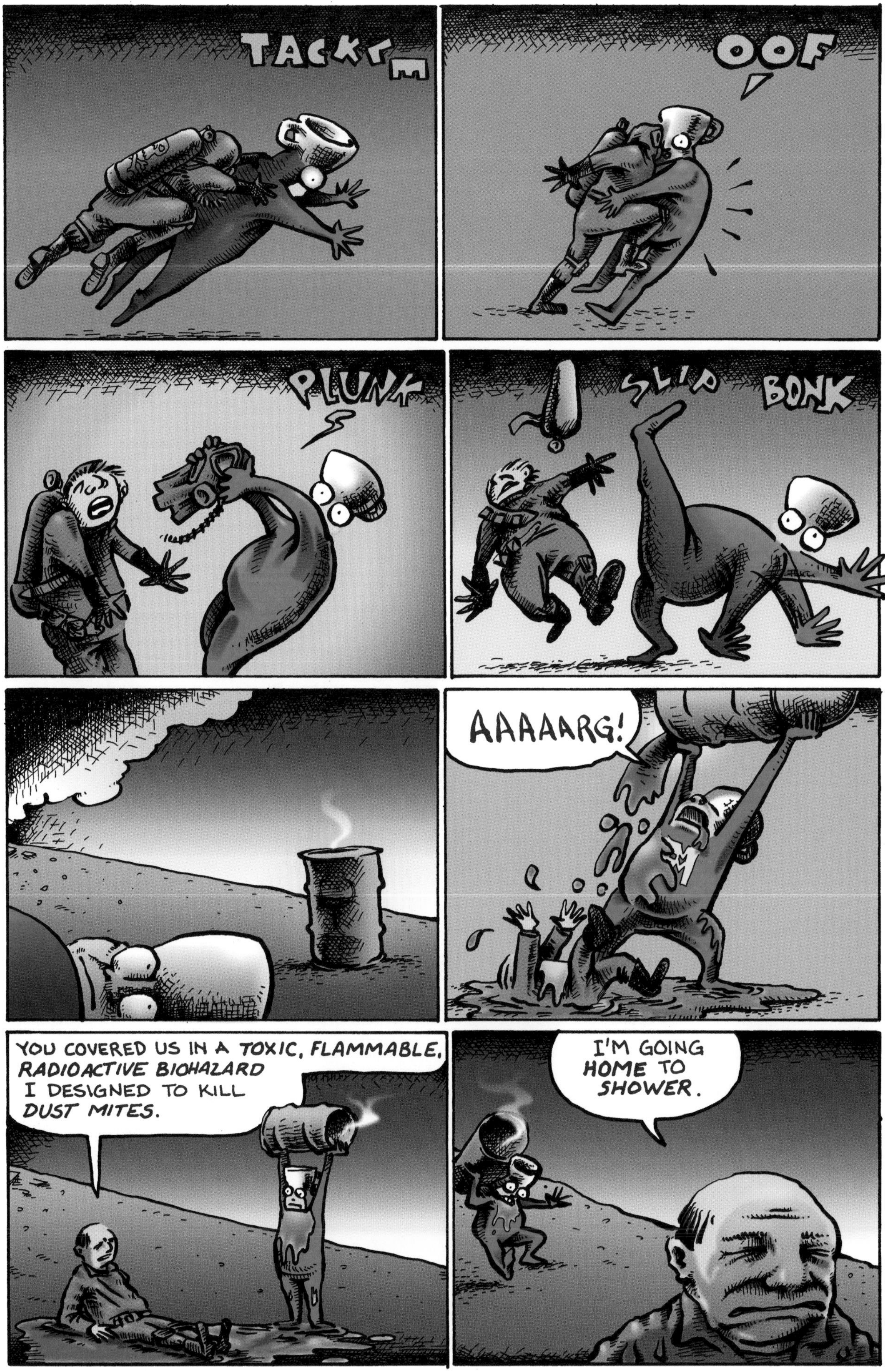
TACKLE
OOF
PLUNK
SLIP
BONK
AAAAARG!
YOU COVERED US IN A TOXIC, FLAMMABLE, RADIOACTIVE BIOHAZARD I DESIGNED TO KILL DUST MITES.
I'M GOING HOME TO SHOWER.

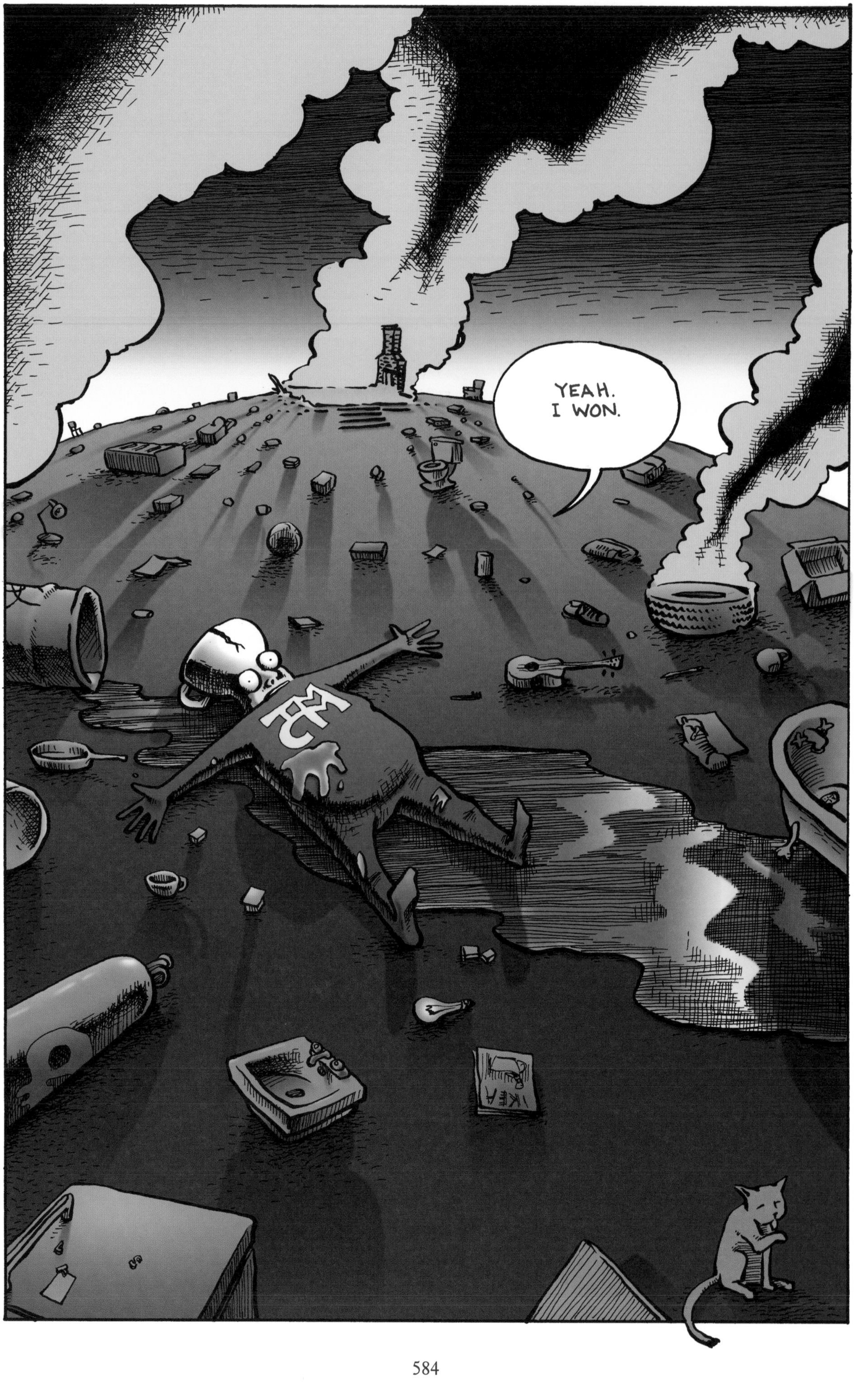
YEAH.
I WON.

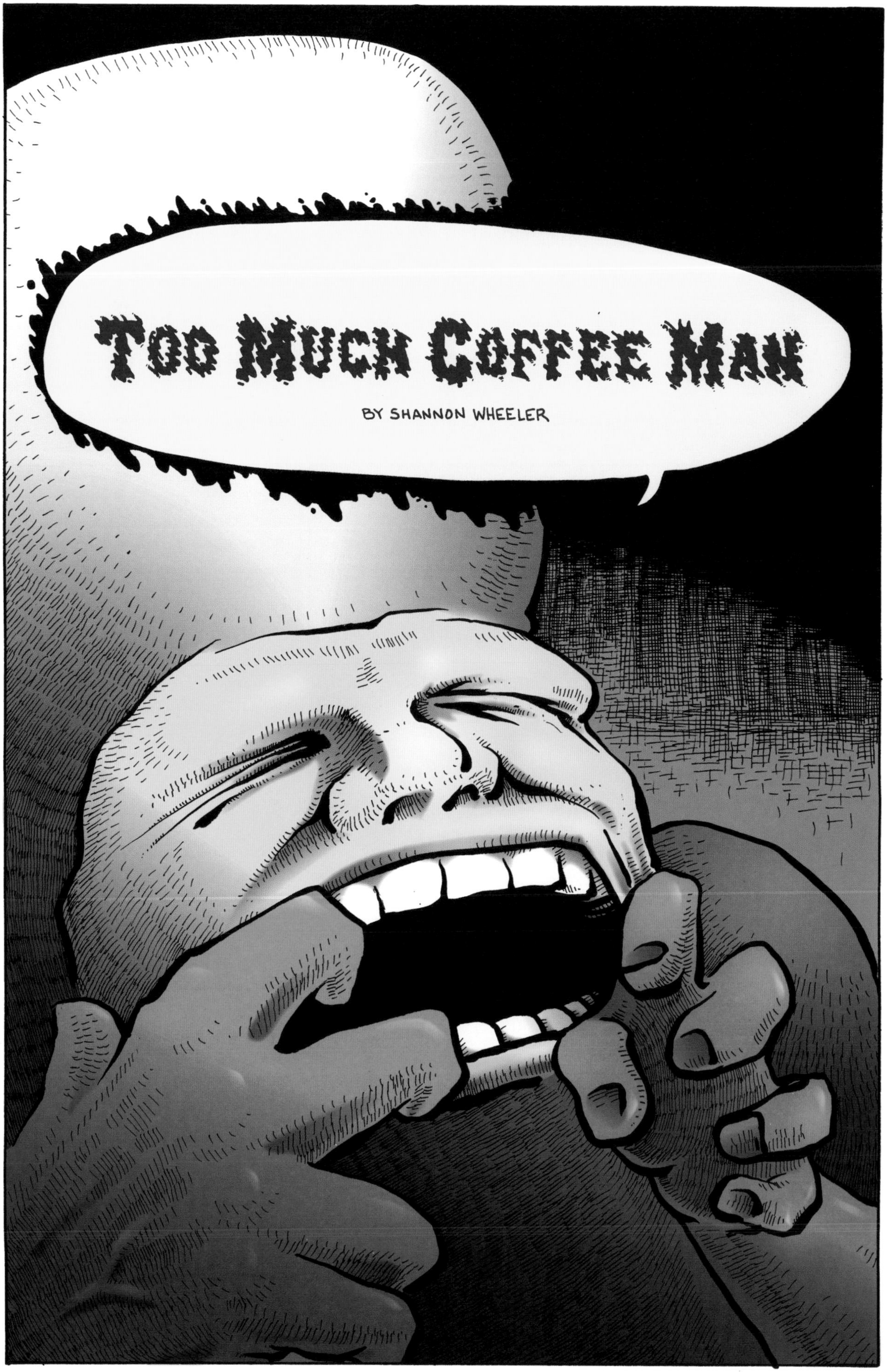
TOO MUCH COFFEE MAN
BY SHANNON WHEELER

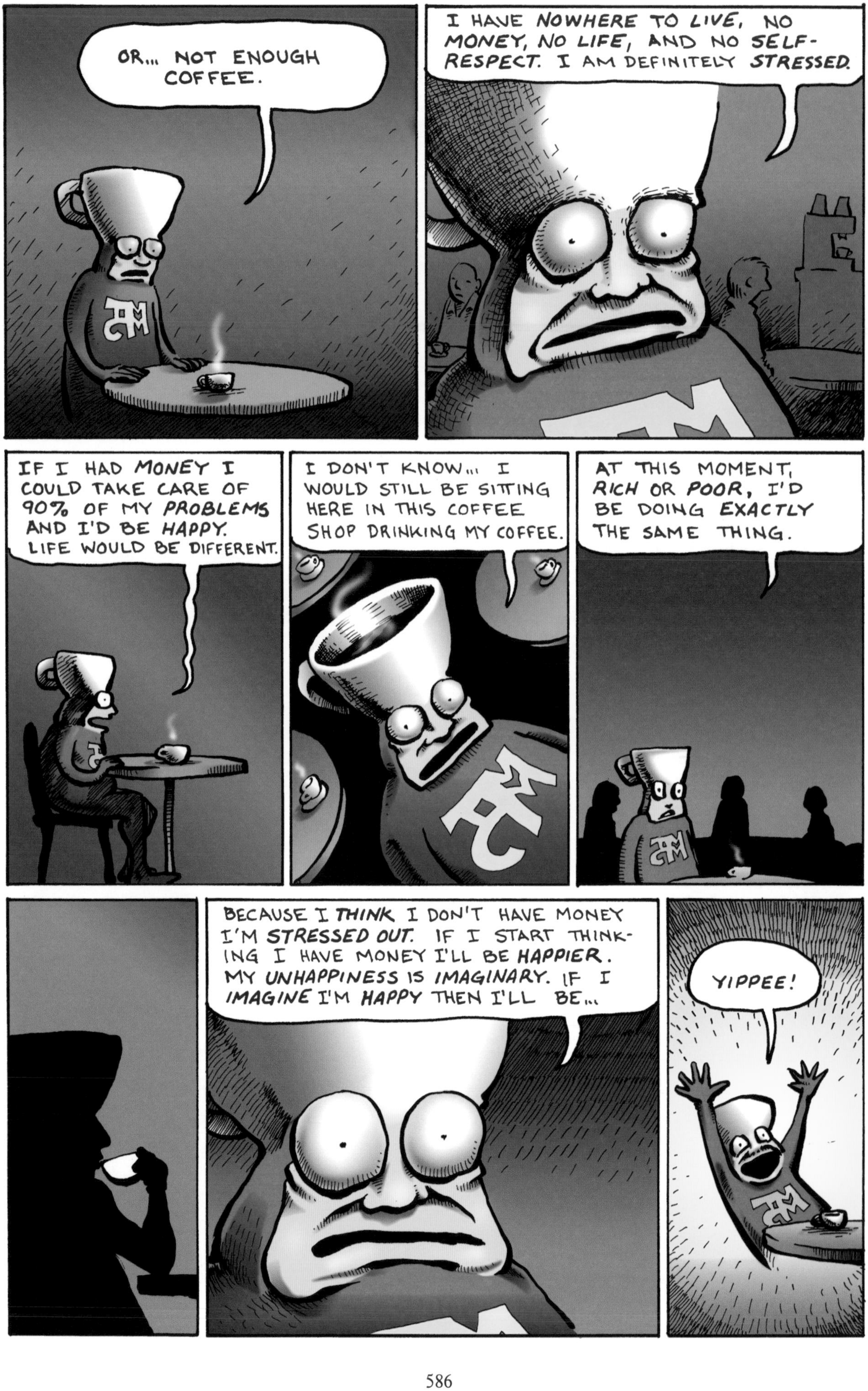
OR... NOT ENOUGH COFFEE.
I HAVE NOWHERE TO LIVE, NO MONEY, NO LIFE, AND NO SELF-RESPECT. I AM DEFINITELY STRESSED.
IF I HAD MONEY I COULD TAKE CARE OF 90% OF MY PROBLEMS AND I'D BE HAPPY. LIFE WOULD BE DIFFERENT.
I DON'T KNOW... I WOULD STILL BE SITTING HERE IN THIS COFFEE SHOP DRINKING MY COFFEE.
AT THIS MOMENT, RICH OR POOR, I'D BE DOING EXACTLY THE SAME THING.
BECAUSE I THINK I DON'T HAVE MONEY I'M STRESSED OUT. IF I START THINKING I HAVE MONEY I'LL BE HAPPIER. MY UNHAPPINESS IS IMAGINARY. IF I IMAGINE I'M HAPPY THEN I'LL BE...
YIPPEE!

I HAVE PLENTY OF MONEY, A GREAT PLACE TO LIVE, AND I'M SURROUNDED BY PEOPLE WHO LOVE ME. I HAVE NOTHING TO WORRY ABOUT.
I AM HAPPY.
BUT... I HAVE NO HOME... A LOT OF BILLS... AND NO MONEY!
CALM DOWN. THERE'S NOTHING TO WORRY ABOUT.
WHAT'S IMPORTANT IS THIS MOMENT.
WE CAN ALL BE HAPPY IF WE SIMPLY CHOOSE TO BE HAPPY!
I SOUND LIKE A CULT LEADER. WHO AM I KIDDING. THIS SUCKS.

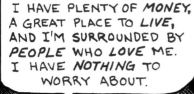

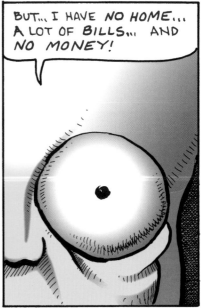

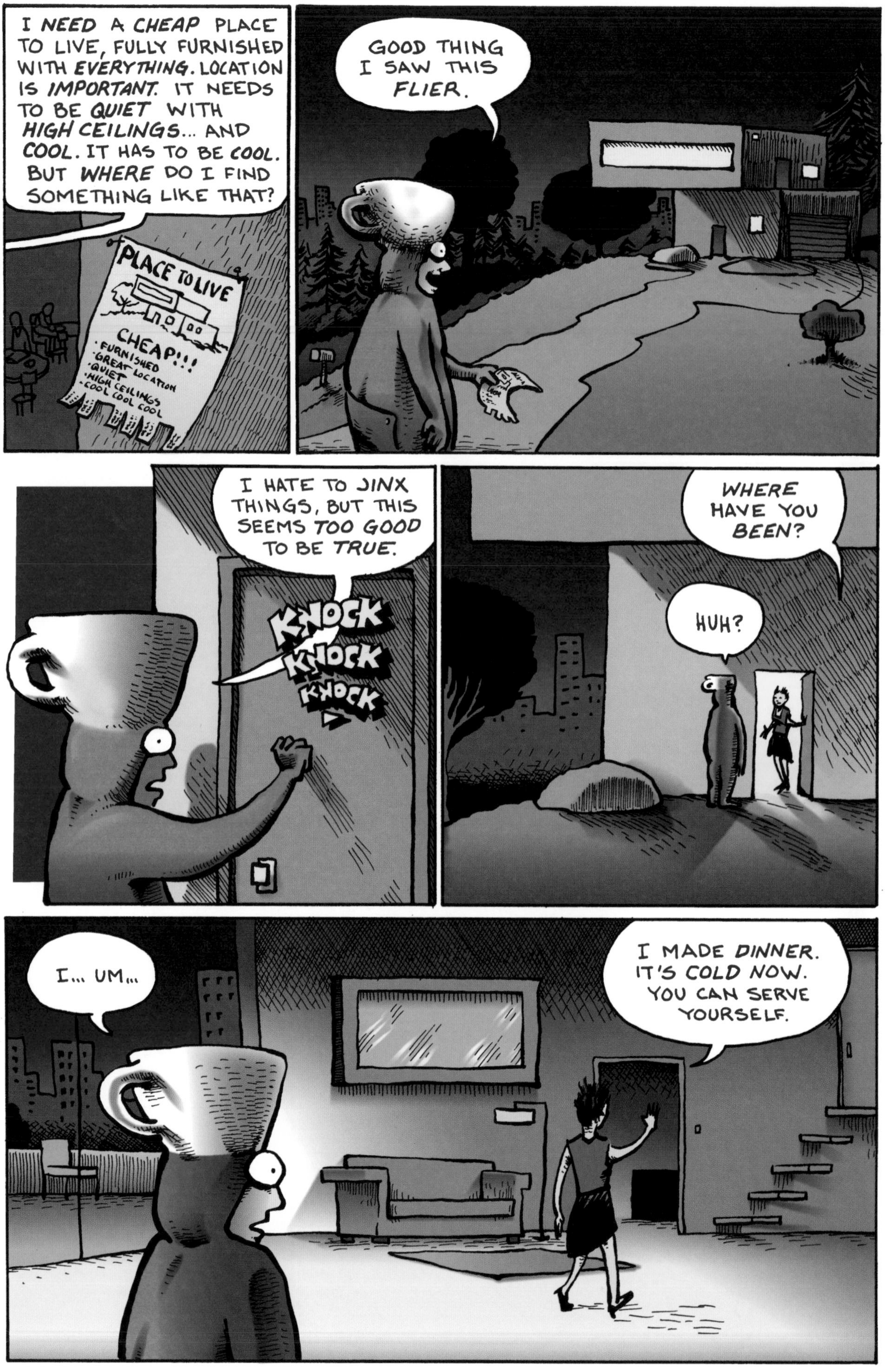
I NEED A CHEAP PLACE TO LIVE, FULLY FURNISHED WITH EVERYTHING. LOCATION IS IMPORTANT. IT NEEDS TO BE QUIET WITH HIGH CEILINGS... AND COOL. IT HAS TO BE COOL. BUT WHERE DO I FIND SOMETHING LIKE THAT?
PLACE TO LIVE
CHEAP!!!
·FURNISHED
·GREAT LOCATION
·QUIET
·HIGH CEILINGS
·COOL COOL COOL
GOOD THING I SAW THIS FLIER.
I HATE TO JINX THINGS, BUT THIS SEEMS TOO GOOD TO BE TRUE.
KNOCK KNOCK KNOCK
WHERE HAVE YOU BEEN?
HUH?
I... UM...
I MADE DINNER. IT'S COLD NOW. YOU CAN SERVE YOURSELF.

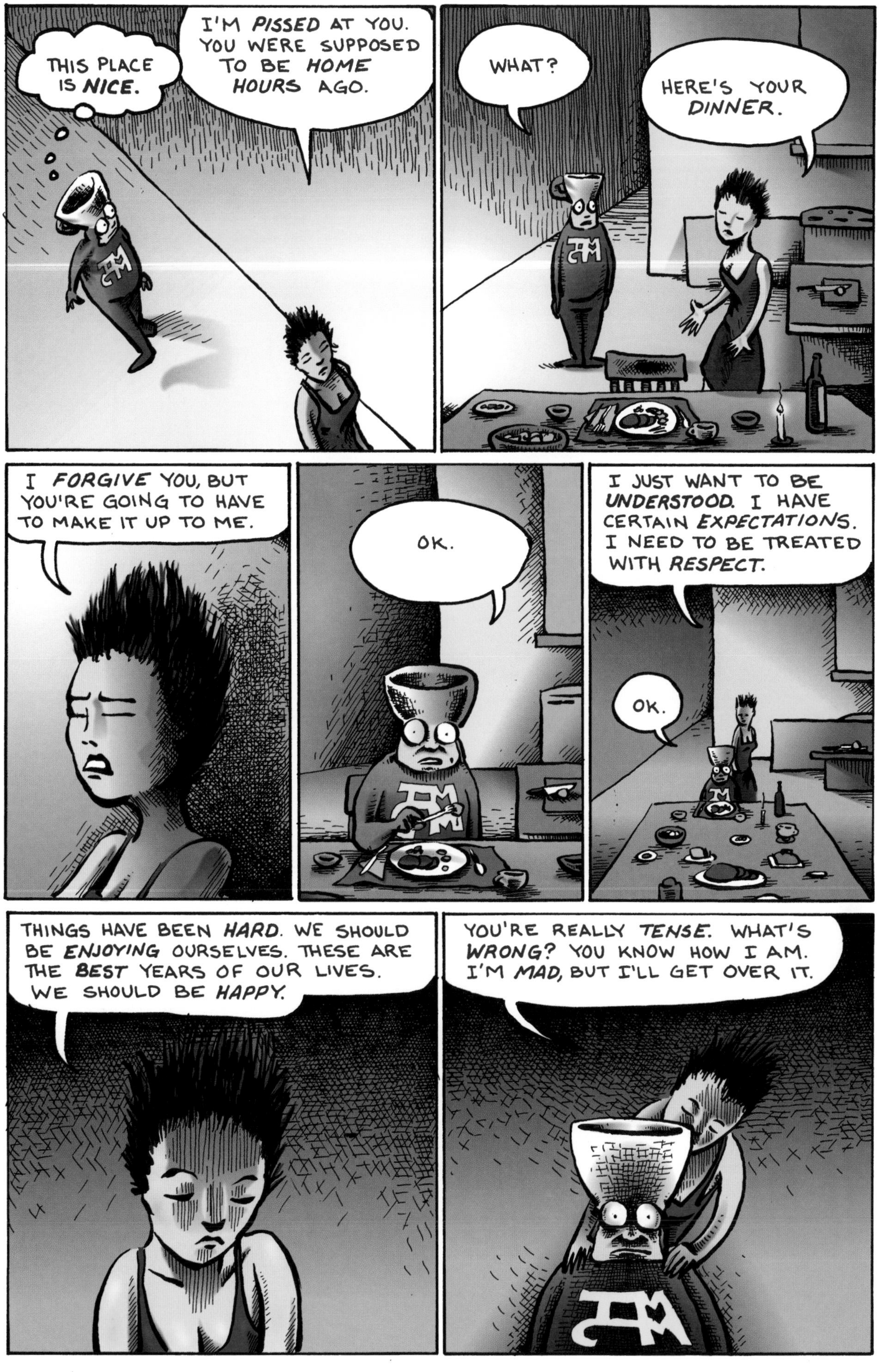
THIS PLACE IS NICE.
I'M PISSED AT YOU. YOU WERE SUPPOSED TO BE HOME HOURS AGO.
WHAT?
HERE'S YOUR DINNER.
I FORGIVE YOU, BUT YOU'RE GOING TO HAVE TO MAKE IT UP TO ME.
OK.
I JUST WANT TO BE UNDERSTOOD. I HAVE CERTAIN EXPECTATIONS. I NEED TO BE TREATED WITH RESPECT.
OK.
THINGS HAVE BEEN HARD. WE SHOULD BE ENJOYING OURSELVES. THESE ARE THE BEST YEARS OF OUR LIVES. WE SHOULD BE HAPPY.
YOU'RE REALLY TENSE. WHAT'S WRONG? YOU KNOW HOW I AM. I'M MAD, BUT I'LL GET OVER IT.

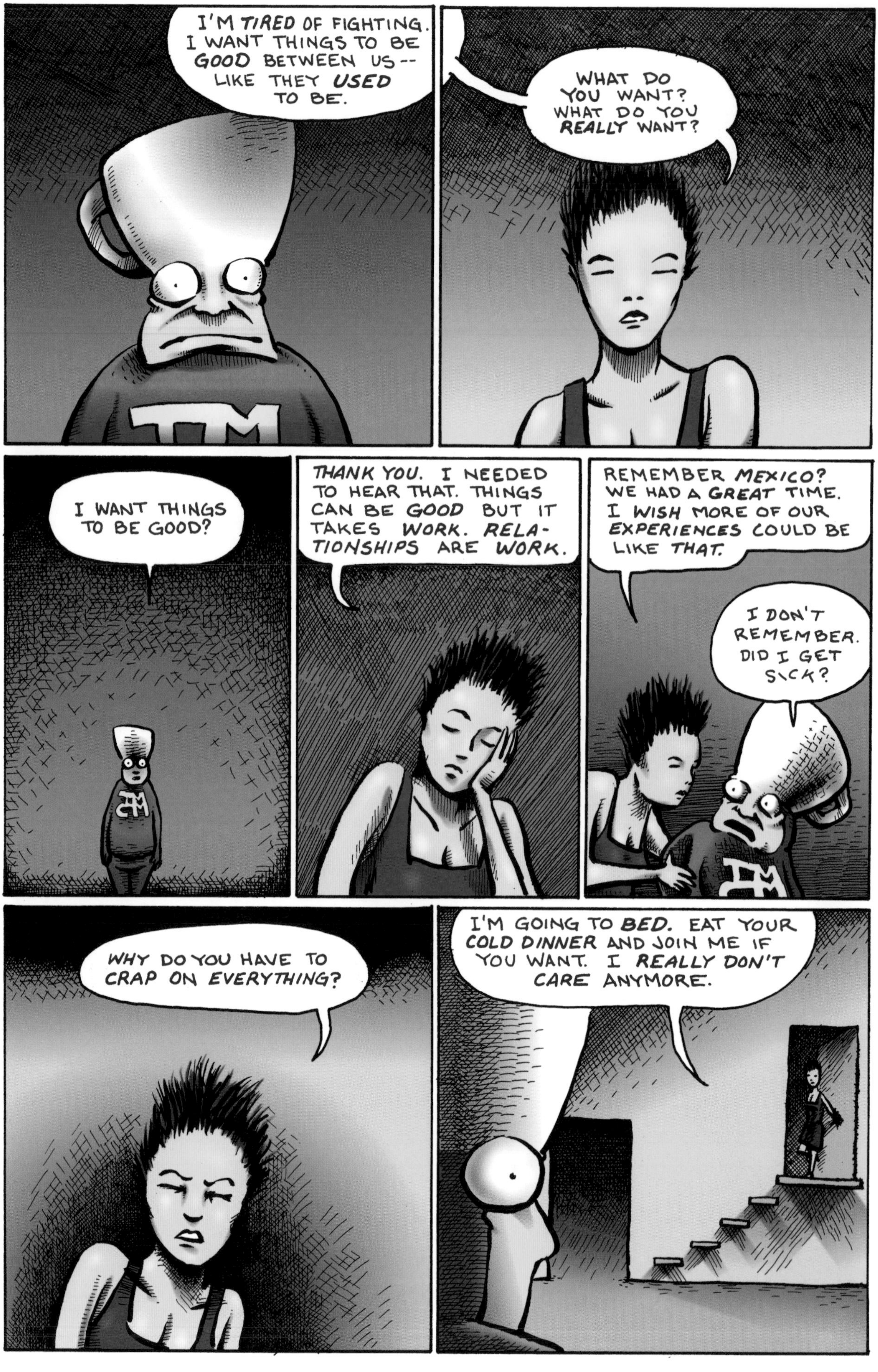

I'M TIRED OF FIGHTING. I WANT THINGS TO BE GOOD BETWEEN US -- LIKE THEY USED TO BE.
WHAT DO YOU WANT? WHAT DO YOU REALLY WANT?
I WANT THINGS TO BE GOOD?
THANK YOU. I NEEDED TO HEAR THAT. THINGS CAN BE GOOD BUT IT TAKES WORK. RELATIONSHIPS ARE WORK.
REMEMBER MEXICO? WE HAD A GREAT TIME. I WISH MORE OF OUR EXPERIENCES COULD BE LIKE THAT.
I DON'T REMEMBER. DID I GET SICK?
WHY DO YOU HAVE TO CRAP ON EVERYTHING?
I'M GOING TO BED. EAT YOUR COLD DINNER AND JOIN ME IF YOU WANT. I REALLY DON'T CARE ANYMORE.

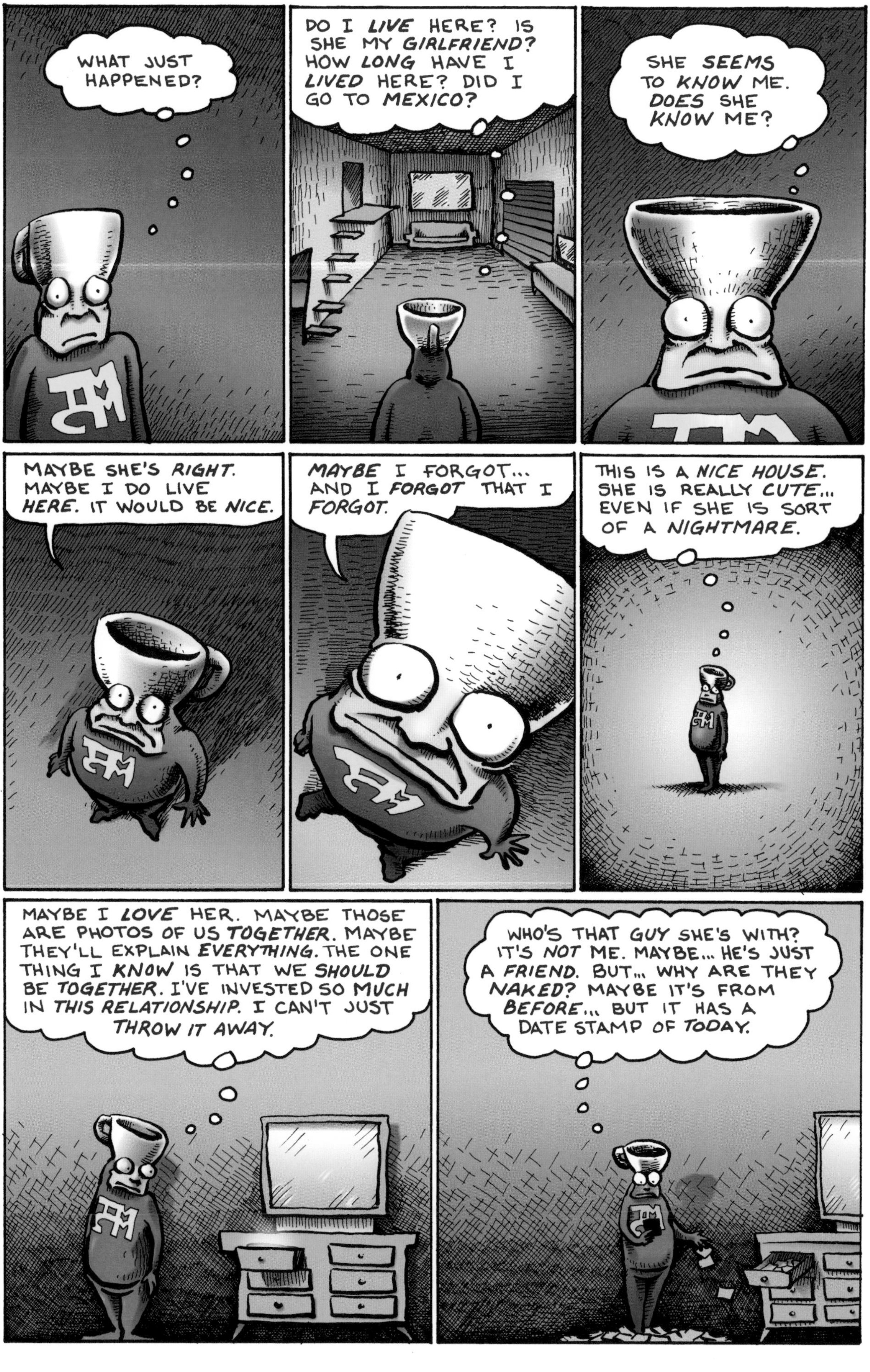
WHAT JUST HAPPENED?
DO I LIVE HERE? IS SHE MY GIRLFRIEND? HOW LONG HAVE I LIVED HERE? DID I GO TO MEXICO?
SHE SEEMS TO KNOW ME. DOES SHE KNOW ME?
MAYBE SHE'S RIGHT. MAYBE I DO LIVE HERE. IT WOULD BE NICE.
MAYBE I FORGOT... AND I FORGOT THAT I FORGOT.
THIS IS A NICE HOUSE. SHE IS REALLY CUTE... EVEN IF SHE IS SORT OF A NIGHTMARE.
MAYBE I LOVE HER. MAYBE THOSE ARE PHOTOS OF US TOGETHER. MAYBE THEY'LL EXPLAIN EVERYTHING. THE ONE THING I KNOW IS THAT WE SHOULD BE TOGETHER. I'VE INVESTED SO MUCH IN THIS RELATIONSHIP. I CAN'T JUST THROW IT AWAY.
WHO'S THAT GUY SHE'S WITH? IT'S NOT ME. MAYBE... HE'S JUST A FRIEND. BUT... WHY ARE THEY NAKED? MAYBE IT'S FROM BEFORE... BUT IT HAS A DATE STAMP OF TODAY.

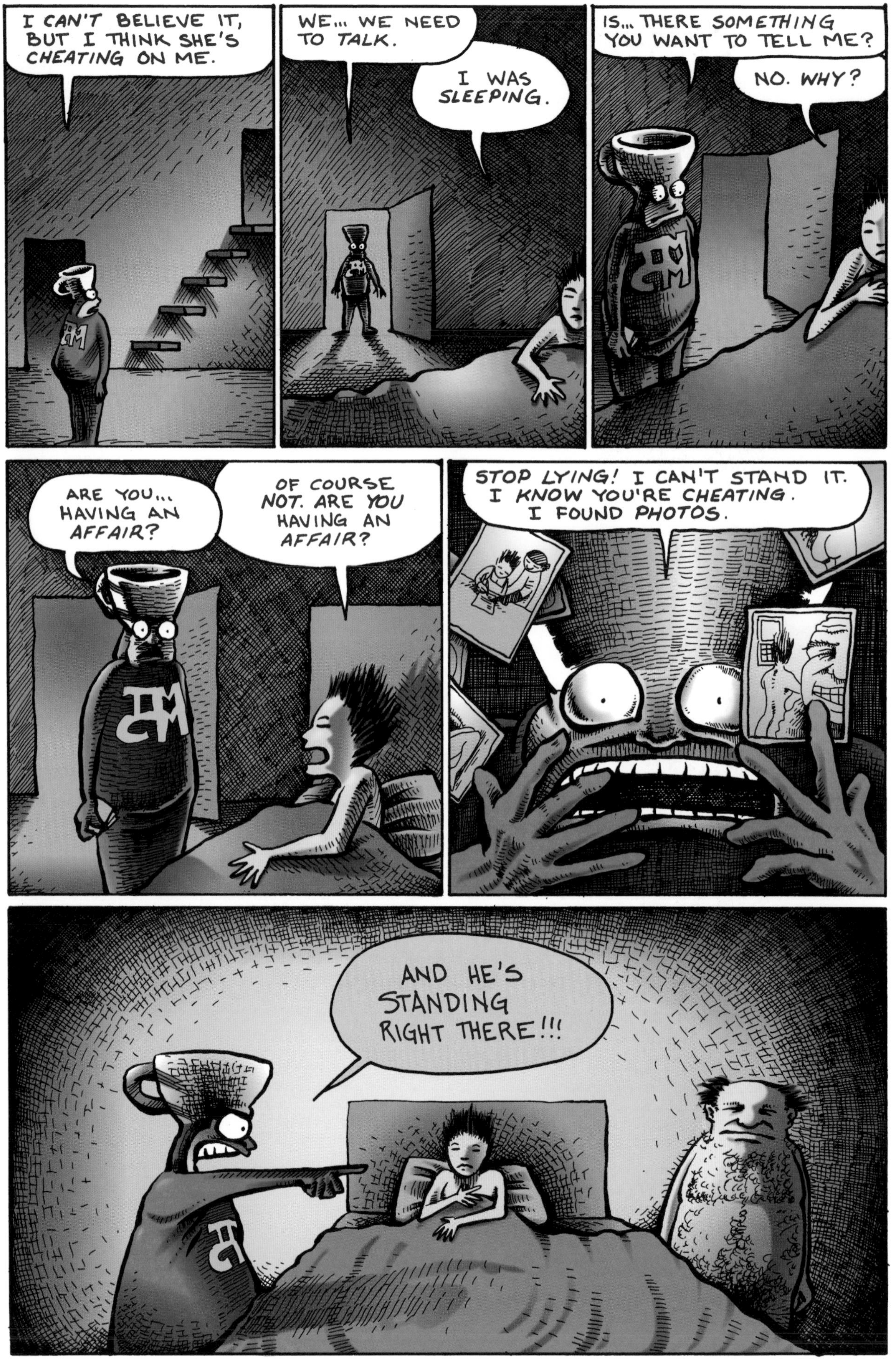
I CAN'T BELIEVE IT, BUT I THINK SHE'S CHEATING ON ME.
WE... WE NEED TO TALK.
I WAS SLEEPING.
IS... THERE SOMETHING YOU WANT TO TELL ME?
NO. WHY?
ARE YOU... HAVING AN AFFAIR?
OF COURSE NOT. ARE YOU HAVING AN AFFAIR?
STOP LYING! I CAN'T STAND IT. I KNOW YOU'RE CHEATING. I FOUND PHOTOS.
AND HE'S STANDING RIGHT THERE!!!

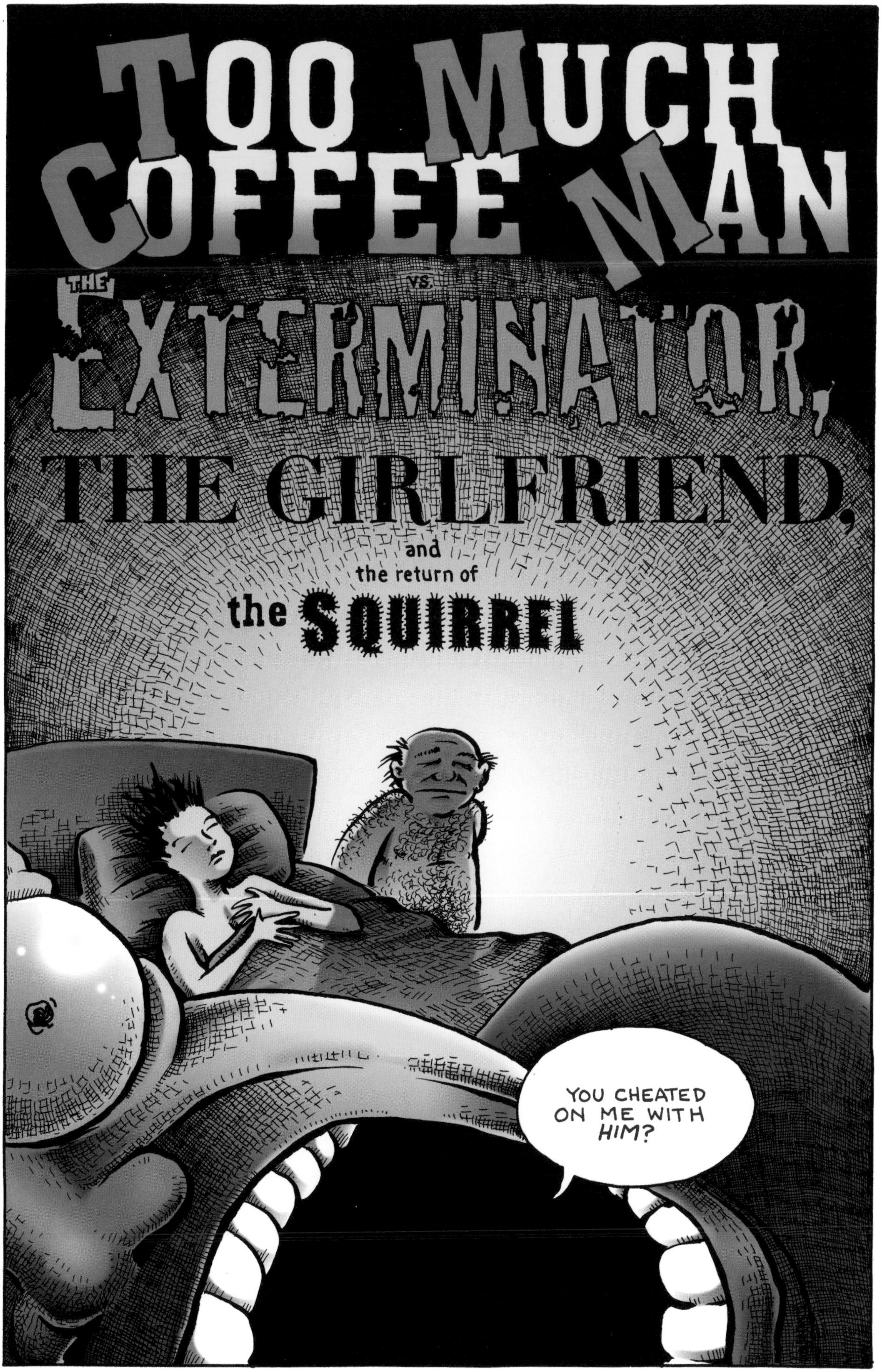
TOO MUCH COFFEE MAN
THE EXTERMINATOR,
VS.
THE GIRLFRIEND,
and
the return of
the SQUIRREL
YOU CHEATED ON ME WITH *HIM*?

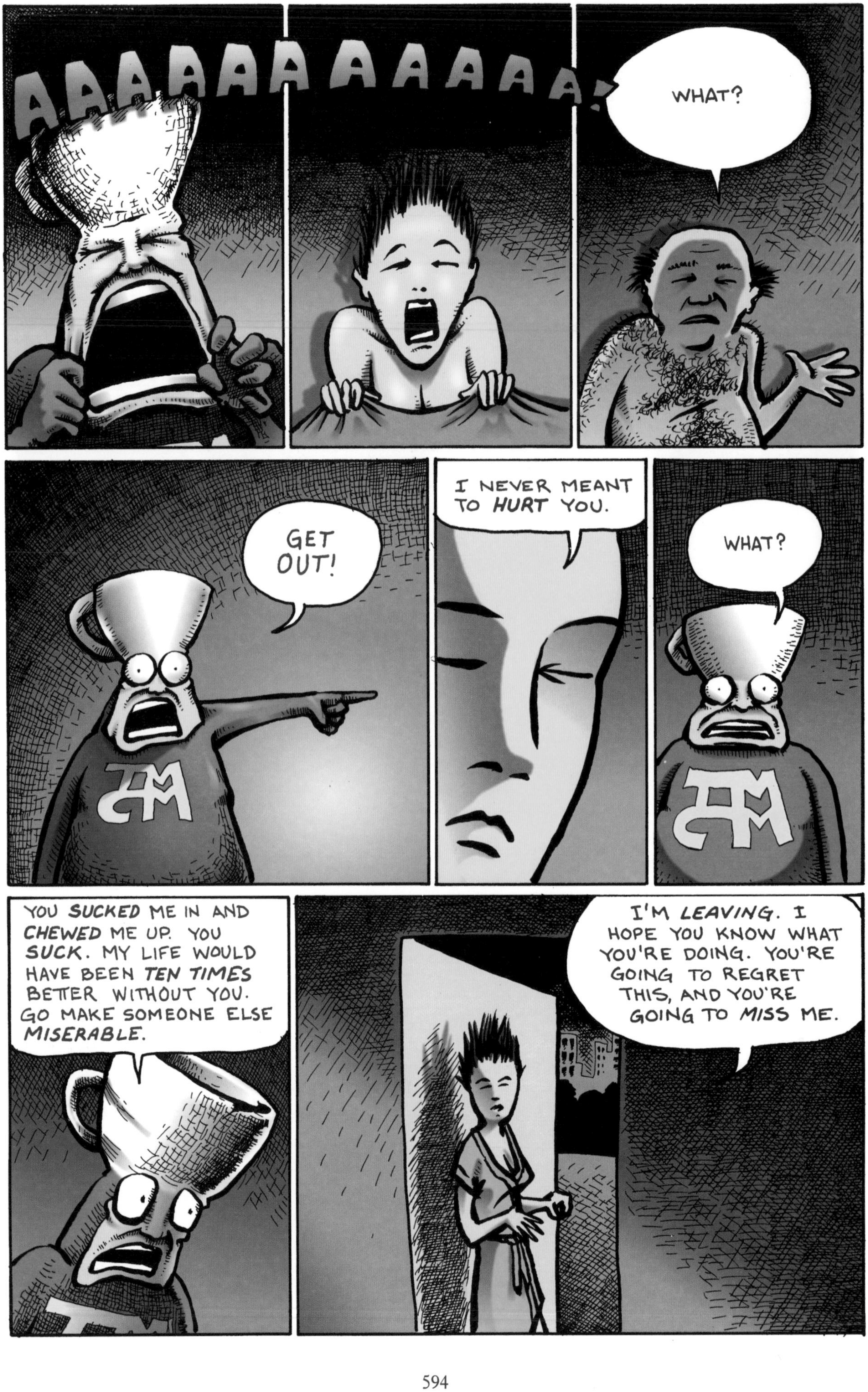
AAAAAAAAAAA!
WHAT?
GET OUT!
I NEVER MEANT TO HURT YOU.
WHAT?
YOU SUCKED ME IN AND CHEWED ME UP. YOU SUCK. MY LIFE WOULD HAVE BEEN TEN TIMES BETTER WITHOUT YOU. GO MAKE SOMEONE ELSE MISERABLE.
I'M LEAVING. I HOPE YOU KNOW WHAT YOU'RE DOING. YOU'RE GOING TO REGRET THIS, AND YOU'RE GOING TO MISS ME.

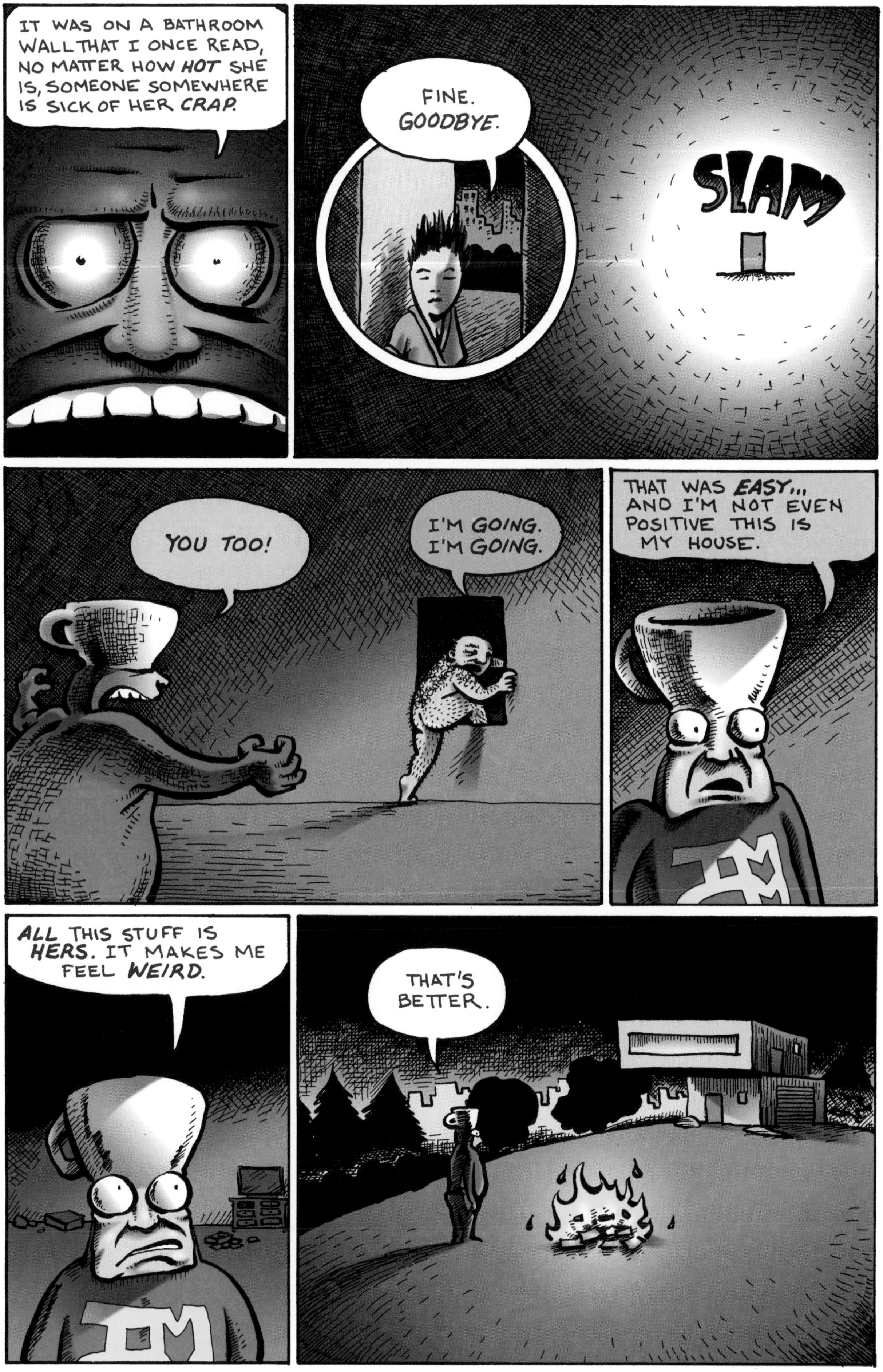
IT WAS ON A BATHROOM WALL THAT I ONCE READ, NO MATTER HOW HOT SHE IS, SOMEONE SOMEWHERE IS SICK OF HER CRAP.
FINE. GOODBYE.
SLAM
YOU TOO!
I'M GOING. I'M GOING.
THAT WAS EASY... AND I'M NOT EVEN POSITIVE THIS IS MY HOUSE.
ALL THIS STUFF IS HERS. IT MAKES ME FEEL WEIRD.
THAT'S BETTER.

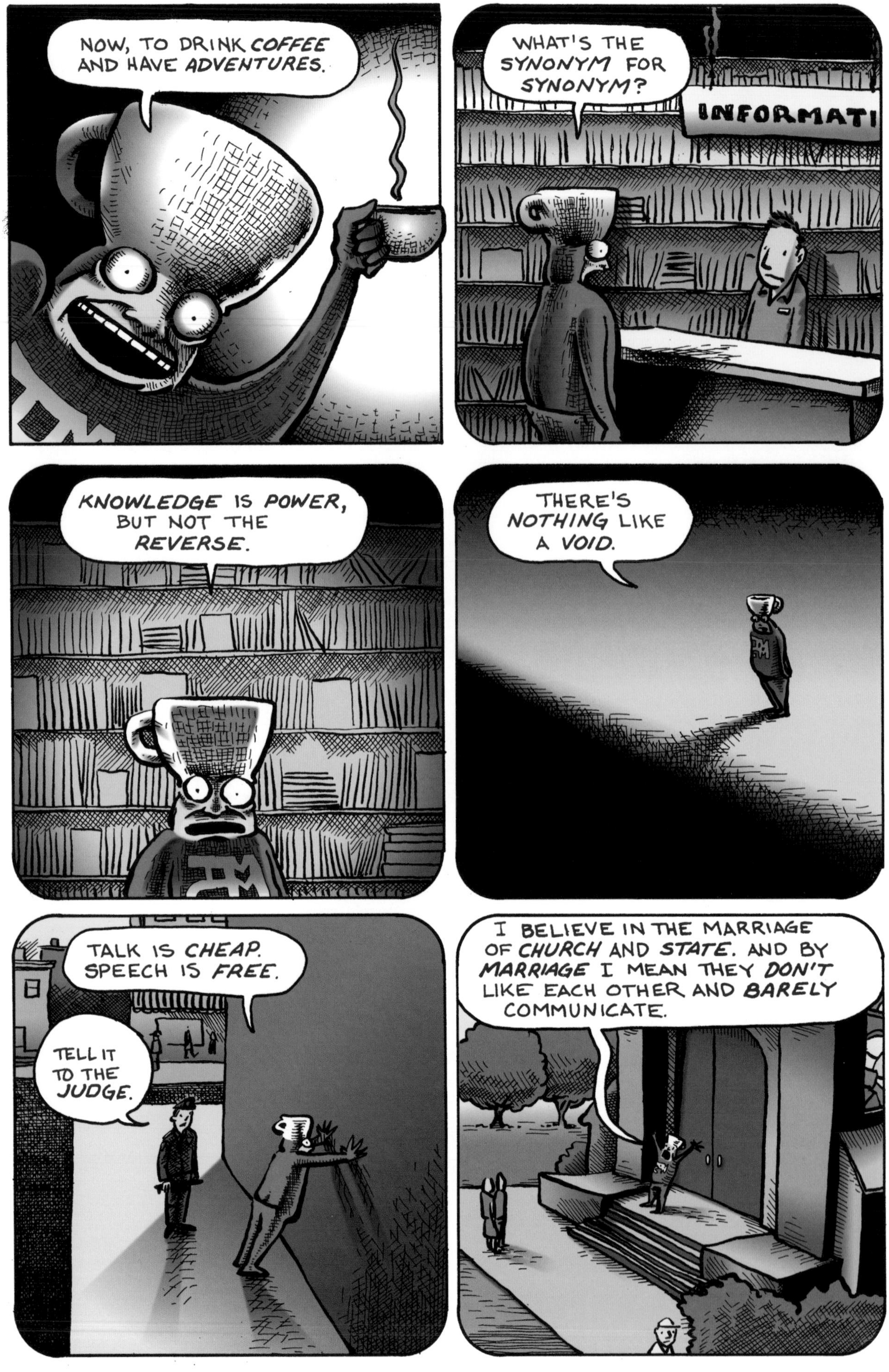
NOW, TO DRINK COFFEE AND HAVE ADVENTURES.
WHAT'S THE SYNONYM FOR SYNONYM?
INFORMATI
KNOWLEDGE IS POWER, BUT NOT THE REVERSE.
THERE'S NOTHING LIKE A VOID.
TALK IS CHEAP. SPEECH IS FREE.
TELL IT TO THE JUDGE.
I BELIEVE IN THE MARRIAGE OF CHURCH AND STATE. AND BY MARRIAGE I MEAN THEY DON'T LIKE EACH OTHER AND BARELY COMMUNICATE.

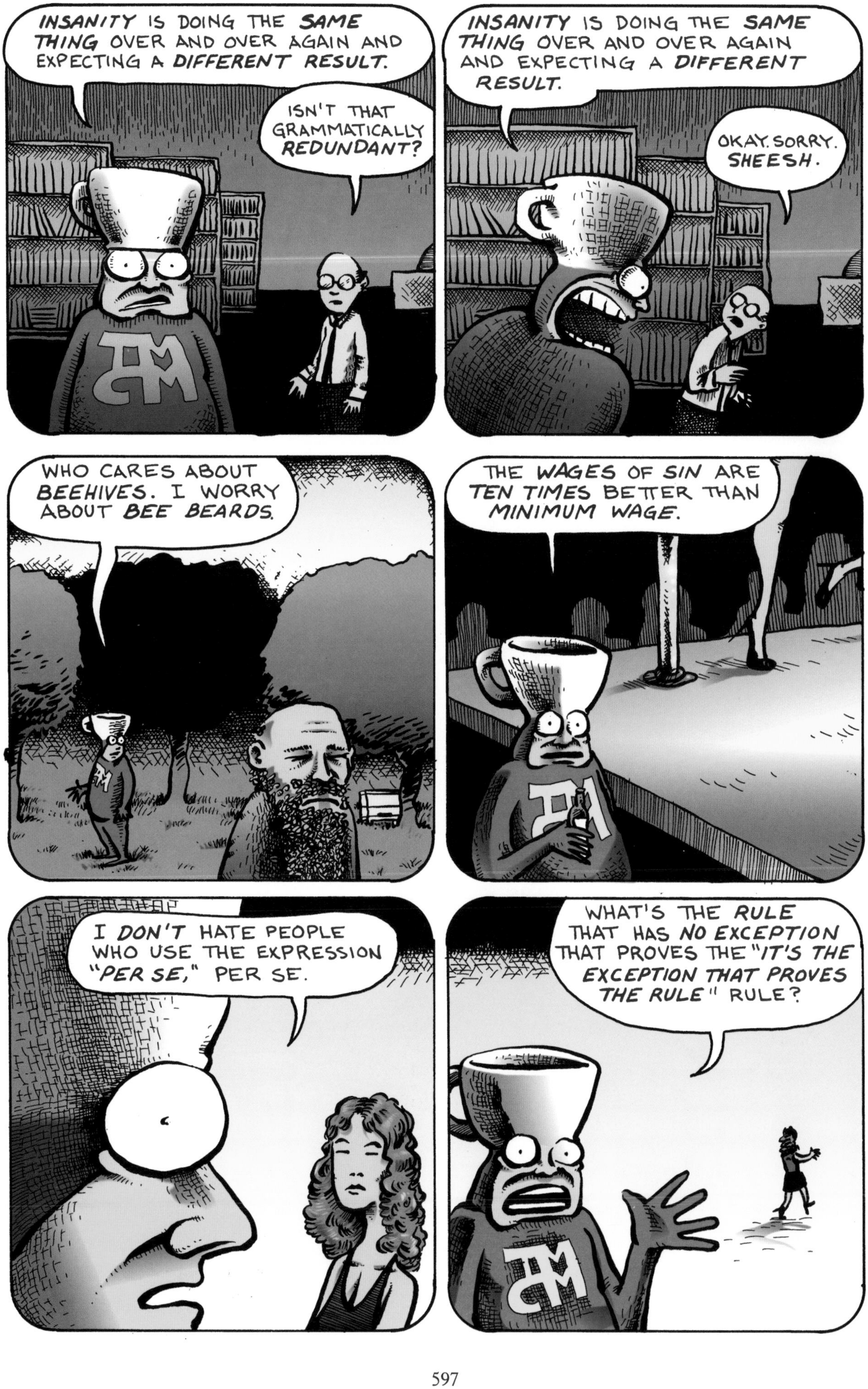
INSANITY IS DOING THE SAME THING OVER AND OVER AGAIN AND EXPECTING A DIFFERENT RESULT.
ISN'T THAT GRAMMATICALLY REDUNDANT?
INSANITY IS DOING THE SAME THING OVER AND OVER AGAIN AND EXPECTING A DIFFERENT RESULT.
OKAY. SORRY. SHEESH.
WHO CARES ABOUT BEEHIVES. I WORRY ABOUT BEE BEARDS.
THE WAGES OF SIN ARE TEN TIMES BETTER THAN MINIMUM WAGE.
I DON'T HATE PEOPLE WHO USE THE EXPRESSION "PER SE," PER SE.
WHAT'S THE RULE THAT HAS NO EXCEPTION THAT PROVES THE "IT'S THE EXCEPTION THAT PROVES THE RULE" RULE?

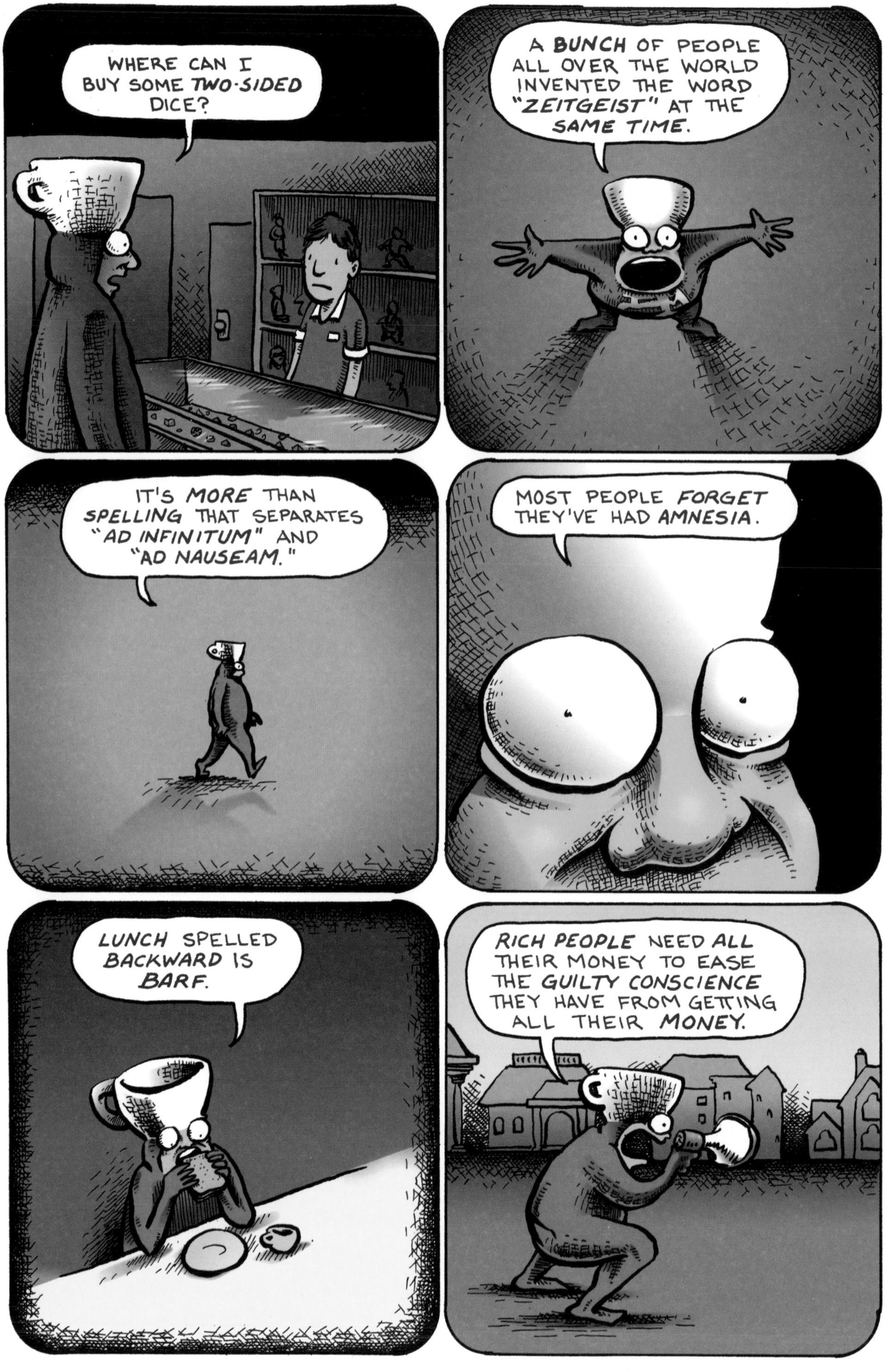
WHERE CAN I BUY SOME TWO-SIDED DICE?
A BUNCH OF PEOPLE ALL OVER THE WORLD INVENTED THE WORD "ZEITGEIST" AT THE SAME TIME.
IT'S MORE THAN SPELLING THAT SEPARATES "AD INFINITUM" AND "AD NAUSEAM."
MOST PEOPLE FORGET THEY'VE HAD AMNESIA.
LUNCH SPELLED BACKWARD IS BARF.
RICH PEOPLE NEED ALL THEIR MONEY TO EASE THE GUILTY CONSCIENCE THEY HAVE FROM GETTING ALL THEIR MONEY.

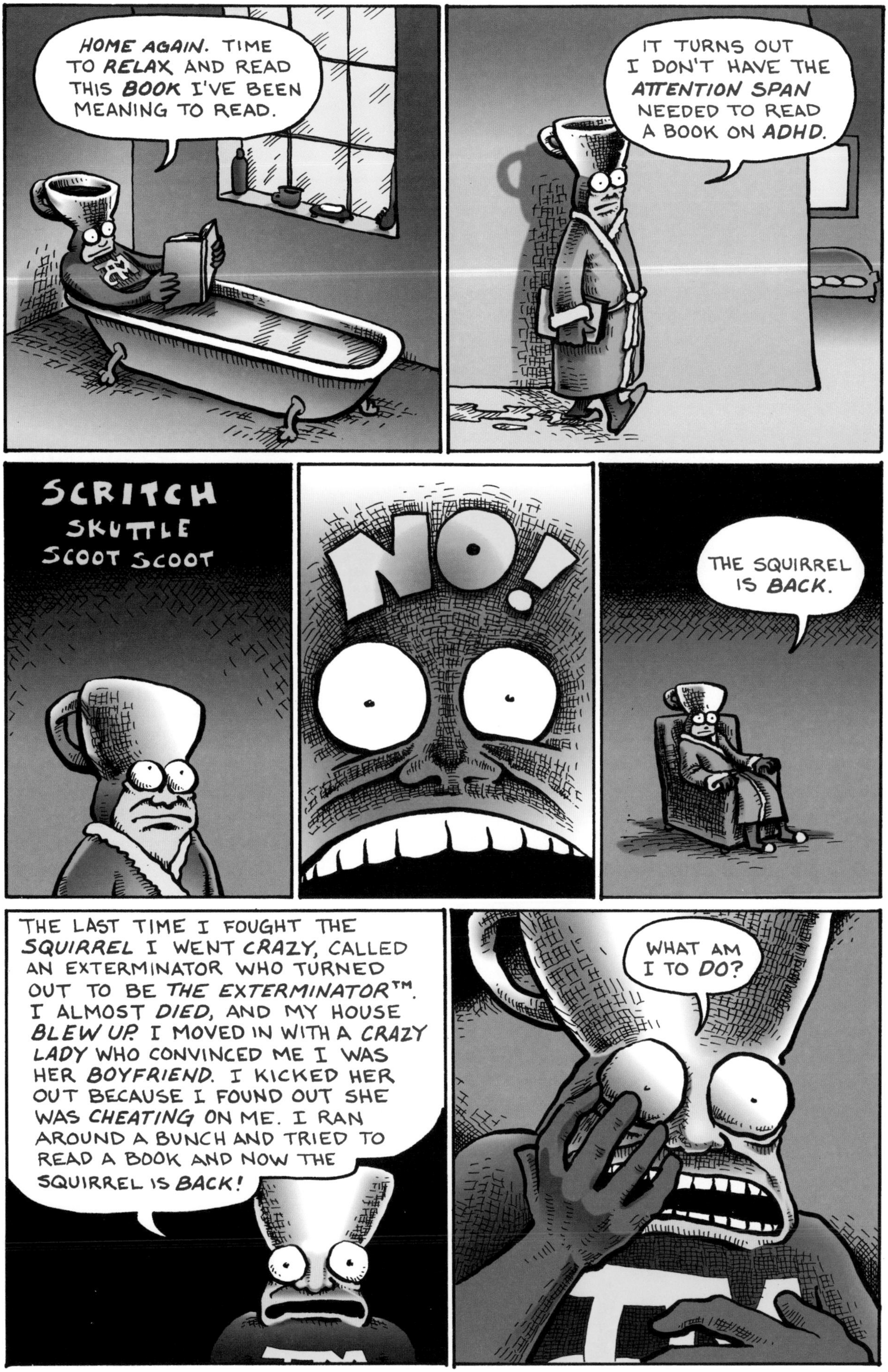
HOME AGAIN. TIME TO RELAX AND READ THIS BOOK I'VE BEEN MEANING TO READ.
IT TURNS OUT I DON'T HAVE THE ATTENTION SPAN NEEDED TO READ A BOOK ON ADHD.
SCRITCH
SKUTTLE
SCOOT SCOOT
NO!
THE SQUIRREL IS BACK.
THE LAST TIME I FOUGHT THE SQUIRREL I WENT CRAZY, CALLED AN EXTERMINATOR WHO TURNED OUT TO BE THE EXTERMINATOR™. I ALMOST DIED, AND MY HOUSE BLEW UP. I MOVED IN WITH A CRAZY LADY WHO CONVINCED ME I WAS HER BOYFRIEND. I KICKED HER OUT BECAUSE I FOUND OUT SHE WAS CHEATING ON ME. I RAN AROUND A BUNCH AND TRIED TO READ A BOOK AND NOW THE SQUIRREL IS BACK!
WHAT AM I TO DO?

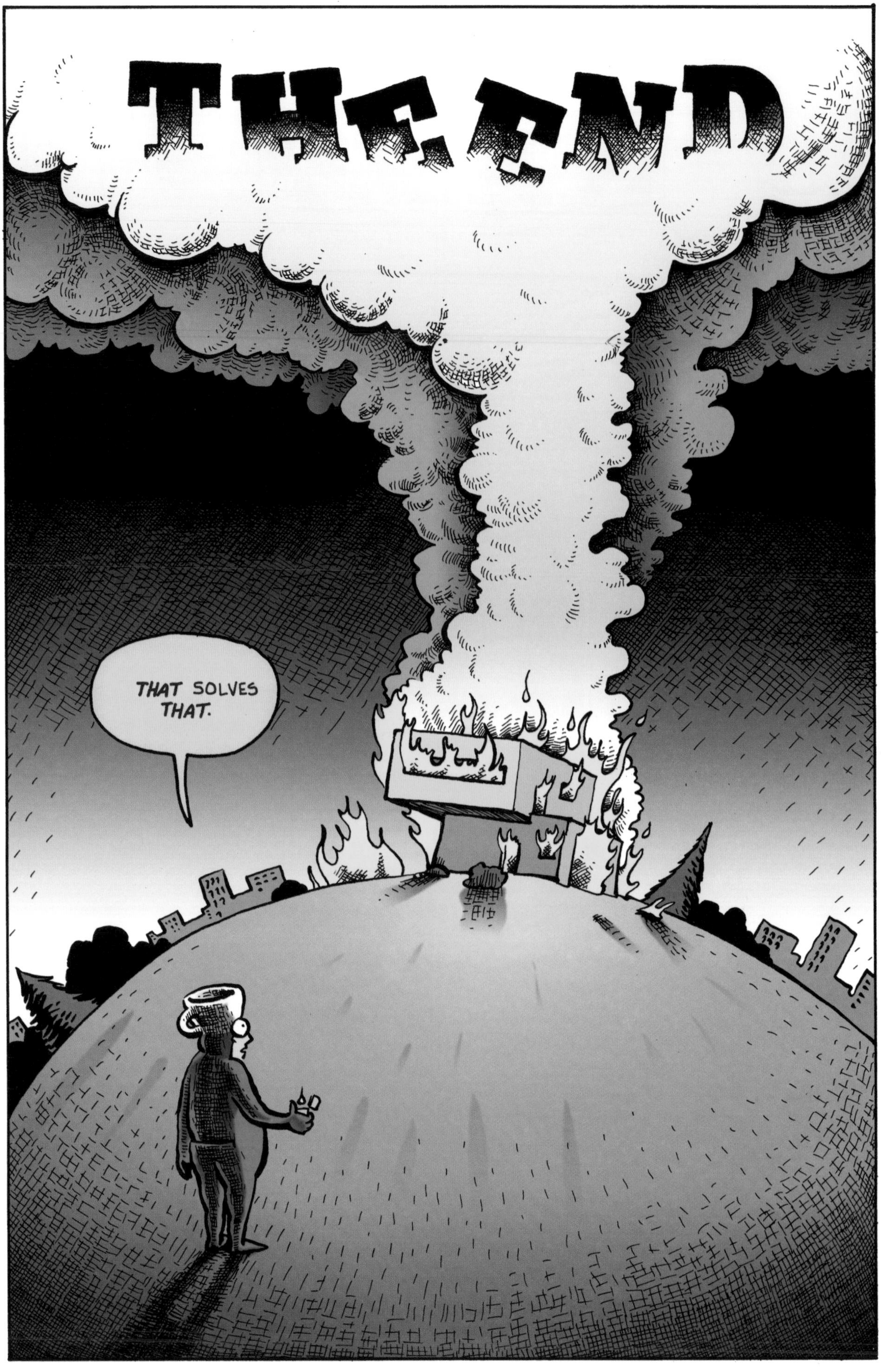
THE END
THAT SOLVES THAT.

TOO MUCH COFFEE MAN
COVER GALLERY

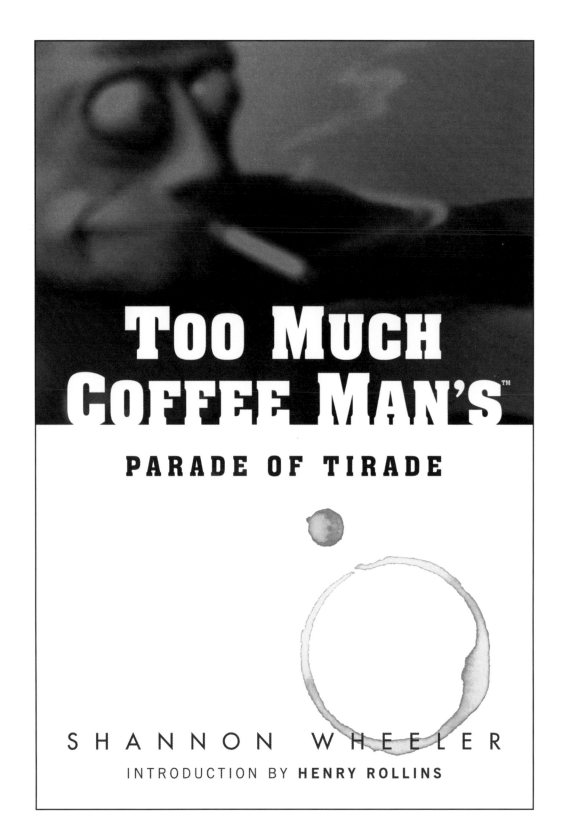

TOO MUCH COFFEE MAN'S™

PARADE OF TIRADE

SHANNON WHEELER

INTRODUCTION BY HENRY ROLLINS

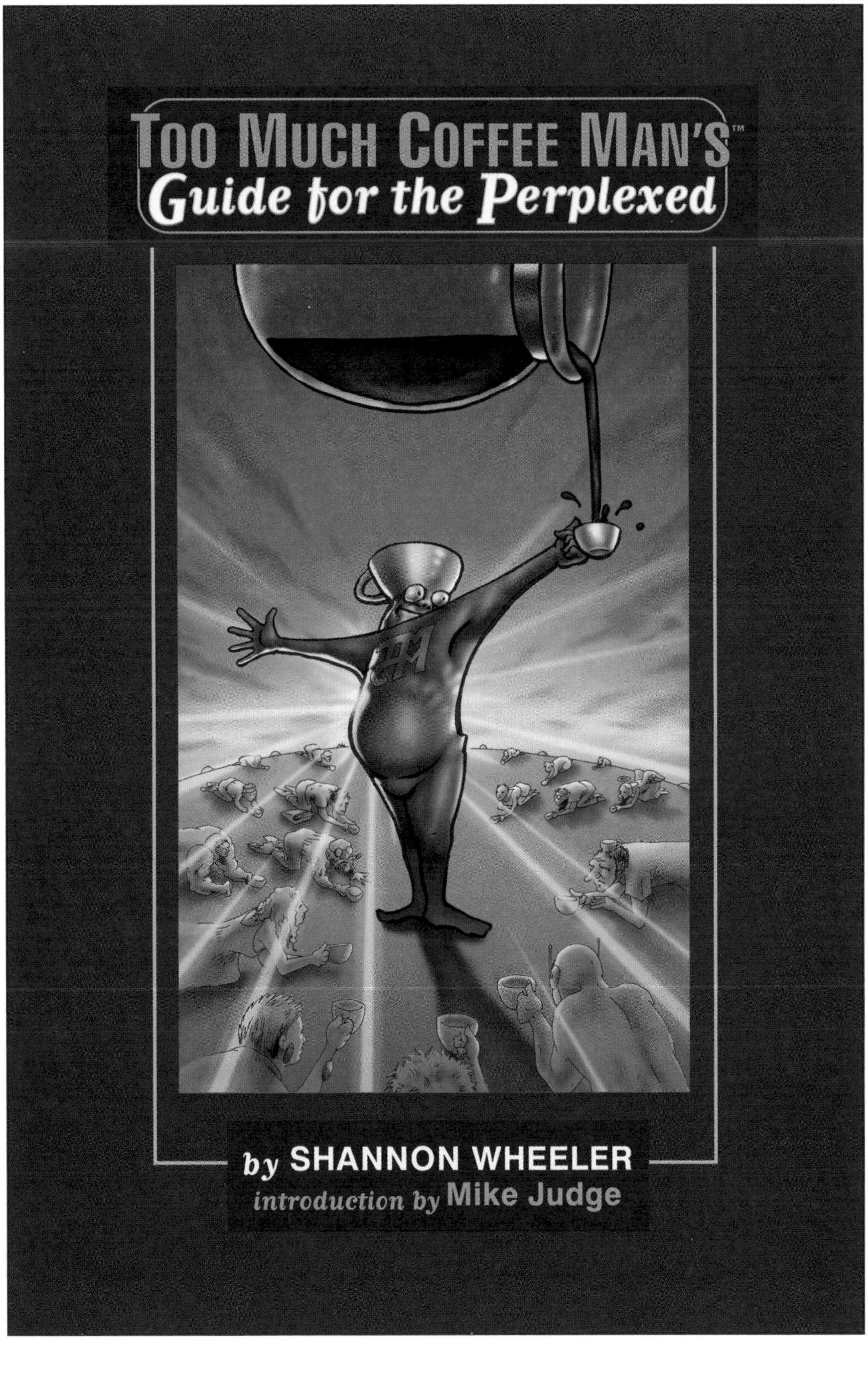
TOO MUCH COFFEE MAN'S™
Guide for the Perplexed
by SHANNON WHEELER
introduction by Mike Judge

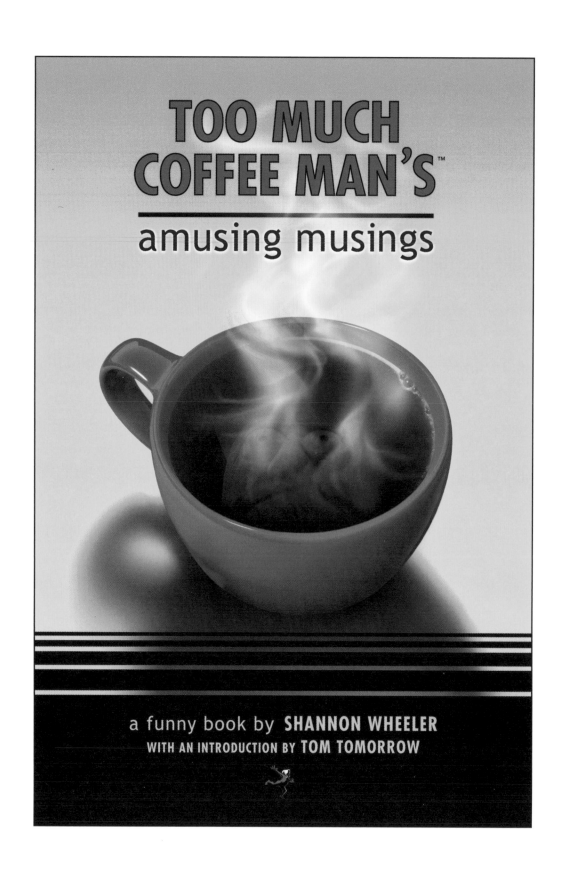

TOO MUCH COFFEE MAN'S™

amusing musings

a funny book by **SHANNON WHEELER**

WITH AN INTRODUCTION BY **TOM TOMORROW**

HOW TO BE
HAPPY

TOO MUCH COFFEE MAN™

SHANNON WHEELER

INTRODUCTION BY TED RALL

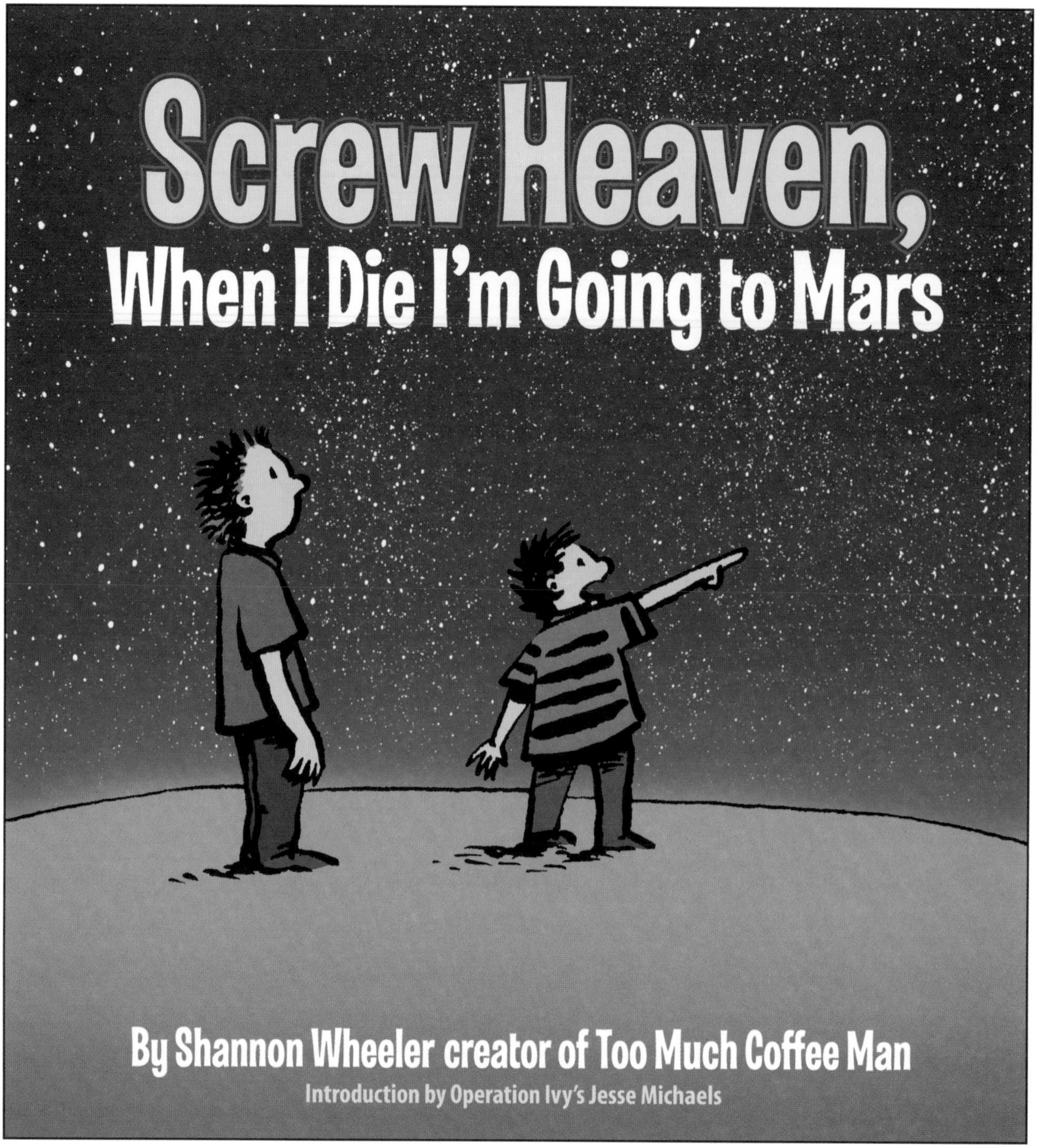
Screw Heaven,
When I Die I'm Going to Mars
By Shannon Wheeler creator of Too Much Coffee Man
Introduction by Operation Ivy's Jesse Michaels

SHANNON WHEELER BIOGRAPHY

It is rumored that Shannon Wheeler drinks too much coffee.

SHANNON WHEELER
~~BIBLIOGRAPHY~~ CHECKLIST

(Collect them all!)

Children with Glue (Blackbird Comics, 1991)
Wake Up and Smell the Cartoon (Mojo Press, 1992)
Guide for the Perplexed (Dark Horse Comics, 1998)
Parade of Tirade (Dark Horse Comics, 1999)
Amusing Musings (Dark Horse Comics, 2001)
How to Be Happy (Dark Horse Comics, 2005)
Postage Stamp Funnies (Dark Horse Comics, 2006)
Screw Heaven, When I Die I'm Going to Mars (Dark Horse Comics, 2007)
I Thought You Would Be Funnier (BOOM! Studios, 2010)
Too Much Coffee Man Omnibus (Dark Horse Comics, 2011)
Cutie Island (BOOM! Studios, 2012)
I Told You So (BOOM! Studios, 2012)
I Don't Get It (BOOM! Studios, 2014)
Too Much Coffee Man Omnibus Plus (Dark Horse Comics, 2017)

WITH OTHER PEOPLE

Oil and Water, with Steve Duin (Fantagraphics Books, 2011)
Grandpa Won't Wake Up, with Simon Max Hill (BOOM! Studios, 2011)
God Is Disappointed in You, with Mark Russell (Top Shelf Productions, 2013)
Apocrypha Now, with Mark Russell (Top Shelf Productions, 2016)

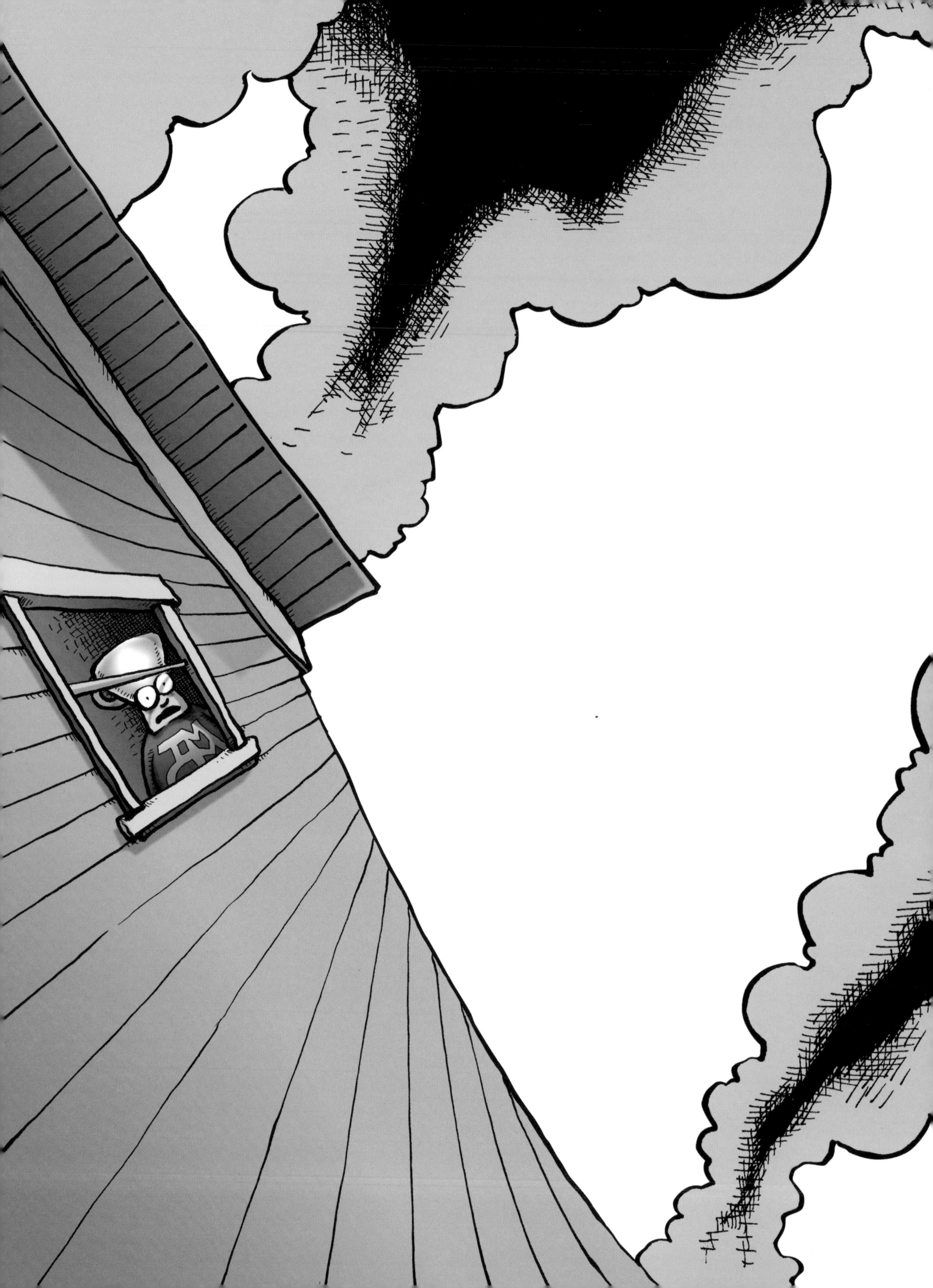

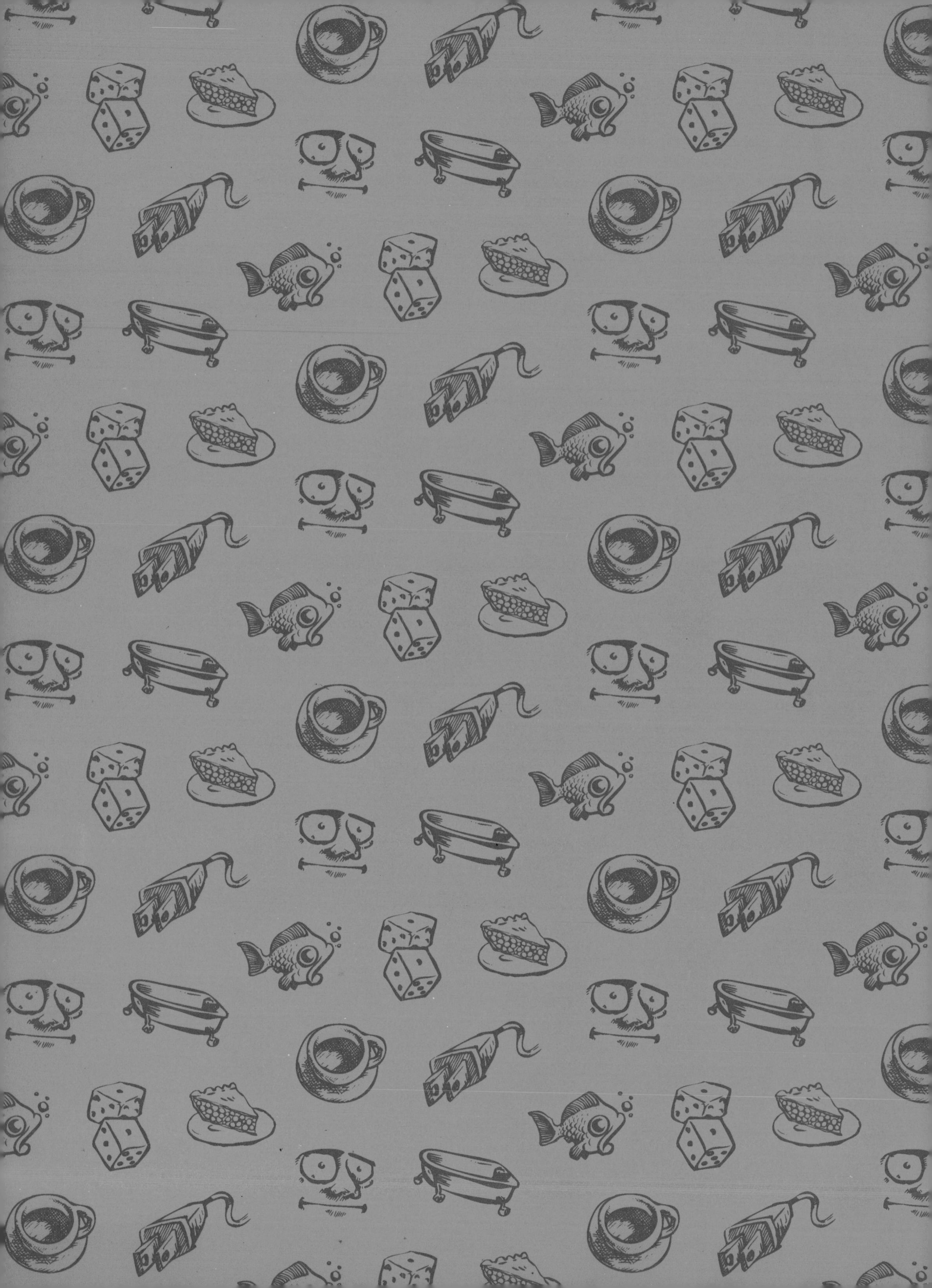